GLOBAL
STUDIES

VOLUME II

GLOBAL STUDIES

VOLUME II

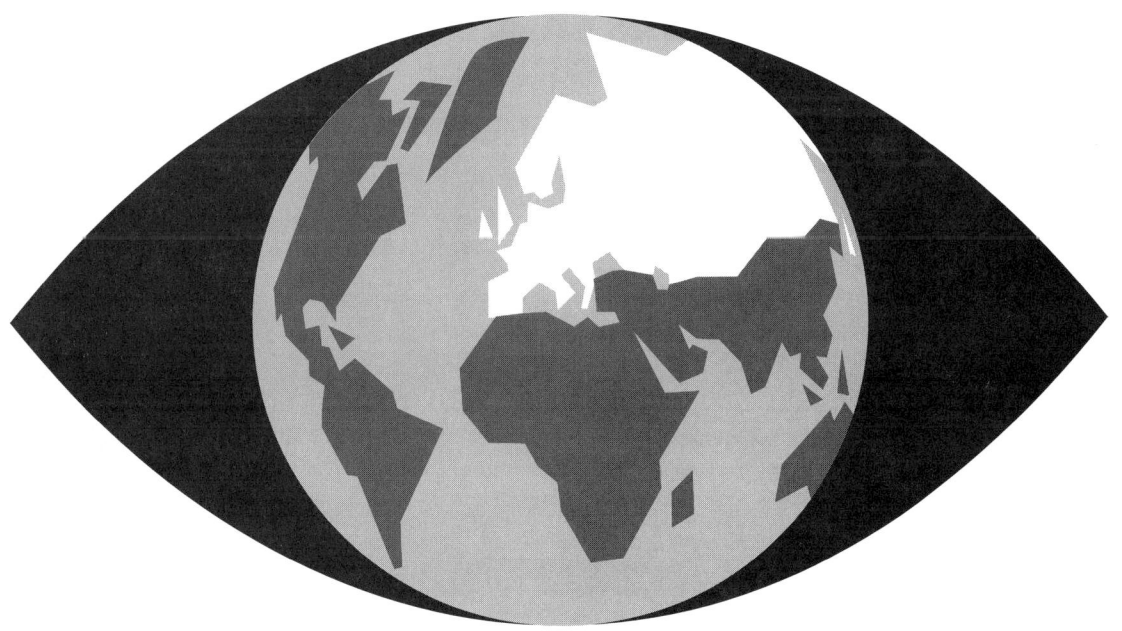

WESTERN EUROPE, EASTERN EUROPE, AND TERRITORIES OF THE FORMER SOVIET UNION

by Mark Willner, M.A.; George Hero, M.A.; and Jerry Weiner, Ph.D.
Consulting Editor: Stanley Kravetz

BARRON'S

All inquiries should be addressed to:
Barron's Educational Series, Inc.
250 Wireless Boulevard
Hauppauge, New York 11788

Library of Congress Catalog Card No.: 87-27079

International Standard Book No. 0-8120-6333-3 (hardcover)
International Standard Book No. 0-8120-3798-7 (paperback)

Library of Congress Cataloging-in-Publication Data
(Revised for vol. 2)
Rosenfeld, Erwin M.
    Global studies
    Vol. 2 by Mark Willner, George Hero, and Jerry Weiner.
    Includes indexes.
    Contents: v. 1. Asia, Africa, and Latin America — v. 2. Europe.
    1. Civilization—History.   I. Geller, Harriet.   II. Willner, Mark.
III. Title.
CB69.2.R67   1987   909   87-27079
ISBN 0-8120-3797-9 (v. 1 : pbk.)
ISBN 0-8120-6333-3 (v. 2)
ISBN 0-8120-3798-7 (v. 2 : pbk.)

Printed in the United States of America
  78   5100   987654

Photo Acknowledgments

Preface

For Which Course Was This Book Designed?

This book was designed to be used as a basic high school text for a one-year, two-term study of Europe—its history and its people. The material is presented in a manner that is appropriate for an introductory survey course. *Europe* refers to the land mass comprising Western Europe, Eastern Europe, and the territories of the former Soviet Union. This text is the logical sequel to *Global Studies: Volume I,* which covers the non-Western world. However, it is not necessary that Volume I be used prior to using Volume II. Volume II stands by itself and provides a comprehensive study of Europe as we approach the conclusion of the twentieth century.

What Are the Special Features of This Book?

The information included here is mainly historical. It is not a world history book, but rather a book about European history. We begin, however, with a general introduction to Europe. This introduction explores physical geography, economic geography, human geography, and prehistoric times. We then embark on a "trip through time" as we "travel" from Ancient Greece and Rome up to the present day. Additional features of the book that you should know about include:

1. *A great deal of attention, more than is usual in a textbook, is given to the history of Eastern Europe and the former Soviet Union.* These areas of Europe have undergone crucial changes during your lifetime. Even with publication of this book, historic events are occurring there that will have an impact into the next century. Americans of your generation need to be well-informed about these areas and how they have changed.

2. *A special section is devoted to the Holocaust, the worst example of man's inhumanity to man in recorded history.* Knowledge of this tragedy is necessary in order to prevent something as terrible as this from happening again.

3. *All the authors of this book are high school social studies teachers.* This is very rarely the case with high school history textbooks. The authors have, combined, more than seventy years of successful experience in teaching European history classes. Much of this book is based upon that experience and therefore contains information that students such as you need to know. The authors also have traveled extensively in Europe, can speak several European languages, and have earned a fine reputation for writing other instructional material on foreign nations.

4. *This book also explains, and has references to, various concepts and issues described in the social studies syllabus of New York State and that of other states.* The fifteen key concepts are: change, choice, citizenship, culture, diversity, empathy, environment, human rights, identity, interdependence, justice, political systems, power, scarcity, and technology. The eleven world issues are: population, war and peace, terrorism, energy resources and allocations, human rights, hunger and poverty, world trade and finance, environmental concerns, political and economic refugees, economic growth and development, and determination of political and economic systems.

5. *Each unit in the book is broken down into chapters.* Enriching the text chapters are questions, maps, timelines, charts, and a unique feature: Profiles in History, which examines the lives of historic figures mentioned within almost every chapter.

Special Message to High School Students Who Will Be Graduating in the 1990s

In this book, you will learn much about Europe's past history. As a result, you will be able to understand the Europe that exists now and the Europe that will exist in the future years of the twenty-first century. The Europe of the 1990s—during your lifetime—is different from the Europe of the twentieth century prior to your birth. During those years, the continent of Europe was the scene of many map changes, two "hot" wars, a "cold" war, and several revolutions—some bloody and some peaceful. This was the Europe that your teachers, parents, and grandparents knew and studied about.

Present-day Europe is a different place, for reasons that you will learn about in this book. In addition, your generation probably knows more about Europe than any earlier generation of American high school students. This knowledge has been acquired mainly from outside of school and may stem from one or more of the following reasons:

1. You or someone you know may have already traveled somewhere in Europe.
2. You may know somebody who works for a European company, or someone who does business with people from Europe.
3. Television, movies, and advertising carry much information about European people.
4. You may have something in your home that was made in a European nation.
5. Through the process of cultural diffusion, you may already be familiar with one or more European languages other than English. You probably know something about music, sports, clothes, cosmetics, and food that are European in origin.
6. The United States is a multicultural society. Throughout our nation, and probably right in your own community, are people who can trace their ancestry to different parts of the globe. Perhaps you are someone who can trace your ancestry to one or more European nations, and if not, you probably know someone whose background is originally from somewhere in Europe.
7. In each year of your lifetime, thousands of European tourists have traveled to the United States. Perhaps you have met some of them in your community.

Summary

Although citizens of the United States, you and your friends are also "citizens of a global community." To understand the European part of this community, you are about to begin a study of the European continent. Europe is that part of the world that has most strongly influenced our own nation's history. And of ironic historical interest, it is the United States that has greatly influenced Europe's history during most of the current century. What will be the nature of the United States' relations with Europe in the twenty-first century? Your generation's actions may well furnish the answer to this question. Upon reading this textbook, you will be better informed about Europe and well equipped to take your place as a citizen of the United States and of the world.

Good luck with this book. It will help you in your travels through Europe—past, present, and future.

Mark Willner

Important Features of This Book

This book's information about Europe begins with an introduction and is then organized into ten units. The ten units contain forty chapters. Each unit has an introduction, while each chapter includes both an introduction and a summary. Other important features of *Global Studies: Volume II* are as follows:

Chronologies. Every chapter has a timeline. This will help you to see quickly, in chronological order, the noteworthy events covered in the chapter.

Profiles in History. These are in-depth descriptions of key people and events. A profile will sharpen your understanding of material in the text.

Maps. Maps throughout the book show locations of significant places. These places include cities, nations, and continents. Many chapters also contain map exercises to sharpen your map comprehension skills.

Glossary. Found at the end of the book, this is an alphabetical listing of important words and their definitions. Familiarity with these words will aid your study of history and will also build up your general vocabulary. Words appearing in boldface in the chapters can be found in the glossary.

Review Exercises. These are found at the end of each chapter. They consist of different kinds of short-answer questions as well as essay questions. By reading the material in each chapter carefully, you will be able to answer all of these questions.

Photographs. You will find photographs in the book of people, places, and events necessary for your understanding of European history. These photographs are accompanied by captions that give helpful information.

Diagrams, Documents, and Charts. These provide additional information to help you understand historic events.

Author Biographies

MARK WILLNER is chairman of the social studies department at Midwood High School at Brooklyn College. He has also taught at Morris High School and at Wadleigh (Harlem) Evening High School and at Temple Emanu-El Religious School. He was selected as the outstanding social studies supervisor in New York State in 1991, and received similar honors in New York City (1984, 1988, and 1992). As a recipient of Fulbright and other grants, Willner has studied and traveled extensively in Asia and Europe. He is a past president of the New York City Social Studies Supervisors Association (S.S.S.A.) and also sits on the executive boards of the New York State S.S.S.A. and the New York City Association of Teachers of Social Studies/United Federation of Teachers (A.T.S.S./U.F.T). He is the chief author of Barron's *Let's Review: Global Studies*.

GEORGE HERO is a teacher in the social studies department at Midwood High School at Brooklyn College, and is also an assistant professor of history at Long Island University. Hero has also taught at Brooklyn College and at the Yeshiva of Flatbush. He is the founder and director of the Westinghouse Social Science Research Program at Midwood High School, and is a co-author of *Let's Review: Global Studies*.

JERRY WEINER, Ph.D., is chairman of the social studies department at Louis D. Brandeis High School, and has also taught at Boys' and Girls' High School. He received his Ph.D. in history from the City University of New York. Dr. Weiner also teaches as an adjunct professor at Columbia University Teacher's College and at Hunter College. In 1989, he was selected as the outstanding social studies supervisor in New York City. He is a past president of the New York City S.S.S.A., and is a co-author of *Let's Review: Global Studies*.

STANLEY KRAVETZ is a former chairman of the social studies department at Syosset High School. He is also past president of the New York State Council for the Social Studies. Kravetz is the author of several books, including *The Holocaust*, *Afro-Asian Studies*, and *European History*.

CONTENTS

INTRODUCTION

UNIT I
THE ANCIENT WORLD

UNIT II
THE MEDIEVAL WORLD

UNIT III
THE BIRTH OF MODERN EUROPE

UNIT IV
EVOLUTION AND REVOLUTION

UNIT V
THE IMPACT OF THE INDUSTRIAL REVOLUTION

UNIT VI

POLITICAL CHANGE IN THE NINETEENTH CENTURY

UNIT VII
IMPERIALISM

UNIT VIII

WAR AND UPHEAVAL IN THE FIRST HALF OF THE TWENTIETH CENTURY

Dit is een foto, zoals
ik me zou wensen,
altijd zo te zijn.
Dan had ik nog wel
een kans om naar
Holywood te komen.
Annefrank.
10 Oct. 1942

(translation)
"This is a photo as I would wish
myself to look all the time. Then
I would maybe have a chance to
come to Hollywood."
Anne Frank, 10 Oct. 1942

UNIT IX

THE COLD WAR AND THE NEW EUROPE

UNIT X

ENTERING THE TWENTY-FIRST CENTURY

PROFILES IN HISTORY

DIAGRAMS, DOCUMENTS, AND CHARTS

MAPS

Introduction

Physical Geography

We begin our study of Europe with its *physical* geography. By studying this topic first, we get to know about the continent's basic land and natural features. We will then be able to understand something about its *economy*. A region's economy is very closely linked to its physical resources. Furthermore, the *human or cultural* features of a region have important connections with its physical and economic features. And finally, the *history and politics* of a region such as Europe are best studied once we know some basic things about its geography, economy, and culture. The first three topics are taken up in this introduction. The historical and political development of Europe begins in Unit I, chronologically, and continues throughout the rest of the book.

Of the six continents on earth, Europe is the fifth largest in physical size. Geographically, Europe refers to the mass of land that goes from the Atlantic Ocean on the west all the way eastward to the western part of Russia. (The eastern part of Russia is in Asia.) Europe is the second most populated continent. As of January 1, 1990, as the last decade of the twentieth century began, the European continent contained thirty-one independent nations. That number has grown during recent years, for economic and political reasons to be explained later in this book.

Europe's physical geography can be understood easily by examining its two general areas: Western Europe and Eastern Europe. The dividing line between the two areas is generally accepted as the line of 15° east longitude. However, even though they lie east of this line, Greece and Finland are considered part of Western Europe for cultural and political reasons.

Western Europe

Overview The part of Europe known as Western Europe consists of twenty-three nations that may be grouped in the following ways:
1. Northwestern Europe: Ireland, United Kingdom (England, Scotland, Wales, and Northern Ireland), France, Monaco, and the Benelux countries (Belgium, the Netherlands, and Luxembourg.)
2. Southern Europe: Portugal, Spain, Malta, Italy, San Marino, and Greece. (We will not include Turkey here, because its capital and most of its land and people are in Asia.)
3. Middle (Central) Europe: Germany, Switzerland, Austria, and Lichtenstein.
4. Scandinavia: Iceland, Norway, Sweden, Finland, Denmark, and Greenland.

Topography   Western Europe has many different kinds of landforms, which have affected political, economic, and cultural ways of life. The major mountains and ranges are the Alps, Appennines, and Pyrenees. The Pyrenees have restricted movement between France and Spain, thereby separating the Iberian peninsula (Spain and Portugal) from the rest of Western Europe. The mountainous terrain in Greece was responsible for the growth of separate city-states in Ancient Greece. The lowlands in the Netherlands made that country's inhabitants concerned about frequent flooding from the North Sea, and many dams and canals have been built for protection. The low plains in the other Benelux nations, as well as those in northeastern France, have been the sites of invasions and battlegrounds throughout European history.

Bodies of Water   The major bodies of water surrounding Western Europe are the Baltic Sea and the North Sea in the north, the Atlantic Ocean to the west and the Mediterranean Sea in the south. The Atlantic Ocean has been a "highway" of commerce and migration between Europe and the Americas, particularly for those nations touching the Atlantic, such as Britain, France, Ireland, and Spain. The proximity to large bodies of water led to the build-up of fishing fleets and eventually to great naval power for several nations. At different times in history, these nations—Britain, France, Holland, Portugal, and Spain—established overseas colonial empires. Historically, the Mediterranean Sea has made cultural diffusion possible between Europe, Africa, and the Middle East, especially by way of the Italian peninsula. In the twentieth century, the North Sea has been developed as an important source of oil. The many warm-water ports on these major bodies of water have helped in the movement of

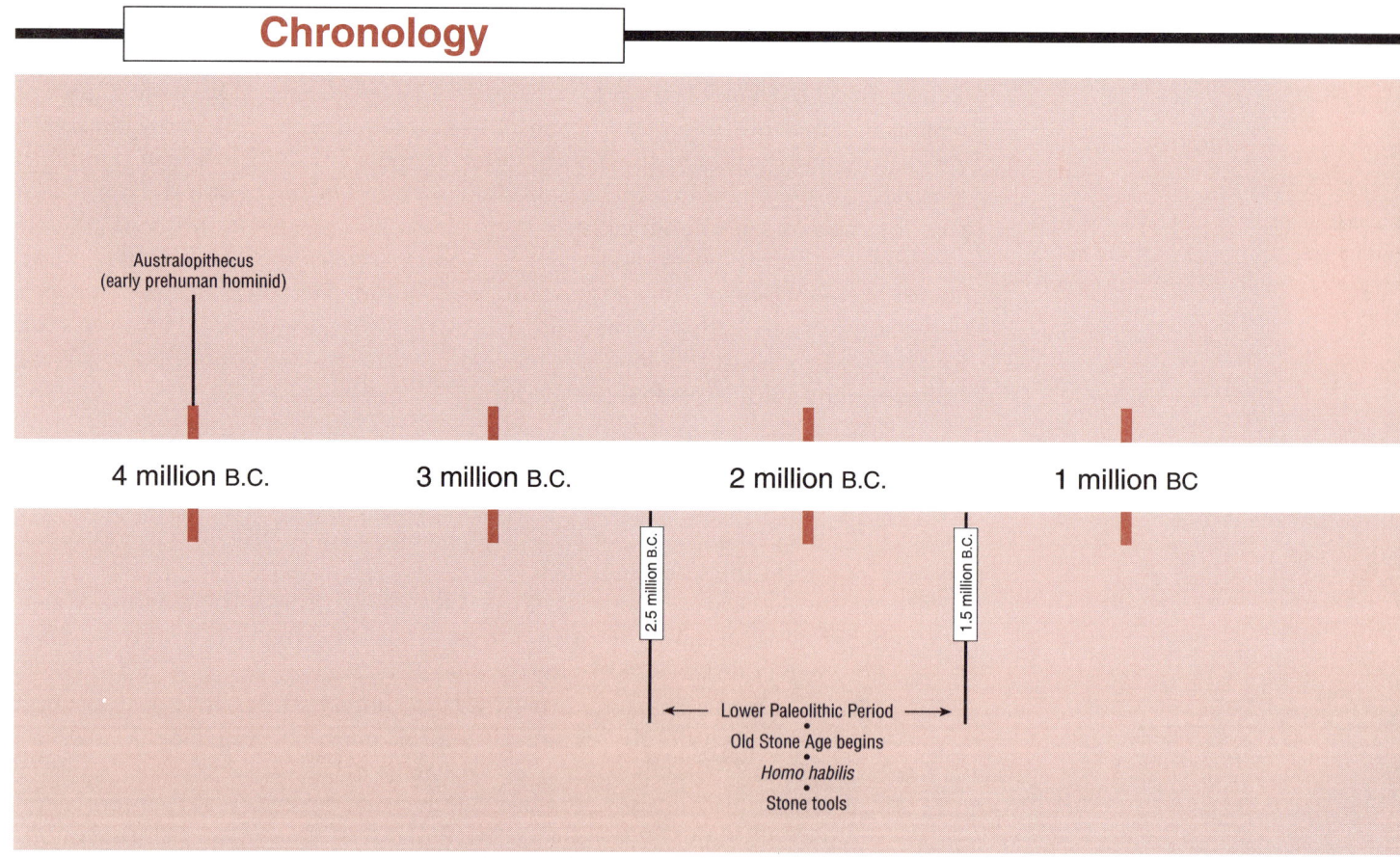

Chronology

Australopithecus
(early prehuman hominid)

4 million B.C.   3 million B.C.   2 million B.C.   1 million BC

2.5 million B.C.   1.5 million B.C.

← Lower Paleolithic Period →
Old Stone Age begins
Homo habilis
Stone tools

goods and people. The Dutch port of Rotterdam, for example, is the largest in Europe and today handles more cargo than even New York City. Several navigable rivers are found in Western Europe, providing easy access between cities and nations. Among these are the Rhine, Po, Seine, Danube, and Thames.

The English Channel separates England from the European mainland, and consequently, it has provided protection for most of British history. However, times change. A good example of this is the construction of the **Chunnel**. This is a newly built railroad tunnel that runs underneath the English Channel. It is a historic "first," connecting Britain with France. Formal opening of the Channel Tunnel occurred in June 1994. The existence of the Chunnel is another reason to explain why the Europe of your lifetime will be different from the Europe of former years and centuries.

The North Atlantic Drift brings moderate temperature patterns to the Atlantic coast nations. The Mediterranean Sea affects the climate in the nations of southern Europe, causing hot, dry summers.

Eastern Europe

Overview Eastern Europe consists of the nations located between Western Europe and Asia. Common religious, ethnic, and cultural ties distinguish the Eastern European countries. Despite a diverse mixture of peoples and influences, the Eastern European

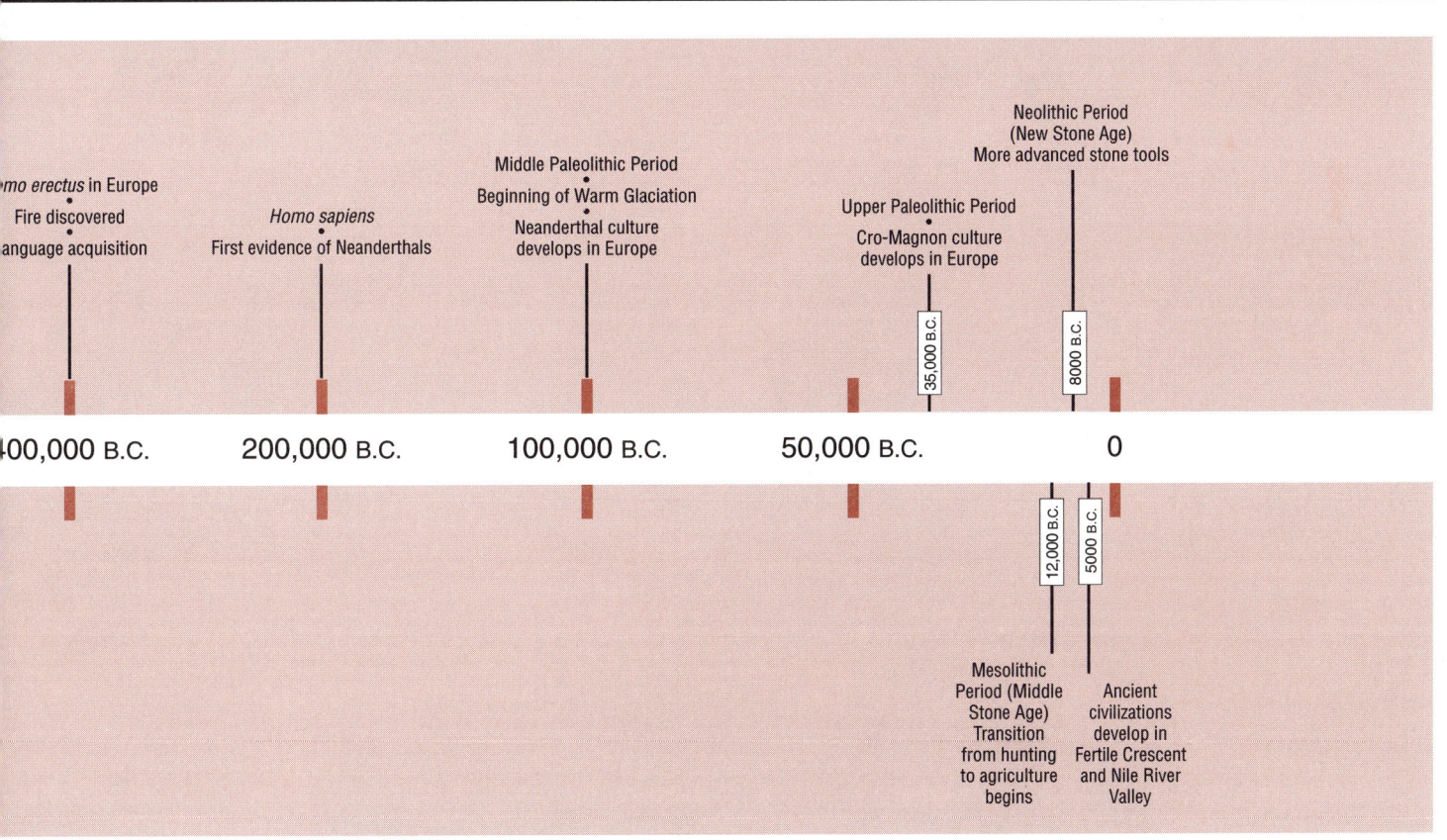

Barents Sea

URAL MOUNTAINS

R U S S I A

KAZAKHSTAN

Aral Sea

Caspian Sea

TURKMENISTAN

FINLAND

Kola Peninsula

White Sea

HELSINKI

TALLINN

ESTONIA

LATVIA

RIGA

HUANIA

VILNIUS

MINSK

BELARUS

ARSAW

UKRAINE

KIEV

MOLDOVA

CHISINAU

ROMANIA

BUCHAREST

BALKAN MTS.

BULGARIA

SOFIA

SKOPJE

EDONIA

REECE

ATHENS

Black Sea

Sea of Azov

Crimea

CAUCASUS MTS.

GEORGIA

TBILISI

AZERBAIJAN

BAKU

Sea of Marmara

ANKARA

Bursa

T U R K E Y

Adana

NICOSIA

CYPRUS

BEIRUT

LEBANON

Mediterranean Sea

Vadso
Murmansk
Monchegorsk
Chupa
Kemi
Oulu
Kajaani
Kuopio
Joensuu
Tampere
Lappeenranta
Lahti
Tartu
Pskov
Velikiye Luki
Hrodna
ARSAW
Lublin
Lutsk
Rivne
Zhytomyr
Lviv
Khmelnytsk'y
Ivano-Frankivsk
Chernivtsi
Cluj-Napoca
Iasi
imisoara
Brasov
Craiova
Ploiesti
LGRADE
Nis
Danube
Ruse
Varna
Burgas
Plovdiv
Kavalla
Thessaloniki
Larisa
Patrai
Kalamai
Irakion
Creta

Nar'yan Mar
Irita
Pechora
Pechora
Nyandoma
Velikiy Ustyug
Syktyvkar
Berezniki
Perm
Kunger
Yekaterinburg
Chelyabinsk
Magnitogorsk
Kudymkar
Izhevsk
Naberezhnyye Chelny
Ufa
Sterlitamak
Salavat
Orsk
Orenburg

Mezen
Mezen
Ukhta
N. Dvina
Archangel
Severodvinsk
Onega
Kem'
Petrozavodsk
Lake Onega
Cherepovets
St. Petersburg
Novgorod
Borovichi
Tver'
Sergiyev Posad
MOSCOW
Elektrostal
Podolsk
Serpukhov
Kolomna
Ryazan'
Kaluga
Smolensk
Orsha
Mohilyow
Bryansk
Orel
Yelets
Kursk
Belgorod
Sumy
Chernihiv
Poltava
Kharkiv
Luhansk
Cherkasy
Dnipropetrovsk
Horlivka
Makiyivka
Shakhty
Kirovohrad
Dniprodzerzhynsk
Donetsk
Kryvyy Rih
Zaporizhzhya
Mariupol
Rostov na Donu
Mykolayiv
Odesa
Kherson
Krasnodar
Stavropol
Elista
Astrakhan
Nal'chik
Cherkessk
Maykop
Sochi
Vladikavkaz
Groznyy
Makhachkala
Derbent
Sumqayit

Rybinsk Res.
Kostroma
Rybinsk
Ivanovo
Kineshma
Vladimir
Nizhniy Novgorod
Cheboksary
Yoshkar Ola
Kazan
Ketchenery
Vyatka
Kirov Chelyabinsk
Saransk
Syzran
Tolyatti
Samara
Penza
Bugul'ma
Balakovo
Tambov
Lipetsk
Voronezh
Saratov
Balashov
Kamyshin
Volzhskiy
Volgograd
Don
Volga

Galati
Braila
Constanta
Istanbul
Izmir
Simferopol
Sevastopol
Yalta
Vinnytsya

Europe

⊛ National capital

• City or village

– · – International boundary

0 100 200 300 400
Scale in Miles

0 100 200 300 400
Scale in Kilometers

Polyconic Projection

BARRON'S ©Copyright 1994 by Barron's Educational Series, Inc.

nations share many historical and cultural roots. They are the nations of Albania, Bulgaria, the Czech Republic, Slovakia, Hungary, Poland, Romania, and the nations that formerly constituted Yugoslavia (Bosnia-Hercegovina, Croatia, Montenegro, Serbia, Slovenia, and Yugoslovian Macedonia, or Skopje). Eastern Europe also includes the nations of the former Soviet Union, now known as the Commonwealth of Independent States or C.I.S. (Russia, Ukraine, Belarus, Moldova, Georgia, Armenia, Azerbaijian, Kazakhstan, Kyrghyzstan, Tadzhikistan, Turkmenistan, Uzbekistan and the Baltic nations of Estonia, Latvia, and Lithuania). Containing over 409 million people, with a wide range of languages and religions, these nations seem to have been constantly brought together by historical events.

Topography Its topography and location have made Eastern Europe an invasion route throughout its history. This has resulted in the mixing of many peoples, languages, and cultures.

Mountains. Mountains have played the most influential role in the development of Eastern Europe's nations. They have acted as barriers and trade routes, both protecting and unifying peoples in this region. Eastern Europe's mountains are low and relatively accessible when compared with other ranges in the world. The Carpathians stretch through Romania, Hungary, the Czech Republic, Slovakia, and Poland; the Balkans run through the southern Slavic lands from northern Bulgaria to eastern Serbia. The Urals, traditionally considered the dividing line between Europe and Asia, stretch across the Eurasian landmass and interrupt the Siberian Plain.

Plains. Plains have also had a profound effect on the history of Eastern Europe. The Northern Plain of Eurasia consists of thousands of miles of flat land. It stretches from the Atlantic Ocean across Western Europe into Eastern Europe, becoming the Siberian Plain upon reaching Russia. It is interrupted only by some low mountain ranges, the most notable of which are the Urals. This geographic feature has made the nations of Eastern Europe susceptible to invasion from both the east and west for centuries. The Great Hungarian Plain, located in the center of Eastern Europe, is an agricultural and horse-breeding region that has attracted invaders as well.

Rivers. Rivers have played an important role in the development of Eastern Europe. As many nations had little or no access to the sea, rivers have served as major trade routes, linking them together and with the rest of the world. This has had great historical significance, especially in regard to contact with the Byzantine Empire in the Medieval Period during which the dominant culture of Eastern Europe was developed. The Danube is one of the most important of these waterways, connecting Hungary, Slovenia, Croatia, Serbia, Bulgaria, and Romania. In addition to trade, it has always been a source of fish, irrigation, and, in modern times, hydroelectric power. Other important rivers are the Morava (linking the Czech Republic, Slovakia, Hungary, Croatia, and Serbia), and the Drava (flowing from Hungary to Croatia).

The rivers within Russia have played an important role in the history and development of the Russian Empire and later the Soviet Union. The Volga (the longest river in Europe) facilitated the internal development of Russia while the Dneiper, Dvina, and Don rivers were essential for trade and commerce, linking Russia, Ukraine, and Belarus. The Neva River still serves as an important route between Russian industrial centers and the Baltic Sea.

Seas and Lakes.   Eastern Europe's seas and lakes are also very important. The Black Sea has historically been essential to trade and commerce for the nations of Bulgaria, Romania, Russia, and Georgia. The Caspian Sea (the largest inland body of water in the world) provides Russia with an important source of food and a passageway for commerce. The Adriatic Sea has provided Albania, Montenegro, Bosnia-Hercegovina, and Croatia with a rich source of fishing, trade and, most recently, tourism. The Baltic Sea has provided Poland, Lithuania, Latvia, Estonia, and Russia with a limited source of trade and commerce. Fresh-water lakes, such as Hungary's Lake Balton or Russia's Lake Baikal (the deepest lake in the world) and Lake Ladoga (the largest inland body of water in Europe), also provide important links in generally land-locked nations.

Vegetation Belts.   As a whole, Eastern Europe is mountainous up to Ukraine and Russia. Yet, there are areas of abundant vegetation: in Serbia and Montenegro, the Pannonian Plain; in Hungary, parts of the Great Hungarian Plain (particularly near Debrecen on the Romanian border); in the Danube Valley and the provinces of Moravia and Bohemia, and in eastern Slovakia; in Bulgaria, the Maritsa Valley, known as "Bulgaria's California" (located between the Balkan and Rhodope mountains), and the Balkan Plateau (in the north, bordering Romania); in Romania, western Transylvania as well as the river valleys of the Danube and the Prut; and in Poland, the Silesian region in the south.

The vegetation belts of the C.I.S. consist of three zones: the tundra, the taiga, and the steppes. The northern rim, including the islands of the Arctic Circle, is known as the tundra and covers about 10 percent of the land. It consists of a thick layer of permanently frozen ground called permafrost. Its severe climate makes the tundra uninhabitable. The taiga, which covers nearly half of Russia, is a great forest that provides wood, but limited crops. These conditions have kept the population there small. The steppes is a very fertile region that has historically attracted both farmers and nomadic tribes. Ukraine, the nation in the southwest, is an important agricultural area known for centuries under tsarist and Soviet rule as the "Breadbasket of Russia." It has the most fertile land in the region. Because of its lack of natural barriers, however, the steppes has always served as an invasion route for armies from both the west and east.

The territories between the steppes and frontier mountains of the southeast are mainly uninhabited desert. The majority of people there, in the former Soviet Union, have always lived in European Russia, particularly in the steppes. Only recently have large numbers of people moved to the north and east, largely to exploit the natural resources in these areas.

Climate   The climate in Eastern Europe is as varied as its many peoples and cultures. The mildest and most beneficial climate is enjoyed by the southern Slavic nations of Serbia, Montenegro, Skopje, Croatia, Slovenia and Bosnia-Hercegovina. The last three have developed a flourishing tourist business on the Adriatic coast. Albania shares this climate, but that nation's internal problems have prevented it from capitalizing on this natural advantage. Warm summers and moderate winters make Bulgaria, Hungary, and Romania ideal for agricultural development. The harsher climate of the Czech Republic, Slovakia and Poland, with very cold winters and cool summers, have traditionally shortened growing seasons.

The climate within the C.I.S. is quite varied. Ukraine, Belarus, Moldova, and the Baltic nations have a climate similar to Poland, the Czech Republic, and Slovakia, with Ukraine's rich soil compensating for the shortness of the growing season.

The extremely h[...] important role in
shaping the char[...] patient. It has also
made them able [...] ocean winds and
the cool Arctic bl[...] ulated world. Even
Russia's warmest [...] Lakes or Canada.

Econo[...]

We will approach the continent's economic geography as we approached its physical geography, by looking first at Western Europe and then at Eastern Europe.

Western Europe

Agriculture

Western Europe's farmers, although declining in number in this century, produce large amounts of food. Careful use of land, pesticides, and modern technology have contributed to food surpluses in many areas. The major agricultural products are wheat, potatoes, meat, wine, and dairy products.

Industrial Production

Western Europe has long been one of the world's leading areas in manufacturing and industrial development. The large deposits of coal in Britain and Germany, combined with scientific technology (beginning with the Industrial Revolution), have been primary factors in this development. Major industrial products are automobiles, chemicals, electronics, steel, and machinery.

Advances in agricultural and industrial production have resulted in a high standard of living for Western Europe's people. Germany has the highest GNP (Gross National Product) on the continent.

The Marshall Plan

The Marshall Plan is named after an American, George C. Marshall, U.S. Secretary of State, who proposed a way in which the United States could help build up Europe's economy after World War II. His plan was passed by Congress in 1947 and was officially known as the European Recovery Act. It made about $12.5 billion in aid available to countries that suffered damage and devastation from the war and called upon the European countries to draw up their own plans for recovery. Most non-Communist European nations accepted the aid offered by the Marshall Plan and, as a result, achieved much economic progress.

Although the plan included all the European nations, the aid was refused by the Communist nations. These were the nations of Eastern Europe and the former Soviet Union. These nations accepted aid from the Council of Mutual Economic Assistance (COMECON), a Soviet version of the Marshall Plan.

Economic Systems and Decision-Making

Today, different types of economic systems exist in the Western European nations. An economic system is a way of making decisions about such basic economic questions as:

1. What should be produced?
2. Who would produce it?
3. How should it be produced?
4. What should the price be?
5. Who should own the land and the means of production?
6. How is the product to be distributed?
7. To whom should it be distributed?

In a **capitalist system**, also known as a free market system, most of these economic questions are decided upon privately and freely by individual citizens. Under capitalism, a society's government has very little to do in making economic decisions. This kind of system permits a free market economy to exist. Historically, societies that have a market economy and economic freedom also allow other kinds of freedom, such as freedom of religion, speech, the press, and so on. In *The Wealth of Nations*, written in 1776, Adam Smith provided a good description of a capitalist system.

In a **socialist** system, most of the basic economic issues are decided by the government. A socialist government is freely elected by the people, and its main goal is to improve the conditions of workers. Democratic freedoms are allowed, as are many political parties.

In a Communist system, an example of a command system, the government makes all the economic decisions. However, Communist governments have usually come to power as a result of violence and revolution. Only one party, the Communist Party, is allowed to exist. *The Communist Manifesto*, written by Karl Marx and Friedrich Engels in 1848, explained certain aspects of Communist theory.

The countries in Western Europe today are said to have a mixed economy; that is, they have elements of both capitalism and socialism. Each nation has a different degree of government ownership (nationalization) of industries. In the field of health and other social services, some nations, such as England, Denmark, and Sweden, have extensive social welfare programs. The British National Health Service provides free dental and medical benefits. The costs of these programs are paid for by taxes on employers and workers.

Although Communist parties have existed in almost every Western European nation, the Communists have been weak and have never won control of a government. These Communist parties claimed to have somewhat different views from those of the former Soviet and East European Communists, thereby hoping to gain more support. In the late 1970s, they were part of a movement called Eurocommunism. However, this movement was not successful.

Attempts at Economic Cooperation

World War II brought economic ruin to Western Europe and also signaled an end to almost 500 years of European economic dominance in the world. During this time, economic rivalry and competition grew among several nations. Since World War II, however, there has been a movement to promote economic unity and cooperation.

The European Economic Community (EEC). The EEC, also known as the **Common Market**, was originally created in 1951 as the ECSC (European Coal and Steel Community). Its aim, as stated by French Foreign Minister Robert Schuman in his Schuman Plan, was to bring together the coal and steel industries of six nations: Belgium, France, Italy, Luxembourg, the Netherlands, and West Germany. This group was also known as the "inner six."

In 1957, the inner six agreed to bring together their economies and reduce barriers such as tariffs. As a result, there was now more free trade among these nations, and they changed their name from ECSC to the EEC. They also created Euratom, to tie together the six nations' research in nuclear power.

The EEC came to be known as the European Community (EC), and was very successful in increasing economic activity among its members. By 1985, six other nations had been accepted for membership: Denmark, Ireland, the United Kingdom, Greece, Portugal, and Spain.

In 1987, the twelve nations of the European Community agreed to bring their economies even closer together by the mid-1990s and to create a "frontier-free" Europe. This plan

- calls for one large common market in which nations can sell their goods more easily to their members,
- allows citizens of a member nation to work in any other member nation of the EC, and
- subjects goods coming into the EC from outside to a high tax (tariff).

The EC's twelve nations would thus make up a single economic unit, with 330 million citizens, that could compete with the world's two current economic giants: the United States and Japan. Eventually, the twelve nations might join together politically, creating a "United States of Europe." Discussions about this took place in Dublin and Rome in 1990, and in Maastricht, the Netherlands, in 1991.

The hopes described above, for greater economic unity by 1992, received a boost with the signing in that year of the Maastricht Treaty. Although the treaty sparked debate in many countries, notably Denmark, England, France, and Germany, it was approved by all members by 1993. These nations were concerned about their voting rights under the treaty as well as the extent to which regulations would affect their sovereignty and the lives of their citizens. The treaty became effective in November 1993. The EC is now known as the **European Union (EU)**. In March 1994, the foreign ministers of the twelve member nations voted to admit four more nations—Austria, Finland, Norway, and Sweden. It is expected, subject to working out further details on the admission, that these four nations will become members as of January 1, 1995. However, in November 1994, Norway voted not to join the EU. (A detailed account of the treaty's provisions and its consequences are given in Chapter 37, "Global Economic Issues.")

The European Free Trade Association (EFTA).   Also known as the "outer seven," this organization, which came into existence in 1960, has had a changing membership. Currently, it has seven member nations: Austria, Finland, Iceland, Liechtenstein, Norway, Sweden, and Switzerland. EFTA has not established as strong links as the EU, but it has similar economic goals. In time it may ask to be admitted into the EU.

Economic Issues   The term "Post-Industrial society" refers to a society in which more people work in service industries (accounting, health, education) than in goods-producing industries (steel, textiles). This situation is becoming more and more common in Western Europe, as it is in the United States.

Inflation refers to rising prices, which have caused a decrease in the value of the European currencies. The increase in oil prices charged by the Middle Eastern nations during the 1970s was one reason for inflation in Western Europe. Another reason was the attempt by the United States to reduce the flow of European imports to the United States and to increase the flow of American exports. Most Western European nations are dependent on outside areas for raw materials, such as oil from the Middle East.

Of increasing importance to Western Europe in the 1990s will be its economic relations with Japan and the United States, as well as with the former Communist nations in Eastern Europe and the former European colonies in Africa and Asia.

Eastern Europe

Agriculture Eastern Europe's economy was almost completely agricultural until the late nineteenth and early twentieth centuries, when the Russian czars began industrialization. With their large growing areas and rich soil, Serbia and Montenegro, followed by Bulgaria and Romania, provide the greatest agricultural output. Serbia and Montenegro produce grains, fruit, tobacco, and wood; Bulgaria provides grains, fruit, rose oil, and tobacco; and Romania grows corn, wheat, and timber. Poland produces limited grain and timber; Hungary provides grain and wine. The Czech Republic, unlike Slovakia, is almost completely industrial, and until recently, Albania's rigid Communist system made its agricultural output barely self-sufficient.

In the C.I.S., Ukraine contains the most fertile regions. It has fed the Russian and later Soviet empires, due to its large production of wheat, rye, barley, cabbage, and potatoes. The Transcaucasusian nations (Georgia, Armenia, and Azerbaijan) supply cotton, tea, and certain subtropical fruit such as oranges and grapes. The nations of the C.I.S. have had agricultural production adversely affected by other factors, both geographic and human. Agricultural output has been traditionally limited by severe droughts, a harsh climate with a limited growing season and its vast size, which often made transportation of goods difficult. As a result of the explosion of the Chernobyl nuclear power plant in 1986 (see Chapter 37, "Global Economic Issues"), much of Ukraine's rich soil was contaminated and its produce became unsafe for consumption. For that reason, the Soviet Union was dependent on outside sources, especially the United States, for much of its wheat. The effects of this disaster still affect the region.

The agricultural production of Eastern Europe was adversely affected in general by the advent of Communist rule from 1917 (in Russia) and 1945 (the rest of Eastern Europe). The recent collapse of these regimes has made clear the extent of the damage done. The policies of **collectivization** (governments forcing farmers to work together on state farms in accordance with Communist philosophy) and Central Economic Planning (state control of what is produced, who should produce it, how much it should cost, and how it should be distributed) have greatly retarded agricultural output and wiped out the industrious, independent farming class that was the backbone of Eastern European society for centuries.

Industrial/Production Resources Outside of the Commonwealth of Independent States, the Czech Republic is Eastern Europe's most industrialized nation. Rich in coal and atomic energy ores, it produces beer, glass, china, machinery, and light aircraft. Poland, with its wealthy deposits of iron ore, coal, zinc, and sulphur, provides iron, automobiles, textiles, and chemicals. Romania, rich in oil (for which it became a target in World War II), produces textiles, machinery, and metals in addition to exporting oil, its greatest resource.

Within the C.I.S., Russia and Ukraine are the world's largest producers of coal and provide the region with 90 percent of its supply. The most important centers of this production are in Ukraine, Urals, and eastern Siberia. Petroleum is a major part of the economies of Russia, Kazakhstan, and Azerbaijan. The largest oil-producing source is the Volga-Ural area, which provides over 70 percent of the region's supply, followed by western Siberia and Azerbaijan. Most natural gas and the production of chemicals come from the Volga-Ural region as well. In addition to its huge supplies of oil and coal, Siberia has immense deposits of iron and other minerals. However, the severe climatic conditions make these resources difficult to obtain. In addition, Siberia provides over 60 percent of all hydroelectric power in the C.I.S. The rich forests of the Russian taiga provide that nation with timber and fur. The Pacific Ocean in the far eastern lands of Russia yields one-third of the fish supply for the region, while areas on the Black Sea and the Baltic nations provide the balance. Ukraine is the world's largest producer of iron and maganese. It is also rich in natural gas and metallic ores, especially precious and semi-precious stones.

Guns vs. Butter Controversy The **gross national product**, or GNP, (total value of goods and services produced in a country) of the nations of Eastern Europe had been severely strained during the years of Communist rule by large military spending. The emphasis on making weapons rather than consumer goods lowered the general living standard for most Eastern Europeans, creating further resentment of the political system. In the former Soviet Union it was estimated that 16 to 20 percent of the total Soviet GNP was spent on national defense. With the fall of communism in Eastern Europe, this "Guns vs. Butter controversy" has already started to resolve itself. Eastern European nations are developing capitalist economies and reducing the part of the GNP spent on the military. However, the political instability and ethnic and religious conflict in parts of the area may threaten these economic changes as well as the attempts to establish democratic governments.

Human and Cultural Geography

Western Europe

Demography Western Europe, with over 300 million people, has a variety of religious, ethnic, and linguistic groups. The largest nations are Germany (79 million), Italy (57 million), and France (56 million). Overpopulation and overcrowding (high population density) are not problems in Western Europe. In fact, population growth rates are among the lowest in the world. One reason for the absence of demographic (population) problems is that Western Europe is thoroughly industrialized and has high standards of living and modern health care. Compared with people in less industrialized areas, such as southern Asia and Sub-Sahara Africa, Western Europeans live longer, marry at an older age, and have smaller families. In addition, women are much more involved in the work force. Urbanization (the movement of people from rural areas to cities) is also characteristic of Western Europe.

Religion Christianity is the predominant religion in Western Europe. The majority of people are Catholic, with the largest concentrations in the south, in Spain and Italy. Members of Protestant denominations are found mainly in the north, in nations such as England and Sweden. (Reasons for the connection between geography and religion are discussed in Chapter 7, "The Reformation.")

Jews have been a minority in Western European nations for centuries. They introduced the concept of monotheism, and from them have come the Ten Commandments. Christians share these beliefs. The combined basic beliefs and ideals of Jews and Christians make up the **Judeo-Christian tradition**. This tradition has influenced life in Western Europe for the last 2,000 years. It has also influenced life in areas that had the greatest number of overseas European settlements, such as those in North and South America. The Jewish bible is known as the Tanach (referred to by Christians as the Old Testament). Christians accept the Tanach but added a part known as the New Testament. The Christian bible, therefore, contains two parts—the Tanach (Old Testament) and the New Testament.

A growing number of Muslims and Hindus live today in some Western European nations, mostly those nations that once had colonies in Africa and Asia. France's Islamic community comes mainly from Algeria and Morocco. Most Hindus and Muslims in England come from the Indian subcontinent (India, Pakistan, and Bangladesh). The Muslims in West Germany are mainly from Turkey and have immigrated for economic reasons.

Ethnic Minority Groups

From Outside Europe. Besides the groups listed in the previous section, people from other areas of the world are found throughout Western Europe. They include people from the Caribbean, Africa, the Middle East, and East Asia. With the British colony of Hong Kong scheduled to come under China's rule in 1997, many Hong Kong Chinese are interested in immigrating to England. However, the British have mixed feelings about whether to admit great numbers of Chinese and other non-British people to their nation. Some of this concern in England (as well as in other European nations) results from prejudice against foreigners. This prejudice is rooted in the issues of race as well as competition for employment, and at times it has even led to riots.

From Inside Europe. The more industrialized nations, such as Germany and France, have "guest workers" from other parts of Europe. These workers often take jobs for short periods of time and send money back to their families. Such workers are from Turkey, Greece, Yugoslavia, Italy, and Portugal. Although there have been attempts by the host countries to assimilate these workers and provide education, instances of ill-feeling and prejudice have also been evident.

Languages

Although numerous languages exist in Western Europe, many have striking similarities. All languages in Western Europe (except Greek) are written using the Roman alphabet. There are also similarities in the ways some words are put together and are spoken. As a result, people in one nation are frequently able to understand the language of another nation. For example, many nouns are spelled somewhat similarly in Spanish, French, and Italian. Because of the similarities between the languages, many Europeans are multilingual. Other reasons for the large numbers of Europeans who are multilingual are the geographic proximity of nations to one another and the frequent travel and economic exchanges between them.

French, Spanish, and Italian are romance languages and have words constructed in a similar pattern. English, German, and Dutch have much in common, and the Scandinavian languages, except for Finnish, are similar. Some nations are officially bilingual because large segments of their populations speak distinct languages. For example, in Switzerland, French, German, and Italian are spoken widely, so all three are accepted as the country's official languages. In Belgium, Flemish and French are primarily used, so the government officially recognizes these languages.

Cultural Achievements

Western European achievements in such fields as art, literature, architecture, sculpture, and music have been very extensive. They are treated in other chapters, in chronological sequence.

Eastern Europe

Demography The population of Eastern Europe is about 409 million, 126 million of whom live outside of the C.I.S. A comparison of the population and area of each individual nation illustrates the breakdown: Albania, slightly larger than Maryland, has a population of roughly 3 million; Bulgaria, as large as Ohio, has approximately 10 million; the Czech Republic and Slovakia, about the size of New York State, have about 16 million; Hungary, roughly equal to Indiana, has a population of approximately 11 million; Poland, about the size of New Mexico, has roughly 39 million; and Romania, twice the size of Pennsylvania, has a little more than 23 million. Due to the present disputes over borders and the conflict over territory in what was formerly Yugoslavia, a breakdown of this sort for the nations of Serbia, Croatia, Slovenia, Montenegro, Yugoslavian Macedonia, and Bosnia-Hercegovina is not possible. The former nation of Yugoslavia was about the size of Wyoming with a population of about 24 million.

The population of the Commonwealth of Independent States is approximately 283 million, slightly more than that of the United States. The Baltic nations and some of the nationalities formerly part of the USSR are not currently members of the C.I.S. However, when one considers that the C.I.S. is twice the physical size of the United States, it is really underpopulated, especially in Russia. In fact, the population density in the Commonwealth is only 33 people per square mile, compared with 68 persons per square mile in the United States and 288 people per square mile in China. Yet, most of the population is located in European Russia and Ukraine. The small populations in Siberia, the taiga, the Asian nations and countries of the Caucasus have only grown slightly in the present century. Most of this increase is largely due to industrialization in these areas.

Ethnic Groups and Languages While many ethnic and linguistic groups make up the population of Eastern Europe, the largest and most dominant is the Slavs (approximately 198 million in the C.I.S., about 85 million outside of it). This includes the Great Russians, Belarussians, Ukrainians, Poles, Serbians, Croatians, Slovenes, Bulgarians, Slovaks, and Czechs. The larger non-Slavic groups in Eastern Europe are the Magyars (proper name for Hungarians), Romanians, Albanians, Greeks, Germans, Balts, Lats, Lithuanians, Finns, Georgians, Armenians, Turks, Tartars, and Gypsies.

Linguistically, the Slavic languages dominate Eastern Europe as well. These include Russian, Ukrainian, Belarussian, Polish, Serbo-Croat, Slovenian, Bulgarian, Slovak, and Czech. All of these came from a common Slavic tongue, which was developed into a written language in the tenth century by the Byzantine missionary Cyril of Thessolonika and his disciples. Adopting letters from the Greek and Coptic (Christian Egyptian) alphabets, the written Slavic languages became known as **Cyrillic**. All early Slavic literature was written in a form of this language known as **Church Slavonic.** (Most Slavic Christians, whether Eastern Orthodox or Catholic, still use this form of **Slavonic** in their religious services.) In later centuries, however, the Poles, Croatians, Slovenes, Slovaks, and Czechs adopted Latin letters in place of the Cyrillic. The Magyar (Hungarian) language is actually an Asiatic tongue similar to that spoken by the Mongols. (The Magyars were Asiatics who invaded and settled in Hungary in the tenth century.) The same is true of the Latvian, Estonian, Lithuanian, Finnish, Turkish, and Tartar languages. The Romanians speak a romance (Latin-based) language, the result of centuries of Roman domination. The ancient languages of Georgian and Armenian are very similar, using the same alphabet. The Albanian language is unique by claiming, like the people who speak it, descent from the Ancient Illyrians. The Gypsies speak their own language, known as Romany, as well as languages of the countries in which they reside. Romany has its origins in the ancient language of northern India. Ethnically, the Gypsies also have northern Indian origins.

Religion The majority of Eastern Europeans are Eastern (Greek) Orthodox Christians. The peoples of Bulgaria, Serbia, the Czech Republic, Romania, Belarus, Ukraine, Russia, and Georgia were Christianized by the Greek Orthodox Church and came under the cultural influence of the Byzantine Empire (the majority of Czechs later became Roman Catholics while under Austrian rule). Poland, Hungary, Slovakia, Croatia, Slovenia, Estonia, Latvia, and Lithuania were converted to Christianity by German Roman Catholic missionaries. In addition, there are groups of Uniates (Eastern Orthodox in practice, but under the authority of the pope). The majority of Estonians and Latvians, along with sizable groups of Czechs and Hungarians, later became Protestants. There have been small numbers of Muslims and Jews in Eastern Europe. Jewish communities have declined, however, due to the Holocaust (1933–1945). Muslim communities have increased in this century, because of immigration and a high birth rate.

Prehistoric Times

Prehistoric tool.

How can we learn about people who lived in Europe long before written records were kept? The term *prehistoric* is used to describe such people *and* the period in which they lived. The earliest evidence of writing dates back only to about 3500 B.C. For this reason scholars have found it necessary to study remains that are unwritten, such as unearthed bones, stones, and pottery to learn about prehistoric times.

The earliest known remains of human culture date from the *Paleolithic Period*, which ranges from about 2 million to 12,000 years ago. The Paleolithic Period, or Old Stone Age, was a time when the first tool-making took place. It was during the early part of this time period that early humans, prehistoric people who had limited powers of speech, began to cooperate with each other in the gathering of food. These early Paleolithic hunter-gatherers probably first made their home in trees. Then, as time passed and prehistoric people developed, they began to walk upright and became nomadic as the climatic conditions changed their environment.

Some scientists who study these traces of early human beings are called archaeologists. If you were an archaeologist you would look closely at artifacts, or objects that have survived, in order to study prehistory. Objects such as stone, tools, bones, and pottery help to tell us about the different types of prehistoric people and their cultures.

Other scientists, such as anthropologists, also study much of the same evidence left from the Paleolithic Period, or Old Stone Age. They try to determine the physical characteristics of prehistoric people and the ways that society was organized. Geologists study fossils and rock formations, which add to the picture and offer evidence of the then existing plant and animal life. This information helps describe the land that prehistoric people inhabited.

The study of prehistory is particularly exciting because new discoveries often help to clear up some of the mystery about the way early people lived and developed.

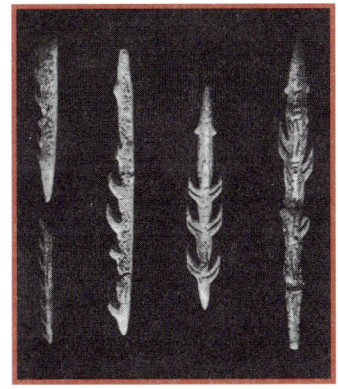

Fishing harpoon from Upper Paleolithic Period.

Arrowhead from Upper Paleolithic Period.

Prehistoric evidence is gathered at sites called archaeological digs, usually chosen because they are likely places to find human bones or artifacts.

Once a site is located and artifacts are found, it is necessary to analyze them. An important step is dating an object, or determining the date in time that the object was used. Dating processes include the carbon-14 method that is reliable for items up to 40,000 years old. Older objects going back to about one million years ago can be analyzed and dated by using other methods.

Despite all the efforts by archaeologists and other interpreters of prehistory, there are still many unanswered questions. Scientists must often speculate based on what they do know to fill in the missing pieces of human history. Interpretations may vary because the evidence found and analyzed in the twentieth century has led to a number of different conclusions by historians and scientists. New discoveries are raising further questions and increasing speculation about our **hominid** ancestors. Nevertheless, a clearer understanding of our prehistoric past in Europe and elsewhere is gradually evolving.

Prehistoric Peoples Enter Europe

The evolution of *Homo sapiens* or the human species is still imperfectly understood. The earliest known remains of our human ancestors have been found in Africa. The bones of a small apelike creature, Australopithecus, were discovered in East Africa, analyzed, and dated to about two million years ago. Australopithecus is classified as a hominid. Hominids are human beings and humanlike creatures that preceded them.

Australopithecus is not generally accepted by scientists as *homo*, a Latin word meaning man. Nevertheless, scientists believe that these remote ancestors of present-day people probably evolved into other hominids. Although some scientists are not absolutely certain if there is a direct relationship in this descent, most researchers believe that enough evidence has been found and analyzed to support this view.

The earliest of the Homo, or human, genus was *Homo habilis* who lived until about 1.5 million years ago. A later Homo in this genus was *Homo erectus*, or person who walks upright, who developed starting 1.4 million years ago. By 400,000 B.C., *Homo erectus*, who had a nomadic life-style, eventually migrated to Europe and parts of Asia. These early human beings adapted to their environment and developed what we call early human culture. They responded to the climatic changes of the Ice Age, a period starting about two million years ago, when huge ice sheets or glaciers spread over and covered large parts of Europe, North America, South America, and small parts of Asia. It was during these four long glacial periods that other more modern people evolved. The last Ice Age, called the Warm Glaciation in Europe, ended 10,000 years ago.

The Emergence of Neanderthal People

During the last glacial period, about 100,000 to 10,000 years ago, an early type of people, generally considered to be of the species *Homo sapiens*, evolved in Europe, North Africa, the Middle East, and Siberia. Fossils of these early people were first discovered in the mid-nineteenth century in the Neander Valley in Germany. Since then, many Neanderthal remains have been found throughout these regions. These human remains are often discovered with artifacts from the Mousterian culture of the Middle Paleolithic Period. This culture used a variety of stone tools that helped in hunting and in the processing of animals for their meat, skin, and bones.

Neanderthal people sometimes inhabited caves and are known to have used fire. They are the first people that we have evidence of who buried their dead. There is also a possibility that Neanderthals had religious ceremonies.

The Neanderthal people, like their ancestors, lived off the food that they could hunt and gather. They ate roots, berries, fish, birds, and larger mammals, such as deer. Moreover, in some caves excavation has shown that communal Neanderthal habitation definitely existed. Large stone fireplaces and enormous quantities of broken bones suggest that organized group activity took place and that food was shared.

Neanderthal people had extreme skeletal features. A large thick skull with heavy brow ridges, a sloping forehead, and a strong jaw characterized their physical appearance. Their brain size averaged 14,500 cc. (cubic centimeters), which is somewhat larger than that of modern people. Neanderthal men averaged over five feet tall and had muscular robust bodies. Women were smaller in stature as in other hominid species. *Homo neanderthalis* became extinct about 35,000 to 30,000 years ago. The exact causes of this disappearance are not known. There is no direct evidence that Neanderthals were exterminated by a more modern species, the Cro-Magnon, who first appeared in Europe about 35,000 years ago.

The Cro-Magnons Settle in Europe

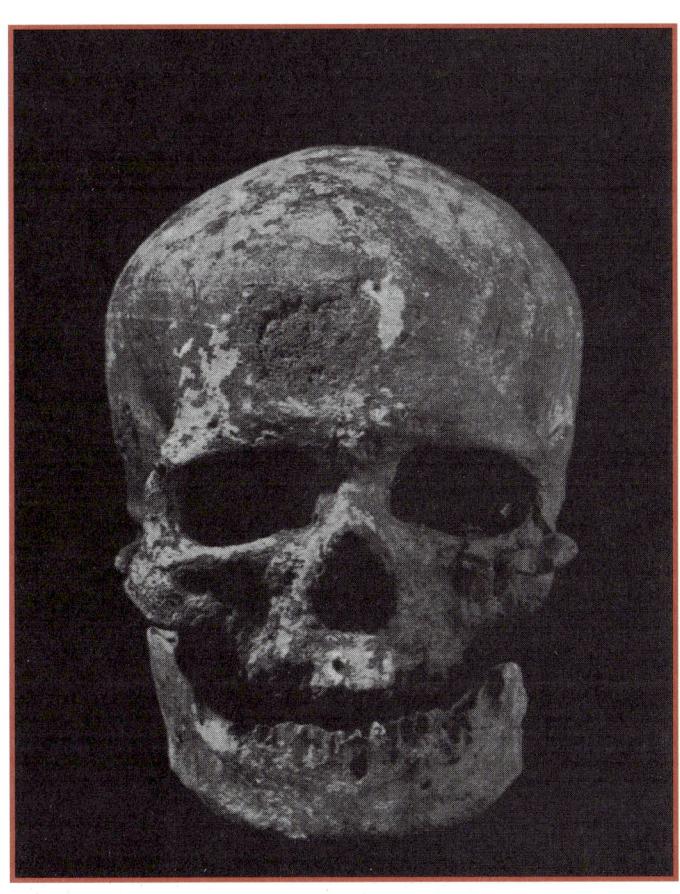

Skull of an old Cro-Magnon man found in Les Eyzies, France, in 1868.

The *Cro-Magnons* were a new group of *Homo sapiens* thought to have first evolved in southwest Asia and spread to other parts of the world. In Europe, the Cro-Magnons completely replaced the Neanderthals. Anthropologists think that the more culturally advanced Cro-Magnons are probably the ancestors of modern *Homo sapiens.*

The name Cro-Magnon comes from the skeletal remains that were found in 1868 in a rock shelter cave of that name. This cave is near the town of Les Eyzies in Dordogne in southwestern France. Later finds in other caverns of the Dordogne Valley, Spain, Germany, Czechoslovakia, and Poland, revealed that the Cro-Magnons had a more advanced culture than the Neanderthals, their predecessors in Europe.

The Cro-Magnons made many important advances in the technology of tool-making. Their use of the stone chisel and knife made it possible for them to work with materials such as bone. They made bone needles, which were used to make leather clothing. Bone fishhooks helped increase their food supply by enabling them to fish in the many rivers and lakes of prehistoric Europe.

Cro-Magnon people lived in complex social groupings that often involved the interaction of a number of different clans. They cooperated in big game hunts and in social gatherings that lasted for weeks. Leaders of Cro-Magnon bands assumed great importance, as can be seen from artifacts found in burials. Certain burial remains of probable Cro-Magnon leaders have artifacts that indicate status and wealth.

The Cro-Magnons are best known for their artistic talents. The Altamira cave in Spain and Lascaux cave in the Vezere Valley of southwestern France are decorated with wall paintings dating to about 16,000 years ago. Scenes of animals being chased in the hunt or just standing quietly are evidence that Cro-Magnon people were accomplished in the art of painting. The cave paintings are thought to be part of a religious event before the hunt in which the "spirit" of the animal is captured. They used natural materials for paint brushes and pigments that were used to depict animals. In Lascaux and elsewhere a large number of sculptures have been found representing animals and abstract objects. Some of these sculptures are the earliest representations of human beings. They are almost all of women with exaggerated sexual characteristics.

There is much speculation about the meaning of these paintings and sculptures. Whether they were meant to be educational, were purely artistic expressions, or had a deeper religious and spiritual significance cannot be definitely determined. Nevertheless, the vivid expressions of movement and elegance of line in this cave art indicate how far Cro-Magnon people had advanced by the time that the Paleolithic Period was coming to an end.

The Paleolithic Period Ends

The long Paleolithic Period was marked by the slow but gradual evolution of prehistoric man. The hominids grew larger. Their intelligence increased. They evolved into more skillful hunters and gatherers and were able to cope with the demands of a nomadic existence during the glacial periods. Paleolithic people learned to dominate and use fire and became increasingly skillful toolmakers.

These predecessors of modern people learned to live together in small groups. Eventually they mastered the ability to cooperate in larger tribal undertakings. Language also evolved, making social development and organization easier. It even became possible for Paleolithic culture to provide for peoples' artistic and spiritual needs.

From 12,000 B.C. to 8000 B.C., there was a significant increase in population. This growth was related to the addition of new food resources. As the Paleolithic Period drew to a close, hunting and gathering began to be gradually replaced by agriculture as the major source of food supply in some regions. This transition period is referred to as the Mesolithic or Middle Stone Age.

The Neolithic Revolution

The term *Neolithic*, or New Stone Age, is used to describe the period of prehistory when people in different parts of the world began to gradually give up hunting and gathering. They started to live in more permanent settlements and began to farm. The Neolithic Period, which lasted from about 8000 BC to 3500 B.C., was a time of cultural evolution and technological development. During the Neolithic Period and immediately thereafter, humans made many of their greatest cultural advances. The development of new agricultural methods led to tremendous changes in life-styles as the Neolithic Period progressed.

The gradual change to an economy based on farming became possible because of the development of new stone tools. For example, hoes to turn over soil were fashioned out of granite, a hard stone that could be sharpened. Sickles were developed to cut the grain crops of wheat, barley, and millet. Pottery shaped on stone wheels made it possible to use hardened clay to store and carry food and water.

The wild plants that Neolithic people domesticated varied depending on the region's climate and the varieties that were available and suitable for the farming of crops. The Agricultural Revolution, which resulted in the domestication of wild plants to crops, meant that farming could be depended upon to feed a larger and more stable population. In Europe and the Middle East, wheat, barley, and millet were domesticated and increasingly became the staples of more permanent communities.

Neolithic people also supplemented their diet by domesticating animals. The food-producing peoples in the New Stone Age raised cattle, sheep, goats, and pigs to add meat and milk products to their diet. They also used the domesticated dog to help them hunt different types of game.

It is generally thought that the Agricultural Revolution and the domestication of animals such as sheep, pigs, and goats began in Asia and the Middle East. The spread of farming techniques and other innovations came about as a result of a gradual cultural diffusion. These cultural and technological developments began during the Mesolithic Era, a time that was the forerunner to the Neolithic Period. The shift to agriculture and more permanent settlements led to a new way of life wherever the more advanced technology and other ideas spread. One result of the increased food supply and more stable communities was an increase in population in parts of Asia, the Middle East, North Africa, and eventually Europe.

The growth of world population to an estimated 90 million people took place mostly in areas where river valleys could be settled. Technological change led to the development of the wheel and its use for transportation. The loom was invented and used for the weaving of textiles and linen. Neolithic people found out how to bake clay bricks that they used in construction. Metals such as copper, lead, and gold were hammered to fashion weapons and jewelry.

The development of more organized communities that depended on the farming of seasonal crops resulted in the establishment of boundary lines, which were defended against intruding peoples. Warfare probably increased over water rights and land use and inheritance. Neolithic people created calendars to measure time, record great events such as victories over enemies, and determine when to plant crops.

Neolithic Culture in Europe

Neolithic culture spread through Europe from about 6000 B.C. to 2000 B.C. The development of European Neolithic cultures resulted from the combining of innovations learned from Middle East sources and local cultural advances. In Europe, particularly in the western regions, the Neolithic or New Stone Age Period continued after 3500 B.C., when other geographical areas, such as the Tigris-Euphrates River Valley in the Fertile Crescent had already begun to develop what historians call the earliest civilizations.

Civilization developed later in Europe than in other world areas. In agriculture, people eventually learned how to cultivate cereals such as wheat and barley. They also adopted the herding of wild pigs, sheep, and goats. The domestication of animals to be used as food sources was not native to Europe. This is also true of agricultural crops like wheat and barley. During the millenniums of the Neolithic

Period there was a gradual cultural diffusion that brought the new changes in the food supply to the far reaches of Western Europe.

In Europe, climatic conditions have destroyed most of the evidence that archaeologists and anthropologists use to determine the developments and cultural changes that took place during the Neolithic Period. Nevertheless, significant surviving artifacts have been found and analyzed. It is generally believed that the peoples living in Europe went through changes in their way of life similar to those of peoples elsewhere.

Remains found at the bottom of European lakes, most notably in Switzerland, indicate the existence of villages built around and over the water. The remains show that the Neolithic peoples in these regions knew how to make pottery, baskets, and wooden furniture. They were skilled at making cloth and linen. Seeds discovered prove that their diet included cereals in addition to foods obtained through hunting, fishing, and gathering.

In northern Europe, archaeologists have found evidence that dogs were among the first animals to be domesticated. The dogs, who helped guard herds and warn the settlement if strangers or wild animals approached, became widespread in Europe.

Neolithic peoples believed in many deities. They worshipped the natural phenomena that surrounded them and transformed nature into gods and goddesses who possessed powers that affected human existence. The Earth Mother, or goddess of fertility, was one of the most worshipped deities during the Neolithic Period. This reverence was probably because the Agricultural Revolution brought an increasing dependency on the crops. Another reason for the worship of the Earth Mother was that she symbolized human fertility and conception. Birth was a miraculous event to the Neolithic peoples. The cycle of the seasons, the creatures of the animal kingdom, and the plant world were also of religious concern to Neolithic people.

Summary

The earlier development of more advanced civilizations in the Middle East and Asia was a result of many factors. Geography and climate played crucial roles. Cultural advances were possible if natural resources could be better used. The discovery of metal and the ability to shape this valuable resource into useful tools and weapons first took place outside of Europe. The Bronze Age was characterized by the use of a technology that combined an alloy of copper and tin to manufacture bronze implements. This technological achievement probably came first in the early civilizations of the Middle East region.

Cultural diffusion led some eastern Mediterranean peoples to shift slowly to a culture that relied more on metals. Some of these cultures, such as the Minoan and Mycenaean civilizations, had trade routes that penetrated into central Europe. They traded for the tin and copper that their people needed. These early civilizations in the eastern Mediterranean region helped spread new ideas and innovations into Europe.

Cultural advances that diffused to Neolithic European peoples led to the gradual development of European civilization. This growth was a natural result of the spread of ideas, discoveries, and innovations among prehistoric peoples.

During the Neolithic Period the first steps took place that led to great changes in the nature of human existence. As time passed, more peoples were affected by these changes. More highly organized societies developed in different world regions. Although this first happened outside of geographical Europe, the knowledge of farming, trade, government, science, and art eventually spread to Europe through cultural diffusion and became the building blocks in the development of European civilization.

Review Exercises

Physical Geography—Western Europe

I. Multiple Choice

Directions: Find the *letter* of the correct answer.

1. Which of the following countries are in northwestern Europe?

   (a) Portugal
   (b) France
   (c) Italy
   (d) Austria

2. Norway and Sweden are in a region known as

   (a) central Europe
   (b) the Iberian peninsula
   (c) the lowlands
   (d) Scandinavia

3. In recent years, the area that has been developed as a source of oil is the

   (a) North Sea
   (b) Baltic Sea
   (c) Mediterranean Sea
   (d) Atlantic Ocean

II. Thought Question

Directions: Answer the following question in essay form.

Geography has affected the lives of people in Western Europe. Explain two ways in which each of the following has affected life in Western Europe.

1. Bodies of water
2. Mountains

Physical Geography—Eastern Europe

I. Multiple Choice

Directions: Find the *letter* of the correct answer.

1. The C.I.S. is physically

    (a) twice the size of the United States.
    (b) more than two and a half times the size of the United States.
    (c) half the size of the United States.
    (d) larger than Europe, but less than the United States.

2. The most fertile region of Russia that has attracted both farmers and nomadic tribes is the

    (a) taiga.
    (b) tundra.
    (c) steppe.
    (d) plain.

3. Covered with permafrost and uninhabitable, Russia's northern rim is

    (a) taiga.
    (b) tundra.
    (c) steppe.
    (d) plain.

4. All of the following are important European rivers *except* the

    (a) Danube.
    (b) Don.
    (c) Vistula.
    (d) Bug.

5. Which is *not* true of Eastern Europe?

    (a) It consists of nations located between Western Europe and the C.I.S.
    (b) There is a diverse mixture of peoples.
    (c) It contains approximately 126 million people.
    (d) There is a unity of religious belief.

II. Thought Question

Directions: Answer the following question in essay form.

The physical geography of Eastern Europe has greatly influenced the lives of its people. Show how this is true by writing about the role of

1. rivers in the area's economic development
2. topography in the physical development of the area
3. geography in making the area interdependent

Economic Geography—Western Europe

I. Multiple Choice

Directions: Find the *letter* of the correct answer.

1. Which nation has the highest Gross National Product (GNP) in Western Europe?

    (a) France
    (b) England
    (c) Holland
    (d) Germany

2. The Marshall Plan provided aid that was

    (a) cultural.
    (b) military.
    (c) financial.
    (d) agricultural.

3. The person most responsible for the growth of the European Common Market was

    (a) Karl Marx.
    (b) Robert Schuman.
    (c) Friedrich Engels.
    (d) George Marshall.

II. Thought Question

Directions: Answer the following question in essay form.

Show one way in which each of the following has affected or will affect economic activity in Western Europe:

1. the European Union
2. social welfare programs
3. the Marshall Plan
4. capitalism

Economic Geography—Eastern Europe

I. Multiple Choice

Directions: Find the *letter* of the correct answer.

1. Called the "Breadbasket of Russia," the greatest agricultural output of the C.I.S. comes from

   (a) Belarus.
   (b) Georgia.
   (c) Siberia.
   (d) Ukraine.

2. The Guns vs. Butter controversy is a disagreement over

   (a) the quality of arms and food production.
   (b) whether or not to nationalize heavy and light industries.
   (c) whether or not to decentralize industry.
   (d) the amount of the GNP spent on arms as opposed to consumer goods.

3. The former Soviet government's policy of forcing farmers to work on state farms was known as

   (a) collectivization.
   (b) cooperatives.
   (c) Russification.
   (d) Perestroika.

4. The Eastern European nations, outside of the C.I.S., that provide the largest agricultural output are

   (a) Yugoslavia, Bulgaria, Romania.
   (b) Poland, Romania, Yugoslavia.
   (c) Bulgaria, Hungary, Czech Republic.
   (d) Albania, Bulgaria, Yugoslavia.

5. The most industrialized Eastern European nation is

   (a) Czech Republic.
   (b) Hungary.
   (c) Poland.
   (d) Romania.

II. Thought Question

Directions: Answer the following question in essay form.

Economic development was a continuous problem for the Communist governments in the USSR and Eastern Europe.

1. What economic problems did they face while they were in power?
2. How did the economic principles they followed help to create these problems?
3. Has the collapse of the Communist system helped to resolve them?

Human and Cultural Geography—Western Europe

I. Multiple Choice

Directions: Find the *letter* of the correct answer.

1. Which nation has the largest population in Western Europe?

    (a) France
    (b) Ireland
    (c) Germany
    (d) Italy

2. In which pair of nations is Catholicism the predominant religion?

    (a) England and Italy
    (b) France and Denmark
    (c) Spain and Portugal
    (d) Sweden and Holland

3. Which pair of nations' people speak romance languages?

    (a) Italy and Spain
    (b) England and Germany
    (c) France and Holland
    (d) Norway and Austria

4. A nation that is officially bilingual is

    (a) Finland.
    (b) Belgium.
    (c) Sweden.
    (d) Austria.

II. Thought Question

Directions: Answer the following questions in essay form.

Overpopulation and high population growth rates are *not* considered to be major problems in Western Europe. Discuss two reasons for this situation.

Human and Cultural Geography—Eastern Europe

I. Multiple Choice

Directions: Find the *letter* of the correct answer.

1. The largest ethnic group in the C.I.S. is the

   (a) Kazakh.
   (b) Georgian.
   (c) Slav.
   (d) Armenian.

2. Most of the population of the C.I.S. lives in

   (a) Central Asia.
   (b) European Russia.
   (c) Siberia.
   (d) the Far East.

3. The largest and most dominant ethnic group in Eastern Europe is the

   (a) Romanian.
   (b) Slavic.
   (c) Magyar.
   (d) Albanian.

4. The Eastern European nation composed of many smaller nations that were formerly and are again becoming independent is

   (a) Romania.
   (b) Hungary.
   (c) Bulgaria.
   (d) Yugoslavia.

5. The religion of the majority of Eastern Europeans is

   (a) Eastern Orthodox Christianity.
   (b) Roman Catholicism.
   (c) Protestantism.
   (d) Islam.

II. Thought Question

Directions: Answer the following question in essay form.

Religion has always been an important part of the culture of Eastern Europe. Show how this is true by

1. discussing the role of religion in the development of two nations in Eastern Europe or the C.I.S.
2. examining how it shaped the culture of the region
3. explaining how religion acted as a factor for disunity

Prehistoric Times

I. Multiple Choice

Directions: Find the *letter* of the correct answer.

1. Archaeologists study artifacts such as tools, bones, and pottery because

   (a) prehistoric writing dates only from 100,000 B.C.
   (b) these objects are records of prehistoric times.
   (c) Paleolithic writing is too complicated to translate.
   (d) prehistoric people put dates on their artifacts.

2. The earliest known remains of human culture date from the

   (a) Paleolithic Period.
   (b) Neolithic Period.
   (c) New Stone Age.
   (d) Mesolithic Era.

3. All of the following are considered by scientists as *Homo* or human genus *except*

   (a) Neanderthal.
   (b) Cro-Magnon.
   (c) Australopithecus.
   (d) *Homo erectus.*

4. Cro-Magnon remains have been found in

   (a) France, Spain, and Germany.
   (b) France, the United States, and Switzerland.
   (c) Poland, Argentina, and France.
   (d) Spain, France, and Australia.

5. Cro-Magnon people

   (a) are not related to present day *Homo sapiens.*
   (b) did not make use of their artistic talents.
   (c) painted cave walls with pictures of animals.
   (d) lived in simple social groupings of nuclear families.

6. The Neolithic Period was a time

   (a) of gradual change to a hunting and gathering economy.
   (b) that occurred prior to the development of agriculture.
   (c) before the domestication of cattle and sheep.
   (d) when prehistoric people developed polished stone tools.

7. Neolithic culture in Europe

   (a) was never influenced by cultural diffusion.
   (b) can be traced in part to the region of the Middle East.
   (c) did not make any advances in farming.
   (d) developed earlier than in other continents.

8. Neolithic people were capable of all of the following *except*

  (a) making pottery and baskets.
  (b) domesticating dogs to help guard herding animals.
  (c) building villages around and above water.
  (d) producing weapons and farm tools made of iron.

9. During the Neolithic Period a common religious belief was that

  (a) a god was to be worshipped only by women.
  (b) a weapon was a symbol of human fertility and conception.
  (c) gods were endowed with powers that affected human existence.
  (d) a tree was to be worshipped by men who wanted a wife.

10. The Bronze Age was characterized by the use of a metal alloy made of

  (a) copper and lead.
  (b) tin and iron.
  (c) copper and tin.
  (d) iron and lead.

II. Matching

Directions: Match the words in Column A with the *correct description* in Column B.

Column A
  1. Australopithecus
  2. *Homo erectus*
  3. *Homo sapiens*
  4. *Homo habilis*
  5. Cro-Magnon
  6. archaeologist
  7. anthropologist
  8. geologist
  9. historian
  10. sociologist

Column B
  (a) name given to present human beings
  (b) first appeared in Europe about 400,000 years ago
  (c) closest ancestor to modern people
  (d) earliest of the Homo, or human, genus
  (e) prehuman hominid
  (f) studies rock formations, fossils, and earth stratification
  (g) studies how individuals function in society
  (h) studies written records to learn the past
  (i) studies physical features, development, and human behavior
  (j) studies prehistoric life by examining artifacts

III. Thought Questions

Directions: Answer the following questions in essay form.

1. We have learned much about prehistoric man due to the work of anthropologists.

  A. State three reasons for prehistoric study.
  B. List three problems that exist in studying the development of hominids.

2. Describe the life-style of Neanderthals.

3. In discussing the Neolithic Period,

   A. explain why it is called a period of "revolution."
   B. explain two reasons why the people may have worshipped the Earth Mother or goddess of fertility.
   C. explain two ways that cultural diffusion affected European development during the period.

Unit I

THE ANCIENT WORLD

Civilization advanced to the Western World in the ninth century. From the river valley civilizations of the Middle East there was a progression across the Mediterranean Sea, first to Greece and then to what is now Italy.

The Greeks were much occupied by war as they were constantly fighting with each other due to the nature of their geographic development. The Greeks invaded Persia and in turn the Persians invaded Greece because of the importance of the peninsula. Despite these constant wars there were advances in politics, with laws being developed. The first steps in the continuing development of democracy took place in Greece. Culturally we owe a tremendous debt to these people. The names of their artists, architects, and playwrights are still famous. The scientific and mathematical advances they uncovered help us better understand our universe today.

The teachings of Socrates, Plato, and Aristotle were discussed by philosophers throughout the Ancient World. Strange to think that Aristotle tutored a young lad destined to become Alexander the Great—conqueror of much of the world.

The Roman Empire began as a minor trading post on the Tiber River during the Estruscan Period and grew to control much of Europe, the Middle East, and North Africa. Going through several stages of development, Rome became a republic and a monarchy.

The Romans were not as innovative as the Greeks. They were more developers and refiners and improvers of what already existed. Their advances in law and political organization remain with us today, however. Our form of government— a republic—can be traced to Rome nearly 2,500 years ago. Architecturally, the Romans built wherever they went. Some of our buildings and monuments in Washington, D.C., are striking copies of Roman structures. Some of our sports arenas are modeled on the colosseums in Rome and Verona. That Romans were the transmitters of Greek innovation can also be seen in their writing, philosophy, and science. It was during the period of Constantine's rule that Christianity became an accepted religion.

So this "Ancient World" is not so ancient if we really think about it. You are involved with it when you use $a^2 + b^2 = c^2$ in math, read Homer in English, and *look at pictures of Greek and Roman sculpture in art. The entrances to your school and to many public buildings, such as post offices, libraries, and court-houses, may have large, Greek-styled columns. The Roman word for laws, "lex," is seen with figures representing justice in courtrooms and courthouses. All around us, therefore, are reminders of the Ancient World's contributions.*

CHAPTER 1

The Ancient Greeks

The Ancient Hellenes (Ninth Century B.C.)

Our study of European history must begin with the Ancient Greeks. Indeed, Greece is known as the "Cradle of Western Civilization." Its inhabitants shaped the development of both Europe and the Mediterranean World. The Ancient Greeks or Hellenes (**Hellas** is the Greek term for Greece) created a unique civilization in the southeastern part of the Mediterranean beginning in the ninth century B.C. Many Greek ideas and institutions were so radically different from those of previous civilizations in the Mediterranean and Middle East that Greece is regarded as the foundation of the Western World. Key concepts and attitudes that came to shape Western society (both European and American) were created in Ancient Hellas.

Hominocentrism

The Greeks changed the way human beings looked at both themselves and the world. A new concept, **hominocentrism**, saw human beings at the center of the universe. To the Hellenes, their gods were superhuman, stronger and greater versions of themselves. The Ancient Greek gods also shared human failings and could become jealous or angry. They often became involved in romance or disputes with human beings.

Geography

Geography greatly influenced the development of Greek culture. The rugged mountainous terrain made Greece unlike other early civilizations in that it did not develop in a river valley. The scarcity of natural resources forced the Greeks to be creative and to overcome nature rather than see themselves as a harmonious part of it. As Hellas was not fertile enough to support a large population, its people were forced to turn to the sea in order to find alternative sources of food. This led to the development of Greek sea power and trade with other peoples. The Greeks became skilled merchants as well as expert sailors. The irregular coastline made for excellent harbors. Greece's proximity to Crete and areas inhabited by the Egyptians (northeast Africa), Hittites (eastern Asia Minor), and Phoenicians (northwest Africa) led to cultural diffusion and economic interdependence. The mountainous topography of the land made farming very difficult. This forced the Greeks to become shepherds and raise livestock. The various obstacles nature placed on the Greeks actually helped them to develop skills and interests that eventually made them both powerful and resourceful.

The rugged nature of the land had an effect on the psychology of the Greek people. They developed a strong sense of individualism, which had both positive and negative results. While this emphasis on the individual made the Hellenes imaginative, daring, and constantly striving for improvement, it also led to disunity and civil wars. These contrasts within the people of Hellas were responsible for both their greatest achievements and their eventual downfall. Greek creations, such as democracy, the Olympics, and philosophy, coexisted with constant fighting between Greek cities and the ancient evil of slavery.

The challenge of everyday living made the Ancient Greeks both creative and strong. An emphasis on developing both the physical and mental side of the individual ("A sound mind in a sound body") and achieving a balance ("Everything in moderation" or "The middle is the best") were seen as the chief goals of each per-

Chapter 1 Chronology

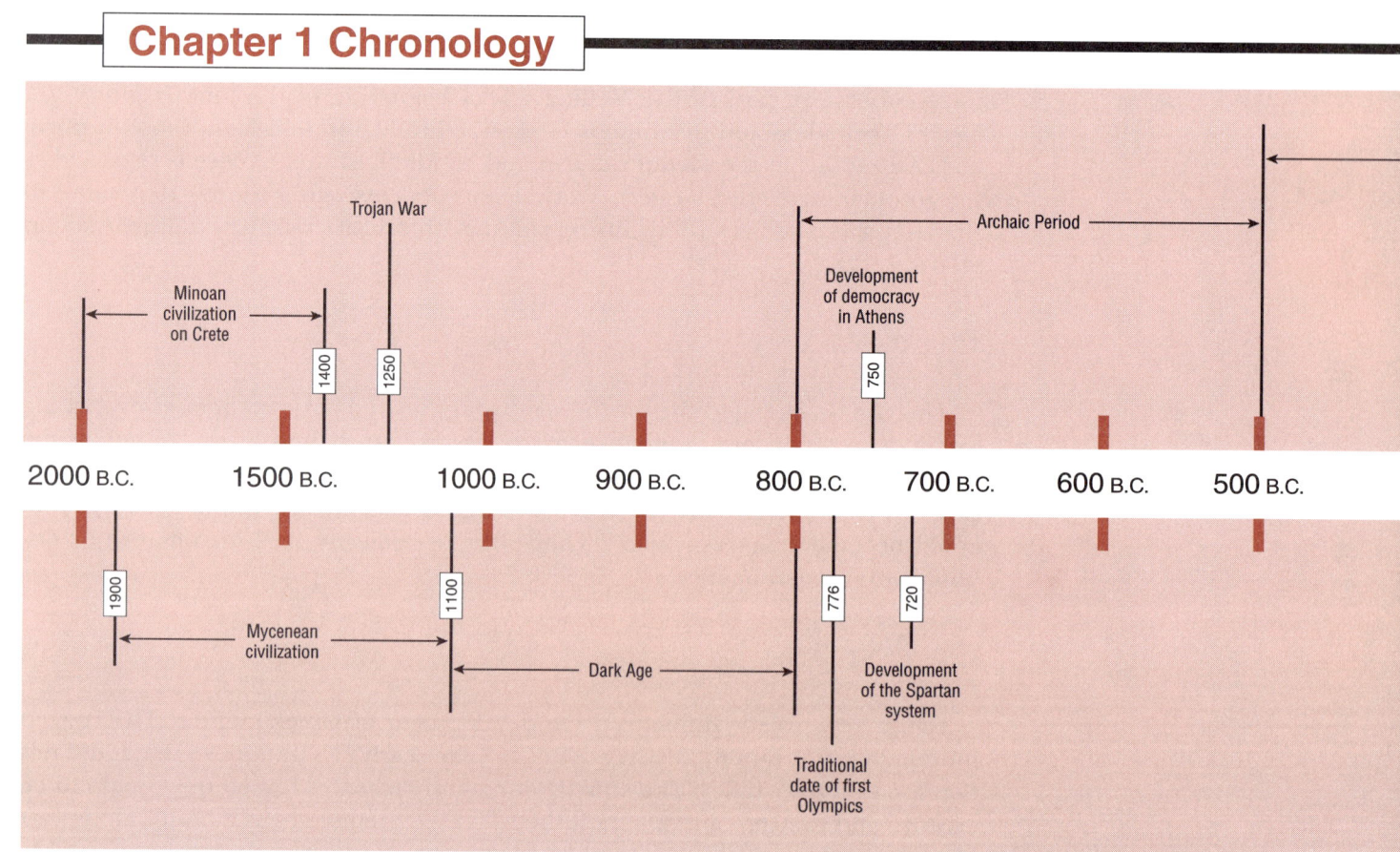

son. The scarcity of luxuries also helped to toughen the Hellenes and make them fully utilize the little they possessed.

The highly competitive nature of the Greeks led to a constant struggle for self-improvement. This made them powerful soldiers in war and aggressive merchants in peace. The Greek determination to achieve all-around excellence raised the level of their civilization and made their many outstanding achievements possible.

The Greek Nation

While the Greeks saw themselves as one "ethnos," or people, they identified with their city rather than a nation. They developed city-states that existed as if they were different countries. The rugged mountainous geography of Greece also contributed to this. The modern concept of nationhood and nationality did not exist in Ancient Hellas. A sense of identity through a common culture, language, and religion could unite the Greeks in times of great crisis. Generally however, they spent more time fighting each other than any foreign enemy. Yet, the Greeks were aware of their achievements and took great pride in them. They referred to all non-Greek peoples as "barbaroi" or "barbarians," seeing their culture as superior to any outside of Hellas. In fact, the term "barbaros" or "barbarian" came from the Greek practice of making fun of the way other languages were spoken and comparing them with the sounds sheep and goats made. Despite the constant

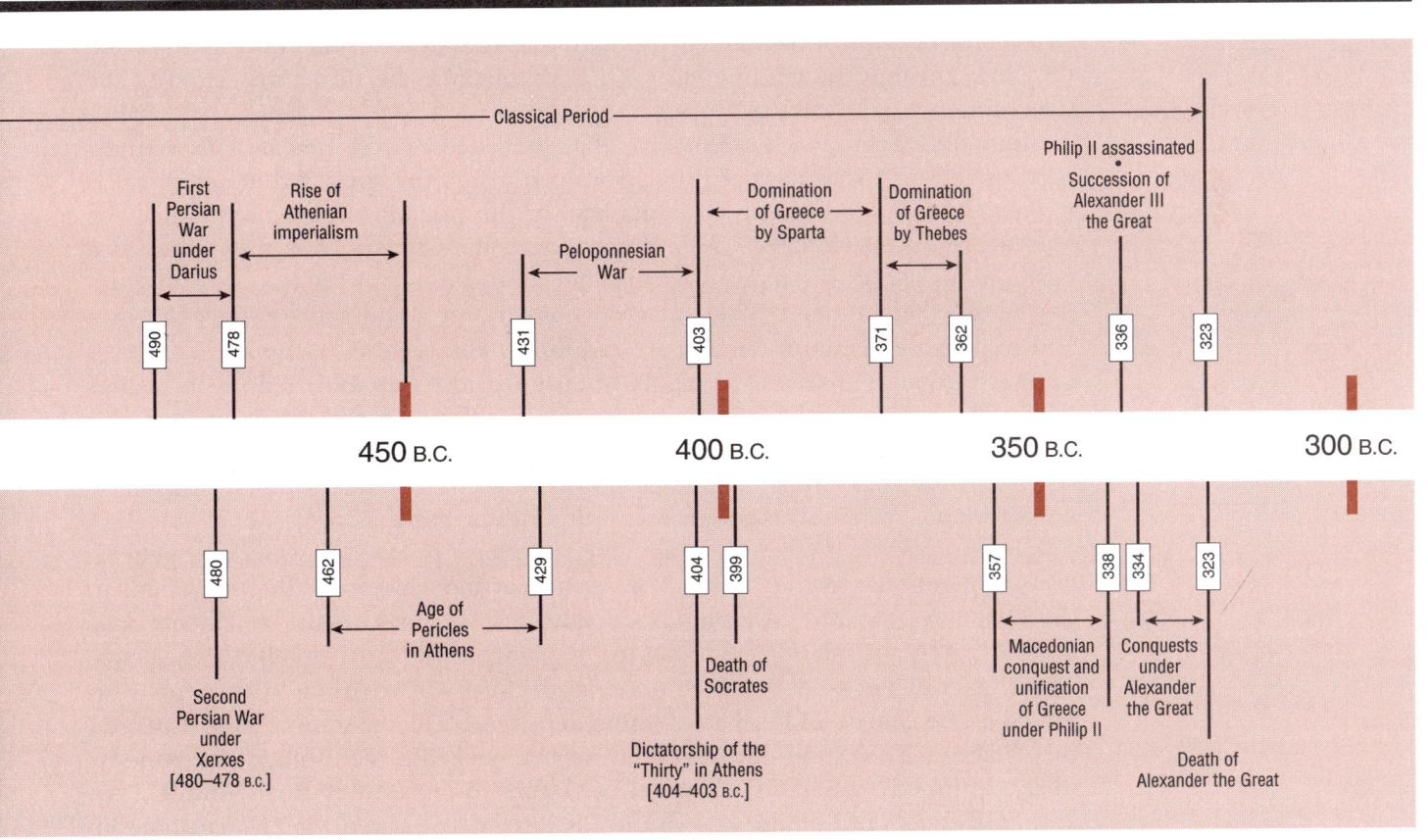

internal warfare, the Greeks did not consider anyone outside of their nation to be civilized.

The definition of exactly who was a Hellene kept changing throughout Ancient Greek history. While the term itself originally referred only to the inhabitants of the southern and central parts of the Greek peninsula, it came to include those of the Greek islands, the western coast of Asia Minor, and northern Greece (Macedonia). As Greek power and influence spread, through colonization by Athens and conquest under the Macedonians, the term eventually came to mean anyone who spoke Greek and adopted Hellenic culture.

Minoan Civilization (2000–1400 B.C.)

The term "Minoan" refers to the unique civilization that flourished on the island of Crete from 2000–1400 B.C. It is named after the mythical Greek ruler of the island. He was punished for refusing to make his promised sacrifice to the gods by having his wife give birth to the Minotaur (a monster that was half-human, half-bull). The name "Minoan" was given to this civilization by Sir Arthur Evans, the British archaeologist who discovered the first Minoan ruins on Crete at the beginning of the twentieth century. He based the name on the art he found, which seemed to suggest the King Minos myth. In fact, the Minoans had been lost to human memory since 1400 B.C., when their civilization was destroyed. Although they may have been the source of the myth of the "lost city" of Atlantis, later Greek civilization was completely unaware that the Minoans had ever existed. Yet, they had an important influence on the Myceneans, the direct ancestors of the Greeks.

Minoan civilization was unlike any that preceded or followed it. The richness and fertility of Crete at that time produced a wealthy society that worshipped nature and indulged heavily in **hedonism**, or the pursuit of pleasure. Unlike the Myceneans and their later Greek descendants, the Minoans saw themselves as a harmonious part of the natural world. They prayed to fertility goddesses and glorified natural phenomena. Their magnificent art and architecture reflect this love and respect for the natural world around them. The religion of the Minoans gives further evidence of this in the bare-breasted priestesses and hedonistic scenes depicted in paintings of religious ceremonies. Although excellent seamen who developed extensive trade and commerce, the Minoans do not seem to have been very aggressive or war-like. They influenced the cultural development on neighboring islands, probably through trade rather than aggression.

Minoan Crete had a central government under a priest-king, who later generations remembered as the "Minos," (a term that may have been the equivalent to the Egyptian pharaoh). A complex **bureaucracy**, or government run by officials, administrated the island from a series of palaces, the most notable at Knossos. These magnificent palaces, which were known for their luxurious apartments, also served as the centers of local production and trade. The most impressive aspect of this "Palace Civilization" however, is their remarkable technology. Apartments were equipped with running water and the equivalent of flush toilets. An advanced system of writing, known only as Linear A, allowed the Minoan bureaucracy to keep records and administer Crete.

As the Minoans developed trade relations with the Greek mainland, they came to influence the Myceneans. While the two civilizations were almost complete opposites culturally, Mycenean and Minoan art show signs of cultural diffusion. This relationship ended however, when the Myceneans invaded Crete (c. 1450 B.C.). After a brief period of Mycenean domination (c. 1450–1400 B.C.) Minoan civilization disappeared.

Mycenean Civilization (1900–1100 B.C.)

The most direct ancestors of the Ancient Hellenes appeared on the Greek peninsula and Asia Minor during the Bronze Age (around 1900 B.C.). Speaking an Indo-European language, which made them the first true "Greeks" to settle in the area, the Myceneans were given their name by the German archaeologist Heinrich Schleimann, who discovered the ruins of their world in the late nineteenth century.

Mycenean Greece was a collection of independent city-kingdoms governed by local rulers. Unlike Minoan Crete with its central government, in Greece each warrior-king administrated his own district and often fought with his neighbors. It was this disunity that led to a civil war among the Mycenean city-kingdoms from 1200 to 1100 B.C., which resulted in the fatal decline of that civilization. The legendary attack on the city of Troy (in Western Asia Minor), which was later immortalized in Homer's epic the *Iliad*, probably took place around 1250 B.C. and marked the beginning of this decline.

The Myceneans developed a strong, flourishing economy based on a combination of "trading and raiding" (commercial relations backed up by force and aggression). They became expert sailors and built strong navies capable of conducting trade and war with equal effectiveness. As trade increased, their art and craft work showed the influence of other civilizations, particularly that of the Minoans.

Unlike any other civilizations of the time, the Myceneans worshipped male sky gods. Their religion is clearly the forerunner of the later Greek hominocentric concept of the gods. It was suited to the feudal warrior society that the Myceneans had developed.

The Mycenean warlords were supported by a palace bureaucracy of scribes who kept records, wrote treaties, and sent messages. Their writing is known as Linear B. Its characters are borrowed from the Minoan Linear A, which has thus far remained a mystery to scholars. Linear B was only diciphered in 1956 by the Greek scholar Michael Ventris, who found it was an early form of Greek. His work proved that the Myceneans were truly the direct ancestors of the Ancient Greeks.

Mycenean culture and power reached its peak around 1300 B.C. The cultural diffusion that resulted from trade contacts with the Hittite Empire and Egypt started to deteriorate around 1250 B.C. The Fall of Troy, which took place about that time, was probably brought about by an economic crisis that seized the entire area. The loss of Minoan Crete as a trading partner, combined with droughts and overpopulation, had probably created the conditions that led to this crisis. The sacking of Troy and records of attacks on both the Hittites and Egyptians are further evidence that this economic depression led to pirating on the part of the Myceneans. By 1200 B.C., wars between Mycenean city-kingdoms had broken out

Heinrich Schliemann

For centuries the story of Troy had excited peoples' imaginations. The abduction of Helen leading to the Greek invasion and attack of the city, the long war, Achilles and Hector in combat, and the account of the Trojan Horse had long been told in story. The Homeric poem, the *Iliad*, was long thought to be a fanciful tale. But not to Heinrich Schliemann, who would use Homer as his guide to uncovering the past.

Young Heinrich (b. 1822) was the son of a poor pastor in what is today Germany. He was put to work at fourteen in a grocery store where he worked long hours. At nineteen he moved to Hamburg and then on to Amsterdam. His quick mind gained him a reputation as a broker and he moved into wider commercial circles. Heinrich also discovered that he had a talent for languages. He would later be able to claim that he was fluent in fifteen different ones.

Schliemann now began making big money and this took him to different parts of the world. In Russia he made more money by trading in indigo. A trip to the American West in 1850 to work for one of his brothers during the gold rush period made him an American citizen when California became a state. Eight years later he sailed up the Nile River to the second cataract, or waterfall. A huge profit from the tea and cotton business allowed him to retire and to set off on his boyhood dream—the unearthing of Troy.

With Homer's *Iliad* in his pocket he prepared himself in Paris by studying the little that was then known about archaeology. While the intellectuals of the day were making fun of him behind his back, he continued to learn what he could from them. Finally he believed he was ready and he set off, in 1869, for the Anatolian Plateau in Turkey. In the spring, Schliemann paced off distances as they were written in the *Iliad* and proclaimed that the Tell of Hissarlik was indeed the site of Ancient Troy.

On and off for the next three years more than 100 men worked to uncover what Schliemann was sure they would find. Many scholars, believing that Homer was only a collection of myths, scoffed at this grocer's attempts. They said that his use of Homer was foolish and he would find nothing. They sat in their easy chairs while Heinrich's fortune was being used in the interests of Classical archaeology. Schliemann's self-confidence was rewarded when the ancient city of Troy was uncovered. Not only was one Troy uncovered, but a number of them were—one on top of the other. Now all the world, including the previous scoffers, hailed his discovery. Today there is a difference of opinion on which level is Homer's Troy, but there is no doubt that it is here and that Troy did exist!

Heinrich Schliemann died on Christmas Day in 1890. It was his imagination that fired an interest in greater archaeological work. Now archaeologists began to look at myths as possible sources of clues to the past. We owe much of what has been discovered to the dreams of a youth that were fulfilled.

and most were either destroyed or declined into obscurity. As these cities disappeared, so did the fundamental patterns of Mycenean culture and society. A wave of northern invaders called the Dorians, possibly led by exiled Mycenean warlords, moved into the Greek peninsula. The Mycenean World came to an end, and with it, the first chapter of Ancient Greek history.

The Dark Age (1100–800 B.C.)

Following the fall of Mycenean civilization, a time of poverty and backwardness took place in the Aegean World. This period (1100–800 B.C.) is known as the Dark Age. With the disappearance of the city-kingdoms and their palace bureaucracies, literacy and art vanished as well. Technical skills declined, and trade was replaced by subsistence farming (producing only enough to survive). A decrease in population, despite the added people brought by Dorian invasions, led to an abandonment of the remaining Mycenean settlements and a return to a more primitive existence. Small farming communities became the basic units of Dark Age Greek society, but many fundamental skills were carried over from the Mycenean World. The lack of traditional leadership allowed the Greeks to reorganize their society in new and different ways.

During the Dark Age, the Ancient Greek World was shaped. The mixture of peoples due to migration formed the ethnic, cultural, and linguistic characteristics that would result in the brilliant Hellenic civilization. As these peoples developed common traits, they expanded into the Aegean islands and Asia Minor. In this way the future foundation of Ancient Greek civilization was established.

The Archaic Period (800–500 B.C.)

The Greek Miracle

By 800 B.C., the various peoples who had mixed together during the Dark Age shared a common language, culture, and religion. This development became known as the "Greek Miracle." A new and revolutionary writing system was created. Using Phoenician letters, the Greek alphabet was based on sound value, like our English alphabet, and allowed greater expression in writing than ever before. Art reflected the creativity of the new culture being formed. Pottery with geometric designs and the gradual reappearance of luxury items signaled the revival of a more sophisticated society. This was further witnessed by the adoption of Iron Age technology.

The Development of Democracy

As the Dark Age progressed, the small farming communities developed into petty tribal kingdoms. Unlike the feudal warrior kings of the Mycenean Period, chieftains were limited in power by their nobles. The ruler met with his nobility to discuss problems and make decisions. Peasants and artisans often voiced opinions in tribal assemblies as well. This development of **oligarchies**, or small elite ruling groups, as opposed to strong monarchies sowed the seeds of Ancient Greek **democracy**.

The Development of the Polis

As the Dark Age came to a close, the tribal groups grew into larger communities. While sharing a common ethnic identity that would be known as Hellenic or Greek by 800 B.C., local tribes maintained rivalries that prevented the creation of a unified Greek nation. These communities would form a new unit, the **polis** or city-state, which would be the basis of Greek life. This concept would later expand through the Greek-speaking World (in the Hellenistic Period), the Roman World, the Byzantine Empire, and the Christian Church in the Middle Ages.

Archaic Greece

The development of poleis (plural of polis) throughout Ancient Greece marked the beginning of the Archaic Period (800–500 B.C.). While each one evolved at its own pace in its own way, the polis created strong bonds between the individual and the community. The concept of citizenship was born as all members of a polis felt personally responsible for helping their city to run efficiently and prosper. Even though each city-state did not necessarily develop into a democracy as Athens did, individuals saw themselves as vital parts of their community, identifying more with their polis than with the Greek nation. Even rural dwellers associated themselves with their local city. The old bonds of family and tribe were replaced by ties to the polis.

Archaic Greek Society Physically and psychologically the polis became the center of Greek life. Each city revolved around two sites: the acropolis and the aghora. Built on the highest point of each community, the acropolis was originally a fortress, which was the ruler's residence and the center of government as well as a place where the population could find safety during an invasion. Temples to the gods were built there as well. Eventually it also became the center of religious life in each polis. The acropolis contained the treasury and armory for its community.

The aghora or marketplace was the site of the city's economic and social life. It was there that both urban and rural dwellers met. As some city-states developed democratic forms of government, the aghora was divided into two parts and became the center of political life as well. In Athens, for example, while merchants and farmers bargained on one side of the marketplace, the Athenian citizens debated and voted on the other. As civic life developed further, many city-states established courts of justice. The development of a legal system led to both written constitutions and trial by jury. These important innovations further strenghtened the bonds that held the individual and community together.

Participation on the part of the citizens also extended to military service. Unlike previous centuries, when warfare was monopolized by nobles, military organization was based on the **phalanx** (roughly equivalent to a regiment) made up of **hoplites**, or infantrymen, who were chiefly citizen volunteers. This system increased the loyalty of the soldiers, as each had a real stake in the effectiveness of the military, and made Greek armies very formidable.

The improvements in military organization and the development of strong navies by many of the city-states resulted in mass colonization outside of Greece itself. This expansion was also a response to economic pressures and population growth in the eighth century B.C. The new Greek settlements became independent poleis and expanded Hellenic civilization further into Asia Minor as well as into the Crimea, southern France, southern Spain, northern Africa, and southern Italy and Sicily (the last two were known as "Greater Greece").

Archaic Greek Art and Architecture

Culturally archaic Greece developed new expressions of creativity as well as expanding on older ones. Greek religion was responsible for much of this. The hominocentric beliefs of Hellenic religion resulted in revolutionary changes in art. Statues took on a realism never before seen. The **kouros** (statue of a nude young man) became an example of the Greek glorification of the human being. The **koura** (statue of a young woman) and sculptures of the gods were further examples of this.

Archaic architects developed a basic style for temples and public buildings (rectangular form with surrounding columns and a low-pitched roof) that applied mathematical principles and the Greek concept of **symmetry** (balance or proportion). Citizens of Greek city-states were keenly interested in beautifying their polis with statues, temples, and decorative public buildings.

The Development of Theater and the Olympics

Greek religious practice also led to the development of two unique and important institutions: the Olympics and theater. Held locally every summer and nationally at Olympia every fourth year, the Olympics were an athletic competition between city-states in which every adult male citizen participated. The contests included footraces (chariot races were later added), field events (discus, javelin), and combat competitions (wrestling, boxing, and a brutal mixture of the two called **pancration**). The event was so important to the Greeks that their calendar was based on Olympiads (years when the Olympics were held), starting in 776 B.C., the traditional year of the first Olympic Games. The Olympics were one of the few examples of widespread cooperation, with warring city-states even signing temporary truces to participate in the competition.

The feast of Dionysius, the god of wine and hedonism, was celebrated by the wearing of costumes and masks. Poems and songs were composed to honor the gods while myths were retold and acted out. These customs eventually developed into full theatrical productions. Contests were held annually in which playwrights competed for awards. Greek drama was divided into tragedy and comedy, performed on alternating evenings during festivals. The most famous Ancient Greek playwrights were Aeschylus, Sophocles, and Euripides (tragedy) and Aristophanes (comedy).

Archaic Literature

Literature was born during the Archaic Period. The *Iliad* and *Odyssey* of Homer are epic poems that glorified the legendary figures of Mycenean Greece. These first pieces of Western literature, written between 800 and 750 B.C., preserved the oral poetry of professional **bards** or traveling singers during the Dark Age. The literary genius of the Greeks came out fully in the writings of the farmer-poet Hesiod, who wrote around 700 B.C. In *Works and Days*, Hesiod objected to the injustice of contemporary society, especially the inequality between the wealthy and the poor. It is, in fact, the first known work of protest ever written. The development of lyric poetry gave literary expression to personal reactions and emotions for the first time. The works of Pindar of Thebes (c. 438 – c. 418 B.C.), who immortalized the accomplishments of athletes, and Sappho of Lesbos (c. 600), the poetess who celebrated nature and the emotional feelings of women, are the best examples of this new style of poetry.

The Development of Science and Philosophy Science and philosophy also began in the Archaic Period. Initially, the two were considered to be part of the same pursuit. Archaic thought centered around explaining and understanding the fundamental forces behind the universe as well as observing the natural world around humankind. This led to a rejection of the traditional myths and attempts to find rational explanations. One group of thinkers, the Materialists, concluded that natural elements (fire, water, and air) were the basic substances of all things. The Materialist tradition is best represented by Democritus (c. 460 B.C.). He first developed the theory that the universe is composed of tiny particles called atoms (Atomic Theory). Rejecting the Materialist school of thought, the mathematician Pythagoras (c. 580 B.C.) believed that the key to the universe lay in a numerical relationship among its parts. The philosopher Heraclitus (c. 500 B.C.) founded a group of thinkers who maintained that a being with perfect intelligence provided the creative force of order in the universe. By the end of the Archaic Period, philosophical and scientific inquiry had separated. Philosophers began to speculate about human nature and scientists continued their investigation of the natural world.

Classical Greece (500–323 B.C.)

Classical Greece marked both the height of Hellenic civilization and its downfall. Although the Greeks had some of their greatest achievements during this period, the independent city-states almost destroyed each other. It was the domination of Macedonia that not only preserved Hellas and its civilization but also spread Greek learning across the known world.

By 500 B.C. most Greek city-states, with the notable exception of Sparta, had developed governments that allowed at least some form of citizen participation. Many others followed the example of the city-state of Athens and established democracies.

The Persian War (490–479 B.C.)

Many Greek cities in Asia Minor came under Persian rule by 500 B.C. The Persian system of **autocracy**, or rule by one king, was imposed on the Greeks. This concept was completely opposed to Hellenic ideas. In addition, the Persians made the Greeks pay monetary tribute. This made Persian rule unbearable. The clash of these two opposing cultures led to the Persian War (490–479 B.C.).

The Persian Invasion Under Darius Some mainland Greek poleis supported unsuccessful revolts by the dominated cities in Asia Minor. King Darius I used this support as an excuse to invade the Greek peninsula. In 490 B.C., a Persian army attacked Attica (central Greece where Athens is located) and was defeated by the Athenian army under the brilliant general Miltiades at the Battle of Marathon. The Spartans did send an army to help, but it arrived too late. This created further tension between the two city-states.

Fearing a Persian reprisal for the humiliating defeat at Marathon, the mainland poleis formed an alliance, the Greek League, which brought together all their armies and navies for a mutual defense of Greece. Due to the efforts of two far-sighted leaders, Themistocles of Athens and King Leonidas of Sparta, the two hostile city-states cooperated in this alliance.

The Persian Invasion Under Xerxes In 480 B.C., King Darius's son Xerxes invaded the Greek peninsula. This time the Persians brought a huge army that left no doubt of the need for unity on the part of most central and southern Greek city-states. Xerxes marched around the northern Aegean coast and first engaged the Greek army at a narrow pass at Thermopolaye. With the assistance of the Athenian navy, the smaller Hellenic forces were able to stop Xerxes's advance. When a local traitor showed the Persians a trail around the pass, the Greek forces were trapped. The Greek commander at Thermopolaye, King Leonidas, managed to evacuate the bulk of his forces and remained with his personal bodyguard of 300 Spartans to fight to the death, delaying the Persian advance. The Persians finally invaded Attica and destroyed Athens, but Leonidas's sacrifice allowed the population to evacuate and gave the Greek forces time to regroup.

In autumn of 480 B.C., the Athenian navy maneuvered the Persians into an engagement in the narrow strait between Attica and the island of Salamis. Unable to use their numerical superiority, the Persian fleet was completely beaten. Their defeat in the Battle of Salamis forced the Persians to retreat to Asia Minor for the winter.

Xerxes renewed his campaign in the spring of 479 B.C., attacking from bases in northern Greece. The Persians were crushed at Platea by the combined forces of the Greek League under the command of a Spartan general and spearheaded by the Spartan army. The Athenian navy sailed across the Aegean and destroyed the Persian fleet at Mycale. The secret escape of Xerxes back to Persia signalled the end of the Persian War.

Athenian Imperialism (478–450 B.C.)

Even though Xerxes's forces had been driven out of mainland Greece, the Persians were still a powerful threat. This danger kept the spirit of unity alive in the Greek World. The Athenians took the lead against Persia as Sparta was no longer willing to remain involved in a project that was so distant from the Peloponnese (southern Greece where Sparta is located). In 478 B.C., under Athens's direction, the Delian League began a campaign to drive the Persians out of the Mediterranean area. By 465 B.C., all the Greek city-states in Asia Minor had been liberated from Persian rule. The Delian League's fleet, which was almost completely Athenian, cleared both the Aegean and Mediterranean of Persian naval power.

The success of the Delian League in ending the Persian threat resulted in a desire by many smaller members to withdraw. Athens, which had benefited economically from its participation, converted the voluntary alliance into an empire to serve its own commercial interests. Using intimidation and military power, the Athenians forced the other Greek city-states to continue their participation in the Delian League.

The Development of Athenian Democracy

Ironically, the rise of Athenian imperialism coincided with the full development of democracy in that polis. Athens began the creation of democratic government about 750 B.C., when absolute monarchy was abolished and replaced with a king elected in an assembly of the **archons** (leaders), of the city-state. These archons, who were originally the heads of tribal clans, soon shared power with the archon-king. Archons were also elected to head the military and to a nine-member body of chief magistrates who carried out Athenian law. Despite growing resentment from the lower classes, the **aristocratic** domination of Athenian politics continued for over two centuries.

The Reforms of Draco and Solon The threat of revolution finally brought change through the work of four reformers beginning with Draco in 621 B.C. He created a legal code (Draconian Laws), which strictly curbed the power of judges. Reform was continued by Solon, who became known as a great lawgiver. He ended slavery of debtors and made it illegal for any Athenian (a free man born in Athens) to be enslaved. Solon promoted economic growth by recruiting skilled artisans from outside Athens. He made wealth, rather than birth, the qualification for citizenship and holding public office. Athenian society was divided into four classes (excluding slaves) based on income, with only the wealthy able to hold public office. Solon's most important reform, however, was his creation of the "People's Court." This court allowed any citizen to bring a case to be heard. Cases were decided by a group of citizens selected by lot (trial by jury).

The Reforms of Pisistratus Despite Solon's reforms, the rivalry between aristocratic groups prevented stability. From 546 to 527 B.C. another reformer, Pisistratus, was given the position of **tyrant** (temporary absolute ruler in an emergency). While he made no constitutional changes, Pisistratus helped to bring economic wealth and stability to Athens. He created a huge public works program in order to provide jobs and stimulate economic growth. This was complemented with long-term loans to farmers to revitalize agriculture and an aggressive foreign policy that promoted Athenian commercial interests. Finally, Pisistratus encouraged the development of civic life with the establishment of a written constitution and the creation of Athenian cults to gods and goddesses.

The Reforms of Cleisthenes In 510 B.C., the sons of Pisistratus (who succeeded their father as tyrants) were overthrown by aristocrats who wished to reestablish the old order. The aristocrats were forced out of power in 508 B.C. by the reformer Cleisthenes, who finally established democracy in Athens. He divided Attica into territorial units, allowing each to elect its own local officials. This helped to expand civic participation. A Council of 500 was established, consisting of fifty representatives from each unit, selected by lot for one-year terms, to decide on policy issues to be voted on by the citizenry. All male citizens over eighteen years of age voted in the Athenian Assembly. Citizenship was hereditary, provided the family maintained its wealth. As women, **metics** (foreigners), and slaves could not vote, final authority in the Athenian state rested with roughly 40,000 males. Although members of the Athenian Assembly were a minority (Attica's population was around 400,000), the assembly was an unprecedented experiment in power sharing.

The Spartan System

Although many Greek poleis followed a pattern similar to that of Athens, the Spartans developed in a very different way. Beginning in 720 B.C., Spartan society took the form of a militaristic state. One reason was to protect itself against revolt by the peoples it ruled over. The peculiar development of Sparta also led to xenophobia (fear of foreigners). The shape of Spartan life was attributed to a legendary lawgiver, Lycurgus. These changes in Sparta took over a century to implement, but ultimately they created a unique society.

Three hereditary classes were created by the Lycurgan Reforms: the Spartans, or citizens, who ran the polis; the **perioeci**, or merchants and artisans; and the **helots**, or slaves, who farmed for the benefit of Sparta. All Spartan males were trained as soldiers from early childhood. They were separated from their parents when they became seven years old and they lived in military barracks until the age of twenty. Spartan boys were given rigorous military training and an education that stressed physical fitness, discipline, obedience, patriotism, and simplicity. Spartan girls were trained at home by their mothers, developing household skills and keeping physically fit. At age twenty, the Spartan male became a regular soldier who trained every day. He was assigned a piece of public land and helots in order to support him. He could marry, but a Spartan could not live with his wife until he reached thirty, at which time he became an "equal," with full rights to participate in political life.

While Spartans were **isolationists** (they did not bother with anyone outside their society) and did not provoke conflict, they were constantly prepared for war, developing the finest army of their day. Religious to the point of superstition, the Spartans rejected all luxuries and decorative arts (**Spartan existence**). They regarded foreigners, especially the Athenians, as sinful, decadent, and a corrupting influence.

The Peloponnesian War (431–403 B.C.)

With such great differences and suspicion between them, it was inevitable that the Athenian policy of imperialism under Pericles (r. 461–429 B.C.) would lead to another Athenian-Spartan conflict. Athens continued to force member city-states to stay in the Delian League, which existed only to enrich Athens further. It tried to impose membership on independent Peloponnesian poleis. This forced Sparta to create the Peloponnesian League, which, unlike its Athenian-dominated counterpart, was a voluntary alliance of southern Greek city-states that did not want to be controlled by Athens. In 454 B.C., the member cities of the Delian League revolted against Athens and were assisted by the Spartans, who had become alarmed at the growth of the Athenian Empire.

Fearing that Athens would be overwhelmed, Pericles made peace with Sparta in 449 B.C. Athens and Sparta agreed not to interfere in each other's **spheres of influence** (areas of domination). In 431 B.C., the peace was broken when Corinth, a member of the Peloponnesian League, convinced Sparta that Athens's attempt to dominate the island of Corcyra (in the Adriatic Sea off the central Greek coast) was a violation of the peace agreement. Arrogant and overconfident, the Athenians plunged into the Peloponnesian War (431–403 B.C.).

Fearing a land war with the Spartan army, Pericles convinced the Athenian population to withdraw behind Athens's walls rather than fight. This left the Spartans free to ravage Attica's countryside in annual raids. A plague behind the city walls in 429 B.C. decimated the Athenian population and claimed the life of Pericles. The Spartan commander, Brasidas, ended the attacks on Attica and encouraged the subject cities to revolt against Athens. The new Athenian leader, Cleon, finally led the army outside the walls and counterattacked. After a period of indecisive fighting, both Brasi-

The Greek World, 431 B.C.

- ▨ Athens and Allies
- ▨ Sparta and Allies
- ▤ Neutral States

0 — miles — 100
0 — kilometers — 200

Map of the Greek world in 431 B.C. The above map shows the division of Greece during the Peloponnesian War (431–403 B.C.). It also shows the importance of Persia in the politics of the Greek city-states.

das and Cleon were killed in 422 B.C. In 421 B.C., the two sides signed a truce, which lasted until 415 B.C., when Athens attacked the powerful Greek city-state of Syracuse on the island of Sicily. The ill-fated and foolish Sicilian Expedition (415–413 B.C.) was conceived by the ambitious politician Alcibiades, who wrongly saw Sicily as an easy target that would build up his reputation.

The disastrous defeat of Athens encouraged Sparta and its allies to renew the war and encourage revolt by the members of the Delian League. Led by the brilliant general Lysander, the Spartans destroyed the Athenian navy and defeated Athens's armies in a series of battles. Sparta also made an alliance with Persia, which supplied money and ships in return for being allowed to reoccupy Asia Minor. By 404 B.C., the Athenians surrendered. Athens was forced to tear down its walls and destroy all but twelve of its ships. A government consisting of fifteen Spartan generals and fifteen exiled Athenian aristocrats (The Thirty) was set up in Athens, guarded by a Spartan army. The Thirty were ousted in 403 B.C., and democratic government was restored. Athens, however, never recovered its former power.

The Unification of Greece Under Macedonia

Sparta tried to dominate the Greek city-states from 403 to 371 B.C., but limited resources and manpower made such control impractical. The polis of Thebes dominated Greece briefly (371–362 B.C.), but an Athenian-led coalition of cities ended Theban domination in 362 B.C. The constant warfare between the city-states weakened the Greek world considerably and made it an easy target for the Persians, who, back in Asia Minor, were once again a great threat.

Realizing the danger and a need for unity, Philip II of Macedonia (r. 359–336 B.C.) began a conquest of Greece in order to create one Hellenic state. Athens tried to lead a coalition to oppose the Macedonians, but was unsuccessful. Despite massive propaganda, especially by the Athenian leader Demosthenes (383–322 B.C.), Philip found much support among the city-states of Greece, who were tired of the Athenian-Spartan conflict. In 338 B.C., the Macedonians defeated the forces of the Athenians at the Battle of Chaeronea. A meeting of all the Greek city-states was called later that year at which a new alliance was created, the Hellenic League. Although the new union was controlled by Macedonia, Philip did allow each polis much freedom in domestic affairs. A common army and navy were created and regular meetings were held at which representatives could discuss and debate league policy. Philip had planned a war against Persia to free the Greek cities of Asia Minor, but was assassinated in 336 B.C. The full potential of a unified Greece was however, realized by his son Alexander III (r. 336–323 B.C.), known as "the Great" (see Chapter 2, "The Hellenistic World").

Culture of the Classical Period

Culturally the Classical Period was one of the most creative in Greek history. The Greeks tried to depict the human being in an idealized way, stressing human potential rather than criticizing human weaknesses. This became known as the "Classical ideal." By the fifth century B.C. Athens had become the center for the arts. Under Pericles (r. 462–429 B.C.) Athens was called the "School of Hellas" because it attracted artists, sculptors, architects, poets, and philosophers from all over Greece. The arts, culture, and intellectual life flourished during this period, which came to be known as the "Golden Age of Athens."

Classical Sculpture and Architecture

Sculpture reached new levels of excellence. Statues realistically portrayed idealized human beauty and physical perfection. Sculptors like Phidias, Polyclitus, and Praxiteles created splendid figures of gods and goddesses. Architecture surpassed anything done before. The greatest examples of Greek Classical building were the temples of the Athenian Acropolis, especially the Parthenon (dedicated to the Virgin Athena), the Erectheum (dedicated to three different gods), and the Nike (dedicated to the Victorious Athena). The architects of these achieved harmony, balance, and proportion, making buildings works of art.

The Development of Historical Writing

In addition to poetry and drama, the first historical works were written during this period. Herodotus (c. 480–c. 425 B.C.), known as the "Father of History," first began the study with his book, *Historia* (literally meaning "investigation"), which examined the political, social, and economic causes of the Persian War. Unlike the chronicles of past civilizations, which merely kept records, Herodotus's purpose was to objectively examine why hostility existed between the Greeks and Persians and how that led to war. This type of writing was continued by Thucydides (c. 460–c. 400 B.C.) in his work, *The Peloponnesian War*, in which the causes and results of the Peloponnesian War were examined. Despite his being an Athenian, Thucydides objectively concluded that Athens was responsible for the conflict.

Philosophy in the Classical Period

Philosophy became a separate study from science in the Classical Period. Shifting from speculation about the nature of the universe to that of human nature, philosophers concentrated on the development of reason and a search for knowledge. This new attitude was reflected in the writings of Protagoras (fifth century B.C.), who believed that thinkers should search for useful knowledge that would make life better. These ideas were adopted by philosophers who became known as Sophists or "Wise Ones." They were primarily teachers who taught the sons of wealthy citizens **rhetoric** (the art of speaking persuasively in public) in order to prepare them for success in political life.

Classical Greek statue of a woman mourning. The Classical Period was known for the realism of its art. This style became a model for later artists. Note the similarity between the above example and later Renaissance statues of the Virgin Mary.

Socrates. The Sophists came under attack from around 400 B.C. from a revolutionary thinker, Socrates (469–399 B.C.), who felt that they had betrayed their duty as philosophers and were more concerned with gaining wealth than with searching for truth. He felt that human ignorance was responsi-

Classical stélé: Ancient Greek graves were usually marked by a stélé or gravestone, decorated with bas-relief. In these depictions, the deceased person is usually seated and saying farewell to his family and friends.

ble for this. He developed a system for discovering truth, the Socratic method, which used questioning with precise definition and exact logic. Socrates would often use this method and embarrass influential citizens in the aghora in order to expose hypocrisy or illogical arguments in Athenian political life. As he developed a following, especially among the younger men, Socrates became a threat to Athenian politicians. He was arrested on charges of "corrupting the youth," found guilty in a prearranged trial, and executed by being forced to drink poison in 399 B.C.

Plato. Socrates's work was continued by his student Plato (428–347 B.C.), who wrote down his teacher's ideas. He established a school, the Academy, in which he taught both Socrates's ideas and his own. Plato developed his own **metaphysical** (dealing with the nonphysical) philosophy. He argued that all the material realities humans experience are really only reflections of a perfect world that exists elsewhere in the universe. For example, if someone looks into a mirror, the reflection they see is close to, but not exactly, what the person looks like. This is because light refraction distorts the image. Plato believed that human beings in this world were like the imperfect reflection in the mirror. The material world of human beings is an imperfect reflection of a perfect world that exists elsewhere in the universe.

Plato also struggled with the questions of justice and political institutions in a series of works on these problems, *The Republic*, *The Politician*, and *The Laws*. Plato concluded that wise laws, created by statesmen with philosophical guidance, were the surest way to provide for justice and good government.

Aristotle. Plato's most brilliant student, Aristotle (384–322 B.C.), rejected his teacher's ideas and developed his own school of philosophy based on **empiricism** (knowledge based on the observable and on experiment). He believed that reality was a combination of form (idea) and matter. Aristotle argued that without matter, form has no reality. He thought that every object in the universe has a "**telos**" (purpose or end), including human beings, which was to be "happy" by achieving a balance between the physical and spiritual. Through his school, the Lyceum, Aristotle and his students copied and cataloged all existing works of human knowledge, which they divided and organized into subject areas. Aristotle was also tutor to Alexander the Great and was very influential in developing a love of Greek culture and learning in his pupil.

Science in the Classical Period Finally, science made great strides in the Classical Period, especially medicine. The work of Hippocrates greatly advanced medical care. Hippocrates argued that the traditional belief that sickness was caused by evil spirits was irrational and nothing could be learned about illness without observation. Since disease was due to natural causes, the cure for a sickness had to be a natural process. He collected information on the curative powers of drugs and the effects of diet on health. An oath still taken by all physicians is attributed to him.

Summary

When we look back at the accomplishments of the brilliant Greek civilization it is difficult to believe that all this happened so long ago. This truly was one of those "golden ages" that happen once in a very great while in history. Our debt to these ancients can never be repaid. The values and ideas they raised influenced the direction future generations would take. Their spirit of curiosity to experiment and progress in the fields of knowledge remain with us today. In political forms, in law, in architecture, in philosophy, and in medicine they are with us. The Classical Period would pave the way for the Hellenistic Age, a time when Greek culture would expand throughout the Mediterranean region and beyond.

CHAPTER 1

Review Exercises

I. Matching

Directions: Match the names in Column A with the achievement or idea for which they are *best known* in Column B.

<u>Column A</u>
1. Socrates
2. Hippocrates
3. Philip II
4. Sappho
5. Plato
6. Hesiod
7. Homer
8. Democritus
9. Pericles
10. Aristotle

<u>Column B</u>
(a) Atomic Theory
(b) knowledge through empiricism
(c) knowledge through questioning
(d) "Golden Age of Athens"
(e) illness is due to natural causes
(f) *The Republic*
(g) female poet
(h) unification of Greece
(i) *Works and Days*
(j) *Iliad* and *Odyssey*

II. Matching

Directions: Match the words in Column A with the *correct description* in Column B.

<u>Column A</u>
1. polis
2. isolationist
3. oligarchy
4. hominocentrism
5. tyrant
6. xenophobia
7. kouros
8. pancration
9. symmetry
10. epic

<u>Column B</u>
(a) temporary absolute ruler in a crisis
(b) balance or proportion
(c) city-state
(d) rule of the few
(e) humans are the center of the universe
(f) statue of a nude young man
(g) one uninterested in foreign affairs
(h) poem that glorified legendary figures
(i) suspicion and fear of foreigners
(j) combination of boxing and wrestling

III. Map Exercise

Directions: Use the map to locate the place associated with each of the following statements. For each statement, write the *letter* of the place.

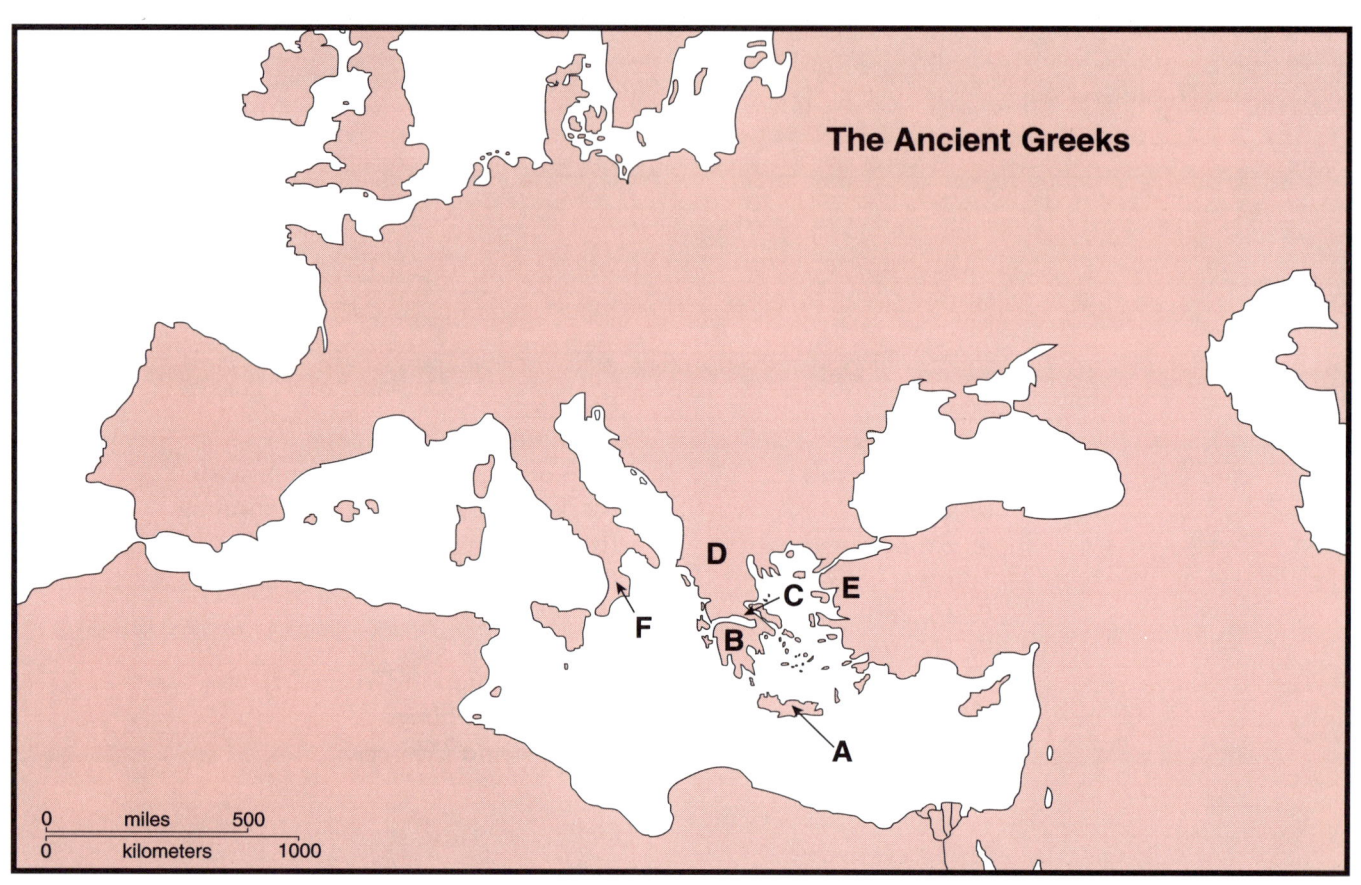

1. _____ Minoan civilization developed here.

2. _____ The legendary war of the Mycenean Period, which was later made famous by Homer, was fought at this site.

3. _____ The city where democracy was first developed is located here.

4. _____ The city of Sparta dominated this area.

5. _____ Philip II and Alexander the Great came from here.

IV. Multiple Choice

Direction: Find the *letter* of the correct answer.

1. Greek civilization was

    (a) monotheistic.
    (b) hominocentric.
    (c) theocentric.
    (d) atheistic.

2. Greece is

   (a) mountainous.
   (b) heavily covered in forests.
   (c) a series of grassy plains.
   (d) blessed with much fertile land.

3. The Greeks became very creative because

   (a) they were inspired by the natural beauty of the land.
   (b) they had to overcome a difficult environment.
   (c) they had a surplus of crops.
   (d) they were more intelligent.

4. The Greeks imagined their gods to be

   (a) spirits.
   (b) half-animal, half-human.
   (c) strange creatures.
   (d) superhumans.

5. Which statement is true of Ancient Greek beliefs?

   (a) Physical strength is all one needs for success.
   (b) Only the development of one's spirit can save the soul.
   (c) A sound mind in a sound body.
   (d) Eat, drink, and be merry, for tomorrow we die.

6. The unique civilization that developed on the island of Crete was the

   (a) Helladic.
   (b) Minoan.
   (c) Hellenic.
   (d) Mycenean.

7. The Bronze Age civilization on the Greek mainland was the

   (a) Helladic.
   (b) Minoan.
   (c) Hellenic.
   (d) Mycenean.

8. All of the following are true of Mycenean civilization except

   (a) the Myceneans were expert sailors.
   (b) the Myceneans worshipped male sky gods.
   (c) the Mycenean economy was based on trading and raiding.
   (d) the Myceneans had a strong central government.

9. The people who invaded Greece from the north after the collapse of the Mycenean World were known as

   (a) Hittites.
   (b) Macedonians.
   (c) Thebans.
   (d) Dorians.

10. The "Greek Miracle" was a unity of

   (a) language, religion, and government.
   (b) language, culture, and government.
   (c) language, religion, and culture.
   (d) religion, culture, and government.

11. The life of a Greek city-state revolved around the

   (a) acropolis and areopagus.
   (b) gymnasium and areopagus.
   (c) gymnasium and aghora.
   (d) acropolis and aghora.

12. Which pair of leaders maintained Greek unity during the Persian War?

   (a) Lysander of Sparta and Miltiades of Athens
   (b) Leonidas of Sparta and Miltiades of Athens
   (c) Lysander of Sparta and Themistocles of Athens
   (d) Leonidas of Sparta and Themistocles of Athens

13. The alliance that the Athenians used to create a commercial empire was

   (a) the Delian League.
   (b) the Hellenic League.
   (c) the Greek League.
   (d) the Peloponnesian League.

14. The "People's Court" had all of the following functions except

   (a) trial by jury.
   (b) allowing any citizen to prosecute.
   (c) deciding the constitutionality of a law.
   (d) acting as a final court of appeal.

15. All of the following were Athenian legal reformers except

   (a) Solon.
   (b) Cleisthenes.
   (c) Cleon.
   (d) Pisistratus.

16. Athenian citizenship was limited to

   (a) wealthy males over twenty-one years of age.
   (b) wealthy males over eighteen years of age.
   (c) wealthy males and females over eighteen years of age.
   (d) any freeborn male over twenty-one years of age.

17. Under Pericles all of the following occurred in Athens except

   (a) an extensive public works program.
   (b) prosperity based on the imperialism of smaller city-states.
   (c) a flourishing of the arts and culture.
   (d) the establishment of a new political system.

18. The "Father of History" was

   (a) Hippocrates.
   (b) Herodotus.
   (c) Thucydides.
   (d) Protagoras.

19. The Socratic method is used by

   (a) physicians.
   (b) teachers.
   (c) politicians.
   (d) historians.

20. Ancient Greek civilization's chief features were its

   (a) hominocentrism and isolationism.
   (b) rationalism and isolationism.
   (c) rationalism and ethnocentrism.
   (d) rationalism and hominocentrism.

V. Thought Questions

Directions: Answer the following questions in essay form.

1. What is meant by the statement, "Ancient Greece is the cradle of Western civilization"? Give three examples of how Greek civilization shaped Western society.

2. How was the geography of Greece responsible for the great accomplishments of its civilization? Show two ways in which the land and its location shaped the Ancient Greek national character.

3. What was the Classical Greek ideal? Give three examples of how this concept was reflected in the art, architecture, and philosophy of Classical Greek society.

4. Imagine that you are an Ancient Greek historian writing a history of the Peloponnesian War. Remembering that you must follow the tradition of unbiased investigation and analysis, give two causes of the Athenian-Spartan conflict and two effects it had on Ancient Greece.

5. Did the Macedonian conquest save or destroy Ancient Greece? Show three ways in which the imposed unification by Philip II affected most Greek city-states.

CHAPTER 2

The Hellenistic World

Do great leaders make history? Or, does history make great leaders? These questions are not easy for us to answer. Nevertheless, in this chapter we meet one such leader. This is Alexander the Great. He was the son of Philip II, who brought about the Macedonian conquest and unification of Greece. Leadership of the Greeks was thus inherited by Alexander. During and after his lifetime, Greek civilization spread into many areas beyond Greece. The Greek language and culture gradually brought the Mediterranean region and the Middle East closer. The conquests of Alexander brought about enormous **cultural diffusion**. This policy, known as Hellenism, combined the dominant Greek culture with the cultures of the other civilizations it came into contact with. We thus refer to this time as the **Hellenistic Period**. Despite political divisions and constant warfare, the Hellenistic Era witnessed many important achievements in the arts, sciences, and technology.

Alexander the Great (336–323 B.C.)

Alexander's Conquests

When Philip II was assassinated in 336 B.C., he was succeeded by his 20-year-old son, Alexander III. The young king, who had been tutored by the philosopher Aristotle, shared his father's love for Greek civilization and his desire to destroy the Persian threat to the Greek World. In 334 B.C. Alexander led a combined Macedonian-Greek army into Asia Minor and defeated the occupying Persian forces. From 333 to 332 B.C. he took control of Asia Minor, Syria, Palestine, and Egypt. Because of its great wealth and central location, Alexander greatly favored Egypt, founding the city of Alexandria on its northern coast. He did not live long enough to retire to it, but his body was entombed there after his death.

In 331 B.C., Alexander invaded Persia, decisively defeating its forces in the Battle of Gaugamela and capturing the capital city of Persepolis. Alexander then continued eastward, conquering the regions of Parthia (modern Iraq and Iran) and Bactria (modern Afghanistan). Pushing across the Hindu Kush Mountains, the

Greeks came into contact with Indian civilization. According to tradition, upon reaching the Indus Valley Alexander's troops, sick with unknown diseases and exhausted from five years of constant marching and fighting, refused to go any further. He was forced to return through southern Persia into Mesopotamia (modern Iraq), where he fell ill and died in June of 323 B.C. His death left a huge empire without any single individual capable of leading it.

Alexander's Goals

Alexander had planned to create a single unified Hellenistic Empire that would bring all the Middle Eastern peoples together with the Greeks to share and expand Hellenic civilization. To encourage this expansion, in 323 B.C. he held a mass marriage ceremony in the city of Susa (modern Iraq), in which Greek soldiers married local women. Alexander himself married a Bactrian princess, Roxanne, in the hopes of creating a new dynasty to rule this multicultural state. Opposition from his Macedonian and Greek commanders, however, prevented him from placing any non-Greeks in important positions. According to some historians, Alexander had developed megalomania (an exaggerated sense of importance in oneself), which both affected his judgment and made him unpopular with many of his officers.

Chapter 2 Chronology

Death of
Alexander the Great

Succession
of Alexander
the Great

Maccabean Revolt

| 336 | 323 | | | 167 |

350 B.C.   300 B.C.   250 B.C.   200 B.C.   150 B.C.   100 B.C.   50 B.C.   0

| 334 | 323 | 275 | | 146 | | 31 |

Creation of
← Hellenistic →
kingdoms

Roman conquest of
Hellenistic kingdoms

Conquests of
Alexander the Great

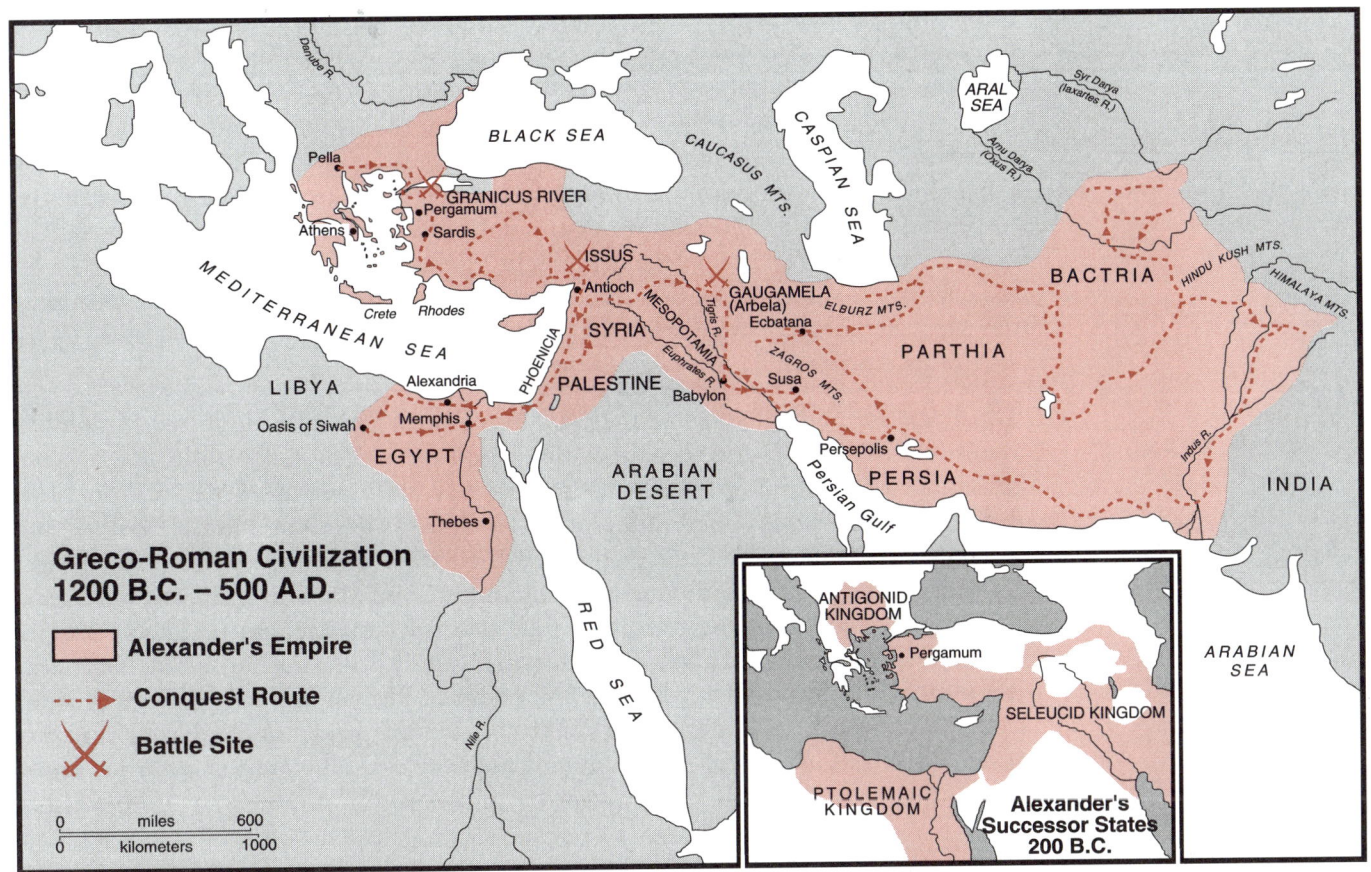

The Empire of Alexander the Great was created by his conquests. This Empire became divided into independent kingdoms after Alexamder's death in 323 B.C. The Hellenistic kingdoms shared a common Greek culture, but fought amongst themselves.

The Hellenistic Kingdoms (323–31 B.C.)

The Foundation of the Hellenistic Kingdoms

Finding a successor for a leader who was seen by many as a god was exceptionally difficult. Soon after Alexander's death, three of his generals began fighting with each other. By 275 B.C., they had carved up Alexander's vast empire and established independent Hellenistic kingdoms: Antigonus in Macedonia and the Aegean World, Ptolemy in Egypt, and Seleucus in Asia Minor and the former Persian Empire.

The Antigonid Kingdom The Antigonid Dynasty ran Macedonia very effectively. It faced problems, however, in keeping out barbarian tribes and controlling the Greek city-states. Around 200 B.C., the city-states appealed to the Romans to assist them in regaining their independence. This resulted in a series of wars that led to Roman domination over Macedonia, Greece, and the Aegean by 129 B.C.

The Ptolemaic Kingdom   Ptolemaic Egypt was the most stable Hellenistic kingdom created. Under the Ptolemies, a traditional Egyptian autocracy was established. It combined the Greek and Egyptian cultures and developed a prosperous economy. Its wealth and political stability allowed the Ptolemaic kingdom to influence and dominate Syria, Asia Minor, and the Aegean. Proof of the economic power of Ptolemaic Egypt was the growth and splendor of Alexandria. It was the largest metropolis of the Ancient World, with a population of about 1 million by the first century B.C. As the influence of the Ptolemies began to decline because of internal unrest, the Ptolemaic Egyptians became dependent on the Romans, who had come to dominate the Mediterranean. They eventually overthrew the dynasty, and Rome made Egypt part of its empire in 31 B.C.

The Seleucid Empire   The huge size and mixture of nations within the Seleucid Empire made political stability and unity extremely difficult to maintain. Unable to hold the eastern provinces of Parthia and Bactria, the Seleucid state consisted of Mesopotamia, Syria, and Asia Minor. Small independent kingdoms developed in the western and northern parts of Asia Minor, some of which were unhappy with Seleucid rule. Among several uprisings, the most successsful was the Maccabean Revolt in 167 B.C. This revolt resulted in the creation of an independent Hellenistic Jewish state in the area of present-day Israel. This kingdom, along with the entire Seleucid kingdom, was finally destroyed in 63 B.C. as a result of Roman and Parthian expansion.

The Hellenistic kingdoms combined Greek ideas and Middle Eastern institutions. Although strong rulers were common, they nevertheless had to prove themselves through effective administration or be swept out of power. No longer could they rely on the Middle Eastern concept of kingship as something sacred. The wealth and power of these kingdoms gave the Greeks great political influence. The cultural influence of Greece upon these kingdoms also prevailed.

Hellenistic Society

Hellenistic society was in some ways different from the Greek World that had inspired it. Greek language and culture provided a common basis, yet the traditions, beliefs, and practices of Middle Eastern civilizations soon became incorporated within it. The result was a multicultural and cosmopolitan society that, despite political tension and wars, both expanded and enriched Greek culture.

The Hellenistic Poleis

The Greeks, who had been divided into small warring city-states before the conquest of Philip II, were now spread throughout the Mediterranean and Middle East. The knowledge, techniques, and ideas of the various peoples the Greeks came into contact with added a new dimension to their civilization. The term *Greek* took on a new meaning, coming to include all "hellenized" or educated (in the new Hellenistic style) peoples. Anyone who did not adopt this new international learning was considered a "barbarian." The polis still remained the center of cultural life. While the old Greek cities continued to flourish, new ones developed throughout the Hellenistic World, most notably Alexandria (in Egypt), Antioch (in Syria), and Pergamum (in Asia Minor).

Because citizen participation in most Hellenistic city-states was limited by the autocratic rulers, a new concern with the arts and private luxury developed. As in

Classical poleis, new buildings and public decorations (temples, statues, and so on) were built to beautify each city. Unlike the attitudes of the previous period however, there was new interest in the decoration of private homes as well. Wealthy citizens competed with each other to acquire art and to commission works by artists. This greatly encouraged the growth of the arts. Libraries and research centers for scholars were created by monarchs who were anxious to show their support of culture and education. This preoccupation with the attainment of wealth and culture also weakened civic participation among citizens, creating the need for large bureaucracies to run each city. The decline of the older concepts also allowed women greater mobility in society.

Art and Architecture

For Hellenistic artists and architects, the artistic works of Ancient Greece served as models. Hellenistic sculptors, however, preferred to show their subjects in a far more realistic way. Unlike the Classical Greeks, who believed that art should idealize human beings by depicting only physically perfect specimens, they sculpted people as they actually looked, with all their flaws and imperfections. Classical artists presented their subjects only at their physical prime of life, but the Hellenistic sculptors chose children and old people as well. The greater social freedom of women was reflected in sculpture as the female nude made its appearance in the Hellenistic Period; the most famous example was the *Aphrodite of Melos* (better known as the *Venus de Milo*). Hellenistic relief carvings and painting reflect a similar development toward realism. Architecture continued to develop, combining Classical Greek models with those of Middle Eastern architecture.

Literature

Literature in the Hellenistic Period grew as well. A simpler form of Greek, known as **Koine**, was adopted by the Hellenistic World for use in government, business, and learning. This simplified language resulted in a growing literacy in a common language that made communication and the sharing of knowledge easier. With the exception of the novel (longer work written in prose rather than poetry), the Classical forms of Greek literature were continued in the Hellenistic Period (epic and lyric poetry, tragic and comic plays, histories). There were also scholars who devoted themselves to the study of earlier Greek literature, writing commentaries on their meaning, style, and grammar as well as establishing and preserving copies of these classics. Other scholars developed rules for grammar, rhetoric, and literary form. They further worked on methods of education and preparation for the ruling elite. Middle Eastern works were also translated into Greek, expanding the general body of knowledge and inspiring new ideas. Many translated works became highly influential, most notably the *Septuagint* or *Hebrew Tanach* (*Old Testament*). These books were put into Greek by Jewish scholars in Alexandria in the third and second centuries B.C.

Philosophy

The philosophers of the Hellenistic Period were not as interested in finding the "absolute truth" about things as their Classical predecessors. They were concerned instead with the problems of human conduct or **ethics** (principles by which people should live). Several schools of philosophical thought developed in this era. The Skeptics doubted everything and argued that there should be no concern with values or truth because neither really existed, and both were only the creation and interpretation of humans. The Cynics mocked society and believed that it should abandon all "civilized" practices in order to return to nature. They wore rags and preached openly against the established authorities and social structure. The Epicureans argued that humans should be concerned only with material happiness, as death was final and there was no evidence of a future existence. Achieving happiness for most Epicureans meant a balance between physical and spiritual development as well as avoiding excessive involvement with the world. The most influential Hellenistic school of philosophy was the Stoic. It was founded by Zeno (c. 300 B.C.), who earned the name "the Stoic" because he taught on his front porch or *stoa*. The Stoics believed that humans had to learn to understand and adapt to the unchanging laws of nature and the universal order. Both good and misfortune had to be accepted because they were the work of a supreme intelligence that ordered the universe. Concern for the material world had to be overcome in order for the soul to reach the "perfect state" of *apatheia* or apathy (absence of feeling). This state would protect the individual from much of the pain that life could bring. The Stoics also stressed the need for community among humans and involvement in public life in order to maintain balance in society.

The Sciences

Science made great progress in the Hellenistic Era. A vast body of scientific information was compiled, based on all the knowledge accumulated by both the Greeks and the Middle Eastern civilizations in the previous centuries. With the advent of the common language of Greek in the Hellenistic World and the greater acessibility of information, Hellenistic scientists had a large base to build upon. Geographic knowledge was expanded by Eratosthenes, who calculated the circumference of the earth as well as developed lines of longitude and latitude that divided the earth into zones. His work is still used by geographers. In the field of astronomy, Aristarchus and Hipparchus made important contributions. Aristarchus argued that the earth revolved around the sun (Heliocentric Theory), but his ideas were overshadowed by those of Hipparchus, who believed that the earth was the center of the universe. While Hipparchus misled Western society on the orbit of the planets for centuries, his work in compiling an atlas of the stars and their movements as well as an accurate calculation of the solar year were valuable contributions.

Mathematics

In the field of mathematics, Hipparchus developed trigonometry. Another Hellenistic mathematician, Euclid, compiled a textbook for geometry that was used for centuries. The scientist Archimedes calculated the value of pi (the ratio between the circumference and the diameter of a circle), devised a system for expressing large numbers, and laid the foundations of calculus. These subjects are still studied in schools throughout the modern world. In physics, Archimedes discovered the laws governing floating. According to tradition he made this discovery while in his bath and cried out, "Eureka!" ("I found it!"). It is not uncommon today for someone who has made a new discovery to use this expression.

Encyclopedias

Most students today would be lost without a set of encyclopedias to refer to. The concept of collecting information in a series of books to make its knowledge accessible to the average person was first created during the Hellenistic Period. Scientific encyclopedias compiled all the knowledge accumulated during this time: in geography by Strabo, in astronomy and geography by Ptolemy, and in medicine by Galen. These works served as resources for later generations to learn from and build on.

Summary

The Hellenistic Period preserved and expanded the culture of the Greeks. The combination of Ancient Greek and Middle Eastern learning made great progress possible in the arts, sciences, and technology. The creation of a common culture that used the best of the Greek and Middle Eastern civilizations provided the structure for an empire in which the entire Mediterranean World would eventually be united. It would be, however, the Romans, not the Hellenistic Greeks, who would finally achieve this unity. The Roman conquest of Hellenistic kingdoms occurred between 146 B.C. and 31 B.C. For all their creative genius and brilliance, the Greeks lacked the political and economic stability to bring about this unification. Yet they provided the foundation on which the imitative Romans would build their Empire. This Empire, as we will see in the next chapter, would act as both a unifying and a civilizing agent for the continent of Europe.

Review Exercises

I. Matching

Directions: Match the names in Column A with the achievement they are *best known* for in Column B.

Column A	*Column B*
1. Aristotle	(a) unified Greece
2. Antigonis	(b) established Hellenistic kingdom of Egypt
3. Archimedes	(c) tutored Alexander III
4. Philip II	(d) discovered laws governing floating
5. Aristarchus	(e) founded Stoic philosophy
6. Euclid	(f) established Hellenistic kingdom of Macedonia
7. Ptolemy	(g) compiled first geometry textbook
8. Eratosthenes	(h) developed Heliocentric Theory
9. Zeno	(i) established Hellenistic kingdom of Middle East
10. Seleucus	(j) calculated the circumference of the earth

II. Matching

Directions: Match the words in Column A with the *correct description* in Column B.

Column A	*Column B*
1. Eureka	(a) defeat of the Persian Empire
2. Alexandria	(b) modern Afghanistan
3. Battle of Gaugamela	(c) creation of Hellenistic Jewish kingdom
4. Alexander III	(d) Greek translation of the *Old Testament* (*Tanach*)
5. Bactria	(e) establishment of Hellenism
6. Maccabean Revolt	(f) capital city of Alexander's Empire
7. *Aphrodite of Melos*	(g) I found it!
8. Parthia	(h) modern Iraq and Iran
9. *Septuagint*	(i) porch
10. stoa	(j) *Venus de Milo*

III. Map Exercise

Directions: Use the map to locate the place associated with each of the following statements. For each statement, write the *letter* of the place.

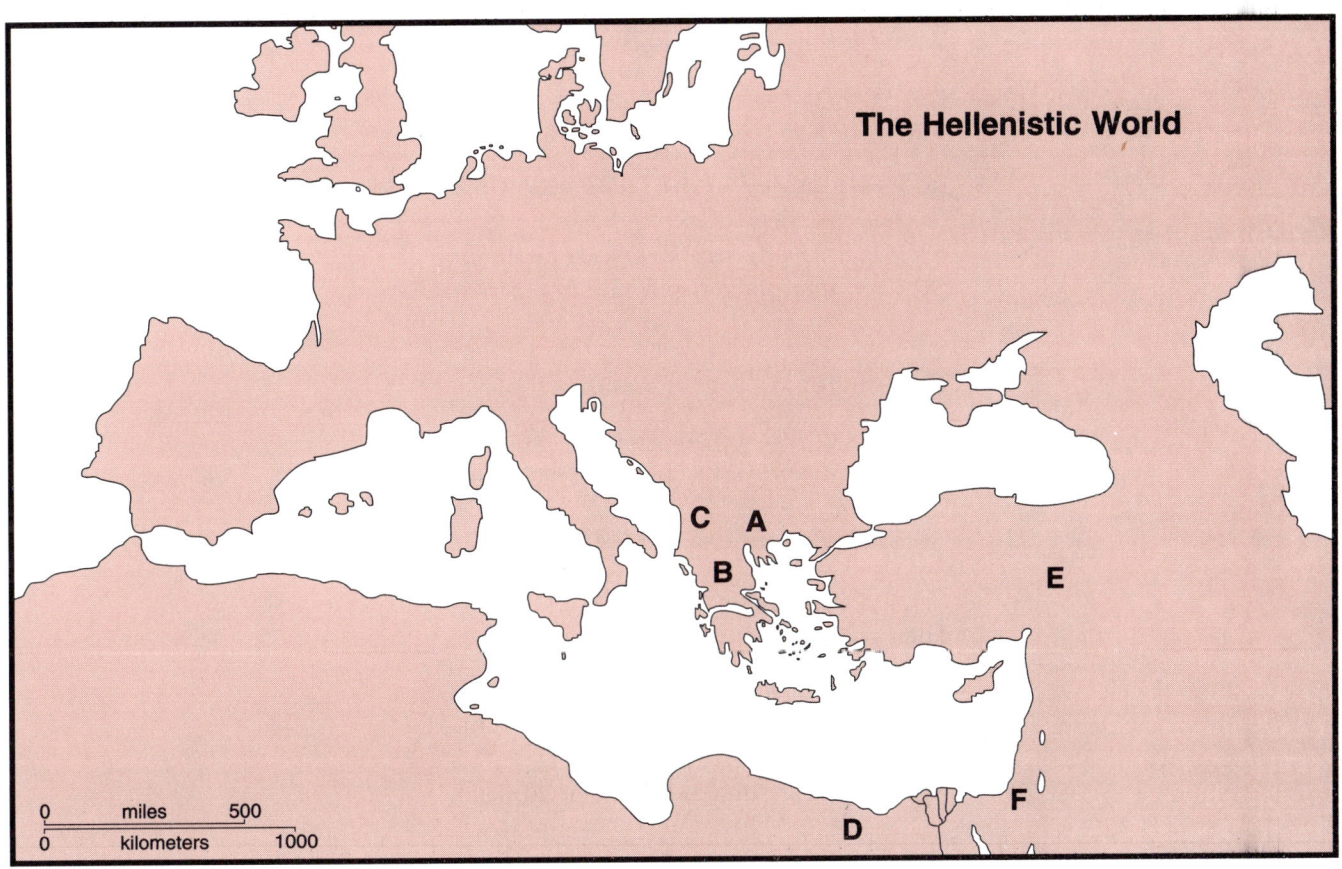

The Hellenistic World

miles 500
0
kilometers 1000
0

1. _____ Philip II's capital city was located here.

2. _____ This is the country that Philip II conquered and unified.

3. _____ Citizens of the Ptolemaic kingdom lived here.

4. _____ The Seleucid kingdom controlled this area.

5. _____ The Antigonid kings held power here. (Give two answers.)

6. _____ The Maccabees created a kingdom here to preserve their religious freedom.

IV. Multiple Choice

Directions: Find the *letter* of the correct answer.

1. Hellenism led to

(a) democracy.
(b) cultural diffusion.
(c) autocracy.
(d) rationalism.

2. Alexander's Empire included all of the following *except*

    (a) Northern Europe.
    (b) the Greek peninsula.
    (c) Asia Minor.
    (d) Mesopotamia.

3. The term *hellenized* referred to someone who

    (a) was educated in the Hellenistic Greek culture.
    (b) had married a Greek.
    (c) was fully or partly Greek by birth.
    (d) lived in a place where the majority was Greek.

4. The Antigonid kingdom consisted of

    (a) Macedonia and the Aegean World.
    (b) Asia Minor and the old Persian Empire.
    (c) Egypt.
    (d) Syria, Palestine, and Mesopotamia.

5. The Ptolemaic kingdom consisted of

    (a) Macedonia and the Aegean World.
    (b) Asia Minor and the old Persian Empire.
    (c) Egypt.
    (d) Syria, Palestine, and Mesopotamia.

6. The Seleucid kingdom consisted of

    (a) Macedonia and the Aegean World.
    (b) Asia Minor and the old Persian Empire.
    (c) Egypt.
    (d) Syria, Palestine, and Mesopotamia.

7. All of the following were reasons for the collapse of the Hellenistic kingdoms *except*

    (a) conflicts among them.
    (b) a lack of internal stability.
    (c) lack of a common language and culture.
    (d) a large mixture of nations within kingdoms.

8. The new and simpler form of Greek used in the Hellenistic Period was

    (a) Macedonian.
    (b) Koine.
    (c) Maccabean.
    (d) Bactria.

9. The following first began in Hellenistic cities *except*

    (a) public libraries and museums.
    (b) decline of civic participation.
    (c) social mobility of women.
    (d) public works to beautify cities.

10. The Hellenistic philosophers were primarily concerned with

    (a) ethics and metaphysics.
    (b) ethics and politics.
    (c) the search for absolute truth.
    (d) the search for absolute beauty.

11. The Epuicureans believed that

    (a) humans had to adapt to the laws of nature.
    (b) humans were too materialistic.
    (c) human should be concerned only with saving their souls.
    (d) humans should be concerned with achieving balance to enjoy life fully.

12. The Cynics argued that

    (a) humans should give up all physical pleasure.
    (b) humans should obey authority blindly.
    (c) humans should develop total apathy in order to avoid pain in life.
    (d) humans should abandon "civilization" and return to nature.

13. The Skeptics

    (a) doubted everything, especially values and trust.
    (b) rejected material happiness in favor of spiritual development.
    (c) preached against established authority and the social structure.
    (d) argued that humans had to return to nature.

14. The Stoics believed that

    (a) absolute truth had to be pursued.
    (b) the laws of nature had to be accepted and total apathy achieved to avoid pain in life.
    (c) material happiness was all that mattered in life.
    (d) a balance between the physical and spiritual had to be achieved.

15. Eratosthenes is famous for his contributions to

    (a) astronomy.
    (b) mathematics.
    (c) physics.
    (d) geography.

16. Aristarchus theorized that

   (a) only some planets orbited around the sun while others floated freely.
   (b) the earth orbited around the moon.
   (c) the earth orbited around the sun.
   (d) the earth was the center of the universe.

17. Hipparchus did all of the following *except*

   (a) develop a theory that the earth was the center of the universe.
   (b) develop calculus.
   (c) accurately calculate the solar year.
   (d) compile an atlas of the stars and their movements.

18. The mathematician Euclid is best known for his contributions to

   (a) geometry.
   (b) algebra.
   (c) trigonometry.
   (d) calculus.

19. Archimedes made all the following contributions to mathematics *except*

   (a) calculating the value of pi.
   (b) developing trigonometry.
   (c) devising a system for expressing larger numbers.
   (d) laying the foundations of calculus.

20. Which pairs of compilers and encyclopedias are *correct*?

   (a) Strabo/geography, Galen/medicine, Ptolemy/astronomy
   (b) Strabo/medicine, Galen/geography, Ptolemy/astronomy
   (c) Strabo/astronomy, Galen/medicine, Ptolemy/geography
   (d) Strabo/geography, Galen/astronomy, Ptolemy/medicine

V. Thought Questions

Directions: Answer the following questions in essay form.

1. To a great extent the conquest of Alexander the Great hellenized the Mediterranean. Give three examples of how Greek culture was mixed with those of other civilizations after Alexander's conquests.

2. Greek civilization improved during the Hellenistic Period.

   A. List three Hellenistic achievements and show how they benefited Greek society.
   B. Explain how each achievement was a change from Greek society during the Classical Period.

3. Why were the Hellenistic kingdoms unsuccessful in realizing Alexander's dream? Was his goal of one unified hellenized world practical? Give three reasons to support your opinion.

CHAPTER 3

Ancient Rome

Introduction

Whereas our greatest debt to Ancient Greece is for the development of philosophy, the debt we owe to Ancient Rome is mainly for its contributions to politics and law. The Romans, however, owe much to Greece. Although not as original or creative as the Greeks, the Romans were masters of imitation and organization. Preserving and improving upon Hellenic and Hellenistic accomplishments, they spread the civilization of Greece throughout Western Europe, Northern Africa, and the eastern Mediterranean. Acting as **civilizing agents** (transmitters of established culture) to the many tribes they conquered, the Romans transformed Western Europe and built foundations on which nations would be formed in the centuries to come. Alexander the Great's dream of forming one united and hellenized world was finally achieved by Rome.

Geography

As with the Greeks, geography influenced the development of Roman culture. When compared with its Hellenic neighbor, the Italian peninsula was richer in resources during the Ancient Period. The Po Valley in the north, the Campania region to the south, and the regions of Apulia and Calabria on the eastern coast of the peninsula along the Adriatic Sea were very fertile. The island of Sicily, south of the Italian peninsula, was agriculturally productive as well, especially in grain. In addition, Italy was rich in raw materials such as iron, tin, gold, and silver. Particularly the land of Ertruria on the northwestern shore along the Tyrrhenian Sea and the island of Elba, directly across from Etruria, contained many desired natural resources. The region of Etruria also had abundant forests.

The city of Rome is located in an area called *Latium*, in the center of Italy, which was somewhat productive, but relatively poor when compared to other regions. Rome is situated inland, with the Tiber River connecting it to the Tyrrhenian Sea. It is cut off from these wealthy areas, except for Ertruria, by the Apennine Mountain range, which extends through the Italian peninsula and connects with the Alps in the northwest. Unlike the mountains of Greece, however, the Apennines did not completely divide the country. If one state could dominate the peninsula, it would control fairly wealthy agricultural and natural resources as well as some excellent harbors. Being in the center of Italy, Rome had many natural land routes, as well as the Tiber, which were used for trade throughout the country. This is probably the origin of the proverb, "All roads lead to Rome." Its central location, accessibility, and relative poverty made Rome's conquest of its neighbors a logical goal.

In addition to encouraging the Romans to be conquerors, the limited agriculture and resources of Latium taught the Romans to be organized and disciplined. A sense of unity and cooperation as well as determination and persistence were developed. Being a mixed population (Etruscans and Latins), they showed a willingness to learn from others, especially from the Greeks. This enabled the Romans to create a political organization that could conquer and administer an empire.

Mythological Origins of the Romans

The two legendary stories of how Rome was created reveal the thinking of the Roman people and the way they viewed themselves. According to the first account, the Romans were descendants of the Trojans. The Trojan hero Aeneas was ordered by the gods to lead the survivors of Troy to Rome and establish a new polis that would rule the world. This story both tied the Romans to the Greeks in their origins and justified their expansionist policy.

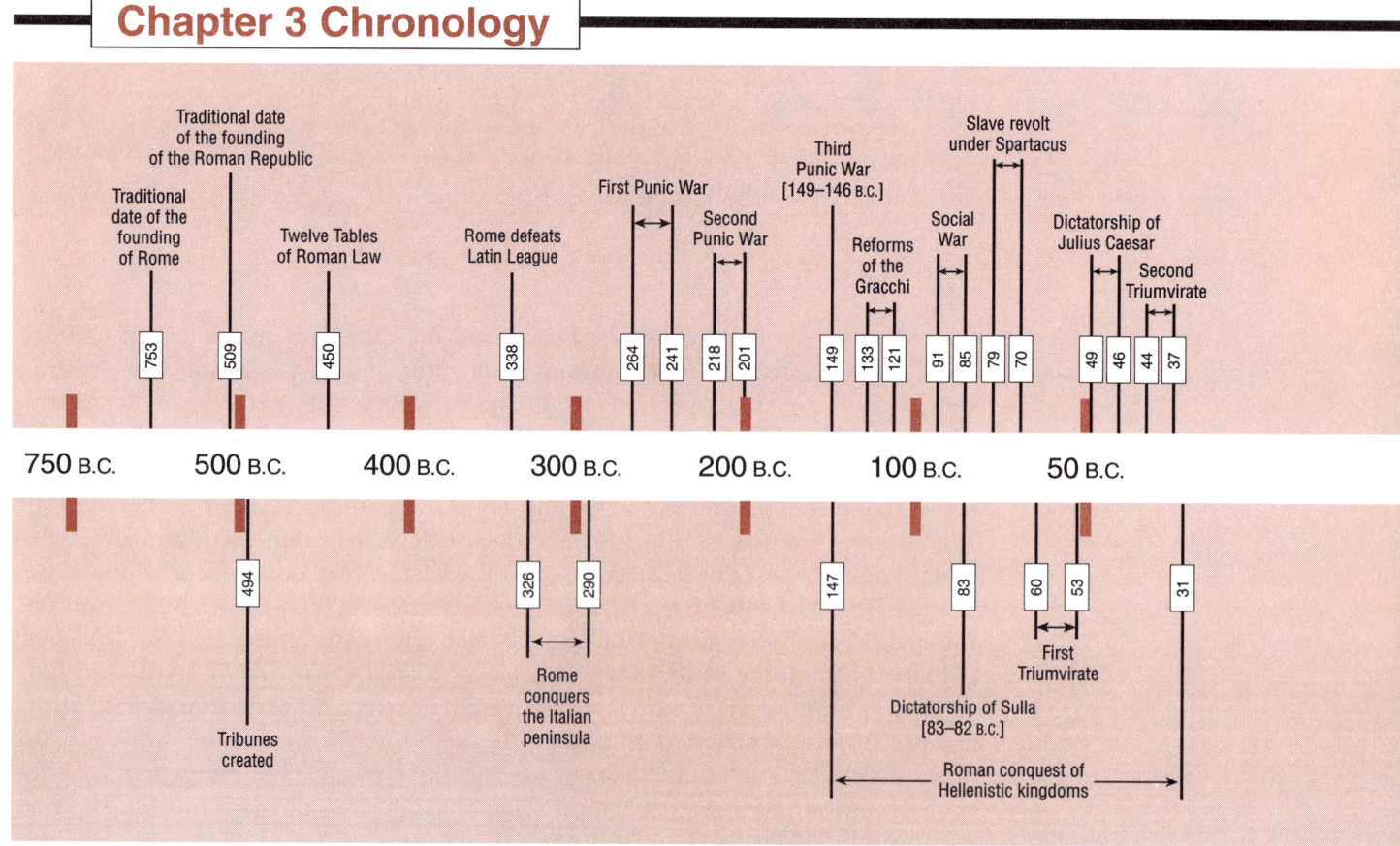

Chapter 3 Chronology

The second story explained the actual founding of the city. The god of war, Mars, fathered twin sons, Romulus and Remus, by the Etruscan princess Rhea Silvia. Their mother was, however, forced to throw the infants into the Tiber. The gods interfered and washed the children ashore. The brothers were protected and fed by a she-wolf, an animal considered sacred by the Latin tribes. Eventually, Romulus and Remus founded a new settlement at the place where they were saved as infants. They quarrelled over who would rule, despite a divine sign that Romulus should be king. The resentful Remus was finally killed by his brother and the new city, Roma, was founded in honor of Romulus.

Early Rome (753–509 B.C.)

How Rome Was Founded

Founded (according to tradition) in 753 B.C., the civitas or city-state (polis) of Roma, or Rome, did not seem particularly suited to possess a huge empire. It was a series of tiny villages built on a group of seven hills on the south bank of the Tiber River in the Latium area. Originally a settlement of farmers and herdsmen, Rome was conquered between 800 and 700 B.C. by the Etruscans, a people who probably migrated from Asia Minor and established a series of cities along the

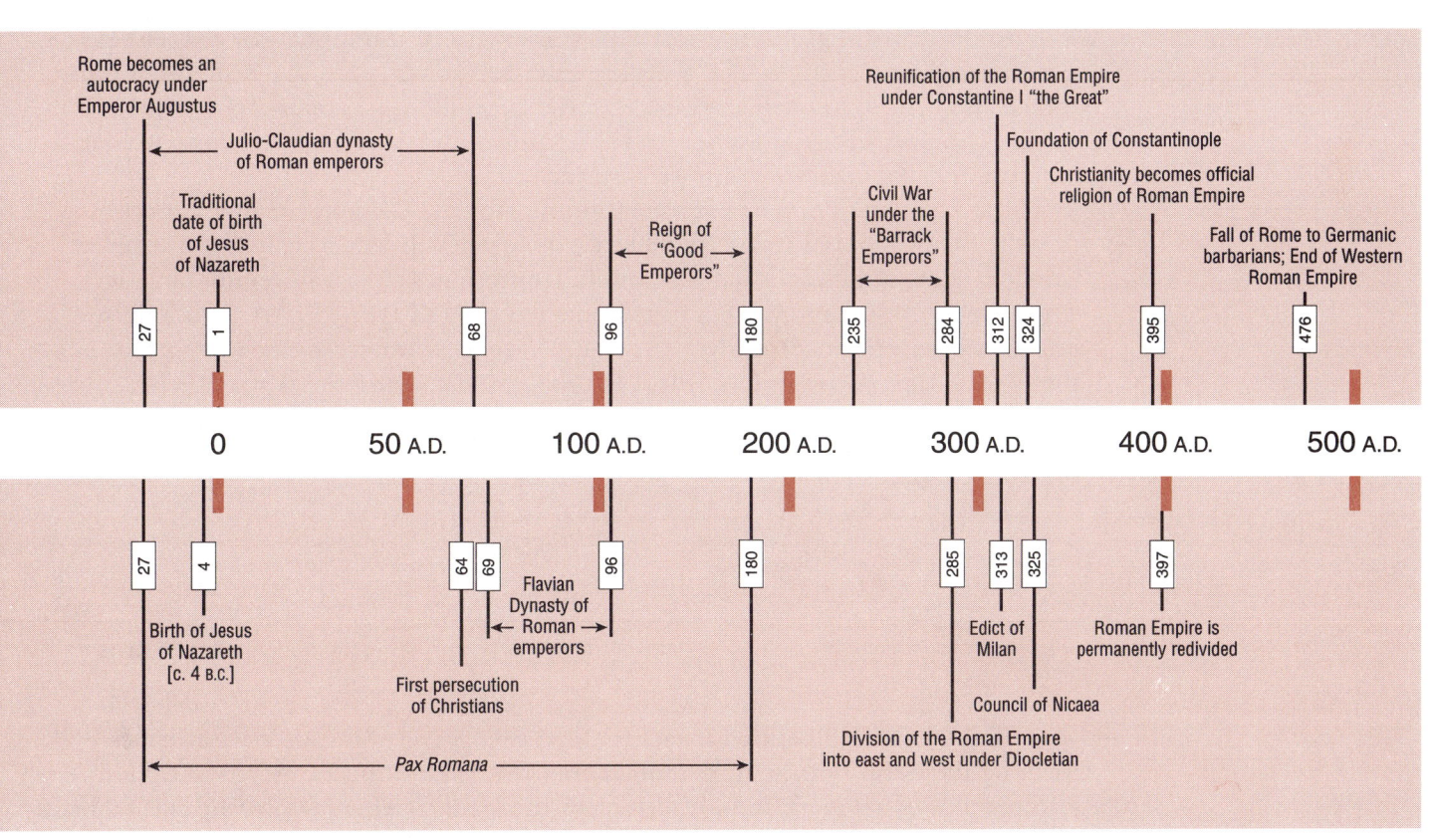

western coast of Italy north of the Tiber River. The Etruscans had a highly advanced civilization, which had been greatly influenced by the Greeks in southern Italy and Sicily (Greater Greece). Dividing their conquered region into independent city-states like the Greeks, the Etruscans came to dominate north and central western Italy between 800 and 650 B.C. After 500 B.C., Etruscan power declined under pressure from the Greeks and Carthaginians (northwestern Africans) as well as native resistance. While they still controlled Latium, however, the Etruscans transformed Rome into a single city-state with a central government under a king.

The Establishment of the Republic

According to tradition, Rome had seven kings from the time of the foundation of the city (753 B.C.) until the establishment of the Republic (509 B.C.). Each king was advised by a council of elders called the Senate, which consisted of about 300 wealthy men who headed powerful families. All Roman citizens—that is, males who were not slaves—belonged to two assemblies, the **Curiae** and the **Centuries**. Membership in the Curiae was based on heredity; members of the Centuries were grouped into military units. Both bodies, however, were severely limited in power and did little more than approve the decisions of the king. The wealthier citizens, from whom the senators were chosen, were known as **patricians**; the rest, who made up the bulk of the population, were called **plebians**. At this time, women and slaves had no place politically and had the same legal status as children (minors). Custom prohibited intermarriage between the two classes; however patricians were often **patrons** (providers and protectors) for plebian **clients** (political supporters). In this way, the patrician class dominated early Rome.

Early Roman religion, art, and architecture were influenced by the Greeks. Greek religious practices and temples served as models for the Romans. Commerce and trade advanced as Rome was transformed into a commercial city. Finally, the creation of an alphabet and a written Latin language brought Roman society a new sophistication and self-awareness.

The development of a new sense of identity for the Romans led to great resentment at Etruscan domination. In 509 B.C., the patricians led a revolt that overthrew Etruscan rule and established a **republic** (representative or indirect democracy). The king was replaced by two annually elected **consuls** (presidents), who held the **imperium** (executive authority). The consuls were, however, selected by and from the Senate, thus keeping the control of the Republic within the patrician class.

The Early Republic (509–265 B.C.)

The Conquest of Italy

At first the newly liberated Romans allied themselves with other Latin tribes by forming the Latin League to defend themselves against the Etruscans and mountain peoples of northern Italy. Invasions by the Gauls (Celtic people who settled in northwestern Europe), beginning around 400 B.C., further threatened the survival of the Roman state. These dangers forced the Romans to develop a strong, disciplined army. By 350 B.C., the success of the Latin League in defeating the northern invaders left the Romans free to begin dominating their allies. By 338 B.C., Rome controlled Latium. From 326 to 290 B.C., the Romans conquered the Samnites, a mountain people living to the southeast of Rome. During these conflicts, the Romans also defeated the Etruscans and Gauls, and occupied northern Italy as well. Finally, Rome captured Greater Greece, putting the Greek colonies of southern Italy and Sicily under their control. By 265 B.C., the Romans were masters of the entire Italian peninsula.

The key to the success of the Romans in unifying Italy was their military organization and political stability. Unlike the Greeks, they were able to develop a successful citizen army and adjust the political system to create loyalty among the conquered peoples. The people of Latium received Roman citizenship, and others were given a more limited political status. Many cities were made **socii** ("Italian Allies") and were allowed local self-government if they met certain military and economic obligations. Colonies of Roman citizens were planted throughout Italy to further the process of Romanization (the spread of Roman culture). As the Romans became obsessed with adopting and imitating Hellenic culture, many Greeks were given the special status of teachers. By giving each conquered people a stake in the new order, the Romans were able to maintain the loose confederation that gave them control of the Italian peninsula.

The Struggle of the Orders

The true genius of Roman organization was shown in the development of the legal system. The Roman constitution, which was constantly modified during the Early Republic, promoted both allegiance and loyalty among the citizens. After the overthrow of Etruscan rule, the patrician aristocrats controlled the Senate as well as the two assemblies, the Curiae and the Centuries. During the following 250 years, however, a conflict between the ruling aristocracy and the plebians developed, which resulted in a gradual, if limited, sharing of power called "the struggle of the orders." The need for the plebians as soldiers gave them a strong bargaining position. By 494 B.C., they gained the right to elect special plebian officials (tribunes), who had the power to veto any law that they thought threatened the interests of their class. A plebian representative body, the Assembly of Tribes, was elected to direct the tribunes and pass plebian laws, which later were recognized by all Roman citizens.

The Twelve Tables

In 450 B.C., the plebians pressured the patricians into writing down and creating a system of Roman law known as the Twelve Tables. Law had previously been kept by oral tradition. Once written down, the Twelve Tables made the law known to everyone and protected the plebians from patrician judges. By 367 B.C., as a result of gradual legal reform and the opening of the major elected offices to all citizens, a law was created requiring that one consul be a plebian. This eventually created a growing number of plebians in the Senate and therefore a threat to patrician power. The aristocrats maintained their control by absorbing these powerful plebians, through economic alliances or marriage, into their own ranks. Although Rome was in theory a fully representative democracy by 265 B.C., a small group of wealthy families, known as the nobiles (ruling nobility), actually held power. Yet the flexibility of the Roman constitution and the ability of the system to provide for its citizens, while at least maintaining the illusion of political equality, made the Early Republic successful.

The Roman Empire Under the Republic (265–31 B.C.)

The First Punic War (264–241 B.C.)

Rome's conquest of Italy had made it a major power and pushed it into the world of Mediterranean politics. Rome soon came into conflict with the Carthaginians about the island of Sicily. Carthage, which had been a northwest African colony of the Phoenicians, became independent about 800 B.C. and proceeded to create an empire of its own. By 300 B.C., the Carthaginians controlled the western Mediterranean and had become serious commercial rivals of the Greeks. In 265 B.C., Carthage attempted to expand its hold on the western part of Sicily. By 264 B.C., the Romans answered the call for assistance from their Greek allies and became involved in a series of conflicts with Carthage known as the Punic Wars (264–146 B.C.).

With no navy, Rome was unsuccessful against Carthage at first. Turning to their traditional teachers, the Greeks, the Romans soon developed an impressive fleet and were able to defeat the Carthaginians decisively at sea in 241 B.C. Victory in the First Punic War gave Rome possession of the islands of Sicily, Corsica, and Sardinia, nations whose cultures were influenced by trade and politics in the Meditteranean region. The Carthaginians began to rebuild their military strength in order to defeat the Romans and reestablish their dominance in the western Mediterranean.

The Second Punic War (218–201 B.C.)

In 218 B.C., the brilliant Carthaginian general Hannibal led his army on a thousand-mile march from its base in Spain through southern Gaul (modern France) into the Alps and down into northern Italy. This attack surprised the Romans, who had been preparing to attack the Carthaginians in Spain. Despite many defeats and fifteen years' occupation of much Roman territory by Carthaginian armies, the Romans were able to defend the city of Rome and prevent Hannibal from gaining control of the peninsula. The key to Rome's survival was that Hannibal was unable to persuade the Italian Allies to turn against Rome. In 203 B.C., under the leadership of the Consul Cornelius Scipio, Rome began a counter-offensive. Launching attacks on Carthaginian bases in Spain and on Carthage itself, Scipio cut off Carthaginian reinforcements in Italy and forced Hannibal to return to North Africa to save his city. His forces divided and, tired from years of campaigning, Hannibal was completely defeated by the Romans in North Africa at the Battle of Zama in 203 B.C. Carthage surrendered in 201 B.C. to Scipio, who was given the title "Africanus" ("Conqueror of Africa") by the Senate. As a result of the Second Punic War (218–201 B.C.), Rome gained control of all of Spain and forced the Carthaginians to destroy their fleet.

The Third Punic War (149–146 B.C.)

The Romans attacked Carthage one last time from 149 to 146 B.C. in what is known as the Third Punic War, because they feared a future threat from another revival of Carthaginian power. They destroyed the city and, according to tradition, poured salt on the site where the city had stood so that nothing could ever grow or be built there. This act marked a turning point in Roman conquest. Thereafter, the Romans followed an aggressive and sometimes brutal policy of conquest. Northwest Africa became part of the Roman Empire, which in 146 B.C., completely controlled the western Mediterranean.

The Conquest of the Hellenistic Kingdoms (146–31 B.C.)

The economic benefits and commercial growth that resulted from the Punic Wars encouraged Rome to expand its empire further. At first occupying territory only to restore peace and prevent conflict, Rome gradually annexed the Hellenistic kingdoms in Greece, Asia Minor, Syria, Palestine, and Egypt between 146 and 31 B.C. This made Rome the master of the Mediterranean, which became known in Latin as *Mare Noster* ("Our Sea"). The conquered areas were divided into provinces and Roman administrators were appointed by the Senate to rule them. Larger provinces, such as Egypt, had governors; smaller areas, such as Palestine, were ruled by procurators. Military forces were needed throughout the Empire to keep peace and discourage rebellion as well as defend its frontiers from barbarian tribes.

The Collapse of the Republic (133–27 B.C.)

Expansion from Civitas to Empire

The expansion of Rome into an empire created new problems and needs as well as luxuries and wealth. The military forces required to protect the Empire's new borders put a great strain on Rome's monetary resources. Political change was also called for, particularly by the Italian Allies, who still made up the bulk of the Roman army. The unfulfilled promise of citizenship for the majority of socii and the domination of the patricians in government created great resentment. The wealth generated by Rome's expansion chiefly benefited the nobilis. Many Romans became part of the **proletariat** (poor laborers), who often turned to crime in order to survive in the city slums. Wealthy Romans, ambitious for political power, began to use the proletariat in planned mob violence to put pressure on rivals and opponents. Another social group, the equites, was made up of patricians who had lost their wealth and were therefore excluded from political power. This group also included wealthy businessmen who lacked the family background to be part of the ruling class. The equites, also struggling for a share of political power, further complicated the situation.

The Reforms of the Gracchi and Marius The inability of the Roman system to adjust to the changes that expansion had brought led to a struggle between two factions for control of the government: the optimates ("the best"), which represented the ruling nobilis; and the populares ("the people"), which was led by reform-minded patricians, but consisted mainly

Hannibal of Carthage

Hannibal of Carthage came from a family of military men. His father Hamiclar had led the Carthaginian armies. His brothers were also generals, but he was to become the most famous of all of them. When Hannibal was a boy of nine, his father took him to the altar of the god Baal and had him swear that he would revenge his country against Rome. Hannibal would fulfill this pledge.

The Romans had already defeated Carthage in what is known as the First Punic War. (Punic comes from *Phoenician*, the people that first settled the area in North Africa.) Rome gained Sicily in that war and soon took over Corsica and Sardinia. Hamiclar believed that the only way to attack Rome was through Spain and he was successful in making Spain a Carthaginian possession. Roman and Carthaginian expansionist plans now clashed in a small Spanish city. Hannibal, now commander of the Carthaginian forces, decided to bring the war home to Rome.

Hannibal was now twenty-eight years old and had been a soldier for nineteen years. His troops followed him willingly because he exhibited all the characteristics a good military leader should have. His athletic ability made him the fastest runner and bravest hunter. He lived in the field with his men and shared hardships with them. The well-being of his men was always important to him.

Hannibal realized that the back door to Rome was through the Alps. He had 40,000 infantry and 9,000 cavalry when he entered southern France. They fought their way through and entered the Alps. Here, the army—with all its equipment, horses, and fighting elephants—began climbing through the passes. After a nine-day climb through snow and ice they reached the top and began their descent. There were many losses during this ordeal. When the army entered Italy, there were only 26,000 soldiers. Hannibal was now able to bring the war home to Rome.

Rome raised a force of 300,000 soldiers, 14,000 cavalry and 456,000 reserves. In a series of battles Hannibal was able to defeat each Roman army sent against him. Hannibal had hoped that some of Rome's unwilling allies would revolt against Rome and join him. A few did, but not enough to be of any significant help.

It was at this point that the Romans decided to change their tactics. They would no longer fight him directly but shadow his forces, picking them off whenever they could. They hoped to wear him down because he was far from his base of supplies and reinforcements. The Romans now decided to leave Hannibal in Italy and attack Carthage directly. The Roman general Scipio landed with a large army in North Africa and threatened the Carthaginian homeland. Carthage had no choice but to call Hannibal home. By now Hannibal and his men had been in Italy for fifteen years and had not won the war.

Hannibal formed a new army with the troops that had returned with him and new recruits. The two armies faced each other at Zama, fifty miles south of Carthage. Despite Hannibal's heroic efforts and generalship, the superior Roman forces were victorious. Scipio was generous in his terms due to his admiration of Hannibal. Carthage was almost destroyed as a military power. Hannibal had won many battles but had lost the war.

of equites and poor urban citizens. The optimates favored the continuation of an **oligarchy** (rule of the few) in government, arguing that the nobilis were the best qualified to rule, while the populares demanded that the political decision-making process be shared by a wider range of classes and that citizenship be given to the Italian Allies. Between 133 and 121 B.C., the brothers Tiberius and Gaius Gracchus, grandsons of Scipio, became champions of the populares and tried to implement reforms, referred to as the Gracchi Reforms. These included:

1. A redistribution of land in order to re-establish independent farms in Italy.
2. The establishment of new colonies to resettle impoverished Romans.
3. The provision of cheaper grain to feed the poor.
4. The granting of full citizenship to the socii.

The optimates, who controlled the Senate, blocked the reforms by provoking violence in Rome and proclaiming a state of crisis for which martial law was needed. They used these crises as reasons to execute the Gracchi as well (Tiberius was killed in 133 B.C. and Gaius in 121 B.C.). The leadership of the populares was taken up in 108 B.C. by Marius, a soldier of common background who had advanced to be elected consul (r. 107–86 B.C.) through his association with a patrician family and his outstanding military record. Marius's victories over rebels in North Africa and in campaigns against the Germanic tribes made him extremely popular and powerful. He adopted a reform program similar to that of the Gracchi, but his poor ability as a politician prevented him from overcoming senatorial opposition and implementing it.

The Social War and the Dictatorship of Sulla The failure of the populares to bring about reform led to great frustration and anger among the Italian Allies, or socii. In 90 B.C., the socii revolted, threatening the existence of the Roman state. The Social War (90–85 B.C.), as the revolt was later known, finally ended when the Senate granted the Allies citizenship in 85 B.C. The optimate Sulla, an impoverished aristocrat who had also advanced through connections and military ability during the socii revolt, seized power in 83 B.C., establishing a military dictatorship. Under Sulla, complete power was restored to the patrician-controlled Senate and the populares were removed from public office. The powers of the tribunes and Assembly of Tribes were also severely limited. While the Senate was enlarged to include the equites and some very wealthy socii, it once again became a highly unrepresentative body. More importantly, it had set a precedent for powerful military commanders seizing control and imposing their personal rule on the Empire.

The First Triumvirate (60–53 B.C.)

As the resentment to aristocratic domination grew, the Senate became increasingly dependent on military leaders to preserve its power. A succession of revolts in Italy, Spain, and Asia Minor, as well as an uprising of slaves, led by the slave rebel Spartacus, from 79 to 70 B.C. frightened the Senate into granting extraordinary powers to three military commanders: Marcus Licinius Crassus, Cneius Pompey, and Gaius Julius Caesar. Crassus was a wealthy and ambitious businessman who became famous for suppressing Spartacus' slave revolt. Lacking nobility and popularity, however, Crassus allied himself with Caesar, an impoverished young commander who had both patrician background and public appeal. Caesar had distinguished himself in the Gallic Wars (58–55 B.C.), a series of military campaigns in which rebellions in Gaul (modern France) were successfully put down and Roman control in that region was expanded. Pompey was a general who won acclaim for putting down the revolts in Italy and Spain as well as expanding Roman control over Asia Minor and the East.

The Senate soon began to regret the power they had given these military leaders. Influenced by the lawyer and orator Cicero, as well as other critics of the decision, the Senate began to oppose them. This resulted in an alliance of the three generals, the First Triumvirate or "rule by three people" (60–53 B.C.).

Using a combination of intimidation (using force to create fear) and popular support, the Triumvirate took control of the government. Alternating as consuls, they pushed through reforms, won great military victories, and spent huge sums of money in order to build popular support. After Crassus's death during a military campaign in 53 B.C., the Triumvirate disintegrated. Pompey, jealous of the popular Caesar, allied himself with the Senate, who gave Pompey dictatorial powers. In 49 B.C., the Senate declared that Caesar was no longer a consul and was to face criminal charges. This authorized Pompey to use the military to enforce this decision. As a result, Rome went into civil war.

The Civil War (49–46 B.C.)

Caesar, who was in Gaul at the time of Pompey's alliance with the Senate, responded by invading Italy. His decision to attack Rome, despite the fact that it was a violation of Roman tradition and would make him a rebel, was symbolized by his crossing of the Rubicon, the river separating Italy from Gaul. The term "crossing the Rubicon" has come to mean someone making an irreversible decision. Caesar's veterans easily defeated Pompey's forces, first on the Italian peninsula and then in Spain and Greece. In 48 B.C., Pompey fled to Egypt to gather a new army but was murdered by the Egyptians, who sent his head to Caesar in the hopes that the proof of his death would prevent Roman forces from crossing their borders. Seizing the opportunity, Caesar used Pompey's death as an excuse to become involved in the affairs of the only Hellenistic kingdom that had not come under Roman domination. Supporting the claim of Cleopatra VII over that of her brother, Caesar made her Queen of Egypt in return for a strong Roman influence in Egyptian affairs.

The Dictatorship of Caesar (46–44 B.C.)

Roman dictator Caesar extended the Empire throughout Gaul.

When Caesar returned to Rome in 46 B.C., he enlarged the Senate with his supporters and used his popularity with the masses to intimidate the nobilis. From 45 to 44 B.C., Caesar ruled as dictator, a title the Senate had been giving him annually since 49 B.C. when he drove Pompey out of Italy. His mistrust and dislike of both the senators and the Republican system grew stronger. The Senate increasingly saw Caesar as power-hungry and a threat to the survival of Roman democracy. The vast majority of Romans, disillusioned with the unrepresentative nature of the Republic, supported Caesar, who used his power to address some of the major problems of the time—financial debt, crime, the decline of small independent farms, and the extension of citizenship. It was rumored that Caesar was not satisfied with the title of dictator and wanted to have the Senate officially declare him king. Convinced they were saving the Republic, a group of senators, including two of Caesar's former supporters, Marcus Brutus and Gaius Cassius, assassinated Caesar in the Senate on March 15, 44 B.C., which became known as the Ides of March.

Caesar's murder was followed by outrage and riots that forced the senatorial conspirators to flee Rome. An alliance, the Second Triumvirate, was formed in 43 B.C. between the two main candidates to succeed Caesar, the military commander Mark Antony and Octavian Caesar (a grandnephew who Caesar adopted as his legal son and heir); and Lepidus, a loyal general who was dedicated to punishing Caesar's assassins.

The Second Triumvirate (43–37 B.C.)

The Second Triumvirate marched on Rome and forced the frightened Senate to give them temporary absolute power. By 42 B.C., the armies of the senatorial conspirators had been defeated and all political opposition to the Triumvirate, including Cicero, were eliminated. While they might have initially intended to rule the Empire jointly, the members of the Triumvirate in fact prepared to remove one another from power. Lepidus, who was given the northwestern African provinces, was exiled by Octavian in 37 B.C. in a struggle for command of Sicily. Antony, who had taken the Eastern provinces, became romantically involved with the ambitious Cleopatra VII. After marrying the Egyptian Queen, Antony tried to establish Caesarion, supposedly Cleopatra's son by Caesar, as the rightful heir to rule the Empire. This gave Octavian who was, under Roman law, Caesar's only heir, an excuse to remove Antony. He declared war on his rivals and defeated the Egyptian forces of Antony and Cleopatra at the Battle of Actium (in Greece) in 31 B.C. Octavian invaded Egypt. This resulted in the suicides of the defeated Antony and Cleopatra. Octavian had Caesarion killed and established Egypt as a Roman province.

The Roman Empire Under the Autocracy (27 B.C.–285 A.D.)

The Establishment of the Autocracy

With the removal of Antony, Octavian became the sole ruler of the Roman Empire. While claiming to restore the Republic, he set up an **autocracy**, or system of one-man rule, that was basically a restoration of monarchy. The Senate was slowly stripped of any real power by Octavian and his successors. Unlike his uncle Julius Caesar, Octavian realized that the title of king was offensive to most Romans and that maintaining the illusion that Rome was still ruled by the Senate would make the transition easier. Having control of the army and chief magistrates as well as inheriting popularity from his uncle, Octavian forced the Senate to make him "First Consul for life." In 27 B.C. he was declared Princeps or First Citizen, which amounted to being made absolute ruler. Changing his name to Augustus or "revered one," he took on the titles of pater patriae ("father of his country") and imperator or emperor ("one who holds the supreme power"). Armed with these titles and the power they represented, he became semi-divine (partly a god) as kings in the Hellenistic East had been, and therefore a new symbol with which all in the Roman Empire could identify.

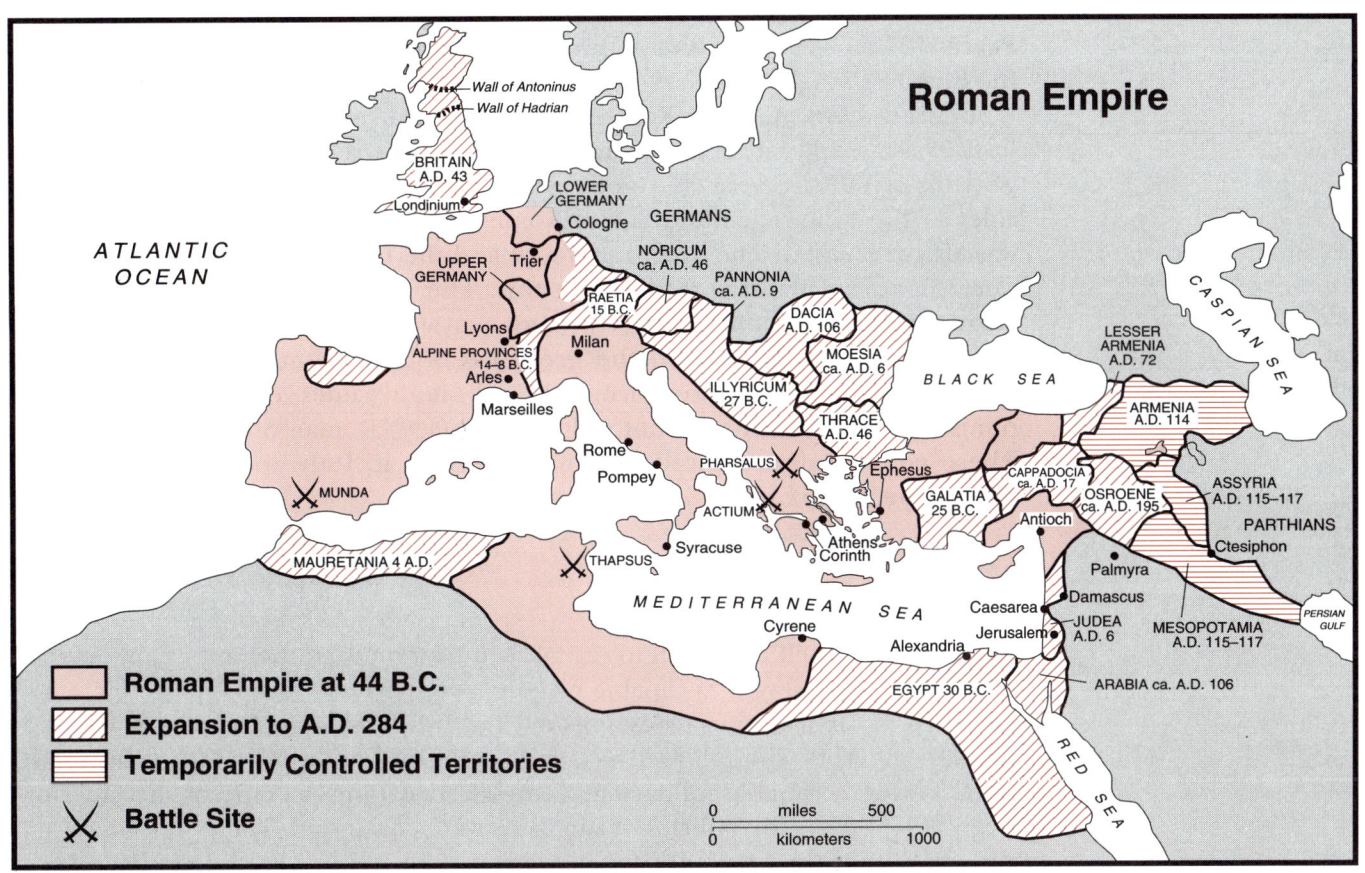

The Roman Empire, 44 B.C.–284 A.D. *This map shows the expansion of the Roman Empire between the death of Julius Caesar in 44 B.C. and the accession of Emperor Diocletian in 284 A.D. The territories annexed during these three centuries brought the Empire to its greatest size; all the peoples living within its vast expanse felt the influence of Greco-Roman civilization. However, by the beginning of the third century A.D. Roman domination of this territory was being threatened by increasing pressure along the frontiers facing the Germans and the Parthians.*

The Reign of Augustus (27 B.C.–14 A.D.)

Augustus's reign (27 B.C.–14 A.D.) restored order in the Roman Empire. This in itself won him enormous support. Trade and commerce were allowed to grow, easing the economic problems and food shortages that had plagued the Roman World during the civil war. The army was brought under control and reassigned to guarding the frontier borders. The navy kept the seas clear of pirates and protected commercial shipping. The government was made into an efficient bureaucracy that offered opportunities for advancement for citizens throughout the Empire. Romanization (adoption of Roman culture and the Latin language) was encouraged, especially outside Italy. Citizenship was likewise extended, which once again gave the population a stake in maintaining the Empire. Augustus pacified the nobilis by giving them important positions within the government and continuing the pretense that Rome was still a republic. In fact, most of the population, which had never had any political power in the Republic to begin with, did not seem to care that Rome was no longer a democracy. The urban poor were given welfare, cheap grain was available for the proletariat, and the reestablishment of independent farmers throughout Italy was encouraged and assisted. Most importantly,

Rome began a period of relative peace known as the *Pax Romana* or "Roman Peace" (27 B.C.–180 A.D.) that improved the standard of living for the majority of the Empire's inhabitants.

Augustus also improved Roman morale and patriotism by developing a pride in the past. He led a revival of the Ancient Roman religion, which included the worship of Julius Caesar as a god, establishing the Emperor as the semi-divine ruler of the Empire. The idea that Rome's conquests were its historical destiny was also developed. The poems of Vergil and the histories of Livy, both of whom were supported by Augustus, reflect this. The Emperor greatly supported and encouraged those Roman writers, poets, playwrights, historians, architects, and artists, whose works praised the greatness of Rome and its people. He also encouraged traditional Roman morals and family values, enacting strict laws to punish individuals who did not follow them (see "Roman Society" on page 83). These policies also inspired citizens, especially in Italy, to join the army and defend the Empire.

The Julio-Claudian Dynasty (27 B.C.–68 A.D.)

Augustus himself did much to revitalize and strengthen the Empire, but his successors were not always as capable or concientious as he was. Hoping to create a hereditary system, Augustus established the Julio-Claudian Dynasty by deciding that all emperors who followed would be from his family. He adopted his son-in-law Tiberius, a capable military man, to succeed him as emperor. In Tiberius's reign (14–37 A.D.) the policies of Augustus were continued. There was, however, a struggle within the family for the succession that resulted in the madman Gaius (nick-named "Caligula" or "Little Boots" because of his small size as a boy) murdering Tiberius and succeeding him as emperor. Caius's incompetent and bloody rule (37–41 A.D.) hurt the prestige of the autocracy and ended only when the Praetorian Guard (personal troops of the emperor) killed him and made his uncle Claudius emperor. Claudius, a handicapped scholar, was a dedicated ruler, but his reign (41–54 A.D.) was hurt by poor advisors.

Claudius was poisoned by his fourth wife and her son by a previous marriage, Nero, who succeeded him as emperor. Nero later had his mother and two wives killed as well. During the reign of Nero (54–68 A.D.), the last of the Julio-Claudians, the image of the Emperor sank to its lowest level. Nero provoked the resentment of many groups in Roman society by:

- Wasting Rome's treasury on personal luxuries and projects
- Posing as an artist despite an obvious lack of any talent
- Humiliating and killing many important senators
- Persecuting Christians
- Forcibly rebuilding Rome by chasing out the population and burning down the city

Despite his policy of "bread and circuses" (feed the poor and give the citizens free shows to prevent them from noticing the poor quality of government), Nero grew extremely unpopular and was overthrown in 68 A.D. by a group of generals. This established the practice that all Roman emperors were to be military men and that the army would control their selection. The Empire, which had grown large and difficult to maintain, could not afford to support incompetent or wasteful rulers. When such leaders appeared, the efficient Roman military machine removed them.

The Flavians and "Good Emperors" (69–180 A.D.)

Beginning with the Flavian Dynasty, which consisted of Vespasian (r. 69–79 A.D.) and his sons Titus (r. 79–81 A.D.) and Domitian (r. 81–96 A.D.), emperors efficiently ruled the Empire, completely ignoring the Senate. The Flavians were succeeded by a group of gifted and brilliant rulers who became known as the "Good Emperors" (r. 96–180 A.D.). They were Nerva (r. 96–98 A.D.), Trajan (r. 98–117 A.D.), Hadrian (r. 117–138 A.D.), Antoninus (r. 138–161 A.D.), and Marcus Aurelius (161–180 A.D.), who was also a noted Stoic philosopher. Under the "Good Emperors," Roman law became universal for the entire Empire, and many humanitarian projects were undertaken to assist the poor. By 180 A.D., however, the army had become overextended guarding the vast frontiers of the Empire. The Romans were finally forced to use paid foreign armies, which were usually unreliable. Money, not patriotism, had become the important factor. Defending Rome's borders became an increasing problem for its emperors.

Roman Society

The Greek Model

The Romans admired the Greeks greatly. Their society was, to a large degree, an imitation of the Hellenic. The four basic forces that shaped the early Roman World were agriculture, family life, war, and religion. Interest in culture developed only after 250 B.C., when Rome was transformed into an empire and came into greater contact with the Hellenistic World. Although the Romans may have physically conquered Greece, they were highly influenced by Hellenic learning and culture. They went to great lengths to become as "Greek" as possible. As a later poet put it, "Captive Greece held Rome captive." This was especially true of the upper classes, who competed to bring Greek slaves, scholars, artists, literature, and art to Rome. One of the earliest and greatest champions of Hellenization (the spread of Greek culture) was Cornelius Scipio, the conqueror of Carthage. He was patron to a group of imported Greek poets, scholars, and artists. This included the historian Polybius (c. 202–120 B.C.), who wrote, in Greek, the first account of Roman history, *The Rise of the Roman Republic*. As they learned from their Hellenic teachers, the Romans developed their own literature in Latin and made great contributions to art and architecture. Not known for their originality, the Romans nonetheless expanded on the Greek models and showed a great talent for imitation.

Roman Architecture

Architecture was one of Rome's two great contributions to world civilization. The Romans perfected both the arch and the dome. These advances allowed them to build larger buildings and expand upon the Greek forms they studied. Although the Romans were not known for their temples, they built the greatest round temple of the Ancient World, the Pantheon (temple to all the gods), noted for its huge dome with an opening in the center. They excelled at secular public buildings such as baths, palaces, basilicas (meeting halls), amphitheatres, aqueducts, bridges, and ceremonial arches. The huge complex of public basilicas and marketplaces in

Roman architecture was an important contribution to world civilization. The sports facility known as the Colosseum (left) and the complex of public basilicas and marketplaces called the Forum (right) are still standing today.

Rome, known as the Forum, and the massive sports facility called the Colosseum were especially impressive examples of the Roman genius for architecture. Roman basilicas and temples later served as models for Christian churches.

Roman Art

Even more than architecture, Roman art was imitative of the Greek, emphasizing the realistic aspect, especially in sculpture. It was, however, in bas-relief (sculptures that are not free-standing but project slightly from a background) and painting that the Romans excelled. Their excellent mosaics (pictures made of small colored pieces of inlaid stone or glass) served as models for early Christian artwork in churches. In public buildings, the Romans preferred historical or natural rather than mythological and religious scenes, which were limited to temples. They also avoided the excessive idealization of Classical Greek art.

Roman Literature

Roman literature produced its own distinctive qualities of realism. The Latin language also developed, especially through poetry. The greatest of Roman poets was Vergil (70–90 B.C.), whose epic poem *Aeneid* gave the Romans a sense of identity by claiming they were descendants of the Trojans. A national saga, it both inspired patriotism and justified Rome's expansion as a matter of destiny. The Roman love of nature and agricultural life was emphasized in Vergil's work, *Georgics*, which reinforced many traditional values. Catullus (c. 85–54 B.C.) wrote lyric poetry about the subject of love and the pain it often causes. Horace (65–8 B.C.), also a lyric poet, presented a picture of reason, intelligence, education, and wit, which was the Roman ideal of a civilized person. Lucretius (c. 95–55 B.C.), in his work *On the Nature of the Universe*, used poetry to instruct his readers to seek fulfillment in philosophy. Ovid (43 B.C.–17 A.D.) translated Greek mythology into Latin poetry in his *Metamorphoses* and amused his readers with his humourous work on seduction, *The Art of Love*. The poetry of Martial (c. 38–102 A.D.) and Juvenal (c. 55–140 A.D.) revealed the flaws of Roman society in satires.

Political Philosophy and Historical Writing

Rome's greatest writer of prose was the lawyer and statesman Cicero (106–43 B.C.). He developed the art of rhetoric in his speeches, which were written down and studied by others. His essays, such as "The Republic" and "The Laws," defended the Republican system of government but argued that a first citizen was needed to lead it.

The Romans excelled most in historical writing. Some of Rome's greatest historians were Greeks, such as Polybius and later Plutarch (c. 46–120 A.D.), who wrote biographies of famous Greeks and Romans in his work *Parallel Lives*. The majority, however, were Romans, writing in Latin. The most influential was Livy (59 B.C.–17 A.D.), whose huge *History of Rome* covered events from Rome's foundation until his own time. Tacitus (c. 55–117 A.D.) wrote about the century following Augustus in his works *Histories* and *Annals* as well as providing detailed information about the German barbarians in his *Germania*. Suetonius (c. 75–150 A.D.) portrayed the Roman rulers from Julius Caesar to Domitian in his history *The Twelve Caesars*. Prominent Romans also produced personal histories, as did Julius Caesar, whose commentaries *On the Gallic War* and *On the Civil War* were standard reading on military strategy. Emperor Marcus Aurelius wrote *Meditations*, a brilliant explanation of Stoic philosophy.

Roman Philosophers Roman philosophers were not original in their thoughts, but they adopted Greek philosophies and expanded on them. Lucretius, who had studied under the Hellenistic philosopher Epicurus, started a Roman school of Epicureanism. Many other Roman Epicureans, however, misinterpreted these ideas and used them as an excuse for a life of sexual pleasure. Stoicism was a far more popular philosophy among the Romans. Its two greatest champions were Seneca (c. 4 B.C.–65 A.D.) and later Marcus Aurelius.

Roman Science

Science also made great progress during the Roman Period. Scholars such as Pliny the Elder (c. 32–79 A.D.), Galen (131–201 A.D.), and Ptolemy (c. 121–151 A.D.) compiled great encyclopedias of scientific knowledge. This store of information was put to practical use in all areas, especially engineering.

Christianity

Lastly, religion became an important part of Roman society. Initially the pagan Roman religion shaped the society's values. As contact with the East grew through conquest, Hellenistic mystery religions became popular and weakened the authority of the family. During the periods of civil war and crisis in the second and third centuries A.D., Christianity began to attract Romans who were searching for a new spiritual meaning in their lives.

Originally a radical sect that broke away from Judaism, Christianity was based on the teachings of Jesus of Nazareth (c. 4 B.C.–29 A.D.). (The traditional year of Jesus's birth, 1 A.D., turned out to be a miscalculation when the Christian system of annual dating was later developed. He was probably born in c. 4 B.C.) Jesus taught his followers to pursue peace and love people, seek spiritual development over material gain, avoid becoming too ritualistic in religious practice, and respect the equality of all human beings. His teachings were firmly based on Judaic tradition. Some Jews saw Jesus as the "Messiah" or "Anointed One" (Christos or Christ in Greek), a leader whose coming was predicted in the Old Testament. Other Jews did not share this view. Jesus also proclaimed that he was the Son of God (God in human form) and had come to prepare humanity for the Kingdom of Heaven, which was spiritual rather than material, through repentence and spiritual renewal. This created much controversy in the Jewish community. Perceived as a threat to the established order, Jesus was arrested and put on trial by the Romans. He was found guilty of blasphemy (disrespectful teaching about God) and sentenced to death by crucifixion. After Jesus's death, his followers claimed that he had risen from the dead, proving that he was both the Messiah and God.

Jesus's original followers consisted of a group of men called **Apostles** or disciples, led by a fisherman named Peter. They preached Jesus's beliefs and gained a small following among the Jews. The Christian Church (body of followers) soon came under the leadership of a Hellenized Jew, Paul of Tarsus, who influenced the movement to accept non-Jews. As a result of this decision, Christianity grew in its appeal, especially among slaves and the poor. The new religion spread rapidly throughout the Mediterranean region—even to Rome itself. By the reign of Nero, Christians were a large enough minority to be viewed as a threat and openly persecuted. Despite a great misunderstanding of Christian teaching and frequent, violent persecution of them by the Roman government, the Christians won many converts. By the time of the reign of Constantine, they were a fairly powerful and influential minority.

The Division of the Empire (284–385)

While Christianity was spreading, the military commander Diocletian became emperor. Diocletian (r. 284–305 A.D.) restored order after a period of civil war (180–284) through the revival of a strong autocracy and central government. Trade and commerce were protected and encouraged in an effort to restore the economy. The losses, however, both of land and people, during the civil war had changed the overall needs of the Roman Empire. Diocletian felt that the Empire was far too large and its borders too vast for one individual to rule alone. In 285 A.D., he divided the Empire into two parts: the East, including Greece, Asia Minor, Egypt, Syria and Palestine, and the West, including Italy, Northwest Africa, Gaul (modern France), Iberia (modern Spain and Portugal), Germania (modern Austria and Germany), and Britain. Each part had an augustus, or emperor, and a caesar, or co-emperor, who would assist him. Diocletian believed the administration of the Empire and the defense of its borders would be far more efficient if it were divided between four leaders. Despite very careful preparation and many determined attempts to assure a peaceful and orderly succession, conflict between the augusti and caesars broke out soon after Diocletian's retirement in 305 A.D.

The Reign of Constantine I (312–337)

Following a series of struggles (306–311 A.D.), the Emperor Constantine (312–337 A.D.) again unified the Empire. In 313 A.D., he issued the Edict of Milan (in Italy), which allowed Christianity to exist freely alongside the official pagan Roman religion. This new freedom encouraged the growth of Christianity, the faith that Constantine himself adopted on his deathbed. (His mother Helen was a Christian and may have had a great influence on him.) He built churches, encouraged Christian clergymen to join state councils, and even presided over the first Christian conference, the Council of Nicaea in 325 A.D. Constantine probably had political motivations as well as religious ones. The borders of the Empire were greatly threatened by this time, especially in the West. Recognizing that the lack of patriotism and religion was in great part responsible for this disintegration, Constantine hoped that the Christian Church would become an institution that would unify the Romans. Christianity did not oppose the existence of the autocracy and might encourage a revival of the Empire.

Recognizing political realities, Constantine erected a new capital city, Constantinople, formerly known as **Byzantium**, in Asia Minor. It had become clear that Rome was no longer in the center of its own empire and was exposed to barbarian invasion. More importantly, it was a recognition that the East was the heart of the Roman World and that the West, outside of Italy and North Africa, was a shrinking frontier full of barbarians.

The Rise of the Christian Church

After the Edict of Milan granted them toleration, the Christians encountered new problems, such as attempts by emperors to dominate the Church, corruption among the clergy, and a lack of devotion on the part of many members. Canon law, rules for proper Christian behavior, were created as were courts to judge and discipline the clergy. Many Christians moved to isolated places, such as deserts and mountains, in order to pray and worship away from the distractions of everyday life. These **ascetics** (people who deny all physical pleasure in order to develop spiritually) were called monastics or **monks** (those who live alone). Living by themselves or in small communities, monastics became heroes for Christians in the Late Roman Period. Beginning with Anthony of Egypt (c. 251–356 A.D.), who founded Christian **monasticism** when he went to live alone in the desert, the movement grew very popular. By 400 A.D., rules had been established for monastic communal life. It soon became an enormously powerful institution, both in the Medieval West and the Byzantine East.

The Fall of the Western Roman Empire (385–476)

Christianity was not able to prevent the collapse of the West, but it did unify the East. By 395 A.D., the Emperor Theodosius I (r. 385–397 A.D.), Constantine's nephew, felt the Christian population had grown substantially enough for him to make it the official religion of the Roman Empire. After Theodosius's reign, however, the Empire was again divided into two parts. In the West, where the erosion of Roman authority was too great, the Empire was overrun by Germanic barbarians. Ironically, these Germanic tribes had initially been given Roman border lands in order to protect the frontier of the Empire, by acting as **foederati**, or "federates." By 450 A.D., they had taken most of Italy. In 476 A.D., the Germanic general Odoacer deposed the last Western Roman Emperor, Romulus Augustulus, and occupied the city of Rome. The Eastern Emperor in Constantinople became the sole ruler of the Roman Empire. This marked the beginning of the Byzantine, or Eastern Roman, period.

There were many reasons for the fall of the Western Roman Empire; no single factor was responsible for its decline from power. The reasons include:

1. The peaceful penetration of Germanic barbarians into the Empire as foederati or mercenaries in the army.
2. The violent penetration of Germanic tribes through invasion.
3. The economic burden of maintaining a large army to protect the borders.
4. The many civil wars between ambitious generals to become emperor.
5. A decrease in the population due to plague and civil war.
6. A greater degree of dependency on barbarians for both labor and military service as a result of the population decrease.
7. Overdependency on slave labor.
8. The decline of Roman cities due to the poor economy.
9. The growth of tenant farmers and serfs replacing small independent farmers.
10. Corruption and inefficiency in the government bureaucracy.

Summary

And so, after so many years the Roman World fell to invaders. We probably can never fully repay our debt to these people who had created, accomplished, and transmitted so much. They had preserved the Greco-Roman culture and had spread it throughout much of the world. They had created a republican form of government that was preserved. While we remember their battles and names of their generals we should not forget that they built beautiful buildings, wrote poetry, recorded history, expanded philosophy, and promoted science. The Roman Catholic Church, which began during this period, remains as a permanent monument to these people. Although the Roman Empire collapsed in the West, the Eastern European Empire continued to thrive for another one thousand years. Rome would later serve as the model and measure by which European leaders judged their own accomplishments.

CHAPTER 3

Review Exercises

1. Matching

Directions: Match the names in Column A with the achievement or name for which they are *best known* in Column B.

Column A
1. Aeneas
2. Romulus and Remus
3. Cornelius Scipio
4. Cleopatra VII
5. Brutus and Cassius
6. Constantine I
7. Octavian
8. Caligula
9. Theodosius I
10. the Gracchi

Column B
(a) made Christianity the official religion of Rome
(b) led the conspiracy to assassinate Julius Caesar
(c) reformer consuls
(d) Augustus
(e) built Constantinople
(f) led the survivors of Troy to Rome
(g) fed and protected by a she-wolf
(h) "Africanus"
(i) last Ptolemaic ruler of Egypt
(j) "little boots"

II. Matching

Directions: Match the words in Column A with the *correct description* in Column B.

Column A
1. curiae
2. centuries
3. patricians
4. consuls
5. equites
6. Twelve Tables
7. Social War
8. tribunes
9. oligarchy
10. imperium

Column B
(a) division of Roman citizens into military units
(b) written and systematized Roman law
(c) impoverished patricians and wealthy mechants
(d) executive authority
(e) rule of the few
(f) membership based on tribe or clan
(g) Roman aristocrats
(h) elected plebian officers
(i) revolt of the Italian Allies
(j) annually elected presidents of the Senate

III. Map Exercise

Directions: Use the map to locate the place associated with each of the following statements. For each statement, write the *letter* of the place.

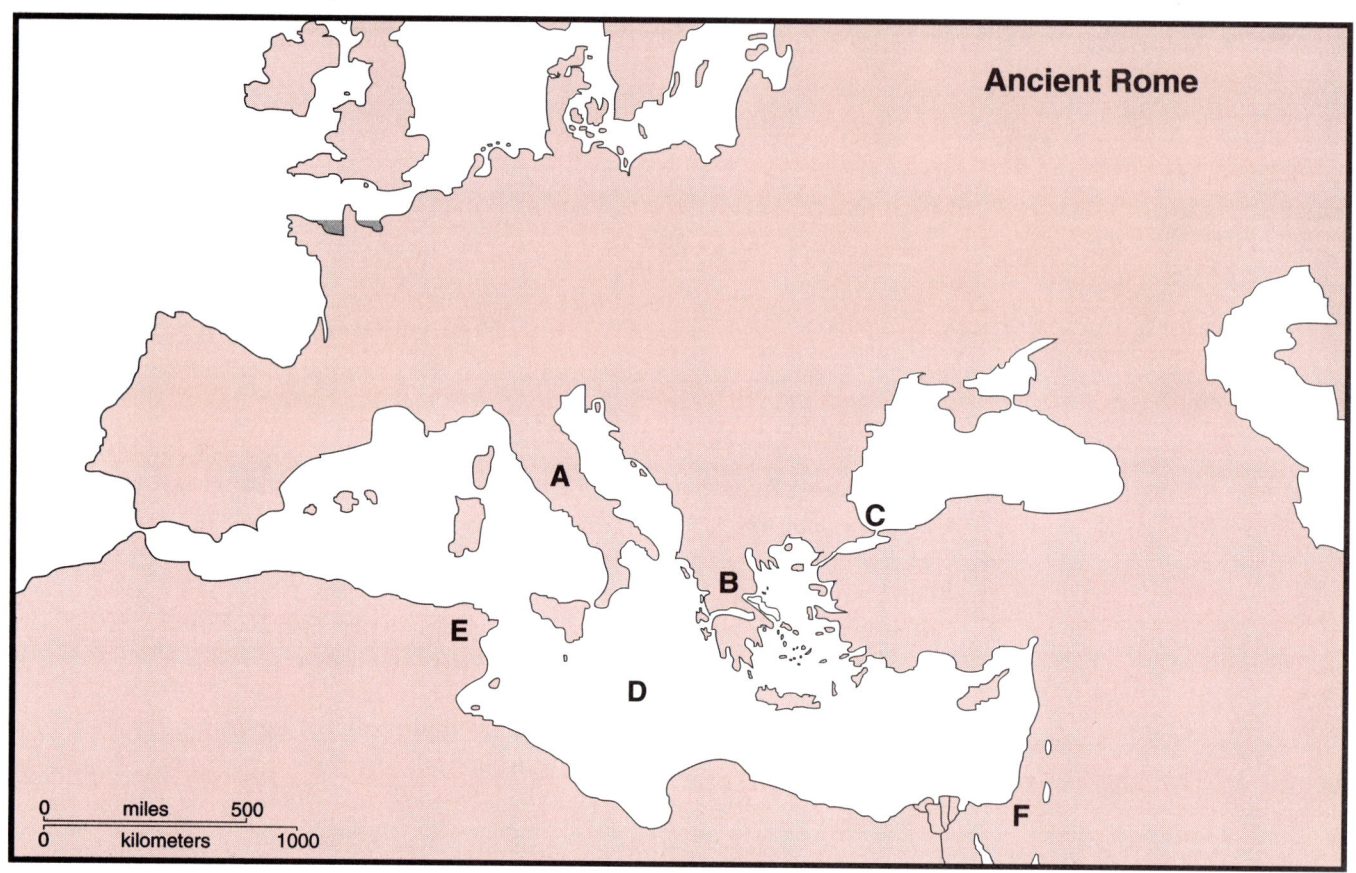

1. _____ Roman civilization was born on this peninsula.

2. _____ The Romans conquered this area in the Punic Wars.

3. _____ The people of this peninsula were looked upon as teachers by the Romans.

4. _____ The Romans called this body of water *Noster Mare* or "Our Sea."

5. _____ Christianity began here.

6. _____ The second capital city of the Roman Empire was located here.

IV. Multiple Choice

Directions: Find the *letter* of the correct answer.

1. Etruscan civilization was greatly influenced by the

    (a) Greeks.
    (b) Egyptians.
    (c) Phoenicians.
    (d) Carthaginians.

2. According to tradition, Rome was settled by

   (a) Numitor.
   (b) Aeneas.
   (c) Romulus and Remus.
   (d) Faustulus.

3. The Romans traditionally believed that their city was founded by

   (a) Numitor.
   (b) Aeneas.
   (c) Romulus and Remus.
   (d) Faustulus.

4. The conflicts between Rome and Carthage were known as the

   (a) Social Wars.
   (b) Numidian Wars.
   (c) Samnite Wars.
   (d) Punic Wars.

5. The military commander who led the armies of Carthage on the famous thousand-mile march across the Alps was

   (a) Julius Caesar.
   (b) Hannibal.
   (c) Cornelius Scipio.
   (d) Marius.

6. All of the following were members of the First Triumvirate *except*

   (a) Pompey.
   (b) Julius Caesar.
   (c) Crassus.
   (d) Lepidus.

7. Julius Caesar was assassinated for all of the following reasons *except*

   (a) He wanted the Senate to proclaim him king.
   (b) The Senate viewed him as a threat to the Republican system.
   (c) The Senate was convinced that his policies had damaged the economy.
   (d) The Senate feared losing its power.

8. The Second Triumvirate consisted of

   (a) Pompey, Julius Caesar, and Lepidus.
   (b) Pompey, Julius Caesar, and Crassus.
   (c) Octavian, Marc Antony, and Lepidus.
   (d) Octavian, Marc Antony, and Crassus.

9. The period of relative peace in the Empire from 27 B.C. to 180 A.D. was known as the

   (a) *imperium.*
   (b) *Noster Mare.*
   (c) *pater patriae.*
   (d) *Pax Romana.*

10. The "Good Emperors"

   (a) divided the Empire up into parts.
   (b) neglected the Empire's borders.
   (c) expanded the Empire's borders.
   (d) restored peace and order to the Empire.

11. The emperor who divided the Roman Empire into east and west was

   (a) Vespasian.
   (b) Septimus Severus.
   (c) Constantine.
   (d) Diocletian.

12. The Edict of Milan

   (a) outlawed the old pagan Roman religion.
   (b) outlawed Christianity.
   (c) tolerated Christianity.
   (d) made Christianity the official religion of the Roman Empire.

13. The First Christian Council was held at

   (a) Rome.
   (b) Constantinople.
   (c) Nicaea.
   (d) Jerusalem.

14. Constantine founded a new capital city in the East for all the following *except*

   (a) Rome was no longer in the center of the Empire.
   (b) Rome was constantly in danger from barbarian attacks.
   (c) The heart of the Empire was in the East.
   (d) Rome had become economically unimportant.

15. The barbarian tribes that were given Roman border lands to protect were

   (a) praetorians.
   (b) foederati.
   (c) socii.
   (d) Centuries.

16. The last Western Roman Emperor was

    (a) Augustine.
    (b) Romulus Augustulus.
    (c) Theodosius I.
    (d) Odoacer.

17. The four basic forces that shaped Roman society were

    (a) agriculture, family life, law, and religion.
    (b) agriculture, family life, war, and religion.
    (c) agriculture, war, law, and religion.
    (d) family life, war, law, and religion.

18. The writer of the first Roman history was

    (a) Livy.
    (b) Polybius.
    (c) Plutarch.
    (d) Vergil.

19. The two aspects of architecture that the Romans perfected were

    (a) the arch and the dome.
    (b) thc arch and thc column.
    (c) the stadium and aqueduct.
    (d) roads and bridges.

20. The life-style that *best* describes Christian monasticism is

    (a) Stoic.
    (b) epicurean.
    (c) ascetic.
    (d) hedonistic.

V. Thought Questions

Directions: Answer the following questions in essay form.

1. Explain the statement, "Captive Greece held Rome captive."

    A. Show two ways in which the Greeks influenced Roman society.
    B. Give two examples of how Rome's relationship with the Greeks is different from that with other conquered peoples.

2. Compare the story of Aeneas with that of Romulus and Remus.

    A. What purpose does each tale serve?
    B. Give two Roman ideals or values that each story emphasizes.

3. Many historians view Rome's accomplishments as the successors of Alexander the Great's achievements.

    A. Give two examples of how the Romans fulfilled the dream of the Macedonian conqueror.

B. List two ways in which the Roman Empire was different from that of the reign of Alexander the Great.

4. Rome made the transition from a city-state to an empire.

A. Did this make the collapse of Roman democracy inevitable?
B. List three problems created by Roman imperialism and why the Republican system was able or unable to deal with each.

5. You are a Roman in 476 A.D. looking back at what had happened to the Empire. In your diary, write and explain those factors that led to the decline of the Western Empire. Give three reasons for the decline of Roman dominance in Western Europe.

Unit II

THE MEDIEVAL WORLD

With the Fall of Rome, the then divided European World followed different paths of progress. The Eastern Roman World became the Byzantine Empire. The development here was different than in the West due to the influence of the Eastern Orthodox Church and not Catholic Rome and the development of an alphabet that is different than the one used in Western Europe. Healing the schism between the two Churches is a continuous goal in today's ecumenical movement. If you visit France, Spain, or Germany, you will be familiar with the alphabet and be able to pronounce the words and read street maps and street signs. In Russia and most Eastern nations, you will have much more difficulty as their letters look different and have different pronunciations than the letters you are used to. Byzantium stood as a protector of Western culture until it was finally defeated by the Turkish invaders in 1453.

In the West after 476 A.D. all was in discord. The unifying force known as Rome was gone, and a long period of stagnation or little development took place. From c. 500 A.D. to c. 1000 A.D. there was a succession of invasions—by Germanic tribes such as the Vandals and the Vikings from the Scandanavian area. The ninth century could well be called "the melancholy century" because there were invasions, storms, plagues, and famines. People looked for protection from marauding bands and pledged their allegiance to anyone who could provide it. Institutions developed that became the basis for some we have today. Early states were created that became the foundations for some that are still on the map. Some of the leaders of the period became the mythical personalities we know as King Arthur of England and Charlemagne of the Holy Roman Empire. Feudalism developed as the political system, and manorialism developed as the economic system. The Roman Catholic Church was dominant during this period and was the major source of learning and hope.

Cultural expansion took place from c. 1200 to 1500 as universities began and great cathedrals were built to glorify God. Men from different social classes went off to fight the Crusades in the Holy Land. Change accelerated during the last decades of the period and provided the basis for the development of a modern Europe.

CHAPTER 4

The Byzantine Empire and the Rise of the Eastern European Nations

Why did the Roman Empire in the West decline? We saw the answers to that question in the last chapter. The question for us to answer in this chapter is about the Roman Empire in the East. Why did it survive beyond 476? Indeed, the Eastern Empire continued for almost another thousand years. To explain the remarkable continuation of the Eastern Roman Empire (476–1453), we must look to such factors as the combination of Greco-Roman and Christian culture, advanced scientific technology, and stable political and religious institutions (the **emperor** supported by an efficient government and the Greek Orthodox Church). The Eastern Roman Empire is commonly referred to as the Byzantine Empire because its capital, Constantinople, was built on the site of the former city of **Byzantium**. Byzantium, as used in this chapter, can thus be either the actual city or the name of the Eastern European Empire (also known as the Empire of New Rome). The unique ability of the Byzantine Empire to recover from crises and to adjust to changes that destroyed other civilizations reflects that great balance of the Classical and Christian cultures. In addition to its numerous contributions to art, architecture, literature, music, theology, and science, Byzantium protected and preserved Greco-Roman civilization. The Eastern Roman Empire also physically shielded the West as it repulsed invaders and enemies from all directions. Byzantine civilization brought together the best elements of the ancient and Christian worlds and created a new society.

The Early Byzantine Empire (476–775)

The first period of Byzantium's history was, in great part, devoted to attempts at restoring the Roman Empire to its former size and power. The idea that the West, particularly Italy and North Africa, could be lost was difficult to accept for most people in the eastern part of the Empire. A series of weak and incompetent rulers in the East from 476 to 527 made any real action to restore the imperial Roman government impossible.

The Reign of Justinian I (527–565)

With the ascent to the throne of Justinian I (r. 527–565), the West was briefly restored to Rome. Known in history as "the last Roman Emperor and first Byzantine Emperor," Justinian managed to reconquer the western part of the Empire, largely through the efforts of two brilliant generals, Belisarius and Narses. This effort, however, drained the Empire of both resources and manpower, damaging the economy and ignoring the growing threat of Persian power in the East. The West itself had also changed. The Roman population had become a minority among the Germanic barbarians who had settled there. Despite all his efforts, within a generation of Justinian's death, the Western Empire was lost again.

The Justinian Legal Code Justinian's efforts domestically had longer-lasting results. He perfected the system of strong monarchy and central government that previous emperors had established. He created a commission, led by the brilliant lawyer Tribonian, to revise

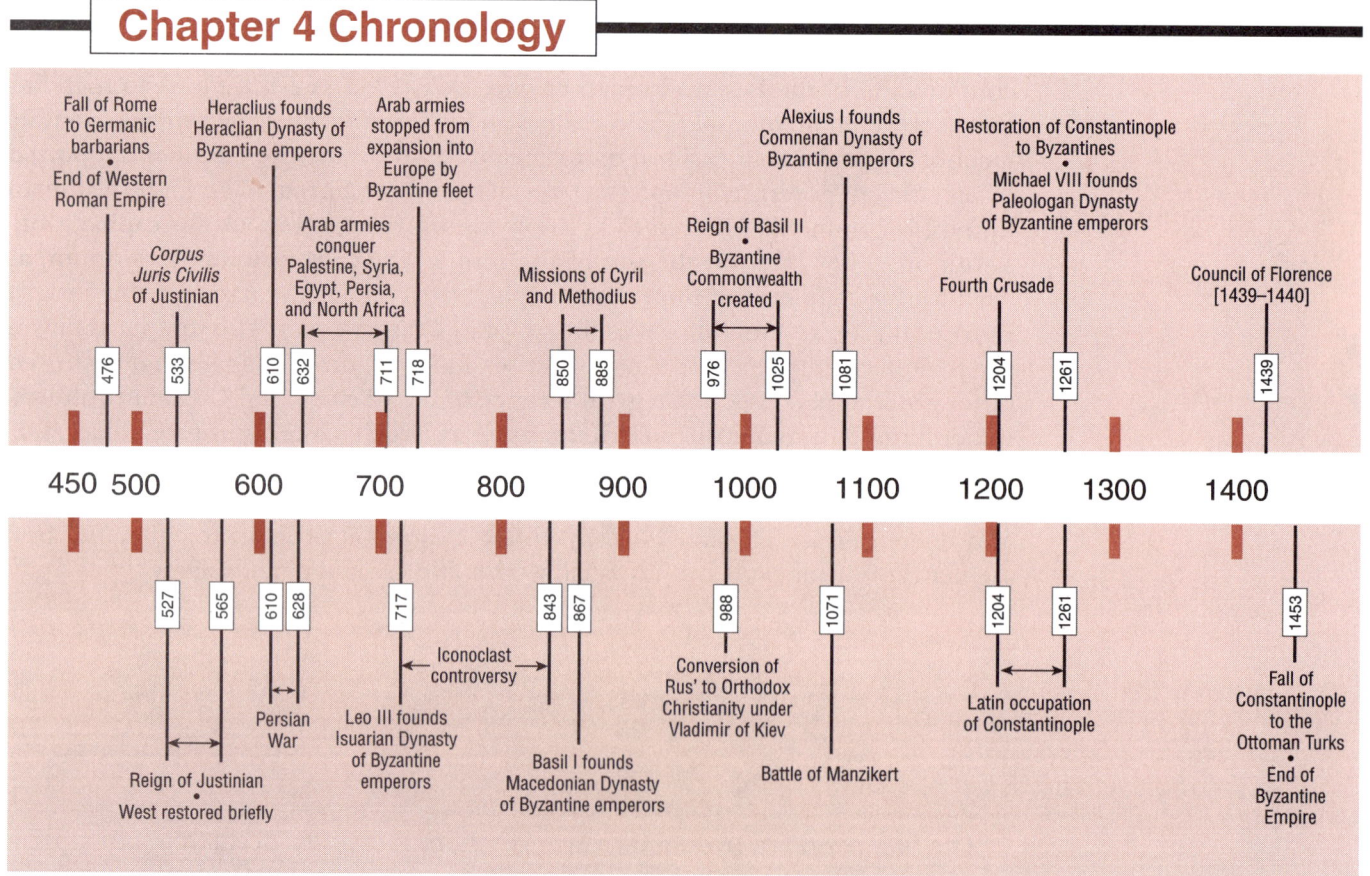

Chapter 4 Chronology

- Fall of Rome to Germanic barbarians
- End of Western Roman Empire
- *Corpus Juris Civilis* of Justinian
- Heraclius founds Heraclian Dynasty of Byzantine emperors
- Arab armies conquer Palestine, Syria, Egypt, Persia, and North Africa
- Arab armies stopped from expansion into Europe by Byzantine fleet
- Missions of Cyril and Methodius
- Reign of Basil II
- Byzantine Commonwealth created
- Alexius I founds Comnenan Dynasty of Byzantine emperors
- Restoration of Constantinople to Byzantines
- Michael VIII founds Paleologan Dynasty of Byzantine emperors
- Fourth Crusade
- Council of Florence [1439–1440]

476 | 533 | 610 | 632 | 711 | 718 | 850 | 885 | 976 | 1025 | 1081 | 1204 | 1261 | 1439

450 500   600   700   800   900   1000   1100   1200   1300   1400

527 | 565 | 610 | 628 | 717 | 843 | 867 | 988 | 1071 | 1204 | 1261 | 1453

- Reign of Justinian
- West restored briefly
- Persian War
- Leo III founds Isaurian Dynasty of Byzantine emperors
- Iconoclast controversy
- Basil I founds Macedonian Dynasty of Byzantine emperors
- Conversion of Rus' to Orthodox Christianity under Vladimir of Kiev
- Battle of Manzikert
- Latin occupation of Constantinople
- Fall of Constantinople to the Ottoman Turks
- End of Byzantine Empire

Roman law. By 533, under Tribonian's leadership the commission produced the *Corpus Juris Civilis* (*Body of Civil Law*). This consisted of:

1. The Codex Justinianus, which organized all the main laws of previous Roman emperors.
2. The Digest, which contained rulings and precedents of Classical Roman lawyers.
3. The Institutes, a handbook for law students.
4. The Novels or New Laws, which presented laws recently added to meet the changing needs of a newly Christian state.

Interestingly, while the first three parts of the *Corpus* were in Latin, the traditonal legal tongue of Rome, the Novels were in Greek. Greek, the language of the East, had now become dominant in the Empire. The *Corpus* remained the basis of Byzantine law until the Empire's collapse in 1453 and influenced the development of later legal systems in both Western and Eastern Europe.

Justinian's Building Program   Justinian also built churches, monasteries, castles, fortifications, palaces, and hospitals, mostly in Constantinople. It was here that he also built the massive Hippodrome (stadium for horseracing) and the magnificent cathedral of Saint Sophia (Holy Wisdom).

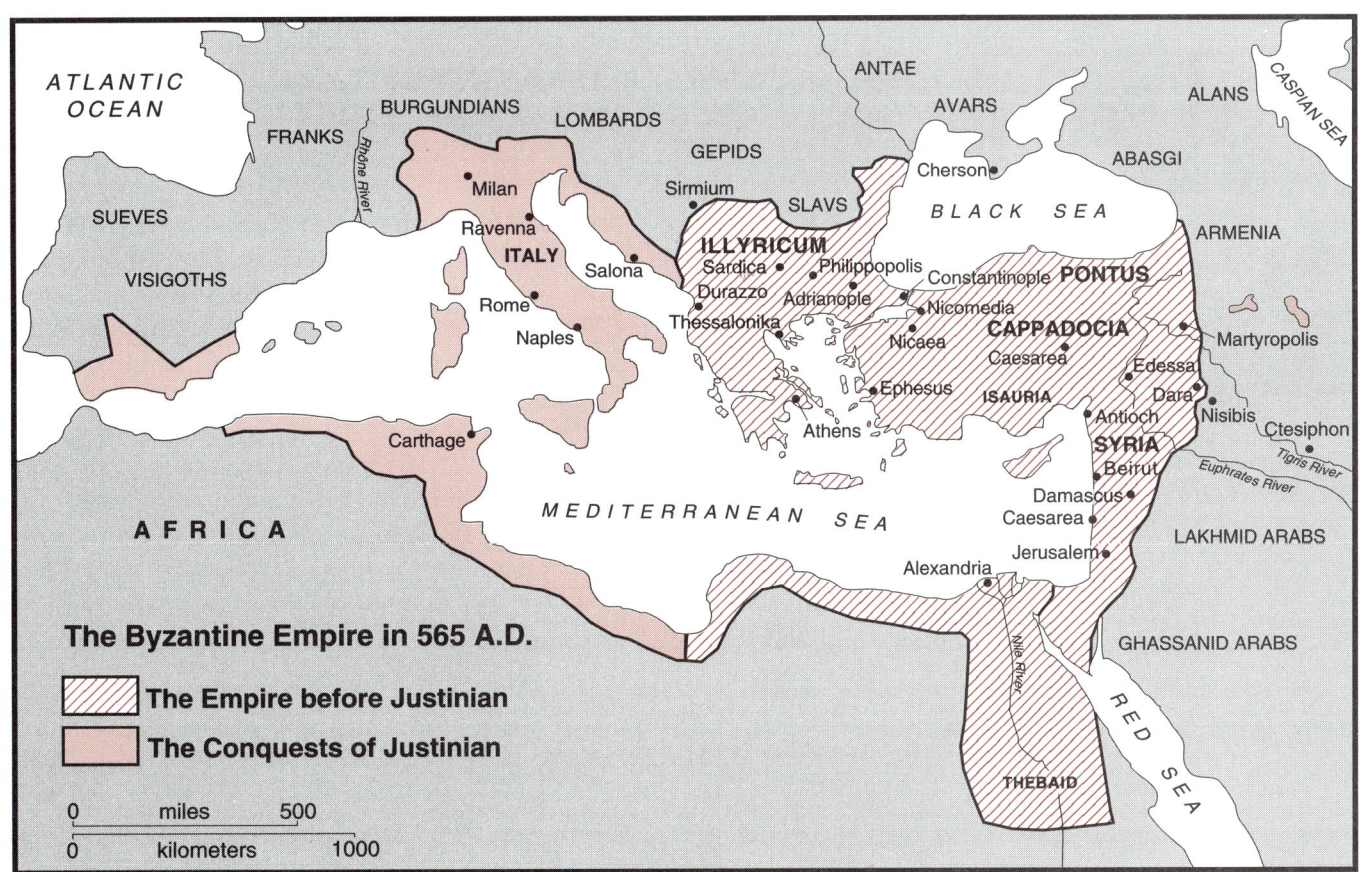

The map above shows the expansion of the Byzantine or Eastern Roman Empire during the reign of the Emperor Justinian (527–565). This expansion was ultimately an unsuccessful attempt to regain the Western Roman Empire from the Germanic tribes.

The Byzantine Empire and the Rise of the Eastern European Nations   **99**

Following the example of Constantine, Justinian saw himself as the protector and defender of Church and Faith. He believed that religious unity was as necessary as loyalty to the emperor and the state. Viewing theological conflict within the Church as dangerous, he attempted to resolve the Monophysite controversy, which had divided Christians within the Empire. The **Monophysites** believed that Jesus was only God and just looked like a man, as opposed to the Orthodox teaching of the Church that he was both fully God and fully human. Justinian's wife, the capable and colorful Empress Theodora, was a Monophysite. Her position gave her husband the trust of the Monophysite community in holding negotiations to end the controversy. Theodora's unexpected death in 548 destroyed any hopes of resolving the division and forced Justinian to persecute the Monophysites. The Monophysites, who were strongest in Egypt, Syria, and North Africa, became enemies of the Empire and were later, in great part, responsible for the loss of these provinces.

The Persian War (610–628)

Justinian's reign left the Eastern Roman Empire physically and economically exhausted. His successors were unable to prevent the loss of the West in 568 to the Germanic barbarians or the invasion of the Balkans by Slavic tribes led by Asiatic nomads in 587. By 610 the Persians had captured Syria, Palestine, Egypt, and much of Asia Minor. Overthrowing an incompetent and unpopular emperor, the dynamic general Heraclius (r. 610–641) seized the throne and led the Byzantine army to defeat the Persians completely. Although Heraclius restored the Eastern provinces to Byzantine control and ended Persian power permanently, the long and costly war left the Empire paralyzed economically and militarily.

The Arab Invasions

In 636 the Arab armies of the Islamic faith, which had started their conquests years earlier, began to invade the territories of the Eastern Roman Empire. The complete exhaustion of the Byzantine military forces and the support of many Monophysites in the Eastern provinces allowed the Arab armies to capture Palestine, Syria, Egypt, North Africa, and part of Asia Minor, as well as the Persian Empire by 711. Jerusalem had been taken by 700. Because of the leadership of Emperor Leo III, the "Isaurian" ("of Syria") (r. 717–741), Constantinople was saved, and the Arab forces were repulsed. The Arab navy was destroyed through the use of a new invention, Greek Fire (a chemical that burned ships and could not be put out with water), which kept the Empire and its ships safe from future Arab attack. By 775 Leo III and his successor, Constantine V (r. 741–775), had restored Asia Minor to the Empire. Byzantium, however, became a strictly European power and had to adjust to this new status.

Icons or holy images of Jesus Christ, the Virgin Mary, and the saints of the Christian Church, were the chief form of art in the Byzantine Empire. The icon shown above is of the Virgin Mary or "Theotokos" ("God Bearer"), as she is more commonly referred to in the Eastern Orthodox Church, and of Christ as a child. Note the supernatural style of the art, such as the odd positions of the hands of the Virgin in relation to her wrists, or the adult head on the infant Jesus.

The High Byzantine Empire (775–1204)

Having lost the Eastern provinces of Palestine, Syria, and Egypt, the Byzantine Empire looked north to Europe. The Mediterranean was no longer the "Roman

Lake," but had become a border dividing the Christian and Islamic worlds. The Slavic nations of Eastern Europe became the focus of Byzantine missions as the Empire's forces reestablished military control of the region. Under a strong series of rulers, Byzantine influence extended into Central and Eastern Europe as well as parts of the East.

The Macedonian Dynasty (867–1055)

Despite great military successes, which included the restoration of Asia Minor and the reconquest of Greece from Slavic tribes, the domestic policies of the Isaurian Dynasty (717–742), particularly iconoclasm (controversy over the use of holy **icons** or religious pictures), created serious internal quarrels. The Isaurian emperors' stand against the use of icons made them extremely unpopular and was ultimately responsible for their downfall. A new Arab threat to Asia Minor and the rise of powerful and aggressive Bulgars (Asiatic–Slavic people) to the north led to the emergence of the Macedonian dynasty (867–1055).

The Conversion of the Slavic Peoples The Macedonian emperors restored the Empire to a position of power and prestige it had not enjoyed since Justinian. This time, however, Byzantium was not economically and physically devastated by the expansion. Beginning with Basil I (r. 867–886), the Empire began a campaign to expand both its influence and its borders. The Byzantines launched a series of successful missions to convert the Slavic peoples to Eastern Orthodox Christianity. There had already been much missionary work done under the leadership of two brothers, Cyril (c. 827–869) and Methodius (c. 815–885), who had converted the peoples of Moravia (in the modern Czech Republic) to Christianity and created the **Slavonic** language and alphabet (used for church services and early historical writing by the Slavic peoples). These nations were extended by the followers of Cyril and Methodius into other Eastern European nations. With the conversion of the leaders of these nations, Bulgaria, Serbia, and Romania, the subjects therein soon became Orthodox Christians as well. The greatest conversion, numerically and geographically, was in 988 in Rus' (present day Belarus', Russia, and Ukraine), under Vladimir of Kiev (r. 980–1015).

The Byzantine Commonwealth Since the rise of the Carolingians in Western Europe (see Chapter 5 "Medieval Europe"), a strained relationship had developed between the Eastern Orthodox Church, under the Patriarch of Constantinople and the Western Roman Catholic Church, under the Pope of Rome. The disagreement arose over the Pope's claim to be the supreme head of the Christian Church. This led to a **schism** or split between Eastern and Western Christianity in 1054.

The two Churches began to compete for the conversion of non-Christian peoples. Eastern Europe soon became divided into two spheres of religious and political influence: the Eastern Orthodox, which included Bulgaria, Serbia, Romania, and Rus', and the Western Roman Catholic, which consisted of Croatia, Moravia, Hungary, and Poland. The Eastern Orthodox nations formed an alliance with the Empire, the Byzantine Commonwealth, which provided mutual military and economic support. The results of this division can still be seen in the political tensions of modern day Eastern European politics.

The Conquest of Bulgaria The rise of Bulgarian aggression in the late tenth century resulted in its conquest by the Empire under Basil II (r. 976–1025) and the annexation of Armenia. By the reign of the last ruler of the Macedonian Dynasty, Byzantium was the greatest

Important Biblical events were often depicted in holy icons. The icon shown above is of the nativity or birth of Jesus Christ, commonly known as Christmas. Note how the important features of the Christmas story (the cave/manger in which Jesus was born, the animals in the manger, the star of Bethlehem) are condensed in a supernatural manner.

power in the Western World. Yet, maintaining the vast borders the Macedonian emperors had created put the Eastern Roman Empire under an enormous pressure. The Western Roman Empire faced the same kind of pressure as it tried to maintain its many borders.

The Crusades

The invasions of the Seljuk Turks (Asiatic nomads) into Asia Minor further strained the Empire's resources. The complete defeat of the Byzantine army by the Seljuks at Manzikert in Asia Minor in 1071 was a blow from which the Empire never fully recovered. By 1081 Armenia and most of Asia Minor had been lost.

With the ascent of Alexius I (r. 1081–1118), the tide of invasion was reversed. Asking the pope for Western European help to remove the Seljuks from Asia Minor, Alexius received an army of **crusaders** (see Chapter 5, "Medieval Europe"), who assisted him in regaining some of Asia Minor (1098). These crusader armies then proceeded further east to regain Jerusalem from the Muslims. Although successive dynasties of emperors managed to maintain these shrunken borders, Byzantium was never able to recover all of Asia Minor or their pre-1071 power.

The relationship with the West and the pope had grown worse due to the actions of the Crusaders. The final break with the West came in 1204 when the knights of the Fourth Crusade attacked and occupied Constantinople. This forced the Byzantine government into exile at Nicaea from 1204 to 1261. The slaughter of fellow Christians by the Crusaders and the installation of a Latin patriarch in Constantinople (with the pope's approval) during the occupation resulted in mistrust and resentment between the Eastern Orthodox and Roman Catholic Churches that has continued until the present day.

The Late Byzantine Empire (1204–1453)

The Paleologian Dynasty (1261–1453)

The restoration of Constantinople under the Paleologian Dynasty (1261–1453) faced overwhelming odds from the start. The successful efforts to remove the occupying Western European Crusaders had exhausted the Byzantines physically and economically. More importantly, new invaders, the Ottoman Turks, had taken most of Asia Minor while the Empire was preoccupied with freeing the capital. To make matters worse, much of the Balkans and Greece had been lost to various Western powers.

The Council of Florence

Beginning with Michael VIII (r. 1261–1282), the Paleologian emperors tried to restore the Empire. Although Byzantium regained most of Greece, the Turks made more gains in Asia Minor. Eventually they controlled the entire area except for Constantinople and its immediate surroundings. Desperate for Western assistance against the Ottoman Turks, the Byzantines entered into negotiations with the **papacy**, which insisted on ending the schism between the Churches as a condition for sending help. There were many attempts at union, the most notable being the Council of Florence (1439–1440), where an agreement was reached, but the clergy and people of the Eastern Orthodox Church would not accept it.

The Fall of Constantinople

By the late fourteenth and early fifteenth centuries, Serbia and Bulgaria had fallen to the Turks, leaving Byzantium encircled. The papacy had lost much of its power and influence in internal battles and was not able to provide the assistance it once could. By 1453 the Turks had captured the area surrounding the capital and lay seige to the city. On Tuesday, May 29, Constantinople fell to the Ottomans. The last Byzantine Emperor, Constantine XI Paleologus (r. 1449–1453), died in the fighting. By 1460 Greece had also fallen. The Ancient World had come to an end.

Byzantine Society

Byzantine society was, in many ways, a continuation of the Roman Empire. We must remember that the region of the Eastern Roman Empire was formerly the Hellenistic kingdoms. Yet, the Christian faith did make some noticcable differences. The population was unified by a common religion (Orthodox Christianity) as well as a common culture (Greco-Roman). They were also often divided by religious issues. For example, even the simplest farmer might get into an argument about theology when he went to market. The disagreements, however, could have very damaging effects, as the Monophysite controversy showed.

Church and State in Byzantium

The influence of religious leaders in the Byzantine Empire was enormous. Basil of Caesarea, a fourth-century bishop, was responsible for the creation of the first orphanages and old age homes. In addition to his philanthropical work, Basil was the author of many theological books, a liturgy, and the first set of rules for monastic life. He was canonized or declared a saint by the Church shortly after his death in 379.

For the vast majority who remained within the official Church, religion gave their lives both hope and meaning. Colorful and impressive religious ceremonies reinforced both their faith in God and the image of the emperor, who became the viceroy or representative of God. It was his duty to protect his people and Church; in turn, the people were expected to cooperate with the government. With the addition of Christian morals and values, governmental responsibilities expanded. Through the monasteries, the government funded orphanages, hospitals, old age homes, and other institutions of social welfare. In fact, Byzantium was the first state to sponsor philanthropic (advancing the care of fellow humans) work.

The relationship between the emperor and Church leadership became a balance of power. Theoretically the two worked side by side, dealing with different needs. While the emperors tended to dominate, they were limited by theology and tradition. Attempts to violate these, as demonstrated by the **Iconoclast** controversy (726–843), ended in failure. This conflict was started when the Isaurian emperors decided to forbid the use of holy icons. The population, led by the monks and many clergymen, refused to accept the decision and protested. The stubborn refusal by the Isaurians to give up on this unpopular policy resulted in their eventual loss of the throne, despite a record of brilliant military successes and good government.

The Patriarchate System

The emperor worked directly with the Patriarch of Constantinople, one of five head bishops who governed the Eastern Church. At the first Christian councils in the late fourth and early fifth centuries, it was decided that the major cities of the Empire (Rome, Constantinople, Alexandria, and Antioch) and Jerusalem (the birthplace of the Christian faith) would have **patriarchs**. They were equals, but the patriarch or pope (meaning Father) of Rome (as the city was the capital of the Empire) was the "first among equals." After the fall of the West in 476, however, the **papacy** took on many special powers, which it later came to regard as its rights.

The Schism of the Eastern and Western Churches

The pope's claim to be the head of the Church brought it into conflict with the other patriarchates, especially Constantinople, which had become the leader of the Eastern Church after the Arab invasions limited the power of the other three. From the ninth to eleventh centuries, theological disputes began to drive a wedge between the two patriarchates. In 1054 a schism occurred between the Eastern (Greek) Orthodox and the Roman (Latin) Catholic Churches. This division was healed soon after, but relations continued to be strained. With the Fourth Crusade of 1204, a final break came. Distrust and resentment followed and continue today, especially in parts of Eastern Europe.

The Improved Status of Women

The legal status of women improved greatly in the Byzantine Empire. Women ruled independently as empresses as well (Irene from 797 to 802, Zoe and Theodora in 1042, and Theodora alone from 1055 to 1056). Women were allowed to own property and became legally independent of male relatives or husbands.

Architecture

The Byzantines expanded on Roman architecture. Continuing to create roads, bridges, aqueducts, palaces, and public buildings, they concentrated on the construction of churches and monasteries. The greatest example of this was the Emperor Justinian's Cathedral of Saint Sophia in Constantinople. Justinian was also responsible for the Monastery of St. Catherine on Mount Sinai (in present-day Egypt).

Sculpture and Painting

Like architecture, art was heavily religious in nature. Although sculpture in the Classical style was practiced, the demand was very limited. Patrons as well as churches commissioned icons, **frescoes** (wall paintings), and mosaics depicting Christ, the Virgin Mary, the various saints, and scenes from the Bible.

The architecture of the Byzantine Empire developed a distinct style, best known by its domed churches. The Cathedral of St. Andrew in the city of Herakleion on the island of Crete is an example of this. Note the combination of architectural styles from the earlier Greek and Roman periods that influenced the Byzantine.

One of the best examples of Byzantine architecture is the eleventh-century church Panaghia Kapnikarea ("Our Lady of the Smoke") in the heart of Athens. Dedicated to the Virgin Mary, it was built on the ruins of a Roman bath.

Carvings and statues were also used at first. They were later forbidden for use in religious worship by the Eastern Church, which decided to allow only flat images. A Byzantine style of religious painting developed; it emphasized the supernatural nature of the subjects. This style dominated Byzantine art, which largely ignored the Western European movement to make artistic depictions more realistic. Unlike the West, where **secular** (nonreligious) art began to appear in the Late Middle Ages, art in Byzantium remained predominantly religious. Monasteries produced the bulk of icons after the Iconoclast controversy, so few names of artists are known because monks did not sign their names to their work.

Literature

Literary forms in Byzantium were dominated, as were all things, by religion. The Byzantines abandoned the simplified **Koine** (Greek used in the Hellenistic Period) for the Classical form of the language. The Classics were studied more for grammar than for content. The three forms of literature that were most developed were history, theology, and **haigiography** (the study of the lives of saints).

Secular poetry disappeared by the sixth century, replaced by the religious poetry used in hymns. Employing the rules and format of Classical poetry, hymn writing became an art. The greatest Byzantine writer was Romanus the Melodist (died c. 555). Responsible for over a thousand hymns (only about 85 have survived), Romanus' work became the model by which future poets would measure their own work. Although secular music was composed as well, religious hymns were in the greatest demand. The Byzantines developed a very stylized form of chant that was used in religious services. As time went on, choirs of singers were used to enhance the beauty of the Eastern Orthodox liturgy. Secular poetry reappeared in the Late Byzantine period with the anonymous epic *Digenes Akritos*, which is about a hero who is half-Arab and half-Byzantine and his romance and struggles. This **humanistic** (study of human beings) work inspired other poets such as Theodore Prodromos (1100–1170), who wrote satires and **panegyrics** (poems of praise) in imitation of the Greeks and Romans.

Historical Writing

In the Roman tradition, historical writing continued to flourish. Despite the strong religious fervor of their civilization, most Byzantine historians tried to be objective and were reliable in their facts. Two schools of history developed: the **monastic**, which consisted of **chronicles** (lists of events in chronological order) that were highly biased toward a religious viewpoint, and the secular, which were written by laymen and reflected a less narrow perspective. The monastics wrote **universal histories**, which started with the Creation in the Bible and went until the present. These writers saw history as part of a predetermined plan by God and read religious significance into every event.

Secular historians were quite varied in their subjects and approaches. The last of the historians trained in the old Roman tradition, Procopius (c. 500–c. 565) wrote on the Emperor Justinian's military successes in *On the Wars*, and the rebuilding of Constantinople in *On the Buildings*. In his last work, *The Secret History*, Procopius unfairly attacked Justinian as an evil ruler, possibly after being denied a government position he thought he deserved. The Emperor Constantine VII "Porphyroghenitos" ("Born in the Purple") (902–959, r. 945–959), wrote two accounts (*On the Imperial Administration* and *On the Cermonies*) of Byzantine government and court life. The historian Michael Psellus (1018–1081) gave fascinating portraits of twelve Byzantine rulers in his *Chronographia* (*Chronography*). One of the most unusual and well written of Byzantine histories was that of Anna Comnena (1083–1154), daughter of Emperor Alexius I. In her *Alexiad*, an account of her father's reign, she analyzed Byzantine society.

Summary

The Byzantine Empire preserved the culture, language, institutions, and customs of the Classical World. More importantly, it reintroduced Western Europe to its Greco-Roman heritage after the Early Middle Ages. Byzantium laid the religious, cultural, and political foundations for the civilizations of the Eastern European nations as well. Islamic civilization also owes much to the Eastern Roman Empire, whose conquered cities introduced much to the Arab invaders. The combination of flexibility and continuity of the Byzantine Empire maintained the Western cultural tradition when it might otherwise have been lost.

CHAPTER 4

Review Exercises

I. Matching

Directions: Match the names in Column A with the achievement they are *best known* for in Column B.

Column A	Column B
1. Tribonian	(a) Cathedral of Saint Sophia
2. Cyril and Methodius	(b) Iconoclast controversy
3. Empress Theodora	(c) *On the Imperial Administration*
4. Justinian I	(d) Monophysite controversy
5. Procopius	(e) *Alexiad*
6. Basil I	(f) conversion of the Slavs
7. Leo III	(g) Byzantine Commonwealth
8. Constantine VII	(h) *Corpus Juris Civilis*
9. Anna Comnena	(i) last Byzantine Emperor
10. Constantine XI	(j) *Secret History*

II. Matching

Directions: Match the words in Column A with the *correct description* in Column B.

Column A	Column B
1. "Greek Fire"	(a) destruction of holy images
2. "Roman Lake"	(b) Byzantine emperor
3. iconoclasm	(c) wall painting
4. patriarch	(d) haigiography
5. "Viceroy of God"	(e) poem of praise
6. philanthropy	(f) Mediterranean Sea
7. study of saints' lives	(g) sack of Constantinople
8. panegyric	(h) defeat of Arab navy
9. fresco	(i) head bishop
10. Fourth Crusade	(j) advancing the care of fellow humans

III. Map Exercise

Directions: Use the map to locate the place associated with each of the following statements. For each statement, write the *letter* of the place.

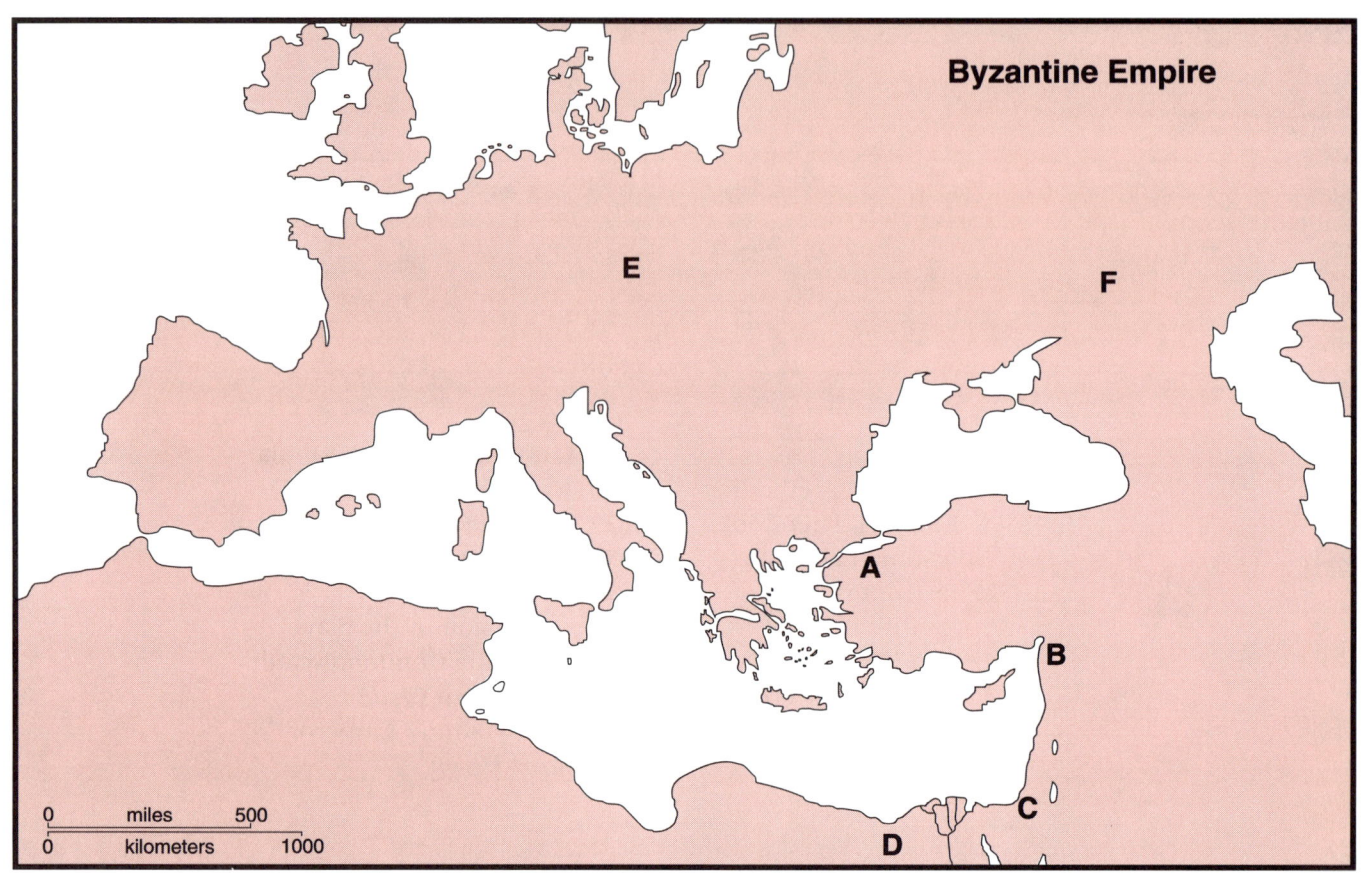

1. _____ The capital city of the Byzantine Empire was located here.

2. _____ This area's Christians were administered by the Patriarch of Alexandria.

3. _____ The Patriarch of Antioch was responsible for the Church of this region.

4. _____ This was the seat of the patriarch who guarded the Christian holy places.

5. _____ The Slavs were first converted to Christianity here.

6. _____ The Russian and Ukrainian cultures developed in this place.

IV. Multiple Choice

Directions: Find the *letter* of the correct answer.

1. The Byzantine Empire was the continuation of the

   (a) Greek Empire.
   (b) Roman Empire.
   (c) Egyptian Empire.
   (d) Persian Empire.

2. The Emperor Justinian accomplished all the following *except*

    (a) the revision of Roman law.
    (b) a massive building program.
    (c) a solution to the Monophysite controversy.
    (d) the temporary restoration of the West.

3. The *Body of Civil Law* consisted of

    (a) Digest, Novels, Institutes, Index.
    (b) Digest, Novels, Codex, Institutes.
    (c) Novels, Codex, Institutes, Index.
    (d) Digest, Codex, Institutes, Index.

4. The Emperor responsible for saving the Empire from the Persians was

    (a) Justinian I.   (b) Leo III.
    (c) Heraclius.   (d) Constantine VII.

5. The success of the Arab invasions in the Empire's Eastern provinces was due to all the following *except*

    (a) poor leadership in the Byzantine government.
    (b) exhaustion of the Byzantine army after the Persian War.
    (c) Monophysite cooperation with the Arab invaders.
    (d) lack of economic resources to begin new military operations.

6. The Isaurian emperors grew unpopular as a result of the

    (a) loss of the Eastern provinces to the Arabs.
    (b) Monophysite controversy.
    (c) corruption in the Byzantine government.
    (d) policy of iconoclasm.

7. The lasting achievement of the Macedonian Dynasty was the

    (a) conversion of the Slavic peoples to Eastern Orthodox Christianity.
    (b) creation of the Byzantine Commonwealth.
    (c) conquest of the Bulgarians.
    (d) annexation of Armenia.

8. The Byzantine Commonwealth consisted of the Byzantine Empire and

    (a) Bulgaria, Moravia, Serbia, and Romania.
    (b) Bulgaria, Serbia, Croatia, and Poland.
    (c) Bulgaria, Serbia, Romania, and Rus'.
    (d) Moravia, Serbia, Poland, and Rus'.

9. All the following were responsible for the schism between the Eastern and Western Churches *except*

    (a) the schism of 1054.
    (b) the concept of papal supremacy.
    (c) the Monophysite controversy.
    (d) the Fourth Crusade.

10. The Byzantine defeat at Manzikert led to the

    (a) Crusades.
    (b) sack of Constantinople.
    (c) rise of the Ottoman Turks.
    (d) schism between the Eastern Orthodox and Roman Catholic Churches.

11. Alexius I was the first Emperor of the

    (a) Nicaean Dynasty.   (b) Comnenan Dynasty.
    (c) Angelan Dynasty.   (d) Paleologan Dynasty.

12. The Fourth Crusade resulted in all the following *except*

    (a) the rise of the Ottoman Turks.
    (b) the sack of Constantinople.
    (c) the restoration of Jerusalem to the Christians.
    (d) the schism between the Eastern Orthodox and Roman Catholic Churches.

13. The last dynasty of Byzantine rulers was the

    (a) Comnenan.   (b) Angelan.
    (c) Paleologan.   (d) Nicaean.

14. In 1453 Constantinople fell to the

    (a) Ottoman Turks.   (b) Seljuk Turks.
    (c) Arabs.   (d) Crusaders.

15. Which of the following statements about Byzantium is most true?

    (a) Their society was unified by a common religion and culture.
    (b) Their style of painting emphasized the natural world.
    (c) The Turks were never able to defeat them.
    (d) Church and state always had a smooth working relationship.

V. Thought Questions

Directions: Answer the following questions in essay form.

1. Explain the statement, "Byzantium was both a continuation of Rome and a new Christian state." Show three ways in which the Empire of New Rome (Byzantium) differed from that of Old Rome.

2. The Arab invasions were both destructive and beneficial for the Byzantine Empire.

    A. Give two examples of how the Empire suffered as a result of the Arab invasions.
    B. Show two ways in which the loss of the Eastern provinces ultimately benefited the Empire.

3. Were the Western Europeans responsible for the destruction of the Byzantine state? Show two ways in which Byzantium's relationship with the West led to the destruction of the Empire.

4. You are a student in a Byzantine university writing to a friend in Rome. In the letter you want to brag a little about the accomplishments and advances that have taken place in the Eastern Empire. Be sure to include the arts, literature, and architecture in your writing.

CHAPTER 5

Medieval Europe

For a long time after 476 A.D., the Byzantine Empire held the Eastern Roman World together. No such unifying force existed in the Western Roman Empire after 476 A.D. The end of Roman government in Western Europe began a period of instability and change. Known as the Middle Ages or the **Medieval** Period (500–1500), it witnessed the transformation of Western Europe into a group of nations that ultimately became among the most powerful on earth. The Middle Ages can be viewed as a period between the ancient and modern worlds. As the Ancient World was vanishing, its knowledge and ideas were passed on to the peoples of the West. They came to regard themselves as the heirs of the Classical World and Greco-Roman civilization. This legacy, passed on by Byzantium, combined with their own unique institutions and became the foundation of modern Western society.

The Early Middle Ages (476–1000)

The Germanic Tribes

The collapse of the Western Roman Empire threw Europe into a state of violent disorder. The Germanic tribes flooded into Roman territory as that Empire's authority was gradually disintegrated. They settled throughout the former Western Empire. These tribes—Visigoths, Ostrogoths, Vandals, Franks, Burgundians, and Anglo-Saxons—were poorly organized and often at war with one other. Between the years of 500 and 750, they divided Western Europe, creating independent kingdoms.

The Rise of the Frankish Kingdom (481–714) Under the leadership of the Merovingian King Clovis (r. 481–511), one of these independent kingdoms, the Frankish kingdom, became very powerful. Building and expanding a strong and organized military, Clovis and his successors conquered all neighboring tribes and expanded their borders. He was also the first

Frankish ruler to convert to Christianity. Clovis hoped that his new religion would eventually unite his kingdom further. A strong monarch, he developed an efficient court of officials. Each local district or county was administered by a royally appointed governor or count, who collected taxes, provided justice, and kept order. Clovis's successors, however, were not very capable rulers. Slowly, royal power and authority disintegrated. The succeeding Merovingian rulers kept dividing the kingdom equally among male children until three weak and disunited subkingdoms existed. Great landowners were depended upon to rule efficiently in place of the central government, which could no longer do so. The local nobles soon grew used to their power and created their own private governments on the lands they ruled. The inability of the royal government to provide protection forced the population to take pledges of loyalty and service to the nobles.

The Early Carolingians (714–768) The vacuum created by lack of leadership on the part of the Merovingian kings was soon filled by the Carolingians. Serving as mayors or chief officers of the Frankish royal court, they built up great power and influence. In 732, Charles Martel (r. 714–741) led Frankish forces to defeat the invading Muslims in the Battle of Tours. His successor, Pepin the Short (r. 741–751), convinced the pope to authorize the transfer of the Frankish crown from the Merovingians to his own family on the grounds that those who exercise power should rule. After deposing the reigning monarch, Pepin was elected king by the Frankish nobles. Once in

Chapter 5 Chronology

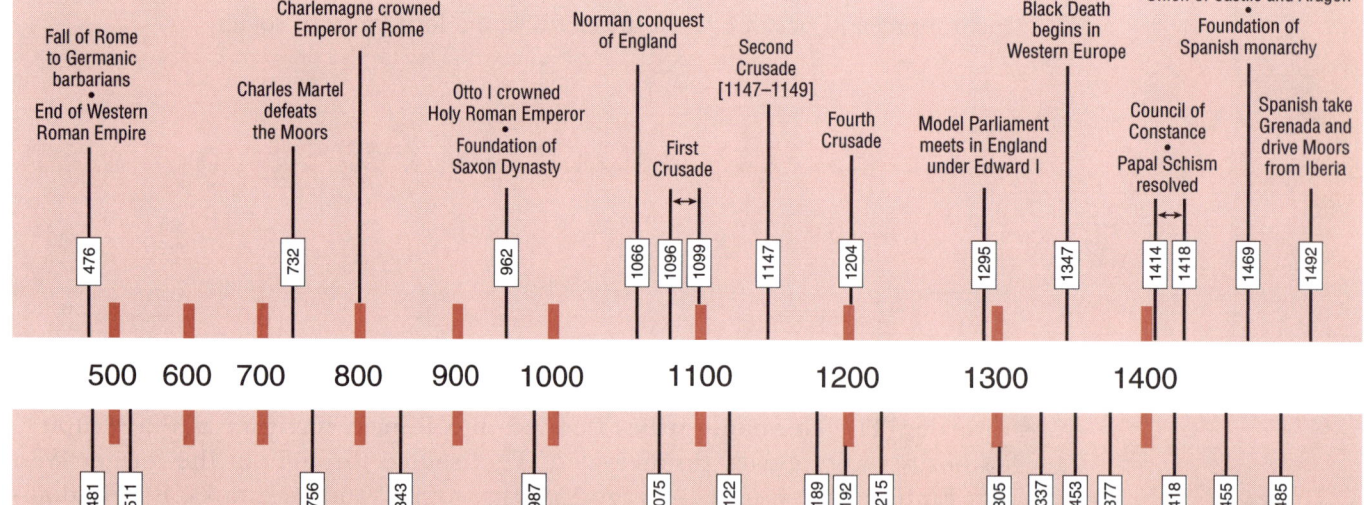

power, he began to rebuild the central authority of the government. Acting as its protector, Pepin defended the papacy from the Lombards and granted captured land to it. Contained in a document known as the "Donation of Pepin" (756), the grant became the basis of the papacy's claim to be an independent state.

Charlemagne and the Creation of the Carolingian Empire (768–814)

Carolus or Charles (768–814), later called Charlemagne or Charles the Great, transformed the Frankish state into the Carolingian Empire. This Empire was to dominate most of Western Europe. Charlemagne conquered all of Italy except the Byzantine territories in the south and the Papal States. He expanded into northeastern Europe, subduing the peoples in that area, and annexed lands in Eastern Europe. Although unable to penetrate Spain, he established a military border beyond the Pyrenees Mountains, which kept his Empire safe from future aggression by the Spanish Moors (Muslims).

Charlemagne restored the strong central government structure established by Clovis. He divided the Empire into some three hundred counties, rewarding loyal counts with personal land grants and punishing any nobles who ignored **royal capitularies** (orders) and regulations. Imperial envoys called *missi dominici* were sent out to investigate and report on the actions of local officials.

Charlemagne enforced uniformity in religion as well as in law, forcing the remaining pagans in the Empire to accept the Christian faith. He encouraged the building of churches and monasteries and imposed a tax of 10 percent of income

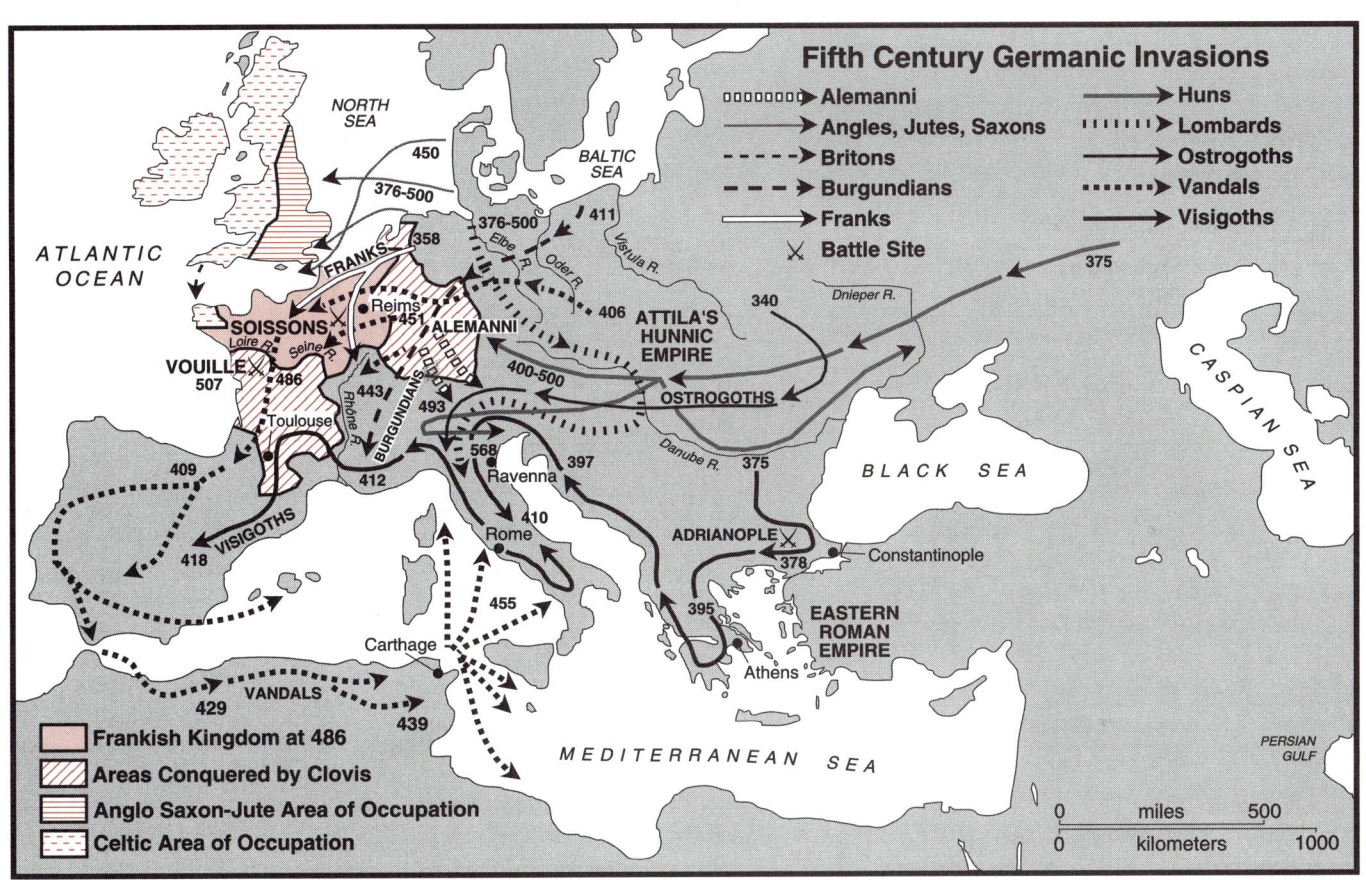

The map above shows the migrations of the Germanic tribes into the Roman Empire in the fifth century. Most of these nations established their own kingdoms within the Empire's borders. The most powerful of these was the Frankish Kingdom in Gaul.

(the **tithe**) to support the Church. Working closely with the papacy, the ruler enforced uniform ritual in religious services.

The Carolingian Renaissance

Within his court, Charlemagne supported a revival of Greco-Roman culture and learning, known later as the "Carolingian Renaissance." This movement established a Palace School at Aachen. All the young men of the court were required to attend the school, producing a generation of educated and efficient administrators.

Charlemagne Crowned Holy Roman Emperor

Charlemagne and his court rediscovered the legacy of the Classical World and attempted to model the Carolingian Empire on the Roman Empire. On Christmas Day in 800, Charlemagne had the pope crown him Holy Roman Emperor. This produced a strong negative reaction from both the Byzantine Emperor and the Eastern Church, straining relations. Yet it was significant because, for the first time, a Germanic ruler adopted Greco-Roman learning and identified himself as a Roman Emperor.

The Disintegration of the Carolingian Empire (814–843)

Charlemagne's son, Louis the Pious (r. 814–840), was a very weak successor. Extremely religious and indecisive, Louis was unable to enforce central authority over the vast Carolingian Empire as his father did. Instead, like the Merovingian kings, he depended on local nobles to rule their own counties. This weakness was

The map above shows the territories conquered by the Frankish King Charlemagne or Charles the Great (766–814). The Carolingian Empire came close to dominating most of Western Europe, a goal later Medieval German rulers would try to imitate.

Charlemagne was the first Holy Roman Emperor.

made worse by the growing barbarian attacks throughout the Empire by Islamic Saracens, Asiatic Magyars, and Scandinavian Vikings. As the invaders did not occupy, but attacked and fled, the only effective method of defense was for each noble to organize an army. This made local rulers warlords. Given these circumstances, the Emperor had little choice but to cooperate with and even reward local nobles who successfully protected their county from attack.

Upon Louis' death in 840, the Carolingian Empire was divided among his three sons. They immediately went to war against each other. The matter was settled in 843 when they signed the Treaty of Verdun, which created three separate and equal kingdoms. The eldest, Lothair, was given Italy and the areas of Burgundy and Provence (Lotharingia); Charles the Bald received the equivalent of modern France (Kingdom of the West Franks); and Louis the German had what is roughly modern Germany (Kingdom of the East Franks). After 843, the rank of Holy Roman Emperor no longer carried any great authority. The imperial title was transferred from one German dynasty to another, but had no real power outside of that of the ruler himself until after the start of the High Middle Ages. After 850, the Saracen, Magyar, and Viking attacks intensified. By 900, the Carolingian Empire had disappeared.

The Rise of Feudalism (850–1000)

Feudalism, a system of local rule based on mutual hereditary obligations, dominated Europe after 850. Peasants turned to the local lords for protection from attack. In return, they provided produce and services for the noble. The need for a strong army forced local lords to offer grants of land (**fiefs**) to warriors or **knights** in order to secure their services. In return, the knights took an oath of loyalty to the noble, becoming his **vassals**, or servants. The noble became their *seigneur* or **lord**, to whom they owed total allegiance. The knights were usually men from the upper levels of society who had been trained to fight and could supply their own armor and horse. They offered their services to more powerful individuals, especially those who owned castles. To be sure that these arrangements would continue, vassalage and fiefs were made hereditary. Elaborate ceremonies for swearing loyalty were developed in order to encourage individual knights to honor their obligations by making them promise in front of witnesses. Many times a vassal would divide part of his own fief to create vassals of his own. Many lords were more powerful than kings, who had become, in reality, little more than local rulers themselves by the tenth century.

Manorialism Feudalism in Western Europe took on the form of **manorialism**, as the peasant population attached itself to self-sufficient agricultural estates run by nobles or the Church, who protected them. The lord of the **manor** and the peasant both had

Viking ships such as this one were used during the invasions that terrorized Western Europe.

hereditary obligations toward each other. In exchange for the use of the land, the peasant became a **serf**, who was bound to stay on the manor and obligated to provide services for his seigneur. These included working the lord's lands, providing skilled labor and repairing roads, fortifications, and buildings. Women were required to perform such duties as spinning, cleaning, and preparing food in the seigneur's house. Those who were not serfs were **villeins**, who were exempt from the obligatory service. For the peasant, the manorial system was usually harsh and cruel, producing, at best, only enough to survive.

The High Middle Ages (1000–1300)

The Decline of Feudalism (1000–1100)

The period that begins with the decline of feudalism is known as the High Middle Ages. It was during this time that Medieval civilization reached its height. The problems that plagued the Early Middle Ages receded after the year 1000. The population actually began to grow, as did the quantity of food produced. Many factors contributed to this:

1. The barbarian attacks ended. The Magyars' expansion was halted and the Vikings settled to form independent Christian nations.
2. There was a great improvement in agricultural techniques that resulted in a surplus of produce. A new system of crop rotation was adopted, in which the land was divided into three fields, rather than the traditional two fields. This improved soil fertility, increased crop yields, provided more food for livestock, and reduced the amount of time spent plowing.
3. The invention of the heavy moldboard plow was a major technological advance that allowed the plowing of heavy soil easily.
4. The improved rigid horsecollar and the adoption of the horseshoe resulted in more efficient use of animals in farmwork.
5. An increased use of iron made agricultural tools more effective.
6. Western Europe's climate improved, bringing about milder winters, better distribution of rainfall, and fewer variations in temperature.
7. Relative peace and the growth in population allowed manors to expand by clearing new lands in order to increase their food production.

Seeking a more peaceful environment in which to pursue their spiritual development, the monks expanded into the northern European wilderness, cutting down forests and draining swamps. They were soon followed by runaway serfs and peasants who were experiencing food shortages due to the increase in population.

These groups eventually established towns in previously uninhabited areas. These combined factors created conditions that encouraged the growth of commerce.

The German Holy Roman Emperors

The revival of trade and the new wealth it produced, especially in the growing towns and cities, destroyed the feudal structure. National kings began to rebuild their authority and power. The earliest and most impressive effort was that of the German Holy Roman Emperors. Until the tenth century, royal power declined in the three kingdoms that had once been the Carolingian Empire. In Germany, local dukes had formed the independent kingdoms of Saxony, Bavaria, Franconia, Swabia, and Lorraine out of the Kingdom of the East Franks. By the mid-tenth century, Otto I (r. 936–973), the Duke of Saxony, ended the Magyars' raids on Germany, gained control over the other independent German kingdoms, and restored the northern parts of Italy once held by the Carolingians. He was crowned Holy Roman Emperor by the pope in 962, founding the Saxon Dynasty of German emperors. Otto "the Great," as he was later known, used **lay investiture** (the appointment of bishops by the ruler rather than by Church officials) to gain control of the German kingdoms. His successors, however, became preoccupied in Italy and allowed feudalism to reappear in Germany. The last ruler of this line, Henry (Heinrich) II (r. 1002–1024), used lay investiture and the influence of the Church to regain imperial control.

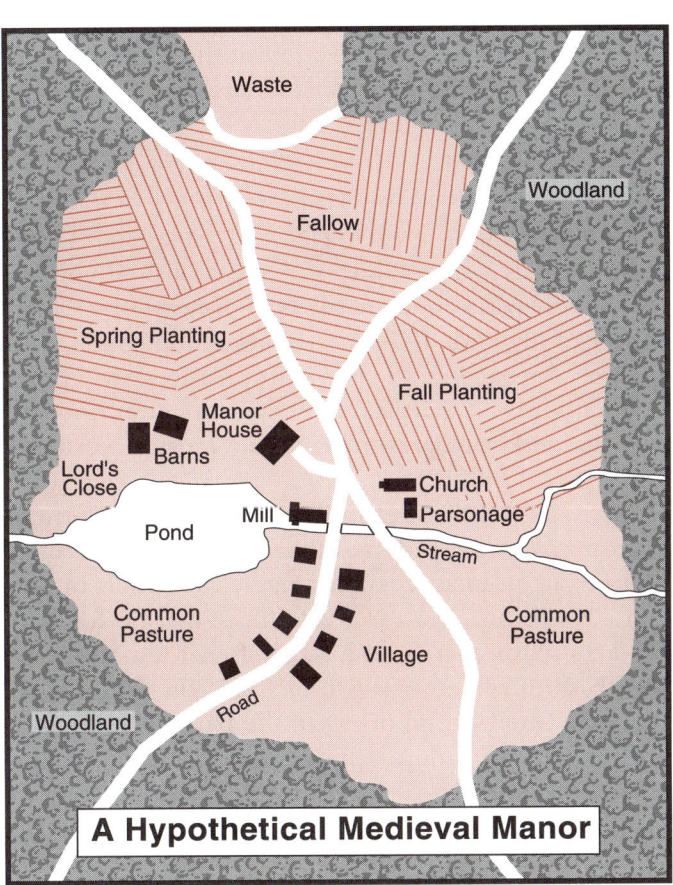

The illustration above shows how a Medieval manor would have been organized in the High Middle Ages. Note the various parts of the manor that combined to make it self-sufficient.

The Lay Investiture Controversy (1046–1122)

In 1024, Konrad II (r. 1024–1039) established the Salian Dynasty of Holy Roman Emperors, also using lay investiture to maintain his power. His son, Henry III (r. 1039–1056), was a reformer who condemned lay investiture. In 1046, he installed his cousin, the dedicated German reformer, Leo IX (r. 1049–1054), as Pope. Under Leo's leadership, a reform movement began within the Roman Catholic Church. This movement opposed corruption among the clergy and lay investiture.

His successor, Pope Gregory VII (r. 1073–1084), pursued these reforms, bringing him into direct conflict with Emperor Henry IV (r. 1056–1105) in 1076. When Henry declared that Gregory VII was no longer Pope, the Emperor was excommunicated, or cut off from participation in Church **sacraments** (holy rites). We must remember that for the Medieval Christian, excommunication meant being damned after death. They believed only the sacraments could save a person's soul. This was the most powerful weapon the Church had at its disposal for defending itself from the attacks of ambitious rulers. In addition, anyone who was excommunicated was no longer a Christian and only a Christian could be Holy Roman

Emperor. Faced with the loss of his crown, he was forced to retract his declaration and seek the Pope's forgiveness in 1077. Henry waited for days for an answer in the snow outside a monastery at Canossa in northern Italy where the Pope was staying. Gregory finally forgave the Emperor after having humbled him. The papacy's victory was, however, a temporary one. In 1084, Henry invaded Italy, forced Gregory into exile, and replaced him. In 1122, a compromise was reached between Emperor Henry V (r. 1106–1125), the German nobles, and the Pope, with the Concordat of Worms. Under this agreement, only the Church could appoint bishops. Yet, the land and powers that came with the position would be given by the Emperor. Ultimately, this weakened the position of the Church.

The Struggle for Italy (1176–1250)

By the mid-twelfth century a new dynasty, the Hohenstaufens of Swabia, attempted to rebuild imperial power. Emperor Frederick I "Barbarossa" ("Red Beard") (r. 1152–1190), pacified the German nobility and reestablished control over northern Italy. In 1176, the Lombard League, an alliance of northern Italian city-states led by the papacy, successfully ended German domination. In 1183, a compromise was reached in which Barbarossa's leadership position was recognized in return for actual independence. Frederick I's successors attempted to restore control over Italy, but in the end were prevented by the most powerful of all the Medieval popes, Innocent III (r. 1196–1216).

Initially, Emperor Frederick II (r. 1198–1250) returned control of the German Church to the papacy and guaranteed papal independence in return for Innocent's support. Frederick II later began an unsuccessful struggle to reassert imperial control over Italy, which ended with his death in 1250. The struggle for Italy between the Hohenstaufens and the papacy created a state of civil war from the late twelfth to the early thirteenth century between two factions; the **Ghibellines** (supporters of the emperor) and the **Guelfs** (supporters of the papacy). Although this struggle established temporary Italian independence, the disunity between the various states led to Italy's domination by foreign powers and a decline in papal power.

Involved with internal struggles, the German nobles could not agree on a successor to Frederick II until 1273, when they elected Rudolf of Habsburg, a weak ruler who would not threaten to dominate them. The fatal flaw of the German Holy Roman Emperors was their determination to create an empire outside Germany, rather than build a national state as other European rulers did. Their obsession with restoring the Roman Empire would later result in the disintegration of their authority and power.

The Creation of France

The Kingdom of France was first established by the Treaty of Verdun as the Kingdom of the West Franks. It was ruled by Charles the Bald and his heirs until 987. Carolingian power, however, declined during that period. Feudalism was stronger in France than anywhere else in Western Europe. While the French kings were officially recognized as overlords of France, real power was held by the great landholding lords. In 987, the French nobles and clergy ended the Carolingian Dynasty and elected one of the chief lords, Hugh Capet (r. 987–996), Count of Paris, as King.

The Capetian Kings (987–1328)

The Capetian Dynasty ruled France for nearly 350 years until 1328. Under the first four Capetians, the kings had no power outside their own domain, the area surrounding Paris known as the Ile de France. The Capetians did manage to establish a hereditary right to the throne and gain the support of the Church, but the rest of the kingdom remained divided in feudal principalities. Even within the Ile de France, Capetian power was limited.

Louis VI "the Fat" (r. 1108–1137), was the first to gain control over the feudal vassals in the domain. Building a strong government and courts, Louis provided order and justice for his subjects. He also ended the monopoly of nobles on royal offices by bringing in men of the middle class who were completely loyal to the king. Louis was so effective that the dying Duke of Aquitane entrusted his daughter Eleanor (1122–1204) and his kingdom to him. She was married to Louis' son and successor, Louis VII (r. 1137–1180), a religious and dedicated ruler, who was not very capable politically. Unable to control the rebellious duchy of Aquitane, Louis secured an annulment (divorce) from the pope and ended the childless marriage. Eleanor married Henry II (r. 1154–1189), King of England, who added the Aquitane to his other French territories. This became known as the Norman-Angevin Empire because Henry was descended from the Dukes of Normandy and Anjou.

Louis' son, Philip (Philippe) II Augustus (r. 1180–1223), soon annexed all the northern Angevin possessions. Philip's successors, especially Louis IX (r. 1226–1270), later canonized as a saint of the Roman Catholic Church, and Philip (Philippe) IV "the Fair" (r. 1285–1314), continued to expand the possessions of the French monarchy. They also developed a strong central government with efficient institutions run by officials devoted to the monarchy. The Capetians gave great financial assistance to the Church in return for its support. This relationship ended when Philip IV became involved in a conflict with Pope Boniface VIII (r. 1294–1303) over the King's power to tax Church property and judge the clergy. Philip turned the French against the papacy, forced the clergy to submit to his authority, and sent agents to Rome to capture Boniface. By 1300, the feudal French monarchy controlled much of the nation under a strong central government.

The Babylonian Captivity and the Papal Schism

After Boniface's death, Phillip used his influence to elect a French bishop, Clement V (r. 1305–1314), as Pope. Clement moved the papacy to Avignon in France. This move gave the kings of France enormous influence over papal decisions. From 1305 to 1377, seven French popes ruled from Avignon. This period became known as the Babylonian Captivity because the papacy, like the Ancient Hebrews held captive in Babylon, were controlled by the French monarchy. In 1377, Pope Gregory XI (1377–1378) returned to Rome. This angered the French Church, which elected a rival pope in Avignon. For forty years a conflict developed between opposing popes in France and Italy known as the Papal Schism. It was finally resolved by the Council of Constance (1414–1418), which elected an Italian as pope and designated Rome as the permanent residence of the papacy.

The Norman Conquest of England

England had been under the control of Anglo-Saxon kings since the Early Middle Ages. In 1066, the Normans conquered the nation. They were led by the Duke of Normandy, William I "the Conqueror" (r. 1066–1087), who claimed that he had a legitimate right to the English throne through his ancestors. William established a centralized form of feudalism in England. He gave large pieces of land as fiefs to his vassals (barons) from Normandy. To avoid the problems that other feudal kings had encountered, he insisted that all sub-vassals (vassals to his barons) take the Salisbury Oath. This was a promise that allegiance to the king would come before loyalty to an immediate lord. This established a stable political environment and a military for the monarchy.

William built a strong central government based on the resources and authority of the previous Anglo-Saxon rulers, claiming to be their rightful successor. He created the **Curia Regis** (Court of the King), which was an assembly of barons and bishops that acted as judges and advisors to the King. William continued the Anglo-Saxon system of local administration, putting the local officials, especially the sheriffs, under the monarchy's direct control. By supporting the Papal Reform Movement, he won the recognition of the pope and control of the English Church. An outstanding achievement of William's government was the Domesday Book of 1086, a detailed survey of his subjects and their property. Compiled in order to examine the kingdom's taxable resources, the Domesday Book illustrates the high level of centralized control and financial expertise of Norman administration.

The Norman-Angevin Dynasty (1087–1272) William's successors, known as the Norman-Angevin Dynasty, were energetic and capable kings who developed royal power. Under Henry I (r. 1100–1135) and Henry II (r. 1154–1189) an effective central government was established. Government departments were created: the **royal exchequer** for tax collection; the treasury, which guarded and dispensed royal money; the chancery, which issued royal orders and composed correspondence; and the royal law courts for the dispensing of justice. Henry I began the **circuit court system**, which sent traveling judges around the nation to hear cases. Henry II established central courts at Westminster to hear more difficult cases and a jury system.

Like Philip IV of France, Henry II came into conflict with the Church over the questions of taxation of Church properties and royal authority to judge the clergy. In 1164 he ordered that clergy accused of civil crimes be tried in royal, instead of Church, courts. Led by Archbishop of Canterbury (highest ranking bishop in England), Thomas Becket, who was previously his friend and chancellor (highest advisor), the King was opposed by the English Church. Becket was murdered, probably on Henry's orders (and later made a saint of the Roman Catholic Church) and popular outrage forced Henry to make concessions to the English Church. Despite this setback, the English kings continued to exercise great control over the Church in England.

Henry also gained vast holdings in France, establishing the Norman-Angevin Empire. His son and successor Richard I "the Lion-Hearted" (r. 1189–1199) kept these territories, but was far too involved with foreign affairs to address domestic problems. His successor, John (r. 1199–1216), lost most of England's French possessions to Philip II Augustus in 1214.

The Magna Carta and the Creation of Parliament Responding to popular discontent with tyrannical policies, John also provoked the Church. In 1215, faced with a rebellion led by the Archbishop of Canterbury and his most powerful nobles, John signed the **Magna Carta** (Great Charter), an agreement to limit royal power. It affirmed the traditional privileges of the nobles, clergy, and townspeople, and the monarchy's privileges of respect, law, and custom. These included:

1. The collection of new taxes only with the consent of the Great Council (nobles and bishops who advised the king).
2. The right of all people to a trial by jury.
3. The rule of law above all other authority, including the king.

It was also an important first step in limiting the power of the monarchy.

King John's concession did not resolve the conflict between the nobility and monarchy. It continued throughout the reign of John's weak and foolish son Henry III (r. 1216–1272). Henry's refusal to work with his barons, use of foreign advisors, concessions to the papacy, and futile military expeditions led the exasperated nobles to rebel. Under Simon de Monfort, the rebels summoned a **parliament**, or representative assembly, made up of nobles, clergy, and townspeople, to decide on a new type of limited monarchy. The rebellion was crushed because of their lack of unity, but Henry's successor, Edward I (r. 1272–1307), established Parliament as a regular assembly of representatives. It was initially only an advisory body to the King, but its powers and rights grew in the following centuries (see Chapter 11, "The Growth of Democracy in England").

The Crusades (1095–1204)

The Crusades began in 1095 when Pope Urban II received a request for mercenaries (paid soldiers) from the Byzantine Emperor Alexius I (see Chapter 4, "The Byzantine Empire and the Rise of the Eastern European Nations"). Urban delivered a sermon at Clermont in France, where he declared a **crusade** or "armed pilgrimage" to restore the Holy Land to Christianity. He claimed that there was hardship and suffering under the Muslims for both the Eastern Christians and pilgrims from Western Europe. The Pope promised salvation for all knights who took up the sword against the Muslims. Urban saw the Crusades as an opportunity to rid Western Europe of the warring feudal knights. The institutions that feudalism had created, particularly knighthood, had become unnecessary. With the changes that had taken place in Western Europe, feudal vassals were nuisances and obstacles to progress. This would also bring greater prestige and power to the papacy and force the Eastern Church to accept **papal supremacy**.

Knights were not the only ones to go on the Crusades. The crusading movement attracted many different types of people. Religious pilgrims, missionary priests, monks and nuns, popular preachers, adventurers seeking wealth, runaway serfs, merchants, impoverished peasants seeking new opportunities, and the families of the knights themselves, often followed the Crusaders. The crusader kingdoms in the Middle East came to resemble their counterparts in Western Europe.

The First Crusade (1095–1099) The response to Urban's request was overwhelming. By 1096, four large armies of the First Crusade, composed mostly of Norman and French knights, arrived at Constantinople to unite with Byzantine forces in a campaign to remove the Turks from Asia Minor and then liberate Jerusalem from Muslim control. The second part of the plan was a surprise to the Byzantine emperor, who was only expecting mercenaries. He was forced to negotiate separately with each crusader group's leader because there was no unity among the knights. Despite their promise to assist Alexius in regaining Asia Minor, the crusader armies separated from the Byzantine forces in 1097 after defeating the Turks in a decisive battle. Once in Syria, the armies split up, each leader anxious to establish his own kingdom. One crusader state was established at Edessa (1097) under Baldwin of Flanders; another at Antioch (1098) under the Norman prince Bohemond; and a third at Jerusalem (1099) under Baldwin, who made people living in Edessa, Antioch, and Tripoli (1100) fiefs of his domain. Disregarding their promises to the Byzantine

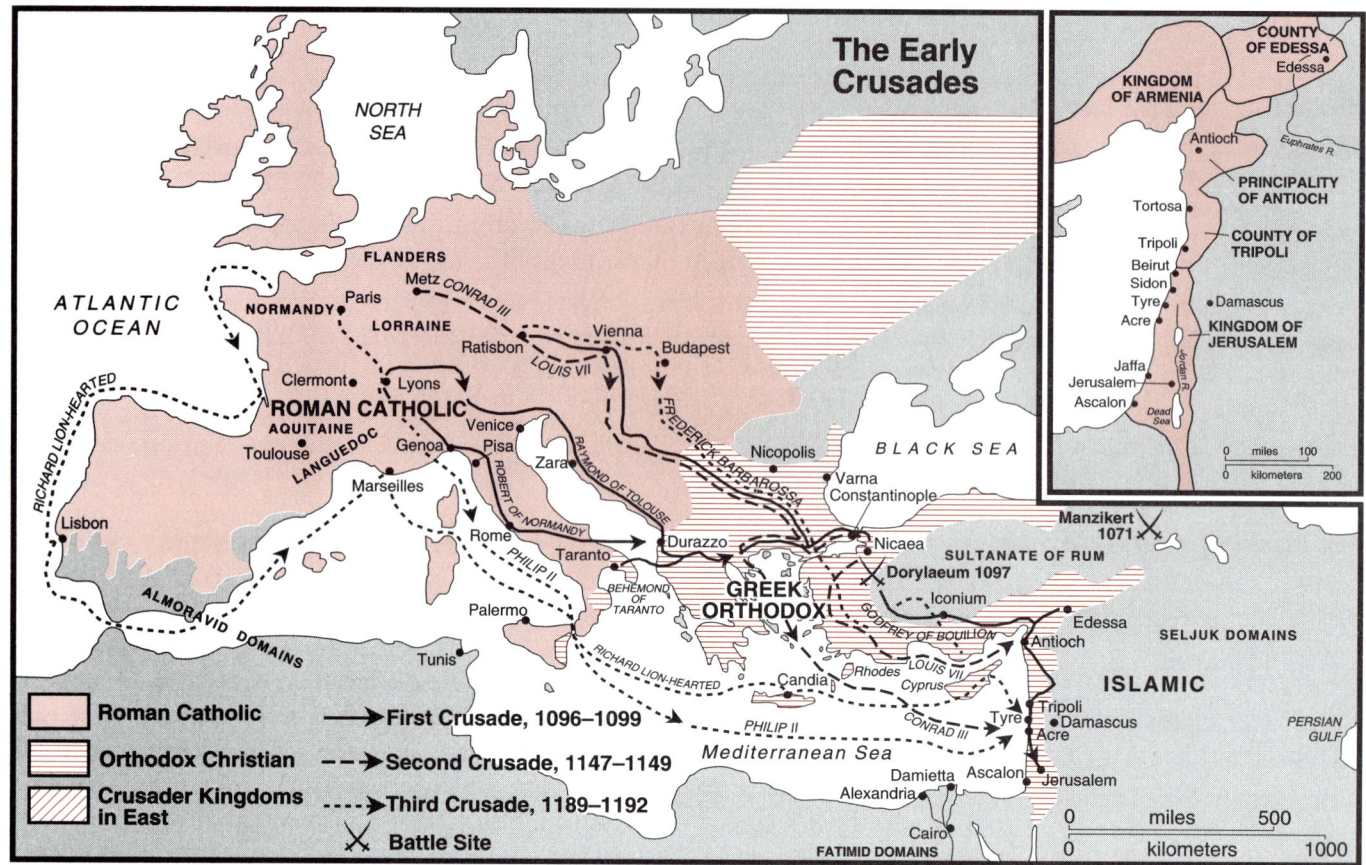

The map above shows the major land and sea routes taken by crusading armies in the first three crusades (1098–1192). The Fourth Crusade (1204) resulted in the capture and occupation of Constantinople by crusaders from 1204–1261. Note the division between Eastern Orthodox Christians and Roman Catholics, that was in great part responsible for the ultimate failure of the Crusades.

emperor and the pope, they established an independent feudal hierarchy of Latin crusader kingdoms under the overlordship of Baldwin, King of Jerusalem.

With the assistance of the Italians, the Crusaders seized the chief Mediterranean seaports in Syria and Palestine, winning control of the sea routes leading to the Latin kingdoms. They also built a series of castles at strategic locations throughout the area. Three crusading orders were established: the Knights Templar, the Knights Hospitaler, and the Teutonic (German) Knights. Modelled on monastic orders, their members vowed to defend and protect Christians living in and **pilgrims** visiting the Holy Land.

Despite all their efforts, maintaining these crusader kingdoms was difficult. To begin with, their numbers were small. They were very dependent on Western Europe for supplies and soldiers. To make matters worse, the crusading knights often abused and committed atrocities against Eastern Orthodox Christians, Jews, and Muslims in the areas through which they passed. The havoc the zealous crusaders brought on the local populations, especially the Jewish communities, made them hated by all groups throughout the region.

The Second Crusade (1147–1149) The Second Crusade was prompted by the loss of Edessa to the Turks in 1144. Appeals by the pope led to the creation of a crusading army under the Holy Roman Emperor Konrad III and French King Louis VII. The force was, however, destroyed by the Turks in Asia Minor and unable to assist the Latin kingdoms. In the years following the Second Crusade, an alliance between the Muslim forces of Egypt and Syria, under the leadership of the dynamic general Saladin (c. 1137–1193), led to the capture of almost all the Latin kingdoms by 1187.

The Third Crusade (1189–1192) Saladin's victories brought another crusade, led by the three most powerful rulers in Western Europe: the Holy Roman Emperor Friedrich I "Barbarossa," the French King Philippe II Augustus, and the English monarch Richard I, "the Lionhearted." Despite its promise, the Third Crusade was also a failure. Barbarossa left first, but died on the way. When the French and English kings arrived, their personal disagreements resulted in Philippe's departure, and Richard was left to lead the crusade alone. After several inconclusive battles, Richard and Saladin agreed to a truce that left Jerusalem in Muslim hands, but allowed Christians free access.

The Fourth Crusade (1204) The Fourth Crusade was a wasteful and destructive event that resulted only in further dividing the Christian world. Started by Pope Innocent III, the crusade did not attract the support expected. Arriving in Constantinople in 1204, the Venetians, who had been hired to transport the Crusaders, and the knights agreed to attack the Byzantine capital instead. The city was savagely taken with many lives lost. The Crusaders proclaimed a Latin empire of Constantinople with its own emperor and patriarch. The Byzantine government went into exile in Nicaea and continued to fight the Latin occupiers until 1261, when they recaptured their capital. After the Fourth Crusade, crusading lost its appeal for most Europeans. Jerusalem remained under Muslim control.

Results of the Crusades

For Christian Europe, the Crusades were a military failure. Yet, they had important results for European history. On the positive side:
1. They exposed Western Europeans to the cultures of Byzantium and the Islamic nations.
2. They brought many new products and technologies to the West.
3. The heritage and learning of the Greco-Roman World was re-introduced to Western Europeans.
4. A new exchange, both economic and cultural, developed between the East and West.
5. Trade and commerce were encouraged, leading to the growth of a merchant class.
6. European exploration advanced through the search for alternative trade routes.
7. The feudal system was effectively destroyed by the flow of knights from Western Europe to the East. This allowed national monarchs to form strong central governments and restore order and stability within Europe.

On the negative side:
1. The Crusades created a permanent split between the East and West, the Western Europeans earning the dislike of Eastern Christians and Muslims.
2. The Eastern (Greek) Orthodox and Roman (Latin) Catholic Churches also divided. (See Chapter 4, "The Byzantine Empire and the Rise of the Eastern European Nations.")

The Late Middle Ages (1300–1500)

Disorder and Strife

The Late Middle Ages saw great disorder and strife. The changes that took place in the High Middle Ages brought conflict to various groups in society. The internal weaknesses and problems within many of the institutions themselves also created instability. Some of the most serious problems were economic and social in nature, the result of limitations and inadequacies within the traditional systems of agriculture, commerce, and industry.

The Decline of the German Emperors

The weak position of the Holy Roman Emperor after the election of Rudolf of Habsburg in 1273 became clearer in succeeding years. In 1356, Emperor Charles (Karl) IV (r. 1347–1378) issued a document known as the Golden Bull, which provided that the Holy Roman Emperor would be chosen by seven princes who would be designated as electors. These rulers were the archbishops of Cologne, Trier, and Mainz, and the princes of Saxony, Brandenburg, the Palatinate, and Bohemia. Each elector was also granted complete independence within his own territory. After 1356, the Empire was decentralized further as other princes demanded and gained the same kind of independence as the electors. The Holy Roman Empire became little more than a loose grouping of hundreds of independent German states. The Emperor could call representatives of this confederation together for an Imperial Diet, but the decisions this body made could not be enforced. As Emperor, he had no army, tax system, or courts other than those within his own kingdom.

The Hundred Years' War (1337–1453)

The histories of France and England are linked from 1300 to 1500 by the Hundred Years' War (1337–1453). This was a conflict over English possessions in France that began in the twelfth century. The first part of the struggle ended with French King Philip II Augustus's annexation of the northern Norman-Angevin Empire in 1214. The English, who still held important southern possessions, were constantly pressured by the strong French kings. A rivalry also developed between the two nations over Flanders, which was dominated politically by France but dependent economically on English wool. In 1328, in France the last Capetian king died without an heir. The French nobles chose a cousin of the Capetians, Philip of Valois, who ruled as Philip VI (r. 1328–1350). King Edward III of England (r. 1327–1377), a grandson of Philip IV, also laid claim to the French throne in 1337. The conflicting claims gave the French king an excuse to deprive the remaining English possessions. These actions led to war.

The First Phase of the Hundred Years' War The first phase of the Hundred Years' War (1337–1360) almost destroyed France. Establishing control over the Channel, the English invaded France and wiped out the French armies in two major battles—Crecy (1346) and Poitiers (1356). Most of the French nobility was killed, and King John (Jean) II (r. 1350–1364) was captured and taken to England. The reason for the victories by the English forces, which were smaller in size, over the French was their use of the accurate and rapid firing longbow. The losses also resulted in forcing the French monarchy to create a new and more loyal nobility and transforming the French army into a paid, better-trained fighting force.

A peasant rebellion known as the Jacquerie followed in 1358, which resulted in groups of unpaid and humiliated French soldiers attacking the French countryside. King John eventually bought his freedom by agreeing to the Treaty of Bretigny (1360), in which he paid a huge ransom and gave Edward more French territories. In turn, the English king rennounced his claim to the French crown.

The Second Phase of the Hundred Years' War   The next part of the war (1364–1380) consisted of limited and indecisive battles. This was due to internal problems in both nations, monetary and political. France faced a struggle for power between two groups within the French court. In England, the kings faced problems over the raising of money. Nevertheless, England invaded France, crushing the French forces in the Battle of Agincourt (1415) and establishing control over most of northern France.

The Third Phase of the Hundred Years' War   In 1422, the French rallied around Charles VII (r. 1422–1461). Starting with the Battle of Orleans (1429), the French armies began using trained archers and cannons, winning great victories. The force behind this recovery was not the timid Charles, who was unable to organize his nation at first, but a young peasant girl, Joan (Jeanne) of Arc. Dressed like a soldier, she inspired both the troops and Charles to take the offensive and drive the English out of France. In 1431, Joan was captured and burned alive by the English. By 1453, England had lost all of its French possessions except the port of Calais.

Results of the Hundred Years' War in France   By this time, the French recognized the need for a powerful central government. Accordingly, the monarchy gained sweeping powers, destroying the feudal basis of French society. When Charles died in 1461, his son, Louis XI (r. 1461–1483), inherited a strong base from which to rule. The growth of royal absolutism, however, seriously retarded France's ability to progress and compete in later centuries.

Results of the Hundred Years' War in England   The defeat in France resulted in an internal conflict between the two most powerful families in England, the Houses of Lancaster and York. The Yorkists, who had a strong claim to the throne through Richard II, blamed the loss of France on the Lancastrians, particularly Henry VI. This struggle, known as the War of the Roses (1453–1485), resulted in the extermination of most members of both families. In 1485, Henry Tudor, a Lancastrian commander, defeated the Yorkist ruler and became King. He assumed the throne as Henry VII (r. 1485–1509), marrying Elizabeth of York and establishing a new dynasty of English kings, the Tudors (see Chapter 10, "The Rise of Nation-States").

Although the English defeat in France and the resulting civil war seemed to be catastrophic at the time, it ultimately made England a great power. The loss of their French territories forced the English to concentrate on developing the resources of the island itself. This resulted in the steady growth of a profitable wool trade and the creation of a navy. England's mastery of the seas and development of industry were the source of its later greatness.

Joan of Arc

It all began like a TV soap opera. The Queen of England, Isabella, and her lover murdered Isabella's husband, Edward II, in 1327 and made his fifteen-year-old son King of England. When the King of France, Charles IV, died without an heir, Isabella, who was his sister, claimed the throne of France for her son. The French refused and the Hundred Years' War was on. For years France and England were locked in combat, with England generally the winner. When things looked darkest for France, a champion came forward to rally France and eventually caused France to win the war. This champion has come to be called Joan the Maid or Joan of Arc.

Joan was born in 1412 in a small village and was raised in a religious setting. During her early teen years she began to hear "voices" which she identified as St. Michael, St. Catherine, and St. Margaret. When Joan was sixteen the voices told her that the Dauphin, the rightful heir to the French throne, had to be made king and that the English should be driven out of France. Joan went to the French court, saw the Dauphin and asked for his support.

The Dauphin, who was to become Charles VII, was willing to grasp any chance of victory. Perhaps Joan was directed by heavenly forces? After all, hadn't she heard the voices? He gave Joan approval to go with the French army to the city of Orleans, where the English were camped. When Joan cut her hair short, which was against custom and practice, and dressed like a man, the court was astonished.

When the army arrived at Orleans with Joan at its head they faced an English army that had already been weakened by disease and lack of supplies. They withdrew in two weeks and France claimed the victory. The Dauphin was now crowned King of France. There was, however, a hostility toward this strange girls who was too popular.

The following year, one of England's allies (Burgandy), captured Joan and turned her over to the English. England wanted her eliminated for they worried that her inspiration would cause their defeat. She was becoming a rallying force for all in France. The English turned her over to a Church court for trial on being a witch. The sorcery charge was a cover for their political action. Charles VII and the court of France did nothing to help her.

Refusing to recant, Joan was found guilty of witchcraft. The "proof" used against her was that she heard voices, claimed inspiration from God, and was in contact with the Devil (because she wore men's clothing). The court decided that she had to be burned alive at the stake. The sentence was carried out.

Twenty-five years later she was retried and found innocent of all charges. In 1920 Joan was cannonized and declared a holy maiden.

The Creation of Spain and Portugal

The Reconquista (or "re-conquering") of the Iberian peninsula from the Moors (Spanish Muslims) by Christian powers in 1492 resulted in the creation of the Spanish and Portuguese nations. This was a slow and discontinuous process that began in 900 when Spanish Christians conquered the land north of the Duoro River, establishing the Kingdom of Leon. About 950, part of the kingdom separated into an independent state, Castile. Rivalries between the two temporarily stopped the progress of the Reconquista until 1031, when the Muslims became involved in a civil war. In 1037, Leon and Castile united into one kingdom, capturing the greater part of the peninsula as far as Toledo by 1085.

The Kingdom of Aragon rose to prominence in the eleventh century. It consisted of the counties of Aragon, Navarre, Saragossa, and Catalonia. While less powerful than Castile, Aragon captured Valencia and the Balearic Islands from the Moors. Its location on the Mediterranean made the kingdom very wealthy and important.

Portugal emerged as an independent state in the twelfth century. Originally part of the Kingdom of Castile, the county was given to Henry (Henri) of Burgundy, a knight who had been instrumental in its capture from the Moors, as a fief by the Castilian king. In 1139, his son, Afonso Henriques (r. 1139–1185), declared himself king of the independent nation of Portugal. With the intercession of the pope, Alfonso VII of Castile (r. 1126–1157) agreed to recognize the new title. The Portuguese gained more territory from the Muslims, including the port city of Lisbon and the southern territory of Algarve. The new nation developed a separate cultural identity and language, as well as a strong national monarchy. During the fourteenth century, Portugal won a series of wars with Castile, thus assuring Portugal's survival as a nation. It then began a program of overseas exploration that brought great wealth and prestige to the country (see Chapter 8, "The Age of Exploration").

Despite the wars with Portugal, the Kingdom of Castile continued to gain territory from the Moors. Castilian forces destroyed the North African Berber armies and captured Cordova and Seville. In 1469, Queen Isabella I of Castile (r. 1474–1504) married King Ferdinand II of Aragon (r. 1458–1516), uniting their kingdoms and creating the nation of Spain. In 1492, Spanish forces conquered the last Muslim stronghold of Grenada. With the unification of the nation complete, the Spanish government turned to overseas exploration and competition with Portugal (see Chapter 8, "The Age of Exploration").

The Black Death (1347–1350)

The political upheaval experienced in Western Europe in the Late Middle Ages was in part the result of social and economic problems. Economic growth from 1000 to 1300 resulted in population growth, which strained the limited food supply. Famines and economic depressions followed in the fourteenth and fifteenth centuries. In addition, a devastating disease known as the Black Death, an epidemic of **bubonic plague**, spread over Europe from 1347 to 1350 and then returned periodically during the following three centuries.

We now know that the Black Death was brought to Europe from the East on ships by rats infested with fleas whose bites transmitted the disease to the human bloodstream. Yet, without microscopes and little scientific knowledge of disease, Europe was at a loss as to know how to fully explain this plague. Many assumed it was the end of the world or the sickness was God's punishment for humanity's sins. Others blamed the Jewish community because they were not generally affected by the plague. (Jews were forced to live separately from the rest of society and were therefore spared the horrors of the Black Death.) It is estimated that a third of Europe's population was wiped out between 1347 and 1350. By the early fifteenth century, there were half as many people as there had been in 1300. It was not until 1450 that the economic and social stresses began to decrease, as royal absolutism restored order and the outbreaks of plague abated.

Medieval Society

The Medieval Church

The greatest influence on Medieval society was the Christian Church. It shaped the culture and organization of the Middle Ages. After the fall of the Western Roman Empire, it was the only institution of the old order left in Western Europe. The Church soon converted Germanic rulers and provided them with guidance in creating a new society. Yet the Germans influenced the Church as well. It had to adjust to meet the needs of its new members, which were often very different from those of the Romans in the Eastern (Byzantine) Empire.

For the average person in the Middle Ages, the Church provided guidance, tradition, and hope. Most people were peasants and lived under very harsh conditions. The Church provided them with a vision of something better in the next world to make up for their suffering in the present. It also gave Medieval society rules to live by. The services of the Church were both educational and entertaining, giving their lives cultural aspects (art, music, poetry, history) to which they would never have otherwise been exposed. The administration of the sacraments, in which almost all people participated from cradle to grave, gave them a sense of identity as well.

The Development of Papal Supremacy

From the start, the pope became the sole representative of the Romans to the new rulers. The papacy took on great responsibilities and powers as well as a role of leadership. As the Germanic tribes converted to Christianity, the pope's flock grew. The concept of papal supremacy (the pope as the leader of the entire Church) and the **petrine theory** (the popes were direct descendants of St. Peter, the leader of Jesus's Apostles) were used to establish the pope's position as the guardian of true doctrine and correct worship.

Under Pope Gregory I "the Great" (r. 590–604), the papacy gained great prestige. An excellent administrator and skillful politician, Gregory strengthened papal political and economic power. Regarded as a Latin Church Father, he wrote important works of theology and outstanding sermons. He is also credited with developing Church music, such as the **Gregorian chant**.

As the Medieval papacy grew in power and prestige, it developed the idea of creating a universal Christian state, which the pope would head. The German Holy Roman Emperors, who saw themselves ruling over a similar type of empire, eventually came into conflict with the papacy. Using their powers of excommunication and interdiction (cutting off an individual or community of Christians from participation in the Church sacraments, which was believed to be essential for salvation) as a means of enforcing their authority, the popes struggled with the German emperors for influence over Medieval Europe. The height of papal power was reached in the thirteenth century, but began to decline in the Late Middle Ages.

Monasticism   The Church's activities were not only religious; the Church was the institution that cared for the poor and weak. It maintained the only hospitals and schools, injecting the concepts of justice, charity, and mercy into the harsh laws of the Germanic tribes. Clergymen often served on the councils of Germanic kings, influencing their policies and administrations. The most influential Medieval Christian institution was **monasticism**. This was a way of life in which monks served as administrators, social workers, and most importantly, missionaries. **Monasteries** became centers of learning, preserving the knowledge and culture of the Greco-Roman past. Unlike those of the East, which were centers of **asceticism** (the practice of denying physical pleasure and comfort in order to develop an individual's spiritual side), the monasteries of the West served the community. Needing guidelines for the different style of monasticism that had developed, Benedict of Nursia (480–543) created the Benedictine Rule. It established an orderly daily routine that consisted of prayer, work, and study, which was particularly suited to the society. The rule became very popular, and monasteries of the Benedictine Order appeared throughout Western Europe.

As Western Europe became Christian, the Benedictines became powerful, accumulating land and wealth through donations and endowments. The efficient maintenance of these holdings often diverted the monks from their spiritual development and community service. Seeking to return to the primitive purity of the Benedictine Rule, a new order, the Cluniac, was created in 910. It emphasized religious ritual and worship as the main duty of monks. The Cluniacs became famous for their elaborate and beautiful **liturgies** (religious services). Their concepts of piety, conduct, and efficient administration influenced reform within the Church during the eleventh century.

As the century progressed, however, the Cluniacs grew increasingly wealthy and worldly as well. In an attempt to return again to the original idea of monasticism, several new monastic orders were established. Located in wild and isolated places to escape the distractions of the world, these orders developed into centers of learning and prayer. They made themselves models of humility and self-denial. In fact, the monk became a folk hero for many in the Medieval World. Men and women from all classes joined monasteries and nunneries (monasteries for women).

By the thirteenth century, **medicant orders** (or begging orders) appeared. Fearing that any monks, no matter how ascetic, would eventually become worldly if they possessed wealth, the medicants adopted a policy of absolute poverty, living by begging. They lived among the people, setting an example of humility and morality. Their preaching had its greatest impact on urban populations. The Dominicans were founded by a Spanish priest, Dominic (1170–1221) to combat heresy in southern France. Their sincerity and lack of wealth made them popular and effective in preaching Roman Catholic Church doctrine. In Italy, a contemporary of Dominic, Francis of Assisi (c. 1182–1226), founded a similar order, the Franciscans, based on absolute poverty and theological simplicity. Unlike the educated Dominicans, the early Franciscans were simple preachers, emphasizing basic Christian values. Despite the initial suspicion and dislike of the medicant orders, especially the Franciscans, both were confirmed by the papacy by 1216.

Medieval Architecture and Art

The Romanesque Style
Like most aspects of Medieval culture, architecture and art were dominated by religion. Although Medieval society regarded artists as craftspeople, some architects attained positions of great authority and respect. Architecture was revived in the eleventh century as Europe came out of the Feudal Period. The term Romanesque, which applies to art and architecture produced during the period between 1000 and 1200, refers to the Roman elements of that style. Romanesque architecture, used mostly in churches, used barrel and cross vaults (arch shaped structures) to support the high ceilings, giving a massive appearance. With the great pressure and weight on the walls, large windows were impossible to include. Therefore, church interiors were very dark. The Cluniac revival and growth of new monastic orders created a demand for churches in the Romanesque style. Examples of this are Notre Dame la Grande in Poitiers, France, and the Cathedral Church of Worms in Germany. Romanesque churches were also built along the great pilgrimage and crusader routes, such as the Cathedral of Santiago at Compostela, Spain.

Romanesque art included sculpture and painting. Walls were decorated with frescoes, and the massive **piers** (supports) were adorned with sculptures. Romanesque sculpture was also noted for its large-scale works.

The Gothic Style
In a desire to achieve height and light in churches, the Gothic style was created. The Gothic church was an attempt to change the darkness and mystery of the Romanesque style. Appearing in the mid-twelfth century, Gothic architecture reflected the intellectual and cultural changes that Western Europe was undergoing. It used slender columns, pointed arches, and huge stained-glass windows, which gave the impression of light, color, and majesty. Supporting arches were also built on the exterior of the church. These became known as flying buttresses, because they gave the impression they were soaring upwards. Outstanding examples of Gothic architecture are the monastic church of Saint Denis, the cathedral of Notre Dame de Paris, and the cathedrals of Chartres and Amiens in France; the cathedrals of Salisbury and York in England; and Cologne Cathedral in Germany. Gothic sculpture was far more proportioned and realistic than was Romanesque. Gothic painting included stained-glass windows, as there was little room for frescoes, and manuscript illumination (illustrations in books).

Medieval Theater in the Round

NORTH
Devil

NORTHEAST
Covetousness

AUDIENCE

The Moat

AUDIENCE

AUDIENCE

WEST
World

EAST
God

Entrance

AUDIENCE

AUDIENCE

The Moat

Actors' Pavilion

SOUTH
Flesh

In Medieval times plays were performed in theaters in the round. The audience watched from hills inside the moat.

Literature

Medieval literature was dominated by religion until the Late Middle Ages, when writing in the vernacular (spoken language) revived **secular** subjects. The majority of written Medieval works were in Latin, chiefly dealing with theology, philosophy, and law. This is not surprising as literacy was limited to clergymen and monastics until the Late Middle Ages. Poetry was limited to hymn writing with its monastic composers remaining anonymous.

Epic Poems   It was the oral poetic traditions of the Germanic and Scandinavian peoples that revived secular poetry. The earliest form of this is the **chanson de geste** (songs of warrior's deeds) or epic poem. The first existing example is the Anglo-Saxon epic *Beowulf*. While it was not written down until much later, it probably dates back to about 800, reflecting the culture of pre-Christian Germanic society. The *Norse Sagas*, which were not written down until the twelfth and thirteenth centuries, also reflect the violence and paganism of a much earlier period in Scandinavian history. The chief Germanic epic, the *Nibelungenlied*, which was composed about 1200, shows evidence of a tradition that dated back to the Germanic invasions of the Roman Empire. The most representative of the chansons de geste were written in France around 1100. The best known was the *Song of Roland*, which tells of a heroic knight's deeds while on Charlemagne's campaign against the Moors in 778. Written by a Spanish contemporary, the *Song of the Cid* dealt with the same subject.

Lyric Poems   The epic was soon rivaled by a new literary form, the lyric poem. This became very popular, especially among the nobility. Its creators, traveling **bards** (singing poets) called **troubadours**, based their works on emotion. They emphasized the longing for love or the suffering from a lack of it, rather than the action and adventure used in the epics. The lyric writers developed a new literary form that examined the self, emotions, and values. Unlike the writers of the epics, the troubadours were not anonymous, composing in very distinct styles.

Romantic Poems   By the twelfth century, the epic and lyric traditions were brought together to produce a new kind of poetry, the **romance**. This was a combination of romance and adventure that usually centered on three themes: the deeds of Charlemagne, the legends about King Arthur (legendary English ruler), and the stories of Greek and Roman heroes. The historical accounts were usually inaccurate and the love story exaggerated, yet the romance was extremely creative. Among the most outstanding examples were Chretien de Troyes' *La Romance de la Rose* (*The Romance of the Rose*), a twelfth century French work that established a model of the ideal knight; Gottfried von Strasbourg's *Tristan und Isolde* (*Tristan and Isolde*) a thirteenth century German examination of two lovers; Wolfram von Eschenbach's *Parzival* (*Parsifal*), another thirteenth century German romance about a knight's quest for the Holy Grail (the legendary cup that Christ used at the Last Supper); and Thomas Malory's *La Morte d'Artur* (*The Death of Arthur*), a fifteenth century English treatment of the Arthurian legend.

Vernacular Literature   Literature in the vernacular developed as well. Stories, often with strong social messages, began to appear by the fourteenth and fifteenth centuries. Society's faults and injustices were pointed out. They examined the life of the common person rather than that of legendary kings or epic heroes. This type of literature often poked fun or harshly criticized Medieval institutions, particularly the Church. Geoffrey Chaucer's *Canterbury Tales* and William Langland's *Piers the Ploughman* are examples of this.

Philosophy

Theology and philosophy were joined together in the Middle Ages. Until the mid-eleventh century, monastic schools were the only centers of learning. They were replaced by the cathedral schools, which were located in urban areas, making education more accessible. During the twelfth century a new institution appeared, the university, which began as a **guild** (Medieval union of artisans) of students and teachers. It grew out of the cathedral schools in northern Europe and, unlike the Italian universities, was run by the teachers, not the students. Founded in 1200, the University of Paris, the first in northern Europe, was soon followed by others (Chartres, Oxford, and Cambridge).

Scholasticism

Medieval cathedral schools and universities produced the Scholastic Movement, which taught that philosophy could be used to better understand theology. Called "Scholastici" or Schoolmen, these thinkers argued that faith and reason were compatible. They believed that God had already revealed truth to humanity and it was the task of the individual to apply reason to ancient texts, such as the Bible, in order to find it. When their sources conflicted, the Scholastics used the **dialectic**, a method of reasoning adapted from the Ancient Greeks, that tried to show logical connections between opposing statements. The Scholastics also looked to classical literature for knowledge. The most famous thinkers of the movement were Anselm of Canterbury (1033–1109), who first developed these ideas and was regarded as the founder of Scholasticism; Peter Abelard (1079–1142), whose work *Sic et non* (*Yes and No*) developed the use of dialectic in theology; and Thomas Aquinas (c. 1225–1274), who applied Scholastic principles to practical issues (politics, justice, social relations) as well as theology. In his work, the *Summa Theologica*, Aquinas attempted to show how all knowledge, both Christian and pagan, can be used to find the truth of Christian belief.

Opposition to Scholasticism Scholasticism was not universally accepted and came under attack by other thinkers. The Franciscan philosopher and scientist Roger Bacon (c. 1214–1294) opposed the use of deductive reasoning and stressed that knowledge of the world must be based on experience. The Franciscan philosopher John Duns Scotus (c. 1266–1308) developed a different philosophical system, Scotism, which taught that faith was more important than reason in order to achieve salvation in the next world. The philosopher William of Ockham (c. 1285–c. 1349) argued that since the existence of God is a metaphysical (beyond nature) belief, it is outside the scope of human reason and must be a matter of faith.

Summary

The Medieval Period was one of enormous change. Western Europe, which had been a collection of Germanic tribal kingdoms, evolved into a group of powerful nations. The Middle Ages saw the violence and disorder of the early period lead to the creation of a new order. The slow re-discovery of the Greco-Roman past, as well as the development of its own institutions, brought Western Europe to a new era, one in which experimentation and exploration would take people beyond their greatest expectations. Once their Medieval childhood ended, the young nations began to grow into world powers that would dominate the world. It is this modern Europe that we encounter in the next unit.

CHAPTER 5

Review Exercises

I. Matching

Directions: Match the names in Column A with the achievement they are *best known* for in Column B.

Column A
1. Edward I
2. Pope Gregory VII
3. Pope Urban II
4. William of Normandy
5. Pope Innocent III
6. King John
7. Charles Martel
8. Geoffrey Chaucer
9. Hugh Capet
10. Clovis

Column B
(a) defeated the Moors at Battle of Tours
(b) first King of France
(c) *Canterbury Tales*
(d) most powerful Medieval Pope
(e) Investiture controversy
(f) conquered Engand in 1066
(g) preached First Crusade
(h) built up Frankish kingdom
(i) forced to sign Magna Carta
(j) established Parliament as a regular assembly

II. Matching

Directions: Match the words in Column A with the *correct description* in Column B.

Column A
1. vassal
2. serf
3. fief
4. *missi dominici*
5. villein
6. baron
7. Ghibelline
8. capitularies
9. tithe
10. Guelf

Column B
(a) supporter of the German Emperor
(b) Carolingian royal edicts
(c) peasant bound to the manor
(d) Church tax of 10 percent of income
(e) grant of land
(f) Carolingian imperial envoys
(g) free peasant on the manor
(h) supporter of the pope
(i) Norman vassal
(j) owed service for land

III. Map Exercise

Directions: Use the map to locate the place associated with each of the following statements. For each statement, write the *letter* of the place.

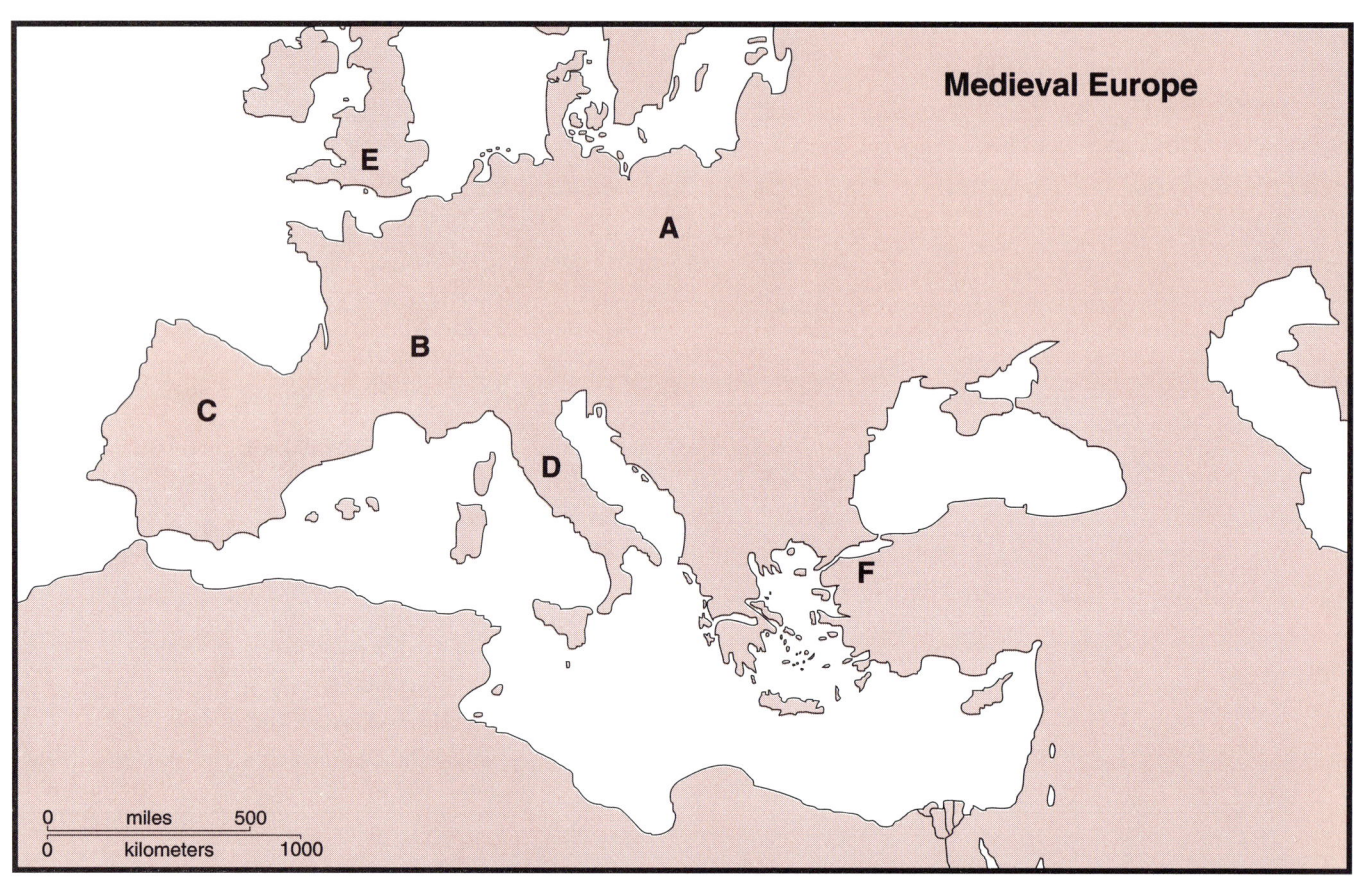

1. _____ The Medieval Holy Roman Emperors came from this place.

2. _____ The papacy controlled the Medieval Roman Catholic Church from here.

3. _____ The Moors were driven from this peninsula.

4. _____ Knights of the Fourth Crusade attacked and occupied this city.

5. _____ The Magna Carta was signed in this nation.

6. _____ This country was the site of the Hundred Years' War.

IV. Multiple Choice

Directions: Find the *letter* of the correct answer.

1. The Germanic kingdom that came to dominate Western Europe was the

(a) Gaulish.
(b) Frankish.
(c) Visigothic.
(d) Ostrogothic.

2. The papacy's claim to be an independent state was based on the document known as the

   (a) "Donation of Constantine."
   (b) "Donation of Clovis."
   (c) "Donation of Pepin."
   (d) "Donation of Charlemagne."

3. Under Charlemagne, all the following were accomplished *except* for

   (a) a uniformity of religion.
   (b) a strong central government.
   (c) the investigation of local officials.
   (d) a revival of learning throughout the Empire.

4. The Treaty of Verdun (843)

   (a) unified the Carolingian Empire.
   (b) divided the Carolingian Empire.
   (c) granted the Carolingian Empire greater territory.
   (d) forced the Carolingian Empire to surrender territory.

5. The breakdown of order in the ninth century was in great part due to the invasions of the

   (a) Saracens, Burgundians, and Anglo-Saxons.
   (b) Magyars, Vikings, and Anglo-Saxons.
   (c) Saracens, Magyars, and Vikings.
   (d) Vikings, Ostrogoths, and Visigoths.

6. Feudalism was based on

   (a) a strong central government.
   (b) a need for unity against barbarian attacks.
   (c) mutual hereditary obligations.
   (d) a balance of power.

7. The form that feudalism took in the Middle Ages was

   (a) agriculturalism.
   (b) seigneurialism.
   (c) manorialism.
   (d) hereditarianism.

8. The following were all reasons for the decline of feudalism *except*

   (a) an improvement in the climate.
   (b) the end of barbarian attacks.
   (c) a decrease in population.
   (d) the invention of better farming equipment.

9. The revival of trade in the eleventh century resulted in the

   (a) development of a single European Empire.
   (b) decline in the influence of the Church.
   (c) growth of independent towns.
   (d) development of democracy in Europe.

10. The reform movement (opposing lay investiture) within the Roman Catholic Church was started by Pope

   (a) Leo IX.
   (b) Gregory VII.
   (c) Innocent II.
   (d) Innocent III.

11. The Concordat of Worms (1122)

   (a) granted all powers of investiture to the papacy.
   (b) granted all powers of investiture to the emperor.
   (c) compromised all powers of investiture between emperor and papacy.
   (d) granted all powers of investiture to a Church council.

12. In looking at Medieval Europe, it is important to remember that

   (a) the division of land among heirs strengthened the kingdoms.
   (b) political vacuums were filled by strong leaders.
   (c) there were no cultural advances during the period.
   (d) the society was never able to establish a class order.

13. The Capetians initially ruled

   (a) Anjou.
   (b) Normandy.
   (c) Lorraine.
   (d) Paris.

14. The King who built a strong central government in France was

   (a) Philip II Augustus.
   (b) Louis VI "the Fat."
   (c) Philip IV "the Fair."
   (d) Louis XI.

15. The French were victorious in the Hundred Years' War after the Battle of

   (a) Crécy.
   (b) Poitiers.
   (c) Agincourt.
   (d) Orléans.

16. All of the following were created by the English king, Henry I, *except*

    (a) the chancery.
    (b) the curia regis.
    (c) the royal law courts.
    (d) the circuit court system.

17. The first established Parliament took place during the reign of

    (a) Richard I.
    (b) John.
    (c) Henry III.
    (d) Edward I.

18. The nation of Spain was created by the union of

    (a) Aragon and Leon.
    (b) Portugal and Castile.
    (c) Aragon and Castile.
    (d) Leon and Portugal.

19. The king who created the independent kingdom of Portugal was

    (a) Henry of Burgundy.
    (b) Afonso Henriques.
    (c) Alfonso VII of Castile.
    (d) Henrique the Navigator.

20. The first Western European monastic order was the

    (a) Benedictine.
    (b) Cluniac.
    (c) Cistercian.
    (d) Franciscan.

IV. Thought Questions

Directions: Complete the following questions in essay form.

1. The Middle Ages were a combination of Classical, Byzantine, and Germanic civilizations. Prove this is true by giving one example of each in Medieval society.

2. Was feudalism the best possible system for Europe in the ninth and tenth centuries? List one benefit this system offered each class in society.

3. You are a merchant in the Late Middle Ages. You are visiting Byzantium on business and are asked about the revival of trade and culture in the West. You explain that political, economic, social, and technological developments in the High Middle Ages made the prosperity and advanced civilization of the Late Middle Ages possible. Give one example of how each of these was responsible for the revival.

4. Why did national monarchies develop during the High and Late Middle Ages? Give one example of how the monarchs of France, England, Spain, and Portugal were each able or unable to consolidate their power.

5. The Crusades had a great impact on Western Europe. Prove this is true by

   A. giving three ideas or institutions that the Crusaders brought to the West.
   B. explaining how each of these influenced the development of Western European society.

UNIT III

THE BIRTH OF MODERN EUROPE

The people of Europe did not simply awaken one morning and see that the modern age was upon them. Change usually takes place over a long period of time and is not evident to those living during the period. The changes that had their start in the Middle Ages began during this period.

Historians generally define modern Europe as the era beginning with the Renaissance. Sculpture, architecture, and literature opened new vistas and a "Golden Age" began in Europe. You will learn why this rebirth began in Italy and what impact it had on all European society. People that you are familiar with such as Michelangelo and da Vinci created great works during this time.

This people-centered, rather than generally heaven-centered, time caused problems for the Roman Catholic Church. The religious uniformity of Europe was torn apart. New religions, such as Lutheranism and Anglicanism, began during the Protestant Reformation. A number of religious wars broke out as nations went to battle over beliefs. The Church counter-attacked through its Counter Reformation with actions designed to meet the objections of the reformers.

Advances in technology, such as new types of vessels and new navigational instruments, allowed European explorers to sail the world. Columbus, Magellan, and Cabot set new courses. Cortes and Pizzaro conquered empires in the Americas. Demand for increased wealth from trade caused Europe to spread its power and influence over the globe. Colonies were established to provide such wealth for individuals and nations.

This commercial growth led to changes in trade and business practices. The old guild system was not capable of meeting the demand for new and better goods that the growing population required. A new class of people, and the attachment to capital, replaced the attachment to the land. Merchants made huge sums of money and developed new business practices from necessity. Checking accounts, new bookkeeping systems, and early forms of corporations were established. The pace of change accelerated during this exciting period.

The Renaissance

The term "renaissance" means "re-birth." When we use it to talk about Western European history, it refers to a period when there was renewed interest in the heritage of the Classical World. Interest in and knowledge of that period had never completely died out even though the Medieval society had been dominated by religion and religious ideas. A series of events renewed interest and respect for what had taken place hundreds of years earlier. A spirited appreciation of art, literature, sculpture, and philosophy developed, beginning in Italy and soon traveling to all parts of Western Europe. The Renaissance Era was not anti-religious, but rather combined the secular features of the Classical World with the religious devotion of the Medieval Period.

The Renaissance Began in Italy

The **Renaissance** began in Italy about 1200. This movement started on the Italian peninsula for a number of reasons. The Italians became interested in Greco-Roman culture through increased contact with the Eastern Roman or Byzantine Empire during the Crusades. This led to a revival of Ancient Greek and Latin languages. Exposure to ancient texts brought the rediscovery of Classical learning. The Italians soon developed an appreciation of their historical past and a new interest in many ancient Greco-Roman ruins. The flow of Byzantine refugees fleeing into Italy to escape the advance of the Ottoman Turks during the fifteenth century further strengthened the revival of Greco-Roman culture.

Many Italian cities grew wealthy through trading with both Western Europe and the Middle East. Successful Italian merchants funded the works of artists, architects, and writers. The art, architecture, and literature of these cities began to reflect the great interest in antiquity that had developed. Many cities and their leaders began to see themselves as the successors to the Greeks and Romans. A new sense of civic pride and rivalry developed. Wishing to restore what they saw as the glory of the Classical World, these cities tried to become modern equivalents of those civilizations.

Humanism and Individualism

By the fourteenth century, Italy saw the rise of **Humanism**, which was the Classical World's glorification of the human form as beautiful and the human mind as capable of discovering truth. The thinkers of the Medieval World distrusted physical beauty and thought of the needs of the body as obstacles to the development of the spirit. They also felt that human wisdom was unable to find truth without guidance from God. This was illustrated by the practice of Medieval artists, usually monks, who did not sign their names to their works, but gave credit to the "greater glory of God." Humanism, on the other hand, emphasized individual and personal achievement. In the Renaissance, not only did artists sign their name to their works, but they became famous and expected to be praised. No longer monastics for the most part, artists in the Renaissance became wealthy and celebrated. In fact, the artist became more important than the patron in that when he became famous, there was a demand for any work by him.

The Renaissance encouraged the individual to pursue a variety of interests. The term **Renaissance man**, meaning a multi-talented person, has its origins here. An excellent example of the type of all-around individual that the Renaissance produced was Benvenuto Cellini (1500–1571). He was an artist (both a sculptor and a goldsmith), a writer (known chiefly for his *Autobiography*), a soldier, and a courtier.

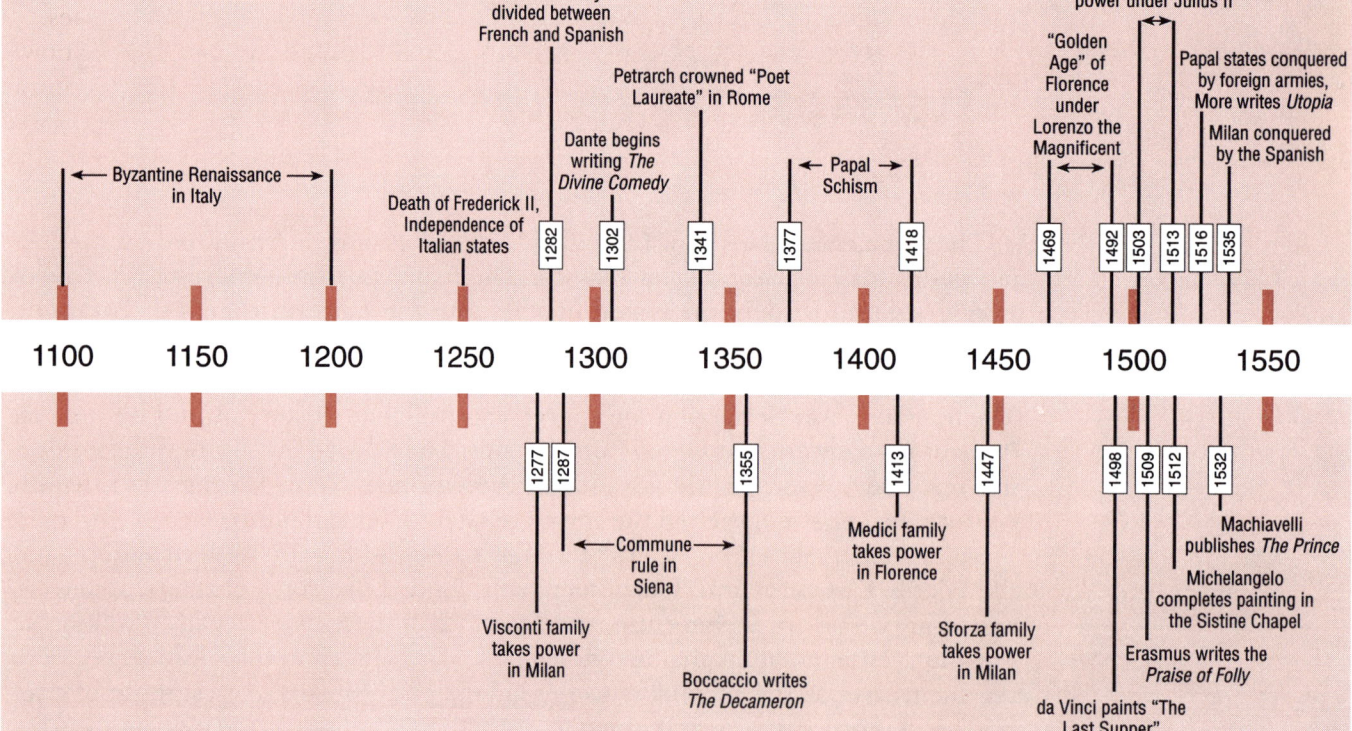

Chapter 6 Chronology

Byzantine Renaissance in Italy

Death of Frederick II, Independence of Italian states

Southern Italy divided between French and Spanish — 1282

Dante begins writing *The Divine Comedy* — 1302

Petrarch crowned "Poet Laureate" in Rome — 1341

Papal Schism — 1377

1418

"Golden Age" of Florence under Lorenzo the Magnificent — 1469

Height of Renaissance, Papal power under Julius II

1492 • 1503 • 1513 • 1516 • 1535

Papal states conquered by foreign armies, More writes *Utopia*

Milan conquered by the Spanish

1100   1150   1200   1250   1300   1350   1400   1450   1500   1550

1277 • 1287 — Visconti family takes power in Milan

Commune rule in Siena

1355 — Boccaccio writes *The Decameron*

1413 — Medici family takes power in Florence

1447 — Sforza family takes power in Milan

da Vinci paints "The Last Supper"

1498 • 1509 • 1512 • 1532

Erasmus writes the *Praise of Folly*

Michelangelo completes painting in the Sistine Chapel

Machiavelli publishes *The Prince*

This type of well-rounded background and **versatility** is still encouraged in contemporary society. The educated person of the Middle Ages was usually a specialist, such as a theologian, artist, and so on, but the individual of learning in the Renaissance was expected to be knowledgeable in many areas, such as poetry, history, dancing, athletics, vernacular languages, theology, art, and Classical languages. Many Renaissance universities expanded their offerings from the traditional seven liberal arts—grammar, rhetoric, logic, arithmetic, geometry, music and astronomy—to include Classical literature, history, and philosophy. One of the most popular books of the period in Europe was the *Book of the Courtier*, which describes the ideal gentleman, by Baldassare Castiglione (1478–1529). The courtier was supposed to be a scholar, athlete, soldier, and statesman—knowledgeable in all areas without appearing to have too great an interest in any one topic. The best example of this ideal was the versatile genius Leonardo da Vinci (1452–1519), who is best known now as a painter, but who also excelled as a sculptor, architect, engineer, inventor, philosopher, botanist, geologist, and anatomist. In fact, Leonardo's drawings of the human anatomy are still used by both medical and art students.

In the fifteenth century, Civic Humanism appeared. This was an interest in the improvement of and the development of civic pride in Italian cities. The Ancient Greek polis and Roman civitas served as models. This attitude led to civic improvement projects, such as better sewerage systems, and works of art to beautify the cities. More importantly, Civic Humanism resulted in a new awareness of and participation in political life by individuals. This was reflected in the attempts to develop a republican form of government in many of the Italian cities. The active life (concern with the present world) became the ideal, replacing the contemplative life (concern with salvation in the next world) that had been dominant in the Middle Ages. The Civic Humanists argued that the individual could be an active citizen with a family and career and still be a good Christian. Civic Humanism therefore made the Renaissance relevant to contemporary problems and issues.

In the sixteenth century, the Italian Renaissance reached its last stage. Known as the High Renaissance (1500–1650), it was a period of high artistic and cultural achievement. Yet, during this century Italy declined politically because of civil war within and invasion from outside.

The Italian City-States

The Renaissance chiefly took place in northern Italy. The Italians were divided into many small city-states, most of which were constantly in conflict with one another. The earliest notable Italian city was Siena, which established a **commune** from 1287–1355. Siena became wealthy through trade and was the first center of Renaissance art and culture. It became a model for the other cities of northern Italy. By the late fourteenth century, Siena declined and was absorbed by more powerful neighbors.

The Importance of Florence

The city of Florence was the "Cradle of Renaissance Culture," producing the greatest artists of the period. It was a wealthy city that grew rich through banking, trade, and the wool industry. Florence began as a self-governing commune in the twelfth century. In 1434, the Medici, a family of wealthy bankers, rose to power. Without altering the Republican structure of government, the Medicis ruled the city. They provided able government, supported building programs, and patronized the arts. The "Golden Age" of culture in Florence was achieved under the rule of Lorenzo de Medici "il Magnifico" ("the Magnificent") (r. 1469–1492), who was himself a scholar, poet, and musician. In 1494, the Medicis were expelled from power for surrendering Florentine possessions to the French. The reestablished republic lasted until 1498, when the Medicis were restored to power. They ruled Florence until the eighteenth century. Despite the competent rule of this family, Florence, like the rest of Italy, declined in the sixteenth century. The influence of the Medici family, however, extended beyond the city they ruled. The Medicis produced three popes, Leo X, Clement VII, and Leo XI, and two queens of France, Catherine de Medici and Marie de Medici.

The Other Northern Italian Cities

Milan The city of Milan also grew wealthy because of its location as a crossroad of trade. Like Florence, it began as a republic. In 1277, the Visconti family seized power and ruled Milan as **despots** until 1447. Despite efforts to restore the Republican system, a new family of despots, the Sforza, took power later that year. While ruthless, the Sforzas provided Milan with competent rule, promoting public works and patronizing the arts. In 1499, the last of the Sforzas, Ludovico "the Moor" (r. 1494–1499), was expelled from the city. By 1535, however, Milan was conquered by the Spanish.

Venice The Republic of Venice was an exception to the Renaissance trend toward despotism. Unlike its neighbors, Venice had been ruled by a powerful merchant oligarchy for centuries. They exercised power through a representative body known as the Great Council, which was limited to the descendants of about 200 families. This system provided Venice with a strong and efficient government that protected and encouraged trade. By the fourteenth century, Venice controlled Mediterranean commerce and had become extremely wealthy. In order to protect the flow of trade, the Venetians conquered territories throughout Italy. This involved them in the power struggles among Italian cities, diverting them from the greater threat of the Ottoman Turks. After the fall of the Byzantine Empire in 1453, trade in the Mediterranean became very limited and Venice entered a period of decline. Along with the rest of Italy, this grew worse after foreign domination began in the sixteenth century.

The Renaissance in Northern Europe

By the sixteenth century, the Renaissance spread to the countries of northern Europe. This was due to the restoration of political stability. National monarchies with strong central governments had replaced the warring feudal states of the Middle Ages. Trade and commerce increased, resulting in the revival of northern Europe's cities. Greater contact with Italy exposed northern Europeans to the Renaissance and the rediscovery of Classical culture and learning.

The Renaissance in northern Europe, however, took a different form. The Italians had been interested in the secular aspects of Greco-Roman civilization. The northern European Humanists tried to "humanize" the Christian religion. Known as Christian Humanism, this movement was an attempt to combine the best values of the Classical World with Christianity. Classical scholarship was combined with Christian concerns. Literature and philosophy were far more important to Christian Humanism than art and architecture. Civic Humanism, with its emphasis on republicanism and civil participation, had no place in the strong national monarchies of northern Europe. Ultimately, northern European Humanism led to an intellectual examination of Christianity, which in turn produced a demand for reform in the Roman Catholic Church. Without realizing it, the Christian Humanists had planted the seeds for the **Reformation** Movement (see Chapter 7, "The Reformation").

Renaissance Society and the Arts

The Renaissance began with the recovery of Classical texts and their study in the original Greek and Latin. The civilizations of Ancient Greece and Rome inspired the efforts of humanists and gave them models to follow. They tried to find the best and most accurate copies of ancient manuscripts and developed new fields of study to assist them in correcting errors and inconsistencies in the texts. Among the new disciplines were philology (study of written texts), grammar, textual and historical criticism, dictionaries, and handbooks on Classical mythology, geography, history, architecture, and art. Classical Latin became the standard by which literary works were judged. The study of Classical Greek also became important, and Greek works were used as models for imitation. For example, the Civic Humanist Lorenzo Valla (1407–1457) reflected this critical spirit when he examined the official Latin translation of the Bible (Saint Jerome Vulgate), and found that it contained errors in translation. This spirit of reevaluation and scholarship was a central characteristic of the Renaissance.

Architecture

Before the fifteenth century, Italian architecture had been a blend of the Byzantine, Romanesque, and Gothic styles. The innovations of the architect Filippo Brunelleschi (1377–1446) brought architecture into a new era. After studying ancient buildings and determining their mathematical proportions, he designed structures that combined these techniques and forms. Brunelleschi is noted for his construction of the dome on the Cathedral of Florence, which was the first attempt on such a large scale since antiquity. Two other Renaissance architects, Donato Bramante (1444–1514) and Michelangelo Buonarroti (1472–1564), were responsible for the design of Saint Peter's Basilica in the Vatican. The Renaissance also made great contributions to domestic architecture, such as ornate palaces and villas (country houses), and urban planning, notably piazzas (town squares), and public buildings. Classic Renaissance architecture is best exemplified by the work of Andrea Palladio (1508–1580), whose villas and churches became models for later generations.

The Dome of The Cathedral of Florence was designed by the architect and artist Filippo Brunelleschi. It is considered a feat of engineering as well as an architectural achievement.

Painting

The genius of the Italian Renaissance is most obvious in its painting and sculpture. In the twelfth and thirteenth centuries, Italian art was greatly influenced by that of Byzantium. Adopting Byzantine forms, it was usually religious in content and made no attempt to be realistic. The subjects depicted were shown in a very supernatural way, which emphasized their holiness rather than their humanity.

The Fourteenth Century With the revival of Humanism in the fourteenth century, however, Italian painting entered a new phase. The revived interest in the Classical World encouraged some artists to paint in secular themes such as history, mythology, and natural scenes. While most continued to depict religious subjects, the work showed both realism and emotion. This style became known as naturalism. Beginning with Giotto (c. 1267–1337), Italian art became more concerned with accurate depictions of the natural world. Religious figures were painted to look like ordinary human beings. They were often placed in natural scenes wearing contemporary clothing. Giotto also introduced the concept of **chiaroscuro**, the use of contrasting light and shade to give the illusion of depth. This made art far more realistic. Considered the true founder of Renaissance painting, Masaccio (1401–1428) gave Giotto's methods a scientific basis. Using Brunelleschi's mathematical laws of architecture, he developed the concept of linear perspective in painting. This gave the work an appearance of distance and space.

The Dome of St. Peter's Basilica, Vatican, Rome: St. Peter's was originally started by the architect Donato Bramante in 1506 and was rebuilt following the designs of Michelangelo Buonarroti between 1546 and 1564. The most impressive part of St. Peter's is the colossal dome which crowns the basilica.

The Fifteenth Century

By the fifteenth century, Italian art had developed a wide variety of individual styles that reflected both the personalities of the artists and the tastes of their patrons. In addition to religious, mythological, historical, and natural subjects, artists painted portraits of their patrons with the same convincing realism. This change is reflected in the work of Sandro Botticelli (c. 1445–1510), who painted scenes from Classical mythology on a scale that was only used previously for religious themes. His two most famous works are "The Birth of Venus" and "Primavera" ("Spring"). Other outstanding Italian painters of this period were Fra Angelico (1387–1455), and Piero della Francesca (c. 1420–1492). In Venice, artists adopted the innovations of the Florentines, but used more color to give the paintings an illusion of radiance. They also began to paint smaller works that could be hung in the homes of wealthy citizens. The best known of the Venetian painters was Titian (c. 1490–1576), whose works went on to influence later generations.

Botticelli's "Birth of Venus" depicts the goddess Venus, having risen out of the sea, standing on a seashell and being blown to shore by wind gods.

The Renaissance   147

The High Renaissance of the sixteenth century produced the greatest artists of the period. Leonardo da Vinci had his greatest impact as a painter even though he finished only a small number of paintings. His most famous is the large fresco "The Last Supper," painted on the wall of a monastery refectory (dining room) in Milan. His other well known works are the "Virgin and Child with Saint Anne" and "La Giaconnda," which is more commonly known as the "Mona Lisa." No less a giant in painting than his Florentine rival da Vinci, Michelangelo Buonarroti distinguished himself with the frescoes on the ceiling of the Sistine Chapel in the Vatican. Working on a scaffold for four years, he covered the ceiling with nine scenes from the Book of Genesis in the Bible. The most famous scene was the "Creation of Adam." A contemporary of both artists, Raphael (1483–1520) painted two famous frescoes on the walls of the Vatican Library, "The School of Athens" and "Disputa."

Northern European Painters Northern Europe produced its own tradition of art in this period. While Italian Renaissance painters studied perspective and anatomy, the northern European artists experimented with real space in their workshops in order to paint realistic images. They are especially famous for their fine detail. In the fifteenth century the Flemish School developed. The most famous of these painters were Jan van Eyck (c. 1390–1441) and Rogier van der Weyden (1400–1464). Both artists were known for their precision, detail, and emotion in their paintings. The German painter Hans Holbein (1497–1543) was famous for his realistic portraits. Two of the most original artists of the northern European Renaissance were Hieronymus Bosch (c. 1450–1516) and Pieter Bruegel the Elder (1525–1569). Bosch's work is full of fantastic creatures and horrifying scenes of violence—reflecting the northern European obsession with sin, hell, and damnation—while Bruegel painted landscapes and scenes from daily life.

Sculpture

Of all the arts in the Renaissance, sculpture was most directly influenced by Classical art. The first Italian sculptor who incorporated Classical sculpture into his work was Nicola Pisano (c. 1220–1278). A southern Italian, Pisano saw numerous examples of ancient sculpture, which he used in his own work. By the late fourteenth century, Italian sculpture adopted the ideas of naturalism. The relief carvings of Lorenzo Ghiberti (1378–1455) achieved both clarity and realism. His most famous work was "The Gates of Paradise" (bronze doors of the Baptistry of Florence). In the fifteenth century, the work of Donatello (c. 1386–1466) brought together the sculpture of the Classical World with that of the Renaissance. Donatello's bronze statue "David" was the first free-standing nude sculpture since antiquity. His work reflected the revival of the Classical glorification of the human body. His "Saint George"

Ghiberti's "Gates of Paradise": Lorenzo Ghiberti won the commission for decorating the doors of the Baptistry of the Florence Cathedral in a competition held by the Florentine Guild of Wool Refiners in 1401.

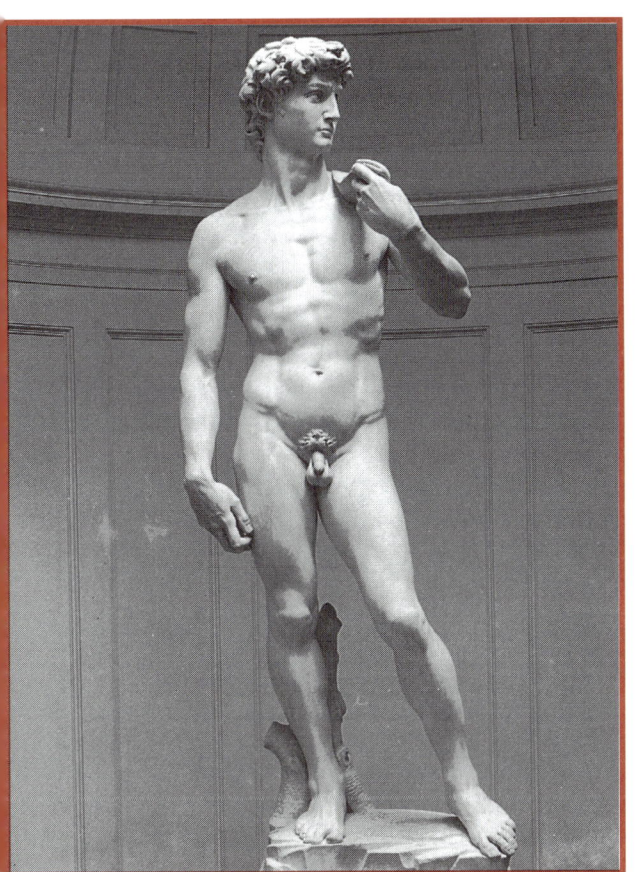

Michelangelo's "David" is considered one of the greatest sculptures ever created. It reflects the Renaissance revival of the Classical admiration of the human body.

applied Classical detail and realism to a Christian subject. The height of Renaissance sculpture was achieved by Michelangelo Buonarroti. His best known work is his sculpture "David," which came closest to the Classical ideal of masculine beauty. His statue "Moses" is also a masterpiece of sculpture, showing great power and emotion, as does his "Pieta," the sculpture depicting the Virgin Mary weeping over the dead body of Jesus.

Literature

Ironically, most of the greatest works of Renaissance literature were written in the **vernacular**, rather than the newly rediscovered Classical languages. The first literary pieces of the Renaissance were in Italian, produced by three writers known as the "Tuscan Triumvirate" because they all lived in Florence in the old Etruscan province of Tuscany. It is for this reason that modern spoken and written Italian is the Tuscan dialect. The first was Dante Alighieri (1265–1321). His masterpiece, *The Divine Comedy*, was an epic poem that combined Classical mythology, Christian theology, and Medieval folklore in an imaginary trip from hell through purgatory to heaven. The combination of references in this work reflect the various influences that created Renaissance society. Dante's other works are entirely secular. The second member of the Triumvirate, Francesco Petrarca or Petrarch (1304–1374), is known as the "Father of Humanism." He was the first writer to abandon the methods and objectives of Medieval thought in favor of the Latin classics. To Petrarch, Classical literature was a source of morality and virtue, despite being the product of a pagan civilization. He searched for ancient manuscripts, studied Classical literature and grammatical style. He wrote poetry in Latin, most notably *Africa*, an epic celebrating the life of the Roman general Scipio "Africanus," as well as beautiful love lyrics in his native Tuscan, known as the *Canzoni* (*Songs*). In 1341, Petrarch was awarded the title of Poet Laureate in Rome. The last member of the Triumvirate was Giovanni Boccaccio (1313–1375), who developed Italian prose. In *The Decameron*, a collection of one hundred tales, Boccaccio examines every side of human nature in a very entertaining narrative style.

Northern European Literary Figures The northern European Renaissance further developed both poetry and prose. England produced some of the most important literature of the period. Sir Thomas More (1478–1535), the Christian Humanist who served as chancellor of England, developed a "blueprint" for a perfect society on earth in his novel *Utopia*. In creating this ideal world, More criticized his own society. Interestingly, utopia (which means either "some place" or "no place" in Ancient Greek, depending on how it is used) is modeled on monastic life, revealing the author's religious spirit. The reign of Queen Elizabeth I (1558–1603) was a period of great literary creativity. Known as the Elizabethan Era, it saw the highest development of English drama in the masterpieces of William Shakespeare (1564–1616), whose plays contain some of the greatest poetry in the English language. These include *Hamlet, Macbeth,* and *Romeo and Juliet*. Equally outstanding are the dramas of Christopher Marlowe (1564–1593), the most famous of which was "Doctor Faustus." The poetry of Edmund Spenser (c. 1552–1599) glorified the ideas of the versatile individual of the Renaissance, particularly in his masterpiece, *The Faerie Queen.* In France, Michel de Montaigne (1533–1592) created the literary form of the essay. His near contemporary, Francois Rabelais (c. 1490–1553), wrote satirical novels, the most famous of which was Gargantua and Pantagruel. Spanish literature entered a Golden Age, as illustrated by the work of Miguel de Cervantes (1547–1616). His masterpiece, which brilliantly criticized Cervantes' society, was *Don Quixote de la Mancha,* a satire about an eccentric gentleman who believes he is a knight.

Historical Writing

The Renaissance also saw the development of modern historical writing. One of the first to write history in secular terms, Leonardo Bruni (1374–1444) was a Civic Humanist who served as chancellor of Florence. His *History of the Florentine People* is considered the first modern historical account, due to its scholarly approach. Bruni, who studied the Roman historians, felt that the past had much to teach the present and that human history was basically a struggle for liberty. This was followed a century later by another Florentine, Francesco Guicciardini (1483–1540), who regarded history as a unique series of events based on human actions that should be studied on its own terms, not for the lessons it could teach. His work, the *History of Italy,* revealed much of the greed, hatred, ambition, and egotism in Renaissance Italy. As a historian of his own time, he made great use of official archives. Guicciardini's concern for factual accuracy and his world view of historical causes set new standards in historical writing. *The Lives of the Artists* by Giorgio Vasari (1511–1574), a series of short biographies about artists by an artist who knew many of them, is indicative of the changes the Renaissance had brought.

Political Philosophy

Political philosophy was highlighted in the Renaissance, most notably by Niccolo Machiavelli (1469–1527). He was a Florentine bureaucrat who had become disillusioned by his experiences serving in the short-lived Florentine Republic of the fifteenth century. A political realist, Machiavelli believed that decisiveness and force were needed for a city or nation to achieve greatness. His most famous work, *The Prince,* was a guidebook for rulers to be successful. He argued that the chief obligation of a prince was to serve his people. This was accomplished by creating a strong state that was safe from enemies. Machiavelli believed that ethics were separate from politics and the ruler should use whatever means were necessary to remain powerful. He coined the phrase "The end justifies the means." While Machiavelli's work was condemned throughout Europe, it served as a model for most rulers of the period and did much to influence the development of strong national monarchies.

The best known northern European Humanist philosopher was the scholar Desiderius Erasmus (1466–1536). Called the "Prince of Humanists," he studied the Classics and applied Ancient Greco-Roman wisdom to Christian belief. Erasmus sought to "humanize" Christianity, instructing individuals to pay less attention to ritual and theology, and seek the "historical" (human) side of Christ, following that example. He also criticized corruption in the Church, calling for religious and social reform. His most famous work was the *Praise of Folly,* which ridiculed the superstition and ignorance of his own time.

Summary

The Renaissance was the result of centuries of cultural and ethnic diffusion. The civilizations of the Classical World (Greek, Roman, Byzantine) and those of the Medieval (Celtic, Germanic, Scandinavian, Slavic) came together to form the modern European nations. The Renaissance removed the cultural limitations that religion had created in the Middle Ages. A new spirit of curiosity and belief in human potential was created. These attitudes would take Europeans far, both in exploration and scientific progress. They would, however, also remove the controls on society, which would result in religious division, war, and the brutal exploitation of other peoples in the New World. Yet, like a child that must get bruised learning how to walk, Europe stood up and took its first steps. It had entered the modern world.

CHAPTER 6

Review Exercises

I. Matching

Directions: Match the names in Column A with the items they are *best associated* with in Column B.

Column A
1. Baldassare Castiglione
2. Desiderius Erasmus
3. Medici family
4. Lorenzo Ghiberti
5. "Mona Lisa"
6. Raphael
7. Michaelangelo
8. Giorgio Vasari
9. Sforza family
10. Botticelli

Column B
(a) "The Gates of Paradise"
(b) "Primavera"
(c) Milan
(d) *The Lives of the Artists*
(e) "Pieta"
(f) *The Book of the Courtier*
(g) "La Giaconnda"
(h) Florence
(i) *Praise of Folly*
(j) "The School of Athens"

II. Matching

Directions: Match the words in Column A with the *correct description* in Column B.

Column A
1. chiaroscuro
2. commune
3. despot
4. Great Council
5. linear perspective
6. utopia
7. piazza
8. canzoni
9. naturalism
10. oligarchy

Column B
(a) tyrannical absolute ruler
(b) rule of the few
(c) realistic art with emotion
(d) some place or no place
(e) town square
(f) appearance of distance and space
(g) contrast of light and shade
(h) shared responsibility of government
(i) songs
(j) Venetian representative body

III. Map Exercise

Directions: Use the map to locate the place associated with each of the following statements. For each statement, write the *letter* of the place.

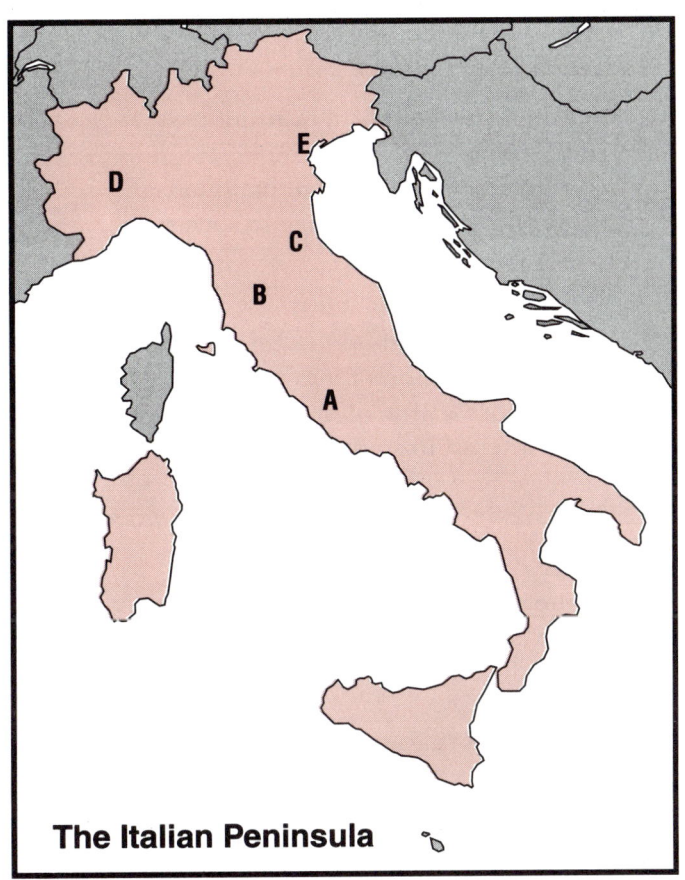

The Italian Peninsula

1. _____ This Italian city was the first to experience the Renaissance.

2. _____ The papacy ruled here.

3. _____ The Medici family came to dominate this Italian city.

4. _____ This Italian maritime republic was an oligarchy.

5. _____ Both the Visconti and Sforza families controlled this Italian city.

IV. Multiple Choice

Directions: Find the *letter* of the correct answer.

1. The term "renaissance" means

    (a) revival.
    (b) restoration.
    (c) re-birth.
    (d) return.

2. The Renaissance was chiefly inspired by

   (a) Hellenistic civilization.
   (b) Medieval Scholasticism.
   (c) Christianity.
   (d) Greco-Roman learning.

3. The Italian Renaissance introduced

   (a) no effective political institutions.
   (b) democratic ideals.
   (c) a strong sense of Italian nationalism.
   (d) no fundamental change in society.

4. Humanism was

   (a) a religion based on the equality of all humans.
   (b) an examination of human values.
   (c) the glorification of humanity and a belief in its potential.
   (d) an interest in studying the variety of human beings.

5. The inability of the Italians to unite into a single nation resulted in

   (a) the domination of the papacy.
   (b) the economic domination of the north.
   (c) the deterioration of political organization.
   (d) the development of independent city-states.

6. The Italian Renaissance was chiefly centered in

   (a) central Italy.
   (b) southern Italy.
   (c) northern Italy.
   (d) Sicily.

7. The term "Renaissance man" refers to

   (a) someone who is well-rounded and versatile.
   (b) an expert in one area.
   (c) an individual who believes in Renaissance Period values.
   (d) a teacher of Classical literature.

8. The Italian city known as the "Cradle of Renaissance Culture" was

   (a) Rome.
   (b) Milan.
   (c) Venice.
   (d) Florence.

9. The first notable Italian city in the Renaissance was

   (a) Rome.
   (b) Siena.
   (c) Venice.
   (d) Florence.

10. The city-state of Siena established a

   (a) republic.
   (b) commune.
   (c) oligarchy.
   (d) monarchy.

11. After 1447, Milan was ruled by the

   (a) Sforza family.
   (b) Medici family.
   (c) Visconti family.
   (d) Valois family.

12. The internal political struggle in fourteenth century Florence resulted in

   (a) the establishment of a republic.
   (b) the establishment of a monarchy.
   (c) the domination of the Medicis.
   (d) the domination of the Viscontis.

13. The Republic of Venice was dominated by an oligarchy of

   (a) aristocrats.
   (b) merchants.
   (c) clergy.
   (d) military leaders.

14. The government of Milan was a

   (a) democracy.
   (b) republic.
   (c) monarchy.
   (d) despotism.

15. Florence became the center of the arts during the Renaissance Period because

   (a) it conquered all the other Italian city-states.
   (b) the climate was better for preserving paintings.
   (c) the pope declared it to be the center.
   (d) it became a wealthy city through trade.

16. The first Renaissance artist to develop the Naturalistic style was

   (a) Giotto.
   (b) Masaccio.
   (c) Fra Angelico.
   (d) Piero della Francesca.

17. All of the following were painted by Leonardo da Vinci *except*

   (a) "The Last Supper."
   (b) "Virgin and Child with Saint Anne."
   (c) "The Creation of Adam."
   (d) "La Giaconnda."

18. The sculpture that came closest to the Classical ideal of masculine beauty was

   (a) Donatello's "David."
   (b) Donatello's "Saint George."
   (c) Michelangelo's "David."
   (d) Michelangelo's "Moses."

19. The "Tuscan Triumvirate" consisted of

   (a) Dante, Petrarch, and Cellini.
   (b) Dante, Boccaccio, and Cellini.
   (c) Dante, Petrarch, and Boccaccio.
   (d) Petrarch, Boccaccio, and Cellini.

20. The "Prince of Christian Humanists" was

   (a) Marsillio Ficino.
   (b) Niccolo Machiavelli.
   (c) Desiderius Erasmus.
   (d) Thomas More.

V. Thought Questions

Directions: Answer the following questions in essay form.

1. The Renaissance was a "re-birth" of Classical civilization.

   A. List four ideas and/or institutions of the Greco-Roman World that were revived by Western European society during this period.
   B. Show how each was influenced by Medieval culture.

2. Humanism was at the center of the Renaissance.

   A. List three ways in which Humanism influenced the basic attitudes of Western Europeans during the Renaissance.
   B. Identify which groups in society were changed by these ideas.

3. The Renaissance was uniquely Italian.

   A. List one political, economic, and social trend occurring in Italy from the twelfth to the sixteenth centuries that influenced the development of the Renaissance.
   B. How does each show that the Italian peninsula was ideally suited for this?

4. You are a Christian Humanist scholar in England during the sixteenth century. You are writing to a friend who is a Humanist in an Italian university to explain the differences between the Renaissance in Italy and northern Europe. Be sure to include political, economic, and cultural differences.

5. The culture of the Renaissance affected the development of society.

   A. Select one writer or poet, historian, artist, *and* architect of the Renaissance.
   B. Show one way each was different from his or her counterpart in the Middle Ages.

CHAPTER 7

The Reformation

Along with the Renaissance, the Reformation contributed to the birth of what we call Modern Europe. And as was also true of the Renaissance, the Reformation can be seen as part of a reaction to the world of the Middle Ages. The Reformation is also called the Protestant Reformation, for reasons that will be explained in this chapter. Simply defined, the Reformation was a movement to reform, or change, certain ideas and practices of the Roman Catholic Church. The movement was successful in some parts of Europe. In addition to affecting religion, the Reformation had an impact on economics and politics in Europe. Ultimately, it was going to have an effect on life in the "New World" of the Americas. Of all the people who played major historical roles during the Reformation, the most important was Martin Luther. His actions in October 1517 marked the start of the Reformation. Let us turn now to him, to understand more about his place in European history.

The Life of Martin Luther

Born in 1483 to a wealthy German peasant family in Saxony, Martin Luther originally planned to study law. But in 1505, during a frightening rainstorm, he was knocked to the ground. He cried out for help from St. Anne and declared, "I will become a monk." Shortly thereafter, he gave up the study of law and entered a monastery. He led a holy life and became particularly concerned with the religious doctrine of salvation of the soul. He did become a monk, and later, a professor of religion at the University of Wittenberg.

His concern with the doctrine of salvation grew to the point that he became disturbed with the current teachings of the Roman Catholic Church about this idea. Those teachings stated that in order to overcome one's sins, and thereby achieve salvation, a person had to have faith and perform good works, along with praying and fasting. It was also permissible to buy an indulgence (a Church pardon to escape punishment for a sin). From Luther's point of view, all that should be necessary to gain salvation was faith in God. Luther rejected the need to

Martin Luther was the main figure responsible for the Protestant Reformation. Although the Reformation was a religious movement at first, it had long-lasting political consequences.

engage in good works, attend elaborate ceremonies, and buy indulgences as signs of good faith. In fact, his doctrine came to be called simply "justification by faith."

These ideas and other beliefs of Luther's eventually became known as Lutheranism. Originally, Luther did not wish to start a new religion, but rather to make some changes in Church practices. Nevertheless, his teachings angered papal authorities in Rome. An additional reason for papal anger was Luther's criticism of the vast amount of wealth accumulated by Church officials. Besides protesting the sale of indulgences, for example, Luther was also against such practices as simony (selling Church offices) and **nepotism**. He felt that these practices were wrongful because they were not in keeping with the spiritual mission of the Church.

Luther's ideas, particularly those on indulgences, attracted unusual public attention when he posted his **95 Theses** on a Wittenberg church door on Sunday, October 31, 1517. The posting of these Theses, or statements, was a specific reaction to the activities of a monk named Johann Tetzel. Tetzel had been sent by Pope Leo X to raise money for construction of the new cathedral of St. Peter in Rome. Tetzel's travels took him to German villages near Wittenberg, where he attempted to obtain money by offering indulgences for sale. He claimed that buyers of indulgences would be making charitable contributions and at the same time

Chapter 7 Chronology

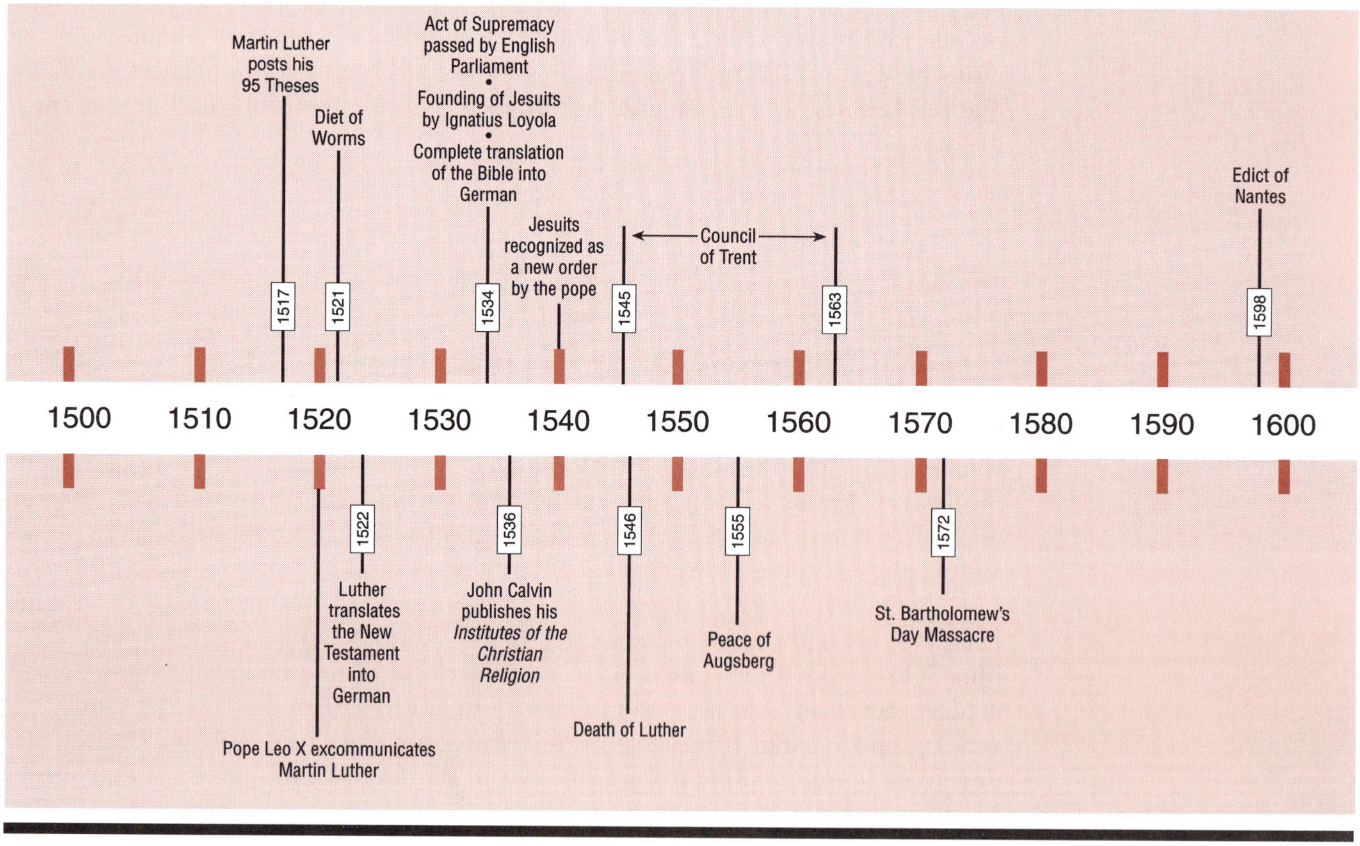

Martin Luther posts his 95 Theses — 1517

Diet of Worms — 1521

Act of Supremacy passed by English Parliament
•
Founding of Jesuits by Ignatius Loyola
•
Complete translation of the Bible into German — 1534

Jesuits recognized as a new order by the pope — 1545

Council of Trent — 1563

Edict of Nantes — 1598

1500 1510 1520 1530 1540 1550 1560 1570 1580 1590 1600

Luther translates the New Testament into German — 1522

Pope Leo X excommunicates Martin Luther

John Calvin publishes his *Institutes of the Christian Religion* — 1536

Death of Luther — 1546

Peace of Augsberg — 1555

St. Bartholomew's Day Massacre — 1572

gaining forgiveness for their prior sins. Luther criticized such claims, stating that indulgences could neither help people escape purgatory nor cancel out their sins, and that it was improper to seek money from people for false promises. Consequently, as was common in those days, Luther wrote his thoughts and nailed them to the church doors. These were the 95 Theses.

In posting these Theses, Luther did not seek to start a revolution or a division in the Catholic Church. Basically, he was questioning the purity of Tetzel's actions and asking scholars to consider the propriety of the claims associated with these practices. Little did he realize or intend the widespread impact of his actions. News about what he had done spread quickly throughout Europe. The 95 Theses were reprinted and aroused much interest. The sale of indulgences began to diminish, while the irritation of the papal authorities began to increase. Although under great pressure from these authorities, Luther refused to recant (take back) his views. In a famous debate in 1519 with John Eck, a noted theologian sent by the pope to confront Luther in Leipzig, Luther maintained his opinions and admitted they were similar to those of John Huss. Huss had preached against the Church in the fifteenth century, was accused of heresy, and was burned at the stake.

Luther now added to his own attacks upon the Church, declaring, for example, that the authority of the Bible and the authority of a person's conscience were more important than the authority of the pope. In June 1520, Pope Leo X excommunicated Luther by issuing a Papal Bull. When Luther received this document, he took the dramatic step of burning it in front of a large crowd in a public square in Wittenberg. He felt confident and fearless in doing this because of the strong support he had been getting in this part of Europe from people who agreed with his views.

In order to carry out the excommunication, and fearing that Luther's teachings and actions would create trouble in the Holy Roman Empire, the large region in central Europe that included present-day Germany, the Emperor Charles V summoned Luther to appear before the Imperial Diet convened at Worms in 1521. Under questioning and through all the attempts to get him to recant his views at this special meeting, Luther stood his ground. A very loose translation of his emotional response has him stating: "Here I stand; I cannot do otherwise. God help me. Amen." Stunned by Luther's firm resistance, Charles V now issued the Edict of Worms. This document condemned Luther as a heretic, forbade the distribution and reading of his works, and ordered his arrest and banishment from the Empire. Fortunately for Luther, several German rulers were willing to protect him from danger. One of these, Frederick the Wise of Saxony, hid Luther in his castle for almost a year. Luther eventually returned to Wittenberg without being bothered by any authorities. He married a former nun and raised a large family. These actions intensified his break with the Roman Catholic Church. In 1529, some of his followers published a protest against the Edict of Worms. Thereafter, his followers became known as Protestants. And what was described generally as the new Protestant religion, based on Luther's teachings, spread rapidly through the northern parts of the Holy Roman Empire such as the German states. Indeed, by the time of Luther's death in 1546, this new religion had been accepted by many princes in this area.

There are now some important questions for us to ask about this Protestant Reformation: What were Luther's basic teachings? What factors were responsible for bringing about the Reformation? What was its impact?

John Huss

John Huss was born in 1369, in the small village of Husinetz, from which his last name originated. John Huss proved to be a problem for the Roman Catholic Church and eventually met his death because of his actions.

John received an education in the city of Prague, in what is now the Czech Republic. He began to teach in the university and became an ordained priest. He lived a simple and austere life and became famous for his sermons.

By c. 1400, the opinions of Wycliffe of England had made their way across the continent and were studied by many in the priesthood. Some of the clergy agreed with certain doctrines put forth by Wycliffe and the Church was forced to take a stand. Huss was one of the clergy that thought Wycliffe was correct and he refused to obey a ruling not to promote what the Church called heretical beliefs.

When Huss continued to preach against the Church, the archbishop excommunicated him and his followers. They paid little attention to this and the archbishop then placed all of Prague under an interdict and ordered that Wycliffe's writing be burned and Huss be silenced. Huss appealed this action to the pope but refused to go to Rome when called.

It was at this time that a new crusade was called—against the king of Naples. As was common practice, indulgences were to be sold to raise money. Huss objected to indulgences as the selling of forgiveness and preached against the shedding of Christian blood by Christians and also said that purgatory did not exist. To top it off he called the pope greedy. The pope branded Huss a heretic and excommunicated him. When this was ignored, the pope placed an interdict on Prague and any city that aided Huss.

At that point, Huss began to write his thoughts. He rejected the worship of images, said that there were too many unnecessary religious practices, and believed that confession should be eliminated. He argued that priests shouldn't be charging for their services. He stated that the Church had too many worldly goods and should sell off what it had. Huss said that the Bible, not the pope, should be the guide for all Christians and that the pope should step down as head of the Church. Furthermore, he claimed that the pope was not infallible and that people should only follow him when he commanded according to God's will.

Huss was given a safe conduct to a council meeting for questioning. Certain points were debated and Huss agreed with those he believed were based on Scripture and recanted his position on these. On other points he would not change his mind, despite the pleadings of his friends. The council was faced with a serious dilemma. How could they allow what they saw as a self-proclaimed heretic to go free? If they allowed a simple priest to oppose them, they would lose their authority. They told him one last time—recant or die. Huss stood on principle and refused. So the council condemned him to death.

In July 1415, John Huss was taken to a spot outside the city. A pile of wood was built around a pole to which John was tied. He was given one last chance—he refused. It is said that John Huss went to a fiery death while singing hymns.

Luther's Teachings

Basic Principles of Protestantism

Most of Luther's basic ideas can be found in his writings. The most important of these were the following, published in 1520: *Address to the Nobility of the German Nation, On the Babylonian Captivity of the Church,* and *The Freedom of a Christian Man.* Their chief ideas, listed below, were accepted by most of the Protestant sects that emerged in Europe. These sects viewed Protestantism as a revision and reformulation of Christian beliefs and traditions. The contrasting views of the Roman Catholic Church at the time are in parentheses.

1. Salvation comes about through faith alone. (Salvation results from faith and good works.)
2. Religious authority rests with the Bible, not with the pope. (The pope and Church officials beneath him are the sources of authority.)
3. Only two **sacraments** are permitted—baptism and communion. (Seven sacraments are practiced—baptism, communion, confirmation, penance, marriage, ordination, and extreme unction.)
4. The clergy, known as ministers, are only guides for the faithful. People should be free to understand and interpret the Bible for themselves. Accordingly, Luther held services in German rather than in Latin, and in 1522, he translated the New Testament into German. His complete translation of the Bible, from Hebrew and Greek texts, appeared in 1534. (Priests were needed to explain writings.)
5. Priests could marry. (Because of their vow of celibacy, priests could not marry.)

Factors Leading to the Reformation

We generally date the beginning of the Reformation to 1517. Its origins and fundamental causes, however, can be found prior to the day when Luther posted his 95 Theses. Such tracing of causes is important whenever studying great historical movements. For example, we realize that the origins of the fall of the Roman Empire can be seen prior to 476, and that the origins of the American Revolution occurred before 1775. Martin Luther's protests against Church practices and beliefs were shared by many people in northern Europe. You may recall that he was concerned about practices such as simony, nepotism, sale of indulgences, and the worldliness of the clergy, as well as teachings about salvation and the role of the pope. These religious reasons by themselves, however, cannot explain why the movement known as the Reformation had such a major historical impact. In many areas, Luther's actions against the Church were supported by people for reasons that had little to do with religion. Nonreligious factors that helped to bring about the Reformation are as follows:

1. *Economic Conflicts:* Many rulers were upset about the economic power and wealth of the Roman Catholic Church. This power and wealth came from taxes imposed by the Church on its worshippers as well as from the vast

amounts of land it owned throughout Europe. Local rulers were angry about the huge amount of money that flowed out of their regions into the papal treasury in Rome. To many rulers, who lived at great distances from Rome, the papacy seemed to be a foreign power interested chiefly in draining wealth from others. And in truth, these rulers hoped to obtain this wealth for themselves and for their people.

2. *Political Conflicts:* It was felt that the pope had too much power over political and other secular, or nonreligious, matters. In the late Middle Ages, many political leaders challenged the pope's claim to be supreme in secular as well as religious affairs. They resisted the Church's claim to power over them and other civil officials and to its interference in political matters concerning their territories. They strongly objected to the Church's authority to remove rulers, to excuse their subjects from allegiance on issues of loyalty and obedience, and to transfer their land to others.

3. *Humanism and Renaissance Thought:* The Renaissance emphasized the ability of humans to think and reason for themselves. Along with this came the questioning of traditional authority. In this atmosphere, many people during the Renaissance began to disagree with certain Church practices and ideas.

4. *Previous Church Problems and Reform Attempts:* Even before Luther, there had been problems within the Church. One example was the Babylonian Captivity of 1309 to 1377, when popes lived in France and were under the control of the king of France. Another instance was the Great Schism of 1378 to 1417, when two popes competed for control of the Church. Other reformers had attacked some of the same practices that Luther protested against. These included John Wycliffe in England, John Huss in Bohemia, and Desiderius Erasmus in Holland.

The Growth and Impact of Protestantism

Luther's movement was to have serious political and religious consequences in the German states. These consequences are discussed in the following paragraphs.

Many German Princes Supported Luther The German princes' attempts to break away from the religious and economic powers of the pope were combined with their attempts to break from the control and power of Charles V, the Holy Roman Emperor. Both the pope and the Holy Roman Emperor were seen as foreigners who had exerted too much control over the German princely states. Feelings of patriotism and nationalism grew, mostly in north German areas. Fighting soon broke out between German princes and Emperor Charles V, as the Emperor wanted to stop the spread of Protestantism, but neither side was able to win decisively. The fighting eventually stopped as a result of the Peace of Augsberg, recognized in a treaty signed in 1555. Two terms of this document were vital in the history of religion in Europe; they were:

1. Lutheranism was recognized as a legal religion.
2. The ruler of an area was the one who would determine the religion for the people of that area. Therefore, if the head of the German state of Saxony chose to follow Protestantism, then his subjects would be Protestant. If the ruler of Bavaria chose to remain as a Catholic, then his subjects would be

Catholic. Subjects who refused to accept the faith chosen by the ruler could not stay in the area. Practically all the north German princes selected the new Lutheran faith.

Protestant Sects Began to Appear

As Protestantism gained popularity, various groups or **sects** appeared that sometimes fought not only with each other, but also with Catholics. Most of these sects did not become large, organized, established Churches, but often united behind a leader and sought to live out their own interpretations of the Bible. One such group was the Anabaptists, eventually to be called Baptists. Among their beliefs were the separation of Church and state, religious tolerance, and baptism and Church membership for adults only. They reasoned that children should not be baptized because of their inability to understand the faith. For these and other beliefs, along with the fact that they were seen as threats to established customs, the Anabaptists suffered persecution; an extreme example occured in the German city of Munster in 1535, where many Anabaptists were executed. Nevertheless, several Anabaptist groups survived, and existed in ways they thought were typical of early Christian communities—by sharing, working, and praying together, and emphasizing ascetism (denial of worldly ways, avoidance of materialism). The spirit of their beliefs can be seen today in the United States in such various groups as the Baptists, Quakers, Mennonites, and Amish.

The Peasants' Rebellion of 1524

Angered with the heavy taxes put upon them by nobles and the Church, south German peasants began to react with violence. Although Luther initially supported the peasants' stand, he soon reversed his support. He was upset with their many instances of burning and killing. Critical of such actions, Luther backed the successful efforts of nobles in putting down the revolt. Consequently, many peasants grew disappointed with Luther and returned to Catholicism.

Luther Supported German Jews

Among Luther's many harsh criticisms of the Catholic Church was its poor treatment of Jews. (See Chapter 34, "The Holocaust.") Laws and actions taken against Jews were wrong, he claimed, as were the Church's beliefs about the Jews and its attempts to convert them. The small community of German Jews initially responded favorably to Luther, welcoming him as a defender and feeling that he respected them. However, when Luther also attempted to convert them, they resisted. Luther then became bitter towards Jews for not accepting entry into his version of Christianity. He made anti-Semitic statements and even suggested extermination. (Fortunately, Luther's **anti-Semitism** emerged late in his life and had little effect on his followers. Indeed, those Scandinavian countries, in which the majority of citizens became Lutherans, were helpful to Jews during the twentieth-century Jewish Holocaust by the Nazis in Germany. See Chapter 34.)

The Growth of Protestantism Beyond Germany

The Protestant Reformation as a movement began in Germany and spread to other parts of Europe. The spread was most evident in northern Europe and to some of the European colonies in North America.

Our survey of the influence of Luther's movement in non-German areas will begin with Switzerland. It was here, in the city of Zurich, that the priest Ulrich

Zwingli was active. Like Luther, Zwingli felt that the Catholic Church had strayed from its original purposes. Both men wished to provide reforms. Until the time of his death in 1531, Zwingli had spoken out against indulgences, and was in favor of simplified church building decorations and allowing priests to marry.

Calvinism

The ideas of Zwingli and Luther spread throughout Switzerland and influenced a Frenchman, John Calvin, who lived in Geneva. Calvin's thoughts about religion are contained in his book, *The Institutes of the Christian Religion*, published in 1536. As Luther did, Calvin opposed the belief that good works would lead to salvation. However, Calvin's emphasis on some issues was different from Luther's. Luther, for example, claimed that people could achieve salvation through faith in God. Calvin maintained that God alone would decide who would be saved; God had already selected those people. This was the theory of **predestination**. According to this theory, God chose certain people, called the elect, to be saved. Those who had not been chosen could never achieve salvation, no matter what they did on earth. While people obviously did not know whether they were among the elect, they should nevertheless behave as though they were among those chosen. This behavior would consist of leading a life according to extremely strict and high moral standards. These standards included careful devotion to the Bible, self-discipline, avoidance of material temptations, living simply, and working hard and honestly in one's occupation.

It was in Geneva, in 1541, that Calvinism became a way of life for citizens there. The city was governed as a **theocracy**. This meant that the government and all laws and rules came under the influence of religious ideas. There was no separation of Church and state. For example, Calvinist regulations against dancing, obscene language, bad manners, and so on were strictly enforced. Geneva became a center for many Europeans who wished to learn about Calvinist ideas. Geneva had become practically a Protestant Rome.

Calvinism could be considered simply one form or pattern within the Protestant Movement against the Catholic Church. Its influence was very great, however. It spread to the Netherlands (Holland), appealing primarily to those living in urban, commercial areas. Calvinism also gained followers in France, particularly among those who were concerned with the worldliness of the Catholic Church. These followers organized churches, mostly in southern France, and were called **Huguenots**. Their attempts to exist were challenged, most critically during the wars of religion that raged in France between 1562 and 1598. A terrible incident of religious violence was the St. Bartholomew's Day Massacre of August, 1572. Thousands of Huguenots were killed in Paris and other parts of France. Religious tension continued until issuance of the Edict of Nantes in 1598, which stated that Protestants in France (as well as other religions) were permitted to practice their faith. This was a victory for religious toleration. (For additional information on this topic, see Chapter 10, "The Rise of Nation-States.")

Protestantism in England

Besides France and the German states, the other major region experiencing religious change in the sixteenth century was England. What has even become known as the English Reformation was begun by King Henry VIII (r. 1509–1547).

However, his motivation and actions leading to change were very different from those of Martin Luther. Henry's protest against the Catholic Church was more for political than for religious reasons. In fact, Henry had been a devout Catholic and had written a criticism of Martin Luther in 1521. This criticism had impressed the pope, who gave Henry the title "Defender of the Faith." This is a title that is still carried by the British monarch.

Henry's problems with the Church stemmed from his wish to have a male heir to his throne. He was unable to have a son with his first wife, Catherine of Aragon. He therefore wanted to divorce Catherine and marry Ann Boleyn. To his dismay, his request to Pope Clement VII for an annulment (voiding) of his marriage to Catherine was denied. Angered by this denial, Henry spoke out against the Pope and authorized the Archbishop of Canterbury, Thomas Cranmer, to annul the marriage in 1533. Henry then married Ann Boleyn. The Pope responded by declaring the divorce from Catherine invalid and by excommunicating Henry. With resentment growing against the Pope, Parliament passed the Act of Supremacy in 1534. This legislation established the King as the head of the Church of England, or **Anglican** Church. Anglicans, as its followers were called, were no longer under the authority of the Pope. Anglicanism became a religion that kept some Catholic ideas and ceremonies but also mixed them with Protestant ways, as in the use of the English language instead of Latin.

Henry's actions were supported by a large majority of English people. They also welcomed his closing down of many monasteries and selling monastery lands. Those who opposed Henry resented the break with Rome. This group included Sir Thomas More, who had hoped to have reforms come from within the Catholic Church itself. Henry feared More and had him executed, along with others who argued against the Act of Supremacy. After Henry died, having married six times, the crown passed to his one son, Edward VI. During his reign (1547–1553), Protestant officials published *The Book of Common Prayer*. This described practices to be observed in Anglican services and was a combination of both Protestant and Catholic ideas. The transformation of England into a Protestant nation was stalled by Edward's successor, Mary Tudor (r. 1553–1558). She tried to make England more Catholic and to restore the authority of the pope. Upon her death, another daughter of Henry VIII became Queen. This was Elizabeth I (r. 1558–1603). She was interested, as had been her father, in devoting her energy to political issues rather than to religious ones. Nevertheless, she did much to make England a Protestant nation. She enforced her belief that the monarch was the head of the Anglican Church, continued her father's policy of seizing Catholic Church lands, and had Parliament pass an act that forced people to pay a fine if they did not attend the Anglican Church. By strengthening both her role and that of the Anglican Church, Elizabeth hoped to bring about a high degree of political unity in England. It can thus be said that by the time of her death in 1603, England had indeed become a leading Protestant nation in Europe. This did not mean, however, that religious controversy and its effect on politics had died down. For almost one hundred years after Elizabeth's death, the English people were to experience much tension and even a civil war. (See Chapter 11, "The Growth of Democracy in England.")

Protestantism Elsewhere

Elsewhere in Europe, Protestantism was making inroads. John Knox brought Calvinism to Scotland, having lived for some time in Geneva. A form of Calvinism,

Presbyterianism, became the national religion of Scotland. In Ireland, Protestants who came over from England became the ruling class. The great majority of Irish people, however, maintained themselves as Catholics. The Scandinavian countries of Denmark, Norway, and Sweden witnessed a spread of Protestant beliefs. Led by royal leaders, Lutheran national state churches were created in these lands.

And in lands overseas, particularly in some New World colonies of North America, the Protestant Reformation had an impact. The Puritans who settled in Massachusetts, for example, had left Europe fearing persecution. Their attempt to "purify" the Anglican Church of all features of Catholicism had caused them problems with English officials. In Virginia, the Church of England became the established Church. Roger Williams, a strong believer in religious freedom and a founder of Rhode Island, is memorialized in a statue of him on "Reformation Wall" in Geneva. In the Dutch colony of New Amsterdam, the settlers were of a Protestant faith. Even today, one can find Dutch Reformed churches and cemeteries in New York City. They are in the borough of Brooklyn, named for the Dutch town of Breukelen. And finally, we should not be surprised to find that the greatest number of Lutherans living in the United States today can be found in the Midwest. The explanation lies in the great emigration of Scandinavian people from, for example, Norway to Minnesota and Iowa.

Lutheranism and Anglicanism were religious offsprings of the Protestant Reformation. So were many other religious groups we have mentioned—the Anabaptists, the Calvinists, and the Presbyterians. Each of these could be considered as one form of Protestantism. Although these various groups or denominations had differences, they shared several things in common. One of these was their refusal to come under the authority of the pope. Obviously, the pope and Catholic Church saw Protestantism as a threat to their view of Christian unity in Western Europe. Their attempts to fight this threat is the topic to which we will now turn.

The Catholic and Counter Reformations

The reaction of the Catholic Church to the Protestant Movement took two basic patterns:

1. The attempt to make some reforms and changes within the Church, maintaining obedience to the pope while recognizing some of the abuses that Luther had attacked. This attempt can be called the Catholic Reformation.
2. The attempt to stop the spread of Protestantism by creating new religious orders. This attempt can be called the **Counter Reformation**.

These reactions by the Catholic Church had the support of political leaders, mainly in southern Europe, as Luther's efforts had from political leaders in northern Europe.

The move to press for changes within the Church came from Pope Paul III (r. 1534–1549). He appointed scholarly figures to high Church positions, such as cardinals and bishops. These leaders sought to maintain a strong devotion to Catholicism. They were willing, though, to make some reforms that would keep people faithful and provide for a spiritual renewal. An opportunity to do this occurred with Pope Paul's call for a Church council at the city of Trent in 1545.

The Council of Trent (1545–1563) upheld the traditional beliefs and practices of the Roman Catholic Church, including the supreme power of the pope over the Church and the necessity of both faith and good works for salvation. It also corrected some abuses, banning the sale of indulgences and forbidding simony. It called for improvement in the training of priests as well as in the keeping of Church finances. New ground was broken by the Council of Trent with the creation of the **Index**. This was a list of books that Catholics were not permitted to read. Books would be placed on the Index if they contained ideas deemed to be heretical by the Church. The Index was seen as an effective weapon to use against the widespread publication of books that had been made possible by the fifteenth century European invention of the printing press. (The Church kept the Index until 1966. In that year, the Second Vatican Council abolished it.) The work of the Council of Trent was designed, in part, to reach some reconciliation with Protestants. Protestant leaders who were invited, however, did not attend.

The establishment of new religious orders, begun in the 1520s, proved to be important. The Capuchins, a branch of the Franciscans, was organized to carry out the ideals of St. Francis and preach to the poor. The Ursuline order of nuns gained an admirable reputation for educating women. But the greatest of these new groups was the **Jesuits**. Known formally as the Society of Jesus, this order was founded in 1534 by the Spaniard, Ignatius Loyola (1491–1556). After receiving a serious wound as a soldier, Loyola became deeply involved in studying about religious issues during his period of recovery. Ultimately, he wrote a book, *Spiritual Exercises*. In it, he emphasized self-discipline and complete obedience to papal leadership of the Roman Catholic Church. These became major characteristics of the Jesuit order, whose followers became known as the "soldiers of the Catholic Church."

The Jesuits were officially recognized as an order by the pope in 1540, and indeed went about their tasks as if they were a finely tuned military organization. Their tasks were to prevent the spread of Protestantism, to help Catholics keep their faith, and to win converts. Their weapons were not guns but devotion, education, and a strong sense of purpose. They were respected for their learning and willingness to engage in debates on religious topics. In southern Germany and Eastern Europe, they were successful in winning some Protestants back to Catholicism. Their efforts, along with the measures of the Council of Trent, were highly welcomed in Spain, France, and Italy. The Jesuits also traveled overseas to East Asia and the Americas, where they proved to be successful **missionaries**. Their great devotion to learning and scholarship is seen in many of the fine colleges they founded in Europe and elsewhere. Even today in the United States, there are several reputable Jesuit institutions of higher learning—Boston College, Fordham University, Georgetown University, Marquette University, Notre Dame University, Loyola University in Chicago, and Loyola University in New Orleans. It should also be noted that those parts of the Americas that were colonized by France, Portugal, and Spain are primarily Catholic in today's world.

Another method used by the Roman Catholic Church to combat Protestantism was the Inquisition, which was a series of Church courts, originally established during the Middle Ages to put heretics on trial. The courts of the Inquisition sought to impose religious uniformity. They proved to be successful mainly in areas of southern Europe, where Protestantism was not much of a threat. The Inquisition had little impact in areas where Protestantism had a firm hold.

Results of the Protestant Reformation

The chief result of the Protestant Reformation was the breakdown of the religious unity of Western Europe. By 1600, the territorial divisions between Protestants and Catholics were clear to see. (See the accompanying map.) The various Protestant faiths were primarily in northern Europe, whereas Catholicism remained dominant in southern Europe. Religious hostility was to continue, one example being the Thirty Years War (1618 to 1648). Additional results were as follows:

1. *Political:* The monarchs and local civil officials, especially in central and northern Europe, gained power as the strength of the Catholic Church declined.

2. *Economic:* The selling of Church property and the abolishment of Church taxes in Protestant areas resulted in an increase of wealth in these areas, although more so for the royal and civil leaders than for the common people.

3. *Cultural:* Progress was made in education and literacy, especially because of the greater interest in reading the Bible. The growth of universities was supported by reformers, and was a continuation of the focus on learning brought about by the Renaissance. For Jesuits, scholastic institutions were instrumental for promoting self-discipline and enriching religious faith.

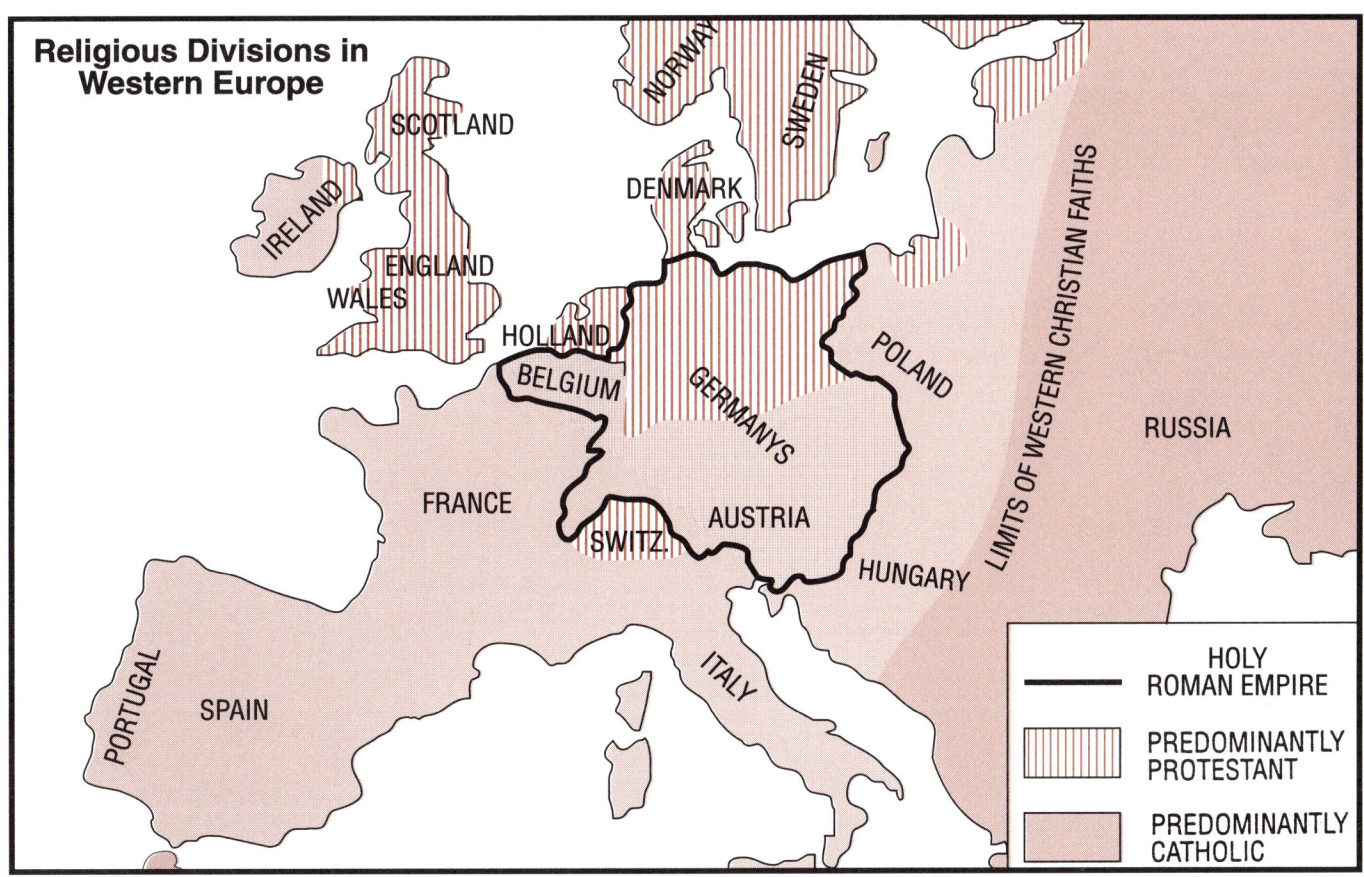

Religious Divisions in Western Europe

HOLY ROMAN EMPIRE
PREDOMINANTLY PROTESTANT
PREDOMINANTLY CATHOLIC

The consequences of the Reformation can be seen in this map. It shows the religious divisions in Western Europe.

Summary

The religious uniformity of Western Europe that had existed for centuries under the Roman Catholic Church was gone forever. Martin Luther had accomplished what Wycliffe and Huss had been unable to accomplish. As a result of Luther's posting of the 95 Theses, the continent would enter a long period of religious wars. New religions resulted from what began in Wittenberg. Switzerland under Calvin became a theocracy and England under Henry VIII became Anglican. Many of the other Protestant denominations that we have today—the Baptist, Quakers, Mennonite, and Amish—began then. Presbyterianism became strong and spread in Scotland under John Knox. The New World inherited some of the difficulties of the Old World when colonies were established. The Catholic Church took steps to remedy some of the problems they faced by eliminating certain excessive practices, but it never regained its previous position.

CHAPTER 7

Review Exercises

I. Matching

Directions: Match the words in Column A with the *correct description* in Column B.

Column A
1. 95 Theses
2. Council of Trent
3. Edict of Nantes
4. Act of Supremacy
5. theocracy
6. indulgence
7. simony
8. Edict of Worms
9. the Index
10. nepotism

Column B
(a) passed by the English Parliament
(b) listed prohibited literature
(c) posted in 1517 by Martin Luther
(d) selling of Church offices
(e) a Church pardon to escape punishment for a sin
(f) condemned Luther as a heretic
(g) the favoring of relatives for high positions
(h) a government organized under religious beliefs
(i) upheld traditional beliefs and practices of the Catholic Church
(j) permitted Protestants in France to have freedom of religion

II. Famous People

Directions: Use the names below to complete the following sentences.

Johann Tetzel	Charles V	Ignatius Loyola
Martin Luther	Henry VIII	John Eck
John Calvin	Leo X	John Knox

1. _____ founded the Jesuits.

2. _____ issued the Edict of Worms, in his role as Holy Roman emperor.

3. _____ established Presbyterianism, a form of Protestantism, in Scotland.

4. _____ wrote *Address to the Nobility of the German Nation*.

5. _____ wrote *The Institutes of the Christian Religion*.

6. _____ offered indulgences for sale throughout the German states.

7. _____ excommunicated Martin Luther.

8. _____ was sent by the pope to debate Luther on religious doctrine.

9. _____ was an English monarch who, although called "Defender of the Faith," was later excommunciated for disobeying papal commands.

III. Map Exercise

Directions: Use the map to locate the place associated with each of the following statements. For each statement, write the *letter* of the place. (An answer may be repeated.)

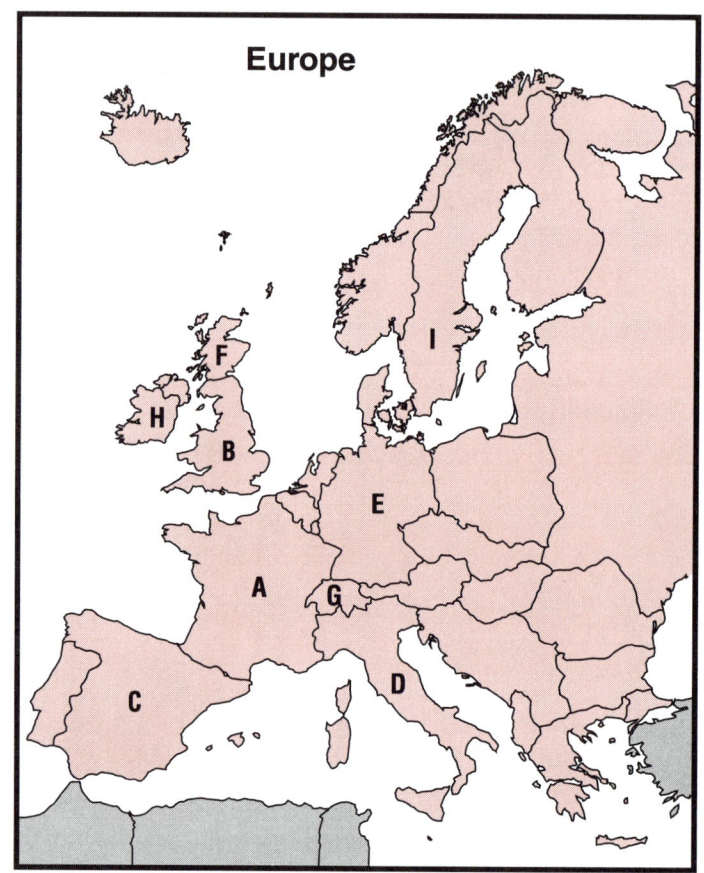

1. _____ Henry VIII ruled here.

2. _____ Where the popes have traditionally lived.

3. _____ John Knox spread a new religion here.

4. _____ Wittenberg is here, where Martin Luther's actions in 1517 helped bring on the Protestant Reformation.

5. _____ Geneva is here, where John Calvin's ideas were put into practice.

6. _____ Site of the Saint Bartholomew's Day Massacre.

7. _____ Birthplace of Ignatius Loyola.

8. _____ Island nation that remained largely loyal to Catholicism, unchanged by the Reformation.

9. _____ The Edict of Nantes was issued here.

10. _____ The Anglican Church was established here.

11. _____ Directly southwest of where Huguenots suffered persecution.

12. _____ This is a Scandinavian country where Lutheranism gained much popularity.

IV. Multiple Choice

Directions: Find the *letter* of the correct answer.

1. Which pair shared the most in common?

   (a) Tetzel and Luther
   (b) Luther and Calvin
   (c) Calvin and Tetzel

2. Who does not belong with the others?

   (a) Knox
   (b) Loyola
   (c) Huss
   (d) Luther

3. Luther was most disturbed by the

   (a) practice of nepotism.
   (b) creation of a theocracy.
   (c) construction of new churches.
   (d) sale of indulgences.

4. Which factor helped most to bring about the Protestant Reformation?

   (a) The Catholic clergy had lost faith in its religion.
   (b) Islam was attracting many converts in Western Europe.
   (c) The nobility in northern Europe resented the power of the Catholic Church.
   (d) Exploration of the Americas led to the introduction of new religious ideas.

5. The development of the printing press helped the success of the Protestant Reformation mainly by

   (a) providing in writing that the Catholic clergy was not completely correct in matters of faith.
   (b) making the spread of new ideas possible.
   (c) describing the evils of simony.
   (d) providing translations of the Bible.

6. Calvinism was brought to North America by

   (a) Jews in New Amsterdam.
   (b) Spaniards in Mexico.
   (c) Frenchmen in Canada.
   (d) Puritans in Massachusetts.

7. The greatest significance of the Reformation for later European history was that

   (a) most Europeans abandoned Catholicism for Protestantism.
   (b) conflict between religious and secular authorities was reduced.
   (c) the Church's control over ideas was diminished.
   (d) Christianity was no longer a powerful force.

8. According to Luther, salvation comes about through

   (a) good works.
   (b) faith.
   (c) indulgences.
   (d) a saintly life.

9. The basic idea in Calvin's religious doctrines was his belief in

   (a) predestination.
   (b) indulgences.
   (c) the basic goodness of man.
   (d) religious freedom.

10. Which of the following did not support Luther?

    (a) German peasants
    (b) German nobility
    (c) Ulrich Zwingli
    (d) Charles V

11. In general, the religious Reformation that occurred under Henry VIII in his country was mainly for

    (a) economic reasons.
    (b) religious reasons.
    (c) political reasons.
    (d) military reasons.

12. The Reformation in Germany resulted in

    (a) a politically weaker Germany.
    (b) a politically stronger Germany.
    (c) no political changes of importance.
    (d) a victory for Catholic clergymen.

13. Luther's success was a result of all of the following *except*

    (a) his appointment by the pope to a high position in Rome.
    (b) the development of the printing press.
    (c) his appeal to the wealthy and middle classes.
    (d) a strong command of language.

14. The chief center of Protestant reformers in the sixteenth century was at

    (a) Paris.
    (b) Geneva.
    (c) Zurich.
    (d) Madrid.

15. One vow of the Jesuits, making them different from other religious orders, was

    (a) chastity.
    (b) poverty.
    (c) obedience to the pope.
    (d) loyalty to Luther.

16. As a result of the Protestant Reformation, Western Europe today can be described as a region that

    (a) is mainly Christian.
    (b) is obedient to the pope.
    (c) had religious diversity.
    (d) has many gods or deities.

V. Thought Questions

Directions: Answer the following questions in essay form.

1. Assume you are Martin Luther. Write a letter to Pope Leo X explaining two reasons for your actions in posting the 95 Theses in Wittenberg.

2. Assume you are a north German prince. Write a letter to Martin Luther, dated in 1522, explaining two reasons why you are willing to support him in his defiance of the pope.

3. Describe one goal of the Catholic Church during the Counter Reformation.

    A. List two methods used to achieve this goal.
    B. Explain whether these methods were successful.

4. Describe two long-range results of the Reformation.

    A. Would Martin Luther have been pleased with these results? Explain.

5. Explain each of the following statements.

    A. The Renaissance contributed to the Reformation.
    B. The Peace of Augsberg was a step toward religious freedom.
    C. Geneva became a "Protestant Rome."
    D. The Reformation had an effect on the history of the United States.

CHAPTER 8

The Age of Exploration

From the mid-1400s for a period of three hundred years, Europeans changed the world as they explored the globe. They were motivated primarily by a search for an all-water trading route to Asia, hoping to find the fabled riches of the East. Ironically they discovered new lands and wealth to the west, in the Americas, which led to further explorations. Rulers, merchants, adventurers, and Christian religious leaders, stimulated by ideas about "God, gold, and glory," settled in what Europeans came to call the New World.

The expression "God, gold, and glory" represented the mixed intentions of the Europeans during the **Age of Exploration**. The European monarchs and merchants wanted to profit from the valuable commercial products—spices, gold, ivory, silk, silver, and slaves—obtained during these voyages. Religious leaders wanted to spread Christianity to peoples previously unknown. The Catholic Church and the European monarchs even hoped to find allies in their struggle against the Islamic Ottoman Empire. The participants in the explorations hoped for heroic adventures that would bring them fame and riches.

European interest in finding a new trading route to Asia grew after the Middle Ages ended. From the 1200s, when Marco Polo's family visited the Chinese Empire of Kublai Khan, Europeans made use of the old established trade routes to Asia. This usually meant traveling to the eastern end of the Mediterranean Sea and joining caravans that followed the "silk route" to the wealthy lands of the fabled East. Merchants from Venice and Genoa dominated the European portion of the Asian trade, but they, too, were dependent on the Turkish and Arab merchants operating out of trading centers in cities such as Antioch and Alexandria. By the time the precious Asian goods reached Western Europe, their prices had increased many times. Moreover, the fact that the Islamic Ottoman Empire played such an important role in this trade troubled the Europeans.

Factors Enabling Exploration There were a number of key factors that enabled Western European nations, primarily Portugal, Spain, Holland, France, and England, to undertake these voyages of discovery. The Renaissance spirit had revived an interest in exploration, geography, and natural science. Many Europeans were increasingly interested in the possibilities of trade with other wealthy areas of the world. Improved sailing vessels and technological advances in navigational instruments made longer voyages of exploration possible. In the fifteenth century, the people of the developing nation-states of Western Europe wanted to find new routes to tap the wealth of the East. In Western Europe, political, economic, and social conditions spurred the growth and organization of a diverse group of individuals who possessed the necessary wealth, knowledge, skills, and willingness to venture overseas to find riches and fame. The desire for God, gold, and glory motivated these merchants, sailors, and adventurers to participate in the often dangerous voyages of exploration.

The need to explore westward in the Atlantic Ocean by Portugal and then Spain, in part, resulted from the control of the older established routes by the Ottoman Empire and the seafaring Italian city-states such as Venice and Genoa. Venturing out into the Atlantic was made easier by use of the new technological advances in determining position and direction at sea, and use of ships and sails more suitable for longer sea voyages.

New Technology Permits Exploration

In the 1400s, a number of technological advances in shipbuilding and navigation made longer sea voyages possible and marked the end of European regional

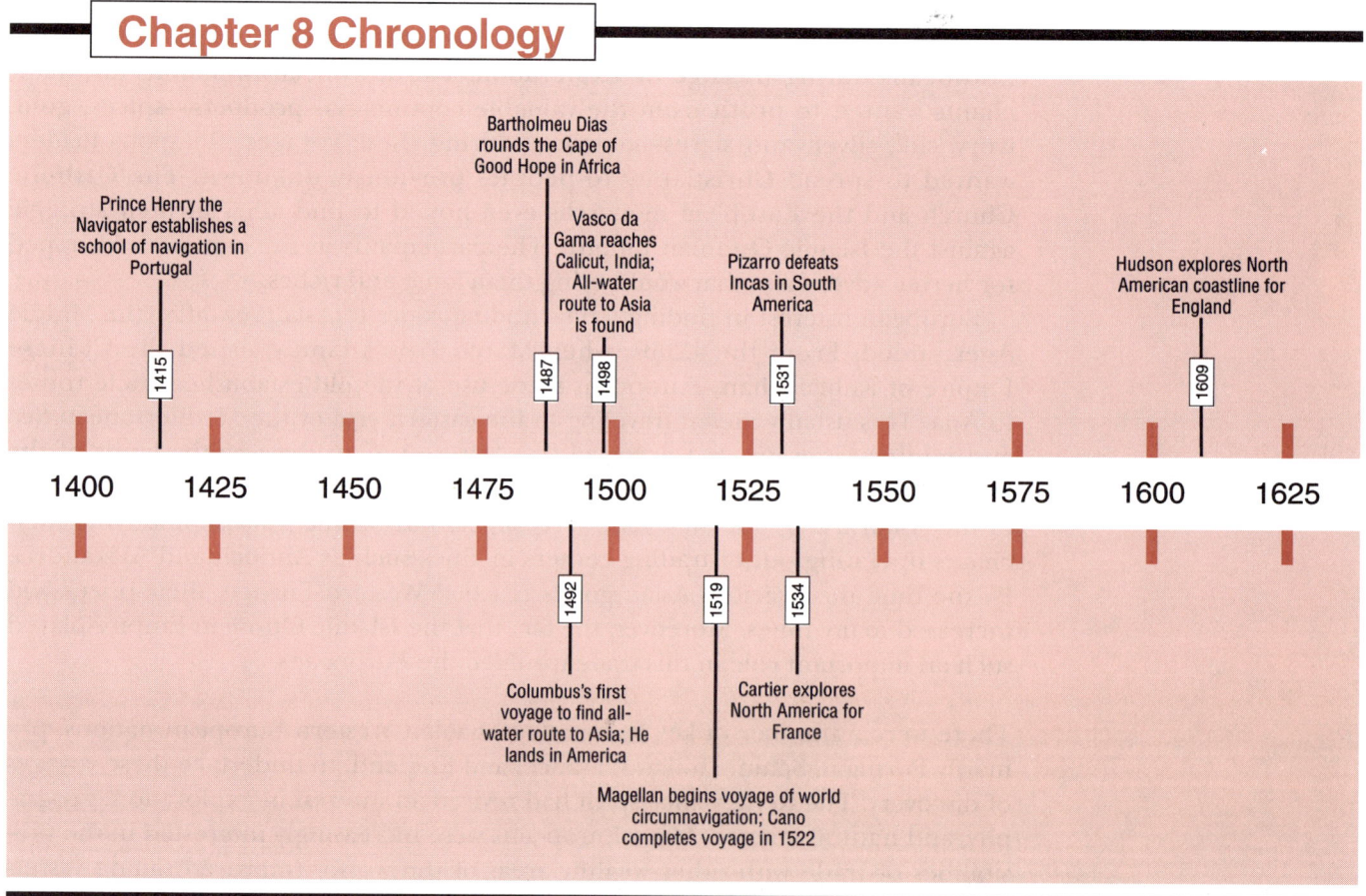

Chapter 8 Chronology

Prince Henry the Navigator establishes a school of navigation in Portugal — 1415

Bartholmeu Dias rounds the Cape of Good Hope in Africa — 1487

Vasco da Gama reaches Calicut, India; All-water route to Asia is found — 1498

Pizarro defeats Incas in South America — 1531

Hudson explores North American coastline for England — 1609

1400   1425   1450   1475   1500   1525   1550   1575   1600   1625

Columbus's first voyage to find all-water route to Asia; He lands in America — 1492

Magellan begins voyage of world circumnavigation; Cano completes voyage in 1522 — 1519

Cartier explores North America for France — 1534

isolation. These voyages would mean the beginning of European global domination. European nations began to carve out colonial empires in the Americas, Africa, Southeast Asia, and later China.

Several of the technological innovations that aided the process of exploration made use of advances that had been perfected by Arabs and Asians. The **compass**, of Chinese origin, helped sailors to better determine geographical direction, and the **astrolabe**, perfected by the Arabs, enabled sailors to determine the altitude of the sun and other celestial bodies. Europeans, particularly the Portuguese, made progress in shipbuilding. The **caravel** type of ship took advantage of advances made in outfitting Islamic sailing vessels. Multiple triangular-shaped lateen sails and masts adapted by European shipwrights enabled ships to travel much faster. The crews of the caravels also made use of European innovations in weaponry, such as cannons and rifles.

European **cartography** skills also gradually improved. The older maps and charts were inaccurate and often based on rumor and legend. During the Renaissance the rediscovered knowledge of the Greek, Roman, Byzantine, and Arab scholars gave Europeans a new and better view of the globe. Europeans later added to this knowledge as they explored more of the unknown world.

Portugal's Early Explorations

Portugal, which bordered the Atlantic Ocean, was the first nation in Western Europe that was capable of venturing out into the Atlantic Ocean in search of new trading opportunities. It began its explorations in the 1420s. Prince Henry (called Prince Henry the Navigator), a younger brother of the king of Portugal, established a school for navigators in Sagres, Portugal, and promoted numerous voyages of exploration. Sea captains flying the Portuguese flag made a number of important discoveries of islands in the Atlantic and pushed farther and farther along the coastline of West Africa during the 1400s in search of a sea route to Asia.

By the mid-1400s, the discovery and settlements on the Azores, the Madeira, and the Cape Verde islands laid the foundation of what would become the Portuguese seaborne empire in the 1500s. The Portuguese established factorias (trading posts) along the African coast and bought gold and ivory from African tribes. In the 1400s, the Portuguese also became increasingly involved in the African slave trade. The capture and sale of slaves was not new in Africa, but the European version of this trade greatly expanded over the next four hundred years. In large measure this led to the ruin of many tribes and devastated the African continent.

After Prince Henry's death in 1460, exploration temporarily slowed. In the 1480s, under the rule of King John II, new ventures were launched, which eventually led to the discovery of an all-water route to Asia. By 1488, Bartolomeu Dias rounded the southern tip of Africa, which was renamed the Cape of Good Hope. In 1497, Vasco da Gama set sail after much preparation. He visited cities along the east coast of Africa and, with the aid of an Arab pilot, crossed the Indian Ocean and reached the Indian port of Calicut in 1498. An all-water route had been found at last, and the profits gained from Vasco da Gama's return cargo of spices gave Europeans an idea of the riches that could be obtained from direct trade with the East.

Columbus's Voyages Lead to Discoveries

In the last decade of the 1400s, under the leadership of King Ferdinand and Queen Isabella, Spain embarked on a series of explorations that led to the establishment of a vast colonial empire. Queen Isabella's support for Columbus's voyage came at a time when a united Spain conquered the last great Moorish state, Grenada, in 1492. The reconquest of the Iberian peninsula from the Muslims did not mean that Catholic Spain gave up its role as a defender of Christianity. After the Catholic monarchs completed the reconquista (reconquest), they continued to make plans to solidify their rule and strengthen Christianity. For example, Catholic Spain was preparing for the expulsion of the Moors and the Jews who would not convert to Christianity.

It is therefore not surprising that in 1492, Queen Isabella also agreed to finance the voyage of Christopher Columbus. A sailor and cartographer by profession, Columbus had for a number of years unsuccessfully tried to convince other European monarchs to finance his voyage to find a westerly all-water route to the East.

Christopher Columbus, explorer for Spain, sailed westward and reached the Americas in 1492. Columbus's voyages led to the European colonization of the Americas and an increase in world trade.

In August 1492, Columbus set sail from Spain with three small ships. Assuming the world was round, Columbus hoped to reach the East by sailing west. He never did achieve his goal of finding a westerly all-water route to Asia on this trip or on his other three subsequent European voyages. Upon his return to Spain after his first voyage, however, Columbus was treated as a hero. He was given the title of Admiral of the Ocean Sea, and Viceroy and Governor of the lands that he discovered. During his remaining voyages, Columbus further explored the Caribbean Islands and sailed along the coast of northern South America.

Columbus was considered to be an excellent navigator, but he miscalculated the voyages' distances. Based on the knowledge that was available then, Columbus thought the trip to the East would be only about 2,200 nautical miles. Although Columbus may have suspected that the real distance to Asia was actually much greater, he refused—right up to his death in 1506—to recognize that the new lands that he explored and began to settle in the Caribbean Sea were not off of the coast of Asia. Columbus never found the great civilizations of Asia. He died a broken man, suffering from his failures as a colonizer and a disease supposedly contracted in the Americas.

The Discovery of the Americas

Columbus's four voyages, however, led to the first major discovery of new lands by Europeans. These lands were later named the Americas, after the minor explorer, the Italian Amerigo Vespucci. Their discovery changed the course of world history by linking the Americas to the rest of the world. Today we know that Columbus was not even the first European to set foot in the Americas. The Vikings from Scandinavia and perhaps other people from Africa and Asia may have reached the Americas earlier. The question of who should be given credit for the discovery of America has caused controversy in recent years. What is really important is that after Columbus's voyages, European interest in the New World grew and the Americas became thereafter linked to other areas across the globe. Columbus should be remembered as a person who was a product and symbol of exploration and global change. This period, during the Renaissance, was a time when Europeans brought the world closer together, sought to spread their ideas to other global areas, and began to make major changes in their economies because of trade.

The Original Inhabitants.   Moreover, there were millions of people already living in the so-called New World who were spread throughout the Americas. The inhabitants whom Columbus first found on the Caribbean Islands were erroneously called Indians by Columbus, and this misnomer has endured to our present day. Some of these first American peoples lived in advanced agricultural and trading civilizations while others hunted and gathered in more primitive tribes. These peoples had developed independently and isolated from the changes that took place in other world areas. After Columbus's voyages, most of these first American peoples underwent enormous changes almost always for the worst. Many of these peoples and their cultures disappeared after contact was made with the Europeans.

Portugal and Spain: Early Colonial Rivalry

As we have just seen, Portugal and Spain played the major roles in the first century of European global exploration. Columbus's early voyages intensified the rivalry between the two Iberian nations. King John II of Portugal rejected Spanish claims to the newly discovered Caribbean Islands. Spain and Portugal steadfastly refused to accept each other's claims and disputed the rights to explore and settle new lands.

The solution to this early colonial rivalry was arranged by Pope Alexander VI, who sought to keep the peace between these two Christian nations. After difficult negotiations and an initial rejection by Portugal, the Treaty of Tordesillas of 1494 was signed, which set the boundary limits or demarcation line separating Portuguese and Spanish interests. Essentially Spain received the right to explore and colonize all newly discovered lands to the west of the treaty line, and Portugal gained the same privileges for lands that were to the east of the demarcation. Spain ultimately gained the lion's share of North and South America and the Caribbean, but Portugal obtained Brazil and claimed the trading rights in the rich Asian lands of India, China, and the East Indies. Despite the papal-sanctioned accord, the Dutch, French, and English refused to recognize the treaty and all soon began to explore and seek to exploit wealth from areas in Asia, Africa, and the Americas.

The Portuguese Seaborne Empire and Brazil

In the 1500s Portugal concentrated for the most part on its trading empire in Africa and Asia. Led by adventurous sea captains such as Pedro Cabral, the Portuguese gained control of the trade in the Indian Ocean from Arab merchants after a bloody war. The Portuguese built naval bases in the Indian Ocean along the east coast of Africa, expanded eastward to the Spice Islands or Moluccas, and eventually established trading ports in China and Japan.

Portugal also explored and began its colonization of Brazil's coast. Pedro Cabral had claimed Brazil for Portugal in 1500. At first Brazil's trade consisted primarily of wood, but in the late 1500s Brazil's importance grew as Portugal lost control of most of its Asian trading bases. The exploitation of Brazil's vast potential for agriculture began with the planting of sugarcane, tobacco, and, later, coffee. Rich deposits of gold and diamonds were later found in the interior of Brazil and made the highland of Minas Gerais another valuable region to explore.

The Native American inhabitants of Brazil—Tupi and Carib tribal groups— could not be employed as a labor force. The majority of this original population either died because of warfare and disease or fled to the interior. Because of this, African slaves increasingly were imported to Brazil to replenish the labor supply. The Portuguese were few in number, and men predominated in the early colonial population. The even smaller number of Portuguese women led to increased racial mixture in Brazil, resulting in the creation of a new racial type, the mestizo.

Spain Conquers the Americas

The 1500s was Spain's golden century. Spain's predominance was in large measure due to the powerful monarchs who ruled its growing empire. (See Chapter 10, "The Rise of Nation-States.") During this time, Spain explored and conquered huge regions in the Americas. The Spanish explorers and conquerors came to the Americas "to serve God and his majesty" and to enrich themselves.

After Columbus's first voyages, Spanish explorers conquered and settled the islands in the Caribbean Sea. By the first decades of the 1500s, Spanish conquistadors began to explore the mainland. Vasco Nuñez de Balboa crossed the jungles of Central America and sighted the Pacific. Ponce de León, who helped conquer Puerto Rico, discovered Florida. The period of Spanish explorations continued for most of the 1500s and resulted in the conquest of the more advanced civilizations in the Americas by the mid-sixteenth century.

Ferdinand Magellan and the Circumnavigation of the Globe

Ferdinand Magellan, a Portuguese soldier of fortune serving the Spanish crown, led a historic three-year sailing expedition that, beginning in 1519, circumnavigated the globe. Magellan's expedition of five ships and a crew of 265 men crossed the Atlantic and explored the east coast of South America, sailing into bays and inlets in search of a route to the South Sea. Magellan overcame a mutiny along the way and sailed past the tip of South America into the Pacific through the dangerous Cape of Storms (Strait of Magellan). The strong currents and severe gales in the strait resulted in the destruction of one ship and the return of another to Spain.

Magellan's ship and two others continued into the South Sea, which Magellan named the Pacific Ocean because he found it to be so calm. The ships sailed on for four months before finally reaching land in the Marianas. Shortly after, in the Philippines, Magellan was killed in a battle between two rival native groups. After Magellan's death, Juan Sebastian del Cano took charge and completed the voyage. Cano eventually arrived in Spain in September, 1522, after a number of adventures with one ship, the Victoria, and a crew of 18 men.

The Magellan-Cano voyage from 1519 to 1522 resulted in the first circumnavigation, or complete circling, of the world by ship. The voyage proved definitely that the world was round, and it revolutionized ideas about the relative proportions of land and water. It also revealed that the Americas were separated from Asia. Magellan's voyage is considered one of the greatest achievements of navigation. Although he did not live to complete the journey, Magellan provided the skill and determination that took his expedition over the great unknown portion of the globe. He justly deserves recognition as a great explorer.

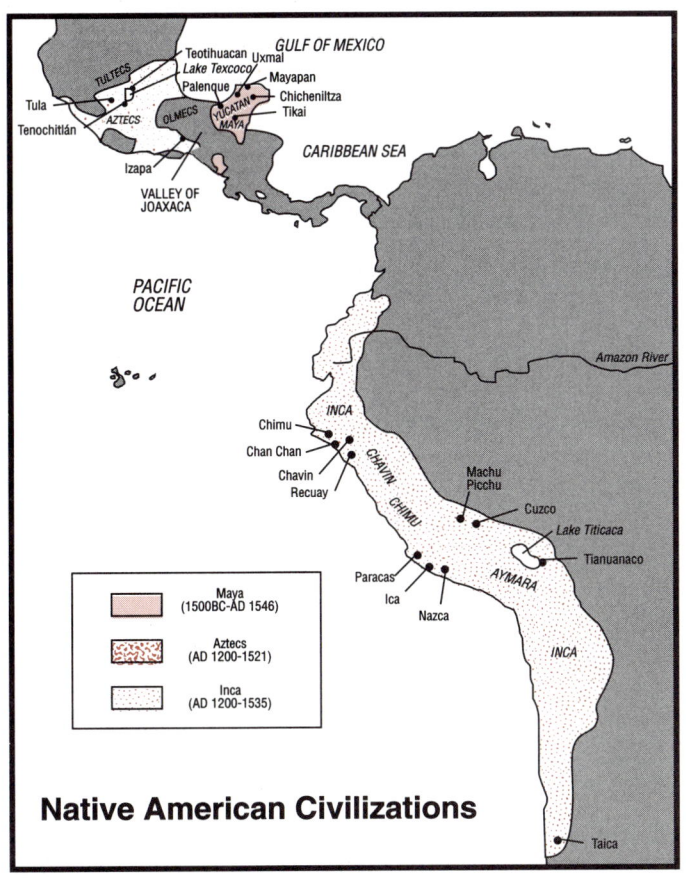

Native American Civilizations

Areas and centers of Native American civilizations prior to the arrival of the Europeans.

Cortés Conquers the Aztecs of Mexico

The exploits of the conquistador, or conqueror, Hernando Cortés excited the imagination of all Europeans who heard the story. *Conquistador* is the Spanish term used to describe the men who took part in the Spanish conquest of Mexico, Peru, and other regions in the sixteenth century. Cortés's expedition to Mexico in 1519 led to the downfall of the Aztec Empire and resulted in an enormous amount of wealth falling into Spanish hands. Cortés, like many Spanish conquistadors, was a minor member of the Spanish nobility, a hidalgo. In Spain, the rule of **primogeniture** (giving all of the land to the firstborn male) had led to the growth of a landless nobility. The hidalgos had the title but little else and thus were interested in heroic adventures that could lead to glory and riches. Cortés's expedition of eleven ships and about five hundred men conquered the Aztec Empire ruled by the all-powerful Montezuma II.

Although Cortés's men were greatly outnumbered, they were able to defeat Montezuma's large armies by means of superior weaponry and tactics that made use of horses, then unknown to the Aztecs. Cortés used a divide-and-conquer strategy and made use of the Aztec's many enemies in his campaign. The Tlaxcalans, who were the Aztec's principal opponents in

Ferdinand Magellan

If you happened to walk along the piers of a certain seaport in Spain on September 19, 1519, you would have not been overly excited by the scene. There were five vessels preparing to sail on a voyage. None of the vessels were large and they were commanded by a man who himself was not an imposing figure.

Ferdinand Magellan was a short man who was from the lower end of Portuguese nobility. His past military adventures had left him with a limp, a broken nose, and a number of scars. Behind this unimpressive exterior, however, dwelt a man who was a thinker and a planner. He was very ambitious and very stubborn. Ferdinand believed that only he had uncovered the truth about a matter, and having discovered it, only he could lead a voyage of discovery.

Ferdinand had spent many hours talking to seafarers, to navigators, and to anyone along the docks from whom he might learn something. He studied the best maps and charts available. He knew about winds and tides and readings. In short, he believed that there was a passage through the newly found continents that would allow him a direct passage west. He was able to convince King Carlos of Spain that the riches of the Spice Islands would be his.

There were some difficulties in crossing the Atlantic but when the flotilla arrived at what is now the Rio de la Plata in Uruguay, those problems were behind them. This *had* to be the passage because it was much larger than anything Magellan and his captains had experienced. Pushing further and further into the estuary, they really believed that this was it. Stubborness kept them looking for a month before Magellan finally had to accept that this was not the passage.

Rather than admitting defeat, Magellan made them push further south along the coast. The weather was turning much colder and they were battered by high seas and sleet. It was winter in the south and the men were in desperate condition. Crew members who had died were buried at sea with regularity and the food supply was getting low.

The situation resulted in an attempted mutiny which needed to be put down—and put down it was. Some of the mutineers were abandoned on a convenient shore and left to the mercy of God. Other mutineers were drawn and quartered and their bodily parts were hung up on poles as a reminder to the rest of the men. The ships continued southwards.

It was on a Sunday in October 1520 when an opening was seen. It seemed to be a strait but, after the disappointment of the previous attempt, Magellan was more cautious. He sent two ships to explore and they reported back five days later that there was, in fact, a passage to the ocean—the one that Balboa had discovered. Some crew members now wanted to turn back, but Magellan refused and he sailed on into the new ocean. He had no idea of how large this ocean was because his maps were inaccurate. He could sail back anyway, as he had no idea of what was there. Finally on March 6, 1521, they reached Guam and reprovisioned.

They sailed on and reached the Philippines. Magellan and his crews now enjoyed a veritable paradise and they rebuilt their ships and bodies. A religious fervor now came over Magellan and he set about converting the Filipinos to Catholicism. A local chieftain that had converted asked Ferdinand for help in conquering an opponent.

Magellan, for the first and certainly the last time, did not make adequate preparations. Trusting too much in God and not enough in man, he took too few troops to oppose a vastly superior force. Magellan was soon surrounded by a vast number of enemies. He was hit by a spear, shot with an arrow, and then hacked with swords. There was not enough left of Magellan to be found when his men tried to bury him.

The voyage was completed by others and they claimed the honors that Magellan really deserved. But history has set that straight. He had proved the earth was round and that Europe was not the center of the earth. A strange thing happened to those that did return—it was the wrong day! This was a puzzlement until it was acknowledged by science and eventually the Vatican that Copernicus and Galileo were right—the earth was a moving object.

the highlands of central Mexico, supplied much of the manpower for the military conquest of such a large empire. The religious beliefs of the Aztecs also helped the Spanish to conquer the leading civilization in Mesoamerica, the land stretching from Mexico to the bottom of Central America. The Aztecs first thought that Cortés and his men were the returning former rulers of this central plateau and valley region of Mexico. The legend of the god Quetzacoatl and the prophecy of his return influenced Montezuma. He allowed Cortés to march up from the coast unopposed toward the Aztec capital of Tenochitlán. The capture of Montezuma resulted in the Aztec ruler giving Cortés huge quantities of gold objects in hope of gaining his freedom. Montezuma was eventually killed, and his golden treasure was melted down into bullion bars. Within three years, warfare and disease destroyed the Aztec trading and tributary empire. Cortés, in the name of the Spanish monarchy, became the new ruler of Mexico. His lieutenants penetrated into other areas of Mesoamerica and repeated the pattern of conquest. The Maya of the Yucatán peninsula and present-day Central America, along with other Native American peoples, could not resist the European conquerors.

Pizarro Conquers the Incas in South America

About ten years after Mexico's conquest, another conquistador, Francisco Pizarro, invaded the Inca Empire and captured its ruler Atahualpa. The land ruled by the Incas was bordered by the Pacific Ocean and Amazon Basin and stretched

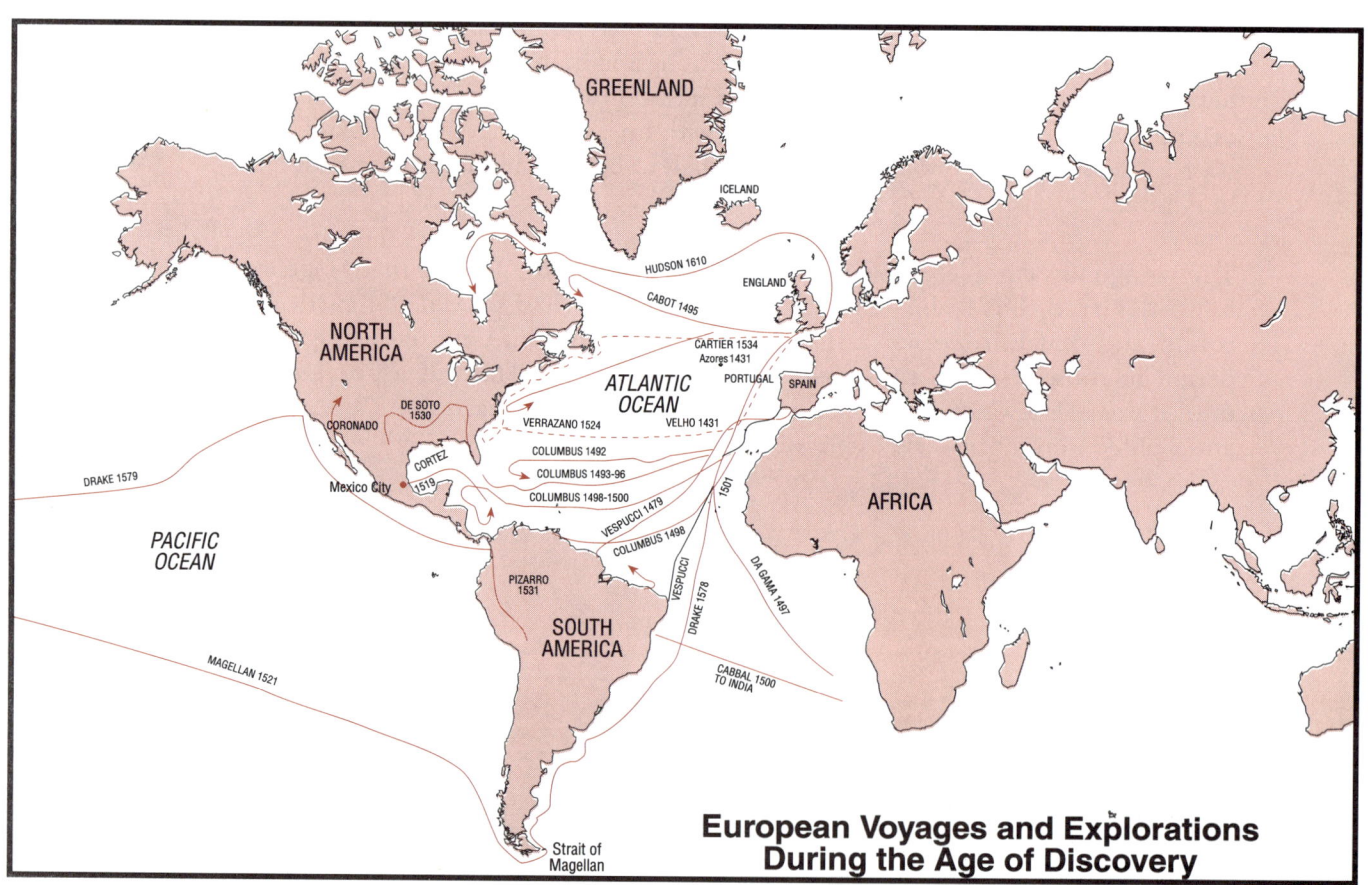

European Voyages and Explorations During the Age of Discovery

from Colombia along the spine of the Andes Mountains into Chile. Pizarro eventually defeated the Inca armies by using the same weaponry and tactics employed by Cortés. The death of Atahualpa soon led to the end of Inca resistance. From their new capital, Lima, in present-day Peru, the Spanish began to rule a vast area of land with many peoples that stretched along the Andes Mountains from Colombia to Chile. As in Mexico, the Native American population was drastically reduced because of the warfare, newly introduced diseases such as smallpox that spread with a deadly rapidity, and mistreatment caused by the abuses in the *encomienda* and *mita* labor systems. The encomienda was tribute granted to some Spanish colonists in the New World. The tribute was often provided in a labor payment by the Native Americans. The mita was essentially a Native American labor obligation for a fixed time period, often in the mines of Peru. Spanish explorers also led expeditions into other regions that resulted in great hardship for the participants and little wealth. Vast areas of northern Mexico and part of the future United States were explored by Hernando de Soto and Francisco Coronado in search of fabled cities of gold.

The Dutch Colonies in Asia, the Americas, and Africa

By the late 1500s, Spain's power in Europe began a long decline. In the Netherlands, the Dutch, who were deeply affected by the Protestant Reformation, gained their independence from Catholic Spain. During these years the Dutch, an industrious people, increasingly depended on commerce with other nations and peoples. By the 1600s, the Dutch Republic established a global trading empire, and Amsterdam became the major commercial city in Europe. During this period, the Dutch had Europe's most powerful navy. By the 1640s, the Dutch had driven the Portuguese out of most of their bases in Asia and gained control of the Spice Islands. The Dutch East India Company, chartered in 1602, monopolized the Netherland's Asian trade. In the Americas the Dutch attacked Spanish and Portuguese settlements and, for a time, controlled Brazil's northern coastal region and its valuable sugar production and trade.

Further north, Henry Hudson, an English navigator working for the Dutch, claimed territory along the Atlantic coast of North America and searched for a northern water route to Asia. Dutch farming and trading settlements were established in New Amsterdam (present-day New York City) and elsewhere in the area. The Dutch West India Company was chartered by the government of the Netherlands to rule the American colonies and regulate the growing trade of farm products and valuable furs. By the middle decades of the 1600s, the Dutch colonies increasingly came under pressure from the British and French, who were busily establishing their own colonial empires.

The French and the Americas

At first the French did not play a major role in the early voyages of exploration and settlement. During the Protestant Reformation and its aftermath, the Catholic Counter Reformation, the French were too involved with religious conflicts and civil wars at home to focus on exploration. However, some French-financed explorations took place, mostly along the North American coast and into the continent's interior waters. French fisheries were set up on the islands of Nova Scotia, Newfoundland, and elsewhere.

In 1524, Giovanni Verrazano tried to find a northwest passage through America to Asia. The northwest passage represented another hope of reaching the East by sailing westward. Jacques Cartier later explored the St. Lawrence River area and claimed eastern Canada for France. By the early 1600s, Samuel de Champlain founded Quebec in Canada. Later in the 1670s, the explorations of the Jesuit missionary Jacques Marquette and the explorer Louis Joliet resulted in French claims in the Mississippi Valley and its valuable fur trade. The French contacts with Native American tribes came mostly through the work of Jesuit missionaries and French fur trappers.

During the 1600s, as political stability at home increased, France expanded into the Caribbean and elsewhere. The French eventually established themselves on the islands of Martinique, Guadaloupe, Haiti, and St. Kitts. The Spaniards were unable to prevent other European nations from taking over these and other islands. The French brought slaves to these islands to work on sugar and tobacco plantations. In Asia, the French gained control of ports along the Indian coastline. In India, the French presence lasted until their defeat by the English in the Seven Years War, fought from 1756 to 1763.

The English Colonize in the Americas

The English showed an early interest in explorations. In 1497, John Cabot, the Italian navigator, was commissioned to find an all-water northern route to Asia. Cabot's voyages took him to Newfoundland, Nova Scotia, and along the New England coastline. However, it wasn't until the later years of Queen Elizabeth I's reign, in the late 1500s, that England sought to establish colonies in North America.

The English first concentrated on raiding Spanish and Portuguese shipping for their gold and silver treasures. Sea captains such as Francis Drake and John Hawkins attacked Spanish ships and ports and engaged in slaving expeditions from West Africa to the European colonies in the Americas to gain from the enormous profits to be earned.

In the 1660s, the English established important colonies in the Spanish Caribbean by taking over Jamaica, the Bahamas, and Barbados. English sugar plantations were soon established, and these were worked by slave labor brought from Africa. The North American continent was initially settled by the English in 1607. The Virginia Company of London financed an expedition that settled in Jamestown, Virginia. Other English colonies were later established in New England by religious dissenters called Pilgrims, who were the first of the Puritan settlers in this colder and less hospitable region. In the 1660s, as a result of a conflict with the Dutch, the English gained control of New Amsterdam, which they renamed New York. By the end of the century, England had colonies along the Atlantic coast of North America from Massachusetts to the Carolinas. England's rise to the position of Europe's most important colonial power came in the mid-eighteenth century after the defeat of their major rival, the French.

Results of the Age of Exploration

Advantages   The Age of Exploration brought far-reaching changes to the peoples of Europe, the Americas, Africa, and Asia. A vast global trading network was created. Colonies and trading posts were established throughout the world and maintained for the benefit of the European colonial powers. Europe, which began the period as one of the poorer and more backward regions of the world, gradually became the center of the world's military and economic power. The wealth of other continents and peoples fueled the economic growth of Western European nations.

Negative Consequences   However, the linking of Africa, Asia, and the Americas to Europe had some serious negative consequences for these regions. Africa was devastated by the slave trade. The enormous loss of population led to political instability that has continued for six centuries. The slave expeditions wreaked havoc on the African tribes, who suffered because of the breaking up of families and exportation of its members. The social and economic consequences for Africa were particularly tragic. Africa's loss of population robbed the continent of the talent and industry of millions of people.

In the Americas, as well, the native populations and cultures drastically declined. The Spanish Empire was controlled through the Council of the Indies in Seville and administered by crown-appointed **viceroys**. The viceroys served as the king's governing agents and they directed the Spanish Empire's interests in terms of military, economic, and social matters. The Spanish officials ignored, for the most part, the injustices inflicted upon the Native American populations. The introduction of African slaves completely changed the population in the West Indies and, to a large measure, on the mainland where the Spanish made use of slave labor. A new people, the Latin Americans, were born out of the resulting racial mixture of Europeans, Africans, and Native Americans.

In Asia, the Europeans had less impact. China and Japan restricted European merchants to a couple of trading ports and severely limited the spread of the Christian religion after the missionaries' early successes. Nevertheless, a European trading presence was established, and the European nations would expand their power and influence in the nineteenth century.

Summary

A number of factors had combined to make the Age of Exploration necessary and possible. Europeans were ready to leave their shores and were curious about what existed across the globe. Each country's desire to control its own trade routes fueled exploration, and technological advances made exploration possible. A period of extraordinarily brave and determined men risked life and limb on their beliefs. To sail off into the unknown calls for a person of great bravery.

Once new lands were uncovered, the nations of Europe competed with each other for colonies to promote both the wealth and grandeur of the mother country. Often, the Native Americans that were already living in these lands were badly treated and suffered at the hands of their new masters. This period was the beginning of what we call today the global economy, and made Europe dominant.

CHAPTER 8

Review Exercises

I. Multiple Choice

Directions: Find the *letter* of the correct answer.

1. The Age of Exploration was spurred on by a European Commercial Revolution because

   (a) countries wishing to increase their trade and wealth supported explorers looking for new trade routes.
   (b) the Italian cities found new trade routes to Asia.
   (c) pirates stopped bothering shipping along trade routes in the Mediterranean.
   (d) the Asian nations were interested in trade with the Americas.

2. The European nation that took the lead in exploring the African coastline for a sea route to Asia in the 1400s was

   (a) Spain.
   (b) Portugal.
   (c) Holland.
   (d) France.

3. European explorers were aided by all of the following technological innovations *except* the

   (a) compass.
   (b) astrolabe.
   (c) lateen sails.
   (d) mechanical oar.

4. The European nation that first became involved in the African slave trade in the 1400s was

   (a) Spain.
   (b) Portugal.
   (c) France.
   (d) Great Britain.

5. The expression that best depicts European interest in exploring other lands is

    (a) divine right of kings.
    (b) God, gold, and glory.
    (c) divide and conquer.
    (d) the victor gets the spoils.

6. Christopher Columbus's voyages of discovery are important because he

    (a) was the first European to reach the Americas.
    (b) found the lost Native American peoples.
    (c) linked the Americas thereafter with other global regions.
    (d) eventually traced an all-water route to Asia.

7. Christopher Columbus should be remembered as a person who

    (a) found the westerly sea route to Asia.
    (b) defended the rights of the native people of the Americas.
    (c) was a product and symbol of the period of global exploration.
    (d) recognized that he found new and unexplored lands.

8. Portugal and Spain sought to settle their early colonial rivalry by means of the

    (a) Treaty of Tordesillas.
    (b) Treaty of Westphalia.
    (c) Seville Demarcation Agreement.
    (d) Madrid Conference Plan.

9. Spain's golden century in the 1500s was assisted by all of the following factors *except*

    (a) strong monarchs who ruled its growing empire.
    (b) conquistadors who were willing to serve God and his majesty.
    (c) the defeat of the last Moorish kingdom of Grenada.
    (d) the expulsion of the Jews and Moors from Spain.

10. All of the following were results of the Age of Exploration *except*

    (a) a vast global trading network was established.
    (b) Europe gradually became the center of the world military and economic power.
    (c) all global regions benefited from the European explorations, which linked the world together.
    (d) other world regions, particularly Africa and the Americas, suffered because of colonization and the slave trade.

II. Vocabulary

Directions: Define the following words, terms, or expressions and use them in a written sentence.

1. God, gold, and glory—
2. New World—
3. Age of Exploration—
4. silk route—
5. compass—
6. caravel—
7. factoria—
8. reconquista—
9. primogeniture—
10. encomienda—

III. Matching

Directions: Match the names in Column A with the achievement they are *best known* for in Column B.

Column A
1. Bartolomeu Dias
2. Vasco da Gama
3. Amerigo Vespucci
4. Vasco de Balboa
5. Ponce de León
6. Ferdinand Magellan
7. Hernando Cortés
8. Henry Hudson
9. Francisco Pizarro
10. Jacques Cartier

Column B
(a) conquered the Aztec Empire
(b) conquered the Inca civilization
(c) reached India in 1498
(d) led expedition that circumnavigated the globe
(e) explored the St. Lawrence River
(f) first European to sight the Pacific
(g) explored area around New York for the Dutch
(h) discovered Florida, conquered Puerto Rico
(i) suggested that discoveries were a new world
(j) rounded the Cape of Good Hope

IV. Map Exercise

Directions: Use the map on the facing page to locate the place associated with each of the statements below. For each statement, write the *letter* of the place.

1. _____ Francisco Pizzaro conquered the Incas here.

2. _____ Hernando Cortés conquered the Aztecs here.

3. _____ Pedro Cabral landed in this nation.

4. _____ Ponce de León discovered this area.

5. _____ Henry Hudson explored this bay.

6. _____ Vasco da Balboa sighted the Pacific from here.

7. _____ John Cabot explored the coastline of this country.

8. _____ Columbus landed on these islands during his voyages.

9. _____ Ferdinand Magellan was the first to round this cape.

10. _____ Bartolomeu Dias was the first to round this cape.

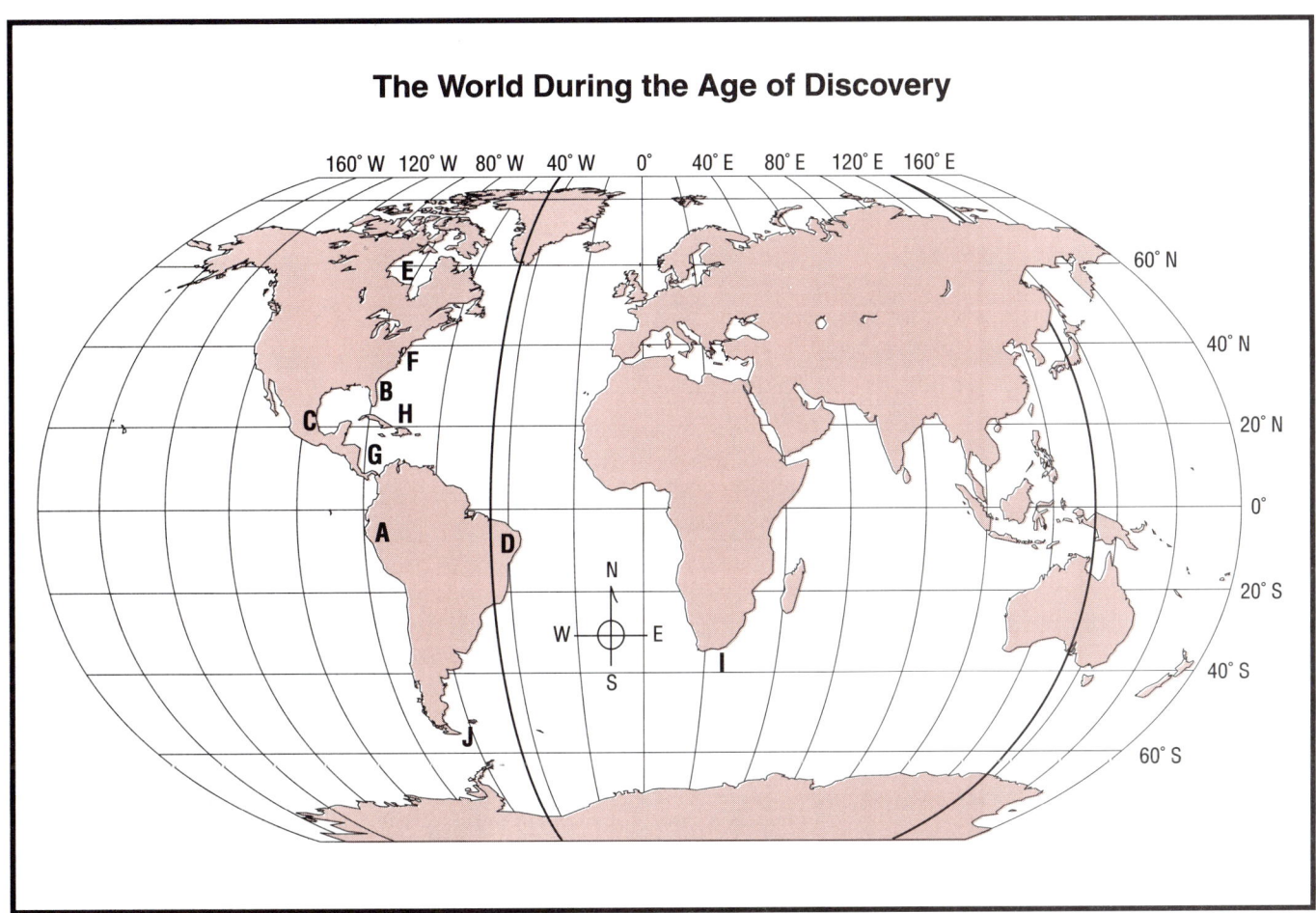

The World During the Age of Discovery

V. Thought Questions

Directions: Answer the following questions in essay form.

1. The fifteenth century saw the expansion of Europe to other parts of the world.

    A. Explain three reasons why Europeans were interested in finding an all-water route to Asia.
    B. Describe three technological improvements that made it possible.
    C. Explain three results of these voyages of exploration.

2. Write a newspaper article about the significance of Christopher Columbus's voyages.

3. Give two reasons why the African slave trade to the Americas began.

4. Prepare both positions—pro and con, or positive and negative—for a debate on consequences of the European discovery and settlement in the Americas.

CHAPTER 9

The Commercial Revolution

Whenever we watch television, we often see commercials. A commercial's purpose is to persuade us to buy something that someone or some company is selling. Buying and selling things, along with producing them, is what commerce and business are all about. Such activities have undergone changes throughout European history. One of those moments of great change has been called the **Commercial Revolution**. This term refers to the changes in trade and business practices that transformed Western European economic life beginning in the seventeenth century and continuing into the eighteenth century. After the Middle Ages, steady economic expansion began to take place. The rise of towns, the beginnings of private banking, the growth of a money economy and trading organizations all signaled the end of the feudal economy in Western Europe. The growth of political and military power by rulers in Spain, Portugal, the Netherlands, France, and England made wider and defensible markets possible.

Commercial expansion was aided by technological improvements in seafaring. By the sixteenth century, European explorations resulted in increased trade with other world regions. The Portuguese voyages down the Atlantic coastline of Africa in the 1400s brought trading opportunities that enriched that nation's monarchy and merchant class. By 1498, the Portuguese navigator Vasco da Gama became the first European to journey by sea to India, thereby opening up sea trade to Asia. An increasing number of European merchants and banking families took part in these economic developments.

By the mid-sixteenth century, Portugal had seized control of the profitable European-Asian trade from the Arabs and Venetians, and goods from the East became more readily available in Western Europe. From Spanish America came huge quantities of gold and silver. This new wealth caused the doubling of prices in Europe but greatly increased economic activity. Portugal and Spain started a transition that led to greater economic development in European nations on the Atlantic Ocean. The defeat of the Spanish Armada in 1588 by the British led to more European nations becoming involved in the trans-Atlantic trade.

The focus of commerce shifted from the Mediterranean to the Atlantic ports as more companies were granted charters to conduct business and trade. A **charter**, issued by a government, was a written agreement by investors who shared ownership in a business or conducted trade. Western European nations formulated economic policies to safeguard their commerce and new colonial possessions. Internal commerce, however, was stimulated by the ending of local trade barriers. By the 1600s, credit facilities, state banks, the stock market, and other economic innovations had become commonplace in the economic life of those nations that became immersed in the growing Commercial Revolution.

Economic Revival in Europe

By the 1400s, the population of Europe had begun once again to rise steadily, and economic recovery started to take place. The decline of population caused by the black death, the bubonic plague, was over. The growth of towns increased as more people moved there from farming areas. They sought work in commercial occupations such as textile production. The monarchs in Western Europe, seeking to expand their power and wealth, supported this process. Political stability made it possible for merchants to travel and trade more freely. The merchant class became more influential as the power of the landowning aristocracy declined. In Italy during the 1400s, the Medici family of Florence became the model for the growing class of wealthy merchants whose financial status led to their increased political power and influence in determining economic policies.

Chapter 9 Chronology

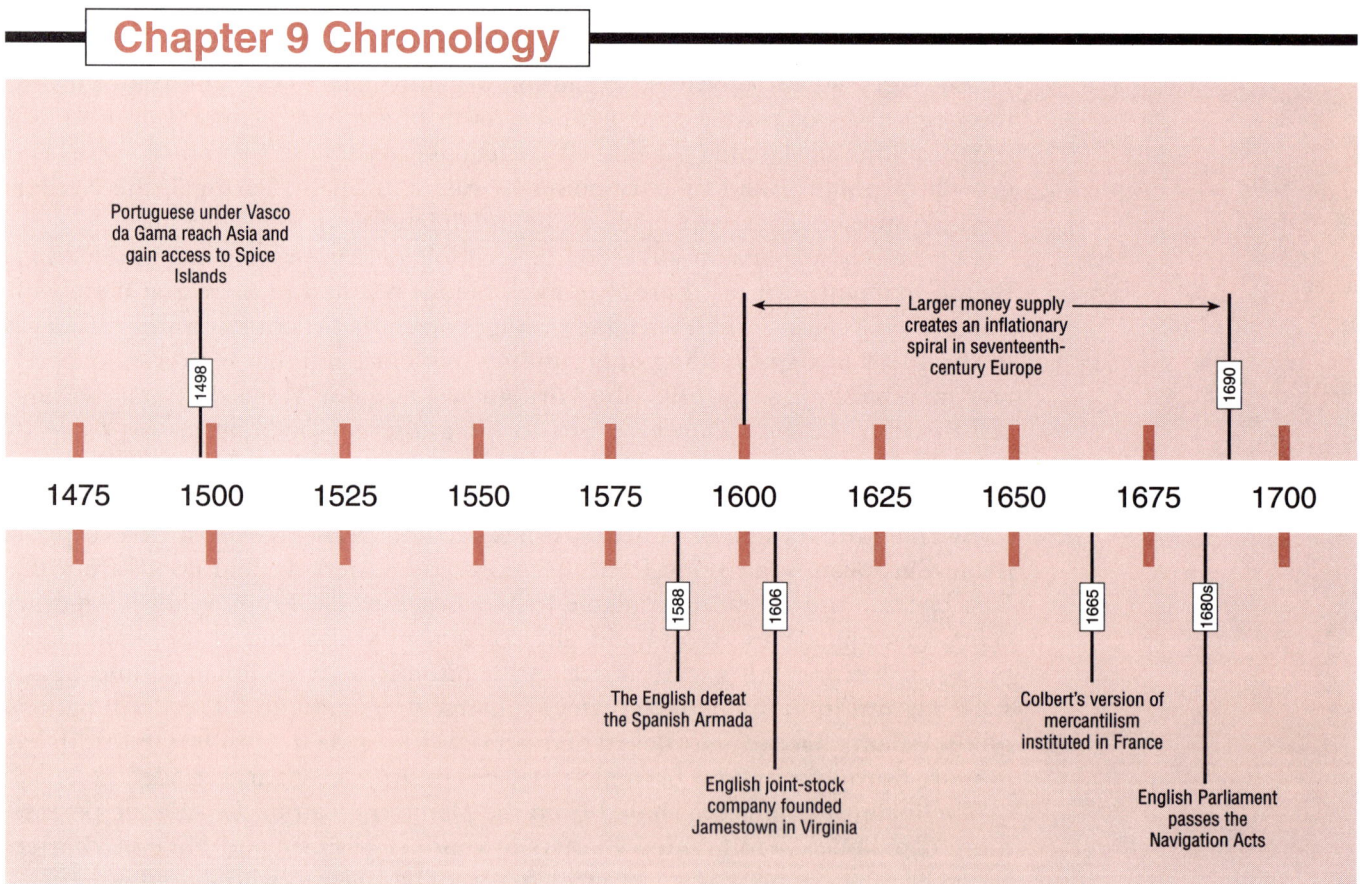

Portuguese under Vasco da Gama reach Asia and gain access to Spice Islands — 1498

Larger money supply creates an inflationary spiral in seventeenth-century Europe — 1690

| 1475 | 1500 | 1525 | 1550 | 1575 | 1600 | 1625 | 1650 | 1675 | 1700 |

1588 — The English defeat the Spanish Armada

1606 — English joint-stock company founded Jamestown in Virginia

1665 — Colbert's version of mercantilism instituted in France

1680s — English Parliament passes the Navigation Acts

Business Methods Change

In Western Europe, the necessary preconditions now existed to achieve the transition from primarily agrarian to more capitalistic types of economies. **Capitalism** is the economic system in which the means of production are privately owned and operated for profit. The rise of a new class of wealthy merchants and bankers powerful enough to initiate commercial exchanges and finance overseas trading expeditions assisted in this transition. Merchants who invested in the financing of a trading vessel's voyage needed to guarantee that there were sufficient funds to hire the captain and crew and to pay for the trading goods and supplies. Trading voyages often lasted years and involved buying and selling at many ports of call long distances from home. Only upon a ship's return could the merchants and the bankers who backed them regain their investment and make a profit. It was not practical for wealthy merchants or even monarchs to provide all of the investment for these trading expeditions alone. Bankers increasingly provided the loans and credit for merchants to conduct their business and trading enterprises.

Starting in the fifteenth century, wealthy families, such as the Medici of Florence and Fuggers of Augsburg, began to finance the merchants who turned to them for **capital**, money used in business. These powerful European banking families grew very wealthy and were able to perform such banking services as accepting deposits, making loans, and transferring funds to other cities. Moreover, the banking families were able to loan European monarchs large sums of money, thereby increasing their political and economic influence.

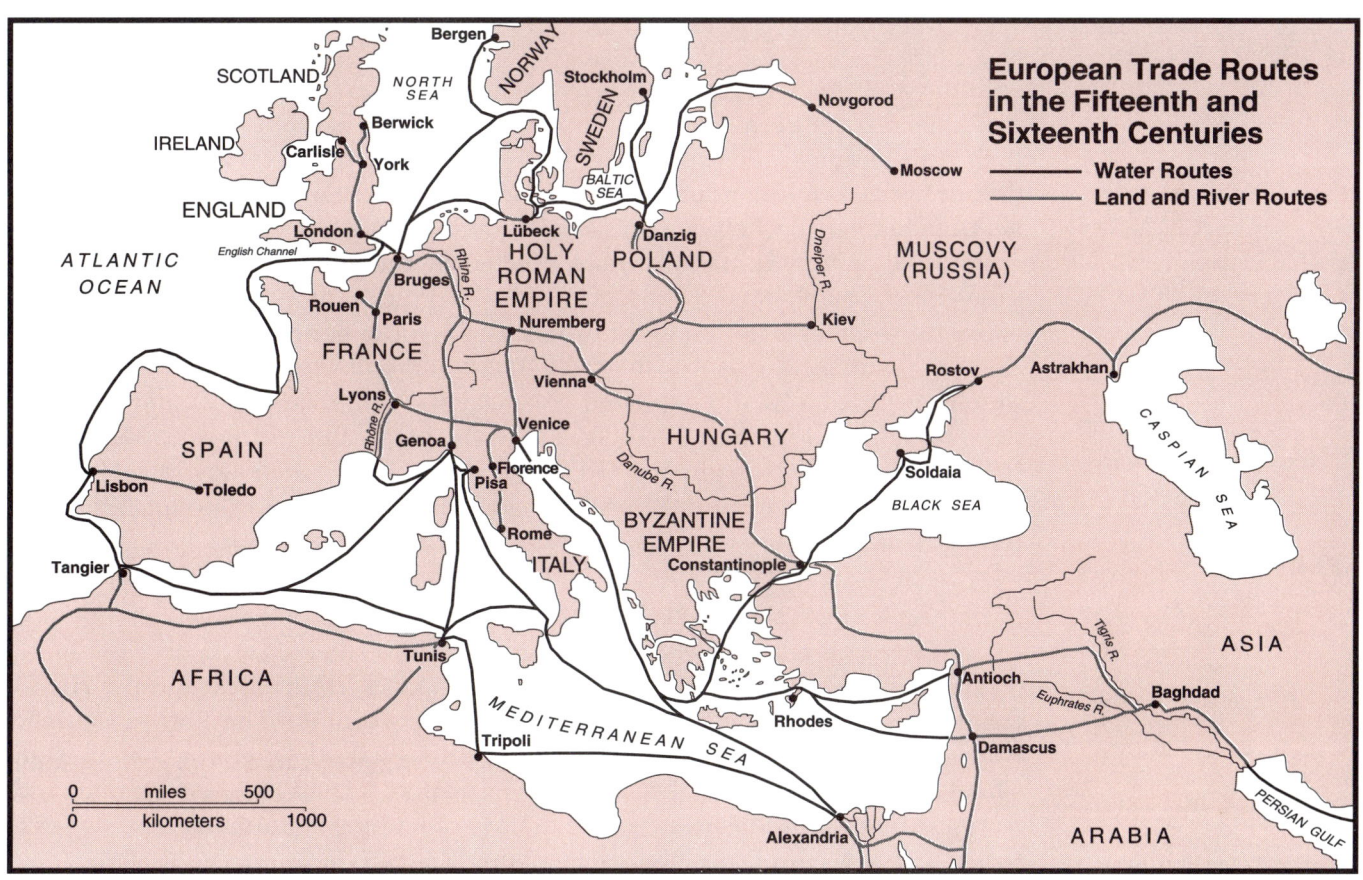

European Trade Routes in the Fifteenth and Sixteenth Centuries

—— Water Routes
—— Land and River Routes

By the 1600s, government-chartered banks began to replace private banking families. New banking services were designed to make trading transactions easier. Bank notes and checks replaced large payments in gold and silver coinage. The government-chartered banks also performed the service of exchanging foreign currencies, often at the official rate of exchange.

The Joint Stock Company

Another important change was the rise of the **joint stock company**. These companies made it possible for individual merchants to invest in organizations that sold shares of **stock** to investors in a trading expedition. In this way, the risks of a venture were shared by a number of investors. The joint stock company, with its shared investment, allowed merchants to put funds into more than one trading opportunity and limit their losses in the event that any one venture failed. Increased capital became available because the joint stock company was a more stable way of financing trading ventures.

Some nations even provided certain joint stock companies with government support. The Dutch East India Company and British East India Company founded in 1600 by Queen Elizabeth I became rich and powerful and acted in the names of their governments in the **colonies** where they operated. These companies could make war, establish forts, seize foreign ships, and monopolize trade. The governments profited from customs revenues collected as result of the companies' trade. In 1606, the Virginia Company of London, a joint stock company, financed an expedition that led to the founding of Jamestown.

The Money Supply Increase

Trade and other commercial activities increased to such an extent that there was a need for a greater money supply. Individuals needed money to conduct their daily business, and the shops that sold goods depended on a large and steady flow of funds. Coins continued to be a medium of exchange for the average business and individual who bought and sold goods.

Fortunately for the nations most affected by the general commercial expansion—most notably Spain, Portugal, Holland, France, and England—large gold and silver shipments flowed into Europe. The Spanish benefited enormously from the Aztec and Inca treasures they plundered and from the mining deposits that were later discovered and exploited. Portugal also found large gold and diamond deposits in Brazil in the late 1600s. Much of this wealth did not remain in the Iberian peninsula, though. Instead, these riches found their way into Holland, England, and France, where they spurred the development of commercial and industrial activities and served as a means of exchange along with copper coinage.

The Rise of the Entrepreneur

The changes in banking, the growth of joint stock companies, and the rise in the money supply created many new business opportunities. The Roman Catholic Church had, through the Middle Ages, prohibited lending money for interest. The declining influence of the Church over matters related to lending money and charging interest was instrumental in the rise of lending institutions. This was particularly true in the Protestant areas where this type of commercial activity was encouraged. Usury, the lending of money for profit by charging interest, became more acceptable and widespread in Holland, England, and elsewhere. The methods of business changed, and it became more acceptable for enterprising individuals to pursue profits. **Entrepreneurs**, individuals who organized, managed, and assumed responsibility for businesses, were able to pursue new ideas and make use of money, raw materials, and labor to produce goods in order to earn a profit.

The textile industries offered some of the best opportunities for entrepreneurs. They were able to combine all the necessary ingredients and take advantage of market conditions. For example, a businessman in England or Holland could buy wool or cotton, hire weavers and dyers to make cloth, and sell the goods on the open market at a profit.

The Beginning of Capitalism

The Commercial Revolution led slowly to the growth of capitalism as the principal economic system in Western Europe. As the capitalist system developed, entrepreneurs, merchants, bankers, and joint stock companies were free to use capital, or money, to generate profits. Property increasingly was privately owned, and the remains of feudalism, such as the fief, faded away. Capitalism also came to be known as the **free enterprise system**. In this system, individual initiative, investment, and risk generated ideas and energy, which resulted in economic activity. Investors with money were free to risk their capital. The banking system developed, in part, to meet the needs of entrepreneurs engaged in capitalistic ventures in commerce and industry.

Another significant change was the decline of the medieval guilds. Guilds were associations of merchants or artisans that governed a town or craft in the Middle Ages. The guilds were gradually replaced by the **domestic system**, which allowed the entrepreneur to exercise greater control over the laborers who produced the goods. Individuals with money to invest in business could, for example, buy raw wool and hire peasants in the countryside to dye and spin it into cloth. The regulations that governed the manner in which the guilds produced and sold goods were no longer adequate for a growing urban population. In an economy controlled in large measure by entrepreneurs who had enough money to invest in a business to make a profit, labor increasingly was paid according to market conditions.

Certain new industries demanded sizable capital investment. In 1445, the German Johannes Gutenberg developed a printing press that used a metal alloy to make movable type. Gutenberg's hand-set type led to the rise of the printing industry. The rapid expansion of the printing industry in the sixteenth and seventeenth centuries required an investment in expensive equipment and supplies. With the backing of banks and joint stock companies, entrepreneurs often provided the necessary investment capital in this industry, similar to the way in which investment capital financed major mining and shipbuilding projects.

Mercantilism Develops in Europe

As trading empires developed, **mercantilism** became the popular economic policy in Western Europe. Mercantilism was based on the belief that national wealth and power were best served by increasing exports and collecting precious metals in exchange for them. **Bullion** (gold or silver) was best acquired by foreign trade and manufacturing or processing. Raw materials were very sought after. Duties, or taxes, on imported goods provided revenue for the government. Colonies were considered beneficial and existed to enrich the mother country, the nation that owned and controlled the settlement in a distant land. Another major aim was to make the mother country independent of other nations.

Increasingly, the monarchs of the Western European countries recognized that their nation's political power depended on controlling its economic wealth. European rulers believed that the most important measure of their nation's wealth was the total amount of bullion—gold or silver—that it owned. The major trading nations, from the sixteenth through eighteenth centuries, sought to increase this national wealth, and thereby their power, by promoting exports and collecting precious metals.

Jean Baptiste Colbert, a French statesman, was one of the leading supporters of mercantilism. Colbert, who became Louis XIV's minister of finance in 1665, sought to make France economically self-sufficient. He was one of the most successful practitioners of mercantilism. Colbert encouraged the growth of industry through subsidies and tariffs, regulated the prices and quality of manufactured goods and agricultural products, sought to break down trade barriers within France, started a serious road-building program, and restricted the use of natural resources. In 1669, as secretary of state for naval affairs, he initiated policies to construct shipyards, arsenals, harbors, and a large navy, one of the first major steps in the development of commerce and colonization.

The period 1500 to 1800 was a time of costly religious wars as well as bitter commercial rivalries. During these years, increasingly large revenues were needed by the developing nations of Western Europe to pay for these wars and the related growing expenses of civil government. The expanding bureaucracies, and government officials, which enabled the monarchs to govern their nations more effectively, added to the need for greater revenues.

Spain and Portugal were the nations that brought most of the bullion to Europe from their mines in the Americas. However, most of this wealth did not remain in the Iberian peninsula because these nations imported more goods than they exported. Spain's economic power also declined because of the ultimate effects of the expulsion of its Jewish and Muslim populations, who were engaged in commerce, trade, and agriculture. Another factor was its fierce Catholicism, which continued from the time of the Catholic monarchs, Ferdinand and Isabella, to Philip II. This took the form of Spain assuming the military role of defender of the Roman Catholic religion and the pope during war with the Ottoman Empire. During the period of the Protestant Reformation and later Catholic Reformation, Spain also sought to defend the interests of Catholicism and suppress a rebellion

Colonial Empires of the New World

VICEROYALTY OF NEW SPAIN

ATLANTIC OCEAN

PACIFIC OCEAN

VICEROYALTY OF NEW GRANADA

GUIANA

VICEROYALTY OF BRAZIL

VICEROYALTY OF PERU

VICEROYALTY OF LA PLATA

Colonial Empires of the New World 1776

Spanish
French
Portuguese
Dutch

0   500   1000

European colonial empires in the Americas during the eighteenth century.

in the future Dutch Republic. The wealth of the Americas ultimately went to France, the Netherlands, and, above all, England, and it provided the capital for these nations' early commercial and industrial development.

Mercantilist theory also supported the idea that it was more profitable to make and sell a finished manufactured product than to market a raw material. For example, English cloth that was exported as woolen blankets was more profitable than English wool as a raw material or even the unfinished cloth. Therefore, it was necessary for mercantilist nations to regulate their trade and control the economies of their colonies. A favorable balance of trade, in which exports were worth more than imports, was a major goal of the mercantilist nations.

The Importance of Colonies

Colonies played an increasingly important role in the mercantilist economies. Their inhabitants not only could supply raw materials for the developing industries, but also were markets for the manufactured goods produced in the mother country. In Western Europe, the competing commercial powers all had mercantilist regulations that were designed to control their trade and thereby maximize their profits at the expense of their economic rivals.

Spain Spain tried to prevent other European nations from trading with its American colonies through a complicated set of trading laws and a system of fleets. This restrictive commercial policy only worked while Spain was capable of enforcing its regulations. Smuggling and piracy were constant problems. By the end of the reign of Philip II and with the defeat of the Spanish Armada in 1588, Spain was no longer Western Europe's leading military and naval power. Spain's decline thereafter was, in large measure, related to its inability to effectively enforce its mercantilist policies.

France In the seventeenth century, France's monarch, Louis XIV, chose Jean Colbert as his finance minister. (See Chapter 10, "The Rise of Nation-States," and page 225.) Colbert was one of the most successful practitioners of mercantilism. While his policies did lead to significant economic growth, his efforts to regulate the French economy were ultimately undone by Louis XIV's extravagances and the expensive wars that the king pursued during his long reign. Heavier taxation, increased borrowing, and the sale of government offices were the result of a constant need for more revenue. Colbert's popularity declined, and he was eventually dismissed from office by Louis XIV.

England England's commercial expansion began during the rule of Elizabeth I in the late 1500s, but grew slowly in the 1600s during the turbulent reigns of the Stuart kings and the Cromwell period. The joint stock company was the principal method that the capital-deficient English used to finance their overseas trading enterprises and early textile industry development. The English colonial ventures to the Atlantic coastline of North America were initially financed by joint stock company investments. English mercantilist policy had a great influence on the economies of the thirteen American colonies. The Navigation Acts passed by the English Parliament during the 1680s were designed to benefit the mother country. The American colonies were prohibited from manufacturing certain finished goods such as iron products. They were restricted in their trade, even with areas under English rule, and were required to use British vessels for the shipment of their goods. Although colonial merchants ignored many of the restrictive regulations, they had to be careful not to arouse the suspicions of the British customs officials. This was particularly true concerning the profitable **triangular trade**. From the Atlantic coast of North America, rum was shipped to Africa for gold and slaves, which in turn were transported to the Caribbean for molasses, which then was taken back to the thirteen colonies to be manufactured into rum. British mercantilist trade regulations, enforced by the powerful royal navy, were a constant problem. Ultimately the colonial resistance to British trading regulations became a major factor in encouraging the independence movement in the thirteen colonies.

The Effects of the Commercial Revolution

The Commercial Revolution in European history led to fundamental changes, which greatly affected economic, political, and social matters in certain nations. By the later Middle Ages, economic expansion became steady and major political changes began to take place with the rise of towns and the development of new national monarchies. The overall effects of the stimulated economic activity led to significant social changes in the European societies and other world areas that experienced these changes. By 1700, these developments or preconditions prepared the stage for the Industrial Revolution.

Economic Effects

The revolution in commerce led to the growth of the economies of a number of Western European nations. The principles of mercantilism were adopted. Increased trade and the control of overseas empires stimulated economic development, first in Portugal and Spain, and then in the Netherlands, France, and England. These nations became competing economic powers as the commercial expansion continued in the following centuries. The advent of private banking, a money economy, and chartered trading organizations increased economic growth. Trade increased as markets grew wider and became more secure. Commercial expansion was supported by technological improvements in seafaring.

Within Europe, quickened commercial activity led to increased economic specialization. This led to the transformation of how goods were produced. A new method of making goods, the domestic system, developed, leading to increased production. The domestic system brought workers together in a cooperative type of manufacturing arrangement. These economic developments contributed to the rise of modern capitalism.

Political Effects

The rivalry that developed concerning commercial matters had major consequences for developments within Europe and throughout the globe where the European nations established colonies. European influence in world affairs continued to increase in the following centuries.

European nations became involved in wars to protect their colonial empires and take colonies and trade away from their rivals. The European nations capable of overseas expansion fought over trade routes, the control of the lucrative slave trade, and colonies in global areas that were vulnerable to European intrusion. These wars were fought in Europe as well as in Asia, the Americas, and Africa. Ultimately, the two remaining rivals, England and France, fought the first world war, the Seven Years War, in the mid-1700s for control of most of the existing global trading network.

Social Effects

The growth in commercial activity led to significant social changes. The development of new economic activities allowed the upper classes, nobles, and rich merchants to acquire great wealth, which they often spent on a lavish life-style. Large palaces and homes were built. New foods were introduced for consumption at European tables. Expensive and exotic clothing such as silks and American furs became more readily available. The upper classes of these nations became patrons of the arts and decorated their homes to display their wealth.

The vast majority of people did not benefit very much from the increased economic activities and expansion. Although the conditions of life that feudalism brought to Europe in the Middle Ages disappeared in the nations where the Commercial Revolution took place, the living conditions of the towns were often harsh. Workers earned low wages, housing was often of poor quality, and health care was inadequate. There was no significant increase in the life span of the majority of urban residents.

Major movements of population occurred because of the European colonization of the Americas. The exportation of millions of African slaves to the Americas to work in agricultural, mining, and other enterprises increased as the centuries progressed. The forced movement of people to locations where the European nations had colonies and needed labor led to the development of new peoples of mixed ancestry. In the process, the Native American population of the Americas drastically declined.

Summary

During this era of economic development, we see where the statement "necessity is the mother of invention" might apply. Now that European nations had spread their flags across distant lands, new business practices were necessary to take full economic advantage of the situation. Two challenges were present: (1) raising and protecting money, and (2) making the mother country independent of other nations. To accomplish the first, new business techniques such as joint stock companies and bank notes and checks were established. To accomplish the second, mercantilism became the dominant economic practice. Colonies were established in the Americas by England, Spain, France, and Holland to enhance the power of the mother country. While Europe became richer as a result of this, it had a negative effect on the inhabitants and resulted in a growing slave trade.

CHAPTER 9

Review Exercises

I. Multiple Choice

Directions: Find the *letter* of the correct answer.

1. European nations adopted mercantilist policies to

    (a) safeguard their commerce and new colonial possessions.
    (b) break down existing trade barriers.
    (c) provide their colonies with financial support to develop industry.
    (d) stimulate the guilds that produced most European goods.

2. By the 1400s, the monarchs of Europe

    (a) sought to limit the growth of towns in their realms.
    (b) began to support urbanization to increase their power.
    (c) created state credit facilities and national banks.
    (d) tried to prevent the disintegration of the feudal system.

3. One reason for the change in business methods was the

    (a) transition from an industrial to an agricultural economy.
    (b) need to finance overseas trading expeditions.
    (c) demand by the landed aristocracy for financial support.
    (d) general decline in trade and industry after 1450.

4. All of the following were associated with the Commercial Revolution *except*

    (a) joint stock companies.
    (b) an increased money supply.
    (c) the rise of the entrepreneur.
    (d) the growth of the manorial system.

5. An inflationary spiral took place starting in the late 1500s because

    (a) entrepreneurs took money out of circulation.
    (b) European nations stopped using coins for exchange.
    (c) the wealth of the American colonies flowed into Europe.
    (d) banking families such as the Medici demanded more stock.

6. Starting in the fifteenth century, European merchants and bankers

   (a) turned to their nations' rulers for trading capital.
   (b) looked to other global centers for capital.
   (c) were successful in curbing mercantilist trading policies.
   (d) increased their political and economic influence.

7. By the mid-1500s, which two European nations had the largest global trading empires?

   (a) England and France
   (b) Spain and Portugal
   (c) Spain and England
   (d) Portugal and Holland

8. Much of the wealth in precious metals transported to Europe from the Americas ultimately

   (a) was invested in landed estates in Spain and Portugal.
   (b) financed industrial developments in England and Holland.
   (c) allowed European monarchs to finance joint stock companies.
   (d) supported costly public works projects in Western Europe.

9. The triangular trade involved which three global regions?

   (a) Asia, Europe, and Africa
   (b) Africa, the Americas, and Asia
   (c) Europe, Africa, and the Americas
   (d) the Americas, Asia, and Europe

10. In the mid-1700s, most English foreign trade was with

   (a) the East Indies.
   (b) Africa.
   (c) North America.
   (d) the West Indies.

II. Vocabulary

Directions: Define the following words, terms, or expressions and use them in a written sentence.

1. Dutch East India Company—
2. Fuggers—
3. Medici—
4. Johannes Gutenberg—
5. Jean Colbert—
6. British East India Company—
7. guild—
8. Navigation Acts—
9. domestic system—
10. colony—

III. Matching

Directions: Match the words in Column A with the *correct description* in Column B

Column A	*Column B*
1. mercantilism	(a) individuals who organized business ventures
2. joint stock company	(b) hurt Africa because of the loss of population
3. capital	(c) group of individuals who invest together
4. entrepreneurs	(d) a method of local home production of goods
5. domestic system	(e) money used for finance
6. triangular trade	(f) economic policies to safeguard commerce, protect new colonial possessions, and pro mote industry
7. capitalism	(g) economic system in which the means of pro- duction are privately owned and operated for profit
8. Commercial Revolution	(h) a written agreement by an investor that grants permission to organize and conduct trade
9. charter	(i) changes in trade and business practices that transformed Europe
10. bullion	(j) gold and silver

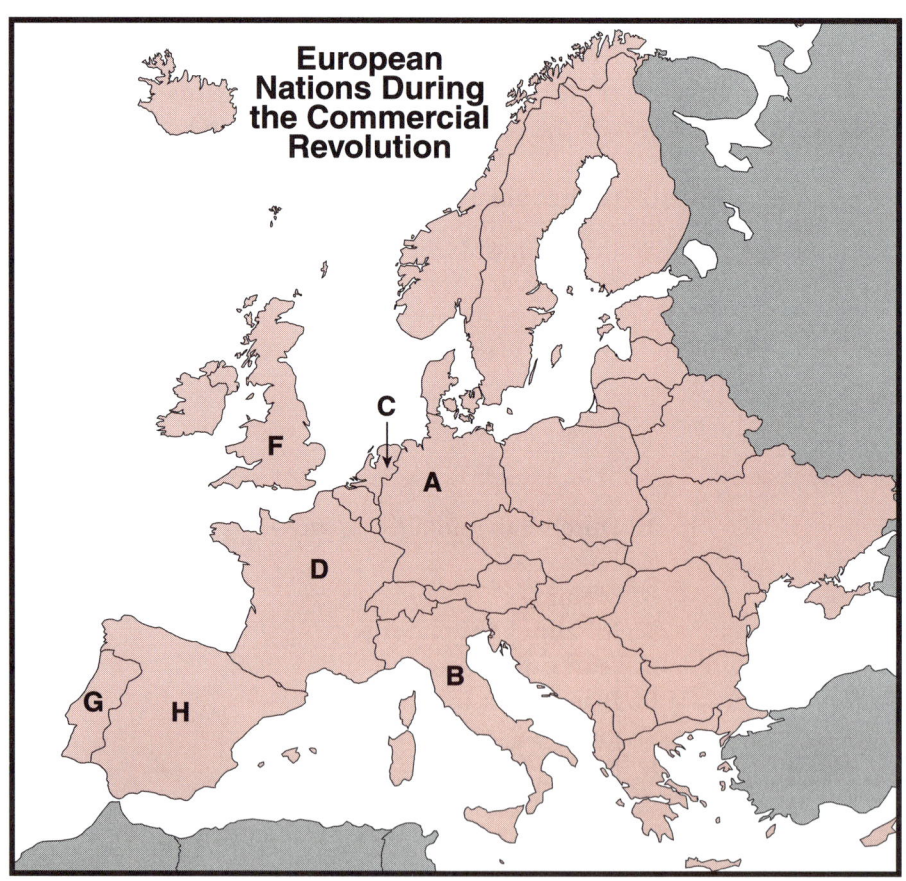

IV. Map Exercise

Directions: Use the map on the previous page to find the place associated with each of the statements below. For each statement, write the *letter* of the place. (An answer may be repeated.)

1. _____ The home country of the Medici family.

2. _____ The home country of the Dutch East India Company.

3. _____ The home country of the British East India Company.

4. _____ Johannes Gutenberg developed the printing press here.

5. _____ Jean Colbert worked for the French government here.

6. _____ Philip II was the King of this nation.

7. _____ The nation that explored the coast of Africa in the 1400s.

8. _____ The Venetian merchants came from this country.

9. _____ The nation that passed the Navigation Acts in the 1680s.

10. _____ The nation that shares the Iberian peninsula with Spain.

V. Thought Questions

Directions: Answer the following questions in essay form.

1. Explain three reasons why the European nations supported mercantilist policies during the Commercial Revolution.

2. Describe three business methods that developed as the Commercial Revolution progressed.

3. You are an entrepreneur during this period and are bragging to your friends about how important you are. Prepare a position paper that you could use to do this.

4. Give two reasons why the free enterprise system, or capitalism, helped cause the decline of the guilds.

5. In an essay explain how the Commercial Revolution increased Europe's economic and military power.

UNIT IV

EVOLUTION AND REVOLUTION

Europe entered into a period of transition in the 1600s and 1700s. Some of the great changes that took place were evolutionary, which means they happened over a period of time in a process of development. Other changes were revolutionary in nature—that is they involved violent and rapid changes in the political and social order.

In Europe during the 1600s and 1700s, evolutionary political processes and changes in thinking gradually led to the development of the concept of nationhood and altered the way that people saw the world. The rise of nation-states was evolutionary in the sense that it took place over long periods of time as monarchs consolidated their power and the idea of the nation became a reality. This evolution of thinking was also part of the Enlightenment and the Scientific Revolution. Although some of these changes in political, economic, and social ideas have been called revolutionary, they were really evolutionary. This was so, because from their introduction to their acceptance, a long period of time passed. This is true of the growth of democracy in England, which had a long evolution as well as an instance of revolution.

Revolution was also a vital part of this time period. The French Revolution and the Napoleonic Era were revolutionary periods in Europe and the Americas. In a sense, the American Revolution that led to the creation of a republic was a forerunner of the revolutionary events that took place in France and Europe after 1789. The changes that occurred in France were truly revolutionary because they resulted in the end of the monarchy, upheaval in the social order, and creation of a republic and later an empire.

In this unit, you will learn about all of these evolutionary and revolutionary events and processes, which helped shape and change Europe during this time period.

In the unit we will also see how many of the nations on the map of Europe came to be. When you look at the map of Europe today you are familiar with many of the names of the countries, their sizes, and their geographic boundaries. You also know something about their forms of government. As you already know it was not always that way. There was constant change taking place, as you saw in the last unit. We continue with this story of change in the unit you are about to study.

The first item of business is to decide what a nation-state is. Then we will turn to some familiar names of places and people. You may have heard of King Henry VIII and his wives, and the fact that he had two of them beheaded. You may have seen a movie about the Four Musketeers of France who were handy with their swords. You probably know that Ferdinand and Isabella of Spain gave Christopher Columbus money, with the result that he would travel and claim to discover America. This was the period of piracy and the Spanish Armada. Some items are not as familiar, such as changes in Austria and Prussia. But, all in all, an exciting time.

We should never forget our debt to England, for we inherited many of our rights from them. Much of our Constitution came from the British, who developed the ideas represented in the document through trial and error. This was not always done peacefully. Along the way we will meet King John—remember Robin Hood?

After this we will go to France and experience its revolution. We will find out why the people were so unhappy that they would begin something that would eventually cause the king and queen and thousands of people to lose their lives. And what a way to suffer these losses—getting beheaded on the guillotine!

Ultimately, a short general from Corsica took over the French government and attempted to take over all of Europe. He fought wars with most of the nations and defeated them all at one time or another. He eventually controlled much of Europe. His big mistake was that he invaded Russia and was stuck in Moscow when the winter came. This led to his eventual defeat in battle and he ended up on a small island in the South Atlantic. The victorious nations then met in Vienna to decide how to make sure revolutions and Napoleons would not happen again.

CHAPTER 10

The Rise of Nation-States

Today, in the 1990s, we say that Europe is a continent of many countries. The word country describes a fixed geographical area and its population, controlled by a government. An example would be modern France or Spain. Countries such as these can also be referred to as nation-states. Their development took place over the course of many centuries, usually under strong rulers, as they grew from small areas to much larger ones. For some of them, the greatest period of development occurred between the late 1400s and the early 1700s.

This was a period of much change in Europe. The changes we have already studied have been cultural (the Renaissance), religious (the Reformation), and economic (the Commercial Revolution and Age of Exploration). It is the major political changes during this period that will be of concern to us in this chapter.

As we will see, those changes that led to the political development of nation-states were most evident in England, France, and Spain. The term nation-state now needs to be defined. It refers to a specific area of land with fixed boundaries, inhabited by people united under an independent central government. The people of a nation-state usually share many common factors, such as language, religion, race, and culture. When all these factors are actually present, we may say that the people have a common **nationality**. This was the situation in England, France, and Spain, and was therefore a key reason for the shaping of unified nation-states under powerful monarchs. In Austria, Prussia, and Russia, however, the population consisted of different nationalities—people who spoke different languages and were of different cultures. As a result, the nation-states that monarchs built in these areas were not characterized by strong feelings of national unity.

We will now examine events in England, France, Spain, Austria, and Prussia. (For Russia, see Chapter 24, "Czarist Russia.")

England

One of the earliest significant instances of royal power and nation-building in England was seen in the reign of William the Conqueror (r. 1066–1087). As Duke of Normandy in France, he laid claim to the English throne. Although opposed by the British King Harold and other Anglo-Saxon nobles, William and his army landed in England and won the decisive Battle of Hastings in 1066. Soon thereafter, he was crowned King William I. The people he ruled over had many customs in common, although they originally belonged to different groups that had invaded the British Isles: Celts, Romans, Germanic Angles, Saxons, Jutes, and Danes. William's actions in 1086, compiling the Domesday Book and making feudal lords and knights take the Salisbury Oath, showed his ability as an effective and commanding ruler. (See Chapter 5, "Medieval Europe.")

William's successors grew increasingly powerful, uniting more of England under their control. As Norman kings of England, these successors had claims to the throne of France and also owned some land in France. French opposition to this situation led to the Hundred Years' War (1337–1453). (See Chapter 5, "Medieval Europe.") Although in this war the English lost all their French territory except for the city of Calais, they increased their feelings of loyalty to their kings. Their sense of patriotism and attention to their own national interests grew stronger. The king could now devote more time to issues within his own nation.

However, conflict over title to the English throne broke out between two families of nobles. This conflict became a series of civil wars known as the Wars of the Roses (1455–1485). This name refers to the crests of the two families—a white rose for the House of York, a red rose for the House of Lancaster. The wars concluded with the victory of Henry Tudor, a member of the House of Lancaster. A

Chapter 10 Chronology

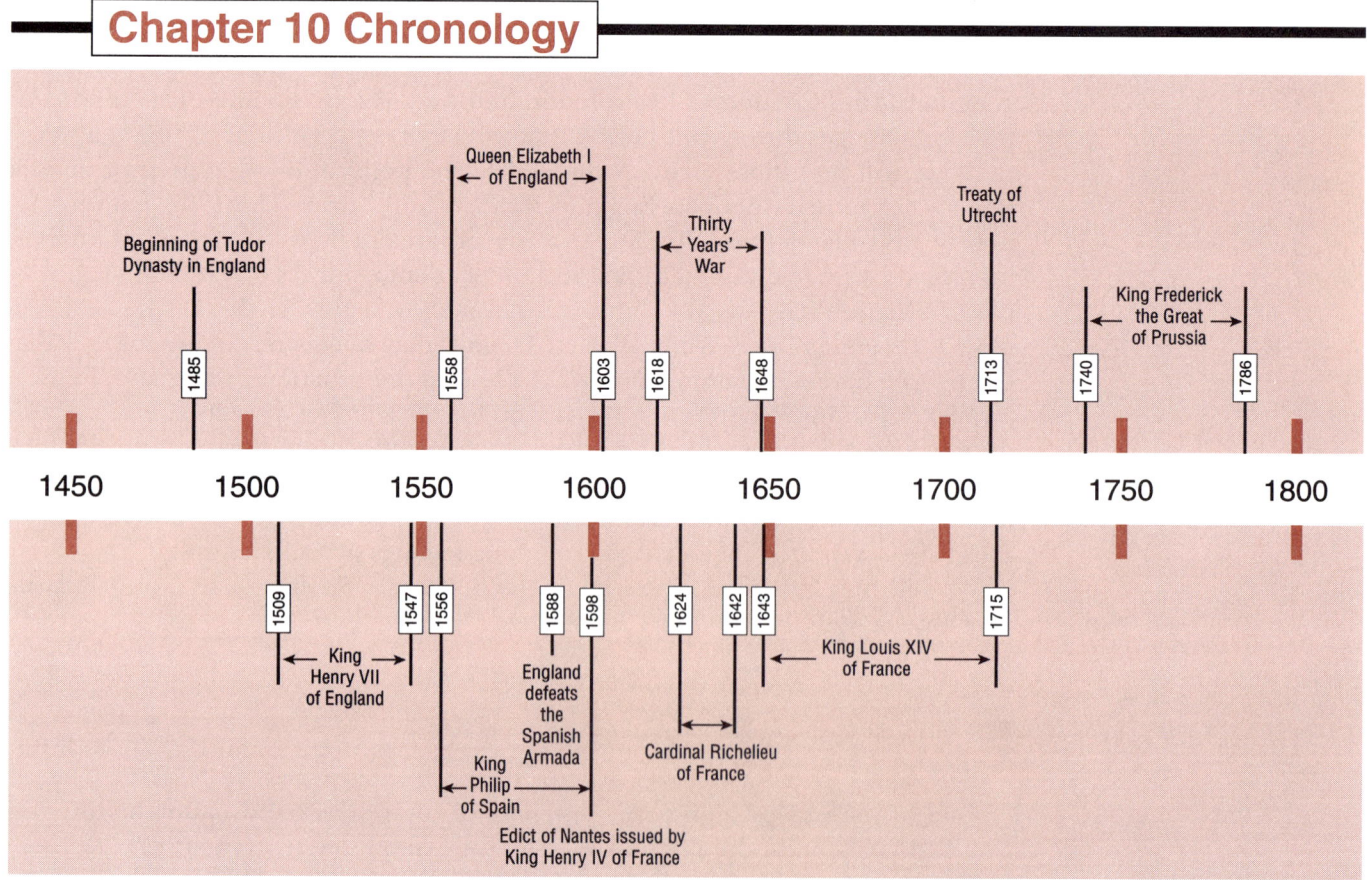

major result of the Wars of the Roses was a strengthening of the position of the monarch at the expense of the nobles because:

- Middle-class merchants, upset with the wars' harmful effect upon commerce, were glad to support the new king.
- The deaths of many nobles reduced the numbers of contenders for the crown.
- The king added to his wealth by taking over the properties of nobles who died and who had opposed him.
- Most people were weary of the long and costly wars and were willing to support the strong central government that the new king created.

The new king, crowned as Henry VII, ruled from 1485 to 1509. His reign began the Tudor Dynasty, which was to consist of five monarchs and lasted from 1485 to 1603. Tudor England, as this period is called, was another step forward in the evolution of both royal power and the nation-state as political forces. This period was the era of strong monarchy. Let us consider the reasons for this.

Henry VII was able to restore order and stability, desperately welcomed after many years of international and civil wars involving his compatriots. Some of this stability was the result of his marriage to Elizabeth of the House of York and his appointment of members of the rising, prosperous merchant class to important positions at his court. He won favor with lawmakers in the Parliament as he rarely asked for a raise in taxes. He had little need to ask, since he was able to add to the royal treasury from properties he seized after the Wars of the Roses. Indeed, when he died, he left to his son a full treasury and a well-managed kingdom.

The Rule of King Henry VIII

That son became Henry VIII (r. 1509–1547). His defiance of the pope, having Parliament pass the Act of Supremacy and creating the Anglican Church, showed him to be an authoritative and powerful figure (see Chapter 7, "The Reformation.") These actions won him the support of the vast majority of his subjects. His taking over land once owned by the Roman Catholic Church helped him to continue the good royal financial record established by his father. Henry VIII got along well with Parliament, being careful to remember the parliamentary limitations on royal power that had been carried over from the Middle Ages—for example, the king could not impose new taxes without Parliament's consent. (See Chapter 5, "Medieval Europe," and Chapter 11, "The Growth of Democracy in England," for a full discussion of these limitations.) Many members of Parliament admired Henry VIII, so he was usually able to get what he wanted from that body. The English economy was prosperous, and Henry encouraged commercial activity. This situation, along with the fact that he kept his nation out of costly overseas wars, helped to make him a popular ruler.

Henry strove to make England great. Historians generally agree, however, that he did this more for his

In this painting by Hans Holbein, Henry VIII has the look of a powerful monarch. His excommunication in 1534 led to passage of the Act of Supremacy, which resulted in the creation of the Church of England.

Edward VI came to the throne as a young boy, upon the death of his father, Henry VIII. During Edward's short reign, Protestant reforms were introduced to the newly created Church of England.

own self-advancement than for love of his people. Personally, he was egotistical, self-centered, and selfish. Although he had many faithful advisers, he did not hesitate to turn against them and have them executed when they displeased him. He had six wives, two of whom he had beheaded for controversial reasons. Some of those who opposed his royal actions concerning religious matters lost their lives and property. Whatever one may think of his moral character, he did leave the nation more united and the monarchy more powerful at his death than when he ascended to the throne.

The Rule of Queen Mary I

The next two Tudor rulers had neither Henry's leadership qualities nor his popularity. Upon Henry's death in 1547, his only son, born of his third wife, became King as Edward VI. He was a ten-year-old, sickly child at the time. Under the influence of strong-willed advisers, his government made England a more Protestant nation. At his death, only six years later, in 1553, his older half-sister became the first woman to sit on the throne of England. Queen Mary I (r. 1553–1558) was Henry's daughter by his first wife, Catherine of Aragon. Although she had some of her father's forceful manner, she used her energies to pursue a policy that angered many people and brought her disfavor. She inherited her mother's devotion to the Roman Catholic faith and proceeded to pursue a policy designed to restore that religion:

- She married Philip II of Catholic Spain.
- She had Parliament repeal (take back) anti-papal laws passed during her father's reign, such as the Act of Supremacy.
- She persecuted Anglican clergymen, burning almost three hundred of them at the stake. Archbishop Cranmer, who had obeyed King Henry VIII and annulled the king's first marriage, suffered this fate. For these actions, the Queen was called "Bloody Mary."

It is a curious twist of history that Mary's religious policy backfired. Her persecutions, for example, designed to spread the Catholic faith and extinguish Anglicanism, dismayed her subjects—both Protestants and non-Protestants. The population was opposed to seeing people burned for their religious opinions. Indeed, Mary's determination to impose her religious beliefs hardened the English public's attitude toward the Roman Catholic Church and probably guaranteed the future of Protestantism in her nation. In the year of her death, 1558, she was a very sad figure. Disliked by her subjects for her religious policies and for engaging England in a brief war that saw the nation lose land in France, she was deserted by her husband after an unhappy marriage. She had no children as heirs, and feared that her probable successor, her Protestant half-sister Elizabeth, would expand upon the religious policies of their common father. Her fears were to be realized.

The Rule of Queen Elizabeth I

As Queen Mary I, Mary Tudor aroused opposition by her actions. These included her marriage to Catholic King Philip II of Spain, and her persecution of Protestants.

Elizabeth I was the daughter of Henry VIII and his second wife, Anne Boleyn. Like her father, Elizabeth had a forceful, compelling personality. She proved to be an authoritative figure who enjoyed flattery and liked to stage big pageants and social events—probably to satisfy her love of display as well as to impress her subjects. It was believed that at the time of her death she owned more than one thousand dresses. Nevertheless, despite these characteristics, she was not perceived in those times to be very "womanly." Possessed of a sharp tongue and what was then considered a masculine toughness, she was said by an advisor, Robert Cecil, to be "more than a man, and sometimes less than a woman." During her reign, 1588 to 1603, she used her skills to promote the power of the throne and to increase pride in the nation. Examples can be seen in her handling of key issues both within her realm and with foreign powers.

In religious matters, she did things that would have pleased her father. She had Parliament repeal laws passed during Queen Mary's reign. England became a more Protestant nation under Elizabeth. English, for instance, became the language of worship, and clergymen were allowed to marry. (See also Chapter 7, "The Reformation.") When the pope excommunicated her in 1570, she and Parliament retaliated by making more harsh laws against Catholics. As Elizabeth did not marry and had no children to leave as heirs, concern grew that her successor would be a devout Catholic—her cousin, Mary, Queen of Scots. Elizabeth imprisoned Mary, and, after learning of Mary's alleged plot to capture her throne, had Mary beheaded in 1587.

The interaction of religion and politics was also seen in Elizabeth's actions toward Ireland. English control over the Irish began as early as 1167. In 1495, the Statute of Drogheda (Poynings's Law) made laws passed by England applicable to Ireland. All Tudor rulers considered themselves to be monarchs of both England and Ireland. Henry VIII tried to introduce into Ireland the religious changes he made in England. Native Irish, who were strongly Catholic, resented English policies. This resentment caused a revolt to break out in 1597, led by Hugh O'Neill. Elizabeth's forces put down the revolt with much bloodshed. This strong-armed action added to the tension between the Irish and English—a tension that continues into the twentieth century. (See Chapter 11, "The Growth of Democracy in England," and Chapter 29, "Independence and Decolonization.")

Elizabeth did not have any deep personal religious feelings. In her private life, she considered herself Protestant while admiring certain Catholic rituals. In her public role as Queen, it was politics that determined her religious policies. She did not want religious issues to harm the stability and unity of her nation. Her ideal was a national church, the (Anglican) Church of England, which would be at once Catholic and Protestant and would claim the loyalty of the majority of her subjects.

Mary, Queen of Scots

She was the great-granddaughter of Henry VII of England, the daughter of James V of Scotland, Queen of France when married to François II, and Queen of Scotland. She was also a pretender for the throne of England and it was this that would get her into trouble. Elizabeth I sat on that throne and would protect it as best she could.

Mary was crowned Queen of Scotland when she was a baby. Her father had died after a battle with the English. Her mother, Marie, was French and realized that the only way Scotland could remain independent of English control was to get a powerful friend. She arranged a political marriage for Mary with the French heir, François.

It is said that Mary loved France when she got there. It had large beautiful castles surrounded by gardens. She was able to travel around and enjoyed meeting the people who seemed to like her. As a devout Catholic in a Catholic nation she was free to practice her religion. François took the throne in 1559 and so Mary became queen in two lands.

Unfortunately, François soon developed a serious fever and then went into a coma. Nothing doctors could do helped him and Mary became a widow one year after becoming queen. She then became unwanted in France and returned to Scotland. She was a Catholic returning to a country that was fast becoming all-Protestant due to the Presbyterian John Knox. An arrangement was made in which Mary would be allowed to practice her religion while others practiced theirs.

Her return was a problem for Elizabeth of England. Many Catholics in the north of England opposed the Protestant Elizabeth and might follow Mary. Mary did have a claim on the English throne by being a descendent of Henry VII. Elizabeth's claim was questioned by some because her mother had been Anne Boleyn and Elizabeth had been called illegitimate by her opposition.

Elizabeth sent Henry Darnley to Mary's court as she knew Mary would be attracted to this handsome man and might marry him. She hoped to control Mary through Darnley. This was a poor choice for Mary but her heart ruled her head and she married him. The leading lords of Scotland opposed the marriage.

In a short time Mary turned against Darnley because of his drinking and other excesses and plotted with others to have him killed. This was accomplished in 1567. Then she turned around and married one of the murderers, James Hepburn, Earl of Bothwell. This was too much for the Scottish lords and they rose in rebellion. Mary ran to England seeking the protection of Elizabeth. Bothwell ran to Scandinavia where he hoped to get aid. Instead he was imprisoned and died there.

Mary, then in England, became involved in plots and conspiracies against Elizabeth. The Counter Reformation was using Mary as a tool for getting England back into the Catholic sphere. Advisers to Elizabeth warned her of this and recommended that Mary be executed. Elizabeth did not have the stomach for the killing of a monarch, as it was too close to her, and so continued to refuse for a long time. Finally there was undeniable proof that Mary was plotting to have Elizabeth assassinated and so she signed the death warrant as a political necessity.

Mary went to her beheading with grace and dignity. She dressed well for the occasion, standing all in red. She knelt on the chopping block and the blow severed her head. Stories tell of how Elizabeth wept for the fate of what truly was an ill-fated queen.

She wanted to keep to a middle ground between what she felt were two extremes—Catholics whose first loyalty was to the pope, and strict Protestant groups, such as the Calvinists and Puritans, who felt the Reformation in England had not gone far enough. In keeping to this middle ground, she did not hesitate to act against anyone from these extremes who might threaten national harmony.

In the field of foreign affairs, Elizabeth acted with similar attitudes regarding politics, religion, and her nation's well-being. Examples can be seen in her policies toward France and Spain, two predominantly Catholic nations who were England's main opponents at the time. When religious wars occurred in France in 1562, she provided encouragement and some help to the **Huguenots** (French Protestants). When the Dutch, who were mostly Protestant, revolted against Spanish rule in 1581, Elizabeth sent them money and a small army. In siding with the Huguenots and the Dutch, Elizabeth did not act as a champion of Protestantism. She supported these groups not because they were Protestants but because they could weaken those powers who were threats to England.

Defeat of the Spanish Armada Tension with Spain reached a peak toward the end of the sixteenth century. Rivalry between the two nations existed on the high seas, where English seamen often attacked Spanish merchant ships, and in the New World colonies of the Americas. More significantly, King Philip II of Spain (r. 1556–1598) wanted to make England Catholic again and to enlarge his territorial domains in Europe. He therefore prepared a fleet of 130 ships to attack England. Called the "Invincible Armada" by Spaniards, the fleet sailed for England in May 1588. Elizabeth and the English were ready, and inflicted a crushing defeat on the Armada in August. The English ships were able to move faster and had superior guns. With several ships sunk in the English Channel and others seriously damaged, and faced with limited ammunition and declining morale among their men, the remaining Armada vessels tried to escape toward the North Sea. Here they faced a violent storm (later called "the Protestant Wind") that destroyed additional ships. Those that survived tried to sail back to Spain around Scotland and Ireland, but not without difficulties. Bad weather and continued attacks by the Irish and English caused more losses for the fleet. Only when the remnant of the Armada reached Spain was the full impact of the disaster understood. Sixty-three ships had been captured or destroyed, with the loss of over ten thousand lives. The crushing defeat of the Armada had three crucial consequences for the English:

The last of the Tudor monarchs, Queen Elizabeth I ruled in an era that saw England's beginnings as a naval and overseas power. Her reign also witnessed a rise in commercial activity and the restoration of Protestantism.

1. As Queen, Elizabeth gained greater prestige and popularity.
2. Protestantism in England was no longer endangered.
3. England was free to continue exploration and settlement overseas, particularly in North America and the West Indies.

In her last years as monarch Elizabeth continued to get along fairly well with Parliament. Yet that legislative body became more active by frequently questioning things that the Queen wanted and by growing concern about the increasing power she had acquired. Parliament also wished to have a greater role in setting government policies. Eventually, after Elizabeth's death in 1603, an outright clash did develop between the throne and Parliament. We will examine this crisis in the next chapter.

It is clear that the Tudor rulers, particularly King Henry VIII and Queen Elizabeth I, increased their authority as monarchs. Nevertheless, strong-willed and domineering as they were, they did not govern as absolute monarchs. **Absolutism**, as we will soon see, was more characteristic of monarchs in France, Prussia, and Austria. An absolute monarch is one who makes all decisions by himself or herself and claims to have complete authority to control the lives of his or her subjects. The absolute monarch does not observe any restriction on his or her power nor consult with any representatives of the people. Answerable only to heaven, he or she would claim to have a "divine right" to rule. This type of ruler can also be described as an **autocrat**.

France

The first major name in the history of absolute monarchy in France is King Louis XI (r. 1461–1483). He was able to increase his power and make his government more wealthy, efficient, and centralized. A chief reason for this was the ending of the Hundred Years' War (1337–1453). The war had seen the deaths of many nobles who might otherwise have challenged his rule. The capture of almost all English territory in France made Frenchmen proud of their nation and also enriched the royal treasury.

The Rule of King Henry IV

The Protestant Reformation that began in 1517 was to affect France and the position of the monarch. A series of religious wars broke out in 1562 between Huguenots (French Protestants) and Catholics. For the next thirty-six years, France suffered much bloodshed and religious bigotry. The kings during these times were weak and ineffective. The fighting ended in 1598, when Henry of Navarre, a member of the Bourbon family, took the throne as Henry IV. Although a Huguenot, he quickly realized that he could not restore peace and unity to his nation nor respect for the monarchy if he maintained his Protestant faith in a predominantly Catholic country. He decided to put the national interests of France above his personal religious beliefs, and converted to Catholicism. In doing this, he is reputed to have remarked, "Paris is well worth a mass."

His decision to convert was one of several politically wise actions taken by Henry IV. Another was his issuing the Edict of Nantes in 1598, a document that was, for that time, a landmark in the history of religious toleration. Its chief provisions were as follows:

1. Huguenots were permitted freedom of worship.
2. They could establish churches in certain places, but not in Paris.
3. They were granted the same civil rights that Catholics had.
4. They could fortify their major cities with their own soldiers.

Curiously, at first the Edict of Nantes was criticized by both Catholics and Huguenots. Catholics felt that the edict gave too much freedom to Huguenots and that its issuance was proof that Henry's conversion was not sincere. For Huguenots, on the other hand, the edict did not go far enough and should have permitted even more religious freedom. Nevertheless, in time, the edict did achieve its purpose. By 1610, the year of Henry's death, a good measure of religious peace and civil order was evident in France.

Two other actions by Henry IV strengthened his government. He was able to reduce the power of the nobles, many of whom had been troublesome for previous kings and had ignored royal directives. Henry placed some of them in his government, while giving bribes to some others. Henry's appointment of the Duke of Sully as his chief minister improved France's financial condition. Sully made the tax collection system much better, and cut down spending by the royal household. The result was a surplus of money in the crown's treasury. Large sums were then used to build roads, bridges, and public buildings. Both agricultural and industrial production improved. France was a prosperous nations in the early years of the seventeenth century.

Henry's reign in that century was cut short by an assassin in 1610. The killer was a religious fanatic, who thought Henry was an enemy of the Catholic Church, and stabbed him on a Paris street. As we have seen, Henry's kingship made France a more stable and powerful nation. And yet, we must note his place in the growth of absolutism in his country. He had the temper of an autocrat. To a meeting of citizens in the town of Toulouse, he once said, "I must insist on being obeyed." He never gave the **Estates-general** (the national legislative body) a chance to challenge his will. Indeed, never once did he summon it to meet. Such royal attitudes were to have serious repercussions in France in the seventeenth and eighteenth centuries.

The Rule of King Louis XIII

Henry's son became King as Louis XIII (1610–1643). As the new King was only eight years old, it was decided that his mother, Marie de Medeci, would rule as regent. This meant that she would rule in his behalf until he came of age. She proved to be ineffective, getting into trouble with the nobles and using up the reserves of money that Sully had created. It was in this setting, in 1614, that a meeting of the Estates-general took place. Almost five hundred members met. They were unable to accomplish anything, as they argued among themselves. The clergy and nobility wanted to retain their special privileges and refused to give into demands from the Third Estate (i.e., commoners, shopkeepers, and peasants). The Estates-general did not meet again until 1789, 175 years later, on the eve of the French Revolution.

The Impact of Cardinal Richelieu When Louis XIII did come of age, he did not appear to be a strong ruler in the mold of his father. However, he appointed as chief minister a man who possessed political skills and substantial leadership abilities. This was Cardinal Richelieu. For almost the entire remainder of Louis XIII's reign, Richelieu was the real power in France (1624–1643). He had two goals:

1. To make the king's power supreme in France; and
2. To make France the supreme power in Europe.

Let us now look at these goals carefully, with particular regard to the methods used in attempting to achieve them.

As chief minister to King Louis XIII, Cardinal Richelieu pursued policies designed to weaken the nobility and the Huguenots. His actions helped in creating the strong, central, absolute authority of the monarchy.

To achieve the first goal, Richelieu aimed to end the rights of the Huguenots and to reduce the power of the nobles. Under the Edict of Nantes, Huguenots were given the right to fortify their towns with their own armies. To Richelieu, this was an obstacle in the way of his desire to build a strong centralized royal government. The Protestant towns were almost states within a state. Accordingly, Richelieu mounted a military campaign against the towns with the backing of the king. With the royal forces successful, the Huguenots were stripped of their special political rights in the towns but were allowed to keep their religious freedoms. As for the nobles, Richelieu had many of their castles destroyed and removed several nobles from positions as governors of provinces. Provinces were subsequently headed by intendants. These were officials selected by the king, forming a kind of civil service, who owed allegiance only to him and who would therefore favor a strong monarchy.

To achieve his second goal, whereby France would become the dominant power in Europe, Richelieu planned to strike at the power of the Catholic Habsburg rulers of Austria and the Holy Roman Empire. A chance to do this came during the Thirty Years' War (1618–1648). This was actually a series of on-again-off-again conflicts that occurred mostly on German soil and that began as a struggle between Protestant and Catholic powers. You may recall that previous bloodshed over religion in Germany had been temporarily settled by the 1555 Peace of Augsberg. (See Chapter 7, "The Reformation.") However, religious issues remained and sparked a Protestant rebellion in Bohemia, which lasted from 1618 to 1620. Its suppression by Habsburg ruler Ferdinand II provoked Danish King Christian IV and soon thereafter Swedish King Gustavus Adolphus to join the struggle on the Protestant side. Protestant Denmark and Sweden fought against Ferdinand for both religious and territorial reasons. Along with Richelieu, they feared the growth of Habsburg power in Europe, especially if that power were to extend to all of Germany. Accordingly, Richelieu gave economic aid to the Swedes. Richelieu did not have France actively enter the fighting until 1635. He made this decision as a result of the failure of Christian IV to invade Germany and the death of Gustavus Adolphus. Here we see how Richelieu gave priority to his political goals over his religious ideals. Although a Catholic clergyman, he now had Catholic France fighting for Protestant forces in Europe against the Catholic Holy Roman Emperor! Cardinal Richelieu had now become statesman Richelieu, trying to make the best of a given situation when it would benefit him. Such a person could be called an **opportunist**, as well as a pragmatist or realist.

Although Richelieu did not live to see the end of the Thirty Years' War in 1648, he would have been pleased with its results. The concluding Treaty of Westphalia recognized victory by the French and Swedes and reduced the power of the Habsburgs. Its main provisions were as follows:

Louis XIV's reign marked the high point of absolutism in France. Known as the Sun King, he ruled in an extravagant manner that planted the seeds for the 1789 revolution.

- France obtained Alsace.
- Switzerland and the Netherlands were recognized as independent Protestant nations.
- German rulers could determine the religion of their people, free from Habsburg influence.

The Rule of King Louis XIV

Like Richelieu, King Louis XIII was not alive when the Thirty Years' War ended. Upon his death in 1643, his son became King as Louis XIV (r. 1643–1715). As the new King was only four years old at the time, rule in France was actually exercised by his mother, Anne, with Cardinal Mazarin as chief minister. Trained by Richelieu to be his successor, Mazarin continued the former's centralizing policies. He was successful in stopping a short series of rebellions called the Fronde (1648–1652). It leaders had hoped to displace Mazarin and weaken the monarchy by securing more power for the nobles. Mazarin's victory added to the absolutism of the crown. The Fronde was to be the last attempt to challenge royal power prior to the revolution of 1789.

At Mazarin's death in 1661, Louis declared that he would rule on his own. His entire reign, covering seventy-two years, was the longest in French history. This reign reached the heights of absolutism, as the result of both the absolutist tendencies that had been growing since the Hundred Years' War and the personality of Louis XIV himself. No monarch ever had a more glorified view of himself and his position. He was convinced, for example that he was "the visible image of God on earth." All his ideas and policies were the result of heavenly guidance and were therefore not open to question or dissent. These beliefs made up the theory of **divine right** of kings. Consequently, it is not surprising that Louis recognized no limits to his authority.

Considering himself to be the greatest of all men, Louis took the sun as his emblem. He became known as the "Sun King" as well as the "Grand Monarch." He is supposed to have said, "**L'état, c'est moi**" (I am the state). Whether or not he made this assertion, it accurately described the conditions of his rule. There was hardly any opposition to his will. Possible threats were held in check. The Estates-general was never summoned. If he wanted to impose new taxes, there was no need to consult with anyone or any group. Fittingly, the right of many cities to choose their own mayor was ended. These posts were sold by the King to those who bid the most and who could prove their loyalty to him. Clearly, Louis XIV was the state—and the state was Louis XIV!

The Palace of Versailles Much of our description about this towering figure would be verified if you could take a trip back in time and visit him at Versailles. This was the site, eleven miles from Paris, where he built a magnificent palace. This became the seat of the French government, taking over twenty-five years to build and requiring more than thirty thousand workers. The expense severely drained the French treasury. The actual figures are not known, as Louis destroyed all construction bills and accounts. You would enter through the palace grounds, amazed at the lovely gardens. You would find the large halls filled with colorful paintings, and named after figures from Greek mythology. You might be dazzled by the 240-foot-long Grand Hall of Mirrors, containing seventeen large windows and as many framed mirrors. Should you wander outside, you would find it easy to get lost among the many fountains, ponds, waterfalls, and marble statues.

You would see many visitors from other countries, astonished at this grand display of wealth and royal power, and hoping to build similar palaces in their own countries. They also hoped to learn to speak French, as well as wear French clothing and adopt French customs. No doubt you would be introduced to many of France's great nobles. Louis wanted them to live at Versailles, especially if they desired favors from him. Also, he could keep an eye on them and their families this way. You shouldn't be surprised to find them happy to have the honor of praying with the King or watching him eat or getting dressed. Finally, if you were not tired at night, you could witness one of the many balls, dances, masquerades, or parties that frequently were held.

Even though he spent huge sums on the Versailles palace and other items that he deemed necessary for a grand monarch, Louis was lucky to have a finance minister generally able to keep the royal treasury full. This minister was Jean Colbert. (See Chapter 9, "The Commercial Revolution.") Colbert wanted to maintain the financial policies of Sully, by making reforms in the tax system and by ending corruption among tax collectors. His decision to raise taxes fell mainly on the middle and lower classes. This was because the clergy and nobles were exempt from paying taxes. He expected large royal revenues to be obtained from trade with other nations and from colonies overseas. He was a firm believer in mercantilism, promoting government regulation of and aid to industry so as to make France self-sufficient. He pressed for high tariffs in order to protect French industries. French agriculture suffered, however, when other nations retaliated against Colbert's high industrial tariffs by placing heavy taxes on French farm exports.

For most of his term of office, Colbert was able to increase the national income. Yet, there were three things that hurt his economic program and that were to seriously affect the French economy. The first of these was the 1685 revocation of the Edict of Nantes. Louis XIV was worried about the Huguenots for political rather than religious reasons. He felt that their existence was a threat to national unity. They began to face mild persecution—their schools were closed, churches attacked, and they were offered bribes and requests to convert to Catholicism. When these measures failed to persuade the Huguenots to give up their Protestant beliefs, the King ordered the Edict of Nantes to be revoked. Little did Louis realize it, but the harshness of this decision was to damage France's prosperity. With their religious freedom now ended, almost two hundred thousand Huguenots secretly fled France. They were among the nation's most energetic, productive, and industrious citizens. Although emigration was forbidden to them, they managed to flee to England, Holland, and the Americas.

The Palace of Versailles was a sign of the splendor of the French monarchy in the seventeenth and eighteenth centuries.

The second and third major blows to the French economy were also the result of actions taken by the King. His personal expenditures for his palace, clothing, and other luxuries drained the treasury. But the most catastrophic shock to France's finances was the series of wars fought with other European nations between 1667 and 1713. The wars of Louis XIV imposed a huge burden on the treasury and saw the nation's productive energies used for fighting rather than for the welfare of the people. The wars lasted off and on from 1667–1713, with the longest being the War of the Spanish Succession (1701–1717).

Why did so many wars take place? The basic answer is that France wanted more land, even if this meant taking it from other rulers. Louis XIV felt that to be safe and secure, France needed to extend to "natural frontiers." This meant taking all the land eastward up to the Rhine River. France already felt protected on the north, west, and south by the English Channel, the Atlantic Ocean, the Pyrenees, and the Mediterranean Sea. The expansionist desires of France worried other countries. Therefore, at one time or another, the French found themselves fighting against England, Spain, Denmark, Sweden, Austria, and several German states. This resistance to French aggression by various combinations is an early example of what we now call balance of power diplomacy.

The most violent conflict was the War of the Spanish Succession. With his grandson inheriting the throne of Spain and all its colonies, Louis hoped to unite France and Spain. This wish was thwarted by an alliance of European nations that wanted to maintain a balance of power and prevent France from gaining a dominant position. Fighting took place in Europe, on the seas, and even in the Americas. The Treaty of Utrecht, 1713, ended the war. The grandson of Louis XIV was recognized as King Philip V of Spain, but Louis agreed that France and Spain would never unite. England received some French territory in North America. France was permitted to retain some of the land acquired prior to the war.

Two years after the Treaty of Utrecht, Louis XIV died. At his death, France was viewed as a political power. Its cultural prestige was the greatest of any European nation. Inside France, however, there were misery, unstable financial conditions, and a population weary of warfare. These conditions were not improved during the reign of Louis XV (r. 1715–1774) and were to be some of the factors that caused the historic revolutionary explosion in 1789 under Louis XVI. The absolutism of Louis XIV extended beyond his life, but eventually, it would tragically affect the life of his nation.

Spain

As you may remember, Spain was the host country for the 1992 Olympic Games. It was ruled under a monarchy then, and still is today. However, you would not call this style of rule an absolute monarchy. Better today to call Spain a constitutional monarchy. This means that the royal power is limited. But this was not the situation several hundred years ago, when the institution of monarchy began and accompanied Spain's emergence as a unified nation.

The Rule of King Ferdinand and Queen Isabella

The marriage in 1469 between Ferdinand of Aragon and Isabella of Castille brought together the Christian communities of Spain. By 1492, their combined

Ferdinand V, also known as Ferdinand the Catholic, completed the unification of the Spanish kingdoms into modern Spain. His reign, with Queen Isabella I, saw the voyage of Columbus, the establishment of the Inquisition, and the expulsion of Jews and Moors.

Isabella I, known as Isabella the Catholic, ruled Spain with her husband for nearly three decades. Prior to her marriage, she was the Queen of Castile.

armies had driven the Muslims from the Iberian peninsula. They were to rule as king and queen together until 1504. During this time, they built a foundation for absolute monarchy as well as for a powerful nation-state. They often put forth laws without seeking approval from the Cortes, the national legislature. Although Catholic, they preferred to appoint Spanish Church officials themselves rather than have these appointments made by the pope. And by demolishing several castles belonging to nobles, they weakened the power of that class.

They felt that religious unity would help achieve political unity. Accordingly, they pursued a policy to make Spain a Catholic country by persecuting minorities such as Jews and Muslims. This persecution took forms that, from a modern democratic point of view, were clear violations of human rights. With authorization from the pope, the Spanish Inquisition was created as a court for detecting and punishing heresy and thus prohibiting religious freedom. It was aimed mostly at Jews, and primarily at those who did not accept offers to convert to Christianity. Accused people brought before the Inquisition and its dreaded head, Tomás de Torquemada, had no procedural safeguards such as the right to have a lawyer. They underwent terrible tortures and were frequently burnt at the stake in a ceremony known as the **auto-da-fé** (act of faith). Another form of persecution was the signing by both monarchs of the Edict of Expulsion on March 31, 1492. Jews were ordered to convert or to leave the kingdom by the following August. Among the thousands who departed were skilled workers, government officials, and merchants. Spain thus lost a valuable group of citizens. (It is of historical value to note that exactly 500 years later, on March 31, 1992, King Juan Carlos of Spain officially revoked the Edict of Expulsion at a Jewish temple in Madrid.)

In foreign affairs, 1492 turned out to have additional significance for Spain. In that year, Christopher Columbus sailed on behalf of the monarchy and landed in the Americas. This voyage, to what from the European perspective was the "New World," soon led to extensive exploration and colonization by other Spaniards. Spain thus gained a large empire and obtained much wealth. Spain also secured an important alliance with the powerful Habsburg family, when Joanna, a daughter of Ferdinand and Isabella, married Philip of Habsburg. Their son became King Charles I of Spain in 1516.

The Rule of King Charles V

In 1519, Charles was also elected as Holy Roman Emperor. As he was the fifth Charles to hold that title, he became Charles V. He thus became one of the most powerful rulers in European history, having the following lands under his authority: Spain and all its colonies in the New World, the Netherlands, the German states, Austria, and part of Italy. During his reign as both King and Holy Roman Emperor, he was successful in defending Christian Europe from invasion by the Ottoman Turks. The key event in this defense was his victory at the Battle of Vienna in 1529. He was less successful in stopping the spread of Protestantism in the

German states, agreeing to the Treaty of Augsberg in 1555. (See Chapter 7, "The Reformation.") These military involvements, along with a short war against France, forced him to spend tremendous amounts of money. As an absolute ruler, he spent freely, never consulting with any group representing his subjects.

In 1556, Charles gave up his throne and retired to a monastery. He determined that his domains were much too vast for control by any one person. Fatigued, and suffering from attacks of gout due to his excessive eating habits, Charles divided his Empire between his brother and his son. His brother became Holy Roman Emperor as Ferdinand I, and began the Austrian Habsburg Dynasty. His son received Spain and all its possessions in Europe and overseas, as Philip II. He began the Spanish Habsburg Dynasty.

The Rule of King Philip II

During his reign, 1556 to 1598, Philip II acted as an absolute monarch in his attempts to increase Spain's role as a world power and to protect Catholicism. By the middle of the sixteenth century, Spain was looked on with great awe. It was said, "When Spain moves, the whole world trembles." Yet by the end of the century, with Philip's passing, a general decline in his nation's fortunes was evident. His style of leadership was such that he trusted no one. Distrustful of even his advisers, he tried to do too many things by himself. His desire for absolute control of all decision-making was seen in his endless reading of long reports and writing replies to various petitions addressed to his government. Decision-making thus became a very slow process. He was unable to distinguish important matters from trivial ones that could be given over to his ministers. These characteristics were not appropriate for the efficient administration of a huge empire. Once, for a period of eight months, he left important messages from his ambassadors unanswered.

He was known to spend lavishly and unwisely, thereby weakening the royal treasury. This could be seen in the huge palace, the Escorial, that he built near Madrid, as well as in the many wars in which he was engaged. Royal expenditures exceeded the income that came in from taxes and his overseas colonies. As a result of creating enormous debts, Philip found himself bankrupt on more than one occasion. Frequently, he had to borrow money from German and Italian bankers. To pay back these loans with their high interest rates, Philip would use the gold and silver taken from Mexico, Peru, and other Spanish colonies in the Americas. This led to an increase in the amount of money in circulation, and ultimately, to a rise in the prices of goods and services. This situation is called inflation. It contributed to a severe decline in the Spanish economy, with suffering for businesses and the middle-class merchants.

A large portion of the merchants and skilled craftsmen were people who faced persecution on the basis of religion. These were **Marranos** (converted Jews who secretly maintained Jewish beliefs and practices) and **Moriscos** (converted Muslims or Moors). If suspected of being insincere in their new beliefs, they risked being subjected to the Inquisition and the auto-da-fé. These institutions had begun in the reign of Philip's great-grandparents, Ferdinand and Isabella, and he did not hesitate to use them against those he deemed heretics. He further issued an expulsion edict against Moriscos in 1570, similar to the one issued in 1492 against the Jews. As a declared upholder of the Catholic faith, Philip said that he "would rather reign in a desert than in a country peopled with heretics." Royal policies stemming from such a pronouncement caused the flight of many

Marranos and Moriscos from Spain, adding further to the country's economic problems.

In the field of foreign affairs, the sad record of Philip was part of Spain's decline as a great power. His goal of protecting Catholicism brought him into conflict with the Muslim Ottoman Turks. Although he was proud of his naval victory against them in 1571 at the Battle of Lepanto, fought near the coast of Greece, he was unable to keep the Turks completely out of the Mediterranean region. He had brief encounters against France on issues concerning religion and land. These struggles, along with other ones, were to place severe drains on his treasury. Serious losses, political and human as well as financial, came about in his relations with England. The frequent raids on Spanish merchant ships and New World colonies by the English were very damaging. And the defeat of the Spanish Armada was a disaster of enormous proportions, as indicated earlier in this chapter.

The most troublesome foreign problem for Philip was the revolt in the seventeen provinces that made up the Netherlands. He inherited this region from his father and was aware of its prominence as a rich commercial center. The taxes he imposed in its people were deeply resented, especially as the people were not consulted and as the monies were used for Philip's expenses, not for the people's benefit. Another cause of resentment was Philip's effort to stop the spread of Protestantism.

In 1566, almost fifty years after Martin Luther's actions had sparked the Reformation, the growth of the Calvinist form of Protestantism so alarmed Philip that he ordered action against the new faith and its followers. The consequence flowing from Philip's policies was an open rebellion. For the remainder of his lifetime, terrible fighting went on, leading to thousands of deaths, destruction of churches, and loss of property. In 1581, under the leadership of William the Silent, the seven northern provinces declared themselves independent from Spain. They were mainly Protestant, while the ten southern provinces were mainly Catholic. However, all the provinces joined in the rebellion. Even after Philip's death in 1598, armed struggle continued. Finally, in 1609, a truce was signed. The seven northern provinces became known as Dutch Netherlands and eventually as Holland. The ten southern provinces, granted limited self-rule by Spain, became known as the Spanish Netherlands and in 1830 became the independent nation of Belgium.

Absolutism in Spain did not end with Philip's passing. But Spain's glorious days as a world power were over. Spanish culture, however, did reach a high level during Philip's reign. During his time and into the seventeenth century many great works were created by Spanish artists and writers: El Greco (painter of saints), Diego Velázquez (a famous royal court painter), Miguel Cervantes (the author of *Don Quixote*), Lope de Vega (a dramatist), and Francisco Suarez (a philosopher).

Austria

The Habsburg family began its control of Austria in the late 1200s. From the sixteenth to eighteenth centuries, its members ruled their lands as heads of the Holy Roman Empire. Absolutism was a key feature of their reign. However, they suffered some loss of power and prestige with their inability to halt the growth of Protestantism in northern Germany and their defeat in the Thirty Years' War. To their credit, they were instrumental as part of a Christian alliance in stopping a

Turkish advance into Europe at the 1683 Battle of Vienna. In the eighteenth century their Empire contained several different subject nationalities: Austrians, Belgians, Croats, Czechs, Germans, Hungarians, Italians, Poles, Romanians, Serbs, and Slovenes. With so many diverse groups—all with different languages and customs—and local nobles who wanted more power, it was not easy for the Habsburg monarchs to build a strong sense of unity. They were worried about revolts by some of the nationalities, as well as threats from other European powers seeking to take parts of their Empire.

The Rule of Maria Theresa

Such worries were on the mind of Austrian ruler and Holy Roman Emperor Charles VI (r. 1711–1740). Accordingly, in order to safeguard the inheritance of his empire to his daughter Maria Theresa, he persuaded many European rulers to sign the Pragmatic Sanction. The signing powers to this agreement promised to let Maria Theresa inherit her lands intact. The year 1740 marked the start of her forty-year reign, 1740 to 1780, as well as an invasion of Silesia by Frederick the Great of Prussia. This was one of Maria Theresa's richest provinces, noted for its iron ore and farmland, and had long been desired by Frederick. Although his father had signed the Pragmatic Sanction, Frederick claimed that he was not bound to honor it. The taking of Silesia by Prussia was contested by Austria and led to a long war known as the War of the Austrian Succession (1740–1748). For a number of reasons, mainly hopes of seizing Austrian land for themselves, several powers allied themselves with Prussia: France, Spain, Sweden, and the German states of Bavaria and Saxony. Weary of France, England supported Austria. The war ended with the Treaty of Aix-la-Chapelle in 1748. It allowed Frederick to keep Silesia, and recognized Maria Theresa as ruler of the other Habsburg lands.

Angered by her loss of Silesia, Maria Theresa sought to regain it and to form an alliance against Prussia. She decided it was in her best interest to ally herself with Bourbon France. England, maintaining its desire for a balance of power in Europe and jealous of France, allied itself with Prussia. This odd changing of alliances between former friends and foes came to be called the Diplomatic Revolution. Shortly thereafter, another war broke out, the Seven Years' War (1756–1763). The causes included disputes over Silesia, other land in Europe, and overseas colonies. This war was the greatest conflict the modern world had seen up to that time. Fighting took place in Europe, India, and the Americas. (In North America, the struggle was known as the French and Indian War.) The Treaty of Hubertusburg, ending the war in 1763, restored matters in Europe much the way they had been prior to the fighting. Prussia, for example, kept Silesia. The Treaty of Paris, signed in the same year, saw England emerge as the dominant power in North America and India.

The Rule of an Enlightened Despot—Joseph II

Maria Theresa's land passed on to her son, who became King Joseph II of Austria and Holy Roman Emperor. As yet another example of an absolute monarch, he single-handedly increased royal authority. He ended local self-government, took control of the Catholic Church and its lands, and taxed nobles heavily and altered their relations with their serfs. Yet Joseph II did try to provide reforms (changes) that he thought would improve the lives of his people. Claiming to rule in the people's best interests as he alone saw them, and declaring that only he knew how best to protect these interests, Joseph was one of several monarchs at the time who became known as **enlightened despots**. He saw himself as paternalistic and fatherly, but not democratic. Although an autocrat, he improved the lot of serfs, and made advances in religious toleration, education, and the judicial system. After his death, most of these reforms were not continued.

Prussia

One of the best-known enlightened or benevolent despots was Frederick II of Prussia. Better known as Frederick the Great (r. 1740–1786), he was a member of the Hohenzollern family. This family of nobles initially ruled the north German state of Brandenburg. Through marriages, alliances, and wars, their holdings came to include Prussia and other German territories. They ruled as absolute monarchs, establishing a powerful centralized government. Although Frederick was the best known of the Hohenzollern monarchs, his predecessors had begun a number of measures that transformed Prussia from a minor kingdom into a strong European power:

1. A civil service was created to make the carrying out of policies more efficient.
2. The army grew to become one of the best trained and most feared in Europe. Officers were selected from the upper class Junkers. The values of obedience, loyalty, and discipline were emphasized in the military as well as elsewhere in society.
3. Primary education was required for most children.
4. The economy prospered, with careful financial planning and development of agriculture and new industries.

As he grew up, Frederick did not appear to have those talents and interests that would enable him to continue the autocratic patterns of his father and grandfather. He played the flute, loved poetry, and enjoyed philosophy. His father, unimpressed by these interests, disciplined his son severely. Curiously, when Frederick came to the throne in 1740, he maintained his involvement with these activities while governing in a manner that was stricter and more authoritarian than that of his father. Hints of this manner, as well as his practice of enlightened depotism, can be seen in his own words. He once said, "The people are not here for the sake of the rulers, but the rulers for the sake of the people." In a letter to the French philosopher Voltaire, he wrote the following: "My chief occupation is to fight the ignorance and the prejudice in this country…I must enlighten my people, cultivate their manners and morals, and make them as happy as human beings can be; as happy as the means at my disposal permit me to make them."

Some of Frederick's achievements within Prussia did show him to be true to his words. He made improvements in the civil-service system, and expanded public education. He placed high taxes on imports in order to encourage and protect Prussian industries, while improving agriculture by giving seeds and money to needy farmers. He encouraged settlers to emigrate from other countries and promoted a high degree of religious toleration relative to his time. His reforms in the court system saw the creation of uniform legal fees, speedy disposition of lawsuits, and reduction in the use of torture. Known as a supporter of literature and the arts, Frederick's rule inspired writers; he was often glorified as a national hero in songs and stories.

In foreign affairs, he sought to increase the power and prestige of his kingdom at the expense of his neighbors. As we have seen, pursuit of his goals involved him in two major European wars—the War of the Austrian Succession and the Seven Years' War. The acquisition of Silesia in these wars, as well as his taking of Polish territory in 1772 in the first Partition of Poland, made Prussia a much enlarged nation by the time of his death in 1786. By this time, it was clear that Prussia had become an equal of Austria, France, and Spain as a power on the European continent.

Summary

You have now finished reading one of the longest chapters in this book. Its length was necessary, as we learned a great deal about the growth of nation-states and the rise of royal absolutism. Knowledge of these changes will help us to understand the history of Europe right up to our own times. Some of the general reasons for these changes can now be summarized:

1. *The powers of nobles had been reduced.*
2. *An increased feeling of national unity made people view the king or queen as an important symbol of the nation.*
3. *In some areas, because of the Reformation, the monarch took over powers traditionally held by the Catholic Church.*
4. *Rising merchants often supported the king or queen to protect their own business interests.*
5. *The establishment of a professional, well-trained army, with a national rather than a purely local loyalty, become a powerful tool in the hands of a monarch. This was a process that had slowly been going on since the Middle Ages.*

It is interesting to note that during this period of time women played a most important role. Isabella of Spain sent out Columbus, and unfortunately began the Inquisition. Maria Theresa was deeply involved in central European political intrigues, which resulted in major conflicts. Mary I of England became known in history as "Bloody Mary" because of her persecution of the Protestants. Elizabeth I of England took over a throne in difficulty and when she died she left her successor a major player in the game of power politics. More than ever power became centered in the hands of what came to be called absolute monarchs. This was exemplified by Louis XIV of France and his "I am the state" statement. Wars were on a world scale because overseas colonies of the major European powers were brought into the fighting.

CHAPTER 10

Review Exercises

I. Matching

Directions: Match the words in Column A with the *correct description* in Column B.

Column A
1. opportunist
2. auto-da-fé
3. nation-state
4. autocrat
5. Marrano
6. nationality
7. intendant
8. Morisco
9. Inquisition
10. Huguenot

Column B
(a) specific area of land, with fixed boundaries, unified under a ruler
(b) resulted in death for heretics, by burning
(c) a Muslim who converted to Catholicism
(d) descriptive of citizens in a country
(e) a Jew who converted to Catholicism
(f) a ruler who makes all decisions by himself/herself
(g) someone who does whatever is thought best at a given moment
(h) a governor or head of a province
(i) a court set up to try and punish heretics
(j) a Protestant in France

II. Famous People

Directions: Use the names below to complete the following sentences.

Henry VIII   Elizabeth I
Frederick the Great   Louis XIV
Cardinal Richelieu   Torquemada
Philip II

1. _____ built the decorative palace at Versailles.

2. _____ sent the Spanish Armada to invade England.

3. _____ sought to end the rights of Huguenots in his or her nation.

4. _____ was the offspring of a king and was the last Tudor ruler.

5. _____ was an English monarch who defied the pope.

6. _____ made Prussia a strong military power.

7. _____ was a religious leader who tried to rid Spain of non-Catholics.

III. Map Exercise

Directions: Use the map to locate the place associated with each of the following statements. For each statement, write the *letter* of the place. (An answer may be repeated.)

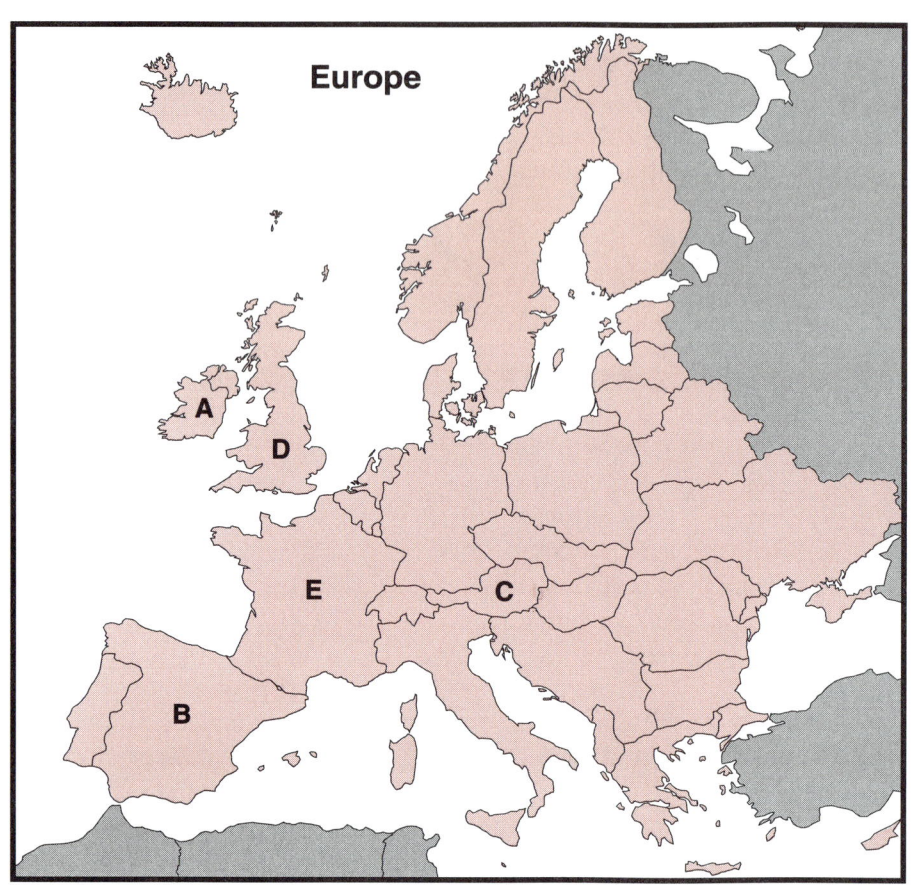

1. _____ Henry VIII ruled here.

2. _____ Jews were expelled in the year Columbus discovered the "New World."

3. _____ Many different subject nationalities lived here, under Habsburg rule.

4. _____ Ferdinand and Isabella combined to drive out Muslim armies.

5. _____ Hugh O'Neill revolts against British rule.

6. _____ The Netherlands successfully revolted against rule by this nation.

7. _____ Henry of Navarre takes the throne as Henry IV.

8. _____ The Escorial is here, built by Philip II.

9. _____ Marranos and Moriscos lived here.

10. _____ Where the "Sun King" ruled.

11. _____ Its power was reduced by terms of the Treaty of Westphalia.

12. _____ Habsburg power was centered here, the site where a westward invasion of Europe by the Turks was stopped.

IV. Multiple Choice

Directions: Find the *letter* of the correct answer.

1. Bourbon, Hohenzollern, and Tudor were names of famous

    (a) castles.
    (b) dynasties.
    (c) capitals.
    (d) battles.

2. Sully, Mazarin, and Colbert were consulted by their kings for advice on

    (a) taxes.
    (b) weapons.
    (c) ships.
    (d) palaces.

3. "L'état, c'est moi," an example of absolutism, was reported to have been said by

    (a) Frederick the Great.
    (b) Henry VIII.
    (c) Cardinal Richelieu.
    (d) Louis XIV.

4. Which was the most important consequence of both the Wars of the Roses and the Hundred Years' War?

    (a) Royal rule weakened.
    (b) A new trade route to the Americas was discovered.
    (c) Royal rule became more powerful.
    (d) Queens replaced kings as rulers.

5. Autocratic monarchs claimed their power to rule was based upon

    (a) the consent of the middle class.
    (b) the support of the Church.
    (c) the theory of mercantilism.
    (d) the theory of divine right.

6. Which family and nation are correctly paired?

    (a) Tudors—England
    (b) Bourbons—Prussia
    (c) Hohenzollerns—Austria
    (d) Habsburgs—France

7. Which was a belief common to seventeenth- and eighteenth-century absolutism?

    (a) Separation of Church and state was encouraged.
    (b) Dissenters are dangerous and should be punished.
    (c) A two-party political system is essential for a stable society.
    (d) The government should establish a strong public-school system.

8. A goal of Cardinal Richelieu's foreign policy was to make France stronger by

   (a) reducing the power of the Habsburgs.
   (b) helping Protestants against Catholics.
   (c) making a Frenchman the king of Spain.
   (d) having King Louis XIII become Holy Roman Emperor.

9. In 1772, Russia, Prussia, and Austria agreed on the first partition of

   (a) Italy.
   (b) Germany.
   (c) Palestine.
   (d) Poland.

10. Revocation of the Edict of Nantes hurt France because

    (a) Huguenots held violent protests.
    (b) Catholics lost their religious freedoms.
    (c) thousands of productive citizens left France.
    (d) other nations formed an alliance against France.

V. Thought Questions

Directions: Answer the following questions in essay form.

1. Describe two factors that led to the rise of nation-states in Europe.

2. Absolutism was characteristic of many European monarchs.

   A. Define absolutism.
   B. Describe one example of absolutism as practiced by each of the following monarchs: (1) Henry VIII, (2) Louis XIV, and (3) Philip II.
   C. Did absolutism help or hinder the growth of nation-states? Explain by presenting two reasons for your opinion.

3. A nation's foreign policy often depends on what it sees as its own self-interest. Support this statement by describing one action taken by each of the following:

   A. Elizabeth I
   B. Cardinal Richelieu
   C. Philip II

4. Define "enlightened despotism."

   A. Name one enlightened despot and his/her country.
   B. Would you like this person as your ruler? Explain.

CHAPTER 11

The Growth of Democracy in England

In the United States the right to vote and the right to enjoy freedom of religion and other basic freedoms are things we seem to take for granted. Such rights are part of the system of government we know as **democracy**. The evolution and growth of this kind of system took place over the course of many centuries, mainly in England. As the twentieth century began, there were very few democracies in the world. Most of the world's people lived under other forms of government. As the twentieth century comes to a close now, during the 1990s, the number of democracies has increased. However, the total number of people living under democratic governments is still less than half of the world's population.

If we go back to the seventeenth century, the comparison between democratic governments and other kinds of governments was even more tilted. Indeed, there were no nations at the start of that century that could be called democracies! Most countries or nation-states were ruled by kings or queens. And as we have seen, several of them practiced absolutism in one form or another. By the end of the seventeenth century, however, there was one nation where the change from government by monarchs to government by the people had taken a bold step forward. This was England. Such a political change was so revolutionary for the 1600s that we can label this development in England the English Revolution. It was followed by similar revolutions in North America and in France in the 1700s.

Because the progress toward democracy in seventeenth-century England was so significant, we will devote this entire chapter to examining it. A good way to begin is to define the word democracy. It may be thought of as a system of government that has two basic features:

1. *Popular Sovereignty:* The people have the freedom to choose those who govern. Generally, they elect representatives to carry out their wishes.
2. *Equality and Respect for the Individual:* Each person has specific freedoms and rights that are protected by the government.

Pre-Seventeenth-Century Historical Background

Like a garden, democracy takes a long time to grow and must be cultivated. It requires care, nourishment, and much attention by both those who govern and those who are governed. Its earliest seeds were planted in Ancient Greece and Rome. Regrettably, its growth was hurt by the rise of tyrannical and autocratic governments later in the Roman Empire and by the feudalism of the Middle Ages. It was unable to blossom under conditions connected with the expansion of royal power and absolutism, as we have just studied. Why, then, did it ever so slowly ripen in England during the seventeenth century, prior to its gaining life elsewhere? Part of the answer lies with the roots planted in English soil prior to that period. Let us review this background.

Jury Systems

The idea of a trial by jury began under King Henry II (r. 1154–1189). The early juries were not strict trial juries in the modern sense, but were rather a group of twelve sworn witnesses who were summoned into a royal court. The royal courts were established originally as a means of strengthening the King's authority.

Chapter 11 Chronology

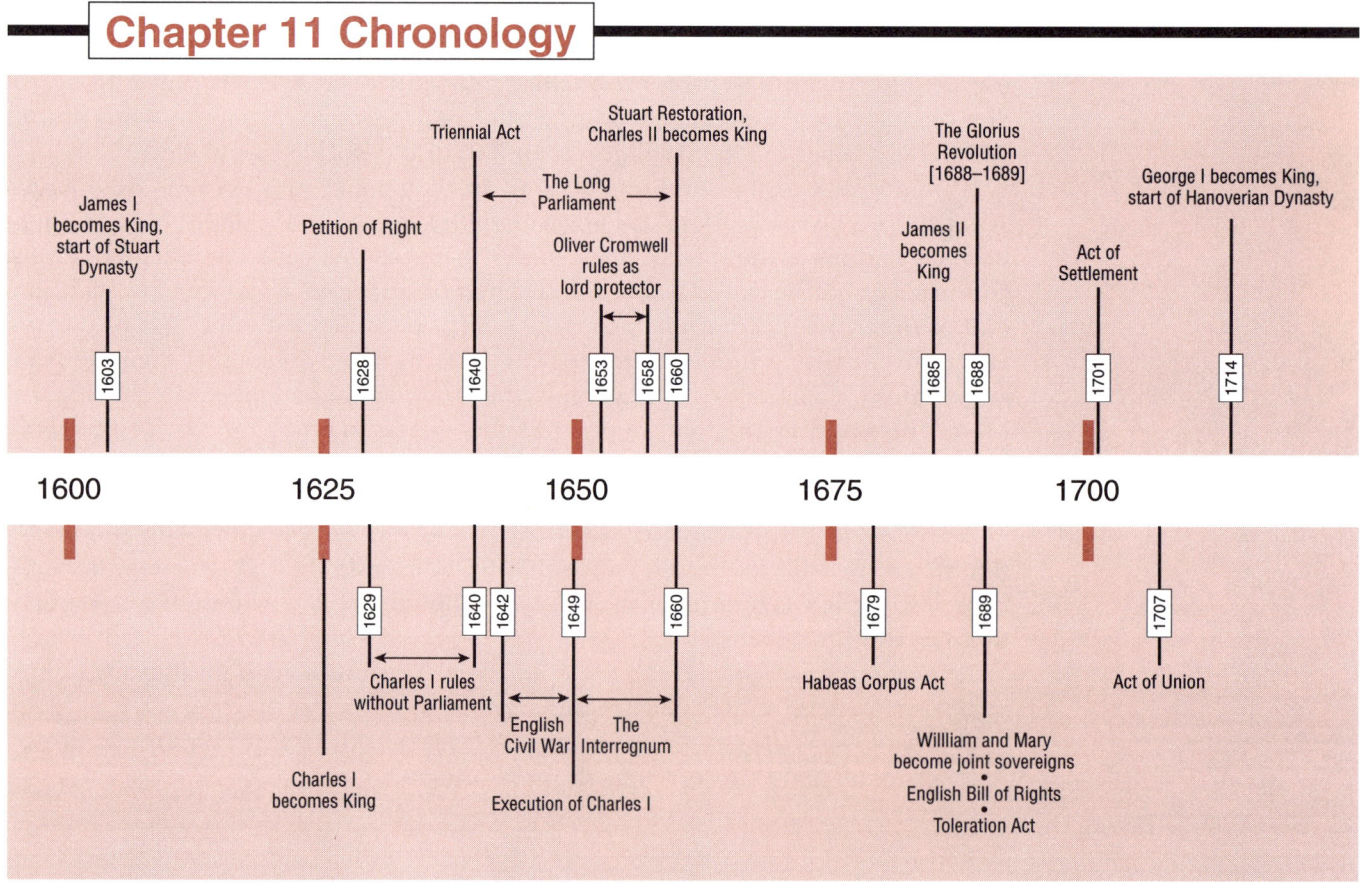

Limit on Royal Power

The **Magna Carta** (Great Charter) was signed by King John I in 1215. (See Chapter 5, "Medieval Europe.") It placed limits on the King's power to imprision people and to levy taxes. It stated, "No freeman shall be imprisoned...unless by the lawful judgment of his peers and by the law of the land." The King needed the consent of the Great Council, an advisory body composed of England's leading nobles and bishops, in order to raise taxes. This body was to evolve eventually into **Parliament**. The Magna Carta established the principle that the King was not above the law; like his subjects, he had to obey the law.

Legislative Power

The Great Council gained more power under the rule of King Edward I. In 1295, he decied to include members of the middle class, the burgesses (representatives of the towns), and knights of the shire (small landowners). When this enlarged Great Council met, it became known as the Model Parliament. For many years afterwards, all parliamentary meetings included representatives of all these groups. Parliament was eventually divided into two parts, the House of Lords (nobles and clergymen) and the House of Commons (burgesses and knights). Even though members of the Lords did not have to face elections and members of the Commons were elected by only a small portion of the population, the very existence of Parliament was nevertheless an important step toward representative government and therefore popular sovereignty in England.

Judicial Power

During the later Middle Ages (1000–1500), the decisions of judges were written down, collected, and became the basis for future legal decisions. These common practices and legal decisions, which were based on judges' conclusions rather than on a code of laws passed by a legislature, formed a body of law known as common law. The English common law, or judge-made law, involving both civil and criminal cases, was held to apply equally to all people.

The Beginning of Stuart Absolutism: Conflict Between the Crown and Parliament

The democratic advances described above did not make England a true democracy. However, they did enable Parliament to have some say in the affairs of the nation. It was generally accepted that passage of laws required the consent of Parliament and agreement by the monarch. And as long as monarchs respected this situation, even though they may not have always liked it, bitter clashes between the crown and Parliament were avoided. Even the most popular and powerful of the Tudor rulers, Henry VIII and Elizabeth I, sought to consult Parliament on important matters. This relationship between the chief parts of the English government worsened after the death of Queen Elizabeth in 1603.

As she died without any heirs, the crown passed to her cousin, King James VI of Scotland. He was the son of Mary, Queen of Scots, and a member of the Stuart family. Mary's grandmother, Margaret Tudor, had married into the Stuart family. And as Margaret was the sister of Henry VIII, father of Elizabeth, Elizabeth and James were therefore related. (See chart below, which shows sovereigns of England and Scotland.) James now became King James I of England as well as King of

THE TUDOR, STUART, AND HANOVERIAN SOVEREIGNS OF ENGLAND AND SCOTLAND

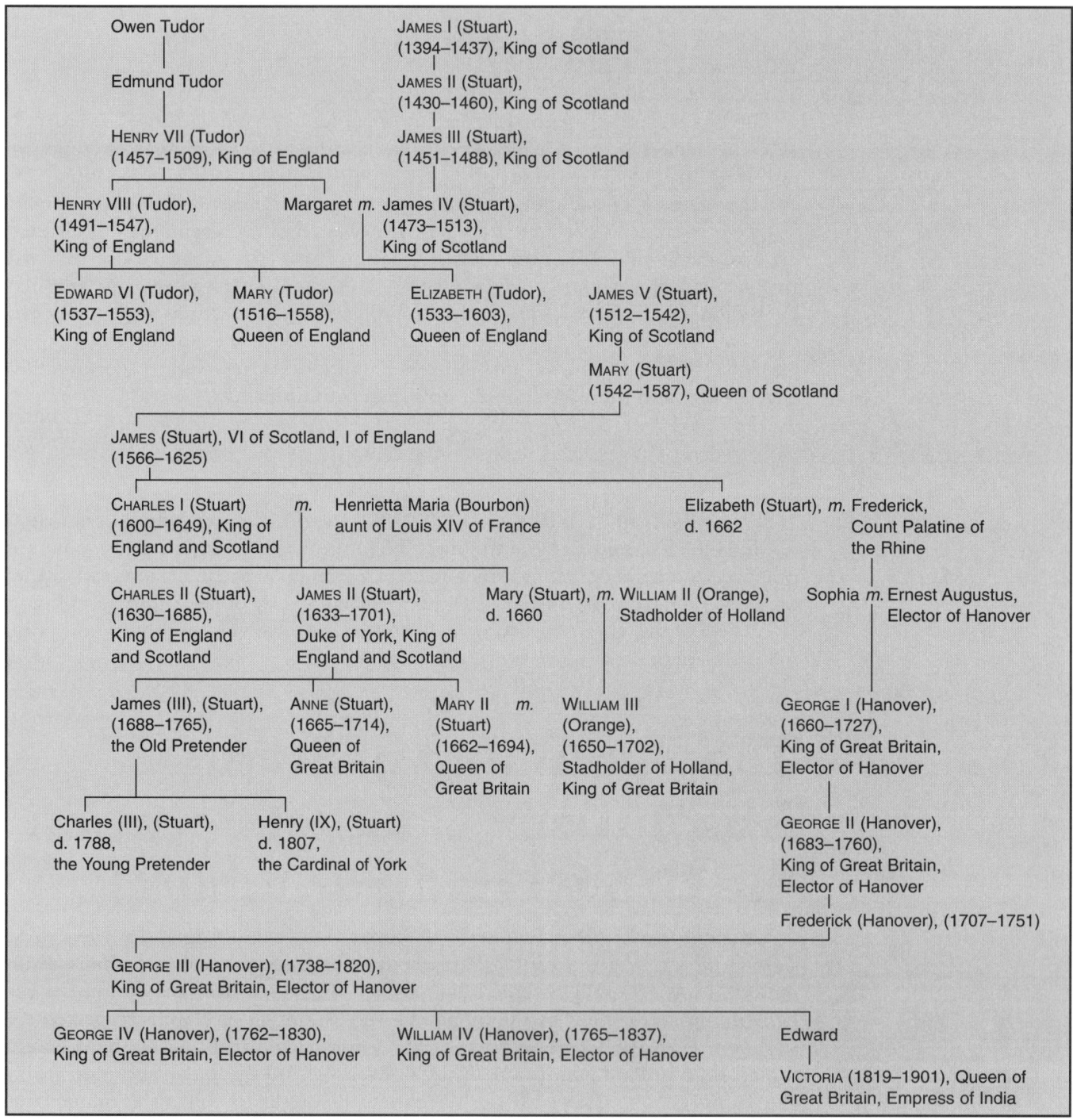

Scotland (r. 1603–1625). The English became distrustful of James soon after he ascended to the throne because he was a foreigner, from Scotland, with a strange accent and undignified manner. Although well educated, particularly in theology, James was not thought to have much common sense. King Henry IV of France had called him "the wisest fool in Christendom."

The Rule of James I

James I ruled as an absolute monarch. He did not respect the democratic traditions that had evolved in England, distrusted Parliament, and claimed to rule by **divine right**. He believed that God had ordained kings to rule. He summarized his concept of government with the Latin phrase, "*a deo rex, a rege lex,*" "the king is from God, and law from the king." With such attitudes, James was to face troubles during his reign. They occurred mainly in three areas: religion, money, and foreign policy.

As head of the Anglican (English) Church, James could appoint all bishops. The bishops wanted a certain amount of uniformity in religious services. Both James and the bishops were concerned about the activities of the Puritans. The Puritans objected to the standards wanted by the bishops, and felt that the Anglican service was too similar to Catholic ways. The Puritans wanted to "purify" the Church of what they considered "popish" practices. James' support of the bishops made the Puritans fear that James was determined to bring the English Church back to Roman Catholicism with control by the pope. James saw the Puritans as a threat to England's political unity and imprisoned Puritan writers who criticized the bishops. Tension increased when James proclaimed that clergymen who refused to conduct services according to the Anglican Prayer Book would be dismissed. With bitterness, thousands of Puritans left England. Some went to Holland and then to North America, where they founded the Massachusetts colony at Plymouth in 1620.

There was one request of the Puritans that James did grant early in his reign. This was for a new translation of the Bible. Upon his orders, the work was completed by a committee in 1611. It was based on original Greek and Hebrew texts, the Latin Vulgate, and various English translations. Known as the King James version, it is considered one of the greatest prose works in the English language and is still used today.

In monetary matters, James was far from being a thrifty monarch. He spent lavishly and frequently found himself asking Parliament for money. Parliament often refused to give him everything he wanted, based on its dislike of him and his ways of ruling. He then angered Parliament by raising money without its approval, increasing taxes on imports and selling titles of nobility.

Some of the tension with Parliament might have been diminished if James had been more agreeable in the field of foreign affairs. Unfortunately, his attempt to create greater friendship with Catholic Spain proved to be very unpopular. His 1604 peace treaty with that country was criticized by Englishmen who bore a general dislike of Spain from the past, and particularly by those merchants in the House of Commons who were profiting from raids on Spanish commerce. In addition, James provoked controversy when he sought to have his son Charles marry a Spanish princess. The House of Commons spoke out against this, preferring that Charles marry a Protestant, and issued in 1621 the Great Protestation. Incensed by this action, James tore up the document, dissolved Parliament, and imprisoned four of its leaders. The marriage never occurred, and Parliament was ultimately called back into session. A basis had now been laid for Parliament's growing power in the making of foreign policy.

The Rule of Charles I

When James died in 1625, there was hardly any sorrow. He was succeeded by his son, Charles I (r. 1625–1649). Little did this twenty-five-year-old new monarch realize it, but his reign was to be the most disastrous in English history. He inherited a harsh set of problems from his father, amid an atmosphere of friction, and he made no attempt to resolve these problems peacefully or to cool down political tempers. Like his father, Charles I was a believer in the divine right of kings and ruled in an arrogant, absolutist manner. His marriage to a French princess, who was Catholic, alarmed Puritans. Under her influence, he relaxed some of the penal laws against Catholics. Parliament began to question whether, even though he was an Anglican, Charles would maintain England as a Protestant nation.

In the first two years of his rule, Charles dissolved Parliament twice. He was upset with its refusal to grant him all the monies he wanted and was worried that his chief adviser would be removed from office. He began to raise money by forcing loans from wealthy subjects and by quartering troops in private homes at the homeowners' expense. Desperate for even more money for his expenditures both at home and abroad, Charles summoned Parliament in 1628. In exchange for granting him more revenues (money), parliament made Charles agree to the Petition of Right. This historic document laid down some of the basic rules of modern constitutional government. With its limitations on royal power, it has even been referred to as the "Stuart Magna Carta." Its main provisions stated that the crown could not:

1. Tax without the consent of Parliament;
2. Place soldiers in private homes without permission; nor
3. Imprison people without a specific charge and a trial.

Hardly had the ink dried on this document than Charles began to ignore it. He began to collect some monies not authorized by Parliament. John Eliot, a parliamentary leader who wrote resolutions of protest against the monarch, was arrested and imprisoned in the Tower of London, where he died. In 1629, Charles dissolved Parliament and did not summon it for the next eleven years. During these years, 1629 to 1640, he continued to violate the provisions of the Petition of Right. One of his more notorious measures was the creation of a royal court called the Star Chamber. Here, he would have his own judges secretly try individuals who disagreed with him. Common law guidelines were not followed, nor were juries used. Many of those who suffered under Star Chamber proceedings were Puritans. Puritans and others who did not conform to Anglican Church practices, as directed by Charles in his role as head of the Church, experienced persecution.

The Long Parliament and the English Civil War

The eventual downfall of Charles I was hastened by events involving both Scotland and Ireland. When Charles attempted to impose Anglican Church organization and rituals in Scotland, he met armed opposition from the Scots. The Scots, who were Presbyterians, stopped Charles's forces from invading their territory. The Scots were willing to fight to preserve their religious freedom. Charles saw their actions as a rebellion and thus summoned a new parliament in 1640 to request funds for an army to fight the Scots. This parliament would meet periodically until 1660 and was therefore called the Long Parliament. It did give Charles, in 1640, the money he wanted, but only after it did the following:

1. Abolished the Star Chamber court;
2. Had two of Charles's chief advisers jailed; and
3. Passed the Triennial Act. This act stated that Parliament was to meet at least once every three years.

These were further checks on the power of royal absolutism and could be seen as additions to the power of Parliament. Such additions came about mainly because Charles recognized Parliament's power of the purse, the ability to raise and provide money.

Although he was able to put down the Scots, Charles then faced a rebellion in 1641 by the Irish. Most of Ireland was Catholic, but under the English crown. Over the years, the northern region of Ulster had been settled by many English and Scottish people. This Anglo-Irish minority grew wealthy, increased its control in the island, and was resented by the majority of native Irish. When this resentment broke out in a rebellion, Charles anticipated leading an army into Ireland to fight the Irish. Uncertain whether to finance an army under Charles for this purpose, Parliament drew up a document, the Grand Remonstrance, containing its many complaints against the king. Charles responded by personally leading an armed force into Parliament in order to arrest five opposition leaders. As the five had been forewarned, they were not present on that day. Having to leave the building without arresting them, Charles reportedly said, "The birds have flown." In the summer of 1642, he moved north of London and raised an army. Parliament took over the government and announced it would raise its own army in preparation for the coming military conflict.

This conflict escalated into the English Civil War, 1642 to 1649. The central issue was whether sovereignty, the power to govern the nation, should be in the hands of the king or Parliament. Although people of every class were on each side, supporters of the king included mostly nobles, wealthy landowners, Anglican and Catholic clergy, and citizens who were against the Puritans for political and religious reasons. Collectively, these supporters were referred to as cavaliers. They were given this name because many leaders of the royal cause were from the king's cavalry, wore fine clothing, and let their hair fall over their shoulders. Parliament's support came primarily from merchants, farmers, small landowners, and the Puritans. They were known as the roundheads, because they cut their hair short and wore it underneath their helments. They received additional support from the Scots. Although the political fate of the nation was at stake, most Englishmen remained neutral. It has been estimated that less than 3 percent of the population was under arms during the fighting.

The fighting at first was a stalemate, but eventually the parliamentary forces won decisively at the battles of Marston Moor (1644) and Naseby (1645). Charles surrendered to the Scots in 1646 and was given over to Parliament in 1647. Why did the cav-

Territory controlled by the king and territory controlled by Parliament, 1642.

aliers lose the war? The chief reason was that Charles's forces really had to fight two armies—that of Scotland and that of Parliament. In addition, there was no one on the royalist side who could match the leadership of the Puritan, Oliver Cromwell (1599–1658). He reorganized most of the parliamentary forces into the new model army. A tall, powerful, heavyset person with a square jaw, Cromwell developed a force of well-trained, disciplined, religious-inspired fighters. He once remarked: "I think that he that prays and preaches best will fight best." His men were known to go into battle chanting psalms.

Even though Charles had surrendered, a serious political problem arose in the victorious Parliament. A split existed between a moderate group and a more radical group. The moderates were willing to place the King back on the throne with strict limitations. They were Anglicans and Presbyterians who wished to have some kind of uniformity and formality. They were opposed by a radical group that severely distrusted Charles. The radicals included Cromwell and many members of the new model army. They were of many different religious beliefs. Known as the independents, they were opposed to the goals of the moderates. They felt that they had fought to establish complete religious freedom. In December 1648, the independents moved in a forceful way. They had Colonel Pride lead soldiers into the House of Commons to exclude all members who did not agree with them. When Pride's Purge was finished, only sixty members remained—all independents. These remaining members, once part of the Long Parliament, were now known as the Rump Parliament. They declared that they represented the people of England, when in reality, their authority rested upon the support of the army.

Moving quickly, they accused Charles I of treason and placed him on trial. Without offering any defense other than to protest his being tried under any authority, Charles was found guilty and was beheaded on January 30, 1649. This act of regicide, the killing of a king, stirred deep emotions throughout the nation. This was particularly so as Charles had shown dignity and courage while quietly praying as he faced his executioner on that fateful January day. Also, it is doubtful whether the Rump Parliament's actions had the support of the nation. Indeed, Charles the Martyr soon became more popular than Charles the King. Curiously, for many people, the sympathetic reaction to his death cancelled out the resentment of his harsh qualities. Already, a wish slowly arose for restoration of the Stuart line. The Rump Parliament, however, would have none of this and proceeded to create a new political order. Clearly, Cromwell had won the day. Royalists had lost their power.

The Interregnum: England as a Commonwealth and then a Protectorate, 1649–1660

The first signs of a new political order came with the decision by the Rump Parliament to abolish the monarchy and the House of Lords. England was now to experience an interruption in the pattern of centuries-old rule by a monarch. This period of interruption was to last for eleven years, 1649 to 1660, and became known as the **interregnum**. In place of a monarchy, England was declared to be a **commonwealth**. In this situation, a commonwealth may be defined as a government that is a

Cromwell, who led an army of well-trained, religious fighters in the new model army. Here he is seen dissolving the Long Parliament.

republic; the power to govern rests with Parliament and a council of state. In reality, the governing power here rested with Cromwell. And his basis of support was the army. England had become a military dictatorship.

Cromwell and the army began to face problems with the Rump Parliament. It was replaced by another parliament that was dissolved in 1653. Thus ended the commonwealth. A constitution was now drawn up by the army, known as the Instrument of Government. It provided for executive power to be exercised by someone in the new position of lord protector. And, of course, it was Cromwell who became lord protector. England now was a **protectorate**. Did the nation benefit from Cromwell's rule during both the commonwealth and protectorate periods?

For answers, we need to look at his deeds, both domestic (within England) and foreign. A strict moral tone was established in England in accordance with Puritan ideals. Outlawed were such things as gambling, dancing, and horse races. Theaters were closed. In matters of religious freedom, his record was mixed, although generally tolerant. He extended protection to the new sect of Quakers, and permitted Jews to return to England by reversing the exclusion policy that had been in effect since 1290. Yet he did give some property of the Anglican Church to Puritans and prohibited use of the Anglican Prayer Book. Roman Catholics were placed under certain restrictions, but penalties against them were rarely enforced in England.

Catholics in Ireland saw a very ugly side of Cromwell as a result of political and religious factors. A rebellion against English rule broke out there in 1650. Cromwell ruthlessly suppressed it, leading an army himself throughout the island. Thousands of Irish people were killed and some were sent into forced labor to British colonies in the West Indies. Hundreds of Catholic priests were, as Cromwell put it, "knocked on the head." Much land was taken and given to followers of Cromwell. Cromwell's acts were bitterly embedded in the Irish people's memory. "The curse of Cromwell on you!" remains one of the worst things you can say to someone you do not like.

In foreign affairs, Cromwell sought to build up English commerce while taking actions against Holland and Spain. He had Parliament pass the Navigation Act of 1651, requiring that imports into England be carried in English ships or in ships from the nation producing the goods. This hurt the Dutch, as their ships had made much profit from carrying goods across the seas. In a short, inconclusive war against the Dutch, the English navy performed ably.

As lord protector, Cromwell never enjoyed support by the majority of his subjects. Insurrections against him occurred in some parts of the country. His ruling under martial (military) law for a while violated the Petition of Right. To finance this and some other actions, he authorized a tax without Parliament's consent. In doing these things, he was committing the kind of injustices that he had criticized when they were committed by the king. Upon his death in 1658, his son Richard became lord protector. Unable to provide effective leadership, Richard resigned his post. The mood in England seemed willing to welcome the return of monarchy. The Long Parliament met and issued an invitation to become king to the son of Charles I who was living in exile abroad. He accepted, and in May 1660, he entered London as King Charles II. The monarchy had been restored.

The Stuart Restoration, 1660–1688

The reign of Charles II (r. 1660–1685) was characterized by a decline in absolutism and a willingness to get along with Parliament. Fully mindful of his father's fate and Cromwell's problems during the Interregnum, Charles promised to abide by the Magna Carta and the Petition of Right. He moved quickly to end the restrictions on activities that had been imposed during Cromwell's rule. Although he had pro-Catholic sympathies, he wisely refrained from letting these influence his public actions. His desire to permit complete religious toleration was not, curiously enough, shared by Parliament. In 1673, with passage of the Test Act, only persons who joined the Anglican Church could vote, hold public office, attend universities, and assemble. Although this legislation narrowed a person's freedom of religion, another law did much to expand a person's rights as an accused in a court of law. The Habeas Corpus Act of 1679 stated that an arrested person could get a writ or court order and be brought before a judge within a certain period of time to hear the charges against him or her. The order was called a writ of habeas corpus. The court would then determine whether the accused should go free or stand trial. The Habeas Corpus Act, which was carried over into American law, provided protection for an individual against unlawful, arbitrary arrest and imprisonment. The purpose of the act was to create a check on the power of the monarch.

In foreign affairs, as in domestic affairs, Charles was careful not to anger Parliament or do anything that would place his crown in danger. He maintained Cromwell's commercial and trade policies and was able to reduce the sea power of the rival Dutch. This was one result of the Anglo-Dutch War of 1664 to 1667; another result was the taking of Dutch New Amsterdam in North America and changing its name to New York, in honor of Charles' brother James, the Duke of York.

Two peaceful political developments that occurred during the reign of Charles II were unwritten but have since become part of both English and American government practices:

1. Charles appointed five men from Parliament to serve as his major advisers. This small group turned out be the forerunner of the cabinet system.
2. In Parliament, two groups emerged with different ideas and interests. These were the Tories and the Whigs. This emergence marked the beginning of political parties.

The Tories were mainly Anglicans, tolerant of Catholics, and preferred a strong but not absolute hereditary monarchy. The Whigs were very anti-Catholic and wanted a weak monarch with a powerful parliament. The formation of these two groups was

Charles II ruled carefully to avoid his father's fate. He made many reforms in England. Here he is welcomed to England by his court.

sparked mainly by the realization that Charles would die without a legitimate child as heir, and that the likely successor would be a Catholic, his brother James.

When Charles died in 1685, his brother did come to the throne as King James II (r. 1685–1688). Although he was taller and more handsome than Charles, he nevertheless lacked his brother's charm as well as his cleverness and respect for history. James had two distinct goals:

1. To rule as an absolute monarch; and
2. To reestablish the Roman Catholic Church in England.

Both of these were clearly unpopular policies; their pursuit by James were the reasons why his reign was one of the shortest in English history.

In 1687, he issued a Declaration of Indulgences without consulting Parliament. Although this document guaranteed religious toleration for all groups, both Tories and Whigs in Parliament viewed it as a cover for promoting Catholicism and felt that the King should have obtained their consent. Further tension was in the air when James ignored the Test Act of 1673 and appointed Catholics to high positions in the army and at Oxford University. Displeasure and fear greeted his creation of a standing army of thirty thousand men, placing it near London in what appeared to be an attempt to intimidate his critics. Fear also gripped Parliament when James's second wife, a Catholic, gave birth to a son. It was assumed that this son's ascent to the throne would lead to a line of Catholic monarchs in a predominantly Protestant nation. To prevent a Stuart Catholic Dynasty, a group of Tory and Whig leaders wrote to the Dutch ruler, the Protestant William of Orange, inviting him to become King of England.

The Glorious Revolution, 1688–1689

William was married to Mary Stuart, a Protestant daughter of James II by his first wife. William himself was the son of the sister of Charles II and James II. (See chart on page 240 that shows sovereigns of England and Scotland.) William accepted Parliament's offer and landed in England with a large army in November 1688. As William advanced toward London, he was greeted by throngs of people and scores of government officials. Deserted by many of his closest followers, James tried to escape on a ship for France but was captured by some fishermen. He was brought to London, and he was afraid that he would be executed. William, having arrived in London without any opposition, now made a smart political decision. He did not have James beheaded, but rather let him flee to France in exile. William did not want to make a martyr and hero of James as had happened when Cromwell had Charles I executed. In France, James received a palace and a pension from King Louis XIV. James was thus permitted to keep his head, but not his throne. Without bloodshed, the English had now made a change in the monarchy—a bloodless revolution had been accomplished.

William's acceptance of the English crown had less to do with his wanting power and more to do with his desire to obtain England as an ally of his native Holland against the France of Louis XIV. On February 13, 1689, he and his wife were officially proclaimed King William III and Queen Mary II (r. 1689–1694). (After his wife's death, William continued to rule until his death in 1702.) Their becoming joint sovereigns, or rulers, was the climax to several active steps taken by

William III and Mary II became joint sovereigns of England through the parliamentary law that became the English Bill of Rights.

Parliament after the initial invitation. It had declared the throne officially vacant as James had "abdicated the government," broken "the original contract between king and people," and had "withdrawn himself out of the kingdom." The crown was then offered to William and Mary on condition that they agree to be bound by a "declaration of right." Having secured agreement, Parliament soon drew up a formal law including this declaration. This law became famous as the English Bill of Rights (1689).

In deposing (removing) James II and placing William and Mary on the throne, Parliament clearly established its right to dethrone and enthrone a monarch. This was the crushing deathblow to the theory of the divine right of kings and queens. From this point on, all authority would be centered in Parliament. This key political concept was authenticated and spelled out in the Bill of Rights, along with rights important for the protection of individual liberties. The chief provisions of this document can be read as restrictions on the power of the king or queen as an absolute monarch. The king or queen may not:

1. Make or suspend laws without the consent of Parliament;
2. Keep a standing army nor levy taxes without the consent of Parliament;
3. Interfere with parliamentary debates and elections;
4. Deny a jury trial to anyone accused of a crime;
5. Inflict cruel or unusual punishments; nor
6. Deny people the right to petition.

Other provisions require that Parliament meet frequently, and that for a person to become the monarch, he or she must neither be a Catholic nor have married a Catholic.

The Bill of Rights now resolved the issue of the relationship beween monarch and Parliament. From 1689 onward, no English king or queen ever tried to govern without the consent of Parliament. Therefore, we can call England a limited or constitutional monarchy. This means that a king or queen sits on the throne, but that person's powers are limited by a written constitution as well as by unwritten traditional practices. The monarch reigns but does not rule.

Although the Glorious Revolution of 1688 to 1689 made some enormous strides, it left certain issues unresolved. Some undemocratic features remained. There were limits, for example, on religious freedom. The Toleration Act of 1689 permitted freedom of worship to all Christians, except for Catholics. This meant that all Protestants, Anglicans, and non-Anglicans could worship freely. And as long as Catholics and other religious groups such as Jews and Unitarians remained loyal to the government, they did not, in reality, suffer any interference. Another undemocratic feature was the makeup of Parliament. Its members were nobles and wealthy landowners and merchants. There were no women or commoners. Very few people had the right to vote. The members of Parliament in the seventeenth century wanted to reduce the monarch's power but were not interested in letting the great mass of people have a voice in choosing and running the government. Also, the House of Lords' membership was based on heredity and the Lords had equal power with the elected House of Commons. For all these reasons, the English Revolution of the seventeenth century may properly be labeled an aristocratic revolution.

In the years following the dramatic events of 1688 to 1689, there were additional political developments of note concerning England. James II went to Ireland, where he led a rebellion against English rule, hoping to retake the throne. After his defeat at the Battle of the Boyne, Parliament enacted severe restrictions on the majority Catholic population of Ireland. Catholics could not buy or inherit property from Protestants and could not run for election to the Irish parliament. That body, under control of London, would consist only of people from the Anglo-Irish Protestant minority. These policies added to the resentment felt in Ireland toward England.

To avoid future problems regarding succession to the throne, the English passed the Act of Settlement in 1701. Passage was prompted by the fact that there were no children born to William and Mary. The chief provisions were the following:

1. Mary's sister Anne would become queen.
2. If Anne should die without heirs, the crown would go to the Protestant Sophia of Hanover and her heirs. Sophia was the granddaughter of James I and had married into the German House of Hanover.
3. All future English monarchs had to be members of the Anglican Church and could not belong to any other Protestant groups.

Although Queen Anne (r. 1702–1714) had seventeen children, none of them survived her. At her death, and with Sophia of Hanover dead, the crown was given to Sophia's son who became King George I (r. 1714–1727). (See chart on page 240 that shows sovereigns of England and Scotland.) Both he and his successor, George II (r. 1727–1760), spoke very little English, were unfamiliar with the workings of English society, and were willing to depend heavily on their advisers—the cabinet. The result was an even further decline in royal power and an increase in the power of the cabinet and Parliament. This pattern, as it progressed in the reign of George III (r. 1760–1820) and thereafter, will be taken up in Chapter 20, "Advances in British Democracy."

The descendants of George I have ruled to the present and have taken the dynastic name the House of Windsor. George's official title at his coronation was King of Great Britain and Ireland. The reason for this was passage of the Act of Union in 1707 by the parliaments of the kingdoms of Scotland and England. Scotland was now merged with England, which also had control over Wales and Ireland; the new kingdom could now be called Great Britain or the United Kingdom (U.K.). The English Parliament could now be called the British Parliament. In the 1990s, for reasons about which we will learn, the United Kingdom consists of England, Wales, Scotland, and Ulster (Northern Ireland).

Political Ideas in Seventeenth-Century England

To understand a writer's ideas about politics and government, we first have to know something about the times when he or she lived. Since we now have learned about the historic political events in seventeenth-century England, we can examine carefully the thoughts of two major writers from that time. They are Thomas Hobbes (1588–1679) and John Locke (1632–1704). They stand at opposite ends of political philosophy from each other.

Hobbes published *Leviathan* in 1651, two years after Charles I was beheaded and amid much political tension. Hobbes was very pessimistic about the behavior of human beings. He felt that by themselves, in a pure state of nature, without any controlling authority, in a condition of anarchy, they were selfish and would do bad things to each other. People would thus be in a continuous state of war. The only way to resolve this bad situation was for people to agree with each other to give up "all their power and strength upon one man, or upon one assembly of men, that may reduce all their wills,…into one will." What would be formed would be a very strong government, a leviathan, with absolute and undivided powers. Hobbes was a defender of absolutism. He was a supporter of Charles I and has even been seen as establishing a set of justifications for twentieth-century totalitarian dictators.

John Locke published the *Two Treatises of Government* in 1690, having lived through the Glorious Revolution. Locke's view of humans differed from that of Hobbes. In a state of nature, Locke thought humans would be basically good and not engaged in constant warfare. They would agree with each other, in a social contract, to set up a government "for their comfortable, safe, and peaceful living . . . in a secure enjoyment of their properties." In creating this government, people would give up some rights but keep many others. These others were natural rights, such as the rights to life, liberty, and property. Government existed to protect these rights, as part of its contractual promises. If government failed in its responsibilities, then the people had the right to resist it and overthrow it. For Locke, the power of government was not absolute. That power was based upon the consent of the governed. These theories would explain why it was proper for Parliament to depose James II and to make itself more powerful in dealings with the monarchy. Although Locke died before 1776, he is considered to be a founding father of the American Revolution. His ideas were known to Thomas Jefferson and found their way into the American Declaration of Independence.

Summary

The growth of democracy in England, particularly as seen in the seventeenth century, has had a worldwide influence. The advances we have described influenced political revolutions in the British colonies in North America (1776) and in France (1789). (See Chapter 13, "The French Revolution.") Democratic ideals also affected the emergence of several nations from imperialism in the twentieth century, India being a good example. A trend toward democracy has also been evident in the closing years of the current century, mainly in Eastern Europe.

In our own nation, we should remember that a major factor in the American Revolution was the emphasis by colonists on their "rights as Englishmen." Indeed, many democratic ideas and political practices developed in England were included in American documents—the English Bill of Rights is similar to the U.S. Constitution and Bill of Rights and Locke's ideas can be found in the Declaration of Independence.

And finally, we should mention two famous American sites that are reminders of the Glorious Revolution. They are both in the state of Virginia. They are Williamsburg and the College of William and Mary. Whether or not you have visited these places, you now know something about the origins of their names.

CHAPTER 11

Review Exercises

I. Matching

Directions: Match the words in Column A with the *correct description* in Column B.

Column A
1. sovereignty
2. roundhead
3. regicide
4. interregnum
5. cavalier
6. lord protector
7. Stuart
8. Hanover
9. cabinet
10. habeas corpus

Column B
(a) supporter of the king during the English Civil War
(b) killing of a king
(c) power to govern a nation
(d) supporter of Parliament during the English Civil War
(e) period of years without a king
(f) the right of an accused person to be told of the charges brought against him/her
(g) title given to Oliver Cromwell
(h) group of advisers to the king
(i) dynastic name for James I and James II
(j) dynastic name for George I and George III

II. Famous People

Directions: Use the names below to complete the following sentences.

Charles I
Charles II
Oliver Cromwell
James I

James II
Thomas Hobbes
William III
John Locke

1. _____ was a King whose period of rule was known as the restoration.

2. _____ as the author of *Leviathan,* was a defender of absolutism.

3. _____ came from Holland to become King of England.

4. _____ ruled England even though he was not a king.

5. _____ was beheaded after the English Civil War.

6. _____ , as the author of *Two Treatises of Government,* believed that the power of a government should be based upon the consent of the governed.

7. _____ was deposed during the Glorious Revolution.

8. _____ was a ruler in Scotland, who became King of England in 1603.

III. Map Exercise

Directions: Use the map to locate the place associated with each of the following statements. For each statement, write the *letter* of the place. (An answer may be repeated.)

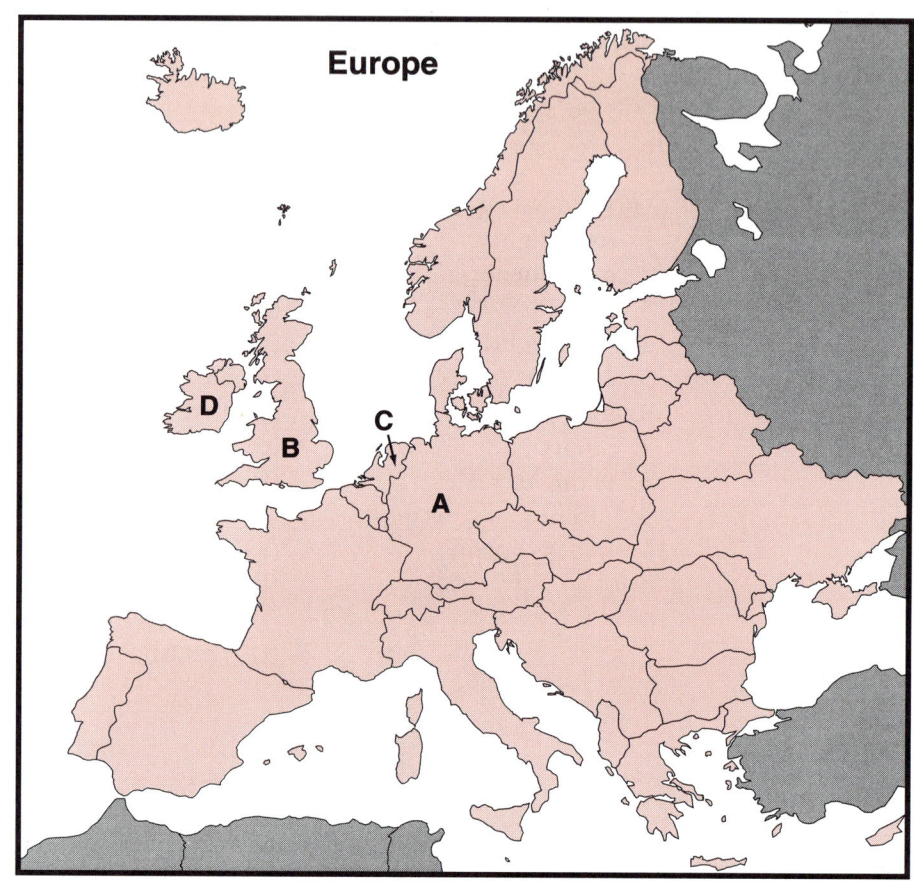

1. _____ Regicide occurred here, in 1649.

2. _____ William and Mary were rulers here, on the European continent.

3. _____ The battle of Marston Moor was fought here.

4. _____ Many Puritans, fearing James I, left here for Holland and for the "New World."

5. _____ The Battle of the Boyne was fought here.

6. _____ Original homeland of King George I.

7. _____ The roundheads and cavaliers fought here.

8. _____ Site of a rebellion against the English, ruthlessly put down by Oliver Cromwell.

IV. Matching

Directions: Match the law in Column A with its *correct effect* in Column B.

Column A
1. Petition of Right
2. Triennial Act
3. Toleration Act
4. Act of Settlement
5. Instrument of Government Act
6. Act of Union
7. Magna Carta
8. Habeas Corpus Act
9. Bill of Rights
10. Test Act

Column B
(a) freedom of worship for all Protestant religions
(b) an arrested person can defend himself/herself
(c) people are protected from cruel and unusual punishment
(d) the king could not quarter soldiers in a home
(e) provided for succession to the throne if William and Mary died without having children
(f) concerned with meetings of Parliament
(g) gave special privileges to Anglican Church member
(h) affected political ties between Scotland and England
(i) earliest check on the power of the monarch
(j) enabled Cromwell to obtain great executive power

V. Multiple Choice

Directions: Find the *letter* of the correct answer.

1. The "divine right" theory of government had its greatest follower in

(a) John Locke.
(b) James I.
(c) Charles II.
(d) George I.

2. In a constitutional monarchy

(a) the king writes the constitution.
(b) the constitution limits the king's power.
(c) the constitution gives the king unlimited power.
(d) the king is free to rule without the constitution if he so wishes.

3. The Glorious Revolution saw parliament

(a) proclaim William and Mary as joint rulers.
(b) declare war against James I.
(c) offer Charles II the title of Lord Protector.
(d) pass the Instrument of Government Act.

4. The greatest influence on the American Declaration of Independence came from

(a) Thomas Hobbes.
(b) Oliver Cromwell.
(c) James II.
(d) John Locke.

5. Star Chamber proceedings were instituted against

(a) sailors who deserted their ships.
(b) soliders of a defeated nation.
(c) political opponents of the king.
(d) clergymen who supported Parliament during the Glorious Revolution.

6. George Santayana said that those who do not learn from the past are doomed to repeat it. Who showed that he clearly "understood" Santayana's comment?

(a) James I
(b) Oliver Cromwell
(c) Charles II
(d) James II

7. English common law grew out of

   (a) decisions by judges.
   (b) acts of Parliament.
   (c) announcements by the monarch.
   (d) jury verdicts made by commoners.

8. The chief reason for the success of Parliament in its seventeenth-century struggles against the crown was its

   (a) calling for demonstrations by farmers, angry with the king.
   (b) power over money appropriations.
   (c) freedom to debate proposed bills.
   (d) control over newspapers.

9. The Stuart Restoration came about mainly because the Commonwealth under Cromwell had

   (a) imposed Puritan ideas.
   (b) weakened English naval strength.
   (c) lost the thirteen colonies in America.
   (d) caused an economic crisis.

V. Thought Questions

Directions: Answer the following questions in essay form.

1. Write a newspaper story for these headlines:

   A. "Civil War Starts in England"
   B. "Charles I Executed"
   C. "William and Mary Become Joint Sovereigns"

2. Write a conversation between Thomas Hobbes and John Locke on the best kind of government for a nation. Each speaker should explain his point of view and give two reasons for it.

3. Define the word "democracy."

   A. Describe two advances in English democracy by 1700.
   B. Describe two undemocratic features in England that still existed by 1700.
   C. Did the coming of George I to the throne help or hinder democracy in England? Explain.

4. Oliver Cromwell was a controversial person, depending upon the perspective from which he was viewed. Give your opinion of him as if you were

   A. Thomas Hobbes.
   B. John Locke.
   C. a Catholic living in Ireland.
   D. a Puritan.
   E. a member of the new model army.

CHAPTER 12

The Enlightenment and the Scientific Revolution

The Enlightenment as the Age of Reason

The **Enlightenment** was a period in human history when new ideas spread and resulted in great change. You have already studied about the Renaissance, a period when Europeans became more interested in worldly matters and less concerned with religion. The Enlightenment was another such period when European intellectuals awakened themselves to the political, economic, cultural, and social problems of their times and the need for change. The writings of philosophers, scientists, and other thinkers were directed towards finding solutions to the serious political, economic, and social issues that they saw around them. The Enlightenment, also called the **Age of Reason**, began in Europe in the last decades of the seventeenth century and continued to the closing years of the 1700s.

Many of the different thoughts that developed during the Enlightenment were a result of the revived learning that had opened up Western European nations to new ideas in the period of the Renaissance. The ideas developed during the Enlightenment represented an attack on the thought that had existed for centuries, which had controlled all aspects of the political, economic, cultural, and social life in Europe. Reason and nature began to be used to study and explain the workings of human behavior. These new ideas led to calls for basic changes in the ways that governments operated and the rights that the individual had in society. Philosophers during the Enlightenment studied the world as if they were looking at it for the first time. They were no longer held back by traditional beliefs, often based on religion. The Enlightenment thinkers fundamentally believed in the use of science to explain the orderly principles governing the universe. They reasoned that the universe ran according to a series of permanent natural laws. Enlightenment figures also held to the optimistic belief that the world and the human beings who inhabited it could be improved. They thought that the triumph of reason would lead to progress.

The Philosophers Promote Science and Reason

During the Enlightenment those individuals whose writings and other works promoted ideas based on science, natural law, and reason were known as philosophes, a French word for philosopher. The ideas of scientists such as Isaac Newton, who provided the well-reasoned mathematical proofs for what other earlier scientists—Copernicus, Kepler, and Galileo—had proposed, excited European intellectuals. The writings of René Descartes and Pierre Bayle on **rationalism**, which is the principle of accepting reason as the authority for any action; Francis Bacon's **empiricism**, which is the search for knowledge based on observation and experiment; and Benedict de Spinoza's **pantheism**, which is the belief that God is all the laws and forces of the universe, had fostered the belief that reason could be used to find the natural laws that governed a universal order. This confidence in human reason gradually became more accepted in Europe during the eighteenth century and found its way into other areas of the world, especially the Americas, by the later decades of the 1700s.

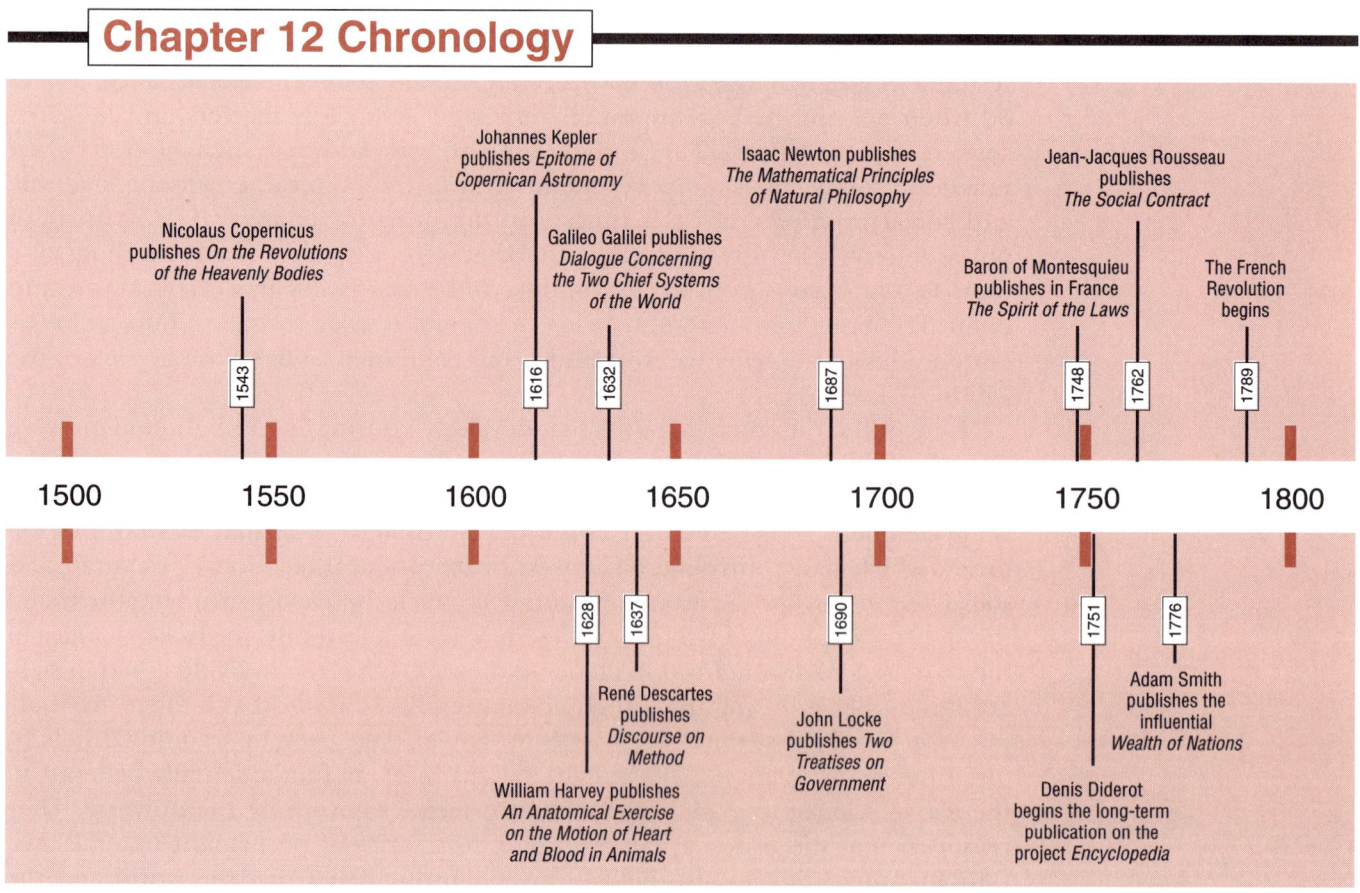

Chapter 12 Chronology

Johannes Kepler publishes *Epitome of Copernican Astronomy*

Isaac Newton publishes *The Mathematical Principles of Natural Philosophy*

Jean-Jacques Rousseau publishes *The Social Contract*

Nicolaus Copernicus publishes *On the Revolutions of the Heavenly Bodies*

Galileo Galilei publishes *Dialogue Concerning the Two Chief Systems of the World*

Baron of Montesquieu publishes in France *The Spirit of the Laws*

The French Revolution begins

1543   1616   1632   1687   1748   1762   1789

1500   1550   1600   1650   1700   1750   1800

1628   1637   1690   1751   1776

René Descartes publishes *Discourse on Method*

John Locke publishes *Two Treatises on Government*

Adam Smith publishes the influential *Wealth of Nations*

William Harvey publishes *An Anatomical Exercise on the Motion of Heart and Blood in Animals*

Denis Diderot begins the long-term publication on the project *Encyclopedia*

The philosophes attacked spiritual authority; dogma, or the arrogant assertion of opinion as fact; intolerance, or the inability to accept other beliefs, particularly about religion; censorship, economic restraints, and social injustices.

France: The Center of the Enlightenment

During the eighteenth century, France was the intellectual center of Europe. The French capital, Paris, was Europe's cultural gathering place. In Paris, at social gatherings called salons, performances of music, readings of poetry, and other cultural events took place. The most important artists, writers, and scientists often met to discuss ideas and dine together at these salons. Influential women played key roles in the spread of Enlightenment ideas. Marie Thérèse Geoffin, Suzanne Necker, Louise de Warens, and Madame de Pompadour, a mistress to Louis XV, are the most famous examples of the patronesses and hostesses at these salon events. These women offered financial support, and their homes and drawing rooms served as the gathering places during the period of the Enlightenment.

Marie Thérèse Geoffin was one of the sponsors of philosophe Denis Diderot. His contribution to the Enlightenment was the ambitious project called the *Encyclopedia*. Diderot symbolized the spirit of the age of the Enlightenment. For more than twenty years, he worked to complete his grand project, which sought to bring together all of the most important knowledge concerning science, technology, art, music, mathematics, law, government, and geography. Diderot, the editor of the *Encyclopedia*, continued to publish his volumes despite government censorship. The contents of a number of the more controversial volumes had angered the Church and the French King Louis XV because they contained criticisms of the Roman Catholic Church and the government.

Between 1751 and 1772, Diderot published a total of twenty-eight volumes, which were eagerly awaited by his many subscribers. In England and Scotland, an English version called the *Encyclopedia Britannica* was produced starting in the 1770s. Diderot and a number of other writers eventually went to prison, but the ideas that they sought to promote in the *Encyclopedia* became widely read and popular throughout Europe and elsewhere.

Political Ideas of the Enlightenment

In France a number of writers expanded upon John Locke's controversial ideas regarding natural rights.

Voltaire

Voltaire, in his writings *Candide* and *Letters Concerning the English,* used wit and satire to promote the concept of a limited monarchy and the importance of freedom of speech and religion. François Marie Arouet, known more familiarly as Voltaire, was a brilliant and satirical writer who came from a French middle-class family. He became very famous in France and elsewhere in Europe for his novels, plays, letters, and other writings in which he attacked prejudice and other evils of society. Voltaire and his intellectual friends believed that reason was a divine force. Through reason society could progress toward liberty and make injustice disappear. Voltaire's writings caused him problems in eighteenth-century France, where absolute monarchy, based on the principle of divine right and a powerful Catholic Church, existed. Voltaire was eventually driven into exile, but his writings and influence could not be suppressed. He symbolized the philosophe whose ideas could not be silenced.

Montesquieu

The Baron of Montesquieu, in his major work *The Spirit of the Laws*, which appeared in two volumes in 1748, was a contributor to the *Encyclopedia* and a learned Enlightenment philosopher. Montesquieu, like Voltaire, was an admirer of England's type of limited government. He believed that only through a system of separation of powers and a system of checks and balances could government be prevented from becoming a tyranny based on the principles of absolutism and divine right. Montesquieu argued that power should be equally divided among the different branches of government. The legislative branch would have the power to make the laws, the executive branch the power to enforce the laws, and the judicial branch the power to interpret the laws and judge if they were violated.

Montesquieu also believed in the rights of the individual citizen and the duty of the government to protect the people's natural liberties. Montesquieu, born to a noble French family, did not live to see how influential his ideas would be later in the writing of constitutions in many nations.

Rousseau

Jean-Jacques Rousseau, who was born in Switzerland, was another important figure of the Enlightenment. Rousseau's most famous work was *The Social Contract*, published in 1762. In this book, Rousseau discussed his political ideas about government and its right to rule, as well as social ideas that were considered to be very radical for their time. (See page 260, Social Ideas.)

Rousseau wrote "man is born free and everywhere is in chains." He stated that liberty was everyone's natural birthright, but most people lived in an oppressed state. Rousseau believed that originally people lived in a state of nature, where they were free and equal even though their societies were primitive. He claimed that in the process of creating a more civilized society, freedom and equality were destroyed because the strongest individuals, who became rulers, forced everyone else to obey unjust laws.

Rousseau argued that it was necessary for all legitimate governments to have the consent of their people. He wrote about the idea of a broader democracy in which the general will of the people was all powerful. Inequality among people could be ended by citizens coming together and agreeing to this general will, which represented what the majority desires and the government should carry out. Rousseau's idea about a broader participation of people as a basis for a truly democratic government was even more advanced than that of John Locke. His concept of the general will of the people greatly influenced the American and French Revolutions. Furthermore, it was an inspiration for the romanticism that flowered in European artistic and literary movements in the late eighteenth and nineteenth centuries. Rousseau's ideas about equality and the will of the majority inspired the revolutionaries who sought to change the manner in which their nations were governed.

Economic Ideas of the Enlightenment

The Physiocrats

Not all of the philosophers concerned themselves primarily with political ideas. One group, the physiocrats, looked for natural laws to explain how an economy could best function. During this period, mercantilism was the most influential theory to which the majority of European governments subscribed in making their economic policies. The physiocrats argued against mercantilism because they reasoned that land, and not gold or silver, was the true measure of a nation's wealth. The physiocrats supported farming and argued for the removal of restrictions on trade in order that farmers could sell their products more freely. They believed that a free market would result in increased trade and more wealth for everybody. The physiocrats wanted an economy in which the government would give merchants and entrepreneurs a free hand to produce and sell their goods in an open market. This idea of government noninterference in the economy is called laissez-faire or let alone.

Adam Smith Adam Smith, an English professor, was the most brilliant defender of the idea of a free economy. In his book *The Wealth of Nations*, first published in 1776, Smith wrote that a free economy without governmental regulations would produce greater wealth for a nation. Smith's ideas were based on what he called three natural laws of economics. They were as follows:

1. *The Law of Supply and Demand:* This law would determine the price of any good that was sold in an open market. Producers would have to adjust their production to meet the demands of the customers. For example, overproduction would lower the price of a good if people did not want it all.

2. *The Law of Competition:* This law would force producers to make better products at a lower price and drive inefficient and selfish individuals, who could not work efficiently and meet the demands of their customers, out of business.

3. *The Law of Self-Interest:* This meant that businesses were primarily created to make profits for their owners. Therefore, the reason for the production of goods was to make money. Left alone this self-interest guaranteed that there would be sufficient goods for customers in an open market.

Essentially Adam Smith believed that if these natural laws were left free to operate without government interference in the economy, a nation would prosper. A large quantity of well-made goods produced at the lowest possible price was essential for economic progress. England was the nation that ultimately paid most attention to Smith's ideas in formulating its economic policies in the late eighteenth and nineteenth centuries.

Cultural and Social Ideas of the Enlightenment

Social Ideas

The ideas of the Enlightenment spread across Europe starting in the mid-eighteenth century and had a significant social and cultural impact. Some of the philosophies of the Enlightenment concerned themselves with ideas that related more directly to the lives of the people.

Rousseau Rousseau's social ideas rejected society's formal structures and rules. In his writings, for example the novel *La Nouvelle Heloise*, Rousseau encouraged people from all walks of life to live humbler lives, closer to nature. His belief that all people were equal under the law made him an opponent of the class system, which controlled social relations throughout Europe.

Rousseau's aim was to give the individual more freedom in a society where the rational general will would enable people to chose for the common good. He looked to education not as a means of imparting things to be known but rather to draw out what was already there. In *Emile*, Rousseau outlined his educational philosophy. He stressed the need to allow the free development of the human potential.

Spinoza Baruch Spinoza was a Dutch philosopher who was educated as an Orthodox Jew. However, his unusually independent thoughts and refusal to observe certain religious ideas and ceremonies led to his excommunication from the Jewish community. He believed that people, as in all aspects of nature, share a common drive for self-preservation. Spinoza equated virtue and power, and he believed in the freedom to be guided by the law of one's own nature. In Spinoza's ethical system, the individual and community could obtain freedom through understanding and the use of an active intellect. He wanted people to think for themselves and not to accept ideas that resulted in loss of social and religious freedom.

Cultural Ideas

More people became educated and capable of reading and writing. These individuals began to read the growing numbers of books, journals, and newspapers that contained the ideas of the Enlightenment. The increase in travel to other countries and the spread of books had far-reaching effects. Despite the efforts of the Roman Catholic Church and government censors in France and elsewhere in Europe to prevent the spread of these new ideas, more people became informed about them. Public lectures, theater presentations, café gatherings, and neighborhood meetings were additional sources of information.

The Enlightenment also brought changes that made it possible for women to take advantage of the opportunities opened by the new ideas. Women acted as art and music patrons, ran intellectual gatherings in salons and public places, increasingly wrote novels and poetry, and were active in the sciences.

Music, literature, and the arts were infused with the ideas of the Enlightenment. The writers, composers, musicians, and artists turned to a classicism that represented order and reason. Musical composers like Johann Sebastian Bach, Joseph

Haydn, and Wolfgang Amadeus Mozart stressed balance and contrast in their symphonies and operas. Literary figures like Jean Baptiste Molière, Pierre Corneille, and Alexander Pope wrote in a style that emphasized form and content in the classical tradition. Painters and sculptors drew their inspiration from the Classical ideas of the Greeks and Romans. The paintings of Jacques-Louis David symbolized the ideas and inspiration that artists took from Cassical subjects and forms.

In architecture, the use of simple Classical forms such as the circle and square contrasted with the more ornate and complicated baroque style. Palaces, opera houses, and other public buildings were designed by architects who attempted to capture the refined and simplified ideas of an earlier Classical Period.

Impact of the Enlightenment on the Americas

The ideas of the Enlightenment traveled across the Atlantic Ocean to the Americas. In the English thirteen colonies, many of the future leaders of the American Revolution and the first American governments were greatly influenced by the new ideas coming out of Europe. The writings of the Enlightenment philosophes were read by the educated members of the English colonies in North America, who often had their own libraries. Discussions of these new ideas took place in homes, taverns, and political meetings.

Benjamin Franklin, the symbol of the enlightened American, was thoroughly familiar with Enlightenment thought. Franklin was a writer, scientist, publisher, and political leader who promoted the ideas that developed in Europe and spread to the Americas. Thomas Paine, the author of *Common Sense*, claimed that Americans possessed natural political rights and had a right to revolt against English tyranny. Thomas Jefferson, James Madison, and other Americans supported the political ideas of the Enlightenment. Jefferson, the principal author of the Declaration of Independence, and Madison, the "Father" of the United States Constitution, were very familiar with the ideas of Locke, Montesquieu, and Rousseau.

In Spanish America, the ideas of the Enlightenment bore fruit in the early nineteenth century during the Napoleonic Era. The ideas of the Enlightenment spread more slowly in the Spanish and Portuguese colonies because the wealthy and educated colonial elite feared the consequences of enlightened thought in Latin America. Francisco Miranda, Simón Bolívar, and José de San Martín, leaders in the various movements for independence in Spanish America, were all influenced by the Enlightenment's political ideas.

The Scientific Revolution and the Scientific Method

With its emphasis on reason, and a willingness to question previously held ideas, the Enlightenment Era produced much change in the ways people thought about themselves and their natural environment. Indeed, the word "change" is the word that perhaps comes immediately to mind when thinking of what we have learned in this chapter as well as in the chapters on the Renaissance and Reformation. Europeans underwent changes in those times that were to have lasting effects into today's world. The same can be said of the ways in which the people of Europe viewed the natural world and the universe itself. Their knowledge of science and mathematics, and the methods used to obtain that knowledge, was transformed dramatically during the sixteenth, seventeenth, and eighteenth centuries. This change in scientific knowledge and methodology is called the scientific revolution.

A new system of ideas and theories was created, based on the direct observation of nature and a belief in the power of reason. These features make up the **scientific method**. This method consists of three stages:

1. Statement of a hypothesis or idea;
2. Experimentation and observation; and
3. Interpretation of results, using reason and mathematics to determine the truth of the hypothesis.

By using this method as well as they could during their lives, a succession of astronomers, physicists, mathematicians, and physicians changed many ideas that had been accepted for centuries. In fact, a twentieth-century philosopher, Alfred Whitehead, labeled the 1600s the "century of genius." His reference was to the scientific advances made during that time. Let us now learn what these advances were, between 1500 and 1800, and who the people were that made these advances possible.

Astronomy and Physics

Nicolaus Copernicus, a Polish astronomer and mathematician, stirred controversy with his claim that the sun was the center of the universe. This was known as the **heliocentric** theory. It was a challenge to an older theory that had been stated by the Ancient Greek scientist Ptolemy. Ptolemy held that the earth was the center of the universe, the **geocentric** theory. This view won long-standing acceptance, lasting well over one thousand years. Known also as the Ptolemaic Theory, it received strong backing from the Roman Catholic Church. Church officials claimed that the Bible supported this view. Copernicus tried, however, using mathematical calculations, to show that this view was incorrect. He asserted that, contrary to Ptolemy's assertation, the earth rotated on its axis and therefore was not stationary. The ideas of Copernicus, appearing in his 1543 book *On the Revolutions of the Heavenly Bodies*, were not widely accepted at the time. Both Luther and Calvin, for example, condemned Copernican theories. The Roman Catholic Church went so far as to place Copernicus's book on the Index of Prohibited Books. The book remained on the Index until its removal in the eighteenth century.

The ultimate acceptance of the heliocentric theory was the result of contributions by other scientists. They were able to prove the truth of this theory by further observations and calculations. This progression of scientific knowledge often follows such a pattern, whereby the ideas put forth by researchers at one point in time form the basis for development and improvement by scientists at a later date. To express this in another way, the accomplishments of a scientist are often dependent upon the efforts of researchers and theorists at an earlier point in history. The theories of Copernicus were the basis for work done by Tycho Brahe, Johannes Kepler, and Galileo Galilei.

Galileo was an Italian mathematician, physicist, and astronomer. Considered one of the world's great scientists, he is regarded as the founder of the experimental method—the cornerstone of modern science.

Brahe (1546–1601) was important for his observations of the planets and stars. This Danish astronomer built an observatory for studying the skies. His conclusions led him to agree with the geocentric theory. His assistant, the German Johannes Kepler (1571–1630), did further investigations to confirm these conclusions. Kepler's book *Epitome of Copernican Astronomy*, published in 1616, contained his findings. Although in general agreement with Copernicus, Kepler described one error in Copernican claims. Copernicus had stated that the planets revolve around the sun in circles. Kepler's calculations convinced him that the planets actually moved in another kind of pattern, an ellipse.

The Accomplishments of Galileo

The next astronomer for us to acknowledge is the Italian, Galileo Galilei (1564–1642). He built a telescope, having learned of a device made in the Netherlands that used lenses to make distant objects seem close. Based upon what he was able to see of the planets and stars, Galileo verified that the planets do indeed move around the sun. His observations made believable the mathematical conclusions arrived at by Kepler. Galileo made these additional discoveries with his telescope:

1. The moon owes its light to reflection.
2. Its surface is not smooth but has valleys and mountains.
3. The sun has movable spots.
4. The planet Jupiter is surrounded by four moons.

All of Galileo's astronomical findings were published in 1632 in his book *Dialogue Concerning the Two Chief Systems of the World.*

Publication of his findings caused trouble for Galileo. They disproved earlier theories proposed by Ptolemy and another famous Greek thinker, Aristotle. It was difficult for many people to discard beliefs of these much-admired men—beliefs that had long been accepted and that had the support of the Roman Catholic Church. The Church ordered Galileo to renounce his views. Upon his refusal, he was summoned to stand trial by the Inquisition in Rome in 1634. Charged as a heretic and facing the death penalty, Galileo humbly submitted to the Inquisition's demand. On his knees, he recanted "... the said heresies and errors as to the movement of the earth around the sun and all other heresies and ideas opposed to the Holy Church." But this admission that the earth was the center of the universe was not enough. He was also made to swear that he "...will never assert or say anything either orally or in writing..." that could make him suspected of being a heretic. There is a legend that soon after he made these statements, Galileo muttered under his breath, "But the earth does move." This is an unproven story, but nevertheless points up the probability that Galileo's Inquisition statements were made under duress.

Isaac Newton was an English mathematician and physicist. His laws of motion and gravitation are thought to be among the greatest achievements of human thought.

In the last few years of his life, Galileo's interest turned to mechanics. This is the physical science concerned with matter in motion. His 1636 publication, *Dialogues on Motion*, summarized his work on this topic. He noted, for example, that without any air friction, objects of different weight will fall at the same speed. This law of falling bodies negated an older theory of Aristotle's and helped set the stage for Isaac Newton's development of his famous laws of motion. Galileo's investigations of the natural world have led many historians to regard him as the founder of experimental science. He showed that reliance upon traditional concepts about nature can not be accepted unless there is clear, definitive, scientific proof of these concepts.

The Accomplishments of Isaac Newton

The year 1642 marked the death of Galileo and the birth of the English scientist Isaac Newton. The former died in January, while the latter was born on Christmas Day in December. Whether an example of destiny or just a coincidence, these events of 1642 point up the passing on of leadership in scientific exploration that has helped human beings to understand the world around them. By the time of his death in 1727, Newton had won wide respect for his accomplishments. His reputation was based mainly on three significant discoveries:

1. Calculus—the basis of modern mathematics. This topic is concerned with examining changing quantities.
2. The law of the composition of light. Newton's demonstrations with light and with color led to the science of optics.
3. The law of gravitation. This law provided humankind with a new insight into the universe and was clearly Newton's most monumental achievement. It is therefore necessary for us to examine it closely.

The concept of gravity, as a force that causes the return of an object to the ground, was recognized prior to Newton's time. However, it remained for Newton to discover the law regulating this force and the attraction it exerts. Briefly stated, the law declares that a force of attraction exists between bodies, and that this force increases as the bodies move closer together. This force can be measured in a mathematical formula. This is the force that pulls objects to the earth and is also the force that keeps planets revolving around the sun. Newton was thus able to *explain* the workings of the solar system—something that Kepler and Galileo had only been able to *describe*. The heliocentric theory could no longer be denied.

Newton's findings were published in 1687 in his book *The Mathematical Principles of Natural Philosophy*, sometimes referred to as *The Principia*. It also contained his three classic Laws of Motion. One of these stated that "a body in motion will stay in motion, unless acted upon by an outside force." It is said that Newton's interest in gravity and motion was initially stimulated by his thinking about an apple that he had watched falling to the ground from a tree. Whether or not this is a true story, Newton's pronouncements had an enormous impact on scientific thinking that continues on to the present. For Newton, the universe was a well-regulated machine that worked in connection with specific laws of nature. His accomplishments helped pave the way for our current ability to travel through and explore outer space. American astronauts are indebted to Newton for his explanations and theories.

Additional Scientific Discoveries

Besides Newton, there were other scientists who sought to find explanations for naturally occurring events. As was true of Newton, these scientists made discoveries that changed older ways of thinking and were thus part of the age's Scientific Revolution. Examples can be found in the field of medicine. The work of Galen, a Greek physician, had dominated thought about health and disease for centuries. He held that chemical changes in a substance were impossible to produce. A Swiss physician, Paracelsus (1493–1541), disproved this theory, however, in his preparation of certain medicines. Some of Galen's notions concerning human anatomy were found to have errors, thanks to the pioneering work of Andreas Vesalius (1514–1564). This Flemish professor gave accurate descriptions of the human brain and the digestive and reproductive systems that he learned about through dissection. These descriptions were presented in his book *On the Structure of the Human Body*, published in 1543.

This drawing of the human body by Vesalius increased human understanding of anatomy.

Knowledge of the human body was expanded with the studies carried out by the English physician William Harvey (1578–1657). By observing humans and by experimenting with the hearts of birds and frogs, Harvey learned much about the circulation of blood. In his 1628 publication, *An Anatomical Exercise on the Motion of the Heart and Blood in Animals*, he described the pumplike features of the heart and the manner in which blood is driven by it in a circulatory pattern. Adding to Harvey's discoveries was the Italian Marcello Malpighi (1628–1694). He described the capillaries and their role in circulation of blood.

The discoveries by people such as Malpighi were made possible by the use of the microscope. Constructed originally in the Netherlands around the year 1600, the microscope enabled scientists to observe things that could not ordinarily be seen by the human eye. The Dutchman Anton van Leeuwenhoek (1632–1723) was thus able to investigate protozoa and bacteria as well as to describe blood corpuscles. In England, Robert Hooke (1635–1703) discovered that living matter was made up of cells.

There were notable advancements in the field of chemistry. The Englishman Robert Boyle (1627–1691), known as the founder of modern chemistry, did pioneering research into the composition of chemical compounds. He was accurate in predicting the discovery of many more elements than were known at his time.

The prediction was validated with the discovery of hydrogen by Henry Cavendish (1731–1810) and the discovery of a gas by Joseph Priestly (1733–1804) that was ultimately named oxygen. The naming was by the Frenchman Antoine Lavoisier (1743–1794).

Growing Support for the Scientific Revolution

Several European philosophers realized the importance of using observation, reason, and careful experimentation when investigating nature. Two of the most prominent were the Frenchman René Descartes (1596–1650) and the Englishman Lord Francis Bacon (1561–1626). Descartes would accept nothing as knowledge unless it could be proven. This may be why he considered mathematics as the "queen of the sciences" and its methods to be useful in all other sciences. His emphasis on applying logic and reason in human affairs led people to describe him as rationalist. According to Descartes, the mere fact that he could think was proof that he existed. This belief was stated in a famous sentence from his *Discourse On Method*, published in 1637: "I think, therefore I am."

Lord Francis Bacon would agree with Descartes on the value of using the scientific method to gain accurate knowledge. However, for Bacon this knowledge would be especially worthwhile only if it could be practical and utilitarian. This meant that it had to benefit mankind in specific ways—fighting disease, conquering suffering, and so on. As he wrote in his *Novum Organum*, published in 1620, science will "…extend more widely the limits of the power and greatness of man."

As advances in scientific knowledge were made, greater interest in science became apparent. A good example of this growing interest was the creation of organizations to help exchange ideas, encourage experimentation, and spread information. Some of the earliest organizations or societies were started in Italy. Galileo, for instance, was a member of the Academia dei Lincei, begun in 1601. In England, King Charles II favored scientific research. In 1662, he granted a charter to a group that became known as the Royal Society of London for Promoting Natural Knowledge. Shortly thereafter, in 1666, King Louis XIV of France approved the founding of the French Academy of Sciences. Within the next one hundred years, similar societies were established in other countries. Scientific journals began to be published by these groups, a practice very much in evidence in our own times.

Summary

This chapter, unlike many of the others before, had no battles, no wars, and no monarchs attempting to expand their territories. Yet the changes that took place probably are longer lasting, further reaching, and had greater impact than we can imagine. Many of the Enlightenment ideas found their way into our Constitution and form of government. They also impacted on France and were a major factor in the French Revolution. Interestingly, some educational policy is based on some of the philosophes' writings. The philosophes attacked the old world of privilege and held out hope for a better time that was attractive to the common person.

In the world of science the advances are all around us today. The centuries of belief that were accepted were now challenged. This caused problems for the scientists and the men of religion. The Church had supported these traditionally held beliefs and it was difficult to change to these new ideas. We see the results of these scientific advances in our everyday lives. Obviously space exploration could not have taken place without Newton. This "revolution" may be said to be continuing today. We are constantly striving to learn more about ourselves and the world in which we live.

CHAPTER 12

Review Exercises

The Enlightenment

I. Multiple Choice

Directions: Find the *letter* of the correct answer.

1. The Enlightenment was a period when

    (a) individuals turned to ideas based on faith.
    (b) philosophers sought to justify the power of the monarch.
    (c) traditional ideas expressed by the Church were most accepted.
    (d) reason and nature began to be used to explain human behavior.

2. The philosophes attacked spiritual authority and intolerance because they supported

    (a) freedom of thought.
    (b) the divine right of kings.
    (c) the Protestant Reformation.
    (d) a more democratic Church.

3. Thomas Hobbes and John Locke differed on the idea

    (a) of a government based on a social contract.
    (b) that the state of nature held back human progress.
    (c) that a government once established could always be changed.
    (d) when people had the right to overthrow a tyrannical government.

4. John Locke believed that people possessed natural rights that included

    (a) liberty, equality, and fraternity.
    (b) life, democracy, and enfranchisement.
    (c) life, liberty, and property.
    (d) equality, paternity, and creativity.

5. Enlightenment thinkers supported all of the following ideas *except*

    (a) separation of powers.
    (b) checks and balances.
    (c) freedom of speech.
    (d) principles of absolutism.

6. The philosophe who believed in a broader democracy based on equality and the general will of the people was

(a) Thomas Hobbes.
(b) John Locke.
(c) Jean-Jacques Rousseau.
(d) Baron de Montesquieu.

7. The physiocrats argued that a nation's wealth was based on

(a) gold and silver.
(b) manufacturing.
(c) land.
(d) restricted trade.

8. The law of supply and demand means that

(a) competition has to be regulated.
(b) overproduction cannot be controlled in an open market.
(c) the price of any good would be determined in an open market.
(d) producers would control the supply and demand of their prices

9. The economic idea that is in opposition to mercantilist policy is

(a) storing bullion.
(b) laissez-faire.
(c) restricted trade.
(d) government subsidies.

10 Artists, musicians, and writers drew inspiration from

(a) Classical traditions.
(b) the Middle Ages.
(c) Gothic styles.
(d) Eastern influences.

II. Matching

Directions: Match the names in Column A with the achievement they are *best known* for in Column B.

Column A
1. Isaac Newton
2. Voltaire
3. Thomas Hobbes
4. John Locke
5. Marie Thérèse Geoffin
6. Denis Diderot
7. Montesquieu
8. Rousseau
9. Adam Smith
10. Simón Bolívar

Column B
(a) defended ideas of free economy
(b) influenced by Enlightenment in South America
(c) argued for a democracy based on general will
(d) wrote about the idea of a separation of powers
(e) compiled *Encyclopedia* of important knowledge
(f) sponsored philosophes; promoted salon gatherings
(g) believed people possessed natural rights
(h) justified rule of absolute monarch
(i) provided well-reasoned mathematical proofs, ideas of gravity
(j) satirical writer, promoted freedom of thought and religion

III. Thought Questions

Directions: Answer the following questions in essay form.

1. How did the Enlightenment philosophes break with traditional values?

2. What were the basic ideas of John Locke?

3. Why were the ideas of Jean-Jacques Rousseau so influential in the late eighteenth and nineteenth centuries?

4. What were Adam Smith's three natural laws of economics?

5. How did the Enlightenment impact on people's lives?

The Scientific Revolution

I. Matching

Directions: Match the scientist in Column A with his publication in Column B.

Column A	_Column B_
1. Nicolaus Copernicus	(a) _The Principia_
2. Galileo Galilei	(b) _On the Revolution of the Heavenly Bodies_
3. Isaac Newton	(c) _Epitome of Copernician Astronomy_
4. William Harvey	(d) _Dialogue Concerning the Two Chief Systems of the World_
5. Johannes Kepler	(e) _Discourse on Method_
6. Andreas Vesalius	(f) _The Structure of the Human Body_
7. René Descartes	(g) _An Anatomical Exercise on the Motion of the Heart and Blood in Animals_

II. Famous People

Directions: Use the names below to complete the following sentences.

Boyle	Harvey
Copernicus	Ptolemy
Galileo	Lavoisier
Leeuwenhoek	Newton
Hooke	Descartes

1. _____ developed the microscope.

2. _____ discovered that living matter consisted of cells.

3. _____ has been called the "father of modern chemistry."

4. _____ considered mathematics to be the "queen of the sciences."

5. _____ contributed to our knowledge of how blood circulates in the body.

6. _____ is credited with naming the gas we now know as oxygen.

7. _____ was a Polish astronomer, initially criticized for proclaiming the "heliocentric theory."

8. _____ had believed that the sun rotates around the earth, the "geocentric theory."

9. _____ built a telescope and was able to verify the "heliocentric theory."

10. _____ was famous for his discoveries concerning calculus, optics, and gravity.

III. Map Exercise

Directions: Use the map to locate the birthplace of each of the following people. For each person, write the *letter* of the birthplace.

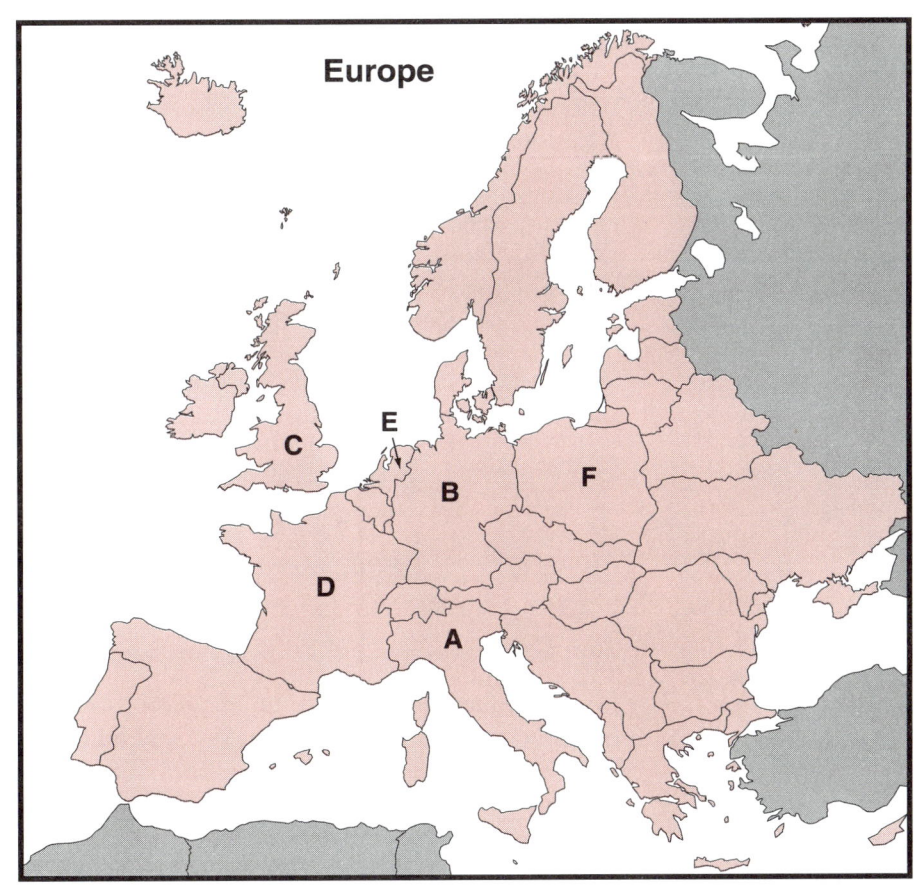

1. _____ Isaac Newton

2. _____ René Descartes

3. _____ Antoine Lavoisier

4. _____ Joseph Boyle

5. _____ Nicolaus Copernicus

6. _____ William Harvey

7. _____ Marcello Malpighi

8. _____ Anton von Leeuwenhoek

9. _____ Galileo Galilei

10. _____ Johannes Kepler

IV. Multiple Choice

Directions: Find the *letter* of the correct answer.

1. The scientific method involves all of the following *except*

   (a) observation of events.
   (b) acceptance of dogma.
   (c) experimentation with theories.
   (d) recording of facts.

2. Who does not belong with the others, in regard to his major area of scientific achievements?

   (a) Copernicus
   (b) Kepler
   (c) Harvey
   (d) Galileo

3. Copernicus was able to disprove the previous theory about the earth's relationship to the sun, as stated by

   (a) Ptolemy.
   (b) Galen.
   (c) Brahe.
   (d) Boyle.

4. Both Galileo Galilei and Francis Bacon were similar in that they

   (a) argued against the statements of Copernicus.
   (b) believed in using the scientific method.
   (c) made discoveries only in the field of astronomy.
   (d) joined the Royal Society of London.

5. "I think, therefore I am," showing the importance of individualism, was stated by

   (a) Vesalius.
   (b) Hooke.
   (c) Descartes.
   (d) Newton.

6. His theory on the law of falling bodies disproved the findings of Aristotle, but was accepted by Newton. This scientist was

(a) Kepler.
(b) Leeuwenhoek.
(c) Copernicus.
(d) Galileo.

7. "The sun is the center of the universe." This assertion was first made by

(a) Ptolemy.
(b) Aristotle.
(c) Bacon.
(d) Copernicus.

8. "A body in motion will stay in motion, unless acted upon by an outside force." This commonly accepted theory was first stated by

(a) Descartes.
(b) Newton.
(c) Harvey.
(d) Bacon.

9. According to medieval thinking, the center of the universe was the

(a) moon.
(b) sun.
(c) earth.
(d) heavens.

V. Thought Questions

Directions: Answer the following questions in essay form.

1. Define the following terms:

   A. scientific revolution
   B. scientific method

2. Write a newspaper story for each of these headlines:

   A. "Copernicus Announces a New Theory About the Earth and the Sun."
   B. "Galileo Faces Charges Before the Inquisition as a Heretic."

3. The lives of people changed because of the discoveries of many of the scientists described in this chapter. Prove this is true by choosing two of them and describing how they changed the world.

CHAPTER 13

The French Revolution

The situation has to be very grim to cause people to revolt. You don't easily put your life in danger and possibly lose everything you have. It may not be much, but whatever it is, it is yours. France, however, underwent quite a violent period of time. When France was one of the great powers of Europe, its citizenry was suffering. By 1789 the people would no longer tolerate the situation. Why didn't the monarchs realize what was going on? Their ignorance of the situation ultimately caused their deaths. Would it have been possible to avoid what happened? It certainly was an exciting and dangerous time to live.

The Ancien Régime

The expression *ancien régime*, or Old Regime, refers to the period, society, and social structure of pre-1789 France. It was a time when those in power were more concerned with their own well-being than with that of the masses of people. King Louis XIV ascended to the throne in 1643, for example, and waged a series of costly wars during his long reign. In addition, he had a lavish palace built at Versailles. Because of the brilliance of his court, Louis XIV is often called the Sun King. By the time of his death in 1715, France was heavily in debt. From his palace at Versailles, Louis XIV had ruled France as an absolute monarch based on the theory of divine right. His long years as King of France enabled him to restructure French society.

Louis XIV ultimately reduced the power and prestige of the French nobility. Nevertheless, the nobility did retain its traditional privileges. Many nobles still had great wealth and land holdings. The nobility served at court and were given the important officers' positions in the powerful French army. Louis XIV had centralized political power in the royal bureaucracy. The royal government officials who administered the King's policies were instructed to exempt the nobility from taxation.

The structure of the Old Regime became more rigid in the 1700s during the reigns of Louis XV and Louis XVI. The nobility became more assertive of its privileges as the eighteenth century progressed. Some of the more enlightened nobles increasingly resented the absolute power of the King. Nevertheless, the nobles did not seek, as in England, to curtail the power of the monarchy.

Causes of the French Revolution

A Highly Structured and Divided Society

The source of French society's problems was its rigid class system, consisting of three estates. An estate was a social group of people. All members of French society belonged to one of the three groups. For example, all members of the Catholic clergy belonged to the **First Estate**, and all nobles were members of the **Second Estate**. The **Third Estate** made up France's largest social group and consisted of all peasants, artisans, and members of the **bourgeoisie** or middle class. A person's estate determined the person's legal rights and status in society. The privileges and exemptions of the First and Second Estates gave rise to a host of inequalities that burdened the vast majority of French people. This majority made up the Third Estate.

In the Roman Catholic Church in France, nobles held the higher offices of the clergy. These high Church officials and the parish priests, who were mostly commoners, controlled religious matters. Church officials determined all issues relat-

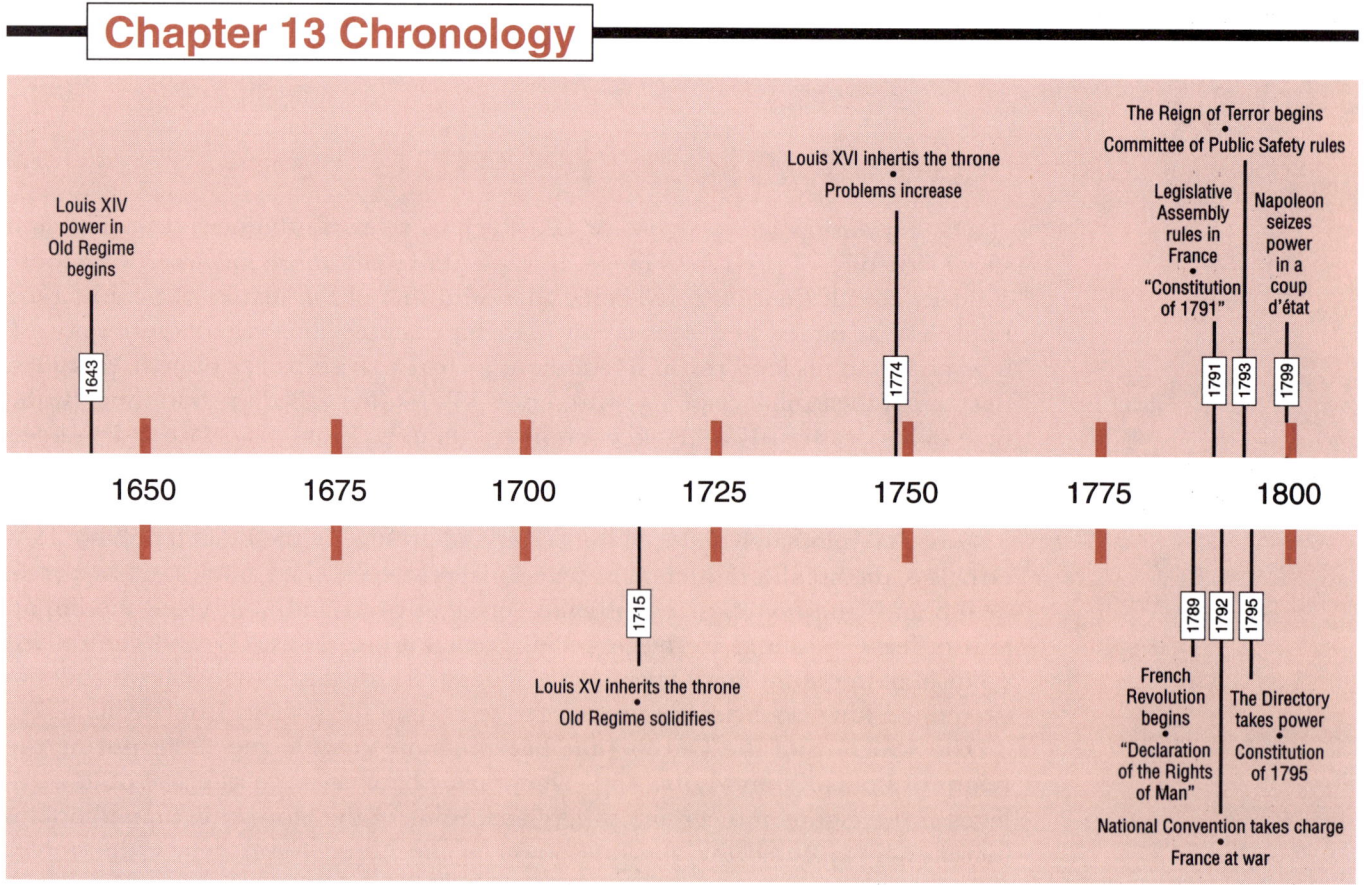

Chapter 13 Chronology

Louis XIV power in Old Regime begins — 1643

Louis XVI inhertis the throne / Problems increase — 1774

The Reign of Terror begins / Committee of Public Safety rules

Legislative Assembly rules in France / "Constitution of 1791" — 1791

Napoleon seizes power in a coup d'état — 1799

1793

1650   1675   1700   1725   1750   1775   1800

1715 — Louis XV inherits the throne / Old Regime solidifies

1789 — French Revolution begins / "Declaration of the Rights of Man"

National Convention takes charge / France at war

1792 — The Directory takes power / Constitution of 1795

1795

ed to the administration of the sacraments, the running of schools, and the care of the poor. The Church possessed large holdings of land and collected a **tithe**, or a tax on income. The Roman Catholic Church was a pillar of French society. The clergy, like the nobility or Second Estate, was exempt from taxes during the Old Regime.

The vast majority of French people did not partake in the politics of power or share the wealth of the first two estates. The commoners of the Third Estate made up approximately 90 percent of the French people. They had no political rights, paid most of the taxes and fees, and had no voice in government. During the 1700s, the Third Estate's economic position considerably worsened because of war, crop failures, and government corruption.

The Third Estate was extremely varied in terms of wealth, education, and occupation. Nevertheless, all commoners suffered because of the unfair social structure. Most of the commoners were either peasants who toiled in France's large agricultural system or poor artisans who lived in squalid conditions in towns and cities. The middle class also belonged to the Third Estate. Its members were the doctors, lawyers, merchants, business professionals, scientists, and philosophers of French society.

The bourgeoisie were all subject to taxation, had no political rights, and increasingly resented their low status. These middle class groups were educated and aware of the new ideas of the Enlightenment. They were increasingly influenced by the philosophes and believed that they deserved more political rights and social justice. Members of the bourgeoisie, along with some allies among the nobility and clergy, ultimately played the leading roles during the French Revolution.

Growing Unhappiness in France During the 1700s

Economic Problems The economic situation was the chief reason for unhappiness. The kings spent extravagantly, leaving the French treasury in terrible financial condition. The kings needed additional funds to meet their enormous expenses and pay their huge debts. The nobles and the higher clergy resisted all efforts by the monarchy to impose taxes on them. The wealthier and more influential members of the aristocracy, the nobles of the robe, had gained their status through service to the royal government. These nobles often held judges' positions. They did not want to ease the financial crisis if it meant a tax on the aristocracy. The noble judges of the *Parlements* or high law courts worked against any of the king's orders that limited their powers and threatened their wealth. The Parlements were not elected bodies but served as law tribunals.

This failure to share the economic burden of supporting an increasingly indebted government meant that any new plan for taxation or fees fell entirely on the Third Estate. The peasants already had to pay a 10 percent tithe on their income to the Church, other heavy taxes, and perform unpaid services for the nobility. They also supplied labor for the crown, the *corvée*, and paid rents to their landlords.

Most city workers, many of whom were artisans, earned low wages. These urban residents faced rising inflation, which made their living conditions extremely harsh, particularly in times of famine. Other urban residents, the middle class groups, increasingly financed the monarchy. The bourgeoisie, most notably the wealthy bankers and merchants, lent the government great sums for most of the eighteenth century. By the 1770s, they were less willing to finance a weak and bankrupt government.

The kings were able to instill fear in the Third Estate and at times the nobility, by the use of *lettres de cachet*, or secret letters, which ordered the arrest and imprisonment of suspected opponents without recourse to any right to be charged and tried. The nobility also helped keep the Third Estate in check through their control of the provincial court system, which safeguarded their inherited rights. The clergy supported the ancien régime by discouraging expressions of dissent, urging acceptance of the established order, and promising a better life in the hereafter for the faithful.

In 1774, Louis XVI, at the age of thirteen, inherited the crown from his grandfather, Louis XV. The financial crisis that Louis XVI faced grew progressively worse. The young King recognized the need for economic reforms; however, his foreign policy only deepened the financial crisis. In his first years as King, Louis XVI supported the American Revolution. This French attempt to gain some revenge on the English for previous humiliation, although successful, only increased the nation's debt.

In 1774, Robert Turgot, Louis XVI's first minister of finance, started a series of economic reforms to reduce the government debt. Expenses at Versailles were reduced, the power of the guilds was limited, and some internal customs duties were removed. Unfortunately for Turgot, his proposed major reform to tax the nobles led to his downfall after two years in office. The nobility of the robe controlled the law courts. Using their judicial power, the judges refused to approve of Turgot's idea to tax the aristocracy. The higher clergy sided with the nobility, and Turgot was soon dismissed by the King.

For a number of years, the French government was able to function because it obtained new bank loans. However, by the end of 1783, the monarchy again found it increasingly difficult to obtain financial support. This worsening economic situation was aggravated by two successively poor French harvests, in 1787 and 1788, which caused severe food shortages.

The nobility stubbornly refused to recognize that they would have to pay taxes if France was to overcome its terrible financial problems. When Louis XVI proposed a new tax law to the Parliament of Paris in 1788, its members, nobles of the Second Estate, steadfastly continued to refuse to pass this law.

The nobility and high clergy were supported in their opposition to any taxation by Queen Marie Antoinette, who had great influence with the King. Marie Antoinette lived a lavish life-style and spent money extravagantly on gowns, balls, and other entertainment. She was more interested in protecting the privileges of her noble and higher clergy friends than in helping her husband solve the desperate French financial situation.

King Louis XVI, the monarch of France at the beginning of the French Revolution, was executed by the nation's revolutionary government in 1793.

The First Stage of the French Revolution: The Creation of a Constitutional Monarchy

The Estates-General Becomes the National Assembly

By May 1789, Louis XVI was left with no choice but to summon the **Estates-general**. The Estates-general, which had not met since 1614, was a representative body composed of delegates from the three estates. Louis hoped to obtain the legislature's approval for the additional taxes that he needed to save France from bankruptcy. The King hoped that this legislative body would cooperate by passing the new taxes on the First and Second Estates, which he believed were the solution to France's economic crisis. This attempt to reform the tax system proved to be the beginning of the end of the Old Regime in France.

The Estates-general operated on the basis of each estate electing its own representatives. Each estate had always met and voted separately and had but one vote. Although the delegates voted as individuals within their estate, ultimately the one vote per estate meant that if the First and Second Estates worked together, they could overcome the more numerous Third Estate. They could also weaken the king's power while protecting their own privileges.

From the time of the call for an Estates-general, members of the Third Estate realized that it was necessary to change the voting procedures of the legislature. They were excited by the prospect of finally passing meaningful reforms that would relieve long-suffered economic, political, and social injustices. Therefore, when the Estates-general met, the members of the Third Estate insisted that all three estates meet as one body with each delegate having one vote. They were supported in their demand for a mass meeting by some of the more enlightened nobility and clergy. The eloquent Abbé de Sieyès played a particularly important role in this early phase of the French Revolution. Sieyès published an influential pamphlet entitled "What is the Third Estate?" in which he attacked the nobility and clergy. He made his chief contributions with the theory of national sovereignty, the idea that political authority to rule rests in the nation and not the king, and also the distinction of active and passive citizens, which restricted the right to vote to men with property.

Despite the King's refusal to heed their request, the Third Estate delegates, who were mostly members of the bourgeoisie, decided not to give in and meet separately. Louis XVI's response was to lock the delegates out of the Estates-general hall in Paris. The King's action did not weaken the determination of the political leaders of the Third Estate. Count Honoré Mirabeau, a noble who had been elected as a delegate to the Third Estate, played a key role in reconvening those delegates who supported the position of only one assembly. Meeting at an indoor tennis court near the closed Estates-general hall, the deputies present named themselves the National Assembly. The delegates took an oath not to disband until they had written a French constitution. This was the Tennis Court

Oath. The intention of Mirabeau and his allies was to create a limited constitutional monarchy.

Louis XVI recognized the danger of a National Assembly in which there were only representatives of the Third Estate. The King reluctantly ordered the First and Second Estates to join in the deliberations of the new legislative body. Louis XVI also took some military precautions and brought more troops to the areas around Paris. The political events began to move at a more rapid pace as the summer of 1789 approached.

The Call for Revolt to Protect the National Assembly

The Tennis Court Oath taken by the National Assembly delegates led to renewed meetings by the delegates. They were unwilling to be denied their right to meet and discuss necessary changes, which they wanted to enact as laws. The debates of the National Assembly had just begun when Louis XVI, acting on the advice of Marie Antoinette and the court faction, dismissed the popular minister of state for finances, Jacques Necker. The departure of Necker, who was considered the most capable financial expert in Louis XVI's government, greatly angered the workers in Paris as well as the French peasants. The Third Estate saw Necker as the hope for relief from taxes and poverty. In addition, word spread throughout Paris that the King was bringing troops to Versailles and was planning to close the National Assembly.

Three days after Necker's dismissal, on July 14, 1789, a Paris mob attacked the infamous Bastille prison fortress, seized its gunpowder supply, and freed the prisoners being held. In Paris, mobs had already rioted over the high price of bread. The attack on the Bastille, which was seen as a symbol of injustice and inequality, led quickly to upheaval in the French countryside.

Peasants throughout France were caught up in the Great Fear. In the summer of 1789, rumors were spread about an aristocratic conspiracy designed to send robbers and bandits to destroy peasants' homes and crops in French villages. The frightened peasants took up arms to defend themselves. When no robbers appeared, the peasants turned their anger on their landlords. Peasants pillaged and burned castles, destroyed tax records, seized granaries, and swore never again to pay feudal dues.

The National Assembly Adopts Reforms

The entry of the lower classes into the revolution, in the summer of 1789, forced the National Assembly to take action. During one particularly long session on August 4, 1789, the nobles and clergy agreed to give up their privileges. In one night the feudal structure of France was abolished. Serfdom and the tax-exempt privileges of the nobility were ended. Church tithes and other feudal customs were abolished. The Old Regime no longer existed by the end of this extraordinary session.

Several weeks later, on August 26, 1789, the National Assembly passed The Declaration of the Rights of Man and the Citizen. In this declaration, all French citizens were guaranteed the rights of liberty, property, security, and freedom from oppression. Other articles of this famous document gave the French people freedom of religion and speech, and the right of equal justice.

The Bastille prison was liberated by a Parisian mob on July 14, 1789 at the beginning of the French Revolution. This prison symbolized oppression during the Old Regime.

The events of the summer of 1789 frightened Louis XVI and his court. Necker was recalled for a time as finance minister. The King went to Paris where he accepted the tricolor, the blue, white, and red ribbon symbol adopted by the newly formed municipal government, which later became the colors of the national flag. He then returned to Versailles.

Soon thereafter, a hungry and angry mob marched to Versailles and broke into the palace. Marquis de Lafayette, a hero of the American Revolution, saved the royal couple from the rioters and safely escorted the king and his family to Paris. Thereafter, the royal family was not allowed to leave Paris.

The Constitution of 1791

The National Assembly continued its work over two years to draft a constitution. After long and difficult sessions, a constitution was completed. It made great changes in the structure of France's government and society. The Constitution of 1791 created a limited monarchy with a unicameral, or one-house, legislative assembly. A system of separation of powers was written into the historic document. A veto power was given to the king, and a judicial branch was set up. The Roman Catholic Church lost its lands and political independence. Church officials were to be elected by property owners and paid as state officials. The changes affecting the Roman Catholic Church led to problems and violence between the bourgeoisie and those peasants who were devout Catholics. The Constitution of 1791 also ended France's traditional territorial division according to provinces. In its place the nation was divided into eighty-three departments, which were to be administered by locally elected officials.

In mid-1791, the first stage of the French Revolution came to a close. The Constitution of 1791 was received with a mixed reaction. For the nobles, clergy, and their peasant supporters, the document went too far, especially regarding the Church reforms. The delegates who were moderates and their mostly middle-class supporters wanted further reforms; however, they accepted the document and hoped to achieve their goal at a later date. The moderates represented those groups that feared further upheaval. The radical delegates opposed the Constitution of 1791 because they wanted a republic and not a monarchy, even if it was a limited one. The radical delegates were supported mainly by the Parisian municipal councils and the working class who joined the increasingly violent mobs.

The nobles and Church hierarchy, increasingly frightened by the angry mobs in the countryside and Paris, fled the country. The growth of mob violence during this time was a result of the worsening economic conditions, which caused hunger in Paris and fear of repression by the nobles in the countryside. The political exiles, *émigrés*, began to urge European rulers to oppose and overturn the changes that had taken place in France.

Louis XVI gave his approval to the Constitution, but he did so reluctantly and under pressure. In June 1791, the King and Queen decided to flee Paris with their family. While in flight, at a road stop in Varennes, the royal family was recognized, arrested, and brought back to Paris under guard. The French Revolution was ready to enter into a more radical and violent phase.

The Second Stage of the French Revolution: The Establishment of a Republic

The Legislative Assembly Defends the Revolution

After the Legislative Assembly was convened in October 1791, it soon split into three political factions. These groupings created a political spectrum in France that divided the legislative members based on their political beliefs. Today this left-to-right political spectrum created in France during the French Revolution is used in all societies to determine where a political party fits in terms of its program. The seating in the Legislative Assembly determined the delegates' political position. The conservatives sat on the right and basically supported the idea of a limited monarchy. They hoped to conserve, or continue, some prior ways, with no changes. The moderates, or centrists, sat in the middle and wanted further reforms. On the left sat the radicals, who wanted extreme changes. From their viewpoint, the conservatives and moderates were too supportive of the Old Regime.

In the early stages of the assembly sessions, the **Girondists**, or moderates, were able to control the workings of the legislature. However, by the spring of 1792, the Paris Commune, a radical grouping that had seized control of the city's municipal government, began to pressure the Legislative Assembly to take more radical measures. The radicals, called the **Jacobins**, gained more influence in the assembly.

The radicals' position in the assembly was strengthened because of the outbreak of war with Austria, which began in April, 1792. Emigrés incited the courts of Europe to intervene. In France, war was advocated by the royalists, who wanted to restore the Old Regime, and republicans, who wished to spread their ideas abroad and rally the nation to their cause at home. The war turned into a disaster for France, and the Jacobins used the deteriorating military situation to further their political ends.

The French armies performed very poorly in the early battles of the war. Austria and Prussia had joined together to attack France. The monarchs of Europe increasingly feared that, unless reversed, the radical political ideas coming out of France, such as republicanism, would spread to their countries. By July 1792, foreign armies were advancing on Paris and threatening to extinguish the revolution. Upset with news coming from the battlefield and other rumors about the king's betrayal, an angry mob stormed the Tuilleries palace and massacred the Swiss guards protecting the royal family. The insurrectionists suspected that the king was plotting with foreign powers to suppress the revolution. The royal couple was imprisoned in a stone tower.

The Jacobins were soon in control of the Legislative Assembly. They were aided by the violent Parisian mobs who increasingly threatened the more conservative and moderate delegates. The idea of a limited monarchy was soon abandoned, and the Constitution of 1791 was set aside. The assembly soon ended its own existence by issuing a call for a new representative body. Fortunately for the radicals, the French army defeated the advancing Austrians and

Prussians. Paris was at least temporarily saved. Thousands of volunteers, stirred by the revolutionary Jacobin orators, had rushed to aid the French army. The resounding victory of the French forces helped the Jacobin leaders in their quest for political control.

The Revolution Takes a Radical Turn

In the summer of 1792, the volatile Parisian mobs demanded greater control over the political direction of the continuing revolution. The Parisian mobs supported the radical Jacobin deputies in the assembly. With the support of the Parisian councils, the Jacobin political leaders turned the revolution onto a more radical and violent path. The Jacobin leaders included Georges Danton, Jean-Paul Marat, and Maximilien Robespierre. During the following months mass arrests of royalist sympathizers, people who were known or suspected to be supporters of the monarchy, took place. In September, angry mobs massacred many of these prisoners.

The newly elected National Convention met in late September 1792. The legislature had been chosen by universal manhood suffrage, which gave all adult male citizens the right to vote. At the first meeting of the National Convention, the monarchy was abolished, a republic was set up, and proceedings were started against the King for treason. The Jacobins greatly influenced these proceedings. The radicals demanded Louis XVI's death. To convict the King of treason, they convincingly used as evidence an iron box of letters containing supposed secret correspondence with foreign monarchs.

The execution of the King in January 1793 was a very momentous event for several reasons. In France, it provoked royalist insurrections in some areas, and led ultimately to a war dictatorship and the bloody repression of any opposition to the radical position. Abroad, Louis XVI's death also led to the formation of a coalition of European powers to crush the revolution.

The National Convention sat from September 1792 until 1795. This political body was responsible for the defense of France's first republican government. Increasingly, the National Convention became the battleground in a power struggle between the Girondists and Jacobins. By June 1793, the moderate Girondists were crushed and eliminated. The deciding votes in this bitter power struggle came from the grouping referred to as the plain. The plain represented the majority of undecided delegates and was very influenced by the sans-coulottes, or people, mostly workers, who wore long pants instead of breeches and who were the backbone of the Parisian mobs. The plain ultimately supported the more radical Jacobin mountain, so called because these delegates occupied the highest benches in the convention.

The defeat of the Girondists, many of whom came from southwestern France, soon led to a bitter attack on the wealthy upper middle class. The Jacobins also adopted a new constitution that furthered their radical aims. The radical leaders, Danton, Marat, and later Robespierre, became the defenders of the people's will in the National Convention.

On the battlefield, France's military opponents—Great Britain, the Netherlands, Spain, Austria, and Prussia—were increasingly successful. Once again Paris was threatened, and the revolution was endangered. Danton issued a call to defend the revolution. An army of volunteers came forward in response to Danton's call. Danton also hoped to bring liberty, equality, and fraternity to other

European nations. It was at this point that the National Convention created a war dictatorship. The deputies created the Committee of Public Safety in the summer of 1793 and gave it operating power.

The Reign of Terror

As the war situation deteriorated, the Committee of Public Safety began to take extraordinary measures. The committee adopted a conscription program, which made all males between the ages of eighteen and forty-five eligible for a military call-up in the summer of 1793. The war was in effect turned into a conflict that involved most of France's population. Within France, the revolutionaries had to contend with a fierce civil war that was being fought against counter-revolutionaries, those people who actively fought or worked against the revolutionary gains. In western France, particularly the Vendée area where religious belief was very strong, violence and revenge led to many deaths. Peasants were angered by the draft, economic hardship, and measures taken against the Roman Catholic Church.

The Jacobins, who controlled the Committee of Public Safety, even faced trouble within the cities. Rioting broke out over food shortages and rising food prices. In Paris, the discontent led to the murder of one of the Jacobin leaders, Marat, by a Girondist supporter. The Jacobins reacted harshly to their opponents in France. They began a campaign to completely crush all opposition to the revolution. This brutal period is referred to as the **Reign of Terror**. The Committee of Public Safety unleashed this campaign of terror in September 1793.

During the following months, domestic enemies, real or imagined, were hunted down. They were turned over to courts that swiftly condemned the accused. Judges handed out harsh sentences to please the angry mobs that followed these trials. Estimations are that about forty thousand people, mostly commoners who were in a large measure tradespeople, workers, and peasants, were executed throughout France. In Paris, there were about three thousand death sentences, usually carried out publicly by guillotine, an execution device that severed the head from the person's body. Many of these victims were falsely accused by their neighbors because of personal reasons. The Queen, Marie Antoinette, was also executed during this period.

Queen Marie Antoinette of France was accused of leading a lavish life-style and having a bad influence on Louis XVI. Marie Antoinette was executed during the Reign of Terror.

The Rise and Fall of Danton and Robespierre

Georges Danton and Maximilien Robespierre were the two leading Jacobin figures in the early months of the terror. As the killings mounted, Robespierre gradually gained dictatorial powers. He was ruthless in his suppression of any

Maximilien Robespierre

It was on July 28, 1794, that a single beheading was greeted with a joyous roar from the crowd. While this head, then held high by the executioner, was not remarkable, it had belonged to a man who was a major player and leader in the French Revolution. History today sees him as a very controversial figure. To some he is a ruthless dictator who was opposed to democracy. Others see him as a man of vision who was ahead of his time and who wanted to install a democratic government in France. However, all see him as a person of honesty and integrity.

Maximilien Robespierre was born in 1758 in Arras, France. His mother died when he was seven and his father soon ran off, never to be heard from again. When old enough Maximilien went to Paris where he eventually entered college and received a law degree. While his oratory was never first rate, his words were appealing and he could sway people with his message. He was sent to the meeting of the Estates-general in 1789.

Physically he was not an imposing figure. He was short, five feet, three inches, with a flat face that had been pitted by smallpox. He had weak eyes and it was necessary for him to wear glasses. All his life he would dress in the old style—an old fashioned tailcoat and knee breeches. He would never wear the long pants that would become the style. Before he left home each morning he would powder his hair.

He lived a simple, almost austere life, living on his deputy's pay. He never stooped to accepting bribes or taking graft. Maximilien believed that all men by nature were good. He would become known as the "incorruptible."

Ideologically he was opposed to the monarchy and was influential in defeating the Girondists when they wanted to establish a constitutional monarchy. He opposed racial and religious discrimination and proposed emancipation of the slaves. He was somewhat anti-Catholic but strongly opposed atheism. He believed that there should be small-scale ownership of property and business so as to promote democracy.

In the dark days of the Republic the Committee of Public Safety was formed and Robespierre became the most influential member. He had a series of laws passed that legislated morality by establishing the death penalty for spreading false news, stealing public property, profiteering, and interfering with the fight against the enemy. His legislation even gave courts power to decide whether the accused would be allowed a lawyer and what evidence would be heard.

And so began the period known as the Reign of Terror, from 1793 to 1794. During this time, thousands of men and women were sent to the guillotine. Social life practically ceased as people were afraid to talk to each other—one might get turned in as an enemy of France! Slowly hostility grew against Robespirerre. Many felt that he was too proud, too powerful, and too dangerous. When he tried to speak to the convention he was shouted down.

An arrest warrant was issued for Robespierre and a force was sent to arrest him. Realizing that the guillotine awaited him, Robespierre attempted suicide. He was so shaky that the bullet went through his cheek and shattered his jaw. Rather than let him die this way, the jailers bound up his jaw so as to keep him alive long enough to take him to the guillotine the next day. There he was, as one historian put it, "shaved by the revolutionary razor."

opposition to what he believed was the Republic of Virtue. In this period, the Jacobins adopted a revolutionary calendar and proclaimed a new cult of the Supreme Being. Robespierre sought to turn the French religious concept of faith in God into the idea of a religion based on reason.

The Committee of Public Safety also was able to overcome the threat of foreign invasion. The new national draft law led to the creation of a revolutionary army that was victorious in the continuing war with the European monarchies. The committee established price and wage controls, decreed food rationing, and forced the acceptance of an inflated currency, the assignat. These and other war measures taken by the Committee of Public Safety were responsible for saving the revolution.

In the spring of 1794, a ideological split, or breakup over serious political differences of opinion, occurred in the committee when Georges Danton and his followers began to call for a relaxation of the emergency measures. This led to the accusation that Danton was disloyal to the revolution. His trial and execution left the committee completely in the hands of Robespierre and the most fanatical Jacobins. By July 1794, the increased use of terror and executions after the death of Danton led the National Convention to order Robespierre's arrest and subsequent execution by guillotine. The Reign of Terror came to an end, to the relief of France's populace.

The Third Stage of the French Revolution: Government by Directory

The Directory Takes Charge

The National Convention briefly took charge of the French government. A new constitution was drafted in 1795, which marked a turn to the right. The constitution ended universal male suffrage by requiring men to own property in order to vote. The wealthy bourgeoisie now controlled the government. The Constitution of 1795 established an executive council of five men called the **Directory** to rule the nation with the help of a two-house, or bicameral, legislature. The Directory managed to govern France from 1795 to 1799. It successfully defended the nation against a royalist uprising and harshly suppressed riots by radical elements caused by the worsening economic conditions, including food shortages and rising prices.

In its last years, the Directory was beset with growing problems and was constantly threatened with bankruptcy. The public began to question the moral character of the Directory's members as scandals affecting their personal lives became known. Corruption and constant intrigues plagued the workings of the Directory and led to rising discontent. As it faced growing charges of ineptness and unpopularity at home, the Directory increasingly depended on the army to maintain control. By late 1799, a popular young army general, Napoleon Bonaparte, joined in a **coup d'état**, or quick seizure of power, thereby ending the Directory's rule in France.

The Lasting Impact of the Revolution

The French Revolution had a deep and lasting impact, and its influence continued into the nineteenth century. The nation would henceforth be the symbol of the fellowship of the French people. This spirit of nationalism became a major factor in Europe and elsewhere. The political slogan "liberty, equality, and fraternity" continued to influence and express the aspirations of peoples throughout the world in the nineteenth and twentieth centuries.

Social Changes

French society and the social structure was permanently changed by the French Revolution. The bourgeoisie and wealthy capitalist class became the dominant political and economic forces in France in the nineteenth century. The Old Regime ended, and the remnants of feudalism were wiped out. Although there would be efforts to restore some of the privileges and trappings of the Old Regime in the nineteenth century, these attempts were short lived.

Political Changes

The French Revolution made some advances toward political democracy; however, in doing so, it resulted in much bloodshed and violence. The revolution brought a temporary end to rule by monarchy. The monarchy was reestablished in the 1800s, but it did not survive the century. Curiously, the English Revolution of the seventeenth century made democratic advances with less bloodshed and the monarchy remained intact. To this day England has a monarch; France has none. Nevertheless, the political system in France did change. The nobility and clergy could no longer dominate political life in France as in the Old Regime. The middle class, particularly the upper or haut bourgeoisie, came to control French political life, especially after the Revolution of 1830. Workers and farmers waited longer to gain their political rights, but they also could not ultimately be denied their rightful voice in determining the nation's politics.

Cultural Changes

Further results of the French Revolution saw the establishment of a uniform system of weights and measures, the metric system. Art and fashion styles changed. People began to dress differently. Long pants and less elaborate dresses became fashionable. France would never be the same as it was before 1789.

Summary

When we look back at the decade we just studied it is hard to believe that all these events took place. When we started, France was an absolute monarchy with the Church and nobility in control. The complaints of the people were never lis-

tented to by the leaders. It is hard for us today to believe that no one was smart enough to see what was happening. The king, separated from the people, didn't have a clue. Those with the power wouldn't give up any part of it—and it often cost them their heads. Neither the Church nor the nobility ever regained the power or position they had. It is also interesting to note that the revolution turned on its own leaders. Additionally, the other nations of Europe were unable to defeat what seemed to be a very weakened France. Could all of this have been avoided? What do you think?

Review Questions

I. Multiple Choice

Directions: Find the *letter* of the correct answer.

1. The Old Regime in France refers to

    (a) the period of the French Revolution.
    (b) pre-1779 French society and social structure.
    (c) the time prior to the regime of Louis XIV.
    (d) when the Directory took power in 1795.

2. The French monarchy prior to 1789 believed in

    (a) constitutional democracy.
    (b) absolute rule.
    (c) constitutional monarchy.
    (d) legislative power.

3. All of the following are true of the class system in France prior to 1789 *except*

    (a) The First and Second Estates paid no taxes or fees.
    (b) The Third Estate was subject to the most taxation.
    (c) The Third Estate was made up of only peasants and artisans.
    (d) The bourgeoisie were part of the Third Estate.

4. Louis XVI was unable to resolve France's financial crisis during his reign because

    (a) the Second Estate was only willing to pay limited taxes.
    (b) the First Estate wanted to increase the labor tax.
    (c) the peasantry and city workers refused to lend money to the monarchy.
    (d) the First and Second Estates blocked all taxation reform affecting them.

5. The Third Estate refused to meet and vote separately in the Estates-general because they

    (a) were less numerous then the first two estates.
    (b) hoped to join with the First Estate and form a majority.
    (c) were following the previous procedures of the French legislature.
    (d) wanted each delegate to have one vote.

6. The National Assembly was responsible for all of the following *except*

   (a) The Declaration of the Rights of Man and the Citizen.
   (b) the abolishment of France's feudal system.
   (c) the Constitution of 1791.
   (d) the Committee of Public Safety.

7. The radical Jacobins wanted a

   (a) limited monarchy.
   (b) republican form of government.
   (c) return to absolute rule.
   (d) coalition with the Girondists.

8. The National Convention served as France's legislature from

   (a) 1774 to 1789.
   (b) 1789 to 1792.
   (c) 1792 to 1795.
   (d) 1795 to 1799.

9. The Reign of Terror refers to the time when

   (a) Jacobin radicals persecuted all suspected opposition.
   (b) King Louis XVI sought to crush the National Assembly.
   (c) the Directory hunted down the radical Jacobins.
   (d) peasants revolted against the Directory.

10. The Constitution of 1795 established

   (a) a Directory of five men to rule the nation.
   (b) a constitutional and limited monarchy.
   (c) universal manhood suffrage in France.
   (d) a military dictatorship to rule France.

II. Matching

Directions: Match the names in Column A with the achievements they are *best known* for in Column B.

Column A	Column B
1. Louis XIV	(a) Louis XVI's first minister of finance
2. Louis XVI	(b) his death ended the Reign of Terror
3. Count Mirabeau	(c) saved Louis XVI at Versailles in 1789
4. Abbé de Sieyès	(d) minister of finance in 1789
5. Jacques Necker	(e) cleric in favor of a National Assembly
6. Georges Danton	(f) assassinated by a Girondist supporter
7. Jean-Paul Marat	(g) King of France in 1789
8. Maximilien Robespierre	(h) the Sun King
9. Robert Turgot	(i) wanted a limited monarchy
10. Marquis de Lafayette	(j) sought to curtail the Reign of Terror

III. Matching

Directions: Match the words in Column A with the *correct description* in Column B.

<u>Column A</u>

1. ancien régime
2. estates
3. bourgeoisie
4. corvée
5. lettres de cachet
6. unicameral assembly
7. émigrés
8. Jacobins
9. sans coulottes
10. guillotine
11. assignat
12. Directory
13. Girondists

<u>Column B</u>

(a) council that ruled France, 1795–1799
(b) French exiles after 1789
(c) radicals of the French Revolution
(d) one-house legislature
(e) labor supplied to the crown
(f) execution method of the French Revolution
(g) middle-class people
(h) people, usually workers, who wore long pants
(i) period of pre-1789 France
(j) French currency during the revolution
(k) moderates during the French Revolution
(l) different social groups in pre-1789 France
(m) secret letters, which ordered the arrest of suspects without rights to a trial

IV. Map Exercise

Directions: Use the map to locate the place associated with each of the following statements. For each statement, write the *letter* of the place.

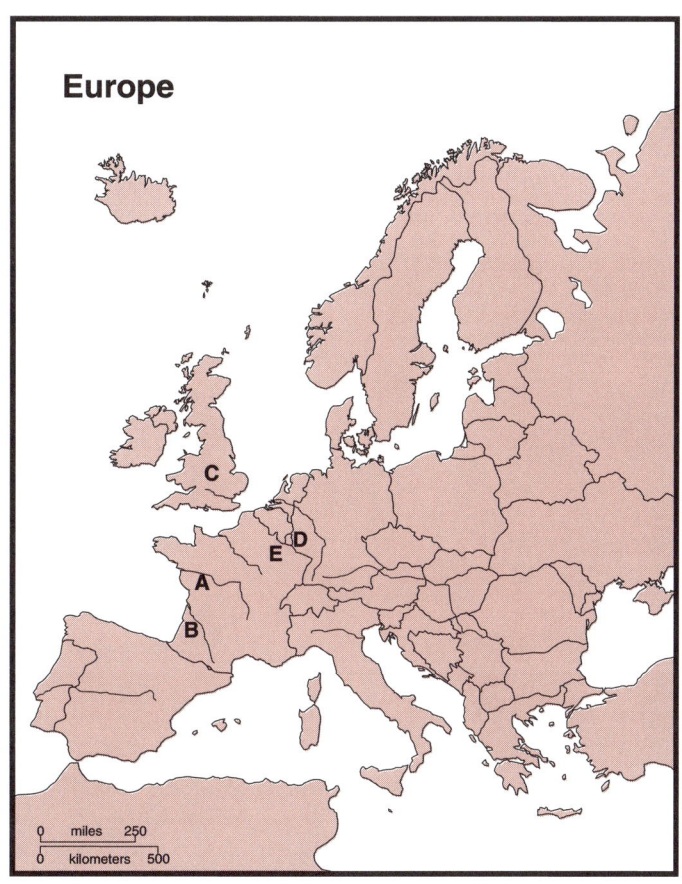

1. _____ The palace where the French kings resided before 1789.

2. _____ The capital of France.

3. _____ The area of France where a counterrevolution took place.

4. _____ The nation to which many émigrés fled after 1789.

5. _____ The area of France that was home to many Girondists.

IV. Thought Questions

Directions: Answer the following questions in essay form.

1. Give three reasons why the French monarchy was unable to solve its financial problems. In your answer cite examples of the reasons that you chose.

2. You have been assigned to write a feature article in a newspaper explaining why the Third Estate wants major economic and political changes.

3. Explain three ways how the French Revolution turned more radical after 1791.

4. During the Reign of Terror you have been arrested and accused of being a monarchist supporter. Write a letter stating your case. Read this letter to the class.

5. Cite three examples showing that the French Revolution had a lasting impact. Give historical evidence to support your examples.

6. Many historians believe that the French Revolution was inevitable. Do you agree with this idea? Support your position by discussing the political, economic, and social situation at the time.

CHAPTER 14

The Rise and Fall of Napoleon

A question is often asked about the ability of an individual to influence the course of history. One person whose name comes to mind when this question is discussed is Napoleon Bonaparte. His name is brought up by those who believe that there are special people who are capable of playing this influential role in history. Factors cited for this ability are the force of a particular personality, favorable circumstances, talent, and even luck. In this chapter, you can answer this question for yourself by reading about the life of Napoleon and the times in which he lived. You can determine if historical events shaped Napoleon's life or if he was one of those special people who caused history to happen.

Early Life

Napoleon Bonaparte was born on the Mediterranean island of Corsica in 1769. Napoleon grew up as a French citizen in a large and traditional Corsican family. At the age of ten, his father decided to send him to France, where he studied at a French military academy. For young Napoleon, his entrance into the academy was decisive because it led to a glorious military career and ultimately his becoming emperor of France.

In 1785, shortly after his graduation, Napoleon was commissioned as a French artillery officer. Napoleon's military career in the last years of the Old Regime offered him little chance for advancement. The French Revolution opened up opportunities to Napoleon; thereafter his military career rapidly advanced. The reasons for Napoleon's new opportunities were a French army that became more open to advancement by men of talent and nonaristocratic backgrounds and Napoleon's extraordinary abilities as a military leader and strategist.

In 1793, his success against a British force brought Napoleon's name to the attention of the Jacobins, who were then in control of the French government. Napoleon's military success drew praise, and he rose quickly in rank. The revolutionary political climate in France led to constantly changing governments. The political instability and threats of invasion by European nations opposed to the revolution made the situation ripe for the rise of a successful and charismatic military figure, that is, a person with a special inspiring quality of leadership.

Napoleon and the Directory

Napoleon survived the reaction after the fall of Robespierre in 1794. He was recalled to duty and resumed his military position as an officer serving the Directory. In 1795, Napoleon demonstrated his skills as an artillery officer when he was called by the Directory to put down a riot by a Parisian mob. Furthermore, his marriage to the influential Joséphine de Beauharnais the following year aided his career. The Directory appointed Napoleon a general and issued orders that assigned him to command the army of the interior. Shortly after, Napoleon became chief of the French army in Italy.

During the next three years, Napoleon distinguished himself as a charismatic leader and strategist in time of war. Napoleon's successes in Italy against the Austrians led to a new command and plans to attack the British Empire. His land campaign in Egypt was at first successful; however, Napoleon's victories were nullified by Lord Nelson's destruction of the French fleet in a decisive naval engagement in the eastern Mediterranean.

Chapter 14 Chronology

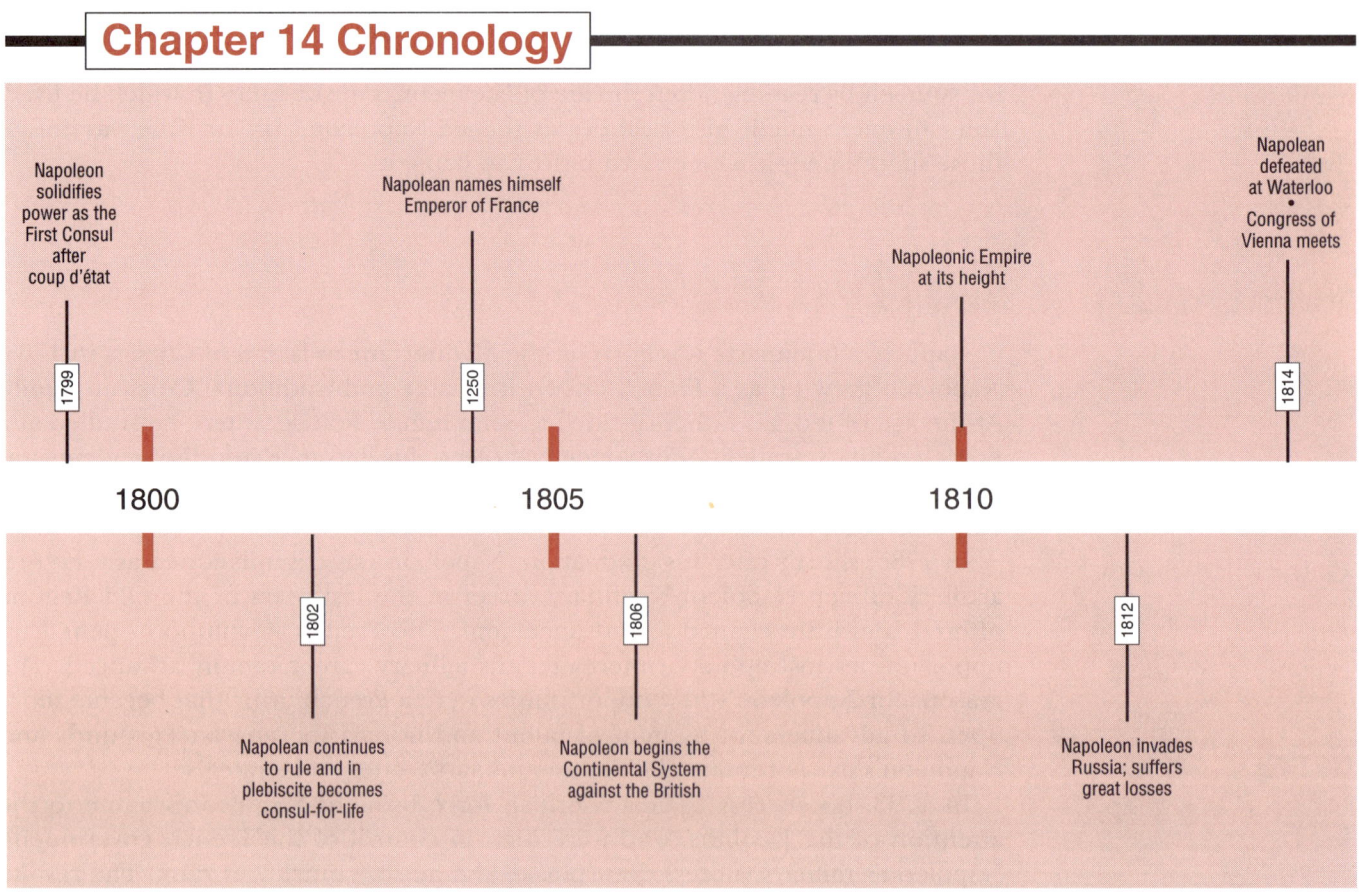

Napoleon solidifies power as the First Consul after coup d'état — 1799

Napolean names himself Emperor of France — 1250

Napoleonic Empire at its height

Napolean defeated at Waterloo
Congress of Vienna meets — 1814

1800   **1805**   **1810**

Napolean continues to rule and in plebiscite becomes consul-for-life — 1802

Napoleon begins the Continental System against the British — 1806

Napoleon invades Russia; suffers great losses — 1812

In 1799, the political status of the Directory in France greatly deteriorated. The French army was defeated in Italy by the Second Coalition—Great Britain, Austria, and Russia. Moreover, at home, the Directory faced accusations of corruption and the threat of bankruptcy. At this juncture, Napoleon decided to return to France. Once in Paris, he joined in a conspiracy against the Directory, which was hatched by one of its own members.

A New Government Takes Power

In 1799, the overthrow of the Directory, by a **coup d'état**, or seizure of power, led to Napoleon's elevation to the position of consul. After a show of military force, the legislature gave political power in France to three officials known as consuls. Shortly thereafter, Napoleon assumed dictatorial powers and the position of First Consul. A new constitution was then proclaimed, which made France a republic. However, the political reality was that Napoleon became France's absolute ruler, and he soon created a dictatorship that violated the spirit of the constitution. Real power was concentrated in the hands of the First Consul, Napoleon.

From 1799 to 1804, Napoleon increasingly used his power to promote his own ends. Although he was aware of the political ideas of the Enlightenment and considered himself a republican and reformer, Napoleon's continued use of dictatorial rule led him away from democracy.

Domestic Policies

Financial Reforms During this period, Napoleon reorganized the state administration and put the government under his personal control. He established the Bank of France, stabilized the currency, and made reforms in the system of taxation. Napoleon required every citizen to pay taxes, placed the collected money into the Bank of France, and used the funds to make government loans. By making these reforms, he brought the financial system under control and stabilized prices.

Educational Reforms By reforming France's educational system, Napoleon created a national system of schools controlled by the government. Furthermore, he established technical and secondary schools or lycées. More students gained access to the educational system, and scholarships were given to poorer, deserving students. These changes toward a more public system open to everyone improved education in France.

The Napoleonic Code Napoleon's greatest achievements during this period were reforms that he made in French law. The **Napoleonic Code** brought all French law into one unified system. Napoleon's law code reflected the ideas of the Enlightenment and took into account the principles of natural law. All men were considered equal under the law, but the state was placed above the individual. In some ways, individual liberties were restricted by curbs on freedom of press and speech. The state reserved the right to censor books and other writings. The codes eliminated the rights that women and children had gained during the early years of the French Revolution. This change in women's rights reflected Napoleon's upbringing and belief in Ancient Roman law. Men, as heads of household, regained legal authority to control the family.

Foreign Policy

The Concordat of 1801 with the Pope   Another of Napoleon's accomplishments as First Consul was the peace agreement made with the Roman Catholic Church. Napoleon was aware of the deep resentment that devout French Catholics felt toward the Civil Constitution of the Clergy passed by the National Assembly in 1790. In western France and other pious rural areas, bloody insurrections against the French Revolution took place in the 1790s. Napoleon negotiated the Concordant of 1801 with Pope Pius VII, which recognized Catholicism as the religion of most of the French people. This historic agreement also provided for continuation of the religious toleration granted to all citizens. The nation's sovereignty was upheld regarding the Church lands seized during the revolution. In addition, bishops continued to be appointed by the French government and had to swear loyalty to the state. In compensation, the state agreed to pay the salaries of the Catholic clergy. By diffusing the Church conflict, Napoleon increased his popularity among the religious French peasantry.

The Rise of the Napoleonic Empire

Napoleon's first steps toward the creation of a French Empire occurred in 1800. He personally conducted a military campaign to avenge the French defeats suffered earlier by armies of the Second Coalition. The withdrawal of Czarist Russia from the European alliance resulted in a weakened coalition that was quickly overwhelmed by Napoleon's masterful military tactics. He crossed the Alps into Italy and defeated Austria. With the Peace of Luneville, Austria was forced out of the war in February 1801.

Only Great Britain remained to offer any kind of military challenge to Napoleon. The proud English were no match for France's mighty army, but under Lord Nelson the British maintained their naval supremacy and protected the war-weary island kingdom. In 1802, the two longtime rival nations signed a peace treaty that was favorable to Napoleon. The Treaty of Amiens restored all of France's territorial conquests in Europe and the Middle East that had been lost in the previous three years. France now became the leading power on the European continent.

Napoleon as Emperor

Napoleon spent the next few years consolidating his political power. In 1802, a **plebiscite**, or direct vote by the people, made Napoleon First Consul-for-life. During this time, Napoleon continued to dictate to his Italian, German, Swiss, and Dutch neighbors concerning land claims, commercial agreements, and other mat-

Napoleon Bonaparte, Emperor of France. Napoleon was able to dominate European affairs from the early 1800s until his defeat by a coalition of European powers in 1814.

ters affecting France's interest. By May 1804, Napoleon was ready to declare himself Emperor of the French. A plot against Napoleon's life was used as an excuse to rid the future emperor of opposition from the French nobility and stifle dissent in the legislature.

A confident Napoleon took the crown from the hands of Pope Pius VII and placed it on his own head. Napoleon at last realized his dream of becoming the Emperor of Europe's strongest military power. Once again by an overwhelming plebiscite the French people approved of Napoleon's decision.

Napoleon soon had French armies on the move. The reasons for this new military campaign in part rested with his ambitions in Italy, Germany, the Netherlands, and Switzerland. It also was a response to Britain's declaration of war after the disagreements caused by the failure of the Treaty of Amiens. Once again Napoleon proved that he was Europe's leading military strategist. The French troops demonstrated their loyalty to Napoleon by their willingness to fight, which led to victories against the hastily formed Third Coalition of Austria, Russia, Great Britain, and Sweden. Prussia joined against Napoleon in 1806 but was also soon thoroughly defeated. On land, Napoleon seemed invincible, but France could not decisively defeat the English. The Royal Navy continued to command the seas and protect Great Britain. In 1805, Lord Nelson completely destroyed the French fleet at Trafalgar.

Napoleon Dominates Europe

The coronation of Napoleon as Emperor meant the death of the French Republic. Although Napoleon had no intention of restoring the Old Regime of prerevolutionary times, he generously allowed the noble émigrés to return to France and created many new titles that were bestowed on favorites. Napoleon pleased the bourgeoisie by slowing inflation, balancing the budget, and creating a national bank. As Emperor, he promoted officials, often from the middle class, according to merit. His popularity among the lower classes of society remained strong particularly after his victories against the Third Coalition.

By 1807, Napoleon was master of Europe. Although France did not seek to militarily conquer Russia, Prussia, or the Austrian Empire, Napoleon dominated these nations through fear and treaties of alliance. Napoleon directly annexed the Dutch republic and a number of Italian states. France also completely controlled Spain after the Emperor forced the Spanish King to reside in France. Napoleon then put his brother Joseph on the Spanish throne. As for the other European nations, France's armies made their rulers subservient to Napoleon's will. In short, they remained independent in name only. Only England, a dangerous military rival, remained beyond Napoleon's reach and influence.

The Continental System

In 1806, Napoleon decided to change tactics against the British. Shortly thereafter, he launched a boycott of British goods on the European continent. This policy was known as the Continental System. Napoleon's decision to cut British trade off with all nations under France's control had two specific goals. One objective of his policy was to make a French-dominated Europe more economically self-sufficient. The other purpose of the Continental System was to weaken and ultimately destroy Great Britain's industrial and commercial economy. The French soon issued a decree that prohibited the entry of British imports into areas of Europe that Napoleon controlled. Russia and Prussia were obliged to cooperate with the ban on imported British products.

The Continental System did not work in the manner that Napoleon intended. The other European nations were able to evade Napoleon's decrees by smuggling cargo in from Britain. Although British trade was reduced, it was not by any means eliminated. In addition, the British responded with a blockade of their own. Suspicious ships on the high seas were stopped and searched. If these ships were found to be carrying goods bound for France, they were forced to sail to British ports where their cargo was taxed. The powerful British navy proved very capable of enforcing the sea blockade.

Britain's policy of stopping all merchant ships caused growing resentment and anger in neutral nations such as the United States. Nevertheless, the British aggressively continued to maintain their blockade. In effect, the French economy was hurt far more than that of Britain. There was a sharp decline in France's maritime trade.

Rising Nationalism in Europe

Napoleon's military successes within continental Europe led to increased problems because of rising nationalist sentiments in the lands that he conquered. France's control of Spain, the Italian kingdoms, and the Confederation of the Rhine resulted in growing local resentment. French taxation and the conscription of soldiers to serve in Napoleon's armies were deeply resented by the local populations who wanted to restore national customs, traditions, and governments. Nationalism stirred the subject peoples of the lands conquered by France to rise up and fight for self-rule.

In Spain, Napoleon's brother, Joseph, was an incapable and increasingly hated ruler. Spanish military forces opposed to Napoleon used guerilla tactics to wage a deadly hit-and-run campaign against the French troops. By 1812, Napoleon had lost the Peninsula War. British troops under command of the Duke of Wellington aided the Spanish forces to defeat Napoleon's dispirited troops and inflict severe losses. The Spanish King was soon restored and a limited monarchy was soon set up with a written constitution.

In Prussia, a country allied to France and forced to support Napoleon's policies, there was a growing spirit of patriotism and nationalism. This support enabled King Frederick William III to rebuild Prussia's army. The Prussian government was reorganized and more political freedom was given to the people. This developing sense of national self-interest resulted in Prussia's military support of Russia after Napoleon's invasion of that nation in 1812.

Napoleon's Downfall

Napoleon's decision to invade Russia with the Grand Army in the spring of 1812 marked the beginning of his downfall. Tsar Alexander I of Russia had reluctantly agreed to support Napoleon's Continental System in 1807. By 1812, the effect of Britain's blockade had severely damaged the Russian economy thus prompting the Tsar to permit a resumption of trade with the British.

Napoleon's response was to invade Russia. The Emperor's campaign strategy was designed to quickly and decisively defeat the Tsar's military forces. Unfortunately for Napoleon, the Russian army did not stand and do battle. Tsar Alexander I ordered his troops to retreat and pursue a Scorched-Earth Policy. The advancing French army, made up in large measure of conscripts from other nations, was increasingly frustrated and demoralized.

In September 1812, the Tsar ordered the burning of the Russian capital, Moscow. Alexander I did not want Moscow to fall into Napoleon's hands and serve as a shelter during the long and harsh Russian winter. A dismayed Napoleon wrote a letter to Alexander I, lamenting the loss of such a beautiful city and in hopes of receiving a peace offer. The Tsar did not respond, and the war continued.

Defeat in Russia

By October, Napoleon recognized that the Grand Army could no longer remain in the open during a particularly harsh Russian winter and ordered a full-scale retreat. "General Winter," with its subzero temperatures and fierce wind-driven snow and ice storms, proved to be too much for Napoleon's improperly dressed and hungry troops. The long brutal march back led to the loss of tens of thousands of soldiers who literally starved or froze to death. Napoleon's victory at the gates of Moscow turned into a disastrous defeat with the elimination of more than 75 percent of France's best army.

Napoleon was never able to recover from the loss of France's most seasoned officers and soldiers. The myth of Napoleon's invincibility finally had been broken. A coalition of France's European enemies soon acted to take advantage of Napoleon's weakened position. Britain, Russia, Prussia, Austria, and Sweden united against Napoleon and formed a powerful alliance.

Napoleon's Exile and Return

Napoleon managed to rush home and raise a new French army. However, at the decisive Battle of Leipzig in October 1813, the combined European armies dealt the French army a stunning defeat. By March 1814, these armies were within Paris and soon forced Napoleon to surrender and abdicate, or leave, as Emperor. The fallen Napoleon was sent into exile on the island of Elba off the Italian coast. The victorious allies brought back Louis XVIII of the Bourbon monarchy, a younger brother of Louis XVI, as ruler of France. Shortly thereafter, the victors reduced France's borders to those existing in 1792.

Napoleon, however, was not finished and made one more desperate attempt to restore the power and glory of his fallen Empire. The French people did not give up hope that Napoleon would return to power and bring back the grandeur of the Empire. Napoleon reentered France in March 1815, amid widespread popular

Europe at the end of the Napoleonic Wars. The victors who participated in the Congress of Vienna redrew the map of Europe.

support. Louis XVIII's army quickly went over to Napoleon. Within days, Napoleon was once again Emperor of France.

Defeat at Waterloo

In the period known as the Hundred Days, the time that Napoleon came back to rule in France, he could not prevent the European governments from reestablishing their powerful alliance. Under the command of the Duke of Wellington, the allied army of the Quadruple Alliance met the French forces led by Napoleon at Waterloo in present-day Belgium in June 1815. After a long and exhausting battle, the allied forces ultimately crushed the French army. The defeat marked the end for Napoleon, who was exiled to St. Helena, a remote island in the south Atlantic controlled by the British. Napoleon lived there as a prisoner for the remaining six years of his life. Prior to Napoleon's death in 1821, the fallen Emperor began to work on his memoirs in which he sought to explain and justify his life's work and accomplishments.

The Congress of Vienna

In the fall of 1814 and lasting into 1815, kings, princes, and diplomats gathered in Vienna, Austria, for a peace conference known as the Congress of Vienna. The

Prince Metternich of the Austrian Empire was the leading figure at the Congress of Vienna. Metternich promoted the principles of legitimacy, balance of power, and compensation.

delegates to the conference had two goals: to restore the political balance in Europe and restore the legitimate rulers to their thrones, and to devise a way to resolve future disputes among the leading powers. There were representatives from most European nations present at this historic gathering. The more important figures were those representing the major powers: Lord Castlereagh (Great Britain), Tsar Alexander I (Russia), King Frederick William III (Prussia), and Prince Klemens von Metternich (Austria). France was represented by Charles Maurice de Talleyrand who spoke for King Louis XVIII. The Congress finished its work over several months, interrupted briefly by the need to fight Napoleon at Waterloo.

The leader of the Congress of Vienna was Prince Metternich. He presided over the Congress and served as its host. Metternich believed that Europe should be restored to the way it was prior to the French Revolution and wanted to establish long-term stability in Europe. He was essentially guided by three principles: legitimacy, compensation, and the **balance of power**. Metternich wanted to restore the rightful hereditary rulers to their thrones, provide payment for those nations that had incurred losses in fighting the French, and create a balance of power in order that no one nation would again dominate Continental Europe as Napoleon had during the preceding years.

In order to accomplish the goals of the Congress, the victors redrew the map of Europe. France was the big loser in terms of loss of territory and payment of war damages. Great Britain took most of France's remaining islands in the West Indies. Austria gained the Italian provinces of Lombardy and Venetia and other territories on the eastern coast of the Adriatic Sea. Attempts by Russia and Prussia to gain territory in formerly held French lands were resisted by Austria and Great Britain. These nations feared an expansion of Russian and Prussian power into central Europe because it would upset the balance of power. Nevertheless, a compromise was reached and Russia received some territory in Poland, and Prussia gained much of the Kingdom of Saxony and land along the Rhine River.

The leading powers at the Congress supported the principle of divine right monarchy as necessary to restore order and stabilize Europe. The Congress reestablished the royal dynasties in France, Spain, Naples, Portugal, Sicily, and Sardinia. Louis XVIII, the Bourbon heir, was made the ruler of France.

In addition, the Congress placed future controls to prevent France from once again threatening the peace in Europe. The French borders were reduced to those that existed in 1790 and a series of buffer states, or neutral lands, were established around France. To France's north, the Netherlands were united under a Dutch ruler. The German Confederation of thirty-nine states under Austrian control was formed to the northeast of France. Switzerland was given back its status of neutrality, and the Italian Kingdom of Piedmont was united with Sardinia.

The agreements made by the delegates at the Congress of Vienna were intended to return Europe to the time of strong monarchies that existed prior to the French Revolution. The delegates to this conference were **reactionaries**, people who wanted to return to the past and who resisted new ideas. The reactionaries hoped to prevent the spread of **liberalism**, a political philosophy that influenced people in Europe in the 1800s. The liberals believed in democratic reforms, accepted the ideas of the Enlightenment, and supported certain freedoms—speech, press, and religion. The reactionaries also wanted to crush the rise of nationalism throughout Europe. Their agreements concerning boundaries reflected the desire to please rulers as opposed to fulfilling the nationalistic aspirations of the people who lived in these lands.

The leaders of Europe were aware that the demand for independence, democratic rule, and national self-determination would lead to revolution and threaten their rule. In order to prevent future problems, Europe's rulers agreed to form new alliances. Austria, Russia, Prussia, and Great Britain joined in the Quadruple Alliance to protect the agreements made in Vienna in November 1815. Several years later, France was admitted to this Alliance. Representatives of the Alliance were to meet regularly to insure the security of Europe, preserve territorial boundaries, prevent the heirs of Napoleon from French rule, and put down any revolutionary movements.

In addition, Czar Alexander I of Russia, seeking to preserve international order based on "justice, Christian charity, and peace," formed a Holy Alliance. The Alliance united the Christian monarchs of Russia, Prussia, Austria, and other nations in an attempt to secure order through cooperative efforts. Great Britain refused to join this Alliance, stating that it needed approval by Parliament, and Pope Pius VII also declined, claiming that no new interpretation of Christian truth was needed. Prince Metternich dismissed the Holy Alliance as a meaningless entity.

Napoleon's Legacy in Europe

Napoleon's legacy is tied to the French Revolution. During the period that he exercised power, Napoleon supported and helped spread many of the ideas of the French Revolution. In the areas of Europe that France controlled, Napoleon instituted important changes and reforms. He decreed the establishment of constitutions and enacted legal reforms based of the ideas of the Napoleonic Code. The recognition of the basic principles of equality before the law and freedom of religion took root in other European nations. In addition, Napoleon either destroyed or reformed the remnants of feudalism wherever his empire ruled.

Napoleon was an excellent administrator who modernized the French government. The Emperor's administrative reforms spread to the lands under France's control. Although those victors over Napoleon, led by the Austrian Prince Metternich, later restored the legitimate monarchs to their thrones, the end of absolutism in Western Europe can be traced to the long-term effects of Napoleon's rule. The monarchs, nobles, and clergy were no longer strong enough to completely regain their former privileges. Limited monarchies and written constitutions were put into place in France and elsewhere. Moreover, the spirit of nationalism that Napoleon awakened could not be completely suppressed. The revolutionary ideas of social justice that spread during the time of the Napoleonic Empire continued to grow and ultimately triumphed in Europe in the nineteenth century.

Napoleon's Legacy in the Americas

Napoleon's legacy also touched the Americas. By 1804, the Emperor had failed in his attempt to reestablish control in Haiti, which had been France's most profitable colony in the eighteenth century. Napoleon sent his brother-in-law, General LeClerc, with a large punitive force to restore order in 1802. LeClerc's goal was to remove Toussaint L'Ouverture, who had become a major obstacle to French colonial ambitions in the Western Hemisphere. The French army was unable to defeat Toussaint's forces in the island's interior, and the revolt continued. By the use of trickery, Toussaint was captured and imprisoned during peace negotiations. However, Toussaint's removal did not end Haitian resistance. The French were eventually forced to withdraw because of their continued heavy losses caused mostly by the ravages of yellow fever. In 1804, Haiti became the second nation in the Western Hemisphere to win independence.

During this period, the United States also became involved with Napoleonic France and its major rival Great Britain. In 1803, Napoleon was in need of funds and recognized that the Louisiana territory was impossible to defend against the British. France sold the land to a surprised U.S. government during Thomas Jefferson's presidency.

Napoleon was also responsible in large measure for growing U.S. involvement in the European wars of the era. The young American nation could not remain isolated from European affairs and untouched by the Napoleonic Wars. The isolationist foreign policy of the United States that called for neutrality conflicted with America's economic interests. Napoleon's Continental System led to increased conflict with the British on the high seas and by 1812, the United States was at war with Britain. Napoleon was comforted by the fact that France's economic policy and diplomacy resulted in the British fighting a war with its former American colonies.

Summary

Europe, despite the attempts of those meeting at Vienna, would never be the same again. The events that took place in France and then "exported" by Napoleon changed the way Europeans thought and acted. It is interesting to see how this man, who came from Corsica, had such an impact. Much of what we will study in the next few chapters is a result of the "Napoleonic Era." From Gibralter on the Mediterranean to Moscow, the French had been masters. Obviously a man of great charismatic quality, Napoleon had the powers of persuasion so as to make people look to him for leadership. He knew when to take advantage of a situation. We may ask if he betrayed the French Revolution, or if he determined events or was determined by them. But whatever the answer, it is sad to realize that he ended his life in exile on a poor isolated island, put there by a Britain that was afraid of him even then.

Review Questions

I. Multiple Choice

Directions: Find the *letter* of the correct answer.

1. Napoleon Bonaparte's early military training prepared him to be

    (a) a military school director.
    (b) an artillery officer.
    (c) a cavalry captain.
    (d) a naval commander.

2. In 1799, Napoleon returned to France and

    (a) took part in the overthrow of the Directory.
    (b) resigned as a military officer to begin a political career.
    (c) became an admiral during a military revolt.
    (d) assumed the title of emperor of the French.

3. During the period 1799 to 1804, Napoleon achieved all of the following *except*

    (a) established the Bank of France.
    (b) reformed France's educational system.
    (c) unified French law under the Napoleonic Code.
    (d) gave women and children more legal rights.

4. The nations that fought against France in the Second Coalition were

    (a) Russia, Great Britain, and Austria.
    (b) Great Britain, Spain, and Prussia.
    (c) Austria, Italy, and Portugal.
    (d) Great Britain, Sweden, and Holland.

5. Great Britain was able to hold off Napoleon's armies because it

    (a) developed an effective artillery weapon.
    (b) maintained its naval supremacy.
    (c) had the nation of Spain as an ally.
    (d) had an army equal to that of Napoleon.

6. After the destruction of the French fleet by Lord Nelson in 1805, Napoleon decided to

   (a) invade Great Britain.
   (b) make peace with Great Britain.
   (c) boycott British goods.
   (d) sell Louisiana to the United States.

7. The Continental System resulted in all of the following *except*

   (a) a sharp rise in France's maritime trade.
   (b) an increase of smuggling in Europe.
   (c) a successful British sea blockade of French trade.
   (d) growing resentment among neutral nations.

8. Napoleon's military success in Europe eventually led to

   (a) rising nationalist sentiment.
   (b) a decline in patriotic sentiments.
   (c) increased support by people in other nations.
   (d) growing support for the French Empire.

9. Napoleon's defeat in the Russian campaign in 1812 was a result of all of the following *except*

   (a) Russia's Scorched-Earth Policy.
   (b) the severe Russian winter.
   (c) a demoralized contingent of foreign troops.
   (d) Russia's ability to stand and fight the Grand Army.

10. Napoleon's defeat by the European Alliance led to the

   (a) restoration of legitimate monarchies.
   (b) creation of a democratically elected government in France.
   (c) re-establishment of feudalism throughout Europe.
   (d) victory of nationalist movements throughout the Americas.

II. Matching

Directions: Match the names in Column A with the achievement they are *best known* for in Column B.

Column A	Column B
1. Joséphine de Beauharnais	(a) Tsar of Russia
2. Lord Nelson	(b) leader of the Haitian Revolution
3. Pius VII	(c) defeated France at Trafalgar
4. Joseph Bonaparte	(d) Pope of Roman Catholics
5. Alexander I	(e) purchased Louisiana
6. Duke of Wellington	(f) leader of Grand Alliance army
7. General LeClerc	(g) wife of Napoleon
8. Toussaint L'Ouverture	(h) placed on the throne of Spain
9. Thomas Jefferson	(i) leader at the Congress of Vienna
10. Prince Metternich	(j) failed to defeat Haitian revolutionaries

III. Matching

Directions: Match the words in Column A with the *correct definition* in Column B.

<u>Column A</u>
1. commission
2. charismatic
3. strategist
4. coup d'état
5. lycée
6. plebiscite
7. blockade
8. peninsula
9. coalition
10. abdicate

<u>Column B</u>
(a) seizure of power
(b) a combination of nations
(c) a direct vote by the people on an issue
(d) to make an officer
(e) inspiring quality of leadership
(f) to give up the throne
(g) capable of planning military operations
(h) secondary school
(i) a strategic barrier
(j) land surrounded by water on three sides

IV. Map Exercise

Directions: Use the map to locate the place associated with the following statements. For each statement, write the *letter* of the place.

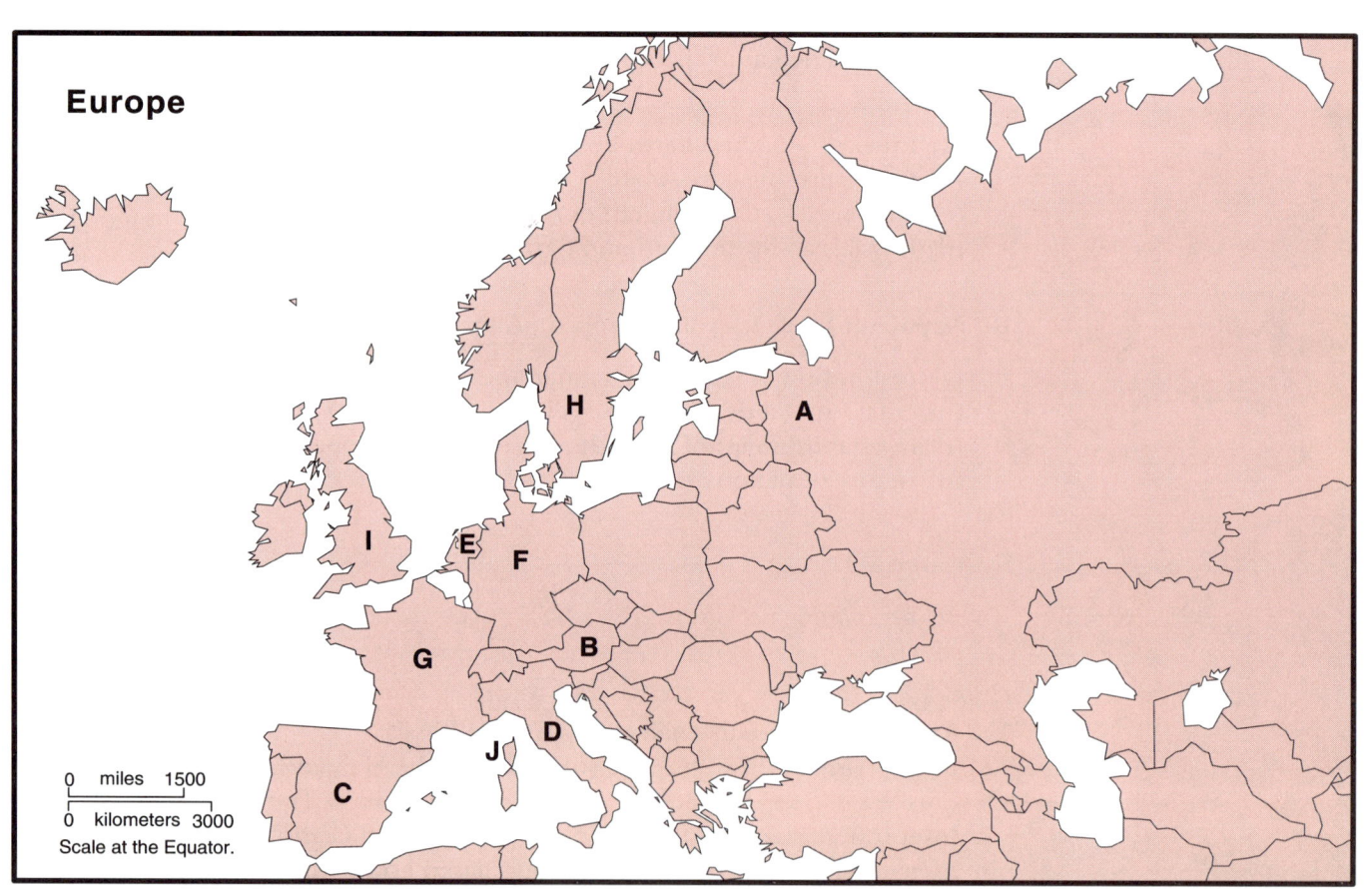

1. _____ The island where Napoleon was born.

2. _____ A harsh winter helped defeat Napoleon here.

3. _____ The Continental System was used against this nation.

4. _____ Napoleon defeated this Empire in Italy.

5. _____ Napoleon's army was defeated here in the Peninsula War.

6. _____ Napoleon annexed the Dutch republic.

7. _____ Napoleon became general of the French army here.

8. _____ Napoleon became the Emperor of this nation in 1804.

9. _____ King Frederick William III built up this nation's army.

10. _____ Joined Great Britain, Russia, Prussia, and Austria against Napoleon.

V. Thought Questions

Directions: Answer the following questions in essay form.

1. Give three reasons and explain how they helped Napoleon become an increasingly popular leader in France.

2. Cite three reforms that Napoleon instituted in France after he became Emperor and explain how they changed an aspect of French life.

3. In an essay explain how Napoleon's Continental System worked and analyze why it failed.

4. List the reasons why the Napoleonic Empire came to an end. Pick one of the reasons that you selected and explain why you think this reason was a major factor.

5. In a speech that you must deliver at the Congress of Vienna, explain how you, Prince Metternich, would return Europe to the pre-French Revolutionary Period.

UNIT V

THE IMPACT OF THE INDUSTRIAL REVOLUTION

We take a lot of things for granted today. When we walk into a room we expect the light to come on when we flip a switch. Our food is kept fresh by the refrigerator and we go to school by bus or car or train. We have hot and cold running water in the sink and take baths or showers inside. Nobody pays much attention when we send a shuttle up into space. Men have walked on the moon and we watched on television. Computers and calculators are now everyday things. We are entertained and enlightened at home by a magic box that takes us around the world in seconds. While it is impossible to give a date when this all started, we can see that most of it began during a period called the Industrial Revolution. It is also impossible to give a date for the ending, because we are still going through it.

We do know that it started in Great Britain. Britain had certain advantages that allowed it to get a head start on the rest of the world. There were important advances in agricultural techniques that resulted in more food, and people were forced off the farms. They moved to the cities amid a shift of population to bigger and bigger urban centers. Life in these cities was not good. People worked long, hard hours and returned home to dirty and dingy places. Despite this, there was a rapid increase in population. There was impact on government, as the merchant class wanted more protection in its pursuit of wealth.

Inventions played an important part in these advances. Old techniques were no longer useful in providing the goods that were needed. New machines were invented that manufactured goods faster and better than ever before. More power was needed and machines replaced human and animal power. Similar advances also took place in transportation and communication. Methods used up until that point became too slow in this new age. Trains replaced horses, engines replaced sails, and telegraphs replaced mail. Obviously these changes are still taking place today.

These changes could not be kept secret by Britain and soon the rest of the continent attempted to join in. The new nation of Germany jumped in in a big way and soon challenged Britain's lead. This later led to difficulties between the two nations.

The market economy that we have today had its start during this time. The operation of the supply-and-demand system created the highest standard of living in history. Factories developed using mass production techniques. The modern corporation had its start, using limited investment techniques that protected investors from risking everything they owned.

But the inequality of the owner and the worker led to demands for changes in the social system. Social scientists discussed ways in which all people could live equally and happily. Some thought that a utopia might be possible. Others, like Karl Marx, saw a coming revolution when the worker would take over industry and the government.

These changes were also reflected in other areas. Advances in medicine attacked diseases. Science progressed as Darwin investigated the evolution of humans and as Freud investigated humans' minds and emotions. These men started controversies that continue today. Art and literature also broke the mold of tradition.

So as you see, this unit is a very important one. Our present lives and standards of living owe much to this period.

CHAPTER 15

Origins of the Industrial Revolution

Historians trace the origins of the **Industrial Revolution** to the agricultural changes that were initiated starting in the fifteenth century. The **Agricultural Revolution** set the stage for the Industrial Revolution that took place in the following centuries. The long-term consequences of the changes in agriculture, such as the closing of lands to farming and the increased movement of people to the cities, were major factors in the rise of industrial growth.

In preindustrial times, most people lived in rural farming communities that had populations of several hundred people. In the countryside, life was harsh for peasants and their families who were employed in agriculture. Although feudalism had for the most part ended in Western Europe after the Middle Ages, the life of the rural peasantry hardly improved. The landlord still reigned supreme and the economic gap between rich, rural landowners and poor farmers, who composed the vast majority of the population in the countryside, remained very wide. Nevertheless, an Agricultural Revolution took place in some countries, helping to spur the Industrial Revolution.

Other factors also fostered the Industrial Revolution. The Age of Discovery led to a Commercial Revolution that increased the availability of capital, trading opportunities, **natural resources**, and labor. The expansion of world trade and the establishment of colonial empires led to the creation of markets for finished goods and a need for raw materials. Technological advances made it possible to produce goods more efficiently and quickly. In addition, the small industries that developed in textiles and other crafts increasingly converted to the domestic system of labor. The mining of coal, often in fields under farmland, provided the needed energy resource to generate power. The domestic system also was employed in mining coal fields.

The Industrial Revolution Begins in Great Britain

The Industrial Revolution began in Great Britain in the 1700s. Great Britain was the nation that combined all of the necessary factors that led to the growth of industry. These factors made the 1800s a British century, and will be examined in this chapter. Other nations of Europe and the United States spent the nineteenth century trying to catch up to Great Britain and duplicating the advances that made the British the world's first industrial empire.

The growth of industry in Great Britain was, in part, due to the political stability of the nation. During the tumultuous years of the seventeenth century, the English beheaded one king and forced another to flee the country. In the 1700s, the British political situation began to stabilize. Britain did take part in the many wars of the eighteenth century, particularly against its rival France, but these international conflicts led to no battles on English soil. A nationalist political spirit gradually developed in Britain.

British industry was thus able to grow and prosper without the interruptions caused by destruction due to warfare at home. In fact, the growth of British industry was assisted by government contracts for cloth to supply the nation's military

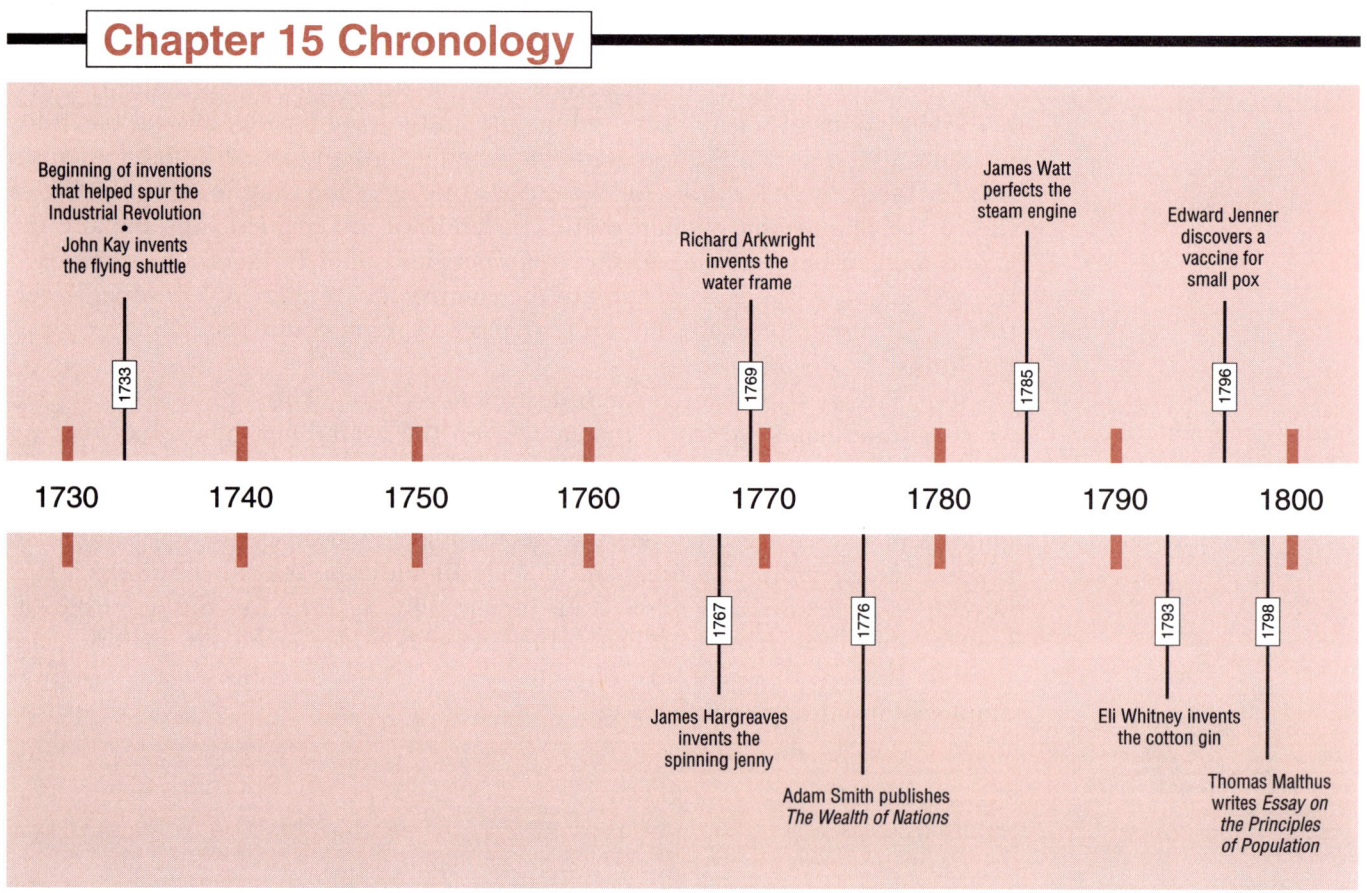

Chapter 15 Chronology

Beginning of inventions that helped spur the Industrial Revolution

John Kay invents the flying shuttle
1733

Richard Arkwright invents the water frame
1769

James Watt perfects the steam engine
1785

Edward Jenner discovers a vaccine for small pox
1796

1730 — 1740 — 1750 — 1760 — 1770 — 1780 — 1790 — 1800

James Hargreaves invents the spinning jenny
1767

Adam Smith publishes *The Wealth of Nations*
1776

Eli Whitney invents the cotton gin
1793

Thomas Malthus writes *Essay on the Principles of Population*
1798

forces. The ordinary citizen, who worked in England's factories and businesses, profited from the century of peace at home.

Business investment grew in a political climate that supported and encouraged economic growth. The influence that the increasingly powerful bankers, merchants, and other professional and business groups had in parliament led to laws that spurred new investment in industry. Throughout this chapter, we will examine other reasons for Great Britain's transformation to an industrial economy.

The Agricultural Revolution

The cast-iron plow aided farmers in preparing the soil for planting in a more efficient manner.

During the 1700s and 1800s, agricultural production increased in Europe because of innovations that changed farming methods. A greater food supply was needed because of an increase in population, particularly in the urban centers that rose as the industrial economy developed. Rapidly growing urban industrial centers stimulated the increased production of food supplies and other farm products.

Small-scale farming declined, in part, because it became more profitable for landowners to push their tenants off the land and enclose it to raise sheep for wool. This enclosure movement led to the migration of farm labor to the cities, particularly in Great Britain. In addition, scientific and technological advances in farming equipment and methods led to the creation of large land holdings, which improved harvests and livestock production.

The Impact of Scientific and Technological Advances in Agriculture

Crop Rotation

Crop rotation changed the method by which farmers kept fields fertile and resulted in increased yields. Crop rotation, perfected through experimentation by Charles Townshend, called for the planting of different crops to allow the soil to replenish itself. Townshend's idea was to grow turnips and clover to replenish the soil with nutrients lost in the growing of such cereals as wheat. In addition, the turnips and clover helped provide feed for animals. Alfalfa, which restored nitrates to the soil, could be grown and fed to animals. The next season wheat could again be planted. Crop rotation revolutionized agriculture. It was no longer necessary to allow fields to lie fallow. More cattle and sheep could be raised for meat, wool, and other animal by-products. And the diets of more people improved as meat became available at a lower cost.

New Inventions Lead to Increased Farm Production

Food production also increased because of the invention of machines and tools that improved farming methods. Jethro Tull symbolized the scientific farmer who used machinery in a well-planted field. Tull planted seeds in a straight row as opposed to scattering them at random. The seed drill was used by Tull to reduce seed loss and better control the weed problem. Other **innovators** perfected the

The seed planting machine made it easier for farmers to plant their crops and increased agricultural production.

iron plow that replaced less-efficient wooden plows. Still other inventions such as mechanical reapers led to further gains in the production of food supplies.

These new methods of farming dramatically changed agricultural production beginning in the early 1700s. The revolution in agriculture was a key to the success of the Industrial Revolution. There was a growing need to feed city workers and an increasingly urban population. The urban centers depended on greater farm production of traditional staples such as wheat and barley. The newly introduced American crops of corn and potatoes also improved the food supply as these staples became more popular.

The small farmer who was concerned with survival lacked the resources to expand food production for markets beyond the village. The harsh struggle to provide food for the family and pay rent and taxes prevented most farmers from taking advantage of increasing production by purchasing or renting more land. Instead the rich, rural landowners and other real estate investors purchased public and private lands and created large estates. The open-field system ended as more land was enclosed. The large landholders possessed the capital to farm by using scientific methods and thereby increased food production. The efficient farming methods made large-scale agricultural production more profitable. Live-

The thresher made it possible for farmers to harvest more crops in a shorter time and cut down on the use of manual labor.

The growth of textile mills during the Industrial Revolution was made possible by investment in new machinery and the increased use of wage labor.

stock raising also grew as a result of the enclosure movement.

The rural laborers were forced off the land and obliged to seek work in the urban centers. Many of the displaced farm workers became the labor force in the manufacturing of textiles and other products.

Industrial Developments

The Textile Industry

The woolen industry had existed for centuries in Great Britain and the Netherlands. In Britain, woolen production was second to farming in people employed and volume of trade. In the 1700s, the demand for woolen goods increased. The need for raw wool was one reason for the enclosure movement. The development of the woolen industry was facilitated by the use of a method of production referred to as the **domestic system**.

The Domestic System In the domestic system, workers were most often hired by entrepreneurs to produce woolens and other finished goods in their homes. Merchants supplied the raw wool, and paid spinners, weavers, fullers, and dyers to make a product that could be sold at market for the highest possible price. This method of production was called the domestic system.

In the domestic system of production, entrepreneurs employed networks of workers, often groups of families. This more efficient labor system increased the profitability of manufacturing. The domestic system worked well during the 1500s and 1600s. Thereafter, it could not keep up with the steady rise in demand for woolens, cotton cloth, leather workings, lace making, and other goods. Starting in the 1700s, a series of technological advances revolutionized cloth production. Cotton entrepreneurs found new ways to expand the textile industry.

Inventions Change the Production Methods of Textiles Advances in machinery changed cloth production. One of the first innovations that speeded the weaving of cloth was the flying shuttle. In 1733, John Kay, a British clockmaker, developed a weaving process that produced thread at a faster pace. Weavers became capable of producing wider fabrics using more materials. Weavers began to use spinner's thread faster than it could be made.

In 1767, James Hargreaves devised the spinning jenny. This machine enabled one person to spin up to seven threads at once. The spinning machine was steadily refined. Later models could produce up to 80 threads at a time. In 1769, Richard Arkwright invented a spinner called the water frame. This machine was capable of holding up to 100 spindles and used water power to continually run machines. The water frame also resulted in an increase in cloth production.

In 1779, Samuel Crompton further improved the cotton business by utilizing the best features of the spinning jenny and water powered frame to devise a machine known as the cotton mule. In a few short years, workers were able to produce high-quality cloth in larger quantities. Then, thread was being spun more

The invention and continual improvement of the loom led to increased weaving of cloth and helped further the production of textiles during the Industrial Revolution.

Eli Whitney's invention of the cotton gin made it easier to remove the seeds from cotton and stimulated the planting of this valuable crop. Whitney was also responsible for the idea of interchangeable parts in machines.

quickly than cloth could be woven. However, in 1785, Edmund Cartwright developed a power-driven machine for weaving called the power loom. Weavers could now produce up to 200 times more fine cloth than before.

The new problem in producing cloth concerned the raw cotton that weavers used in the spinning machines or power looms. The difficulty in separating out the seeds led to a shortage of cotton. However, by 1793, an American, Eli Whitney, invented the cotton gin. Whitney's labor-saving machine greatly aided the British cotton industry. The cotton gin cleaned the seeds from the fibers and the end result was a greater production of raw cotton, particularly in the United States during the 1800s. British importations of raw cotton in huge quantities enabled textile production to expand rapidly.

The Development of New Sources of Power and Transportation

Abundant Natural Resources and Favorable Geography Great Britain's rich supply of natural resources and excellent geographical conditions aided the start of the Industrial Revolution. Fine harbors and swiftly flowing rivers helped spur British trade. Access to raw materials and markets enabled British merchants and entrepreneurs to promote industrial growth. Shipment by water in a growing British merchant marine allowed overseas commerce to expand. Raw materials and finished goods flowed continuously on the nation's water transportation system. In addition, water provided the initial power for the development of industry.

Great Britain also possessed large supplies of coal and iron that were accessible. These key raw materials were essential for industrial development. Coal was also used as a power source to fuel industrial machinery. By the 1760s miners could use canals to ship coal more cheaply and easily to developing factories.

Iron production also improved because of technological changes. In the 1700s new processes were developed that increasingly made more efficient use of coke fuel to produce stronger iron. The ability to utilize coal instead of charcoal resulted in expanded iron production and more machinery for industry.

The Harnessing of Steam Power The early textile mills were built near flowing streams and rivers to take advantage of this source of water power. The ability to use the tremendous potential of steamed water finally became a reality when James Watt first developed the steam engine in 1785. By building upon earlier innovations, Watt made it possible for textile machines to be driven by steam engines. The harnessing of steam allowed entrepreneurs to build factories in more convenient locations. Freezing water during the cold winter was no longer a problem because of steam power.

Steam power also helped in coal mining. In 1698, Thomas Savery developed a steam-driven pump that helped in removing water from mines. By the 1700s, Savery's pump was improved upon by Thomas Newcomen. The innovative Newcomen pump was safer, but it often broke down and required lots of coal to generate the steam. Watt's steam engine greatly expanded the power of the earlier steam pumps, did not consume more fuel, and was safe to use.

James Watt's invention of a reliable steam engine resulted in the increased use of machines to provide the energy needed during the Industrial Revolution.

Capital, Commerce, and Labor

The Development of Commerce and Capital

The Commercial Revolution that began earlier in the 1500s led to an accumulation of money, or capital. Overseas trading empires that were financed by joint stock companies and banks created new wealth. This capital was reinvested and helped make the growth of industry possible. Fortunately for Great Britain, the nation's expanding overseas trading empire enabled British merchants and bankers to become more prosperous. More money became increasingly available for investment in industry.

In addition, the wealthy land-holding aristocracy and gentry profited greatly from the new large-scale farming. Landowners also earned money in overseas commerce, including the slave trade. The aristocracy and landed middle class often took advantage of investment in the growing industries.

The English banking system also began to modernize by the early 1700s. More efficient financial services such as loans at reasonable interest rates spurred investment in industry. Money became more readily available to improve machinery, construct factories, and increase production. The British government assisted in this process by encouraging business investment with favorable laws passed by Parliament.

The Growing Supply of Labor

One of the crucial factors in the development of industry was the availability of a large labor supply. The overall rise of European population after the Middle Ages was slow but steady. After the catastrophic demographic, or population, drop caused by the **bubonic plague**—a disease spread by black rats infested with fleas that carried a deadly bacillus—population growth resumed. By the mid-1700s, Western European population was approximately 135 million, or twice what it had been four centuries earlier. Within the next century, or by 1850, there was a phenomenal burst of population growth. For a variety of reasons, the number of Europeans rose to approximately 255 million. The new farming methods led to a rapid growth of food supplies to feed the expanding urban population.

Advances in medicine led to a declining death rate, particularly from the dreaded disease of smallpox. In 1796, Edward Jenner discovered a vaccine that was effective against smallpox. The control of this highly contagious disease, and other advances such as improved sanitation, resulted in people living longer. The survival of children through the perilous years from birth through early childhood reflected the better living conditions, more abundant food supplies, and improved health conditions of this period.

In 1798, Thomas Robert Malthus, a British economist, predicted that Europe was on the brink of another population catastrophe in his *Essay on the Principles of Population*. Malthus stated that European population was growing geometrically, while the available food supply was only increasing arithmetically. This prediction of dire consequences was based on Malthus's belief that European nations would soon outstrip their resources. Fortunately for Europe, the Industrial Revolution enormously expanded the productive capacity of Great Britain and other countries. It was now possible for the economies of industrial nations to support larger populations.

In Great Britain, it is estimated the population tripled from 1750 to 1850. By the mid-1800s, there were about 18 million people living in England. This rapid population growth spurred industrial progress by adding to the labor force in Great Britain. Other factors were also at play that made it possible to absorb these extra workers into the new factories and businesses. The rising demand for manufactured products required a growing labor supply. Expanding retail businesses also employed more workers.

Great Britain's Industrial Advantages

There was no single reason why Great Britain became Europe's leading industrial power by the nineteenth century. However, Britain did combine all of the necessary factors for industrial development. England was a politically stable nation whose government supported economic growth. The nation combined abundant natural resources, a favorable geography, and a business and scientific climate that encouraged new and innovative ideas. Most of the important inventions and innovative ideas that resulted in an increased capacity for industrial production in the 1700s and the first part of the 1800s originated in Great Britain.

The British also developed a banking system, which was capable of supporting industrial growth and handling the increased amount of financial transactions. Great Britain had a growing labor supply available for industry because of the movement of people to urban areas as a result of the agricultural enclosure movement and an increase in population.

During the 1700s and 1800s, British industrial growth profited from all of these favorable conditions that encouraged its rapid development. Great Britain was ripe for the economic changes that transformed the nation into the world's first industrial power. The ideas advocated by Adam Smith in *The Wealth of Nations* about free enterprise and laissez-faire economics proved to be the correct formula for British industrial expansion. A noninterventionist government policy was an important factor in Britain's economic transformation.

Summary

As is often said about periods of history, there was good news and bad news. The good news was that there was a greater production of food than before. The bad news was that people were forced off the land and had to uproot themselves and move to the cities. There is also another example of necessity and invention. The demand for increasing quantities of textile goods resulted in a series of inventions that sped up production. This in turn led to the need for more reliable and greater power, and so Watt developed a much-improved steam engine. This had an impact on mining operations. Great Britain was fortunate that it was in a position to lead in this, as it made the country the dominant power in Europe for the nineteenth century. This also impacted the social situation in England. Change took place at a rapid rate. The question of whether this is good or bad is one we will investigate as we go on.

CHAPTER 15

Review Exercises

I. Multiple Choice

Directions: Find the *letter* of the correct answer.

1. In Great Britain, the migration of farm labor to the cities was assisted by the

   (a) domestic system.
   (b) enclosure movement.
   (c) decline in urban population.
   (d) open-field system.

2. Food production increased for all of the following reasons *except*

   (a) the invention of machines and tools for farming.
   (b) crop rotation to increase yields.
   (c) the increase of the open-field system.
   (d) large land owners possessed more capital.

3. The production of finished goods at home is called

   (a) the domestic system.
   (b) scientific production.
   (c) the assembly line.
   (d) labor-saving production.

4. The invention of the cotton gin

   (a) led to the development of the power loom.
   (b) greatly stimulated textile production.
   (c) decreased the need for raw cotton.
   (d) led to a decline in the use of slave labor.

5. Great Britain's Industrial Revolution was aided by all of the following *except*

   (a) a rich supply of coal and iron ore.
   (b) excellent geographical conditions.
   (c) a growing trading empire.
   (d) the availability of petroleum.

6. The harnessing of steam power

   (a) led to a decline in the need for coal.
   (b) did not solve the problem of freezing water in winter.
   (c) led to the development of steam-powered textile machines.
   (d) only aided industrial growth after 1800.

7. The development of commerce in England was aided by

   (a) more efficient financial services.
   (b) the decline of joint stock companies.
   (c) workers investing more capital in stocks.
   (d) the use of mercantilist policies after 1776.

8. Starting in the mid-1700s, Western European populations

   (a) remained stable for 100 years.
   (b) declined 10 percent by 1850.
   (c) almost doubled within a century.
   (d) recovered after four centuries of decline.

9. In his *Essay on the Principles of Population*, Thomas Malthus predicted

   (a) Europe would have a sufficient food supply.
   (b) Europe was on the brink of a population catastrophe.
   (c) that the population of Europe would grow arithmetically.
   (d) that the economies of industrial nations could support larger populations.

10. Political stability in Great Britain

   (a) increased during the reign of the Stuart kings.
   (b) encouraged economic growth by the mid-1700s.
   (c) had no real effect on the growth of industry.
   (d) led to a resurgence of the aristocracy in the nineteenth century.

II. Matching

Directions: Match the person in Column A with the achievement they are *best known* for in Column B.

Column A	Column B
1. James Watt	(a) developed the system of crop rotation
2. Eli Whitney	(b) perfected the use of the seed drill
3. Jethro Tull	(c) invented the water frame
4. Charles Townshend	(d) invented the spinning jenny
5. Richard Arkwright	(e) invented the flying shuttle
6. Edmund Cartwright	(f) perfected the cotton mule
7. Thomas Savery	(g) invented the cotton gin
8. John Kay	(h) invented crude steam pump for mining
9. Samuel Crompton	(i) developed the steam engine
10. James Hargreaves	(j) developed the power loom

III. Matching

Directions: Match the words in Column A with the *correct description* in Column B.

Column A
1. natural resources
2. enclosure movement
3. crop rotation
4. innovator
5. spinning jenny
6. cotton gin
7. gentry
8. bubonic plague
9. noninterventionist
10. vaccine

Column B
(a) dead bacteria used to produce immunity to a disease
(b) people of good birth and social standing
(c) the practice of fencing off common lands by wealthy landowners in the 1700s
(d) materials found in nature and used by people
(e) a person who makes changes or introduces new methods
(f) machine that spun several threads at the same time
(g) a person who does not interfere
(h) a terrible disease, carried by fleas on rats, which killed many people in the fourteenth century
(i) machine that separated seeds from cotton
(j) the system of alternating different crops in a field to keep land fertile

IV. Skills Practice: Time Placement

Directions: Place the following items on a timeline.

1. cotton gin
2. water frame
3. flying shuttle
4. spinning jenny
5. steam engine
6. smallpox vaccine

V. Thought Questions

Directions: Answer the following questions in essay form.

1. The Agricultural Revolution had both positive and negative effects on the lives of people. Prove this is true by explaining two positive and two negative effects on people.

2. List three inventions in the textile industry that led to greater production. For each invention explain how it resulted in increased production.

3. You are an editorial writer for the *London Times*. Write an editorial that will persuade the British people to start an Industrial Revolution. In your editorial give three examples of Britain's advantages.

4. Cite three reasons why the urban labor force increased in Western Europe. For each reason explain how it resulted in more urban residents and workers.

5. Compose a speech to a group of investors in which you explain to them why they should abandon the domestic system and invest in a factory that you are building.

CHAPTER 16

Development of an Industrial Economy

Industrialization spread rapidly to other countries. As was true in Britain, the factory system became the center of the industrial economy in France, Germany, the United States, northern Italy, Belgium, and the Netherlands during the 1800s. Industrial growth was characterized by large-scale manufacturing that took place in factories. After the 1870s, smaller-scale industrial development began to spread to other global areas.

Improvement in transportation and communication helped industry to grow. The digging of canals in Great Britain, France, the United States, and elsewhere provided water links that made the shipment of raw materials and finished goods easier and cheaper. Roads linking urban areas were constructed by private companies. The arrival of the steam-powered locomotive made railroad transportation possible. In the nineteenth century, a railroad boom began in the industrializing countries. Scientific inventions also led to the development of better communications. The telegraph, wireless, and telephone all assisted commerce and industry to expand and operate more efficiently.

The spread of industry was facilitated by the expansion of the **capitalist system**. The rise of big business in turn spurred the development of industrial **capitalism**. **Mass production** of cheaper goods resulted in higher profits but required greater investment in machinery. Individual and family businesses, **partnerships**, and **corporations** flourished in the expanding industrial world of the nineteenth century.

The Spread of Industry to Other Nations

Great Britain

Great Britain sought to prevent the spread of industrial knowledge and technological advances to other countries. Parliament passed laws to prohibit the exportation of British industrial secrets. Laws making machinery export illegal and prohibiting British technicians and mechanics from moving to other countries were enacted. The English goal was to safeguard its position as the world's leading industrial and trading nation. Despite the severe restrictions enacted, however, Great Britain could not maintain its industrial monopoly.

France

In the 1800s, the French government pursued policies that encouraged industrialization. France at first promoted its textile manufacturing. From the 1830s to the mid-1860s, cotton textile production doubled. The invention of the silk loom by Joseph-Marie Jacquard led to the rise of a dynamic silk manufacturing industry. French industry tended to specialize in the fabrication of luxury items. Carpets, tapestries, fashion clothing, excellent wines, and porcelains were not mass produced in large factories. These craft-oriented goods were manufactured by artisans in limited-sized businesses.

French railroad development aided industrial growth. A railroad network was built that radiated out of Paris in all directions. Banking and commercial interests influenced the French government to reduce high tariffs and other trade barriers. Trade and commerce thereafter expanded. In the decades after the Revolution of

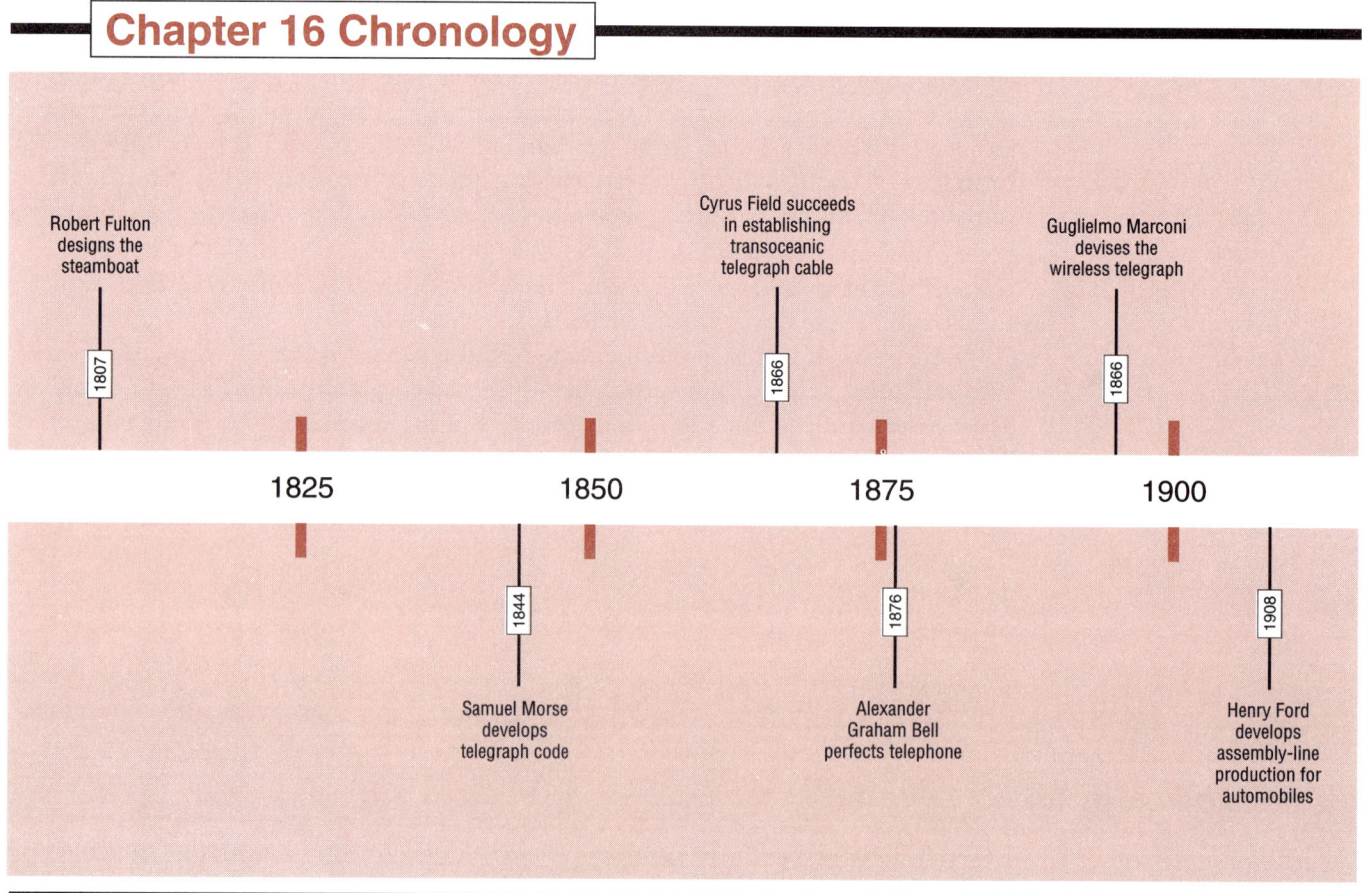

Chapter 16 Chronology

Robert Fulton designs the steamboat — 1807

Cyrus Field succeeds in establishing transoceanic telegraph cable — 1866

Guglielmo Marconi devises the wireless telegraph — 1866

1825   1850   1875   1900

1844 — Samuel Morse develops telegraph code

1876 — Alexander Graham Bell perfects telephone

1908 — Henry Ford develops assembly-line production for automobiles

1848, French industry tended to remain as primarily small-scale, craft-oriented enterprises. Agricultural production also continued to be characterized by the traditional system of limited-sized family farms.

Germany

In Germany, an industrial economy began to develop in the post-Napoleonic Period. British investment was the initial source for industrial capital. German industrial pioneers such as Krupp, Stinnes, and Mannesman later provided much of the national capital to finance industrial growth. The combination of government funding with national and international investment capital led to a boom in railroad development after 1840.

The German textile and metallurgy industries flourished by the mid-1800s. Advanced mining techniques led to the exploitation of the Ruhr and Saar iron and coal fields. After the 1840s iron production in Germany significantly increased.

Under the leadership of Prussia, the German states created a customs union called the **Zollverein** in 1834. This free-trade area included all the major German states. The removal of trade barriers encouraged industrial expansion. By the 1850s, Germany had the European continent's most powerful industrial economy. Within a generation, Germany would challenge Great Britain's industrial leadership.

Other European Countries

Industrialization spread elsewhere in Europe in the 1800s. Belgium profited from its commercial relations with the Netherlands and rich deposits of coal for fuel to build textile factories. In northern Italy, the combination of a skilled and urbanized labor force, plentiful deposits of coal and iron, and good transportation and communication links led to industrial growth. Later, the manufacturing of textiles on a large scale spread to Eastern Europe and czarist Russia.

Developments in Business and Industry

Industrial Capitalism Leads to Mass Production

The development of the capitalist system aided the rise of large factories and mass production. Capitalism was the economic system that made it possible for more individuals to invest in and own manufacturing enterprises. The possibility of earning more profits motivated people to invest in all types of manufacturing businesses. Capitalism contributed to the growth of bigger business enterprises and increased production.

Capital investment greatly aided the expansion of the factory system. Increased financial investment in new factories and equipment accelerated during the 1800s. In order to make very high profits, industrial capitalists sought control of all aspects of the means of production. Manufacturers exploited the labor force and determined the range of consumer choice.

Preindustrial capitalism first led to the growth of a global trading economy. By the nineteenth century the Industrial Revolution resulted in a manufacturing economy that incorporated gains made earlier during Europe's commercial expansion.

Investment capital was utilized to purchase costly machinery that replaced more expensive and less efficient labor. The development of mass production technology enabled factory owners to produce large quantities of identical goods by using fast-working and precise machinery. The mass production of similar goods received a boost when the concept of **interchangeable parts** was introduced. By the early 1800s, Eli Whitney's contribution of replaceable parts made it easier to assemble machinery and change worn-out parts.

During the nineteenth century, the idea of industrial efficiency increasingly became popular because it led to more production at a cheaper cost and higher profits. In the later decades of the 1800s, factories adopted a **division-of-labor** system. Workers were assigned specialized tasks and took responsibility for a particular job. As the product moved down the **assembly line** each worker was responsible for completing a task. The success of the assembly-line system increased the quantities of manufactured goods and lowered production costs. The industrialist had greater ability to sell at a cheaper price and thus expand the market for the particular product. Assembly-line production spread in Europe and the United States.

The American Henry Ford utilized the assembly-line system to mass produce automobiles in 1908. A conveyor belt transported an auto body, and workers alongside all completed their specialized tasks to finish the car. The Model T Ford became the symbol of efficient assembly-line production.

Business Organizations Modernize

The need to finance industrial development led to the growth of more complex business organizations. The expansion of industry and trade resulted in larger-sized businesses. Individual and family-owned enterprises continued to grow, but other types of business organizations became popular because they proved more capable of raising capital and limiting risk.

Partnerships were formed by two or more individuals who agreed to share management responsibility and work together to raise capital. Debt liability was thus limited for each partner, and more business could be taken on by a group of partners. The partnership form of business grew in the 1800s.

The corporation, or enterprise owned by many investors, became the favored form of business organization of most larger companies by the mid-nineteenth century. Corporations or **joint stock companies** had played a pivotal role since the Commercial Revolution in financing expeditions and trading ventures. During the 1800s, entrepreneurs increasingly offered shares of **stock** or ownership in new companies to raise the necessary capital to launch a manufacturing enterprise. Investment in the stock of an enterprise made the holder of that company's shares a part owner of the business.

Stockholders could earn income based on the number of shares that were held, if the company was profitable. In addition, a stockholder could also profit if the share price increased, and the stock was sold for a higher price than that for which it was originally purchased. Losses were limited to the amount of shares owned and did not exceed the purchase price for the stock. In the 1800s, industrial countries began to pass laws that eliminated the stockholder's responsibility if the company failed and could not pay its debts.

The success of big business corporations in Great Britain, Germany, the United States, and elsewhere in Europe was often at the expense of smaller enterprises that could not compete on a larger scale. Corporations, when possible, bought out smaller companies and tried to establish a **monopoly**, or complete control, of the market for a particular product. The Standard Oil Company, organized and controlled by the American John D. Rockefeller, established total domination of the oil industry in the United States. In Europe and the United States large corporations sought control of the companies that contributed to their final products. This form of monopoly was called **vertical integration** and was used in Europe and the United States to eliminate competition.

Banks increasingly played a key role in financing industrial development. In Europe, the House of Rothschild based in Paris became one of the world's leading investment banks. The Rothschild bank worked with other investment institutions to organize companies and finance overseas business ventures in transportation, mainly railroads, and communication systems. As the 1800s progressed, international investment ventures by private banks became more commonplace. Governments also became involved in helping protect investments and secure markets.

Fluctuations in the Business Cycles

In the era of the Industrial Revolution, business cycles increasingly determined the fate of entire national economies. The business cycle included periods of prosperity and boom times as well as **recession** and **depression**. Industrialization made related businesses increasingly dependent on each other. If the economy was expanding, one industry might contribute to the growth of another. For example, the railroad boom led to increased coal and iron production.

Business cycles followed predictable sequences, although the length of time of each expansion and decline varied. During a boom phase there was high employment, increased production, and more buying and selling; however, prosperous times did not last forever. Inevitably a period of recession or even bust followed. Decreased business activity and unemployment resulted. If the decline was severe enough, it was called a depression. Business fluctuations often led to widespread suffering in times of depression.

Before the nineteenth century most people in Europe lived in the countryside or small towns and farmed for a living. By the twentieth century, there was an enormous growth in the cities. The numbers of factory workers in the industrialized nations of Western Europe grew during this period. Agricultural employment and rural populations declined while industry expanded. The development of the industrial economy brought great changes for the urban factory worker.

Workers were naturally dependent on their salaries to support themselves and their families. The arrival of hard times particularly hurt the urban industrial worker. Unfortunately, the capitalist system of production could not guarantee workers jobs all of the time.

Scientific Advances Further Industrial Development

Industrial development benefited from advances in science and technology. Transportation and communication improvements made businesses easier to run and more profitable. The harnessing of steam power revolutionized water and land transportation. In 1807, the American Robert Fulton perfected a steam-powered boat, which was able to travel on the Hudson River. By the late 1830s, steamships were crossing the Atlantic Ocean carrying passengers and goods.

Richard Trevithick, a British engineer, developed a steam-powered locomotive that ran on rails in 1804. A railroad boom took place first in the industrial nations and later worldwide as design improvements made the steam locomotive more workable. Railroads and steamships made it possible to move more goods faster and cheaper. Transportation advances helped spur the growth of a world economy and led to increased overseas investment.

In the late 1800s, a new type of engine was developed that used gasoline and petroleum oil for fuel. This internal combustion engine ultimately replaced the steam engine in the 1900s because it was easier to operate and more dependable. The combustion engine eventually powered cars, trucks, ships, and locomotives.

The elevator was one of the modern urban conveniences that made it possible for people and goods to be transported within a building.

The increased production of land vehicles led to the building of better road networks.

Scientific advances also played an important part in speeding communication. The development of faster communications made the operation of businesses easier. Samuel Morse, an American inventor, is credited with developing the telegraph in 1844. Morse code, based on a system of dots and dashes, was transmitted over telegraph wire. The industrial nations of Europe and the United States were soon linked by the telegraph lines that carried information at high speeds over great distances. In 1866, Cyrus Field completed a transatlantic cable that linked Europe and North America. In the 1870s, it became possible to send a cable around the world from New York to Paris to Tokyo and elsewhere in a matter of minutes.

Another communication advance was the invention of the telephone in 1876 by Alexander Graham Bell. The telephone used small electrical wires to carry the sound of people's voices and enabled people to speak over long distances. In 1895, the Italian Guglielmo Marconi perfected a system to transmit electric signals without the use of cable or wire. Marconi's wireless was called the radio in the United States.

The advances in harnessing electricity made the powering of streetlights and the use of electric-current motors practical. Thomas Edison's invention of the incandescent light design for electric generating plants brought cheap lighting to factories, streets, and homes. By the early 1900s electricity began to replace coal as the primary source for industrial energy to power machines.

Technological innovations in transportation, communication, and electricity led to dramatic changes in the ways people lived and worked. The pace of life quickened wherever the new technology spread. Industrialization brought an ever-increasing **mechanization** and modernization to the world economy.

Summary

Increased industrial production in Europe was the result of a combination of factors. Great Britain served as a model for other European nations to follow. The growth of transportation and communication networks was also important for the growth of industry. The rise of big business concerns, particularly corporations, which were capable of raising large sums of capital for investment in factories and equipment, enabled manufacturing to expand. By the end of the nineteenth century, a number of nations in Western Europe and the United States had launched their Industrial Revolutions.

I. Multiple Choice

Directions: Find the *letter* of the correct answer.

1. The Industrial Revolution began in the late 1700s in

   (a) Germany.
   (b) Great Britain.
   (c) Italy.
   (d) the United States.

2. Early industrialization in France was characterized by the

   (a) development of heavy industry.
   (b) specialization in the fabrication of luxury goods.
   (c) mass production of goods in large factories.
   (d) conversion from small-scale to large farms.

3. The German states created the Zollverein in 1834 to

   (a) promote a military alliance in Germany.
   (b) facilitate the development of a free-trade area.
   (c) restrict trade between Prussia and the rest of Germany.
   (d) challenge Great Britain's economic superiority in Europe.

4. The development of capitalism contributed to all of the following *except*

   (a) the rise of large factories and mass production.
   (b) more money available for investment in industry.
   (c) the growth of a global trading economy.
   (d) more workers laboring in safer conditions.

5. Industrial efficiency in the nineteenth century was aided by

   (a) monopolies.
   (b) vertical integration.
   (c) assembly lines.
   (d) partnerships.

6. Corporations became popular as a form of business because they

   (a) prevented investment by foreigners.
   (b) limited risk and raised more capital.
   (c) gave stockholders managerial responsibility.
   (d) always earned shareholders a profit.

7. Business cycles have a tendency to

   (a) vary in the length of expansion and decline.
   (b) always have longer boom phases.
   (c) rarely have periods of decline.
   (d) increase employment in times of depression.

8. The capitalist system of production

   (a) guarantees workers jobs all the time.
   (b) has always benefited the industrial worker.
   (c) led to greater agricultural employment while industry expanded.
   (d) made it possible for more people to invest in and own businesses.

9. Great Britain would be most afraid of

   (a) French increased food production.
   (b) American support of Spanish industry.
   (c) German rapid industrial growth.
   (d) Russian investment in Austria.

10. One result of the changes during this period was the

    (a) increased harmony among nations.
    (b) shrinking of the world.
    (c) move back to farming areas.
    (d) control of nations by banking concerns.

II. Matching

Directions: Match the names in Column A with the achievement they are *best known* for in Column B.

Column A	Column B
1. Henry Ford	(a) development of telegraph code system
2. Robert Fulton	(b) steam-powered locomotive in Great Britain
3. Richard Trevithick	(c) wireless communication
4. Guglielmo Marconi	(d) developed steamboat in United States
5. Samuel Morse	(e) assembly-line production of automobiles

III. Vocabulary

Directions: Define the following words, terms, or expressions and use them in a written sentence.
   1. mass production—
   2. vertical integration—
   3. capitalism—

4. assembly line—
5. monopoly—
6. division of labor—
7. partnership—
8. corporation—
9. interchangeable parts—
10. mechanization—

IV. Thought Questions

Directions: Answer the following questions in essay form.

1. Explain three ways in which the development of capitalism spurred the Industrial Revolution.

2. Describe in an essay how industrial efficiency increased production in the nineteenth century. Give at least three examples.

3. In a written speech to potential stock investors explain the advantages of a corporation as a business organization.

4. Cite three advances in science and technology and explain how they aided industrial development.

5. List the nations to which the Industrial Revolution spread in the nineteenth century. Select one country and explain the conditions that aided its industrial development.

V. Activities

Directions: Complete the following activities.

1. Chose an invention that was made in the nineteenth century. Explain in an essay how this invention helped change your life.

2. Go to a museum that has a photograph collection of industrial production in the nineteenth century. Use the photographs to do a research report on what a factory was like during this time period.

CHAPTER 17

Changes in Social and Economic Conditions

How did the lives of people change when some European societies underwent the transformation from an agricultural to an industrial-based economy? Why did some people benefit from these changes while other people only exchanged one difficult existence for another? How did people live in the developing cities? What were the living conditions in the growing industrial centers? These are some of the questions that will be discussed in the following pages. In this chapter, you will read about how the lives of people were changed as urban centers expanded in the Industrial Age. You will also read about what the cities were like in the 1800s as they rapidly grew.

The Industrial Revolution had an enormous impact on the way people lived and worked. The working and living conditions in the nations that developed industrial economies experienced dramatic changes as cities grew larger. In the 1800s, industrialization radically altered the life of those people who left rural agricultural areas for the urban centers where they could find factory work. The expansion of the industrial economy transformed the social structure in Great Britain and elsewhere in Western Europe. This shift from a rural agricultural economy to an urban industrial economy led to major societal changes that had profound long-term consequences.

For the most part, traditional life on the farm had never been easy and was far from what may be thought of as a rustic or pastoral dream. The farmer historically worked throughout the year from sunrise to sunset, in all types of weather, performing difficult agricultural tasks. Conditions in farming villages were horrible. To quote Thomas Hobbes from his 1651 book *Leviathan*, life was "nasty, brutish, and short."

Young children were called upon to help out with chores around the farm at an early age and later worked alongside their parents to do whatever had to be done to help their family survive. Marriage took place at an early age, and the newlywed couples were fortunate if they could farm their own land right away. Life was rustic and pleasures were few and simple. Nevertheless, everyone shared the same lifestyle and families lived and usually remained together or in the same general locality. Families were better able to take care of their older members when they ceased to be economically productive.

The Industrial Revolution caused major alterations in the traditional life-styles and ways of making a living for those people who came to the urban centers from rural areas. In the European nations where industrialization took place, economic and social problems arose in these urban areas.

Industrialization was a contributing factor in the population explosion and rapid growth of large cities. The rise of the factory system created a need for more workers in the urban centers. Although working and living conditions for the industrial and mining workers were often difficult, people continued to flock to the cities in search of work. City living was destructive to the working-class family because its members no longer functioned as a cohesive unit. The urban family had to adapt to patterns of labor and life-styles that were ruinous to its health and social well-being.

Radically different ways of living and working developed in the industrializing countries as people moved to larger towns and cities. There were new opportunities for people to improve their status in society. Prior to the Industrial Age, a person's position in life was determined at birth. There was little possibility for people to rise above the level of their families' status. In a social structure determined by the traditional agricultural economy, upward mobility was limited.

Chapter 17 Chronology

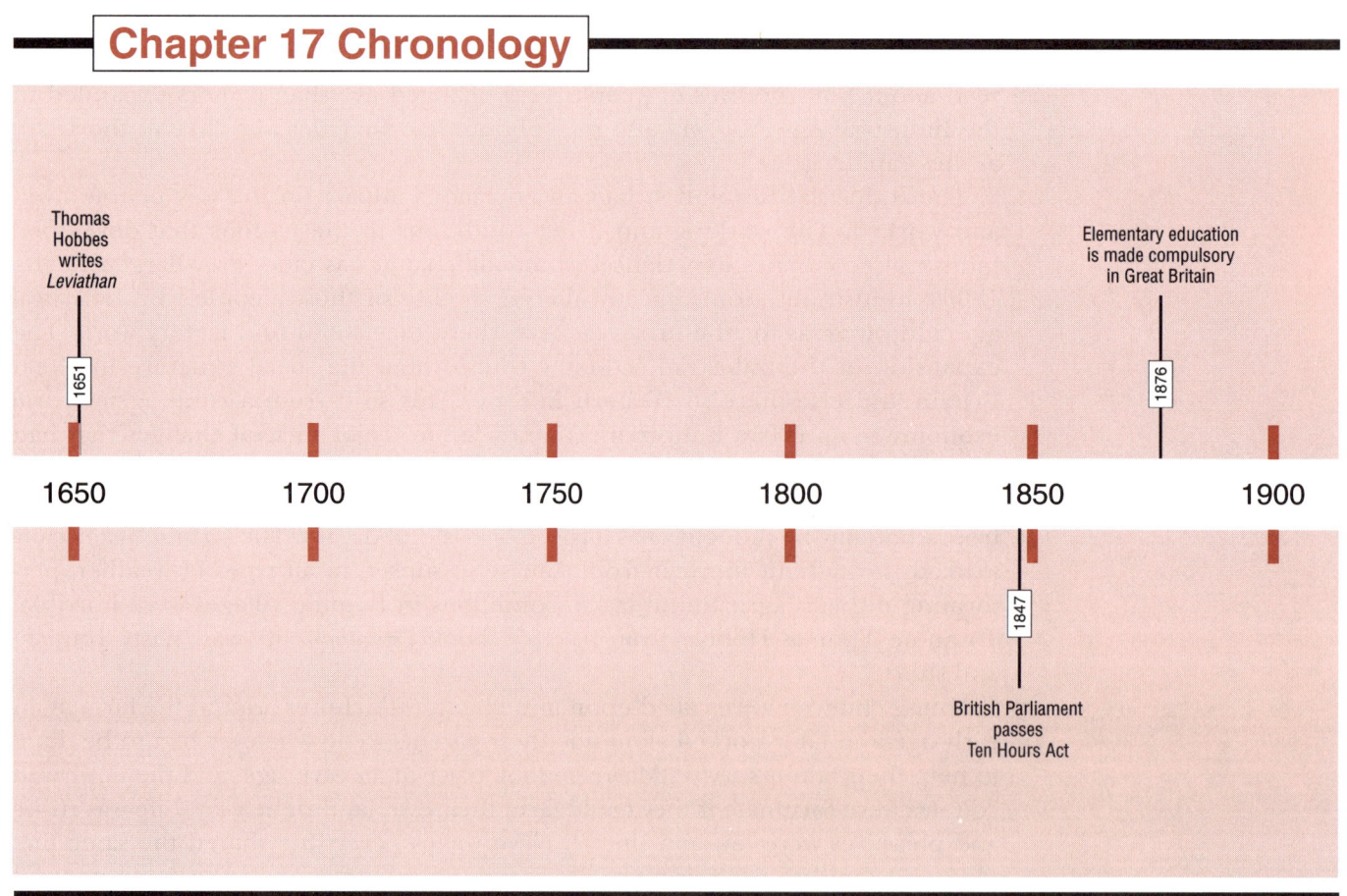

Thomas Hobbes writes *Leviathan*
1651

Elementary education is made compulsory in Great Britain
1876

1650 1700 1750 1800 1850 1900

1847
British Parliament passes Ten Hours Act

The Growth of the Middle Class

The growth of industrial centers resulted in the expansion of the middle class. The middle class comprised the **social class** between the aristocracy, or very wealthy, and the workers, or lower groups in society. People in urban areas had more of an opportunity to use their initiative and talent to achieve material success and a higher status in a more flexible and fluid society. The industrial and business elite grew rich and the middle class prospered. Nevertheless, not everyone benefited from the opportunities presented by the Industrial Age.

The development of a middle class in Western Europe had been limited by an agricultural-based economy. There were not enough opportunities for advancement in agriculture, particularly in European countries where farm ownership and employment began to decrease. The growth of industrialization and the rise of the urban centers gave more opportunities to an expanding middle class.

In the Preindustrial Era, the middle class was primarily composed of a small number of doctors, merchants, lawyers, and bankers. Industrialization enabled new groups of people to enjoy the benefits of middle class life. Successful owners of mines, railroads, and factories gained upper-middle-class status. Increasing numbers of professional workers such as managers of companies and stores, teachers, clerks, and owners of small businesses achieved middle-class status.

The middle-class life-style led to changes in the family. In the agricultural economy men and women shared the responsibility of providing for the family. However, in the industrial economy men increasingly became the sole providers for their families. In the growing cities, middle-class women devoted themselves to bringing up their children and maintaining the home. A husband's success was often measured by his ability to hire domestic help to relieve his wife's burdens at home. Servants were employed for low wages to perform the tedious household chores, enabling middle class women to escape the drudgery of washing laundry, cleaning, and other unpleasant household tasks.

In the 1800s few middle-class women worked outside of their homes. Nevertheless, many women who no longer had to work took the opportunity to improve their lives. Freed from the household chores, middle-class women used the time to educate their children and themselves at home. These women taught their daughters how to embroider, sew, cook, and act like refined young ladies. Some women also instructed themselves in the natural sciences, geography, gardening, and ways to improve their homes.

The urban middle-class family was very conscious of its social position. It did not identify with the other growing social class, the industrial workers. The middle class, particularly its more wealthy members, sought to copy the life-styles of the aristocratic upper class. Much of their wealth went into the purchasing of large homes and even estates that were lavishly furnished and decorated. Even those middle-class families who lived a more moderate life-style were conscious of their status in society. They sought to show their social position by dress and other mannerisms that set them apart from the working class. A respectable appearance and polite manners were among the expected social norms that the middle class displayed in society.

Middle-class boys had more opportunities than girls outside of the home. Boys were sent to school for the training needed to succeed at work and to maintain their family's social position. Higher education for young men from good families became increasingly possible. Some middle class young men were educated to take over their fathers' positions in the family business. Girls and young women had limited job opportunities. Middle-class women were not expected to be wage earners or pursue professional careers. An important change came about in 1876, when elementary education was made compulsory.

The Urban Working Class Expands

The vast majority of working-class families that labored in factories and lived in the urban industrial centers faced harsh economic and social conditions. Workers and their families often suffered as a result of the terrible economic and social problems that industrialization created for the labor force.

The largest growth of population in the industrializing nations of Western Europe was in the cities. The population explosion that began in the mid-1700s resulted in expanding urban centers where people flocked to find work in factories and mills. As the population increased, the living conditions that the workers confronted steadily worsened despite gains made in medicine and the improved food supply.

The growth of cities during the Industrial Revolution was a result of increased trade and factory production, and the rise of urban areas as job centers. The growth of industrial centers expanded the middle class.

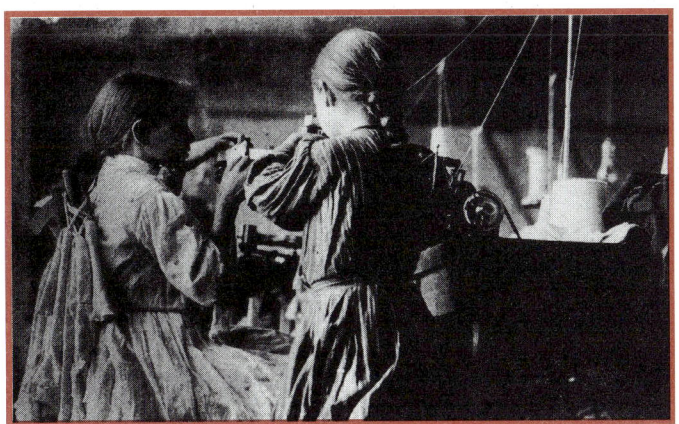

During the Industrial Revolution, women and girls were increasingly employed in textile factories. The use of women and child labor was popular because they earned lower wages.

The majority of people who came to the cities ended up working in factories. This working class became known as the **proletariat**. Working conditions in the industrial plants were often extremely difficult. The early efforts by Europeans, namely the British industrialists, to create decent working conditions and establish model factory towns ended as competition increased.

The increased supply of skilled and unskilled workers led to a favorable labor situation for the factory owners, who were able to keep wages very low. Poor salaries made it necessary for an entire family, including young children who started to work as early as age six, to search for employment. Finding a job for all of its members made it easier for the family to survive. Children and women were particularly sought after because they worked for lower wages than men. Young children who labored in mines and factories often did dangerous jobs. Many of them were your age or younger.

General working conditions were dangerous and unhealthy. Workers labored twelve to sixteen hours daily, six days a week. Much of the labor involved operating noisy machinery that lacked safeguards. The long hours of monotonous and repetitive labor often resulted in accidents that seriously injured working men, women, and children. There was no compensation for the loss of a finger, limb, or even the life of a worker.

Workers followed their rigid schedules throughout the year. There were no vacations, sick leaves, or paid holidays. Ventilation and lighting were often very poor, and workers suffered in an atmosphere where the air was full of fumes and smoke. Horrible environmental conditions led to serious health problems for workers in factories, mills, and mines. For example, coal miners, particularly children, breathed in coal dust that blackened their lungs, thus shortening their lives. The crowded conditions in the factories and poor ventilation caused the easy spread of diseases such as tuberculosis and pneumonia, which killed many workers.

Time became more of a factor in the lives of the industrial workers. The rhythms of the seasons and the sun's daily path determined the work cycle of farmers. However, the industrial worker found that time ruled their lives in a more structured manner. Workers were required to report to their jobs and follow rigid schedules that were designed to maximize production. The factory workers moved to the sound of the bell that signaled the beginning and the end to a shift as well as periods allowed for activities such as lunch. To a large measure, the workers became dehumanized as they lost their ability to function as independent human beings. Some progress in their condition was made, however, with passage of the Ten Hours Act in 1847.

Living Conditions in the Cities

The living conditions of workers and their families differed greatly from that of the upper- and middle-class city residents. The comfortable life-styles of the upper-class families were increasingly shared by the more wealthy middle-class members. Professionals such as lawyers and bankers and business owners were better able to provide their families with conveniences and luxuries previously only available to the upper class. Even middle-class parents who were not very affluent had comfortable lives and offered their children the advantages of education, health care, and proper sanitation. Workers and their families, for the most part, did not share in these advantages of city life.

Nevertheless, it should be remembered that the city served as an escape from the terrible conditions that existed in farming villages and agricultural work and the authoritarian rule of the landlord who dominated rural life. Despite its harshness, city life broke down the rigidity of the class system and offered more hope for advancement. The living conditions of the workers and their families in the cities were too often miserable. The rapid growth of cities throughout the period of industrialization resulted in the construction of tenement-type housing for working-class families. In the poorer city neighborhoods in Great Britain, France, Germany, Belgium, and elsewhere, crime, disease, and other problems plagued the life of the urban family.

Prior to the 1800s, most cities developed in places that were convenient to land and water trading routes. The Industrial Revolution, however, led to an explosive growth of cities in areas that were not natural marketplaces. Cities grew near sources of power, such as coal fields, and other raw materials. The building of factories or mills often led to a rapid rise in the surrounding population as people flocked in to find work. Factory owners and middle-class families took the best available housing and constructed new and more lavish homes on private estates. The workers and their families were forced to make due with whatever was offered to them or was available.

In the early stage of the Industrial Revolution, some of the enlightened factory and mill owners sought to establish towns in which the living conditions of the workers were tolerable. In factory towns such as Manchester and Sheffield there were attempts to provide workers with better living conditions.

As industrial competition heightened in the 1800s, however, less care and thought went into planning city growth. In fact, urban cities grew so quickly that housing, sanitation, and other conditions of urban life became increasingly dangerous and unhealthy. The owners of factories, mills, and mines were more concerned with profits and industrial competition than they were with the living conditions of the workers and their families. Even though some mill owners provided their laborers with housing and were instrumental in raising health standards, most industrialists opted not to improve the general living conditions of their workers.

Life at Home

The vast majority of workers and their families had a miserable home life. The long work day of twelve to sixteen hours kept workers away from their homes six days a week from sunrise to sunset. After dark, the exhausted workers returned to their crowded, poorly constructed tenement buildings. Often living space was limited to one or two rooms for a family of six to ten people. The lack of ventilation and adequate heating made these apartments too hot in the summer and too cold in the winter. The poor health conditions resulted in the spread of communicable diseases such as typhoid and cholera.

The tenements were built either out of wood or brick and little attention was given to the common areas. Courtyards, halls, and alleyways were often dark. Large piles of garbage and other filth including excrement made these areas unsightly and unhealthy. The stench that rose from these tenements was often overwhelming.

Neighborhood Conditions

Street conditions were hardly any better. The majority of streets were unpaved and had no drainage facilities. When it rained, the mud combined with garbage and other filth, making walking in the streets difficult. Horse-drawn carriages and wagons added to the problem. The air was often heavy with black smoke from the coal-burning factories and mills. At times there were attempts to clean larger avenues, but in general few cities did much to improve the quality of the streets. Crime became commonplace on dark and isolated city streets and alleys. Some changes were made with the introduction of gas street lamps, paved streets, and drainage systems, but the deplorable conditions of the industrial city streets for the most part continued throughout the nineteenth century.

The factory, mill, and mine owners operated with a free hand. Industrialists did not concern themselves with improving the conditions of city life. Essentially, they lacked a sense of social responsibility. Rivers that flowed through industrial cities were used to dump industrial and mining wastes. The water in rivers and streams became increasingly contaminated and unusable for drinking, cooking, and even washing.

Not surprisingly, the terrible living and working conditions in the cities had a negative impact on the average worker's life span. Disease was rampant in the factories and tenements. The ravages of pneumonia, tuberculosis, cholera, and typhoid reduced the life span of the working class. Children were particularly vulnerable and suffered greatly if they worked in the dark, damp, and poorly ventilated mines.

Workers had flocked to the cities in hopes of finding work and creating a better life for themselves and their families. Unfortunately, for most workers this did not happen. Although most workers did find jobs, their lives rarely improved. In rural areas, families were used to working on farms from dawn to dusk. Farm life was hard, but at least the family worked, ate, and rested together in conditions that proved to be far more sanitary than those in the industrial city. They shared life as a social unit. However, in the city all the social conditions were different. Increasingly, the working-class family ceased to be a cohesive social unit. Industrial labor called for the same long hours, but factory work was more impersonal and dangerous. Accidents and sickness added to the miserable conditions. The harsh economic situation trapped most working families into a life of poverty.

Changing Economic and Political Conditions

As the 1800s progressed, the Industrial Revolution transformed the economies of Great Britain and the other European nations to which it spread. Industrial capitalism was profit driven and totally unregulated. **Materialism**, or the tendency to be more concerned with money or luxury goods rather than spiritual or intellectual values, became more prevalent. A materialist culture developed in the Industrial Age, which the manufacturing and business elite increasingly embraced. This belief in materialism was supported by the upwardly mobile middle class. The growing middle class sought status and prosperity. They overwhelmingly supported economic ideas that allowed entrepreneurs and industrialists to maximize their control over industry and capital without governmental interference.

The growth of stock exchanges during the Industrial Revolution made more money available for business investments and facilitated the rise of capitalism.

The Industrial Revolution that thereafter shaped Western European economic life heightened the differences between the middle class and the lower class. The gap between rich and poor widened and created new tensions. Industrial capitalism created unanticipated problems. Alongside the upper- and middle-class prosperity, there also existed widespread poverty among the working class.

Large financial organizations such as banks and business corporations increasingly gained influence and power in the prospering industrial economies of Western Europe. The huge sums of money and great profits earned gave the wealthy upper and middle classes control of the political process. Political decisions almost always reflected the interests of the wealthy business class.

Summary

In this chapter, we have seen that industrialization and urbanization led to major changes in the way people lived. People came to the urban centers in search of work and a place to live. Some people benefited more than others from the changes that took place. Those who benefited were members of the upper class and the growing middle class. Most people, however, had more difficult lives. These people were the working class and their families.

Despite scientific and technological achievements that led to improvements in city life, most urban city residents did not benefit from these advances. Workers faced a number of problems that were not easily resolved. Housing and sanitation inadequacies, communicable diseases, industrial pollution, and rising crime continued to affect the overall quality of life for most city residents.

The Industrial Age also had an impact on European economic development. Industrial capitalism triumphed in the nineteenth century. Laissez-faire attitudes regarding industrial and business enterprises led to the acquisition of great fortunes. The middle class supported industrialization because it led to its prosperity. The working class benefited the least from the changed economic conditions. Factory workers' lives were full of drudgery and poverty. The terrible conditions under which most workers lived led to demands for the reform of industrial capitalism and the political system that supported it.

Residents of urban environments today, particularly those living in major cities, might recognize many of the problems that plagued the earlier urban centers. In some modern-day cities new issues could be added to the earlier problems of city life. To paraphrase an often-quoted French saying, "the more that things change, the more they remain the same."

CHAPTER 17

Review Exercises

___

I. Multiple Choice

Directions: Find the *letter* of the correct answer.

1. Prior to the Industrial Age

   (a) people could easily rise above their families' social status.
   (b) upward mobility was not limited by the traditional agricultural economy.
   (c) there were many opportunities for people to improve their status in society.
   (d) a person's position in life was often determined at birth.

2. The growth of industrial centers resulted in

   (a) the decline of the middle class.
   (b) government control of the industrial elite.
   (c) harsh economic and social conditions for workers.
   (d) large numbers of middle-class women in the work force.

3. All of the following groups were part of the middle class *except*

   (a) doctors.
   (b) lawyers.
   (c) artisans.
   (d) store owners.

4. The middle-class life-style led to the following change:

   (a) Men and women shared equally in providing for the family.
   (b) Women did all of the housework without the help of servants.
   (c) Young women were expected to prepare themselves for university education.
   (d) Women were expected to remain at home to care for the household and children.

5. The industrial worker was expected to work

   (a) a forty-hour and five-day week.
   (b) twelve to sixteen hours daily, six days a week.
   (c) for a salary that paid a dollar an hour.
   (d) part of the year in a factory for no wages.

6. All of the following are examples of nineteenth-century working conditions *except*

    (a) workers received only a one-week paid vacation.
    (b) child labor was used in mines and factories.
    (c) factories often had poor ventilation, which helped spread disease.
    (d) there was no compensation for physical injury or a worker's death.

7. Living conditions in the late nineteenth-century industrial city were

    (a) basically the same for the different social classes.
    (b) quite good because of improvements made by the upper class.
    (c) particularly difficult for working-class families.
    (d) free of most of the problems that cities face in the twentieth century.

8. In the nineteenth century, municipal governments

    (a) sought to closely regulate the effects of pollution.
    (b) increasingly sought to improve the living conditions of workers and their families.
    (c) followed a laissez-faire policy regarding industrial abuses by mill and factory owners.
    (d) tried to bring all social classes together in a compact to improve city life.

9. Which of the following statements about the impact of urban life is true?

    (a) Most urban workers found jobs that improved the quality of their families' lives.
    (b) Life in the city was more family oriented than in rural areas.
    (c) Working-class families ceased to be cohesive social units.
    (d) Tenement life provided families with a safe and healthy environment.

10. Changing economic conditions due to nineteenth-century industrialization

    (a) were the result of a profit-driven and unregulated capitalist economy.
    (b) resulted in a growing acceptance of the need to aid the worker.
    (c) caused a decline in population growth in Western Europe.
    (d) took place without any significant improvement in science and technology.

II. Matching

Directions: Match the words in Column A with the *correct description* in Column B.

Column A	Column B
1. laissez-faire	(a) working class in the industrial society
2. social class	(b) position in society based on birth, education, and job status
3. proletariat	(c) idea that government does not interfere or regulate business
4. materialist	(d) ability to move up in status in society
5. upward mobility	(e) person who values having possessions

III. Thought Questions

Directions: Answer the following questions in essay form.

1. In a dialogue that you and another student will write and then read in class discuss why the middle class identified with the upper, as opposed to the lower, class.

2. You are a union organizer. You are assigned the task of writing a leaflet to workers during the Industrial Revolution listing the reasons why they should attend a union meeting.

3. Describe in an essay the living conditions of most industrial workers in the nineteenth century.

4. You are a social worker. Prepare a report explaining the difficulties for an urban industrial worker and a cohesive family unit, and asking legislators to pass a law reducing the hours worked per day to a maximum of ten and limiting a work week to five days.

5. For a debate in class, take a position pro or con in a prepared speech that the changes in the middle-class life-style made the role of men more important in the family than women during the Industrial Revolution.

IV. Activities

Directions: Complete the following activities.

1. Imagine that you are living in a factory town in the 1880s. A new factory has opened. Create a diary-type journal describing the changes that have taken place in your town over the period of one year.

2. Imagine that you are working in a new factory in your town during the nineteenth century. Write letters to your family describing your life and your work.

CHAPTER 18

New Economic Theories and Ideas

Industrialization brought prosperity and benefits to the European nations that transformed their economies. The Industrial Revolution also created problems that resulted from the wide-ranging economic and social changes that it caused in Great Britain, France, Germany, and elsewhere. In Europe, there were increasing demands for political and economic reform during the 1800s. Workers' associations began to develop into labor unions. Slowly, unions became more commonplace, and their right to represent workers was gradually accepted in Western Europe. As the century progressed, workers rose up in violent revolution to struggle for reforms to improve their job and living conditions.

There were also attempts to reform the political system in Great Britain and elsewhere in Europe. Political repression, however, became the rule in the post-Napoleonic Period. Under the leadership of Prince Metternich, at the Congress of Vienna, 1814–1815, the European continental powers sought to defend absolute monarchies, prevent liberal reforms, and repress outbreaks of nationalist movements.

The stable political climate that the Metternich system tried to establish in Europe did not last long. By 1830, a number of revolutions swept over different European nations such as Greece, the Netherlands, Poland, Italy, and parts of the Austrian Empire. The Concert of Europe, which the great powers created to preserve the peace, broke down. These revolutions were mainly political in nature and over issues such as nationalism and demands for democratic reforms. Great Britain was the exception where reforms were made toward greater democracy that were evolutionary rather than revolutionary. In France, the July Revolution brought the middle-class liberals to power under a constitutional monarchy.

New economic theories and ideas about the organization of society were advanced by reformers and revolutionaries, but it was later, beginning with the revolutionary movements that took place in 1848, when the deep divisions separating the middle-class liberals, who wanted moderate reforms, and the workers and their intellectual supporters, who demanded radical changes, were revealed. The widespread poverty and harsh labor and living conditions of the working class resulted in criticism of the existing political, social, and economic order and called for change.

The Growing Call for Reform

Economic Theories

The Industrial Revolution had its earliest impact in Great Britain. Industrialization led to material progress and higher social status for the British middle class. The wealthy owners of factories, mills, mines, and railroads were joined by the middle class in the belief that government should not interfere with business. Business leaders supported Adam Smith's ideas about **laissez-faire** economics. Smith's *The Wealth of Nations* (see Chapter 12, "The Enlightenment and the Scientific Revolution") also supported the capitalist viewpoint on the value of labor. Workers had to sell their labor in a free and competitive market. According to Smith, labor, not money, was the true source of wealth, and a person's motive for labor was self-interest.

Smith had been the first to explain the relationship between capitalism and laissez-faire economics. He theorized that an "invisible hand" would guide compe-

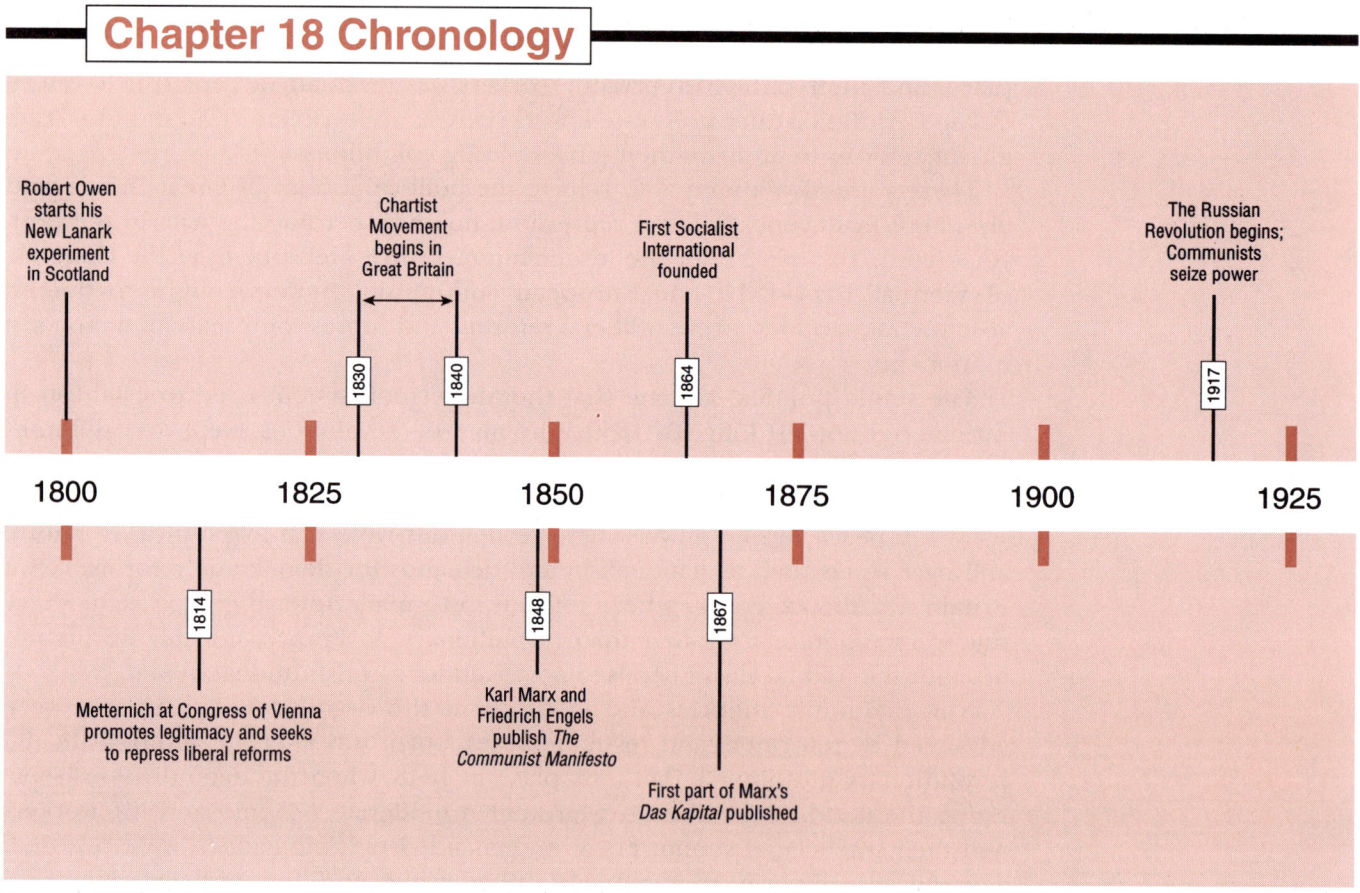

Chapter 18 Chronology

Robert Owen starts his New Lanark experiment in Scotland

Chartist Movement begins in Great Britain

First Socialist International founded | 1864

The Russian Revolution begins; Communists seize power | 1917

1830   1840

1800   1825   1850   1875   1900   1925

1814

Metternich at Congress of Vienna promotes legitimacy and seeks to repress liberal reforms

1848

Karl Marx and Friedrich Engels publish *The Communist Manifesto*

1867

First part of Marx's *Das Kapital* published

tition and free-market pricing and allow for resources to be put to the most productive use. By allowing people to act in their own self-interest they would ultimately bring about economic progress and social harmony.

Smith argued that the economy followed the law of supply and demand. Without governmental interference, the cheapest and best-made products would attract consumers. Efficient producers would make more profits, hire more workers, and expand their businesses, thereby benefiting everyone.

The lack of business regulations led to an industrial society of haves and have-nots in Great Britain and elsewhere in Western Europe. Workers were exploited and often lived in miserable conditions. There were economists who believed that the terrible working and living conditions that developed in industrial societies could not be avoided and were a direct result of overpopulation and an inefficient food supply.

Malthus and Ricardo: Two Pessimistic Economic Theories

In 1798, Thomas Malthus, in his *Essay on the Principles of Population*, took a gloomy view about the workings of the economy. Malthus wrote that misery and poverty were natural outcomes because population grew at a faster rate than the food supply. Malthus saw this as a law of nature and was against any interference in this process. He believed that nothing could be done to prevent natural disasters such as famine and disease. In Malthus's view these unavoidable outcomes were the only real checks on unwanted population growth.

Another English economist and banker, David Ricardo, writing twenty years later, linked the persistence of poverty to what he referred to as the "iron law of wages." Ricardo, in his most famous work, *The Principles of Political Economy and Taxation*, theorized that as the population increased so did the labor supply. Wages tended to stabilize around the subsistence level. Any rise in the price of labor would cause the working population to increase to the point that it heightened competition because of a glut of workers whose market price, or wages, would fall back to the subsistence level. In other words, increased competition for jobs kept wages low. Ricardo also stated the value of almost any good was the function of the labor that produced it. According to Ricardo—like Adam Smith—government interference would only make matters worse. In addition—like Malthus—Ricardo theorized that poverty was inevitable.

Bentham and Mill: Ideas About Economic Reform

There were other people, however, who believed that poverty could be controlled if reforms were made. Laissez-faire economic ideas were attacked by these early reformers. They argued that governments should be required to bring about changes to improve society. In Great Britain, many of these early reformers were religious figures or **humanitarians** who worked to have Parliament pass legislation to abolish slavery and regulate working conditions.

Other reformers sought to change ideas about government involvement in solving society's problems. Jeremy Bentham, who developed the idea of **utilitarianism**, argued that the true test of any institution or action was its usefulness. Bentham and his pupil John Stuart Mill believed that a useful government should influence the distribution of wealth. Mill proposed a tax on income that would allow government to bring the greatest happiness to the largest number of people.

Bentham and Mill criticized laissez-faire economics. They were among those reformers who were concerned with correcting economic abuses such as monopolies and other business actions that brought harm to society. Utilitarians did not condemn the capitalist system. Instead they sought to reform it by means of corrective legislation. Bentham and Mill also supported the ideas of a good public education and the right to vote for men and women. Both men wanted to politically reform society to serve the needs of the many, as opposed to the few.

The Beginning of Worker Movements

Worker associations also tried to improve the harsh labor conditions and low wages through protests and strikes. In the 1800s, workers' associations began to transform into labor unions. Despite the opposition to unions by owners of large businesses and government laws against worker combinations, laborers continued to organize to fight for better hours and wages. In Great Britain, workers had to overcome the Combination Acts of 1799 and 1800 to keep their labor union cause alive. By the 1820s, British workers gained parliament's acceptance and were allowed to meet and discuss labor issues such as wages and hours. Labor organizations also sought to expand political rights of workers and called for reforms in the qualifications for voting.

In the 1830s, a workers' movement called the **Chartist** Movement developed in Great Britain. The Chartists wanted real political reform. They argued for **universal suffrage** for men, a secret ballot, annually elected Parliaments, and equal electoral districts. Chartists supported payments for members of Parliament and opposed property qualifications for office. The Chartists managed to continue as a force in Great Britain through the 1840s despite the fact that the movement failed to convince Parliament of the need for political reform.

Socialism

There were some reformers, called socialists, who believed that the capitalist economic system itself was the real cause of society's problems. **Socialism** called for a society in which workers own, manage, and control production. These socialists argued that the Industrial Revolution led to a fierce competition by owners of businesses to make profits, thus causing misery for the working class. Some socialists believed that production should be only controlled, and not necessarily owned, by the government whereas others argued for worker control and ownership. Many of these socialists believed in a political system in which there was a democratic means of gaining power and promoting their ideas. They respected the idea of individual values. Other advocates of socialism argued that the government should control production and distribution so that people could share equally in society's abundance.

Utopian Socialism

A number of the early socialists were often referred to as utopians. The **utopian socialists** envisioned the creation of an ideal society in which all people would share equally in its benefits. One of the first of the utopian socialists was Robert Owen, a wealthy Scottish cotton manufacturer. Owen had experienced firsthand the misery of the working class in his youth. At age ten, Owen worked in the textile industry, but by the age of 23, he had become a successful factory owner. Conscious of the workers' plight, Owen decided to create an industrial community where people could work in a more just and healthy environment.

In 1800, in a Scottish mill town called New Lanark, Robert Owen established his industrial community. Owen strived to give his workers better working and living conditions. Owen did not give production control to his workers, but he did pay higher wages, provided for education by constructing schools, and offered affordable and decent housing. The New Lanark experiment was a profitable success and encouraged other utopian socialists.

In France, Charles Fourier also worked to create model communities in which cooperation would replace competition and improve workers' lives. Fourier's ideas resulted in the establishment of communities known as **phalansteries**. The Fourier plan called for an organization of five hundred to two thousand workers in which each person would do the job for which he or she was best suited and share in the profits. All of the utopian communities set up in France and later in the United States that followed Fourier's ideas ultimately failed.

Another Frenchman, Louis Blanc, sought to promote a production system based on labor-run cooperative workshops that would be financially supported by the government. In a widely read book, *The Organization of Labor*, Blanc proposed the socialization of all major economic services such as banking and transportation. The cooperative factories were to be operated for and by the workers.

The utopian socialists did not adequately deal with the issue of who controlled the political system. These socialist reformers had no plan for workers to take control of political power from the traditional nobility, industrial elite, and middle class in Western European societies such as Great Britain and France. By ignoring the reality of actual power, these early socialists left government control in the hands of a combination of aristocrats and members of the bourgeoisie. These economic groups bitterly opposed the idea of giving real political power and authority over production to workers and their supporters.

Radical Socialism

Other socialists proposed ideas that sought to revolutionize industrial society. Radical socialists such as Pierre Proudhon and Louis Auguste Blanqui were revolutionaries who called for more drastic solutions to relieve the terrible labor and living conditions of the working class. Proudhon demanded the abolition of the state, the government controlled by the aristocrats and bourgeoisie. He called for the establishment of a dictatorship of the **proletariat**, or working class, a government that would rule in the name of the workers until they were ready to assume power. Despite these calls and ideas for a more militant approach to achieve social change, the radical socialists lacked a credible theory of social action to overthrow the existing order.

Karl Marx and Scientific Socialism

Karl Marx is credited with developing the theoretical basis for scientific socialism, the economic and political philosophy that came to be known as Marxism. Marx dismissed the earlier theories of socialism, particularly its utopian version, as impractical. Marx and his close friend and collaborator Friedrich Engels devoted their lives to the formulation of economic theories and political analysis based partly on the work of earlier theorists and historians, most notably George Hegel, David Ricardo, and Louis Blanc; nevertheless the Marxist philosophical method, dialectical materialism, as fully developed by Marx and Engels, was unquestionably original. They wrote that the exploited working class would rise up and ultimately gain control of society. Marx challenged the laws of economics that supported capitalism. He argued that capitalism was unstable and in the course of history would eventually self-destruct.

Early Life of Karl Marx

Karl Marx was the son of a prosperous German lawyer who had converted from Judaism to Christianity to further his career in the legal profession. In Germany, Marx earned a doctorate in history and philosophy. Beginning in his student years, Marx gained a reputation as someone with radical views who was deeply concerned with the miserable working conditions created by the factory system. In his early writings, Marx blamed industrial capitalism for society's political, economic, and social problems.

By the 1840s, Marx's political and religious views led to problems with the Prussian government. As a result, Marx left Germany and settled for a time in Paris, where he met and collaborated with Engels. In 1848, they published their socialist theories in a work entitled *The Communist Manifesto* (see page 353). This critical historical analysis of society became the basis for scientific socialism or communism.

Marxist Theory of Communism

Marx dismissed the writings of the utopian socialists as impractical ideas that would never work. The utopian socialist ideas that existed prior to Marxism were not based on the premise of the history of the **class struggle**. There was a fundamental belief that society could be reformed by working within the existing economic and political systems for change, which would be evolutionary. Instead, Marx argued for a more practical and scientific analysis of society's problems. Only then, Marx believed, would socialism become the path for the working class to follow. Essential to Marx's interpretation of history was the importance he placed on the idea of class struggle. Marx wrote that the historical process could be divided into different stages of a political struggle for control of society's economic benefits by competing social classes.

Marx stated that the four stages of history were in effect economic conflicts among the classes to determine ownership of the **means of production**, labor and machinery. The social group that controlled production was the ruling class in the four different stages of history. Marx argued that in all societies throughout history, there had been power struggles between two economic groups, the haves and the have-nots.

In ancient society, Marx declared that production was based on slavery. In the Medieval West, the principles of feudalism determined production. The industrial capitalist stage was based on the system of wage labor. In the present stage of industrial capitalism the struggle to control society was between capitalists, or the bourgeoisie, and the workers, or proletariat.

Marx saw this division of society into classes as a natural result of existing economic forces. According to Marx, the ruling class never gave up control of society or production without conflict. Therefore, Marx believed that history only moved forward because of class struggle. Marx believed this conflict was inevitable and predicted that the working class or proletariat would rise up in revolution. The proletariat would ultimately replace the bourgeoisie and take control of the means of production.

In his interpretation of history, Marx placed emphasis on economic conditions. According to Marx, society's laws, customs, religions, social systems, and art all developed in response to existing economic forces. Humanity's historical struggle for a better material life and living conditions could only be understood by using an economic analysis of the factors that determined political and social issues. Marx's economic interpretation of history was based on the idea that history followed scientific laws just as in nature.

In the nineteenth-century industrialized societies, Marx stated the proletariat suffered because it was exploited by the bourgeoisie or capitalist class seeking to maximize its profits. Marx allowed for the worker to earn a living wage, but he believed that the worker, because of the owner's control of the means of production, labored more hours than he or she would in order to live. This extra work was surplus value. Marx wrote that surplus value was the difference between the price of a good and the wage paid to a worker.

The Communist Manifesto

The history of all hitherto existing society is the history of class struggles. Freeman and slave, patrician and plebeian, lord and serf, guildmaster and journeyman, in a word, oppressor and oppressed, stood in constant opposition to one another, carried on an uninterrupted, now hidden, now open fight, a fight that each time ended, either in a revolutionary reconstitution of society at large, or in the common ruin of the contending classes....

The modern bourgeois society that has sprouted from the ruins of feudal society, has not done away with class antagonisms. It has but established new classes, new conditions of oppression, new forms of struggle in place of the old ones.

Our epoch, the epoch of the bourgeoisie, possesses, however, this distinctive feature: It has simplified the class antagonisms. Society as a whole is more and more splitting up into two hostile camps, into two classes directly facing each other—bourgeoisie and proletariat....

The bourgeoisie, wherever it has got the upper hand, has put an end to all feudal, patriarchal, idyllic relations. It has pitilessly torn asunder the motley feudal ties that bound man to his "natural superiors," and has left no other bond between man and man than naked self-interest, than callous "cash payment." It has drowned the most heavenly ecstasies of religious fervor, of chivalrous enthusiasm, of philistine sentimentalism, in the icy water of egotistical calculation. It has resolved personal worth into exchange value, and in place of the numberless indefeasible chartered freedoms, has set up that single, unconscionable freedom—Free Trade. In one word, for exploitation, veiled by religious and political illusions, it has substituted naked, shameless, direct, brutal exploitation.

The bourgeoisie has stripped of its halo every occupation hitherto honored and looked up to with reverent awe. It has converted the physician, the lawyer, the priest, the poet, the man of science into its paid wage-laborers.

For example, according to Marx, if the workers needed to labor four hours a day in order to live, they were paid wages for their work during this working time. The money earned constituted a living wage, although it was basically a subsistence wage. The employer believed that this was the wage to which the worker was entitled. However, the factory owner wanted the worker to labor for more than four hours in order to make profit for the owner. If workers wanted to keep their jobs, they had to labor ten or more hours a day. These extra hours were not really paid for and resulted in the owner stealing hours of labor from the workers. Marx believed that the worker was exploited in this unequal relationship between capital and labor.

According to Marx's surplus value theory, the capitalists sought to keep as much of the profit as possible. Marx wrote that this was wrong because the profit motive resulted in the industrial capitalist paying the workers low wages. On the other hand, Marx believed that this basic economic injustice was a natural and inevitable outcome of the present capitalist stage of history.

Marx regarded labor as the only source of productive value or capital. Although he praised the bourgeoisie for having expanded the material basis of civilization by industrialization and urbanization, Marx also blamed this ruling class for the miserable working and living conditions of most of the population. Marx theorized that as capitalist competition continued to increase, profit margins would shrink. This competition would inevitably result in more people living in poverty. The contradiction of an industrial society based on the prosperous few and the poverty of the many would ultimately lead to revolution. Marx wrote, "workers of the world unite; you have nothing to lose but your chains."

Marx predicted the inevitability of violent revolution by the workers to seize economic and political power. He realized that the capitalists would never peacefully give up economic and political power. Marx saw the Communist Revolution first resulting in a **dictatorship of the proletariat**, or a government that would be more just and would rule in behalf of the working class. This workers' government would bring economic, political, and social justice. Eventually a classless society would emerge. There would be no need for governments. The government would wither away when it was no longer needed to protect the proletarian revolution.

The Impact of Communism

Karl Marx spent the later part of his life in Great Britain. Marx's large and needy family was for the most part supported through the generosity of his friend, Friedrich Engels. The failed revolutions of 1848, in their attempts to promote political and economic reforms, did not end Marx's work to promote scientific socialism. In 1867, the first part of his major economic work *Das Kapital* was published. In Great Britain, Marx continued his activist role to promote scientific socialism. Increasingly, this type of socialism became known as communism. In the 1860s and 1870s, Marx worked and argued with other leading socialist and trade union activists. He helped found the First Socialist International in 1864. The International sought to promote the causes of the worker or proletariat in Europe and the United States.

By the time of his death in 1883, Marx was the most prominent figure in European socialism. In the 1880s, a number of the socialist parties that formed in European nations adopted Marx's ideas. These socialist parties based their goals on Marx's prediction that Communist revolutions would occur in the Western European industrialized societies or in North America.

Failure of Marxism in Western Europe

The socialist parties that followed Marx's ideology in Western Europe did not experience the inevitable revolution that Marx predicted. In the decades after Marx's death, most of the industrialized countries initiated economic and social reforms. In Western Europe, the standard of living rose from the late 1800s into the early 1900s. Many of the most flagrant abuses seen in the first stages of the Industrial Revolution were ended.

Governments began to initiate reform that led to improvements in working and living conditions. Public health improved, and public education became more commonplace. Labor unions were increasingly allowed to organize. This resulted in gains for workers in terms of health and accident insurance, unemployment insurance, higher wages, safer working conditions, and fewer hours. Child labor abuses were gradually ended in most countries.

Marx underestimated the workers' identification with their own countries. Nationalism was a strong force in the Western European industrialized societies. Marx's idea of an international community of the proletariat did not appeal to the vast majority of industrial workers. The gains made by labor as a result of reforms caused workers to support their national governments. Most workers hoped to change the capitalist system through peaceful methods and not by overthrowing the established order.

Despite the failure of Marx's prediction that Communist revolutions would ultimately occur in Western Europe's industrial societies, his ideas did eventually have a major impact on the course of human history.

Marxism in Eastern Europe

In the early 1900s, a small group of Communists used Marx's ideas to bring revolution to Russia. Although czarist Russia did not fit Marx's description of an industrial society where proletarian revolution was inevitable, a determined number of radical Russian Marxists seized power in 1917. Russia had been primarily an agricultural society that had not completely shed the traces of feudalism. Nevertheless, the **Bolshevik** seizure of power in Russia, and the use of Marx's ideas to create a Communist society, had an enormous impact on the course of historical developments in the twentieth century.

Marxism did not come to pass in the same way that Marx had predicted it would in Russia, later in Eastern Europe, or the other places it developed. In part, this was due to certain weaknesses in Marx's analysis of the capitalist system. Marx did not foresee the ability of the capitalist system to change and adapt to new conditions. Marx wrote his theories when laissez-faire capitalism was the rule of the day. He thought that capitalism was a temporary stage and could not predict the variant forms of state-sponsored capitalism, which developed in the twentieth century.

Marx failed to recognize the pivotal and irreplaceable role played by the capitalist class, and the captains of industry, in the creation of an economy that satisfied the demands of people who wanted to be consumers and have a more material life. Marx underestimated the role that self-interest played in determining economic choices. In addition, Marx could not predict that even when his economic theories were put into practice they would be distorted by a ruthless dictatorial and essentially nonproductive ruling class and bureaucracy, which exploited the people in the guise of a benevolent dictatorship of the proletariat.

The Legacy of Socialism and Marxism

The legacy of socialism was not limited only to the ideas of Marx and Engels and the rise of Communist systems based on totalitarianism. In the twentieth century, democratic forms of socialism were developed in Western Europe. In Britain, Sweden, and elsewhere greater emphasis was given to the democratic means of gaining government control of important aspects of the means of production to benefit the public. The democratic socialists gained power through elections and were respectful of individual values and political rights. They were willing to give up political power if they lost the support of the electorate.

In the Soviet Union and the other Communist nations, which adopted the system of a dictatorship of the proletariat after gaining power through violent revolution or by other nondemocratic means, Marxist ideas interpreted by Communist rulers dominated the lives of the people. Throughout most of the twentieth century, Communist governments believed that they were the best hope of the working class and prophesied that capitalism would eventually collapse because of its fundamental weaknesses and contradictions. (See Chapter 31, "Rise of Totalitarianism: in Russia, Italy, and Germany.")

Summary

In this chapter, we see a clear connection between historical forces at work and philosophical thought and debate. Clearly the standard of living of most Europeans was increasing, but there were costs involved. These costs included poor living and working conditions for most people. Children worked long, hard hours in factories and mines. Wealth was being concentrated in a few hands. A critical question was asked by thinkers in the 1800s: was this suffering a necessary result of the capitalist system? There were thinkers who answered "no." A group of these were called utopians because they believed that the government had an obligation to intervene in order to create a better society. These utopians, some more utopian than others, wanted to design what to them was a perfect community.

Other thinkers were more harsh in their condemnation of the capitalist system. They believed that change would only come through the workers rising up and overthrowing the present system and taking control for themselves. Karl Marx and his followers had an impact on Europe that we are still feeling today.

CHAPTER 18

Review
Exercises

I. Multiple Choice

Directions: Find the *letter* of the correct answer.

1. A main idea of Karl Marx and Friedrich Engels' *The Communist Manifesto* is that the proletariat

   (a) would need foreign help to achieve its revolutionary ends.
   (b) had to cooperate with capitalists to gain economic rewards.
   (c) should allow the capitalists to control the means of production.
   (d) must unite to overthrow the capitalist class.

2. The iron law of wages stated that

   (a) the state should intervene to regulate wages.
   (b) job competition would lead to higher wages.
   (c) natural laws did not play a role in determining wages.
   (d) wages should be left to free-market competition.

3. A number of the early reformers believed that

   (a) capitalism would have to be completely overhauled.
   (b) governments should be required to make changes to improve society.
   (c) natural forces in society would eventually improve the workers' lives.
   (d) any government involvement in the economy was not necessary.

4. The proponents of utilitarianism believed that

   (a) private education would bring more equality for workers.
   (b) the capitalist system was totally unfair to workers.
   (c) only educated men should have the right to vote.
   (d) a useful government should influence the distribution of wealth.

5. The Chartist Movement in Great Britain wanted all of the following reforms *except*

   (a) universal suffrage for men.
   (b) annually elected parliaments.
   (c) proper qualifications for voting.
   (d) a secret ballot.

6. The socialists believed that the real cause of workers' problems was

    (a) the failure to follow the ideas of Adam Smith.
    (b) fierce competition by owners of businesses to make profits.
    (c) workers' involvement in owning and managing businesses.
    (d) government efforts to regulate businesses in Europe.

7. The utopian socialists were criticized because they

    (a) did not deal with the issue of who controlled the political system.
    (b) sought to exploit workers instead of improving their lives.
    (c) never put their ideas into practice in experimental communities.
    (d) only sought to create workers' communities where competition existed.

8. The scientific socialists argued that

    (a) the key to improving society was safeguarding property.
    (b) the state should be abolished and replaced by the dictatorship of the proletariat.
    (c) armed revolution would only lead to further state repression.
    (d) the terrible living and working conditions were the fault of the proletariat.

9. Karl Marx believed in all of the following ideas *except*

    (a) capitalism was unstable and would self-destruct.
    (b) industrial capitalism was to blame for society's problems.
    (c) history should be interpreted as a class struggle.
    (d) religious organizations should do more to relieve society's problems.

10. Karl Marx's surplus value theory stated that

    (a) capitalists sought to keep as much profit as possible.
    (b) the profit motive kept wages artificially high.
    (c) production was the responsibility of the bourgeoisie.
    (d) the bourgeoisie was exploited by the proletariat class.

II. Matching

Directions: Match the names in Column A with the achievement they are *best known* for in Column B.

Column A	Column B
1. Prince Metternich	(a) sought cooperative workshops supported by governments
2. Louis Phillipe	(b) set up communities called "phalansteries"
3. David Ricardo	(c) first to call for dictatorship of the proletariat
4. Jeremy Bentham	(d) demanded abolition of the state and opposed to the idea of property
5. Robert Owen	(e) Marx's friend and collaborator
6. Charles Fourier	(f) devised the iron law of wages
7. Louis Blanc	(g) conducted utopian experiment in Scotland
8. Friedrich Engels	(h) believed in the concept of utilitarianism
9. Pierre Proudhon	(i) sought to restore legitimacy and prevent reform
10. Louis Auguste Blanqui	(j) citizen monarch of France

III. Vocabulary

Directions: Define the following words, terms, or expressions and use them in a written sentence.

1. class struggle—
2. proletariat—
3. utopian socialist—
4. humanitarian—
5. utilitarian—
6. universal suffrage—
7. phalansteries—
8. Chartist—
9. means of production—
10. capitalist class—

IV. Thought Questions

Directions: Answer the following questions in essay form.

1. Give three reasons why workers in the 1800s increasingly demanded more reforms.

2. Write a dialogue with another student about the ideas of Jeremy Bentham and John Stuart Mill, which will be presented orally in class.

3. Give three reforms that the Chartists sought in Great Britain, and explain why the Chartists wanted these reforms.

4. Describe the experiments of two utopian socialists, and explain why they were either a success or failure.

5. You are a reporter for the *Manchester Guardian* and have just returned from a meeting at which Marx and Engels have explained their theories. Write an article explaining why their ideas are dangerous for existing capitalist societies. Remember you are living in the 1860s.

V. Activities

Directions: Complete the following activities.

1. You are a participant in a *debate* about the need to reform the capitalist system. Assume the role of one of the following persons and prepare for an in-class debate in which you will defend that person's ideas.

   A. Jeremy Bentham
   B. Karl Marx
   C. Pierre Proudhon
   D. Louis Blanc
   E. Robert Owen

2. You are assigned a research report to write about the life of one of the persons listed below.

    A. David Ricardo
    B. John Stuart Mill
    C. Pierre Proudhon
    D. Robert Owen
    E. Louis Blanc
    F. Friedrich Engels

CHAPTER 19

Changes in the Arts and Sciences

The cultural and scientific achievements of any society can tell us much about the people in that society. This is true of our own society, in the 1990s. It was also valid for European society in the 1800s. In that time the work of artists, musicians, and writers increasingly reflected the new social, economic, and political conditions brought on by the Industrial Revolution. European artists and composers sought to express the feelings of societies that were in the process of undergoing great changes. The Industrial Revolution spurred the growth of a middle class that provided a new and larger audience for the arts, literature, and music.

During the nineteenth century, advances in science dramatically improved people's lives in some Western European nations. The scientific discoveries in biology and medicine led to the adoption of innovative medical techniques and resulted in people living longer. Diseases that were previously deadly claimed fewer lives because of new medical breakthroughs.

There were also important improvements made in transportation and communication, based on a steady stream of scientific inventions and technological achievements. Discoveries in the fields of biology, chemistry, and physics unraveled some of the mysteries of science. Psychology and sociology rose in importance as a result of research.

The scientific achievements and the revolution in the arts, literature, and music were in part related to a greater freedom to express new and controversial ideas. A society that encourages and welcomes new ideas in industry is also likely to foster and accept new ideas in other areas. Reason and natural law were combined with emotion, imagination, and intuition, that is, knowing something without reasoning, to bring major advances in science and new inspiration to the arts.

Science Explores New Ideas

Medical Discoveries

During the 1800s, a number of medical advances resulted in people living longer and healthier lives. Prior to the nineteenth century, doctors had less knowledge of the causes and prevention of deadly diseases. For example, smallpox and diphtheria had killed millions of people over the previous centuries. New discoveries in medicine helped gain more control of these and other fatal diseases in Western Europe and elsewhere.

As we learned earlier, Edward Jenner, an English doctor, discovered in 1796 a cure for one of the world's most dreaded diseases—smallpox. Jenner's discovery of a vaccine that would prevent smallpox was based on his observation of natural phenomena. He noticed that dairy workers in England who had contracted cowpox, a nondeadly disease, were immune from catching smallpox. Jenner theorized that there was a connection between the two diseases. By the later decades of the nineteenth century, the widespread inoculation, that is, the injection of a mild form of the virus into the body, of people in Western Europe with a smallpox vaccine practically wiped out the disease.

The combined work of a German physician, Robert Koch, a French chemist, Louis Pasteur, and a British surgeon, Joseph Lister, led to significant advances in medicine. Pasteur found that tiny organisms called bacteria caused **infectious**

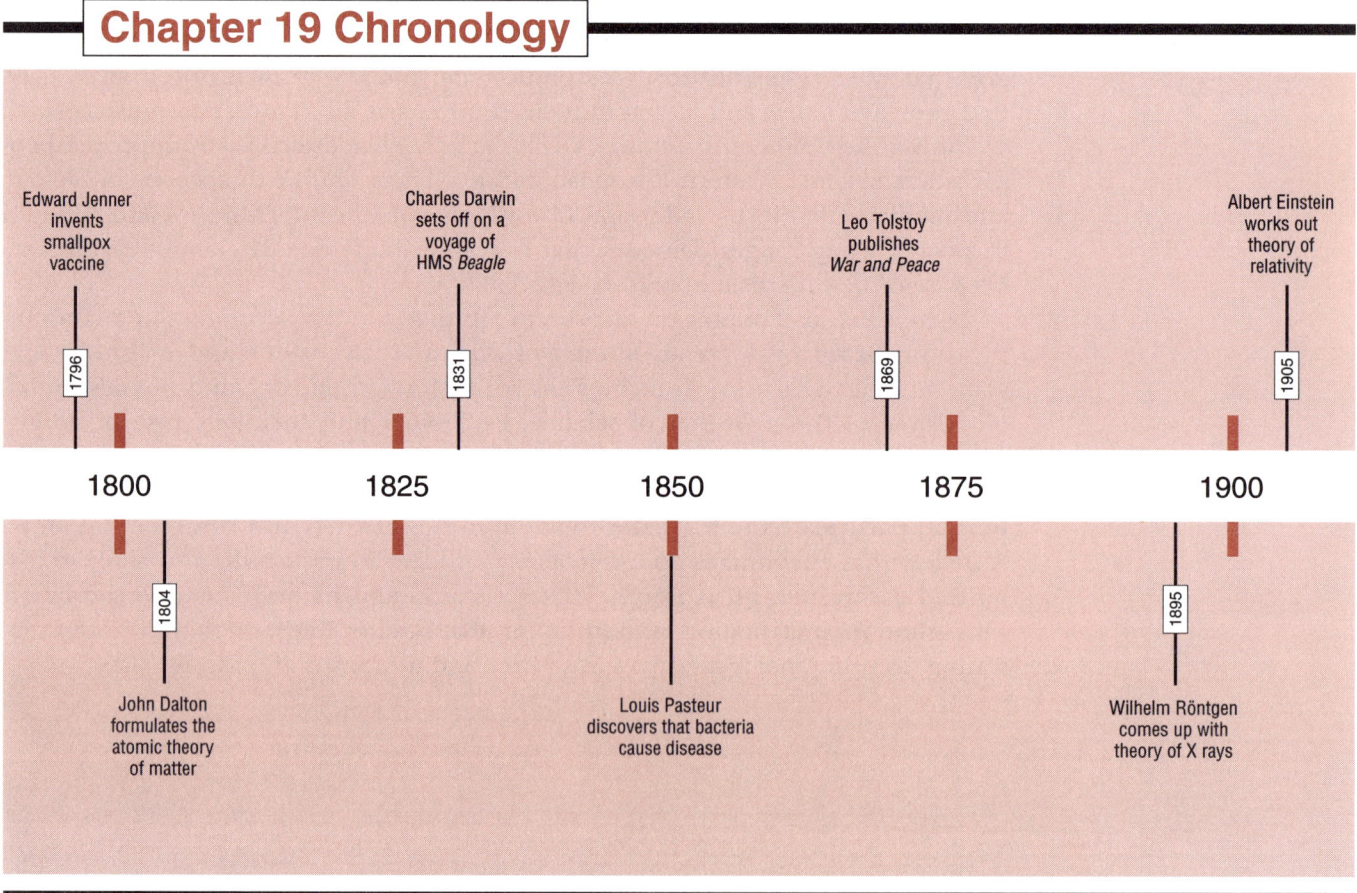

Chapter 19 Chronology

Edward Jenner invents smallpox vaccine — 1796

Charles Darwin sets off on a voyage of HMS *Beagle* — 1831

Leo Tolstoy publishes *War and Peace* — 1869

Albert Einstein works out theory of relativity — 1905

1800　　1825　　1850　　1875　　1900

John Dalton formulates the atomic theory of matter — 1804

Louis Pasteur discovers that bacteria cause disease

Wilhelm Röntgen comes up with theory of X rays — 1895

diseases. In the 1850s, he proved that people could prevent infectious diseases if they were properly immunized by means of a vaccination. Pasteur had discovered that a weakened strain of anthrax bacteria could be injected into sheep to allow the animal to build resistance to a more deadly form of the disease.

In the 1880s, Pasteur applied his methods to the organisms that caused rabies. By a series of inoculations, Pasteur was able to save the life of a young boy who was bitten by a rabid dog. Prior to Pasteur's discovery, rabies was a fatal disease. Pasteur also developed the process of heating a liquid to kill bacteria. The process is called **pasteurization** in his honor.

Robert Koch's experiments also proved that bacteria caused infectious diseases. Koch found the specific bacteria that caused tuberculosis and cholera. Koch also collaborated with Pasteur in studying anthrax. Joseph Lister applied the discoveries of Pasteur and Koch about bacteria and germs to surgery. Despite advances in surgery made through the use of anesthesia, about half of all surgical patients died. The high death toll was caused by infectious diseases, which resulted from medical procedures. Lister connected the filthy conditions of hospitals to the spread of germs that caused people's deaths after surgery.

Lister began a program in the hospital where he operated to improve standards of cleanliness. He insisted on the use of clean medical instruments and a hospital environment that no longer tolerated the filthy conditions, which had been considered normal up to this time. The survival rate of Lister's patients increased enormously. By the 1890s, other European nations as well as the United States adopted Lister's methods.

New Ideas About Living Things

There were major discoveries in biology that resulted in new ways of looking at life. By using microscopes in the 1600s, scientists had observed that cells make up all life. (See Chapter 12, "The Enlightenment and the Scientific Revolution.") However, it wasn't until the mid-nineteenth century that the cell theory was formulated. The work of a biologist, Theodore Schwann, and a botanist, Matias Schleiden, proved the theory that all living matter was composed of cells. These German scientists discovered that cells created other cells and had lives of their own. Previously, nonliving matter was thought to be the source of live cells.

In the 1870s, another German biologist, August Weismann, studied the question of how living things passed on their biological characteristics. His research showed that reproductive-type cells transmitted people's biological characteristics to the next generation. A decade earlier, Gregor Mendel, an Austrian monk, had discovered that there was a pattern for the characteristics of traits that were inherited. Mendel's experiments with plants led him to conclude that tiny particles, later called genes, were responsible for the transmission of traits. Although Mendel's ideas were not widely known until the twentieth century, his work laid the groundwork for **genetics**, the science of heredity.

Darwin's Theories Challenge Existing Ideas

The most controversial scientific ideas came from the work of the British naturalist and biologist Charles Darwin. Darwin believed that there was a need to explain the existence of the great variety of plants and animals, which resulted in the enormous diversity of life. He also wondered why some plants and animals became extinct while others lived on. Darwin's research thereafter sought answers to these challenging questions.

In 1831, Darwin set off on a world voyage on the HMS *Beagle*, a British naval vessel. During these travels, he studied a wide variety of plant and animal life. The research only increased Darwin's curiosity about why certain plants and animals survive whereas others die off and disappear.

Darwin's initial research led him to hypothesize that most animal groups increase more quickly than their food supply and therefore they are in a constant struggle for survival. Those plants and animals better adapted to their environment are the ones who survive. The survivors who lived on passed on these characteristics to their offspring. Darwin named this process of struggle **natural selection**.

Darwin wrote two ground-breaking books, *The Origin of the Species by Means of Natural Selection*, published in 1859, and *The Descent of Man*, published in 1871. They were considered radical because they challenged previously held ideas about how species arose and how human beings originated. Darwin rejected the idea that species arose spontaneously. In addition, his theory of evolution was viewed as an attack on the religious ideas of his day because it contradicted the biblical account of creation.

In his work, *The Descent of Man*, Darwin theorized that humans and apes had a common ancestor. The belief that human beings descended from an ancestor that was apelike led to a long and bitter controversy. Supporters of Darwin's theory of evolution were heatedly challenged by religious people who believed that God created man and woman. The scientific study of Darwin's theories gradually led to their acceptance and changed people's understanding about the origins of life and human evolution. Nevertheless, this controversy still exists today in such ideas as "creationist science," which emphasizes the role of God in the origin of living things.

Social Darwinism

Darwin's theories were later utilized to explain economic and social issues. In the late 1800s, Herbert Spencer, a British philosopher, applied Darwin's ideas to develop a social theory about people's struggle for existence. This was called **Social Darwinism**. Spencer wrote that only the strongest humans survive. Social Darwinism justified aggressive business practices that enabled strong competitors to drive out weaker ones. Industrial leaders were involved in an economic competition for the survival of the fittest in the capitalist system.

Social Darwinism also was applied to theories of racial superiority, extreme nationalism, and imperialism. Strong European nations justified their use of military power against weaker nations as necessary to protect their industrial trading economies. The Englishman Rudyard Kipling claimed that European nations, in practicing imperialism, had a responsibility to improve the lives of people overseas. (See Chapter 26, "The New Imperialism.") Some European composers such as the German, Richard Wagner, created musical works that stimulated pride in a national and ethnic identity. It should be noted that many of these ideas, which seem racist today, were considered in this time period to be the reality of the then existing world situation.

The Development of the Social Sciences

Sigmund Freud was a pioneer in the field of psychiatry. Freud helped modernize the treatment of mental illness.

In the mid-nineteenth century, the study of human behavior in society, or sociology, became more accepted in Europe. The French philosopher, Auguste Comte applied scientific methods to theorize laws that governed human behavior. In Europe and elsewhere, Comte's ideas were adopted by those who wanted to bring a more scientific rationale to the organization and workings of government and society.

Another new social science that developed was psychology, or the study of human behavior. In Russia, Ivan Pavlov conducted experiments with dogs that proved that animals could be conditioned to act in certain ways. Pavlov's theory about unconscious responses to certain stimuli influenced other scientists. Other psychologists applied Pavlov's ideas to design training programs that could change a person's behavior.

The writings of Sigmund Freud had the greatest influence on the study of human behavior. Based on his work with mentally ill people, Freud theorized that an unconscious part of the mind governs much of human behavior. He believed that the unconscious at times masked the reasons for a person's behavior. Freud pioneered the development of a method of treatment to help people discover the motives for their actions and thoughts. Psychiatry and psychoanalysis gradually came to be accepted as proper methods of treatment for increasing numbers of people with mental problems.

Advances in Physical Sciences

Marie Curie and her husband Pierre were pioneers in the study of radioactive radium. Madame Curie won Noble Prizes for her work in physics and chemistry.

Albert Einstein was responsible for the theory of relativity. Einstein theorized that the motion of one object could only be measured by comparing it to the relative motion of another object. His ideas challenged Newtonian physics.

In the early 1800s, the work of the British teacher John Dalton also helped to revolutionize the study of chemistry. Dalton theorized that invisible particles called atoms made up all matter. He concluded, in 1804, that atoms were the basic elements of all things and that similar atoms were in fact identical. Later in the century, a Russian chemist, Dimitry Mendeleyev, worked out the theory that similar atoms had the same properties. Mendeleyev drew up a periodic table of the known elements, which was ordered according to their atomic structures.

Physicists also worked to discover other mysteries of the atom. In the 1890s, Wilhelm Röntgen conducted experiments with electromagnetic waves. Röntgen's work with high-energy electric waves led to the discovery of unknown emissions, thereafter called X rays, that could penetrate the body tissue and other matter.

Other physicists such as the German Max Planck, Marie and Pierre Curie of France, and Albert Einstein furthered the study of the laws of physics. Einstein eventually developed the theory that energy and matter were interchangeable. He also theorized that all matter was in constant motion. Einstein's 1905 theory of relativity stated that matter could only be measured by comparing it to the motion of other objects or matter. The work of these and other early physicists led to an era of scientifically applicable ideas based on the laws of physics. The use of atomic energy for peaceful and military purposes in the twentieth century was made possible by this early pioneering work.

Art, Literature, and Music Take New Forms

A Revolution in Artistic Expression

Vincent Van Gogh was a Postimpressionist painter. Van Gogh employed short, heavy brush strokes and very bright colors to depict a sense of intense energy.

In the 1800s, art and music were greatly influenced by the changes that transformed society. There was a creative reaction to the order and reason that the Enlightenment had brought to artistic and musical expression. This led to the presentation of new forms of art and music to a wider audience.

Romantic artists looked to nature, themes of the glorified past, and heroic rebellion for subjects to paint. Romanticism stressed imagination and human emotion instead of reason. The French painter Eugène Delacroix's works mirrored the brighter colors and sweeping paint strokes, which symbolized the romantic artists' emotional style of art.

In England, other romantic artists emphasized the love of nature in their works. John Constable and J. M. W. Turner revolutionized British landscape painting. Through the use of color, these artists reflected their sensitivities to the beauty of nature. The individual's awe in face of the power of nature was captured in their paintings.

By the mid-nineteenth century, some artists turned back to realism. The canvases of the French painter Gustave Courbet reflected real and concrete objects and rejected sentimentality. Other realistic artists portrayed life honestly and sought out themes that reflected daily existence. The paintings of Frenchmen Honoré Daumier and Camille Corot depicted life objectively and did not hide its blemishes.

In the later decades of the 1800s, other forms of artistic expression developed. Some artists turned away from romanticism and realism. They looked to fleeting impressions for their ideas, as opposed to static forms. French Impressionists such as Camille Pissarro, Claude Monet, Auguste Renoir, and Edgar Degas were inspired by the color spectrum and how light reflected the brilliance of the placement of colors. Their paintings showed the effects of light at a given moment. Natural light that made the most of the pure colors of the spectrum—oranges, reds, yellows, and bright blues—inspired the Impressionist artists.

By the close of the 1800s, another group of painters called Postimpressionists even took the emphasis on

Auguste Renoir was an Impressionist painter. Impressionists were intrigued with color and light. They experimented with placing colors side by side on a canvas to create an impression.

bright light and color to greater extremes. The paintings of Paul Cézanne, Vincent van Gogh, and Paul Gauguin reflected an effort to experiment with new ways to show form. Shapes were used along with color to depict mood and express emotion.

Literature Reflects Romanticism and Realism

By the late nineteenth century, many writers' works reflected a literary style that valued emotion, imagination, and intuition. English poets such as Percy Shelley and John Keats glorified nature and a simpler life in their poems. Henry Wadsworth Longfellow expressed the romantic poet's belief that there was a universal spirit that united all things in nature. Romantic literature often reflected the theme that industrialization was to blame for the ugliness in society and the decline of traditional values.

Other writers stressed ideas of romance and adventure in their literary works. The German writer Johann von Schiller wrote about the legendary hero William Tell. The Frenchman Victor Hugo portrayed tales of human suffering in a powerful and moving manner in *The Hunchback of Notre Dame* and *Les Misérables*. The French writer George Sand depicted peasants and workers with compassion in her fiction. Another well-known writer, Madame de Staël, sought to express the reality of historical action in her brilliant writings. Madame de Staël, the daughter of the French economic minister, Jacques Necker, wrote about the French Revolution and the Napoleonic Period. The Scottish writer Sir Walter Scott wrote historic novels such as *Ivanhoe*, exciting the imagination of people who looked romantically back to the Middle Ages as a time of adventure and heroism.

Other nineteenth-century writers and poets expressed the romantic ideals of individual liberties and nationalism in their writings. The English poet Lord Byron mixed his poetry with a real-life involvement with the Greek fight for independence from the Ottoman Turks. The Russian writer Aleksandr Pushkin looked to the traditional Russian peasant for his inspiration.

Literature also reflected realistic views of life by the mid-nineteenth century. The French writer Honoré de Balzac in *The Human Comedy* realistically showed how aspects of French bourgeoisie life was based on greed and stupidity. Balzac was particularly critical of the failures and foibles of the growing middle class.

English writers such as William Thackeray ridiculed the displays of wealth by the upper and middle classes in their novels. Mary Ann Evans depicted a British social order that lacked common sense in her novels. Charles Dickens wrote about the horrible conditions of the hospitals, prisons, and poorhouses. In his fictionalized account of urban life, *Hard Times*, Dickens realistically portrayed the evils that materialism and industrialism caused in the city.

The Russian writer Leo Tolstoy painstakingly recounted and analyzed social customs and peasant lives. Tolstoy's 1869 historical novel, *War and Peace*, depicted the lives of five families in the time of Napoleon's invasion of Russia. Another Russian, Theodor Dostoievskii, presented a clear view of the Russian judicial system in *Crime and Punishment.*

Romanticism Influences Music

In the 1800s, music reflected the romanticism that stirred the emotions of many composers. The romantic composers sought to express their feelings in a freer musical manner. They rejected the form and order that the Enlightenment brought to musical composition. The symphonies of the German Ludwig van Beethoven bridged the transition from a more classical to a freer romantic style. Beethoven used themes of freedom and liberty when he composed his revolutionary Third Symphony, the *Eroica.*

Other romantic composers, such as the Austrian Franz Schubert, the Russian Pyotr Tchaikovsky, and the Czech Antonín Dvořák, used melodies that gave vent to their powerful emotions. Nationalism found expression in the music of the romantic compositions of such artists as the German Richard Wagner. His cycle of four operas, *The Ring of the Nibelungen,* used a German epic of the Middle Ages to evoke strong feelings of nationalism.

Opera also flowered in the 1800s. The works of the Italian Giuseppe Verdi reflected the growing popularity of operatic music. Public concert halls in Italy and elsewhere were packed to hear Verdi's *Aida* and *Rigoletto.*

The range of power of instruments grew during the 1800s. The piano became an important instrument in concert halls. A growing number of middle-class people began to attend piano recitals featuring the works of Poland's Frédéric Chopin. The size of orchestras increased and attending a musical concert to hear the romantic works of Europe's great composers became almost commonplace.

The Legacy of Advances in the Arts and Sciences

The growth that took place in the areas of the arts and sciences carried into the twentieth century. People in industrializing European nations began to live longer and healthier lives. They had more time to enjoy a life that afforded them some leisure time. This was particularly true of the growing middle class, which could take advantage of the new opportunities for cultural enrichment and had the means to benefit from advances in science and medicine.

Summary

As change was taking place in the economic and political spheres, it was also taking place in the field of science and the arts. Scientific investigation provided us with the early vaccines that protect us against disease. We found that if we protect ourselves against bacterial infection we would live longer and better lives. When Darwin proposed his natural selection and origin of the species theories he created a storm that is still with us in certain circles. That his theories were applied to the business and political worlds certainly seems an odd change of his intent. Psychology and psychiatry looked into people's motivations and actions. Mental illness came to be treated like other illnesses. In the arts, romantic adventure and nationalism dominated. This was reflected in the works of a number of writers, artists, and musicians. Unfortunately, the worker had little time to enjoy all of this. While the workers did benefit from many of these advances they had to wait well into the twentieth century to enjoy them.

CHAPTER 19

Review Exercises

I. Multiple Choice

Directions: Find the *letter* of the correct answer.

1. In the 1800s the work of artists, writers and musicians reflected

    (a) the influence of religion in worldly affairs.
    (b) new conditions brought on by the Industrial Revolution and nationalism.
    (c) the growing sense of internationalism in the world community.
    (d) strong influences from the ideas of the Middle Ages.

2. During the nineteenth century, medical advances helped prevent and cure

    (a) cancer and heart attacks.
    (b) smallpox and rabies.
    (c) AIDS and polio.
    (d) pneumonia and syphilis.

3. Pasteur proved that an infectious disease could be

    (a) prevented if people were immunized by vaccination.
    (b) cured if people had massive blood transfusions.
    (c) resisted if people drank mineral water and castor oil.
    (d) beneficial to society because it eliminated weaker people.

4. The theory of evolution conflicted with the previously held idea that

    (a) all living things were created by God.
    (b) only the fittest members of a species survive.
    (c) human characteristics are passed on through genes.
    (d) apes and humans have a common ancestor.

5. Social Darwinism was used to justify all of the following *except*

    (a) aggressive business practices.
    (b) theories of racial superiority.
    (c) demilitarization and internationalism.
    (d) extreme nationalism and imperialism.

6. Sigmund Freud theorized that

   (a) bacteria is the cause of disease.
   (b) the unconscious mind governs much human behavior.
   (c) natural selection is determined by survival of the fittest.
   (d) psychiatry was harmful to people's mental health.

7. Artists and musicians in the 1800s sought inspirations from

   (a) order and enlightened reason.
   (b) romantic themes and nature.
   (c) religious and classical ideas.
   (d) abstract and surrealistic expression.

8. In the 1800s, writers were often critical of

   (a) materialism and senseless displays of wealth.
   (b) ideas that were based on heroism and adventure.
   (c) the ideas of nationalism and romanticism.
   (d) real depictions of how most people really lived.

9. In the nineteenth century many musical composers

   (a) embraced the form and order of the Enlightenment.
   (b) looked to classical times for their themes.
   (c) used melodies to express a broad range of feelings.
   (d) abandoned operatic music as a relic of the past.

10. All of the following statements are true of the 1800s *except*

   (a) the piano became an important instrument in music halls.
   (b) a growing number of middle-class people attended concerts.
   (c) the size of European orchestras decreased by 10 percent.
   (d) the range and power of musical instruments grew.

II. Matching

Directions: Match the names in Column A with the achievement they are *best known* for in Column B.

Column A	*Column B*
1. Ludwig van Beethoven	(a) writings justified imperialism
2. Giuseppe Verdi	(b) French Impressionist painter
3. Charles Dickens	(c) wrote the heroic adventure *Ivanhoe*
4. Sir Walter Scott	(d) realistically depicted city life in *Hard Times*
5. Henry Wadsworth Longfellow	(e) composed *Eroica* Symphony
	(f) Italian opera composer
6. Claude Monet	(g) poet who believed in universal spirit
7. Honoré Daumier	(h) artistic themes expressed daily existence
8. Ivan Pavlov	(i) laid groundwork for genetics
9. Rudyard Kipling	(j) theory of unconscious response
10. Gregor Mendel	

III. Vocabulary

Directions: Define the following words, terms, or expressions and use them in a written sentence.

1. immunize—
2. vaccination—
3. bacteria—
4. rabies—
5. pasteurization—
6. anesthesia—
7. surgery—
8. germs—
9. hospital—
10. infectious—

IV. Thought Questions

Directions: Answer the following questions in essay form.

1. Cite three examples describing how the work of artists, musicians, and writers changed in the 1800s.

2. List three medical advances or scientific discoveries and explain how they improved people's lives.

3. You are assigned to write an essay for or against Charles Darwin's ideas about evolution. In your essay, give three arguments supporting your position.

4. Write a newspaper article about Sigmund Freud and how he modernized the study of human behavior.

5. List five writers, poets, composers, or artists of the nineteenth century who are considered exponents of romanticism. For one of the five persons who you have chosen explain why his or her work is considered to be that of a "romantic."

V. Activities

Directions: Complete the following activities.

1. You are a young person growing up in the late 1800s. Write a report on the different types of popular entertainment available to your friends and family.

2. You are assigned a museum research project. Go to a local museum and locate five paintings that are by artists listed in this chapter. For each painting describe how the artist expresses ideas about life in the nineteenth century.

POLITICAL CHANGE IN THE NINETEENTH CENTURY

You often hear the statement that if you don't learn from history you are bound to repeat its mistakes. During your reading of this section (and those to follow) you well may ask, "Does anyone learn anything from history?" In many situations you will wonder why the persons or nations did this or that. Didn't they realize it would cause trouble? You will also meet charismatic leaders who were able to influence people to take actions not in their best interests. You will also meet leaders who attempted to lead by using tactics of hundreds of years ago.

We will first visit Great Britain, which in the nineteenth century was the greatest single power in the world because of its lead in industrialization. The impact of industrialization is seen in the might of a nation. As we move east across Europe, from Britain to Russia, you will notice that the power of a country is related to its progress in industrial development. It is also interesting to note that democratic advances take the same path. British democratic advances were evolutionary. This is not to say that there was not some disruption, but compared to that occurring on the Continent it was little. The established constitutional monarchy was working well, and the two major political parties seemed to have the interests of the nation as the most important item. Both parties favored increased democracy for reasons of their own and worked to improve the lives of the people. Unfortunately the situation in Ireland was not improved and still continues well into the twentieth century.

The story of France reads like a modern soap opera. This nation seemed to be constantly in and out of trouble. It tried to turn the clock back to before the French Revolution and establish a system like the British one. The problem is that the French had no real tradition for this type of government. It took Britain two hundred years to develop its system, yet France wanted to accomplish this end overnight. What developed were confrontations in 1830 and 1848—into a republic and out, into an empire and out, finally turning to another Napoleon. But you can't bring back the good old days, and this Louis Napoleon was nothing like his uncle. While everything went well in the beginning, and Paris became the "city of lights" that it still is today, Louis soon got into foreign policy disasters.

During our previous study we used the names Italy and Germany to designate certain geographical areas on the map. In reality these are both relatively new nations that were formed little more than 150 years ago. In this unit you will meet romantic figures from there, such as Mazzini and Garibaldi. You will also meet hardheaded ones, such as Cavour and Bismarck. In fact, probably the most controversial figure of his day was Bismarck, who used "blood and iron" to unify his nation. There was no parliamentary tradition in Germany, and with a weak king, Bismarck could do as he wished.

As we travel further east you will find a land that was little changed by time. It took longer for both industry and democracy to get here. The Russian and Austro-Hungarian empires were not major players in the game of power politics. Russia eventually became involved when it was in the best interests of Britain and France. Britain was on Russia's side at one time and against Russia at another, depending on the needs of its own foreign policy. Russia could be seen going down the path to revolution, but little could be done to stop it. The Balkan area was viewed as the backwater of Europe. The continuing ethnic feuds have caused war after war. While Vienna danced the waltz, the people in this area suffered. The Ottoman Empire, which reached to the gates of Vienna in 1683, was reduced in the nineteenth century to a small piece of land because Britain did not want Russia to control a very important body of water.

This was a complicated time. But it is important to know and understand it because the events and changes that took place during this period had a direct impact on the twentieth century.

CHAPTER 20

Advances in British Democracy

We have traced the growth of **democracy** in Great Britain through both revolutionary and evolutionary periods. At the beginning of the nineteenth century, Britain was the most democratic nation in Europe; yet the British political system had a long way to go to be called truly *democratic*, as we use the term today. There were still a number of practices that had to change to allow Britain to become what it is at the present time. Let us now trace these further evolutionary changes that began about 1800. We will pay particular attention to the ongoing Irish problem, a problem yet to be solved.

Nondemocratic Characteristics in Britain

Our discussion will begin by reviewing our definition of democracy. As we noted on the first page of Chapter 11, "The Growth of Democracy in England," democracy may be defined as a system of government that has two basic features:

1. **Popular sovereignty**; and
2. Equality and respect for the individual.

The British system in 1800 had some characteristics that conflicted with these features and was therefore nondemocratic. These characteristics were as follows:

- *Open Ballot*: People voted in the open, not in private or secretly. Thus, they did not always vote the way they may have wanted and may also have been subject to bribery and intimidation.
- *Voting Restrictions*: The only citizens allowed to vote were those who owned a certain amount of property. Because of these restrictions, only 5 percent of the British population were eligible to vote in parliamentary elections. Women could not vote, and neither could those men who were middle-class merchants, workers, and farmers.

- *Officeholding Requirements*: Very few people were eligible to hold public office. Eligibility requirements were based on property, religion, and gender (sex). You could hold office if you owned a certain amount of property, belonged to the Anglican Church or some other Protestant group, and were a man. Government positions were thus denied to women, Catholics, Jews, and poor people.
- *Unfair Representation in the House of Commons*: An area of land on which many people lived was marked off with boundaries and was called a political district or borough. Each borough in Britain was allowed to elect representatives to the House of Commons. Because of the **Industrial Revolution**, big population changes occurred, with people leaving rural areas to live in urban areas. This meant that boroughs in rural areas lost population, while boroughs in urban areas such as Manchester gained population. However, the number of representatives from all these boroughs remained the same! The "losing" boroughs should have had reductions made in their representatives. This was not done, and such boroughs became known as *rotten boroughs*. Some urban boroughs became underrepresented, whereas others weren't represented at all. And in some districts, wealthy landowners who were in the House of Lords were able to choose representatives to the Commons. These districts were called *pocket boroughs*. The political power in such districts was, figuratively, in the "pocket" of the wealthy landowners.

Chapter 20 Chronology

Catholic Emancipation Act

Slavery abolished in British possessions

Chartists draw up the People's Charter

Labor party founded

Act of Union

Second Reform Bill

Redistribution Bill

Fourth Reform Bill; universal manhood suffrage

Parliament Act

1801 · 1829 · 1833 · 1838 · 1867 · 1885 · 1901 · 1918 · 1949

1800   **1825**   **1850**   **1875**   **1900**   **1925**   **1950**

1807 · 1832 · 1837 · 1848 · 1872 · 1884 · 1901 · 1911 · 1928

Slave trade outlawed

First Reform Bill; Tories and Whigs become known as Conservatives and Liberals

Worst year in Irish potato famine

Secret ballot

Third Reform Bill

Parliament Act

Fifth Reform Bill; universal suffrage as women gain the right to vote

← Reign of Queen Victoria I →

- *Power of the House of Lords*: Members of the House of Lords were not elected. Their seats were appointed, based on heredity; this process was not an example of popular sovereignty. In addition, since passage of laws needed agreement by both parts of Parliament, the House of Lords could vote down a bill favored by the House of Commons.

The Reform Bills

The Reform Bill of 1832

A movement to change or reform some of the above nondemocratic characteristics began to grow, particularly among middle-class merchants and workers. Their efforts were stalled during the period of the Napoleonic Wars. But a few years after these wars ended in 1815, the movement gained strength. When the Whig party came to power in Parliament in 1830, its **cabinet** members wanted the House of Lords to agree to a bill passed in Commons that would provide for some political reforms. To make sure that the Lords, controlled by the Tory party, would do this, the Whigs got King William IV (r. 1830–1837) to threaten to appoint more Whig nobles as Lords' members. The ultimate result was passage of the Reform Bill of 1832.

This bill, also called the *First Reform Bill*, was a partial step along the path toward more democracy. It provided for the following:

- More than fifty rotten boroughs were abolished, as were many pocket boroughs. Urban, industrial boroughs got more seats in Commons.
- The right to vote (**suffrage**) was extended to the middle class, as property qualifications were lowered.

By obtaining the right to vote (also called the **franchise**), people connected with the Industrial Revolution—bankers, merchants, factory owners—were going to have a greater role in the nation's political affairs. Many of these new voters became supporters of the Whig party, thankful for the liberal political changes it brought about. The Whig party soon changed its name to the Liberal party. The opposition Tory party, consisting primarily of landowners, and not wanting to make sweeping political changes so quickly, changed its name to the Conservative party.

Citizen interest in election results. A crowd gathers at the "Daily Graphic" office, to watch the progress of the 1892 British parliamentary elections.

Democratic Progress Between the First and Second Reform Bills

It would be thirty-five years later, in 1867, before a second major reform bill was passed in Parliament. But before we examine that legislation, we should consider some other early nineteenth-century democratic advances made in Britain. In 1807, the slave trade was outlawed, while, in 1833, slavery was abolished in all British possessions. Specific religious qualifications for serving in Parliament were done away with in 1829 and in 1858. With passage of the Catholic

Benjamin Disraeli was an able British prime minister in the nineteenth century. He labeled himself as "a conservative to preserve all that is good in our constitution and a radical to remove all that is bad."

Emancipation Act in 1829, Catholics were permitted to serve in Parliament if they recognized the Protestant rulers as the true heads of the kingdom and denied the authority of the pope to interfere in the kingdom's affairs. In 1858, Jews were given the right to serve in Parliament.

A group of Englishmen concerned with making democratic changes were active in the 1830s and 1840s. In 1838, they wrote their proposals in a document called the *People's Charter*. Known as the **Chartists**, they wanted Parliament to provide for:

- Ending property qualifications for service in Parliament;
- The secret ballot;
- Universal manhood suffrage—giving the right to vote to all males;
- Yearly elections of Parliament; and
- Salaries for members of Parliament.

The Chartists held parades and meetings to publicize their demands. They were not successful, as these demands were considered too extreme for the times. Although the Chartist Movement faded away in the 1850s, by 1918 all of their demands except annual elections had been adopted.

The Reform Bill of 1867

By the 1860s, the desire for parliamentary reform had grown. The Tory (Conservative) party, led by Benjamin Disraeli (1804–1881), wanted to gain the credit for fulfilling this desire. Accordingly, the conservatives obtained passage of the Reform Bill of 1867. Also known as the *Second Reform Bill*, this legislation lowered property qualifications for voting even further than did the 1832 bill. Almost all male workers in cities were *enfranchised* (given the vote or franchise), as were men who paid rent for or owned their homes in urban areas. Consequently, the number of men now allowed to vote was almost doubled what it had been. This newly enfranchised population, so hoped Disraeli, would now support the Conservative party. This desired result did not come about, particularly as most city workers voted for liberals. Eventually, in 1901, workers and others would form a new party, the Labor party.

Further Increases in Voting Rights

The issue of voting rights was the subject of additional legislation in the late nineteenth and early twentieth centuries. In 1872, the *secret ballot* system was adopted by Parliament. Also called the *Australian ballot*, because it originated in Australia, it replaced the open ballot system. The bill providing for the new system was enacted under the leadership of the liberal prime minister William Gladstone (1809–1898). In three additional reform bills, the franchise was again extended:

1. In the Reform Bill of 1884 (the *Third Reform Bill*) agricultural workers were given the right to vote.
2. Universal manhood suffrage was achieved with passage of the Reform Bill of 1918. This *Fourth Reform Bill* gave the franchise to all men over twenty-one years of age.
3. True popular sovereignty, an aspect of a complete democracy, came about with enactment of the Reform Bill of 1928. By this bill, the right to vote was given to all women over twenty-one years of age.

Many suffragists, like this one, were arrested for their outspokenness about gaining women's voting rights. They were successful, however. The passage of the Reform Bill of 1928 gave all women over the age of twenty-one the right to vote.

The goal of **universal suffrage** was now achieved. This achievement was largely due to the efforts of several women who were active in leading a movement to improve the position of women in British society. These women were called *suffragettes*. Among their leaders were Emmeline Pankhurst and her daughters, Christabel and Sylvia. Their actions carried forward the hopes of Mary Wollstonecraft, an eighteenth-century pioneer in the struggle for equality for women in England.

Additional Parliamentary Reforms

While the measures described above did much to affect who could vote for members of Parliament, other laws were enacted that produced changes concerning Parliament. The *Redistribution Bill* of 1885 divided the nation into political districts that were approximately equal in population. Of historic importance for the functioning of Parliament were two laws that limited the power of the House of Lords. The House of Lords was not an elected body and was controlled by the conservatives. It could prevent a bill passed by the House of Commons from becoming law, as consent was needed by both houses for a bill to become a law. This situation did not seem right, as the House of Commons was a more representative body, elected by the people. The issue reached a head with the 1909 budget. Under Liberal Party leadership, the Commons passed a budget bill that the Lords defeated. In new elections for the House of Commons, the liberals won. These results showed that voters supported the original budget bill. The House of Lords now agreed to pass it.

This incident set the stage for the famous Parliament Act of 1911. Again under Liberal party leadership, the Commons passed a bill that would weaken the legislative power of the Lords. It was defeated in the House of Lords, and new elections were held for the Commons. The liberals won a majority of seats and claimed that they had the nation's support for the original bill. When the Lords still refused to consent to the bill, King George V (r. 1910–1936) threatened to appoint more liberals to the House of Lords to insure passage of the bill. In 1911, the bill was passed. It effectively weakened the power of the Lords over legislation by providing that:

- any money bill passed by the Commons would become law, even if the Lords were against it, after thirty days; and
- other bills passed by the Commons three times over a two-year period would become law, even if opposed by the Lords.

The House of Lords, therefore, had merely a temporary or *suspensive veto* over legislation. Of added significance in 1911 were measures that required elections to the House of Commons every five years and that gave salaries to members of the Commons. Finally, it should be noted that the Lords' suspensive veto over legislation was reduced to one year, as stated in the Parliament Act of 1949.

Growth of Cabinet Power

The government of Great Britain can be described as a *constitutional monarchy* as well as a *parliamentary democracy*. The cabinet consists of members of Parliament who act as advisers or ministers to the monarch. They include the chief adviser or *prime minister* and other people, all of whom are chosen by the majority party in Parliament. The majority party is that party which has won a majority of seats in the House of Commons, through elections by the population. The practice of the cabinet being selected from and being responsible to the majority party is called *cabinet responsibility to the parliament.* As we noted in Chapter 11, "The Growth of Democracy in England," the practice of a ruler relying on advisers from parliament began in the years following the **Glorious Revolution** of 1688–1689. The first two Hanoverian kings, George I (r. 1714–1727) and George II (r. 1727–1760), spoke English poorly and were content to trust the business of running the government to the cabinet. George III (r. 1760–1820) spoke English very well and was serious about his role as King. He frequently met with his cabinet. The role and prestige of the cabinet grew during these first hundred years after the Glorious Revolution and was to continue during the nineteenth century. This was particularly evident in the distinguished careers of two renowned prime ministers, Benjamin Disraeli and William Gladstone.

They were key figures in British politics from 1866 to 1894. In addition to their brilliance and popularity, they were trusted and respected by the **monarchy**. The British ruler during these times was Queen Victoria (r. 1837–1901). The granddaughter of George III, (see chart showing sovereigns of England and Scotland in Chapter 11, "The Growth of Democracy in England"), she reigned for the longest period of any British monarch. This period became known as the *Victorian Era* or *Victorian Age*, celebrated for its advances in social, economic, and political affairs. Queen Victoria was careful to stay within the limits of her power, leaving her cabinet ministers, such as Disraeli and Gladstone, the freedom to push through the kind of reform legislation we have already described.

The expansion of cabinet responsibility and the passage of reform democratic legislation are very important parts of the British system of government. They came about over a long period of years, in a peaceful manner, and thus were achieved through **evolution** rather than through violence and **revolution**. The system has managed to combine continuity with necessary changes and has attempted to guarantee human rights to all its citizens. However, unlike the situation in the United States, there is no written **constitution** in Britain that forms the basis of its democracy. What does pass for a British constitution is really a combination of the following:

- Actual written documents and laws, such as the Magna Carta and the Reform Bill of 1832; and
- Unwritten customs and traditions, such as cabinet responsibility.

From what we have now learned, it is clear that politics in nineteenth-century Britain led to significant democratic changes. However, there was one political issue that grew more critical and controversial in the 1800s and early 1900s. Failure to resolve it peacefully in those times has led to problems even in our own era. This issue was the Irish Question.

The Irish Question

The onset of problems between England and Ireland prior to 1800 has been described already. (See Chapter 10, "The Rise of Nation-States," and Chapter 11, "The Growth of Democracy in England.") The English Protestants who settled in Northern Ireland (Ulster) were a minority, but they had dominated political and economic affairs. The majority of people, Irish Catholics, were very upset with the conditions under which they lived. Under English rule ever since being conquered in the twelfth century, the Irish people had wished to become independent. As the nineteenth century opened, Britain tried to ease tension. By the Act of Union, passed in 1801, parliament joined Ireland and Great Britain to form the United Kingdom of Great Britain and Ireland. The Irish were given representation in the British Parliament but were angry at the little real power they had in that body. They were also angry at having to pay taxes to the Anglican Church and high rents to absentee Protestant landlords. One of their leaders, Daniel O'Connell, the "Great Emancipator," organized people to demand reforms and some kind of **home rule** or independence.

Amidst this atmosphere, a terrible tragedy struck Ireland, the potato famine of the 1840s, with 1848 being the worst year. Because of natural conditions, the potato crop, a mainstay of the Irish diet, was ruined. Tens of thousands died of starvation, while other thousands migrated to the United States. Survivors pressed for land law reforms as well as home rule legislation. The British generally resisted these demands, fearful that the Protestant minority in Ireland would suffer. Nevertheless, legislation was enacted in 1869 that freed Catholics from paying taxes to the Anglican Church. The 1870 and 1881 land acts eased restrictions on evictions, rents, and purchases of land. Elected as an Irish representative to Parliament, Charles Parnell tried to gain the help of both liberals and conservatives in obtaining more benefits for Ireland. Critical moments came in 1886 and 1892 when Gladstone and the liberals introduced home rule legislation. These efforts were unsuccessful. In 1895, the conservatives did get some land reform laws passed but stayed away from any home rule bills. A short-lived achievement occurred in 1912, when Parliament did pass a home rule bill. However, Protestants in Ulster were so alarmed at the passage that they set up an armed force of more than one hundred thousand men to resist the carrying out of the bill. The bill was never enforced. When World War I broke out in 1914, with Britain as one of the powers involved, the Irish Question faded into the background. Yet, when the war was over in 1918, attempts were again made to "answer" this troublesome question. In Chapter 29, "Independence and Decolonization," we will look at these attempts to decide whether or not they were satisfactory.

Summary

As the chapter ends, we see a far more democratic Britain than opened the century. What is important to realize is that the changes took place over a long period of time in a fairly peaceful manner. Few changes that last are accomplished quickly. You have only to look at the French Revolution to realize that. It is also interesting to note that most of the demands of the Chartists, a "third party," were incorporated. You will often find in history that when third parties have rea-

sonable demands, existing parties "claim" these demands themselves in order to eliminate the third party. The queen or king continued to reign but no longer ruled as power shifted to the House of Commons, the body that now represented the people. While there are many similarities between the United States and Great Britain, there are two important differences to remember. First, Britain does not have a written constitution. Second, the British parliamentary system is considerably different from our own presidential/congressional system. There are many arguments for the advantages of each. Can you think of some?

CHAPTER 20

Review Exercises

I. Matching

Directions: Match the words in Column A with the *correct description* in Column B.

Column A
1. rotten borough
2. House of Lords
3. home rule
4. House of Commons
5. constitutional monarchy
6. suffrage
7. Chartists
8. Whigs
9. Tories
10. suspensive veto
11. pocket borough

Column B
(a) independence wanted by the Irish
(b) an area underrepresented in the House of Commons
(c) members chosen by elections
(d) the right to vote
(e) also known as liberals
(f) also known as conservatives
(g) representation from here was influenced by wealthy landowners
(h) members were chosen by the monarch
(i) a power given to the House of Lords
(j) Parliament can limit the power of a queen
(k) a movement of city workers pressing for political reform

II. Famous People

Directions: Use the names below to complete the following sentences.

Benjamin Disraeli   Charles Parnell
Queen Victoria   Daniel O'Connell
William Gladstone   Emmeline Pankhurst

1. _____ was an Irish representative to Parliament who tried to gain benefits for Catholics in Ireland.

2. _____ led a movement that resulted in universal suffrage, as reflected in the Reform Bill of 1928.

3. _____ was the Tory leader credited with passage of the Reform Bill of 1867, hoping to get city workers to support his party.

4. _____ organized the Irish people to demand home rule from Britain.

5. _____ headed the Liberal party and was prime minister when Parliament adopted the secret ballot system.

6. _____ showed restraint by not interfering with the legislative activities of Parliament.

III. Multiple Choice

Directions: Find the *letter* of the correct answer.

1. A law to extend the franchise would concern the right of people to

   (a) run for office.
   (b) enjoy freedom of religion.
   (c) own property.
   (d) vote in elections.

2. The main reason for the population change in early nineteenth-century Britain resulting in unequal representation in Parliament was the

   (a) War of 1812.
   (b) Napoleonic Wars.
   (c) Industrial Revolution.
   (d) Chartist Movement.

3. Emmeline Pankhurst and her daughters were active mainly in the movement to give women the opportunity to

   (a) serve in the House of Lords.
   (b) vote for members of Parliament.
   (c) obtain the position of prime minister.
   (d) become members of the cabinet.

4. An undemocratic feature of the British government at the start of the nineteenth-century was

   (a) the lack of a cabinet system.
   (b) the inability of Parliament to pass laws.
   (c) the House of Lords being as powerful as the House of Commons.
   (d) the monarch's power over Parliament.

5. Democracy in Britain grew as a result of

   (a) violent revolution.
   (b) peaceful evolution.
   (c) cultural diffusion.
   (d) decisions by the monarch.

6. Why did the House of Lords, although resistant at first, finally agree to passage of the Reform Bill of 1832?

   (a) The king was about to dismiss its members.
   (b) The House of Commons threatened to take over all of Parliament.
   (c) The liberal prime minister was going to replace half of its members.
   (d) The king was likely to appoint new liberal lords.

7. The potato famine of the 1840s most seriously affected people living in

   (a) England.
   (b) Scotland.
   (c) the United Kingdom.
   (d) Ireland.

8. The Chartist Movement

   (a) was declared illegal by Parliament.
   (b) successfully worked to limit royal power.
   (c) had demands that eventually became laws.
   (d) failed in its attempt to expand the power of the House of Lords.

9. In Britain, a person becomes a cabinet member upon being

   (a) elected by popular vote.
   (b) chosen by the prime minister.
   (c) appointed by the monarch.
   (d) nominated in the House of Lords.

10. The Reform Bill that most pleased the suffragettes was the one passed in

    (a) 1832.
    (b) 1867.
    (c) 1884.
    (d) 1928.

11. Which long-term effect did the Magna Carta and the growth of Parliament have on England?

    (a) Royal power was limited.
    (b) The House of Commons lost its power to tax.
    (c) The influence of the middle class was reduced.
    (d) The number of political parties decreased.

12. The House of Lords was weakened by the Parliament Act of 1911, because its

    (a) ability to choose cabinet members was taken away.
    (b) power over legislation was reduced.
    (c) members would now be elected.
    (d) control over suffrage rules was abolished.

13. The Catholic Emancipation Act of 1829 made it possible for Catholics to

    (a) vote for members of Parliament.
    (b) serve in Parliament.
    (c) practice their religion freely.
    (d) pay fewer taxes.

14. Which of the following was *not* affected by the Act of Union (1801)?

   (a) Great Britain
   (b) Ireland
   (c) North America
   (d) The United Kingdom

15. What was one result of the Parliament Acts of 1911 and 1949?

   (a) The House of Lords lost some power.
   (b) The House of Commons lost some power.
   (c) Members of Parliament did not have to pay any taxes.
   (d) Parliament had to get royal approval for all legislation.

IV. Thought Questions

Directions: Answer the following questions in essay form.

1. Define the following terms:

   A. the British constitution
   B. secret ballot
   C. universal manhood suffrage
   D. universal suffrage

2. For many years in England, property, religion, and gender were barriers that were used to deny many people their full rights as citizens in political affairs. For each barrier, do the following:

   A. Explain one measure that was taken to abolish it.
   B. Describe one group of people who benefited from this measure.

3. Draw a "staircase" of advances in British democracy from 1832 to 1928, with each "step" representing one of the five Reform Bills. In each step, describe one way in which a democratic advance was provided for.

4. For each of the following draw a poster or a sign that a person would march with in a demonstration if the person wanted

   A. home rule for Ireland.
   B. woman suffrage.
   C. an end to rotten boroughs.
   D. the franchise for factory workers.

5. What was the Irish Question?

   A. How did the British try to answer this question in the nineteenth century?
   B. Were these answers satisfactory to the Irish people? Explain.

CHAPTER 21

Changes in France

The defeat of Napoleon at Waterloo left France in chaos. The twenty years of almost constant warfare had caused great damage to the French nation and its people. The **monarchy** was overthrown, and the nation was invaded by armies that destroyed valuable property. After the final defeat of Napoleon, the victorious Allies determined how France was to be treated at the Congress of Vienna, which met in 1814 and 1815. (See Chapter 14, "The Rise and Fall of Napoleon.") During the Congress of Vienna, a number of other important issues were also settled. The French royal family was restored to power, and France's borders were reduced to those that existed in 1790. The leaders of Europe hoped to return to the past and erase the changes made after the **French Revolution**.

In this chapter, you will learn if the leaders of Europe were successful in determining the future of France. You will see if it is possible to turn back the clock once change has taken place. By the end of the chapter, you can evaluate whether the French Revolution and the **Napoleonic Era** brought lasting changes to France.

The Bourbon Restoration

Louis XVIII's restoration in 1814 was a crucial test for postwar stability. In an effort to insure domestic tranquility, peace, and order at home, the King and his advisers designed a political compromise. A balance was sought between the heritage of the old regime and the changes that followed the French Revolution. Louis XVIII granted a **charter** that allowed for a two-house legislature. The Chamber of Peers was hereditary, and the Chamber of Deputies was limited to men of landed wealth. Napoleon's centralized administration and tax system were enthusiastically maintained by the restored monarchy.

The King and his ministers pursued a course of political restraint and administrative efficiency. Louis's moderate policies proved effective in preventing a revival of radicalism in France. However, after the assassination of the Bourbon Duke of Berry in 1820, the King did impose restrictions in an effort to smother radical ideas printed in the press and taught in universities.

The Count of Artois, the King's younger brother, succeeded to the throne after Louis XVIII died in 1824. Charles X was an **ultraroyalist** (extreme royalist), who sought to revive the symbols of **divine right**. During his reign, public criticism of the monarchy grew, particularly after the election of 1827.

This election brought more liberals into the legislature. The liberals in France favored a republican form of government, restrictions on the Catholic Church, and an economic policy that supported free trade and other **laissez-faire** ideas. Charles reacted to his increasingly hostile opposition with firmness. In 1830, the King's ministers issued a set of secretly drafted decrees, the *July Ordinances*, which dissolved the recently elected chamber, further restricted **suffrage**, and increased press censorship.

Public reaction to the July Ordinances was negative and soon turned violent. In Paris alone, seven hundred people died in three days during a popular uprising. Charles X tried to appoint a more acceptable ministry, but it was too late. Liberal leaders started to plan for a new regime. By August, Charles decided to abdicate. The **restoration** had provided political stability for fifteen years, but France's ruling Bourbon monarch fell in 1830. During this time period, ideas of **liberalism**

Chapter 21 Chronology

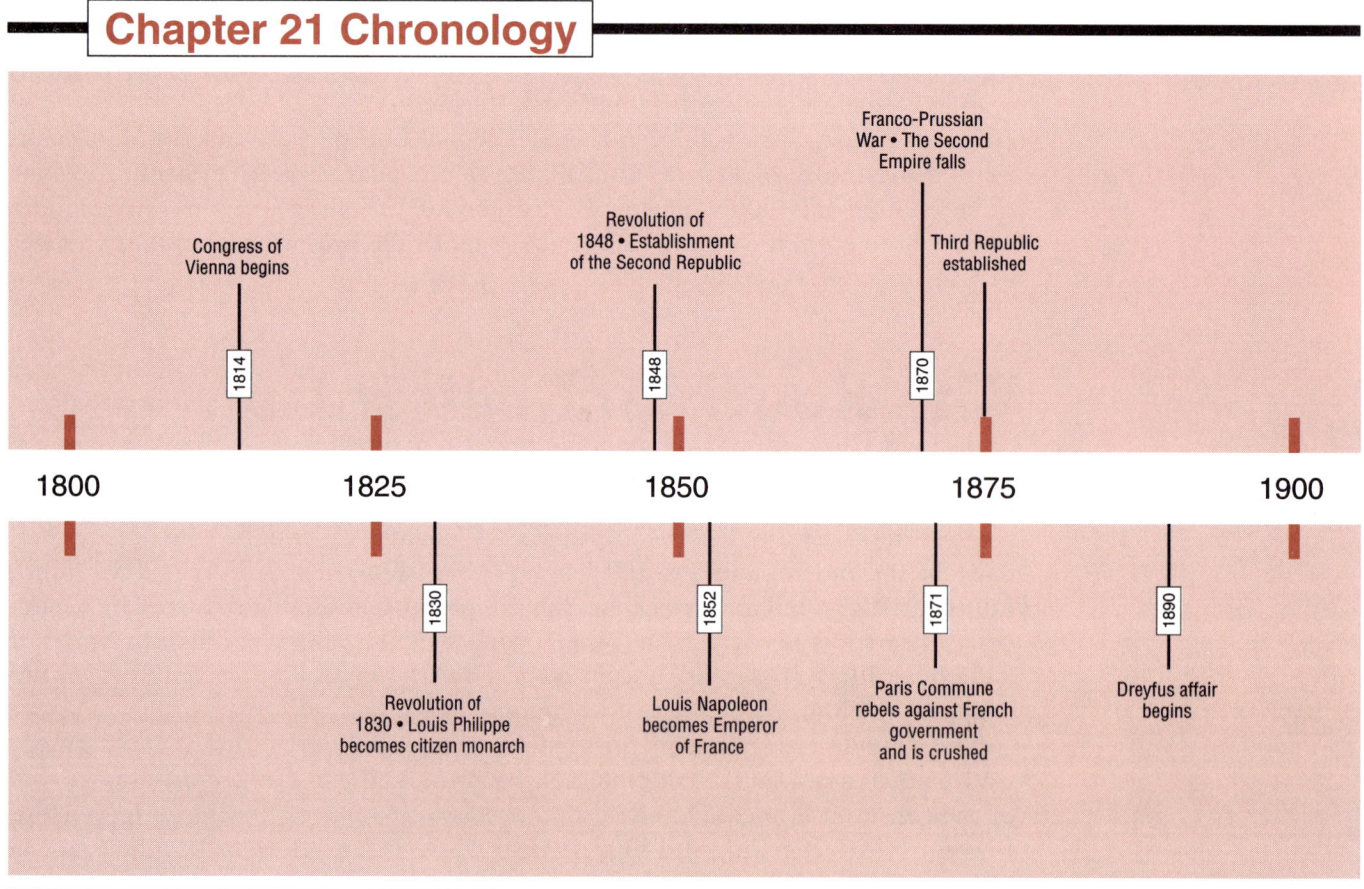

Congress of Vienna begins — 1814

Revolution of 1848 • Establishment of the Second Republic — 1848

Franco-Prussian War • The Second Empire falls

Third Republic established — 1870

1800   1825   1850   1875   1900

Revolution of 1830 • Louis Philippe becomes citizen monarch — 1830

Louis Napoleon becomes Emperor of France — 1852

Paris Commune rebels against French government and is crushed — 1871

Dreyfus affair begins — 1890

began to sweep over Europe. England's liberal political system, which preserved the monarchy, served as the model for France.

The Liberal Monarchy in France

The **revolution** that shook France in 1830 resulted in the establishment of a liberal monarchy. Louis Philippe, who traced his descent in the royal line to the House of Orléans, became the new King. Louis Philippe considered himself a citizen king and chose the revolutionary tricolor as France's flag. Nevertheless, the King assured other monarchs that France would not export revolution, thereby heading off a possible European reaction.

The Revolution of 1830 in France was led by the middle class. The growing political influence of the middle class reflected this group's increasing economic power. Many members of the middle class were liberals who believed in the individual's right to liberty and wanted laissez-faire economic policies that favored their industrial and commercial interests. The liberals also supported constitutional government, basic individual freedoms, and the separation of Church and state.

The July Monarchy

Louis Philippe's regime is referred to as the July Monarchy. A new **constitution** was presented to the French people as a contract that could not be broken. The old **aristocracy**, which was influential during the previous two regimes, thereafter lost political power to the middle class. Despite opposition from both the right, the pro-Bourbon legitimists, and the left, the advocates of a **republic**, the July Monarchy established itself as a symbol of political stability. Even the Bonapartists, who were led by Louis Napoleon, the Emperor's nephew, could not stir up a serious revolt against the citizen monarch. Louis Philippe remained as King of France for eighteen years.

Louis Philippe's rule in France concentrated on economic growth and an efficient and stable administration. In 1833, a national system for public education was established, which greatly benefited the growing middle class. In addition, beginning in the 1830s, the July Monarchy enthusiastically supported the growth of railroads. The monarchy benefited from the stability and progress that it offered to the middle class. Visions of economic development and political order encouraged the expanding **bourgeoisie** to support Louis Philippe.

In the 1840s, political conflict in France essentially involved a struggle between two middle-class factions. The differences separating the two groups led by Adolphe Thiers and François Guizot were not great and basically involved the interpretation of the existing constitution. Guizot, who was French premier from 1840 to 1848, emphasized the rule of law and parliamentary government in order to insure stability and make progress. Louis Philippe supported Guizot's faction until the end of the July Monarchy in 1848. In that year, revolutionaries with more radical visions of democracy and social justice swept away the Guizot government. The faltering French economy enabled revolutionaries to attract support, and by 1848, the French people, particularly the working class, became increasingly discontent. They demanded various political reforms, especially voting rights.

The Revolution of 1848 Louis Philippe's attempt to use troops to control the demonstrations that broke out in February 1848 resulted in the weakening of the King's power. The French soldiers sympathized with the working-class protesters and joined them. Over the next number of days, bloody disturbances took place in Paris and other French cities. On February 24, the Parisian workers broke into the Chamber of Deputies and forced the proclamation of a republic. Louis Philippe fled into exile in Great Britain. The February Revolution was at first distinctly radical.

A **provisional government** was set up and a new constitution was drafted. In the spring of 1848, a French government was elected by an expanded electorate that included all adult males. The constitution enacted many democratic reforms, including a constituent assembly and a president elected by **universal** manhood suffrage.

The Second Republic

The idea of a republic was not new to France. During the period of the French Revolution, the First Republic was established and it lasted until the creation of the Napoleonic Empire. The Second Republic did not last very long because of basic disagreements that divided the middle class and the workers. The social gulf separating the moderate middle class, who were the majority in the constituent assembly, and the working class could not be bridged. Class-oriented violence now marked the political strife in France.

The provisional government took power immediately after the proclamation of the Second Republic and represented some of the more radical and **socialist** factions. The socialist Louis Blanc was a member of the provisional government. Blanc outlined his ideal for a new social order based on the principle of "from each according to his needs, to each according to his abilities." In the first stage, Blanc argued for the immediate relief of the unemployed through a ministry of progress, which would establish his social workshops system. The social workshops were to be controlled by the working men and supported by the state.

When the newly elected constituent assembly met on May 4th, it immediately replaced the provisional government with a five-man executive council of its own containing no socialists or radicals. Discontent among the radicals and socialists led to an unsuccessful coup headed by the radical thinker and revolutionary Louis Auguste Blanqui. The government reacted by dissolving the Blanc-inspired workshop program. The workers' reaction was immediate and violent. A class war began in the streets of Paris. For three days the government's troops were pitted against armed workers. An estimated ten thousand people were killed and wounded in a struggle without quarter until government troops regained control of the city.

The June Days of Terror frightened the wealthier bourgeoisie, **nobility**, and other middle-class citizens. In the December 1848 election for president of France, all four candidates campaigned as republicans. Louis Napoleon Bonaparte was the candidate who received the greatest support from the members of French society. The electorate was disillusioned with the course of events in France and wanted a return to order, stability, and renewed economic progress. French people thought back to the glory days of Napoleon I and longed for a return to those times of national greatness. Louis Napoleon won 70 percent of the votes and became the first and only president of France's Second Republic.

Louis Napoleon Bonaparte and the Second Republic

Louis Napoleon's term as president of the Second Republic brought him into political conflict with the monarchists who controlled the Chamber of Deputies. Nevertheless, in his first years of office, Louis Napoleon's popularity grew as he continued to appeal to public opinion as a democratic reformer and increasingly gained the support of the powerful groups in France—the army, the middle class, the Church, and the peasants. The future Napoleon III also won the confidence of the largely Catholic French population. He helped the pope suppress an attempt by Italian nationalists to establish a republic in Rome and gave the Roman Catholic Church control over French education.

When the Chamber of Deputies rejected a constitutional amendment that would have allowed him a second term, Louis Napoleon decided to engineer a **coup d'état**. On December 2, 1851, Louis Napoleon called the Republic a failure and took control of the government. Victory was assured by the arrests of opposition deputies and other potential opponents and by the use of troops to take effective control of the Parisian streets. The concentration of both the executive and legislative powers in his hands was part of Napoleon's shrewd plan to use dictatorial authority to win popular support.

Louis Napoleon then used a **plebiscite** to have the people grant him the power to create a new constitution. In this first plebiscite, he boldly reestablished universal suffrage for all French men and received a strong show of support. In a second plebiscite shortly thereafter, about 95 percent of the electorate approved of transforming France from a republic to a hereditary **empire**. In 1852, Louis Napoleon became Napoleon III, Emperor of France.

The Second Empire

The Second Empire, created by the nephew of Napoleon Bonaparte, who established France's first empire, brought important changes. In the 1850s, Napoleon III benefited from an economic boom in France, which his government helped stimulate by acting to foster growth. The state created special investment funds and tax incentives, and launched huge public works projects. Paris changed enormously and assumed more of an aura of grandeur. The *prefect*, or appointed mayor of Paris, Baron Georges Haussmann, created broad boulevards and ornate public buildings, and rid the city's center of slums. The state support of **entrepreneurs** engaged in public works projects gave rise to rumors of political spoils and speculation.

The court of Napoleon led by Empress Eugénie achieved a measure of brilliance. French prestige in the arts and sciences increased, and the talented received the Emperor's rewards of honors and promotions. The Emperor sponsored social and educational reform and publicly took credit for his works.

Foreign Policy Napoleon III's foreign policy was designed to increase his popularity. One way that Napoleon sought to prove his greatness was by becoming involved in foreign wars and risky overseas adventures. Napoleon saw the Crimean War as an opportunity to show the world that France was once again a military power to be respected and to increase his own stature. The Russian attempt to take advantage of the weakness of the Ottoman Empire and expand toward the warm-water ports of the Mediterranean Sea was opposed by France. Joining with Great Britain, the French were soon involved in war. The French success in the Crimean War, 1854–1856, brought the Emperor great prestige when the Russians asked for peace after the fall of Sebastopol. France also profited from measures to protect its trade and financial interests in the Middle East.

Napoleon III's **intervention** in Italy had less success because it resulted in the loss of papal territory. His support of Italy had antagonized French Catholics, and the Emperor subsequently tried to strengthen his domestic popularity by an adventure in Mexico. Using the initial pretext of a joint British, French, and Spanish intervention in the country to force payment of foreign debts, France kept its troops in Mexico after the other nations withdrew. The Emperor then sought to impose French control over Mexico. This led to a war in which the liberal Mexican government was defeated. France then installed Archduke Maximilian of Austria as Emperor in Mexico. Unexpected strong Mexican resistance and United States opposition forced the French to withdraw and abandon Maximilian. Napoleon's prestige suffered greatly after Maximilian was defeated and then executed.

The Second Empire Falls

The Empire's changing fortunes caused it to lose support at home as the 1860s progressed. Even Napoleon III's successful colonial ventures in Indochina and Africa began to be regarded as a very expensive military burden. The French public became concerned with the high cost of military glory. Napoleon III sought to turn public opinion in his favor by taking measures to liberalize the Empire. In 1868, freedom of the press and the right to assembly were once again permitted. Members of the legislature were also allowed to question ministers. Workers were allowed to organize and even strike. The government also established public secondary schools for girls. The Emperor's belated attempts at **liberalization** did not satisfy his critics and even served to alienate some of his old supporters. In 1870, facing an increasingly difficult political situation at home and in Europe, the Emperor permitted the establishment of a full-fledged parliamentary system. A republican was then allowed to be chosen as prime minister.

In foreign affairs, Louis Napoleon, looking to regain public favor and support in the legislature, took a nationalist stand regarding France's growing differences with Prussia. The main issues were France's concern over the growth of German strength on its borders and competition over influence in Spain. The Prussians, led by Otto von Bismarck, were well prepared for battle and maneuvered the French into a declaration of war. The German military machine quickly crossed into France and in a period of six weeks decisively won the Franco-Prussian War. (See Chapter 23, "Unification of Germany.") The German capture of Louis Napoleon soon led to the collapse of the Second Empire.

Peace with Prussia and the Paris Commune

In early 1871, the newly elected French **National Assembly** made peace with Prussia. In the peace treaty, France lost the provinces of Alsace and Lorraine and agreed to pay Prussia the equivalent of a one-billion-dollar war reparation. A further humiliation was the staging of a Prussian victory march in Paris.

These actions angered many people in France and led to demonstrations and calls for renewed war with Prussia. The French legislature reacted by seeking to restore order in Paris, but its actions had the opposite effect. The provisional government suspended payments to the national guard, which had many Parisians in the ranks. The national guard had played a prominent role in defending Paris during the German siege. In addition, Parisians were angered by the government's declaration that all debts and rents suspended during the siege now be paid. These unpopular measures led to unrest and an uprising in Paris.

During the revolt, workers who wanted a socialist form of government established the **commune** of Paris. The leaders of the Paris Commune operated as a government and were soon in conflict with the National Assembly. The commune refused to recognize the assembly, and the communards called for the conversion of France into a decentralized federation of independent cities. The Paris Commune also declared itself against the Roman Catholic Church and propertied classes.

A bitter and bloody civil war broke out in Paris. By the time that the troops loyal to the National Assembly regained control of the city, more than twenty thousand people had been killed and more than forty thousand arrested. That bloody week in May 1871 left a legacy of class bitterness and further polarized French politics. The intensification of the social divisions between the middle class and the workers continued into the twentieth century.

The Third Republic

After the destruction of the Paris Commune, a political struggle developed over what form the new government should take. Royalists and republicans fought over this vital political issue. Finally, in 1875, another constitution was agreed upon, which gave France a republican government. The Third Republic proved politically unstable and unpopular. Political parties in the modern sense did not exist. Instead, political groupings held together by immediate concerns continued to the end of the century. Royalist sentiment remained strong but was divided along Bourbon, Orléanist, or Bonapartist lines. Republicans were equally divided over issues related to liberalism. Radical republicans were stridently anticlerical and antiroyalist, whereas the moderates sought to compromise on key issues.

The Constitution of 1875 provided for a two-house legislature that elected a president for a four-year term. The real political power was in the hands of the legislature, which had to approve of all acts before they officially became law. A cabinet of ministers was created with the post of premier to handle all executive business.

Crisis in the Third Republic

The 1880s and 1890s were periods of crises for the Third Republic. One of its greatest threats came from a popular war hero, General Georges Boulanger. Chosen as war minister in 1886, Boulanger championed revenge against the Germans. He was supported by royalists and other antirepublicans. In 1871, after launching a losing campaign calling for a new legislature and constitution, Boulanger began to plan a coup d'état. His goal was to establish a more authoritarian regime, but he lost his nerve and fled to Brussels. The Boulanger Movement soon collapsed without the direction of its popular leader.

A second threat to the Republic in the 1890s involved the construction of a canal through Panama. The failure of the French Panama Company and the loss of money invested by thousands of stockholders led to a scandal that shook the government. Charges of corruption, poor management, and dishonesty resulted in trials that further embittered the public. The socialist movement benefited from this scandal and won nearly fifty seats in the legislature for the first time.

The Dreyfus Affair The Third Republic's gravest crisis in the 1890s was the Dreyfus affair. Captain Alfred Dreyfus, a Jewish army officer, was arrested and charged with treason for selling military secrets to the Germans. The French army, a stronghold of monarchists and Catholics, was permeated with **anti-Semitism**. The officer corps knew that Dreyfus was innocent. Nevertheless, to cover up their general incompetence and to protect the guilty party who was one of their own, the French army sacrificed Dreyfus. After his conviction by a French court-martial, Dreyfus was sentenced to degradation and deportation for life. He was sent to Devil's Island, a notorious prison off the northeast coast of South America. In general, public opinion applauded the conviction.

Captain Alfred Dreyfus, a Jewish officer in the French army, was unjustly convicted of selling military secrets to the Germans. He served twelve years before his innocence was proven.

Dreyfus's family and many supporters continued to maintain his innocence. By 1897, growing evidence indicated that Dreyfus was convicted through the use of forged documents. The military, however, remained adamant and refused to go along with a reversal of Dreyfus's sentence despite new evidence indicating that a Major Esterazy was responsible for the treasonous acts. Esterazy was tried by court-martial and acquitted within minutes. Army leaders argued that military authority would be undermined if Dreyfus was retried.

Emile Zola, a French writer and leading supporter of Dreyfus, sent an open letter to Felix Faure, the president of the French Republic, accusing the judges of acting on orders of the war ministry. The case became a major issue in France. Catholics, monarchists, militarists, and conservatives joined together in patriotic indignation against socialists, republicans, anticlericals, and Jews, whom they accused of selling out the country and weakening the army.

The Dreyfus affair continued through the late 1890s into the first decade of the twentieth century. Dreyfus was retried in 1899, but the military court was unable to admit its error. He was once again found guilty, this time with extenuating circumstances, and sentenced to ten years. Faced with worldwide indignation, France issued a pardon to Dreyfus. In 1906, he was readmitted into the army with the rank of major and given the Legion of Honor after he was completely exonerated by the supreme court of appeals. The support of republicans, socialists, artists, and writers was eventually successful, and justice was served.

The Dreyfus affair was an important test that proved the Third Republic could survive despite the deep split it caused among a generation of French citizens. After the Dreyfus affair, republican supporters began to demand reforms that were beneficial to the working class. The Dreyfus affair continues to influence France to our present day. The problem of anti-Semitism remains a serious issue in French society.

Summary

This chapter reminds us of the saying, "You can't tell the players without a scorecard." The last chapter, which involved change in Britain, had evolution as

Le Petit Journal

Le Petit Journal

Le Supplément illustré

SUPPLÉMENT ILLUSTRÉ

Huit pages : CINQ centimes

ABONNEMENTS

DIMANCHE 13 JANVIER 1895

Numéro 217

The Dreyfus affair gained much public attention when world-famous author Emile Zola published an open letter in newspapers to the president of France. The letter, known as "J'Accuse," charged the war ministry with using Dreyfus as a scapegoat for the actions of another officer.

a theme. What theme would you give to the changes in France? We looked at constant conflict between monarchists and republicans, liberals and conservatives, and workers and owners. There were violent demonstrations and blockaded streets and another in a series of constitutions. There seemed to be no tradition for the orderly settling of differences, and so upheaval was the answer. The people were willing to surrender their liberties for the security they saw in another Napoleon. His foreign policy proved to be a disaster for France and another republic was declared. This republic experienced its own problems—the Boulanger crisis, the Canal crisis, and the Dreyfus affair. It is difficult to believe that it lasted until 1940!

Review Exercises

I. Multiple Choice

Directions: Find the *letter* of the correct answer.

1. After the defeat of Napoleon, the victorious European powers restored which of the following royal families to the French throne?

   (a) Romanovs   (b) Bourbons
   (c) Habsburgs   (d) Stuarts

2. The ruling monarchy was overthrown in 1830 because

   (a) Charles X was too liberal a ruler.
   (b) the July Ordinances were popular in France.
   (c) the French aristocrats demanded power.
   (d) middle class groups wanted a more liberal regime.

3. The main support of Louis Philippe's liberal monarchy came from the

   (a) old aristocracy.   (b) working class.
   (c) middle class.   (d) ultraroyalists.

4. In the Revolution of 1848, political conflict in France led to the creation of a

   (a) legitimist monarchy.
   (b) short-lived republic.
   (c) radical democracy.
   (d) Paris Commune.

5. The Second Republic failed because the

   (a) working class demanded a more conservative government.
   (b) constituent assembly supported socialist reforms.
   (c) the middle class gave up control of the government.
   (d) French people wanted stability and economic progress.

6. During the Second Empire, Napoleon III was successful in all of the following *except*

   (a) the Crimean War.
   (b) the renovation of Paris.
   (c) social and educational reform.
   (d) intervention in Mexico.

7. The Second Empire came to an end in 1870 because of the

   (a) Mexican intervention.
   (b) fall of the Paris Commune.
   (c) Franco-Prussian War.
   (d) unification of Italy.

8. The Paris Commune was supported primarily by the

   (a) propertied classes.
   (b) Roman Catholic Church.
   (c) working class.
   (d) legitimists and royalists.

9. Prior to the twentieth century, the Third Republic was politically unstable because

   (a) there were no clear-cut political parties.
   (b) the French Republic had no written constitution.
   (c) the president was directly elected by the people.
   (d) military leaders seized power in a coup d'état.

10. The Dreyfus affair was a grave crisis for all of the following reasons *except*

   (a) the military's authority was at stake.
   (b) the affair involved charges of anti-Semitism.
   (c) French society was divided over the issue.
   (d) the army helped Dreyfus's supporters.

II. Matching

Directions: Match the names in Column A with the achievement they are *best known* for in Column B.

Column A	*Column B*
1. Archduke Maximilian	(a) renovated Paris during the Second Empire
2. Charles X	(b) citizen monarch
3. Louis Philippe	(c) Bourbon ultraroyalist King
4. Louis Napoleon	(d) workshop program
5. Louis Auguste Blanqui	(e) ruled France in Second Empire
6. Louis Blanc	(f) believed in violent revolution
7. Georges Haussmann	(g) wrongly convicted of treason
8. Georges Boulanger	(h) popular general in Third Republic
9. Alfred Dreyfus	(i) government leader in the 1840s
10. François Guizot	(j) French-installed Emperor of Mexico

III. Vocabulary

Directions: Define the following words, terms, or expressions and use them in a written sentence.

1. ultraroyalist—
2. anti-Semitic—
3. provisional government—
4. liberal monarchy—
5. renovation—

6. commune—
7. intervention—
8. treason—
9. middle class—
10. suffrage—

IV. Thought Questions

Directions: Answer the following questions in essay form.

1. Give three reasons why the middle class supported Louis Philippe as the French monarch after the Revolution of 1830.

2. You are a working-class supporter of the Revolution of 1848. Write an essay explaining why you are in favor of the revolution. Give three reasons for your position.

3. Write a newspaper article about the results of the Franco-Prussian War.

4. You are a member of the Paris Commune. Write a leaflet listing the goals of the commune.

5. Write an essay about the Dreyfus affair. In your essay, analyze two reasons why Dreyfus was accused and explain how he was eventually exonerated.

V. Activities

Directions: Complete the following activities.

1. You have been chosen as a spokesperson for the revolutionaries in the events listed below. Make a list of demands that your fellow revolutionaries will support, and prepare a list of arguments to support your demands. Read this list to your class as a basis for discussion.

   A. The Revolution of 1830
   B. The Revolution of 1848
   C. The Paris Commune

2. You have been chosen as the lawyer to defend Alfred Dreyfus at his military trial. Prepare a list of arguments that you will use to defend him.

3. You are assigned a research project to prepare a report on one of the persons listed below. This research requires you to go to the library to get the necessary information. For the person assigned, you must report on the role that he or she played in France during the nineteenth century.

   A. Louis Philippe
   B. Louis Napoleon
   C. Adolphe Thiers
   D. François Guizot
   E. Georges Haussman
   F. Empress Eugenie
   G. General Boulanger

CHAPTER 22

Unification of Italy

Do you know anyone who is Italian? If so, perhaps that person, or others of his or her family, were born in a nation that can be identified today on a map as Italy. Have you ever gone to an Italian restaurant? The food was prepared and named from traditions originating in a nation that can be identified today on a map as Italy. This nation occupies land in southern Europe, mainly on a peninsula surrounded by three seas. Although Italian people have lived on this land for centuries, the nation-state we locate today on a map as Italy came into existence only in the second half of the nineteenth century. The history of the creation of this nation at that time will be the topic for us to learn about in this chapter.

The desire of the Italian people to form their own nation, free of rule by others, is an example of **nationalism**. Nationalism is the belief that a group of people who share a common **culture**, language, and historical tradition should have their own country in a specific area of land. Nationalism is also a feeling of pride in and loyalty to one's country. When people who were ruled by outsiders finally accomplish their nationalistic goals and form a nation-state, they can then make their own laws and have their own government. Such people are said to be sovereign and to have independence or **autonomy**.

The spirit of nationalism greatly influenced the political history of Europe in the nineteenth century, particularly with the unification movements that led to the births of modern Italy and Germany. And in the last years of the twentieth century, it has been a factor in the breakup of the former Soviet Union. This spirit has been a force for both good and evil. Nationalism can be viewed favorably when it brings people together for common, shared peaceful purposes. It is also a force for good when a person becomes proud to do good things for his nation, or carries out peaceful responsibilities, or feels happy at the accomplishments of his fellow citizens. On the other hand, it can be a force for evil when it brings people together for the purpose of committing wrongful acts. This is also true when a person does things under the name of nationalism that cause harm to others. Extremely intense and passionate nationalistic pride, as shown by individuals who think their nation is always right and can never do anything wrong, is called *chauvinism*. Such intense nationalism can also be evident when a nation thinks its ways are superior and attempts to impose them on others or even destroy the ways of others. This may be called excessive **ethnocentrism**.

Background to Italian Unification

The modern nation of Italy was formed by the uniting of several Italian-speaking regions. For this reason our study of nationalism in Italy requires that we see how this process of unification occurred.

There was no united Italian nation in 1815, due to the decisions of the **Congress of Vienna**. As you may recall, this meeting was held at the end of the Napoleonic Wars in order to remake the map of Europe. (See Chapter 14, "The Rise and Fall of Napoleon.") The Austrian minister at this meeting, Prince Metternich, had no desire to promote unity in the Italian peninsula. For him, Italy would simply be a "geographic expression"—a place, not a free united nation. To guarantee this situation, this "place" was divided as follows:

1. Lombardy and Venetia, two provinces in the north, were to be governed by Austria.
2. The **duchies** of Tuscany, Parma, and Modena, along with the Kingdom of the Two Sicilies, would be under local rulers controlled by Austria.
3. Rome and the Papal States would be under the authority of the Catholic Church.
4. Only the Kingdom of Sardinia (which included Sardinia and Piedmont) would be under Italian control. Therefore, the vast majority of Italian peo-

Chapter 22 Chronology

Congress of Vienna — 1815

Sardinia defeated in an uprising against Austria — 1848

Austro-Sardinian War
•
Sardinia acquires Lombardy — 1859

Victor Emanuel II becomes King of Italy — 1861

Rome annexed after the Franco-Prussian War
•
Unification is completed
•
Rome becomes the capital of the nation — 1870

1800   1825   1850   1875

Mazzini organizes Young Italy — 1831

Cavour becomes prime minister of Sardinia — 1852

Garibaldi conquers the Kingdom of the Two Sicilies — 1860

Venetia annexed after the Seven Weeks' War — 1866

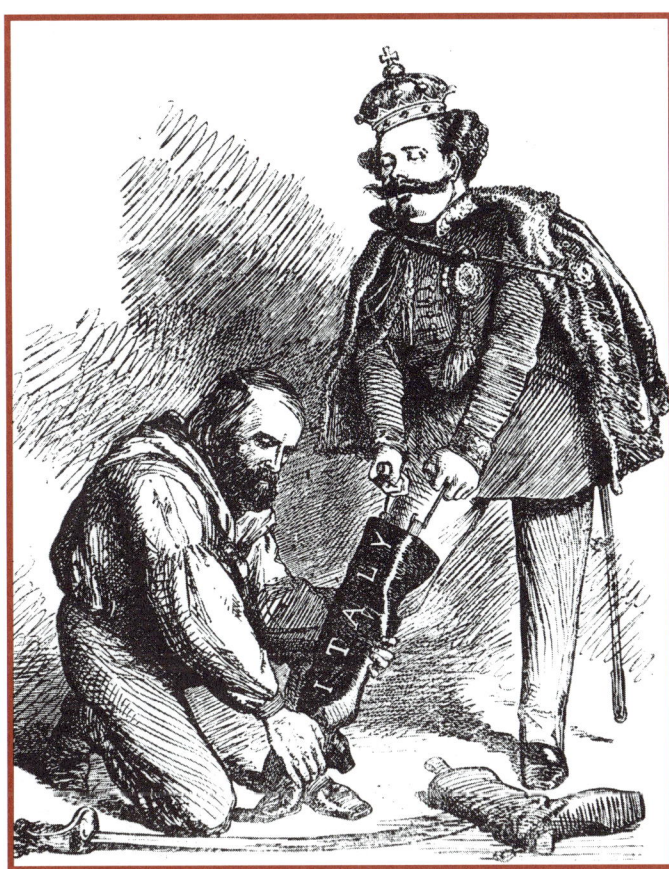

The success of the movement for Italian unification. Garibaldi assists in measuring King Victor Emmanuel for fitting into the boot of a unified Italy.

ple were under some sort of foreign domination not of their own choosing.

The domination of Austria was the biggest obstacle to Italian unification. The Austrian military crushed uprisings against its rule in 1820, 1821, 1831, and 1848. Another obstacle was the Catholic Church. It feared that a united Italy would interfere with the **pope's** authority in Rome and the Papal States. Still another roadblock in the path to unification was a political disagreement among Italian nationalist leaders themselves. Giuseppe Mazzini and Giuseppe Garibaldi wanted an autonomous Italy to be set up as a democratic republic. Camillo Cavour preferred Italy to become a constitutional monarchy, similar to that in Great Britain.

As we will soon see, these three men were to play important leadership roles in promoting unity. Additional factors helping the cause of Italian nationalism were the following:

- The influence of the French Revolution's ideals of liberty and nationalism.
- Remembrance of the great achievements on the Italian peninsula during the Roman Empire and the **Renaissance**.
- Growth of patriotic societies such as the *Carbonari* and *Young Italy*. In their speeches, writings, and other activities, they spread ideas of unity.
- The active role of Sardinia and its royal House of Savoy.

Nationalist Leaders

Giuseppe Mazzini   Mazzini (1805–1872) was a thin man, fond of poetry and philosophy. He was more an idealist and a thinker than a doer and a man of practical affairs. His plans for Italy called for a democratic government led by and responsible to the people. These goals, along with his fear of **monarchy**, put him at odds with Cavour. He was a member of the Carbonari and was a founder of Young Italy (1831). He was active in the short-lived uprising of 1848 and spent several years in prison and exile. His propaganda efforts on behalf of unification were carried on both in Italy and abroad. More than anyone else, he inspired Italians with hopes for unity and autonomy. For these reasons he has been called the "soul" of unification.

Giuseppe Garibaldi   Garibaldi (1807–1882) was an adventurous person, often unpredictable, very hot-headed, and willing to take risks. In dress he was a nonconformist, known particularly for his famous red shirt. He had a reputation for military skill and daring, having escaped capture from both Austrian and French armies. He lived in exile for a number of years, working once as a candlemaker in Staten Island, New York. Although distrusted by Cavour, his bravery as a soldier in the cause of Italian nationalism made him popular as the "sword" of unification.

Camillo Cavour   Cavour (1810–1861) was a master statesman of the nineteenth century. A short man, his eyes and manner made him seem shrewd and clever. For this educated, well-traveled man, Mazzini was too much of an unrealistic dreamer, and Garibaldi, a good but reckless soldier. In 1852, Cavour became prime minister of Sardinia, a kingdom ruled by Victor Emmanuel II of the House of Savoy. It was Cavour's intention to have Sardinia lead the fight for Italian unity. A man of action and cool planning, he once remarked, "I cannot make a speech, but I can make Italy." The movement for Italian unity became known as the **Risorgimento**, the Italian word for resurgence or revival. It was also the name of a newspaper that Cavour had once edited. For his efforts as a diplomat in working with or against other European countries to aid Italy, he has been called the "brain" of unification.

Steps in the Unification Process

The years 1859 to 1870 were the crucial ones in which the various parts of the Italian peninsula and islands were united into one nation. During this time, Cavour's planning proved to be effective. He wanted Austrian power removed, while adding land to Sardinia, so that Victor Emmanuel would be proclaimed king of a unified country. These goals could not, he felt, be accomplished solely by the Italians. Foreign help was needed. Such help would be forthcoming if Sardinia showed it was a stable, prosperous kingdom with armed power. In other words, Sardinia wanted to get enough respect so that major powers, such as France, would be willing to take her side in future struggles. With Victor Emmanuel's help, Cavour built railroads, helped farmers, assisted banks, and made the army stronger. Although Sardinia's assistance to France and Britain was not needed in the Crimean War (1854–1856), Cavour sent troops. He was thus invited to the peace conference, where he made a brief but impressive speech about the need for Italian unification.

Having become friendly with Napoleon III of France, Cavour persuaded him to agree to a secret alliance against Austria. France wanted to weaken Austria's position as a European power and was willing therefore to see Austria lose land in Italy. Cavour, of course, wanted to see Austria out of Italy so that unification could be promoted. France would send forces to Sardinia if Sardinia could draw Austria into a war. On the assumption that the combined Sardinian-French forces would drive Austria out of Lombardy and Venetia, Sardinia would give France the territories of Nice and Savoy. When Sardinian protest provoked Austria into declaring war in 1859, the plan was hatched. With the promised French help, the Austro-Sardinian War lasted just two months. Having suffered severe defeats at the battles of Magenta and Solferino, Austrian forces left Lombardy. Italian nationalists gained inspiration from this and overthrew Austrian rulers in several states. As preparations were being made to invade Venetia, Cavour was shocked to learn that Napoleon III had dropped out of the war and had signed a peace treaty with Austria.

Why had Napoleon done this? The answers rest upon what France now saw as its own best interests. In matters of foreign policy, a nation will usually act on the basis of its own self-interests. In this case, Napoleon feared that a long war with Austria would tempt mighty Prussia to come to Austria's side. This he did not want. Secondly, he did not anticipate armed Italian anti-Austrian uprisings in other parts of the peninsula. He was worried that a large united Italy would become a Mediterranean rival to France. Finally, Napoleon was pressured by French Catholics to get out of the war. They claimed that a united Italy under Cavour would lessen the power of the Roman Catholic Church and take away much of its property.

The Austro-Sardinian War of 1859 was now over. Sardinia kept its word and *ceded* (gave up) Nice and Savoy to France. Austria permitted Sardinia to *annex* (add) Lombardy to its territory. Austrian rulers who had been overthrown in the states of Modena, Tuscany, Parma, and Romagna were restored. However, in the next year, 1860, the people in these states voted in a **plebiscite** to be annexed to Sardinia. (A plebiscite election is one where a population votes yes or no on the issue of political self-determination.) So it was that in April 1860 an enlarged Sardinian **parliament** met. Represented was all of Italy except Venetia, the Papal States, and the Kingdom of the Two Sicilies.

The Crucial Years of 1860–1861

As notable as this meeting was, it was not the only reason that 1860 was a momentous year in Italian history; for it was in May 1860 that Garibaldi began a series of military conquests that led him to be called the "sword" of unification. With approximately one thousand armed men, wearing red shirts and slouch hats, he sailed from Piedmont to invade the island of Sicily. He had secret financial support from Cavour, even though Cavour's wish for an eventual monarchy in Italy conflicted with Garibaldi's preference for a **republic** without a king. Although the two men disliked each other, they did share a common dream of an autonomous Italy and realized that each could help the other. Garibaldi's *Red Shirts* easily defeated the Austrian-backed ruler of Sicily and then sailed to southern Italy, where they were again victorious. In these newly conquered areas, the former Kingdom of the Two Sicilies, people welcomed Garibaldi enthusiastically and joined his army.

Garibaldi was now poised to move forth, to take Rome and the Papal States. This was of concern to Cavour, still fearful about Garibaldi's republican ideas and worried that an attack on the French troops protecting Rome might provoke France into declaring war. Aware that Garibaldi disliked him, Cavour cleverly advised Victor Emmanuel to lead Sardinian troops southward by himself, take some of the Papal States but not Rome itself, and meet with Garibaldi. Victor Emmanuel did all this, parading with Garibaldi through the streets of Naples to cheering crowds. In a plebiscite, people in the former Kingdom of the Two Sicilies agreed to be united with the Kingdom of Sardinia. Garibaldi, willing to give up his hope of an Italian republic, refused the many titles and honors Victor Emmanuel offered him and retired to his farm. In March 1861, the Kingdom of Italy was proclaimed with Victor Emmanuel as King.

The Impact of the Seven Weeks' War and the Franco-Prussian War

The only parts of Italy not under Victor Emmanuel were Austrian-controlled Venetia and French-controlled Rome. Based upon two events soon to happen outside of Italy, the new kingdom would add these parts in a bloodless manner. In the *Seven Weeks' War* of 1866 between Austria and Prussia, Italy joined the side of Prussia. Austria was defeated and ceded Venetia to Italy. By plebiscite, the Venetians became part of the nation of Italy. During the *Franco-Prussian War* of 1870, France withdrew her troops from Rome. In September, Italian forces entered the city. In a plebiscite, Rome's citizens voted 134,000 to 1,500 to join Italy. Rome now was designated as the capital of Italy—a "place" that was no longer a "geographical expression," but a unified nation destined to have an important role in European affairs.

A United Italy Faces Problems

A unified nation as it approached the last thirty years of the nineteenth century, Italy faced problems that were economic, social, and political. It was without large deposits of coal and iron and thus did not have a strong industrial base to compete with other countries. The south was much poorer than the north. The relationship between the Catholic Church and the new government was very controversial; becoming known as the *Roman Question*. Pope Pius XI had never agreed to the annexation of Rome and the Papal States and did not at first accept the legality of the new kingdom. He even went so far as to forbid Catholics from participating in politics. The Roman Question continued to pose a serious problem until 1929. In that year, an area in Rome, Vatican City, was set up as a sovereign state in an agreement between the Pope and the dictator Mussolini.

Another source of irritation between the south and north was the dominance of northerners in the new government. The government was created as a constitutional monarchy, hopefully to function as did Great Britain's. These hopes were imperfectly realized, as Italy lacked a long tradition of representative self-government. The regional variations and frequent bad feelings between local areas held back a workable democratic central government. In addition, the growth of many political parties made compromises difficult to achieve and often led to instability and government crises. Finally, there were many Italians who felt that additional territory belonged to Italy for cultural and traditional reasons and therefore ought to be added to the new nation. This territory was called *Italia irridenta* (Italy unredeemed) and included Trieste, Trentino, and Istria. This issue was partially settled after World War I. Italy soon joined in the race by European countries for **colonies** overseas. In Africa, by 1900, she had obtained Eritrea, Italian Somaliland, and Libya while failing to conquer Ethiopia.

Summary

We now have a united Italy in southern Europe. It was a long time in the making but when a hardheaded practical man involved himself—Cavour—the job got done! It seems that dreamers are interesting in history but that you need practical people as leaders. (In the next unit this is very evident!) Garibaldi was one of history's more colorful characters, ready for adventure at any time. He fought in both the Old and New Worlds, and a movie of his life would be fun to see. But it was the step-by-step planning of Cavour that got the job accomplished. He "used" other nations, when he could, to help him toward his goal, but he was ready to step aside if necessary. He did not seek personal glory: the creation of Italy was his aim. Italy, however, had a number of continuing problems: the industrial north against the agricultural south; the opposition to the Church in many areas against the followers of the papacy; the monarchists against the liberals. We will look at these issues again in the future.

CHAPTER 22

Review Exercises

I. Matching

Directions: Match the words in Column A with the *correct description* in Column B.

Column A
1. chauvinism
2. excessive ethnocentrism
3. nationalism
4. sovereign
5. constitutional monarchy
6. democratic republic
7. plcbiscitc

Column B
(a) a belief that people with a common culture and set of traditions should have their own country
(b) political autonomy
(c) a vote by people on the issue of independence
(d) desired by Mazzini and Garibaldi
(e) desired by Cavour
(f) a belief that one's society and culture are superior to those of others
(g) an intense loyalty to one's nation, believing that it is always right in its actions

II. Famous People

Directions: Use the names below to complete the following sentences. (An answer may be repeated.)

Camillo Cavour
Prince Metternich
Giuseppe Mazzini

Victor Emmanuel II
Giuseppe Garibaldi
Napoleon III

1. _____ wanted Italy to remain as a *geographic expression* under Austrian domination.

2. _____ was known as the "sword" of Italian unification.

3. _____ planned to have Sardinia lead the fight for unification.

4. _____ was known as the "soul" of Italian unification.

5. _____ did not keep fully his promise to send military forces during the Austro-Sardinian War.

6. _____ was known as the "brain" of Italian unification.

7. _____ was seen by Cavour as a unifying symbol for Italian sovereignty.

8. _____ helped in the founding of Young Italy.

9. _____ had followers known as the Red Shirts.

III. Multiple Choice

Directions: Find the *letter* of the correct answer.

1. The *Roman Question* involved politics and

   (a) economics.
   (b) geography.
   (c) religion.
   (d) language.

2. Chauvinists would most likely claim that their nation's people

   (a) are as good as any other people.
   (b) have a backward culture.
   (c) have a tradition of democracy.
   (d) constitute a master race.

3. Nationalism may be defined as

   (a) a feeling of unity within a country.
   (b) the desire to rule other people.
   (c) a respect for law and order.
   (d) opposition to absolute monarchy.

4. Which of the following believed that Sardinia-Piedmont should lead the fight for unification?

   (a) Cavour
   (b) Garibaldi
   (c) Mazzini
   (d) the pope

5. The reason for believing that Sardinia-Piedmont should lead the fight was that Sardinia-Piedmont

   (a) was friendly with Austria.
   (b) had the support of the pope.
   (c) had rulers who were Italian.
   (d) was an ally of Britain.

6. Which best describes Italy's form of government in 1871?

   (a) Republic
   (b) Kingdom
   (c) Dictatorship
   (d) Colony

7. Italy was able to add Rome to its territory as a result of the

    (a) Franco-Prussian War.
    (b) Seven Weeks' War.
    (c) Austro-Sardinian War.
    (d) Napoleonic Wars.

IV. Map Exercise

Directions: Use the map to locate the place associated with each of the following statements. For each statement, write the *letter* of the place. (An answer may be repeated.)

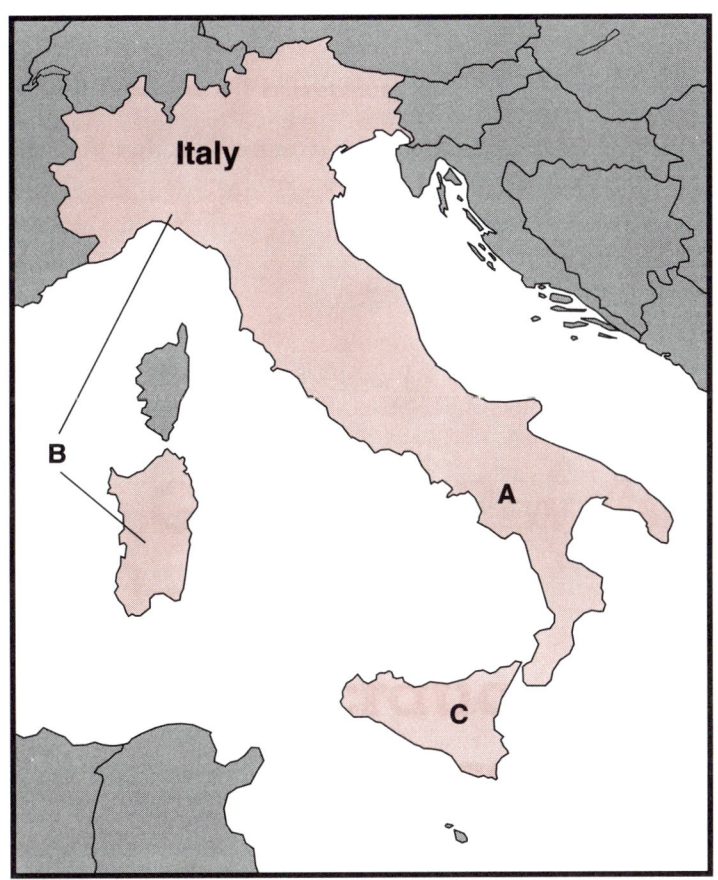

1. _____ Cavour was from here.

2. _____ Furthest area from Prussia.

3. _____ Earliest conquest by Garibaldi.

4. _____ The House of Savoy ruled here until 1861.

5. _____ Vatican City is here.

6. _____ It had help from France during a war with Austria.

7. _____ Last area to become part of the Italian nation.

8. _____ Closest area to France.

V. Thought Questions

Directions: Answer the following questions in essay form.

1. The ideas and actions of certain persons had great impact on Italian unification. They were Camillo Cavour, Giuseppe Garibaldo, Giuseppe Mazzini, Napoleon III, and Victor Emmanuel II. For each person, do the following:

   A. Identify one idea or action of this person that had an impact on Italian unification.
   B. State one way this idea or action had an impact on Italian unification.

2. In the nineteenth century, Italy changed from being a "geographic expression" to a nation-state.

   A. Explain the difference between a "geographic expression" and a nation-state.
   B. Describe two factors (not people) that inspired Italians to form a nation-state.

3. Write a conversation between Cavour and Mazzini, taking place in 1850, on the topic of Italian unification. Each person should explain his goal and one reason for wanting this goal.

4. Draw a postage stamp design, to be issued by the Italian government, honoring the accomplishments of each of these people: Cavour, Garibaldi, Mazzini.

5. Draw a cartoon showing three obstacles that faced the Italian people in their desire to become unified.

6. A. Identify three problems faced by Italy in its first fifty years as a united nation.
   B. For each problem, describe one reason for its existence.

CHAPTER 23

Unification of Germany

In the first half of the nineteenth century, Germany was, like Italy, a "geographic expression." There were several German states, but no unified country with a central government. The nation of Germany that we can find today on a map did not come into being until 1871. It is located on land that for centuries prior to this time was inhabited by people who spoke a common language and who shared many common traditions. Until 1806, the German states were part of the Holy Roman Empire. The Napoleonic Wars had brought an end to that **Empire**. But when Napoleon himself was defeated at Waterloo in 1815, the **Congress of Vienna** met to remake the map of Europe. Its plans regarding the German states included the creation of the German Confederation, under the authority of Austria. Fifty-six years later, by 1871, the confederation had passed out of existence, Austria's role was weakened, and a united Germany had arisen under the leadership of the state of Prussia. How did all this occur? Who was responsible? This chapter will provide the answers. German unification was similar to Italian unification in some ways but was also very different. Try to discover the similarities and differences as you read the chapter.

Obstacles to German Unification, 1815–1862

The presence of Austria as one of the thirty-nine states in the German Confederation was the main obstacle to unification of the German people in 1815 and in the years immediately thereafter. The word *German* in these times described an **ethnic group** and a **nationality**, not a **nation**. There were, for example, German people in both Austria and Prussia. Austria was ruled by Germans but was also an empire that included many other non-Germanic nationalities. Examples were Italians, Hungarians, Serbs, Croats, Czechs, Poles, and Romanians. Each of these nationalities, in fact, wanted to form its own nation. Austria sought to put down any nationalistic attempts by these groups, as we saw in the case of the Italians. Austria was also against any nationalistic or unification actions by other German states, such as Prussia and Saxony. If they were to unite, Austria would lose its commanding position over German people in Europe and would be faced with a rival power on its northern border. Therefore, we should not be surprised that Austrian Minister Metternich pressured the German Confederation to issue the *Carlsbad Decrees* in 1819. These were designed to silence people from speaking, writing, or teaching about nationalist and liberal ideas. Under these decrees, for example, newspaper editors and university professors could be jailed for expressing thoughts about unification. Such laws were examples of censorship.

Opposition to a unified German nation was also held by France. France felt secure with having weak neighbors on its borders and would thus have been upset by any hint of nationalism shown by the German states. Even among some of the non-Austrian German states, there was concern about a unified nation. This was especially so in Bavaria and other south German states. The people here, who were outnumbered by the north German states, were mainly Catholic and mostly farmers. A united Germany would be under greater influence by the northern states. These areas, such as Prussia, were primarily Protestant and were more interested in commerce and manufacturing.

Chapter 23 Chronology

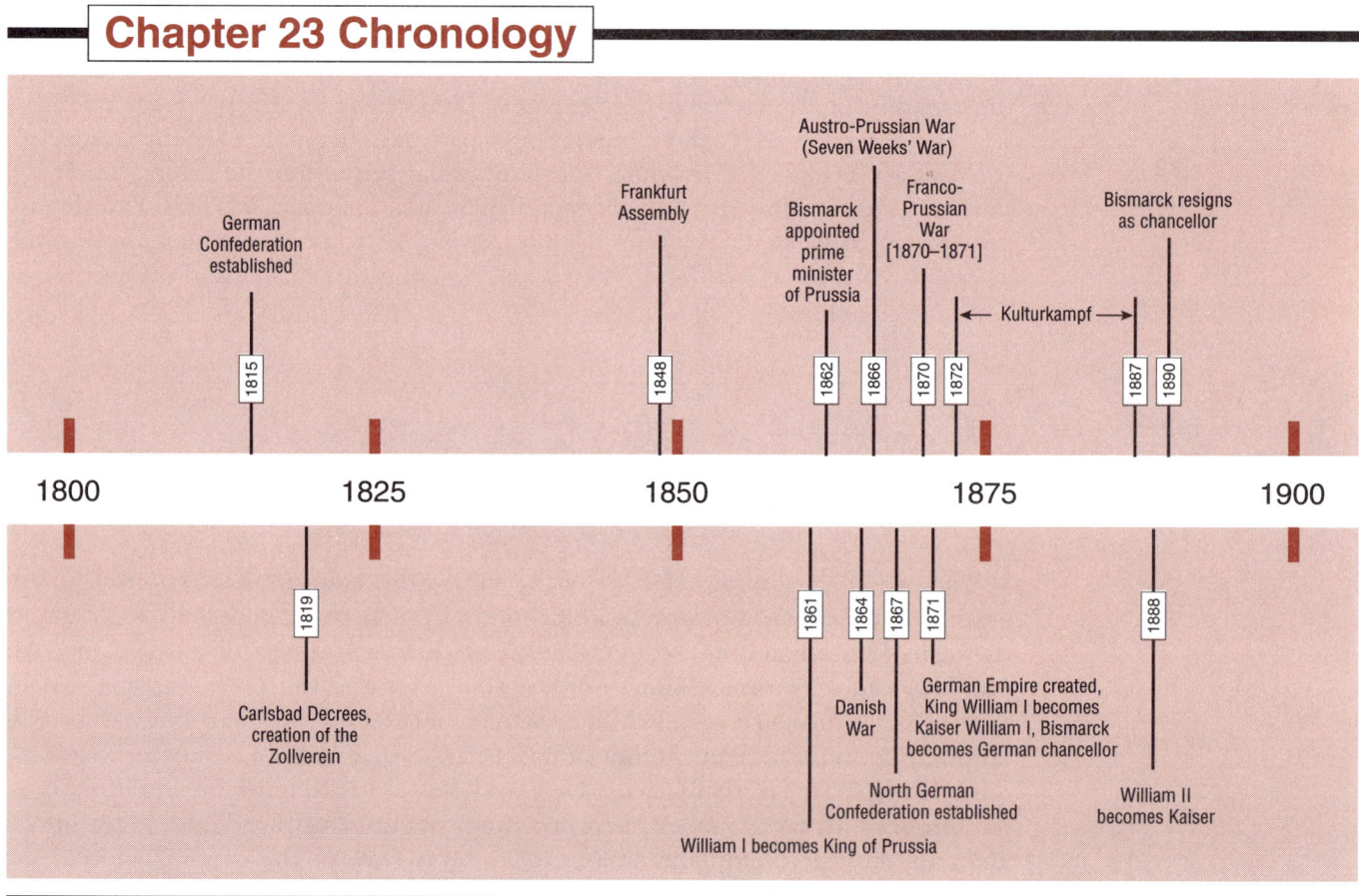

Factors Favoring German Unification

In spite of the many obstacles described above, there were a number of factors favoring German unity in the first half of the nineteenth century. Curiously, the Napoleonic Wars were an indirect factor. Napoleon's conquests had provoked a cohesive, nationalistic reaction among Germans, as they fought against him. As you may recall, both Austria and Prussia had troops at Waterloo and were represented at the Congress of Vienna. That 1815 meeting created the German Confederation, as we have seen. However, the Confederation was ineffective and disappointed German nationalists. They now considered other means of achieving unity.

A form of economic unity was achieved by some German states with the formation of the **Zollverein** in 1819. This was a tariff or customs union that included Prussia and several states, but not Austria. Members of this union would not place tariffs (special taxes) on goods coming from other members. Before 1819, many states would tax goods highly from other states. This would make products more expensive and slow down trade. With the Zollverein in existence, prices were lower, trade grew, and manufacturers, workers, and merchants prospered. This free trade association brought Prussia and the other member states closer together economically but had little immediate political effect. It was apparent to industrialists, however, that even greater prosperity would come about with unification under a national government. Existence of the Zollverein added to tension between Prussia and Austria.

Another factor encouraging a feeling of national unity as well as pride among Germans was the work of philosophers and historians. Johann Fichte (1762–1814) was a philosopher who declared the Germans to be the greatest of all people, with the need to unite and become the leader among civilized nations. Additionally, he claimed that German was superior to other languages. The philosopher Georg Hegel (1770–1831) was a strong supporter of the Prussian **monarchy**, emphasizing the value of a powerful central government. A group of Prussian historians arose who claimed that it was Prussia's great mission in history to unite the German people. The most famous of these historians was Heinrich von Treitschke (1834–1896). Treitschke considered himself an intense patriot, believing that the Germans were the best of all peoples and that the Prussians were the best of all Germans.

The Importance of 1848

Very soon, we will meet those Prussian figures who shared the above thoughts and were prominent in weaving together a fabric of nationhood from separate pieces of geographical cloth. Before we do so, we will talk about two events between 1815–1862 that were attempts at unification. One of these was the Revolution of 1848. In that year, German liberals pressed for certain goals that were similar to goals being sought in other parts of Europe:

- a written **constitution** to limit autocratic monarchs; and
- expansion of the right to vote.

And in the German states, there was a wish to create a nation from the German Confederation but without Austria. The movement for both liberal and nationalistic goals resulted in the election of the *Frankfurt Assembly* in 1848. The assembly drew up a constitution, modeled after features from the American and British political systems, and offered the position of **emperor** of a united Germany to King Frederick William IV of Prussia (r. 1840–1861). He refused the offer, afraid that Austria would go to war against him if he accepted the proposal. Also, as a believer in the "**divine right**" theory, he felt that any crown that he could accept "…is not one created by an Assembly born of revolutionary seed [but] must be a crown set with the seal of the Almighty…" Frederick's actions sealed the doom of the Frankfurt Assembly and the Frankfurt Constitution. It was against his principles to "pick up a crown from the gutter," as he described the offer of the Frankfurt Assembly.

In 1850, however, Frederick William IV did try to unite several German states by speaking with the rulers of those states. He was told by Austria to stop doing this. While in the town of Olmutz, he made the decision to obey this command. This "*humilation of Olmutz*" was yet another Austrian action that angered Prussia.

Unification Leaders

Otto von Bismarck The most important figure in the history of German unification was Otto von Bismarck (1815–1898). Standing more than six feet tall, and possessed of a powerful build and a rough-looking face, Bismarck came from a rich, noble landowning family in the Brandenburg section of Prussia. Such families formed the aristocratic class of people known as **Junkers**. A strong-willed person, he could not stand to be criticized and scorned those who he felt were his social and intellectual inferiors. He also looked down on the ideals of **democracy** and **liberalism**. For him, an elected parliamentary government was useless and ineffective; a written constitution was simply "a sheet of paper" and should never be allowed to limit royal power and governmental action. From 1851 to 1862, he held several political positions: as Prussian delegate to the German Confederation, and as Prussian spokesman to Russia and France. In 1862, King William (Wilhelm) I of Prussia (r. 1861–1888) appointed him to be the Prussian prime minister.

In this post, he moved to strengthen Prussia and make it the centerpiece around which other states would be added to create a German nation. In this respect, Prussia was to become a "German Sardinia." He proved to be bold, daring, and willing to lie and deceive and to use force when necessary to accomplish his goals. He denounced the democratic efforts of the Frankfurt Assembly, declaring that Germans do "…not look to Prussia's liberalism, but to her power. The great questions of the day are not to be decided by speeches and majority resolutions—but by blood and iron."

Otto von Bismarck, known as the "Iron Chancellor," was responsible for the unification of Germany. Here, towards the end of his life, he is pictured with several decorations.

King William I King William I came to the throne of Prussia in 1861, as a member of the Hohenzollern **Dynasty**. As was true of some of his predecessors, he wanted Prussia to be a powerful, militaristic, and authoritarian kingdom. Under him, Bismarck became prime minister and enjoyed his support of the "**blood and iron**" policies.

Helmuth von Moltke Von Moltke (1800–1891) became head of the Prussian army. He made it the best-trained and most efficient fighting force in Europe. Unlike Garibaldi, he was a quiet, calm military planner. He was one of the first generals to use modern scientific methods of warfare, regarding careful use of new weapons, battlefield formations, and detailed strategies. His love for Prussia, his interest in the army, and his obedience to Bismarck and King William were unquestioned.

Steps in the Unification Process

The years 1862 to 1871 were the crucial ones in which various German states, under Prussia's leadership, were unified into a German nation. The steps involved in this process were carried out according to Bismarck's goals. These were to strengthen Prussia and then take appropriate measures against Austria and France. Pursuit of these goals led Prussia to fight in three wars: in 1864 with Denmark, in 1866 with Austria, and in 1870 to 1871 with France.

Strengthening Prussia

When Bismarck was appointed Prussia's prime minister in 1862, he found the kingdom to be enjoying economic prosperity. He wanted to maintain this, while increasing Prussia's military might. Accordingly, he frequently asked the Prussian parliament to raise taxes and approve funds for reorganizing the army and giving it more weapons. And just as frequently, parliament turned him down. Many of its members were liberals who distrusted Bismarck and opposed his obvious militaristic policies. Not to be outdone, Bismarck would often dissolve parliament, raise taxes with the king's consent, and call for elections to a new legislature. His collection and spending of monies violated the Prussian constitution, as did his censorship of newspapers and restrictions on anyone who criticized him. With the support of an expanding army, many of whose officers were Junkers, and the cooperation of the king, Bismarck practically rulled Prussia as a dictator. Much of his success in ruling with a weak—sometimes without any—parliament was due to a strong public feeling of nationalism that made

King William I of Germany, also known as Kaiser Wilhelm I. Berlin, the capital of his Prussian homeland, became the capital of the new German Empire—the Second Reich.

many overlook his autocratic behavior. In addition, his successes in foreign policy overshadowed any concerns about domestic policy.

The Danish War, 1864

This brief war illustrated the shrewd and deceptive diplomatic maneuvering of Bismarck to achieve both short-term and long-range goals. In the short run, he wanted to obtain more land for Prussia and increase its prestige; in the long run, he wanted to reduce Austria's status. Strangely, this war began with Prussia and Austria as allies against Denmark in a dispute over the states of Schleswig and Holstein. Holstein was populated mainly by Germans and belonged to the German Confederation. Schleswig had a mix of both Germans and Danes. Although not actually part of Denmark, both sides had been ruled by the Danish King. Under a new constitution in 1863, the King claimed that the states belonged to him, and he announced that he was about to **annex** Schleswig first. He dismissed the protests about his intentions from Prussia and Austria, whereupon they both declared war against Denmark. Denmark was no match against their combined armies and surrendered after only three months of fighting.

In the treaty ending the war, Denmark agreed to give up both Schleswig and Holstein. Austria assumed that Prussia and Austria would jointly control the two states. Austria also moved to have both states combine into a single state and then become part of the German Confederation. Bismarck contested this, standing up to Austria. After bitter arguments, it was decided that Prussia would administer Schleswig and Austria would administer Holstein. This decision was not to Austria's liking, as Bismarck well knew, and was part of his anti-Austrian policy.

The Seven Weeks' War (Austro-Prussian War) 1866

Bismarck's anti-Austrian policy was not aimed at destroying Austria, but at isolating it and reducing its power among the German states. He would then be free of Austria as an obstacle in his path toward establishing a Prussian-dominated German nation. He felt that war was bound to occur and that he had to be ready, both militarily and diplomatically. Military preparedness progressed well under von Moltke. Diplomatically, Bismarck made some wise arrangements. He signed a secret treaty with the new Kingdom of Italy, promising to give it Austrian-controlled Venetia if Italy helped Prussia in a war with Austria. Bismarck did this, aware that he was violating a rule of the German Confederation that prohibited one member from signing a treaty of alliance with a foreign nation against another member. Concerned that France might aid Austria in a war, Bismarck convinced France to stay out of any conflict. He vaguely suggested to France that he would not stand in France's way if it were to annex Belgium. France agreed, assuming that a German civil war would weaken both Prussia and Austria and thus leave France with limp, disunited neighbors on its eastern border. Bismarck had also paved the way to keep Russia out of any conflict, as he had previously signed a treaty with that country promising Prussian help if Russia had to put down a revolt in Poland.

Another dispute between Prussia and Austria arose over the Schleswig-Holstein Question. This dispute led to the Austro-Prussian War of 1866, in which most German states, afraid of Prussian might and sharing a common religious tie of Catholicism with Austria, took the Austrian side. A few states took Prussia's side. In what thus amounted to a German civil war, Prussia won a quick, stunning victory.

The war was over so soon that is has also been called the Seven Weeks' War. Von Moltke's troops fought with advanced weapons, while making effective use for that time of such technology as the railroad and the telegraph. His forces were much better trained and organized than were those of Austria. The most crushing Prussian victory was the Battle of Sadowa. The *Treaty of Prague* ended the war and contained these provisions:

1. The German Confederation was dissolved. A new association was to be created of most German states, but without Austria and four south German states. (In 1867, the association became known as the North German Confederation.)
2. Schleswig-Holstein was to be added to Prussia.
3. Venetia would be added to Italy.
4. Austria was to pay Prussia a small **indemnity** (amount of money for losing the war).

Austria was treated leniently in this treaty. Such was Bismarck's intent, even though Prussian King William fiercely opposed him and wanted to humiliate Austria. Bismarck's generosity was not the result of any special kindness nor humanitarian gesture. He reasoned that Prussia might need Austria's help at some future time. And as the 1860s drew to a close, Prussia comfortably found itself as the leader of the twenty-one-member North German Confederation—a union of almost all the German states. Yet, it realized that the last obstacle remained on the path to a fully united nation.

The Franco-Prussian War, 1870–1871

In his book *Reminiscences*, written sometime after the 1870s, Bismarck says: "I assumed that a united Germany was only a question of time, and that the North German Confederation was only the first step in its solution...but I did not doubt that a war with France must take place before a united Germany could be realized." The war that Bismarck felt was inevitable would be important to him in two specific ways:

1. It would produce a patriotic feeling and a sense of nationalism among all Germans in a struggle against a common enemy.
2. It would persuade the four south German states, mainly Catholic and somewhat concerned about being part of a nation led by Protestant Prussia, that they would be better off, more prosperous, and safer in union with Prussia.

As much as Bismarck was edging toward a confrontation with France, he was aware that the French themselves were thinking about going to war. France was growing extremely worried about the growth of German unity and power to its east. Some Frenchmen even took up the cry "Revenge for Sadowa," angered at Prussia's defeat of Austria in that battle. Others felt that, during the 1860s, France had suffered a loss of prestige in foreign affairs. A war might now help to regain prestige and respect.

An air of tension was evident among French and Germans as the 1870s began. In newspapers and speeches, bitter words and accusations were exchanged. In such an atmosphere, Bismarck did not want to appear as the aggressor. Better, he felt, to make France look like the one responsible for a conflict. The opportunity to do this arose in a very unlikely manner, regarding the throne of Spain. With their throne vacant, the Spaniards offered it to Prince Leopold, a Hohenzollern relative of Prussian King William. If Leopold accepted this offer, it would anger

France for fear of a possible Spanish-Prussian alliance. Leopold at first accepted the offer but then changed his mind. This would have ended the matter, but the French wanted to be sure that no Hohenzollern would ever become king of Spain. To achieve this goal, France wanted such a promise from the head of all the Hohenzollerns, Prussian King William. The French minister made this demand upon the King at the town of Ems. The King refused to give into the demand and sent a telegram to Bismarck describing the events at Ems. Bismarck now edited the telegram in such a way that it appeared as if the French minister and the Prussian King had insulted each other. Bismarck then released the telegram for publication by the press. It became known as the *Ems Dispatch* and had the effect of inciting both French and Germans. It was timed to be published July 14, 1870. As this was France's Independence Day, French patriotism was duly aroused, with crowds in Paris shouting for war with Prussia and screaming, "À Berlin, À Berlin" ("on to Berlin"). On the same day in Berlin, having heard about the dispatch, crowds emotionally spoke out for war with France. On July 19, 1870, France declared war on Prussia. The Franco-Prussian War had begun!

France boasted that its army was prepared, with its war minister stating that all was ready even "down to the last button…of the last soldier." The mood in Paris was that French forces would easily cross the Rhine River and that the Catholic south German states would warmly welcome them. Tragically for France, these expectations proved to be completely unrealistic. Its army was disorganized and was short of ammunition, food, and transportation. It never reached German soil.

King William I is proclaimed Emperor of a united Germany, in 1871, at Versailles. Bismarck, standing at the bottom of the steps, became chancellor of Germany.

The south German states immediately sided with Bismarck, adding to his already impressive military forces. Under von Moltke, these well-equipped forces moved quickly to the French border and won several battles. One of the most significant was at Sedan in September 1870. A French army of 120,000 men was defeated, with Emperor Napoleon III of France taken as prisoner. Prussian forces soon thereafter surrounded Paris.

On January 18, 1871, with Paris facing starvation and collapse, a historical event occurred in the nearby Palace of Versailles. In its famous Hall of Mirrors, built and often walked through by King Louis XIV, the German Empire was proclaimed. Prussia's King William I became Emperor William I (Kaiser Wilhelm) in the presence of Bismarck and many German princes and statesmen. The North German Confederation was abolished. The new union, the German Empire, contained both northern and southern states. Unification had been achieved. The nation of Germany was a reality.

Less than two weeks later, on January 28, 1871, Paris surrendered. Negotiations for peace were concluded with the Treaty of Frankfurt in May. Its harsh provisions were dictated by Bismarck:

1. France would cede Alsace and Lorraine to Germany.
2. France would pay to Germany an idemnity of $1 billion.
3. France would support a German army of occupation until the entire amount of the indemnity was paid.

The treaty was a humiliation for France, stirring in its people a quest for revenge. The bitterness they felt went very deeply into their souls. Accordingly, tension between France and Germany continued right up to the moment of their next confrontation less than fifty years later, in World War I.

The New Nation of Germany

The Germany that was born with "blood and iron" in the second half of the nineteenth century began to build itself up as a major European power. It did things that had roots in the pre-1871 history of the German people, and also did things that would prove to be the basis for twentieth-century activities. We will now look at some of these things from 1871 to 1900 in terms of political, economic, and social policies.

Political Policies

The government was headed by Kaiser William I, who appointed Bismarck as chancellor (prime minister). A two-house parliament was created, consisting of the *Bundesrat* and the *Reichstag*. The Bundesrat was the upper house, whose members were appointed by the rulers of the twenty-five states. It had greater power than did the Reichstag, whose members were elected by the few people eligible to vote. Although there were several political parties in both houses, the Kaiser and the chancellor controlled enough members to affect parliamentary decisions. Bismarck, in fact, was referred to as the "Iron Chancellor." Both the Kaiser and the chancellor had very few limits on their power; Germany was thus more an autocracy than a limited monarchy. In addition, as Prussia was more than half of the nation, it had enough representatives in both the Bundesrat and the Reichstag to influence legislation.

Bismarck rides to meet Napoleon III, 1870, after the Prussian victory at Sedan. He enjoyed a dominant role in state affairs until 1890 when he was forced to resign as chancellor by King William II.

The government wanted Germany to be known as a great empire, or **reich**. The kaiser was, therefore, the head of the Second Reich. (The Holy Roman Empire that had ruled the German people for centuries, until 1806, was considered to be the First Reich.) As we will see, the Second Reich was to last for forty-seven years, 1871 to 1918. During that time the government adopted policies that it felt were necessary for Germany to be regarded as a major power—militarism and imperialism. Militarism could be seen in the continued buildup of the army and navy. Imperialism referred to acquiring **colonies** oveseas, something that several other European nations had begun to do in the nineteenth century. In Unit VII we will examine Germany's role in the race for colonies. Both militarism and imperialism would be underlying factors for the terrible conflicts in 1914 and 1939 that became World Wars I and II.

In 1888, when William I died, his sickly son continued the Hohenzollern line as Frederick III. After Frederick's brief reign of three months, his son became Kaiser William II (r. 1888–1918). Although William I had been content to let Bismarck act on his behalf, this was not true for his grandson. William II and Bismarck did not get along very well. William was unwilling to let Bismarck continue to have a dominant role in affairs of state. Bismarck, in turn, was upset at this attitude. Both men disagreed on issues concerning Russia and laws dealing with the Social Democrat political party. Finally, in 1890, the Kaiser forced Bismarck to resign as chancellor.

Economic Policies

In the years prior to his resignation, however, Bismarck was active in promoting the rapid industrialization of Germany. A high tariff policy kept out goods from other nations and helped protect German manufacturers. The steel industry progressed, based upon the rich coal and iron resources in the Ruhr Valley. Germany became very prosperous and was an economic rival of Britain and France. Nevertheless, workers wanted improvements in their poor living and working conditions. Many of them looked to the Social Democrat party to pass laws that would help them. This political party, along with other socialist parties, believed in greater involvement by government in the nation's economic affairs. Bismarck feared these parties and the many reforms affecting workers that they hoped to enact. He had laws passed that restricted their expression of ideas in speeches and in print. Still, the social democrats were able to add to their strength in the Reichstag. Bismarck now changed his views and pushed for passage of many reforms asked for by the socialists, hoping to weaken their popularity and thereby reduce their numbers in the Reichstag. As a result, the German government voted into law several measures that were beneficial to workers. These included health, accident, and old-age insurance—a kind of social security system. Other laws provided for limited working hours, holidays, and pensions. These laws became models for other nations, in attempts to better the lives of workers.

Social Policies

One of the bitterest issues for Bismarck to deal with in the new Germany was his relations with the German Catholics. Unlike the disputes that another German, Martin Luther, had with the Catholic Church, Bismarck's chief problems dealt more with political and economic issues rather than religious ones. Most German Catholics lived in the south and favored a weak central government. They formed a political party, the Center party, which opposed Bismarck's wish to create a strong centralized government. The Catholics also had ties to the pope and felt that Church lands in Germany should be controlled by him rather than by the predominantly Protestant German government. For Bismarck, therefore, such attitudes by Catholics were threats to German unity and showed a lack of nationalism. He thus mounted a nonviolent attack on the Catholic Church, called the **kulturkampf** (struggle for civilization). In 1872, severe laws were enacted to control activities of Catholics: priests were put under government authority and were not allowed to criticize the government, Catholic schools were closed, Jesuits were expelled from Germany, and only civil marriage ceremonies were permitted. In spite of these actions, Catholic resistance increased as did the number of Reichstag seats won by the Center party. As was the case with the Social Democrat Party, Bismarck now began to change his views. Between 1878 and 1887, he had almost all the anti-Catholic legislation **repealed** (removed as laws). Even many Protestants had urged him to do this, alarmed at some features of the kulturkampf.

Although no kulturkampf was carried out against other minorities in Germany, there existed prejudicial and at times harsh attitudes toward such peoples. They included Germans who were of Danish, French, and Polish descent, as well as German Jews. Citizens of non-German descent were often pressured to adopt German ways. Jews were falsely accused as threats to the nation by an adviser to the kaiser, Adolf Stocker, while Bismarck tried to blame Jews for his problems with the kulturkampf. These examples of **anti-Semitism** were to reach ghastly levels in the **Nazi Holocaust** of the twentieth century. (See Chapter 34, "The Holocaust.")

Summary

If we referred to Cavour as hardheaded in the last chapter, then the term certainly applies to Bismarck as well—if not more so! Here is a man who dominated European politics during the last half of the nineteenth century. Nations were not able to act without taking into consideration the position of Bismarck and of a new and powerful nation in the center of Europe—Germany. He was totally dedicated to the accomplishment of unifying the German states into a nation that would become a dominant force on the continent. Every action he took was dedicated to that goal. He was able to accomplish what he wished because the people followed him, because he was able to dominate a weak king, and because there were not strong democratic traditions to overcome. He was shrewd enough to defeat Denmark quickly and not punish this small nation so that it wouldn't hate him; he was also smart enough to realize that Austria wasn't much of a military power and gained it as a friend after defeat; and he tricked a foolish Louis Napoleon into declaring war on him! (As you know from Chapter 21, there was no way France could win.) The legacy of hatred he earned in France would come back to cause problems in the future, after a jealous William II finally forced Bismarck to resign.

CHAPTER 23

Review Exercises

I. Matching

Directions: Match the words in Column A with the *correct description* in Column B.

Column A
1. Zollverein
2. Reichstag
3. Ems Dispatch
4. Bundesrat
5. Carlsbad Decrees
6. Junker
7. kulturkampf
8. reich
9. Frankfurt Assembly
10. Sadowa
11. Olmutz
12. chancellor
13. kaiser
14. Sedan

Column B
(a) upper house of German legislature
(b) reduced tariffs among German states
(c) crucial battle in Franco-Prussian War
(d) prohibited expression of nationalist ideas
(e) framed a constitution using British and American ideas as models
(f) lower house of German legislature
(g) a title for William II
(h) angered France, prompting her to go to war against Prussia
(i) site of humiliation suffered by Prussia
(j) a title for Bismarck
(k) aristocratic Prussian supporter of Bismarck
(l) title for nation or empire
(m) struggle between Bismarck and the Catholic Church
(n) crucial battle in Austro-Prussian War

II. Famous People

Directions: Use the names below to complete the following sentences.

Napoleon III
Otto von Bismarck
Johann Fichte
Helmuth von Moltke

Prince Metternich
Heinrich von Treitschke
William I

1. _____ made the Prussian army a powerful fighting force.

2. _____ was a historian who believed Prussians to be the best of all Germans, and the Germans to be the best of all people.

3. _____ used "blood and iron" to promote unification of Germany.

4. _____ wanted Prussia to be a weak member of the German Confederation.

5. _____ failed in an attempt to defeat Prussian forces in a war.

6. _____ was a philosopher who believed in German unity and felt that the German language was superior to other languages.

7. _____ became known as Emperor (Kaiser) after 1871.

III. Multiple Choice

Directions: Find the *letter* of the correct answer.

1. The common theme in the writings of Fichte and von Treitschke was German

   (a) militarism. (b) imperialism.
   (c) ethnocentrism. (d) socialism.

2. The greatest roadblock to German unification between 1815 and 1860 was the

   (a) threat of war with England.
   (b) tension between Austria and Prussia.
   (c) power of the pope.
   (d) existence of high tariffs in the German states.

3. War between France and Prussia was prompted by statements in the

   (a) Ems Dispatch.
   (b) Zollverein agreement.
   (c) Carlsbad Decrees.
   (d) Frankfurt Assembly Constitution.

4. The Revolution of 1848 was an attempt to establish a government that would advance the ideas of

   (a) divine right monarchy.
   (b) Catholicism.
   (c) democracy.
   (d) autocracy.

5. German unification was proclaimed after Prussia's war against

   (a) Denmark. (b) France.
   (c) Austria. (d) Italy.

6. The Seven Weeks' War is also known as the

   (a) Napoleonic War. (b) Danish War.
   (c) Franco-Prussian War. (d) Austro-Prussian War.

7. Hohenzollern was the name of the

   (a) Prussian ruling family.
   (b) army unit created by von Moltke.
   (c) Zollverein organization.
   (d) book written by Fichte.

8. Bismarck's fall from power resulted from his disagreements with

(a) Kaiser William I.   (b) Kaiser William II.
(c) Adolph Stocker.   (d) Heinrich von Treitschke.

9. Religion as an issue

(a) brought on the Danish War.
(b) divided the north and south German states.
(c) caused distrust between Austria and France.
(d) led to the Fall of Paris.

10. The period that saw the passage by Germany's government of social security and other laws designed to help workers was from

(a) 1848 to 1868.   (b) 1864 to 1884.
(c) 1866 to 1886.   (d) 1871 to 1891.

IV. Map Exercise

Directions: Use the map to locate the place associated with each of the following statements. For each statement, write the *letter* of the place. (An answer may be repeated.)

1. _____ Lost Alsace-Lorraine after defeat in a war.

2. _____ Shared a common language and religion with the people of Bavaria.

3. _____ The Second Reich was proclaimed here.

4. _____ Victorious in the Seven Weeks' War.

5. _____ Lost Schleswig-Holstein after defeat in a war.

6. _____ Pledged to aid Prussia in a war, in return for territory.

7. _____ Its armies won three wars between 1864 and 1871.

8. _____ The kulturkampf occurred here.

V. Thought Questions

Directions: Answer the following questions in essay form.

1. The ideas and actions of certain persons had a great impact on German unification. They were Kaiser William I, Johann Fichte, Georg Hegel, Henrich von Treitschke, Helmuth von Moltke, and Otto von Bismarck. For each person, do the following:

   A. Identify one idea or action of this person that had an impact on German unification.
   B. State one way this idea or action had an impact on German unification.

2. In the nineteenth century, Germany, like Italy, changed from being a "geographic expression" to a nation-state.

   A. Describe two factors that were obstacles to German unification, 1815–1866.
   B. Describe two factors that favored German unification, 1815–1866.

3. Humiliation can affect a group of people as deeply as it can affect an individual. Examples of national humiliation occurred at Olmutz in 1850 and at Versailles in 1871. For each of these examples, do the following:

   A. Describe the humiliation that took place, naming the individuals and groups involved.
   B. Explain one reason for what happened.
   C. Describe how the humiliation affected German unification.

4. Draw a postage stamp design, to be issued by the German government, honoring the accomplishments of each of these people: Bismarck, von Moltke.

5. "Bismarck is to be admired for his actions, on and off the battlefield, in bringing about German unification."

   A. Write a position paper arguing for this statement, giving at least two specific actions or events.
   B. Write a position paper arguing against this statement, giving at least two specific actions or events.

CHAPTER 24

Tsarist Russia

The importance of Tsarist Russia in European history, particularly in the nineteenth and early twentieth centuries, was enormous. A vast empire that stretched from Eastern Europe to the Pacific, it produced a fascinating civilization full of contrasts and contradictions. A combination of many cultural influences, the Russian Empire created its own unique identity. The impact of Russia on Eastern Europe was especially important as it shaped the development of that region. Tsarist Russia's cultural contributions were to have an impact on modern Western civilization.

Early History (600–1689)

Kievan Rus' (879–1237)

The earliest settlers in Russia were Slavic tribes who migrated there between 600 and 700. In developing trade (furs, beeswax, and honey) rather than agriculture, their settlements grew from towns to prosperous cities. These cities depended on Scandinavian Vikings, whom the Slavs called **Varangians**, to protect them and their trade routes. The Varangians became the ruling class, intermarrying with the Slavs, founding a new state, **Rus'**, and a royal dynasty, the House of Rurik. By 879, a loose union of semi-autonomous (partly independent) city-states under the leadership of a prince at Kiev was established. The Kievan state became a center of trade. It was located in Ukraine, the most fertile region of Russia, with excellent river transportation. It became powerful and wealthy, establishing a close relationship with the Byzantine Empire. (See Chapter 4, "The Byzantine Empire and the Rise of the Eastern European Nations.")

The Conversion of Russ

In 988, Prince Vladimir (r. 978–1015) was converted to Eastern Orthodox Christianity, bringing Kiev and all Rus' with him. With the adoption of the Byzantine faith came cultural, artistic, and social influences. Rus' was also brought into the political orbit of Byzantium and its Eastern European allies, known collectively as the Byzantine Commonwealth. (See Chapter 4, "The Byzantine Empire and the Rise of the Eastern European Nations.") Under Byzantine influence, Kievan culture attained a high level of sophistication, with a highly educated upper class.

Appanage Russia (1237–1480)

In 1237, Kievan Rus' was invaded by **Mongol** armies under Batu Khan, a grandson of the legendary Genghis Khan. Called *Tartars* by the Russians, these nomadic Asiatic horsemen conquered most of Russia and ruled it for more than two hundred years. Only the city of Novgorod (founded by the legendary Rurik) was able to remain independent by repulsing the attacks of the Mongols, as well as those of the Swedes and the Teutonic (German) knights. Known as the *Khanate of the Golden Horde*, the Mongol princes ruled from their capital city of Sarai, located in the steppes (a vast plain in southwest Russia). Mongol rule was indirect and usually consisted of little more than collecting tribute from its subjects. Local Russian princes were granted **appanages** or served as representatives of the Mongol government. They ruled their principalities with little, if any, interference. For this reason, the period is called **Appanage Russia**.

Mongol domination did not last, as uprisings by Russian princes over-extended Mongol military forces. By 1395, every major Mongol city, including Sarai, had

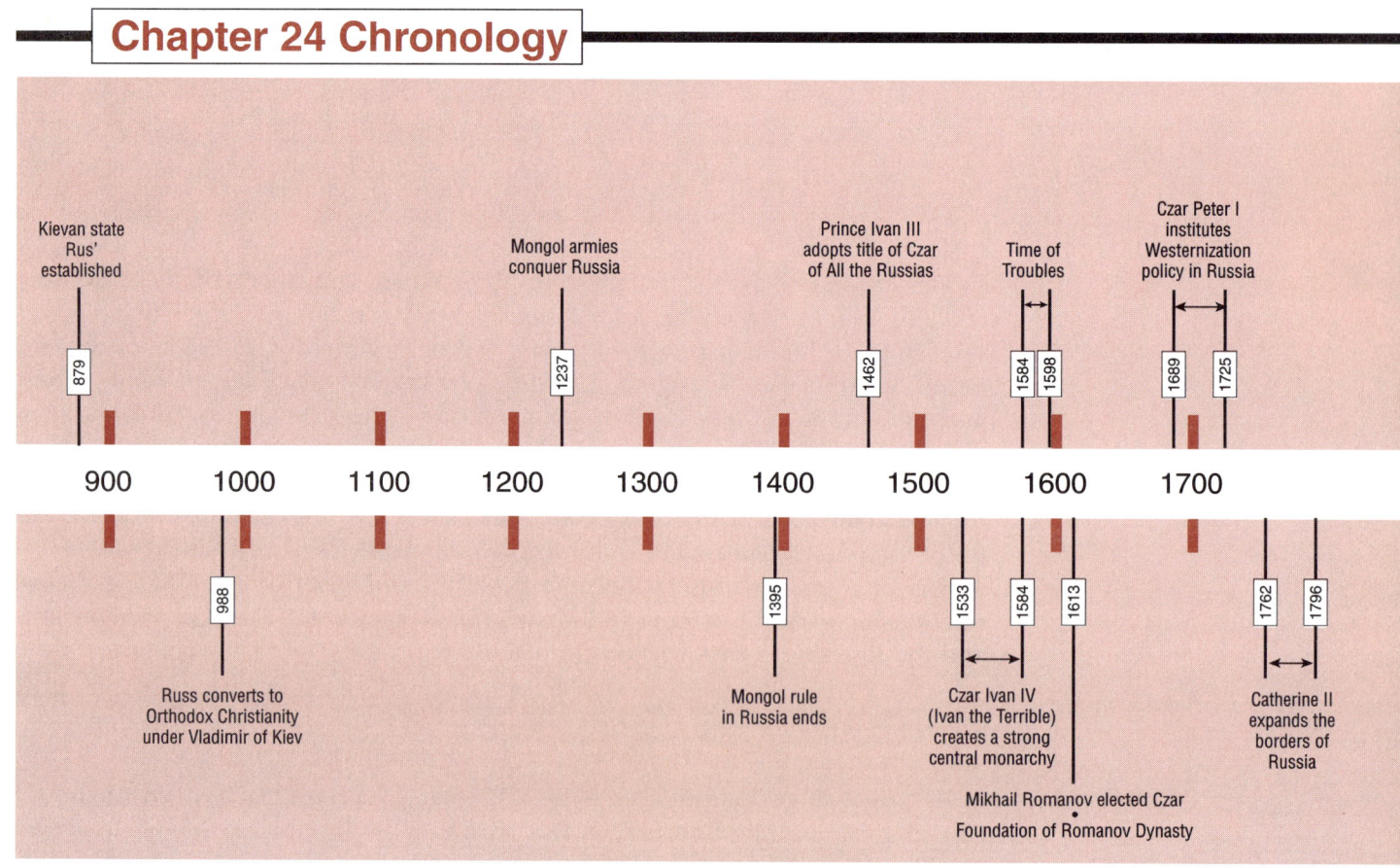

Chapter 24 Chronology

Kievan state Rus' established — 879

Mongol armies conquer Russia — 1237

Prince Ivan III adopts title of Czar of All the Russias — 1462

Time of Troubles — 1584 / 1598

Czar Peter I institutes Westernization policy in Russia — 1689 / 1725

900   1000   1100   1200   1300   1400   1500   1600   1700

988 — Russ converts to Orthodox Christianity under Vladimir of Kiev

1395 — Mongol rule in Russia ends

1533 / 1584 — Czar Ivan IV (Ivan the Terrible) creates a strong central monarchy

1613 — Mikhail Romanov elected Czar • Foundation of Romanov Dynasty

1762 / 1796 — Catherine II expands the borders of Russia

been destroyed. Between 1450 and 1480, the last remains of Mongol rule were wiped out by the princes of Moscow. Mongol domination had cut Russia off from contact with the West just as the **Renaissance** started, thus isolating it. It had also made the Russians extremely conservative and protective of their religious and social traditions. This attitude is the reason that later rulers who tried to carry out reforms met with so much stubborn opposition on the part of the nobility, clergy, and peasantry.

The Muscovite State (1462–1689)

Moscow soon rose to prominence among the Russian cities, especially after it became the seat of the Russian Orthodox **Patriarchate**. The **Patriarch's** presence enhanced the image of the city. When the Byzantine Empire fell to the Ottoman Turks in 1453, Prince Ivan (John) III (r. 1462–1505) declared Moscow to be the "Third Rome" or center of the Byzantine tradition and Eastern Orthodox Church (Constantinople had taken the title of "Second Rome" after the fall of the original capital city of Rome in 476). In 1462, Ivan married Sophia Paleologus, niece of the last Byzantine **Emperor**, and adopted the imperial Byzantine coat-of-arms (the double-headed eagle), declaring himself **Tsar**, or Caesar (emperor) of All the Russias. The claim to be the sole ruler of Russia was a recognition of the power the princes of Moscow had in fact accumulated.

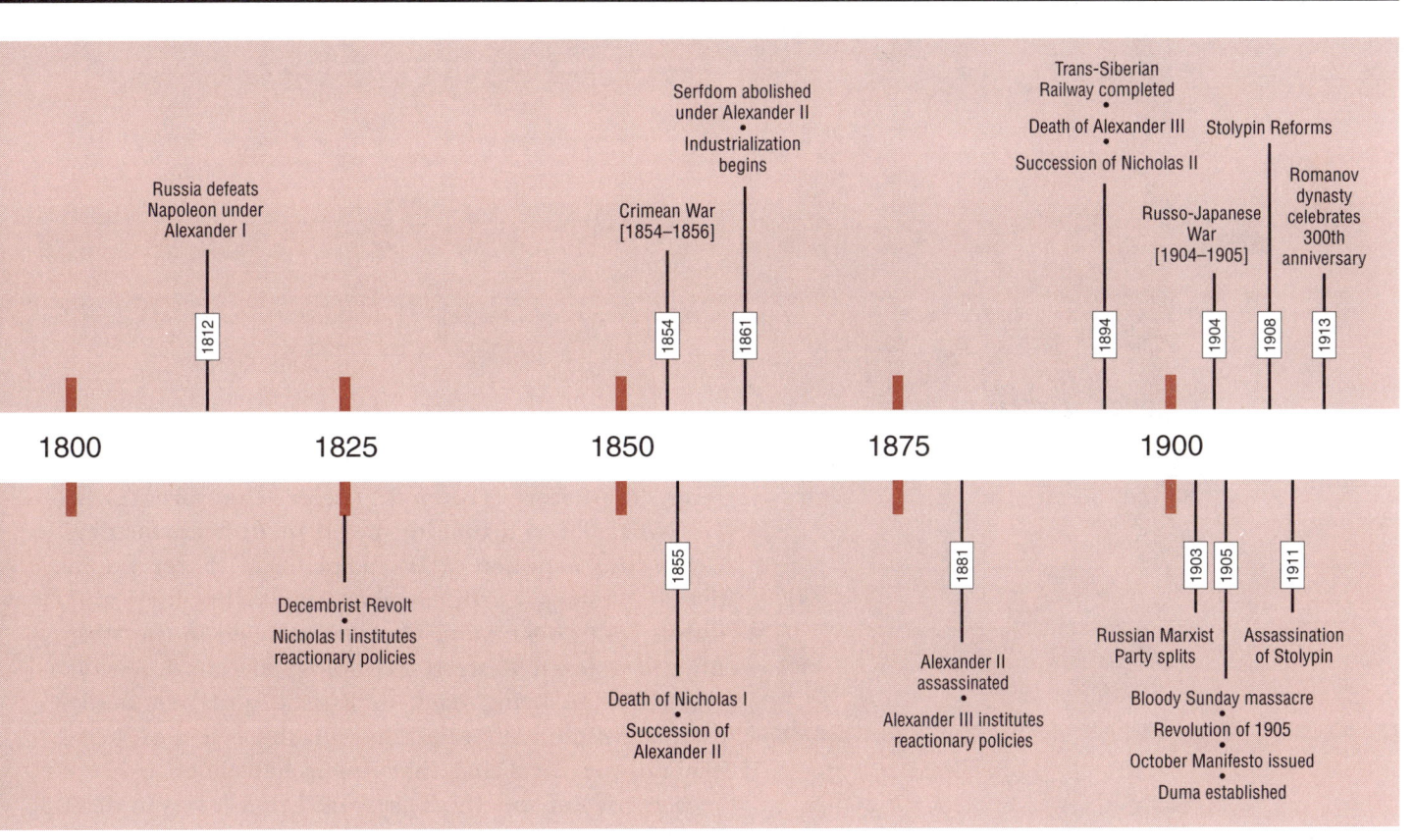

Timeline (1800–1913):

Above the line:
- 1812 — Russia defeats Napoleon under Alexander I
- 1854 — Crimean War [1854–1856]
- 1861 — Serfdom abolished under Alexander II; Industrialization begins
- 1894 — Trans-Siberian Railway completed; Death of Alexander III; Succession of Nicholas II
- 1904 — Russo-Japanese War [1904–1905]
- 1908 — Stolypin Reforms
- 1913 — Romanov dynasty celebrates 300th anniversary

Axis marks: 1800, 1825, 1850, 1875, 1900

Below the line:
- 1825 — Decembrist Revolt; Nicholas I institutes reactionary policies
- 1855 — Death of Nicholas I; Succession of Alexander II
- 1881 — Alexander II assassinated; Alexander III institutes reactionary policies
- 1903 — Russian Marxist Party splits
- 1905 — Bloody Sunday massacre; Revolution of 1905; October Manifesto issued; Duma established
- 1911 — Assassination of Stolypin

Under Tsar Ivan IV (Ivan the Terrible) (r. 1533–1584), the dream of the Muscovite princes to rule all of Russia was finally fulfilled. Always a person who brought out both admiration and fear in people, the reign by Ivan was key to the establishment of a powerful central government and absolute **monarchy**. In the earlier part of his reign, he was a popular Tsar who regained much of European Russia from the Mongols. The later part of his rule was one of terror. Ivan used brutal and ruthless force against the local princes and **boyars** (nobles). By the end of his reign, he had ended their independent authority and made them subservient to the monarchy. He also created a new *service nobility* that was loyal to the Tsar Suffering from depression and paranoia in his last years, Ivan killed his eldest son and heir in a fit of rage. This left Russia with a weak and possibly mentally defective successor, Tsar Theodor (Theodore) (r. 1584–1598) who died without an heir.

This began a period of **anarchy** (disorder) known as the *Time of Troubles*. Theodore's chief minister, the boyar Boris Godunov, became Tsar after his death. Rumors soon circulated, however, that Boris had murdered Theodore's younger brother Dimitrii in order to take the throne. Despite being an effective leader in both foreign and domestic affairs, Godunov became unpopular and a target for ambitious nobles who wanted power. In 1604, Russia was invaded by a Polish army led by an individual pretending to be the dead Prince (Tsarevich) Dimitrii. This began a period of civil war during which Godunov died and Poland temporarily dominated Russia. This situation ended in 1613 with the selection of a new Tsar, Mikhail (Michael) Romanov (r. 1613–1645), by the Council of Nobles (Zemskii Sobor). The Romanov Dynasty ruled Russia for the next three hundred years.

The Reign of the Romanov Tsars (1689–1917)

Westernization Under Peter the Great (1689–1725)

Under the first Romanovs, the monarchy grew even stronger and Russia's borders expanded. The reign of Peter (Piotr) I (Peter the Great) (r. 1689–1725) was a turning point in Russian history. Beginning a policy of Westernization, Peter introduced Western European customs, technology, and industries to his nation. He even traveled to the West himself to learn Western technology firsthand, recruit craftsmen to bring back to Russia, and personally establish diplomatic relations with the rulers of Western Europe. Realizing that Russia had fallen behind the rest of Europe, the Tsar feared that it was in danger of being conquered by neighboring nations with

Peter the Great began a policy of Westernization in Russia. He feared that Russia was in danger of being conquered by neighboring nations who had more modern armies.

Catherine the Great was a popular member of the Russian court. With the help of guards, she overthrew her husband Peter III to become Tsaritsa.

modern armies, particularly Sweden. Peter modernized Russia's military and managed to defeat the Swedes, gaining the coastal regions along the Baltic Sea and the Gulf of Finland.

Peter adopted the bureaucratic system of Western European monarchs to make government more efficient and absolute. When the patriarch opposed these policies, the Tsar abolished the patriarchate and established the Holy Synod (Council of Bishops), tying the Church closer to the autocracy. Peter built a new capital city, St. Petersburg, on the shores of the Baltic, giving his new navy a limited sea route to Europe. He intended the city to be a *Window to the West*, as it was modeled on the cities of Western Europe. Despite great opposition from the nobles and the Church, Peter did transform Russia into a modern power. However, the **Petrine Reforms** only changed the upper classes and the government. The bulk of the population, who were peasants, remained uneffected by the reforms, many tied down in serfdom.

Peter was a larger-than-life figure in many ways. He stood almost seven feet tall, possessing boundless energy and a violent temper. He was relentless in pursuing his goals and ruthless in putting down opposition. Like Ivan the Terrible, he was responsible for the deaths of many, including his own son. His goal was to bring Russia "kicking and screaming" into the modern world. He did this at high cost to both his country and his family.

Russia's Expansion Under Catherine the Great (1762–1796)

Peter the Great was followed by a series of weak and incompetent rulers, yet the system he created continued to function. The reign of Catherine (Ekaterina) II (Catherine the Great) (r. 1762–1796) restored strong leadership. German by birth, Catherine married the weak and unpopular Peter III (r. 1762). Unlike her husband, her intelligence, energy, and personality made her popular with many in the Russian court. Catherine was well educated in the French language and culture as well as the ideas of the **Enlightenment**. (See Chapter 12, "The Enlightenment and the Scientific Revolution.") She was also very ambitious and possessed a legendary sexual appetite. With the assistance of the imperial guards, Catherine overthrew Peter and became **Tsaritsa** or Empress.

With many allies in both the military and nobility, Catherine established a strong and stable government. An "**enlightened despot**," she addressed the need for domestic reform by attempting to make changes regarding Russian law, serfdom, and the status of women. The reforms were interrupted by the widespread and violent peasant revolt led by the cossack Emelian Pugachёv, which lasted from 1773 to 1774. Although the rebellion was unsuccessful, it threatened the established order and put an end to any further reform.

Catherine the Great

A daughter, named Sophia, was born in 1729 to the prince of a small German principality named Anahlt-Zerbst. No one would care about this event except that this princess will go down in history as Catherine the Great, Tsaritsa of Russia.

The story begins with Elizabeth, then Czarina of Russia. As she had no direct heirs and there were no specific rules over the succession, she chose her nephew Peter to succeed her. Elizabeth now began to look for a wife for him. Love was not involved with the choice because this was a matter of state importance. Peter was not every young girl's dream. He is described as stupid, ugly, and bad-tempered, with a face that had been scarred by smallpox. Sophia was chosen because Elizabeth believed that she could be controlled inasmuch as her family would be grateful for the honor given her. Sophia is described as being as intelligent as Peter was not, as attractive as Peter was not, and as lively as Peter was not. She had no voice in the decision and so set off for St. Petersburg with her mother.

Deciding to make the best of the situation, Sophia plunged into studying about Russia, learning the language, and becoming a member of the Russian Orthodox Church. It was at her conversion that she changed her name to Catherine.

After the wedding Catherine attempted to create a blissful union, but Peter, who was most happy when dressing as a military officer and playing soldier, was a poor husband and Catherine led an unhappy life. Finally Elizabeth died and Peter assumed the throne. He was a poor Tsar, and his actions both in policies at home and in foreign affairs angered those in the palace. A small group of nobles decided to assassinate Peter. The leader of the conspirators was a very close friend of Catherine's, and it was decided to make her the solitary ruler. There is little doubt that Catherine knew about and was in full agreement with the murder of her husband. In July 1762 the deed was done and Catherine was crowned in Moscow.

Catherine was not democratic. She believed that monarchs ruled by **divine right**. She could, however, be called an "enlightened despot," for she ruled in what was, for those days, an enlightened manner. She had read widely of the French **philosophes** such as Voltaire and Diderot. She wrote plays, built libraries, and constructed schools for the daughters of the Russian nobility. She restricted lawful torture and allowed a degree of religious toleration. There was even talk of her reducing the burden of the **serfs** and reforming the law codes. She communicated with the philosophes in Paris and was highly praised by them.

Unfortunately for Catherine and Russia at this point, another in a series of serf rebellions took place. A **cossack** named Pugachëv claimed that he was the true tsar and that the people should rise up and unseat Catherine. He issued decrees abolishing serfdom, taxes, and military service. Realizing the danger, Catherine called out the army and savagely surpressed the revolt. After this episode Catherine no longer trusted the serfs and hence gave the nobility more power. This ended any further attempts at reform.

Catherine was far more successful in her actions in the field of foreign affairs. Her policies and actions filled out Russia's borders to the extent we are more familiar with. Interestingly, the American hero John Paul Jones lead the Russian navy in one of the battles.

Catherine died in 1796, leaving a far more Westernized Russia than she inherited. Legend says that she lived a zestful and generally happy life surrounded by those she loved and the many who loved her.

Catherine was more successful in foreign policy. She renewed Russia's drive to expand its borders. In two successful wars against the Ottoman Empire between 1769 and 1792, she captured all the Turkish territory north of the Black Sea as far as the Balkan peninsula. This included the Crimea, which gave Russia a limited warm-water port. Catherine established Russia as the protector of Eastern Orthodox Christians in the Ottoman Empire. This policy was aimed at gaining Constantinople in order to free access from the Black Sea to the Mediterranean. Although the Tsaritsa fell short of this goal, she established it as an objective for her successors and made interference in Eastern Europe a traditional feature of Russian foreign policy. (See Chapter 25, "Discontent in the Austro-Hungarian and Ottoman Empires.") In addition, much of Siberia was explored and settled by the Russians in her reign. When she died in 1796, Russia had become a vast empire and a major factor in world affairs.

Russia in the Napoleonic Wars (1801–1814)

After the brief reign of Catherine's incompetent son and successor Paul (Pavel) (r. 1796–1801), Alexander (Aleksandr) I (r. 1801–1825) carried on the Russian policy of expansion, gaining Georgia and Finland. In his early years, the Tsar made some attempts at internal reform, but he was forced to abandon them as they were too far-reaching for the time.

Alexander's fame rests in Russia's victory in the Napoleonic Wars (1799–1815). The Russian policy of the *scorched earth* (retreating and burning anything that could be used by the enemy) forced Napoleon to overextend his forces, resulting in his ultimate defeat. This brought both the Tsar and his nation great prestige.

Reaction Under Nicholas I (1825–1855)

Alexander's brother and successor, Nicholas (Nikolai) I (r. 1825–1855) began his reign with the suppression of the *Decembrist Revolt*, an unsuccessful attempt by a group of reform-minded army officers to overthrow the **autocracy** and replace it with a constitutional monarchy. This made the new Tsar a *reactionary* (someone who is extremely opposed to change), with an exaggerated fear of revolution. He opposed any kind of internal reform and established a policy called **Official Nationality**, which promoted Russian **nationalism** and stressed its culture ("Orthodoxy, Nationalism, and Autocracy"). A program called **Russification** was also followed, which forced non-Russian minorities to adopt the dominant culture or face discrimination. He ignored Russia's domestic problems, especially serfdom, which created great discontent among the population.

Nicholas also pursued the traditional policy of expansion and interference in Eastern Europe. Russia's disastrous involvement in the Crimean War (1854–1856) (see Chapter 25, "Discontent in the Austro-Hungarian and Ottoman Empires") made it very clear that both modernization and internal reform were badly needed if Russia was to continue to remain a world power. Nicholas' death in 1855 brought an end to the conflict.

Reform Under Alexander II (1855–1881)

The reign of Alexander II (r. 1855–1881) brought much-needed reforms to Russia. In 1861, he officially ended serfdom with the *Emancipation Edict*. Along with their freedom, the newly emancipated (freed) serfs received land, which they would pay for over a period of 49 years. The government also compensated the landownwers for their losses. Full ownership of the land was given to village **communes (mir)**, until the individual peasant paid his loan to the government. The land received by the peasants after emancipation was, however, insufficient to support their numbers, while their loan payments placed a tremendous financial burden on them. Unable to compete with large landowners in a free market, many lost their farms and were forced into the cities, where they became factory workers.

The tsar also established a system of elected rural assemblies **(zemstvo)**, which were responsible for running local government (schools, orphanages, roads, bridges) and collecting taxes. This first Russian experiment in representative government was fairly successful. The legal system was also changed as the concepts of equality before the law and trial by jury were adopted. Reforms were also made in education and the armed forces. The Russian military was modernized as well.

Alexander II ended Russian serfdom with the Emancipation Edict, through which newly freed serfs could purchase land.

Industrialization in Russia

Alexander began a program of industrialization in order to bring Russia's economy and technology up to date. With the benefits of industrialization, however, came its evils; slums, exploitation of workers, and urban unrest. The growth of a **proletariat** (workers) class in Russia brought new support to the revolutionary movement, which had been growing since the 1870s. Beginning with the unsuccessful radical middle-class group called "S Narod" ("To the People") or *Narodniks*, the revolutionary movement turned to violence as fanatical intellectuals and students took charge. A new revolutionary organization, "The People's Will," began committing acts of terrorism to force the government into further reforms. In 1881, terrorists assassinated Alexander.

Alexander III (1881–1894)

The Tsar Liberator's successor, Alexander III (r. 1881–1894), was a determined autocrat who reacted to his father's assassination by crushing any revolt with force. With the **Okhrana** (czarist secret police), he arrested, executed, or drove the bulk of the revolutionary movement into exile. The policies of official nationality and Russification were revived and increased. Censorship and controls on education

Nicholas II, son of Alexander III, lacked his father's will and determination, so he was unable to stop radical movements.

and the arts were tightened as well. There was a rise in persecutions of non-Russian minorities, especially against Jews. Bloody **pogroms** (anti-Jewish riots) caused many Jews to immigrate to the United States.

Alexander continued to develop the Empire's industries. Under the guidance of Finance Minister Sergei Witte (1849–1915), Russia went on the gold standard, attracted foreign investment, expanded its industrial output, and completed the construction of the Trans-Siberian Railway (an engineering feat for that time), which connected European Russia with the Pacific.

Nicholas II (1894–1917)

Alexander III was succeeded by his well-intentioned but weak son Nicholas II (r. 1894–1917). Nicholas tried to pursue the policies of his father but lacked Alexander's will and determination. His German-born wife, the Tsaritsa Alexandra (1872–1918), was domineering and superstitious, often interfering in her husband's affairs and influencing his decisions. Their son, the Tsarevich Alexis (1904–1918), suffered from **hemophilia** (disease of excessive bleeding), which was kept a secret to maintain confidence in the continuity of the monarchy. This often resulted in behavior on the part of the royal couple that made them appear irresponsible and unfeeling. It also gave enormous influence to a corrupt and fraudulent "holy man," Grigorii Efimovich, known as *Rasputin* (one who is given to immoral behavior), who was able to control the bleeding of the young boy. Rasputin was often the cause of scandal and embarrassment for the royal family.

The Establishment of Marxist Revolutionary Parties

Nicholas was unable to repress the radical movements as effectively as his father. During his reign, revolutionary groups continued to develop. In 1898, Russian Marxists formed the *Social Democratic party*, hoping to organize industrial workers into a revolutionary force. In 1903, they divided into two rival factions, the moderate **Mensheviks**, which means "minority," and the extremist **Bolsheviks**, or "majority." Ironically, the majority of Social Democrats were Mensheviks, whereas the Bolsheviks were few in number.

Led by Vladimir Illich Ulianov, known as Nikolai Lenin (1870–1924), the Bolsheviks were determined revolutionaries who believed in using any means to achieve their goals. Lenin believed that the workers were not capable of **revolution**, which would ultimately be for their greatest benefit. It was therefore the duty of the Bolshevik party to organize and lead them toward a complete overthrow of the existing order. In contrast, the Mensheviks believed that their duty was to represent the wishes of the workers. They worked toward peaceful change within the system, rather than advocating violent revolution. Unlike the Bolsheviks, who were a small and secret organization based on strict discipline, the Mensheviks were an extensive group divided into many disunified branches.

Nicholas II and his wife Alexandra kept their son Alexis's hemophilia a secret to maintain public confidence that the monarchy would continue. Their behavior had the opposite effect and made them look irresponsible and unfeeling.

Despite the efforts of the government, these revolutionary groups were able to organize strikes and agitate workers in factories.

Bloody Sunday and the Revolution of 1905

In 1904, Russia went to war against Japan over possessions in Korea. Despite a superior military force, Russia was defeated because of the overextension of its supply lines. The loss in the Russo-Japanese War (1904–1905) aggravated the discontent that existed within the nation, especially in the cities. In January 1905, a peaceful demonstration to petition the tsar for reforms was fired upon by troops. This resulted in a massacre that became known as *Bloody Sunday*. The tsar was blamed for the deaths (although he knew nothing about the event until afterwards) and was given the name *Bloody Nicholas.*

This event, combined with the humiliating defeat in Korea, discredited the monarchy and led to an uprising in Russia's cities known as the Revolution of 1905. The government was able to put down the rebellion, but with great difficulty. Hoping to stem the tide of revolution, the tsar issued the *October Manifesto of 1905,* which established a parliament, the **Duma**, and granted a constitution. Although the October Manifesto officially made Russia a *constitutional monarchy,* the Duma had limited powers and the nation continued to remain an autocracy.

The Stolypin Reforms

Fearful of future revolutions, Nicholas began to adopt reforms. Working with Prime Minister Peter Stolypin (1863–1911), he passed several laws that encouraged the creation of independent farms and a conservative class of landowning peasants. Known as the *Stolypin Reforms*, these measures reduced revolutionary activity considerably. Stolypin's assassination in 1911 by revolutionaries prevented further reforms. The movement leading toward revolution reached a climactic moment in 1917. (See Chapter 31, "Rise of Totalitarianism in Russia, Italy, and Germany.")

Tsarist Society

Kievan Culture

Early Russian society was dominated by religion. The architecture, art, and music of the Kievan, Appanage, and pre-Petrine Russia were exclusively **ecclesiastical** in nature. The magnificent Russian Orthodox **cathedrals**, churches, and monasteries reflect the brilliant style of early architects. The **secular** buildings, such as the palaces in the **Kremlin** fortress of Moscow, also reflect this religious influence in its architecture and decoration. Literature consisted of theology, **hagiography**, and poetry. Historical writing was limited to monastic chronicles, the most famous of which was *The Russian Primary Chronicle*.

The Westernization of Russian Culture

After Peter the Great, Russian culture also developed along Western European lines. Although the quality of Russia's architects and artists was excellent, their work was highly imitative of the West. Russia's greatest contributions were in literature and music. It was in these fields that the Russians showed the most originality and creativity.

Literature   The most famous of Russian poets was Aleksandr (Alexander) Pushkin (1799–1837), whose poetry and prose won him great distinction. Among his most famous works are the poems "Eugene Onegin," "The Bronze Horseman," and "Poltava," and the stories *A Captain's Daughter* and *Boris Godunov*. Many Russian novelists won great fame as well. The earliest was Nikolai Gogol (1809–1852), whose short stories and novels are known for both their humor and creativity in satirizing contemporary Russian society. Among his more famous tales are "Taras Bulba," "The Diary of a Madman," "The Inspector General," and "The Overcoat." His novel and greatest masterpiece is *Dead Souls*, which exposed the evils of serfdom. The two greatest Russian novelists were Theodor Dostoievskii (1821–1881) and Count Lev (Leo) Tolstoi (1828–1910). Dostoievskii was acclaimed for his psychological novels, *Crime and Punishment*, *The Idiot*, *The Possessed*, and *The Brothers Karamazov*, which is considered by many to be the greatest novel ever written. Tolstoi's contributions are no less impressive including *Anna Karenina*,

Aleksandr Pushkin earned fame for his poetry and stories, including "Eugene Onegin."

Theodor Dostoievskii wrote The Brothers Karamazov, *believed to be the greatest novel ever writtten.*

Resurrection, and the massive work on Russia during the Napoleonic Wars, *War and Peace*. Russia also produced many outstanding playwrights, the best known of which was Anton Chekhov (1860–1904). His dramas and comedies have become classics, especially *The Cherry Orchard*, *Uncle Vanya*, *The Seagull*, and *Three Sisters*.

Music Russian contributions to music are also of great importance. Russian composers often combined traditional church and folk music with Western European styles to produce some of the greatest pieces ever written. Among the most famous of these composers in the Tsarist Period were Aleksandr Borodin (1833–1887), Modest Moussorgskii (1839–1881), Piotr (Peter) Ilich Tchakovshii (1840–1893), and Nikolai Rimsky-Korsakov (1844–1908). These musical giants composed operas, choral works, symphonies, concertos, and chamber music. Some even composed traditional liturgical music for use in the Russian Orthodox Church.

Summary

Tsarist Russia was a brilliant civilization with many contrasts. The poetry, music, and literature existed next to serfdom and autocracy. The growth of the Russian Empire, which had an enormous effect on the development of European history, was initially motivated by a fear of invasion. The policies of the tsars were often the result of a desire to "keep up" with Western Europe in order to be safe from attack. Yet, in its desire to imitate the West, Russia faced unique problems that made its leaders realize that it was different. Indeed, the failure to adopt Western-style democratic reforms was to have a shattering impact on Russia in the early and late twentieth century.

Russia's vast size and the strong conservative traditions of its people made change difficult. The population, which was basically peasants, was never affected by the changes until much later, if at all. It is not difficult to understand why Russia was never completely part of the Western European community. Its importance in that development, however, cannot be denied.

CHAPTER 24

Review Exercises

I. Matching

Directions: Match the names in Column A with the achievement they are *best known* for in Column B.

Column A
1. Prince Vladimir
2. Vladimir Illich Ulianov
3. Alexander II
4. Theodor Dostoievskii
5. Count Lev (Leo) Tolstoy
6. Nikolai Gogol
7. Tsar Ivan IV ("the Terrible")
8. Count Sergei Witte
9. Tsar Nicholas I
10. Batu Khan

Column B
(a) Russification
(b) Russian industrialization
(c) *War and Peace*
(d) *Dead Souls*
(e) Conversion of Russ to Eastern Orthodoxy
(f) *The Brothers Karamazov*
(g) Nikolai Lenin
(h) the Golden Horde
(i) "Scorched Earth" Policy
(j) service nobility

II. Matching

Directions: Match the words in Column A with the *correct description* in Column B.

Column A
1. Varangians
2. S Narod
3. Moscow
4. Rus'
5. Duma
6. Zemskii Sobor
7. mir
8. Okhrana
9. zemstvo
10. Holy Synod

Column B
(a) Russian parliament
(b) Kievan Russia
(c) Council of Nobles
(d) village commune
(e) tsarist secret police
(f) Council of Bishops
(g) "Third Rome"
(h) elected provincial assemblies
(i) Scandinavian Vikings
(j) "To the People"

III. Multiple Choice

Directions: Find the *letter* of the correct answer.

1. The earliest Russian state was ruled from

   (a) Kiev.
   (b) Novgorod.
   (c) Moscow.
   (d) St. Petersburg.

2. The first Russian ruler to adopt the title of Tsar was

   (a) Vladimir.
   (b) Ivan III ("the Great").
   (c) Ivan IV ("the Terrible").
   (d) Mikhail Romanov.

3. Peter the Great was best known for his policy of

   (a) Westernization.
   (b) Russification.
   (c) official nationality.
   (d) Pan-Slavism.

4. The Petrine Reforms mainly affected the

   (a) peasants.
   (b) clergy.
   (c) middle classes.
   (d) upper classes.

5. The foreign policy of Catherine the Great focused on

   (a) Western Europe and the Mediterranean.
   (b) Eastern Europe and the Mediterranean.
   (c) Eastern Europe and the Middle East.
   (d) Western Europe and the Middle East.

6. Alexander I is best known for Russia's victory in the

   (a) Russo-Turkish Wars.
   (b) Napoleonic Wars.
   (c) Crimean War.
   (d) Balkan Wars.

7. Which did *not* take place in the reign of Nicholas I?

   (a) the Congress of Vienna
   (b) the Decembrist Revolt
   (c) the Crimean War
   (d) Russification

8. Alexander II accomplished all of the following *except*

    (a) the emancipation of the serfs.
    (b) Russian industrialization.
    (c) the implementation of the official nationality program.
    (d) the creation of the *mirs* and *zemstvos*.

9. The policies of Alexander III were most similar to those of

    (a) Peter the Great.
    (b) Alexander I.
    (c) Nicholas I.
    (d) Alexander II.

10. The revolutionary organization that used terrorism to force reform was

    (a) "To the People."   (b) "The People's Will."
    (c) "The People's Party."   (d) "For the People."

11. The Russian Social Democratic party divided into two rival factions, the

    (a) Bolsheviks and Narodniks.
    (b) Mensheviks and Narodniks.
    (c) Bolsheviks and Mensheviks.
    (d) Socialists and Narodniks.

12. Under Finance Minister Sergei Witte all of the following were accomplished *except*

    (a) an improvement of working conditions in Russian factories.
    (b) Russia's going on the gold standard.
    (c) the completion of the Trans-Siberian Railway.
    (d) the expansion of Russian industrial output.

13. Which event did *not* lead to the Russian Revolution of 1905?

    (a) the "Bloody Sunday" massacre
    (b) the Russo-Japanese War
    (c) the activity of revolutionaries in factories
    (d) the influence of Rasputin over the Russian royal family

14. The October Manifesto of 1905 made Russia officially

    (a) an autocracy.
    (b) a constitutional monarchy.
    (c) a democratic republic.
    (d) a socialist state.

15. The Stolypin Reforms were chiefly aimed at assisting

    (a) the peasantry.
    (b) industrialists.
    (c) the upper classes.
    (d) the clergy.

16. Russia's most original cultural contributions were in

    (a) architecture and art.
    (b) music and art.
    (c) literature and music.
    (d) literature and art.

17. To understand Russia, it is important to realize that

    (a) it has had close ties with Western Europe during its development.
    (b) the Russian Orthodox and Roman Catholic Churches have always been united.
    (c) the Mongol Period prevented Russia from having a Renaissance and Enlightenment.
    (d) the people of the Russian Empire all shared a common ethnicity and culture.

18. The writer best known for the development of the psychological novel was

    (a) Nikolai Gogol.
    (b) Theodor Dostoievskii
    (c) Count Lev Tolstoi.
    (d) Anton Chekhov.

19. Find the *incorrect* pair of author and work.

    (a) Count Lev Tolstoi, *The Possessed*
    (b) Theodor Dostoievskii, *Crime and Punishment*
    (c) Nikolai Gogol, *Dead Souls*
    (d) Anton Chekhov, *The Cherry Orchard*

20. Russian foreign policy was usually determined by its

    (a) continuous expansion westward.
    (b) having friendly neighbors on its borders.
    (c) following a policy of noninvolvement.
    (d) having no natural defensible borders in the West.

IV. Thought Questions

Directions: Answer the following questions in essay form.

1. Peter the Great attempted to transform Russia into a Western nation. Show how he tried to do this by explaining two examples of change for each group in Russian society.

2. You are an American diplomat at the Russian Imperial Court in St. Petersburg during the early twentieth century. You are writing a report on Russian foreign policy. Explain three main objectives of tsarist foreign policy and three historical reasons for their development.

3. How successful were the Romanovs in modernizing Russia through reform? Explain two ways in which they were successful and two in which they failed.

4. Russia's acquisitions made it into an empire. Explain:

   A. two ways they helped, and
   B. two ways they hindered Russia's development.

5. Throughout Russia's history, determined rulers have significantly changed their nation's course. For each of the following, evaluate their contribution to Russia's development.

   A. Prince Vladimir of Kiev
   B. Tsar Ivan III ("the Great")
   C. Tsar Ivan IV ("the Terrible")
   D. Tsar Peter I ("the Great")
   E. Tsarina Catherine II ("the Great")
   F. Tsar Alexander II ("Tsar Liberator")

Discontent in the Austro-Hungarian and Ottoman Empires

By the end of the nineteenth century a number of nation-states had been established in Western Europe. In the East there were still three **empires**. We looked at the Russian Empire in the last chapter. In this one we will look at two others, the Ottoman and the Austro-Hungarian. Once they had been very powerful, but at this time they could be called "doomed **dynasties**." Many of the nations we now recognize on a map of Eastern Europe were formed after these two were dissolved. This area has many **ethnic groups** that live intermixed with each other. The differences that separate them have often been the case of hatred and bloodshed.

The Austro-Hungarian Empire

The Austrian Empire ruled by the Habsburgs was the largest one in Europe, except for Russia. Its peoples were divided into three major geographical divisions: Austria, Bohemia (modern Czech Republic and Slovakia), and Hungary. The population was composed of different **nationalities**: Germans, Czechs, Magyars, Poles, Serbians, Croatians, Slovenes, Slovaks, Ruthenians (Ukrainians), Romanians, Dalmatians, and Italians. In some parts of the Empire the nationalities lived in blocs, but in many regions they were mixed together, often producing tension and conflict. The Germans occupied all of Austria and considerable parts of Bohemia. Yet, this ruling group was not a majority within this multinational empire.

The Sites of the Different Ethnic Groups

The Asiatic Magyars were dominant in Hungary but accounted for only about half the population, which contained many Slavs and Romanians. The Italian population was limited to the parts of northern Italy controlled by the Austrians. The

Czechs occupied Bohemia and the adjoining Moravia. In addition to the Czechs, the Serbians, Croatians, Slovenes, Slovaks, Dalmatians, Poles, and Ruthenians were the Slavic peoples of the Empire, both united and divided by religious, cultural, and ethnic ties. The Serbians, Croatians, Slovenes, and Dalmatians were Yugoslavs, or southern Slavs, occupying the southeastern part of the Empire. They were separated from their fellow Slavs in the north by the Germans, Magyars, and Romanians, who stretched across central and Eastern Europe. The Romanians, who had religious, cultural, and ethnic ties to both the Latin and Slavic peoples, were extremely proud of their unique background. The Empire was divided religiously as well as culturally. Although most of the population was either Roman Catholic or Eastern Orthodox Christians, there were substantial minorities of Protestant Christians, Muslims, and Jews. Despite all the differences, the Habsburg Empire managed to stay together. However, many of these groups, subject nationalities such as the Serbs and Romanians, hoped to break away and create their own nations.

The Austrian Revolution of 1848

In 1848, the Austrian Empire was ruled by the weak and incompetent Emperor Ferdinand I (r. 1835–1848), who had given the running of the government to the reactionary Prince Klemens von Metternich (1773–1859). Metternich was dedicat-

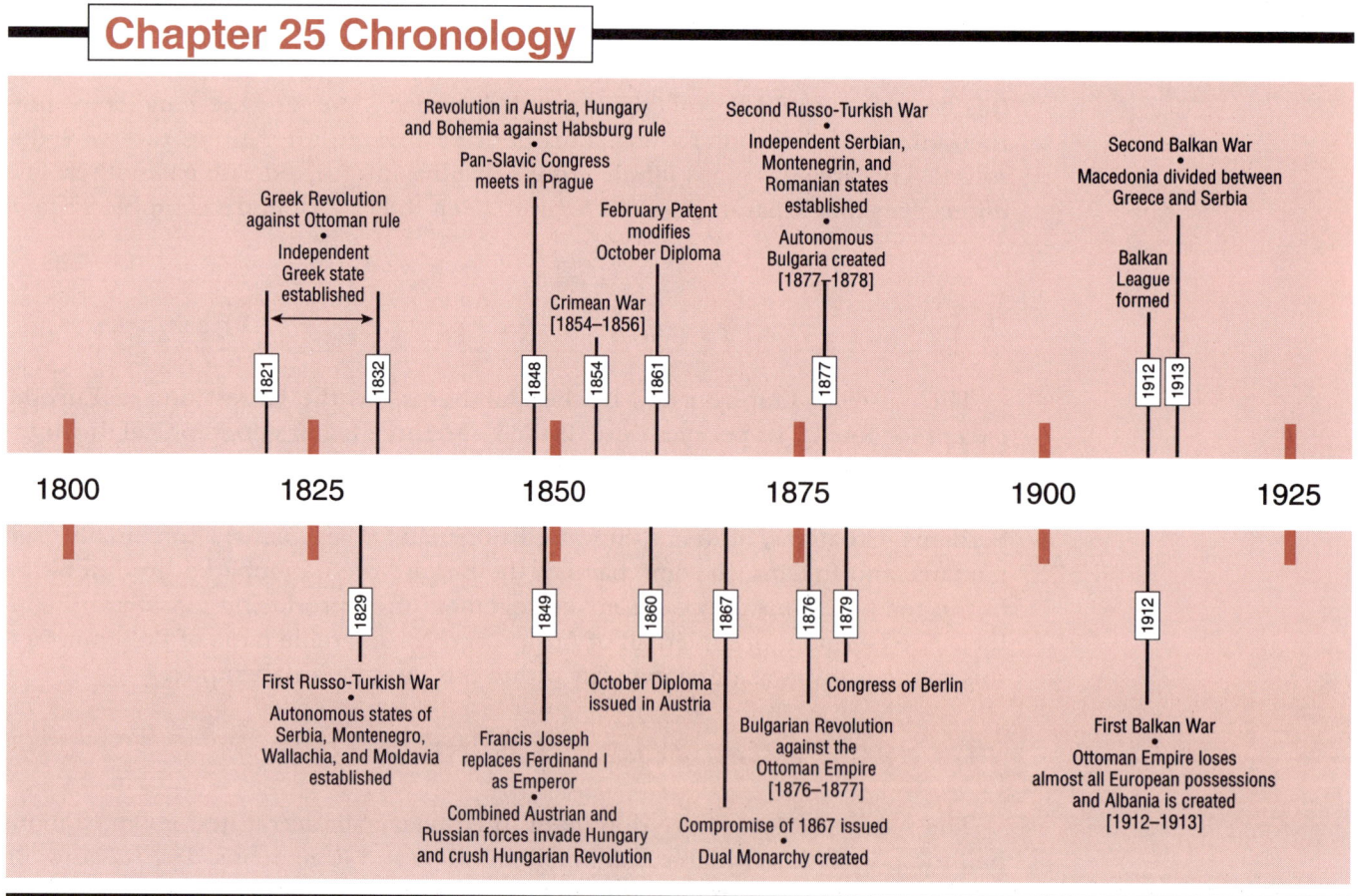

Chapter 25 Chronology

Revolution in Austria, Hungary and Bohemia against Habsburg rule

Pan-Slavic Congress meets in Prague

Greek Revolution against Ottoman rule

Independent Greek state established

February Patent modifies October Diploma

Crimean War [1854–1856]

Second Russo-Turkish War

Independent Serbian, Montenegrin, and Romanian states established

Autonomous Bulgaria created [1877–1878]

Second Balkan War

Macedonia divided between Greece and Serbia

Balkan League formed

1821   1832   1848   1854   1861   1877   1912   1913

1800   1825   1850   1875   1900   1925

1829   1849   1860   1867   1876   1879   1912

First Russo-Turkish War

Autonomous states of Serbia, Montenegro, Wallachia, and Moldavia established

Francis Joseph replaces Ferdinand I as Emperor

Combined Austrian and Russian forces invade Hungary and crush Hungarian Revolution

October Diploma issued in Austria

Compromise of 1867 issued

Dual Monarchy created

Congress of Berlin

Bulgarian Revolution against the Ottoman Empire [1876–1877]

First Balkan War

Ottoman Empire loses almost all European possessions and Albania is created [1912–1913]

ed to preserving the established order and regarded both **nationalism** and **democracy** as threats to the Empire. (See Chapter 21, "Changes in France.") While ignoring the various problems of the dissatisfied nationalities, which had been multiplying in Austria since the beginning of the nineteenth century, he put down any attempts at political and social reforms. The **bourgeoisie** (middle class) became impatient with government policy, which served the interests of the landowning **aristocracy**. Intellectuals and students were dissatisfied with the autocratic system and desired democratic reforms. The peasantry was discontented with the **robot**, the system of obligatory **peasant** labor. Metternich's policies only made this resentment stronger.

The revolution in France in February of 1848 sparked a similar reaction in Austria a month later. Rioting forced Metternich, and later the Emperor, to flee the capital, Vienna. In July, a constituent assembly met in Austria to write a new **constitution**. The group consisted of writers, editors, professors, and students, with few members of the bourgeoisie or the **proletariat** (workers), making it highly unrepresentative. The assembly abolished the robot, an action that ended both the peasants' discontent and their interest in revolutionary reform. The disagreement among revolutionary leaders and the loss of widespread support resulted in the restoration of imperial power by October. In order to pacify the dissatisfaction created by the restoration of absolute monarchy, Emperor Ferdinand was replaced by his nephew, Francis Joseph (Franz Josef) II (r. 1848–1916), and a promise of future reform was given. In March of 1849, a demand was made for the establishment of a decentralized system, but this was suspended by the government on the grounds that a crisis with the national minorities of the Empire existed.

The Hungarian Revolution of 1848

Revolution erupted in Hungary as well in 1848. In March the radical Magyar journalist Louis (Lajos) Kossuth (1802–1894) led a revolutionary government that demanded independence. The Magyar leadership was divided, because moderates, such as the great landowner Count Stefan (Istvan) Szechenyi (1791–1860), favored the development of cultural and economic independence while remaining within the Habsburg Empire. The Magyars approved the *March Laws*, which established an elected Hungarian parliament and abolished serfdom. In the autumn of 1848, the Austrians tried to invade Hungary and restore imperial control. The nationalistic Magyars, despite disagreements among the leadership, successfully defended their land. In April of 1849, the Magyar Diet, or parliament, declared Hungary an independent **republic**, electing Kossuth as its first president. In June, Francis Joseph enlisted the assistance of the Russians in suppressing the new Hungarian state. By August, the Austrians controlled Hungary, and Kossuth was forced to flee.

The Czech Revolution of 1848

There was also revolution in Bohemia in 1848. The Czechs revolted in April, seizing the capital city of Prague. To prevent the Czechs from establishing an independent kingdom, the Austrian government promised them a constituent assembly and reforms. In June, the first Pan-Slavic Congress met in Prague, trying to establish Slavic solidarity against Austria. Only a few days after, however, Austrian forces invaded Bohemia and crushed the Czech Revolution, establishing a military government there.

The Compromise of 1867

Following the upheavals of 1848, the Austrian government re-established centralized rule. Power was given by the distrustful Emperor to loyal German-speaking officials. In an effort to regain popular support, Francis Joseph experimented with decentralization by issuing the *October Diploma* in 1860. It created aristocratic assemblies in Hungary and Bohemia that would elect representatives to the Imperial Diet. The Magyars refused to participate, demanding the restoration of the March Laws. In 1861, the Emperor modified the October Diploma by issuing the *February Patent*, which established a parliament for the Empire known as the **Reichstrat**. The Reichstrat consisted of an Upper House, which was appointed by the Emperor, and a Lower House, which was elected by the Austrian upper class and bourgeoisie. The Magyars also refused to participate in this new structure.

The Dual Monarchy

In 1866, Austria's defeat by Prussia and the successful unification of Italy (see Chapter 22, "Unification of Italy"), greatly weakened the prestige of the Habsburg monarchy. The Magyars, led by Francis (Istvan) Deak (1803–1876) and Julius (Gyula) Andrassy (1823–1890), demanded independence from Austria. Francis Joseph was forced to agree to the *Ausgleich* or Compromise of 1867, which created the *Dual Monarchy* of Austria-Hungary. The compromise divided the Habsburg Empire in two, the Austrian Empire and the Kingdom of Hungary. Austria was governed under the February Patent of 1861, whereas Hungary followed the March Laws of 1848. Domestically, each state operated separately but, nationally, they were still ruled by the Emperor, who had control over the military and foreign affairs. More importantly, Austria and Hungary were bound by the need to keep the national minorities under control. The attitude toward the Slavs was especially hostile, creating a desire among them for unification with their fellow Slavs who were gaining independence from the Ottoman Empire. Slavic nationalism and Austro-Hungarian repression grew as the century progressed.

The Ottoman Empire

The Ottoman Empire ended its conquests in Europe in 1683, when the Turkish army was stopped by the Habsburgs outside of Vienna. Throughout the seventeenth and eighteenth centuries, the Turks were slowly pushed back toward Asia. By the nineteenth century, the Ottoman Empire was known as the "Sick Man of Europe," as a result of its long process of territorial disintegration. Beginning with the Greek Revolution of 1821, in which southern and central Greece won independence, a rise in Balkan and Slavic nationalism started to eat away at the remainder of Ottoman possessions in Europe.

The Ottoman System

The internal system of the Ottoman Empire contributed to its disintegration. Unlike the other states of Europe, it had no strong central government. The **sultan**, in the capital city of Constantinople (formerly the capital of **Byzantium**), ruled his empire like a feudal lord, exercising little control over regional areas. The local Turkish rulers usually did as they pleased, especially if they controlled areas where there was a sizeable population or majority of non-Turks. Treatment of non-Turkish peoples, especially Christians and Jews, was often extremely harsh. In the Balkans and Eastern Europe, the rise in Slavic nationalism created greater tension and hatred between the Turks and their subjects. Rebellions were answered with massacres and great destruction, resulting in terrorism and equally violent responses from the local populations. In addition, the Russians had adopted a policy of assisting their fellow Slavs and Orthodox Christians (the Greeks and Romanians), in order to drive the Turks from Europe and secure a free route from the Black Sea to the Mediterranean. (See Chapter 24, "Tsarist Russia.") Russian ambitions in Eastern Europe and the Mediterranean created concern among the other great powers, especially the Austrians and British. This created a potentially explosive international scene.

The First Russo-Turkish War (1829)

Lacking advanced European weaponry and scientific technology, the relatively backward armies of the Ottoman Empire were unable to prevent the secession (breaking away) of Slavic states. After the First Russo-Turkish War (1829), Serbia, Montenegro, and the Romanian provinces of Wallachia and Moldavia became autonomous (self-governing) states under the protection of Russia.

The Crimean War (1853–1856)

In 1853, the Russians began a campaign to drive the Turks out of Eastern Europe by occupying the Romanian provinces. Alarmed by the action, Great Britain and France went to war on behalf of Turkey. They wanted to prevent the Russians from succeeding in their traditional goal of capturing the Dardanelles (the water passage that connects the Black Sea with the Mediterranean). This conflict became known as the Crimean War (1854–1856) because the French and British forces concentrated on capturing the Russian fortress of Sevastopol in the Crimea on the northern coast of the Black Sea. The war is best remembered for the tragic charge of a British cavalry unit known as the *Light Brigade*. (More than six hundred British soldiers were massacred in this unsuccessful attack.) The fortress was finally taken in 1855 and Russia was forced to withdraw from both the Crimea and Romania. Despite the Russian loss, nationalism and a desire for independence on the part of the Slavic and Orthodox Christian peoples in Eastern Europe continued. Although the Russians had failed to achieve their goals, they maintained a strong presence in Eastern Europe.

The Second Russo-Turkish War (1877–1878)

In 1876, a revolt against Ottoman rule broke out in Bulgaria. The Turks suppressed it by slaughtering thousands of Bulgarians. The two autonomous Balkan states of Serbia and Montenegro responded by declaring war on the Ottoman Empire. Once again asserting themselves as protectors of the Slavs and Orthodox Christians, the Russians went to war on their behalf. The Second Russo-Turkish War (1877–1878) resulted in the complete defeat of the Ottoman Empire. The

Florence Nightingale

The hospital was dark at night with little light available for the patients as they lay wounded from the battles. After eight o'clock each night a woman carrying a lamp would go to each bed, offering the occupants some words of comfort and tending to the wounds. The nurse that made these rounds was soon called "The Lady with the Lamp."

Florence Nightingale was born (1820) into an upper middle-class family. Her father had comfortable homes in London and in the country. In fact, she was born in Florence, Italy, while the family was vacationing on the Continent. Unusual for the day, she was taught Greek, Latin, French, German, Italian, history, philosophy, and mathematics. Rather than enter the social scene that was available to her, she remained with her studies. In 1837, according to Florence, she heard the voice of God informing her that she would have an important mission. What it was, was not made clear.

She became interested in nursing, completed the training course, and in 1853 was appointed Superintendent of the Hospital for Invalid Gentlewomen. Dissatisfied with this position, she was looking for a wider field for her work when the Crimean War broke out in 1854.

After the British and French armies landed on the Crimean peninsula, reports began to come back to London of the terrible conditions that the wounded had to endure. Women were then asked to serve the cause by going to the area to help. Florence Nightingale saw this as her opportunity. With the aid of a friend, she put together a staff of nurses and was given charge of a hospital in Turkey.

When the group arrived in Scutari, they found a rat- and bug-infested, overcrowded military hospital with hostile doctors. There were no beds; the wounded lay on straw on the floor. The nurses' first act was to wash the patients and scrub clean their clothing. Once the hospital was in smooth, sanitary running order, Florence transferred herself to Balaklava in the Crimea. Although stricken with fever, she took over supervision of the military hospitals there and was able to achieve an improvement in both sanitary conditions and medical care.

After the war she returned to an England that wanted to give her the honors she deserved. Rather than accept them, however, she entered into another battle with the establishment: to improve the health, living conditions, and food of the average British soldier. She was unsuccessful until an audience with Queen Victoria was arranged. The queen took up Nightingale's cause and ordered that a royal commission be appointed to investigate. Their findings resulted in the founding of the Army Medical School.

At the same time, Florence Nightingale was busy establishing the first school for nurses in the world. It trained midwives, placed nurses in hospitals, and reformed the workhouses.

In her later years she became reclusive, rarely leaving her home, and eventually died at the age of ninety in 1910. Although entitled by her accomplishments to be buried among the famous in Westminster Abbey, she chose instead a simpler resting place.

The Treaty of Berlin confirmed the independence of Serbia, Montenegro, and Romania, but reduced the size of Bulgaria.

Turks were forced to sign the Treaty of San Stefano, which established the independence of Serbia, Montenegro, and Romania, and granted **autonomy** to an expanded Bulgaria. The substantial increase in Russian power as a result of the treaty alarmed the other nations of Europe, who refused to accept it. In order to avoid war, the Russians, French, Austrians, and Germans met at the Congress of Berlin (1878) in order to find an acceptable solution. The Treaty of Berlin replaced the Treaty of San Stefano. It confirmed the independence of Serbia, Montenegro, and Romania but reduced the size of the autonomous Bulgaria. In addition, the Ottoman province of Bosnia-Herzegovina was given to Austria to "administer." This angered Serbia, which lost its access to the sea, and created a rivalry between the Austrians and the Russians in the Balkans, ending the traditional alliance among Russia, Austria, and Germany. (See Chapter 30, "World War I.")

The Balkan Wars (1912–1913)

Under Russian patronage, Bulgaria, Serbia, Montenegro, and Greece formed the *Balkan League* in 1912. In the First Balkan War (1912–1913), they easily defeated the Ottoman Turks. Under the Treaty of London (1913), the Ottoman Empire lost all its European possessions except the area adjacent to the Turkish Straits. Serbia, still angry over the division of its lands in the Treaty of Berlin, demanded access to the Adriatic Sea. To avoid giving Serbia territory, Austria created the new

Balkan state of Albania. This further created tensions between Austria and Serbia. Having been denied access to the sea, Serbia demanded Bulgarian Macedonia (which had been divided between Greece, Serbia, and Bulgaria) as compensation. This action resulted in a dispute between the two nations that led to the Second Balkan War (1913), in which Serbia, Montenegro, Romania, and Greece joined tho Ottoman Empire to defeat Bulgaria. The Treaty of Bucharest (1913) forced Bulgaria to give up land to Romania and divided Macedonia between Greece and Serbia. The Balkan League, however, also ended. Serbia, Montenegro, Romania, and Russia turned their attention westward, to their fellow Slavs and the Orthodox Christians under Austrian rule.

Summary

The discontent in both the Austro-Hungarian and Ottoman Empires had a great effect on the development of European history. In Austria-Hungary, this discontent was evident in the growing desire of subject nationalities to become independent. Although the Compromise of 1867 was able to satisfy the Germans and Magyars, it worked to the common disadvantage of the Slavs. The poor attitude of the ruling groups toward the Slavic population destroyed the fabric of the multinational Habsburg Empire. The dissatisfaction of the Serbians, in particular, would have far-reaching consequences for Austria-Hungary, especially in 1914. In the Ottoman Empire, discontent meant the end of their European possessions. Outside of a small area surrounding Constantinople, the Turks were driven into Asia Minor. The inability of the Ottoman system to rule efficiently made it clear that great change was needed. Its poor performance as a world power made that clearer. Unlike the neighboring Russian Empire, the Austro-Hungarian and Ottoman Empires lacked any widespread internal unity, whether in the area of religion, culture, or ethnicity. The Austrians depended on a tradition (Holy Roman Empire) that was unknown or no longer important to the majority of the population. The Ottomans, who won their empire through conquest, ruled by force over an extremely diverse and often hostile population. The collapse of both empires after World War I, however, would have even greater consequences for the peoples living in them.

Review Exercises

I. Matching

Directions: Match the names and words in Column A with the *correct description* in Column B.

Column A
1. proletariat
2. Reichstrat
3. "Sick Man of Europe"
4. robot
5. Louis Kossuth
6. Ausgleich
7. Treaty of Bucharest
8. bourgeoisie
9. Treaty of San Stefano
10. Czech Revolution

Column B
(a) middle class
(b) Pan-Slavic Congress
(c) Compromise of 1867
(d) division of Macedonia
(e) workers
(f) Bulgarian autonomy
(g) president of Magyar Diet
(h) Ottoman Empire
(i) Austrian parliament
(j) system of obligatory peasant labor

II. Map Exercise

Directions: Use the map on the following page to locate the place associated with each of the statements below. For each statement, write the *letter* of the place.

1. _____ The Pan-Slavic Congress met briefly in this city.

2. _____ This Magyar nation tried to become independent in 1848.

3. _____ The October Diploma and February Patent were issued here.

4. _____ This nation was the first to achieve independence from the Ottoman Empire.

5. _____ The Second Russo-Turkish War was started by a revolt against Ottoman rule in this country.

6. _____ The Congress of Berlin gave the Austrians this region to "administer."

7. _____ The Treaty of London (1913) created this Balkan nation.

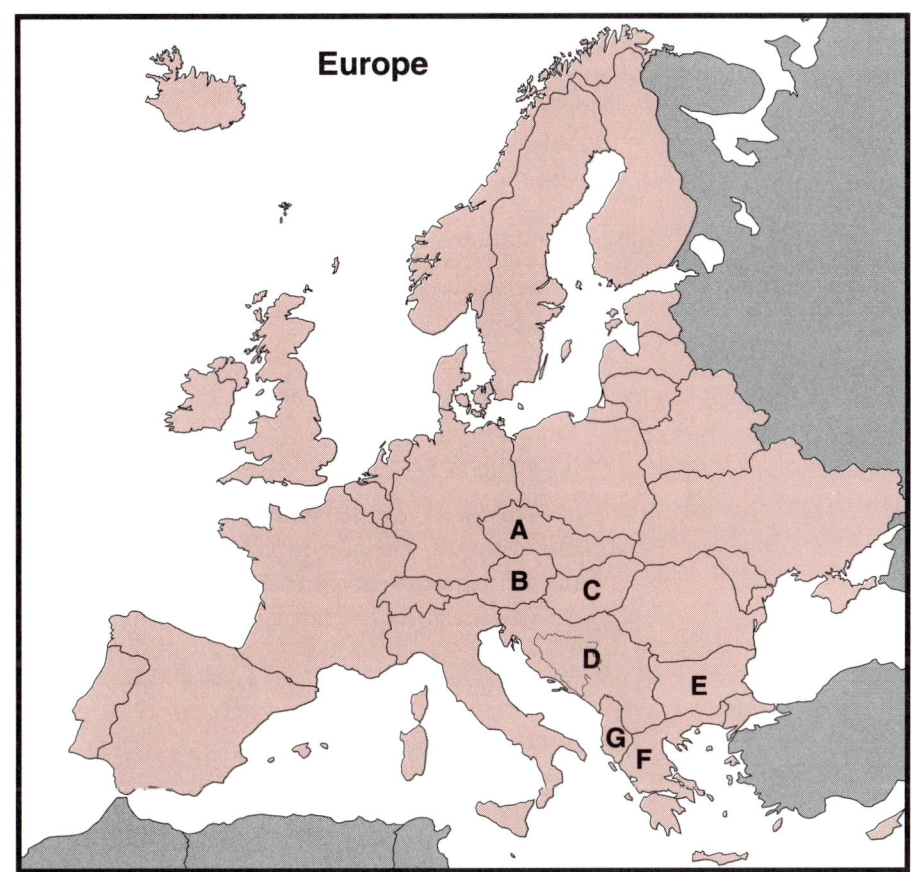

Europe

III. Multiple Choice

Directions: Find the *letter* of the correct choice.

1. The ruling ethnic group in the Austrian Empire was the

   (a) Magyar.
   (b) German.
   (c) Czech.
   (d) Slavic.

2. All of the following groups are ethnically Slavic *except* the

   (a) Polish.
   (b) Czechs.
   (c) Romanians.
   (d) Ruthenians.

3. The Yugoslav peoples of the Austrian Empire were the

   (a) Croatians, Slovaks, Slovenes, and Dalmatians.
   (b) Croatians, Slovenes, Ruthenians, and Dalmatians.
   (c) Serbians, Czechs, Slovaks, and Slovenes.
   (d) Serbians, Croatians, Slovenes, and Dalmatians.

4. The Magyars were

   (a) Asiatic.
   (b) Greek.
   (c) Latin.
   (d) Ukrainian.

5. The Romanians were proud of their heritage, which was

   (a) Latin and Slavic.
   (b) Greek and Slavic.
   (c) Latin and Greek.
   (d) Latin, Greek, and Slavic.

6. The Balkan area developed differently from that of Western Europe because

   (a) the Austrians and Russians divided it between them.
   (b) the Ottoman Turks controlled the area for centuries.
   (c) the British wanted control over the area.
   (d) Austria wanted Orthodox Christianity to spread in the area.

7. Prince Metternich's policies were

   (a) liberal.
   (b) conservative.
   (c) reactionary.
   (d) radical.

8. The Austrian constituent assembly in 1848 failed because the leadership was

   (a) not unified.
   (b) highly unrepresentative.
   (c) lacked strong peasant support.
   (d) all of the above.

9. Emperor Ferdinand I was replaced by his nephew

   (a) Francis Joseph II.
   (b) Francis Ferdinand.
   (c) Ferdinand II.
   (d) Klemens von Metternich.

10. The president of the revolutionary Hungarian Republic of 1848–1849 was

    (a) Julius Andrassy.
    (b) Count Stefan Szechenyi.
    (c) Louis Kossuth.
    (d) Francis Deak.

11. The Pan-Slavic Congress tried to establish

    (a) Slavic unity against Austria.
    (b) a union of Slavic nations.
    (c) one unified Slavic nation.
    (d) a Slavic political party in the Austrian parliament.

12. Emperor Francis Joseph experimented with decentralization by issuing the

   (a) February Patent.
   (b) March Laws.
   (c) October Diploma.
   (d) December Declaration.

13. The leaders of the Hungarian Independence Movement were

   (a) Julius Andrassy and Francis Deak.
   (b) Louis Kossuth and Francis Deak.
   (c) Louis Kossuth and Count Stefan Szechenyi.
   (d) Julius Andrassy and Count Stefan Szechenyi.

14. After the Compromise of 1867, Austria and Hungary were governed *respectively* by the

   (a) October Diploma and March Laws.
   (b) February Patent and March Laws.
   (c) March Laws and October Diploma.
   (d) March Laws and February Patent.

15. The Ottoman Empire was a

   (a) centralized autocracy.
   (b) decentralized autocracy.
   (c) constitutional monarchy.
   (d) republic.

16. As a result of the First Russo-Turkish War (1829), the following nations became autonomous states:

   (a) Serbia, Montenegro, Wallachia, and Moldavia.
   (b) Serbia, Croatia, Montenegro, and Slovenia.
   (c) Bulgaria, Romania, Wallachia, and Moldavia.
   (d) Bulgaria, Croatia, Slovenia, and Slovakia.

17. As a result of the Second Russo-Turkish War (1877–1878), the following independent nations were created:

   (a) Montengro, Croatia, and Bulgaria.
   (b) Montenegro, Bulgaria, and Romania.
   (c) Serbia, Montenegro, and Romania.
   (d) Serbia, Wallachia, and Moldavia.

18. The Congress of Berlin gave Austria-Hungary the "administration" of

   (a) Bosnia-Herzegovina.
   (b) Montenegro.
   (c) Croatia.
   (d) Serbia.

19. The Ottoman Empire lost almost all its European possessions after

    (a) the Crimean War.
    (b) the First Balkan War.
    (c) the Second Balkan War.
    (d) World War I.

20. The Balkan League ended as a result of

    (a) the Crimean War.
    (b) the First Balkan War.
    (c) the Second Balkan War.
    (d) the World War I.

IV. Thought Questions

Directions: Answer the following questions in essay form.

1. How did the political system and ethnic makeup of the Austrian Empire determine its ability to function effectively? Explain two negative and/or positive examples.

2. The Compromise of 1867 was to solve the discontent in the Austrian Empire.

    A. Describe the compromise.
    B. Explain three reasons for its success or failure.

3. The Ottoman Empire was called the "Sick Man of Europe."

    A. Explain three reasons for this name being given to the Turkish Empire.
    B. Determine whether or not each could have been solved through reforms.

4. The end of Turkish domination did not mean the end of problems in Eastern Europe. Explain

    A. three differences before Ottoman rule and
    B. three differences after Ottoman rule.

5. You are a Slav living in Austria-Hungary answering a letter from relatives in the Ottoman Empire. Compare and contrast three ways your life under the Habsburgs is different from that of your family under the Turks.

UNIT VII

IMPERIALISM

In this unit we will enter a new period of exploration and colonization, which is directly tied to the Industrial Revolution. It became important for the European nations to have these colonies both as sources for natural resources and as markets for European products. If the amount of steel production is tied to a nation's amount of power (and it is) then it is important to secure the raw materials for such production. It is not surprising then that Great Britain led the way in this "New Imperialism." The application of industrial technology to the development of military weapons made it possible for Europe to rule much of Africa and Asia. The populations of those areas may have been brave, but no spear will ever defeat a rifle.

Britain, of course, used its navy to control the world. Without a large population to provide them with a large army, the British turned to their traditional strong area—the navy. British policy was to control certain points along the major shipping lanes so that it could control the waterways of the world. New areas became the objects of British foreign policy: the ports of Hong Kong, Singapore, and Aden; the islands of Ceylon (now Sri Lanka) and Cyprus; and the state of Egypt, in order to control the Suez Canal. France also engaged in this race to acquire possessions overseas. It "grabbed" much of North and West Africa and Southeast Asia. Portugal claimed areas on the eastern and western coasts of Africa where its explorers landed. Little Belgium controlled a huge area in central Africa far larger than itself. Italy and Germany, late in becoming nations, were late in acquiring overseas possessions and often had to settle for what they saw as the crumbs of colonization. National honor was very much involved in the race for possessions.

Along the way we will meet the explorers who braved the unknown to explore and claim lands for their nations. Some went because of greed and others went because they wished to bring the Christian religion to the people of the area. There is no doubt that most Europeans believed they were superior to the people who occupied the areas and thought of themselves as bringing "civilization" to residents.

China was divided because it refused to realize that it was no longer the "center of the world." A lack of leadership and an attempt to remain isolated proved its undoing. It was not a proud moment in British history when the British forced opium addiction on the Chinese. The Japanese, looking at what was happening, began to modernize themselves after the visit by the American Commodore Matthew Perry. They adopted the techniques and technologies of the West and so became an imperialist aggressor country themselves. They looked upon China, Korea, and Manchuria as their natural spheres of influence. Similar happenings took place in the Middle East, India, and Southeast Asia.

After World War II, the ease and success with which independence was accomplished in many areas was mainly due to the actions taken by the Europeans before freeing the possessions. In the long run, however, there have been major problems in most of the new nations, having to do with ethnic hatreds, artificial boundaries, and race problems. And, the Irish problem is still with us.

It is important to your understanding of the twentieth century that you learn what happened during this period. There is a direct connection between events here and what we will study in the next unit.

CHAPTER 26

The New Imperialism

Nations in Europe were eager for expansion, but had no place to go on the Continent without starting a war with a neighbor. This new nationalistic feeling led directly to the New Imperialism. With the advances of the Industrial Revolution, even the smallest of nations could think about conquering large areas of Arica and Asia. These new colonies would then serve the Europeans' need for raw materials and markets for their products. The Europeans could feel good about taking them over because they could justify their actions as "humanitarian." Lessons had been learned from the older Imperialistic Period. New forms of control were soon developed.

Imperialism can be defined as the intentional control by a powerful nation over a weaker region or nation. This control is usually political, economic, and social or cultural. As many of the regions under this kind of control were colonies, the practice of imperialism can also be referred to as colonialism. Imperialistic policies have been carried out in history by European as well as non-European peoples. We will concern ourselves only with the imperialism of Western European nations.

The Old Imperialism and the New Imperialism

There have been two distinct periods of imperialism. The Old Imperialism lasted from about 1500 to 1800. It was a feature of both the Age of Exploration (see Chapter 8) and the Commercial Revolution (see Chapter 9). It was concerned initially with establishing trade routes and obtaining resources, and soon thereafter with the actual acquisition of lands and control over the people in those lands. It was carried on by private individuals and companies, and also by nation-states. This older form of imperialism took place mainly in the Western Hemisphere—North America, South America, and the Caribbean region.

The New Imperialism began in the second half of the nineteenth century and lasted a few years past the middle of the twentieth century. It was concerned with establishing trade routes and obtaining resources, but also sought to create markets and to find places worthy of large financial investments. It was carried out mainly by governments as official policy and took place mostly in the Eastern Hemisphere—Africa and Asia. Imperialistic nations desired to rule over other lands and people and to establish empires for reasons that went beyond those characteristics of the older imperialism. Let us now see what the reasons were for the New Imperialism.

Reasons for the New Imperialism

There were many reasons for the New Imperialism. As with any historic development that affects large numbers of people in different global regions, we must examine reasons for imperialism from economic, political, and social viewpoints. It is also necessary to understand the particular time in history when a given development such as imperialism occurs. Two of the most important aspects of nineteenth-century European history that we have learned about— the Industrial Revolution and nationalism—have a connection with the New Imperialism.

Chapter 26 Chronology

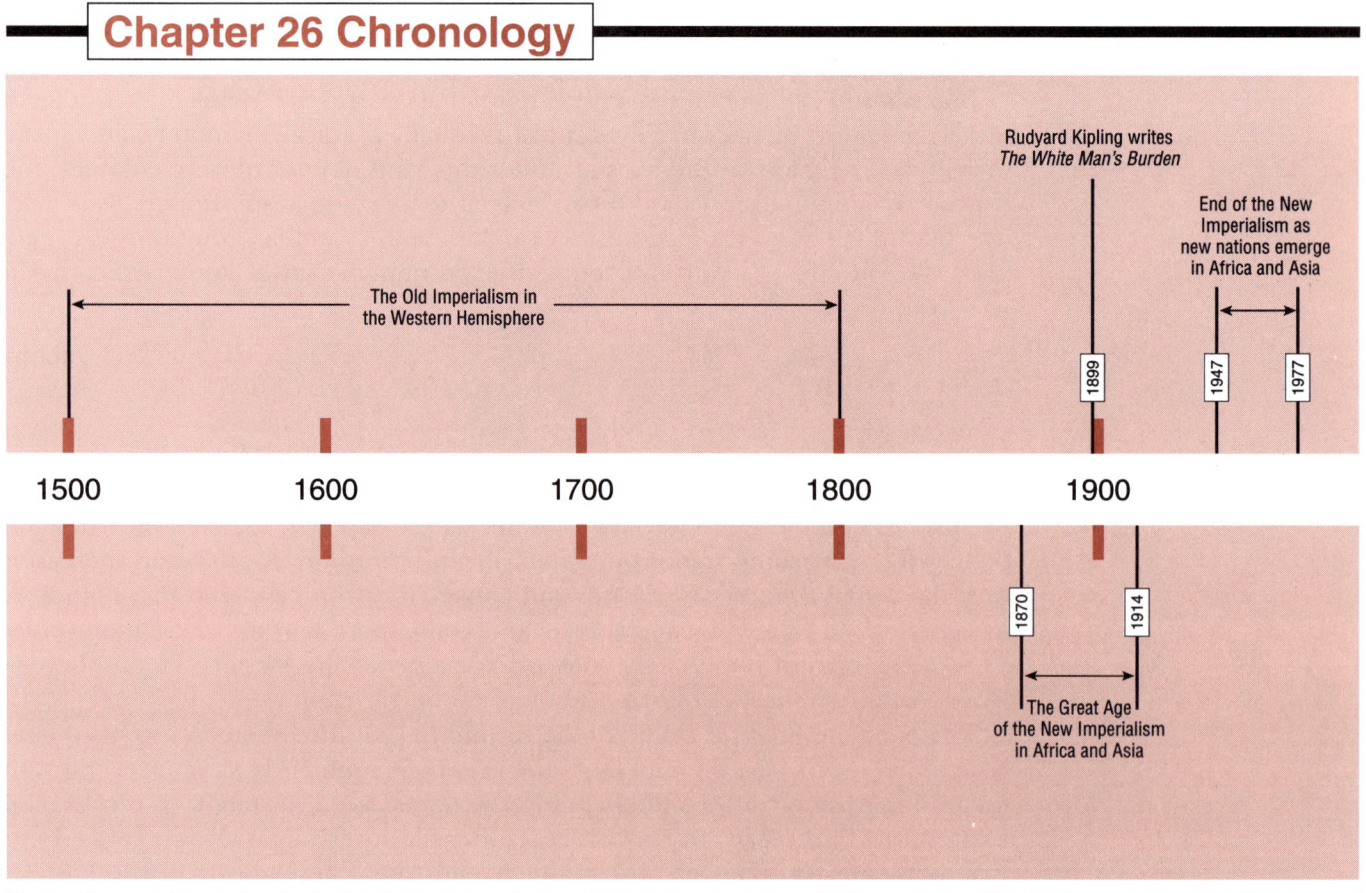

Rudyard Kipling writes *The White Man's Burden*

End of the New Imperialism as new nations emerge in Africa and Asia

The Old Imperialism in the Western Hemisphere

1899

1947 1977

1500   1600   1700   1800   1900

1870   1914

The Great Age of the New Imperialism in Africa and Asia

Economic Reasons

The increased supply of manufactured goods produced by the Industrial Revolution encouraged European nations to find new markets for these goods. A new market meant a part of the world where there would be an opportunity for people there to buy goods produced by the European nations. These nations would also seek out resource-rich regions in order to exploit (make use of) the region's raw materials. These raw materials would be turned into a finished, manufactured product. The Industrial Revolution also saw a rise in the number of wealthy business professionals, merchants, and large companies. With surplus capital available to them, they looked overseas for places to invest their money. As investors, they would hope to make a profit. They would also expect their own national governments to send soldiers to protect their investments, such as rubber plantations, from interference by natives of the region as well as by other imperialistic nations.

Political Reasons

Nations hoped to gain prestige and glory by expanding their power globally. These nationalistic desires sparked nations to seek a balance of power with other nations who were also trying to build colonial empires. New nations such as Germany and Italy wanted to achieve their own "place in the sun" and catch up with longtime colonial powers such as France, Great Britain, and the Netherlands. Imperialistic rivalries in some instances grew intense. Strong-willed leaders who urged the use of armed forces to pursue their nations' claims were engaging in **jingoism**. Nations also wanted overseas territories as places for military bases and coaling stations for their navies. In addition, a colony was a potential source of manpower for the imperialistic nation's army.

Social Reasons

European nations thought their way of life to be superior to other global areas. Consequently, they felt both an obligation and a right to spread their culture into these areas. These feelings of **ethnocentrism** can be seen in the 1899 poem, *The White Man's Burden*, by the Englishman Rudyard Kipling (1865–1936). It was about the obligation of carrying Western civilization to those people in other parts of the world, who were considered to be "backward" and less fortunate. These feelings were also the result of nineteenth-century notions of white racial superiority and the theory of **Social Darwinsim**. Such beliefs held that social progress depended on competition among human beings, resulting in the "survival of the fittest." And as Europeans saw themselves as more powerful and more advanced technologically, they regarded it as natural for stronger societies to conquer weaker ones.

Certainly, there were those European missionaries, educators, doctors, engineers, and scientists who went to Africa and Asia with such fixed, rigid views. Yet, among them were many who traveled overseas for purely humanitarian purposes, and with respect for the native peoples they met. Thus, for example, there were those missionaries whose emphasis was simply on seeking converts to Christianity; and there were those missionaries who were interested less with religion than with matters of health and living conditions. In addition, there were explorers who mainly wished to learn more about the physical geography of regions that were unknown to them.

Forms of Imperialist Control

The European nations that became imperialistic powers established their control and authority in different ways. The various forms or types of such authority and control are described below.

Sphere of Influence

By claiming a **sphere of influence**, a nation gained sole economic power in a region and had exclusive economic rights to trade, to invest, and to develop mines, factories, or railroads. Other nations could not interfere with its activities. This form of imperialism was used in China, where each foreign nation active there, such as Germany, had economic control in a specific region. In general, other foreign nations would respect this kind of arrangement.

Concession

A **concession** consisted of a foreign nation's obtaining special privileges. An underdeveloped region gave permission to a technologically advanced country to do something of economic value in the region. For example, the Arabs let the British drill for oil and build a railroad in the Middle East. Ultimately, while Arab rulers in the Arabian peninsula would gain part of the profits from the sale of the oil, it would be the British who would keep most of the profits and expand their economic and political control in the region.

Protectorate

Under a **protectorate** system, a colonial nation would allow the native ruler of a region to remain in office as a figurehead, while in reality the colonial power made all major decisions. The colonial nation, as a "protecting big brother power," would prevent other nations from coming into the region. For example, the French held Morocco and Tunisia as protectorates. Also, the Eastern European **satellite nations** controlled by the Soviet Union after World War II can be thought of as protectorates. (See Chapter 32, "World War II," and Chapter 35, "The Cold War.")

Colony

To set up a **colony**, an imperialistic nation would achieve total control over a region through settlement or conquest. The nation then would annex the region, or add it to its territorial belongings, with the region becoming part of a colonial empire. The colony would have the flag of the imperialistic power or mother country flying over it, just as if the colony were a piece of land situated in Europe within the boundaries of the mother country itself. French annexations of Algeria and Indochina, and Portuguese control over Angola are examples of colonial acquisitions.

Mandate

A **mandate** describes a region that is placed under the temporary control of a nation by an international organization. Such a situation is rare, but did occur after World War I. Turkey, a losing nation, was forced to give up its control of Palestine, Iraq, Syria, and Lebanon. The League of Nations, the forerunner of the United Nations, agreed to let Britain have a mandate over Palestine and Iraq, and to let France have a mandate over Syria and Lebanon. Britain and France were victorious nations in World War I, and gained control over the mandated territories for a limited amount of time.

Summary

As we saw, the key terms in our definition of imperialism are "control," not "own"; "powerful," not "big"; "weaker," not "smaller." The prestige of the European nations was tied up with this new movement. There is no doubt that the Europeans felt superior to their "newly conquered peoples," and considered the Asians and Africans inferior in culture and advancement. The fact that these centuries-old societies had their own cultures and own ways of doing things did not matter. To the Europeans, their way was the only way. Their drive was primarily economic, but there were those who truly did believe that they should, as Kipling wrote, "take up the White man's burden" and "send forth the best ye breed."

CHAPTER 26

Review Exercises

___

I. Multiple Choice

Directions: Find the *letter* of the correct answer.

1. A word meaning the same as imperialism is

   (a) communism.
   (b) racism.
   (c) socialism.
   (d) colonialism.

2. A chief reason for the ability of European nations to practice imperialism throughout the nineteenth century was their

   (a) technological development.
   (b) cultural patterns.
   (c) use of natural resources.
   (d) agricultural achievements.

3. *The White Man's Burden* by Rudyard Kipling was seen as an argument for imperialism because of its belief in European

   (a) economic practices.
   (b) cultural superiority.
   (c) political ideals.
   (d) military achievements.

4. In order to influence a nation's claim to overseas land, a jingoist leader would most likely want to send

   (a) missionaries.
   (b) doctors.
   (d) soliders.
   (d) teachers.

5. "All great nations . . . have desired to set their mark upon barbarian lands, and those who fail to do participate in this rivalry will play a pitiable role in time to come." This quotation least supports the concept of

   (a) capitalism.
   (b) imperialism.
   (c) Social Darwinism.
   (d) ethnocentrism.

6. Which pattern best describes the development of colonial power in the 1800s?

   (a) imperialism, nationalism, industrialization
   (b) nationalism, imperialism, industrialization
   (c) nationalism, industrialization, imperialism
   (d) industrialization, imperialism, nationalism

II. Matching

Directions: Match the words in Column A with the *correct description* in Column B.

Column A
1. sphere of influence
2. colony
3. protectorate
4. concession

in

Column B
(a) France allows a Moroccan leader to rule, but really makes all the key decisions
(b) England gains sole economic power in China and has exclusive rights to all mineral resources
(c) Germany receives permission to drill for oil

   Iran
(d) Portugal takes over Angola and controls all activities, making Angola part of the Portuguese Empire

III. Time Periods

Directions: Read each of the following descriptions carefully. Write "O" if the description applies to the Old Imperialism. Write "N" if the description applies to the New Imperialism.

1. _____ Took place mainly in North and South America.

2. _____ Spain and Portugal were the early, leading nations.

3. _____ Concerned mostly with securing trade routes.

4. _____ Was a result of the Commercial Revolution.

5. _____ Occurred mainly from 1870–1914.

6. _____ Affected the Caribbean region.

7. _____ Took place mainly in Africa and Asia.

8. _____ Interested in finding new markets and places to invest surplus capital.

IV. Thought Questions

Directions: Answer the following questions in essay form.

1. Describe one way in which each of the following was a reason for European imperialism in the nineteenth century.

   A. The Industrial Revolution
   B. Nationalism

2. Describe four ways in which a nation exercised imperialistic control in an overseas territory.

CHAPTER 27

Imperialism in Africa

When the twentieth century began, over 90 percent of the African continent was controlled by Europeans. This control took the various forms that we learned about in the last chapter. The only parts of Africa that were not under European rule were the countries of Ethiopia and Liberia. And yet, just one hundred years earlier, at the start of the nineteenth century, there was no part of Africa under control by a European nation.

What then had brought on this historic change that saw European power extend into Africa? The general reasons were given in Chapter 26. In this chapter we will see how this power was extended and how it was maintained. Several European nations become involved in the "scramble for Africa," a competition for land and resources in this huge continent. The scramble for Africa was most intense from 1880 to 1910 and resulted in a **partition** of Africa, meaning a division of its land without any consent given by the African people.

There had been earlier contact between Europe and Africa, during the age of the Old Imperialism. In that period, 1500 to 1800, however, Africa was not viewed as a target for conquest and takeover. The European interest in Africa at that time was focused on specific economic goals:

1. To trade for ivory, gold, and other items;
2. To establish bases as stopovers for ships sailing to South and East Asia; and
3. To obtain slaves for work in the Americas, the "New World" of the Western Hemisphere.

Moreover, the European contact with Africa was limited mostly to coastal areas.

The European nations that developed the largest colonial empires in Africa from 1880 to 1910 were Britain and France. We will look at the imperialistic roles they played in Africa's history as well as the roles played by Germany, Italy, Belgium, and Portugal.

Great Britain

In time, of all the European nations active in Africa, Britain came to rule over the largest number of African people. Britain's colonies were scattered all over the continent. In the north, Britain gained dominance in Egypt. Egyptian rulers in the mid-1800s borrowed much money from British banks. Unable to pay back all their loans, the rulers piled up large debts and were subject to pressure from bankers to follow various economic policies. Additional British interest in Egypt emerged with construction of the Suez Canal in 1869. A French company, headed by Ferdinand de Lesseps, had built the canal with the permission of the Egyptian government. The Egyptian government, in fact, was the biggest stockholder in this company. However, the head of the government, Ismail Pasha, had added to his country's foreign debt because of his excessive spending and fancy life-style. To pay off his debts, he sold large amounts of stock in the Suez Canal Company to the British government in 1875. Britain thus became a part owner of the canal. This was important to Britain, as it was the biggest user of the canal and considered it part of its "lifeline to India." In fact, the trade route from Britain through the Mediterranean Sea, the Suez Canal, and the Red Sea to India and Britain's Asian possessions, became known as the "lifeline of the British Empire."

With Egypt's financial problems growing worse, the British sent in troops in 1882. The reasons were supposedly to protect investments and the Suez Canal, and to reorganize Egypt's monetary system. Although Egyptian officials remained in power, it was the British, who, by setting up a protectorate, really ruled the country.

Chapter 27 Chronology

France occupies Algeria
•
Great Trek in Southern Africa

Suez Canal completed

France establishes a protectorate in Tunisia

Berlin Conference [1884–1885]

Italians defeated at Adowa

Belgium takes over the Congo

1830 1869 1881 1884 1896 1908

1825 1850 1875 1900 1925

1840 1870 1873 1882 1898 1911

Arrival of Cecil Rhodes in Cape Colony

Britain establishes a protectorate in Egypt

Fashoda Incident

Italy takes over Libya [1911–1912]

Travels of David Livingstone in Africa

British Involvement in Central and East Africa

British interests also reached south of Egypt, into the region known as the Sudan. Whoever controlled the Sudan, site of the upper Nile River, would be able to control the flow of Nile waters into Egypt. In 1898, British forces in the Sudan defeated the forces of the Mahdi, the Islamic ruler, and captured Khartoum. Moving further south, the British reached the town of Fashoda only to find a French army that had recently arrived there. The French had raised their flag in this part of the southern Sudan, hoping to expand eastward from their empire in West Africa. The two European armies faced each other for almost two weeks, poised to begin a territorial war. However, since neither Britain nor France really wished to go to war, an agreement was signed that prevented fighting. It stated that France would recognize British authority over the Sudan, while Britain would respect France's colonization in West Africa.

This settlement of what became known as the Fashoda Incident, made without asking the Sudanese for their opinion, resulted in the addition of the Anglo-Egyptian Sudan territory to the British Empire. The Fashoda Incident also showed how overseas competition could lead to a war between colonial powers. It also demonstrated how great powers could compromise, under certain "face-saving" conditions. Finally, it signaled a growing friendliness between two former enemies—a friendliness that would be important in the world wars of the twentieth century.

In East Africa, another possible confrontation between colonial powers grew as England, Germany, and Portugal laid claims here. A settlement was reached in the Berlin Conference of 1884–1885. Recognition was given to a region labeled British East Africa and a region called German East Africa, and to Mozambique as a Portuguese colony. No Africans were involved in these agreements. As British East Africa had much undeveloped land and had a cooler climate than many other parts of Africa, it attracted many Englishmen to come and settle there. They were mainly from the poorer classes and saw an opportunity to better their lives at the expense of the native Africans. These Englishmen and their descendants came to look upon this territory as their homeland and thus developed a "settler mentality." This was to be a factor in their resistance to East African independence movements in the 1960s.

The British government's takeover in East Africa, as well as in some other regions, did come across some obstacles. One of these was the armed resistance of African people. Both the Shana and Matabele tribes, for example, fought two wars against the foreigners before being subdued. The British cause was helped by superior weapons, as well as general disunity among tribal groups. East African societies were also disrupted by a large slave trade, begun by Arabs, that lasted into the nineteenth century. Another factor that weakened these societies and made them vulnerable and open to a takeover was a famine caused by rinderpest. This is the name of a cattle disease. The death of many cattle caused malnutrition and starvation for East Africans.

British Involvement in Southern Africa and the Influence of Cecil Rhodes

Southern Africa was another region that experienced British imperialism. The great attractions here were the rich deposits of gold and diamonds along with the geographically strategic locale of the tip of Africa. The tip of Africa had been settled by the Dutch in 1652 and was called Cape Colony. It was taken by the British in 1815, at the end of the Napoleonic Wars. In 1870, an Englishman whose activities were to shape the history of the region arrived in Cape Colony. This was Cecil Rhodes (1853–1902). As a financial investor who was to become a prime minister of Cape Colony and an "empire builder," Rhodes acquired control of the diamond production in Southern Africa by the 1890s. The methods used to obtain land with diamond deposits included armed force, bribery of local chieftains, and treaties.

The use of treaties stirred controversy, because Europeans and Africans would view them differently. Controversy stemmed from a clash between English legal traditions and age-old African customs. A good example of this was the 1888 treaty signed by the Englishman Rudd, an agent of Cecil Rhodes, and Lobengula, chief of the Matabeles. By the terms of this document, Lobengula gave to Rudd (unknowingly) all the mineral rights of his tribal region. In return, he was to receive rifles, cartridges, a yearly income, and a steamboat. When Rhodes's company, the British South Africa Company, began to develop gold and diamond mines, Lobengula protested and even wrote a letter of complaint to Queen Victoria. The British position was that the 1888 treaty was a perfectly legal document that transferred title to and ownership of the land to them. In England, it was common for ownership of property to be exchanged by the signing of a contract. It was not so in Africa. From Lobengula's point of view, and that of tribal African societies, ownership of land was sacred and certainly could not be exchanged according to a piece of paper. Nevertheless, Lobengula lost his land. It soon became the English colony of Rhodesia, named after Cecil Rhodes.

Rhodes became an extremely wealthy man. He dreamed of a huge British Empire in Africa, hoping to complete a "Cape to Cairo" railroad. His dreams, if they had been realized, would have added to British power as well as to his own wealth. By the terms of his will, large sums of money, obtained from his gold and diamond mines, were left to establish scholarships at Oxford University for Englishmen and Americans. Indeed, even now, it is an outstanding honor to be granted a Rhodes scholarship.

Although Rhodes was the key economic and political figure in the growth of British dominance in Southern Africa, this dominance could not have been achieved without the deployment of British soldiers. They were needed to win over the Zulus, a tribal people who were highly disciplined warriors who fought courageously. The soldiers were also needed to fight against the Boers. The Boers were descendants of the Dutch settlers who had come to Southern Africa in 1652. They resented the British takeover of Cape Colony in 1815 and migrated northward in 1830. This migration, known as the Great Trek, resulted in the establishment of the Republics of Transvaal and the Orange Free State. Tension between the Boers and Britain was aggravated when more Englishmen came to these areas following the news of the discovery of valuable gold and diamond deposits. This tension resulted in the Boer War, 1899–1902. Upon winning the war, Britain promised the Boers some form of self-government. In 1910, the Transvaal and the Orange Free State were combined with the British territories of Cape Colony and Natal to form the Union of South Africa. The region now became a self-governing dominion within the British Empire.

The colonial policy Britain followed in most of its African settlements as well as in most of its Asian colonies was called **indirect rule**. This policy permitted local rulers to maintain some power in their region, although they actually followed the directions given by the British. A good example of British colonial rule can be seen in Nigeria. Under the British administrator of this colony, Sir Frederick Lugard, local tribal chiefs were allowed to retain their authority as long as they obeyed general guidelines concerning such items as prohibitions on slavery and on warfare among themselves. Native Nigerian laws, religion, and traditions could be maintained in so far as they did not sharply conflict with British standards. The British sought to build railroads, improve commerce and agriculture, fight disease, and educate selected natives. As the British felt that their values and ways of life were superior to those of Africans and should be spread, the British even brought some Africans to schools in Britain in order to educate them. The hope was that these individuals would plant British political and social ideas in Africa.

British Explorers

A great deal of interest about Africa grew from the travels and publications of British explorers. Businessmen, missionaries, and government officials gained knowledge about what they previously thought was an unknown or "dark" continent. Among the famous explorers were the following:

David Livingstone was a Scottish missionary and explorer. He conducted extensive explorations of Africa's interior. Thought to be missing in his travels, he was found by the American reporter Henry Stanley.

- Mungo Park was the first Westerner to travel along the Niger River in West Africa.
- David Livingstone, a physician and missionary, was the best-known European explorer of the nineteenth century. Between 1840 and 1873, he traveled extensively in Central Africa. His writings received wide publicity in Europe. He came across a magnificent waterfall in 1855, naming it Victoria Falls, in honor of Queen Victoria. In 1869, a New York newspaper reporter, Henry Stanley, tracked down Livingstone near Lake Tanganyika. They then jointly explored areas of East Africa.
- Richard Burton and John Speke journeyed south along the Nile River and throughout East Africa, helping to establish British claims to the region.

The maps drawn by these explorers provided new information about Africa. Their books described several well-organized and developed native civilizations. Similar information appeared in the writings of some missionaries. However, there were also prejudiced accounts by Europeans, which pictured Africans as "savages" and were the basis for negative myths and stereotypes.

France

During the nineteenth century, France was able to build a colonial empire in Africa that covered more territory than Britain's. The first major French penetration was in North Africa. Upset with actions taken by the Barbary pirates from North African Islamic regions, France complained to the ruler of Algeria. Dissatisfied with his response, France sent a military force in 1830 that arrested the ruler and took over the region.

In neighboring Tunisia, the ruler, known as the Bey, was a poor financial manager. He lived beyond his means, and borrowed heavily from French bankers and the French government. In 1881, wanting to reform Tunisia's monetary system, protect its investments, get repayment of loans, and expand its role in North Africa, France established a protectorate in Tunisia. France improved transportation and education and built up several industries.

Sir Richard Francis Burton

His life had enough adventure in it for three people. He went to places, visited cities, and met people that we can only dream about. He was a military man, a discoverer, a linguist, and an author. If you saw Richard Burton's life in a movie you might think that it was fiction.

Burton was born in England in 1821 into a family that had English, French, and Irish ancestry. His father had attempted a military career but had failed and moved, with Richard, to France. The young boy spent much of his early life there, and returned to England to attend Oxford when he was 19. By this time he could speak Italian, Greek, Latin, and of course French. In his memoirs Burton wrote that he never truly felt at home anywhere. Perhaps that is why he had the desire to go to many places on the earth—no place was home to him.

Two years after entering Oxford, Burton was expelled. He joined the military as an officer and was posted to the Eighteenth Regiment of the Bombay Native Infantry in India. In that assignment he fought in a number of skirmishes in what is today Pakistan. While there he learned Arabic, Hindi, and six other Indian languages. (Eventually Burton was able to speak twenty-five languages and a large number of dialects.) His commanding officer used his talent for languages and had him disguise himself as a Muslim merchant so as to obtain information. Although the head of intelligence had use for him, Burton had a talent for making other people dislike him. After the death of the commandant, an unfriendly officer destroyed Burton's potential career and he resigned.

In 1853 Burton disguised himself as an Afghan Muslim and visited Cairo, Suez, and Medina. He was one of the first Europeans to visit the holy Muslim shrine in Mecca. Non-Muslims were not allowed in this sacred city and thus to visit was to put one's life in danger. While there he made the first accurate sketches of the mosque and the holy shrine, the Kabbah. He then became the first European to enter the holy city of Harar and leave it alive.

By 1855 English explorers were searching for the source of the Nile. As you know the Nile is the life-supporting thread of Egypt. The question of its source was important because if it dried up, all life in Egypt would be threatened. England had great interest in the area because of the potential for a canal to be built there and its imperialist goals in the area.

In that year Burton joined with John Hanning Speke and others to find the source. The party was attacked by Africans, Speke was wounded, and Burton had a javelin thrown through his jaw. Since he was seriously wounded, he had to return to England for medical attention and recuperation. But Burton was unable to stay out of action. He then went to the Crimea to train Turks in their war against Russia.

In 1857 he rejoined Speke to again attempt to find the source of the Nile. Two methods were generally being tried at the time. One was to sail up the Nile into the heart of the continent. The other was to start at Zanzibar and cross East Africa. Burton and Speke chose the second way. Their trip across the continent was filled with incredible hardships. There were attacks by African tribes, disease, and the lack of adequate supplies. They arrived at what would eventually be called Lake Tanganyika and were disappointed to find that it was not the source of the Nile. By then Burton had malaria and Speke was almost blind. Speke, however, recovered and set out without Burton. Speke discovered Lake Victoria and claimed this as the source of the Nile. Burton denied this claim but Speke returned to London and received recognition as the discoverer of the source. Burton received no recognition. A debate was set up between the two of them. However, before the debate could take place, Speke died in a freak shooting accident. Many think he committed suicide because he did not want to debate Burton.

The Foreign Office used Burton's talent for languages and he served in Brazil, Syria, and Trieste. He wrote a number of books on the cultures of the areas he was familiar with. Some of these were considered pornographic at that time. After his death, his wife, a religious woman, burned all his diaries and journals. The destruction of this forty-year collection was a great loss to sociologists who could have used it to better understand other peoples.

Who was right about the source of the Nile? As they say: you can look it up!

With the acquisition of Algeria and Tunisia, France then felt it was necessary to protect these holdings by taking over Morocco. A dispute with Germany, which also desired a foothold in Morocco, was resolved in 1911. France secured a protectorate in Morocco while Germany gained land in West Africa.

French Involvement in Central and West Africa

French interest in Central and West Africa was spurred by economic and "national honor" factors, as well as by the accounts of the explorer René Callie. A railroad was constructed from Dakar, on the west coast, into the interior regions of the continent. Commercial settlements were set up along various parts of the west coast, the "bulge" of Africa. The French push from the coast inward was often met with strong resistance. Only superior armed forces and weaponry enabled victory to be achieved over Samori Toure, King of what is now Senegal, and King Behanzin of Dahomey.

The colonial policy France followed in most of its African settlements as well as in its Asian colonies was called **direct rule**. France exercised much more control over its territories than was the case with Britain's indirect rule policy. France often removed local rulers, replacing them with French officials. Decisions for the colonies were made directly in Paris. Since the French language and culture were considered by the French to be preferable, all people were supposed to learn them in colonized regions. These attitudes formed the basis for France's claim to carry out a "civilizing mission" and to accomplish **assimilation** of native peoples into French culture. Successful assimilation would be achieved with people giving up their local culture and replacing it with French culture. France viewed colonies such as Algeria and the Ivory Coast as part of France, the same way Paris was part of France. Some overseas areas were even allowed to send representatives to the French National Assembly in Paris.

Germany

As a latecomer to national unity (see Chapter 23, "Unification of Germany"), Germany was also a latecomer to imperialism. Even though Chancellor Bismarck himself was not very interested in gaining colonies, Kaisers William I and William II, along with other Germans, felt that colonial acquisitions were necessary for Germany to be considered a great power and to enjoy a "place in the sun" with other European nations. The four scattered German colonies in Africa covered very little land. These were Togoland, Cameroon, German East Africa, and Southwest Africa. Unlike Britain and France, which were able to strengthen their colonial empires well into the twentieth century, Germany never really had a chance to do this. It lost all its possessions after its defeat in 1918 in World War I.

One of the few reversals for European imperialism occurred at the Battle of Adowa in 1896. There, the Ethiopian Emperor Menelik II defeated a force of Italians.

Italy

As was true of Germany, Italy was a latecomer both to national unity (see Chapter 22 "Unification of Italy") and the race for colonies. As a result, there was very little land left for Italy to gain. It was thwarted in its efforts to take Abyssinia

(Ethiopia), suffering a crushing defeat by the forces of Emperor Menelik II at Adowa in 1896. Italy did obtain the small desert lands of Eritrea and Somaliland near the Horn of Africa. With the gradual weakening of Ottoman Turkish rule in North Africa, Italy was able to send in troops and acquire Libya in 1911–1912.

Belgium

Another latecomer to the "scramble for Africa" was Belgium. Its "Empire" consisted of only one region—the Congo. Nevertheless, it was, and still is, one of the most resource-rich parts of the continent. Eager to obtain rubber and ivory from this part of Central Africa, Belgian King Leopold II (r. 1865–1909), acting as a private citizen, formed a company with several Belgian capitalists in 1876. The company made huge profits but did little to improve the lives of the people of the Congo. The native population was terribly mistreated. Many were forced to work on rubber plantations amid harsh conditions, and they were often subjected to torture. The company looked upon the Congo simply as an investment and followed a policy of **exploitation**. This meant that the company took unfair advantage of its position and cared only for itself.

News about the inhumane treatment of natives along with news of financial scandals resulted in the Belgian government taking formal control of the Congo in 1908. From that point on, the region was known as a colony, the Belgian Congo. Under the Belgian government, exploitation was somewhat reduced and an attempt was made to copy the British system of indirect rule. The Belgians also followed a policy of **paternalism**. With this attitude, the Belgians viewed the Congolese as if they were children needing to be led and instructed, unable to care for themselves. Such an attitude was demeaning and racist, and was a factor in causing problems for the Congo when it became independent in 1960.

Portugal

Portugal was one of the earliest European nations to have commercial contacts and settlements in Africa. Using its advanced nagivational skills in the fifteenth and sixteenth centuries during the Age of Exploration (see Chapter 8, "The Age of Exploration"), Portuguese sailors on the way to Asia would stop along the east and west coasts of Africa to trade and to set up supply bases. Eventually, these stopovers became the Portuguese colonies of Angola, Mozambique, and Portuguese Guinea. In the late nineteenth century, Portugal was fortunate in being able to have its colonial status in Angola and Mozambique recognized by the other European powers. By this time, it was a weak nation and could not have competed for land with England, France, and Germany. Yet, because all of these other nations feared each other, with each wanting to prevent the other from gaining more land in Southern Africa, Portugal was allowed to retain Angola and Mozambique. This was one of the decisions reached concerning the partition of Africa at the Berlin Conference of 1884–1885.

Portuguese colonial policies were examples of both exploitation and paternalism. As was generally true of France's attitudes toward its colonies, Portugal viewed its African possessions as if they were, like Lisbon, part of Portugal itself.

With such attitudes, as we will see in discussing the end of imperialism (see Chapter 29, "Independence and Decolonization"), Portugal was very reluctant to grant independence to its colonies.

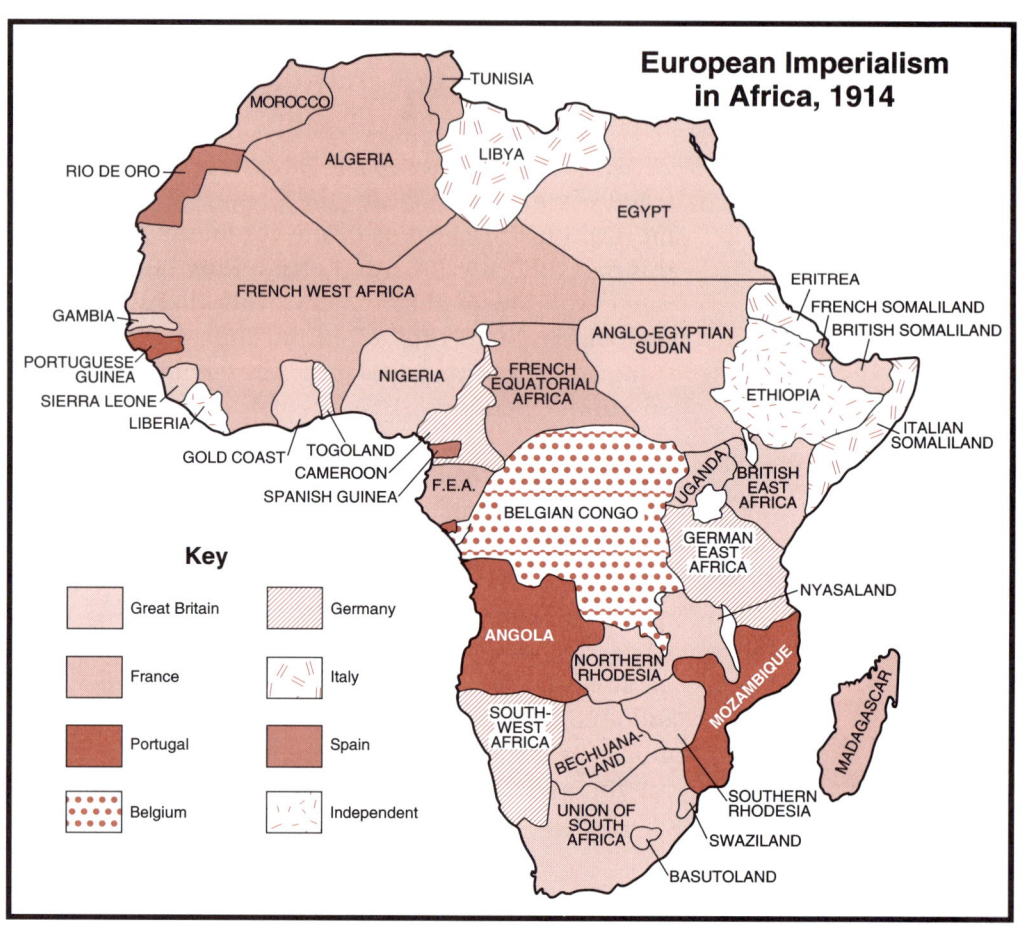

European Imperialism in Africa, 1914

TUNISIA
MOROCCO
ALGERIA
LIBYA
RIO DE ORO
EGYPT
FRENCH WEST AFRICA
ERITREA
FRENCH SOMALILAND
BRITISH SOMALILAND
GAMBIA
ANGLO-EGYPTIAN SUDAN
PORTUGUESE GUINEA
NIGERIA
FRENCH EQUATORIAL AFRICA
ETHIOPIA
SIERRA LEONE
LIBERIA
ITALIAN SOMALILAND
GOLD COAST
TOGOLAND
CAMEROON
F.E.A.
UGANDA
BRITISH EAST AFRICA
SPANISH GUINEA
BELGIAN CONGO
GERMAN EAST AFRICA
NYASALAND
ANGOLA
NORTHERN RHODESIA
MOZAMBIQUE
SOUTH-WEST AFRICA
BECHUANA-LAND
MADAGASCAR
UNION OF SOUTH AFRICA
SOUTHERN RHODESIA
SWAZILAND
BASUTOLAND

Key

Great Britain	Germany
France	Italy
Portugal	Spain
Belgium	Independent

Summary

As we look at the map of Africa above, we see a new map of the continent. At the beginning of the century there were a few outposts along the coastline but little else. One hundred years later, almost the entire continent was divided up. Great Britain and France got the major share with the newcomers, Germany and Italy, having to settle for what was left. Belgium and Portugal were allowed to keep their colonies because it was not in the interest of the other European countries to take them away. Each of the European countries ruled its area as it saw best. Boundaries were drawn by the Europeans without taking into consideration what was good for the Africans or what the Africans wanted.

It was also a period of high adventure. We should not slight the accomplishments of the brave men and women who risked their lives in opening new lands. They often had little idea where they were going or if they would come back alive. They went through hardships that would stop all but the bravest. Some, like Rhodes, went for fortune; most went for fame.

CHAPTER 27

Review Exercises

I. Matching

Directions: Match the words in Column A with the *correct description* in Column B.

Column A
1. direct rule
2. Great Trek
3. assimilation
4. rinderpest
5. paternalism
6. indirect rule
7. partition of Africa
8. scramble for Africa
9. "lifeline to India"

Column B
(a) British method of control in its colonies
(b) a goal of France in its colonies
(c) involved Boers in Southern Africa
(d) French method of control in its colonies
(e) attitude of Belgium and Portugal toward their colonies
(f) a cattle disease causing malnutrition in East Africa
(g) division of Africa by European powers
(h) influenced British interest in building the Suez Canal
(i) race for colonies in Africa by European powers

II. Famous People

Directions: Use the names below to complete the following sentences.

Cecil Rhodes
Lobengula
Mungo Park
Ismail Pasha
Henry Stanley
Menelik II

Frederick Lugard
David Livingstone
Ferdinand de Lesseps
the Mahdi
Leopold II
René Callie

1. _____ dreamed of building a "Cape to Cairo" railroad.

2. _____ found Livingstone near Lake Tanganyika.

3. _____ was a British administrator in Nigeria.

4. _____ was the first Westerner to travel along the Niger River.

5. _____ was the best-known European explorer of the nineteenth century.

6. _____ defeated Italian forces in Ethiopia.

7. _____ , as King of Belgium, helped to exploit the Congo region.

8. _____ gave up land, unknowingly, to an agent of Cecil Rhodes.

9. _____ built the Suez Canal.

10. _____ suffered defeat by the British in his attempt to maintain his rule in the Sudan.

11. _____ sold large amounts of Suez Canal Company stock to Britain, to help pay off some of his debts.

12. _____ explored much of Central and West Africa, on behalf of France.

III. Map Exercise

Directions: Use the map to locate the place associated with each of the following statements. For each statement, write the *letter* of the place. (An answer may be repeated.) Use the Africa map for questions 1–8, and the Europe map for questions 9–15.

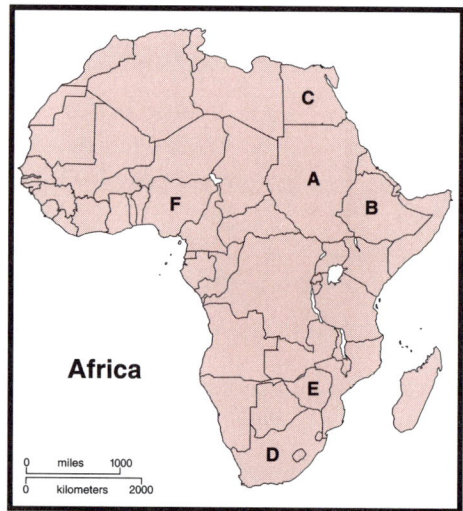
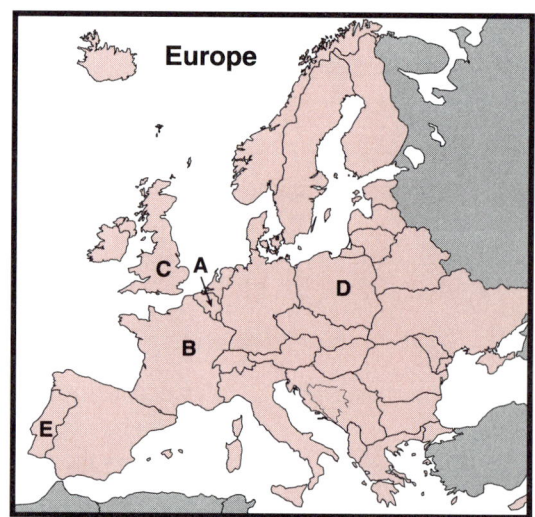

1. _____ The Battle of Adowa took place here.

2. _____ The Fashoda Incident occurred here.

3. _____ This is the closest nation to the Suez Canal.

4. _____ The Great Trek happened here.

5. _____ This is where Zulus fought the British.

6. _____ This was once a colony named after Cecil Rhodes.

7. _____ Place where Frederick Lugard was a colonial administrator.

8. _____ This was a free nation in the nineteenth century, not taken over in the "scramble for Africa"

9. _____ Country that almost went to war with France at Fashoda.

10. _____ This nation was concerned with protecting its "lifeline to India."

11. _____ Country that occupied Morocco, Tunisia, and Algeria.

12. _____ This nation colonized most of the Congo region.

13. _____ This country established a policy of "indirect rule" in its colonies,

14. _____ Nation that embarked on a "civilizing mission" in its colonies.

15. _____ Country that established colonies in Angola and Mozambique.

16. _____ This nation was a late starter in the race for colonies in Africa.

IV. Multiple Choice

Directions: Find the *letter* of the correct answer.

1. Which nation never acquired colonies in Africa?

   (a) Italy   (b) Belgium
   (c) the United States (d) France

2. Taking unfair advantage of a region's resources by a foreign power is known as

   (a) annexation.   (b) administration.
   (c) assimilation.   (d) exploitation.

3. From 1880–1910, which nations were most involved in colonizing Africa?

   (a) oil-rich Middle Eastern nations
   (b) East Asian nations, trying to create new markets
   (c) industrialized Western European nations
   (d) Eastern European nations under Russian control

4. The nations involved in the "scramble for Africa" wanted colonies there mainly because these nations were

   (a) competing for raw materials and markets.
   (b) determined to spread Christianity overseas.
   (c) in need of land for growing populations.
   (d) wanted to complete their geographic knowledge of Africa.

5. The planned partition of Africa occurred at a conference in

   (a) Berlin.   (b) Paris.
   (c) London.   (d) Khartoum.

6. Which is a correct statement about the partitioning of Africa by imperialist nations?

   (a) The continent was divided equally among these nations.
   (b) African unity was encouraged.
   (c) The cultural and ethnic diversity of Africans was disregarded.
   (d) Divisions were based on traditional tribal boundaries.

7. France was not an active colonial power in which part of Africa?

    (a) Northern   (b) Central
    (c) Southern   (d) Western

8. The clash between Western legal traditions and traditional African tribal patterns could be seen in the land arrangement between

    (a) Cecil Rhodes and Logengula.
    (b) Ferdinand de Lesseps and the Zulus.
    (c) Leopold II and Ismail Pasha.
    (d) David Livingstone and the Mahdi.

V. Thought Questions

Directions: Answer the following questions in essay form.

1. European contact with Africa from 1880–1910 was different from the contact between 1500–1800. Describe two differences. For each difference, give one reason.

2. Explain how each of the following either influenced, or was affected by European imperialism in Africa:

    A. Cecil Rhodes
    B. David Livingstone
    C. Ismail Pasha
    D. Lobengula
    E. Boers
    F. Zulus
    G. René Callie
    H. Leopold II

3. Each of the following represents an imperialist policy followed by one or more European nations in Africa. For each policy, give a definition; name one European nation that followed this policy; and give one reason for, or one goal of, this policy.

    A. indirect rule
    B. direct rule
    C. exploitation
    D. civilizing mission
    E. paternalism

CHAPTER 28

Imperialism in Asia

As we now turn to Asia we see very similar patterns to those in Africa. The military might of Europe due to the Industrial Revolution allowed it to take advantage of a militarily weaker area. The British flag was seen around the globe. The saying, "The sun never sets on the British Empire," was certainly accurate. The French were also active in their imperialistic goals, with holdings in many parts of the world. The Spanish, Dutch, and Portuguese held on to their small pieces. Germany and Italy were forced to play a smaller game due to their late arrival on the scene. A new player, the United States, obtained the Philippines after defeating Spain. The European nations also took advantage of the fact that there was little unity in the areas where they took control. The peoples that lived there were culturally intermixed and so a feeling of true nationalism did not really exist.

The Middle East was divided between Britain and France after World War I. The League of Nations gave over this area on the pretext that the area would be prepared for independence. The area that was Palestine was promised as a homeland to the Jewish people by the British, who then reneged on that promise. It was not in the British interest to anger the Arabs who had the oil. This area saw four wars after the state of Israel was created in 1948.

South Asia

Who was Lord Cornwallis? Most Americans know him as the English general who surrendered to George Washington in 1781, at the Battle of Yorktown. This surrender marked the end of the American Revolution and thus the end of British control over its thirteen colonies in North America. As you know, these thirteen colonies went on to form the United States of America. You also know that George Washington went on to become the country's first president. But, do you know what happened to Lord Cornwallis after the Battle of Yorktown?

Most Americans cannot answer this question, probably because U.S. history textbooks usually do not mention him after the chapter on the Revolution. However, people in England and India know about him. This is because he had an important position in India, having gone there on behalf of the British East India

Company. He was a governor-general there as well as a military commander, at a time in the late 1700s when the British were slowly gaining power in South Asia. Although today, with the British no longer in control of India, it is of interest to find a Cornwallis Road in downtown New Delhi—India's capital city!

The India that Cornwallis saw was not an independent united nation-state. It was a geographic expression, a place, just like Italy was, prior to becoming a unified nation. British authority in this place called India reached a point where India became the largest colony in the British Empire. It was even termed the "jewel of the Empire" as well as the "jewel of the crown." It covered a huge area in South Asia, geographically called the Indian Subcontinent, from which the present day nations of India, Pakistan, and Bangladesh were carved.

Early British Involvement, 1600–1858

The British East India Company was formed as a private company in 1600, under a charter granted by Queen Elizabeth I. In 1613, it received permission to trade in India from the ruling Mughals. From this time until 1858, the company exercised powers usually associated with a government. It had, for example, its own private army. One of its employees, Robert Clive, led military forces to victories over both French and native armies. The French had competed with Britain for influence in South Asia, just as was the case in North America. The victories

Chapter 28 Chronology

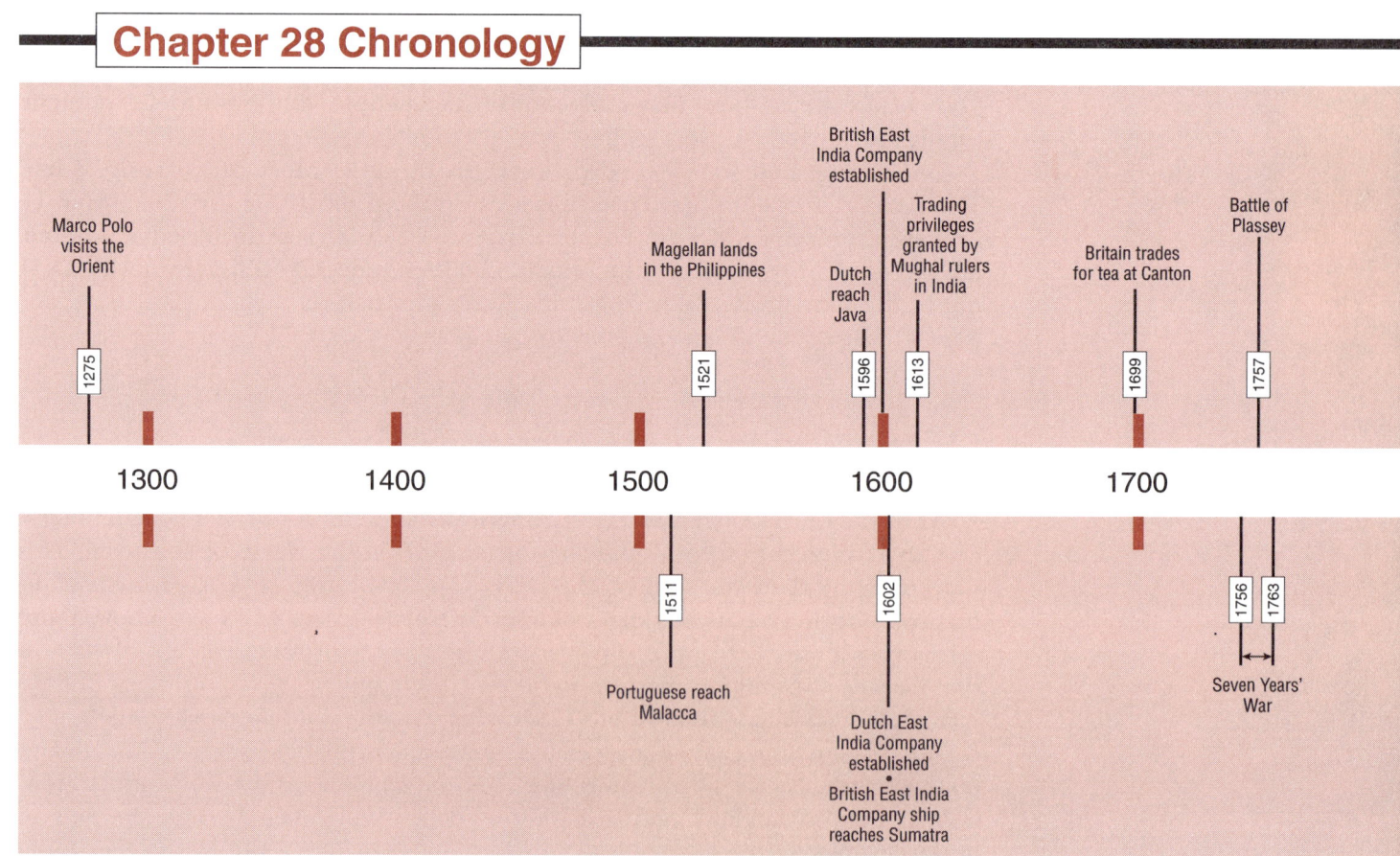

Marco Polo visits the Orient — 1275

Magellan lands in the Philippines — 1521

Dutch reach Java — 1596

British East India Company established / Trading privileges granted by Mughal rulers in India — 1613

Britain trades for tea at Canton — 1699

Battle of Plassey — 1757

1300   1400   1500   1600   1700

Portuguese reach Malacca — 1511

Dutch East India Company established / British East India Company ship reaches Sumatra — 1602

Seven Years' War — 1756–1763

over the French came during the Seven Years' War (1756–1763), a true world war, as fighting occurred in both America and Asia. The most famous of these victories in India was at Plassey, in 1757. Consequently, the British became the dominant and unofficial political power in the subcontinent. It was soon thereafter that Lord Cornwallis came to India.

Under his leadership, up to 1793, and that of succeeding governors-general, into the 1800s, the East India Company expanded its control in South Asia. It was able to do this for a number of reasons:

1. The region had hundreds of small states and no central government. The Mughal rulers controlled much, but not all, of the vast region.
2. There was religious divisiveness among the Indians. Tension existed between the two major groups, Hindus and Muslims, thereby restricting any cooperation among them against the British.
3. Linguistic divisiveness also existed. There was no common language; several languages and hundreds of dialects were spoken in the region.
4. Militarily, the Indians were unable to stand up to superior British arms and organization.

The Sepoy Mutiny In 1857, a key event took place in India that was to affect sharply the relationship between the British and the Indians. This was the Sepoy Mutiny. Also known as the Sepoy Rebellion, it was fought against the British for both religious and politi-

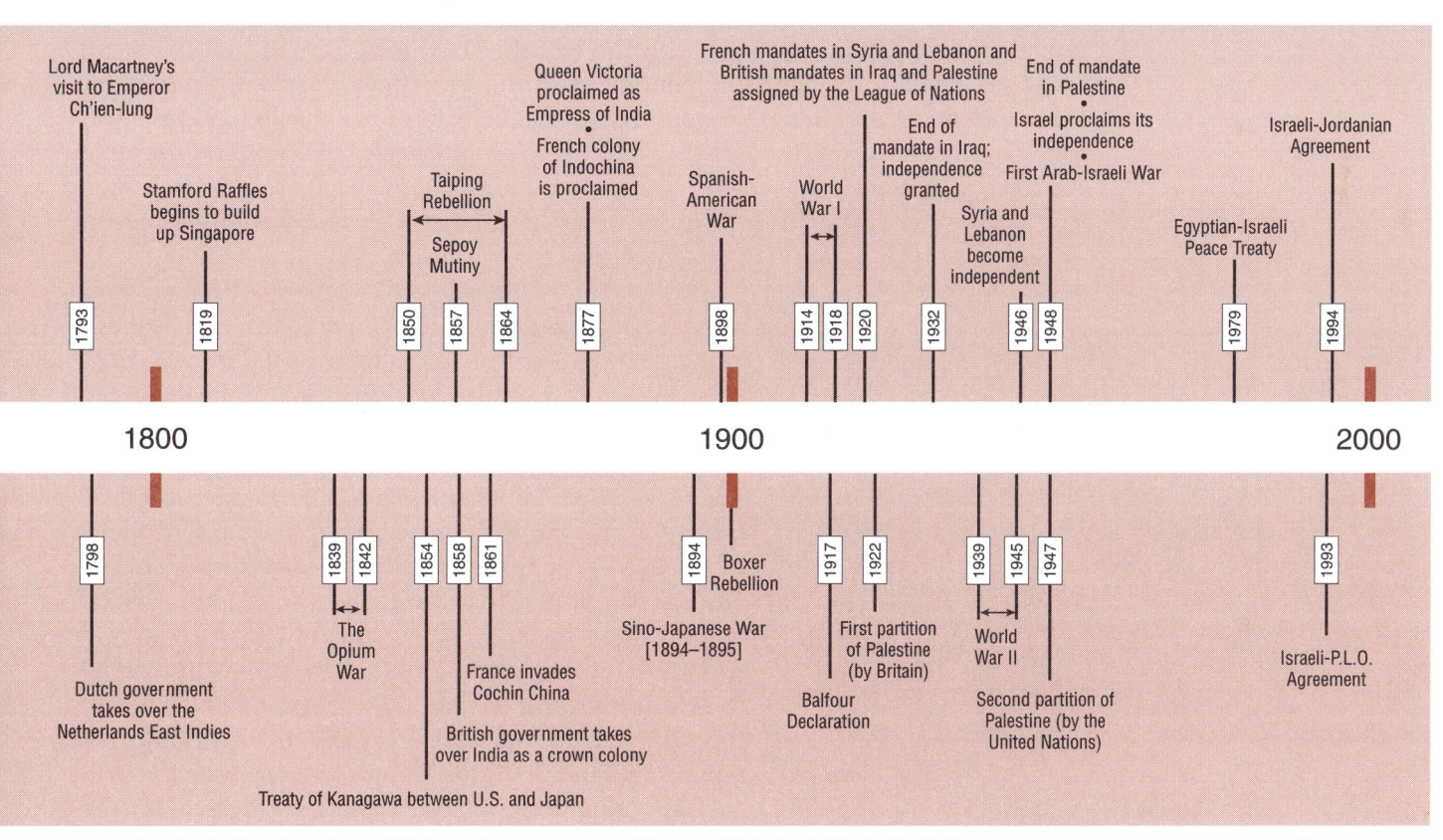

cal reasons. It began when Indians in the British army (**sepoys**) suspected that the grease used on bullet cartridges came from cows and pigs. If so, to bite into these cartridges, as was necessary when loading them, would have violated Hindu and Muslim beliefs, as Hindus believe cows are sacred and Muslims are forbidden from eating pork. These beliefs led to a mutiny that gradually spread beyond the armed forces and grew into an anti-Western movement. It attracted Indian princes and peasants. (In fact, some Indian historians view the Sepoy Mutiny as a war of independence.) Eventually, it was severely put down. Nevertheless, the East India Company was abolished. In 1858, it was replaced as a governing body by the British crown along with Parliament. India then became a crown colony.

The British Government's Colonial Policy in India

British authority following the Sepoy Mutiny covered almost 70 percent of the subcontinent. The British raj (rule) expanded, using a variety of methods. In some instances, outright military subjugation (forcible takeover) occurred. Treaties and alliances were often made between the British and a prince of a state, who was an enemy of another prince. Special favors were also given to "cooperative" princes. These were successful examples of "divide and conquer" tactics.

Indirect rule was the general policy in India, as had been the case with British possessions in Africa. In London, a minister from Parliament was given responsibility for Indian affairs. Under the minister was a viceroy in India who carried out directives. And under the viceroy were several British officials, or advisers, who watched over local matters but also left a large measure of control with the local rulers or princes. All of these people, British and Indian, were indirectly responsible to Queen Victoria. In 1877, she was recognized by Parliament as Empress of India.

For Britain, India was viewed as a source of economic wealth. Manufacturers of textiles, machines, and other products looked upon India as a vast market for their goods. This development of a market, however, harmed those Indian producers who could not compete with the British. Many local Indian industries suffered as they did not have the technology of the foreigners for mass production, nor could they sell items at competitive prices. British investment helped build up tea plantations as well as the steel and cement industries. The colonial government improved transportation by constructing railroads, bridges, and roadways. The number of hospitals and schools increased. A civil service system was introduced that provided for efficient government operations.

In social and cultural matters, the British sought to impose their own ways. They introduced the English language, wanting Indians to learn it. Those who mastered it could aspire to positions in the civil service system. The growth of churches was evidence of missionary activity. British style in architecture and gardens was soon apparent. The British attempted to make "brown Englishmen" out of selected Indians, who would be given a British-style education in England. It was hoped that these few would adopt British cultural customs and values and return to India and spread them in the population. The British also acted to stamp out those Indian cultural practices that they thought were wrong. Such an ethnocentric attitude resulted in the abolition of suttee. This was a Hindu custom whereby a widow would burn herself on the funeral pyre of her dead husband. To the British,

Many British officials lived very well in India. As an example, the wife of a British judge is here being attended to by two Indian women who served as maids.

such an act was considered to be suicide and contrary to Christian ideals and therefore was outlawed. Attempts were also made to end the Indian custom of killing unwanted baby girls (female infanticide).

British involvement in India grew rapidly, especially after completion of the Suez Canal in 1869. The trip there by ship was still, however, long and difficult. Life in India, with different climate and health conditions from those of Europe, could be challenging. British tombstones, for example, found as far north as Peshawar (in present-day Pakistan) and as far south as Madras (in present-day India), tell of English men, women, and children who died of cholera, malaria, and other diseases. Some of these tombs in Madras can be found in a historic building, St. Mary's Church, built by the British. It still stands today, with a sign outside proclaiming it as "the oldest Anglican church east of Suez." Inside the church, among several paintings, is a portrait of a famous member of the British East India Company, Elihu Yale (1649–1721). This is the same person for whom Yale University in New Haven, Connecticut, in the United States is named.

Thus, we can see how British imperialism brought a connecting link between three continents. Elihu Yale, a man from England, part of *Europe*, traveled to British India, in *Asia*, and is remembered for being a benefactor at a great university in a British colony in *North America*. The final note in this tri-continental historical drama occurred in the 1950s when Chester Bowles, a Yale graduate and the American ambassador to India, went to St. Mary's Church to place a plaque near the portrait of Elihu Yale. Thus, a citizen of the United States of America (a nation whose roots were as British colonies) traveled to India (a nation that was once a British colony) to honor a native of the former mother country of both colonial settlements. The connecting link involving Chester Bowles in the twentieth century had roots in the connecting link involving Lord Cornwallis in the eighteenth century, whom we mentioned at the start of this chapter.

East Asia

When people gather to have big, fancy dinners, they may do this at home or in a large restaurant, or a catering hall. The occasion may be a happy family event, or a celebration of a holiday, or an important event such as a wedding or graduation. The food that is eaten may very well be served on expensive and beautiful dishes called china. This name was originally used by Englishmen over two hundred years ago to describe the skillfully designed porcelain and pottery made in China. Such items were much in demand by Europeans at the time. The desire to obtain these and other items was one of many reasons for European interest in China. This interest was eventually to grow into imperialistic activities.

China, along with Japan and Korea, is in a part of the world referred to as East Asia, the Orient, or the Far East. The region to the south of China can also be called the Orient, but is better known as Southeast Asia. European imperialism was to affect this part of the world also. In this section, we will trace the European contact with East Asia.

China

The major European imperialistic involvement in China occurred primarily in the nineteenth and twentieth centuries. However, interest in China goes back much earlier. In 1275, for example, Marco Polo's trip to the Orient stirred much excitement among Europeans. During the Age of Discovery, ships of Portugal were able to sail to China. They reached there in 1514 and set up a trading station at Macao in 1557. In 1699, the British were purchasing tea at the port of Canton (known today as Guangzhou). The British East India Company was very active in the tea trade, as the demand in London and elsewhere in the British Isles for tea increased enormously.

For the Chinese, trade with the British and other Europeans in the eighteenth century was very profitable. Along with tea, the chief Chinese exports to Europe were silk, sugar, and ginger. Yet, the Chinese did not want Europeans to trade outside of the Canton area. This restriction, as well as the many regulations imposed upon the European traders by the Chinese government, aroused resentment. The Chinese looked down upon the Europeans, considered them to be barbarians, and had little desire for European goods.

These kinds of Chinese ethnocentric attitudes were evident in the reaction to a visit in 1793 by Lord George Macartney, a representative of King George III of Britain. Macartney had come to see the Emperor Ch'ien-lung, of the Ch'ing Dynasty, hoping to get increased trade and better contacts for British businessmen. He was shocked and saddened by the Emperor's response. The Emperor refused the foreigner's requests, noting that China had no need "to import any product produced by barbarians." This refusal, conveyed in a letter to King George, was upsetting to the British. Another reason for their discontent with the Chinese was the fact that they had to pay for Chinese goods with large amounts of silver. This form of payment was necessary, as the Chinese did not want to buy British products. For the British, an outflow of silver was considered harmful to their economy.

The Opium War (1839–1842) This commercial relationship began to change dramatically in the early 1800s. The British realized that there was a market for opium in China. This narcotic drug was mass produced in India, and sold by British merchants to the Chinese. Payment for the opium was made in goods and in ever-increasing amounts of silver. This drain of silver, as well as the injurious effects of opium-smoking on the Chinese population, angered the Chinese government. Accordingly, it banned all commerce in opium. Unable to enforce the ban, the government destroyed a stockpile of opium at a Canton warehouse in 1839. The British responded by sending warships to China. The Opium War (1839–1842) had begun!

The Chinese forces were no match for the British. Superior weaponry and organization led to a British victory. The resulting Treaty of Nanking in 1842 completely changed China's relations with the Western World. The chief provisions were as follows:

1. China consented to open five ports for trade, including Canton and Shanghai;
2. The British were given the island of Hong Kong;
3. China was to pay an **indemnity** (an amount of money for wrongdoing) to Britain to make up for destroyed opium;
4. British merchants and government officials could live in the five "treaty ports"; and

During the Opium Wars, British naval and ground forces overwhelmed the Chinese. Superior arms and military tactics resulted in many victories for the British.

5. The British were granted the right of **extraterritoriality**. This meant that a British person in the treaty ports would be subject to British law, not Chinese law. In addition, if such a person was accused of committing an offense, he or she would be tried in British courts, not Chinese courts.

These provisions were humiliating for the Chinese. The Treaty of Nanking was the first of what would be called "the unequal treaties," for other nations forced China to sign treaties granting them the same trade rights Britain had gained. These other nations included France, Russia, and Germany. During the remainder of the nineteenth and into the early twentieth centuries, each of these four nations acquired a **sphere of influence** in different areas of China. They forced the Manchu rulers (leaders of the Ch'ing Dynasty) to give them economic privileges in these areas. These privileges included the right to build mines, factories, and railroads, and to search for minerals. They also obtained land on which to build military bases to protect their spheres of influence.

The Sino-Japanese War

Non-European nations were also active in China. These were the United States and Japan. The United States was granted commercial privileges, although it did not acquire a sphere of influence. It did propose an "Open Door Policy," whereby all foreign nations would enjoy equal trading rights in China. The other nations accepted this idea in theory, but did not really honor it in practice. One of these, an Asian newcomer to imperialism, was Japan. Having built up its economic and military power in the late 1800s, Japan was able to defeat China in the 1894–1895 Sino-Japanese War. Japan took over the island of Taiwan along with other Chinese territory.

The Boxer Rebellion

China's inability to defend itself against imperialism caused unrest among its people. The government, headed by the Empress Tz'u-hsi, (r. 1898–1908) was also perceived to be corrupt and incapable of improving the lives of the people. Consequently, violence broke out in 1900, led by a secret Chinese society called the "Society of Harmonious Fists" or Boxers. This Boxer Rebellion, secretly supported by the Empress, was aimed mainly at driving out foreigners from China. Many foreigners were killed by the Boxers before a combined army from six nations put an end to the fighting. Further agony followed for China, as the Manchu government was forced in a 1901 treaty to pay large indemnities and to let foreigners have expanded military and commercial powers. The United States returned most of its indemnity money to China, thereby earning some measure of goodwill.

Why Did China Become a Victim of Imperialism?

As a result of all the imperialistic activity described above, China appeared to be a humiliated and partially dismembered country at the start of the twentieth century. It became a victim of imperialism for several reasons:
1. Its mineral resources attracted investors.
2. Foreigners visualized its large population as both a market for the sale of goods, as well as a source of cheap labor.
3. A great demand existed in the West for China's silk and tea.

4. The Manchu rulers did not have sufficient military power to repel the foreigners. Their rule was inefficient and corrupt. The country lacked the unity and centralized control necessary to protect itself.

5. The Taiping Rebellion (1850–1864), the longest and bloodiest war anywhere in the world during the nineteenth century, caused great devastation in China. It was led by Southern Chinese, who, for economic, political, and religious reasons, wanted to overthrow the government. Although the Ch'ing Dynasty was able to put down this revolt, the dynasty was severely weakened. Its inability to protect foreign citizens during the fighting gave yet another excuse for foreign troops to come to China and take advantage of the country. Military skirmishes took place, followed by more "unequal treaties," and more acquisitions of land and economic privileges.

6. The broadest and most profound reason contributing to China's victimization was, indirectly, its strong sense of pride and ethnocentrism. For centuries, China had been an advanced and prosperous country. Its achievements in science, politics, literature, and the arts were notable. It saw itself as the most powerful and civilized region on earth, and isolated itself. It looked down upon others, not wanting to be affected by any outside "barbarian" customs. Such attitudes, however, prevented it from learning from others and caused it to be hostile rather than open to contact with foreigners.

How Did Japan Avoid Becoming a Victim of Imperialism? China's neighbor Japan, however, adopted a different attitude toward relations with Westerners in the nineteenth century. While Japan also viewed Westerners as "barbarians," it nevertheless recognized their superiority in weapons, transportation, and technology. It realized that there was much it could learn from them. In addition, it was fearful that hostility to foreigners and a refusal to open commercial contacts with them might subject it to the kind of victimization that China had suffered. Accordingly, in 1854, it signed the Treaty of Kanagawa with the American, Commodore Matthew Perry. This treaty opened up Japanese ports for trade, and was soon followed by similar treaties with Britain, France, Holland, and Russia.

With the Meiji Restoration of 1868, Japan embarked on a policy of modernization. It had avoided becoming a victim of imperialism. Indeed, as its economy improved, and as it sent young men overseas to learn Western ways in arms, government, and technology, it soon became a colonial power itself. Appropriately, it viewed neighboring Korea and China as targets. Japan's subsequent desire to extend its colonial domains to all of East and Southeast Asia would bring it into conflict with the United States and other Western nations. This conflict was a cause of World War II. (See Chapter 32, "World War II.")

Southeast Asia

The name "Southeast Asia" is a relatively recent one. Prior to the twentieth century, various parts of the region had been known by other names—i.e., the Spice Islands, the East Indies, and Indochina. Some parts of Southeast Asia are on the Asian mainland, while others are islands in the form of **archipelagoes**. The best known of the latter are the present-day nations of Indonesia and the Philippines. Most mainlanders of Southeast Asia live on either the Malay or Indochina peninsulas.

Malaysian money shows British influence. English words are mixed in with Malay words.

Burma (now Myanmar) issued currency that included a typical fishing scene, along with Burmese and English words.

This Hong Kong stamp shows both British and Chinese influences. After Hong Kong reverts to Chinese control in 1997, it is doubtful that new stamps will have any sign of British impact.

Prior to Malaysia's independence, it was known as the British colony of Malaya. Accordingly, Britain issued stamps such as this one.

The Dutch queen is pictured on a stamp used in the former Dutch West Indies. The colony became the nation of present-day Indonesia.

In the twentieth century, even after it became free, the Philippines issued stamps that contained language of both its former colonizer and occupier. These were Spain and the United States.

Indonesian currency has reflected a mixture of Indonesian history, both as a Dutch colony and as a free nation. The picture is of Sukarno, the first president. There are also some Dutch words.

European nations were initially interested in the spices from the region. One of the aims of Christopher Columbus in 1492 was to reach the "Spice Islands" in the "Indies." In later years, European interest was focused on mineral deposits such as tin and oil, and agricultural products such as rubber, tobacco, tea, and coffee. During the age of the New Imperialism, Europeans also sought to control land in Southeast Asia in order to protect and have better access to their holdings in other parts of Asia. While Portugal and Spain were the first European nations to establish contact here, the major colonization was done by the Dutch, British, and French. Among non-European nations, the United States and Japan were colonial rulers for short periods of time.

There are ten independent nations today in Southeast Asia. With the exception of Thailand, every one of these was colonized at one point in its history. The colonizers were, as we have just seen, from different nations. This is one reason why this corner of Asia is sometimes described as a cultural "patchwork quilt." The sequence and pattern of involvement by European nations in Southeast Asia is similar in some ways to their involvement in the Americas, Africa, and other parts of Asia.

Portugal and Spain

Marco Polo's writings about his trip to Asia in the second half of the thirteenth century excited readers with accounts of both East and Southeast Asian lands. The Portuguese, navigational leaders in the Age of Exploration, reached India in 1498 as a result of Vasco da Gama's historic voyage. They soon moved on to the East Indies, reaching the Malay peninsula in 1511 and some other areas shortly thereafter. They were able to put down resistance by Muslims who had controlled the sea routes, and were able to profit handsomely from the trade in spices such as nutmeg, cloves, pepper, and mace. The Portuguese had then pioneered an all-water route eastward from Europe to the Indies. Although they gained some small amounts of land, they were unable to construct large-scale colonial settlements.

The Spanish also wished to establish an all-water route to the region. They did so, thanks to the voyage of Magellan. Sailing westward across the Pacific Ocean, he landed in what is now the Philippines in 1521, and claimed the islands for Spain. The Spaniards were to rule here for over three hundred years, spreading Christianity and Spanish customs. Spanish governance over the Philippines was made chiefly from Mexico, Spain's major colony in the Americas. Following its pattern of colonial rule in the New World, the king of Spain gave large amounts of land to religious orders and other Spaniards. Natives who worked these lands endured much exploitation and hardship. Spain lost the Philippines to the United States as a result of the Spanish-American War of 1898.

The Netherlands

The first Dutch sailors to reach Southeast Asia arrived in 1596. They landed on the island of Java, part of present-day Indonesia. Their trade in spices was profitable, and grew quickly. To conduct these commercial transactions, the Dutch East India Company was formed in 1602. The Dutch were able to keep away Portuguese and Spanish competition. However, because of severe mismanagement, the company went bankrupt in 1799. The Dutch government then took over control in Java, Sumatra, and neighboring islands, thus creating the colony called the Dutch East Indies or Netherlands East Indies.

The Dutch then introduced a practice known as the culture system. It was designed as an economic policy whereby crops would be cultivated for export. It required native farmers to grow export crops such as tea, quinine, coffee, and sugar on portions of their land. Local chieftains would assign quotas as ordered by the Dutch, and gather the crops for sale. The Dutch would pay very low prices, some money then going to the chieftain and hardly anything to the farmers. The Dutch would then sell the crops on the world market for high prices and thus make tremendous profits. The system really became a policy of forced labor. In addition, it denied farmers the opportunity to use the land as they wished. They were not able to produce sufficient crops for their own local markets nor much food for themselves.

At the start of the twentieth century, Dutch colonial administrators sought to improve the lives of Indonesians by creating the ethical policy. This was planned to make certain welfare services available. Better schools and health facilities were built, along with paved roads and irrigation projects for rice cultivation. Politically, the Dutch pursued a policy of direct rule. Indonesians were given little say in the affairs of their land. Dutch rule was interrupted in 1942, during World War II, when the Japanese occupied the colony. The Japanese exploited the land for its resources and left in 1945, upon their defeat in the war. The postwar developments in Indonesia will be examined in Chapter 29, "Independence and Decolonization."

Great Britain

In 1969, the nation of Singapore, near the Malay peninsula, had huge celebrations of what it labeled its one hundred and fiftieth anniversary. Although this island nation became independent in 1963, Singapore dates it birth to the year 1819. This was when Sir Stamford Raffles, an employee of the British East India Company, established the site as a trading post. The site was strategically vital, as it commanded the Straits of Malacca. This waterway was part of the sea route to China.

However, the British had already been in Southeast Asia for over two hundred years prior to Raffles's presence. A British East India Company ship had reached Sumatra in 1602. The British competed with the Dutch for domination of the spice trade. Eventually, they focused their attention on the region of the Malay peninsula and left Sumatra and Java to the Dutch.

The nineteenth century witnessed significant British colonial advances in the region. Singapore and former Dutch Malacca became the Straits Settlement in 1824. In the 1870s, four sultans who ruled small areas on the Malay peninsula, fearful of attacks from Siam (current-day Thailand), entered into agreements with the British. The British agreed to give them protection, while obtaining greater commercial privileges. This action by the British was similar to the "divide and conquer" patterns that had occurred in India. In 1895, the sultans agreed to unite their areas as the Federated Malay States under British authority. Other sultans did not join the federation, but agreed to some form of British control while retaining their powers. Thus, another form of indirect rule was established.

In a short period of time, the Straits Settlement, the Federated Malay States, and the unfederated states became known as Malaya. The total British effort in the region—political, economic, and military—yielded rewards. The tin and rubber produced in Malaya led to much prosperity.

The other British possession in Southeast Asia was Burma. The western part of Burma was subdued with military force in 1826, in order to protect India's border. The rest of Burma was taken over in 1885, as the British were concerned about possible French penetration into the area and wanted to further shore up protection of eastern India. A British governor administered Burma, with hereditary rulers keeping some control over local affairs.

France

As was the case with Britain and Holland, France organized an East India Company in the 1600s. Early on in that era, France was active in Cochin China. This is in present-day Vietnam. Both traders and missionaries were on the company's ships. In 1627, Alexandré de Rhodes, a French missionary, adapted the Vietnamese language to the Roman alphabet. With his knowledge of the region, he paved the way for further French influence. Both commercial and missionary activities slowly increased until the early 1800s. However, persecution by the Vietnamese emperors of both missionaries and their converts rose alarmingly. In the 1850s, the Emperor Tu-duc refused France's request for religious liberty and a trading post at Hue. As a result, in 1861 French forces invaded Cochin China, captured the main city of Saigon (now Ho Chi Minh City), and established a colony. In 1863, France announced itself to be the protector of Cambodia as well as other parts of what is now Vietnam.

Imperialistic activity then quickened with the designation of a French civilian governor in Cochin China in 1879, and the creation of a protectorate over Annam and Tonkin (other parts of present-day Vietnam) and Laos. In 1887, France declared all these regions together to be the colony of Indochina. As was true in its African colonies, France pursued a policy of direct rule in Indochina. The powerful French governor-general followed directives from superiors in Paris, and made sure that these were carried out by French subordinates. Rice and rubber cultivation enriched the Frenchmen who came to Indochina while very little of the wealth reached the native workers. France considered Indochina to be an actual part of French territory and even built parts of Saigon to make it look similar to Paris. This colonial attitude of the French was to spell trouble for it in the 1950s.

France had thoughts about moving into Siam (Thailand), as did Britain. The Siamese recognized this, and would frequently alternate their favoritism toward one nation and then toward the other. Because of this clever maneuvering, and because neither France nor Britain wanted the other to dominate the region, Siam was able to remain independent. It was the only part of Southeast Asia to escape colonization.

The growth of European power in East and Southeast Asia was similar in several ways to what we saw happen in Africa and South Asia. The "scramble" for land in the Orient occurred over a long period of time, for a host of reasons. While major wars did not erupt there between the European powers themselves, those powers nevertheless did have to confront a non-European power in the 1940s who also sought land there—Japan. The nature of that struggle and its consequences for independence movements will be studied shortly (Chapter 29, "Independence and Decolonization"). However, we have one more "stop" to make in Asia in the current chapter. That will be westward, in the region generally referred to as the Middle East.

The Middle East

The Middle East is a geographic term that refers mostly to the areas of West Asia and Northeast Africa. European contact with these areas has been ongoing for thousands of years, examples being the periods of the Punic Wars, Alexander the Great, the Roman Empire, the Byzantine Empire, the Crusades, and the Ottoman Turks. The major European imperialistic involvement in modern times was within the last one hundred years. It is this time period that we will now study. Our study will only concern the Asian portion of the Middle East, as we have already "traveled" to the African portion. (See Chapter 27, "Imperialism in Africa.")

Among many factors that made the Middle East a target for European Imperialism were two specific ones:

1. The Middle East was a strategic location as the crossroads of three continents—Europe, Africa, and Asia. With completion of the Suez Canal in 1869, the Middle East became a vital link in the water route between Europe and Asia.

2. The Middle East was also a source of oil. The world's greatest oil reserves are in the lands near the Persian Gulf.

Over a period of time, these lands and other regions of the Middle East had become part of the Ottoman Empire (1453–1918). The Empire gradually weakened during the 1800s, becoming known as the "sick man of Europe." (See Chapter 25, "Discontent in the Austro-Hungarian and Ottoman Empires.") The ruling Ottoman Turks were corrupt, inefficient, and unresponsive to the needs of the many different peoples under their authority. The final blow to the Empire came in 1918 with the end of World War I. The Turks had fought on the side of Germany and Austria-Hungary and lost the war. Consequently, the Middle Eastern lands that belonged to the Empire, and which were mainly inhabited by Arabs, were taken away. They were placed under the control of the newly formed League of Nations. From 1920 onward, the league created **mandates** in some of these lands: Palestine, Iraq, and Syria. A mandate was permission given to a nation to rule over a region temporarily, until the region was considered ready for independence. Mandates in the Middle East were given to Britain and France.

Great Britain

Britain received mandates over Iraq and Palestine. Although the mandate in Iraq did not begin officially until 1922, Britain had already developed contact with this region several years earlier. It had obtained **concessions** for oil in Iraq, as well as in present-day Kuwait and Iran. This arrangement permitted Britain to explore for and produce oil, while sharing the profits with the region's local rulers. At the time of such arrangements, prior to World War I, the British were well aware that the native Arabs did not like being under the authority of the Ottoman Turks. As a result, Britain befriended the Iraqis by supporting their anti-Turkish sentiments.

Lord Balfour was the author of the famous declaration that bears his name. He attempted to promote a policy in Palestine that would be acceptable to both Arabs and Jews.

As long as Britain was able to extract profits from oil, it made little attempt to impose its culture on the Arabs in Iraq. Indirect rule was the policy. The mandate ended in 1932, although British advisers continued to maintain a role in Iraqi political and economic affairs.

The Balfour Declaration and the British Mandate in Palestine

The British mandate in Palestine proved to be very troublesome, presenting serious problems not found in the mandate in Iraq. This was because both Jews and Arabs had wanted to create nation-states in the region. During World War I, British forces defeated the Turks and took over Palestine. Britain made territorial promises to both Jews and Arabs, and issued an important document in 1917 called the Balfour Declaration. Named after Lord Balfour, the English statesman, the document proposed that Great Britain would view "...with favor the establishment in Palestine of a national home for the Jewish people, ...it being understood that nothing shall be done which may prejudice the civil and religious rights of...non-Jewish communities."

Zionists, those Jews who pressed for some part of Palestine as a Jewish homeland, saw hope in the Balfour Declaration. Arab nationalists wanted the land for their own, and were against giving any part to Zionists. Fighting broke out between both groups, as well as between each group and the British. In 1922, Britain partitioned Palestine by itself, taking about 77 percent of it and establishing this as the Arab kingdom of Transjordan. To sever such a large area for a new Arab nation was a surprising decision, especially as no Jewish homeland was established. Transjordan was given limited freedom, and was promised eventual independence by the British. This promise was fulfilled in 1946, with the region to take the name of Jordan. The British stayed on good terms with the Jordanians, helping to train an armed force known as the Arab Legion.

The United Nations Partition Plan for Palestine

Chaim Weizmann was a brilliant chemist who worked with the British in World War I. He helped to draw up the Balfour Declaration and became the first president of Israel (1948–1952).

In 1922, the remaining 23 percent of Palestine, lying to the west along the Mediterranean Sea, was still a mandate under British control. It remained so until 1947, without any Jewish homeland being created. By that time, fighting had increased and Britain decided to let the new international organization, the United Nations (U.N.), resolve the political status of the region. The United Nations decided to partition this remaining portion of Palestine in November 1947, giving part to the Zionists as a Jewish state and part to be a Palestinian Arab state. The city of Jerusalem, holy to both Jews and Muslims, was to be under U.N. supervision.

Jews accepted the partition plan and declared the state of Israel in May 1948. The British mandate in Palestine had come to an end. However, Arabs both in Palestine and in the nations neighboring Palestine rejected the partition plan. In May 1948, twenty-four hours after Israel proclaimed its independence, six Arab nations declared war on Israel. Although the combined Arab forces were larger and better equipped, they were unable to accomplish their goal of destroying Israel. A truce arranged by the U.N. ended the fighting temporarily.

Since 1949, three other major wars have been fought between the Israelis and the Arabs. Israel maintained its existence, successfully defending it in each of these. In 1979, Egypt became the first Arab nation to sign a peace treaty with Israel and to grant it recognition. In 1994, Jordan became the second Arab nation to act similarly. The other Arab nations, however, are still technically at war with Israel. In the last decade of the twentieth century, some optimistic signs of peace in the area appeared on the horizon. Peace talks between Israel, Palestinian Arabs, and some Arab nations were held in Spain and the United States in 1991,

King Hussein of Jordan (1935–present) is seen here reviewing soldiers of his Arab Legion. Having suffered devastating defeats by Israel when he sent troops to attack that nation in 1948 and 1967, he signed a peace treaty with Israel in 1994.

Between 1945 and 1948, Jewish immigrants such as these Holocaust survivors hoped to settle in Palestine. Very often, pro-Arab British mandate authorities refused them entry.

1992, and 1993. A historic agreement between Israel and the Palestine Liberation Organization (P.L.O.), claiming to represent Palestinian Arabs, was signed in September 1993. By allowing a limited amount of self-rule to the Palestinians in some areas, the agreement did much to ease tensions in the Middle East. If other Arab nations follow the examples of Egypt and Jordan, and recognize Israel, hopes for settlement of what has become known as the Arab-Israeli dispute may be realized by the end of the 1990s.

France

In 1920, France was given mandates in Lebanon and Syria. However, French involvement in these regions goes back to the sixteenth century. France's commercial and cultural ties to the region became so strong, that by 1900, her economic involvement in the area was the greatest of any European power. In addition, the Ottoman rulers had let France become the protector of all Catholics in the regions; the French language was also widely spoken.

Nevertheless there was resistance to French mandatory control in Syria and Lebanon. An independence-seeking resistance movement was put down by French troops in the 1920s. Consequently, France established overall colonial control of both Syria and Lebanon. The two regions, sometimes referred to as the Levant, became part of the French Empire. All education in public schools was conducted in French. French was substituted for Arabic as the official language. Under the French-controlled economy Beirut became a prosperous city. French authority was easy to impose because of the various religious and ethnic groups in Syria and Lebanon, including the Kurds, Maronite Christians, Druze, and diverse Muslim groups. The French befriended each of these, thus following a policy of "divide and conquer" as well as "divide and rule."

Health services, transportation, and communication were improved with the French presence. Yet, the desire for independence lingered into the 1940s. In

Jordanian officials met with Ralph Bunche (fourth from left) in 1949, to discuss Arab-Israeli issues. Bunche was an African-American who acted upon behalf of the United Nations to bring peace to the Middle East.

1946, France granted independence to both colonies. Factors leading to this included the impact of World War II (1939–1945) on a weary France, the wishes of the colonized peoples, and pressure from the United Nations and France's allies.

The Middle East of today bears effects of European Imperialism. These are not as pronounced, however, as they are in Africa and other parts of Asia. The main reason for this contrast is that European colonialism in the Middle East came later and ended sooner than was the case elsewhere. The decline of European colonialism in Asia, as well as in Africa, was most evident in the years following World War II. In almost all instances, this decline was accompanied peacefully. It was not marked by widespread outbreaks of violent rebellion, as was true of the American Revolution, when the thirteen American colonies fought against British rule in the eighteenth century. In the twentieth century, the struggle against various forms of imperialism, along with the emergence of new, independent nations, was a crucial turning point in world history. To appreciate its significance, we move on to the next chapter. Appropriately, its title is "Independence and Decolonization."

Summary

If any lesson should be learned from this chapter it is that a nation cannot stand still. As you know, China at one time was way ahead of Europe in intellectual development, but at a certain point decided that further advancement was no longer necessary. So China stagnated while the Europeans went through their Renaissance and Industrial Revolution. If you stand still, you go backwards in relation to others; a nation cannot afford to do that. It is interesting that Japan exists as a model for us to look at. The Japanese had also closed themselves off to Western influences. After Perry arrived they soon adopted the ways of the West and became imperialists on their own. Their history during the late nineteenth and twentieth centuries was very different than that of their neighbors.

We can also see possible problems starting to develop. There were jealousies among nations as France was envious of Britain, Germany was envious of France and Britain, and Japan wanted to have sole control over what it saw as its area. Nations seemed not to care about the people's welfare in the areas they controlled. These people were pawns in a nationalistic power play. As we move ahead in our study this will become more evident.

CHAPTER 28

Review Exercises

Imperialism in South Asia

I. Matching

Directions: Match the words in Column A with the *correct description* in Column B.

Column A
1. raj
2. mutiny
3. suttee
4. sepoy

Column B
(a) a rebellion
(b) period of British rule in India
(c) Indian soldier in the British army
(d) custom whereby a widow would hurl herself onto her husband's funeral pyre

II. Famous People

Directions: Use the names below to complete the following sentences.

Queen Victoria   Lord Cornwallis
Elihu Yale   Robert Clive
Queen Elizabeth I

1. _____ became a governor-general of the British East India Company.

2. _____ granted a charter to the British East India Company.

3. _____ was proclaimed Empress of India.

4. _____ led British forces to victory over the French.

5. _____ was an official of the British East India Company whose portrait can be found in St. Mary's Church in Madras.

III. Multiple Choice

Directions: Find the *letter* of the correct answer.

1. In the 1600s, the British East India Company received trading privileges from the

(a) Hindus.
(c) Brahmans.
(b) Mughals.
(d) sepoys.

2. The Battle of Plassey showed the military superiority of the

    (a) Mughals.
    (b) Pakistanis.
    (c) British.
    (d) French.

3. Which of the following is an example of a cause-and-effect relationship?

    (a) Battle of Plassey—charter given to the British East India Company
    (b) the Sepoy Mutiny—India becomes a crown colony
    (c) Queen Victoria ascends the throne—Lord Cornwallis sent to India
    (d) outlawing of suttee—construction of St. Mary's Church

IV. Thought Questions

Directions: Answer the following questions in essay form.

1. British involvement in India after 1858 was different from earlier involvement.

    A. What was this difference?
    B. Give one reason for this difference.

2. The British East India Company was able to expand its control in India during the seventeenth, eighteenth, and nineteenth centuries. Discuss three reasons for this expansion.

3. Was the Sepoy Mutiny a religious war or a war for independence?

    A. Present one argument for each view.
    B. Which view do you personally accept? Why?

4. Were the British correct for abolishing suttee? Present both a positive and negative answer to this question, with one reason for each answer.

5. Assume that you are an Englishman or Englishwoman living in India in 1877. Write a letter to Queen Victoria, explaining two reasons why the British are in India and what they hope to accomplish. In your letter, you must use each of the following terms at least once. The term may be used in any grammatical form you wish. Underline the term each time you use it.

    divide and conquer   ethnocentric   raj   suttee market
    geographic expression   Mughal

6. Explain how the life of Elihu Yale was an example of the impact of British history in both South Asia and North America.

Imperialism in East Asia and Southeast Asia

I. Matching

Directions: Match the words in Column A with the *correct description* in Column B.

Column A
1. extraterritoriality
2. indemnity
3. archipelago
4. Orient
5. Spice Islands
6. peninsula
7. "patchwork quilt"

Column B
(a) another name for East Asia
(b) land surrounded by water on three sides
(c) another name for the East Indies
(d) money paid for committing wrongful actions
(e) the right of a person who is accused of a crime in a foreign country to be tried in the courts of his or her own country
(f) another name for all Southeast Asian nations
(g) islands in a particular pattern

II. Famous People

Directions: Use the names below to complete the following sentences.

Marco Polo
Emperor Tu-duc
Lord Macartney
Stamford Raffles
Manchu
the Ch'ien-lung Emperor

King George III
Matthew Perry
Christopher Columbus
Meiji
Ferdinand Magellan

1. _____ founded the British colony of Singapore.

2. _____ exhibited ethnocentrism to a British ambassador.

3. _____ was the name of a Chinese ruling dynasty.

4. _____ traveled to China, hoping to establish relations there for his nation.

5. _____ established a Spanish colony in the Philippines.

6. _____ referred to the royal family in Japan.

7. _____ traveled to the Orient in the thirteenth century.

8. _____ established commercial relations between his nations and Japan in the nineteenth century.

9. _____ hoped to sail to the Spice Islands in the fifteenth century.

10. _____ denied France's request for special privileges in Cochin China, thereby provoking a French armed attack.

11. _____ sent a representative to China to arrange for relations with his nation.

III. Matching

Directions: Match the colony with the European nation that controlled it.

Colony
1. Indonesia
2. Singapore
3. Indochina
4. Philippines
5. Vietnam
6. Malaysia
7. Burma
8. Macao
9. Hong Kong

European Nation
(a) France
(b) England
(c) the Netherlands
(d) Spain
(e) Portugal

IV. Map Exercise

Directions: Use the maps to locate the place associated with each of the following statements. For each statement, write the *letter* of the place. (An answer may be repeated.) Use the Asia map for questions 1–8 and the Europe map for questions 9–13.

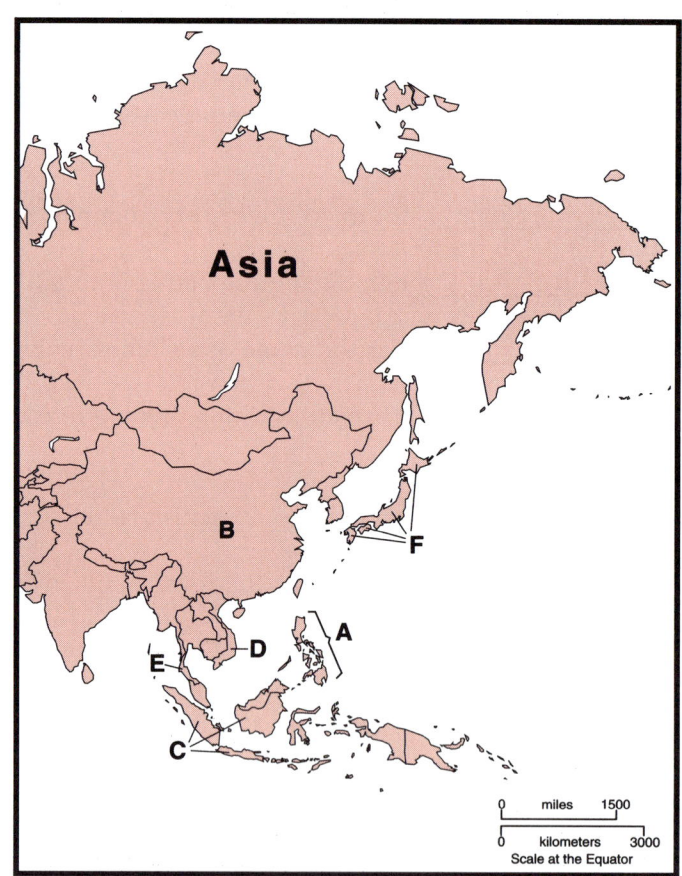

1. _____ The Boxer Rebellion took place here.

2. _____ This area was ruled by both Spain and the United States.

3. _____ This country was subjected to colonization by France.

4. _____ It was once known as the Dutch East Indies.

5. _____ This is the largest nation directly north of the Straits of Malacca.

6. _____ The Treaty of Kanagawa was signed between this nation and the United States.

7. _____ The Taiping Rebellion occurred here.

8. _____ This country was subjected to its colonial power's "culture system."

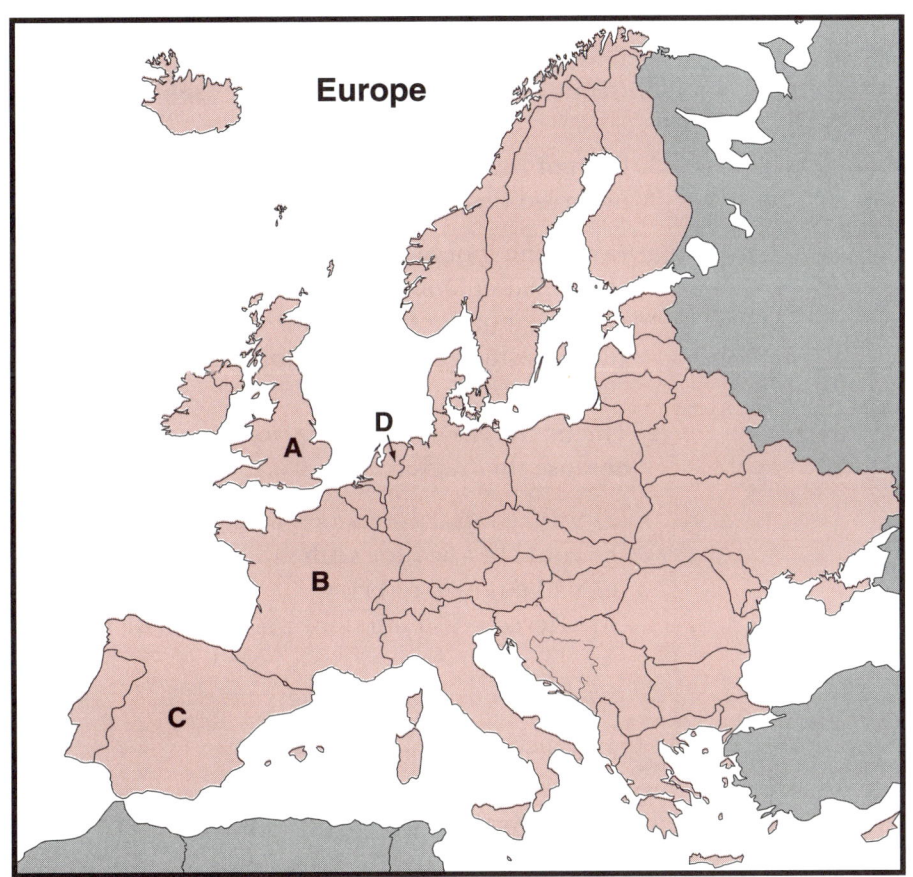

9. _____ This nation signed the Treaty of Nanking with China.

10. _____ Its only colony in Southeast Asia was the Philippines.

11. _____ It forced China to open up "treaty ports."

12. _____ This country was the major power in the Indochina peninsula.

13. _____ It controlled the largest archipelago in Southeast Asia.

V. Multiple Choice

Directions: Find the *letter* of the correct answer.

1. Which pair lists the opponents in the Opium War?

    (a) France and Vietnam
    (b) the United States and the Philippines
    (c) Britain and China
    (d) Holland and Java

2. As a result of the Opium Wars

    (a) Saigon was controlled by France.
    (b) Hong Kong became a British colony.
    (c) Canton became a "treaty port," open to Portugal.
    (d) Burma came under a German sphere of influence.

3. Each of the following happened to a nation in East Asia. Which event occurred first?

    (a) opening of Shanghai for trade
    (b) defeat in Sino-Japanese War
    (c) defeat in the Opium War
    (d) imposition of extraterritoriality

4. The main reason for European interest in the Orient in the 1880s was because that region

    (a) was an attractive market for agricultural machinery.
    (b) could be used for settling Europe's growing population.
    (c) had large oil reserves.
    (d) offered possibilities for profit in trade and commerce.

5. The Boxers in China wanted

    (a) a democratic government.
    (b) increased migration to Europe.
    (c) the overthrow of the Manchus.
    (d) expulsion of foreigners.

6. Which was a result of the Boxer Rebellion?

    (a) England withdrew from China.
    (b) China received an indemnity from France.
    (c) The United States returned part of its indemnity to China.
    (d) China took over land in Japan.

7. Which of the following does not belong with the others?

    (a) Spice Islands
    (b) East Indies
    (c) Indochina
    (d) Indonesia

8. The lives of Indonesia's people were supposed to improve under the "ethical policy" adopted by the

(a) Dutch. (b) British.
(c) French. (d) Spanish.

9. The greatest challenge to British colonial rule in Southeast Asia in the 1940s came from

(a) France. (b) Japan.
(c) China. (d) the Netherlands.

VI. Thought Questions

Directions: Answer the following questions in essay form.

1. Why did China become a victim of nineteenth-century European imperialism while Japan did not? Give three reasons.

2. Assume that you are the author of a book on Chinese history that will be published in the next few months. Your chapter on the Opium War promises to be read with much interest. Please write a summary of that chapter now, indicating the following:

   A. one cause of the Opium War
   B. two results of the Treaty of Nanking
   C. one reason explaining whether or not this treaty was unfair to China

3. Each of the following had an effect on European contacts with Southeast Asia. Identify each of the following and describe the contact that each had with a specific part of Southeast Asia. Be sure to name the specific part.

   A. Stamford Raffles
   B. Ferdinand Magellan
   C. Dutch East India Company

Imperialism in the Middle East

I. Matching

Directions: Match the words in Column A with the *correct description* in Column B.

Column A	*Column B*
1. Levant	(a) control over an area for a limited amount of time, as decided upon by an international organization
2. mandate	
3. partition	(b) permission give by one nation to a foreign nation to work on the land for economic purposes
4. concession	
5. Zionism	(c) desire to establish a Jewish homeland
	(d) refers to modern-day Syria and Lebanon
	(e) division of an area into two or more parts

II. Famous People

Directions: Use the names below to complete the following sentences.

Lord Balfour   Chaim Weizmann
Ralph Bunche   King Hussein

1. _____ was the first president of Israel.

2. _____ made promises to both Arabs and Jews concerning the future of Palestine.

3. _____ was the first ruler of Jordan.

4. _____ was a United Nations official who helped to arrange a truce in the first Arab-Israeli War.

III. Map Exercise

Directions: Use the map to locate the place associated with each of the following statements. For each statement, write the *letter* of the place.

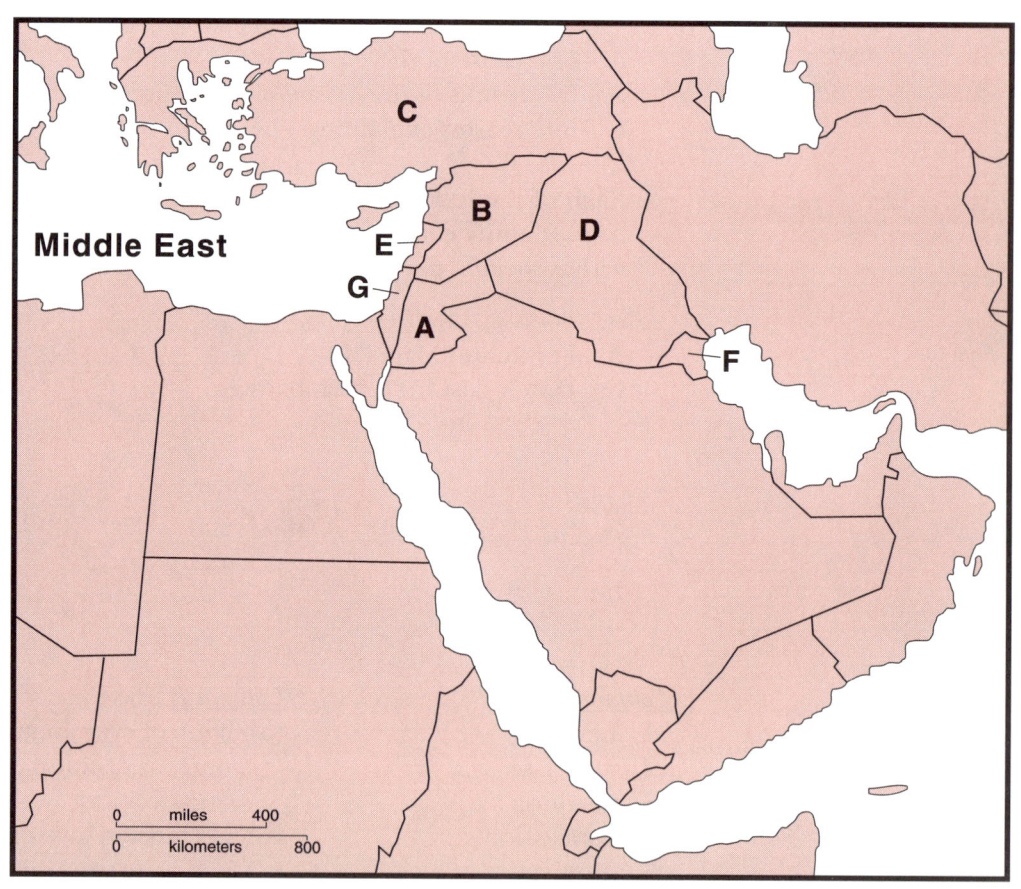

Middle East

1. _____ This country has King Hussein as its leader.

2. _____ This country is located directly south of all that remains of the Ottoman Empire.

3. _____ These two nations were part of French mandate in the Middle East. (Give two answers.)

4. _____ As a former part of a British mandate, this country was attacked by six Arab nations in 1948.

5. _____ These two nations make up the Levant. (Give two answers.)

6. _____ This area was once known as Transjordan.

7. _____ These two nations were once parts of the British mandate Palestine. (Give two answers.)

8. _____ This is the site of a former British mandate that touches the Persian Gulf.

9. _____ This country is the smallest area to grant oil concessions to the British.

10. _____ This nation controlled Palestine prior to World War I.

IV. Multiple Choice

Directions: Find the *letter* of the correct answer.

1. The Balfour Declaration was issued by

   (a) Francc.
   (b) England.
   (c) Turkey.
   (d) the League of Nations.

2. The Balfour Declaration affected people in

   (a) Iraq.
   (b) Iran.
   (c) Syria.
   (d) Palestine.

3. Which of the following once controlled the greatest amount of land in the Middle East?

   (a) Ottoman Turks
   (b) English
   (c) French
   (d) Iraqis

4. In which time period did the greatest number of European mandates in the Middle East come to an end?

   (a) 1915–1924
   (b) 1925–1934
   (c) 1946–1954
   (d) 1955–1964

5. A European nation that obtained a concession for oil in the Middle East could

   (a) colonize the land.
   (b) explore for oil.
   (c) keep all profits from the sale of oil.
   (d) sell oil only in the Middle East.

6. Which of the following were involved in the two partitions of Palestine?

   (a) England and the League of Nations
   (b) France and the League of Nations
   (c) England and the United Nations
   (d) France and the United Nations

7. Arab nationalism was most insistent in its desire to

   (a) increase oil sales.
   (b) side with England against France.
   (c) rid the Middle East of foreign control.
   (d) expand the mandate system.

IV. Thought Questions

Directions: Answer the following questions in essay form.

1. Describe two reasons for European interest in the Middle East.

2. Describe two reasons for the end of English and French control in the Middle East after World II.

3. Why has European imperialism had less effect in the Middle East than in Africa and other parts of Asia? Give two reason, with specific examples.

CHAPTER 29

Independence and Decolonization

What's in a name? Well, plenty—especially if you trace the end of European imperialism in this century in both Africa and Asia. Consider the following. If you compared two maps of Africa in the twentieth century, one drawn between 1900 and 1945, and one drawn today, you would see several contrasts. The first map would show the colonies of the Gold Coast, Rhodesia, and the Belgian Congo, as well as the cities of Leopoldville and Salisbury. On a current map, you would not find these names. Instead, you would find the nations of Ghana, Zimbabwe, and Zaire, and the cities of Kinshasa and Harare. On contrasting maps of Asia, you would find that the cities of Batavia and Saigon have been replaced by Djakarta and Ho Chi Minh City.

These changes can be explained as decisions made by people who became free from colonial domination. A free people may wish to change names that were given to them and their land without their consent. Such changes can be interpreted as a rejection of an Imperialistic Era in their history. On the other hand, a free people may wish to retain certain features of their colonized past. The nation of Singapore retained its colonial name and Malaysia has a name similar to its colonial name of Malaya. Pakistanis adapted so well to the British sport of cricket, introduced during the British colonial era, that they are said to have a better team today than Britain itself has!

World War II lasted from 1939 to 1945. The period after the war was a time when all the African and Asian nations mentioned above, along with many others, emerged from their colonial status to become free peoples. Therefore, the post-World War II period can be called a time of **decolonization**. In this chapter we will learn why decolonization occurred in Africa and Asia. In addition, we will evaluate the positive and negative aspects of imperialism.

General Reasons for Decolonization and the Growth of Independence

In the years after World War II, over fifty nations in Africa and Asia became independent. For some of them, the transition from a colony to a free, sovereign nation was peaceful. For others, the transition was marked by violence and bloodshed. There were many general reasons for the end of imperialism since 1945:

1. Nationalist movements in the colonies had become very powerful. Some of these movements had even started before the Second World War. They gained support from native people as well as from some people in the mother country (the imperial nation itself). Ironically, the native leaders of several independence movements were educated in European countries and the United States. Some of them would become the heads of the newly formed nations.

2. The Western European nations were weary after fighting World War II. The tremendous loss of life and property among both winners and losers in this war contributed to a weakening of the desire to maintain colonial empires.

Chapter 29 Chronology

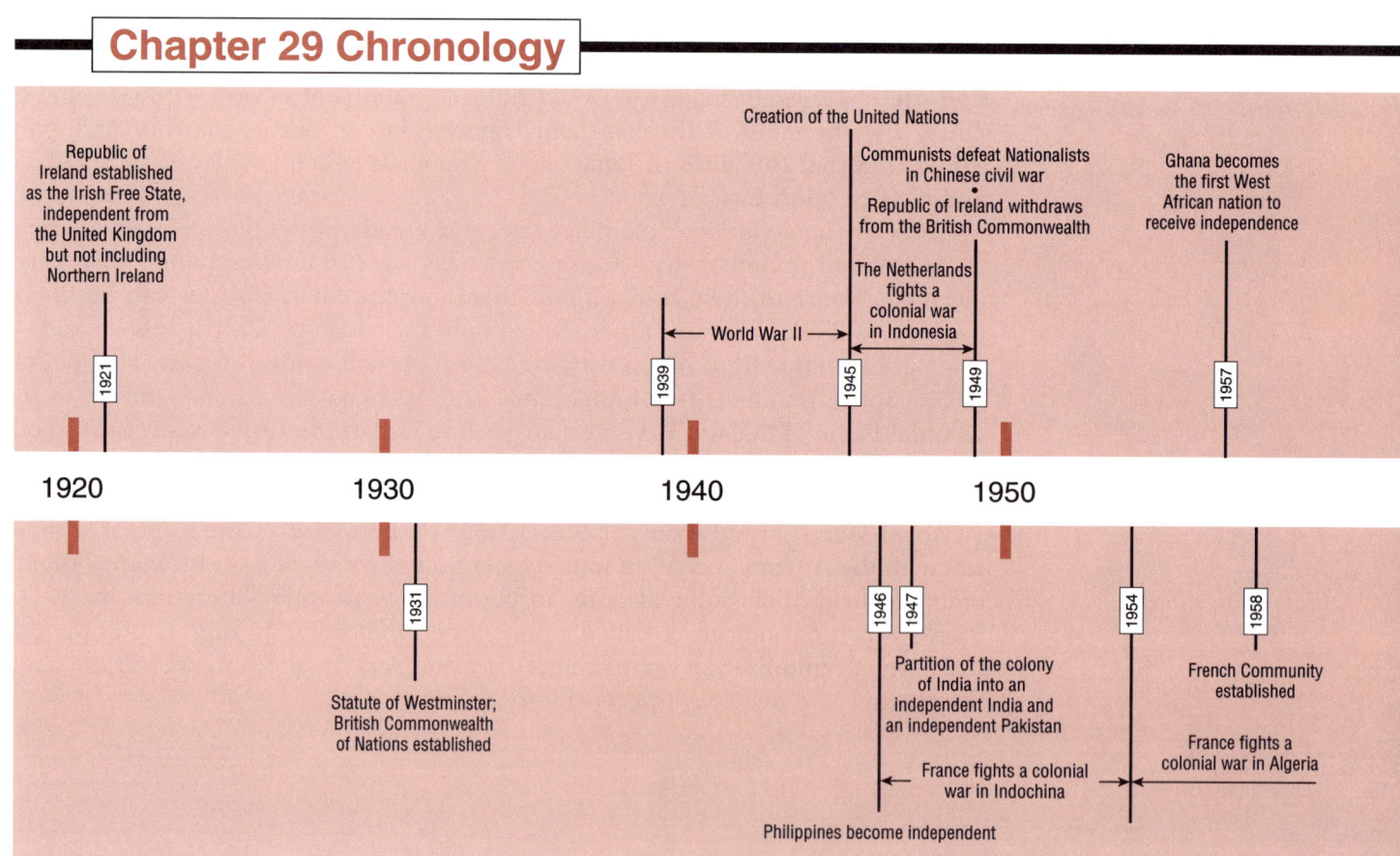

Republic of Ireland established as the Irish Free State, independent from the United Kingdom but not including Northern Ireland — 1921

Creation of the United Nations

Communists defeat Nationalists in Chinese civil war

Republic of Ireland withdraws from the British Commonwealth

The Netherlands fights a colonial war in Indonesia

Ghana becomes the first West African nation to receive independence — 1957

1939 ← World War II → 1945 — 1949

1920   1930   1940   1950

1931 — Statute of Westminster; British Commonwealth of Nations established

1946 — Philippines become independent

1947 — Partition of the colony of India into an independent India and an independent Pakistan

France fights a colonial war in Indochina

1954 — France fights a colonial war in Algeria

1958 — French Community established

This West African scene reflects action taken during an early period of self-government.

Some of the victorious nations that had colonies questioned whether they could afford the money and humanpower needed to keep their possessions.

3. The Western concepts of democracy were powerful arguments for promoting independence. The ideals of freedom and self-determination, prized by Western democracies in their wartime struggle against Nazi Germany, fascist Italy, and imperial Japan, became goals aspired to by people in the African and Asian colonies. Indeed, if such ideals were features of "superior" societies, then, argued nationalist leaders, why shouldn't they all be applied to colonized people. These leaders also pointed to the countless soldiers from several colonies that fought in the armies of the mother countries during the war. Not only did soldiers from, for example, Algeria and India shed blood for France and Britain, but they were also told that they were fighting for noble democratic values. For them to claim these values for their own societies after the war seemed only natural.

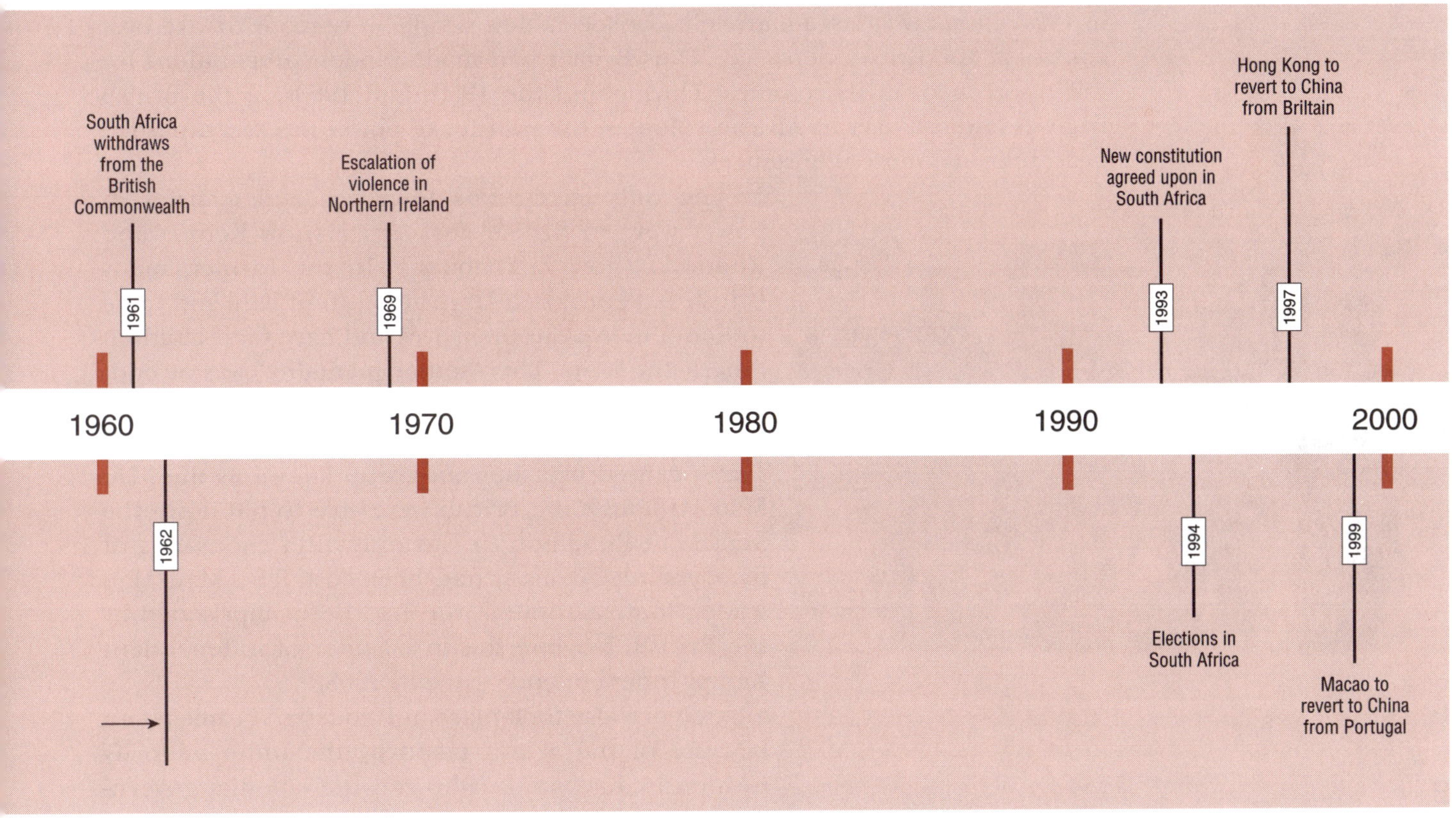

South Africa withdraws from the British Commonwealth — 1961

Escalation of violence in Northern Ireland — 1969

New constitution agreed upon in South Africa — 1993

Hong Kong to revert to China from Briltain — 1997

1960   1970   1980   1990   2000

1962 →

Elections in South Africa — 1994

Macao to revert to China from Portugal — 1999

4. The United Nations. A fourth reason to explain the post-World War II surge in independence was related to the values and ideals mentioned above. To advance and foster them, as part of an effort to achieve world peace, the United Nations was created in 1945. The existence of the U.N. furnished colonial people with yet another source of hope for seeking a change in their political status.

As we now move to examine these changes in different geographic locales, we should be aware that some changes occurred faster than others. It was not until 1975, thirty years after the war ended and the U.N. was formed, that the vast majority of colonies had attained freedom. A primary reason for this long and uneven transition to independence rests with the different policies of the colonial powers. (See Chapter 27, "Imperialism in Africa," for full explanations of these policies.)

Decolonization in Africa

In 1945, there were only four independent nations in Africa—Egypt, Ethiopia, Liberia, and South Africa. The rest of the continent was part of the colonial empires of European nations. Those with the largest possessions were Britain, France, Portugal, and Belgium.

Great Britain

Britain's policy of indirect rule permitted local rulers to retain some power. In addition, it enabled selected Africans to receive a British-style education in Britain. One of these was Kwame Nkrumah, who became the first head of Ghana in 1957. In many cases, a native elite or special few people were ready to take over control as the British departed. Thus Britain had made modest preparations for self-government in its colonies. Throughout the 1950s and 1960s, as the British flag was lowered over its African colonies, the transfer of power was accomplished peacefully in almost all instances.

The only exceptions to a peaceful transfer of power were in British East Africa (now Kenya) and Rhodesia (now Zimbabawe). In the former, many British settlers owned large amounts of land and came to Kenya to live out their lives and have their children inherit the land. This "settler mentality" was at odds with the desire of Kenyans to own land and to become independent. Violence over theses issues began in the 1950s, caused by a Kenyan group known as the Mau Mau. Although the British were able to put down the Mau Mau Rebellion, it was only after thousands of lives, mainly African, had been lost. The Mau Mau leader, Jomo Kenyatta, who had been imprisoned by the British, became the first leader of independent Kenya. Independence came in 1963.

Violence also took place in Rhodesia. It came about because of the action taken by the white minority headed by Ian Smith, who ran the colonial government. In 1965, the white government, fearing eventual

Jomo Kenyatta was a renowned leader in the struggle to gain independence for Kenya. As was true of many such leaders against colonial rule, he became his nation's first head of

Many of the new nations in Africa sought to build cooperation between each other. Here, Kenya's Jomo Kenyatta (second from the right) meets with other heads of new nations—Milton Obote of Uganda, Julius Nyerere of Tanzania, and Kenneth Kaunda of Zambia (from left to right).

Ghana's independence was further recognized when it gained membership in the United Nations. Here, at a meeting of the General Assembly in New York City, sits Kwame Nkrumah and other Ghanaian officials.

Many former French colonies maintained ties with France, often seeking economic and military aid. In 1966, French President Charles de Gaulle met with African members of the French Community.

black rule that had been promised by the British, declared its independence from Britain. Britain was upset with this decision, as were the black Rhodesians. A civil war broke out, with the black Rhodesians, headed by Robert Mugabe and Joshua Nkomo, fighting Ian Smith's government. Eventually, a cease-fire was reached. Free elections, held under British supervision in 1979, resulted in Robert Mugabe becoming prime minister. In 1980, the name of the nation was officially changed to Zimbabwe. This was the name of the site of a former African kingdom in the region, prior to the arrival of Cecil Rhodes and the area becoming a British colony.

France

France's policies of direct rule and assimilation established close links with its African colonies. These policies were to provide some basis in preparing for self-government. The colonies sent many soldiers to fight under French General Charles de Gaulle in World War II. They were also allowed, unlike the British colonies, to elect representatives to the French legislature in Paris. However, independence movements arose. Often, they were led by Africans who were educated in France and who eventually would become leaders of new nations. These included Félix Houphouet-Boigny (Ivory Coast) and Léopold Senghor (Senegal). In the 1950s, the North African colonies of Tunisia, Morocco, and Libya achieved independence peacefully. In 1960, twelve new independent nations were peacefully formed from French territories in West Africa and Equatorial Africa.

The only nonpeaceful transition to independence occurred in Algeria. Many French people had settled there and developed the kind of settler mentality we have previously described. They viewed Algeria as if it were part of France. So did the French government. Unwilling to give up Algeria, the French were faced with a bloody rebellion led by Ahmed Ben Bella. From 1954 to 1962, a colonial war enveloped France and Algeria. Peace and independence finally came in 1962, with Ben Bella as the new nation's leader.

Portugal

Portugal's policy of paternalism viewed colonies as though they were children. Portugal did very little to prepare them for independence. As was true of France in regard to Algeria, Portugal looked upon its African possessions in Angola, Mozambique, and Guinea as if they were parts of Portugal. Consequently, it was unwilling to grant independence freely. Colonial wars thus broke out, ending in

In an effort to assist those emerging nations facing economic problems, the United Nations often sends in food.

1975, with the colonies gaining their independence. Mozambique's first leader was the head of the anti-Portuguese forces, Samora Machel.

Belgium

Belgium's policies of paternalism and exploitation in the Congo did little to pave the way for independence. Unwilling to leave this resource-rich region, Belgium faced riots and a determined nationalist movement in the 1950s and 1960s. The leaders were Patrice Lumumba and Joseph Kasavubu. In 1960, Belgium consented to independence. However, because of instability in the new government and fighting among the Congolese, Belgium and the United States sent in troops to bring calm and order to the nation. In 1971, the Congo changed its name to Zaire.

Decolonization in South Asia

British policy in India was to inadvertently lay the seeds for growth of a strong independence movement. The Indians, having been taught to value British political values, learned them only too well. The first organized political movement to reduce Britain's authority began in 1885 with creation of the Indian National Congress. It eventually became known as the Congress party. In the twentieth century, leading political figures associated with the Congress party were Mahatma Gandhi, Jawharlal Nehru, and Indira Gandhi. In 1906, the Muslim League was created by those Muslims who feared that the Congress party was becoming too strongly dominated by Hindus. One of its founders was Mohammad Ali Jinnah. As was true of the Congress party leaders, Jinnah and the leaders of the Muslim League had been educated in England. All of these figures began to press, peacefully, for independence.

Mahatma Gandhi's boycotts and other nonviolent activities were designed to shame the British and have them "quit India." Indian participation in World Wars I and II, fighting for Britain, as well as Parliament's passing legislation to increase local self-rule, raised hopes for independence. With the end of World War II, Britain moved more quickly to make these hopes a reality. However, even though the British had aimed to leave behind them a single united country, there was much tension between Hindus and Muslims. The Congress party and the Muslim League were unable to solve all their political differences over the future of India. Britain had hoped that the huge colony of India would be transformed into the nation of India. Many Muslims, fearing that such a nation would have a Hindu majority and might act against their interests, talked of having a nation of their own.

The differences between the two groups led to much bloodshed and numerous migrations of people throughout the subcontinent. Each group sought to be where its members were in a majority. Civil war loomed as a distinct possibility if there was no agreement on a partition plan of the colony. Finally, on August 15, 1947, independence came with the creation of two new nations, India and Pakistan, formed by a partition of what had been the British crown colony of India. India, with a majority of Hindus, chose Nehru as its first president. Pakistan, divided into western and eastern regions separated by India, became a Muslim-dominated nation with Jinnah as its first head. A further partition in the subcontinent took place in 1971, when East Pakistan separated from West Pakistan due to political and economic disputes. East Pakistan mounted a successful rebellion, helped by India, and became a new nation known as Bangladesh.

Decolonization in East and Southeast Asia

World War II witnessed a temporary halt in European control in East and Southeast Asia. The halt was the result of conquests by Japan. Japanese imperialism replaced Western imperialism as Japan's forces defeated British, French, and American troops wherever the Westerners had possessions. These lands were eventually retaken, as Allied Western forces pushed Japan back to its original territory. The Japanese surrender in 1945 ended the war, and left open the issue of whether or not Western colonial control would resume.

East Asia

China's struggle against Japanese occupation in World War II was helped by Britain and the United States. By war's end, China had become an ally of the Western nations and one of the prominent nations in the United Nations. It thus regained, with two small exceptions, all territories that had been taken as colonies or spheres of influence prior to the war. One of these exceptions was Hong Kong, where Britain retained its colonial control. This control had begun after the Opium War. (See Chapter 28, "Imperialism in Asia.") China, under the nationalist rule of Chiang Kai-shek in the late 1940s, was not very concerned about the retention of Hong Kong as a colony. It was much more concerned with fighting off the Chinese Communists in a civil war.

The Communists were victorious in 1949, led by Mao Zedong. The new leaders objected to continued British control over what they considered to be Chinese land. From 1982 to 1984, Britain and China had negotiations to determine the colony's future. It was finally decided that Hong Kong would revert to Chinese control in 1997. The 1984 agreement further declared that for a period of fifty years thereafter, Hong Kong could continue to keep its legal, educational, and economic system.

Not far from Hong Kong is the Portuguese colony of Macao. Having become a Portuguese possession in 1557, it is the oldest European settlement in East Asia. It will revert to China in 1999, under an agreement that permits it to keep its present capitalist system for fifty years.

Southeast Asia

The emergence of independent nations in Southeast Asia after World War II followed a pattern similar to that in Africa. There were examples of both peaceful and violent transitions from colonial subjugation. The first transition, a peaceful one, occurred with recognition of Philippine independence by the United States in 1946. The other Western nations that gradually loosened their imperial ties were the Netherlands, Britain, and France.

The Netherlands   With the Japanese surrender in 1945, the people of the Netherlands East Indies proclaimed their independence from Holland and declared their new government to be the Republic of Indonesia. The Dutch refused to accept this state of affairs and sent troops to regain control. From 1945 to 1949, bitter warfare took place. The Indonesians were led by Achmed Sukarno, a Dutch-educated engineer. With intervention by the United Nations, a cease-fire was put into effect. In December 1949, the Dutch formally recognized Indonesian independence. Sukarno became the new nation's first head of state.

Great Britain   The end of British rule in Southeast Asia was characterized by nonviolence. With its decision to withdraw from nearby India and without any wish to remain in Burma, Britain recognized Burma (now Myanmar) as a free nation in 1948. Britain retained its authority in Malaya after the war, and was able to defeat a Communist-led rebellion. The colony attained sovereignty peacefully in 1963, taking the name Malaysia. It was controlled by its major ethnic groups, Malays. Worried about such a situation, Singapore, inhabited mainly by people of Chinese extraction, broke away from Malaysia to become a separate nation in 1965. The final curtain call for British colonialism in Southeast Asia came with the granting of independence to the small oil-rich kingdom of Brunei in 1984.

France   The French exit from its colonies in Southeast Asia was made only after a bitter and long war, 1946–1954. French Indochina, taken by Japan during the war, consisted of the present-day countries of Laos, Vietnam, and Cambodia. In Indochina, as in other regions ruled by Japan, native leaders formed a resistance group to fight for independence. Ho Chi Minh was the head of such a group, the Viet Minh. After the war, he declared Vietnam to be an independent country. France disregarded this, seeking to regain control and subjugation in Indochina. In 1946, the Viet Minh, an openly Communist organization, began fighting the French. This conflict was to become the bloodiest colonial war in Asia.

By 1954, with French public opinion torn over the struggle, and with major victories by the Viet Minh such as at Dien Bien Phu, France agreed to negotiations for peace. The Geneva Accords, ending the war, were signed in 1954. They resulted in independence for the countries of Laos and Cambodia. Vietnam was to be divided into two independent parts: a Communist-led North Vietnam and a South Vietnam under anti-Communist leaders. A vote was scheduled to be held in 1956 to decide on a single government for the two Vietnams. This never took place.

By the early 1960s, widespread fighting had broken out in South Vietnam. This resulted from discontent of some of its citizens as well as attempts by the North Vietnamese to establish one unified nation. Fighting against the South Vietnamese government were the Viet Cong (South Vietnamese Communists) and ultimately the army of North Vietnam. The Viet Cong and the North Vietnamese received material assistance from China and the Soviet Union. The South Vietnamese received help from the United States in the form of equipment as well as over five hundred thousand combat troops. In 1973, President Richard Nixon withdrew American forces in the hope that North and South Vietnam could work out their differences peacefully. The South Vietnamese government, under President Nguyen Van Thieu, grew weak and very unpopular. Fighting resumed, resulting in a North Vietnamese takeover in 1975 and the proclamation in 1976 of a unified country. Hanoi became the country's capital, while Saigon, the former capital of South Vietnam, had its name changed to Ho Chi Mihn City. In 1993, the first year of President Bill Clinton's administration, the United States and Vietnam began to consider the possibility of establishing diplomatic relations. In 1994, tourism and economic contacts were promoted. Vietnam also turned over more information on American servicemen killed or missing in the war.

The British Commonwealth of Nations

As we have seen, decolonization was achieved in both violent and nonviolent ways. Several former colonies retain ties today to their former foreign rulers. Many of Britain's colonies, after achieving independence, voluntarily chose membership in the British Commonwealth of Nations.

This is an organization with forty-nine members. It includes Great Britain and most of its former colonies in Africa, Asia, North America, Central and South America, the West Indies in the Caribbean region, Australia, New Zealand, and scattered islands in the Mediterranean Sea, Indian Ocean, and Western Pacific Ocean. The Commonwealth was created with passage of an act by the British Parliament, called the Statute of Westminster, in 1931. It provided that Britain and those former colonies who were independent as of that year—Australia, Canada, South Africa, and New Zealand—were equal partners in the organization. Membership would be voluntary, without any interference by Britain in the affairs of the other members. Each member would, however, declare loyalty to the British crown and recognize its cultural links to Britain. Membership increased in the post-World War II era, as new nations chose to become part of the Commonwealth.

Into the 1990s, Commonwealth members would usually meet once a year to discuss matters of mutual interest. The organization also provides some economic privileges for its members. There are scientific and educational exchanges of information as well as sporting and cultural events. Critics of the Commonwealth claim that it has little purpose, saying the membership is too large and represents too many diverse geographical areas and conflicting political and economic interests. Canada, Australia, and New Zealand, original Commonwealth members, are still active. Two former British possessions, South Africa and Ireland, however, chose not to remain as members.

Canada

Although once held by France, Canada came under British rule in 1763 after the French and Indian War. A revolt against the British was put down in 1837. As more and more English people migrated to Canada, and as a wave of democratic reforms were taking place in the mother country itself during the first half of the nineteenth century, Canada was to experience important political changes. The Durham Report of 1839, written by Lord Durham of Britain, recommended self-government for the Canadians. This recommendation was adopted in 1867, with passage of the British North America Act. Canada became a dominion. It enjoyed self-government, but remained part of the British Empire. A governor-general from Britain represented the monarch, and in theory, had a veto power. This was hardly used, however. Canadians consider 1867 as their year of independence.

Australia and New Zealand

A continent in itself, Australia became a British possession in 1770 with the arrival of Captain James Cook. Up until 1840, it was used by Britain as a place to send debtors and criminals. The discovery of gold in 1851 spurred immigration there. It received dominion status in 1901. New Zealand, to the southeast of Australia, was also explored and settled by Captain Cook. It became a dominion in 1907.

South Africa

This southernmost region of Africa had become a dominion in 1910. It joined the Commonwealth in 1931. Although greatly outnumbered by black South Africans, the white population controlled the nation and discriminated against blacks. The policy of **apartheid**, keeping the races apart, was an example of this discrimination. Within the white population were both English-speaking people and Afrikaans-speaking people. They were descendants of Europeans who had begun arriving there in the seventeenth century. The Afrikaners, mainly of Dutch extraction, won control of the government in 1948. In 1961, subjected to harsh attacks on its apartheid policies from other Commonwealth members, South Africa withdrew from the Commonwealth. It declared itself to be a republic.

Into the 1980s, the government continued its discriminatory practices against blacks. However, in the early 1990s, as a result of worldwide condemnation of these practices and of protests by black South Africans, the government began to make some changes. Apartheid laws were relaxed, interracial marriages were allowed, the ban on the black-controlled African National Congress political party was removed, and greater political participation for nonwhites was granted. In 1992 and 1993, President Frederik W. de Klerk and black African leader Nelson Mandela met frequently to consider a further easing of tensions and more political involvement of blacks in the nation's government.

These efforts resulted in a historic agreement, reached without violence, announced in November 1993. Signed by the major political groups in the nation, this agreement spelled out a death warrant for apartheid. Its major features were as follows:

1. A new constitution, guaranteeing equal rights for all citizens, became the supreme law of the land until such time as an elected legislature writes a permanent version. Discrimination by race was forbidden.
2. Free elections for a legislature, to be called the parliament, were scheduled for April 1994. The parliament would consist of an assembly and a senate.
3. The office of a president, who is to be chosen by the assembly, was designated.

Although the agreement was not signed by extreme white separatists groups, most South Africans appeared ready to support it. As expected, historic parliamentary elections were held in 1994 in a peaceful atmosphere. Mandela was chosen the nation's president.

Southwest Africa

The early 1990s witnessed another political change in southern African affairs. This involved the nearby territory once known as Southwest Africa. Southwest Africa had been a German colony from the late nineteenth century until the end of World War I in 1918. After the war, the League of Nations made it a mandate under South Africa. South Africa exploited the region and imposed its apartheid laws there. Facing criticism from the United Nations and frequent raids from a resistance movement, the South-West Africa People's Organization, South Africa finally agreed to grant independence to the region in March 1990. The new nation changed its name to Namibia, with Sam Nujoma, a former head of the resistance movement, as its president.

Ireland

The Irish Question has been a source of controversy between Ireland and Britain for centuries. (See Chapter 11, "The Growth of Democracy in England," and Chapter 20, "Advances in British Democracy.") By 1600, Protestant England had gained control over Catholic Ireland. From that time until the twentieth century, British imperialist treatment of the Irish had been cruel and harsh. When Oliver Cromwell ruled England in the seventeenth century, many Irish were killed by his forces; in addition, Protestants from England and Scotland took over large areas of land in Northern Ireland. Until the 1800s, Irish Catholics could not hold political office and were taxed to support the Anglican (Protestant) Church.

Division of Ireland In 1905, the Sinn Fein party was formed as a nationalist group to press Britain for Irish independence. Its leader was Eamon de Valera. Although the Easter Rebellion in 1916 against the British was unsuccessful, with many rebel leaders executed, the Sinn Fein continued its campaign for home rule and independence. This campaign was conducted peacefully as well as through guerrilla warfare against British forces. In 1921, the southern four-fifths of the island of Ireland became a free nation known as the Republic of Ireland. The remaining one-fifth, Northern Ireland, also known as Ulster, decided to remain as part of the United Kingdom (the official name for the united nation of England, Scotland, Wales, and Northern Ireland). The division of the island was completed in 1922. In 1949, the Irish Republic ended its membership in the British Commonwealth.

Political and Sectarian Strife Catholics in Northern Ireland wanted the area to be united with the Irish Republic to the south, as did the new Republic of Ireland itself. These requests were turned down by Britain, particularly because the majority of Ulster citizens were Protestants and wanted to stay under the British crown. Extremist groups, both Catholic and Protestant, began to fight an undeclared civil war in Northern Ireland. This kind of religious conflict is known as sectarian strife. This violence escalated in 1969 and has continued to the present. The Irish Republican Army (I.R.A.), along with its political component, the Sinn Fein, spoke for many Ulster Catholics and demanded a united Ireland. Militant Protestants, headed by the

Reverend Ian Paisley, were against unification. British troops have been sent to Ulster since 1969 to help maintain peace and stop the killings and terrorist actions of both sides. Most of the violence, often directed against civilians, has been carried out by the I.R.A. and a Protestant group, the Ulster Freedom Fighters (U.F.F). British efforts to reduce the violence have not been very successful.

Attempted Solutions A political solution to what had been called "the Troubles" was attempted in 1985, with the Hillsborough Agreement. This provided for greater cooperation against extremist groups, stopping discrimination toward the Catholic minority in the north, and giving the Republic of Ireland some involvement in the governing of Northern Ireland. The agreement has had mixed results, and has been criticized by both Catholics and Protestants. For Protestants the agreement went too far. For Catholics, it did not go far enough.

In 1992, another political solution was attempted as officials from Britain, Ireland, and Northern Ireland met in the Irish capital of Dublin. They hoped to stem the violence and terrorism that had taken over three thousand lives during the previous twenty-three years. Lives were lost in Ulster, as well as in Britain itself. One hopeful sign for peace in Dublin was the presence at the talks for the first time since 1922, of a leader from one of the major Protestant political parties of Northern Ireland. That party, the Ulster Unionist party, was nevertheless in favor of continuing the region's link to Britain. This contrasted with the wish of Ulster Catholics for more say in the Ulster government and eventual unification with Ireland, as well as the Irish government's wish for unification of the island. Neither the I.R.A. nor the Sinn Fein were invited to the Dublin talks, as they refused to give up their campaign of violence to end British rule in the north.

The 1992 talks in Dublin were suspended, however, as little progress was made on the issues. Violence continued on both sides in 1993, thus hampering the chances of holding further talks. An additional troublesome item concerns a request made by Protestant political leaders. They say they will not attend any talks until the Irish government promises to change its constitutional claim of sovereignty in the north. The Irish government, in turn, has said that this can only be accomplished as part of an overall negotiated agreement.

In 1994, another relevant item made the news. As a result of talks between Gerry Adams, president of Sinn Fein, and John Hume, head of a Catholic political party in Northern Ireland, a plan was considered whereby the Sinn Fein would be allowed to take part in peace negotiations if it promised to halt acts of violence by the I.R.A. Yet, such a plan would have to be weighed carefully and agreed to by other key figures: Irish Prime Minister Albert Reynolds, British Prime Minister John Major, and Ulster leaders such as Reverend Paisley.

The French Community

France wished to create a relationship with its former colonies, similar to the British Commonwealth of Nations. Accordingly, in 1958, the French Community was established. Several new African nations joined, under provisions that treated them as equals with France, and aimed at consultations on various economic and defense policies. However, as many members began to withdraw, the organization ceased to function. Nevertheless, France still gives economic aid and provides military support upon request when it feels it is necessary. For example, French troops were sent to the African nations of Chad and Gabon in recent years. This was done to suppress armed opposition to the governments there.

Evaluation of Imperialism

European Imperialism had both positive and negative effects for those nations who acquired land overseas. On the positive side, it was obvious that the growth of an empire gave a nation prestige, wealth, and a way to spread its culture. The mother country's standard of living improved, while careers in the military and foreign service were made available. Investors and business leaders were furnished with raw materials and expanding markets.

On the negative side was the reality that imperialistic ventures could draw nations into wars. These might be with rival colonial powers or with the colonies themselves. Taxpayers in the mother country would have to pay for wars and imperialistic consequences. Poor images of the colonial nation and bad feelings toward it could result in overseas colonies.

The effects of Imperialism upon the colonized regions were also a mix of the positive and the negative.

THE EFFECTS OF IMPERIALISM ON COLONIZED REGIONS

Consequence	Positive	Negative
Political	Brought stability and unification; training for independence; promoted the nation-state idea	Colonial wars, discrimination; drew boundaries without consulting native peoples
Economic	Introduced modernization; improved means of transportation and communication; created industries; taught new skills; improved the standards of living; provided employment	Took wealth away from colony; treated workers badly; did not provide for advancement and management for colonized people; destroyed traditional industries and patterns of trade
Social	Introduced Christianity and other aspects of Western culture; built schools and hospitals; introduced modern medicine	Looked down upon native cultures; promoted racism and a sense of cultural inferiority; introduced Western vices and diseases

Summary

So we have come to the end of an era of European history. Never again did the nations of Europe impact on the world the way they had. The end of World War II saw the end of Colonialism. France and Great Britain were too weakened to try to keep control of their possessions. The movement into independence was very uneven. There was some relationship between the manner in which the colony was treated and how independence was achieved. The newly emerging nations of Britain and France, for example, generally made a smoother transition and kept up relationships with their former rulers. Those colonies controlled by Belgium and Portugal had a far more difficult time.

On the Asian continent there were more difficulties. When the Indian subcontinent split into two nations, with Pakistan and India divided on religious lines, bloodshed resulted. The religious difficulties continue to exist. The Chinese underwent a civil war that resulted in a Communist victory. The United States became involved in a land war in Southeast Asia when they involved themselves in a long, drawn-out conflict in Vietnam.

There are still problems to be resolved. The change from an apartheid system in South Africa could have a difficult time. Many whites there are not accepting of the changes that give the Africans equality. The on-going problem of Ireland is still with us, like a festering sore that refuses to heal. The lines between the Catholics and Protestants in the north are so hardened that solution seems impossible.

This last section was an evaluation of the period of Colonialism. Did the European nations benefit? Did the African or Asian people benefit? What do you think?

Review Exercises

I. Matching

Directions: Match the words in Column A with the *correct description* in Column B.

<u>Column A</u>
1. sovereignty
2. subjugation
3. apartheid
4. decolonization
5. sectarian strife

<u>Column B</u>
(a) under the control of a foreign power
(b) policy of separating races in South Africa
(c) achieving independence from foreign rule
(d) describing interreligious conflicts
(e) freedom to make one's own decisions

II. Map Exercise

Directions: Use the map to locate the place associated with each of the following statements. For each statement, write the *letter* of the place.

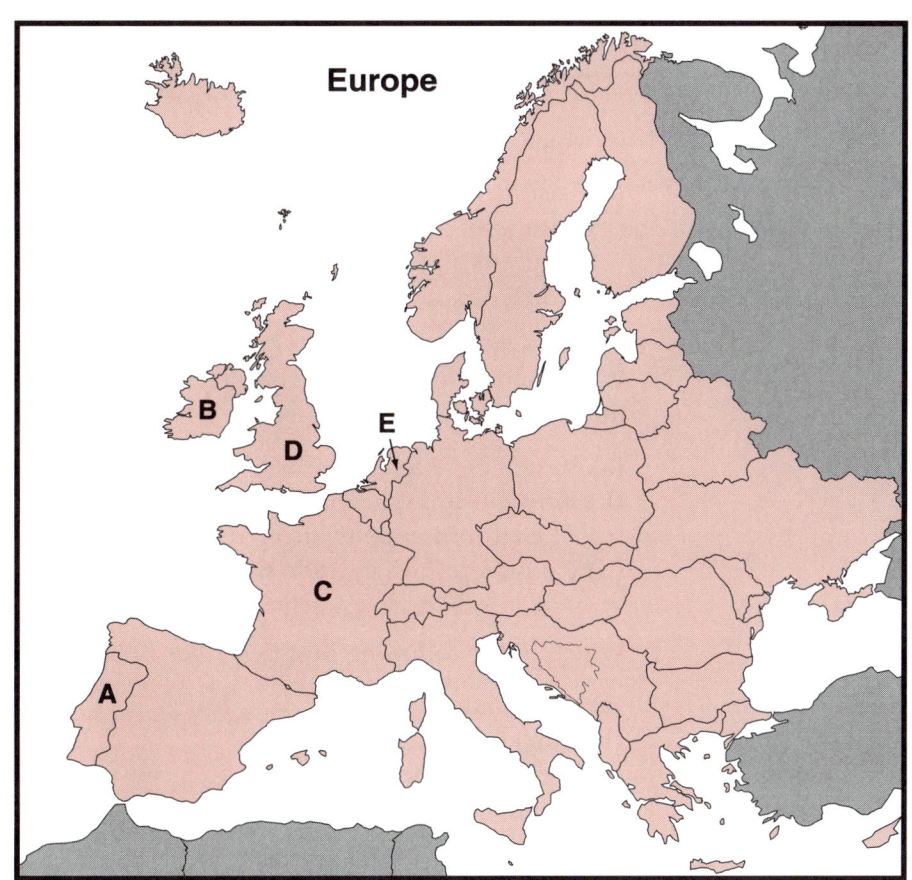

1. _____ a colonial war in Indochina

2. _____ the Mau Mau Rebellion in Kenya

3. _____ a colonial war in Algeria

4. _____ the Statute of Westminster

5. _____ a colonial war in Indonesia

6. _____ a colonial war in Angola

7. _____ The government of this country will give up Hong Kong to China in 1997.

8. _____ This nation will give up Macao to China in 1999.

9. _____ issued the Durham Report, concerning Canada

10. _____ The "Easter Rebellion" occurred here.

11. _____ partition of India

12. _____ The Sinn Fein party wanted independence from this nation.

13. _____ Eamon de Valera was active here as a nationalist leader.

14. _____ This nation formed a Commonwealth association with many former colonies.

III. Multiple Choice

Directions: Find the *letter* of the correct answer.

1. In which area was decolonization most peaceful?

   (a) East Africa
   (b) Southeast Asia
   (c) South Asia
   (d) North Africa

2. Which action indicates a negative reaction by a former colony against its colonial past?

   (a) Judges in Ghana wear British-style wigs.
   (b) Kenya invites Queen Elizabeth for a visit.
   (c) The city of Leopoldville changes its name to Kinshasa.
   (d) Pakistan refuses to trade with France.

3. Which of the following best describes Belgium's colonial policy?

   (a) exploitation
   (b) humanism
   (c) Westernization
   (d) democracy

4. If an imperialist nation follows a policy of strict paternalism toward its colony, the colony will probably

   (a) have little contact with the mother country.
   (b) have a high standard of living.
   (c) not be protected in a war against an invading nation.
   (d) have little preparation for independence.

5. In Africa and Asia, a major result of World War II was

   (a) an increased feeling of nationalism.
   (b) a general decline in the standard of living.
   (c) an increase in colonization by European nations.
   (d) a rapid decline in population.

6. The withdrawals of France from Indochina and Holland from the East Indies illustrate that nations

   (a) discard traditional foreign policy goals after military struggles.
   (b) tend to base foreign policy decisions on what they believe to be their self-interests.
   (c) use warfare as the best way to resolve international disputes.
   (d) tend to refer foreign policy conflicts to the United Nations.

7. Which was an important reason for India achieving independence?

   (a) British losses in the Sepoy Mutiny
   (b) the revolt of Bangladesh against Pakistan and England
   (c) the military victories of Mahatma Gandhi's armed forces
   (d) Indian participation in World Wars I and II

8. Which time period saw the greatest amount of decolonization in Africa and Asia?

   (a) 1492–1878
   (b) 1878–1914
   (c) 1914–1945
   (d) 1945–1975

9. "The sun never set" on the Empire once ruled by

   (a) Britain.
   (b) France.
   (c) Portugal.
   (d) Belgium.

10. The boundaries of modern African nations do not usually follow tribal boundaries mainly because

   (a) African nations are trying to limit tribal influence.
   (b) most tribes are unwilling to cooperate with the new national governments.
   (c) tribes have lost their importance in the lives of modern Africans.
   (d) modern national boundaries tend to follow former colonial boundaries.

11. Which statement best explains why the British partitioned India in 1947?

   (a) Britain feared a united India.
   (b) One part of India wanted to remain under British control.
   (c) Religious differences led to political division.
   (d) Economic disputes caused separation of regions.

12. The existence of a "settler mentality" was a critical factor in the struggle for independence in

   (a) Algeria.   (b) Pakistan.
   (c) Ghana.   (d) Malaysia.

IV. Thought Questions

Directions: Answer the following questions in essay form.

1. Describe three reasons for the decolonization and emergence of independent nations that occurred after 1945.

2. Colonial policies differed among European nations.

   A. Describe the colonial policies of any two nations.
   B. Describe how each policy affected the transition to independence of one colony controlled by the nation.

3. The emergence of independent nations from imperialism has been both peaceful and violent.

   A. Describe one example of each kind in Africa.
   B. Describe one example of each kind of Asia.

4. Professor Yes and Professor No have often debated, giving their views on this statement: "Imperialism has been more beneficial than harmful." Write down the debate that they recently had, in which they carefully explained their different views and each gave two reasons for these views. The debate can be written in the form of a conversation, as indicated below. Specific facts and names of specific places must be mentioned.

   Y:
   N:
   Y:
   N:

WAR AND UPHEAVAL IN THE FIRST HALF OF THE TWENTIETH CENTURY

During your lifetime, in the second half of the twentieth century, nations have been at peace more than at war. This was not the case in the first half of the twentieth century. Indeed, those fifty years, from 1900 to 1950, saw the world plunge into two horrible wars, World War I and World War II. The peace that followed the Second World War has been generally maintained, mainly because the fear of a third and more deadly world war has led most nations to try to resolve disputes without coming to blows on the battlefield.

Both wars, along with the Holocaust brought on by Nazi Germany, showed the darkest side of human nature. A brighter side was shown in the creation of the United Nations and the realization by the Western democracies of the important role they must play to prevent the spread of tyranny and war.

Tyranny, war, and threats to democracy were clearly on the agenda of the dictatorships that rose to power in Russia, Germany, and Italy. These three nations are no longer under dictatorial rule.

The actions affecting war and peace in the first 50 years of our current century will be examined in this unit.

This unit, therefore, is very long. It begins with World War I, in 1914. In that year, the shots of an assassin brought an end to the world of Victorian values. Industrialization brought weaponry to the front lines. Machine guns ended mass charges, submarines prowled the seas, and airplanes engaged in combat. After the war, the question of a peace treaty faced the victors in Paris.

World War I pushed Russia over the brink. Men of determination overthrew the 200-year reign of the Romanov Dynasty. There were two of these revolutions in 1917. First Nicholas II abdicated, with Lenin and the Bolsheviks seizing control. Stalin, rightfully called the Man of Steel, took over after the death of Lenin.

Not concerned with ideology, he established totalitarianism in all its forms. Millions died because of his actions.

In central Europe, two men became dictators. The political and economic situation in Italy and Germany allowed two charismatic individuals to gain control of their governments. Mussolini and Hitler led their nations into the worst war the world had ever seen.

When the war ended, the world was stunned by the horrors revealed in the opening of the concentration camps. The evidence of the mass killing of millions of human beings continues to be difficult to believe. Part of the Nazi policy was the planned systematic elimination of the Jewish people. Six million Jews were eliminated along with six million other persons that the Nazis considered to be "less than human." If no other lesson is learned from World War II, humankind must resolve that never again can genocide be attempted, nor can a man like Hitler be allowed to hypnotize a nation and to move an entire world to war.

As part of the settlement after the war, an organization was established to try to insure that such an event would never occur again. The United Nations has had its successes and its failures; but today, almost 50 years later, it still exists and there has been no major conflict.

World War I

Causes of World War I

Why do nations go to war? This is a question that is not easily answered. Indeed, there may be many answers. Historians themselves may disagree on the answers and often disagree on the chief reason that led to a particular war. Perhaps each war should be examined separately, as the reasons for one conflict may indeed be very different from the reasons for another. This section will examine the reasons for the conflict that became known as World War I (1914–1918).

After learning about these reasons, you may wish to think about whether or not this war was **inevitable** (bound to happen). Viewed against the background of the preceding years, however, its outbreak in 1914 seemed surprising. There had not been a major European war involving so many nations in almost 100 years. With the end of the Napoleonic Wars in 1815, the **Congress of Vienna** laid the foundation for a near-century of peace. This "Pax Europa" was broken only by a few brief and local wars (the Austro-Prussian, Franco-Prussian, Russo-Turkish, and Crimean wars). Beginning in the 1870s, however, a series of forces and events combined to move Europe toward a major war. These included a growing spirit of **nationalism**, increasingly dangerous colonial conflicts, a complex system of entangling alliances, and a rising tide of **militarism**.

The war that was to sweep across Europe, and even draw in the United States would last for four years. It was far more destructive of lives and property than any previous conflict and was the first so-called total war. Civilian populations became military objectives and targets along with soldiers. Terrifying weapons were used for the first time. It is no wonder that this terrible conflict was originally called the Great War. After it was over, President Woodrow Wilson of the United States hoped that the world would see it as "the war to end all wars."

It is time now for us to see why this war occurred. In doing so, we will look at both underlying and immediate causes. Many factors contributed to the start of World War I. All of the major powers shared some blame, although historians disagree on whether one nation was more at fault than the others.

Underlying Causes

Causes that build up over a long period of time, leading to an argument or dispute, can be called underlying. They can also be described as basic or fundamental causes.

Imperialism The desire to control overseas regions (i.e., imperialism) led to sharp competition and rivalry among the nations of Europe. Examples included the following:

1. Britain and Germany in East Africa, where their colonies bordered on each other.
2. Britain and Germany in the Middle East. Germany wished to construct a Berlin-to-Baghdad railroad. For the British, this would pose a threat to their "lifeline to India" through the Suez Canal.
3. France and Germany in Morocco, where Germany had contested France's establishment of a **protectorate**.
4. Austria-Hungary and Russia in the Balkans (southeast Europe), where Russia's support of Serbia was seen as a threat to the unity of the Austro-Hungarian Empire.

Nationalism Strong ties to a nation and/or ethnic group (i.e., nationalism) stirred deep emotions. Many groups of people wanted to be free of control by other nations. For

Chapter 30 Chronology

Franco-Prussian War [1870–1871]	1870
Alliance formed between Germany and Austria-Hungary	1879
Triple Alliance formed with Germany, Austria-Hungary, and Italy as members	1882
Dual Alliance formed between France and Russia	1894
Fashoda affair	1898
Entente Cordiale formed between France and Britain	1904
Entente formed between Britain and Russia; Triple Entente formed with Britain, France, and Russia as members	1907
Balkan Wars [1912–1913]	1912
Assassination of Austrian Archduke Francis Ferdinand and his wife in Sarajevo; Start of World War I	1914
Battle of Verdun	1916
Russian revolutions; United States enters the war; Treaty of Brest-Litovsk	1917
Armistice agreement; End of World War I	1918
Paris Peace Conference; Signing of Treaty of Versailles; U.S. refuses to join the League of Nations	1919
Other peace treaties	1923

example, Bosnia and Herzogovina, which consisted of Slavic people, as did Serbia, wanted to be free from Austria-Hungary so they could be unified with Serbia and thus be with others of their own kind. As Russia was a Slavic nation, it backed the nationalist wishes of Bosnia, Herzogovina, and Serbia. Obviously, this angered Austria-Hungary. Austria-Hungary and the Ottoman Turks ruled over many different **nationalities**, who wanted to break free and form their own nations. Some of these subject nationalities, besides the ones mentioned above, were Czechs, Slovaks, Poles, and Arabs.

Nationalism was also a source of anger and antagonism (opposition to someone or something) between France and Germany. Ever since France's defeat in the Franco-Prussian War (1870–1871), France had resented Germany. French pride was especially hurt by the loss of Alsace-Lorraine to Germany at the end of the war. France's passionate desire to regain this territory was reflected in the often-heard cry for *revanche* (revenge). This wish was ingrained in students your age and younger in schools throughout France in the late nineteenth and early twentieth centuries.

Alliances Otto von Bismarck, chancellor of Germany, was well aware of France's antagonism toward Germany. Accordingly, to assist Germany in case of a French attack, and also to isolate France, he formed an alliance with Austria-Hungary in 1879. In 1882, Italy allied herself with these two nations because she was upset with France's seizure of Tunisia in North Africa. Thus was born the **Triple Alliance** of Germany, Austria-Hungary, and Italy. Known as the Central powers, these nations stated that their alliance was purely defensive and that they would not start a war. The parties to a defensive alliance, however, usually promise to help each other if any one of them is attacked by someone else. Formation of the Triple Alliance shows how a nation's self-interest influences its dealings with other nations. Anti-French feeling brought Italy and Germany together; then, as Germany was already allied with Austria-Hungary, Italy found herself an ally of that nation. This was ironic, however, as Italy had long feared Austria-Hungary and had wanted to get Austrian land that was inhabited by Italians. Italy may have felt that it was more in her interest to ally herself with the two German-speaking nations than to stay isolated.

The French and British were aware of the linkages put together in the Triple Alliance and became disturbed. France's wish to regain Alsace-Lorraine, along with her fear of being alone in a possible showdown with Germany and that nation's allies, prompted France to seek allies of her own. An opportunity arose when the tsar of Russia faced economic troubles. France lent him money for both industrial and military projects, and the two nations also signed a treaty, forming the Dual Alliance in 1894. For reasons of self-interest, each felt good about this alliance: it gave France, lying to Germany's west, an ally on the eastern side of Germany, and it gave Russia an ally against Austria-Hungary, a competitor with Russia for influence in the Balkans.

Although Britain had a long history of warfare with France, Britain was now growing much more alarmed about Germany. German naval power was seen as a threat on the seas, while German industries were challenging British products on the world market. Also, as we have seen, the two countries had clashing imperialistic ambitions in both East Africa and the Middle East. For these reasons, and because of British fear of being alone in case of conflict with the Triple Alliance, it entered into an entente (understanding) with France in 1904. This Entente Cordiale, although not a strictly military alliance, nevertheless brought these two historic enemies closer together. It was also another instance of how self-interest affects a nation's foreign policy. Only six years earlier, in 1898, Britain and France had almost gone to war over the Fashoda affair in Africa, but now both nations were more afraid of Germany than of each other. Also, the Anglo-French Entente of that year settled another colonial issue in Africa. It provided that Britain would recognize French control in Morocco in return for French recognition of British control in Egypt.

In 1907 Britain and Russia entered into an "understanding." Russia, weakened and shocked by her defeat in the Russo-Japanese War (1904–1905), was willing to smooth over with Britain the conflicting imperialistic claims of both nations in Central Asia (i.e., Afghanistan and Persia). Britain saw in Russia another counterweight to Germany, geographically. Indeed, the agreement with Russia in 1907, and that with France in 1904, reflected a traditional British foreign policy goal in dealings with other European nations—to maintain a **balance of power**. As a country lying apart from the European continent, Britain would traditionally stay out of the disputes among continental countries. She would act differently, however, when events might, in her opinion, appear threatening to her interests. Thus, in the Napoleonic Wars, Britain sided with Prussia to stop General Napoleon. Less than 100 years later, however, Britain found that her self-interest lay in aligning herself with France and Russia against Germany, the nation united by Prussia!

This 1907 agreement between Britain and Russia, along with the Dual Alliance of 1894 and the Entente Cordiale of 1904, now aligned Britain, France, and Russia as the **Triple Entente**. The result was that, fewer than ten years into the twentieth century, Europe had become an armed camp. Two powerful alliances, representing six nations, had emerged. Although these alliances were supposedly formed to keep peace, we have to wonder whether their creation provided a balance of power or a balance of terror. We can also ask, in general, whether alliances tend to promote peace or war. In the early 1900s, the danger existed that the slightest dispute between any two nations in opposing alliances could expand into a confrontation among all six nations. This is what happened in 1914.

Militarism　As the alliance system divided Europe into opposing groups, each member nation began to increase its military strength. Indeed, one German officer had said, "In time of peace, prepare for war." The growth of armies and navies, as well as the development of advanced weaponry, added to the **belligerent** (warlike, get-tough) mood. Belligerent and hostile nations have a tendency to settle arguments by fighting. As governments sought to build up their military arsenals, arms manufacturers such as Krupp in Germany and Schneider in France increased production.

Lack of Any World Peacekeeping Machinery　Prior to World War I, no strong global organization existed to foster peace or to settle disputes between nations. There was no United Nations. Some historians have described the tense period from the 1870s to 1914 as one of international **anarchy**. (The term *anarchy* refers to the absence of any overriding political organization, able to set and enforce rules.)

Immediate Cause

The immediate cause of World War I was the assassination of Francis (Franz) Ferdinand, archduke of Austria, on June 28, 1914. He was killed in Sarajevo, the capital city of Bosnia and Herzogovina, by Gavrilo Princip. Bosnia and Herzogovina were Balkan parts of the Austro-Hungarian Empire, and had Slavic people

Austrian Archduke Francis Ferdinand.

who wished to be free. Princip was from nearby Serbia, an independent Slavic nation, which wanted unification with Bosnia and Herzogovina and was opposed to rule by Austria-Hungary. Although Princip was not a Serbian government official, and acted as a member of the Black Hand, a secret society of Serbian nationalists, Austria-Hungary nevertheless blamed Serbia for the killing. Although Serbia claimed it was not responsible, its government had known of the assassination plot beforehand.

The shots fired by Princip not only killed the archduke and his wife, but also would indirectly cause the deaths of almost ten million other people during the next four years. The event of June 28 has been likened to a "spark setting off the Balkan powder keg." The term *powder keg* referred to the crisis that had been smoldering in the Balkans for several years prior to 1914. Tension had existed since the 1870s, when Serbian nationalists with Russian backing strove to create a Slavic state from parts of Austria-Hungary and the declining Ottoman Turkish Empire. Subject nationalities under Austria-Hungary protested the treatment they received. Austro-Hungarian opposition to these movements was intense. In 1912–1913, two Balkan wars were fought over land claims in the area. These wars would prove to be mere preludes to what would take place all over Europe from 1914 to 1918.

Events Following the Archduke's Assassination

In the six weeks between the assassination on June 28 and the outbreak of war on August 4, 1914, events developed in a way that showed how jealousies, rivalries, bitterness, and underlying causes discussed previously would destroy the Pax Europa. The key events that saw the firing of a revolver in June lead to the blasting of guns in August were as follows:

1. Between June 28 and July 23, Austria-Hungary decided to take action against Serbia. However, knowing that Russia might aid Serbia, Austria-Hungary wanted to be sure that Germany would stand behind her. Germany indicated her willingness to do so. The German agreement to support any policy to be pursued by Austria-Hungary has been interpreted as Germany giving her ally a "blank check to be filled in for any amount."

2. On July 23, Austria-Hungary sent Serbia an **ultimatum** (a set of demands that must be accepted). This required Serbia to put down all writing, teaching, demonstrating, and so on that was against Austria-Hungary. The ultimatum also demanded that Serbia fire any officials opposed to Austria-Hungary, and that Austria-Hungary be allowed to send her own judges to Serbia to conduct a trial of those involved with the archduke's shooting. If the ultimatum was not answered positively within 48 hours, war would be declared on Serbia.

3. On July 25, France assured Russia of support in the crisis.

4. On July 26, Serbia, having received some assurance of support from Russia, responded affirmatively to all parts of the ultimatum except the last part.

Five minutes after this photograph of the archduke and his wife, Sophie, was taken on June 28, 1914, they were assassinated by Gavrilo Princip.

Gavrilo Princip

If you had happened to pass the young man on the street, you most likely would have paid little attention to him. He was short and very thin, with a high forehead. The only noticeable aspect was his strikingly blue eyes. If you had come closer, you might say that they had an almost hypnotic quality. Perhaps they shone with the idealism of youth—the passionate desire to drive the Austrians from his beloved Serbia and to create an independent nation. Gavrilo Princip opposed Church domination, custom, and tradition, hated the Austrian regime, and sought the creation of a south Slav state. Like many other zealots, he did not smoke, drink, or seek the company of women.

Princip decided that the best way to accomplish his goal was through the assassination of Francis Ferdinand, the archduke of Austria. Francis Joseph, who had been Emperor of Austria, was reaching the end of his days and Francis Ferdinand would be the successor. A band of three men, with Princip as their leader, planned to kill the archduke when the time was right. They formed a secret society, the Black Hand, and took an oath. We would find it difficult today to take this seriously, but it was not foolish to them. They swore that "...from this day until the moment of my death, I shall remain faithful to every law of this organization; I shall be ready to sacrifice for it, to die for it, and to take its secrets to the grave." After the oath was completed, each of the three conspirators was given a little box containing a cyanide capsule that he was to take if captured.

The newspapers reported that the archduke and his wife were to visit Sarajevo on June 28. The Austrians could not have picked a worse time. June 28 was a day held sacred by all Serb nationalists. It was St. Vitas Day, named for a Serbian hero who had stabbed a sultan that was leading a Turkish army. To have the successor to the throne of the Austrian oppressors visit on that day was a slap in the face of all Serbian nationalists.

Princip and his followers prepared themselves for the visit by practicing their markmanship. Princip became a skilled man with a gun.

The three arrived in Sarajevo on June 4, 1914, and stayed pretty much to themselves. They studied the route that the newspapers said would be taken by the archduke. Princip gave each man a position along the route so that the three would have a number of opportunities to kill Francis Ferdinand as he passed.

While waiting at the post he had assigned to himself, Princip heard a bomb go off. Each of the conspirators had a pistol and a bomb. Elated, he ran to see what had happened. Finding that one of his followers had been arrested, Princip was going to shoot both his partner and himself so as to avoid capture. The crowds were so great, however, that he could not get a shot off. He then heard that the attempt had failed and the archduke had driven off safely.

What happened then is one of the strange twists of fate that sometimes occur in history. Believing that it was all over, that they had lost their opportunity to strike a blow for Serbian nationalism, Princip looked up and saw the archduke in a car five feet away. The archduke had insisted on going to see an aide who had been wounded by the bomb blast. Another aide, believing that, if another attempt was made, it would come from a certain side, now stood on the running board of the car on that side—opposite from Princip. The driver of the automobile drove down the wrong street to get to the hospital and had to stop to turn around. He chose to do this directly in front of where Princip was standing. It was too close to use the bomb, so Princip took out his pistol and shot twice, killing both the archduke and his wife.

Princip then attempted to shoot himself, but the gun was ripped from his hand by the crowd. He tried to bite down on the cyanide capsule, but a blow to his head knocked it out of his mouth. The conspirators were all arrested and sentenced to death—except for Princip. Too young for the death penalty, he was sentenced to 20 years at hard labor. Four years later, on April 28, 1918, he died in prison as a result of harsh treatment and tuberculosis. Princip did not live to see the end of the war he did so much to bring about.

5. On July 26, Britain called for an international conference.
6. On July 27, Germany rejected the invitation to attend.
7. On July 28, Austria declared war on Serbia and bombed the city of Belgrade, having begun **mobilization** (getting ready for war) during the summer.
8. On July 29, Russia began to mobilize. Germany tried to soften and moderate Austria-Hungary's reactions to the ultimatum's response.
9. On August 1, France announced that she would do what her interests dictated.
10. On August 2, Germany declared war on Russia.
11. On August 3, Germany declared war on France and invaded Belgium in order to attack France. Britain, not legally bound by her entente with France to assist that nation, pondered a decision to go to war.
12. On August 4, Britain declared war on Germany. What finally swayed Britain's declaration was the invasion of Belgium. In a treaty signed in 1839, Britain, the German state of Prussia, and other European powers had agreed to respect and guarantee the neutrality of Belgium. Germany's actions in 1914 were seen as a violation of this treaty. The fact that Germany was indifferent about Belgium's status and Britain's reaction was evident in the sarcastic statement made by Chancellor Bethmann-Hollweg of Germany. He dismissed Britain's action by stating that Britain had gone to war simply for "a scrap of paper." This remark, printed by presses all over the world, was a major reason for the charge of war guilt made against Germany after the war.
13. On August 6, Austria-Hungary declared war on Russia.

By the first week of August, all members of the two alliances had gone to war except Italy. That nation did not consider itself bound by the Triple Alliance agreement, and had always been uneasy about aligning itself with Austria-Hungary. In May 1915, Italy joined the Allies (Britain, France, Japan, Russia, and Serbia), having signed a secret agreement with them for a promise of land. Japan joined the Allied side in 1914, while the United States would join in 1917. By the time the war was over, other nations, as well as colonies of nations, had become involved as belligerents (participants in a fight).

In *Origins of the World War*, a book about World War I written in 1928, the American historian Sidney Fay states, "None of the Powers wanted a European War. Their governing rulers and ministers, with few exceptions, all foresaw that it must be a frightful struggle in which the political results were not absolutely certain, but in which the loss of life, suffering, and economic consequences were bound to be terrible." Since then, some other historians have supported Fay's thinking. Others have laid the blame on one or more of the major belligerents. All of them, however, have agreed on how shocking and unprecedented were the human and economic consequences. In the next section we will see why these tragedies occurred as we survey the conduct of the war.

Conduct of World War I

The terrible loss of life and property during World War I can explain why this conflict was originally called the Great War. New weapons and technology were used that made warfare more deadly than it had ever been before. With almost 30 nations and colonies involved, World War I had more participants, both military and civilian, than any prior war on our planet. The actual conduct of the war will concern us in this section.

New weapons and technology caused more human losses than any prior war in what was termed the Great War. Here British soldiers fight from the trenches.

Women played a valuable role on the home front during the war. Skilled workers are shown in a French munitions factory.

New Weapons

The warfare from 1914 to 1918 produced unprecedented numbers of casualties as innovative (new) weaponry was employed on land and in sea and air. Ground forces were equipped with machine guns able to fire many bullets in quick succession over a wide area. The use of machine guns eliminated the traditional stand-up-and-charge tactics. Tanks were armored vehicles containing lethal guns, and maneuvered by soldiers seated inside. These fierce-looking vehicles could easily break through enemy lines and move over different kinds of terrain (land). Exploding canisters released poison gas that caused injuries never experienced in prior conflicts between nations. The threat of gas warfare required infantry units to carry gas masks and to learn how to use them within seconds of an attack.

Naval warfare expanded with the construction of faster and more powerful battleships. Besides engaging in combat and troop transport, these ships were effective in maintaining blockades of water routes. An innovation was the submarine, first used by Germany. Also called U-boats, from the German word *unterwasser* (underwater), submarines inflicted enormous damage throughout the war.

Warfare in the air was introduced as belligerents on both sides sought to use the newly invented airplane. Aircraft were initially utilized to observe troop movements. Pilots also engaged in bombings and "dogfights," but on a very limited scale. Aerial combat here was in its infancy and had little impact upon the course of the Great War.

The management and care of these new weapons called for extensive training. The training had to be given not just to professional soldiers, but also to the thousands of civilians who were drafted to fight for their countries. The drafting of civilians for combat had been relatively rare in previous wars. Most fighting had been done by individuals who had voluntarily chosen military careers and were thus professional soldiers. World War I, with so many civilians in uniform and so many others at work in factories and at home in the war effort, became known as the first total war.

Military Aspects

The war was fought almost entirely in Europe and surrounding waters, although there was some action in the Middle East. From 1914 to 1916 the fighting resulted in a **stalemate**, with neither side gaining much ground. In 1917, even though Russia dropped out of the war, the entry of the United States helped the remaining Triple Entente nations to secure victory in 1918. In Europe, the war was fought on two fronts, the western and the eastern, described in relation to the

War posters from the United States and Germany were used to build up morale and patriotism.

geographical position of the Central powers. The major battles resulting from military strategic planning are listed below in chronological order, as are other key events of the war.

1. *Marne River* (1914): Lying to the southeast of Paris, the Marne River was the site of a strong defense effort by French forces against the Germans. After overrunning Belgium, Germany had hoped to score a quick victory against France by taking Paris. At the Marne River, both sides dug trenches in the ground, trying but unable to advance against each other. This kind of trench warfare was common along the western front.

2. *Tannenberg* (1914): This battle, fought on the eastern front, in Germany, proved to be a crushing defeat for the Russian army.

3. *Gallipoli* (1915): In 1914, the Ottoman Turks, fearing Russia, joined with the Triple Alliance powers. Turkey was in a geographical position to prevent Russian ships from reaching the Mediterranean Sea. Britain and France landed troops on Turkey's Gallipoli peninsula in an attempt to capture the capital of Constantinople and connect with Russia. After eight months of combat, the Allies withdrew. They could not break through the Turkish lines, commanded by Turkish and German officers.

4. *Jutland* (1916): This was the largest naval battle of the war, occurring off the coast of Denmark in the North Sea, between Britain and Germany. Although neither belligerent could claim complete victory, the German attempt to break the British blockade remained unsuccessful.

5. *Verdun* (1916): Scene of the bloodiest battle of the war, this area in northeastern France locked France and Germany into an indecisive struggle. A famous example of dangerous, dirty, and at times boring trench warfare, the six-month-long encounter at Verdun saw almost 600,000 men killed.

6. *Russian Revolution of March* (1917): Russian forces had suffered disastrous losses in the war. The resulting discontent, along with other factors, led to the overthrow of Czar Nicholas II. However, the new provisional government, led by Aleksandr Kerensky, wanted Russia to stay in the war.

7. *United States Entry into the War* (April 1917): Although the United States had declared itself neutral at the outbreak of the war in 1914, and wished to follow a policy of **isolationism**, it changed its mind during the next three years. For a number of reasons dealing with economics, politics, geography, cultural ties, and **propaganda**, Congress sided with the British and French and declared war on the Central powers. This was done at the request of President Woodrow Wilson.

8. *Capture of Jerusalem by British Forces* (1917): This victory in Palestine by British General Edward Allenby helped protect British interests in the Middle East and was a severe blow against Ottoman Turkish rule in the region. It laid the basis for the British Mandate in Palestine, to begin after the war. (See Chapter 28, "Imperialism in Asia.")

9. *Russian Revolution of November* (1917): In the second Russian Revolution of 1917, the provisional government was ousted by Vladimir Ilyich (Nikolai) Lenin and the Communists. Lenin had stated that he wanted to take Russia out of the war. This was accomplished with the signing of peace treaties with the Central powers at Brest-Litovsk in 1918.

10. *Chateau-Thierry and the Argonne Forest* (1918): One result of the Brest-Litovsk treaties was that Germany was now free to take troops from the eastern front to the western front. She did this, mounting a large offensive push in

France. However, she was stopped at the battles of Chateau-Thierry and the Argonne Forest and was pushed back all the way to her own borders. These battles saw American forces under General John Pershing fighting with the French troops of General Ferdinand Foch.

End of the War

The skies were darkening for the Central powers in the fall of 1918. In September, the Turks requested peace. Austria-Hungary was coming apart, as some subject nationalities had declared their independence from the Empire. On November 9, Kaiser William II of Germany abdicated (quit his office) and fled to Holland. A new German government was established and agreed to stop fighting the war. Accordingly, an **armistice** was signed in a railroad car in France on November 11, 1918, between Germany and the Allied forces. The armistice stated that all combat would cease at the eleventh hour of the eleventh day of the eleventh month of 1918. There was rejoicing then in many parts of the world. In the United States, November 11 has since been a national holiday, referred to also as Veteran's Day or Armistice Day.

With peace now on the horizon, the world could breathe easier. In November 1918, nobody had yet called this war World War I. That title came later in the century, for reasons we will discuss in Chapter 32 ("World War II"). The key problems for consideration in the winter of 1918–1919 were how to arrange a suitable peace, what to do with the defeated countries, and how to prevent another "Great War" from occurring. These problems were on the agenda at the peace conference that took place in Paris in January 1919. The resolution of these problems, as well as the general results of the war, will be the next topic for us to examine.

Results of World War I

What is the purpose of a peace conference? This is an important question to ask as we prepare to study the peace conference that took place after World War I. Delegates to this kind of conference may agree on its purpose, but may disagree on how to achieve that purpose. They may not even agree on the purposes. Some other questions to consider are those raised at the end of the last section: How can a suitable and just peace be arranged? How should the defeated countries be treated? How can another war be prevented?

In this section you will see how each of these questions was answered by delegates at the Paris Peace Conference of 1919, and will also learn the general results of World War I.

The Delegates and Their Goals

The Peace Conference opened in Paris in January 1919, with delegates from almost all the victorious Allied powers. Russia was not present, as she was involved in a civil war. (See Chapter 31, "The Rise of Totalitarianism in Russia, Italy, and Germany.") Other absentees were the defeated nations. (It had been decided to call in Germany and her allies only after treaty terms had been drawn up.) The major participants in Paris were the four most powerful Allied victors, known as the **Big Four**: France, Great Britain, Italy, and the United States. They were represented by their respective leaders: Premier Georges Clemenceau of France, Prime Minister David Lloyd George of Great Britain, Premier Vittorio Orlando of Italy, and President Woodrow Wilson of the United States.

Each of these men came to the conference with specific goals and objectives. So did delegates from other nations, such as Belgium. Every delegate's goals represented the foreign policy desires of his nation. As we said previously, the foreign policy of a nation is influenced by its own self-interests. Foreign policy is also influenced by geography and a nation's past relations with other nations. These factors must be kept in mind to order to understand why there were disagreements among the Big Four at the 1919 Peace Conference.

France   Premier Clemenceau spoke for a nation that had been seriously hurt by Germany in this most recent war, as well as in the Franco-Prussian War some 47 years earlier. France wanted revanche for the loss of Alsace-Lorraine, and security against possible German **aggression** in the future. France hoped to severely weaken Germany by making that nation limit her military, give up land in Europe and overseas, and pay for damages during the war.

Great Britain   Although Britain was further away from Germany than was France, and although British soil had not been trod upon by German troops, Britain nevertheless wanted to see a weakened Germany. For Lloyd George, this would mean a reduced German navy, loss of colonies, and German reparations (payments) for the war. These goals would benefit British self-interests. Prime Minister George would be less harsh on Germany than would France. He may have remembered a slogan about Germany from a fellow countryman: "Hang the Kaiser, but preserve a balance of power."

Italy   Italy hoped to add to her territory in Europe, particularly with acquisitions from Austria-Hungary. She also wanted land overseas and claimed that many areas had been promised to her in secret treaties. Premier Orlando argued with Lloyd George about some of these claims, and left the conference in anger. The Big Four then became the Big Three.

The United States   President Wilson arrived in Paris with goals that were entirely different from those of his fellow delegates. Much more idealistic than they, and coming from a nation whose soil was untouched by the war and was furthest from the Central powers, he did not seek punishment. His overall goal was a "peace without victory." His specific goals were outlined in a speech he gave to Congress in January 1918 that contained the famous Fourteen Points. While eight of these concerned specific regions and nations, the remaining six dealt with broad issues and spelled out objectives that Wilson hoped to see adopted at the peace conference:

1. Freedom of the seas;
2. Self-determination for all people;
3. Open diplomacy and the end of secret treaties;
4. End of tariffs and other economic barriers;
5. Limitations on weapons; and
6. Establishment of a League of Nations to settle international disputes peacefully.

The signing of the Treaty of Versailles at the Hall of Mirrors on June 28, 1919, exactly five years after the assassination of Archduke Ferdinand.

It would almost seem that Wilson viewed war as a disease. And with a disease, doctors hope to cure it and ultimately find the reasons for it. If the reasons are known, then perhaps sufficient methods can be created to prevent its recurrence. Did the other "doctors" at the Paris Peace Conference agree with Wilson? Let us turn now to the provisions of the peace treaty that was put together and eventually signed at the Palace of Versailles in June 1919.

Provisions of the Versailles Peace Treaty

After much arguing and many compromises among the delegates, the Treaty of Versailles was drawn up in May 1919. At this point, representatives from the new German republic were summoned to appear and told to sign the treaty. Viewing the document as too harsh, the Germans at first refused to sign it. But when the Allies threatened to renew the war, the representatives had no choice. They signed the treaty on June 8, 1919, precisely five years after the assassination of Archduke Francis Ferdinand in Sarajevo! Another event from the past was called to mind at the signing ceremony. In the Hall of Mirrors, site of the ceremony, almost 50 years earlier after the Prussian victory in the Franco-Prussian War, the Prussian leader Bismarck had proclaimed the birth of the German Empire.

Although the treaty was a long document, its chief provisions can be summarized as follows:

1. Creation of a League of Nations.
2. Loss of German territory in Europe. Alsace-Lorraine would be returned to France. The resource-rich Saar Valley would be under League of Nations authority for 15 years. During that period, France could have all the coal mined in the region as part payment for German war damages. The recreated nation of Poland received much German territory, including a strip of land that would give Poland a seaport on the Baltic Sea. This strip of land, known as "the Polish corridor," separated German East Prussia from the rest of Germany. Danzing, formerly a German city, would be a free city administered by the League of Nations for Polish use.
3. Loss of German territory overseas. All German colonies would be held as **mandates** by the League of Nations.
4. Military restrictions on Germany. Germany was restricted to an army of 100,000 volunteers and prohibited from practicing **conscription** (drafting people into the armed forces). The Rhineland was to be demilitarized, and the navy limited to a few ships. Germany could not build submarines, military aircraft, or other instruments of war.

5. War guilt and reparations. Germany was forced to admit guilt for the war, and therefore required to make huge monetary payments called reparations.

Other Peace Treaties and Territorial Changes

Separate treaties were signed with the other Central powers.

1. With Austria in 1919, the Treaty of St. Germain; with Hungary in 1920, the Treaty of Trianon. In the last year of the war, the Austro-Hungarian Empire under Habsburg rule had ceased to exist. In its place were the independent nations of Austria and Hungary and the new nations of Czechoslovakia and Yugoslavia. Both consisted of subject nationalities that had long clamored for independent nationhood, free of Habsburg domination. The new Yugoslavia contained both Serbia and Sarajevo. Limitations were placed on the armies of both Austria and Hungary. They also had to pay reparations, though not as severe as those imposed on Germany. Also, Austria was forbidden from any future union (*anschluss*) with Germany.

2. With Turkey in 1923, the Treaty of Sevres. This treaty officially reduced the once powerful Ottoman Empire to the sole nation of Turkey. Non-Turkish areas in the Middle East were taken away and became mandates; two examples were Palestine and Syria. Turkey did not have to pay reparations, nor was her army restricted.

Other territorial arrangements saw Poland re-established as a nation. It had undergone several partitions since 1795. The three Baltic regions of Lithuania, Latvia, and Estonia became free. They had been taken by Germany from Russia in the Treaty of Brest-Litovsk, which was canceled after the war.

A summary of major territorial changes after World War I is given below. Also, see the contrasting maps of Europe to locate these changes.

MAJOR TERRITORIAL CHANGES AFTER WORLD WAR I

Change	Nation(s) from which land was taken
Poland was recreated, with a "corridor" to the sea.	Germany and German-conquered areas of Russia
Romania was enlarged.	Austria-Hungary
Yugoslavia and Czechoslovakia were created as new nations.	Austria-Hungary
Austria and Hungary became separate nations.	Austria-Hungary
Finland, Estonia, Latvia, and Lithuania were created.	Russia
Alsace-Lorraine was returned to France.	Germany
Syria, Lebanon, and Palestine become mandates under the League of Nations.	Turkey

General Results of World War I

As we have seen, World War I was labeled the Great War for many reasons. An additional reason lies in the fact that the war changed the course of world history. It brought short-range results as well as long-range outcomes that affected future

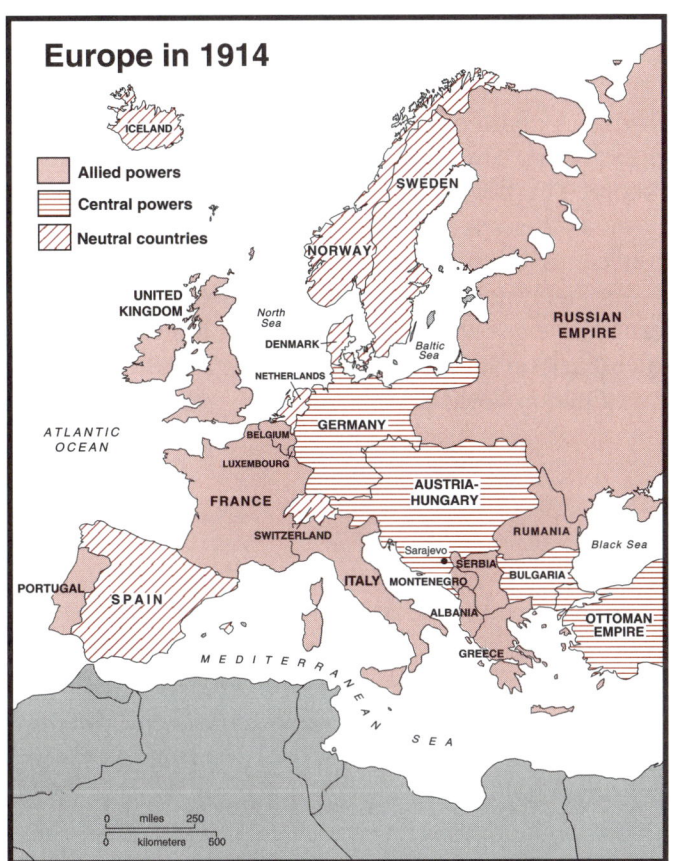

Europe in 1914

- Allied powers
- Central powers
- Neutral countries

ICELAND
SWEDEN
NORWAY
UNITED KINGDOM
North Sea
DENMARK
Baltic Sea
NETHERLANDS
RUSSIAN EMPIRE
ATLANTIC OCEAN
GERMANY
BELGIUM
LUXEMBURG
FRANCE
AUSTRIA-HUNGARY
SWITZERLAND
RUMANIA
Black Sea
Sarajevo
SERBIA
ITALY MONTENEGRO
PORTUGAL
SPAIN
BULGARIA
ALBANIA
OTTOMAN EMPIRE
GREECE
M E D I T E R R A N E A N S E A

miles 0 250
kilometers 0 500

Europe in 1919

- New countries
- Countries with border changes

ICELAND
SWEDEN
NORWAY
FINLAND
ESTONIA
UNITED KINGDOM
IRELAND
North Sea
DENMARK
Baltic Sea
LATVIA
LITHUANIA
SOVIET UNION
NETHERLANDS
ATLANTIC OCEAN
E. PRUSSIA
GERMANY
POLAND
BELGIUM
LUXEMBURG
CZECHOSLOVAKIA
FRANCE
AUSTRIA HUNGARY
SWITZERLAND
ROMANIA
ITALY
YUGOSLAVIA
Black Sea
BULGARIA
PORTUGAL
SPAIN
ALBANIA
TURKEY
GREECE
M E D I T E R R A N E A N S E A

miles 0 250
kilometers 0 500

events and generations. The economic chaos and radical social changes in its wake were accompanied by historic political developments. Some of the most powerful European nations lost their influence and began to decline. Many monarchs lost their thrones. Some empires came to an end, while others expanded. A Communist government came to power in Russia. The general results, seen from economic, social, and political perspectives, are discussed below.

Economic The war was very costly to the participants. Costs were estimated at close to $400 billion. In all belligerent nations, taxes had to be raised while living standards fell. The losers became debtor nations, some of them finding it difficult to make reparation payments while rebuilding their economies. Many of the economic problems arising from the war were partly responsible for the worldwide Great Depression that began in 1929.

Social Casualties were heavy. Estimates are that ten million soldiers were killed and another 31 million wounded. Civilian population losses were also in the millions, caused to a large degree by the deadly weapons used for the first time in warfare. Most Europeans failed to understand the destructive power of these weapons until they had been used, and to realize how horrible modern warfare had become. Displacement of people as refugees and changes in boundaries brought resentment. This was true, for example, in western Poland and Czechoslovakia, where large numbers of Germans now found themselves living. Ethnic tensions also existed, for a variety of reasons, between Turks and Greeks and between Turks and

Armenians. Between 1915 and 1922 almost two million Armenians were killed by the Ottoman Turks in a campaign of **genocide**.

Political New nations arose, and boundaries changed, as shown in the preceding table. Ownership of some colonies changed. The long-standing Ottoman and Austro-Hungarian Empires were no more. The League of Nations was formed in an effort to secure world peace and to watch over specified areas as mandates. Three traditional royal **dynasties** saw their centuries-long rule ended: the Hohenzollerns in Germany, the Habsburgs in Austria-Hungary, and the Romanovs in Russia. The world's first Communist government came to power in Russia as a result of a revolution. Germany was about to embark on her first experience as a democracy. The United States was not viewed as a major world power.

Summary

Europe would never be the same after World War I. The results left the world uncertain about the future. As coming events would suggest, it may have been easier to achieve a victory on a battlefield than to gain a lasting peace at a conference table. The League of Nations was the first large international forum to design a peace plan for Europe since the 1815 Congress of Vienna. As we will see, however, the league lacked powers of enforcement and did not have the United States as a member. (In 1920, the U.S. Senate refused to let the United States join the league.)

*The Treaty of Versailles stirred controversy. Critics claimed that it was too harsh on Germany and thereby planted the seeds of World War II. The Germans certainly were bitter about it, claiming that its provisions amounted to a **diktat** (dictated peace). Adolf Hitler and the Nazi party were able to use this issue as an effective argument in their rise to power in 1933. Treaty critics in Germany and elsewhere believed that all of Wilson's Fourteen Points should have been incorporated into the treaty. In their view, the failure to do so created a peace with vengeance rather than with justice.*

Whether or not we accept these opinions, we should pause to consider a situation that, although simplistic, nevertheless raises a fundamental issue of human nature. Assume that two longtime enemies, A and B, have a fistfight. A wins decisively. To make sure that B will never again bother A, how should A act toward B? Should A continue to beat up B, inflicting additional punishment? Or should A treat B kindly, helping him up and shaking hands? Critics of the Versailles treaty would probably choose the second course of action, and proponents of the treaty the first.

Those who favored the treaty felt that Germany deserved what she received. For them, Germany was seen to have been a hostile, militaristic nation for decades that needed to be taught a lesson now that it was defeated in war. German land in Europe was taken mainly on the basis of nationality; lands taken overseas were to be administered as mandates under the League of Nations with the promise of eventual independence. The treaty by itself cannot be blamed for the rise of Hitler and the Nazis. And if all the treaty provisions had been fully enforced, particularly the military ones, argued the proponents, Germany would have been unable to engage in another world war.

You have now seen the answers to the question posed on page 527. These answers make us realize how troubling these questions are. Indeed, some of the decisions respecting territorial changes, as well as some other changes occurring in the World War I era, have become undone in our own times. The first few years of the 1990s, for example, have witnessed a new Germany, a disunited Czechoslovakia, a surprisingly reformed Russia, and a dismembered Yugoslavia facing a bitter civil war. The twentieth century began with trouble in the Balkans, and now seems to be ending in the same way. Yet no one foresees a major war emerging from the Balkan crisis of the 1990s.

From the upheavals and discontent immediately after World War I, however, there did emerge totalitarian dictatorships in Russia, Italy, and Germany. It is this emergence that will concern us in the next chapter.

Review Exercises

Causes of World War I

I. Matching

Directions: Match the words in Column A with the *correct description* in Column B.

Column A
1. belligerence
2. mobilization
3. anarchy
4. ultimatum
5. revanche

Column B
(a) lack of government or other legal authority
(b) warlike, hostile attitude
(c) final, forcible demand for some action to be taken
(d) preparations to fight a war
(e) French term indicating a desire to right something that is perceived as wrong

II. Map Exercise

Directions: Use the map on the next page to locate the place associated with each of the following statements. For each statement, write the *letter* of the place.

1. _____ This nation traditionally sought a balance of power in Europe.

2. _____ This country became part of the Triple Entente, with England and Russia.

3. _____ This was the place where Archduke Francis Ferdinand was assassinated.

4. _____ This country wanted revanche for Alsace-Lorraine.

5. _____ This country was the Triple Entente member most worried about German naval power.

6. _____ This nation aligned herself with Austria-Hungary and Italy as part of the Triple Alliance.

7. _____ This country was resented by several subject nationalities, who wanted to form their own nations.

8. _____ The Battle of Verdun was fought here.

9. _____ This nation issued an ultimatum to Serbia in 1914.

10. _____ This country was the victor in the Franco-Prussian War.

11. _____ This country was southeast of the area of the Balkan Wars of 1912–1913.

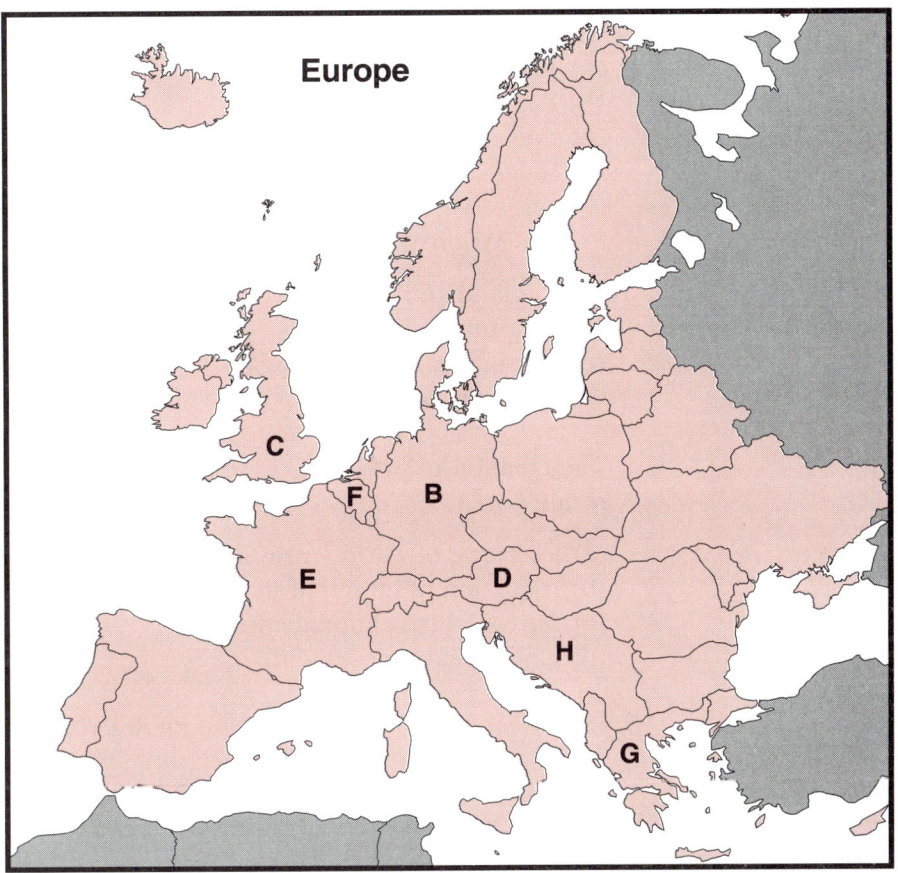

Europe

12. _____ This country gave Austria-Hungary a "blank check" after the archduke's assassination.

13. _____ This nation was the neutral country whose invasion by Germany finally made England a belligerent in World War I.

III. Multiple Choice

Directions: Find the *letter* of the correct answer.

1. The formation of the Triple Entente and the Triple Alliance was an attempt to

   (a) encourage war.
   (b) end imperialism.
   (c) achieve a balance of power.
   (d) group nations according to their attitudes toward democracy.

2. The immediate cause of World War I was the

   (a) imperialist rivalry in Africa.
   (b) assassination of the Austrian archduke.
   (c) Fashoda affair.
   (d) dispute over Alsace-Lorraine.

3. Austria hesitated before attacking Serbia in 1914 because of fear of

   (a) Russia.
   (b) England.
   (c) the United States.
   (d) Italy.

4. Prior to World War I, the main rivals for influence in the Balkans were

   (a) England and France.
   (b) Belgium and Italy.
   (c) Russia and Austria-Hungary.
   (d) Germany and Turkey.

5. The creation of two alliances of European powers in the years before 1914 resulted in a

   (a) lessening of world tensions.
   (b) reduction in imperialism.
   (c) series of international crises.
   (d) global peace movement.

6. Underlying causes of war can also be described as causes that are

   (a) basic.
   (b) inevitable.
   (c) immediate.
   (d) natural.

7. The Central powers in World War I included all of the following *except*

   (a) Turkey.
   (b) Germany.
   (c) France.
   (d) Austria-Hungary.

IV. Thought Questions

Directions: Answer the following questions in essay form.

1. There were several causes for the outbreak of World War I.

   A. Explain the difference between an underlying cause and an immediate cause.
   B. Describe three underlying causes, and give an example of each.
   C. Which one of the three that you described in (B) was the most responsible for bringing on the war? Explain your answer.

2. A nation's perception of its self-interests will often affect its foreign policy. Describe two examples that illustrate this statement, with reference to the growth of alliances prior to World War I.

3. Explain this statement: "Gavrilo Princip's bullet ended almost 100 years of a Pax Europa."

Conduct of World War I

I. Matching

Directions: Match the words in Column A with the *correct description* in Column B.

<u>Column A</u>
1. stalemate
2. abdication
3. armistice
4. trench

<u>Column B</u>
(a) removing oneself from a high position of authority
(b) truce in fighting
(c) referring to a form of warfare, fought from a fixed, dug-in site
(d) indecisive outcome in a war, where no side has made any major gains

II. Famous People

Directions: For each person listed below, write TA if the person was from a nation or an ally of the Triple Alliance. Write TE if the person was from a nation or ally of the Triple Entente.

1. _____ Ferdinand Foch

2. _____ John Pershing

3. _____ Kaiser William II

4. _____ Woodrow Wilson

5. _____ Tsar Nicholas II

6. _____ Edward Allenby

7. _____ Aleksandr Kerenshii

III. Famous Places

Directions: At each of the places listed below, an event took place that was important in World War I.

1. Argonne Forest
2. Brest-Litovsk
3. Gallipoli
4. Jerusalem
5. Jutland
6. Marne River
7. Verdun

For each place, do the following:
A. Identify the country in which the place is located.
B. Describe what happened there, naming any nation that was involved in the event.
C. Explain the significance of the event in regard to World War I.

IV. Thought Questions

Directions: Answer the following questions in essay form.

1. World War I was called the Great War, in terms of weapons and participants. Discuss four specific reasons to justify this statement.

2. Identify each of the following by showing its relationship to World War I:

A. trench warfare
B. eastern front
C. western front
D. "eleventh hour of the eleventh day of the eleventh month"

Results of World War I

I. Matching

Directions: Match the words in Column A with the *correct description* in Column B.

<u>Column A</u>
1. reparations
2. conscription
3. debtor
4. anschluss
5. genocide
6. refugee
7. diktat

<u>Column B</u>
(a) union between nations
(b) German view of the Versailles treaty's provisions that affected Germany
(c) monetary payment for war damages
(d) person or nation that owes money
(e) intentional killing of an ethnic group
(f) one who is forced to flee from his or her native land
(g) drafting of civilians into a nation's armed forces

II. Map Exercise

Directions: Use the map to locate the place associated with each of the following statements. For each statement, write the *letter* of the place.

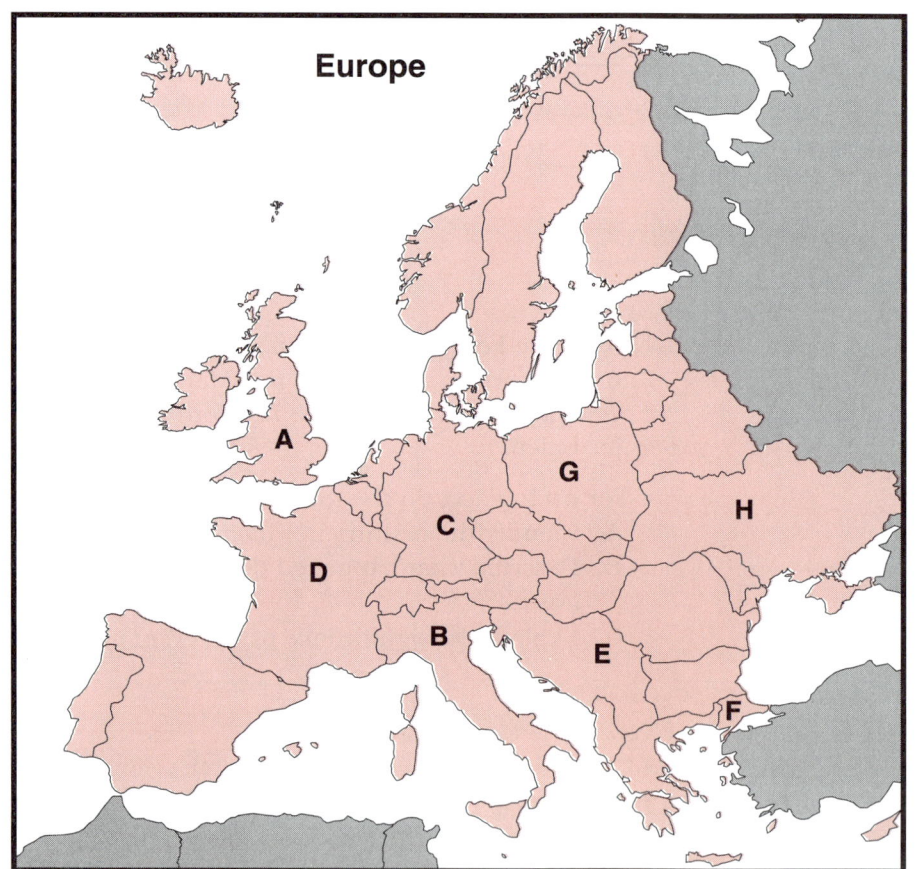

1. _____ This country was represented by Vittorio Orlando at the Paris Peace Conference.

2. _____ This country was defeated in the war and forced to admit "war guilt" and to pay reparations.

3. _____ This area was represented by Georges Clemenceau at the Paris Peace Conference.

4. _____ This nation regained Alsace-Lorraine after the war.

5. _____ This area was created after the war as a new nation containing Serbia, Sarajevo, and some Balkan nationalities.

6. _____ This country was represented by Lloyd George at the Paris Peace Conference.

7. _____ This area was closest to the nation that was given a mandate over Palestine, as a result of Turkey's defeat in World War I.

8. _____ This country was recreated after World War I, with a "corridor" to the Baltic Sea.

9. _____ This area was the place where the Habsburg Dynasty lost power after the war.

10. _____ This area was the place where the Hohenzollern Dynasty lost power after the war.

11. _____ This country was the place where genocidal actions were carried out against Armenians.

12. _____ This was the easternmost nation from the nation represented by Woodrow Wilson at the Paris Peace Conference.

13. _____ This area separated Germany from East Prussia.

III. Multiple Choice

Directions: Find the *letter* of the correct answer.

1. The Big Four at the Paris Peace Conference did not include

   (a) France. (b) England.
   (c) Russia. (d) Italy.

2. At the conference a "peace without victory" was the goal sought by

   (a) Lloyd George.
   (b) Woodrow Wilson.
   (c) Georges Clemenceau.
   (d) Tsar Nicholas II.

3. Which is a valid statement concerning *both* the Congress of Vienna (1815) and the Paris Peace Conference (1919)?

   (a) France attended as a victorious nation.
   (b) Kings were restored to their thrones.
   (c) Many boundaries were changed.
   (d) A League of Nations was created.

4. A political result of World War I was that in some European nations

   (a) living standards improved.
   (b) dictators came to power.
   (c) trade with the United States increased.
   (d) migration to overseas colonies decreased.

5. President Wilson's hopes were best reflected in the part of the Versailles treaty that concerned

    (a) splitting Germany's colonies among the Allies.
    (b) war guilt.
    (c) reparations.
    (d) the League of Nations.

IV. Thought Questions

Direction: Answer the following questions in essay form.

1. Assume that tape recordings have been recently discovered concerning two conversations held in Paris in 1919, and that you have listened to these tapes. Those taking part in the conversations were Lloyd George (LG), Georges Clemenceau (GC), Woodrow Wilson (WW), and Gavrilo Princip's ghost (GPG). Conversation 1 was held on the first day of the Paris Peace Conference, at a private party. Conversation 2 was held at another party, just after the signing of the Versailles peace treaty. It is necessary that you write down what you heard in these conversations, as the tapes are very old and may soon disintegrate.

   As you listened to conversation 1, you learned much and heard *three* of the people named above. Choose two persons that you heard, and for *each one* describe the following:

    A. the area or territory represented by the person;
    B. one goal the person hoped to achieve at the Paris Peace Conference, and one reason for this goal;
    C. the person's reaction to the goal of one other person.

   As you listened to conversation 2, you learned what all *four* people thought of a portion of the Versailles treaty.

   Write down both conversations, labeling each one and skipping a line between them. The format of the conversations should use the initials given above, and might begin like this:

   LG: Good evening, friends. It's nice to see you in Paris tonight.
   WW: Yes, indeed. We have some important business to transact.
   GC: We surely do. As soon as this party is over, we can work on the map of Europe.
   GPC: Yes! I am very concerned about this matter. I wish slower music was being played. I'm too old for these fast numbers.

2. The Treaty of Versailles significantly affected Germany.

    A. Describe three provisions that had important effects on Germany.
    B. Explain two reasons for German criticism of the treaty.
    C. Do you agree with the treaty's provisions affecting Germany (i.e., was Germany treated properly or too harshly?)? Explain.

3. Describe three results of World War I, including one in each of these categories: political, economic, and social.

    A. Which result most seriously affected Europe? Explain.
    B. Which result would, in your opinion, have the most significance for the future of Europe? (Make a prediction and explain your answer.)

CHAPTER 31

The Rise of Totalitarianism in Russia, Italy, and Germany

The world had little time to breathe after the Treaty of Versailles before it seemed that trouble was again on the horizon. Profound changes in three nations would affect the rest of the world for the remaining years of the century.

It is interesting that in Russia, Italy, and Germany three men used similar tactics to rise to power and solidify their positions. Stalin, Mussolini, and Hitler, while different in many ways, also had much in common. They came from unimpressive backgrounds, but they were shrewd about human nature. Seeing a political vacuum, they filled it and then eliminated opposition. Promises were made to people who were suffering economic hardships and welcomed the hope of a better future. All three leaders were single-minded men who used a small band of dedicated followers to frighten the masses of people. Each had a simple, easily understood plan. Each appealed to the nationalistic spirit of the people and was successful because good people did nothing.

Because of these three, millions died. Ask yourself, "What would I have done?" as you read this chapter.

Communism in Russia

The rise of **totalitarianism** in Russia began a trend that was to be followed throughout many parts of Europe in the twentieth century. Totalitarianism is a form of government in which one person or group, usually a political party, has complete control and does not tolerate (allow) any opposition. With World War I, the traditional Russian tsarist system collapsed and left a vacuum in its place. It was the **Bolsheviks**, or Communists, who seized the opportunity.

When the war began, the tsarist government was trying to correct the many problems and widespread unrest created by Russian industrialization. The inability of the regime to fight a modern war made the faults and weaknesses of the **monarchy** even more apparent, and the lack of any democratic experience left the nation vulnerable to any group ruthless enough to seize power. Throughout the nineteenth century, the tsars had failed to respond adequately to the need for political reform. That failure was about to doom the Russian monarchy.

Russia in World War I (1914–1917)

The Last Years of the Czarist System

For Russia, World War I was a devastating experience. It was the worst possible time for Russia, still trying to industrialize and solve many internal problems, to go to war. The magnitude of World War I, which destroyed many stable governments, was even more damaging for the tsarist regime. Russia's limited industry, agriculture, and communications could not sustain a major war effort. Despite advice to the contrary, Tsar Nicholas (Nikolai) II (1868–1918) took personal command of the army in the autumn of 1915. The retreating Russian forces, demoralized (discouraged) by more than a year of terrible defeats, expected the Tsar's leadership to turn the tide of battle. Instead, the continuing losses undermined the image of the Russian ruler, who had left his unpopular wife, Tsarina Alexandra (Aleksandra) (1872–1918), in charge of the government while he was away. (See Chapter 24, "Tsarist Russia.") The civilian population also was demoralized

Chapter 31 Chronology

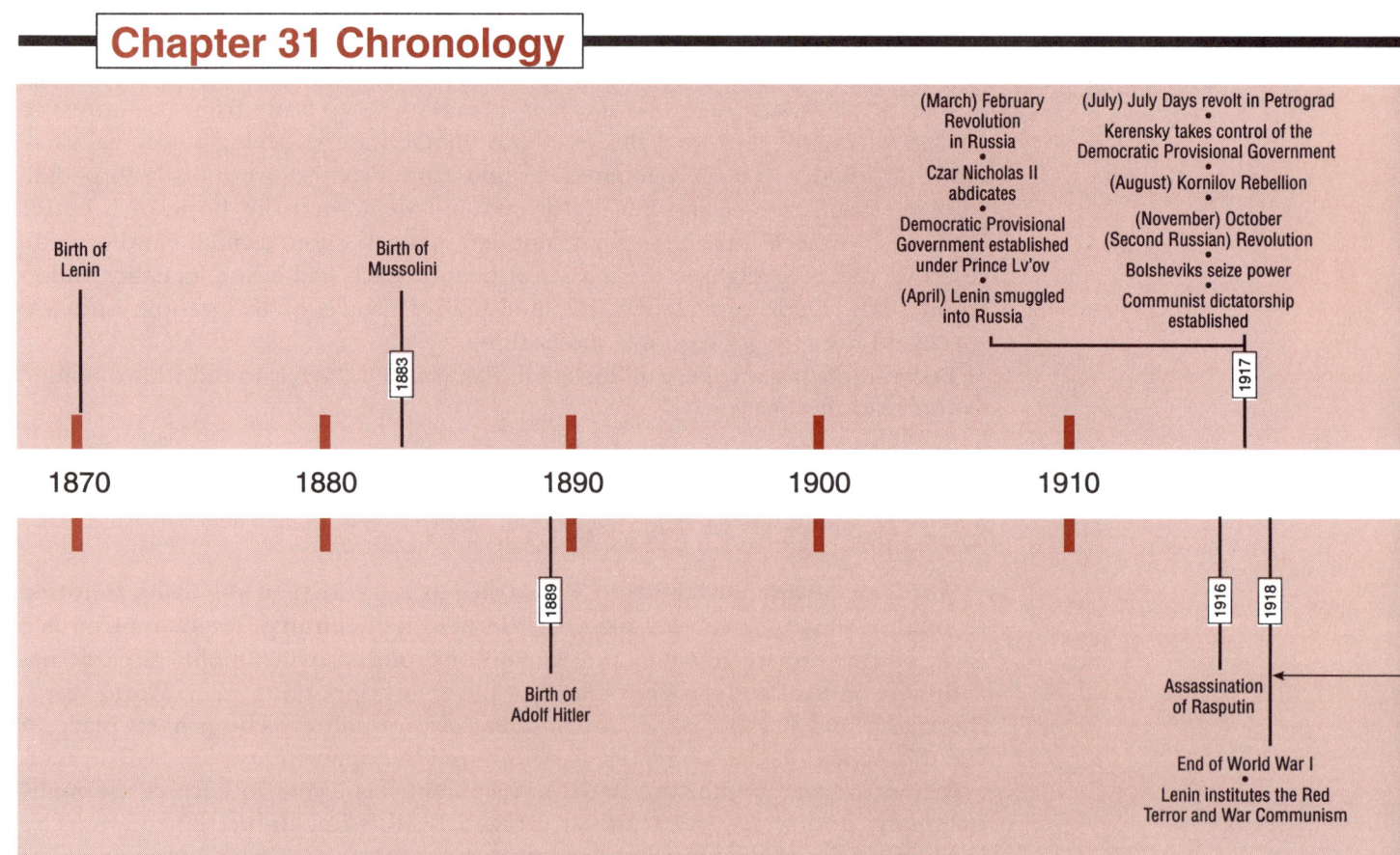

Birth of Lenin	Birth of Mussolini 1883		(March) February Revolution in Russia • Czar Nicholas II abdicates • Democratic Provisional Government established under Prince Lv'ov • (April) Lenin smuggled into Russia

(July) July Days revolt in Petrograd • Kerensky takes control of the Democratic Provisional Government • (August) Kornilov Rebellion • (November) October (Second Russian) Revolution • Bolsheviks seize power • Communist dictatorship established

1917

1870   1880   1890   1900   1910

1889

Birth of Adolf Hitler

1916   1918

Assassination of Rasputin

End of World War I
•
Lenin institutes the Red Terror and War Communism

by defeat and began to blame the German-born Alexandra for Russia's military performance. Russia was hopelessly unable to supply her troops with weapons or food. The fragile industrial structure was near collapse. Revolutionaries agitated workers into striking, creating even greater shortages for the army. As hunger, suffering, and humiliation grew, soldiers refused to follow orders, revolted against their commanders, or simply deserted.

The February Revolution of 1917

By February 1917, the Tsar's army was either retreating or deserting, while riots erupted in Russian cities. Returning to the capital city of Petrograd (St. Petersburg had been renamed at the start of the war), Tsar Nicholas was captured. The **Duma** (Russian parliament) had already declared a new government, under the leadership of the liberal nobleman Prince Georgii Lv'ov (1861–1925). In March 1917, 300 years of rule by the Romanov **Dynasty** came to an end when Nicholas abdicated (resigned) as the Tsar of Russia. He also abdicated for his son and thereby ended the centuries-old autocratic monarchy that had ruled Russia. The well-meaning but weak and incompetent Tsar never fully understood what had happened or why. He merely observed that the date on the letter of abdication was March 15, or the Ides of March, the day on which Julius Caesar had been assassinated in the Roman Senate (*tsar* means "Caesar" in Russian). He accepted his fall from power as fate.

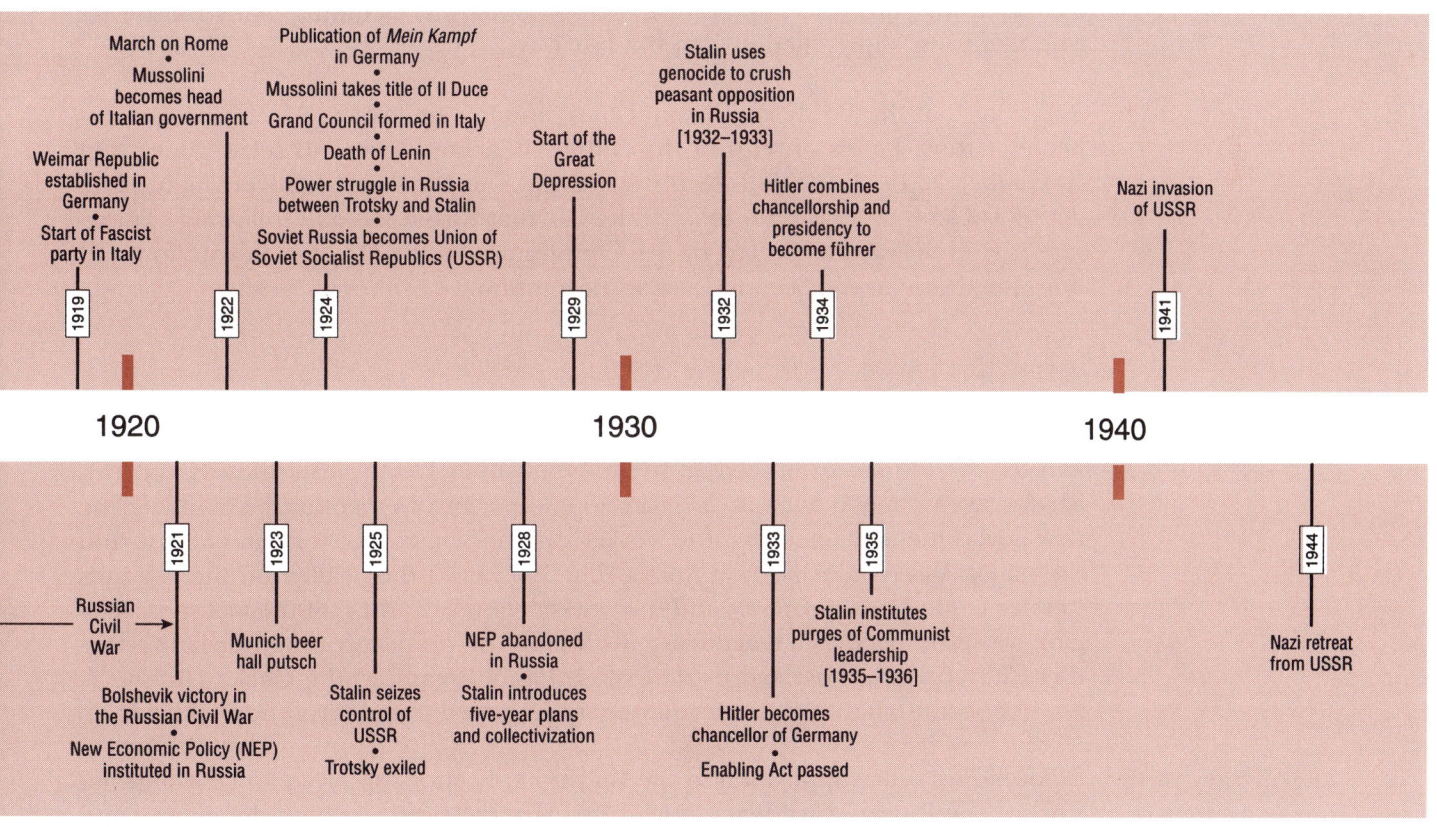

The Provisional Government (March–October 1917)

The Program of the Provisional Government. The **Democratic Provisional Government**, as the new administration was called, declared that Russia was a democracy and announced plans to hold elections. It consisted, however, of the **bourgeoisie** (middle class), liberal nobles, and intellectuals, and did not end Russia's involvement in the war. The defeats continued. The leadership showed that it did not understand how desperate and tired the Russian people were from the war. The Provisional Government's goal to transform Russia into a **democracy** by allowing elections and freedom of speech was well intentioned, but impracticable during a major war. Also, the program of democratic reform was unfamiliar to most Russians, who had known no other form of government other than **autocracy**.

The Rise of the Soviets. In the meantime, the workers, soldiers, and sailors in the cities responded to the leaders of worker's parties, in particular the Socialists (see Chapter 24 "Tsarist Russia"). These parties formed their own councils, called **soviets**. In April, the leader of the Bolsheviks, or Communists, Vladimir Lenin (1870–1924), returned to Russia from exile in Switzerland and presented his radical program of proletarian (worker) Socialist **revolution** called the April Theses. Despite the program's appeal to the masses (it called for "bread, land, and peace"), the extremist Bolsheviks did not attract a majority of workers.

The July Days. In July came a revolt against the unpopular Provisional Government. Known as the July Days, the uprising in Petrograd was the result of frustration over Russia's continued participation in the war. In an attempt to appease the populace, Lv'ov was replaced by Aleksandr Kerenskii (1881–1970), a member of the Socialist Revolutionary party. In September, General Lavr Kornilov (1870–1918), commander of the Russian army, attempted to seize power from the provisional government and establish a military dictatorship. Desperate for troops, Kerenskii was forced to free all of the revolutionaries, including many Bolsheviks who had been imprisoned during the July Days.

The October Revolution of 1917

Realizing that the Bolsheviks did not have enough support to win in the December elections, Lenin organized the Bolshevik armed forces to seize power. On November 7, 1917, the Bolsheviks overthrew the Provisional Government. The date was October 25 on the Julian calendar that Russia was still following. Therefore, the event was celebrated by the Communists as the October Revolution, but it is also known as the Second Russian Revolution.

The Russian Civil War (1918–1921)

The Establishment of Soviet Russia

After the October Revolution, Lenin and his followers made peace with Germany and removed Russia from the war. In the humiliating Treaty of Brest-Litovsk (1918), Russia gave up much territory in order to end her involvement in the conflict. The new government claimed that the worker's parties, or soviets, were in control, and the nation was renamed Soviet Russia. The Bolsheviks then called on the peasants to seize landowners' property, and the workers to take control of the factories. Religion was prohibited as a **reactionary** institution. All property of the Russian Orthodox Church was confiscated or destroyed. Lenin organized the **Cheka** (Bolshevik secret police) to fight counterrevolutionary (opposed to the revolution) activity.

The Victory of the Red Army

Before long, active opposition to the Bolshevik dictatorship broke out throughout Russia. The Russian Civil War (1918–1921) that followed was both destructive and bitter. The Bolsheviks, or Communists as they began to call themselves, created the Red Army to combat the counterrevolutionary armies, which were called the Whites. Atrocities were committed on both sides (Tsar Nicholas and his family were brutally murdered in 1918 by the Bolsheviks). Despite greater support on the part of the populace, the Whites did not have strong lines of supply or communication. Also, the Bolsheviks had Russia's remaining industry under their control, whereas the White Army was dependent on assistance from the British and Americans. At the beginning the anti-Communist forces captured large areas of Russia. However, as the conflict dragged on, overextension and lack of unity among the diverse leadership resulted in the loss of territory to the Reds. The Red Army, under the leadership of the ruthless Bolshevik leader Lev Bronstein, known as Leon Trotsky (1879–1940), became an effective fighting force. By 1921, the Whites had been defeated and the Communists controlled Russia.

War Communism

During the civil war the Bolsheviks established a policy known as War Communism. Major industries, banks, and all utilities were nationalized. Private trade was prohibited, and food was seized from the peasants. The transportation and communication systems broke down. As the economy declined and fuel shortages followed, opposition to the Bolshevik government arose. To control the population, Lenin instituted the Red Terror, a systematic brutalization of the population. The Bolsheviks arrested and executed thousands of innocent people to promote an atmosphere of terror. Spies were planted to create mutual suspicion and to divide the populace, thus preventing unified opposition.

Soviet Russia Under and After Lenin (1921–1925)

Marxism-Leninism

Lenin had adopted the ideas of Karl Marx into his own system (Marxism-Leninism). He believed that the Communist party was the vanguard or forefront of the Russian Revolution. There had to be a period, the **dictatorship of the proletariat** (workers), when the party ruled without opposition in order to create the conditions for a Communist society. The government had this power because the Bolsheviks represented the proletariat, who were the majority. The ultimate goal was to create a society of workers all sharing equally the burdens and the profits of their labors.

The New Economic Policy

After the civil war, Russian discontent with Communist rule began to grow. Fearing the collapse of his newly established government, Lenin introduced the New Economic Policy (NEP) in 1921. This allowed a partial restoration of **capitalism** on a local level to avoid the disintegration of the economy. Lenin justified this radical departure from **communism** as, "one step backward to go two steps forward." He also imported foreign capitalists to provide technical expertise in rebuilding Russian industry. During this period, Soviet Russia invaded and occupied Ukraine, Belarussia, and the nations of the Transcaucasus. In 1924, under a new constitution Soviet Russia became the Union of Soviet Socialist Republics (USSR). That same year, Lenin died, leaving no successor in the Soviet leadership.

The Struggle Between Trotsky and Stalin

A struggle for power developed between Trotsky, who was Lenin's designated successor, and Joseph Stalin (Iosif Dzhugashvili), called the Man of Steel (1879–1953). Although less well known than Trotsky, Stalin had held several key positions in the Soviet regime and was able to take over the leadership of the Communist party and Soviet Russia. By 1925, Stalin had forced his rival into exile. Trotsky was later assassinated in Mexico by Stalin's agents.

Anastasia

It is 1920 in Berlin, Germany. A young woman is seen climbing over the rail on a bridge and jumping into the canal, attempting suicide. She is pulled out and taken to a clinic for treatment and recovery. In the clinic she tells an amazing story. She claims to be the daughter of Nicholas II of Russia. The world believes that the entire family, the Tsar, his wife, and their children, as well as some of their servants, had been murdered by the Communists three years ago. What is the truth? Let's look at the facts.

We know that Anastasia was the tsar's youngest daughter. She had a pleasing personality, and everyone seemed to like her. She wasn't the pretty one, but she was vivacious. She was described as fond of jokes, able to mimic people and make them laugh. Anastasia was a tomboy and could climb trees with the best. In fact, on one occasion her daring almost caused her to drown; her father had to dive under the water and grab her hair to save her life. In a snowball fight she packed snow around a rock and hit her sister in the face, knocking her out.

When the Bolsheviks took control of Russia, they had the Romanovs arrested and eventually moved them to a town named Ekaterinburg. They decided that the entire family should be killed so that no one would be left to claim the throne. Studies and investigations, which are still going on, seem to verify this story.

The traditional account of the Romanovs' last hours is as follows. The family was awakened on the night of July 16–17, 1918. They were told to dress and go downstairs for their own safety as there were disturbances in the streets. The tsar carried the heir, Alexis, followed by the tsarina, the four daughters, and a few servants. Seeing no furniture in the room, the tsarina called for a few chairs as she had difficulty standing. Meanwhile a detachment of 12 men had been created, and each man had been told which person to aim at. The men began shooting, and soon bullets were ricocheting around the room. (Some reports say that this was due to the jewels that had been sewn into the ladies' corsets.) There was so much shooting that a haze developed in the room. When it was believed that all were dead, the detachment brought in stretchers on which to take the bodies out for burning and disposal. A tremendous shock—some of the daughters were still alive! Some men then took bayonets and stabbed the young women. The bodies were then removed, burned, and thrown into a pit.

When the woman that had attempted suicide saw a picture of the tsar's family in the clinic (what was it doing there?) she became almost hysterical. She remembered being shot and falling senseless. She was taken away in a wagon and eventually ended up in Romania.

She did look a lot like pictures of the tsar's daughter. She had a mark similar to one that Anastasia was known to have. The shape of her ears and her handwriting also added to the evidence. She also seemed to know a great many intimate details about the family. When questioned in Russian, however, the woman could not understand the language. Psychiatrists stated that perhaps the trauma of that night and what followed had driven the language from her memory.

She eventually went to court attempting to establish what she claimed was her true identity and the Romanov inheritance. The court ruled against her, and she faded from the newspapers.

The question still exists. Was she a survivor, or were there any other survivors, of that night in Ekaterinburg? Investigations still continue.

The USSR Under Stalin (1925–1941)

The Purges Stalin proved to be one of the most brutal and ruthless **dictators** in modern history. He was responsible for millions of deaths, starting with the elimination of all possible rivals. Creating his own secret police (the **NKVD**, which eventually became the **KGB**), Stalin spied on, arrested, tortured, and executed party members, government officials, artists, writers, clergy, workers, and even peasants whom he suspected of not supporting his policies. In time, he became subject to paranoia (fear and suspicion of others, often without cause), and even close friends and relatives were killed. From 1935 to 1936, Stalin conducted a series of "show trials" (hearings where the verdicts were predecided), known as the purges. Hundreds of leading Communists were arrested, forced to confess to crimes they had never committed, and executed.

The Five-Year Plans In 1928, dissatisfied with the slow growth rate of Soviet industry, Stalin abandoned Lenin's NEP in favor of centralized economic planning. Goals for agriculture and industry (often unrealistically high) as well as the means for achieving them, were laid out in a series of five-year plans. These were designed to enable the USSR to catch up with the other industrialized nations by emphasizing the development of steel, iron, coal, and oil. The population was expected to sacrifice and do without consumer goods until the Soviet Union could reach the level of industrial development attained by capitalist nations. Opposition to these plans was quickly and brutally put down.

Collectivization and Genocide To pay for the imported technology needed to institute the five-year plans, farms were collectivized. **Collectivization** was the policy of forcing peasants to farm on state land and to allow the government to decide on the distribution of profits. Many peasants were opposed to this policy and refused to surrender their land. To end the opposition, Stalin began a series of **genocides** (mass killings) between 1932 and 1937. He claimed that he was eliminating the **kulaks** (wealthy peasants who supposedly exploited their neighbors). In fact, few of the at least 14.5 million peasants who died by execution, perished in Siberian labor camps, or starved in Stalin's government-created famine in Ukraine (1932–1933), were kulaks. Other groups who opposed Stalin were also crushed. In spite of these harsh measures, the peasants did not fully cooperate, and the Collectivization Program failed to achieve its goal. When World War II interrupted the Third Five-Year Plan in 1941, only heavy industry had made any progress. The loss of life and the human suffering that these modest gains had cost were enormous. It is understandable that many Russians, especially the Ukrainians, first saw the invading German armies as liberators.

The USSR in World War II (1941–1945)

When Nazi Germany invaded the Soviet Union in 1941, the government was completely unprepared. (See Chapter 32, "World War II.") Stalin's purges had eliminated most of the USSR's best generals. Also, despite all the suffering, Soviet industry was unequal to that of Nazi Germany. The only advantage the Soviets had was that the Germans had stretched their supply lines. Once again, the population was forced to resort to the "Scorched Earth" Policy that had been used so effectively against Napoleon. (See Chapter 24, "Tsarist Russia.") By 1944, overextension of supply lines, the harsh Russian winter, and stiff military resistance by the Russians, despite heavy losses, had worn down the German forces. By 1945, the Red

Army had pushed the Nazis out of Russia and Eastern Europe back into Germany and had occupied the eastern portion of that nation.

The decision to enter World War I was disastrous for Russia. Not fully industrialized, the Russians were unable to fight a modern war on such a large scale. While Tsarist Russia had adopted industrialization from Western Europe, the democratic system of government was absent. Russia's attempt to adopt the Western economic model without the political reforms that should come with it brought great problems. The nation's involvement in a conflict that strained fully industrialized nations resulted in revolution.

Once in power, the Communists encountered the same problems. They were able to rule only through force and terror. The Soviet regime's achievements were modest when the death and human suffering involved are considered. Much greater progress could have been achieved with far less loss of life if democratic reforms had been made. The actions of Lenin and Stalin were as bad as, if not worse than, those of the cruelest tsars in Russian history. The Communist attempt to put "old wine in new bottles" produced an era of suffering for the Russians and other peoples of the Soviet Union.

Fascism in Italy

From 1922 to 1943, Italy experienced totalitarian rule under a fascist government headed by Benito Mussolini. The word *fascist* comes from the Latin *fasces*, an axelike weapon that was a symbol of the Ancient Roman Empire. Mussolini wanted Italians to feel a strong sense of **nationalism** and to remember that glory of the Roman Empire. Mussolini and his "**Black Shirts**" came to power for a number of reasons. It is necessary for us to examine these reasons.

Reasons for the Rise of Fascism in Italy

1. *Economic:* Although considered a victor in World War I, the costs of the war for Italy had been staggering. After the war, there was much unemployment, many strikes, and severe inflation. Along with city workers, farmers grew more and more dissatisfied with the hard economic conditions.

2. *Political:* The weak and divided parliamentary government of King Victor Emanuel III was unable to provide leadership or to inspire confidence in its ability to solve post-World War I crises. The multiple-party system in the legislature often caused a deadlock in the passage of laws. No one political party had a majority. Also, there was no strong democratic tradition in Italy. Moreover, the fear of communism and of a Communist-led revolution was exploited (used to advantage) by Mussolini, who promised to defend Italy and thereby won many followers. The failure by Italy to gain all the land she wanted at the Paris Peace Conference contributed to annoyance with the government. In short, many Italians hoped for a strong leader who could bring stability and pride to the nation.

3. *Social:* Italy was suffering from low morale and was saddened by the almost 700,000 deaths incurred in World War I. Pensions for families of those killed, as well as for wounded veterans, were frequently delayed, causing aggravation and anger. Mussolini promised the Italian people security, order, and economic progress in exchange for their liberties and freedom.

The Role of Benito Mussolini

Benito Mussolini (1883–1945) was born in central Italy. He worked as an elementary school teacher and as a journalist before being drafted to fight in World War I. Formerly he had favored **socialism** and atheism, while being opposed to the Italian monarchy and all forms of nationalism. These views and many others were to change as he ultimately came to champion private property, make his own peace with the monarchy and the Catholic Church, and advocate (call for) a chauvinism that made people proud to be Italian. This frequent shifting of viewpoints was common with him. He was an opportunist, someone without any really consistent beliefs who would change his views whenever it appeared advantageous to do so.

In 1919, Mussolini founded the *fasci di combattimento* (groups for combat). This organization was to become a powerful political and terrorizing force, tripling its membership to 300,000 between 1920 and 1922.

Mussolini organized his supporters for a march on Rome in the fall of 1922. Fearing a coup, King Emmanuel III named him premier of Italy.

The Rise to Power of the Fascists

Mussolini's party attracted unhappy people from various segments of Italian society. Businessmen and the middle class were willing to give him financial support. His promise of full employment and calls for patriotic pride won him many city workers and army veterans. The fascists wore black shirts as uniforms, and became known by this clothing. They began to engage in violent tactics and street demonstrations. Property and officials of other political parties, certain newspapers, and labor unions were attacked. Police often looked away from these incidents, while judges were pressured to release any fascists who had been arrested for violent behavior. These patterns were similar to those used in later years by Hitler in Germany.

In 1921, the fascists won some seats in the Italian parliament and expanded their activities. Mussolini felt encouraged to put added pressure on the government and to organize his supporters for a bold step. In the fall of 1922, the **March on Rome** took place. Fascist followers, claiming that they wanted to save Italy from a Communist takeover, went to Rome by railroad, car, carriage, and foot. King Victor Emmanuel III, fearing a coup (a quick, nonviolent takeover of government) sent a telegraph message to Mussolini in Milan on October 29, 1922, asking him to form a new government. The next morning, having taken a sleeping-car train, Mussolini arrived in Rome. He thus became the premier of Italy, without having been elected to the office or even thinking about it three years earlier.

Mussolini in Power

In short order, the premiership became a dictatorship. Although the king remained in office, Mussolini was given emergency powers. A law was passed that made sure the fascists would control the weakened parliament. Other laws restricted freedom of the press and civil liberties. Critics were silenced, usually by threats

All males from age eight to eighty-three were ordered by Mussolini to get military training. Here young soldiers march in Rome.

and terror. Giacomo Matteotti, publisher of a book exposing Mussolini and his tactics, was murdered. In 1924, Mussolini took the title **Il Duce** (the leader). He established himself as head of the Grand Council of the Fascist party, the most powerful group in Italy. His picture could be seen in many places. So could signs that urged Italians to *credere, combattere, obbedire* (believe, fight, obey).

In the area of economics, Italy became a **corporate state**. This was a system in which most of the important industries, such as manufacturing and transportation, were formed into organizations known as syndicates. Each syndicate was like a corporation. From each syndicate, managers and workers came to meet with government officers chosen by Mussolini to decide on issues such as wages, prices, and working conditions. Private property was allowed, however, in keeping with Mussolini's strong anti-communist stance.

Political power had now become authoritarian. This situation was not what those who helped to unify Italy in the nineteenth century had struggled for. (See Chapter 22, "Unification of Italy.")

Mussolini had little respect for democracy. Dictators such as he often use other means, such as force, fear, and fabrication to gain power. They will be successful if three conditions exist:

1. Discontent is widespread.
2. Those in power are weak and also insensitive to the nation's problems.
3. The majority of people are **apathetic** and do nothing to oppose the seizure of power.

To preserve power, dictators resort to some of the same means used to acquire that power. This was true, as we have seen, of Joseph Stalin in the Soviet Union. Other leaders who were cut from similar cloth in post-World War I Europe were Marshal Pilsudski in Poland (1926), Antonio Salazar in Portugal (1932), Adolf Hitler in Germany (1933), John Metaxas in Greece (1936), King Carol in Rumania (1938), and General Francisco Franco in Spain (1939).

The use of armed force at home was a strong thread in this cloth. The international community of the 1930s stood still while force was used domestically. When its use crossed international boundaries, however, force eventually led to severe conflict that broke out in the 1930s; something which will soon concern us. (See Chapter 32, "World War II.") However, we will first learn about the totalitarianism that arose in the nation most responsible for that war—Nazi Germany.

Nazism in Germany

Dictators Benito Mussolini of Italy and Adolf Hitler of Germany used terrorizing tactics to control their countries' citizens.

Totalitarianism is a political philosophy that has emerged in the twentieth century. The term *totalitarianism* describes a government in which one political party, or a single group of like-minded persons, monopolizes all power and exercises complete authority over the masses of people and their activities. This system involves total control of all features of an individual's life by the government, with both civil and political rights being curtailed. Although various forms of totalitarianism exist in parts of the world today, the earliest examples were evident in three European nations during the 20-year period following World War I. These nations were the Soviet Union (under Communism), Italy (under fascism), and Germany (under Nazism). Totalitarian societies look down upon individual human rights and civil liberties. The values of democracy are not found in such societies. Totalitarian states emphasize four factors:

1. Glorification of the whole community (i.e., the state);
2. Authoritarian rule by a dictator or by selected members of the one political party allowed to exist;
3. Control of the individual citizen's life; and
4. Belief that the individual should serve the state and exists solely to promote the state's interests.

In Western Europe, these features of totalitarianism were most characteristic of Germany under the control of Adolf Hitler and the Nazi party, from 1933 to 1945. This government, known as the Third Reich, arose after the period of the Weimar Republic.

Germany Under the Weimar Republic (1919–1933)

The Weimar Republic was the German government established after World War I. It was a democratic government, with a constitution drawn up in the city of Weimar. There were many political parties that would campaign for seats in the government, which was headed by President Friederich Ebert. This was the government that had sent representatives to sign the Versailles peace treaty. However, this experiment with democracy in Germany faced many problems. These included economic chaos, street violence, and political threats from the left and right.

The five main reasons why the Weimar government was unsuccessful are as follows:

1. In the early 1920s, the Weimar government printed paper money with little hard currency to back it, resulting in severe inflation. (Inflation occurs when there is such a great amount of money in circulation that its value decreases.) This situation devastated the German economy and resulted in severe unemployment and street violence.
2. When Germany was unable to meet her reparation payments in 1923, France sent troops to occupy the Ruhr Valley, Germany's chief industrial area. Ill will grew against the French, while the Weimar government's response was simply to print more money. This action, of course, added to the inflationary crisis.
3. The terrible unemployment in Germany in the 1920s and again in the 1930s caused severe suffering and unrest.
4. The German economy was restored somewhat after 1923, and conditions temporarily improved. However, in 1929, a worldwide economic depression that threatened the stability of democratic governments everywhere again brought much suffering to Germany. Unemployment rose to six million in 1932, and Germans lost faith in their political leaders. This further fueled the anger that had been caused by the Treaty of Versailles.
5. The government was unstable because no one single party was able to achieve a majority in the Reichstag, the more powerful of the two legislative houses created by the Weimar constitution. As a result, German political leaders seemed helpless to deal with the challenging economic problems.

These problems led many Germans to conclude that democracy was ill suited to their nation, and that a strong, bold autocracy would be preferable. The desire for such a political system grew as people remembered that it had brought Germany, under Bismarck's leadership, political unification, economic growth, and respect as an international power. Furthermore, a strong democratic tradition did not exist in German history. The evolution of representative elected government and respect for human rights, which over the centuries had taken place in such countries as Britain and France, had not occurred in Germany.

The Role of Adolf Hitler

Adolf Hitler (1889–1945) was born in Austria and served in the German army during World War I. Afterwards, he joined the **Nazi** (National Socialist German Workers) Party. He spoke out against the Weimar government and was arrested for his role in the Munich beer hall putsch of 1923, an unsuccessful attempt to overthrow the government. While imprisoned, he wrote the book *Mein Kampf* (*My Struggle*), which was not immediately popular in Germany. It explained Hitler's ideas for a stronger and more powerful German nation. It also revealed his racist beliefs concerning the alleged superiority of Aryans as a "master race" and the need to eliminate all groups he considered inferior, such as Jews, Slavs, gypsies, and blacks. Hitler was released from prison in 1924 and resumed efforts to expand support for his ideas and those of the Nazi party. He showed himself to be a stirring and charismatic (appealing) speaker when addressing large crowds, thereby attracting many people to the party.

The Rise of the Nazis to Power

The Nazis began to run candidates for seats in the legislature and were able to win some, although they never gained a majority of seats. In addition to the problems of the Weimar government and the powerful role played by Hitler, a number of other factors also led to the eventual rise of the Nazis to power in Germany.

1. *Economic Problems:* The Nazis offered simple explanations for both the causes of and the cures for Germany's economic problems. These problems, as described above, affected millions of Germans (six million workers were unemployed in 1932). Reparations demanded by the Versailles treaty were condemned as unjust and were blamed for causing the economic crisis.
2. *Patriotic Appeals:* The Nazi program stirred German nationalism by emphasizing several points. Among the measures it called for were the following:
   - A large increase in the armed forces;
   - Expansion of the German fatherland to include territory in Europe where people of German descent lived (i.e., Austria and parts of Poland and Czechoslovakia);
   - Control over educational and cultural institutions in order to teach Nazi principles of **racism** and physical fitness for the glory of the state;
   - Ignoring the Versailles treaty and refusing to accept the war-guilt clause;
   - Regaining land that Germany had held in Europe prior to World War I and its overseas colonies;
   - Use of violence as a legitimate means to achieve domestic and international goals; and

- Glorifying the mythical German race (the so-called *Volk*) as the source of all strength and power. The Nazis also claimed that Nordic Germans were destined to rule the world and to eliminate undesirable people. This attitude was an example of excessive **ethnocentrism**. Hitler and his followers blamed the Weimar government for accepting the Versailles treaty, and said it had been forced to do so by Jews, Communists, and others. Finally, the Nazis stated that German forces had not been defeated in World War I but rather had been "stabbed in the back."

3. *Anti-Semitism:* The term **anti-Semitism** refers to prejudice and hatred directed toward Jews only because they are Jews. Prejudiced attitudes toward Jews had existed in Germany and Austria for hundred of years, resulting in persecution, exile, and loss of life and property. However, Hitler's prejudice against Jews was fanatical. He used them as **scapegoats** for his own personal failures in Vienna and elsewhere, and also for Germany's problems. These false ideas became persuasive parts of Nazi **propaganda**, especially when they were blended with "master race" theories. Hitler claimed that the Aryans (Germans of Nordic descent) were a master race who were naturally entitled to control and rule people of less "pure" blood, such as Slavs and Jews. (The **Holocaust**, in which six million Jews were systematically and intentionally murdered after Hitler came to power, was the tragic consequence of these misguided ideas. See Chapter 34, "The Holocaust.")

4. *Fear of Communism and of Soviet Russia:* The Nazis played upon these fears with great success, and portrayed themselves as the only ones capable of protecting Germany from foreign beliefs and potential aggressors. In this way, they were able to win the support of large segments of the German population, including such influential groups as bankers and industrialists. In addition, because Karl Marx was of Jewish origin, Hitler was able to link his own anti-Semitic propaganda with his anti-Communist position.

5. *Use of Private, Illegal Armed Groups:* Many of Hitler's followers were organized into private armies. One such group was the Storm Troopers, or **"brown shirts."** They employed scare tactics and violence to terrorize Jews and other opponents of the Nazis. Many were thugs and gangsters who took matters into their own hands and beat up people for little or no reason.

6. *Lack of Meaningful Opposition:* Few strong voices inside Germany spoke out against the Nazis. Many Germans came to gradually support Hitler, while others were apathetic. A third group feared to speak against him; indeed, many who did were later intimidated. Internationally, there was little awareness of or concern about the Nazi Movement.

The Nazis Come to Power

The formal takeover of Germany by the Nazis occurred in January 1933, when the president of the Weimar Republic, Paul von Hindenburg, appointed Hitler as chancellor. By this time, the Nazis had become the largest political party in Germany and formed the single largest block in the Reichstag, the German parliament. Yet they had never won a clear majority in any national election. (In 1932, for example, they won slightly less than 40 percent of the seats in the Reichstag. To control the government, a party had to win a majority of the seats.) At first, Hitler promised to preserve the Weimar constitution with all its democratic features and protections. However, he soon instituted (set in place) policies that ended the experiment in democracy that had been introduced in 1919 under the Weimar Republic.

In February 1933, he began to transform himself from a chancellor to a dictator. He called for new elections to the Reichstag for March 4. However, on February 27, a fire of unknown origin destroyed the Reichstag building. Hitler blamed the Communists, predicting that they were about to lead a revolt. He then persuaded President von Hindenburg to issue orders ending freedom of speech and assembly. A mentally retarded Dutch Communist was eventually brought to trial and convicted of setting the fire. It is generally assumed, however, that the Nazis themselves had done so. To falsely and maliciously hold others responsible for acts they did not do is to use them as scapegoats and to employ the "**big lie**" technique. Both of these notorious tactics are frequently used by dictatorial and totalitarian governments.

In the March elections, the Nazis won only 44 percent of the seats. Nevertheless, with Hitler's followers applying various kinds of intimidation, almost the entire Reichstag voted to pass the Enabling Act. This act suspended the constitution and gave Hitler dictatorial powers. He shortly thereafter abolished all opposition parties. Labor unions and opposition newspapers were banned. Radio stations were placed under government control, with Joseph Goebbels as minister of propaganda. To carry out all these policies, Hitler established a secret police force called the **Gestapo**. People arrested by the Gestapo would often be sent to large prison areas called **concentration camps**. These, however, were not the **death camps** that were built in the 1940s.

Hitler's Government Becomes Known as the Third Reich

With the death of President von Hindenburg in 1934, Hitler became president as well as chancellor, adopting the title of **der führer** (the leader). He proclaimed his government as the Third Reich and predicted that it would last for 1,000 years. For Hitler, the Third Reich was the successor to both the Holy Roman Empire (First Reich) and the German Empire begun by Bismarck (Second Reich).

The rules and policies of the Nazis now were spread throughout Germany, in schools, churches, social clubs, sports programs, and a special Hitler youth organization. Young children were encouraged to wear the swatiska, the twisted-cross symbol for the Nazi party, and to inform authorities about their parents and any friends who were not following Nazi rules and regulations or who did anything else that could be regarded as antigovernment behavior. Books were burned that contained writings of Jews or any others who were deemed "undesirable." Large meetings and rallies were held where Nazi followers made emotional speeches praising Hitler and condemning Jews and the Treaty of Versailles, and where hundreds would shout approval of Hitler and give the Nazi salute. This situation was a far cry from the hopes of those who had brought forth the Weimar Republic, a chance for Germany to become a democratic nation.

Summary

Hitler's coming to power resulted in a totalitarian dictatorship that eventually resulted in World War II and brought devastation to Germany and to most of the rest of Europe. His distorted ideas, along with his antidemocratic beliefs and tactics, unfortunately found a receptive audience in post-World War I Germany.

In that audience were those who genuinely believed in him. Many other Germans tolerated him without much enthusiasm, assuming that he would not stay in power. For those who were apathetic, we are reminded of a famous comment by the eighteenth century British statesman Edmund Burke: "All that is necessary for evil to triumph is for good men to do nothing."

The same comment would also be applicable, in various ways, to events in Russia and Italy that we have described. The dictatorial power that had become characteristic of Russia, Germany, and Italy by the 1930s was a threat to the citizens of those nations. The antidemocratic features of the totalitarian regimes in Italy and Germany also proved to be a menace to their neighbors and, indeed, to the world at large. This danger became apparent when these regimes, for a variety of reasons, attempted to expand beyond their borders. It took a world war to hold this expansion and to bring these regimes to an end.

In the 1930s, the world stood on the brink of another disaster. Europe was divided between the driving ambitions of the dictators in Germany, Italy, and the Soviet Union and the lethargy of the democracies of Britain and France.

The Russian people had traded the cruelties of the tsars for the far greater oppression of Stalin, who stood out as the greatest mass murderer in history. Millions died because of his cruelty. Mussolini proved to be a pompous leader of little merit. Hitler became infamous as one of history's greatest villains.

Yet should we blame these three men alone, or do the people who stood by and allowed them to proceed share the responsibility? We keep asking the same question in this study of European history: "Are there lessons to be learned, or are we destined to continue to repeat the same mistakes?" What do you think?

CHAPTER 31

Review Exercises

Communism in Russia

I. Matching

Directions: Match the names in Column A with the achievement they are *best known* for in Column B.

Column A
1. Tsarina Alexandra
2. Stalin
3. Prince Lv'ov
4. Lenin
5. Lev Bronstein
6. Aleksandr Kerenskii
7. General Kornilov
8. Napoleon
9. Iosif Dzhugashvili
10. Tsar Nicholas II

Column B
(a) defeated by "Scorched Earth" Policy
(b) April Theses
(c) Leon Trotsky
(d) tried to overthrow the Provisional Government
(e) Joseph Stalin
(f) second leader of the Provisional Government
(g) Man of Steel
(h) blamed for Russian military losses in World War I
(i) last Romanov ruler of Russia
(j) first leader of the Democratic Provisional Government

II. Matching

Directions: Match the words in Column A with the *correct description* in Column B.

Column A
1. Petrograd
2. Duma
3. Cheka
4. Red Army
5. Whites
6. genocide
7. soviet
8. KGB
9. Bolsheviks
10. kulaks

Column B
(a) worker's council
(b) Bolshevik secret police
(c) Communists
(d) St. Petersburg
(e) Bolshevik term for wealthy peasants
(f) Bolshevik army
(g) Russian parliament
(h) Soviet secret police
(i) anti-Communist forces
(j) mass killing of people of a particular race or nationality

III. Multiple Choice

Directions: Find the *letter* of the correct answer.

1. Russia was unprepared for World War I because of a lack of

   (a) men to serve as soldiers.
   (b) protection against its cold climate.
   (c) capable commanders.
   (d) industrial capacity to produce sufficient arms.

2. Tsar Nicholas II's decision to take personal command of his armies

   (a) left his unpopular wife in charge of the government.
   (b) effected no change in the losses of the Russian army.
   (c) undermined his image as the divinely appointed monarch of Russia.
   (d) all of the above.

3. Tsar Nicholas II abdicated because he

   (a) was tired of being ruler of Russia.
   (b) was not reelected in the national elections.
   (c) realized he was no longer in control of his government or army.
   (d) had been overthrown in favor of another member of the royal family.

4. The Provisional Government of 1917 officially declared Russia to be a

   (a) constitutional monarchy.
   (b) democracy.
   (c) Socialist state.
   (d) dictatorship until the war ended.

5. Lenin promised the Russian people

   (a) bread, peace, and wealth.
   (b) bread, peace, and land.
   (c) bread, peace, and security.
   (d) bread, peace, and freedom.

6. During the February Revolution, workers, soldiers, and sailors in the cities organized

   (a) dumas.
   (b) zemstvos.
   (c) mirs.
   (d) soviets.

7. The appeal of the Provisional Government was limited because most people

   (a) were unfamiliar with democracy.
   (b) were unwilling to accept political change.
   (c) were in favor of continuing the war.
   (d) disliked the leadership.

8. Which did *not* occur during the July Days?

   (a) There was a revolt against the Provisional Government.
   (b) Aleksandr Kerenshii replaced Prince Lv'ov.
   (c) Kerenshii used jailed revolutionaries to defend Petrograd.
   (d) General Kornilov successfully established a dictatorship over Russia.

9. The Bolsheviks gained power by

   (a) winning the December elections.
   (b) taking control of the army.
   (c) overthrowing the government in Petrograd.
   (d) leading a popular overthrow of the Provisional Government.

10. After the October Revolution, the Bolsheviks

    (a) continued the war effort.
    (b) made peace with Germany and withdrew from the war.
    (c) pulled Russian troops out of World War I, but continued to supply the Allies.
    (d) held elections to decide on continued participation in the war.

11. Lenin organized the Cheka to

    (a) defend Russia's borders.
    (b) patrol the countryside for criminals.
    (c) fight against counterrevolutionary activity.
    (d) replace the Russian army in national defense.

12. The Bolsheviks declared that the Russian Orthodox Church

    (a) represented the national faith of Soviet Russia.
    (b) was to become a government agency.
    (c) was to be tolerated, but was not a state institution.
    (d) was prohibited as a reactionary institution.

13. Which of the following did *not* occur during the Russian Civil War?

    (a) There was bitter and destructive fighting.
    (b) The Bolsheviks used the Red Terror to control the population.
    (c) The Russian royal family was brutally murdered.
    (d) The White Army gained control of the major Russian cities.

14. Under War Communism, Lenin

    (a) privatized all industries and utilities.
    (b) allowed private trade.
    (c) seized food from the peasantry to feed the cities.
    (d) built up Russia's transportation and communication system.

15. The New Economic Policy of 1921

    (a) fully restored capitalism.
    (b) imported foreign capitalists for technical expertise.
    (c) privatized all industries and utilities.
    (d) encouraged the growth of new corporations.

16. After Stalin took power in 1925, he conducted the purges in which he

    (a) fired all incompetent or corrupt civil servants.
    (b) arrested all counterrevolutionaries.
    (c) arrested and executed hundreds of leading Communists.
    (d) arrested and deported all the Russian Orthodox clergy.

17. Stalin created his own secret police, initially called the

    (a) Okhrana.   (b) KGB.
    (c) NKVD.   (d) NEP.

18. Collectivization was the policy of

    (a) forcing the population to work for the state during harvest season.
    (b) forcing the peasantry to work together on state farms.
    (c) seizing land and giving it to loyal Communists.
    (d) seizing a large percentage of produce from all private farms.

19. To end peasant opposition to collectivization, Stalin

    (a) allowed the peasants to share government profits.
    (b) lowered taxes.
    (c) sent troops to intimidate the peasants.
    (d) began a series of genocides, using deadly force and a man-made famine.

20. The Soviet Union was able to defeat Nazi Germany by resorting to

    (a) guerrilla warfare.
    (b) the "Scorched Earth" Policy.
    (c) using peasants as decoys in ambushes.
    (d) planting deadly minefields throughout the nation.

IV. Thought Questions

Directions: Answer the following questions in essay form.

1. World War I made the Russian Revolution inevitable. Give three examples that explain how the war led to revolution.

2. Was democracy possible in Russia? If the Bolsheviks had not seized power, could a democratic system have been established? Give three reasons to support your argument.

3. You are the Russian correspondent for an American newspaper in 1917.

    A. Give two reasons why the Bolsheviks succeeded in seizing power.
    B. Explain whether the takeover was a revolution or a coup d'etat, giving two reasons for your opinion.

4. Did the Bolsheviks succeed in establishing a Communist state?

    A. Explain two policies of Lenin and two of Stalin.
    B. Discuss whether either leader was successful in bringing about communism.

5. Stalin is considered to be one of history's great murderers. Explain how his policies led to this evaluation.

Fascism in Italy

I. Matching

Directions: Match the words in Column A with the *correct description* in Column B.

Column A
1. Il Duce
2. opportunism
3. *fasces*
4. black shirts
5. coup

Column B
(a) changing one's opinion, whenever it is an advantage to do so
(b) symbols of the Ancient Roman Empire
(c) Mussolini's followers
(d) a sudden, bloodless takeover of a government
(e) the title that Mussolini took for himself

II. Multiple Choice

Directions: Find the *letter* of the correct answer.

1. The fascists used all of the following means to obtain power *except*

(a) skillful propaganda.
(b) violent intimidation.
(c) legal elections.
(d) street demonstrations.

2. Mussolini became premier

(a) by winning a majority of seats in the Italian parliament.
(b) through disruption and threats.
(c) by overthrowing King Victor Emmanuel III.
(d) upon the death of the former premier.

3. One reason for Mussolini's rise to power was that he

(a) promised to rebuild Rome.
(b) had the support of business leaders.
(c) promised to establish a democratic system of government.
(d) agreed to work with Italian Communists.

4. Once Mussolini and the fascists achieved power,

(a) all other political parties were dissolved.
(b) the king fled from the country.
(c) the fascists adopted democratic policies.
(d) the Grand Council was abolished.

5. The most immediate result of the March on Rome in 1922 was

(a) social.
(c) military.
(b) economic.
(d) political.

6. The "corporate state" idea reflected which area of Mussolini's policy?

  (a) military   (b) economic
  (c) foreign   (d) educational

III. Thought Questions

Directions: Answer the following questions in essay form.

1. A. Describe three factors in post-World War I Italy that made possible the rise of fascism.
   B. Which of these was most likely to enable a dictator to come to power? Explain your answer.

2. A. Describe two tactics used by Mussolini and his Fascist party that helped them rise to power.
   B. Explain why you think these tactics could or could not be used in the United States today.

Nazism in Germany

I. Matching

Directions: Match the words in Column A with the *correct description* in Column B.

Column A	*Column B*
1. Reichstag	(a) someone wrongfully blamed for a harmful problem or event
2. scapegoat	
3. swatiska	(b) symbol of the Nazi party and the Nazi government
4. Aryan	
5. apathetic	(c) political philosophy practiced by the Nazis
6. inflation	(d) official name of the Nazi government
7. totalitarianism	(e) the title that Hitler took for himself
8. excessive ethnocentrism	(f) the "master race," according to Nazi theory
9. Gestapo	(g) economic situation in which prices rise and the value of money declines
10. Third Reich	
11. der führer	(h) German parliament
12. anti-Semitism	(i) Hitler's secret police force
	(j) indifferent, uncaring
	(k) attitude of superiority over all other human groups
	(l) prejudice against Jews

II. Famous People

Directions: Use the names below to complete the following sentences.

Joseph Goebbels   Friederich Ebert
Adolf Hitler   Paul von Hindenburg

1. _____ was arrested for his role in the Munich beer hall putsch.

2. _____ became the first president of the Weimer Republic.

3. _____ wrote *Mein Kampf.*

4. _____ became minister of propaganda in the Nazi regime.

5. _____ was given increased powers under the Enabling Act.

6. _____ was the last president of the Weimar Republic.

7. _____ became chancellor of Germany in 1933.

III. Multiple Choice

Directions: Find the *letter* of the correct answer.

1. The Nazis used all of the following means to obtain power except

   (a) skillful propaganda.
   (b) violent intimidation.
   (c) legal elections.
   (d) street demonstrations.

2. Hitler became chancellor

   (a) by winning a majority of seats in the Reichstag.
   (b) through disruption and threats.
   (c) by overthrowing President von Hindenburg.
   (d) upon the death of the former chancellor.

3. Which of the following occurred after all the others?

   (a) Reichstag fire
   (b) Munich beer hall putsch
   (c) passage of the Enabling Act
   (d) writing of *Mein Kampf*

4. Blaming a Dutch Communist for the Reichstag fire

   (a) was an example of the "big lie" technique.
   (b) hurt the reputation of the Storm Troopers.
   (c) resulted in the dismissal of Joseph Goebbels.
   (d) was the idea of the Gestapo.

5. The earliest concentration camps had people sent there by the

   (a) Storm Troopers.   (b) brown shirts.
   (c) Gestapo.   (d) Hitler youth organization.

6. Which pair of leaders suffered a common fate in their political careers and were victims of forces beyond their control?

   (a) Hindenburg and Hitler
   (b) Mussolini and Hindenburg
   (c) Hindenburg and Victor Emmanuel III
   (d) Hitler and Victor Emmanuel III

7. All of the following post-World War I conditions contributed to the rise of dictatorial governments in both German and Italy *except*

    (a) unemployment.
    (b) reparations.
    (c) inflation.
    (d) fear of communism.

8. In a totalitarian state

    (a) all industry is owned by the government.
    (b) the state controls every aspect of the lives of the people.
    (c) the state guarantees civil liberties for everyone.
    (d) a free election occurs every four years.

9. In general, a dictator

    (a) encourages critical thinking on political matters in schools.
    (b) encourages laborers to strike.
    (c) permits only two political parties.
    (d) takes over the means of communication.

10. Dictatorships do not accept the idea that

    (a) might makes right.
    (b) strict censorship is necessary.
    (c) the state serves the individual.
    (d) uniformity of thought is very important.

IV. Thought Questions

Directions: Answer the following questions in essay form.

1. A. Describe three factors in post-World War I Germany that made possible the rise of a totalitarian dictatorship.
   B. Which of these was most likely to enable a dictator to come to power? Explain your answer.

2. A. Describe two tactics used by Hitler and his Nazi party that helped them come to power.
   B. Explain why you think these tactics could or could not be used in the United States today.

3. A. Define totalitarianism.
   B. Describe two examples of totalitarianism in Nazi Germany.
   C. Explain why the Nazis thought each example was correct or necessary.
   D. Explain why you think similar examples would or would not be possible in the United States today.

World War II

Here we go again! Less than a generation has passed since the Treaty of Versailles marked the end to the "war to end all wars," and nations are once more on the march. We must ask the question, "Why?" As we look at the attempts at peacekeeping during the 1920s and 1930s, what weaknesses will we see? How could a Hitler get the world involved in another war, and how could he almost win it? Was there a certain point at which, if the democracies had said, "Stop," Hitler would have retreated?

This time we have two new major players in the game—the United States and Japan. Japan will play the bully in the East, while the United States will attempt to use the oceans on her borders to stay out of the conflict. Japan will force the United States into action and will eventually pay a high price for doing so. New and more terrible weaponry that has the capacity for mass killing will be developed by both sides. Hitler will make the same mistake that Napoleon did, and the Soviet Union will make him pay for it.

The saying "Politics make strange bedfellows" is exemplified when the democracies of the United States and Great Britain join with the totalitarian Soviet Union against a common enemy. Finally an exhausted world will see the destruction of two entire cities with the atomic bomb. The years from 1939 to 1945 will be a terrible period with terrible results.

Causes of World War II

If you stand before a house and look at it carefully, you will see its front and its top. What you cannot see is the foundation. If the foundation is sturdy and supports the house well, then the house will be stable. If, on the other hand, the foundation is weak, then the house is in danger of crumbling and cannot fulfill one of its chief purposes—to provide shelter. Indeed, the house may become unsafe for those who dwell within it.

After World War I, many nations hoped to prevent another war by building what could be called a house of peace. The foundations of this house were the Treaty of Versailles, the League of Nations, disarmament conferences, and international pacts (agreements). Unfortunately, the house of peace crumbled for a number of reasons, most of them due to the action of the Axis powers (Germany, Italy, and Japan). The cracks they made in the foundations, along with the failure of other nations to repair them immediately, led to destruction of the house. The consequence of this destruction was World War II.

Although the war started in Europe, it soon became a global conflict. Fighting took place on three continents—Europe, Africa, and Asia. More nations (over 50) were belligerents than in any other war in history. In this section we will look at the attempts to maintain peace in the post-World War I Era. We will then turn our attention to the underlying and specific causes of the Second World War in our century.

Attempts at Peace in the Post-World War I Period

In the period between the two world wars, the major powers tried to create firm foundations to preserve peace and thereby reduce the chances of another huge conflict. These foundations were built with noble efforts; but, as we now can see, they had weak spots.

1. *The Treaty of Versailles, 1919:* This treaty (see Chapter 30, "World War I") produced bitterness that Hitler and the Nazis were able to exploit. Germany felt that she had not been defeated, that she had voluntarily surrendered,

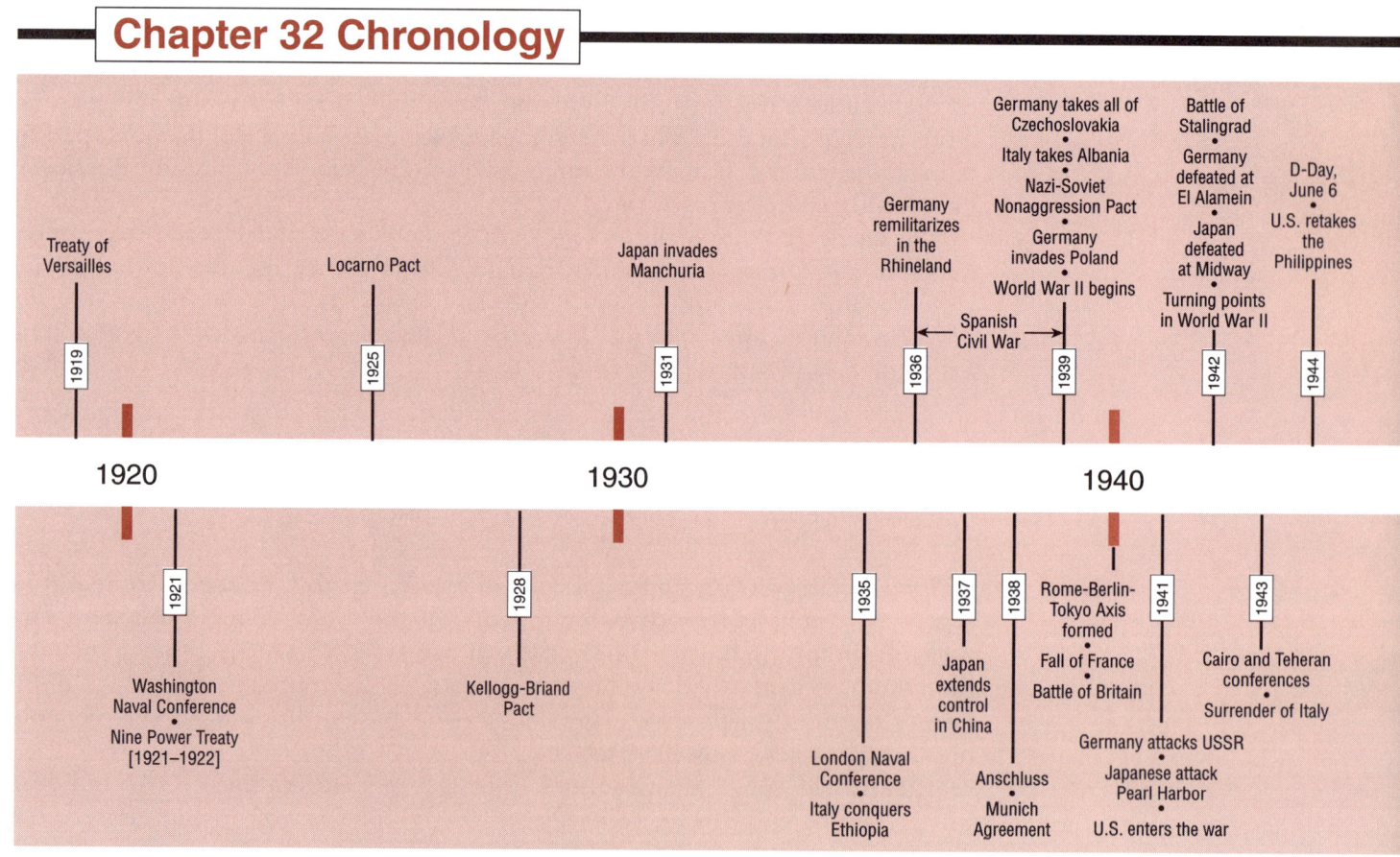

Chapter 32 Chronology

Treaty of Versailles — 1919

Locarno Pact — 1925

Japan invades Manchuria — 1931

Germany remilitarizes in the Rhineland — 1936
Spanish Civil War

Germany takes all of Czechoslovakia
Italy takes Albania
Nazi-Soviet Nonaggression Pact
Germany invades Poland
World War II begins — 1939

Battle of Stalingrad
Germany defeated at El Alamein
Japan defeated at Midway
Turning points in World War II — 1942

D-Day, June 6
U.S. retakes the Philippines — 1944

1920

1930

1940

1921 — Washington Naval Conference
Nine Power Treaty [1921–1922]

1928 — Kellogg-Briand Pact

1935 — London Naval Conference
Italy conquers Ethiopia

1937 — Japan extends control in China

1938 — Anschluss
Munich Agreement

Rome-Berlin-Tokyo Axis formed
Fall of France
Battle of Britain
Germany attacks USSR
Japanese attack Pearl Harbor
U.S. enters the war

1941

1943 — Cairo and Teheran conferences
Surrender of Italy

and that the provisions of the treaty were very harsh. Also, as the treaty did not indicate specific means of enforcing its restrictions, its impact became meaningless.

2. *The League of Nations:* The League of Nations was not created to be, nor did it act as, a world government. It met in Geneva, Switzerland, and did record some achievements in its brief history. It resolved crises involving Sweden and Finland, and Greece and Bulgaria. Issues of health, trade, and labor were addressed by the league; for example, it sponsored the International Labor Office. However, the league was never a truly universal organization. While it did reach a membership of 57 nations by 1933, the fact that the United States never joined was a blow to the organization's prestige. When the league first convened in 1920, none of the defeated nations from World War I were members. Germany was admitted in 1926 but withdrew, along with Japan, in 1933. Italy withdrew in 1936. The league was without power to tax, raise an army, or enforce its decisions. Its inability to respond effectively to Axis aggression in the 1930s signaled its doom. The requirement that all decisions receive the unanimous consent of its members hindered its functioning.

3. *Disarmament Conferences:* Recognition of arms competition as a factor leading to World War I led to a series of conferences that attempted to limit armaments. At the Washington Conference, 1921–1922, Britain, the United

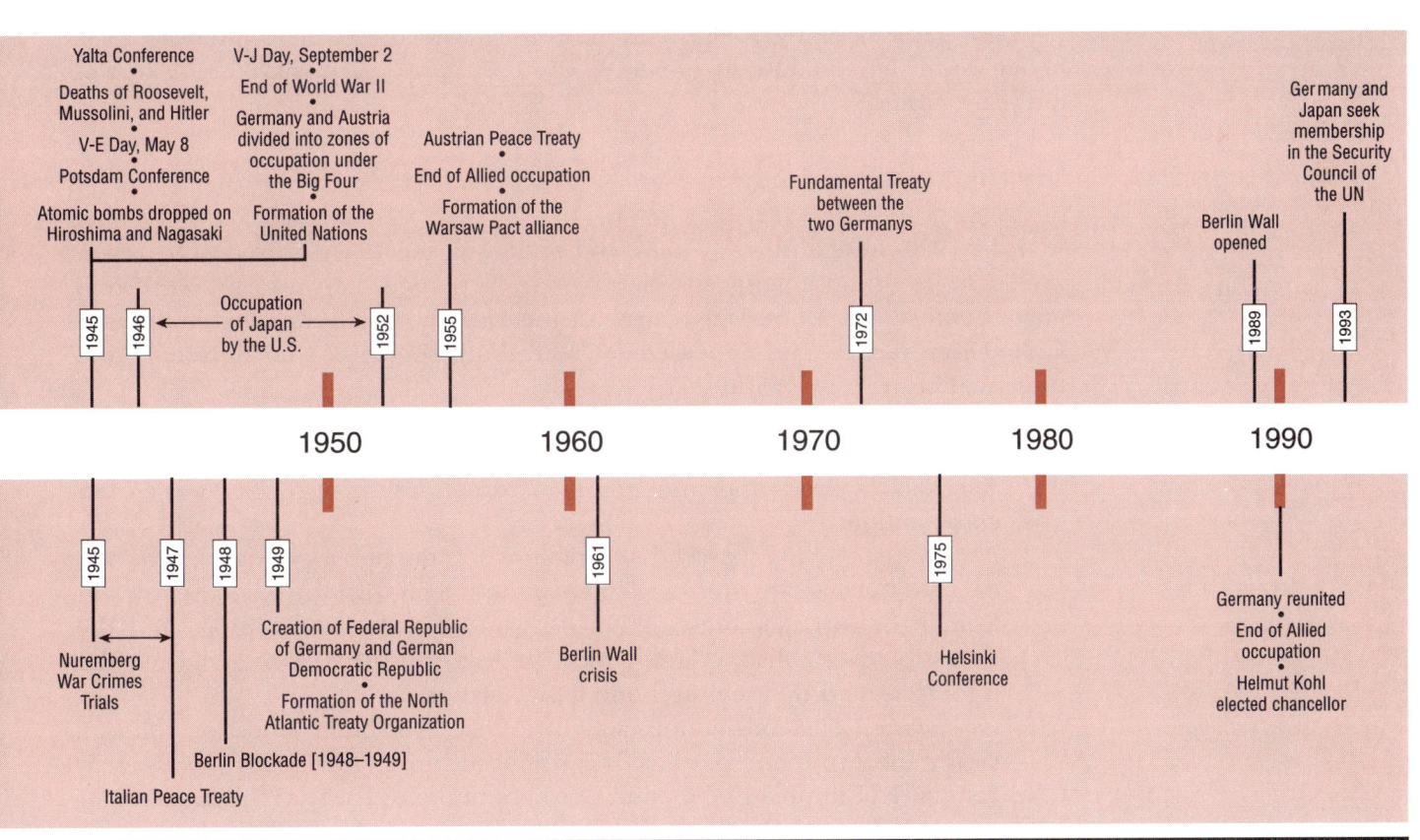

States, Japan, France, and Italy agreed to halt construction of capital (large) warships for ten years. They also promised to maintain capital ships in a ratio of 5 : 5 : 3 : 1.67 : 1.67. At the 1930 London Naval Conference, Britain, the United States, and Japan compromised on a 10 : 10 : 7 ratio for a five-year period. This was to cover destroyers and cruisers as well as capital ships. At the London Conference of 1935, however, Japan's request to Britain and the United States for a 10 : 10 : 10 ratio, or **parity**, was turned down by the Western powers. The conference ended without an agreement, and Japan soon expanded her navy.

4. *International Pacts:* The 1920s witnessed several agreements among groups of nations hoping to strengthen their idealistic resolve for peace.
   • Nine-Power Treaty at the Washington Conference (1921–1922). The United States, Britain, Japan, and other nations wished to avoid any imperialist conflict in China. They therefore agreed to respect an **Open Door Policy** in China, providing equal trading rights and respecting China's independence.
   • Locarno Pact (1925). This was an agreement signed by the Western European Allies with Germany. It provided for Germany to accept permanently its boundaries on the west with Belgium and France, and to seek a peaceful settlement of any disputes regarding its Polish and Czechoslovakian boundaries in the east.
   • Kellogg-Briand Pact (1928). Also known as the Pact of Paris, this document was signed by more than 60 nations, including the United States, France, Germany, Italy, and Japan. They promised to resolve disputes in a peaceful manner, outlawing war "as an instrument of national policy." Although the treaty was not backed by any threat of force, the signers hoped that world moral influence would make it work.

These pacts gained global attention, as they reflected noble aspirations for a better world. The mood they evoked in the 1920s contrasted sharply with that of ten years earlier.

Underlying Reasons for World War II

If the 1920s were a time for hope and optimism, the 1930s proved to be otherwise; a series of movements and events were to plunge the world into a second major conflict. The underlying causes of this tragedy, which included **militarism**, **nationalism**, **racism**, and **appeasement**, were both similar to and different from those that brought on World War I.

1. *Militarism:* Large amounts of money continued to be spent on weapons. Military strength was seen as a source of nationalistic pride. The leaders of the Axis nations always appeared in military dress, and they glorified war as necessary and just.
2. *Nationalism and Racism:* The Axis nations saw themselves as superior to others (the German "master race" theory, the Italian wish to revive the Ancient Roman Empire, Japanese self-pride based on Shinto teachings and the necessity to establish a "new order" in Asia) and therefore as having the right to extend their cultures and their borders.
3. *Imperialism:* The Axis nations sought to take over other lands for political, racist, and economic reasons. Japan moved into China (1931, 1937), Italy conquered Ethiopia (1935), and Germany annexed Austria (the *anschluss*, or union, 1938) and Czechoslovakia (1938, 1939).

4. *Economic Tensions:* Economic problems, brought on mainly by the worldwide depression of the 1930s, contributed to the rise of aggressive dictators. Germany also experienced difficulty in making reparation payments and in trying to overcome severe inflation.

5. *Failure of Collective Security:* No united stand was taken by the democracies when the Axis powers took their imperialistic actions. Little was done to curb the aggressive policies of Germany, Italy, and Japan. The League of Nations condemned some of these actions but was unable to take any other measures.

6. *Appeasement:* To give in to a potential aggressor, hoping that the aggressor will then be content and not commit any further harmful acts, is called appeasement. During the 1930s the term came to mean the policy of accepting territorial **aggression** against small nations in the hope of avoiding a general war. The Munich Agreement of 1938 was an example of this meaning. It will be discussed below, along with other specific events leading to war.

Specific Events Leading to War in Europe

The 1930s saw the house of peace that some nations had hoped to build fall apart. It was not strong enough to withstand the many "rocks and projectiles" thrown at it by the three Axis aggressors. We will now examine the destructive acts of each one of them.

Italy Even though Mussolini stirred his countrymen's pride by frequent references to the Roman Empire, little available unoccupied land overseas was left for him to conquer. He saw an opportunity in Ethiopia in 1935, when he took advantage of a border dispute to send in an invasion force. Ethiopian soldiers under Emperor Haile Selassie were no match for the Italian army and were easily defeated. The League of Nations branded Italy as an aggressor and voted for sanctions (economic restrictions), but had no way to enforce them. The league's actions were ignored by Mussolini, who proclaimed Ethiopia to be part of the Italian Empire. Additional **belligerent** actions taken by Mussolini were his aiding General Franco in the Spanish Civil War (1936–1939) and his annexation of Albania in 1939.

Germany The most serious acts of destruction aimed at the so-called house of peace were carried out by the Third Reich, Hitler's Nazi government. As did Mussolini, Hitler engaged in actions that went directly against both the spirit and the letter of the documents signed in the 1920s that aspired toward a peaceful world. The following is a chronology of his actions:

1. *1935:* Germany had begun to remilitarize. Factories were building war-related products. "Hunting clubs" were teaching people how to use weapons. **Conscription** was reintroduced. These activities were in violation of the Versailles treaty.

2. *1936:* Flexing his muscles, and stating his right to control all German territory, Hitler ordered troops into the Rhineland. Although such action also violated the Versailles treaty, and sparked an angry reaction from the French prime minister, nothing was done to stop Hitler.

Ethiopian Emperor Haile Selassie spoke at the League of Nations in 1936 about Mussolini's attack on his country.

General Francisco Franco greets supporters during the Spanish Civil War.

3. *1936–1939:* The Spanish Civil War presented Hitler with an opportunity to test some of his newly trained soldiers and newly developed weapons. He used these to help General Franco in his revolt against the Spanish government. A republican government had been elected in Spain, including Socialists, Communists, and liberals. The monarchy, the army, and the Catholic Church had lost some of their status and prestige in the nation. To remedy this situation, and to strike against what he feared was a possible growth of **communism**, General Franco and his followers, the Nationalists, struck against the government. While Russia supplied the Loyalists, those on the government side, Mussolini and Hitler helped the Nationalists. Ultimately the Nationalists triumphed, with Franco establishing a fascist dictatorship in Spain.

   The fact that no democratic nation stepped in to fight Franco and try to prevent his dictatorship was a sign of encouragement to Hitler. Perhaps he too could strike at some region without fear of resistance. The early cooperative efforts by Hitler and Mussolini in 1936 led to their forming a military alliance known as the Rome-Berlin Axis. The term *Axis* was introduced by Mussolini, from his theory that the world of the future would turn on an imaginary line drawn from Rome to Berlin. Soon after this agreement, Germany signed the Anti-Comintern Treaty with Japan. Endorsed also by Italy, this treaty aimed at cooperation against the expansion of Russian communism. From this moment on in 1936, Germany, Italy, and Japan would be known as the **Axis powers**.

4. *1938:* In March 1938, Hitler again violated the Treaty of Versailles by achieving anschluss (union) with Austria. In the 1920s, a Nazi party was started in Austria. It gained strength through terror, assassination of opponents, and other means similar to those used by the Nazis in Germany. By 1938, Austrian Chancellor Kurt Schuschnigg, pressured to include Nazis in his cabinet, had intended to hold a **plebiscite** (a nationwide yes or no vote) on the issue of anschluss with Germany. But before he could do this, Hitler sent German troops into Austria, had Schuschnigg arrested, and installed a Nazi as chancellor. As a sign of expanding Nazi policies, Hitler's Storm Troopers forced elderly Jewish men and women to clean the streets of Vienna. Again, nothing was done by Western nations in response to the events of March 1938.

   Hitler tried to justify anschluss with Austria by declaring that his soldiers were needed to help keep order, and that all German-speaking people should be united. Austria was now part of the Third Reich. By 1938 almost all of central Europe was controlled by the continent's two Axis powers.

5. *1938:* Hitler next turned his attention to Czechoslovakia. Approximately one half of this new nation, formed after World War I, was surrounded by the Third Reich on three sides. Over three million Germans lived in its western region, called the Sudetenland. Hitler declared that it was only natural for the Sudeten Germans to be united with other Germans. The same theme was trumpeted by the Nazi party that had been organized in the Sudetenland. The call for German unity provoked riots and demonstrations against the Czech government in May and June of 1938. The Czechs placed the region under martial law, sending troops to quell disorders. Hitler then maintained that the Sudeten Germans needed "protection" by the Third Reich. Nazi **propaganda** told of alleged Czech atrocities against these Germans. Hitler also described Czechoslovakia as a "dagger aimed at the heart

of Germany," and asserted that Germany needed to expand its own borders to acquire *lebensraum* (living space).

In light of these events and statements, tension grew in Europe during the summer of 1938. On September 22, 1938, Hitler announced that Germany would occupy the Sudetenland. Fear gripped Czechoslovakia, even though it had a defensive military alliance with the Soviet Union. This agreement stated, however, that the Soviet Union would offer assistance only if France did so. France consulted with Britain, hoping for its support if matters came to a head. On September 29, a meeting to resolve the Sudeten crisis was held in the German city of Munich. Attending were Hitler, British Prime Minister Neville Chamberlain, French Premier Edouad Daladier, and Italy's Benito Mussolini. Czechoslovakia was not represented. Toward midnight, an agreement was reached.

The Munich Agreement provided for a partition of Czechoslovakia. Hitler would be allowed to annex the Sudetenland without interference. The other delegates to the Munich Conference agreed to the annexation, based upon Hitler's promise that he would not make any other territorial demands. Britain and France decided not to defend Czechoslovakia, and were thus willing to sacrifice the Sudetenland, in the hope of avoiding a full-scale war. Their decision was an act of appeasement. When Neville Chamberlain arrived back in London after the conference, he said that the Munich Agreement meant there would be "peace in our time." In October, German troops moved into the Sudetenland. The Axis powers had secured control of central Europe without having fired a shot.

6. *1939:* In March 1939, Hitler, disregarding his prior statements about Czechoslovakia, sent in troops to occupy the rest of the country. Thus another addition was made to the lands held by the Third Reich. Chamberlain's policy of appeasement had been a failure. Hitler's boldness increased as he grew more and more certain that the Western powers were too fearful and too weak to put up any show of force against him. This boldness was apparent in the threats he began to make to Poland in the spring and summer of 1939.

7. *1939:* In August 1939, to the world's amazement, Hitler announced the signing of a treaty with the Soviet Union, the Nazi-Soviet Nonaggression Pact. It came as a surprise because Hitler detested communism, disliked the Soviet leader Joseph Stalin, had often talked about taking over the soil-rich Soviet region of Ukraine, and considered Slavs to be an inferior race of people. Nevertheless, he put aside these sentiments and thoughts, temporarily, in order to prevent the Soviets from fighting him over Poland. If Britain and France were to resist him, he did not want to worry about waging a war on two fronts.

France and Britain were surprised and upset over the treaty. Along with the rest of the world, they knew that Hitler and Stalin were antagonists and therefore felt that the two dictators could not possibly agree on anything. The two Western nations had now lost a potential ally, as they had assumed that they could count on Soviet help against Hitler if a war broke out. They also now feared that Poland would be a likely target for Hitler's army, with the Soviets promising not to fight him.

By the terms of the treaty that were disclosed publicly, Germany and the Soviet Union promised not to attack each other and to remain neutral if the

Hitler (center) boldly ignored the Munich Agreement he signed with (from left) Chamberlain, Daladier, and Mussolini.

other was involved in a war. The secret parts of the treaty provided that the Soviets would not interfere with Hitler's move into western Poland in return for Hitler's not interfering with Soviet moves into eastern Poland and the Baltic nations of Finland, Lithuania, Latvia, and Estonia. Unknown to the world, Poland was about to undergo **partition**, and much of Eastern Europe was to be carved into German and Soviet zones of occupation.

In April 1939, prior to the Nazi-Soviet Pact (also called the Molotov-Ribbentrop Pact, named for the foreign ministers from the USSR and Germany), Britain and France had signed a mutual assistance pact with Poland. They had thus let Hitler know that they were prepared to use force should he continue his moves eastward. Hitler's awareness of this pact (although he probably still doubted British and French resolve to fight) was a factor prompting him to sign the nonaggression pact with the Soviets in August.

Immediate Cause of War in Europe

On September 1, 1970, an American tourist in Warsaw, the capital of Poland, woke up to find Polish soldiers standing quietly at attention in several parts of the city. There was a small monument where each soldier stood, and a strange silence prevailed that had not been present on the previous day. The tourist soon learned the reasons for what he saw. These scenes were part of the Polish government's annual observance of the horror that had occurred 31 years earlier, on September 1, 1939. On that day, Germany invaded Poland, marking the start of World War II in Europe.

The buildup to the German invasion had begun a number of years earlier, but it intensified in the summer of 1939. Germany had been outraged at the 1919 Versailles treaty's award to Poland of the city of Danzig as well as a strip of German territory for access to the Baltic Sea. This territory, known as the Polish corridor, separated most of Germany from its region of East Prussia. Ever since 1933, Hitler had seized upon these issues as one of his appeals to German nationalism. A Nazi party had been established in Danzig, and it campaigned for linkage with the fatherland (Germany). Now, in the last week of August 1939, with the ink barely dry on the nonaggression pact with the Soviets, Hitler demanded the return of Danzig and protection for Germans living in the Polish corridor. The Nazi propaganda machine had turned out stories of atrocities against these Germans. On August 19, Hitler requested the presence in Berlin of a Polish official to discuss a "German solution" to the "Polish question." No representative appeared. On August 31, during the night, German soldiers, masquerading as Poles, attacked a German radio station on the German-Polish border. Hitler, stating that Poland had attacked German forces, ordered the German army into Poland the next day, September 1. By breakfast time, German troops were on Polish soil, while German planes were bombing Warsaw and other parts of Poland.

On September 3, Britain and France demanded German withdrawal. Upon Hitler's refusal, they backed up their guarantees to Poland and declared war on Germany. World War II had begun.

At first the United States was not a direct participant, although it gradually came to support the British and French. It was not until late 1941, two years after the invasion of Poland, that America entered the war. The immediate reason why it became a belligerent in the third year of the war is explained in the next section.

Specific Events Leading to War in Asia

In Asia an aggressive, militaristic Japan moved to destroy the European "house of peace" during a ten-year period beginning in 1931.

1. *1931–1932:* During this time, Japan invaded parts of Manchuria, in northern China, wanting to possess the region's coal, iron, and fertile soil. With few resources on its crowded islands, and with a growing population, Japanese imperialists looked down upon China as a natural target. Japan's action was a violation of the Nine Power Treaty of 1921–1922. Japan ignored criticism from the League of Nations and withdrew from the organization. The United States, wanting to maintain an Open Door Policy in China, issued the Stimson Doctrine, which stated that no recognition would be given to land taken by force. This had little affect on Japan, as it experienced no attempt to enforce the doctrine. Japan excluded all foreigners and exploited the mineral resources of Manchuria for its own use. The Chinese were unable to stop this from happening.

2. *1937:* In 1937, Japan sought to invade other areas in China. Many historians regard these invasions as the opening battles of World War II in Asia. Although Japan's military might brought much suffering to the Chinese, by 1939 Japan had not been able to conquer the entire nation.

3. *1940:* In 1940, with the fall of France and Holland to Germany, Japan took over French Indochina and claimed "protective custody" over the Dutch East Indies. With these advances in Southeast Asia, Japan was on the way to establishing its East Asian co-prosperity sphere and a "new order." In truth, these were simply masks for Japan's expanding colonial empire. In September 1940, Japan signed a military alliance with Germany and Italy, officially creating the Rome-Berlin-Tokyo Axis.

4. *1941:* With Britain now struggling in Europe as the only remaining Western power against Germany, and unable to send reinforcements to the Orient, it appeared likely that Japan would be able to take over such British colonies as Hong Kong and Malaya. The United States, having bases in Hawaii and the Philippine Islands, was the sole power left in the way of Japanese expansion in East Asia. When General Hideki Tojo became prime minister of Japan in October 1941, tension increased between Japan and the United States. Japan refused American requests to leave China, while the United States stopped exports to Japan and moved its Pacific fleet to Pearl Harbor in Hawaii.

On December 7, 1941, Japan launched a surprise attack against U.S. forces in Pearl Harbor. More than 2,000 Americans were killed, and many battleships and planes were destroyed. On December 8, 1941, U.S. President Franklin D. Roosevelt asked Congress to declare war on Japan, predicting that December 7, 1941, would become "a date that will live in infamy." Congress honored the president's request, and on the same day Britain declared war on Japan. In the following week, Germany and Italy declared war on the United States, while Congress answered with a war declaration against them. Less than 25 years after the end of World War I the world was engulfed in a second major conflict.

By 1939, as we have seen, there was no longer a "house of peace." One may argue that its foundations should have been made more secure by its builders or even that it should have been constructed in a different manner. On the other hand, its destroyers acted in ways that were not fully anticipated. And even if these ways had been anticipated, what should the builders have done as "preventive maintenance" or "repairs"?

In the period between the two world wars, the victorious nations in World War I, as democracies, were committed to goals other than preparing for war. They were attempting to improve the economic and civic well-being of their populations. The Great Depression, beginning in 1929, had produced serious setbacks to these attempts. The totalitarian governments of Germany, Italy, and Japan were less interested in the material well-being of their citizens, and more inclined to focus money and energy on "guns" than on "butter." Without any long tradition of **democracy**, they were able to use their people as instruments of their own policies and grandiose ambitions.

The Western democracies also found it difficult to understand the ugly proportions of totalitarian aggression. To average British, French, and American citizens, people such as Hitler and Mussolini seemed to be apart from the mainstream of humane and intellectual progress that Western Europe had been achieving ever since the **Renaissance** and the **Enlightenment**. Never did one imagine that these leaders, heirs to cultures that had produced great writers, artists, and scientists, would pursue goals that would result in a world war.

That war was fought in even more horrible fashion and in more locales than was World War I. The conduct of World War II will now concern us.

Conduct of World War II

While it was being fought, World War I had been called the Great War. Although World War II produced more casualties and was fought in wider geographical areas than the First World War, it was never called the greater war. Yet it may go down in history as, to borrow terminology from President Woodrow Wilson, the war that ended all wars. Perhaps we may, at the very least, call it the last great war of the twentieth century. One reason for this hope is the terror evoked by the new weaponry used in the war's final phases. Another reason is the peacekeeping machinery that was created at the war's end. The actual conduct of the war will be our topic in this section.

Churchill replaced Chamberlain as Britain's prime minister. Here he reviews the American 101st Airborne Division with Generals Dwight D. Eisenhower and Maxwell D. Taylor.

The War in Europe, 1939–1941

This early part of the war saw many German successes. Poland surrendered on September 27, 1939. The German victory was marked by a new kind of warfare, called *blitzkrieg*, or lightning war, that involved coordinating swift, simultaneous attacks by air and land. The land forces included tanks, artillery, and infantry. In accord with the Nazi-Soviet Nonaggression Pact, the USSR moved to seize "its areas" of eastern Poland, along with Estonia, Latvia, and Lithuania. In November 1939, Soviet forces attacked Finland and ultimately took it over in March 1940.

For several months after the conquest of Poland, German forces were busy building up their strength without engaging in any major hostilities. A lull was apparent on the western front, as the Germans dug in behind their fortified position in the Rhineland, the Siegfried line. France massed forces at the Maginot line, along its eastern border. The lack of any action in this part of Europe led to the name the "phony war." No one used this term after April 9, 1940, however, when Germany began to launch a series of successful blitzkrieg attacks. By May 1940, Denmark, Norway, Luxembourg, the Netherlands, and Belgium had fallen. These victories gave Hitler greater access to the North Sea and to Britain, and afforded him the opportunity of attacking France without going through the Maginot line. They also led to the resignation of British Prime Minister Neville Chamberlain, a symbol of the failed policy of appeasement. His place was taken by Winston Churchill.

The Fall of France By the end of May 1940, the German strategy of invading France through Belgium, north of the Maginot line, became clear. Avoiding the temptation to move immediately toward Paris, Hitler's troops sought to secure all of northeastern France by splitting the main French army in the south from a combined Belgian, British, and French force in the north. This was accomplished by moving quickly against the combined armies and forcing them to evacuate France at the English Channel seaport of Dunkirk. The evacuation of over 300,000 soldiers from Dunkirk in late May and early June of 1940 was astonishing. British ships, small boats, yachts, and other kinds of vessels rushed across the English Channel to save the soldiers. The

Dunkirk evacuation of so many men, although necessitated by a clear military gain for the Germans, proved to be a powerful morale builder for the British.

A study of German documents after the war reveals that Hitler had purposely held back from crushing the Allied forces, overwhelmingly British, at Dunkirk. He had the power to do so, but may have thought that Britain was no longer a threat to him and may have wanted to save his tanks, infantry, and air force for conquering France. The conquest became a reality with the Fall of Paris in June 1940. The Wehrmacht, the Germany army, had advanced toward Paris with little difficulty; French forces were not well prepared. A popular French leader from World War I, Marshall Philippe Pétain, took over the government on June 16, 1940, and on the same day signed an **armistice** with the Germans in a railroad car in the French village of Compiegne. To the shame of the French, this was the same car in the same village where the Germans had signed the armistice that ended World War I. Further shame was heaped upon France when Italy declared war on it in June. With France already on its knees, this "stab in the back" from its southeastern neighbor shocked public opinion in Britain and the United States. Italy now became a belligerent in World War II.

By the terms of the armistice, France was divided into two parts. Northern France was to be governed by the Germans, as occupied France. The southern region was to be under German supervision, but administered by a French government located in the city of Vichy and headed by Marshall Pétain. Vichy France, as this region was called, had in its government several collaborators. These were French citizens who were willing to work with the Nazis and carry out their wishes. Other French people continued to secretly fight the Germans as part of the resistance forces; they acted in small groups to sabotage German installations. Frenchmen who escaped to Britain after Dunkirk formed the Free French forces, under General Charles de Gaulle. They refused to have anything to do with the Vichy government and prepared for the day when they could return to France and drive out the Germans.

The Battle of Britain With the surrender of France in June 1940, Britain stood alone. It was the only remaining anti-Axis belligerent. The United States, though alarmed at the Fall of France and willing to give material aid to the British, wanted to continue her policy of **isolationism** rather than committing herself to fighting. Hitler now assumed, in these circumstances, that Britain would be willing to make peace, thereby leaving him in control of the European continent. He is even alleged to have sent out some peace feelers to London, promising to leave Britain alone, along with her colonial empire, if she dropped out of the war. The British would have none of this. Throughout her long history of trying to maintain a **balance of power** in Europe, Britain had often gone to war to prevent the kind of dominance by a single nation that Hitler achieved after defeating France.

In August 1940, Hitler and his air marshal, Herman Goering, decided to bomb the British Isles as prelude to an invasion. Thus began the Battle of Britain, which was to last until November 1940. Under Prime Minister Winston Churchill, the mood of the population was defiant. He told the nation he would offer his "blood, toil, tears, and sweat." On June 4, 1940, after the evacuation from Dunkirk, Churchill set a courageous tone with an emotional speech that included these words:

> *We shall go on to the end . . . . we shall fight with growing confidence and with growing strength in the air, we shall defend our Island, whatever the cost*

may be. We shall fight on the beaches, we shall fight on the landing grounds, we shall fight in the fields and in the streets, we shall fight in the hills; we shall never surrender . . . .

Later in the month, he pleaded with his fellow citizens to "stand up to" Hitler. Otherwise, "the whole world . . . will sink into the abyss of a new Dark Age." With a ringing voice he further said: "Let us therefore brace ourselves to our duties, and so bear ourselves that, if the British Empire and its Commonwealth last for a thousand years, men will say, 'This was their finest hour.'"

Such Churchillian oratory strengthened the people for the frightening warfare to be waged by the Luftwaffe (the German air force). Day and night, mostly from August to November, German planes bombed airports, military bases, and industrial centers. The most terrifying moments came whenever there were attacks, referred to as the "blitz," often in the night, on heavily populated civilian centers. This kind of total war was worse than what had occurred in World War I. However, Britain's civilian defense procedures during the bombing raids of 1940 proved reasonably effective in protecting people. Thousands slept in underground shelters, subways, and basements. Many fled their city homes for the countryside; parents in targeted urban areas such as London and Coventry evacuated many of their children to the country.

The most crucial factor in Britain's successful defense against the German onslaught was her air force. Royal Air Force (RAF) planes dueled with German pilots in the skies all over southern England. Britain's air war was significantly assisted by the use of radar. Invented in the 1930s, this scientific device could detect aircraft miles away. Its use was instrumental in the destruction of more than 1,700 German aircraft; British losses numbered approximately 1,000. As the air war continued, the Germans were preparing for an invasion along the French coast. Called Operation Sea Lion, the invasion could not begin as long as the RAF was still flying. With the Luftwaffe encountering unexpectedly high losses, Hitler called off Operation Sea Lion on the advice of Air Marshall Goering on September 17, 1940.

Although the Germans were to continue occasional bombing raids until 1941, the Battle of Britain was a defeat for them. In a glowing tribute to RAF pilots, Churchill proclaimed, "Never in the field of human conflict was so much owed by so many to so few."

Wartime air raids became part of the lives of Londoners. Thousands of them slept in the city's underground (subway) system, which served double-duty as bomb shelters.

Aggression in the Balkans and the Soviet Union With a stalemate in the west, Hitler now turned his attention to the Balkans and to Eastern Europe. Although Mussolini had failed to take Greece in the fall of 1940, German forces put down strong resistance there and finally occupied the country in May 1941. Prior to this advance, Hitler had added Romania, Bulgaria, Hungary, and Yugoslavia to his domain. He had hoped to reach the Suez Canal, to disrupt British commerce, and to seize nearby oil fields. Unable, however, to go through neutral Turkey, he failed in an attempt to seize Egypt by attacking through Libya. Elsewhere in the Middle East, the Axis suffered a loss when British and Free French troops took over areas held by Vichy France, such as Syria.

The other military goal of Hitler in mid-1941 was the conquest of the Soviet Union. Unworried about his western front, with a weakened Britain and an isolationist America, he eyed with envy the rich soil of eastern Poland and the Russian oil fields in Ukraine and other areas, all essential to the fulfillment of his lebensraum policy. He was certain that Russia could be taken quickly, before the winter months. Willing to ignore the 1939 Nonaggression Pact and to risk the possible danger of a two-front war, Germany attacked Russia on June 22, 1941. The code name for the invasion was Operation Barbarossa, named for a Germanic king. The attack startled the world. Both Britain and the United States said they would try to send supplies to the Russians. Although they distrusted Soviet leader Stalin and feared communism, they considered it important to help any nation that was fighting Hitler.

The fighting by Soviet forces against the almost three million German troops did not go well at first. Retreating on several fronts, the Russians sought desperately to hinder enemy advances by following the Scorched Earth Policy. Accordingly, they destroyed farm and industrial equipment, blew up roads, and burned crops. The strategy was partially successful, as the Wehrmacht was unable to get any further than the approaches to Leningrad and Moscow by the end of 1941. With winter now setting in, and a successful counterattack near Moscow by Soviet General Georgi Zhukov, Hitler's war machine was forced to hold its lines.

Zhukov's attack on December 5, 1941, gave a welcome boost to Soviet morale, as did the events of the next several days. Japan's attack on the American naval base at Pearl Harbor on December 7, 1941, led to a declaration of war by the United States on Japan on December 8, 1941. On December 11, Germany and Italy, honoring their agreement with Japan, declared war on the United States. With its own declaration against these two nations, the United States became an active participant in the struggle against Axis aggression. As 1942 began, events in Europe were about to take a different turn.

Victory in Europe, 1942–1945

Some of the most horrible combat ever seen on our planet occurred in the years between 1942 and 1945. This was true in Europe, as well as in Africa and Asia. For Hitler, the war in Europe now, with America's entry, had two fronts. This situation, with reminders of World War I's tragedy for Germany, was just what he had wanted to avoid. Throughout 1942, therefore, he increased the pressure on the USSR in the hope of quickly closing down the eastern front in order to meet the expected thrust from the Americans, British, and Free French on his west. Additional troops were sent to besiege Leningrad, while a major offensive was launched against Stalingrad.

Stalingrad The battle for Stalingrad lasted six months. It became exceptionally brutal as German soldiers penetrated into the city and faced hand-to-hand combat with the Russians. Fierce weather, starvation, and disease took a terrible toll on both armies as well as on the civilian population. At Stalingrad the Russians lost more men than the United States lost in the entire war! In late 1942, "General Winter," the same foe that had contributed to Napoleon's defeat in Russia in 1812, was to spell disaster for the Germans. This factor, along with continuing counteroffensives by the Soviets, resulted on January 31, 1943, in the surrender of a German army of almost 350,000 men. Spurred by this victory, Soviet forces pushed the Germans out of their land by early 1944. The siege of Stalingrad had ended. With Hitler's battered soldiers retreating, the Russians seized previously Nazi-controlled territory in Eastern Europe—Latvia, Poland, and Hungary. The drive toward Berlin now gained momentum, and the Soviets began to envision an end to what they were to call the Great Patriotic War.

Allied Summit Meetings On the western and southern fronts, the United States and its Allies became active. In 1941, President Roosevelt and Prime Minister Churchill signed the Atlantic Charter. This was an idealistic document, similar to former President Woodrow Wilson's Fourteen Points, describing the war aims of the two major Atlantic democracies. Among other things, they pledged to do the following:

1. Seek no territories;
2. Respect the right of people to practice self-determination and choose their own governments;
3. Insure freedom of the seas;
4. Provide access to equal economic opportunity; and
5. Work for an end to aggression by all nations.

In January 1942, twenty-six nations, as Allies fighting the Axis powers, sent delegates to a meeting in Washington, D.C. They promised to work together, not sign separate peace treaties, and adhere to the principles of the Atlantic Charter.

At another international meeting, held in Teheran, Iran, in December 1943, the **Big Three** (Roosevelt, Churchill, and Stalin) discussed plans for dealing with Germany. Stalin was emphatic that Germany must be divided and kept divided. His additional wish for a second front to be opened in the west with an invasion of occupied France was agreed to by Roosevelt and Churchill. However, Churchill, fearing Stalin's future designs on Eastern Europe, proposed a major offensive by American and British forces from the Mediterranean into the Balkans and then northward. Stalin's opposition to this proposal, supported by Roosevelt, prevented it from being carried out, with troublesome consequences after the war. The leaders at the Teheran Conference agreed to meet again.

North Africa and Italy On the military scene, a combined American and British force under U.S. General Dwight Eisenhower landed in North Africa in 1942 and inflicted heavy losses on German units. A momentous victory that prevented the Germans under General Erwin Rommel, "the Desert Fox," from reaching the Suez Canal occurred in November 1942 at El Alamein. This was accomplished by British troops led by General Bernard Montgomery. The first significant Allied military venture in Europe occurred on July 10, 1943. Deciding to strike at the European Axis powers through their "soft underbelly," a combined American, British, and Canadian force landed in Sicily to begin an invasion of Italy. At this point Marshal Pietro Badoglio took over the Italian government from Mussolini, who fled and was taken to the north of Italy by German parachutists. Badoglio supported the Allied nations, surrendered to them, and welcomed their landing on the Italian mainland in September 1943 to fight the

An Allied victory at El Alamein in Egypt prevented the Germans from reaching the Suez Canal.

remaining German soldiers. After heavy fighting at such places as Anzio, the Allies marched into Rome on June 4, 1944.

D-Day With the victories in Italy by 1944, Germany was being hurt on her southern front, and the Russians were advancing on the east. What now remained to be done was a drive on Germany's western front. Such a drive, known as Operation Overlord, had been planned for months, under the overall command of General Eisenhower. It culminated in an immense show of force on June 6, 1944, D-Day, with an invasion on the beaches of Normandy, France. Thousands of ships transported American, British, Canadian, and Free French soldiers across the English Channel. In France they met determined resistance from entrenched German forces, but were able to take the beaches and march inland. Allied warplanes successfully battled German aircraft. Other Allied landings in France were made in August 1944, and the Wehrmact began retreating eastward from these onslaughts. Finally, on August 25, 1944, Paris was liberated. Amidst cheers and prayers, General Charles de Gaulle led a victory parade into the city.

The Allies were now ready for a drive to Berlin. One last major German stand took place in Belgium, in December 1944, at the Battle of the Bulge, but after a bitter ten-day struggle the victorious Allies were able to step foot on German soil. As 1945 approached, it was evident that this would be the final year of the war.

The Yalta Conference In February 1945, the three main Allied leaders—Roosevelt, Churchill, and Stalin—met at Yalta to make postwar plans. They represented the most important members of the Grand Alliance of nations fighting the Axis powers. At this meeting, held in the Crimea region of the Soviet Union, the Big Three agreed on six points:

1. Germany should be demilitarized and divided into zones of occupation after the war.
2. Trials for war criminals should be held.
3. Arrangements would be made for a new international peacekeeping organization.
4. Poland was to be restored with new boundaries, getting some German land for her west while letting Russia have some of Poland's land to her east.
5. The USSR would permit free elections in the Eastern European regions it had taken from the Germans.
6. The USSR would enter the war in Asia against Japan once Germany had surrendered. In return, Stalin would get control of some northern Japanese islands, the Kuriles.

The agreements reached at the Yalta Conference were to cause problems after the war. (See Chapter 35, "The Cold War.") Roosevelt was more willing than was Churchill to reach accord with Stalin. One reason was the U.S. President's strong wish to have the Soviets enter the war against Japan. As it happened, Roosevelt never lived to see the war's end; he died on April 12, 1945. He was succeeded in office by former Vice-President Harry S Truman.

Stalin (in uniform) is seated with Churchill and an ailing President Roosevelt at the Yalta Conference.

V-E Day In that same eventful month of April 1945, the German army in Italy gave up. Mussolini was captured and killed by Italian guerrillas. He was then taken to Milan, where his corpse was shot five times by a mother who had lost five sons in the war. He was then hung by the ankles in front of a small shop. Later that month, American soldiers met their Soviet counterparts in eastern Germany. On April 30, Hitler committed suicide in his Berlin underground bunker. His body was then soaked with gas and burnt. Even though his remains were never found, there is no serious disagreement about his death. The Russians were attacking Berlin at the time and were permitted to march into the city first, on May 2, 1945. On May 7, U.S. General Eisenhower received a formal unconditional surrender by German forces; on May 8, a formal surrender was also made to Soviet General Zhukov. The date May 8, 1945, has since been proclaimed as V-E Day, the day of victory in Europe. To the relief of millions, the war in Europe had come to an end.

General Eisenhower was the supreme commander of Allied forces in Europe. Here he gives a "full victory, nothing else" order to paratroopers.

Women air force pilots, or WASPs, regularly ferried American war planes across the United States during WWII.

One unanticipated horror of the war shocked the Allies as they marched through Europe while attacking German soldiers. This was the discovery of the torture and death inflicted on innocent civilians by the Nazis in **concentration camps** and **death camps**. The most seriously targeted of these civilians were Jews, victims of the **Holocaust**. This word refers to the intentional persecution and murder of European Jews by the Germans from 1933–1945. Six million were exterminated, mostly in camps such as Auschwitz, Dachau, and Treblinka. The planned extermination of a group of people because of their religion, race, or ethnicity is called **genocide**. The genocidal tactics of the Nazis were a horrible extension of Hitler's anti-Semitic attitudes. Although there were instances of Jewish resistance, such as the uprising of 1943 in the Warsaw Ghetto, the outside world stood by and did nothing while these deadly tactics—gas chambers, ovens, firing squads—were being used. Among other groups who suffered in the camps because the Nazis had labeled them as inferior human beings were homosexuals, Jehovah's Witnesses, gypsies, Slavs, and mentally retarded persons. (See Chapter 34, "The Holocaust.")

Victory in Asia and the Pacific, 1942–1945

From December 7, 1941, the date of the Pearl Harbor attack, until mid-1942, Japan achieved major success in Asia and the Pacific. Among its conquests during this time were Hong Kong, Malaya, Singapore,

U.S. forces in Rome, riding by the colosseum in 1944.

MacArthur, commander in chief of the southwest Pacific during World War II, was able to recapture the Philippines as he had vowed in 1942.

the Philippines, the Dutch East Indies, and Burma. Having already taken Korea and parts of eastern China and French Indochina, Japan seemed destined to carve out its so-called co-prosperity sphere in Asia. However, from May to August 1942, Japan was defeated in three major engagements that were to limit its imperial expansion:

1. The Battle of the Coral Sea, where American and Australian naval forces prevented an invasion of Australia.
2. The Battle of Midway Island, where the U.S. navy broke Japanese codes, destroyed four carriers, and thereby prevented an attack upon Hawaii. This battle proved to be the turning point in the Pacific.
3. The Battle of Guadalcanal, where, at the most southerly point gained by the Japanese, American marines achieved a bitter and costly victory.

U.S. forces were now ready to take the offensive, and began to mount an "island-hopping" campaign. The goal was to slowly capture Japanese-held islands in the Pacific, on the way to attacking Japan itself. Meanwhile, on the Asian mainland in 1942 and 1943, Japanese troops began to retreat under pressure from the Americans, British, Chinese, and several native resistance groups. At the Cairo Conference of November 1943, Roosevelt, Churchill, and Chinese nationalist leader Chiang Kai-shek signed the Cairo Declaration. They pledged to continue fighting Japan until that nation made an unconditional surrender. Japan would lose all territories it had taken, with Korea to become independent.

Another major American success was gained in 1944 at the Battle of Leyte Gulf, near the Philippines. In October, U.S. General Douglas MacArthur was able to recapture the Philippines. He had escaped from there in 1942 with the promise "I shall return." Combined U.S. land, sea, and air forces now edged closer to Japan with fiercely fought encounters at Iwo Jima in February-March 1945, and at Okinawa in April-June 1945. In Tokyo itself, a single bombing raid took the lives of more than 80,000 people. These advances did much to weaken Japan's fighting ability, while boosting Allied morale. The cry "Remember Pearl Harbor" was a stimulus for American forces. So were the grim discoveries about indescribable Japanese treatment of soldiers and civilians of all ethnic backgrounds in prisoner-of-war camps.

The Potsdam Conference

In July 1945, with Germany and Italy out of the war, and Japan's defeat a virtual certainty, American, British, and Russian leaders met at Potsdam, a town near Berlin. Attending this meeting were Truman, Churchill, and Stalin. (During the Potsdam Conference, held from July 17 to August 2, Clement Attlee became British prime minister and replaced Winston Churchill.) The three Allies issued a declaration concerning the future control and occupation of Germany, while calling for Japan's unconditional surrender. Much distrust was evident at Potsdam, as Churchill and Truman were upset at Stalin for not keeping his Yalta promises concerning free elections in Eastern Europe. Because of this feeling, Truman did not want to tell Stalin about the successful testing of an American atomic bomb.

Atomic Bombs and V-J Day

The Potsdam Conference ended on August 2. Although the United States warned Japan about suffering terrible destruction if it did not surrender, the Japanese turned down the **ultimatum**. On August 6, 1945, unwilling to risk untold numbers of American lives in invading Japan, President Truman ordered that an atomic bomb be dropped on the city of Hiroshima. Loss of life and property from this bomb was greater than the casualties and damage in any city ever bombed previously in wartime. On August 8, 1945, the USSR declared war on Japan and raced to fight

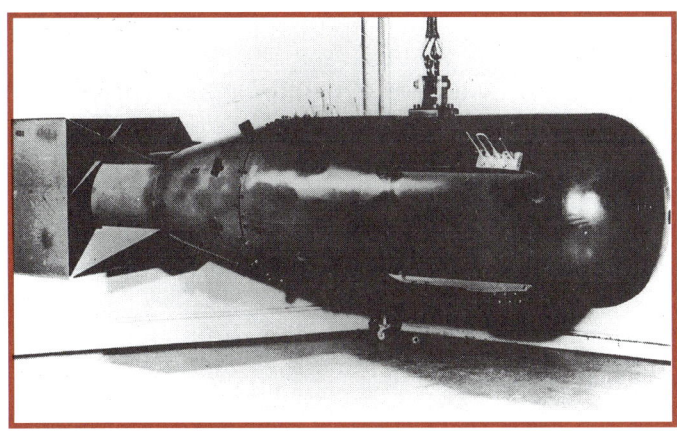

Atomic bombs like the "Little Boy" brought tremendous losses to Japan—and an end to World War II.

U.S. troops raising their flag at Iwo Jima in 1945.

dwindling Japanese forces in northern China. As Japan still refused to surrender, the United States dropped a second atomic bomb on August 9, 1945, on the city of Nagasaki. The additional losses from this bombing finally compelled the Japanese to surrender. Speaking for the very first time to his people on the radio, Japanese Emperor Hirohito told them of his decision. The formal surrender took place on September 2, 1945, on board the battleship USS *Missouri*. The Japanese surrender was accepted by Supreme Allied Commander General Douglas MacArthur. World War II had finally come to a close. To this day, September 2, 1945, is remembered as V-J Day, the day of victory over Japan.

This section on the conduct of World War II is much longer than its counterpart on the conduct of World War I. (See Chapter 30, "World War I.") This is due to the greater numbers of belligerents, weapons, combat zones, and deaths, as well as the sheer length of time involved. The results of the Second World War were staggering and historic, as will be seen in the next section. Only 21 years elapsed between the end of one world war and the start of the second. More than 45 years have now elapsed since the end of World War II without any significantly similar global confrontations. Let us hope that the absence of widespread strife will continue.

Results of World War II

The world of 1945 bore little resemblance to the world of the 1930s. Europe was shattered and lay in ruins, its peoples facing an uncertain future. Japan's reign as an imperial power was over. Some of the questions that faced the victors of World War I now confronted the victors of World War II. How should the defeated nations be treated? Could any kind of machinery be established that would prevent another world war?

The answers to these questions will be indicated below, as we describe the general results of the Second World War. We will then focus on matters related mainly to Europe.

Economic Results

World War II proved to be the most costly war ever fought. The loss of life and property far surpassed that in any previous conflict. Military costs alone were said to range into hundreds of billions of dollars. The economies of many European nations were destroyed. The industrial productivity necessary to support warfare provided jobs to many, but did not really add to the economic wealth of nations. Indeed, resources such as rubber, steel, oil, and wood had to be used for military purposes rather than for consumer goods. The money and material needed to transport, equip, clothe, and feed the armed forces of a belligerent nation were staggering. Civilians who were drafted or who volunteered for military duty had to leave their jobs and learn new skills.

Communism spread into Eastern Europe because of the occupation of this region by the Soviet Union. The Communists promised high standards of living and a better distribution of goods and services than had existed under capitalistic systems prior to the war.

Social Results

More people, soldiers and civilians, were killed than in any other war. Much of this high casualty rate was due to refined and newer weapons, as well as to the racist policies of the Axis powers. Another factor was the wide-ranging fighting in the war, taking place on three continents—Africa, Asia, and Europe. More than 22 million died, in both civilian and military populations; more than 34 million survived the war with wounds. At war's end, millions of people had become refugees and displaced persons. Homelessness, broken families, and poverty were constant reminders of the upheaval caused by the war. As a total war, involving all groups in a nation, the Second World War was of greater scope than World War I.

Scientific Results

By the end of the war, the use of radar had become much more sophisticated. Faster and more complex airplanes were built as knowledge of the science of aeronautics increased. Successful warfare at sea required advances in battleship and submarine design, as well as newer navigational equipment.

Weapons research resulted in newer and more deadly products. German scientists were able to manufacture a pilotless, jet-propelled bomb, the V1, and a rocket-propelled bomb, the V2. These brought much suffering to British civilians in urban areas. The most lethal weapon to come out of the war, however, was the atomic bomb. Its development reflected the pioneering work done by many scientists in discovering aspects of nuclear reactions. Chief among them were Enrico Fermi (an Italian who fled to the United States in 1938), Niels Bohr (from Denmark), Leo Szilard (a refugee from Hungary), and Albert Einstein (a German Jew who came to the United States in 1932). Fearful of an atomic bomb's destructiveness, but also worried that the Germans might produce one during the war, U.S. President Roosevelt committed much money and other resources to a secret project to develop the bomb. The **Manhattan Project**, as it was called, resulted in the production of two atomic bombs. Their use in World War II ushered in the nuclear age.

The war also saw the development and application of new medicines to help save lives on the battlefields. These included sulfa drugs and penicillin. Along with better use of blood plasma, they reduced the number of combat-related deaths from what it had been in World War I.

Political Results

These results were the most dramatic and had consequences that have continued to our own times. Some will be discussed here; others, in the chapters identified below.

1. The United States and the Soviet Union became the two leading **superpowers** and eventually clashed on many issues in what became known as the **Cold War**. (See Chapter 35, "The Cold War.")
2. The totalitarian systems of Germany, Italy, and Japan ended with the complete defeat of these nations.
3. Colonized peoples in Africa and Asia quickened their desires for independence. Their nationalistic movements were factors that would usher in the end of Western imperialism and the age of **decolonization**. (See Chapter 29, "Independence and Decolonization.")
4. France and Britain, although victorious nations in the war, gradually gave up their empires and declined as world powers.
5. To maintain peace and address issues that could lead to conflicts, as well as issues affecting global social and economic concerns, the Allies established the United Nations. (See Chapter 33, "The United Nations and Postwar Western Europe.")
6. Peace treaties and territorial changes involved several nations. As agreed to in the 1945 Potsdam Conference, a Council of Foreign Ministers was created to draw up the peace treaties on behalf of the five major victorious Allies: the United States, the Soviet Union, France, Great Britain, and China. In 1947, a treaty was signed with Italy whereby she was to pay some reparations and to lose any colonies she had acquired. In other treaties, Bulgaria, Finland, Hungary, and Romania also had adjustments in their boundaries, losing some land acquired during the war.
7. Most Eastern European countries became **satellite nations** in a sphere of influence controlled by the Soviet Union. (See Chapter 35, "The Cold War.") Many Soviet actions were in violation of the Yalta agreements. The Soviet Union kept the Baltic states of Estonia, Latvia, and Lithuania, having annexed them in 1940. It also obtained an eastern region of Czechoslovakia and substantial territory from Poland. The Soviet border was now moved further west. Poland's border, called the Oder-Neisse line for two rivers, was also moved further west with land taken from Germany. Germans who lived in what was now new parts of Poland, the USSR, and the Sudetenland area of Czechoslovakia, were expelled and forced to go to Germany.
8. Austria, which had become part of the Third Reich in 1938, was divided into four zones of occupation, administered by the United States, France, Great Britain, and the USSR. This situation continued until 1955, when the four Allies signed a formal peace treaty with Austria. By the treaty's terms, Austria became an independent nation with its pre-1938 boundaries. It was forbidden to have any political or economic union with Germany.
9. Germany was also divided into four zones of occupation—American, British, French, and Russian. However, Germany's postwar history and status were to be different from those of the other defeated Axis powers.
10. Japan was occupied until 1952 by the United States. Emperor Hirohito was allowed to stay in power. War crimes trials were held for key figures in Japan's military, such as Admiral Tojo, responsible for planning the Pearl

Harbor attack. Convicted as a war criminal, he was subsequently executed. Under U.S. General Douglas MacArthur, the Japanese put together a new **constitution** modeled on a democratic structure. The United States also aided Japan in its industrial recovery from the war.

The Nuremberg War Crimes Trials

From 1945 to 1947, the Allied powers held a series of trials for several Nazi officials. Conducted at the German city of Nuremberg, these were known as the Nuremberg War Crimes Trials. The judges formed an international tribunal; the prosecutors were from the victorious nations. The defendant Nazis were permitted to have lawyers and to defend themselves, rights that they had never granted to the millions whose deaths they caused. Among the charges against the Germans were these three:

1. "Crimes against the peace";
2. "Conspiracy to wage aggressive war"; and
3. "Crimes against humanity."

The first two charges related to the aggression that Germany had unleashed toward other nations. The third charge was based specifically on the atrocities committed by Germans against Jews and others considered to be "inferior human beings."

The trials exposed the terrible actions taken by the Nazis, with evidence and testimony that shocked a wartorn world. Of the 22 defendants tried, 19 were found guilty and three were acquitted. Twelve of the guilty were sentenced to death; seven, to life imprisonment. The Allies wanted the trials to serve as a warning to potential aggressors and as a means of encouraging respect for international law. They also hoped to promote the growth of democratic political organizations in Germany.

In addition to the Nuremberg trials, many other trials were held throughout Germany into the late 1940s. Among hundreds who were prosecuted as war criminals were doctors and nurses who had conducted outrageous "medical experiments" on concentration camp prisoners, camp guards, and officials in various war-related activities. These trials were part of a policy of denazification, which sought to cleanse Germany of Nazism by banning the Nazi party and not allowing any former Nazis to hold positions in government, education, or industry. Some former Nazis escaped detection by changing their names and hiding or by secretly leaving Germany. A few others, who were accomplished scientists, may have been helped to leave Germany by Western officials, with the expectation that these scientists would be helpful in the research and development of weapons systems in the growing Cold War against Communist nations.

Occupation of Germany, 1945–1990

The division and occupation of Germany soon became a source of tension among the four occupiers. Three fourths of the country, in the west, was controlled by the three Allied democracies, the United States, Britain, and France, while the eastern part was occupied by the Communist Soviet Union. The city of Berlin was in the eastern part of Germany. Although this entire area of Germany was under Soviet control, Berlin was to be a divided city separated into four zones of occupation. The three zones held by the United States, Britain, and France were known as West Berlin, and the Soviet zone as East Berlin. The Berlin Blockade of 1948–1949, imposed by the Soviets, challenged Western rights in West Berlin. Access to the city from the western parts of Germany was denied. The subsequent Berlin airlift by the United States and an Allied military buildup persuaded the Soviets to back down to end the blockade.

The Two Germanys

With the four World War II Allies unable to agree on a plan for German reunification, the Western nations permitted their zones in western Germany to come together in 1949 as the Federal Republic of Germany (West Germany); with its capital at Bonn. West Berlin was part of this new nation. The eastern part of Germany, under the Soviets, became the German Democratic Republic (East Germany); its capital was East Berlin. Thus, as the 1950s began, a strange, tense, and unexpected atmosphere engulfed central Europe. While Germany itself was no longer a military threat, those who had defeated her as friendly Allies were now at odds. The emerging hostile attitudes between the United States and the rest of the free world on the one hand, and the Soviet Union and the rest of the Communist world on the other, made for a very uneasy post-World War II peace. The division of Germany, of course, was an example of the attitudes that existed between the two sides in this confrontation known as the Cold War.

Tension increased with a strengthening of military forces. Both Germanys were allowed, with restrictions imposed by their occupiers, to build up their armies. The Allied nations also maintained troops in the two Germanys. The creation of two military alliances, the **North Atlantic Treaty Organization (NATO)** in 1949, and the Warsaw Pact in 1955, along with the crisis over the Berlin Wall in 1961, added to a mood of belligerence. (See Chapter 35, "The Cold War.")

Fortunately, from the 1970s onward, the bitterness in and over divided Germany eased somewhat. Normalization between the two Germanys was achieved in 1972 with the signing of the Fundamental Treaty, whereby West and East Germany recognized each other and established formal diplomatic relations. Both nations were admitted to the United Nations in 1973, and the United States recognized East Germany in 1974. At the Helsinki Conference of 1975, thirty-three European countries, along with the United States and Canada, signed the Helsinki Pact. By its terms, the signers recognized all post-World War II boundary changes in Germany and elsewhere in Europe. They also agreed to recognize the importance of promoting human rights throughout Europe and to investigate any governmental actions that violated these rights. A Helsinki Watch Committee was established to conduct such investigations. This historic meeting in Helsinki was the largest gathering of European nations since the 1815 **Congress of Vienna**. The meeting's primary goals can be seen in its official title—the Conference on Security and Cooperation in Europe (CSCE).

West Germany slowly began to function as a democracy, while enjoying great economic growth. It adopted a constitution providing for elections to a two-house parliament and protection of civil liberties. Political parties emerged, the most popular being the Christian Democrats and the Social Democrats. Some of the important heads of the government, known as the chancellors, have been Konrad Adenauer, Willy Brandt, Helmut Schmidt, and Helmut Kohl. West German industries expanded, particularly in automobiles and machinery. Its business leaders utilized technological advances and a well-educated labor force, while benefiting

The Berlin Wall divided Germany, as well as Europe, for 28 years, and was a physical symbol of the Cold War.

from the financial aid provided by the United States under the Marshall Plan. Over the years, a true "economic miracle" took place in West Germany.

East Germany, as a satellite of the USSR, became a Communist dictatorship. Its economy lagged behind that of West Germany, while its political system denied civil liberties and created a police-state atmosphere. Hundreds of its citizens tried to escape from the country, with several being shot as they tried to cross the border into West Germany. From 1946 until 1989, its only leaders were Communist party chiefs Walter Ulbricht and Erich Honecker. Starting in 1989, however, East Germany's history was to change drastically.

Reunification of Germany

In 1989, the unhappiness and distraught of East German citizens toward their government reached alarming proportions. During the summer months, thousands fled into Czechoslovakia, Hungary, and Austria in attempts to travel from these countries into West Germany. Prodemocracy demonstrations and confrontations with police broke out in Leipzig and other large cities. These actions forced the leader, Erich Honecker, to resign; Gregor Gysi replaced him. Gysi, in turn, was replaced by Hans Modrow, who suggested that some aspects of **capitalism** be introduced into East Germany. The ban on political parties was lifted, with new groups then challenging the Communists for control of the government and demanding free elections. In October, the celebration of East Germany's fortieth anniversary

East and West Berlin were reunited on November 9, 1989 when the hated Berlin Wall was opened.

stirred little enthusiasm. Ironically, it provoked further antigovernment demonstrations. These were signs that historic events would soon occur. Less than a month later, on November 9, 1989, the hated Berlin Wall was opened! This was done by the East German authorities. Once a blatant (conspicuous) symbol of divided Germany, restricting free movement of people and ideas, the wall now lost its significance as a political, economic, and social barrier. Throngs poured through the many openings in the wall, past the East German guards who previously would have prevented such movement by using force. It now seemed that the reunification process would be speeded along.

In March 1990, East Germany held its first-ever free and open elections. A government was chosen that promised to work for unity with West Germany. In May, a series of crucial meetings, known as the "**four-plus-two negotiations**," took place. These talks involved the four occupying powers (Britain, France, the Soviet Union, and the United States) plus the two German states. The delegates deliberated on the future of a united Germany. In July, an economic merger occurred when the West German mark became the unit of currency in East Germany. This meant that, even though the German people were still living in two separate nations, all Germans would use the same money. East Germans were allowed to move into West Germany; West German companies were permitted to set up capitalist-style businesses in East Germany.

A degree of economic unity had now been achieved, and the talks planning for political unity were continuing. Poland wanted to be included in the four-plus-two negotiations because it had suffered more from German occupation in World War II than any other European nation. Poland wanted assurance that a reunited Germany would respect Polish sovereignty and would not seek to retake any land given to Poland after the war. Specifically, Poland wanted to be sure that the Oder-Neisse boundary line between East Germany and Poland would remain intact. A promise to maintain this boundary was made by West German Chancellor Helmut Kohl in mid-1990, on the assumption that he would be the first head of a united German nation.

Unity talks proceeded now at a fast pace. The Big Four Allied nations of World War II agreed to end their status as occupiers. The talks culminated with the formal act of reunification on October 3, 1990. As that day began, at the stroke of midnight, near the Reichstag (parliament) building in Berlin, a ringing sound came from a replica of the American Liberty Bell—a gift from the United States. The black, red, and gold flag of West Germany was raised as the flag of the reunited nation. The president of what up to that moment had been West Germany, Richard von Weizsacker, read a proclamation of unity. When he had finished, a crowd of more than one million sang the West German—now the national—anthem. They sang from the third stanza of what had been the prewar national anthem, the first verses of which had been banned in the postwar period. Divided for 45 years, Germany was now reunited. Although the Germany of 1990, with a population of 78 million, was now the largest nation in Western Europe, it was the smallest German nation in the 119 years since Bismarck had completed the first movement for unification.

The All-German Elections

In December 1990, the first all-German elections were held. The winners were the Christian Democratic Union (CDU) coalition party and its leader, Helmut Kohl. Kohl had campaigned on hopes for a new prosperity for all and a promise not to raise taxes to pay for reunification. By June 1991, however, the economic picture in the new Germany had darkened, and Kohl was forced to break his promises. Taxes had to be raised to finance the cost of reunification and to fight the economic depression that was engulfing the eastern part of the new nation. Many of the former Communist-state-controlled industries there had now closed down, leaving thousands unemployed. Untold numbers of these unemployed traveled westward, hoping to find jobs. This migration led to tensions between westerners and easterners. There has even been talk of a "wall in the head" that still divides the country.

These predicaments caused trouble for Chancellor Kohl and his ruling coalition. Demonstrations were staged against him, with the CDU losing some local elections in 1991. Kohl was plagued by his hesitancy to send German soldiers to assist in the 1991 Persian Gulf War. He also faced domestic unrest in 1992–1993 that saw violence directed against new immigrants and long-time non-German residents in eastern Germany, as well as scattered outbreaks of **anti-Semitism**. As his popularity declined, that of the chief rival political party, the Socialist Democratic party (SPD), increased. Some commentators even predicted that the SPD would win control of the nation in the elections scheduled for 1994. They were wrong, as Kohl and the CDU emerged victorious. In light of this peaceful election, the world assumes and hopes that the two main postwar developments in Germany—its unity as a nation and its democratic structure—will continue into the twenty-first century. One change scheduled to occur by that time will be the movement of the government from Bonn back to Berlin. Political leaders agreed to this change, in principle, in January 1994.

Summary

Almost 50 years have passed since the end of World War II. For the first time in this century, a generation of Europeans has grown up without being involved in warfare on the continent. This generation has benefited from the postwar peace; and, as its members move into leadership positions, it will try to learn from the past and to insure the continued absence of war. Nevertheless, the impact and the memory of the Second World War linger, as two incidents in 1992 attest.

Early that year, a ceremony was held in London at the unveiling of a statue to Sir Arthur Harris. Known as "Bomber Harris," he was head of the British Bomber Command in World War II and directed the intensive bombing of the German city of Dresden in February 1945. This saturation bombing killed 135,000 people and is remembered to this day with horror by all Germans. Consequently, there was anger in Germany when the monument to Harris was dedicated. Upon learning that members of the British royal family had attended the dedication, a German newspaper in Munich protested the erection of the statue as "unnecessary and tasteless."

In September 1992, the German aerospace industry planned to celebrate in October the fiftieth anniversary of a major scientific achievement—the develop-

ment of the V2 rocket. Development of this rocket at the German city of Peenemunde represented a tremendous breakthrough in space technology. The V2 could carry a warhead for a distance of 200 miles and reach an altitude of 60–70 miles. The V2 was unlike any previous weapon of war and was used in German aerial attacks on British cities from 1942 to 1945. Almost 3,000 people were killed in 1944 and 1945 alone. With memories of the V2 attacks, as well as the German bombings during the Battle of Britain, British protests about the upcoming October 1992 celebration spread. A strong voice of condemnation came from Winston S. Churchill, a member of the British Parliament and a grandson of the wartime prime minister. Even some Germans criticized the celebration, as it reminded them of the Nazi Era and the fact that the underground factories in Peenemunde had been built with slave labor. The celebration was ultimately canceled.

These incidents concerning the Harris statue and the V2 rocket are signs that the past is remembered. Another issue that has made headlines concerns Germany and its future. When the United Nations opened its forty-seventh session in September 1992, Germany's foreign minister let it be known that his nation would like a permanent seat on the Security Council. As we will see in the next chapter, the Security Council is a very powerful and prestigious group in the United Nations. Germany's request was based upon its strong economic position in world affairs. Ironically, its plea came just one day after Japan's foreign minister suggested that his nation be given a permanent seat on the UN Council. That the two major aggressors in World War II should now, toward the end of this century, seek stature in a peacekeeping organization shows how much the world has changed since 1945! We will now move on to learn about that organization and the ways that it functions.

CHAPTER 32

Review Exercises

Causes of World War II

I. Matching

Directions: Match the words in Column A with the *correct description* in Column B.

Column A
1. appeasement
2. aggression
3. plebiscite
4. lebensraum
5. antagonism
6. remilitarization

Column B
(a) harmful action against a person or a group of people
(b) living space
(c) situation in which people do not like each other and are liable to engage in harmful actions
(d) giving in to a potential aggressor, in the hope of reaching peace
(e) policy denied to Germany by terms of the Treaty of Versailles
(f) nationwide vote whereby people are asked to take a stand on a specific issue

II. Famous People

Directions: Use the names below to complete the following sentences.

Francisco Franco
Adolf Hitler
Edouad Daladier
Kurt Schuschnigg

Neville Chamberlain
Haile Selassie
Joseph Stalin
Franklin D. Roosevelt

1. _____ had his country taken over by Italy in 1935.

2. _____ was helped by Germany and Italy in winning the Spanish-Civil War.

3. _____ signed the Munich Agreement, claiming that it would lead to "peace in our time."

4. _____ accepted the Munich Agreement on behalf of France.

5. _____ agreed to a nonaggression pact with Nazi Germany.

6. _____ argued against creation of the Polish corridor.

7. _____ was viewed by Hitler as an obstacle to anschluss with Austria.

8. _____ predicted that December 7, 1941, would be "a date that will live in infamy."

III. Map Exercise

Directions: Use the map to locate the place associated with each of the following statements. For each statement, write the *letter* of the place.

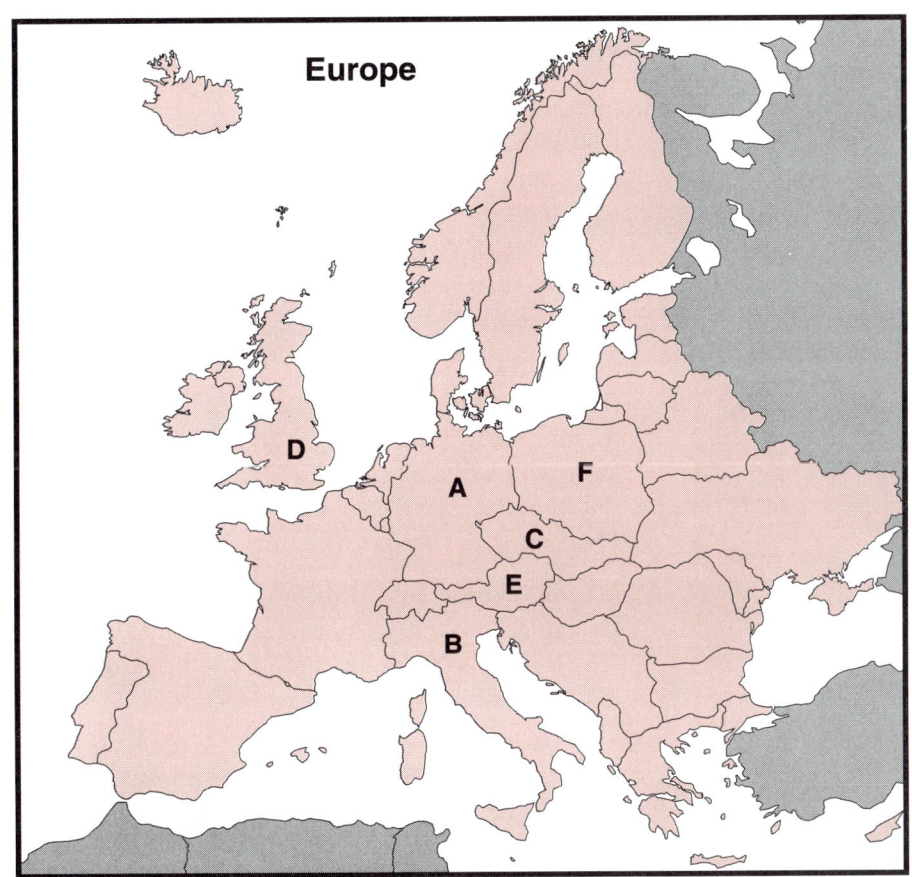

1. _____ The country's leader was condemned by the League of Nations for taking over Ethiopia.

2. _____ The Sudetenland is here.

3. _____ The Munich Agreement was signed here.

4. _____ Neville Chamberlain represented this nation at the Munich Conference.

5. _____ The country was subjected to anschluss with Germany, in violation of the Treaty of Versailles.

6. _____ Danzig is here.

7. _____ The Molotov-Ribbentrop Pact was signed between the USSR and this nation. (Give two letters.)

8. _____ This nation's aggression in September 1939 was the immediate cause of World War II.

9. _____ The Rhineland is here.

10. _____ These countries were the two Axis powers in Europe. (Give two answers.)

IV. Multiple Choice

Directions: Find the *letter* of the correct answer.

1. The Axis powers included nations

   (a) only in Europe.
   (b) only in Asia.
   (c) in Europe and Asia.
   (d) on all the continents.

2. The German land demanded that immediately preceded the start of World War II was for

   (a) Alsace-Lorraine.
   (b) the Sudetenland.
   (c) the Rhineland.
   (d) the Polish corridor.

3. The first major strike affecting the prestige of the League of Nations was

   (a) Italy's invasion of Ethiopia.
   (b) Japan's attack on Manchuria.
   (c) Germany's move into the Sudetenland.
   (d) Japan's bombing of Pearl Harbor.

4. Between the two world wars, nationalism was a force that

   (a) weakened the League of Nations.
   (b) strengthened the league.
   (c) had no effect on the league.
   (d) was promoted by the league.

5. The Washington and London disarmament conferences from 1921 to 1935 sought to limit the power of

   (a) armies.
   (b) air forces.
   (c) navies.
   (d) marines.

6. German rearmament in the 1930s was

   (a) supported by France.
   (b) encouraged by the Weimar government.
   (c) stopped by Hitler.
   (d) in violation of the Treaty of Versailles.

7. Germany's main argument for wanting the Sudetenland was to

   (a) reduce British commercial influence in Europe.
   (b) protect the area's German-speaking people.
   (c) prevent Czechoslovakia's expansion.
   (d) diminish the impact of communism.

8. From today's vantage point, the Munich Agreement is important because it

   (a) helped create the Rome-Berlin-Tokyo Axis.
   (b) symbolized the consequences of appeasing an aggressor.
   (c) was responsible for the anschluss between Germany and Austria.
   (d) prevented Czechoslovakia from becoming a League of Nations mandate.

9. Which of the following was least evident on a global scale during the 1930s?

   (a) collective security   (b) nationalism
   (c) militarism   (d) racism

10. A common situation in the years prior to the start of World Wars I and II was

   (a) Russian imperialism.
   (b) a set of international crises.
   (c) the failure to create an international peacekeeping organization.
   (d) instanccs of appcasement by Britain and France.

11. The fall of France and Holland to Germany in 1940 contributed to their loss of colonies in

   (a) Southeast Asia.   (b) the Middle East.
   (c) South America.   (d) Africa.

V. Thought Questions

Directions: Answer the following questions in essay form.

1. There were several causes for the outbreak of World War II.

   A. Describe three underlying causes, and give an example of each.
   B. Explain which one of these was most responsible for bringing on the war.

2. A. Draw and label the "house of peace" that was built after World War I, with four "pillars."
   B. Describe two specific actions (but not by the same nation) that weakened the house of peace. For each action, give (i) the name of the nation responsible, (ii) the action taken by this nation, (iii) the pillar that was weakened by this action, (iv) the lesson or moral to be learned from the situation you have described.

3. A. Read each of the following statements carefully:
      (i)   Appeasement of potential aggressors can maintain peace.
      (ii) Preparation for war is the best way to preserve peace.
      (iii) A system of collective security would have prevented World War II.
   B. Tell whether or not you agree with each statement, and in each case give one specific reason for your opinion.

Conduct of World War II

I. Matching

Directions: Match the words in Column A with the *correct description* in Column B.

<u>Column A</u>
1. blitzkrieg
2. Wehrmacht
3. isolationism
4. collaborators
5. Maginot line
6. Siegfried line
7. Luftwaffe
8. RAF

<u>Column B</u>
(a) German air force
(b) lightning war
(c) natives of occupied nations who assisted the German armed forces
(d) fortified position in western Germany
(e) German army
(f) fortified position in France facing eastward, toward Germany
(g) noninvolvement in world affairs
(h) British air force

II. Famous People

Directions: Use the names below to complete the following sentences.

Winston Churchill
Philippe Petain
Herman Goering
Dwight Eisenhower
Erwin Rommel
Douglas MacArthur
Harry S Truman

Joseph Stalin
Charles de Gaulle
Georgi Zhukov
Franklin D. Roosevelt
Bernard Montgomery
Pietro Badoglio
Emperor Hirohito

1. _____ ruled Vichy France, in collaboration with the Germans.

2. _____ ordered atomic bombs dropped on Japan.

3. _____ led British forces in North Africa.

4 _____ succeeded Il Duce as a national leader.

5. _____ rallied his nation after the evacuation at Dunkirk.

6. _____ planned to bomb Britain, prior to an invasion.

7. _____ planned Operation Overlord, leading to D-Day.

8. _____ commanded a successful counterattack against the Germans, after they had invaded his nation in 1941.

9. _____ accepted the surrender of Japan in 1945.

10. _____ was the only Communist member of the Big Three during World War II.

11. _____ failed in his efforts to have Germany capture the Suez Canal.

12. _____ was head of the last Axis power to surrender in World War II.

13. _____ led a victory parade into Paris, as head of the Free French forces.

14. _____ represented the United States at the Yalta Conference of 1945.

III. Map Exercise

Directions: Use the map to locate the place associated with each of the following statements. For each statement, write the *letter* of the place.

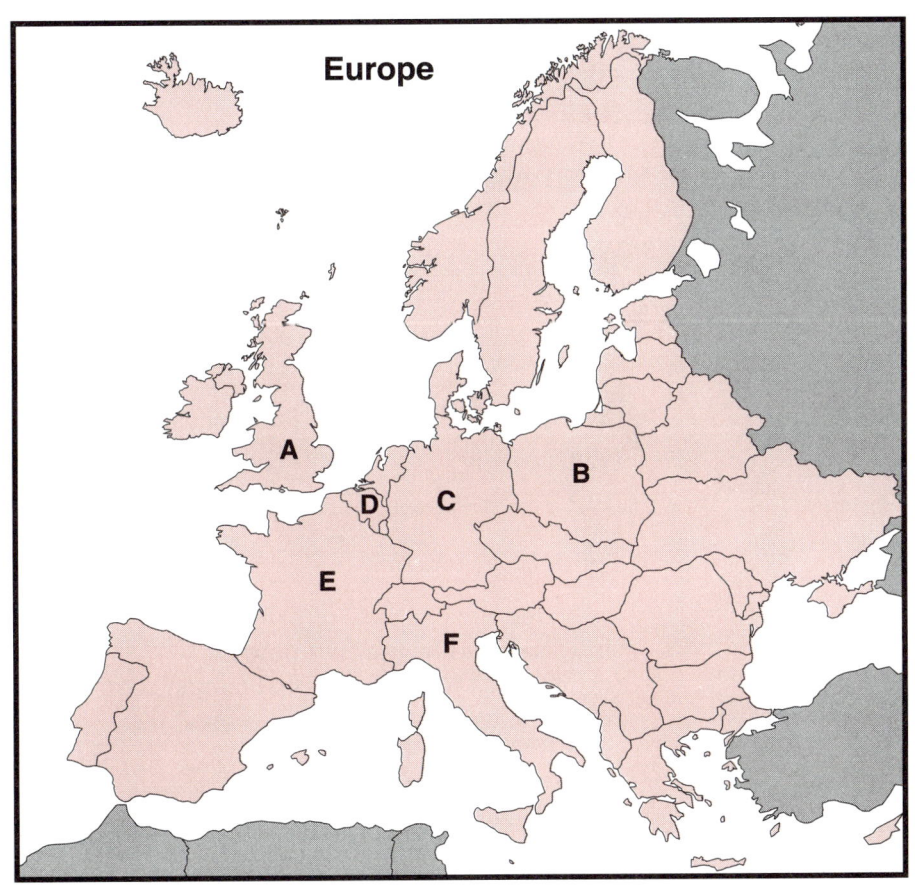

1. _____ Directly west of the country that put into effect a "Scorched Earth" Policy upon being invaded.

2. _____ This nation conducted Operation Barbarossa, in violation of the Molotov-Ribbentrop Nonaggression Pact.

3. _____ Closest nation to where the Battle of El Alamein was fought.

4. _____ This country was victorious in the "Battle of Britain."

5. _____ The Battle of the Bulge occurred here.

6. _____ The leader of this country surrendered to Allied forces on May 8, 1945.

7. _____ The Normandy invasion occurred here.

8. _____ Has referred to World War II as "the Great Patriotic War."

IV. Multiple Choice

Directions: Find the *letter* of the correct answer.

1. The campaign of "island-hopping" occurred off the coast of

   (a) North Africa.
   (b) east Asia.
   (c) southern Europe.
   (d) western Europe.

2. The immediate cause of World War II in Europe was the

   (a) bombing of Britain.
   (b) invasion of Poland.
   (c) attack on the Soviet Union.
   (d) landing in Normandy.

3. Which occurred after all the others?

   (a) V-E Day   (b) V-J Day
   (c) the Yalta Conference   (d) D-Day

4. "General Winter" most seriously hurt the military goals of

   (a) Germany.   (b) Italy.
   (c) France.   (d) Japan.

5. The Atlantic Charter

   (a) stated the war aims of Britain and the United States.
   (b) was signed by the Axis powers.
   (c) provided for international cooperation in constructing an atomic bomb.
   (d) was written by de Gaulle and Stalin.

IV. Famous Places

Directions: At each of the places listed below, an event occurred that was important in World War II.

1. Anzio   6. Normandy
2. the Bulge   7. Potsdam
3. Dunkirk   8. Stalingrad
4. Guadalcanal   9. Yalta
5. Leyte Gulf

For each place, do the following:
   A. Identify the country in which the place in located.
   B. Describe what happened, naming any nation or nations involved in the event.
   C. Explain how the event affected World War II.

V. Famous Quotations

Directions: Below are quotations from famous people in World War II.

1. [I can offer only] "blood, sweat, toil, and tears."
2. "I shall return."
3. "Never in the field of human conflict was so much owed by so many to so few."
4. "This was their finest hour."

For each quotation do the following:
   A. Name the person who made the statement, and give his nation.
   B. Describe one reason or one circumstance to explain why the person made the statement.
   C. Interpret what the person meant by the statement.

Results of World War II

I. Matching

Directions: Match the words in Column A with the *correct description* in Column B.

Column A	*Column B*
1. denazification	(a) development of weapon used against Japan
2. satellite nation	(b) policy directed against Germany
3. reunification	(c) Soviet-occupied nation
4. Manhattan Project	(d) term descriptive of the two Germanys in 1972
5. normalization	(e) term descriptive of the two Germanys in 1990
6. Federal Republic of Germany	(f) the United States and the Soviet Union from 1945 to 1989
7. German Democratic Republic	(g) former name of West Germany
8. superpower	(h) former name of East Germany

II. Famous People

Directions: Use the names below to complete the following sentences.

Albert Einstein   Helmut Kohl
Enrico Fermi   Erich Honecker
Niels Bohr

1. _____ became the first head of a united German nation in the post-World War II Era.

2. _____ was a German Jew who immigrated to the United States and did important scientific work that led to construction of the atomic bomb.

3. _____ was a Danish scientist involved with research on nuclear reactions.

4. _____ became the Communist head of East Germany.

5. _____ was an Italian immigrant to the United States, known for his work on the Manhattan Project.

III. Multiple Choice

Directions: Find the *letter* of the correct answer.

1. The Oder-Neisse line separated German territory from

    (a) Poland.   (b) France.
    (c) the Soviet Union. (d) Italy.

2. Which of the following ended after all the others?

    (a) U.S. occupation of Japan
    (b) the Berlin Wall
    (c) Allied occupation of Germany
    (d) the Berlin Blockade

3. At the Nuremberg war crimes trials, charges were brought against officials from

    (a) Japan.
    (b) Germany.
    (c) Italy.
    (d) all the Axis nations.

4. The Helsinki Conference was designed to bring to European nations improvement in

    (a) trade relations.
    (b) human rights.
    (c) economic cooperation.
    (d) arms control.

5. Which of the following did not become a satellite of the Soviet Union?

    (a) Lithuania
    (b) Latvia
    (c) West Germany
    (d) East Germany

6. The Marshall Plan meant that Western Europe would

    (a) have to depend on American nuclear protection.
    (b) have a chance to receive financial aid.
    (c) restore democracy as a system of government.
    (d) be able to influence American foreign policy.

7. The Berlin War was built

    (a) with the help of the United Nations.
    (b) to prevent people in East Berlin from escaping to West Berlin.
    (c) to stop any West German forces from reaching the Soviet Union.
    (d) with the cooperation of the two Germanys.

8. Which was a major result of World War II?

   (a) Military alliances were abolished.
   (b) Efforts to develop new weapons decreased.
   (c) European colonialism began to decline.
   (d) Democracy spread throughout Eastern Europe.

9. A political result of World War II was

   (a) the emergence of the United States and the USSR as superpowers.
   (b) an expansion of German colonies in Africa.
   (c) the election of a military government in Japan.
   (d) the withdrawal of all U.S. forces from Europe.

IV. Thought Questions

Directions: Answer the following questions in essay form.

1. Describe four results of World War II, giving one for each of these categories:

   A. political
   B. economic
   C. social
   D. scientific

2. Which of the results described in your answer to question 1 affected Europe most seriously? Explain.

3. The Nuremberg war crimes trials were unlike most courtroom trials. Explain the unusual nature of these trials by describing one feature of each of the following:

   A. judges
   B. defendants
   C. charges against the defendants

4. Several events were historic in the reunification of Germany. For each date below, describe a significant event that occurred, and explain its importance for German reunification:

   A. 1972
   B. November 1989
   C. May 1990
   D. July 1990
   E. October 1990

CHAPTER 33

The United Nations and Postwar Western Europe

We will look at two different themes in this chapter. In the first half we will view the development of the United Nations, which came into being as a result of World War II. The founders hoped that this body would be a more effective world forum than the League of Nations was and that it would be able to settle international differences before a major war started. They hoped also that certain reasons for war would be eliminated. From 1945 until now there have been a number of localized wars but no global conflicts such as World Wars I and II. Can the United Nations take credit for this situation?

In the second half of the chapter we will trace the development of certain nations in Western Europe from 1945 until today. The devastation caused by World War II was enormous. The people involved in the conflict had to rebuild their lives and their nations. They had to do this with the threat of Soviet domination hanging over them. With the aid and protection of the United Nations each proceeded along its own path to the development of a sound political and economic system.

The United Nations

The year 1945 was a significant date in the history of our planet. It marked the end of World War II, which may have been the war that ended all wars. It also marked the birth of the United Nations (UN). The fact that, from 1945 until now, there have been no large-scale global wars such as World War II is due in part to the work of this organization. Although the United Nations has not always been able to prevent conflicts, it has had some success in bringing them to a halt and in curbing aggressive tendencies. Examples have been the Arab-Israeli wars, the Korean War, and the Persian Gulf War. Today, almost all the world's nations are members of the United Nations. They look to that organization as a place to attempt the settlement of disputes as well as a source of help in solving difficult social and economic problems.

Historical Background

The League of Nations, founded after World War I, was the predecessor of the United Nations. The league proved, however, to be very weak, and it failed to function after 1939. (See Chapter 32, "World War II.") Two years later, in 1941, U.S. President Franklin D. Roosevelt and British Prime Minister Winston Churchill signed the Atlantic Charter. Among other items, this document spoke of the need to create an international peacekeeping organization. At a 1942 conference in Washington, D.C., several Allied nations upheld the principles of the charter and agreed to call the organization the United Nations. At the Yalta Conference of 1945, the **Big Three** leaders, Roosevelt, Churchill, and Stalin, considered procedures for voting in the organization. They also called for a meeting in San Francisco to write a charter for the organization.

At the San Francisco Conference, held from April to June 1945, delegates from 50 nations drafted the UN charter. The same year, in sharp contrast to its refusal to join the League of Nations in 1920, the United States became the very first nation to approve the UN charter. This contrast reflected a change in American foreign policy from **isolationism** to **internationalism**. In addition, the United States consented to the establishment of UN headquarters in New York City. The UN came into actual existence on October 24, 1945, and October 24 has since been recognized as United Nations Day.

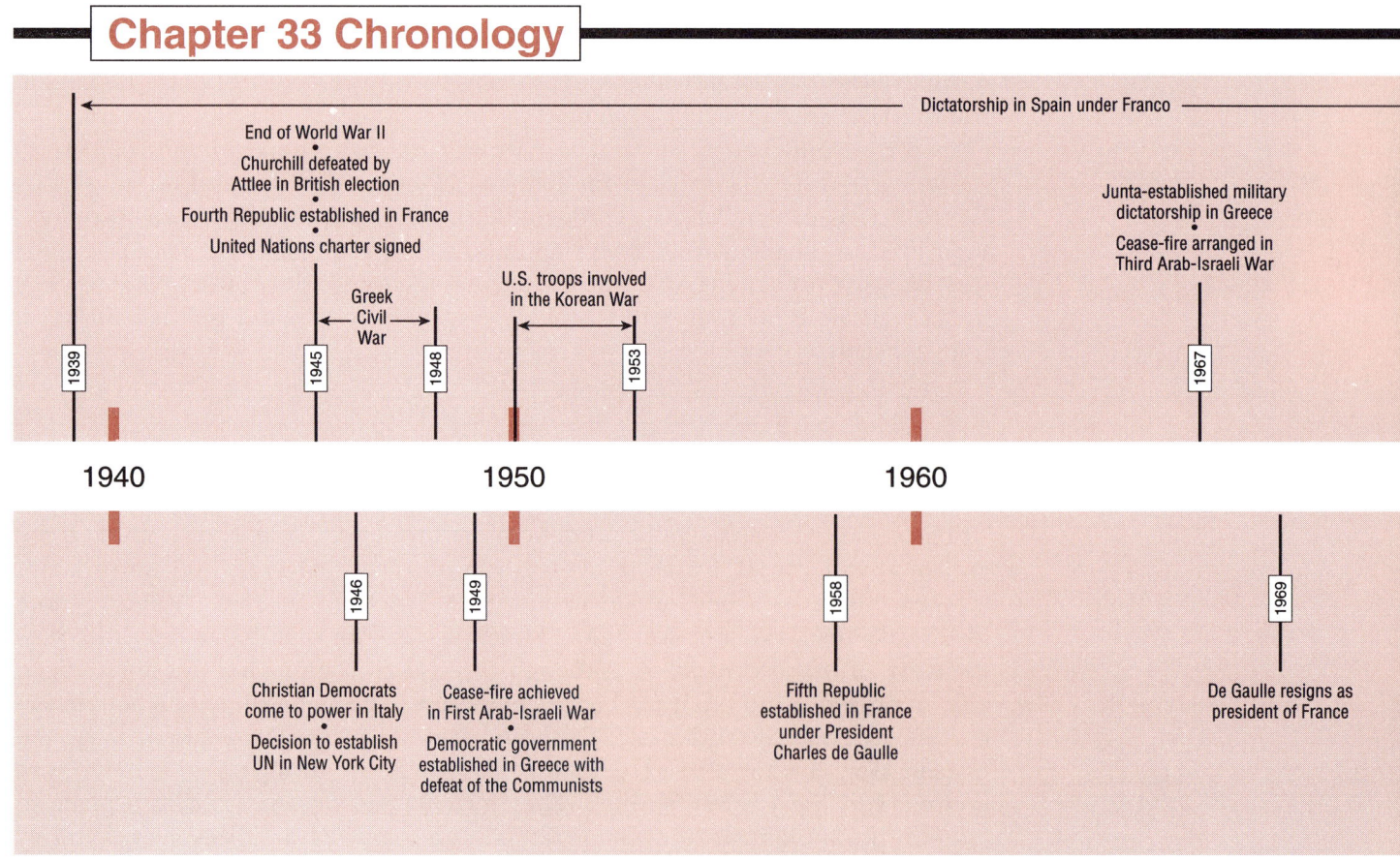

Chapter 33 Chronology

Dictatorship in Spain under Franco

End of World War II

Churchill defeated by Attlee in British election

Fourth Republic established in France

United Nations charter signed

Greek Civil War

U.S. troops involved in the Korean War

Junta-established military dictatorship in Greece

Cease-fire arranged in Third Arab-Israeli War

1939 · 1945 · 1948 · 1953 · 1967

1940 · 1950 · 1960

1946 · 1949 · 1958 · 1969

Christian Democrats come to power in Italy

Decision to establish UN in New York City

Cease-fire achieved in First Arab-Israeli War

Democratic government established in Greece with defeat of the Communists

Fifth Republic established in France under President Charles de Gaulle

De Gaulle resigns as president of France

Purposes and Organizational Structure

The general purposes of the United Nations are stated in its charter: to maintain peace and to construct friendly relations among nations. In addition, the organization has these specific goals:

1. To put down acts of aggression by using collective force;
2. To encourage respect for human rights; and
3. To improve social and economic conditions through international cooperation.

In order to achieve these noble aims, the United Nations is organized into six major bodies and several specialized agencies.

The General Assembly The General Assembly consists of all member nations, the total having reached 178 by early 1994. Each member has one vote. The General Assembly meets once a year for about three months, starting in September. On occasion, it can be called into special session. It considers international problems and can make recommendations to other UN bodies. Although most matters are decided by a majority vote, on issues considered to be "important questions" a two-thirds vote is required for any decision. The General Assembly elects the secretary-general and other heads of the various UN bodies. It also determines the UN budget and spreads the expenses among the member nations. Also, it has the power to admit

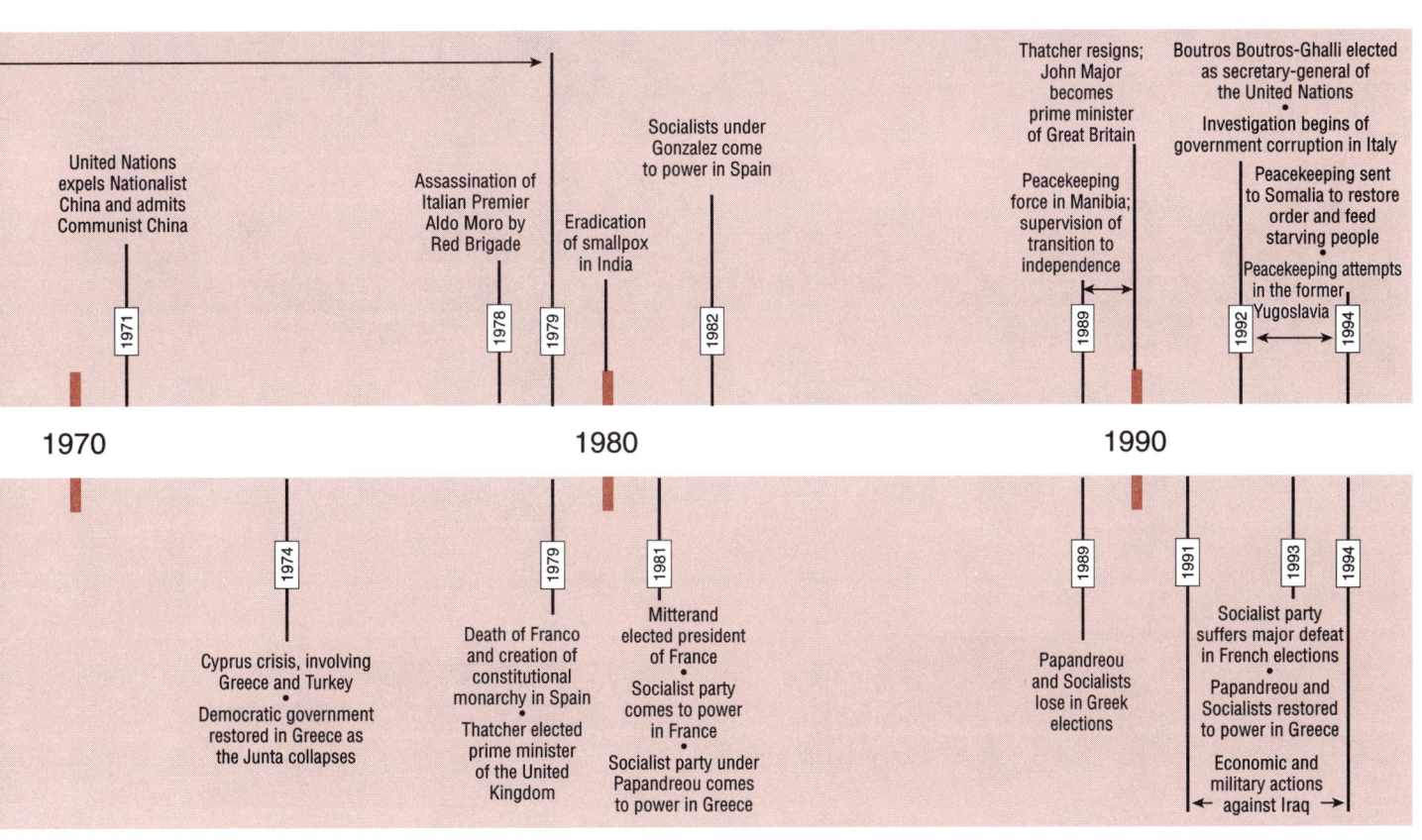

1970

United Nations expels Nationalist China and admits Communist China — 1971

Assassination of Italian Premier Aldo Moro by Red Brigade — 1978

Eradication of smallpox in India — 1979

Socialists under Gonzalez come to power in Spain — 1982

1980

Thatcher resigns; John Major becomes prime minister of Great Britain
Peacekeeping force in Manibia; supervision of transition to independence — 1989

Boutros Boutros-Ghalli elected as secretary-general of the United Nations
Investigation begins of government corruption in Italy
Peacekeeping sent to Somalia to restore order and feed starving people
Peacekeeping attempts in the former Yugoslavia — 1992–1994

1990

1974 — Cyprus crisis, involving Greece and Turkey
Democratic government restored in Greece as the Junta collapses

1979 — Death of Franco and creation of constitutional monarchy in Spain
Thatcher elected prime minister of the United Kingdom

1981 — Mitterand elected president of France
Socialist party comes to power in France
Socialist party under Papandreou comes to power in Greece

1989 — Papandreou and Socialists lose in Greek elections

1991

1993 — Socialist party suffers major defeat in French elections
Papandreou and Socialists restored to power in Greece
Economic and military actions against Iraq — 1994

and expel members. For example, in 1971 the Communist People's Republic of China, which was in control of mainland China, was admitted to take the UN seat previously held by the Nationalist Republic of China, which controlled only Taiwan. More recently, in 1992, Yugoslavia was expelled because of the bitter fighting in that former country. Prior to Yugoslavia's expulsion, General Assembly membership had reached an all-time high of 179 nations.

In its early years, the General Assembly was dominated mostly by Northern Hemisphere nations; the Western bloc (the United States and her allies) and the **Soviet Bloc** (the USSR and her allies). By the mid-1990s, however, the Assembly's configuration has now shifted dramatically. With the end of the Soviet Union and the collapse of communism in many parts of the world, the Soviet Bloc ceased to exist. In fact, the majority power in the General Assembly today rests with the nations of Africa, Asia, and Latin America, lying primarily in the Southern Hemisphere and containing most of the world's population. This Third World bloc consists of several nations that were colonies at the time the United Nations was founded. Although they do not always vote together on issues, their combined strength would account for more than 120 votes.

The Security Council The Security Council has 15 members. Five are permanent, while ten are nonpermanent. The 1945 UN charter listed the five permanent members as the United States, Great Britain, France, the USSR, and China. These **Big Five** were the original Security Council permanent members because they had been the chief victorious Allies in World War II. Since that time, however, two significant changes have

The UN Security Council investigates problems and takes actions to maintain world-wide peace.

occurred among these five members. In 1971, as stated in the preceding section, the China seat was given to the People's Republic of China. In January 1992, as a result of the dissolution (breakup) of the USSR, its seat was given to Russia. Further changes may take place toward the twenty-first century, as Germany and Japan have indicated a desire to sit on the Security Council. In addition, some Third World members have begun to question whether Britain and France should be allowed to retain their memberships on the Council. That such changes should even be considered shows how much the world has evolved between the end of World War II in 1945 and today. During that time, Germany and Japan have risen from wartorn devastation to become major economic powers. Ironically, Britain and France have declined from the major status they once held.

The Council's ten nonpermanent members are elected by the General Assembly for a two-year term. They can be reelected, but not immediately after completing a term.

The Security Council functions as the UN's executive body. This means that it can do the following:

1. Investigate problems; and
2. Take action to maintain international peace. It has the power, for example, to call for UN members to take measures, military or economic, against an aggressor nation or nations.

The council meets continuously in order to resolve serious international disputes. It can not, however, force members to agree with its decisions. Resolutions for action in the Security Council require nine votes, including the votes of all five permanent members. Therefore, each permanent member has veto power over Security Council proposals.

The Secretariat The Secretariat is the organization responsible for all the administrative work of the United Nations. With a staff of several thousand workers, including experts and advisers, it assists in carrying out the decisions reached by the Security Council and the General Assembly. The head of the Secretariat, who is the most important UN official, has the title of secretary-general. He or she is nominated by the Security Council, is voted on by the General Assembly for a five-year term, and can be reelected immediately. The secretary-general presents an annual report on UN activities to the General Assembly and attends all its meetings, as well as all meetings of the Security Council. He or she can act as a mediator in crises and is often assigned specific diplomatic activities. Six people have served in this post:

1. Trygve Lie of Norway (1946–1953);
2. Dag Hammarskjold of Sweden (1953–1961);
3. U Thant of Burma (1961–1971);
4. Kurt Waldheim of Austria (1972–1981);
5. Javier Perez de Cuellar of Peru (1981–1992); and
6. Boutros Boutros-Ghali of Egypt (1992–present).

These men, like all other people who work in the Secretariat, act as international civil servants. They are not to take partisan, self-interested roles as representatives of their home nations, but rather to function as neutral figures in fulfilling the goals of the UN charter. This is the primary reason why each of the six secretaries-general in UN history was chosen from a nation that was not directly allied with either of the Cold War **superpowers**. Indeed, Boutros-Ghali's election was meaningful in that he was the first secretary-general from the Arab world as well as from the continent of Africa.

The International Court of Justice The International Court of Justice considers questions of international law. The 15 judges, coming from different nations, decide cases by a majority vote. Countries that consent to have the International Court hear a case must agree in advance to accept its decision.

The Trusteeship Council The Trusteeship Council was created to control and safeguard areas under UN trust or supervision. Such areas at times may have contained colonial people or may have been in transition from colonial rule to independence. In recent years some Western Pacific islands have been under administration by the Trusteeship Council. The five Security Council members make up the Trusteeship Council.

The Economic and Social Council The 54 members of the Economic and Social Council (ECOSOC) are elected by the General Assembly and serve for three years. They are concerned with achieving progress in economic, social, cultural, and health-related conditions. This organization works with groups such as the UN Commission on Human Rights to improve the status of people whose poor standard of living may lead to tension and wars.

The Specialized Agencies These are bodies in the United Nations that carry out specific social and economic tasks. Six of these agencies are as follows:

1. UNESCO (United Nations Educational, Scientific, and Cultural Organization);
2. WHO (World Health Organization);
3. FAO (Food and Agriculture Organization);
4. UNICEF (United Nations International Children's Fund);
5. The World Bank (also known as the International Bank for Reconstruction and Development); and
6. The IAEA (International Atomic Energy Agency).

Successes and Failures of the United Nations

The United Nations has been more successful in dealing with social and economic issues than with political issues. Examples of success can be seen in eliminating smallpox, fighting famines, protecting the environment, and drawing attention to women's rights and the status of young children. In October 1993, for example, the United Nations reported that it had made significant progress in meeting health goals, such as immunization programs, that are expected to prevent some two million infant deaths a year by 1995.

On political matters, the United Nations has had mixed results. Most of its effectiveness has been due to U.S. involvement. Six examples of positive action are the following:

1. Imposing economic sanctions against Rhodesia (1966) and Iraq (1990–1994);
2. Armed intervention in the Korean War (1950–1953) and the Persian Gulf War (1991);
3. Sending peacekeeping units to Lebanon (1980s), Arab-Israeli borders (1949, 1973), and Cyprus (1963);
4. Overseeing the transition to independence in Namibia (1989–1990);
5. Supervising free elections in Angola (1992); and
6. Sending a peacekeeping force to restore order and feed starving people in Somalia (1992–1994).

The United Nations buildings in New York.

In other instances, however, UN decisions and resolutions have been disobeyed or defied. Here are six examples of nations that flouted UN resolutions:

1. Arab nations by attacking Israel (1948);
2. The USSR in refusing to remove troops from Hungary (1956) and Afghanistan (1979–1980);
3. India, by not honoring a cease-fire in its war with Pakistan (1971–1972);
4. Iran, for refusing to release American hostages (1980);
5. Israel, by annexing the Golan Heights (1981); and
6. Iraq and North Korea, by interfering with UN nuclear weapons inspectors (1991–1994).

Both proponents and critics of the United Nations recognize some of its limitations. It does not have its own military force and must depend on requests for help from member nations. It has a huge budget, and often runs short of money when some members refuse to pay assessed expenses. Countries may simply refuse to heed UN resolutions and decisions when these conflict with what the parties involved perceive to be their own national interests. During the Cold War, the two major superpowers bypassed the United Nations or otherwise frustrated UN policy attempts when they so wished.

Nevertheless, it is important to remember that the United Nations is not, and was not set up to be, a world government. Rather, it serves as a place where crucial world issues can be raised and discussed. Nations and individuals come to it when in need, valuing its role as a forum and its influence on public opinion. Ultimately, it will be effective to the extent that its member nations want it to be.

Postwar Western Europe

World War II left Western Europe devastated. The devastation was physical, economic, and emotional. The combined problems of rebuilding shattered nations and meeting the threat of Soviet domination from Eastern Europe made the task of preserving a stable democratic order even more difficult. Although economic, technical, and military assistance from the United States was a great help, the new Western European governments had to face strong opposition from the many left-wing (pro-Socialist/Communist) political parties that sprang up. The creation of the **North Atlantic Treaty Organization** (**NATO**) and the constant threat of military, possibly nuclear, confrontation with the USSR made the task of political reconstruction even more challenging. While every Western European nation had to face this complication, each had to first tackle its own particular domestic political and economic problems.

Great Britain

After World War II, Great Britain had the dual problem of rebuilding an exhausted economy while dismantling its vast empire. This was exceedingly difficult as those colonial possessions had been vital sources of that island's great wealth in the nineteenth and early twentieth centuries. In addition, Britain had been willing to accept many immigrants from those possessions. They came from such diverse areas as East Africa, Southeast Asia, and the West Indies, seeking economic improvement or fleeing the chaos that independence had brought to their native lands. In some instances, these migrants added an even greater burden to an already weak economy.

Movement Toward a Welfare State

The elections in 1945 led to the replacement of Winston Churchill's Conservative party wartime coalition with a liberal Labour party government led by Clement Attlee. The Conservatives lost because of voter concern with the economy, which was rapidly deteriorating. It was this new administration that negotiated the **partition** of India in 1947 and began a process of **decolonization** that removed Britain's primary source of wealth. The result was a reduction of the military, further contributing to the mass unemployment created after the war. Domestically, the labour government followed a policy of **socialism** that made Britain a welfare state, that is, a political system in which a government provides for the total care of its citizens. In the belief that the economy could not be dependent on **capitalism**, the Bank of England, coal mines, gas and electric companies, and the iron and steel industries were **nationalized** (put under the control of the government). However, as most British industries were still privately owned, a mixed economy (combination of socialism and capitalism) was created. The Labour government also extended insurance coverage for unemployment, old age, and sickness and set up a national health care program to provide free medical treatment for all Britons. These extensive reforms, however, necessitated a sharp increase in taxation, and the high cost for these social programs resulted in popular dissatisfaction and the loss of the Labour party to the Conservatives in the 1951 elections.

The Conservative government, which remained in power until 1964, restored some industries to private control and modified the health insurance program. Nevertheless, the cost of maintaining the welfare state was a further strain on the British economy, which was having great difficulty rebuilding because of the loss of its colonies and the competition in its domestic market from American and Japanese products. Inflation and the rise of trade unions demanding higher wages for workers also contributed to the problem. From 1964 to 1979, alternating Conservative and Labour governments were unable to create a strong and stable economy.

Thatcher and Major Move Away from the Welfare State

In 1979, a Conservative government led by Margaret Thatcher, Britain's first woman prime minister, began a program of radically reducing the welfare state. This policy, known as Thatcherism, restricted the power of unions, cut government spending, lowered taxes, dismantled many welfare programs and returned a number of industries to private ownership. Although these measures improved the growth of the British economy, they could not reduce the high rate of unemployment that had long been a great problem for many Britons. It was, however, Thatcher's opposition to increased British participation in the **European Community** that led to a split in the Conservative party and her resignation in 1990. Her successor as prime minister, John Major, continued her domestic policies, but supported a role for Britain in the movement for European unity. Narrowly winning the 1992 elections, the Major government has faced continued economic problems and strong opposition from both the Labour party and extremely nationalist Conservatives.

France

After the collapse of the Nazi-controlled Vichy government and the liberation of France in 1945, a democratic coalition government was established under the presidency of General Charles de Gaulle. The new government, known as the

Fourth Republic, consisted of three leftist parties: the Socialists, the Communists, and the Popular Republic Movement (MRP), which was a Roman Catholic progressive (favoring reform) party. The Fourth Republic was, however, politically divided and ineffective. Disgusted with the disunity and angry over the lack of power of the presidency, de Gaulle resigned in 1946. In 1947, the Communists were expelled from the coalition government after they had encouraged a series of strikes.

The Fall of the Fourth Republic Although the Socialists and the MRPs remained divided over many issues (there were 25 different cabinets from 1946 to 1958), they did manage to create a mixed economy. Despite the political instability, the French economy grew. It was the strain of trying to maintain the old colonial empire that eventually caused the downfall of the Fourth Republic. After 12 years of unsuccessful fighting to preserve French possessions in North Africa and Southeast Asia, popular dissatisfaction with the Fourth Republic led to civil unrest. Amid fears of a complete breakdown of order, a new government was formed in 1958 under the leadership of de Gaulle.

The Fifth Republic The Fifth Republic, as the new administration was called, gave President de Gaulle final authority over foreign policy and national defense, as well as the right to name the prime minister, dissolve the National Assembly, call for new elections, and assume emergency powers. This new arrangement reflected the popular anger over the disunity and instability of leadership in the Fourth Republic. De Gaulle ruled until 1969, restoring political stability and creating economic prosperity. He settled the colonial question by granting independence to all former French possessions. By 1960, France had become a nuclear nation as well. In 1968, however, student riots and strikes by workers devastated the French economy. Despite an overwhelming victory by de Gaulle in the 1969 elections, voter rejection of reforms later in that year lead to his resignation.

Socialism Under Mitterand De Gaulle's successors, Georges Pompidou and Valery Giscard d'Estaing, concentrated on building up the French economy and industry. The worldwide economic crisis of the 1970s crippled these efforts. In 1981, a Socialist government under Francois Mitterand was elected. Mitterand nationalized major industries and banks as well as increased taxes for new social programs. These measures, however, created high inflation and forced Mitterand to cut spending, resulting in popular discontent. Support for increased participation in the European Comunity further hurt the government, resulting in a Socialist party defeat in the 1993 elections. Opposition to a greater French role in the movement for European unity, especially from farmers, will present future governments with great challenges.

Italy

The fall of the Italian fascist government in 1943 resulted, as in France, in the rise of leftist parties. In the 1946 elections the nation narrowly voted to abolish the **monarchy** and establish a **democracy**. Despite strong showings by the Socialists and Communists, the Christian Democrats emerged as the dominant party under the leadership of Alcide de Gaspari. Under a series of coalition governments, Italy's economy was rebuilt and expanded. Despite strong opposition by the Communists, who were excluded from the government in 1947, the Christian Democrats continued to lead coalitions after de Gaspari's retirement in 1953. There was, however, division within the party after its leader left.

Terrorism in Italy In the 1960s, the Socialists and Communists gained strength. Although the leftist parties often won election to local positions, the Christian Democrats continued to control the national government. Italy's economy, which had grown until this time, experienced a slowdown because of high inflation and strikes by trade unions. The result was a period of political and economic instability. Adding to Italy's problems was the rise of **terrorism** in the 1970s by a leftist group known as the Red Brigade. This crisis reached its height with the assassination of former Prime Minister Aldo Moro in 1978. By the 1980s the terrorist activities had subsided as a result of strong countermeasures by the Italian government.

The War on Organized Crime The 1980s and 1990s brought new political instability as the government mounted an attack on organized crime. Known as the Mafia, organized crime became the target of public criticism especially in regard to its influence over both local and national government. This situation forced the Italian political leadership to take legal and military action against leading criminal figures. Despite attempts by crime bosses to intimidate and assassinate government officials, the government has had some success in limiting the Mafia's power.

Criticism of Government Corruption Despite many elections and changes of leadership in Italy since World War II, little changed in the way the Italian government operated. During the 1990s public criticism of the traditional corruption in government resulted in scandals that created further political instability. Committed to increased participation in the European Community, the Italian government faces great challenges from both internal criticism of traditional problems and a changing world economy. The 1994 elections saw the dominance of a coalition of right-wing parties, including a few Neo-Fascists, under a new prime minister, Silvio Berlusconi.

Greece

Following World War II, Soviet-supported Greek guerrillas attempted to overthrow the constitutional monarchy and establish a Communist regime in Greece. After the devastating civil war in 1945–1948, the Greek government faced both economic and political challenges. The Greek constitutional monarchy, led by a Conservative government, made great economic progress during the 1950s. By 1967, however, popular dissatisfaction with the traditional corruption in Greek government and the rise of leftist parties had led to overthrow of the monarchy, exile of the king, and establishment of a dictatorship by a group of generals in 1967.

Greece Under the Junta The Junta, as the military regime became known, brought economic growth and internal stability to the nation. In 1974, however, it became involved in an unsuccessful attempt to reunite the predominantly Greek island of Cyprus with Greece through a military invasion. This resulted in a counterinvasion by Turkey, in which that nation took over 40 percent of the island, massacring and displacing much of the Greek population in the name of the Cypriot Turkish minority. The corrupt Junta, having sold much of its arms to foreign powers, was unable to mount an adequate military response. The Cyprus debacle resulted in the collapse of the military regime and the restoration of a democratic government under the conservative New Democracy party led by Konstantinos Karamanlis.

Karamanlis and Papandreou

Under Karamanlis, Greece enjoyed new economic growth and political stability. In 1981, the nation joined the European Community. Greece's lack of social programs and the traditional government corruption led however, to the election of a Socialist government under Andreas Papandreou later that year. The Socialists nationalized key industries and created a social welfare program. Fearing popular discontent if taxation increased, Papandreou illegally used European Community funds intended for building Greek industry to offset the costs of his social reforms. This action led to charges of corruption that toppled his government in 1989. A new government was formed by the New Democracy party under Konstantinos Mitsotakis.

The Reforms of Mitsotakis and the Return of Papandreou

The Mitsotakis government was forced to adopt severe measures to undo the damage done to the Greek economy by the Papandreou social reforms. The spending cuts and modifications in social programs that were needed resulted in great unpopularity for the government. In 1993 a split within the New Democracy party itself, led by Antonios Samaras, forced the collapse of the Mitsotakis government. It was replaced by a new Socialist regime under an aging Papandreou. The open corruption and incompetence of the restored Papandreou government brought criticism from all political parties, including many within the Socialist party. The new Greek government must face the challenge of balancing economic realities with social and political needs.

Spain

Spain was ruled for 36 years by the **dictator** Francisco Franco after the fascists won the Spanish Civil War in 1939. Upon Franco's death in 1979, power was transferred to a constitutional monarchy under King Juan Carlos I. Thus began a new era of democratic rule in Spain.

Spain's Success as a Mixed Economy Under Gonzalez

In the 1975 elections, a coalition government under Adolfo Suarez was elected. The Suarez government was able to establish democratic institutions, but could not create the political unity needed to address Spain's economic problems. In 1982, a Socialist government under Felipe Gonzalez was elected. Establishing a mixed economy, the Gonzalez government was able to balance the creation of a social welfare system with a market economy. Spain's entrance into the European Community in 1986 further strengthened the growth of the Spanish economy. In fact, Spain's economic strategy was so successful that it was viewed as a model by many Eastern European nations after the collapse of communism in 1989.

Terrorism and Basque Independence

A major problem faced by the Spanish government has been terrorism by the Basques, an ethnic group in Spain fighting for independence. Despite attempts by King Juan Carlos to grant measures of Basque self-rule, separatist extremists have continued attacks against both government officials and civilians.

Challenges for the Spanish Government

Despite this problem, the economic recovery of Spain has helped that nation to become a force on the European scene, as became evident when Spain was selected as the site of the 1992 Olympic Games. Nevertheless, challenges still face the Spanish government, both in dealing with internal problems and in connection with its increased participation in the European Community.

The rise of European unity and the collapse of communism have changed the goals of European governments. As the Cold War becomes a memory, new challenges await the nations of both Western and Eastern Europe. Experiments with socialism have left many people skeptical about the modern welfare state. Yet, with the growing concern over population size, economic growth, and environmental pollution, the role of government in solving these problems cannot be ignored. Discontent with traditional corruption in many European governments has created a movement for reform. Finally, the role of each nation in the new European Community, which will probably soon include the nations of Eastern Europe, must be determined. The growing **nationalism** within many countries may prove a formidable (causing doubt or fear) obstacle to this goal. However, the transformation of most Western European nations from imperial powers to individual countries has made unity an economic necessity. In short, as the twenty-first century approaches, the nations of Europe are discovering new possibilities and facing new problems.

Summary

Obviously, the United Nations has not lived up to all that its founders expected. In certain political situations it has been unsuccessful, but in others there has been a degree of accomplishment. In the humanitarian area the United Nations has brought hope to many parts of the world by fighting disease and hunger. Peacekeeping forces have kept small conflicts from getting larger. The organization also remains an important forum for the discussion of world issues. Without real police powers, however, it will be only as effective as its members want it to be. How would you evaluate the United Nations?

Despite the seeming removal of the threat of Soviet domination, the Western European community still faces problems of expanding populations, inadequate economic growth, and environmental pollution. What should be the role of government in attempting to solve these problems? While there are forces within each nation moving it toward a real "community" of states, a nationalistic spirit still exists. Since it is obvious that a return to the "good old days" of imperialism is not possible, each nation must find a new role for itself in a new world.

Review Exercises

The United Nations

I. Matching

Directions: Each of the three major parts of the United Nations has specific powers and responsibilities. Read carefully the following statements, and match each with the appropriate part of the United Nations.

(a) the General Assembly
(b) the Security Council
(c) the Secretariat

1. _____ It has five permanent members.

2. _____ It can elect the secretary-general.

3. _____ It had 178 members in early 1994.

4. _____ Its head is the secretary-general.

5. _____ It has 15 members.

6. _____ The Third World bloc of nations constitute a majority in this part.

7. _____ It has ten nonpermanent members.

8. _____ Its chief officer is the UN's most important official.

9. _____ It functions as the UN's executive body.

10. _____ A veto by a permanent member of this part can defeat a resolution.

11. _____ It expelled Nationalist China and Yugoslavia from UN membership.

12. _____ It decides matters that are "important questions" by a two-thirds vote.

13. _____ It has primary responsibility for investigating situations that threaten world peace.

II. Multiple Choice

Directions: Find the *letter* of the correct answer.

1. In the General Assembly, each nation has a vote that is

   (a) based upon its population.
   (b) dependent on its physical size.
   (c) equal to that of each other nation.
   (d) in proportion to its financial contributions to the United Nations.

2. U Thant, Kurt Waldheim, Javier Perez de Cuellar, and Boutros Boutros-Ghali have all held the position of

   (a) president of the General Assembly.
   (b) head of the Security Council.
   (c) secretary-general.
   (d) head of the World Health Organization.

3. According to the UN charter, the Security Council has the power to

   (a) veto resolutions passed by the General Assembly.
   (b) choose the secretary-general.
   (c) admit new members.
   (d) recommend the use of force to halt aggression.

4. The United Nations finances its activities mainly by

   (a) selling property throughout the world.
   (b) taxing citizens of member nations.
   (c) selling stocks and bonds.
   (d) assessing dues on member nations.

5. The League of Nations and the United Nations were both created for the purpose of

   (a) stopping the spread of communism.
   (b) eliminating military dictators.
   (c) maintaining international peace.
   (d) building a single world culture.

III. Thought Questions

Directions: Answer the following questions in essay form.

1. Explain how each of the following played a role in the formation of the United Nations:

   A. the Atlantic Charter
   B. the Yalta Conference
   C. the San Francisco Conference

2. The United Nations was formed in order to achieve several goals.

   A. State three of these goals.
   B. Describe one way in which the United Nations has tried to achieve each goal.
   C. For each goal, discuss whether these efforts have been successful.

3. Give two specific examples of how the United Nations is an improvement over the League of Nations.

4. The United Nations has sent peacekeeping forces to many parts of the world in the last 45 years.

   A. Name three parts of the world where this has been done.

B. For each of these parts, describe briefly the circumstances that led the United Nations to send peacekeeping forces.

C. For each part, state whether or not the peacekeeping goal has been achieved. (It will be necessary to do some independent research in order to answer this question.)

5. Write a brief letter to the secretary-general of the United Nations, giving your view of the UN's greatest strength and its greatest weakness. Give one reason for each viewpoint.

Postwar Western Europe

I. Map Exercise

Directions: Use the map to locate the place associated with each of the following statements. For each statement, write the *letter* of the place.

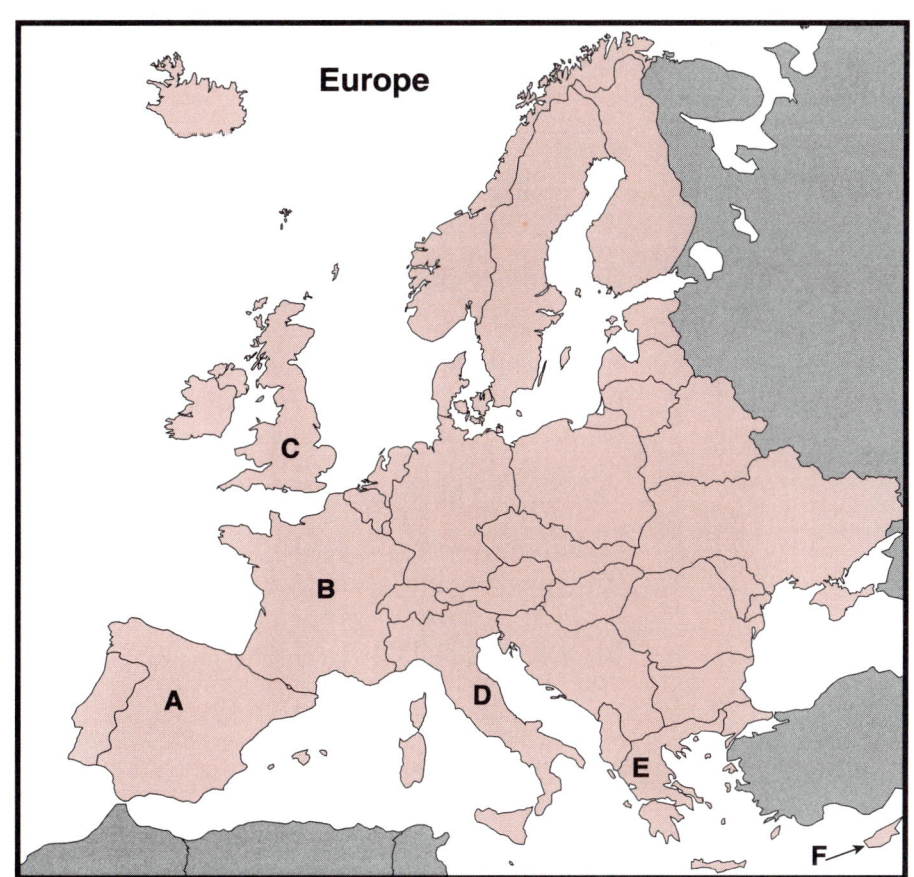

1. _____ Margaret Thatcher was formerly the prime minister of this nation.

2. _____ In this country there is a war between the government and organized crime.

3. _____ This country's economic growth is a model for Eastern European nations.

4. _____ There was a military dictatorship in this nation from 1967 to 1974.

5. _____ The Fifth Republic was established here in 1958.

6. _____ This island has been the source of ongoing tension between Greece and Turkey.

II. Multiple Choice

Directions: Select the *letter* of the correct choice.

1. The Labour party under Clement Attlee did all of the following *except*

   (a) nationalize the Bank of England.
   (b) create a national health care program.
   (c) lower taxes.
   (d) begin the process of decolonization.

2. Under Thatcherism

   (a) taxes were raised.
   (b) government spending was cut.
   (c) the national health care program was expanded.
   (d) the rate of unemployment was reduced.

3. Under the leadership of de Gaulle, France

   (a) expanded its imperial possessions.
   (b) became a nuclear power.
   (c) experienced a severe economic crisis.
   (d) became politically unstable.

4. The Socialist government of Mitterand did all of the following *except*

   (a) support increased participation in the European Community.
   (b) nationalize major industries.
   (c) increase taxes to create new social programs.
   (d) build up the French military.

5. The political party that has dominated Italian politics since 1946 is the

   (a) Christian Democratic.
   (b) Italian Nationalist.
   (c) Socialist.
   (d) Communist.

6. The assassination of Aldo Moro in 1978 was a result of

   (a) political rivalry.
   (b) terrorism.
   (c) the government's war on the Mafia.
   (d) religious fanaticism.

7. At the conclusion of the Greek Civil War (1945–1948),

    (a) Greece became a satellite of the USSR.
    (b) a Fascist dictatorship was established.
    (c) a constitutional monarchy was restored.
    (d) Greece was divided into two parts.

8. The Greek Junta fell from power in 1974 because it

    (a) failed to prevent the Turkish invasion of northern Cyprus.
    (b) was repressive and violated human rights.
    (c) was corrupt and unable to run the country efficiently.
    (d) had ruined the economy through wasteful spending.

9. After Franco's death in 1979, Spain became

    (a) a constitutional monarchy.
    (b) an absolute monarchy.
    (c) a Socialist state.
    (d) a fascist dictatorship.

10. Terrorism has become a problem in Spain because of

    (a) the rise of revolutionary political parties.
    (b) the country's foreign policy.
    (c) the desire of the Basques for independence.
    (d) the repressive attitude of the government toward workers.

III. Thought Questions

Directions: Answer the following questions in essay form.

1. Some Western European nations have created economic systems that have been termed *mixed economies.*

    A. Define mixed economy.
    B. Select two Western European nations that have created such an economic system, and assess the success of each.

2. The European Community is an attempt to unify the nations of Western Europe for their common benefit.

    A. Explain the concept of the European Community, and discuss how it is supposed to work.
    B. Select two Western European nations that have joined the European Community and assess how beneficial membership has been to each.

CHAPTER 34

The Holocaust

Introduction

The worst international tragedy to affect Europe in this century was World War II. In Chapter 32, we saw how Nazi Germany, under the leadership of Adolf Hitler, was responsible for the conflict that tore apart that continent from 1939 to 1945. Hitler and the Nazis were also responsible for another tragedy that shocked the world's conscience, one that lasted from 1933 to 1945, during the lifetime of the Third Reich. This was the **Holocaust**. In its simplest definition, the Holocaust refers to the intentional murder of six million European Jews. It also included the attempt by the Nazis to destroy Judaism as a religion.

The proper noun *Holocaust* must be distinguished from the word *holocaust*, with a lowercase *h*. The latter can be used to describe *any* great, massive destruction, usually by fire. It is actually a Greek translation of a word used in the Bible, a word that means a total burning and describes a sacrifice. Today, the reduction to ashes of several large skyscrapers filled with people, such as those at New York City's World Trade Center, could be termed a holocaust, as could the destruction caused by the dropping of atomic bombs on Hiroshima and Nagasaki during World War II. People also speak of a nuclear holocaust, fearful of the growth of nuclear weapons throughout the world today. So while *holocaust* could refer to any one of a number of terrible acts of destruction, *Holocaust*, with an uppercase *H*, refers solely to the *very specific* destruction of a *specific* group of people by another *specific* group of people and its government at a *specific* time in history. What happened to the Jews of Europe at the hands of the Nazis from 1933 to 1945 was not just "a holocaust," but is referred to as "The Holocaust."

The Holocaust was a unique event in world history. It was the most cruel and bloody attempt by a government to carry out a policy of **genocide** (a word coined after World War II to mean the planned **annihilation** or destruction of a people because of its religion or race or nationality). The unusual aspects of the Holocaust can be seen in a portion of a report made in the United States by the President's Commission on the Holocaust in 1979:

The Holocaust was the systematic, bureaucratic extermination of six million Jews by the Nazis and their collaborators as a central act of state during the Second World War; as night descended, millions of other peoples were swept into this net of death. It was a crime unique in the annals of human history, different not only in the quantity of violence—the sheer numbers killed—but in its manner and purpose as a mass criminal enterprise organized by the state against defenseless civilian populations. The decision was to kill every Jew everywhere in Europe: the definition of Jew as target for death transcended all boundaries.

The concept of the annihilation of an entire people, as distinguished from their subjugation, was unprecedented; never before in human history had genocide been an all-pervasive government policy unaffected by territorial or economic advantage and unchecked by moral or religious constraints.

The genocide practiced by the Nazis was a war. Indeed, a book about the Holocaust by the historian Lucy Dawidowicz calls it *The War Against the Jews*. In this chapter, we will try to understand why and how that war was carried out. We will also learn about the world's reaction, acts of resistance by Jews and non-Jews, and implications for our own times.

Chapter 34 Chronology

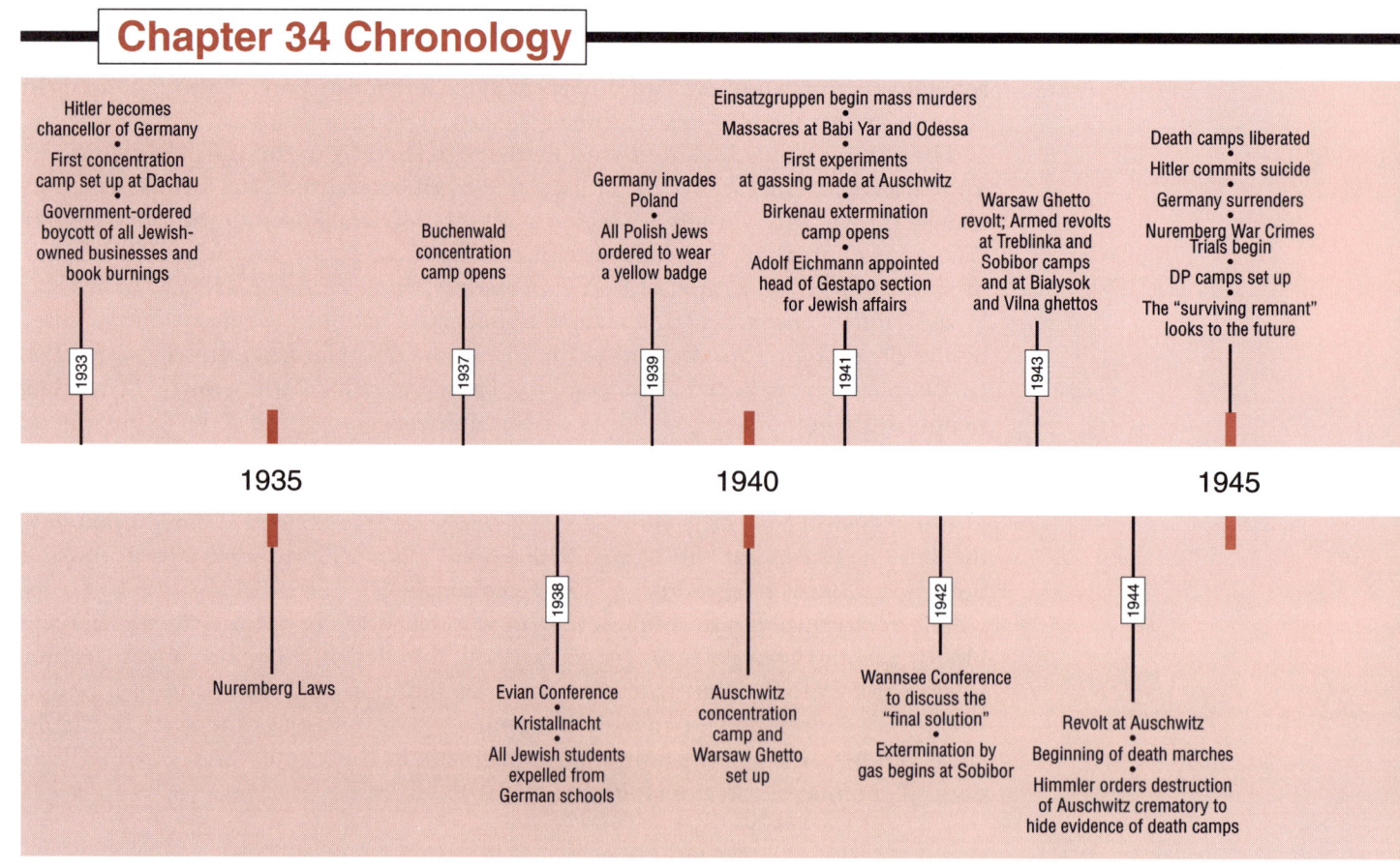

1933
- Hitler becomes chancellor of Germany
- First concentration camp set up at Dachau
- Government-ordered boycott of all Jewish-owned businesses and book burnings

1935
- Nuremberg Laws

1937
- Buchenwald concentration camp opens

1938
- Evian Conference
- Kristallnacht
- All Jewish students expelled from German schools

1939
- Germany invades Poland
- All Polish Jews ordered to wear a yellow badge

1940
- Auschwitz concentration camp and Warsaw Ghetto set up

1941
- Einsatzgruppen begin mass murders
- Massacres at Babi Yar and Odessa
- First experiments at gassing made at Auschwitz
- Birkenau extermination camp opens
- Adolf Eichmann appointed head of Gestapo section for Jewish affairs

1942
- Wannsee Conference to discuss the "final solution"
- Extermination by gas begins at Sobibor

1943
- Warsaw Ghetto revolt; Armed revolts at Treblinka and Sobibor camps and at Bialysok and Vilna ghettos

1944
- Revolt at Auschwitz
- Beginning of death marches
- Himmler orders destruction of Auschwitz crematory to hide evidence of death camps

1945
- Death camps liberated
- Hitler commits suicide
- Germany surrenders
- Nuremberg War Crimes Trials begin
- DP camps set up
- The "surviving remnant" looks to the future

Reasons for Studying the Holocaust

The period of the Holocaust was one of the ugliest and darkest moments in the history of mankind. One reason for studying this topic is to prevent a tragedy like the Holocaust from ever happening again, to any group of people anywhere on earth. We can also learn about the danger of apathy (not caring) and about the consequences of hateful behavior toward people because of religion, **race**, or **nationality**. Knowledge of the Holocaust exposes us to an evil side of human beings, a side that we have to be aware of in order to prevent it from influencing harmful behavior toward other human beings.

Study of the Holocaust also makes us aware of how precious and fragile life can be. A threat to the life, well-being, and freedom of one of us is a threat to all of us. As was said by John Donne, a sixteenth-century English poet, "No man is an island, entire of itself; every man is a piece of the continent, a part of the main . . . Any man's death diminishes me, because I am involved in mankind; and therefore never seek to know for whom the bell tolls; it tolls for thee."

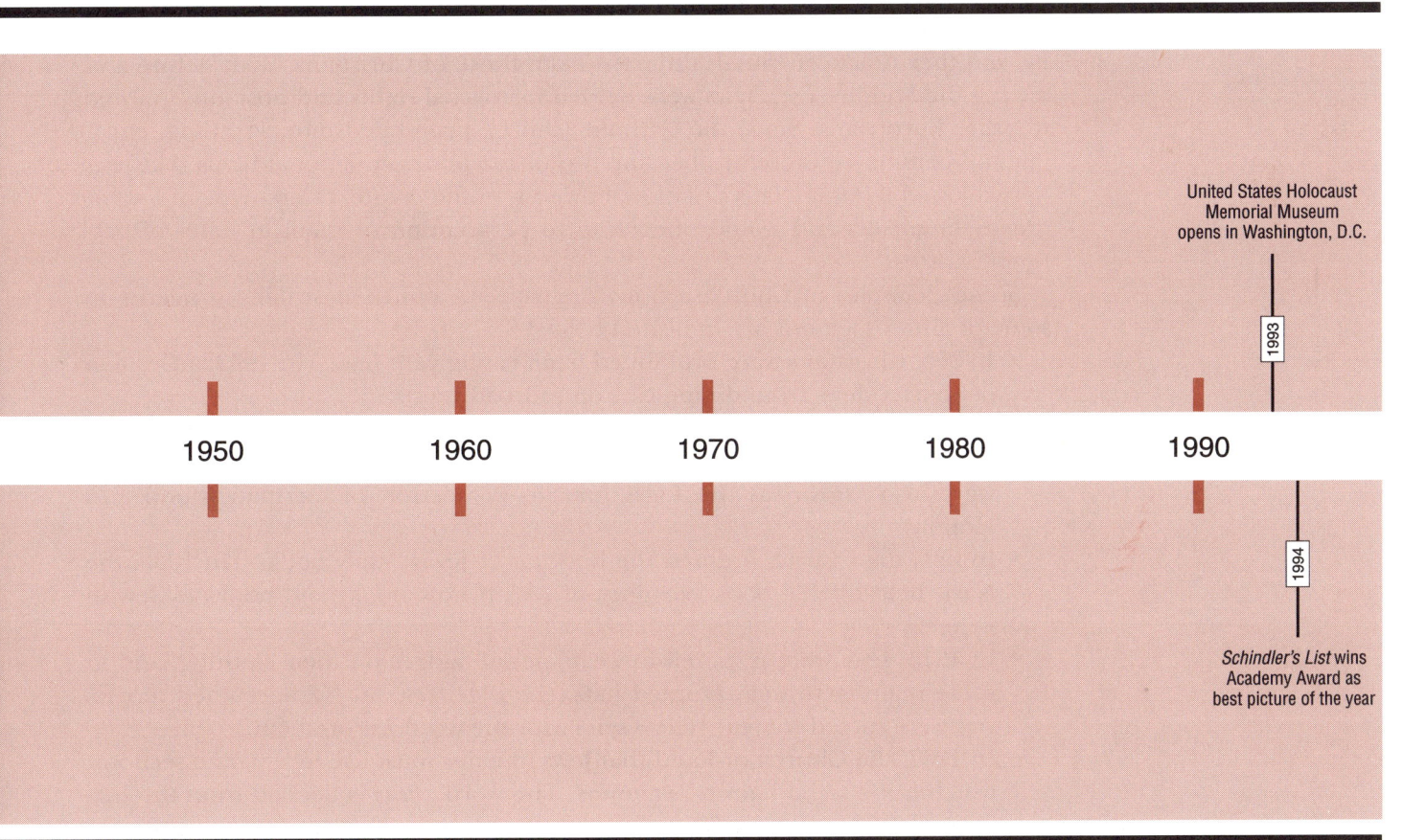

United States Holocaust
Memorial Museum
opens in Washington, D.C.

1993

1950   1960   1970   1980   1990

1994

Schindler's List wins
Academy Award as
best picture of the year

Anti-Semitism in Europe Prior to Hitler

Anti-Semitism can refer to any hostile actions taken against Jewish people only because of their being Jewish. These actions throughout history have included religious **prejudice**, separation and expulsion, economic and social restrictions, and attacks and killing. Anti-Semitism was a constant theme, perhaps the most prejudiced one, throughout European history for almost two thousand years. This fact was the basis for a book published in 1992 by Professor Robert Wistrich and seen as a television series in 1993: *Anti-Semitism: The Longest Hatred*. Although Hitler and his Nazis were among the most notorious anti-Semites ever, they were not the first ones to practice this horrible form of hatred. However, many of their anti-Semitic actions were similar to ones practiced in earlier times in Europe.

Religious Anti-Semitism

The earliest and longest-lasting form of anti-Semitism has been religious anti-Semitism. Its origins rested in Christian beliefs about Jews. (Happily, these beliefs have been declared false by Church authorities in this century and are no longer taught as Christian doctrine.) Among these beliefs were that Jews were responsible for the death of Jesus Christ (**deicide**), and that they used the blood of Christian children in ceremonies (the "blood libel" accusation). Jews were also singled out because they refused to accept Jesus as the Messiah and be converted to Christianity, and they practiced rituals different from those of Christians. Both before and during the Middle Ages, Jews were denied many civil rights and positions granted to other Europeans. Since the Catholic Church prohibited moneylending, banking and commerce therefore became two of the few occupational fields that Jews were allowed to enter. This situation, however, would create a **stereotype** of Jews as greedy financiers and would often lead to persecution of them in times of economic distress.

Some examples of Church actions against Jews and their striking similarity to some of Hitler's actions are indicated below:
- In 306, Christians were prohibited from eating with Jews. (In 1939, a German law barred Jews from dining cars on railroad trains.)
- In 309, the Church forbade marriages between Christians and Jews. (In 1935, the Nuremberg Laws said that Jews could not marry non-Jews. These laws were also known as the Laws for the Protection of German Blood and Honor.)
- In 681, the Church ordered the burning of Jewish holy books. (In 1933, the Nazis held official book burnings of Jewish holy books and books by Jewish writers.)
- In 1215, Jews were required to wear special badges on their clothing, and in some regions, to wear pointed hats. (In 1941, Jews in Nazi-occupied territories were forced to wear yellow stars with the word *Jew* on them.)
- In 1267, the Church ordered that Jews in cities must live in separate sections, which came to be known as **ghettos**. The word *ghetto* is derived from the Italian word *geta*, an iron factory in the neighborhood where Jews were forced

to live in Venice in 1516. (In 1939, the Nazis began to force Jews to live in ghettos throughout Europe, with one of the biggest being the Warsaw Ghetto in Poland.)

In general, the later Middle Ages, 1000–1500, proved to be a very difficult period for Jews. During the Crusades, 1095–1204, for example, Christian armies slaughtered whole communities of European Jews while traveling to fight the Muslims in Palestine. Although their chief aim was to recapture the Holy Land from Muslims, the crusaders nevertheless were full of such zeal and bigotry that they considered Jews, as well as Muslims, to be **heretics**—and if heretics refused to accept conversion, they deserved to be killed. One of the worst massacres by crusaders occurred in the German city of Worms in 1098.

Expulsions and Scapegoating

Expulsions of Jews from western European domains were common. Examples were in England (1290), France (1394), German lands (1300s), Spain (1492), and Portugal (1495). The expulsions were usually based on religious reasons as well as on desires to obtain Jewish property. An additional reason was the belief that Jews were somehow responsible for various problems affecting these societies—for example, economic distress, spread of disease, and bad weather conditions. Indeed, European people has come to believe that whenever bad times befell them, Jews were responsible. Jews thus became **scapegoats**, in that they were falsely blamed for bad situations. These were situations for which Jews were not responsible but were held to be, since the accusers could not otherwise explain why these situations occurred. To accuse a person or a people falsely of something, without knowing the true facts, or even refusing to accept the true facts, is an example of **prejudice**. An instance of prejudice and scapegoating during the Nazi Era was Hitler's blaming German Jews for Germany's defeat in World War I and for the humiliating provisions of the Versailles treaty.

Of all the expulsions during the Middle Ages, the most tragic was from Spain. Jews had lived there for hundreds of years prior to the expulsion order of King Ferdinand and Queen Isabella in 1492. This order was part of several long-standing efforts to rid the Iberian peninsula of Jews and Judaism. One of these efforts, the dreaded **Inquisition**, resulted in the deaths of thousands of Jews. Headed by the priest Tomas de Torquemada, the Inquisition sought to cleanse Spain of heretics. Acting as a court, it would condemn to torture and death those who, like the Jews, were deemed to be nonbelievers in Church laws and doctrines. Death was often by burning at an elaborate ceremony called the **auto-da-fé** (act of faith).

Jews could avoid persecution in Spain by converting to Catholicism or by leaving for lands where they could find refuge. There were not many of these. Thus grew the legend of "the wandering Jew," a stranger who supposedly had no land of his own, a foreigner who would be subject to prejudice and restrictions wherever he went. Some lands did prove willing to accept Jews, during and soon after the Middle Ages. Among these were Holland, the Ottoman Turkish Empire, Poland, and Russia. These last two regions, making up most of eastern Europe, would emerge as the most populous areas of Jewish settlement by the start of the twentieth century, even though, by that time, historic expulsion orders had been lifted and Jews were free to settle anywhere in Europe. On the eve of the Holocaust, in the 1930s, approximately half of the world's seventeen million Jews lived in eastern Europe. And tragically, it was in these regions where the greatest number of Jews were killed because of the Nazi fury between 1939 and 1945.

Secular Anti-Semitism

Although religious anti-Semitism was a main factor for hostility toward Jews prior to the twentieth century, two other forms of anti-Semitism began to take shape in the eighteenth and nineteenth centuries: *secular* anti-Semitism and *racial* anti-Semitism. **Secular** anti-Semitism was not based on religious reasons, but was a prejudice against Jews based on economic and social factors. They were seen as a minority group who did not deserve all the rights and privileges of other groups. They might be perceived as objects of fear and resentment. Accordingly, they were discriminated against in housing, schools, and certain occupations. Often, from the seventeenth century on, in parts of central and eastern Europe, Jewish communities, in both urban and rural areas would be subject to bloody attacks called **pogroms**. These violent attacks resulted in murder, rape, and the destruction of property. They were carried out by unruly mobs of non-Jews and would last from a few hours to several days. Examples were those conducted by Bogdan Chmelnitzki in Poland (1600s) and by Cossacks in Russia (1800s).

These examples of secular anti-Semitism were fueled by scapegoating, myths, distortions, and superstitions. One such false notion about Jews was described in a book titled *The Protocols of the Elders of Zion*. Written in the late nineteenth century in eastern Europe, it claimed that Jews were involved in a worldwide conspiracy to take over the governments of Christian nations. It became a popular book in Europe in the 1920s and 1930s, even though it was proved to be a forgery and without factual basis. Diabolically, Hitler and the Nazis made use of the myths created by both religious and secular anti-Semitism. Once they occupied areas of eastern Europe and elsewhere during World War II, they were successful in getting large numbers of native non-Jews to assist them in extermination campaigns against Jews.

Racial Anti-Semitism

As wrongful as was secular anti-Semitism, it did not have the potential for indescribable evil that was true of racial anti-Semitism. Also known as *scientific* anti-Semitism, this belief emerged in the nineteenth century and would be used by Hitler to support Nazi genocide. An unproven theory, it held that, because of heredity and gene structure, Jews were an inferior and dangerous race of people. Considered to be as dangerous to society as bacterial and viral infections would be to the human body, such a race, said Hitler's propagandists, should be removed from society and eventually be done away with. Because of this false notion, as well as other beliefs we have discussed, six million Jews would be killed on orders from the leaders of the Third Reich between 1933 and 1945.

We have now examined three forms of anti-Semitism. A summary of the harsh messages communicated in these forms is described by the American professor Raul Hilberg in his book *The Destruction of the European Jews:* religious anti-Semitism—you may not live among us as Jews; secular anti-Semitism—you may not live among us; racial anti-Semitism—you may not live.

Anti-Semitism in Germany Prior to Hitler

Throughout the long history of the German people, some great figures have emerged. In music, we know of Bach, Beethoven, Brahms, Handel, Mendelssohn, Schubert, and Wagner. In science and technology, we learned about Gutenberg, Roentgen, and Einstein. And in religion and politics, we have studied the accomplishments of Martin Luther (see Chapter 7, "The Reformation") and Otto von Bismarck (see Chapter 23, "Unification of Germany"). Yet, German society also brought forth Hitler and the Holocaust. Why? Is it possible to explain why a particular people has produced individuals who made noteworthy contributions to culture and progress as well as those who were responsible for evil and despicable acts? This is a difficult question to answer. Nevertheless, we can point to a lengthy record of anti-Semitism in German territory prior to Hitler's rise to power in 1933.

This history is in addition to the general examples in pre-1933 Europe described earlier in this chapter. Typical were the following laws passed in Germany in the 1300s:

- The property of dead Jews would become public property.
- If a Christian owed money to a Jew, the government could collect the money and keep it.

The Black Death

By far, however, the most notorious instance of fourteenth-century German anti-Semitism focused on the spread of a disease known then as the *Black Death*. A deadly, highly contagious illness, it killed hundreds of thousands of people from 1348 to 1350. Modern medical science has determined that these deaths were caused by the bubonic plague. The plague was probably spread by infected rats and fleas, amidst the common unsanitary conditions found in many towns and villages. However, fourteenth-century Europe was ignorant of the germ theory of disease as well as ways by which infections could be transmitted.

This ignorance, combined with an understandable fear of the unknown, provided a ripe setting for seeking a scapegoat for the plague. The Jews were blamed, even though there was no scientific evidence for this. One reason for heaping blame upon them was that they did not suffer as much from the plague as did others. This was probably due to the strict dietary and hygienic laws observed by many Jews, as well as to the fact that they often lived apart from and had little contact with their Christian neighbors. However, these facts were not within the mindset of the Medieval European community. Rather, the fact that Jews lived apart and did not suffer greatly gave rise to the belief that they were poisoning well water and spreading the plague in order to wipe out the Christian population. This erroneous belief seemed to fit in logically with the centuries-old assertion by the Church that Jews were allied with the devil so as to bring about bad times. The consequences of the Black Death "situation" for German Jews were bloody and horrible. The anger and prejudice directed against them led to more than half their numbers being slaughtered by the end of the century.

The Impact of Martin Luther and Richard Wagner

Less than two hundred years after the ravages of the Black Death, another instance of anti-Semitism occurred. Although it did not lead to any deaths, it provided further fuel for the flames of prejudiced thinking. It took the form of sermons and writings by Martin Luther, the leading figure in the Protestant **Reformation**. Luther had hoped to convert German Jews to Protestantism, having admired them in his early years as a priest. Upon the refusal of Jews to convert, Luther's admiration turned to hatred. He now termed Jews as "children of the devil." In a widely read publication of his in 1543, he condemned Jews for their religious and economic practices. Ironically, this publication was reissued by the Nazis almost four hundred years later, even though they officially were against religion in general and religious leaders.

In addition to Luther, another revered German figure from the past who was used by the Nazis in their anti-Semitic propaganda was the composer Richard Wagner. Gaining fame in the nineteenth century, Wagner wrote operas that had stirring music and that pictured the German people as superior to all others. He was also known for his outspoken anti-Semitic views. Shortly before his death in 1883, he wrote of the Jewish race as "the born enemy of true mankind and of everything that is noble." Although he died six years before Hitler was born, Wagner's music along with his theories (now considered erroneous) about Germans and about Jews were to have enormous influence on Hitler and all of Nazi philosophy.

By the dawn of the twentieth century, the fact that Jews and their religion were able to survive in Europe throughout the many prior years of persecution was a minor miracle. The reasons for this are varied, based on factors of faith, devotion, perseverance, adaptations, intellectual and commercial skills, and mutual self-help. Those many years of persecution and false accusations, however, had resulted in Jews being marked as enemies of the state and of religion. Hitler and his Nazi supporters thus grew up with and were inheritors of anti-Jewish thinking. While they did not create hatred of Jews, they nevertheless fed upon that hatred, added to it, and were to do things that went far beyond what previous generations of anti-Semites had done.

Hitler's War Against the Jews, 1933–1939

Hitler's anti-Semitic attitudes were well-formed by the time he became chancellor of Germany in 1933. He blamed Jews for his personal failure early in life to become a successful painter and also felt that Jews were responsible for Germany's defeat in World War I. Although neither of these charges was true, he nevertheless wrote about them in his autobiography *Mein Kampf* (*My Struggle*), published in 1924. In 1919, he joined a political party that was against the democratic Weimar government and preached anti-Semitism. This was the German Workers' party. Soon thereafter he rose to become party leader, with the name changed to the National Socialist German Workers' (**Nazi**) party. Eventually, he and his party would come to rule Germany as the Third Reich. (See Chapter 31, "Rise of Totalitarianism in Russia, Italy, and Germany.")

Aryan Supremacy

Nazi philosophy became the philosophy of the Third Reich. Central to this way of thinking was the belief that the German people formed a *master race*, whose destiny was to rule the world and whose members were of "pure Ayran blood." By *Aryan*, the Nazis meant a superior, white, Nordic, heroic person, having a particular brain size and certain facial features. This doctrine of Aryan supremacy, although biologically false, had no room for Jews, blacks, or other groups who were deemed to be of "impure" or "mixed" blood. It thus became a basis for a policy of exclusion, excluding from society and eventually exterminating those non-Aryans who would now be considered *untermenschen* (subhumans). This racial theory added a new and tragic dimension to European anti-Semitism. Up to this point in the long and sad history of anti-Semitism, Jews could usually avoid persecution by converting, and by assimilating into the Christian world. But under Nazism, these possibilities no longer existed. German Jews would remain Jews and non-Aryan no matter how long they and their ancestors had lived in Germany and no matter how much they had contributed to German society. German Jewish families in the 1930s suffered persecution, for example, even though members of their previous generations had helped Bismarck in the Franco-Prussian War and had fought for the kaiser in World War I. Also targeted for mistreatment would be someone who claimed not to be a Jew but who had converted to Christianity, as well as someone who, if the Nazis could prove it, had a Jewish ancestor and thus was a "carrier" of "impure blood."

Mistreatment of Jews began soon after Hitler became chancellor on January 30, 1933. In April, for example, a **boycott** against Jewish stores and businesses was staged by Nazi party members. They would stand outside these places with signs, urging people not to enter and buy things. The chief organizer of the boycott was Julius Streicher, editor of the notorious anti-Semitic newspaper *Der Sturmer*. Later in April, the government passed a series of laws that did the following:

- Expelled Jews from civil service jobs.
- Prohibited Jews from practicing law.
- Denied payments from the national health service to patients who had gone to Jewish doctors.
- Restricted Jewish enrollment in high schools.

Book Burnings On May 10, 1933, an event took place in Berlin, and in other cities as well, that was directed more toward Judaism as a religion and as a culture than against individuals. This was a public book burning. Thrown into the flames before cheering crowds were Jewish holy books as well as books written by Jewish authors. Delighted with such devastation, Josef Goebbels, Hitler's minister of propaganda, stated that "these flames not only illuminate the final end of an old era, they also light up the new." An ironical contrast to this statement is one made by Heinrich Heine, a German-Jewish poet whose works were among those consumed in the fires. Almost one hundred years ago, he had said: "Where books are burned, in the end men will burn as well." The horror of this prophecy would come true during the Holocaust.

All book burnings were supervised by members of the *SS*. This was an abbreviation for the *Schutzstaffel*, a small specially picked armed group created by Hitler in 1925 to protect him. It was to grow into a powerful political and military organization in the Third Reich, headed by one of Hitler's friends, Heinrich Himmler.

Originally having only two hundred men, the SS rose to more than four million by 1940. It was to have direct responsibility for the concentration, labor, and death camps. Specially trained to hate and take action against all "enemies of the Reich," especially Jews, the SS included a feared secret police unit known as the **Gestapo** (*Geheimnis Staats Polizei*). Gestapo agents would frequently drag people from their homes in the middle of the night and also engaged in kidnapping and murder. The Gestapo became a law unto itself, with the SS becoming practically a government within the government.

The Nuremberg Laws   The attempt to isolate Jews from German society took a major step forward in 1935. In a mass rally and meeting in September, Nazi party leaders enacted the Nuremberg Laws. These measures effectively stripped from Jews their rights as citizens and transformed them into mere subjects. Jews could not, for example, enjoy the rights, privileges, and protections of other Germans. They could not marry non-Jews nor employ Aryans in their households. Prohibitions were placed on their entering public places such as parks, owning dogs, and going to swimming pools and health spas. By the end of the year, it was common to see the sign "Juden Verboten" ("No Jews") in restaurants, villages, and towns throughout Germany. The Nuremberg Laws made Nazi racism part of the government's legal system and thus made possible the passage of much more anti-Semitic legislation. Such state-sponsored prejudicial decrees widened the psychological gap between Germans and Jews. German society looked upon Jews as aliens or even worse, whereas Jews felt severely handicapped and shamed by being singled out for unfair treatment. Lifelong relationships between Jews and non-Jews—in business, in school, and among families—were now being shattered.

   The destruction of friendships, particularly among students in schools, was devastating. Imagine that, if because of your religion or your race, you were suddenly shunned and isolated by teachers, and by other students in your school with whom you had been friendly for several years. You ran the risk of being beaten up after school, spat upon, having your parents cursed, while also learning from class lessons and from textbooks that you and your kind were no good, unfit to be citizens, and responsible for your nation's problems and its defeat in a recent war! Such were the heartrending and haunting challenges facing Jewish youth your age in their formative years of adolescent growth. Some of the worst challenges on a one-to-one human level came from boys who were members of the Hitler Youth and from girls who belonged to the League of German Girls. These organizations trained their members in sports and military ways, while instilling anti-Semitic attitudes. The youth were assigned booklets to read that contained hateful stores about Jews, accompanied by ugly and distorted pictures. One of the most popular of these publications bore the suggestive title "Don't Trust the Fox in the Green Meadow."

The Year 1938 as a Turning Point   The year 1938 was a critical one for the Third Reich, in regard to both its expansionist and its anti-Semitic policies. In March, Hitler achieved *anschluss* with Austria, followed by acquisition of the Czech Sudetenland in September as a result of the Munich Agreement (see Chapter 32, "World War II"). Austrian and Sudetenland Jews would now be subject to the restrictive and harsh laws of the Nazi Reich. For these Jews, as well as for those in Germany, however, these developments would prove to be overshadowed by others that made 1938 a bitter year.

The Evian Conference

In July, an international conference was convened at the French city of Evian. The purpose of the Evian Conference was to deal with the problem of growing numbers of people wanting to flee from the Nazis. The majority of these refugees were Jews. Many nations at the conference, including France, Canada, Australia, the United States, and Great Britain, deplored Nazi actions against Jews and stated that safe havens should be found for them. However, most of the nations, for a variety of reasons, either refused to open their doors or were willing to accept only a small number of refugees as immigrants. Holland, Denmark, and the Dominican Republic were more willing than others to accept refugees.

Although the Evian Conference gave little hope for Jews suffering under the Nazis, it could not be described as a definite case of anti-Semitism. Such a description, however, clearly applies to three other events in 1938, brought on by German authorities. The less harmful of these were two decrees issued in October that, in effect, were additional ways of treating Jews as subjects and outcasts rather than as German citizens. The first decree ordered that, from then on, Jews would have to add another "identifying" name, such as Israel or Sarah, to their names. The second decree directed that their passports be stamped with the letter *J* for *Jude*, the German word for Jew. As dehumanizing as these rules were, they would be a far cry from the vicious physical attacks on Jews, their homes, and their holy places that took place nationwide on the evening of November 9, 1938. That date has since been referred to as **Kristallnacht** (night of the broken glass). As the worst anti-Semitic action since Hitler's rise to power in 1933, and as a shocking sign of the genocide yet to come, and finally as a terrifying example of a totalitarian government's group-directed violence, the details surrounding Kristallnacht must be carefully examined.

Kristallnacht What happened on Thursday night, November 9, 1938, and continued on through November 11, 1938, was an *aktionen* (a planned action) against German Jews that really became a pogrom. All over Germany, Nazi gangs, Gestapo members, and masses of citizens killed 92 Jews, set fire to almost 200 synagogues while destroying 76 of these, broke into and looted more than 7,000 Jewish shops and businesses, and attacked untold numbers of people in their homes and in the streets. The local police did nothing during the attacks. More than 35,000 Jews were arrested and sent to concentration camps. The breaking of so much glass, most of which had been made in Belgium, is the reason the aktionen is called Kristallnacht. Indeed, so much glass was broken that it would supposedly have taken all the plate glass factories in Belgium almost two years to make replacements!

Why did Kristallnacht occur? Nazi officials such as Propaganda Minister Joseph Goebbels claimed that the violence was a spontaneous outpouring of anger based on the killing of a German official in Paris by a Jewish teenager. This was a lie, and Goebbels knew it was a lie. In fact, it was a "**big lie**." From documents shown at the Nuremberg Trials in 1945, it is clear that the events of November 9 to 11, 1938, had been well-planned. Secret notices had been sent before and during these dates from Gestapo headquarters all over Germany, under direct orders from Reinhard Heydrich and Heinrich Himmler, two Nazi officials close to Hitler. Use of the "big lie" technique, however, was a common feature of the Third Reich and has been characteristic of all totalitarian governments. The true background and aftermath of Kristallnacht are as follows.

Kristallnacht, also known as the "night of the broken glass," was an evening of planned violence against Jewish people living in Germany, which the police did nothing to stop. So many windows were broken that it is estimated it would take plate glass factories two years to replace all of them.

During the early years of the twentieth century, thousands of eastern European Jews had come to Germany. In his wish, however, to make Germany *Judenrein* (free of Jews), Hitler gave an order to expel these people. In October 1938, more than eighteen thousand were forcibly taken to the German-Polish border, beaten, robbed, and sent into Poland. In this group was Zindel Grynszpan and his family. They wrote about their expulsion to their seventeen-year-old son, Herschel Grynszpan, who was studying in Paris. Angered at learning of his family's ordeal, Herschel went to the German embassy in Paris on November 6, 1938, where he shot Ernst von Rath, an embassy official. The Nazis claimed that this assassination was part of an international plot against Germany, blaming all Jews for the killing. This accusation of "collective guilt," holding all Jews responsible for the actions of one of them, was an example of the "big lie" technique. A cry for revenge arose from German newspapers, Nazi officials, and even some Church leaders. This revenge became the violence that allegedly occurred "spontaneously" a few days later on November 9, 1938. This allegation was of course another part of the "big lie." To add insult to injury, the Nazis now claimed that since Jews were responsible for causing the violence and resulting damage, they would have to pay a penalty of more than one billion German marks!

The terror unleashed on November 9, 1938, does not deserve to be called Kristallnacht, because the literal translation of this word refers to crystal, something pleasing, delicate, and refined. Clearly, none of these adjectives applies to what the Nazis and their followers did on that night. Truer descriptions are contained in these German words: *Reichspogromnacht, Novemberpogrom,* and *Judenpogrom.* In fact, these words are used today in Germany and, most significantly, in history textbooks read in German schools.

Attempts to Emigrate from Germany

As 1938 drew to a close, the majority of Jews remaining in Germany now tried to emigrate. From 1933 up to this point, some had already left, mostly in fear of Hitler. Yet those numbers had been small; in 1933 only 10 percent of the total population of five hundred thousand Jews had fled. (In that year, only one person out of every hundred Germans was Jewish.) Even though Hitler had hoped that Jews would emigrate voluntarily between 1933 and 1938, most did not. Why? The reason is that most German Jews belonged to families that had lived in Germany for generations and thus identified strongly with German culture, considering Germany their homeland. They were Germans who happened to have been born as Jews. To many of them, emigration would be a symbol of weakness and disloyalty. They viewed Germany as an advanced, modern society, placing their trust in the German people as logical, reasonable, and compassionate. Even though Jews in the Nazi Era up to 1938 were aware of prior instances of anti-Semitism in German history, they felt that Hitler and his followers would soon pass out of power. Indeed, most people throughout the world shared the belief that the Third Reich would last for only a short time. In addition, we should recognize that neither the world nor Germany's Jews had any idea or warning about the genocide that would be attempted in the 1940s.

After 1938, it became harder for Jews to leave Germany. And even those who did leave during the 1930s had no guarantee that they would gain entry into another nation. For a variety of reasons, many nations shut their doors to these refugees.

- Several, like the United States, had restrictive immigration laws.
- Many were still suffering unemployment problems stemming from the world-wide Great Depression and did not want any newcomers.
- Some nations, possibly because of anti-Semitism, felt that if they accepted Jewish refugees from Germany, they might thereby encourage refugees from other parts of Europe to come to their lands.
- Jews who hoped to travel to Palestine and build a Jewish state there faced restrictions from Britain. Britain held a mandate over that area and was afraid of hostile reactions from Arabs toward Jewish immigration there.

A sad story concerned the ship *St. Louis* and the nine hundred Jews who sailed on it from Hamburg, Germany, in 1939. Their attempt to settle in Cuba was rejected and the ship had to return to Europe. Most of the passengers would eventually die in the Holocaust.

Hitler's War Against the Jews, 1939–1945

With Germany's attack on Poland in 1939, World War II began. The conquests of Poland and other nations in Europe made the Jews in these areas subjects of the Third Reich. The Nazis were now to extend their anti-Semitic policies to these areas. They would also adopt practices that would be more shocking than those they had carried out between 1933 and 1938 in the territories they occupied in that time. To understand these practices more fully, we will examine events mostly in eastern Europe. It was here, particularly in Poland, that Hitler's war against the Jews was more ferocious than in Nazi-occupied areas of western and southern Europe.

The Ghettos The ghettos were sealed-off, restricted areas of cities, into which Nazis forced Jews to live. These areas were different from Jewish ghettos in earlier centuries. In those ghettos, people could still get on with their lives in a limited manner. In the Nazi-imposed ghettos, however, the aim was not to create a permanent setting, but to have a temporary arrangement for people prior to sending them away as slave laborers or on to **death camps**. Isolation of Jews from non-Jews was another reason for the ghettos.

Heavily populated ghettos were established in Lodz and Krakow in Poland, Vilna in Lithuania, and Bialystok in Russia. The largest was Poland's Warsaw Ghetto, created in 1940 in a run-down neighborhood and surrounded by a newly built wall topped with barbed wire and cut glass. It was to have a population of almost 450,000 people. The buildings, food, water, and sanitary services here were inadequate to take care of so many people. Fully aware of this, however, the Nazis forced Jews there from other sections of Warsaw as well as from outlying rural vil-

An unknown German photographer took this picture of families being led out of the Warsaw Ghetto at gunpoint for deportation.

This photo was used as evidence of Nazi terrorism at the Nuremberg War Crimes Trials. It shows women and children being removed from the Warsaw Ghetto.

lages. This overcrowding, often with several people confined to one room, created very harsh living conditions. Contributing to this inhuman existence were additional measures dictated by the Germans:

- Rationing of food and water below minimum health standards.
- Removal of radios and telephones in order to cut off Jews from the outside world.
- Stationing of armed guards to prevent people from leaving the ghetto.
- Reducing heat in the winter.
- Requiring all Jews to buy and wear a six-pointed yellow star on their clothing.

At unpredictable moments, there might be roundups and arrests for no legitimate reason, as well as beatings, rapes, and shootings.

Such conditions were to be found, with minor differences, in ghettos all over Europe. The impact of these conditions was devastating, particularly in Warsaw. In psychological terms, depression among inhabitants led to an alarming number of heart attacks and suicides. In physical terms, life become a struggle for existence. Hunger caused tens of thousands of deaths. Common were diseases such as typhus, tuberculosis, and dysentery. Parents faced terrible ordeals when trying to explain to their children what was happening and when deciding whom to feed first with meager and rotting food. Young people your age often resorted to smuggling food from outside the ghetto, while running the risk of getting caught by the Germans or by the Polish guards they often employed. If successful in smuggling food, you might face the emotional crisis of deciding how to share it with your parents and any starving grandparents who were still alive.

The Judenrat In each ghetto, the Nazis set up a Jewish council known at the *Judenrat*. In most instances, this council would consist of Jews who were respected leaders in Jewish communities. The Judenrat in a ghetto would have several functions:

- To act as an administrative government in obeying and carrying out Nazi regulations.
- To be responsible for basic services such as employment, sanitation, health, and education, and to establish a police force and jails.
- To represent Jews in dealings with the occupation authorities.

Jews who were Judenrat members had mixed feelings about their roles. On the one hand, they feared the shame of collaborating with the Nazis and worried about being seen by their fellow Jews as tools and puppets. On the other hand, they stood to obtain benefits and protection for themselves and their families, gain status, and do what they could to help their fellow Jews.

Clearly, they faced a dilemma. If they were too obedient to Nazi demands concerning food, arrests, laborers, and so on, they risked charges of condemnation and betrayal by their brethren. If they sought to bargain with the Nazis or refused to carry out demands, the risked torture and even death. Indeed, most Judenrat officials either were ultimately killed by the Nazis or were among the last Jews to be deported to death camps. A sad exception to these fates was Adam Czerniakow, a Judenrat leader in Warsaw who found it increasingly difficult to enforce Nazi orders while trying to soften restrictions on his people. In July 1942, he refused to sign a mass **deportation** order for the death camps. Soon thereafter, he committed suicide by taking poison.

The existence of these camps was probably not known to Czerniakow when he first became head of the Warsaw Judenrat. His eventual awareness of them was certainly a factor in his refusal to sign a deportation order. What he probably did not know, however, was the overall reason for the death camps: They were the central part of the "**final solution**," the horrible Nazi plan to kill all Jews in Europe.

The "Final Solution" The word *solution* does not often appear when you study history. You are most likely to encounter it in a science or mathematics class. Math teachers will use the word in trying to answer a problem. This kind of thought process was diabolically applied by the Nazis in their treatment of Jews. Jews were seen as a "problem" that needed a solution. Just what to do with them became known as the *Jewish Question*. This anti-Semitic phrase, the Jewish Question, first crept into the minds of Europeans in the nineteenth century. For Hitler, from 1933 to 1939, in the areas making up the Third Reich—Germany, Austria, and Czechoslovakia—the three answers or solutions to this question were humiliation, separation, and expulsion. After 1939, with the German occupation of other parts of Europe, a fourth and final solution was agreed upon—the total annihilation of European Jews. The final solution to the Jewish Question would thus be mass murder, or genocide.

When was this incredible decision made? It is difficult to point to a specific date or document with instructions. However, historians believe that sometime in 1941 Hitler spoke to Heinrich Himmler, head of the SS, about the extermination of the Jews of Europe. In July 1941, the SS second-in-command to Himmler, Reinhard Heydrich, was placed in charge of planning this extermination, this final solution. On December 8, 1941, the day the United States entered World War II, the first extermination camp was opened at Chelmno in Poland. It is possible that Hitler had thoughts about genocide prior to coming to power in 1933. Yet, it was only in the early 1940s that exact plans were made to carry out this gruesome policy. By 1941, for example, the war had been going well for Germany and the other **Axis powers**. Any human restraints inside the **reich** had weakened; there were also no concerns now about reactions from democratic nations. These countries had been very reluctant, as we have seen, even to admit fleeing Jews into their lands.

The Wannsee Conference

In January 1942 at Lake Wannsee, outside of Berlin, a conference was held to determine various ways of achieving the final solution. Heydrich, known for his fiery anti-Semitism, presided. Among others attending were Adolf Eichmann, a

Gestapo officer who was assigned now as supervisor of Jewish Affairs and Evacuation Affairs. All participants in the Wannsee Conference were shown charts and maps by Heydrich, indicating the numbers and nationalities of Jews who were to be included in the final solution. Basic logistical (behind-the-scenes) items were discussed, such as the locations of death camps, the cheapest and most efficient means of transporting Jews there from all over Europe, who would be responsible for the roundups and deportations, what should be done at the camps, how to identify "half-Jews" and what should be done with them, and so on.

It is astonishing to realize that Heydrich and his colleagues were discussing very matter-of-factly the destruction of millions of human beings. The Wannsee Conference could just as well have been a meeting of the board of directors of a corporation, considering the transportation costs and other business issues connected with the manufacture and sale of a product. All the Nazis present at Wannsee considered themselves to be refined, cultured, and well-educated individuals. At the conference, they listened to classical music and enjoyed a fine meal. And yet, not one of them protested against the diabolical overall plan of wiping out a whole group of people from the face of the earth!

The implementation of the final solution would lie in the hands of the SS, not the regular German army. The latter, known as the Wehrmacht, was a well-trained professional military force. Assisted by other land, sea, and air fighters, the Wehrmacht had conquered Belgium, France, Poland, and many other parts of Europe by 1942. They were more concerned with fighting and defeating other nations' armies than with killing innocent civilian Jewish men, women, and children. It was not that the Wehrmacht would act to protect Jews; rather, it was that the SS who, in the aftermath of Wehrmacht victories in a region, were the ones to move in and begin to organize ghettos and implement other aspects of the final solution. In fact, there was much competition and bad feeling between Wehrmacht and SS commanders over such things as weapons, equipment, trucks, use of roads, and obtaining money and favors from Hitler.

The SS became such a huge and powerful organization under Himmler that it existed almost as a state within a state. While it did have some renowned fighting units, it also had recruited many Germans who had been criminals, army rejects, and other social outcasts. Other members were drawn from occupations such as dock workers, laborers, waiters, truck drivers, and other ordinary civilian jobs. Once in the SS, they became trained as bigots, torturers, and cold-blooded killers. On their uniforms was the SS symbol, twin lightning flashes that were really a double zigzag of the letter *S* from the runic alphabet. This alphabet had been devised by an ancient Germanic tribe, in whose mystical rituals Himmler was deeply interested. An additional SS symbol, worn mostly by Death's head units at **concentration camps**, was a skull and crossbones.

The Einsatzgruppen

One of the most feared components within the SS was the **Einsatzgruppen** (Special Duty Groups). Eventually known also as "mobile killing units," their members were handpicked for "special actions" primarily in Poland and Russia—areas containing the great majority of European Jews. Among the many anti-Semitic lies put forth by Heydrich was that Jews were responsible for the rise of communism and must therefore be liquidated (killed) in accordance with Hitler's wishes. The Einsatzgruppen were given three specific tasks:

1. To encourage local peoples to stage pogroms against Jews.
2. To transfer Jews to ghettos that were being created.
3. To commit mass murder by shooting and other means.

These tasks were usually not difficult to achieve. Large numbers of native people in areas taken by the Germans would often do the bidding of their occupiers. This was due in part to their fear of the Germans and willingness to accept German propaganda but was mainly due to their own feelings and traditions of anti-Semitism. Thus, for example, there were hundreds of Poles, Latvians, Lithuanians, Ukrainians, and other eastern European people who contributed to the final solution. They carried out Nazi requests regarding pogroms, transports, and shootings. Many volunteered for training at the notorious Trawniki camp in Poland. All of these individuals were **collaborators** with the Germans. (It should be noted that there were Nazi collaborators in other conquered European nations. Frenchmen in the Vichy government sent Jews to death camps; Croatians who became fascists in Yugoslavia and members of the Iron Guard in Romania committed acts of slaughter against Jews in those nations.)

Collaborators in eastern Europe made the work of the Einsatzgruppen easy. While certainly not all people in this region aided the Germans, there were more than sufficient numbers who pulled triggers, performed unspeakable acts of torture and humiliation, or stood by when bloody actions occurred. Such actions would take place in a number of ways. One such incident, typical of many others, was described by Otto Ohlendorf, an Einsatzgruppen commander:

> *[A unit assigned to kill Jews] would enter a village or town and order the prominent Jewish citizens to call together all other Jews for the purpose of resettlement. They were requested to hand over their valuables to the leaders of the unit, and shortly before the execution to surrender their outer clothing. The men, women, and children were led to a place of execution which in most cases was located next to a more deeply excavated anti-tank ditch. Then they were shot kneeling or standing, and the corpses thrown into the ditch.*

The victims of this kind of brutality might often be forced to dig their own ditches/graves and would then be shot in the back of the neck. Administering what the Germans called "neck shots" became so sickening and frightful for some of the executioners that they asked to be "excused." Their places would be taken by the Trawnikis, those non-Germans trained at the Polish camp for such tasks. Shootings might also be done by a firing squad or by a single machine gunner. The largest single massacre committed by an Einsatzgruppen squad was by machine gun at Babi Yar. At this site, near the city of Kiev in the former Soviet Union, more than thirty-five thousand Jews met death.

Shootings were not the only lethal horror visited upon Jews by the Einsatzgruppen and their collaborators. Sealed trucks, buses, and vans were used in ways that did not require the killers to see their victims at the moment of death. Elderly Jews in a Polish town, for example, would be herded into a van that was deceptively painted by the Germans to look like a Red Cross vehicle. They might be told that they were going to be "resettled" or "relocated," or were being taken to a "hospital." (These were, or course, additional examples of German "big lie" techniques.) Before the van drove off, and unbeknown to the occupants, a special pipe was used to connect the van's exhaust with the interior. The van would then drive on, until all passengers died of carbon monoxide gas.

This woman is being led to her execution. Many like her were shot in the back of the neck and then thrown in a ditch.

Would killing by gas in this fashion be more efficient, expensive, and honorable than killing by bullets? German leaders in Poland would argue about such matters, without any sensitivity, as if they were discussing destroying diseased animals rather than human beings! It has been estimated that of the six million Jews murdered during the Holocaust, almost two million were killed by the Einsatzgruppen and their collaborators. Untold numbers of others died from epidemics, hunger, terrible suffering, and forced death marches. The site may have been a ghetto, forest, transport, railroad car, or collection point anywhere in German-controlled Europe. The majority of the six million, however, met their end in the death camps and the concentration camps. The creation of these camps and all that occurred within them defies the imagination. Their existence, as part of the final solution, is yet another reason for the Holocaust being the greatest crime in human history.

The Death Camps

In 1942 in Poland, the Nazis finished building six large sealed and guarded facilities, chiefly for the purpose of killing Jews. They were located at Chelmno, Treblinka, Maidanek, Sobibor, Belzec, and Auschwitz, and can be referred to as death camps or extermination camps. There were many other camps where Jews were killed, although they were not originally intended to be places for mass murder. These were called concentration camps, as their purpose was to concentrate enemies of the reich in one place. The first of more than one hundred of these was opened at Dachau, Germany, in March 1933. Most of its original inmates were non-Jews and included supporters of the Weimar Republic, Socialists, Communists, and others who spoke out against the Nazis. Some other large concentration camps that were opened between 1933 and the start of World War II in 1939 were Belsen, Buchenwald, and Ravensbruck in Germany and Mauthausen in Austria. Many of these had subcamps, with increasing numbers of Jews and other imprisoned populations that included homosexuals, the mentally retarded, the physically handicapped, Gypsies, and Jehovah's Witnesses. Along with Jews and Hitler's political enemies, all these groups were considered "unfit" and "undesirable" by him. Some concentration camps, such as Mauthausen, became slave labor camps for the purpose of helping the German war effort. Hundreds of thousands perished there, from outright killing as well as from overwork under inhuman conditions.

Planet Auschwitz Of all these horrible places, Auschwitz was the worst. In March 1941, after Auschwitz had already been opened as a concentration camp, Himmler chose it as the primary site for the murder of Europe's Jews. The world inside this camp would become so far removed from ordinary human existence that one inmate described life there as being on another planet. Many of the things that happened on "planet Auschwitz" happened at other camps, but not with as much grotesque intensity nor with the large numbers of affected people as at this site in southwestern Poland. It is thus necessary for us to focus on Auschwitz to understand what all the camps were like.

Auschwitz was actually divided into thirty-nine camps within a radius of fifty miles. There were three main camps, each one capable of housing thousands of prisoners and having a separate function. Auschwitz I was a concentration camp; Auschwitz II was known officially as Birkenau and was a death camp that claimed the lives of three million people; Auschwitz III, known as Monowitz, was a slave labor camp. From 1942 on, transports, mainly railroad freight cars, would arrive daily. They were crowded with Jews, jammed in tightly, without food, water, or toilet facilities. Some transports took days to complete their journeys. The occupants, with only the belongings they could carry, had no idea where they were going. They were deported from almost all the European nations, from as far west as France and as far south as Greece; the greatest number of deportations were from parts of Poland and the former Soviet Union. With cool-headed efficiency, Nazi "desk-murderers" such as Adolf Eichmann routinely planned time schedules, made sure that transports were in good working conditions, assigned train engineers, and acted in a businesslike fashion as if they were arranging for shipments of cattle rather than human beings.

Auschwitz was considered the worst of all concentration camps where people were treated like cattle and subjected to medical experiments.

The Selection Process

Untold numbers of people did not survive the transports' journeys to Auschwitz. At the camp's entrance was a sign in German, "Arbeit Macht Frei" (Work will make

THE CONCENTRATION CAMPS

Between 1939 and 1945, six million unarmed and innocent Jewish civilians – men, women, children and babies – were murdered in Nazi-controlled Europe, as part of a deliberate policy to destroy all traces of Jewish life and culture. As many as two million of these were killed in their towns and villages, some confined in ghettoes where death by slow starvation was a deliberate Nazi policy, others taken to be shot at mass-murder sites near where they lived. The remaining four million Jews were forced from their homes and taken by train to distant concentration camps, where they were murdered by being worked to death, starved to death, beaten to death, shot, or gassed.

Auschwitz concentration camp in which more than 2 million people were murdered between 1941 and 1944, including Jews, Gypsies, and Soviet prisoners.

Among the hundreds of thousands of non-Jews sent by the Nazis to concentration camps were anti-Nazis, Jehovah's Witnesses, homosexuals, the mentally ill, and the chronically sick. In addition, more than 250,000 Gypsies were murdered, in a Nazi attempt to eliminate Gypsies as well as Jews from the map of Europe.

In many of the camps shown here so-called "medical" experiments were carried out, without anaesthetics, soley to satisfy the curiosity and sadism of the doctors. Hundreds of otherwise healthy "patients" were tortured and murdered during these experiments.

BELZEC Camps set up solely for the murder of Jews.

Other camps in which Jews and non-Jews were put to forced labor, starved, tortured and murdered in conditions of the worst imaginable cruelty. Most of these camps had "satellite" labor camps nearby.

NORTH SEA

BALTIC SEA

LATVIA

LITHUANIA

USSR

Vaivara

Klooga

Stutthof

Neuengamme

Ravensbrück

Bergen-Belsen

Sachsenhausen

CHELMNO

TREBLINKA

Mittelbau Dora

Gross Rosen

POLAND

SOBIBOR

Buchenwald

AUSCHWITZ

MAIDANEK

GERMANY

Plaszow

BELZEC

Flossenberg

Natzweiler

CZECHOSLOVAKIA

FRANCE

Dachau

Mauthausen

SWITZERLAND

AUSTRIA

HUNGARY

RUMANIA

BLACK SEA

ITALY

Jasenovac

Gospič

Sajmište

YUGOSLAVIA

MEDITERRANEAN SEA

| 0 | miles | 200 |
| 0 | kilometers | 400 |

When people arrived at concentration camps, they had to endure a selection process. The strongest were sent to work camps and those determined weak, the elderly, women, children, and babies, were killed in the gas chambers.

you free). As yet another example of the "big lie" technique, this sign was supposed to inspire camp inmates with hope and make them feel welcome. What really happened upon arrival of the transports was very unwelcome and frightening. Their doors would be flung open by SS guards with dogs. Exhausted, tired, hungry, and thirsty, the surviving Jews were yelled at and forced to line up on a long railroad platform. Without knowing where they were nor what awaited them, they now underwent the "selection process." This hideous procedure was carried out by SS officials and medical doctors, among them the notorious Dr. Josef Mengele. They would look at the deportees and decide which ones seemed capable of work and which would be "nonproductive." As a result of this selection process, usually made with a casual flick of the thumb, nod of the head, or pointing with a cane, two columns of people were formed. On the right of the German officials might be healthy-looking males, from perhaps the late teens to forty-five years of age, and some women; on the left would be children, the elderly, the sick, and the infirm, and the remainder of the transport's women. Mothers clutching babies would be on this line. Members of a family were often separated, while screaming, crying, and desperately reaching out to each other. Their anguish had no impact on their status. SS guards would beat them, while dogs would bark and threaten to bite; the two columns would be moved further apart. This moment would be the last time that those who survived the selection process, such as healthy teenagers, would ever see any parents and other relatives who were placed on the "nonproductive" line. Those placed on this line were sent immediately, unknowingly, to gas chambers. Here, they would be killed in a horrible manner, to be described later in this chapter.

For those designated as "productive," slave labor became their assignment. Some were given backbreaking factory jobs to aid the German war effort; others would be sent to kitchens or latrines as part of the camp administration. Inmates needed by the SS, such as physicians, engineers, or carpenters, might be spared from some of the dirtier jobs. Among the dirtier jobs were those performed by the *Sonderkommando*, special units of prisoners who were assigned to take dead bodies from the gas chambers and elsewhere to be burned in a **crematory**. Auschwitz had four crematories, containing forty-six ovens. Sonderkommando units were responsible for cleaning up the gas chambers and ovens. Workers in these units were usually killed within three months, probably to prevent them from spreading information about their duties. They would be replaced by other inmates.

Another unsavory task would be performed by those selected by German guards to be *kapos*. Kapos (short for *Kameraden Polizei* or "Comrade Police") were prisoners, both Jewish and non-Jewish. Their task was to be in charge of other prisoners regarding labor and housing. In carrying out their orders, kapos often became as violent as, and at times more violent than, their German masters. Had they not behaved in these ways, they too might have been murdered.

Daily life for inhabitants of "planet Auschwitz" was nightmarish, both emotionally and physically. They were isolated from all features of a normal society. When deportees entered Auschwitz, as well as any other camp, they were stripped of their humanity; lost were their names, employment, social status, friends, family, and identity. Each of them would be recognized only as a number, burned into an arm as a never-to-be removed tattoo. Inmates would wear ragged uniforms, be watched constantly, and be beaten and punished for any reason, and sometimes for no reason. They lived in crude, unsanitary barracks, crowded together with as many as four hundred other prisoners. They were purposely underfed, often with unfit and rotten food. SS physicians had determined a specific number of calories to be consumed. Food was rationed in such a way that prisoners would rarely survive for more than three months. These conditions often resulted in savage behavior among inmates and a breakdown of any civilized contact between them. Some might steal food from others, fight for scraps and crumbs, and rummage through garbage heaps for something to eat.

Medical Experiments

Another unique horror visited upon selected prisoners at Auschwitz was medical experiments. Never before on planet earth had human beings been forced to undergo sadistic tests and experiments by medical professionals under official governmental authority. On planet Auschwitz, however, the SS did not consider inmates to be human or worthy of life. Accordingly, Himmler, and SS doctors such as Mengele, saw nothing wrong in "advancing scientific knowledge" by using Jews and other "subhumans" as guinea pigs. In one experiment, designed to help the German air force learn about the effects of high altitudes on pilots, inmates were placed in a decompression chamber. Here, they were subjected to air becoming so thin that their eardrums would often burst. It was common for many subjects to die from these tests.

Some other torturous experiments were conducted to find out how people could endure cold—for example, having them standing naked in ice water or outdoors in bitter snow. Mengele, hoping to learn what caused eye color in twins, would kill them and then dissect the eyes. Various viruses, cancer cells, and typhus germs would be injected into prisoners to observe the effects. Newly developed drugs would then be administered to test their effectiveness. Surgical experiments, often without anesthetics, were carried out on sex organs. In addition, a group of healthy prisoners might be subjected to heavy doses of radiation, making them sterile. Specimens would then be taken from their affected tissues for laboratory analysis. Probably more for sports entertainment than for medical knowledge, prisoners would be tested to see how fast they would run when being chased by starving dogs.

Needless to say, many tens of thousands died from these ghastly practices. Most of the experiments carried on in Auschwitz and other camps contributed nothing of value to medical research. A few documents containing results of some experiments have been preserved. Yet, the medical profession today faces ethical questions over whether these documents should be destroyed or not. In addition, we have to question whether certain results, even if important, should be published and disseminated. Another lingering and troublesome question about the medical experiments concerns the behavior of the participating doctors and nurses. In a profession dedicated to healing, why some of its members did things to hurt and kill people can only strain the imagination and shock the conscience.

And if the discussion about experiments causes us such sadness and agony, what do we dare ask about the gas chambers? As the very least, we have a responsibility to learn about them. Their use represented, in all recorded human history, the worst abuse of technology by a government and the most hideous extermination process, ever, of a group of people.

The Gas Chambers Gas chambers, such as those at Auschwitz, Belzec, Treblinka, and other extermination sites, were used mainly for two reasons: they were the least expensive and the most efficient means of mass murder. Experimentation with gassing at Auschwitz took place in September 1941, with large-scale exterminations underway by the summer of 1942. Gas had been used even earlier by the Nazis, as part of their **euthanasia** (mercy killing) program. In 1939, Hitler had ordered that "imperfect Aryans" (i.e., German children who were physically handicapped or mentally ill) should be put to death. It is not surprising that such methods would soon be employed against Jews on a massive scale, as part of the final solution.

Gas chambers were considered inexpensive and efficient ways to commit large-scale extermination of Jews.

By 1942, German scientists, having experimented with different gasses, decided upon using **Zyklon B**, an insecticide. It was discovered that cans with pellets of the gas, when dropped through windows in the chambers' roofs, would soon poison the air inside the chambers. Death would occur within three to five minutes, upon inhalation of the gas. Between ten and fifteen thousand people would be killed this way at Auschwitz, in any given day. The events occurring on such a day, carefully arranged by the SS, would unfold in a deceptive yet gruesome manner.

Jews selected for the gas chambers were never told the truth about what was going to happen. They would be marched to a sealed, harmless-looking building, where they were instructed to remove their clothes and place them on numbered hooks. They

Wedding rings were just some of the belongings taken from the corpses of victims who died in the gas chambers.

were given bars of soap and told that they would be taking a shower in order to be disinfected. These "instructions" were designed to comfort both the people who had just come off transports after days of traveling and the camp inmates who had been living in dirty barracks. Prior to being herded, with hundreds of others, into a large room with shower heads, the unaware victims would be told to remember their numbers so as to reclaim their clothing. They might also be spoken to reassuringly by guards, and even be accompanied by musicians, who, at a distance, would play soft and melodious music. Once the room was full, guards would lock the doors and drop the gas pellets into ventilation shafts. The resulting hissing sound from the pellets' bursting was quickly drowned out by the cries, screams, vomiting, and pounding on walls by the trapped Jews. SS officers would maliciously look through peepholes. When they were satisfied that no one was left alive, they would order Sonderkommandos to open the doors, remove the bodies, and get the chamber clean and ready for its next victims!

Such was the ruthless, cold-blooded inhumanity of the camp officers, acting as if they were managing an assembly-line process at a manufacturing plant. Evidence of this insensitive, horrible mentality, fully endorsed by Hitler and Himmler, was next seen in the disposition of the fallen bodies. Using special hook-tipped poles and large ice tongs, Sonderkommandos would drag the corpses into a wagon or truck. The bodies of mothers and children who died clinging to each other were pried apart. It was not easy to wipe away the blood nor to remove the scratches on walls made by the deceased with their fingernails during their final moments. According to a fixed schedule and routine, the camp workers would next use pliers to extract teeth containing gold. Heads were shaved, with the removed hair slated to be used in boots for German soldiers, as well as in pillows and clothing. The clothing, luggage, eyeglasses, jewelry, and any other belongings of the victims were stored in a mountainlike stake called the *Brezhinka.* Usable items from the Brezhinka were sent to Germany.

The Crematory The bodies would then be taken to the crematory, for burning in ovens and furnaces. Two thousand bodies could be incinerated every twenty-four hours. So many burnings took place at Auschwitz that, periodically, several inches of human fat had to be scraped from the chimney walls of the crematory. The ashes would be discarded. At times when the camp's furnaces were inoperative, the bodies would be burned in open pits. The stench of burning flesh would often spread for miles, thereby producing complaints from nearby townspeople. These complaints were at odds with statements by these same townspeople after 1945 that they "did not know" what was happening at Auschwitz.

A heartbreaking partial summary account of extermination processes at Auschwitz is contained in the 1979 report issued in the United States by the President's Commission on the Holocaust:

> At Auschwitz was a [company], a division of I. G. Farben. This . . . petro-
> chemical complex brought human slavery to its ultimate perfection by reducing

human beings to consumable raw materials, from which all mineral life was sys-
tematically drained before the bodies were recycled into the Nazi war economy;
gold teeth for the treasury, hair for mattresses, ashes for fertilizer. In their relent-
less search for . . . [extermination methods], German scientists discovered Zyklon
B, which could kill 2,000 persons in less than 30 minutes at a cost of one-half-
cent per body. Near the end of the war, in order to cut expenses and save gas,
"cost-account considerations" led to an order to place living children directly in
the ovens or throw them into open burning pits. The same type of ingenuity and
control [used in] modern industrial development was . . . applied to the process
of destruction.

The horrors perpetrated on the Jews of Europe, as we have now seen, were shameful, revolting, and inexcusable. While many of these horrors were also perpetrated on other groups, such as Gypsies, Slavs, and others we have mentioned, none suffered as much nor were intended for as much suffering as Jews. As Elie Wiesel, an Auschwitz survivor, has stated, "While not all victims were Jews, yet, all Jews were victims."

Did the Jews do anything to resist being victimized? Were they able to do anything? The complex answers to these questions will now be examined.

Jewish Resistance

Yes. There were many instances of Jewish resistance to the Nazis. In fact, these instances were some of the most heroic in human history. They occurred under conditions never experienced by other groups facing oppression, let alone the uniqueness of intended mass annihilation. These conditions, described below, made any decision to offer resistance a very difficult one:

- The physical, armed strength of the Germans and their collaborators was overwhelming. The Jews had no weapons of their own.
- Amidst the frightening quality of life imposed by the Germans in ghettos and camps (starvation, disease, forced labor, overcrowding, random shootings, and separation of families), mere survival from day to day became the chief goal. It required all of one's energy just to stay alive. Physical weakness and emotional demoralization had devastating effects on peoples' ability and will to survive.
- A small number of Jews felt that their suffering was God's will and that they should accept their fate.
- Attempts to have any organized leadership among Jewish communities was impossible, given the lack of means of communication and transportation.
- The Jews were alone, all alone. No help could be expected from anybody. No nation fighting the Germans during World War II offered aid to Jews. Most, as we have seen, did not even want to accept Jews as refugees fleeing Hitler. While the French and Dutch underground resistance groups were linked with sovereign nations fighting the Germans, and could expect help from the surrounding native population and even from the United States and its allies, the position of Jews in European countries during the war years of 1939 to 1945 was completely different. There was no Jewish nation, as Israel was not yet in existence. Palestine, part of which was to become the site of a Jewish homeland in 1948, was controlled by the British. They refused to let Jews

come there to settle. Traditional anti-Semitism in German-occupied countries, as shown by frequent instances of collaboration and refusal to fight for and with Jews, proved to be obstacles for Jews willing to share in resistance efforts. Who then would aid the Jews, protect them, and give them weapons with which to fight?

- Deception and the "big lie" technique were used often by the Germans to mask their goal of genocide. Not wanting to publicize the truth about the camps, the Germans would state that the camps were merely labor camps, that life there would be more healthy and free than in crowded ghettos. Jews in western European countries were often told, for example, that they were going to be "resettled in farmland to the east." Whether or not such promises were truly believed, it is clear that they offered hope for something better than the wretched, deprived life of the ghettos. In addition, we must remember that most Jews in Europe were often isolated from contact with the rest of the world. The could only know what the Germans wanted them to know. Certainly, very few of them were aware of or could even imagine the horrors of the camps.

- Psychologically, human beings recoil from the unthinkable and the unknown. For Jews to believe that Germans, who were considered to be highly cultured and civilized, would now seek to kill off a whole people was difficult if not impossible to grasp. Most of those killed in the Holocaust could not conceive that innocent people would be murdered just because they were Jewish. For centuries, as we have seen, Jews faced persecution, Yet, they were able to survive, sometimes by making accommodations with the oppressors. Indeed, this may have been one reason for the actions of those who became Judenrat members in the ghettos and those who became kapos in the camps. Yet, even Judenrat leaders and kapos were eventually killed. The Nazis acted with a malicious mindset that produced far more terrible conditions for Jews than had ever existed previously.

Given all these factors, there were still several instances of resistance by Jews. These occurred in ghettos and camps and were both violent and spiritual. All of them were examples of bravery, courage, and heroism.

The Warsaw Ghetto Uprising, 1943

Of the many armed revolts by Jews against Germans, the most famous was in Warsaw, Poland. Sealed off from the rest of the city in 1940 by construction of an encircling wall, the Warsaw Ghetto became a terribly overcrowded area by 1941. Its peak population of 450,000 Jews in that year dwindled to 70,000 by April 1943. The drop was due primarily to the deportation of more than 300,000 Jews to the Treblinka death camp, where almost all were sent to the gas chambers. Countless other thousands had died in the ghetto itself, either from hunger, from the cold, from disease, or in massacres by the Germans and their collaborators. The final deportation of Jews was to begin on April 19, 1943. The date was significant for two reasons:

1. The evening of this day would mark the start of the Jewish holiday of Passover. The Nazis were aware of this and, fully knowing the dates of Jewish holidays, would often carry out sadistic and deadly actions at such times.
2. As April 20 was Hitler's birthday, SS head Himmler had hoped to present Hitler with a "birthday gift" on that day—an announcement that the Warsaw Ghetto was free of Jews and had been burned to the ground.

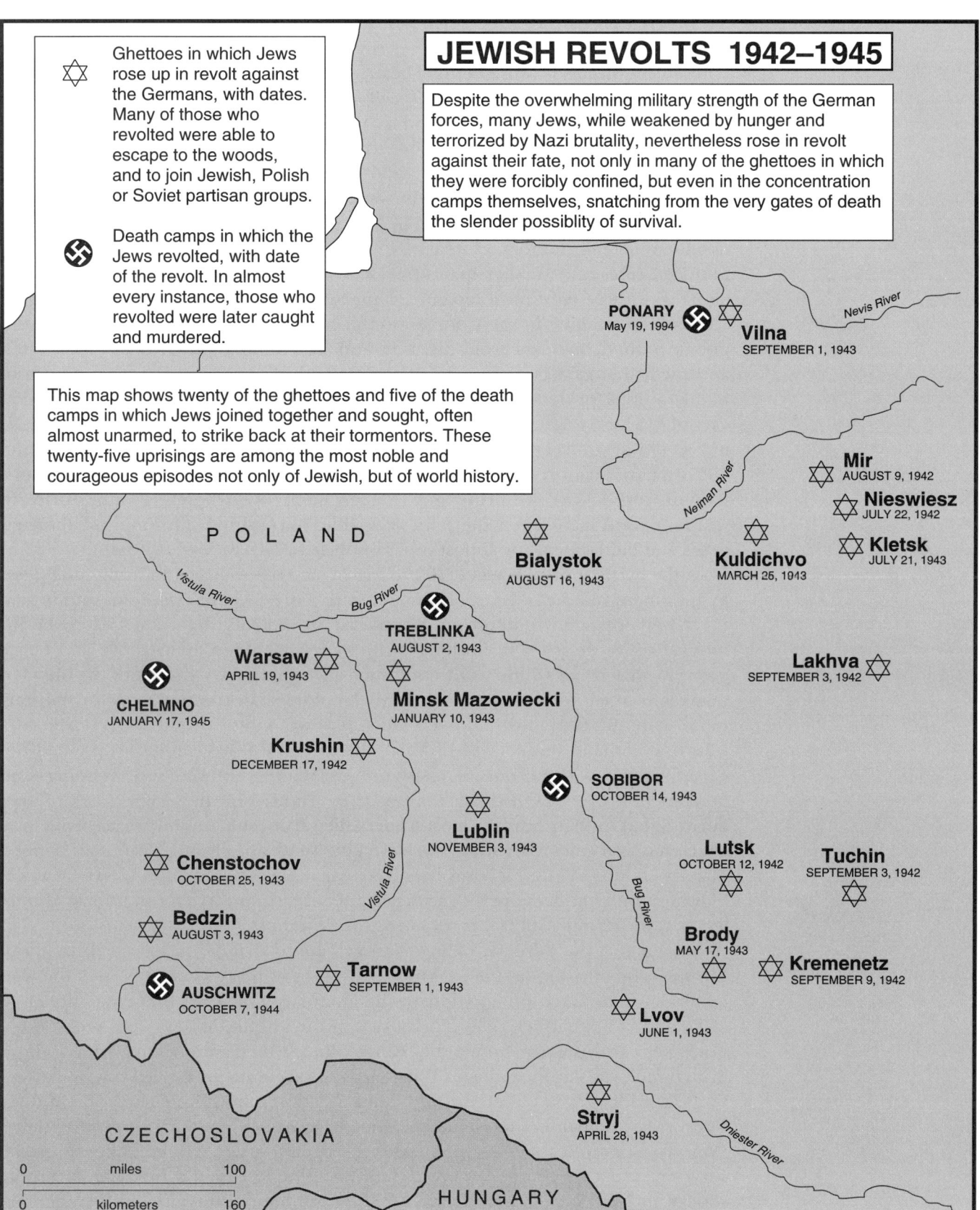

JEWISH REVOLTS 1942–1945

Despite the overwhelming military strength of the German forces, many Jews, while weakened by hunger and terrorized by Nazi brutality, nevertheless rose in revolt against their fate, not only in many of the ghettoes in which they were forcibly confined, but even in the concentration camps themselves, snatching from the very gates of death the slender possiblity of survival.

Ghettoes in which Jews rose up in revolt against the Germans, with dates. Many of those who revolted were able to escape to the woods, and to join Jewish, Polish or Soviet partisan groups.

Death camps in which the Jews revolted, with date of the revolt. In almost every instance, those who revolted were later caught and murdered.

This map shows twenty of the ghettoes and five of the death camps in which Jews joined together and sought, often almost unarmed, to strike back at their tormentors. These twenty-five uprisings are among the most noble and courageous episodes not only of Jewish, but of world history.

Nevis River

PONARY
May 19, 1994

Vilna
SEPTEMBER 1, 1943

Neiman River

POLAND

Vistula River

Bug River

Mir
AUGUST 9, 1942

Nieswiesz
JULY 22, 1942

Bialystok
AUGUST 16, 1943

Kuldichvo
MARCH 25, 1943

Kletsk
JULY 21, 1943

TREBLINKA
AUGUST 2, 1943

Lakhva
SEPTEMBER 3, 1942

Warsaw
APRIL 19, 1943

CHELMNO
JANUARY 17, 1945

Minsk Mazowiecki
JANUARY 10, 1943

Krushin
DECEMBER 17, 1942

SOBIBOR
OCTOBER 14, 1943

Vistula River

Lublin
NOVEMBER 3, 1943

Lutsk
OCTOBER 12, 1942

Tuchin
SEPTEMBER 3, 1942

Chenstochov
OCTOBER 25, 1943

Bug River

Brody
MAY 17, 1943

Kremenetz
SEPTEMBER 9, 1942

Bedzin
AUGUST 3, 1943

Tarnow
SEPTEMBER 1, 1943

AUSCHWITZ
OCTOBER 7, 1944

Lvov
JUNE 1, 1943

Stryj
APRIL 28, 1943

Dniester River

CZECHOSLOVAKIA

miles	100
0	
kilometers	160
0	

HUNGARY

However, Hitler did not receive any "gift" on his birthday. What he did receive was news about a violent and bloody struggle that broke out when German forces entered the streets of the ghetto. These forces were met with gunfire from members of the ZOB (*Zydowska Organizacja Bojowa*, Jewish Fighting Organization). Led by 23-year-old Mordechai Anielewicz, the ZOB killed six SS soldiers and six Ukrainian guards. Such action by armed Jews shocked SS General Jurgen Stroop—he was surprised to learn that "inferior people" could and would offer resistance to the "master race." He was also unaware that some sort of revolt against Germans had been planned by Jews for the past few months. The ZOB had obtained a small number of weapons from the Polish underground, almost one hundred rifles and smaller quantities of pistols, hand grenades, and explosives, along with three light machine guns. Numbering no more than 1,500 young men and women, ranging in age from ten to the early twenties, the Jewish fighters were poorly trained, suffered from diseases, and had limited amounts of food, water, and medicine. In a David vs. Goliath contest, they were up against thousands of highly trained professional soldiers from the strongest European armed force at the time. These soldiers were healthy and well-supplied and had access to modern means of warfare. These means, all of which were used against Jews in the ghetto, consisted of armored trucks, heavy machine guns, tanks, aircraft, artillery, flamethrowers, and chlorine gas. Facing such overwhelming superiority in weaponry and manpower, the Jews were able, astonishingly, to hold off the Germans and battle them for almost one month (April 19 to May 16, 1943).

As the battle for the Warsaw Ghetto was in an urban setting, fighting took place in apartment buildings, on rooftops and street corners, from windows, and in sewers, basements, and underground bunkers. Stroop found gas and fire to be his most effective weapons in flushing out Jews from hidden areas above and below ground. Nevertheless, the ZOB continued to inflict heavy casualties on the Germans and to capture weapons from fallen soldiers. In the first week of fighting, more than 150 Germans had been killed and wounded. Yet the ZOB leadership, with its command bunker at #18 Mila Street, realized that, militarily, it could not exist for long. With no outside assistance, decreasing ammunition, buildings and bunkers destroyed, ZOB resistance began to crumble in the second week of May. Surrounded in their bunker, most leaders died from suffocation by gas, while others committed suicide. A scant few were able to escape through infested, dangerous sewers out of the city and then to nearby forests. On May 16, 1943, upon blowing up the unoccupied Warsaw synagogue, Stroop was able to inform Himmler that the Warsaw Ghetto "is no longer in existence."

News about the heroism of the Warsaw Ghetto defenders spread throughout Europe. The uprising became a symbol of courage and resistance. It took the Germans almost as much time to destroy the ghetto as it took for them to conquer all of Poland in September 1939. The efforts of the ghetto fighters were recorded in notes kept by historian Emmanuel Ringelblum, which were found after 1945 in buried milk cans in the ruins of Warsaw. Other accounts of the fighting were kept by ZOB leaders Zivia Lubetkin and Vladka Meed. Along with her husband and fellow survivor Benjamin Meed, Vladka Meed became active after the war in WAGRO (Warsaw Ghetto Resistance Organization). Formed in the United States by ghetto survivors and their American-born children, WAGRO held a fifty-year memorial service in New York City in April 1993, to commemorate the ghetto rebellion. With Stroop and other SS officials in captivity after the war, this service is proof that, in the battle for the Warsaw Ghetto, David had ultimately defeated Goliath.

Uprisings in Other Ghettos

Armed resistance occurred in many other ghettos, notably in Bialystok (Poland) and Vilna (Lithuania). In 1943, Jews in both cities attacked Nazi forces. The attackers had little ammunition and were eventually defeated. Most were hunted down and killed. A few were able to escape to the forests, where they formed partisan units and continued to fight the Germans.

Uprisings in the Camps

It was much more difficult for Jews to offer armed resistance in the camps than was the case in the ghettos. As the ghettos were sections of cities, there was always the possibility of obtaining smuggled weapons and food, and of establishing some contact with local anti-German forces. The situation in the camps was much different, as these were usually built in the countryside and were completely cut off from the outside world. In addition, the frightening physical and emotional hardships in the camps made any coordinated resistance practically impossible. Yet, there were revolts in the camps. Three of these courageous episodes occurred in Treblinka, Sobibor, and Auschwitz:

1. *Treblinka:* On August 2, 1943, the Treblinka death camp witnessed fires, explosions, and gunfire that stunned the camp guards. Many of them were killed, as a rebellion planned by Jewish inmates became a reality. A much-feared camp, Treblinka had been the site where more than eight hundred thousand Jews had perished since its opening in June 1942. In the summer of 1943, however, among the deportees arriving here from all over Europe were several survivors from the Warsaw Ghetto. They brought with them news of the uprising there as well as some concealed weapons. Able to steal rifles, ammunition, grenades, gasoline, and knives, the Jews blew up buildings and attacked guards on a planned signal at 3:45 P.M. Fierce fighting resulted in many Jewish and German deaths. While almost two hundred Jews escaped from the camp, several others were hanged by the Germans after the revolt was eventually put down. Later in the year, the camp was closed.

2. *Sobibor:* On October 16, 1943, the Sobibor death camp was dismantled on orders from Himmler. Two days earlier, on October 14, 1943, Jewish prisoners had staged a revolt that took the lives of several Nazi officers. Armed with hatchets and a few guns, they initially overpowered the camp guards. Four hundred were able to run out of the camp and head for the woods. Yet, almost half of these were killed in a minefield surrounding the camp. Sobibor was then closed, and the SS feared that the camp's secrecy would be exposed by the escapees.

3. *Auschwitz:* On October 7, 1944, a daring event occurred in Auschwitz. A revolt was begun by a Sonderkommando unit of Jewish prisoners. Working in Crematorium IV, where bodies from the gas chambers were to be burned, they turned on the SS guards, throwing one of them into the flames while killing four others. As part of their plan, they then blew up the crematorium and ran for the camp fence. About six hundred actually broke out of the camp but were soon caught and shot. Two days later, four women were charged with smuggling explosives to the Sonderkommando unit. They were horribly tortured and then hanged in front of some inmates. The destroyed structure was never rebuilt, although the three remaining crematoria in the

camp continued to function. Soon thereafter, on November 24, 1944, Himmler ordered the destruction of all the Auschwitz creamatoria and gas chambers in an attempt to hide evidence of the death camp.

Spiritual Resistance

The resistance efforts just described were aimed at violently hurting the Nazi oppressors and their collaborators, escaping from them, and rescuing other Jews. Another form of resistance, not using armed weapons, sought to preserve a sense of human dignity and identity. We may describe this form as *spiritual resistance*. Amidst environments of isolation, deprivation, and death imposed by the Germans, conditions under which human beings could not live or exist, Jews nevertheless found many ways to express this powerful manner of fighting back and maintaining their cultural heritage. This was true in both the ghettos and the camps.

In ghettos such as those of Warsaw and Vilna, examples of underground and illegal activities were as follows: self-help organizations to aid the weak and the poor; secret gatherings to recite prayers, hold religious services, and observe religious holidays; schools that taught both secular and religious subjects; poetry readings, dramatic presentations, and art exhibits; lectures and concerts; libraries, study groups, and various publications. One of the most important publications in Warsaw was organized by the historian Emmanuel Ringelblum. Under the code name *Oneg Shabbat* (Pleasure of the Sabbath), its aim was to compile documentation about Jewish life in the ghetto under German occupation. These documents included diaries, posters, announcements, photographs, jokes, and other material gathered by a large staff, hidden in crates, and discovered after World War II.

Writers in the ghettos of Bialystok, Lodz, and Vilna also put together materials to portray Jewish survival. To document a record of hardship, heroism, and daily life for the sake of history and future generations was an inspiration for Jews throughout eastern Europe in both the ghettos and the camps. If nothing else, a diary was a desire of the will to live, a willingness to bear witness and present testimony, and even to seek a form of immortality. Uncertain whether they would survive Nazi cruelty, diary writers looked to the future. They hoped that their words would tell humanity how dreadful were their experiences, trusting that nothing like these experiences would happen to anyone ever again.

To the extent that the ghetto Jews were able to maintain their culture in the ways described above, historian Lucy Dawidowicz, writing in 1975, claimed that "they triumphed over the Germans." She also noted that "the strategy of the . . . leadership in the . . . welfare, religious, educational and cultural groupings was to hold back the tide of barbarism and create islands of civilization, normality and decency. Operating under terror, amid hunger and disease, they succeeded in helping those they reached to retain and enrich their humanity."

In the camps, where it was obviously impossible to do what was done in the ghettos, spiritual resistance was evident, nevertheless. Each day of survival in a place like Auschwitz, just by washing one's hands and doing the simplest of things, was an act of resistance. If anything, it signified a way of holding back the Nazi genocide. Some prisoners attempted acts of sabotage by, for example, tearing up clothes in the Brezhinka and placing sand in machinery they were forced to work on for the German war effort. Preserving religious faith and traditions in any way possible was another means of opposing the dehumanization process in the camps. Examples, always done secretly and at great risk, were as follows:

- Inmates reciting portions of the Bible to each other.
- Writing down or scratching on discarded scraps of paper stories about Jewish heroes and procedures for observing holidays.
- Staging mock religious services and whispering the spoken parts for events such as the Passover Seder.
- Teaching songs and prayers.

Frequently, according to German documents captured after the war, Jews prayed, sang, and comforted each other in the gas chambers. Mothers were known to calm their children, to smile at them and speak softly. Many Nazi officials were surprised at how such "inferior people" could die with dignity.

Januscz Korczak   One of countless acts of spiritual resistance, attempting to maintain some dignity and delay news of the inevitable, involved Dr. Januscz Korczak. A famous Jewish pediatrician in Warsaw, he was the founder and director of an orphanage for very young Jewish children in the ghetto. His care and love for these children was boundless. This was probably why, at the age of sixty-four, he accompanied them when they were ordered by the Germans, in August 1942, to leave the orphanage for the Umschlagplatz (the central train station in Warsaw). Even though, as a physician, he could have been exempt from this deportation order, Korczak chose to stay with "his" children. He did not tell them the truth about the journey they were to take. Rather, he had them dress up in their best clothes and told them they were going to enjoy a day of sunshine in some open, green fields.

What an astonishing sight this was to see, amidst the ugliness and misery of German-occupied Warsaw—an orderly march of two hundred small boys and girls, led by an old man carrying a sick child! One eyewitness noted that the children were

> . . . *emaciated, weak, shriveled and shrunk. They carry shabby packages, some have schoolbooks, notebooks under their arms. No one is crying. Their little eyes are turned toward the doctor. They are strangely calm; they feel almost well. The doctor is going with them, so what do they have to be afraid of? They are not alone, they are not abandoned.*
>
> *Dr. Korczak busies himself with the children . . . He buttons the coat of one child, ties up the package of another, or straightens the cap of a third.*

At the Umschlagplatz, another observer sadly watched the children remove their yellow stars as ordered. He remarked that the procession was like a "field of buttercups." The children were last seen boarding the train with Dr. Korczak. From the Umschlagplatz, as would be true for hundreds of thousands of Jews, they went on to Treblinka, to face death in the gas chambers.

Did Januscz Korczak act wisely? Is *spiritual resistance* an accurate term to describe what he did? Should he have told the children the truth? What would you have said to a child, younger than yourself, in such a situation? And further, on another day when a deportation was carried out, what should a mother and father have told their little son when he asked this question: "Why does Hitler hate me when he doesn't even know me?"

The agony of trying to answer these questions makes us more sensitive, today, about the horrors associated with the Holocaust. But we must also ask how sensitive was the world itself, from 1933 to 1945, when these horrors were being perpetrated against the Jews of Europe. The possible answers, neither easy nor satisfying, await us below.

World Reaction to the Holocaust

In the 1980s, the world learned about mass killings occurring in Cambodia (formerly Kampuchea), believed what it learned, and tried to end the bloodshed. In the 1990s, the world learned about mass killings in the former Yugoslavia, believed what it learned, and tried to end the bloodshed. In the 1940s, the world learned about the mass killings of Jews, hesitated to believe initially what it learned, and did nothing to end the bloodshed. And even when convinced that the reported slaughter of innocent millions was true, the world still failed to take strong action. Recognition of its failure in the dark days of the 1940s may explain why the world was willing to do something about the mass murders of the 1980s and 1990s.

Reports about the worst of the Nazi atrocities began to leak out from Germany and German-controlled lands in 1941 but were not fully accepted until 1942. On December 18, 1942, the *New York Times* carried a story about a joint declaration by eleven nations fighting Hitler in which they acknowledged and condemned his "bestial policy of cold-blooded extermination" of "the Jewish people in Europe." Among those signing the declaration were the United States, Britain, France, Greece, and Russia. Their willingness to issue this declaration was based upon information from several sources. Three of these were as follows:

1. Published articles in London newspapers of a report received from Polish Jews describing the death of seven hundred thousand people.
2. A meeting of American Jewish leaders with President Franklin D. Roosevelt, called after the U.S. State Department confirmed the truth of a telegram sent to these leaders by Gerhard Riegner. Riegner, a German Jew living in Switzerland, wrote about the "final solution," having heard about it from other Jews and from a German citizen.
3. Reports and testimony delivered personally to President Roosevelt and to British Foreign Minister Anthony Eden by Jan Karski. Karski was a member of the Polish underground who had witnessed mass murders in the Belzec death camp.

From 1942 onward, newspapers around the world printed stories about the killings. On March 1, 1943, in New York City's Madison Square Garden, a "Stop Hitler Now" rally was held. Among the speakers addressing an overflow crowd were New York Governor Thomas E. Dewey, Mayor Fiorello LaGuardia, Supreme Court Justice William O. Douglas, and several Jewish and Christian clergymen. A program was announced calling on the Allied nations to negotiate for the release of Jews, to send food to the ghettos and camps, to accept Jewish refugees, and to punish German leaders after the war. This New York rally and program, along with similar ones, had little effect in provoking Allied action nor in reducing German activities. Indeed, no help was given in April and May of 1943 as Jews battled in the Warsaw Ghetto and as deportations continued from all over Europe. In 1944, the War Refugee Board was created by President Roosevelt, for the purpose of negotiating for the rescue of Jews and other victims of Nazi persecution. However, it was established too late and with such limited powers that it was unable to accomplish very much. It was in 1944, also, that Allied pilots took photographs of Auschwitz and the rail lines leading into it. Yet, no attempt was made to drop bombs on the crematoria nor on the rail lines.

Why didn't the Allies mount any specific military action to stop the Nazi persecutions and mass killings between 1942 and 1945? Clearly, as we have seen, increasing evidence had led to increased awareness. In the Allied nations, Jews and others had requested that bombing raids be made. And in July 1944, British Prime Minister Winston Churchill himself labeled the Holocaust as "probably the greatest and most horrible single crime ever committed in the whole history of the world." The failure by the Allies to take any collective military action is generally explained by one or more of the following reasons:

- Many people felt that the best way to rescue the Jews and stop the mass killings was to win the war against the Germans. Accordingly, it would be more advantageous to use weapons and manpower against military targets than to destroy camps and railroad lines.
- Some government officials who learned of the atrocities simply refused to believe that such inhuman acts took place. Many ordinary private citizens, both Jewish and non-Jewish, initially refused to accept as true the reports of massacres and other beastly crimes.
- There were officials who, because of their own prejudice toward Jews, held back information and refused to take any action.
- The Nazis were fairly successful in practicing both delay and deception. From time to time, for example, the Gestapo would fake a willingness to enter into negotiations to save Jews. Meanwhile, the murders would continue. Nazi propaganda, rather than make any mention of gas chambers, would point out the benefits for Jews of being transported from grimy ghettos to camps "in the countryside." The camp at Theresienstadt (also known as *Terezin*) in Czechoslovakia was set up as a "model showcase," where newsreels and pictures were made by the Nazis to show Jews living freely and eating well. Invited visitors from such groups as the International Red Cross were able to observe pleasant scenes, without ever realizing or being told that the camp was built as a deception and as a stopover for inmates on their way to Auschwitz.

These Nazi "successes" should not, however, excuse the failures of the Allies. Those failures, as summarized by historian Martin Gilbert in his book *Auschwitz and the Allies*, "were those of imagination, of response, of intelligence, of piecing together and evaluating what was known, of coordination, of initiative, and even at times of sympathy."

Denmark, Sweden, and Raoul Wallenberg

Two nations that did take specific measures to show solidarity with Jews, by making heroic rescue efforts, were Denmark and Sweden. Having occupied Denmark since 1940, the Germans decided to send the small number of Danish Jews to Auschwitz in September 1943. SS troops had to be sent from Germany to arrange this, because the Danish police, armed forces, and King Christian X, refused to cooperate with the Germans and become collaborators. The Wehrmacht commander in Denmark also refused to cooperate, claiming that rounding up Jews was not a military matter.

With the roundup scheduled for October 1943, the Danes made a secret agreement with neighboring Sweden for the transfer of Jews. Sweden promised to give *sanctuary* (a safe place) to Danish Jewish refugees. In what was to become one of the most extraordinary rescues in history, the Danes helped more than seven thousand Jews to escape secretly over the 15-mile waterway separating their nation from Sweden. Danish people from all walks of life hid Jews in their homes, drove them to coastal areas, posted lookouts to watch for Germans, provided stimulants to keep people awake, and smuggled them into all kinds of fishing boats and pleasure craft for the trip to Sweden. After the war, the Danes welcomed back their former fellow citizens.

As a neutral country in World War II, Sweden could offer refuge to anyone claiming Swedish citizenship. One of its diplomats in German-occupied Hungary was Raoul Wallenberg. From 1944 to 1945, he worked brilliantly and courageously to place thousands of Jews under Swedish government authority in order to protect them from both the Nazis and their Hungarian collaborators. His main method was to issue "protective passports," certificates containing the Swedish embassy stamp and his signature. He had given out twenty thousand passports by January 1945 and had at times handed them directly to Jews who were about to be transported to Auschwitz. In addition, he was known to bring food and medicine at night to needy people. Wallenberg's efforts were truly humanitarian, having saved so many people from the gas chambers. Yet when Hungary was freed of German occupation by the Russians in 1945, he was taken prisoner by them for unknown reasons and never seen again.

The Role of the Churches

Another person helpful to some Hungarian Jews was the Budapest representative of the pope, Angelo Roncalli. Roncalli, who later became Pope John XXIII, was one of the countless Christian clergymen who provided assistance to entrapped Jews. Nevertheless, the general attitudes of the Churches in Europe (Catholic, Protestant, and Orthodox) to the plight of the Jews were varied and complex. Pope Pius XI, the Catholic leader at the time of Hitler's rise to power, wrote that myths of "race" and "blood" were contrary to Christian teaching. However, he neither mentioned nor criticized anti-Semitism. He was succeeded in 1939 by Pius XII, who learned by 1942 of the murders in the camps and elsewhere. His public statements, though, were limited to expressions of sympathy for sufferers of injustice and pleas for humane conduct of the war. Although Jewish leaders did not get from the Pope a requested specific condemnation of Nazi anti-Semitism, the Jews of Rome did gain refuge in Vatican buildings during the Nazi occupation of the city. Some historians felt that the Pope's public silence was a sign of anti-Semitism within the Church. Others claim that his silence was due to a genuine fear that, if he spoke out, European Catholics might themselves be subjected to a "final solution."

The Catholic Church in Germany did little to oppose Nazi anti-Semitism and was alleged to have given documents to authorities in order to detect people of Jewish origin. One of the very few clergymen to denounce the mass murders of Jews was Bernard Lichtenberg. Throughout western Europe, Catholic clergy often spoke out against persecution of Jews and aided in rescue work. Indeed, many convents and monasteries protected young Jewish children by converting them temporarily to Catholicism. In eastern Europe, however, Catholic officials were less willing to take a strong public stance and in some cases actually cooperated with the Germans.

Orthodox leaders in some eastern European nations were more responsive, heeding the pronouncement by the **Patriarch** of Constantinople. He urged his bishops to help Jews and to proclaim in their churches that to conceal Jews was a sacred duty.

The response by Protestant churches was generally mixed. In many German Protestant congregations, there were Nazi supporters who acquiesced in anti-Jewish legislation and other measures. Rarely did any church protest against the persecution. Christians who had converted from Judaism were excluded from some churches but were protected by others. Within German-occupied nations, the position of Protestant communities varied. In Denmark, France, Holland, and Norway, there were examples of local churches and individual clergymen issuing public protests when deportations of Jews started. Few such protests were made in Austria, Belgium, Finland, Poland, and the Soviet Union.

When people began to realize the horrors the Jews were subjected to, many risked their own lives to rescue them. Jewish children were often concealed by Christian families, who raised them as Catholics. The X marks a Jewish altar boy.

Christian Rescuers—the "Righteous Among the Nations"

Christians who sought to help Jews during the Holocaust did so at great risk. Their efforts took several forms, such as smuggling weapons, arranging hiding places, and organizing rescues. They acted for reasons of friendliness, compassion, and their view of humane Christian teachings about helping those in need. For their actions, such individuals were honored by the state of Israel with the title "righteous among the nations." Their names and deeds are documented in the major Holocaust study center in Israel, the Yad Vashem Martyrs' and Heroes' Memorial Museum. Some of those so honored were the following:

- In France, Mother Maria of Paris produced false identification papers in her convent. She organized an underground network of Orthodox and Catholic clergy who gave shelter to Jews and smuggled many out of Paris. She was subsequently arrested and sent to die in a gas chamber.
- Near Vilna, Lithuania, Benedictine nuns were able to smuggle guns and knives into the ghetto. On occasion, they were even able to dress up men in nuns' habit and have them pass out of the ghetto under the eyes of the unsuspecting Germans.
- In the French town of Le Chambon sur-Lignon, Magda Trocmé and her husband, Protestant minister Andre Trocmé, arranged to hide adults and children. They persuaded the entire town to help these Jews evade the Germans.
- In Amsterdam, Dutch Christians Jan and Miep Gies hid Jews in an attic. Among those in hiding there from 1942 to 1944 were Otto Frank and his family. A young girl in this family, Anne Frank, kept a daily account of her life. Although she was eventually arrested and sent to a concentration camp where she died, her account was published after the war and became internationally famous, with the title *The Diary of a Young Girl.*

- In Germany itself, one of the very few Protestant clergymen who eventually protested against the Nazis was Pastor Martin Niemoller. He was arrested and sent to several concentration camps. Somehow, he was able to survive. After the war, he made a revealing statement that shows the danger of apathy (not caring):

> *First they came for the Jews. I was silent. I was not a Jew. Then they came for the Communists. I was silent. I was not a Communist. Then they came for the trade unionists. I was silent. I was not a trade unionist. Then they came for me. There was no one left to speak for me.*

The efforts of these people, as well as those of Raoul Wallenberg, the Danes, the Swedes, and others, were noble and courageous. Yet, such efforts were isolated ones, and far too few. The sad fact is that these efforts saved, at most, only a few thousand Jewish lives. The Nazis took six million.

Dit is een foto, zoals
ik me zou wensen,
altijd zo te zijn.
Dan had ik nog wel
een kans om naar
Holywood te komen.
Annefrank.
10 Oct. 1942

(translation)
"This is a photo as I would wish myself to look all the time. Then I would maybe have a chance to come to Hollywood."
Anne Frank, 10 Oct. 1942

The Diary of Anne Frank is a true, bittersweet story of a young Jewish girl's years in hiding before she was sent to the concentration camp, Bergen-Belsen. She died there two months before Holland was liberated.

The Holocaust Ends—Defeat of Nazi Germany in 1945

By early 1945, it was clear that the Allied forces were going to defeat the Germans and that the war in Europe would soon end. The horrors of the camps would also come to an end. As the Russians pushed closer on Germany's eastern front, they liberated (freed) the camp at Maidanek in July 1944 and reached Auschwitz the following February. The Germans had already fled, having blown up several crematoria and gas chambers. The destruction had been ordered by Himmler, in an attempt to wipe out evidence of Nazi atrocities. The effects of the atrocities were nevertheless obvious to the Russians, as they initially found hundreds of corpses and eight thousand weak and emaciated survivors. In the main camp alone, there were two hundred starving children your age and younger. The Russian army gave little aid to these survivors, mostly because its chief goal was to reach Berlin.

The Death Marches

Three weeks prior to the Russian discoveries at Auschwitz, the Germans burned thousands of bodies, organized forced marches of more than sixty-five thousand prisoners out of the camp, and shot hundreds who were too sick and lame to walk. The forced movement of prisoners westward toward Germany became rightly known as the "death marches." Long columns of Jews and others were herded through snow and freezing weather, subject to humiliation and beating by the guards. Those inmates who were unable to keep up were either shot or left to die along the way. The fact that the Nazis continued to murder Jews, even when it was certain that the Allies were going to win the war, is further evidence of their inexplicable malice.

American and British forces attacking Germany's western front were able to liberate several camps. When they came to places such as Buchenwald and Bergen-Belsen in April 1945, however, they were completely unprepared for what they saw. To view unburied corpses and skeletonlike survivors amidst a horrible stench was enough to cause physical and mental disorders among the Allied soldiers. Inmates had to be disinfected and "deloused"; they were unable to digest normal food, having suffered from malnourishment for months, if not years. The American general, Dwight D. Eisenhower, commander of the Allied forces in Europe, was accompanied by U.S. generals George Patton and Omar Bradley on an inspection of the Ohrduf camp in May 1945. They were shocked to find corpses of Jewish inmates scattered throughout the camp. German citizens who lived near camps such as Dachau and Buchenwald, and who claimed to be ignorant of what went on in the camps, were forced to march through them by the Allies, and on occasion to bury corpses.

The Surviving Remnant

Approximately two-thirds of Europe's Jews died during the Holocaust. The remaining one-third, many of whom were barely alive in 1945, became known as the "surviving remnant." Their immediate future did not look promising. Some had fled the camps as the Germans themselves fled the Allies; others were found in the camps as well as in cities and the countryside. Countless numbers had lost family, property, and homes. Where were they to go? What would happen to them? Some sought to return to their birthplaces. The majority were relocated in displaced persons camps (DP camps) set up by the Allies. Some of these survivors, unable or unwilling to return to their homelands, stayed in DP camps as refugees for up to four years. Some were able to realize their wish of migrating to Palestine, part of which became Israel in 1948, or to the United States.

The world's response to the surviving remnant was mixed. Although the German armies had surrendered on May 8, 1945, anti-Semitism in some parts of eastern Europe did not cease in the ensuing months and years. Its existence posed a threat to the already decimated Jewish communities there. The worst example occurred in July 1945 in Kielce, Poland, where a pogrom took the lives of forty-two Jews. The fear prompted by this and similar incidents can explain why many survivors from eastern European lands such as Poland, Romania, and Lithuania refused to return and why some who were there now tried to leave. In many instances, returning Jews were not allowed to regain their homes and businesses. The situation for survivors from western Europe wishing to return and get on with their lives was somewhat brighter. A heartwarming welcome, for example, was given in Denmark. All remaining possessions were given back to returning Danish Jews. Countless survivors who reestablished themselves in France and Holland, as well as those who entered the United States, led distinguished lives and enriched their communities. Yet, even for them, and certainly for those survivors unable to resume normal lives, the horrors of their past could not be forgotten.

The Death Toll

The greatest and most unspeakable horror of that past—the twelve years from 1933 to 1945—was the intentional murder of more than six million innocent people simply because they were Jewish. The approximate numbers of those killed, along with the percentage of the prewar Jewish population they represent are as follows:

JEWISH DEATH TOLL IN THE HOLOCAUST

Austria	40,000	20%	Hungary	200,000	50%
Belgium	40,000	67%	Italy	8,000	16%
Czechoslovakia	315,000	88%	Latvia	80,000	84%
Denmark	500	8%	Lithuania	217,000	97%
Estonia	1,500	33%	Luxembourg	700	23%
Finland	8	1%	Norway	760	42%
France	90,000	30%	Poland	2,850,000	88%
Germany	170,000	32%	Romania	425,000	50%
Greece	60,000	80%	Soviet Union	1,252,000	44%
Holland	105,000	75%	Yugoslavia	60,000	80%

Source: Figures are from "36 Questions Asked About the Holocaust" (Simon Wiesenthal Center, New York, 1979), 1.

These numbers stagger the imagination. Even to contemplate the figure of six million is bewildering. It is likely that the greatest number of people you have ever seen together was at a sports complex. Some baseball stadiums and football arenas in the United States can hold a hundred thousand people. It would take sixty of them to hold every person who died in the Holocaust!

Further examination of these numbers reveals additional shocking conclusions. Almost one and one-half million of the dead were children. Thus, almost an entire generation had been destroyed. And at the other end of the life spectrum, it has been estimated that almost no one over the age of thirty-five had survived the Holocaust. The continued existence of European Jewry over the previous two thousand years had suffered a terrible blow. This can be seen in the following statistics, showing the number of Jews in Europe in a particular year and the percentage that number represented of all Jews in the world at the time:

JEWISH WORLD POPULATION

Year	Number of Jews	Percentage
1840	3,950,000	88%
1900	8,900,000	81%
1939	9,500,000	57%
1946	2,850,000	26%

Source: Figures are from Y. Gutman and C. Schaztker, "The Holocaust and Its Significance" (The Zalman Shazar Center, Jerusalem, 1983), 228.

With such a loss of life, European Jewish culture faced an uncertain future. Did this mean that the "final solution" was a success?

The Nuremberg War Crimes Trials, 1945–1949

What should be done with those Germans who were responsible for planning and carrying out the "final solution?" This became a challenging question in November 1945, when twenty-two high-ranking Nazi officials went on trial in the city of Nuremberg before an international military tribunal (a court with judges from the four major Allied victors—the United States, Great Britain, France, and the Soviet Union). Several charges were brought against them, including committing war crimes and committing crimes against humanity. This last charge was the only one that had some connection with the attempted genocide against the Jews of Europe. Yet, the killing of Jews only because they were Jews was not considered a crime. Rather, the charge of crimes against humanity was applied specifically to acts of violence committed against civilians of occupied nations—for example, Hungarians, French, Russians, and Poles. However, evidence of genocide was presented to the judges. It consisted of oral testimony, documents, films, and photographs. Some of it consisted of such horrible material that one British official considered the material too terrible to present to the judges. Nevertheless, its presentation was vital in making the world aware of how inhuman were the Nazi actions against Jews and many other people.

The accused Nazis were allowed to hire lawyers and to defend themselves, privileges they had never granted to those they had once accused and victimized. Hermann Göring (Hitler's closest aide and head of the German air force), Hans Frank (governor-general of Nazi-occupied Poland), and the other Nuremberg defendants raised several issues in their defense. They knew they could not claim that the Holocaust never happened, and there was too much evidence to prove that it did occur. Yet, two of their issues were pressed strongly upon the judges in an attempt to support their claim of innocence:

1. One issue was that they were "just following orders." The tribunal rejected this by stating that duty to such basic human laws and laws against murder, enslavement, and extermination take priority over any obedience to nation or government.

Simon Wiesenthal

If you met him on the street, you would probably pass him by without a glance. There was nothing about him that made him stand out in a crowd. If you began a conversation with him, he would respond with traces of a European accent in a voice filled with sadness and determination. It would be difficult to figure this man out.

Simon Wiesenthal was born in 1908 in what is now Russia. Deciding to become an architect, he attended the university in Prague, Czechoslovakia, and after graduation opened a business in today's Lvov, Poland. When the Soviet army invaded in 1939, he was forced to close his business and was arrested. The penalty for owning a business, according to the Soviet secret police, was to be sent to a forced labor camp in Siberia. However, by bribing a member of the police, he was able to escape being consigned to that frozen wasteland.

When Germany attacked the Soviets in 1941, Wiesenthal found himself in a forced labor group. He was sent to one camp, his wife to another. During the war, he was transferred from one concentration camp to another, one forced labor group to another. When the war ended, he and his wife were reunited. Together they had lost eighty-nine members of their families in the horrors of the Holocaust.

The question then facing Wiesenthal was whether to go back to his old occupation of architect. He found, however, that he was unable to forget the horrors of the camps and to return to a previous life as if nothing had happened. Instead, he decided to dedicate himself to tracking down and arresting Nazis that had escaped into hiding. This search would be in the spirit of justice, not vengeance. He knew there were many ex-Nazis that had "vanished" during the chaos after World War II. Because there were so many refugees and displaced persons, these criminals were able to change their identities and vanish into anonymity. The governments of West Germany, the United States, and the Soviet Union had joined in a search for them. Later, when Israel became a nation, it too would enter the hunt for these war criminals.

Wiesenthal began by helping the U.S. army gather evidence with which to prosecute the Nazis. At the same time, in Linz, Austria, he and a staff of thirty volunteers opened a center to help Jewish refugees and to find evidence for war crimes trials.

In 1954, with the closing of the Linz office, the files were sent to Israel for safekeeping. Meanwhile, information came to Wiesenthal that one of the greatest war criminals, Adolf Eichmann, was alive and living in Argentina. It seems that a number of ex-Nazis had been able to obtain false papers and had moved to South America. Eichmann had been a key figure in the horrible "final solution." Wiesenthal gave the information to the Israeli government, which formed a team to capture Eichmann. They knew that going through official channels would probably be useless, so they captured him instead and smuggled him into Israel. There he was placed on trial and his crimes were exposed to the world. He was found guilty and executed according to the law.

In 1961 Wiesenthal opened the Jewish Documentation Center in Vienna in order to continue seeking out ex-Gestapo agents, SS officers, and other Nazis for trial. In 1967 he was responsible for locating Fritz Stangl, the former commandant of the Treblinka and Sobibor death camps.

More than eleven hundred Nazi war criminals have been captured and brought to justice because of this man who just couldn't forget. The Simon Wiesenthal Center for Holocaust Studies, in Los Angeles, still continues the work of exposing prejudice and anti-Semitism.

2. Another issue raised by the defense rested upon the *Führer-prinzip* (the Nazi "leadership principal"). This theory held that, since all commands were ordered by Hitler as a dictator and refusal to obey them would be punished by death, therefore only Hitler could be held responsible and all other Nazis were innocent of any wrongdoing. The Nuremberg judges rejected this contention, noting that individuals are responsible for their actions and that ordered acts of brutality and torture cannot be excused, as such acts violate the international law of war.

In October 1946, the court gave its verdict. Of the twenty-two defendants, nineteen were found guilty, three were acquitted. Twelve were sentenced to hang and seven received varied prison sentences ranging from ten years to life. There were many other trials of Nazi officials, held in Nuremberg as well as in the different parts of Germany under Allied occupation and in countries where war crimes and civilian atrocities were committed. Placed on trial were those Germans, and their collaborators, responsible for conducting medical experiments and for administering and carrying out evil acts in the death camps, concentration camps, and ghettos.

Recent Events

Although the specific events of the Holocaust ended in 1945, their consequences continue right up to our own time. This fact can be seen in several issues that still haunt the world, in lessons to be learned, and in attempts at remembering this era. Let us consider some examples that have occurred within the past ten years.

- *The Trial of John Demjanjuk:* As an immigrant to the United States after the war, John Demjanjuk had lied about his background as a death camp guard in Poland. Because this action violated American law, Demjanjuk was stripped of his U.S. citizenship in 1981 and sent to Israel to stand trial. In 1988, he was tried, convicted, and sentenced to die for murders in Sobibor and Treblinka. In 1993, however, the Israeli Supreme Court reversed his conviction.

- *"Ethnic Cleansing" in the Former Yugoslavia:* In 1992 up to 1995, Serbian forces in the former Yugoslavia murdered or imprisoned thousands of Muslim civilians in Bosnia. (See Chapter 36, "The Collapse of Communism in the Soviet Union and Eastern Europe.") The Serbs also sought to drive Muslims away and thus expand Serbian territory. Such actions directed against a specific **ethnic group** rekindled sad memories of the Holocaust.

- *Neo-Nazism and Anti-Foreigner Violence in Germany:* The early 1990s have witnessed a small but alarming increase of young Germans joining movements that hold views similar to those of the disbanded Nazi party. Many of these young people were unemployed and were known as "skinheads," based upon their shaved heads. These movements have been responsible for acts of violence, including murder, against Turks and other foreigners of European origin living in Germany. The German government has now banned neo-Nazi parties and has condemned the anti-foreigner violence. The government's actions appear to have the support of a majority of Germany's population. In January 1993, in marking the sixtieth anniversary of Hitler's rise to power, thousands of Germans stopped working for 15 minutes to commemorate the date and to protest against neo-Nazi violence.

- *Germany Agrees to Finance Auschwitz Restoration and to Compensate Holocaust Survivors:* In late 1992, the German government said that it would provide $6 million to restore the Auschwitz death camp and to preserve it as a memorial site. The government also signed an agreement to pay compensation to Holocaust survivors who previously had received little or nothing from the government.
- *France Creates a National Day of Remembrance:* In February 1993, French President François Mitterand signed a decree that established a national day of remembrance to recall the anti-Semitic crimes carried out by the Vichy collaborationist regime and the occupying German forces between 1940 and 1944. The date chosen was July 16, as it was on this date in 1942 that the first of several mass arrests of Jews was made by French police officers. Thousands of those arrested were eventually deported to German death camps through Europe.
- *Opening of the U.S. Holocaust Memorial Museum in Washington, D.C.:* On April 26, 1993, this museum was formally opened and dedicated in our nation's capital. The collection of historical items here includes a railroad car that transported Jews to Auschwitz, as well as empty canisters of Zyklon B poison gas. At the dedication were President Bill Clinton, many world leaders, and thousands of Holocaust survivors. In his remarks, President Clinton noted that "the Holocaust reminds us forever that knowledge divorced from values can only serve to deepen the human nightmare, that a head without a heart is not humanity." He also praised Resistance fighters, Allied soldiers, and private individuals who "manned the line of righteousness, who risked and lost their lives to save others."
- *Showing of the Holocaust Movie* Schindler's List: In 1993, *Schindler's List* opened in theaters across the United States. It told how Oskar Schindler, a German Christian factory owner tried to protect Jews in Poland from the Nazis. It received favorable reviews and won an Academy Award for best picture in 1994.

Summary

The official actions taken by France and the United States (national day of remembrance and establishment of Holocaust Museum) serve as powerful reminders of one of the worst instances in history of man's inhumanity to man. Such thoughts and remembrances about the Holocaust will also lead us to bear in mind the tragedies suffered by other groups of people because of prejudice. Examples include the racism against blacks in South Africa and during slavery in the United States, and the attempted genocide committed by the Turks against Armenians. There are lessons to be learned, with implications for all of us, from remembering and studying bias-related actions against any ethnic or racial group of people. Knowledge of the Holocaust makes very vivid these lessons and their consequences.
- Dehumanization: *To reduce any group to something less than human is to consider them unworthy of respect and, ultimately, unworthy of life itself. Isn't this what happened in the gas chambers?*
- Apathy: *Not caring about the persecution of others will encourage the tormentors and can destroy hope in the persecuted. It can also affect one's own*

sense of morality and guilt. Finally, its full meaning becomes frightfully clear when those who are apathetic find themselves to be targets of persecution and have no one to lift a helping hand or raise a voice in protest. The story of Pastor Martin Niemoller comes to mind.

- **Individual Responsibility:** *People must think about the consequences and results of their actions. Otherwise, they are responsible for what may come to pass. Nazi desk clerks who arranged for Jews to be crowded in transports as well as scientists who manufactured Zyklon B gas are not free of guilt for the deaths in the camps.*

- **Wrongful Use of Science and Technology:** *Advances in knowledge about the natural world and in the ability to control it have the potential for good as well as evil. Germany was well-known, prior to the Holocaust, for its scientific and industrial achievements. Yet, scientists and industrial concerns abused their talents by seeking to destroy life instead of trying to preserve it.*

- **Individual Courage:** *The willingness of some non-Jews to act as rescuers has much to tell us. Their actions, amidst severe dangers, showed their ethical priority in putting human life ahead of concerns about status, personal safety, profit, and submission to wrongful authority. Recent research on such people revealed that they shared a spirit of independence, as well as empathy, compassion, and an intolerance for injustice.*

The history and lessons of the Holocaust are instructive. The uniqueness of this man-made tragedy rests in a combination of events, personalities, and factors that had never occurred previously. It is hoped that they will never occur again, to Jews nor to any group, anywhere in the world. This hope will be realized through education, awareness, respect for human rights, and a consistent willingness to maintain safeguards against all forms of prejudice and bias. These tasks will not be easy, for as President Clinton, in speaking at the Holocaust Memorial Museum's dedication in 1993, commented, "How fragile are the safeguards of civilization." Can we maintain these safeguards? Will we?

CHAPTER 34

Review Exercises

I. Matching

Directions: Match the words in Column A with the *correct description* in Column B.

Column A
1. euthanasia
2. deportation
3. apathy
4. genocide
5. deicide
6. stereotype
7. scapegoat
8. ghetto
9. pogrom
10. refugee
11. boycott
12. "final solution"
13. collaboration
14. selection process
15. crematorium
16. prejudice

Column B
(a) indifference, not caring
(b) killing of a god
(c) organized refusal to buy products
(d) Nazi term for the murder of all Jews in Europe
(e) the planned killing of a whole people or nation
(f) section of a city, where Jews were forced to live
(g) ovens and furnaces where inmates' bodies were burned
(h) forced removal of Jews to concentration and death camps
(i) a policy of mercy killing
(j) a violent attack on Jews by non-Jews
(k) someone who has been forced from or has lost his or her home
(l) a person or group unjustly blamed for bad things
(m) used to determine who would live and die at the camps
(n) an attitude toward a group of people that is based upon false information and unproven opinions
(o) a fixed view or idea about the behavior of all members of a religion or race
(p) cooperation by non-Germans with Germans in carrying out anti-Semitic actions

II. Famous People

Directions: Use the names below to complete the following sentences.

Vladka Meed   Martin Niemoller
Raoul Wallenberg   Heinrich Heine
Josef Goebbels   Adolf Eichmann
Adam Czerniakow   Heinrich Himmler
Josef Mengele   Januscz Korczak
Mordechai Anielewicz

1. _____ led the ZOB in its revolt against the Germans in the Warsaw Ghetto.

2. _____ was the German minister of propaganda.

3. _____ performed medical experiments at Auschwitz.

4. _____ prophesied that the burning of books would lead to the burning of people.

5. _____ was the leader of the SS.

6. _____ faced dilemmas as a Judenrat leader.

7. _____ organized deportations of Jews, in his role as a Gestapo officer.

8. _____ fought in and survived the Warsaw Ghetto revolt.

9. _____ was a pediatrician who chose to accompany Jewish orphans to Treblinka.

10. _____ saved thousands of Hungarian Jews in his role as a Swedish diplomat.

11. _____ was an imprisoned Protestant pastor who came to realize the danger of apathy.

III. Multiple Choice

Directions: Find the *letter* of the correct answer.

1. Which pair of words or phrases best describe a cause-and-effect relationship in connection with the "final solution"?

   (a) master race theory—genocide
   (b) putsch—Nordic supremacy theory
   (c) Kristallnacht—rise of the Third Reich
   (d) Babi Yar massacre—passage of the Nuremberg Laws

2. "At first they came for the Communists and I did nothing. Next, they came for the Jews, and I did nothing. Then, they came for the Catholics, and I did nothing. And then, they came for me." This speaker's actions were examples of

    (a) exploitation.   (b) charisma.
    (c) apathy.   (d) prejudice.

3. The group that has suffered as a result of anti-Semitism has been

    (a) Russians.   (b) Catholics.
    (c) Communists.   (d) Jews.

4. Which pair of people shared similiar attitudes toward Jews?

    (a) Reinhard Heydrich and Julius Streicher
    (b) Josef Goebbels and Adam Czerniakow
    (c) Adolf Eichmann and Januscz Korczak
    (d) Bogdan Chmelnitzki and Mordechai Aneliewicz

5. Hitler's "final solution" was aimed directly at extermination of

    (a) blacks.
    (b) Communists.
    (c) Jews.
    (d) Jehovah's Witnesses.

6. Which event occurred before the others?

    (a) Kristallnacht
    (b) Invasion of Poland
    (c) Passage of Nuremberg Laws
    (d) Wannsee Conference

7. Which sign was placed at the entrance to German concentration and death camps?

    (a) "Mein Kampf"
    (b) "Arbeit Macht Frei"
    (c) "Untermenschen"
    (d) "Judenrein"

8. The sign in question 7 could be translated as

    (a) "Jews are welcome."
    (b) "Be proud of yourself."
    (c) "My struggle is your struggle."
    (d) "Work will make you free."

9. Jews were often used by Hitler as scapegoats for Germany's

    (a) death rate.
    (b) many problems.
    (c) birth rate.
    (d) loss of overseas colonies.

10. Concerning the treatment of Jews, which of the following had a goal that was different from the goals of the other three?

   (a) Einsatzgruppen
   (b) Judenrat
   (c) Schutzstaffel (SS)
   (d) Gestapo

11. Zyklon B was used by the Nazis at

   (a) Auschwitz.
   (b) Nuremberg.
   (c) Vichy.
   (d) Theresienstadt.

12. All of the following performed assigned tasks in the death camps except for the

   (a) kapos.
   (b) Iron Guard.
   (c) Sonderkommandos.
   (d) SS.

13. Which was a major result of the Nuremberg War Crimes Trials?

   (a) National leaders were held personally responsible for crimes against humanity.
   (b) The State of Israel was created as a home for the surviving remnant.
   (c) Soldiers were required to pay for property damages caused during Kristallnacht.
   (d) Germany was ordered to build memorial monuments at Sobibor, Buchenwald, and Dachau.

IV. Speakers

Directions: Read carefully what each of the following speakers has to say. Then, for each question below, write the *letter* of the speaker who is best described by the question.

SPEAKER A: "The Aryans are to blame for the crime in the streets and for the severe unemployment we are facing."

SPEAKER B: "We must get rid of people who are Aryans, simply because they are Aryans."

SPEAKER C: "All these Aryans are wealthy, they are robbing our nation of its money, and they all have the same smell."

SPEAKER D: "The only two Aryans I know are lazy. Therefore, all Aryans must be lazy."

1. This speaker is considering genocide.

2. This speaker's thinking clearly shows much more prejudice than that of the other speakers.

3. These two speakers have created a stereotype. (Give two answers.)

4. Instead of sending Jews to concentration camps, this speaker would clearly send Aryans, since he views them as scapegoats.

5. This speaker would most likely recommend a "final solution" to the "Aryan Question" in his nation.

6. This speaker's statement is an example of pronouncing collective guilt.

V. Thought Questions

Directions: Answer the following questions in essay form.

1. Write a letter to the principal of your school about the Holocaust. In the letter, give two reasons why it is important for students to learn about the Holocaust.

2. Describe three examples of or reasons for anti-Semitism in Europe prior to Hitler's coming to power.

3. Explain how each of the following was a step toward the "final solution."

   A. Book burnings
   B. the Nuremberg Laws
   C. Kristallnacht
   D. the Wannsee Conference

4. There were many times between 1933 and 1945 when the Germans used the "big lie" technique in their dealings with European Jews. Describe two examples of this technique. For each example, state

   (a) the "big lie" itself.
   (b) one reason it was used.
   (c) one result of its use.
   (d) the true facts concerning the "lie."

5. Resistance by Jews during the Holocaust took many forms.

   A. Describe one example of violent resistance.
   B. Describe one example of spirtual or nonviolent resistance.
   C. State two reasons to explain why it was difficult for Jews to maintain any form of resistance.

6. The following statements raise controversial issues about the Holocaust. Read each statement carefully. For each, explain with one reason whether you agree or disagree.

   A. The Allies were correct for not bombing the crematoria and the railroad tracks leading to the death camps.
   B. Holocaust survivors who came to the United States and had children here should tell their children about their experiences.
   C. A Jewish person alive today should not visit Germany.
   D. An SS guard at Treblinka who followed orders and controlled operation of the gas chambers is not responsible for his actions.

E, Results of medical experiments performed in concentration camps should not be published.

F. A Judenrat leader who carried out German demands was acting correctly.

7. A headline in a German newspaper some years ago said the following: "GERMAN YOUTHS FOUND IGNORANT OF HITLER AND THE HOLOCAUST." This headline was the conclusion reached after a private study had been conducted in a few high schools. Assume that you are applying for a grant of money to spend a year in Germany, seeking to wipe out this ignorance in these few schools. Write a letter to the German minister of education in support of your application, explaining

A. The two most significant ideas (or lessons or morals) about Hitler and the Holocaust that you think German students should know about.

B. Your reasons for selecting these ideas.

C. One activity or assignment that these students should be given, to learn about Hitler and the Holocaust.

D. One thing that these students should do if someone like Hitler tries to start something again in Germany that is similar to the Holocaust.

Unit IX

THE COLD WAR AND THE NEW EUROPE

The worst war that the world had ever seen was now over and all mankind hoped that there would be peace forever. The first fifty years of the twentieth century had been the bloodiest in all recorded history and everyone wanted to go on to a better life. Whereas people living during the next period would not see the "hot" wars that had been fought previously, they would now live through the period that is known as the Cold War.

While the Western nations had been allied with the Soviet Union for the common goal of defeating Nazi Germany, there was little other reason for friendship between the West and the East. Historically, there was a list of reasons that the two had not been on friendly terms. Many of these you have studied in previous chapters. After World War II it seemed to the West that the Soviets had intentions of controlling all of Europe. They refused to remove their troops from the nations in Eastern Europe and imposed a Soviet-controlled system in almost all of them. The United States, the only Western nation strong enough to stand against the seemingly expansionist intentions of the USSR, developed a policy to contain their expansion. This policy caused a major change in traditional American foreign policy—that we would become militarily involved in Europe if a nation there was attacked.

As the differences hardened between West and East, the period came to be referred to as the "Cold War." We did not fight, but we were not friends. At certain times we stood, as they say, eyeball to eyeball, waiting for the other to blink. The world held its breath when we blockaded Cuba and demanded that the missiles installed by the Soviets be removed. They "blinked" and the missiles were removed. The peace seemed to have been kept by a doctrine of mass retaliation called "mutually assured destruction" (MAD). There was a tremendous buildup of weapons on both sides. Missiles were developed that could be fired from above and below both land and sea that were capable of destroying the entire planet.

With the death of the dictator Stalin and the coming to power of Khrushchëv, a thaw began to take place. Through a series of talks during a period known as détente, both nations took steps to back away from the edge of disaster. This proceeded unevenly with two steps forward and one step back. But these were steps that would help to warm the chill.

Khrushchëv made some reforms in the military situation. He attempted changes politically as well. He allowed greater freedom of expression than had been practiced. Writers could now print articles that were somewhat critical of the government. This breath of fresh air was eliminated when Khrushchëv was forced to resign and Brezhnev took his place. The long period of his rule was one of stagnation and repression. After him, there were two "ancients" that soon died. The Soviets then turned to the younger generation with the appointment of Gorbachëv.

What Gorbachëv soon realized was that the USSR was going bankrupt. Their economy was a disaster so they could not afford to continue to spend on the military and hope to raise the people's standard of living. In reality, the Soviet Union was a "Third World" nation with major military power. Gorbachëv's policies of Glasnost and Perestroika were to change all of this. Once, however, you open the box of freedom it is hard to close it. In quick succession, there were calls for greater freedom, attempted coups, the rise of Yeltsin, and the fall of Gorbachëv. This resulted in the breaking apart of the Union of Soviet Socialist Republics into fifteen independent units at the start of this decade.

All this will not be easy as both in the former USSR and the newly freed Eastern European nations there must be a transition to a more democratic state with a market economy. Age-old ethnic hostilities will emerge to cause many problems. We are living through this today. The daily newspaper and TV reports will help, along with your textbook.

The Cold War

In 1945, the victorious Allied leaders were faced with creating a lasting peace. From the start, mistrust between the Soviet Union and the West made this difficult. While this mistrust grew into hostility, it never heated up into another conflict such as World War II. Yet, this "cold" struggle between East and West was no friendly rivalry. The **Cold War** was a battle of words and propaganda, involving competition in science, weapons, and in seeking allies among the emerging nations of Africa, Asia, and Latin America. It was a war in every way. The two new superpowers, the United States and the Soviet Union, had conflicting philosophies about politics, economics, and human rights. The nations of Europe were divided between them, and the rest of the world became the arena in which these two sides would wrestle for influence and control.

Agreements During World War II (1943–1945)

The Mistrust Between the Allies

Although they were allies, the great mistrust between the Soviet Union, the United States, and Great Britain made them uneasy partners against the Axis powers. The reasons were mainly philosophical, political, and historical:

1. Communist theory viewed the capitalist nations as enemies, claiming that communism would one day spread over the earth.
2. Since the Communists came to power in 1917, the leaders of the Western capitalist democracies viewed them as threats and said so.
3. Allied support of the White Army during the Russian Civil War (1918–1921). The United States and Great Britain had landed troops on Russian soil during the conflict, thus adding to the Soviet fear of invasion.
4. The United States did not officially recognize the USSR until 1933.
5. The dictatorial, police-state policies of the USSR contrasted with the democratic ideals of the Western nations.

Opposition to Nazi Germany was the only bond that held them together. Once that was gone, the old suspicions reappeared. The decisions made during the peace settlements in the years immediately following the war laid the groundwork for the Cold War by dividing Europe into two specific spheres of political influence (communist and democratic).

The Teheran Conference (1943)

The first conference took place in Teheran (Iran) in 1943 between the Soviet dictator Joseph Stalin, United States President Franklin Roosevelt and British Prime Minister Sir Winston Churchill (see Chapter 32, "World War II"). At that meeting, Stalin agreed to bring the USSR into the war against Japan after the defeat of Germany, while the United States and Great Britain agreed to open a second front in France, forcing the Nazis to divide their army. Stalin rejected a proposal that they open another front in Eastern Europe, which would have given the British and Americans greater influence in the region.

The Yalta Conference (February 1945)

The second conference took place at Yalta (Crimea) in February of 1945. While they agreed on the establishment of the United Nations (see Chapter 33, "The

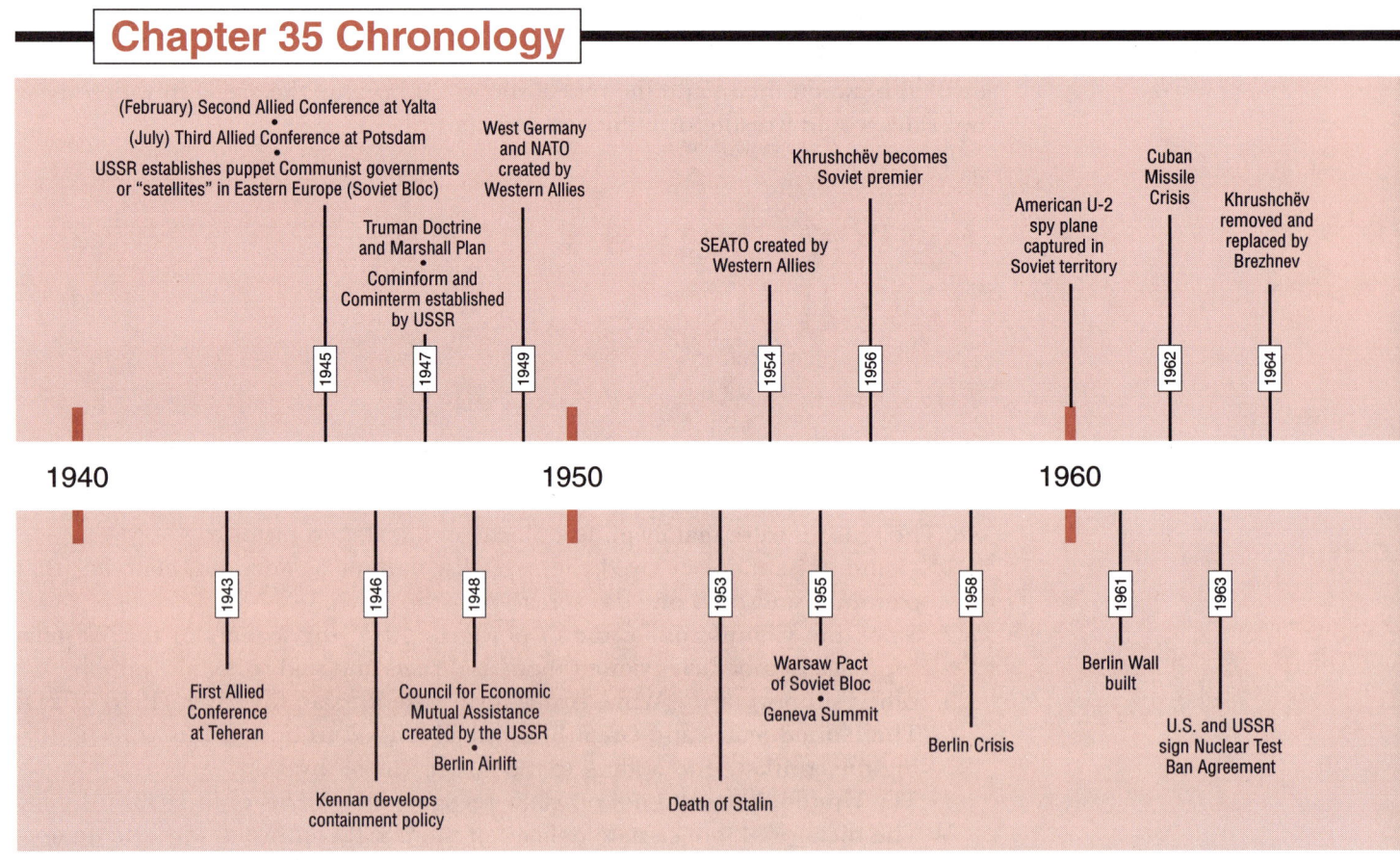

Chapter 35 Chronology

(February) Second Allied Conference at Yalta
(July) Third Allied Conference at Potsdam
USSR establishes puppet Communist governments or "satellites" in Eastern Europe (Soviet Bloc)

West Germany and NATO created by Western Allies

Khrushchëv becomes Soviet premier

Cuban Missile Crisis

Khrushchëv removed and replaced by Brezhnev

Truman Doctrine and Marshall Plan
Cominform and Cominterm established by USSR

SEATO created by Western Allies

American U-2 spy plane captured in Soviet territory

1945 1947 1949 1954 1956 1962 1964

1940 **1950** **1960**

1943 1946 1948 1953 1955 1958 1961 1963

First Allied Conference at Teheran

Council for Economic Mutual Assistance created by the USSR
Berlin Airlift

Warsaw Pact of Soviet Bloc
Geneva Summit

Berlin Crisis

Berlin Wall built

U.S. and USSR sign Nuclear Test Ban Agreement

Kennan develops containment policy

Death of Stalin

United Nations and Postwar Western Europe"), the complete "de-Nazification" of Germany, and the creation of four occupation zones (United States, Great Britain, France, and the USSR) within that nation, the Allies soon disagreed on the postwar fate of Eastern Europe. Stalin argued that Eastern Europe, which was already occupied by Soviet troops, was vital to the USSR's security as Russia had been invaded through these countries for centuries. He insisted that the Soviet Union be given some measure of control over the region. Both Roosevelt and Churchill objected, and it was finally agreed that free general elections be held in these nations as soon as possible.

The Potsdam Conference (July 1945)

The last meeting of the three Allies took place in Potsdam (Germany) in July of 1945. At this conference, the only original member left was Stalin, as Roosevelt had died and Churchill had lost that year's election in Britain. The United States was represented by the new president, Harry Truman, and Great Britain by its new prime minister, Clement Attlee. Even though they once again agreed on matters concerning Germany, Eastern Europe was still a sensitive issue. The vague assurance of free elections in the near future was all the Western Allies could obtain from Stalin.

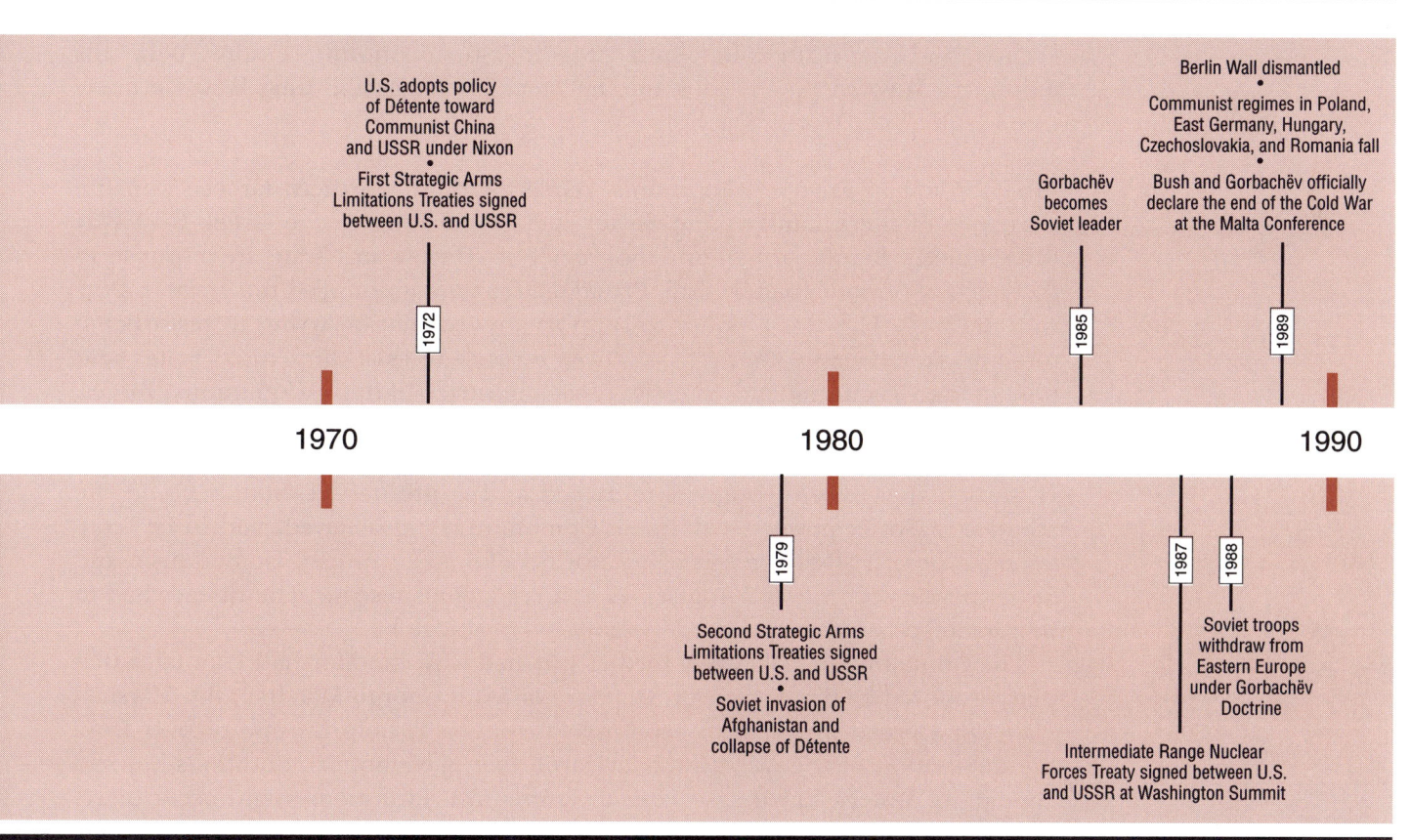

The Soviet Satellites in Eastern Europe

The Descent of the Iron Curtain

With the spirit of cooperation already disappearing after the Potsdam Conference, Stalin ignored the previous agreements and forced Communist dictatorships on the Eastern European nations of Poland, Romania, Bulgaria, and Hungary, beginning in 1945. Independent local Communist regimes had established themselves in Yugoslavia, Czechoslovakia, and Albania, initially appearing as friendly to the USSR. The Allies were infuriated at the creation of these Soviet **satellite nations** (smaller nations controlled by a larger one). Truman denounced the new governments and Churchill added a new term to the political vocabulary when he warned of an "**Iron Curtain**" dividing a free and democratic West from an East under totalitarian rule. Stalin retaliated by calling the Western democracies the enemies of communism. While not all the Eastern European Communist leaders were obedient to Stalin, their nations nevertheless became known as the **Soviet Bloc**, or Eastern Bloc. This grouping, also called the Communist bloc, stood in contrast to the Western Bloc, or the "Free World" bloc.

The Division of Berlin The breakdown of cooperation was felt most strongly in Germany, which was still divided into zones of occupation. Berlin, the former German capital city, which was within the Soviet zone, was itself divided into four occupation sectors. Access to the individual sectors was only through the Soviet zone. In 1947, the British, French, and American zones joined together for economic reasons. With this union, the Western powers took the first steps toward establishing West Germany (see Chapter 32, "World War II").

The Policy of Containment After the war in Europe, Communist rebels captured northern Greece with the assistance of the Albanians and Soviet backing, leading to the Greek Civil War (1945–1948). Similar rebellions took place in Turkey and Iran. In response to these acts of Soviet expansionism, President Truman announced the Truman Doctrine in 1947. This was a policy to support any free nation trying to resist being forcibly taken over by another power. As a result of this, the United States sent military and economic aid to assist those countries fighting Communist forces. The Truman Doctrine was part of new American policy known as Containment. Developed in 1946 by American diplomat George Kennan, the Containment theory argued that only through determined and continued resistance could the advance of Soviet power be stopped. Communism, he believed, had to be "contained" where it already existed and not be allowed to spread. Communism and Soviet power were viewed, in a sense, as a contagious disease. The disease had to be contained before it "infected" other parts of the globe.

The Containment policy was further pursued with the Marshall Plan later that year. Proposed by the American Secretary of State George Marshall, the Marshall Plan was a broad program of economic assistance to help Europe recover from the devastation of the war. Marshall feared that if economic conditions got bad enough in Western Europe, successful Communist revolutions might occur there. Both the Truman Doctrine and the Marshall Plan were highly successful. By 1948, the Communist rebellions in Greece, Turkey, and Iran had been defeated and the Western European nations underwent a remarkable economic recovery.

Cominform and the CEMA. In 1947, as a way of countering U.S. economic involvement in Western Europe, the Soviet Union established the Communist Information Bureau or **Cominform**. This was an organization designed to better coordinate the policies of the Soviet Union and the nations of Eastern Europe. In reality it was a restoration of the **Cominterm** or Communist International, which worked for world revolution. The following year a Soviet version of the Marshall Plan, the Council for Economic Mutual Assistance, was created. In reality, these policies merely tightened the USSR's grip on its Eastern European satellites.

The Division of Germany As tensions in Germany grew greater, the Soviets cut off all access routes between Berlin and the Western occupation zones in June of 1948. This trapped the Westerners living in the city. In response, the United States established the Berlin Airlift, which flew food, fuel, and supplies to the Western sectors. With the Berlin Airlift making the blockade ineffectual, the Soviets decided not to escalate the crisis and re-opened the access routes in May of 1949. A month later, the Western Allies established the Federal Republic of Germany or West Germany as it came to be known. The Soviets responded by creating an East Germany, the German Democratic Republic, in their zone.

The Creation of NATO The mounting tension between the East and West gradually led to military alliances. In April of 1949, representatives of twelve Western nations signed the North Atlantic Pact. This was a mutual defense agreement (if one nation is attacked, the others will come to its aid) between the United States, Great Britain, France, Belgium, the Netherlands, Luxembourg, Denmark, Norway, Iceland, Canada, Italy, and Portugal. In 1952, Greece and Turkey joined, followed by West Germany in 1955. The **North Atlantic Treaty Organization (NATO)** was established to coordinate the activities of the alliance, and be ready to respond to any acts of Soviet expansion in Europe.

The Creation of the Warsaw Pact The Soviets responded to West Germany's joining of NATO with the creation of the **Warsaw Pact** in 1955. This was a military alliance of the Soviet Union with Albania, Bulgaria, Czechoslovakia, East Germany, Hungary, Poland, and Romania. Yugoslavia, under the independent Communist leader Tito, refused to join. (In 1961, Albania left both the Warsaw Pact and the Soviet Bloc.)

The Arms Race

Both alliances now began to stockpile huge quantities of arms. They enlarged their armed forces, increased military spending, and sent spies into each other's member nations. Thus, as the 1950s came to a close, it appeared that a frightening repetition of history was occuring. The two military alliances were reminders of the "two armed camps" of the alliances that existed before World War I (see Chapter 30, "World War I"). Both the Triple Alliance and Triple Entente claimed to be merely defensive in purpose. That is, that each would fight only if attacked by the other. A similar policy was echoed by NATO and the Warsaw Pact. Yet, the existence of these two groupings made the world more alarmed than was the case with the earlier alliances, for these reasons:

1. NATO and the Warsaw Pact had many more member nations, spanning three continents.
2. Their armed forces were larger.
3. Their weapons were newer and more deadly. Air forces, intercontinental missiles, and atomic power came to be possessed by both sides.
4. Fear and distrust on both sides was enormous. The West was upset with the USSR's post-World War II expansion into Eastern Europe, Stalin's treachery, and the messianic belief of the Communists that spoke of inevitable world domination. The Soviets claimed that the Western powers were "ganging up" on them. NATO was seen as a threat to the Soviets, reminiscent of two previous invasions of Russia from the West (Napoleon in 1812 and Hitler in 1941).

Amidst such tensions, we should not be surprised to find their effect on many other global areas.

The Creation of SEATO   The rise of Communist regimes in China under Mao Zedong and North Korea under Kim Il-Sung in 1949 created panic in the West. These nations were friendly with the USSR, taking a similar anti-Western and anti-American stance. When North Korea attacked South Korea in 1950, United Nations forces, led by the United States, went to war. The conflict became known as the Korean War (1950–1953). An armistice brought the fighting to a temporary halt. However, no peace treaty formally ending the war was ever signed. North Korea received weapons from the USSR, as well as both arms and manpower from Communist China. Yet, the North Koreans failed to take the South. This was considered a successful application of the Containment Policy by the United States and its allies as it had stopped Communist expansion and re-established the status quo (existing state of affairs) before the war.

The United States, in the forefront of having successfully protected a nation from Communist domination, became more convinced of the importance of practicing Containment. In 1954, U.S. President Eisenhower expanded the Western anti-Communist alliance system with the creation of the **Southeast Asia Treaty Organization (SEATO)**. This included the United States, Great Britain, France, Australia, New Zealand, the Philippines, Thailand, and Pakistan.

The Policy of Peaceful Co-Existence   In 1953, Stalin died and control of the USSR government went to much more moderate leadership. The new Soviet leader, Nikita Khrushchëv (r. 1956–1964), adapted a doctrine called "Peaceful Co-existence." This was a policy of peaceful competition between the East and the West that would be based on greater achievement as a means of influencing non-allied nations. In the USSR, Khrushchev had begun several reforms in domestic policy and had a reputation for being a reformer (see Chapter 36, "The Collapse of Communism in the Soviet Union and Eastern Europe").

In July of 1955, President Eisenhower, British Prime Minister Anthony Eden, and French Premier Edgar Faure met with Khrushchëv in Geneva, Switzerland. Known as the Geneva Summit, it was a breakthrough in Soviet-Western relations since the start of the Cold War in 1945.

The Berlin Crisis (1958)   The tension soon returned, however, as Khrushchëv began a campaign to demilitarize and neutralize West Berlin in November of 1958. He demanded that the Western powers pull out all military personnel and equipment from Berlin in six months or he would turn the city over to the East Germans (The GDR was a government that the West did not recognize). When the Western powers refused to give in, Khrushchëv let the deadline pass, ending the Berlin Crisis of 1958. This event was viewed internationally as an embarrassment to the Communists. The Soviet premier agreed to meet with Eisenhower at a summit in Paris in 1960, but the capture of an American U-2 spy plane carrying out surveillance operations over Soviet territory resulted in its cancellation.

In early 1961, Khrushchëv renewed his pressure on the Western powers about West Berlin. In August, the Soviets and East Germans closed the border between East and West Berlin and began the construction of a wall that divided the city. The Berlin Wall, which was built to prevent East Germans from escaping to the West, became a symbol of Communist oppresssion in Eastern Europe. Even though the crisis subsided, relations between East and West began to deteriorate.

The Cuban Missile Crisis (1962) When the revolutionary leader Fidel Castro took power in Cuba in 1959, he was at first welcomed as a relief to the military dictatorship of General Fulgencio Batista. By 1960, however, Castro had made it clear that he was clearly within the Communist camp and strengthened his ties with the USSR and Communist China. Seeing Castro as a threat to American security, the United States responded by arming and preparing a military force composed of Cuban exiles to overthrow the regime. The failure of this group at the Bay of Pigs in 1961 drove Castro to seek assistance from the Soviet Union. The Soviets provided Castro with conventional arms, but also began to construct missile launching pads for intermediate range missiles. United States President John Kennedy demanded that the missiles be dismantled. He ordered a blockade to prevent Soviet ships from bringing further equipment to Cuba. After tense negotiations, Khrushchëv removed the missiles. Kennedy pledged not to invade Cuba and to pull NATO missiles out of Turkey.

After the Cuban Missile Crisis of 1962, the Washington-Moscow hotline (telephone that linked the U.S. president with the premier of the USSR) was established in case of another crisis. Following the crisis, the United States and the USSR signed the first Nuclear Test Ban in July of 1963, which agreed to stop the testing of nuclear weapons in the air. This was the first agreement of its kind, indicative of the changes the Cuban Missile Crisis had created. In October of 1964, however, the reform-minded Khrushchëv was removed from office and replaced with the hard-line Communist Leonid Brezhnev (see Chapter 36, "The Collapse of Communism in the Soviet Union and Eastern Europe"). This resulted in a return to a more antagonistic Soviet foreign policy and a renewal of strained relations between the two superpowers.

The Decline of the Cold War (1972–1991)

The Policy of Détente

As the decade progressed, there was an improvement in East-West relations. Beginning with the presidency of Richard Nixon, a "thaw" in the Cold War began. Relations improved between the United States and its Western Allies, and the Sovi-

Europe During the Cold War

- NATO Alliance, 1955
- ★ Original EEC Members, 1957
- Communist Bloc (Members of Warsaw Pact and COMECON)

Map of Europe during the Cold War: the above map shows the division of Europe during the Cold War (1945–1991). Note that the democratic and Communist alliances are roughly equivalent to the traditional cultural divisions between Eastern and Western Europe.

et Union. A policy of **Détente** (understanding) was adopted and new conferences on arms control followed. In 1972 and 1979, two Strategic Arms Limitations Treaties (SALT I and SALT II) were signed, which put limited restrictions on weapons production.

Détente declined in the early 1980s due to the Soviet invasion of Afghanistan in 1979 and the imposition of military government by the Soviet Union on Poland in 1981. To the West, these actions seemed to be a return to the expansionist policies of Stalin's rule. However, both policies met with great resistance within the Soviet Bloc. The war in Afghanistan cost thousands of lives and became very unpopular in the USSR, sparking desertions in the army and protests at home. The crackdown in Poland only served to unify the Polish people in their opposition to Soviet domination (see Chapter 36, "The Collapse of Communism in the Soviet Union and Eastern Europe").

The End of the Cold War

After Mikhail Gorbachëv (r. 1985–1991) became the Soviet leader in 1985, relations with the West, particularly the United States, improved. Gorbachëv's policies of **Glasnost** (openness) and **Perestroika** (restructuring) brought political and economic reforms which were viewed with admiration in the West (see Chapter 36, "The Collapse of Communism in the Soviet Union and Eastern Europe"). In December of 1987, American President Ronald Reagan and Gorbachëv signed the Intermediate Range Nuclear Forces Treaty (INF) at the Washington Summit. This was an agreement to destroy all American and Soviet missiles within a range of 315 to 3,125 miles within three years. It was the first American-Soviet agreement to actually reduce the level of arms.

In 1988, Gorbachëv began to pull out Soviet troops from Eastern Europe (the Gorbachëv Doctrine). This was followed by the fall of the Berlin Wall in 1989 and with it almost all the Communist regimes of Eastern Europe (see Chapter 36, "The Collapse of Communism in the Soviet Union and Eastern Europe"). With the collapse of the Soviet Bloc in Eastern Europe, the need for the NATO alliance lessened. In December of 1989, American President George Bush and Gorbachëv officially declared the end of the Cold War at the Malta Conference. The struggle that had divided both Europe and the world for 45 years was finally over.

Summary

The Cold War had divided the post-World War II world into hostile camps for almost half a century. The fear, suspicion, and hatred this struggle created has left three legacies. The first is a vacuum of power as the nations once dominated by the USSR become independent. Many ancient hatreds have resurfaced because the common enemy that controlled them is gone. The second is the excess supply of arms, including nuclear weapons, that are available to these warring nations, as well as others throughout the world. The last is the environmental, economic, and psychological damage done to the individual nations on both sides. The ideological struggle of the Cold War has been replaced by nationalism, on the one hand, and a desire for greater global cooperation on the other. The military alliances created during the Cold War were not designed to handle the new conflicts that have arisen throughout Europe and the world in recent years. Creating a new order will be an enormous challenge for leaders in the future.

CHAPTER 35

Review Exercises

I. Matching

Directions: Match the names and words in Column A with the *correct description* in Column B.

Column A
1. Cominterm
2. Richard Nixon
3. Cominform
4. German Democratic Republic
5. Sir Winston Churchill
6. Mikhail Gorbachëv
7. Warsaw Pact
8. Nikita Khrushchëv
9. Harry Truman
10. Federal Republic of Germany

Column B
(a) Yalta Conference
(b) West Germany
(c) Détente
(d) Communist International
(e) East Germany
(f) Potsdam Conference
(g) Communist Information Bureau
(h) Soviet Bloc
(i) Berlin Crisis of 1958
(j) Washington Summit

II. Multiple Choice

Directions: Find the *letter* of the correct answer.

1. The Cold War resulted in all of the following *except*

   (a) military confrontation between the superpowers.
   (b) great mistrust between the East and West.
   (c) mistrust resulting in hostility between the USSR and the West.
   (d) smaller nations fighting in place of the superpowers.

2. The Allies were held together during World War II by mutual

   (a) doctrines of democratic government.
   (b) desires to expand their territories.
   (c) opposition to Nazi Germany.
   (d) opposition to Communist ideology.

3. The proposal for an Allied front in Eastern Europe was rejected at

   (a) Geneva.
   (b) Teheran.
   (c) Yalta.
   (d) Potsdam.

4. The decision to divide Germany into four zones of occupation was made at

   (a) Geneva.
   (b) Teheran.
   (c) Yalta.
   (d) Potsdam.

5. The initial agreement that free elections be held in Eastern Europe after its liberation was made at

   (a) Geneva.
   (b) Teheran.
   (c) Yalta.
   (d) Potsdam.

6. The vague confirmation of the agreement to hold free elections was made at

   (a) Geneva.
   (b) Teheran.
   (c) Yalta.
   (d) Potsdam.

7. The three Eastern European nations that did not have Soviet-imposed Communist governments were

   (a) Poland, Bulgaria, Romania.
   (b) Poland, Hungary, Romania.
   (c) Yugoslavia, Albania, Czechoslovakia.
   (d) Yugoslavia, Hungary, Czechoslovakia.

8. The leader who coined the phrase the "Iron Curtain" was

   (a) Harry Truman.
   (b) Winston Churchill.
   (c) Joseph Stalin.
   (d) Dwight Eisenhower.

9. Berlin was divided into four zones of occupation under the

   (a) Americans, British, Germans, and Soviets.
   (b) Americans, British, French, and Soviets.
   (c) Americans, British, French, and Italians.
   (d) British, French, Germans, and Soviets.

10. After World War II, Soviet-backed Communist forces tried to seize power in

   (a) Greece, Italy, and Turkey.
   (b) Greece, Albania, and Turkey.
   (c) Greece, Turkey, and Iran.
   (d) Greece, Albania, and Iran.

11. The policy of Containment was developed by

    (a) Harry Truman.
    (b) Winston Churchill.
    (c) George Marshall.
    (d) George Kennan.

12. The Truman Doctrine provided

    (a) economic aid to Western Europe.
    (b) military aid to Western Europe.
    (c) medical assistance to Western Europe.
    (d) technology to Western Europe.

13. The Marshall Plan provided

    (a) economic aid to Western Europe.
    (b) military aid to Western Europe.
    (c) medical assistance to Western Europe.
    (d) technology to Western Europe.

14. The Truman Doctrine and Marshall Plan resulted from the policy of

    (a) agressive action against communism.
    (b) Containment.
    (c) peaceful co-existence.
    (d) Détente.

15. The Council for Economic Mutual Assistance was the Soviet version of

    (a) NATO.
    (b) SALT.
    (c) the Truman Doctrine.
    (d) the Marshall Plan.

16. The Warsaw Pact was the Soviet version of

    (a) NATO.
    (b) SALT.
    (c) the Truman Doctrine.
    (d) the Marshall Plan.

17. The nations known as "satellites" were

    (a) under U.S. control.
    (b) under NATO control.
    (c) under Soviet control.
    (d) under Warsaw Pact control.

18. The Western European response to the Berlin Blockade was

    (a) a threat to use nuclear weapons.
    (b) the Berlin Airlift.
    (c) an economic blockade.
    (d) an invasion of East Germany.

19. Which of the following was *not* a Cold War conflict?

    (a) the Korean War
    (b) the Berlin Crisis of 1958
    (c) the Cuban Missile Crisis
    (d) the Soviet invasion of Afghanistan

20. The Cold War was officially ended at the

    (a) Yalta Conference.
    (b) Malta Conference.
    (c) Geneva Summit.
    (d) Washington Summit.

III. Thought Questions

Directions: Answer the following questions in essay form.

1. World War II was followed by a different type of conflict known as the Cold War.

    A. Define the term "Cold War."
    B. Explain three ways in which this conflict was different from previous wars.

2. Both sides—East and West—must bear responsibility for the Cold War. Agree or disagree with this statement based on the following.

    A. Describe three events that led to the Cold War.
    B. Explain the Soviet point of view in relation to each event.
    C. Explain the Western point of view in relation to each event.

3. You are a television journalist investigating how the attitudes and actions of the superpowers in the Cold War were changed by the Cuban Missile Crisis. Give three examples of how the event led to efforts to improve relations between the superpowers.

4. Economics ended the Cold War. The cost of maintaining this conflict was responsible for its end. Give three reasons for agreeing or disagreeing with this statement.

5. Did the Cold War transform Europe and the world? Show three ways in which the conduct of world affairs and international relations were changed by the Cold War.

CHAPTER 36

The Collapse of Communism in the Soviet Union and Eastern Europe

The Soviet Union emerged from World War II as a superpower. While Stalin's successors tried to reduce repression after his death, the USSR remained a totalitarian state. Involved in the Cold War with the West, the Soviet and Eastern European Communist systems proved unable to maintain their military machine and improve the standard of living for their people. By 1989, being a world power was too costly for the Soviet Union to continue indefinitely. It was also becoming clear that communism was a failure. In 1991, after 70 years of communism in Russia and 45 years of Soviet domination in Eastern Europe, the Communist system behind the Iron Curtain collapsed. That this occurred with little violence or bloodshed is remarkable. However, enormous damage had been done. The people under the former Communist regimes in Eastern Europe—politically inexperienced, and with their countries polluted, technologically backward, and economically damaged—now began to stumble forward toward democracy and capitalism.

The Decline and Collapse of the Soviet Union (1945–1991)

The USSR After World War II

After World War II, the USSR gained control over most of Eastern Europe. This brought greater territory for the Soviet Empire, as well as larger strains on its devastated economy. The cost of maintaining troops in the Eastern European nations and keeping a strong military made it necessary for emphasis to continue to be on the development of heavy industry. Consumer goods and housing were neglected and food shortages were common. The new series of Five Year Plans continued to promote industrial production primarily for military expansion.

As Joseph Stalin's dictatorship (r. 1925–1953) wound down to its last years, the Soviet Union remained a police state. Intellectuals and artists were prevented from free expression. Stalin developed a cult of personality, by which he was officially worshipped through government propaganda. In early 1953, it appeared that he was about to launch another purge (see Chapter 31, "Rise of Totalitarianism in Russia, Italy, and Germany"), but his death in March of that year prevented it.

The Great Thaw

From 1953 to 1958, a collective leadership consisting of Georgii Malenkov (1902–1988), Nikita Khrushchëv (1894–1971), and later Nikolai Bulganin (1895–1975), ruled the Soviet Union. They put an end to the government terror, arresting and executing the hated Lavrentii Beria (1899–1953), head of the secret police. By 1958, Khrushchëv had removed his partners and taken power by himself. In February of 1956, Khrushchëv delivered a powerful speech at the 20th Congress of the Soviet Communist party, denouncing Stalin, his crimes, and his cult of personality. He later cleared the names of many innocent people, both living and dead, who Stalin had wrongly arrested, condemned, and imprisoned. Millions of political prisoners were released from the Soviet concentration camps in

Chapter 36 Chronology

Death of Tito in Yugoslavia

USSR establishes puppet Communist regimes or "satellites" in Eastern Europe (Soviet Bloc)

Soviet troops invade Hungary

Khrushchëv becomes Soviet premier

Khrushchëv removed and replaced by Brezhnev

Policy of Détente with the West established

Martial law declared in Poland

Solidarity trade union declared illegal

1945 — 1956 — 1964 — 1972

1950 **1960** **1970** **1980**

1953 1961 1968 1979 1982

Death of Stalin

Albania leaves Soviet Bloc

"Prague Spring" under Dubček crushed by invasion of Warsaw Pact troops

Death of Brezhnev and succession of Andropov

Soviet invasion of Afghanistan and collapse of Détente

Siberia. Intellectuals and artists were also given greater freedom of expression. This period became known as the Great Thaw. The writings of dissidents (people who disagree with or reject accepted beliefs), which could not be read during Stalin's rule, were published for the first time. The most notable example was Vladimir Dudinstev's *Not By Bread Alone* (1957), which sharply criticized the Soviet bureaucracy. Khrushchëv originally allowed Boris Pasternak's (1890–1960) masterpiece, *Doctor Zhivago* (1958), to be published as well, but gave in to pressure from the Soviet censors and banned the work. Pasternak was not allowed by the Soviet authorities to accept the Nobel Prize he won for the novel.

Reforms Under Khrushchëv (1956–1963)

Khrushchëv tried to institute reforms to improve the economy. While he did not abandon the emphasis on heavy industry, he encouraged the production of consumer goods and the construction of housing. Despite great efforts to catch up with Western production, the Soviet economy began to lag during the 1960s. In an effort to increase agricultural production, Khrushchëv combined collective farms into larger units, hoping to improve efficiency. He also initiated the Virgin Lands Program, which tried to cultivate semi-arid land in Western Siberia and Central Asia. Despite some early successes, a series of droughts turned the area into a desert and the Virgin Lands Program was an embarrassing failure.

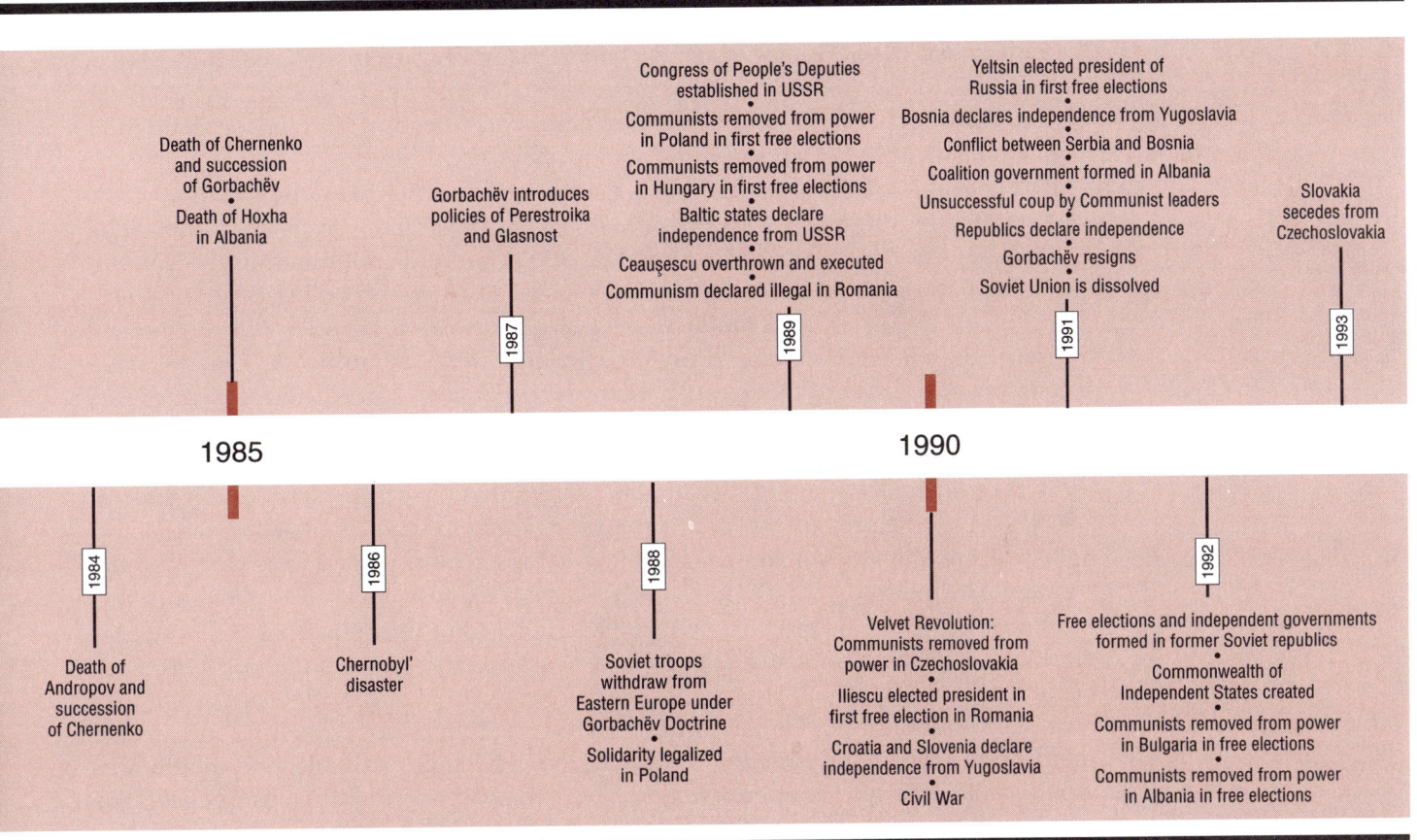

Most of the Soviet Union's resources went into an arms race (competition to build weapons) along with space research. In the autumn of 1957, the Soviets launched Sputnik I, the first artificial earth satellite. This landmark achievement was followed by the successful sending of a rocket to the moon in 1959. In April 1961, the first orbital flight with an astronaut aboard was made by Yurii Gagarin (1934–1968). Although these accomplishments brought great prestige to the USSR, they were an expense the Soviets could not afford. Khrushchëv's foreign policy shifted from one of reconciliation with the West to an aggressive attitude that led to serious confrontations (see Chapter 35, "The Cold War").

Opposition to Khrushchëv gradually increased within the Soviet leadership. He was criticized for his failures in agriculture and foreign policy. Viewed by many as a "rude peasant" who was incompetent, Khrushchëv was removed from his position in October 1964. Aleksei Kosigin (1904–1980) replaced him as premier and Leonid Brezhnev (r. 1964–1982) became general secretary of the Communist Party. By 1977, Brezhnev became dominant in the Soviet government, taking on the title of president (1977–1982).

The USSR Under Brezhnev (1964–1982)

Brezhnev ruled the USSR with a strong hand. His leadership was a period of great stagnation. Stubbornly, and without much regard for his people's welfare, Brezhnev refused to depart from the traditional Soviet goals or methods of rule. For intellectuals and artists it was a return to repression. All literature and art were censored and human rights were abused openly. An underground dissident movement began that included writers, poets, journalists, clergy, professors, students, and scientists. Publishing their works in underground presses known as **samizdat**, they exposed the injustices of the Soviet system and protested their continuation.

The Dissidence of Solzhenitsyn and Sakharov The most famous figures of this movement were the dissident writer Aleksandr Solzhenitsyn (1918–) and the emminent scientist Andrey Sakharov (1921–1989). Under Stalin, Solzhenitysn had been imprisoned in a Siberian labor camp, which he wrote about in a short novel, *One Day in the Life of Ivan Denisovich* (1962). His subsequent works were banned under Brezhnev and only published in the West or by samizdat. Like Pasternak, he was not allowed to accept his Nobel Prize for literature in 1970. When he completed a massive three-volume history of the Siberian camps, the *Gulag Archipelago* (1974), it was banned. Its publication in the West resulted in Solzhenitsyn's expulsion from the Soviet Union the following year. Audrey Sakharov was a prominent physicist and "father of the Soviet hydrogen bomb." He also joined the ranks of the dissidents with the publication of his book, *My Country and the World* (1974), in which he called for greater freedom of expression and the reform of the political system. In 1975, he was awarded the Nobel Peace Prize, but was not allowed to accept it. Sakharov's contacts with Western journalists resulted in his internal exile in the city of Gorky, which was not open to foreigners. In 1987, Sakharov was released and allowed to return to Moscow, where he was elected a member of the Congress of People's Deputies and died in 1989.

Economic Decline In economic affairs, the Brezhnev years were a period of decline and decay. Although more consumer goods and housing became available, the quality was poor and the output could not keep up with the growing population. The levels of agricultural production declined and the USSR was forced to depend on imports from the United States and the West. The increased contact with the West due to **Détente** (see Chapter 35, "The Cold War") made the Soviet consumers aware of how poor their standard of living was compared with nations in the West and the United States. Most people had to stand on long lines for hours to get the most basic items. A privileged class of Communist party elites had also developed under Brezhnev. They lived a luxurious life-style, able to get any product they wanted, including much sought-after Western goods, in "special" stores with no lines. This antagonized many Soviet citizens further. Finally, the repressive nature of the Brezhnev regime and the inefficiency of the Soviet system made them both angry and cynical. The Soviet invasion of Afghanistan in 1979 further angered the population, especially youths (see Chapter 35, "The Cold War").

Andropov and Chernenko (1982–1985)

Following Brezhnev's death in 1982, there was a succession of leaders with brief administrations. Yurii Andropov (r. 1982–1984) became seriously ill after taking power. While he tried to institute basic economic reforms, his sudden death in February of 1984 prevented any serious changes from being implemented. His successor, Konstantin Chernenko (r. 1984–1985) was a reactionary who wished to continue the policies of Brezhnev. Already declining in health when he took Andropov's place, he died in March of 1985.

Reform Under Gorbachëv (1985–1989)

With the rise of Mikhail Gorbachëv (r. 1985–1991), a younger generation of Soviet leaders took control. Even though he wanted to begin reforms, Gorbachëv was hesitant at first. The meltdown of the nuclear reactor at Chernobyl' in 1986 made the need for reform clear. The accident was a major disaster that contaminated entire areas of Ukraine, poisoning thousands of people and animals. It greatly reduced the capability of one of the world's most fertile regions to produce crops. The slow reaction of the government to the disaster and its clumsy attempt to cover it up resulted in an angry population. This gave Gorbachëv the excuse he needed to seek reforms. In 1987, he introduced two new radical programs: **Glasnost** and **Perestroika**.

Glasnost The policy of Glasnost ("openness") was aimed at reducing the intellectual, political, and cultural repression that had been part of the Soviet system. The media were given more freedom in their reporting. For the first time, dissenting opinions could be expressed openly. Glasnost also led to the publication of books that had been banned, such as Pasternak's *Doctor Zhivago*. Gorbachëv also released dissidents who were imprisoned or in exile, including Sakharov. He even invited Solzhenitsyn back to the USSR.

Perestroika Perestroika ("restructuring") was created to promote greater productivity in both industry and agriculture. It also was designed to improve the quality of Soviet goods. Gorbachëv began by reforming the USSR's command economy (a system in which government planners make all economic decisions). Gorbachëv decentralized Soviet industrial and agricultural management (the Enterprise Law of 1987), by which factory and farm managers were given greater control over determining both the production and the distribution of profits. Worker incentives,

Andrey Dmitryevich Sakharov

His nation had given him honors, prestige, and position. In a Soviet Union in which few were privileged, he stood out as a member of the elite and therefore lived well. Everyone knew and respected him and he was greeted wherever he went. We may ask the question "Why did he give all this up?" We don't know if we can really answer this question.

There is no doubt that Sakharov was a brilliant scientist. He received a doctorate at the age of twenty-six and became a member of the prestigious Soviet Academy of Sciences at thirty-two. He developed the hydrogen bomb for the Soviets and researched the basis for controlled thermonuclear fusion. It seemed that he had it all when he went against the government in 1961 at the age of forty. He openly opposed Khrushchëv's plan to test a 100-megaton hydrogen bomb in the atmosphere. A few years later he called for nuclear arms reduction and opposed the suppression of Soviet citizens who criticize the government. He was told to be silent about these things, but refused. He continued to speak out against what he considered to be Soviet curtailment of human rights.

He was married (his second time) to Yelena Bonner in 1971 and she joined him in his struggle against Soviet oppression. In December 1979 he denounced the invasion of Afghanistan and, in an open letter to the world, called for nations to boycott the Moscow Olympics. He was isolated and ostracized by his former friends and colleagues. Academicians would no longer communicate with him. He was shunned by his former wife and even by his children.

He continued to join those citizens who opposed government policies (dissidents) by speaking out, writing, and standing in silent protest before government buildings. He became the conscience of the Russian people.

The Communist party finally reacted in January of 1980. Afraid to take drastic action because of world opinion, they stripped Sakharov of all the honors they had previously given him and sent him to live in exile in the closed city of Gorky, about 275 miles west of Moscow. His wife Yelena followed four years later. In Gorky they were cut off completely from all communication with the outside world. Guards were always around them. When they went to the stores they were accompanied so that nobody would speak to them. Besides, it was dangerous for the person who would try. They went on a hunger strike demanding decent medical care and had to be force-fed by doctors and guards.

It is difficult to say exactly what Sakharov wanted for the Russian people. You can say he wanted them freed from the oppressive dictatorial rule of the Communist party and its leaders. He wanted to bring a liberal parliamentary democracy to a nation that had not experienced one. He saw a relationship between democracy and a market economy as the only hope for the future of the Russian people.

The heavy hand of Communist oppression was lifted when Gorbachëv came to power. We will have to wait for the historians to accurately tell us of Gorbachëv's motivations, but there is little doubt that he began to change the system. He called the KGB guards in Gorky in December 1986 and instructed them to install a telephone in Sakharov's quarters. Two months earlier Sakharov had written Gorbachëv complaining of his illegal exile. In a telephone conversation, Gorbachëv attempted to negotiate with Sakharov conditions for his and Yelena's release. They agreed that Sakharov would speak out only in those cases that he felt he could not remain silent. He then asked for the release of all political prisoners. Gorbachëv refused. (It is interesting to note that 300 political prisoners were released in the next three months.)

Sakharov was elected to the Congress of People's Deputies where he and Gorbachëv opposed each other. He, by now, was worn out and old before his time. He died of a heart attack on December 14, 1989, while preparing a speech to give the next day.

Perhaps the best way to sum up his life is to quote a Russian, Leonid Batkin, who said, "The fact is that in our country there have not been and currently are not any democratic institutions. But we had Sakharov. We did not have people who have declared themselves openly in opposition, without which normal political life is impossible. But we did have an opposition, because we had Sakharov!"

such as a pay increase for greater individual productivity, were adopted. The goal of this law was to make factories and farms independent, self-sufficient, and profitable, so that they would no longer need government **subsidies** (money to make up losses). The Law of Cooperatives of 1987 allowed Soviet citizens to set up private businesses, free of state control, and keep the profits. This was intended to encourage more production of better products and services, and beginning a system of individual enterprise. The Agricultural Reform Law of 1988 broke up the state and collective farms, replacing them with a private leasing system. Individual farmers were able to own and profit from their farms once they paid off a long-term lease. The goal of this reform was to promote greater productivity through the private ownership of land.

Clearly, the changes described above, while commonplace in our own society, were monumental for the USSR. The reason was that they completely violated traditional Communist theory. Yet, Gorbachëv was willing to try such "violations" if they could result in a more productive economy for the Soviet Union.

The Gorbachëv Doctrine Politically, Perestroika reduced the direct involvement of the Communist party leadership in the day-to-day governance of the country and increased the authority of local government agencies. This angered the **nomemklatura**, or ruling group of the Communist party. Religious freedoms were also granted and the Russian Orthodox Church celebrated its **millennium** (one thousandth anniversary) with the support of the government. Jews were permitted greater freedom, with an increasing number allowed to migrate to other countries. In foreign affairs, Gorbachëv implemented the Gorbachëv Doctrine, a policy of noninterference in Eastern Europe and the world. By autumn of 1988, he began to reduce the number of Soviet troops in some of the satellite nations, encouraging the collapse of the Communist regimes in those nations a year later.

Köhl and Gorbachëv: The photograph above shows the leader of the newly unified Germany, Helmet Köhl, meeting with the leader of the USSR, Mikhail Gorbachëv. The meeting was held in 1990, a year before communism's collapse in the Soviet Union.

The Decline of the Communist Party of the Soviet Union (CPSU)

Faced with growing opposition from a number of older bureaucrats, military leaders, and party officials, Gorbachëv took the title of president and removed his opponents from positions of power in 1988. In 1989, he instituted a Soviet parliament, the Congress of People's Deputies. Members would be chosen by free elections, a new procedure for the Soviet Union. Despite enormous advantages and influence over the election process, a number of prominent Communists were nevertheless defeated. The majority of representatives were, however, Communists who ran unopposed. Yet, this panicked Gorbachëv. Despite being dedicated to reform, he feared that if this trend continued, the dominance of the Communist party would slowly disappear.

The election of dissidents, such as Sakharov, and officials who were openly critical of the regime, such as Boris Yeltsin, was seen by Gorbachëv as a threat to the survival of the system. Yeltsin had risen to power by promoting Russian nationalism and downplaying the Soviet Union. The population, which had always seen

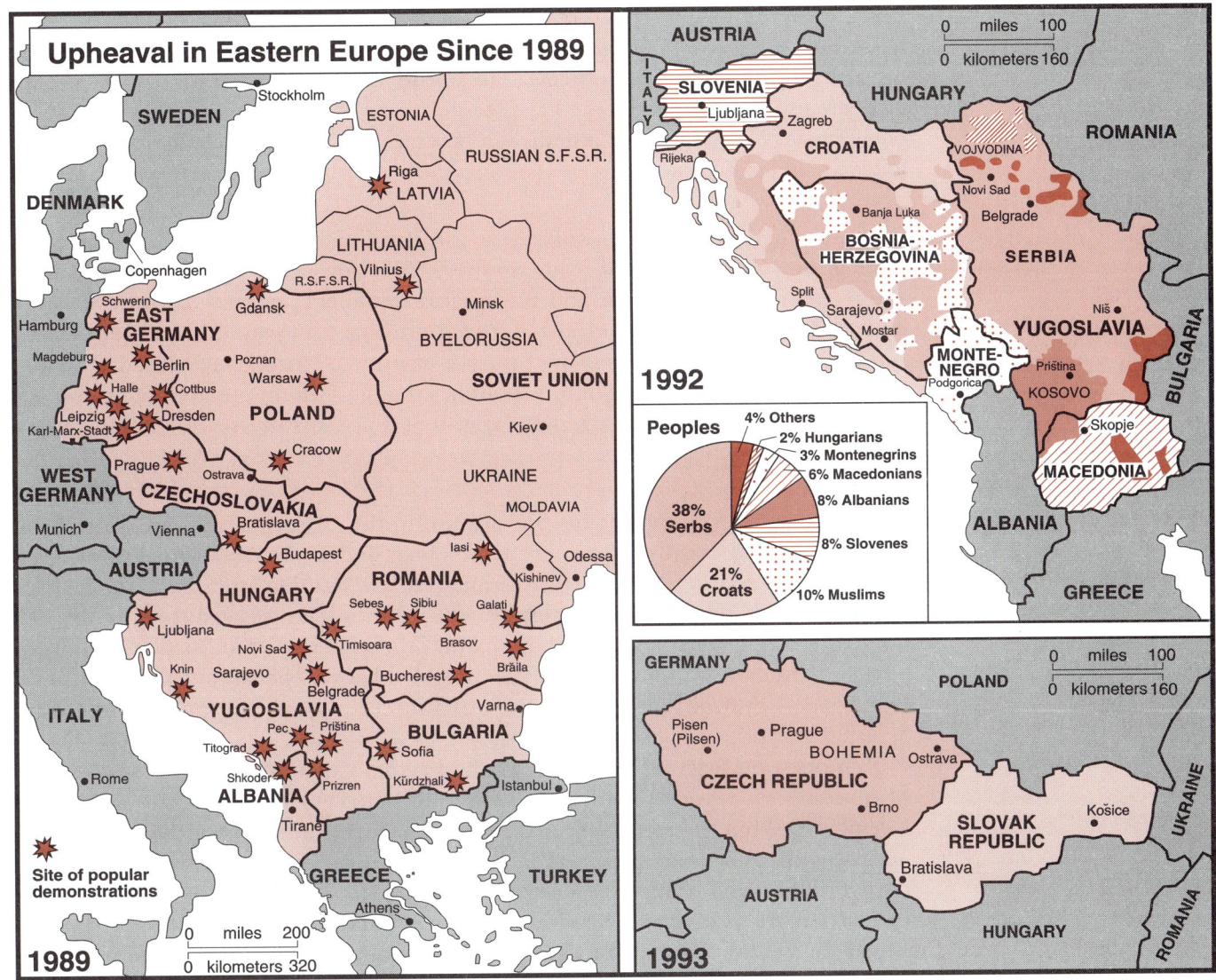

Upheaval in Eastern Europe Since 1989

1989

Site of popular demonstrations

1992

Peoples

- 38% Serbs
- 21% Croats
- 10% Muslims
- 8% Slovenes
- 8% Albanians
- 6% Macedonians
- 3% Montenegrins
- 2% Hungarians
- 4% Others

1993

Map of Eastern Europe: The above maps show the changes in Eastern Europe after the collapse of communism in 1989. Note that most of the new countries are actually nations that existed before World War II.

the two as the same, took a new pride in their nation and directed their anger directly at the Soviet government. Gorbachëv, who never understood this, continued to remain a strong supporter of communism and became as unpopular as the system he defended. He also came under heavy criticism from conservative hardline Communists for allowing the election.

Gorbachëv's Retreat from Reform (1989–1991)

In March of 1989, the Baltic Sea satellite nations of Lithuania and Estonia declared their independence. Neighboring Latvia followed later in the year. These declarations were encouraged by the withdrawal of Soviet domination in Eastern Europe that was taking place under the Gorbachëv Doctrine. That same month, the Congress of People's Deputies repealed the Communist party's monopoly of political power. This meant that the Communists could no longer be the only political party allowed by law. At the May Day celebration on May 1 (the traditional day of celebration worldwide for all socialists and Communists), Gorbachëv and the other Soviet leaders were jeered at by protesters. At the Communist party

Congress in July, Boris Yeltsin resigned dramatically from the party. With the resignation of foreign minister Eduard Shevardnadze in December, Gorbachëv began to back down from his reforms. He chose hard-line Communists Gennadii Yanayev and Valentin Pavlov as vice-president and premier. By February 1991, Gorbachëv was calling himself "a dedicated Communist" and criticizing many former allies as "radicals."

The Union Treaty of Republics

With Yeltsin's election as president of the Russian Republic, the largest nation among the 15 republics that made up the USSR, Gorbachëv now had a rival. Soon strains between the Russian and Soviet governments appeared. In July, Shevardnadze also quit the Communist party, founding a movement for democratic reform. Totally overwhelmed by the turn of events, Gorbachëv agreed to sign a union treaty with the heads of ten republics that gave them greater autonomy. His agreement to the new arrangement frightened conservatives into calling on the military to "save the country."

The Russian Revolution of 1991

In August, while Gorbachëv was on vacation in the Crimea, a military **coup d'etat** (an unexpected seizure of power) took place, led by Yanayev and Pavlov. Gorbachëv was put under house arrest and martial law was declared. Lacking any public support, including military support, the coup was unsuccessful and collapsed after three days. Yeltsin, who had appeared on the steps of the Russian Republic's government building and defied the illegal takeover, became a national hero. Gorbachëv returned and the leaders of the coup were disgraced. Some were arrested and others committed suicide.

Rumors soon began that Gorbachëv had actually planned the takeover as a way of undoing his reforms before the Communist party leadership had completely lost power. While these accusations were never proven, the coup had made him appear weak and incompetent. The failed overthrow discredited the Communist party and the KGB. This turn of events became known as the Russian Revolution of 1991. Disregarding the previous unsigned union agreement, Yeltsin declared Russia an independent state. One by one, the other republics also claimed independence. Gorbachëv tried desperately, but unsuccessfully, to stop the swift breakup of the Soviet Union. On December 25, 1991, he resigned from the presidency of an empire that no longer existed. That evening, the Soviet flag was lowered from the Kremlin for the last time. This historic episode now meant that both communism in Russia and the Soviet Union were over. The revolution that had shook the world seventy years earlier ended not with a bang, but a whimper.

The Commonwealth of Independent States (1991–)

With the USSR disbanded, each republic held its own elections and established its own independent government. Russia, as the largest and most populous of these states, took a leadership position in creating a new union of autonomous nations, the Commonwealth of Independent States. The United Nations recognized each new nation, giving them their own representatives.

Some republics did not make a smooth transition. Civil war flared up in Georgia between the newly elected government under Eduard Shervardnadze and rebels who refused to recognize it. Fighting between the Christians of Armenia and the Muslims of Azerbaijan also began. This conflict, which had started in the last years of Gorbachëv's rule, grew worse without the Soviet government to mediate.

While Russia tried to take the role of leader of the new Commonwealth, the other republics were still fearful of once again being dominated by them. This was especially true in Ukraine, where strong feelings of nationalism had risen. In 1992 and 1993, Russia and Ukraine negotiated a compromise over the Black Sea fleet in the Crimea, an area in the southern Ukraine that was a very important naval base for the Russians. The two nations finally agreed that it would belong to Ukraine, but the Russian fleet would be allowed to use it.

The Conflict Between Yeltsin and Parliament

In the fall of 1993, President Yeltsin dismissed the Congress of People's Deputies. Composed mainly of Communists from the Gorbachëv Period, this former Soviet parliament had blocked all of his efforts to reform the Russian economic system into a capitalist free market. Yeltsin demanded that new elections be held. He pointed out that most of the parliament's deputies had never really been elected by the people as they ran unopposed in most cases in the first elections of 1989. Realizing that they probably would not be returned to office in a fair election, the majority of representatives refused to stop meeting and barricaded themselves in the parliament building. After a brief standoff between the parliament and their supporters, Yeltsin ordered troops to re-take the parliament building and arrest the rebellious deputies. These decisive actions were successful and added to Yeltsin's popularity.

Yeltsin also took steps toward creating a new constitution wherein the presidency would gain greater power. While this move was seen by some as the first step to a dictatorship, others saw it as necessary to push through economic reforms. Not

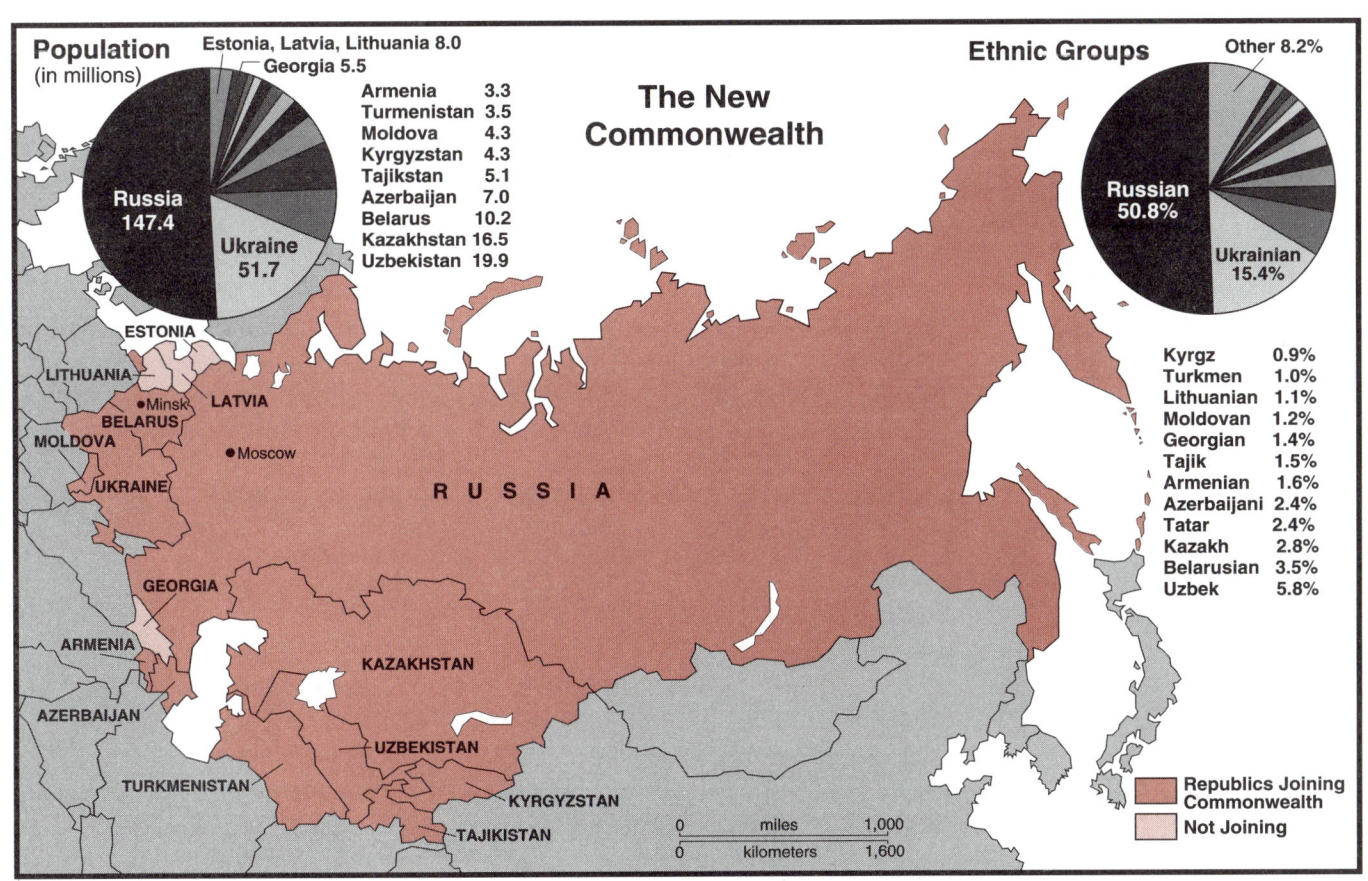

Population (in millions)

Estonia, Latvia, Lithuania 8.0
Georgia 5.5

Armenia	3.3
Turmenistan	3.5
Moldova	4.3
Kyrgyzstan	4.3
Tajikstan	5.1
Azerbaijan	7.0
Belarus	10.2
Kazakhstan	16.5
Uzbekistan	19.9

Russia 147.4

Ukraine 51.7

The New Commonwealth

Ethnic Groups

Other 8.2%

Russian 50.8%

Ukrainian 15.4%

Kyrgz	0.9%
Turkmen	1.0%
Lithuanian	1.1%
Moldovan	1.2%
Georgian	1.4%
Tajik	1.5%
Armenian	1.6%
Azerbaijani	2.4%
Tatar	2.4%
Kazakh	2.8%
Belarusian	3.5%
Uzbek	5.8%

RUSSIA

ESTONIA
LITHUANIA
LATVIA
•Minsk
BELARUS
MOLDOVA
UKRAINE
•Moscow
GEORGIA
ARMENIA
AZERBAIJAN
KAZAKHSTAN
UZBEKISTAN
TURKMENISTAN
KYRGYZSTAN
TAJIKISTAN

0 miles 1,000
0 kilometers 1,600

Republics Joining Commonwealth
Not Joining

Map of the C.I.S. in 1991: The map above shows the Commonwealth of Independent States. After the disintegration of the Soviet Union, most of the newly independent nations formed a federation in order to promote economic growth and provide mutual security. It is interesting to see how dependent these nations have become on each other, especially Russia, which is the largest and most populated.

The Collapse of Communism in the Soviet Union and Eastern Europe 707 suprisingly, in a nation that has only known autocracy throughout its history, Yeltsin's bid for greater power has given many Russians new confidence in him as a strong leader. This perception, along with his great popularity, continues to keep him in power despite the great suffering the economic transformation is creating.

As 1994 began, a spirit of cooperation existed between most nations of the Commonwealth (C.I.S.). Each was still struggling, however, to solve its economic problems and make a smooth transition to capitalism and a free market. The success of these efforts may well decide the extent to which they will become and remain democracies. The damage done by the dominance of a command economy and a corrupt bureaucracy (when part of the Soviet Union) will be difficult to correct. A very difficult road lies ahead.

Eastern Europe (1945–1992)

Soviet Domination (1945–1988)

The end of World War II brought a considerable extension of Soviet power in Eastern Europe. It imposed Communist-dominated governments on the Baltic States (Estonia, Latvia and Lithuania), Poland, Romania, Bulgaria, Hungary, and East Germany. In Czechoslovakia, Yugoslavia, and Albania, local Communist governments took control and worked in accommodation with the Soviets (see Chapter 35, "The Cold War").

The End of Soviet Domination (1988–1990)

With the announcement of the Gorbachëv Doctrine in 1988 and the withdrawal of the Soviet presence in Eastern Europe, the Communist regimes began to fall. The first signs were in Poland and Hungary where dissatisfaction with the regimes had reached crisis proportions. The loss of Soviet economic and political support forced these governments to begin backing down. By the end of 1989, most of those nations had already overthrown, or were in the process of overthrowing, the governments placed there by the Soviets. Yugoslavia and Albania, the two countries whose Communist governments had not been imposed by the Soviet Union, would undergo political change a year later.

East Germany

The Berlin Wall, the hated symbol of Communist domination and the Cold War, was torn down as the East German regime under Eric Honecker was overthrown. East Germany's re-unification with the West in 1990 marked the end of the Communist Era in Eastern Europe and the start of a turbulent period of reorganization (see Chapter 32, "World War II").

Poland

When Poland regained its independence after World War I, it became a democracy. Such was its political status until 1926, when an authoritarian regime under

Marshal Joseph Pilsudski was begun. In 1939, the nation was invaded and occupied by Nazi Germany. (This marked the beginning of World War II in Europe.) In 1945, with Soviet forces driving the Nazis out, Poland came under Stalin's control. A Soviet-supported Polish Communist regime was placed over the country. Poland now became a satellite of the USSR.

The Rise of Solidarity In 1980, the anti-Communist labor union Solidarity began to challenge the authority of the Polish Communist government under General Wojciech Jaruzelski. Solidarity's leader, Lech Walesa, led the union in an eight-year struggle against the regime, despite the fact that it was officially banned in 1981. In the summer of 1988, strikes throughout the nation forced Jaruzelski to agree to negotiations with the workers of the still illegal trade union. The government agreed to legalize Solidarity and hold partially free elections that would divide power in the Polish parliament between the Communists and their opposition.

The Collapse of Communism in Poland In the June 1989 elections, Solidarity won all the opposition seats in the parliament (35 percent of the total) and 99 out of 100 senate seats in the newly created two-chamber legislature. The Communists also lost most of their "safe" seats as they failed to receive the mandatory 50 percent of the vote. Jaruzelski was elected president and appointed Tadeusz Mazowiecki as the nation's first non-Communist prime minister since Soviet domination. In December, the Polish parliament eliminated the Communist party's constitutional guarantee of leadership, officially transforming Poland into a republic, and forcing Jaruzelski to resign. He was replaced by Walesa, who led his country as it began its struggle to transform its economy into a capitalist system.

Hungary

After World War I, Hungary lost two thirds of its land and population in peace settlements. The Habsburg monarchy was replaced by a military dictatorship under Admiral Nicholas Horthy. He sided with Germany in World War II in hopes of regaining its lost territories. After the war, the Soviet Union installed a dictatorship under Matyas Rakosi, who had been trained in Moscow. Hungary now also became a satellite of the USSR. The Hungarian people never accepted this imposition. Stalin's death in 1953 gave Hungary and the nations of Eastern Europe the false impression that they could develop independently.

The 1956 Hungarian Revolution In 1956, Imre Nagy, a Hungarian Communist, became party leader. In an atmosphere of great nationalism, Nagy announced that Hungary would reestablish a multi-party system and pursue a neutral foreign policy. This would mean abandoning its connection with the USSR. Such a striking announcement angered the Soviets. They responded by mounting an invasion of the country in October. Nagy was removed from power and later executed. This harsh policy of not permitting independent actions by Soviet satellites became known as the Brezhnev Doctrine.

The Collapse of Communism in Hungary Janos Kadar was installed as Hungary's new Communist dictator. While Kadar ruthlessly supressed dissent, he gradually introduced reforms that permitted limited private economic enterprise and greater cultural expression. In May of 1988, Kadar fell from power and was replaced by Karoly Grosz. He began to democratize the nation and introduce reforms to revitalize its economy. A year later, the Hungarian government dismantled the barbed-wire fence on the German border that had come to symbolize the Iron Curtain. It had long prevented many East Germans, who were tired of the harsh government control and poor living standards in their country, from crossing through Hungary to the West. In an act of defiance, refugees were allowed through.

The Establishment of Democracy in Hungary　In September 1988, as a multi-party system began to appear, negotiations were held between the Communist leaders and representatives of the new political parties that had formed to assure an orderly transition of power. It was decided that Hungary would become a democratic republic with a one-chamber legislature elected by universal suffrage (the right of all citizens to vote), and a weak presidency. In the October elections of 1989, despite a change in name to the Hungarian Socialist party, the Communists were badly defeated. In December, parliament dissolved itself. New elections in 1990 swept the remaining Communists from power. The new parliament ended the Communists' control through legislation and put Hungary on the path to a fully capitalist economy. In June 1990, Imre Nagy was re-buried with honors as a hero of the failed 1956 Hungarian Revolution.

Czechoslovakia

Czechoslovakia, the union of Bohemia, Moravia, and Slovakia, was created at the end of World War I from the Austro-Hungarian Empire. It was the only Eastern European nation to maintain a parliamentary democracy from 1918 to 1938. The Czech experiment with democracy ended sadly in 1938, due to the attack by Nazi Germany (see Chapter 32, "World War II"). In retaliation, the Czech government expelled 2.5 million ethnic Germans in 1945, after Germany's defeat. With strong support from the Soviet Union, the Czech Communist party was able to gain 38 percent of the vote and some key government positions in the 1946 elections. In February of 1948, working with the Soviet Union, the Communists seized power from the Czechoslovakian president, Eduard Benes, and began Stalinist purges of dissidents. By the end of the year, Czechoslovakia was a Soviet satellite. Its people were severely distressed as a result of coming under Soviet control.

The Prague Spring　After 20 years of Communist rule, discontent reached a crisis level. This resulted in the removal of the president and party leader Antonin Novotny. He was replaced by Alexander Dubček, who immediately initiated a reform program. From January to August of 1968, Dubček abolished censorship, allowed greater cultural and intellectual freedom, began to improve relations with the West, and discussed further democratization. Calling his policies "Socialism with a human face," the brief period of Dubček's rule became known as the "Prague Spring" (Prague was the capital of Czechoslovkia). The Dubček reforms were seen in Czechoslovakia as a welcome change, just as spring is enjoyed after winter. Fearing they were setting a bad example, the Soviets ordered the leaders to limit the reforms. When they refused, the Soviet Union invaded Czechoslovakia with Warsaw Pact troops. Dubček was forced out of office, to the dismay of the Czechoslovakian people. His successor, Gustav Husak, restored strict Communist control over the nation. Husak remained in power until Milos Jakes replaced him in December of 1987.

The Velvet Revolution   Twenty years after the Soviet invasion, the deteriorating economy in Czechoslovakia and events in other Soviet satellites, most notably Poland and Hungary, encouraged dissent. The violent reaction of the police to student demonstrations and the arrest of the popular dramatist/political essayist/human rights advocate Vaclav Havel in 1989 sparked even greater waves of protest. Havel was the co-founder of the Charter 77 reform movement, a group based on a document developed by the Helsinki Conference and an international organization that monitors and reports on human rights violations. He was released within five months due to public pressure. By summer of 1989, student demonstrations had started again.

In November, their numbers reached 25,000 and the authorities reacted by clubbing the students off the streets. Two days later, a demonstration of hundreds of thousands filled Wenceslas Square in Prague. It brought together the two largest groups opposing the Communist government; the Czech Civic Forum (led by Havel) and the Slovak Public Against Violence in Slovakia. After several days of equally huge demonstrations, the Jakes government resigned. This was the beginning of what became known as Czechoslovakia's Velvet Revolution. Starting in December, the Communist-dominated parliament voted to shift to a free market economy and a Western-type parliamentary system, hoping to maintain their power in the face of widespread dissatisfaction. Dubček was named chairman of the National parliament and Havel was elected interim president of Czechoslovakia, the first non-Communist leader in more than forty years. In June of 1990, Havel was re-elected president and the Communists were swept out of power in the national elections, receiving only 13 percent of the vote. The new government began the transition from a command economy to a free market. It also had to undo forty years of economic mismanagement and environmental damage from heavy industrialization without pollution controls.

Czechoslovakia Becomes Two Nations   By 1991, there was discontent in Slovakia. The Slovak people, who had long felt dominated by the Czechs, became resentful of Havel's intention to wind down Slovakia's chief industry, the production of arms. The Slovak prime minister, Vladimir Meciar, announced that the Republic would continue to sell arms without seeking the national government in Prague's approval. A national hero in the Czech republics of Bohemia and Moravia and a respected figure internationally, Havel became highly unpopular in Slovakia, largely due to Meciar. Adopting a nationalist doctrine, Meciar mounted a campaign to promote Slovak secession from Czechoslovakia. Slovak opposition leaders in the capital of Bratislava, including Dubček, called for his resignation. Despite a fierce battle, Meciar succeeded in gaining a vote for independence in the summer of 1992. Havel resigned as president in disgust, warning against the division of the nation. On January 1, 1993, Czechoslovakia legally separated into the nations of the Czech Republic and Slovakia. With the wisdom of the split still in question on the part of many Slovaks as well as Czechs, the two countries face an uncertain future.

Romania

The nation of Romania, combining Wallachia, Moldavia, Bessarabia, and later Transylvania, was formed in the early nineteenth century. It gained independence from the Ottoman Empire in 1878. After World War I, the Romanian monarchy supported a fascist dictatorship under Marshal Ion Antonescu. He joined his nation to the Axis powers in World War II. Toward the end of the war, Romania became disgusted with the Nazis and made a separate peace with the Allies. Subsequently, Romania became an independent constitutional monarchy under King Michael V. The monarchy lasted from 1945 until 1948, when a Soviet-supported Romanian Communist party took control of the government. The Communists ousted the king and established a harsh dictatorship under Gheorghe Gheorghiu-Dej.

The Dictatorship of Ceausescu After Gheorghiu-Dej's death in 1965, Nicolae Ceauşescu replaced him as leader of the Communist regime. While he appeared to be a reformer, Ceauşescu was in reality a brutal dictator. Although Romania seemed to enjoy a measure of independence from the Soviet Union, Ceauşescu secretly cleared all his actions with Moscow. Under his rule, Romania's economy and environment were seriously damaged through waste, incompetence, and corruption. His racist dreams of creating a dominant Romanian people inspired anti-contraceptive and anti-abortion policies. These resulted in a high infant mortality rate and cruel and unsanitary state orphanages that often sold children to foreigners. The extravagant and wasteful life-style of the Ceauşescu further antagonized the Romanian people. They were upset with the dictator's image abroad as a reformer and independent Communist leader. Pressure for reform finally exploded in December of 1989 when the Ceauşescu regime was violently overthrown. Ceauşescu and his wife were arrested, tried, and then executed on Romanian national television.

The National Salvation Front The new government, called the National Salvation Front, was composed of ex-Communists. The new interim president, Ion Iliescu, was formerly a close associate of Ceauşescu. The new government outlawed communism, disbanded the Romanian secret police, and began the privatization of collective farms. In Romania's first free elections in May of 1990, Iliescu was re-elected president by an overwhelming majority. During the campaign, however, anti-government demonstrators were brutally suppressed and opposition leaders were physically attacked. There was also a question of possible fraud in the election itself. By 1991, there was growing dissatisfaction with the government, whom many saw as a thinly disguised continuation of the Ceauşescu regime. Protests and demonstrations forced the National Salvation Front's vice president, Claudiu Iordache, to resign, charging that the government was protecting former Communists because of information that could associate the leaders with Ceauşescu. Dissatisfaction with the Iliescu government continued into 1994.

Bulgaria

Bulgaria was created in 1878 as a result of the Russo-Turkish War. In both World War I and World War II, it sided with Germany in hopes of regaining control of territories lost during the Second Balkan War of 1913 (see Chapter 25, "Discontent in the Austro-Hungarian and Ottoman Empires"). In 1944, Soviet troops entered the country and installed a Communist-dominated coalition. A brutal Communist regime under Georgi Dmitrov ruled Bulgaria until 1954.

The Zhivkov Regime Dmitrov was replaced by Todor Zhivkov, who attempted to divert the growing discontent with the Communist system by emphasizing Bulgarian nationalism. During the 1980s, Zhivkov persecuted the Turkish minority in Bulgaria, forcing them to adopt Bulgarian names and culture—or face deportation. Despite a massive campaign that appealed to Bulgarian history and culture, the Communist dictator did not succeed. The continuing decline of the economy combined with the persecution of minorities created unrest throughout the country. Anticipating an overthrow, Zhivkov abruptly resigned in November of 1989 as both head of state and Communist party leader.

The Collapse of Communism in Bulgaria In January of 1990, the Bulgarian parliament, the National Assembly, agreed to end the constitutionally granted dominance of the Communist party of the Bulgarian government. The Communists also lost their control over the armed forces. In February, the new premier, Andrei Lukanov, appointed a cabinet and a new all-Communist government. By March, the National Assembly had passed laws permitting ethnic Turks to reassume their Islamic names and the practice of their faith. The Communist party, renamed the Bulgarian Socialist party, won control of the new parliament after elections were held in June. Despite their strong showing, the Socialists faced growing opposition. In November, a wave of demonstrations forced Lukanov and his one-party cabinet to resign. A new coalition government was formed by the Socialists and the Union of Democratic Forces, a group made up of 19 political parties in favor of establishing a democratic government. The Union of Democratic Forces was divided into two internal groups, one promising gradual economic reform, the other favoring faster-paced reforms. In the summer of 1991, a new constitution was created. Yet, the former Communists still remain the dominant political force in the nation.

Albania

Albania was ruled by the Ottoman Empire from the fifteenth century until 1912, when it was established as an independent nation after the First Balkan War (see Chapter 25, "Discontent in the Austro-Hungarian and Ottoman Empires"). A nation with a Muslim majority, it was ruled by an Eastern Orthodox Christian monarch, King Zog, as a compromise with the other nations surrounding Albania. In 1939, fascist Italy invaded the country, ousting the King and establishing a military dictatorship. After World War II, Albania became a satellite of the Soviet Union under the independent and hard-line Communist dictator Enver Hoxha (1908–1985).

Albania Under Hoxha Albania suffered under Hoxha's brutal and destructive regime. Albanian Communist rule forced the tiny nation into political and economic exile from the rest of the world. All religion was savagely repressed and the country had the worst living standards of all of the Eastern European nations. A dedicated Stalinist, Hoxha thought the Soviet dictator's successors were far too liberal and mild. Disillusioned with the USSR, Albania broke its ties with the Soviet Bloc and became allied with Communist China and its equally hard-line leader Mao Zedong in 1960.

The Collapse of Communism in Albania Following Hoxha's death in 1985, the Communist domination of Albania slowly began to crumble. Hoxha's successor, Ramiz Alia, was forced to begin political and economic reforms in March of 1990, as he saw the rest of Eastern Europe abandoning the Communist system. Faced with internal unrest and economic collapse, Alia slowly began to decentralize the economic system. In March of 1991, Europe's poorest country finally ended its isolation by establishing diplomatic ties with the European Community, the United States, and the Soviet Union. The government also legalized labor strikes and ended the ban on religious practice. In addition, Albania held its first multi-party elections since the Communist takeover.

Despite the Communists' victory with a two-thirds majority in a questionably run election, by June the unpopular government was forced to step down. A multi-party coalition was formed to temporarily run the nation. In the spring of 1992, new elections were held, after which the Communists were removed from power. The new Albanian government faced enormous domestic problems in trying to undo the damage of the previous Communist regime. It also faced great external pressures, especially from Serbia, which is at odds with the Albanian-dominated independent republic of Kosovo, in the former Yugoslavia.

Yugoslavia

Unlike the other nations of its region, Yugoslavia was a mixture of nations and religions. It emerged as a nation after World War I, known as the Kingdom of the Serbs, Croats, and Slovenes (the three Slavic peoples it united). In 1929, it was renamed the Kingdom of Yugoslavia (Southern Slavs). It was ruled by the Serbian monarchy until World War II, when the Germans ousted the king and established a military dictatorship. A similar fascist regime was created by the Nazis in Croatia. After the war, the Soviet Union occupied the nation, where the Yugoslavian Communists, under Josip Brodz, known as Marshal Tito (r. 1945–1980), had already seized power.

Yugoslavia Under Tito Tito divided Yugoslavia into the Republics of Serbia, Croatia, Slovenia, Montenegro, Macedonia, and Bosnia-Hercegovina, with the two autonomous (self-governing) provinces of Vojvodina and Kosovo. In March of 1948, Tito, who did not owe his power to the Soviets as other Eastern European Communist regimes did, left the Soviet Bloc. Yugoslavia became a Communist dictatorship under Tito that was free of Soviet control. Tito ruled Yugoslavia until 1980, using a combination of force, the development of a Yugoslavian nationalism, and limited capitalism. The nation's ability to remain independent of the Soviet Union was beneficial.

The Disintegration of Yugoslavia After Tito's death, the forces of local nationalism began to resurface. The dictator's personal appeal and use of force had prevented the various nationalities that composed Yugoslavia from traditional territorial disputes. Many Serbians felt that the Croatian-born Tito had deliberately broken up the Serbian population, which was numerically larger, into many independent Yugoslav republics in order to weaken their political influence.

War in Slovenia and Croatia. By 1990, the nations of Croatia and Slovenia declared themselves independent. Trying to prevent the disintegration of the country, the Serbian-dominated Yugoslav government and military sent troops into Slovenia and Croatia. The well-organized Slovenian government was able to successfully repulse the government troops with its volunteer army. The Yugoslav government was forced to recognize Slovenia's independence. However, in Croatia, it was a different situation. Croatia's declaration of independence prompted a violent response from its sizable Serbian minority. The Serbians and Croatians became involved in local conflicts which grew larger when the Yugoslavian army interfered in support of the Serbian minority. While outwardly claiming that they were trying to prevent Croatia's break from the Yugoslav union, it soon became clear that the Serbian-dominated army had taken sides in what had become an ethnic war between Serbs and Croats. Acts of violence and brutality were committed on both sides, with the term "ethnic cleansing" (killing with the intention of wiping out a whole race of people) being used to describe the extent of the violence there.

Conflict in Bosnia-Hercegovina.   As a truce was finally reached between Croatia and Serbia in 1991, conflict broke out between Serbians and Muslims of Bosnia-Hercegovina, a heavily Muslim republic with large Serbian and Croatian populations (whereas the Muslims are the largest, no group is over 50 percent). This was the result of the Bosnian government's declaration of its independence from Yugoslavia. The Serbs of Bosnia-Hercegovina feared the Muslim-dominated government and wanted union with the other Serbian areas of Yugoslavia. The Bosnian Serbs soon were supported by Yugoslav army units sent to stop the fighting and prevent Bosnia-Hercegovina from leaving Yugoslavia. As in Croatia, it soon became an ethnic war between the Serbs and Bosnian Muslims. The Croatians soon became involved as well with Croatian army units invading parts of Bosnia-Hercegovina. By 1993, Serbia and Croatia controlled large parts of Bosnia-Hercegovina.

The conflicts among all three of these groups are religious and ethnic, since all have historical roots in that region. The Serbians, the largest of the major ethnic groups of Yugoslavia, believe that both the Croatians and the Bosnian Muslims will persecute them wherever they are a minority. This fear is based on past massacres the Serbians suffered from both groups. The conflict was also encouraged by nationalist politicians such as the Serbian President Slobodon Milosevic and the Croatian President Franjo Tudtman. Finally, there is much religious conflict between the Eastern Orthodox Serbs, the Roman Catholic Croatians, and the Muslim Bosnians.

Despite efforts on the part of the United Nations and the European Community, the conflicts have not yet been resolved. In late 1992, the nation of Yugoslavia officially disappeared as the remaining republics (Montenegro, Macedonia) and autonomous provinces (Vojvodina and Kosovo) declared independence. As of 1994, the killing continued in the bloodiest tragedy of the decade.

Summary

It was difficult to believe that the Soviet Union had disintegrated so rapidly. After half a century of confrontation between East and West, the West emerged as "victor." The reforms placed into motion by Khrushchëv ended in the fall of Gorbachëv and the rise of Yeltsin. It now all seems so obvious—the USSR had been unable to meet the demands required of a superpower at home or abroad. It again showed that a leader cannot allow people limited "openness." Once the door is opened it must be opened all the way—the people will demand it. Gorbachëv was carried along on the tidal wave of reform that he initiated.

There are many problems facing the ex-Soviet Empire. We must remember that its people are attempting to reform both the political and economic areas at the same time. Without a long tradition of democracy, this will take time. The failure of the Communist system and transition to a market economy will be difficult. Ethnicity has raised its ugly head in a number of areas, resulting in bloodshed. This new situation will pose important questions for the United States. What should our role be—a participant in change or a bystander?

Review Exercises

I. Matching

Directions: Match the names in Column A with the achievement they are *best known* for in Column B.

Column A
1. Lavrentii Beria
2. King Zog
3. Boris Pasternak
4. Eric Honecker
5. Nikita Khrushchëv
6. Marshal Joseph Pilsudski
7. Andrey Sakharov
8. Vladimir Meciar
9. Marshal Ion Antonescu
10. Vladimir Dudinstev

Column B
(a) fascist government of Romania
(b) pre-war Polish dictator
(c) *My Country and the World*
(d) Slovak independence
(e) *Doctor Zhivago*
(f) *Not By Bread Alone*
(g) last leader of East Germany
(h) KGB
(i) only Albanian king
(j) 20th Soviet Communist party Congress

II. Matching

Directions: Match the words in Column A with the *correct description* in Column B.

Column A
1. Gulag Archipelago
2. Kosovo
3. National Salvation Front
4. nomenklatura
5. Détente
6. Glasnost
7. Solidarity
8. Charter 77
9. National Assembly
10. Perestroika

Column B
(a) replaced Ceauşescu regime
(b) Bulgarian parliament
(c) Czechoslovakian reform movement
(d) openness
(e) ruling elite
(f) understanding
(g) Siberian concentration camps
(h) territory disputed by Serbia and Albania
(i) restructuring
(j) Polish trade union

III. Map Exercise

Directions: Use the map to locate the place associated with each of the following statements. For each statement, write the *letter* of the place.

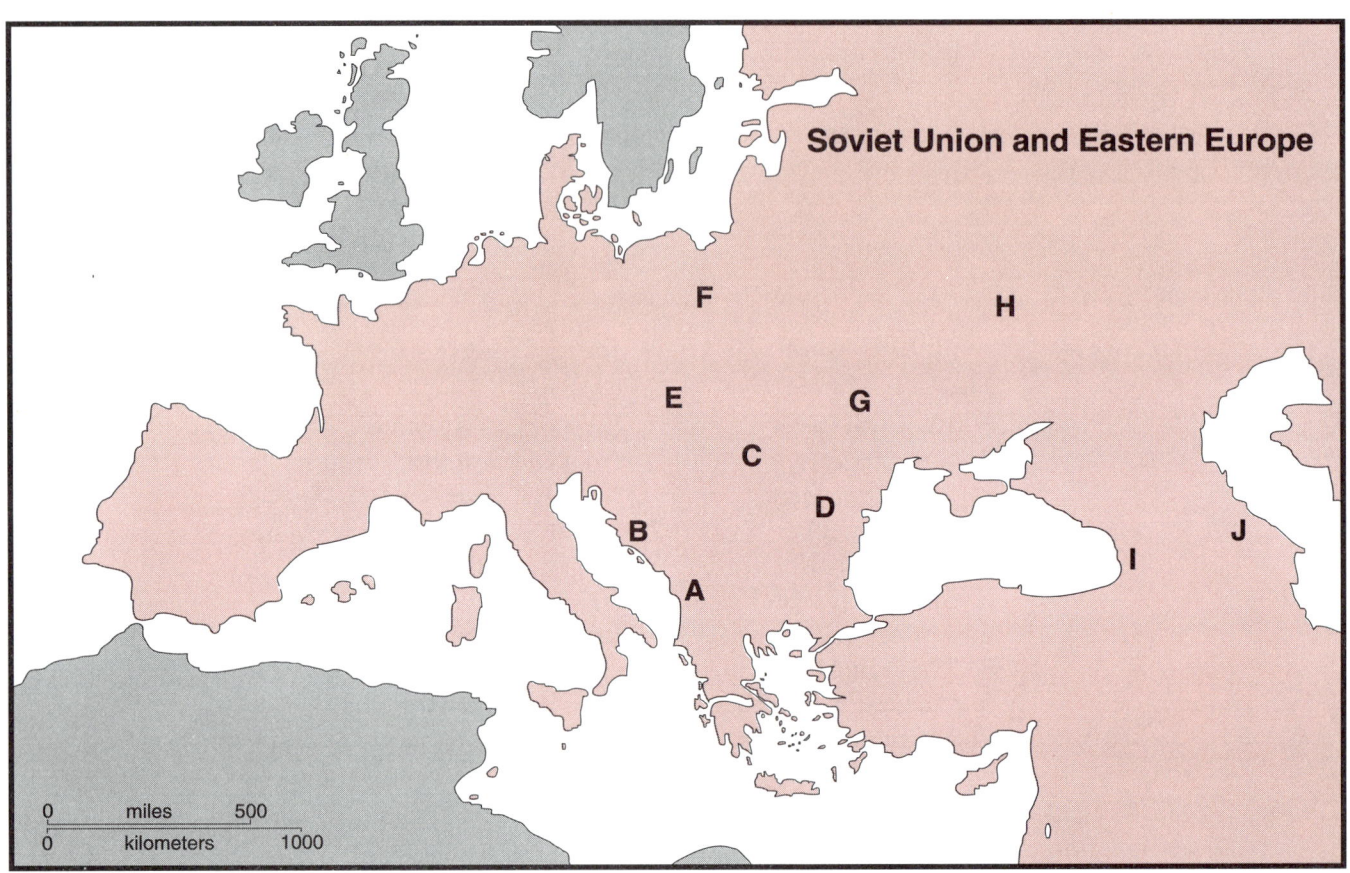

1. _____ The cities of Moscow and St. Petersburg are here.

2. _____ The Chernobyl' disaster took place in this nation.

3. _____ There has been a civil war in this country since the collapse of the USSR.

4. _____ This nation continues to fight with Azerbaijan.

5. _____ Soviet troops invaded here in 1956.

6. _____ Solidarity led workers of this nation.

7. _____ Ceaușescu dominated this country.

8. _____ This was where the Prague Spring and Velvet Revolution took place.

9. _____ Civil war has divided this country into conflicting nations.

10. _____ This nation was created in 1913 as part of the Balkan Wars.

IV. Multiple Choice

Directions: Find the *letter* of the correct answers.

1. Which of the following is not true of the USSR after World War II?

   (a) Soviet troops occupied Eastern Europe.
   (b) Despite an increase in housing construction, it was not enough.
   (c) Food shortages were common.
   (d) Soviet industry concentrated on consumer goods.

2. The period following Stalin's death was known as the

   (a) purge.
   (b) Great Thaw.
   (c) samizdat.
   (d) millennium.

3. All of the following individuals were prevented from receiving Nobel Prizes *except*

   (a) Aleksandr Solzhenitsyn.
   (b) Boris Pasternak.
   (c) Andrey Sakharov.
   (d) Vladimir Dudinstev.

4. The Virgin Lands Program failed because

   (a) the government refused to spend the money needed.
   (b) droughts turned the area into a dustbowl.
   (c) Soviet technology was not advanced enough.
   (d) there was mismanagement by the bureaucracy.

5. The Brezhnev regime was characterized by its

   (a) extension of political reform.
   (b) economic stagnation.
   (c) departure from traditional Soviet foreign policy goals.
   (d) improvement in the quality of consumer goods.

6. Increased contact with the West under Brezhnev resulted in the policy of

   (a) Détente.
   (b) Glasnost.
   (c) Perestroika.
   (d) samizdat.

7. The immediate crisis that allowed Gorbachëv to make his reforms was the

   (a) failing military efforts in Afghanistan.
   (b) Chernobyl' meltdown in Ukraine.
   (c) poor economy of the USSR.
   (d) unrest of the nationalities in the Soviet Republics.

8. Which of the following was *not* an example of Perestroika?

    (a) the Enterprise Law of 1987
    (b) the Law of Cooperatives
    (c) the Agricultural Reform Law of 1988
    (d) the Gorbachëv Doctrine

9. The most important result of the Gorbachëv Doctrine was

    (a) economic reform.
    (b) greater freedom of personal expression and the press.
    (c) improved relations with the West.
    (d) the collapse of the Communist regimes in Eastern Europe.

10. Gorbachëv's reforms were ultimately ineffective because

    (a) he was undermined by the nomenklatura.
    (b) they were overshadowed by the unrest in the Republics.
    (c) the Soviet people were unwilling to cooperate.
    (d) he was unable to allow the Communist party to lose its dominance.

11. The greatest challenge Russia will face under Boris Yeltsin is

    (a) creating a new union of independent republics.
    (b) solving the dispute with Ukraine over the Black Sea fleet.
    (c) transforming Russia's economy to free market.
    (d) ending the fighting between individual Republics.

12. Opposition to Communist domination in Poland was led by

    (a) the Roman Catholic Church.
    (b) Solidarity.
    (c) Polish intellectuals.
    (d) dissatisfied peasants.

13. The Hungarian nationalist leader removed by Soviet troops in 1956 was

    (a) Matyas Rakosi.
    (b) Imre Nagy.
    (c) Janos Kadar.
    (d) Karoly Grosz.

14. The Czechoslovakian nationalist leader ousted by Warsaw Pact forces in 1968 was

    (a) Eduard Benes.
    (b) Antonin Novotny.
    (c) Alexander Dubček.
    (d) Gustav Husak.

15. The "Prague Spring" refers to

   (a) the brief period of progressive government under Dubček.
   (b) a rise in the Czechoslovakian economy under Kadar.
   (c) improvement in the economy since the fall of communism under Havel.
   (d) the especially beautiful weather in Bohemia at that time of year.

16. The overthrow of communism in Czechoslovakia was known as the

   (a) Havel Revolution.
   (b) Wenceslas Revolution.
   (c) Second Czech Revolution.
   (d) Velvet Revolution.

17. Which was *not* true of the Ceauşescu regime in Romania?

   (a) It promoted a false image abroad of independence from the USSR.
   (b) The government enforced birth control and created humane orphanages.
   (c) Mismanaged industry resulted in pollution and environmental damage.
   (d) Romania's economic resources were squandered on wasteful projects.

18. Bulgarian Communist leader Todor Zhivkov tried to preserve his regime by

   (a) using military force.
   (b) appealing to nationalism.
   (c) allowing limited capitalism.
   (d) making sweeping social reforms.

19. The Albanian dictator Enver Hoxha

   (a) established a Stalinist regime.
   (b) experimented with limited capitalism.
   (c) tolerated religion.
   (d) traded heavily with the West.

20. Marshal Tito maintained the unity of Yugoslavia through

   (a) military force.
   (b) nationalism.
   (c) limited capitalism.
   (d) all of the above

V. Thought Questions

Directions: Answer the following questions in essay form.

   1. It has been stated that Soviet leadership has been a contest between reformers and reactionaries.

      A. Examine the domestic policy of the Soviet leaders Stalin, Khrushchev, Brezhnev, and Gorbachëv.
      B. Discuss the accuracy of the statement. Base your argument on the policies of each leader.

2. You are a Soviet dissident during the last years of the Brezhnev Era. You are writing secretly to a Western newspaper in order to show the outside world how difficult life has become in the USSR. Briefly identify three of the greatest problems faced by the average Soviet citizen. Discuss whether a continuation of the established system was possible indefinitely.

3. Gorbachëv attempted to make those changes he felt were necessary for the success of the Soviet system.

   A. Discuss Gorbachëv's two major reform policies.
   B. Explain why he thought these were necessary.
   C. Why did these reforms eventually lead to the demise of the Soviet system?

4. The reforms in the USSR led to changes throughout Eastern Europe.

   A. Select two Eastern European nations and describe the events that led to the collapse of communism.
   B. Explain the effect of Gorbachëv's policy on the events in those countries.

UNIT X

ENTERING THE TWENTY-FIRST CENTURY

We are almost finished with our journey through European history. In this unit we will reflect on where we are as we prepare to enter a new millennium. If we ever learn anything from history it is time to realize that nations have to put aside hatred and settle their differences without going to war. With modern weaponry, a wide-scale war might well mean the end of life as we know it. We must also learn that hatred within a country, neighbor against neighbor, is self-destructive and will make any national improvement impossible.

The world is now a global village in many ways. Rapid communication and transportation have made us interdependent. The developed and developing nations must establish a trading relationship that benefits both partners. The isolation and self-sufficiency of the manor is not possible when the world comes into your living room on television. Peaceful development is not possible when there are a few rich nations and many poor ones.

In Europe an extraordinary event is taking place. We studied that first Rome, then the leaders Charlemagne, Napoleon, and Hitler attempted to unite all the parts of Europe. But this was done by conquest. Europe today is attempting this through peaceful means. In a series of small and big steps, progress has been made. It is a difficult process and there are still antagonisms and distrust between nations, but little by little advances have been made. The next century might see a "United Europe."

The fall of the Iron Curtain has complicated things. The former Soviet Bloc and the C.I.S. wish to be included in the picture. These nations tend to be behind the West economically and so will need its support. The East will be a fertile field for investment but it must solve its own political problems in order to get ahead. The problem of trade is a complex one involving political, social, and economic issues.

Many believe that the single greatest problem facing us is the rapid increase in world population that has taken place. With a fairly fixed amount of resources and an increasing number of people to share them, a decent standard of living is not only impossible, but increasing misery is almost guaranteed. The developed nations have almost reached zero population growth. This must be reached by the developing, or Third World, nations also, where hunger affects a significant total of the population. They must take steps to curb their ever-increasing population or be destined never to attain a decent standard of living. Food shipments from the agriculturally advanced nations is a humanitarian effort but not the long-term answer.

The world's scientists must reach an understanding about common goals. When the atomic energy plant exploded in Ukraine, not only the local population was affected. The fallout did not stop at the border but spread into the atmosphere and impacted other nations near and far. A line on a map did not stop this. Neither will it stop acid rain, global warming, or other global problems facing us.

While we have these problems, not all is gloom and doom. We are developing a world culture that will bring future generations closer together. You have much to look forward to as you prepare to become a citizen in the twenty-first century.

CHAPTER 37

Global Economic Issues

When people shop today, they often have many different choices to select from before purchasing the item they want. This is true of automobiles, clothing, electronic equipment, and most other products. There is an increasing number of foreign-made goods in the stores. Think about the products that your family buys. Was the clothing you are wearing manufactured here or abroad? Was the stereo equipment that you have at home produced in Japan, Korea, the United States, or elsewhere? Should you buy an American-made automobile or an import?

The marketplace today has become increasingly global. In this chapter, you will examine how global economic development brought about by scientific and technological progress has led to a growing interdependence. The world has become more economically interrelated, and there is an increasing trend to form mutually beneficial regional trading associations. No longer are nations and regions self-sufficient in terms of their economic needs. The standard of living of almost any country depends on its involvement in the global financial and trading system. Nations can no longer completely control their economic independence and financial health; there are many outside factors.

Most countries have become more involved in the expanding network of world trade. The prices of raw materials, such as petroleum, and competitive manufactured goods, such as automobiles, are now international economic issues. Trade barriers, **multinational corporations**, aid to developing nations, the value of national currencies, the interrelated world stock markets, and foreign investment are among the concerns of the expanding global economy. The drug and arms trade are also important issues for the world economy.

International Trade and Economic Cooperation

The growth of international trade in the second half of the twentieth century has been phenomenal. All nations, developed and developing, are now—more than ever—dependent on the global trading network to improve the standard of living of their citizens. This is an example of **global interdependence**. Some of the industrialized nations, such as the United States, Germany, and Japan, possess advantages that give them enormous power in the world trading system. Nevertheless, even those nations with the largest and most dynamic economies depend on many other countries for raw materials and markets for their products.

The European Community (The European Union)

In Europe in the post-World War II Era, the idea of a common economic community took root. A French banker, Jean Monnet, had a vision of a European common market. Monnet envisioned one enormous European market in which there would be no trade barriers among the continent's diverse nations. Beginning in the 1950s, six European countries joined together to form an economic community. The European Community (EC) has continued to add new members in the 1990s. This regional trading community has the potential to become the world's leading economic bloc.

The Maastricht Treaty   Using a slow but steady approach, the expanded European Community has begun to remove troublesome trading barriers. In 1992, member nations of the EC voted to complete the last steps of economic integration. In Maastricht, Holland, the EC member nations agreed to further reduce trading barriers, eventually create a

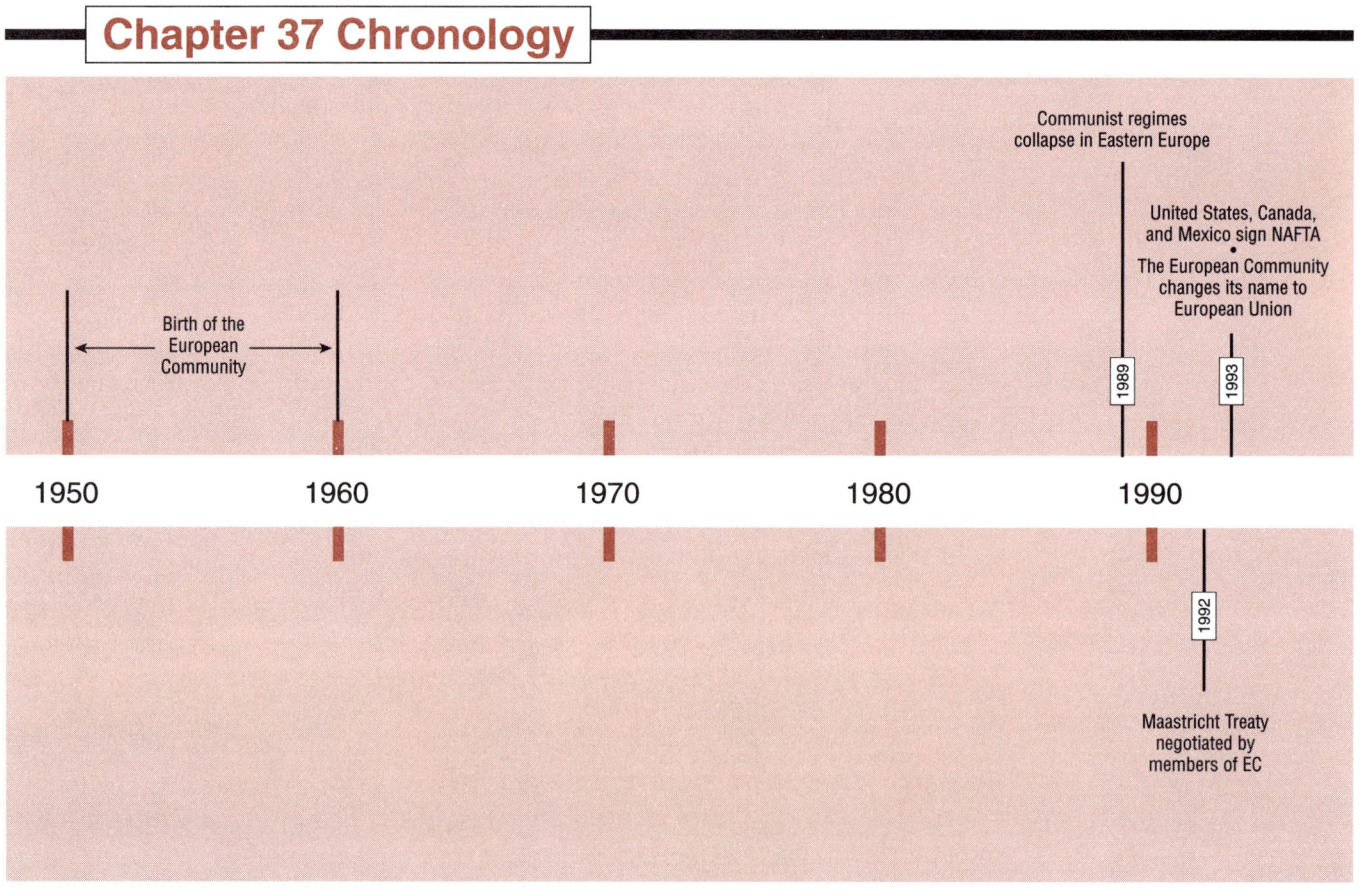

Chapter 37 Chronology

Birth of the European Community

1950   1960   1970   1980   1990

Communist regimes collapse in Eastern Europe

United States, Canada, and Mexico sign NAFTA

The European Community changes its name to European Union

1989   1993

1992

Maastricht Treaty negotiated by members of EC

French banker Jean Monnet envisioned a European common market that has opened trade barriers among the Continent's nations since the 1950s. In 1993, it became known as the European Union.

common European currency, and give more of each nation's control of its economy to the central EC governing body, which is based in Brussels, Belgium. Each nation put the Maastricht Treaty to a vote for approval or rejection. The Maastricht Treaty sparked strong debates in EC member nations, particularly in France, Denmark, Germany, and Great Britain, concerning its acceptability. Those for the treaty's approval argued that unless Europe unites economically, it will not be able to effectively compete in the changing world markets. They claim that European production would ultimately become more efficient and less costly. Those against approval argued that their nations will lose control of their economies and that certain producers, such as French farmers, would be negatively affected.

By the end of 1993, the EC members voted to approve the Maastricht Treaty. The treaty is a concrete step towards economic cooperation. For example, it will now be possible for a member nation such as Germany to manufacture automobiles and sell them in the markets of European Community countries without any import duties or other trade restrictions being imposed. The creation of a powerful European trading community has important consequences for world trade. In 1993 also, the EC officially changed its name to the EU or European Union.

The agricultural and industrial products of EU member nations have an advantage over the same type of goods produced elsewhere. Elimination of import duties means that it is often cheaper to buy and sell agricultural produce, raw materials, and finished goods within the trading community. The plan to create a common currency and a central bank to regulate the monetary system would make the European Union a competitive rival of the United States and Japan.

General Agreement on Tariffs and Trade

Global trade permits nations to specialize in the manufacture of products if they have the necessary resources. Within a common market such as the EU or NAFTA (the 1993 North American Free Trade Association, which joins the United States, Canada, and Mexico together in a trading bloc), consumers can produce and purchase more goods at a lower cost than if each country sought to be self-sufficient. Also, resources that are scarce can be used more efficiently if only certain nations produce a particular product.

The Western European nations, the United States, Japan, Canada, China, and Brazil have the greatest volume of trade. These nations have dynamic industrial economies in which many people earn enough money to buy large quantities of goods. They are all concerned with the issues of having access to other regional markets and safeguarding their own national production.

In 1993, the world's leading trading nations reached compromise on trade issues and avoided a disastrous global economic war. The outcome of negotiations for a **General Agreement on Tariffs and Trade (GATT)** resulted in big cuts in tariffs on most goods. The United States and the European Union will, on average, cut tariffs in half on each other's goods. Tariffs on goods from the rest of the world will be cut less. Agricultural tariffs will be reduced by 36 percent in industrial nations and 24 percent in developing nations.

The agreement is expected to stimulate business and investment activity by opening markets and encouraging countries to specialize in producing whatever goods they can make efficiently. There are still unresolved issues relating to movies, television, and financial services. Nevertheless, the GATT is crucial for the future of trade among the industrial nations, and also for the developing countries of the world.

Multinational Corporations

Multinational corporations are companies that operate and have investments in more than one country. These companies manufacture and market products in more than one country to help link the world trading network together. Multinational corporations control an expanding volume of trade in all global regions. These businesses are very competitive and seek to penetrate new markets whenever an economic opportunity presents itself. For example, General Motors, the SONY Corporation, and Volkswagen are companies that began respectively in the United States, Japan, and Germany, but which now have become multinational because they operate and invest in other nations. Multinational companies can have positive and negative effects within the global economy and in individual nations.

Advantages of Multinational Corporations

Multinational corporations often have access to enormous financial resources, such as bank loans and stock issues, which allow them to invest in costly industrial expansion and technology. These companies bring new manufacturing facilities to developing countries that do not have sufficient national funding to increase their industrial production. Jobs are created, workers earn and spend salaries, and the standard of living rises, especially for those people involved in the employ of these companies. Another benefit is the use of a nation's natural resources in the multinational corporations' factories. An improved transportation and communication network generally results from these companies' need to have reliable connections to the global market.

Disadvantages of Multinational Corporations

In developing countries, national industries can suffer from competition from multinational corporations. And, the exploitation of raw materials can have a negative ecological impact if national regulations or safeguards are not present. Furthermore, the outflow of capital, money that leaves a nation, to foreign-based corporations is another serious problem. Corporations often send profits abroad in dollars or other currencies, such as the Japanese yen or German deutschemark. This can lead to a major devaluation, loss of value, of the national money. Multinational companies often act in their own self-interest, particularly regarding the remittance of profits, the sending of money abroad.

Present and Future Activities

Even economic blocs, such as the European Union, cannot completely control multinational companies. The international business outlook of corporations that have ventured beyond their original national borders makes them increasingly independent, self-sufficient, and adaptable to changing conditions. International companies can evade import restrictions by investing in manufacturing to produce their product within a market that penalizes the importation of goods.

The European automobile market is an example of what is now happening. Germany, Italy, France, and Great Britain are all major European automobile producers. Within the EU, these nations are no longer subject to import restrictions. In

Great Britain, there is growing Japanese corporate investment in automobile plants to produce Toyotas, Mitsubishis, and other cars. The European-made Japanese automobiles are not considered foreign exports (whereas Japanese automobiles made in Japan and sold in Europe would be considered foreign exports) and therefore do not face the usual import restrictions that limit imports and raise prices. The excellent quality of these cars and their competitive prices will make them an increasing threat to the community's automobile industry. The United States automobile market has suffered from this type of economic penetration.

In the 1990s, there is the danger that multinational corporations serving their own interests can ignite a trade war that would be disastrous for the global economy. The inability to control international companies can have long-term negative economic consequences for many nations. The identification of multinational corporations with particular countries can cause rifts that have economic repercussions. For example, the environmental disaster in Bhopal, India in 1984 at the Goodyear-operated plant caused severe strains between that nation and the United States. In Bhopal, a chemical plant owned by a multinational company, the Union Carbide Corporation, leaked a large quantity of poisonous gas, which killed 2,000 people and severely injured 150,000 others. The Indian government sued the Union Carbide Corporation for damages, but the case was complicated by the fact that Union Carbide operated in India through a subsidiary, or company that controlled another company.

Problems caused by international companies because of the lack of effective controls can lead nations to take economic measures designed to hurt countries that are considered the home country of the multinational corporation. This action is called an economic reprisal, a kind of "revenge." Ultimately, it can pit one trading bloc against another and depress world economic growth. This means that unless some international agreement is made about the way multinational corporations invest and operate, global manufacturing and trade could even decrease.

The Growing Number of Developing Nations

Most nations are still trying to meet the basic needs of their citizens in a world that has become more interdependent. One important long-range issue is the growing economic gap between the limited number of rich nations and the much larger group of poor countries. During the 1980s, poorer nations, particularly those dependent on the sale of raw materials to earn foreign exchange, found themselves increasingly in debt to richer nations, private banks, and international lending agencies.

Investment capital is difficult for people in these nations to obtain because the political climate in developing nations is often unstable. The "revolving door" governments in many of these nations makes investing in them too risky. In addition, corruption and outright thievery in Third World nations have discouraged people in more stable and wealthier countries from investing there. Problems occurred even in nations whose leaders were successful in obtaining capital to develop mixed economies that combine free market ideas and government controls. Nations such as Brazil and Mexico learned that huge borrowing to finance infrastructure projects and basic facilities, such as power plants and communication systems, led to enormous debt. The debt owed was impossible to ever repay without severely damaging national interests.

The road to a more diversified economy, one more varied in terms of goods produced, and a higher standard of living is long and difficult. The negative impact of a large national debt, money owed by a country, is the loss of economic independence to international financial institutions. Private banks and other lending institutions want to be repaid and can place restrictions on the debtor nation, which can adversely impact the people and overall economy of that nation.

To make the necessary economic transformation, nations require funding from outside international sources. The International Monetary Fund (IMF), the World Bank, private banks, and industrial nations supply the financial assistance to support attempts by developing nations for economic diversification.

In Europe, the collapse of communism in the Soviet Union and Eastern Europe, beginning in 1989, resulted in a widening of the economic gap within Europe. Western Europe's economic growth and cooperation is in sharp contrast to the former Communist bloc nations' shattered economies. Huge investments will be necessary in Poland, Hungary, Russia, Ukraine, and elsewhere if these countries are to develop diversified economies and raise the standard of living of their people.

The danger of failing to develop the economies of the poorer European nations is enormous. There is the risk of a massive migration from the developing nations of Eastern Europe, where desperate workers who cannot find employment in their own countries will seek a brighter economic future in the industrialized nations of Western Europe. Germany, France, Great Britain, and Italy all confront this problem in the 1990s, and perhaps beyond.

Unemployment is a complicated issue because there is an increasing problem of finding work for all of the people in the countries of the EU. For example, in the fall of 1993, in Germany, Volkswagen changed the schedule of a number of automobile plants to a four-day work week to increase the total number of jobs for workers. There is also the problem of "guest workers." These laborers from foreign countries were invited by EU countries to come and work in jobs that could not be filled in the 1970s and 1980s. They have worked for a number of years and now find that they are less in demand and no longer welcome. Often these workers have brought their families to the host country and cut ties to their countries of origin.

Most of the nations in developing global regions are facing growing economic problems. As the twentieth century ends, poorer nations find it more difficult to attract **investment capital**, money needed to start or expand a business. This is in large part due to the end of the Cold War. The costly competition between the capitalist and Communist blocs for Third World support has ended. The Communist bloc has disintegrated, and the nations that have emerged in the 1990s are now part of the vast group of developing countries. The poorer nations of Africa, Asia, Latin America, the Caribbean basin, and the Middle East face competition from Eastern Europe and the countries of the Commonwealth of Independent States for international funding and general economic support.

The International Financial System

The 1980s was a period of growing international financial cooperation by the wealthier nations. The Group of Seven, the leading industrial countries, increasingly worked together as a financial community to control the international monetary system. These nations—the United States, Japan, Germany, France, Canada, Great Britain, and Italy—find that coordination of monetary policies is essential for their mutual economic health. The Group of Seven now meets whenever there is a need to resolve a critical monetary issue that affects the global economy. Recently, Russia has attempted to join the Group of Seven.

One issue of concern is whether the value of a particular national currency, that is, how much it should be worth, should be supported by the group. The other possibility is to allow the value of a money to be determined by market conditions (supply and demand), which is called allowing a currency to float.

The decline in value of a currency can have a dramatic impact on trade. For example, a cheaper dollar makes it easier for other nations to buy more American products. However, the export of products to the United States becomes more difficult because foreign goods are then more expensive. Therefore, each country sends representatives of its national bank to international meetings to try to keep currency fluctuations (changes in a money's value) within reasonable limits.

International Economic Problems

The Global Drug Trade

Drug trafficking is an international economic concern. In addition to the severe political, social, and health problems caused by the widespread and growing use of illegal narcotics, the global financial system is negatively affected by the vast sums of money that are earned by the international **drug cartels**, business associations that are monopolistic in their actions. It is estimated that the United States alone has more than a multibillion dollar annual market for drugs such as cocaine, heroin, and marijuana. The long-term economic consequences for the United States and other major drug-consuming nations are enormous and, unfortunately, growing.

The drug cartels have become powerful international business organizations. The drug traffickers control large transportation and communication networks and have gained entrance into the international financial system. Huge sums of money are laundered (made "clean," or seemingly legal, by investing in legal businesses). The banks that accept deposits from drug traffickers are corrupted by associating with these people as well as by the profits earned in these financial transactions.

The tremendous sums of money that drug cartels control poses political and social problems for all nations involved in the narcotics network. In Colombia and Peru, the consequences have led to more violence and political instability. Guerrilla organizations often make alliances with drug traffickers to earn money for revolutionary activities. Police officers and the military leaders are bribed to look the other way or stage meaningless headline-producing raids.

In South America, the struggle against the powerful drug cartels demonstrates that a local or regional approach will not work to reduce or eliminate drug production. It is obvious that increased international cooperation is needed to fight what has become one of the world's most serious economic problems—the global drug trade.

The Arms Trade

The sale of weapons to nations that can ill-afford to waste needed financial resources expanded enormously during the 1980s. The competitive arms trade has been estimated to be worth more than fifty billion dollars annually. The United States, France, Russia, and Great Britain are the world's largest sellers of weapons. However, these nations are not the only producers of arms for export. Developing nations, such as Brazil, China, and Israel, have large weapons industries that earn foreign exchange for other economic needs.

The breakup of the former Soviet Union and the changes in Eastern Europe have complicated the arms problem. There is now a terrible danger that sophisticated military technology to make missiles, fighter planes, and even nuclear weapons will become increasingly available. Government officials and military leaders in Russia, Ukraine, and elsewhere may sell military technology and equipment for needed cash for their developing nations to Iran, Libya, or any nation that can pay for them.

The Gulf War in 1991 is proof of what can happen if advanced military technology falls into the wrong hands. The former Soviet Union built up the Iraqi military to the point where the leader of this nation, Saddam Hussein, became an international threat. Other nations also sold Iraq military technology and equipment. Iraq's invasion of Kuwait, motivated by the desire to gain control of that nation's oil resources, led to a war between Iraq and a military force led by the United States (and consisting of soldiers from other countries) and sponsored by the United Nations. Saddam Hussein thought that he could win because of the huge investment made in his military forces. He was proved wrong, but the price in lives lost and property destroyed was enormous.

The use of financial resources to purchase weapons by poor nations has a negative impact on the people of these countries. The economic consequences of such misguided actions means that less money is available in the budget for education, public health, housing, and the creation of jobs.

The wealthier nations, such as the United States and France, often justify the arms trade as an economic necessity. For the United States, arms production has been an integral part of the American economy since the Cold War began. In the 1990s, the United States faces economic problems because there is no longer as great a need to build up an arms supply since the collapse of the Soviet Union and since other Eastern European Communist countries have become more democratic. Therefore, the United States must find employment for those people who were employed by defense companies, because the market has decreased for weapons. France, another leading supplier of world arms, also uses its earnings from weapons exports to help pay for oil imports, and faces a similar problem.

The real cost of arms sales can be seen in the political instability in a growing number of developing nations in Africa, Asia, and Europe. The problem is compounded by the sale of weapons by private arms dealers to terrorist organizations and revolutionary groups. Unless greater international cooperation and restraint is shown by the weapons-exporting nations and the increasing number of developing nations that participate in the destructive arms trade, this problem will continue in the 1990s.

Summary

The United States cannot isolate itself from the rest of the world. For example, as you look around your house you may note that many of the goods you enjoy have come from overseas. Your standard of living is directly tied to international trade. Yet, we cannot continue to increase our debt through a negative balance of trade. We must increase our exports to the nations we import from. This affects jobs here. It is a complicated problem with complex solutions.

The European Union is removing barriers to trade and expanding economic cooperation and integration. There are nationalistic difficulties involved. In addition, the "emerging" nations of Eastern Europe want to play a larger role because their economies need to be expanded in order to achieve a greater standard of living for their people. Political uncertainties in these countries makes accomplishing this difficult.

Problems that will have to be solved, such as those of arms trade and currency fluctuation, pose important problems for the United States. We live in an economically interdependent world. A frost in Brazil raises the price of our coffee, a stronger yen in Japan raises the prices of our automobiles. Our elected leaders will be facing these real challenges to policy. What should the role of the United States be?

I. Multiple Choice

Directions: Find the *letter* of the correct answer.

1. Global economic development had led to

    (a) decreased foreign investment.
    (b) multinational interdependence.
    (c) increased trade barriers.
    (d) declining world trade.

2. All of the following nations are members of the European Union (EU) *except*

    (a) Great Britain.
    (b) France.
    (c) Germany.
    (d) Russia.

3. The primary goal of the European Union is to

    (a) achieve economic integration of the member nations.
    (b) form an economic organization along the lines of NATO.
    (c) prevent nonmember nations from manufacturing in Europe.
    (d) create a completely self-sufficient trading network.

4. In the 1990s, all of the world's leading trading nations will probably

    (a) increase the volume of their agricultural exports.
    (b) try to avoid a disastrous global economic war.
    (c) erect trade barriers to protect their national production.
    (d) give up the idea of forming economic trading blocs.

5. All of the following are positive effects of multinational corporations *except*

    (a) creating jobs where they set up manufacturing plants.
    (b) establishing new manufacturing facilities in developing countries.
    (c) helping national industries by increasing competition.
    (d) contributing to raising the standard of living of their workers.

6. Multinational corporations have a tendency to

    (a) serve the interests of the nation where their headquarters are.
    (b) try to remain within the areas of the United States and Western Europe.
    (c) be increasingly independent and have an international outlook.
    (d) invest their profits within the nations where they earn them.

7. During the 1980s many developing nations

    (a) reduced the amount of foreign debt they owed.
    (b) happily complied with austerity measures called for by the IMF.
    (c) avoided borrowing to finance infrastructure projects.
    (d) became more burdened with unpayable debts.

8. The collapse of communism in the Soviet Union and the nations of Eastern Europe

    (a) made more financial aid available for developing nations.
    (b) led to a growth of employment in these countries.
    (c) caused greater competition for limited financial aid.
    (d) resulted in more investment capital for Africa and Asia.

9. The decline of the United States currency (the dollar) would result in

    (a) United States goods becoming expensive in Europe.
    (b) foreign automobiles becoming cheaper in the United States.
    (c) no real change because the dollar is still powerful.
    (d) American products being cheaper in other world markets.

10. The global drug trade is a problem for all of the following reasons *except:*

    (a) huge sums of drug money are laundered by drug cartels.
    (b) drug money increases political instability and violence.
    (c) profits from the drug trade are used mostly for philanthropic purposes.
    (d) some international banks and businesses cooperate with the drug cartels.

II. Vocabulary

Directions: Define the following words, terms, or expressions and use them in a written sentence.

1. Group of Seven—
2. developing nation—
3. European Economic Community—
4. remittance of profits—
5. currency devaluation—
6. import restrictions—
7. global interdependence—
8. unemployment index—
9. exchange rate—
10. arms trade—

III. Thought Questions

Directions: Answer the following questions in essay form.

1. Global economic development has made the world more interdependent. Explain three reasons that prove this statement true.

2. List three goals of the European Union, and describe how they will help EU integration.

3. Multinational corporations are increasingly important in the global economy. Explain three positive and three negative aspects of multinational corporations.

4. Developing nations have a number of problems confronting them. Chose four of these problems and then explain how the developing nation is overcoming them.

5. Two problems that continue to face the world community are the drug trade and arms trade. For each problem, explain why they need to be solved.

IV. Activities

Directions: Complete the following activities.

1. Write a research paper on one of the following topics. Use library resources to complete your research.

   A. General Agreement on Tariffs and Trade (GATT)
   B. European Union (EU)
   C. International Monetary Fund (IMF)
   D. North Atlantic Treaty Organization (NATO)

2. Create an in-class debate team and assume one of the points of view listed below. Prepare arguments stating your assigned position.

   A. Free Trade versus Restricted Trade
   B. Legalization of Drug Use versus Restricted Use of Drugs
   C. Unrestricted Arms Sales versus Restricted Arms Sales
   D. No Control of Multinational Corporations versus International Control of Multinational Corporations

CHAPTER 38

Global Environmental and Social Issues

There are new words and expressions that people your age are used to but were not known to your parents. Some of these expressions are *global warming, acid rain, AIDS,* and *ozone depletion.* In this chapter, you will read about the global environment and social issues that are important in the 1990s. The answers to the concerns raised by these global environmental and social issues will determine how you live in the future and the quality of life that you enjoy in the twenty-first century.

The explosive growth of world population in the twentieth century is largely responsible for many of the environmental and social problems that exist today. Our future existence is threatened unless solutions are found to better utilize the earth's resources and safeguard the global environment from the ravages of pollution. For example, dramatic climatic changes caused by the **greenhouse effect** (the heating of the earth's atmosphere caused by pollution), uncontrolled forest burnings, and other causes, will be a major concern for future populations in the twenty-first century if pollution continues to heat up the earth's atmosphere.

Associated with climate change is the issue of the destruction of **rain forests**. The increasing exploitation of tropical rain forests has led to the clearing of large zones in Latin America, Asia, and Africa for farmland. Population pressures have resulted in the decline and extinction of numerous plant and animal species.

The failure to properly control and dispose of industrial pollution and waste has caused severe environmental damage and devastating human health problems. The poisonous gas leak in Bhopal, India (1984), and the nuclear accident in Chernobyl', Ukraine (1986), are examples of how important it is to have safeguards to prevent industrial disasters.

Sexually transmitted diseases, such as AIDS and other illnesses, are threatening the present and future populations of many developing nations. The lack of an adequate health system adds to the devastating effects of diseases that are rapidly spreading. Unless cures are found and social behavior changed, the death rate will increase. Women and children are particularly vulnerable in regions where environmental factors such as drought have led to widespread malnutrition and lower resistance to disease.

Many of the environmental and social problems discussed in this chapter have led to conflicting opinions about their real causes, proposed solutions, and the seriousness of the issue. These differences have resulted in controversies among reputable scientists. Not all scientists agree about the problems and the proposed solutions, which you will read about in this chapter.

World Population Growth

The growth of world population has accelerated in the twentieth century. The estimated global population of 1.5 billion at the end of the nineteenth century is now approaching 6 billion. The 400 percent increase in the number of human beings inhabiting the earth in about a century has created strong pressures to curb future population growth. Today the world is facing a situation that Thomas Malthus stated would happen earlier. Malthus, writing at the end of the 1700s, predicted that food production would not keep pace with population growth thereby causing increasing poverty. There are too many people to adequately feed, house, clothe, and provide for in a humane manner.

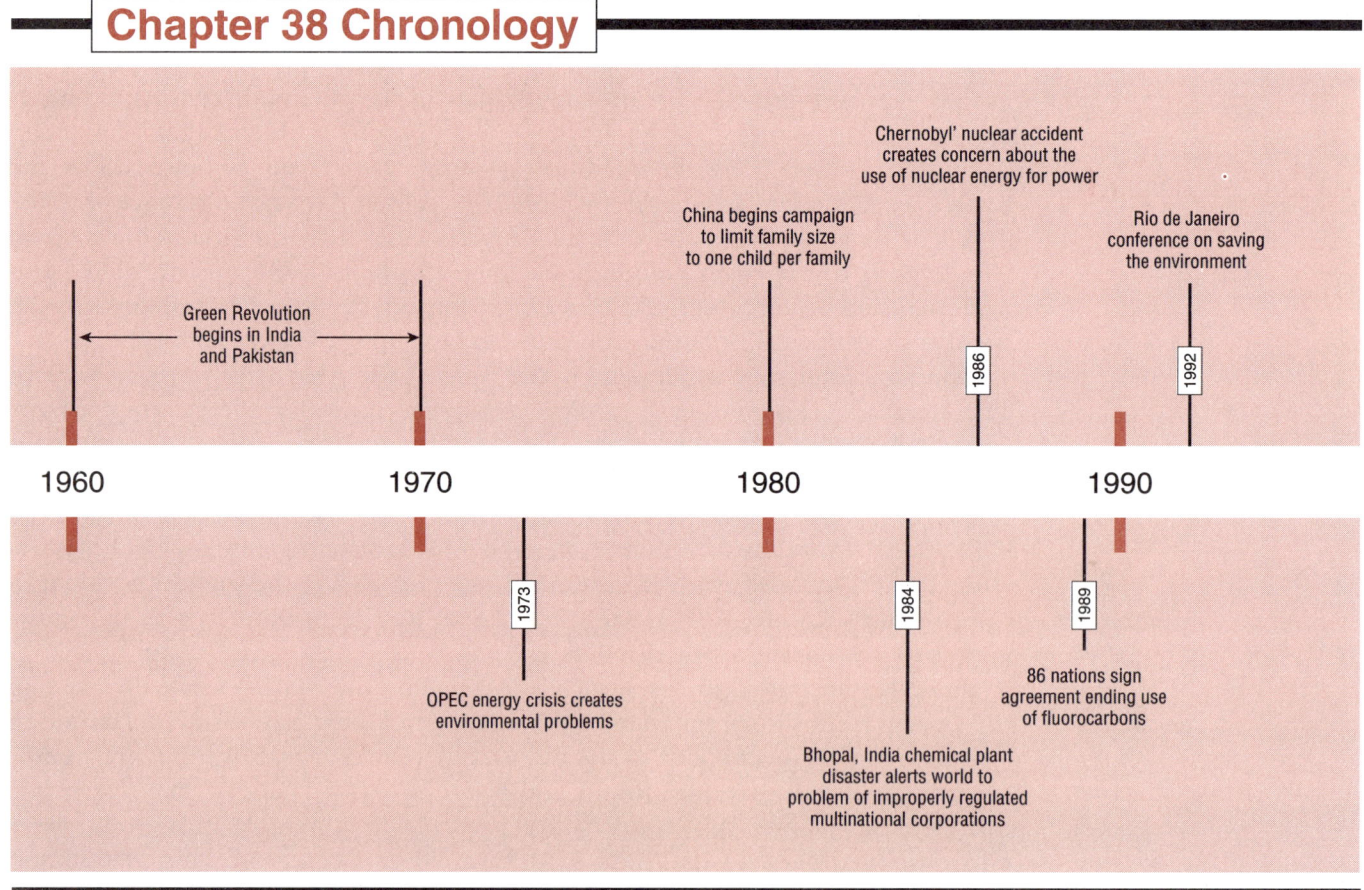

Chapter 38 Chronology

Green Revolution begins in India and Pakistan

China begins campaign to limit family size to one child per family

Chernobyl' nuclear accident creates concern about the use of nuclear energy for power — 1986

Rio de Janeiro conference on saving the environment — 1992

1960   1970   1980   1990

1973 — OPEC energy crisis creates environmental problems

1984 — Bhopal, India chemical plant disaster alerts world to problem of improperly regulated multinational corporations

1989 — 86 nations sign agreement ending use of fluorocarbons

Reasons for Population Growth

Today, people live much longer than they did in the past. The control of deadly diseases, including smallpox, tuberculosis, and polio through vaccines and effective medical treatment, has allowed more children to survive into adulthood. The declining infant mortality rate, measured by the number of deaths per thousand infants, and the corresponding high birth rate has led to a doubling of population every twenty to thirty years in many developing countries. This population growth has caused considerable problems. Food supplies, housing, schools, and jobs are increasingly needed to maintain and improve the standard of living. Unfortunately, in too many developing nations, considerable obstacles exist to meet even the basic needs of growing populations.

Consequences of Population Growth

At the present rate of growth, the population of the earth is expected to top 10 billion by the third decade of the twenty-first century. The highest rate of rapid population growth is taking place in Asia, Africa, and Latin America. The explosion in population has forced many people to abandon rural areas and flock to cities. Urban centers in developing nations are threatened because overpopulation has resulted in slum conditions for ever larger numbers of people. For example, a Peruvian farmer who comes to Lima to escape horrible political and economic conditions in the countryside finds life in the big city to be dehumanizing, unhealthy, and deadly in other ways. The slums of the cities in developing nations often lack sewers, toilets, and safe drinking water. In Europe, particularly the EU countries, population growth has been less rapid. Industrialization, the change from an agricultural to a highly urban society, and the belief that too many children prevent the improvement of the quality of a family's life have resulted in reduced population growth.

The problems caused by overpopulation mean that lowering or at least stabilizing the birth rate is essential. The goal of controlling the birth rate often conflicts with religious ideas and traditional social customs. A large family is frequently prized by parents in rural areas who need more hands to help work the land. Religious leaders with large followings often prevent family planning programs from successfully working. The concept of birth control remains a controversial issue. The Roman Catholic religion remains vehemently opposed to all efforts to legalize abortions. These religious leaders believe that population control and abortion are against the teachings of their religion.

China is an example of how difficult it is to establish an effective birth control program. In the 1980s, the population of China was estimated to be between 900 million and 1 billion. The totalitarian Communist government then began a campaign to limit family size to one child per couple. Parents who violated the official limit faced community pressures and heavy penalties. Despite some early successes, the imposed limit is being violated by families who refuse to settle for one child, particularly if it is a girl. China's growing population is once again threatening to wipe out gains made in food production and health services. In addition, despite its efforts, China is looked down upon by those in the West who see a violation of individual human rights in this mandatory program to control births.

Thomas Robert Malthus

You may find it strange to bring up this nineteenth-century thinker at this point. After all, you did read about him when you studied about the Industrial Revolution earlier. Why bring him up now when you are looking ahead to the twenty-first century? The reason is that what he had to say is so important to us today. His writing may give us a clue to what the standard of living may be in the future for you, and for all citizens of the world.

Thomas Malthus was the son of an eccentric member of the English upper middle class. He had his own tutor who prepared him for university life. Malthus spent his life in academic research and lived on the college campus. It is interesting that rather than becoming a dreamer living in what we call an "ivory tower," Malthus became a hard-headed realist when it came to problems as he saw them. He was tall and handsome and had a speech defect because of a cleft palate. This made him somewhat difficult to understand. He never made a great deal of money, and married somewhat late in life.

His major work is titled "An Essay on the Principle of Population as It Affects the Future Improvement of Society." Simply put, he said that population, if it keeps growing, will soon outstrip the food supply that is available. He studied the growth patterns of areas in England and saw that the number of people doubled every twenty-five years. At that time the population of the United States was doubling every fifteen years. But it really doesn't matter if it's fifteen, twenty-five, or fifty. Land that was suitable for the production of food, while it will increase, will increase at a much slower rate. If we want to show this mathematically it would look like this:

population	1	2	4	8	16	32	64	128
land increase	1	2	3	4	5	6	7	8

Therefore it seems to make sense that a large number of people will always be miserable. No matter how hard it tries, humanity will always be shoved down by the lack of a proper diet. His predictions were very pessimistic.

He feared that the pressure to seek food for growing populations could lead to wars among nations. Wars would thus be tragically one means of reducing population. Other reductions in populations could happen due to epidemics, plagues, or pestilences. If these do not "work" then the only result will be premature death due to famine. You can certainly see why he is a picture of gloom and doom!

The question facing us is, is he right? Historically what he forecast has not happened up until now. The improvements in the productive capacity of the land and what we call the *Green Revolution*, begun in the 1960s, has made greater amounts of food available. When we see severely malnourished people on TV in some parts of the world we are not seeing Malthus's thoughts come true but the result of a local condition. As for population, we see zero population growth (ZPG) in Western Europe, the United States, and Japan. China has strict controls on the number of children allowed in a family. It is in other parts of the developing world that the problem of overpopulation exists. If the world cannot or does not come to grips with the problem, then Malthus will be proven right and people in developing countries will face a future of poverty and misery, that aid from the more developed nations alone will not alleviate.

World Hunger and Health Issues

Population growth is the underlying cause of hunger and malnutrition in many parts of the world. Despite the gains made in food supplies due to the **Green Revolution**, many nations do not produce enough food to adequately feed their expanding populations. Other factors at work that make the solution of the growing world hunger problem more complex are:

1. Political instability often aggravates the problem of malnutrition. Revolutionary warfare and tribal strife have caused a decrease in food production in many developing nations.
2. In parts of Eastern Europe and Russia, the difficult transition from a command economy and collective farm system to a market economy and private land ownership has led to food shortages.
3. In the 1990s, an increasing number of food-deficient nations need more direct aid and credits to meet the basic nutritional requirements of their people.
4. Changing climatic conditions have also added to world hunger.

In Africa, south of the Sahara, the Sahel, a semiarid belt, has expanded because of drought conditions. Other regions in Africa are suffering from the effects of a long period of little rainfall. Dry conditions cause people to dig deeper wells, thereby lowering the water table. Further, because wood is the main source of fuel for cooking, many Africans also burn the available trees and other vegetation for firewood. This causes erosion of arable land (land that can be tilled and planted in). Overgrazing by herds in many marginal areas compounds the erosion problem.

United Nations agencies and food-exporting countries, such as the United States, Canada, and France, are donating food supplies and offering technical assistance to stimulate agricultural production. Private aid organizations, such as CARE, help coordinate the distribution of food and provide some health services. Nevertheless, corruption, the lack of adequate transportation networks, and other regional problems often hamper the distribution of food supplies.

A related problem is the lack of financial resources to invest in improving agricultural production. Many developing countries concentrate investment in the industrial sector. They do not have sufficient funds to industrialize and at the same time invest in improved seed varieties, chemical fertilizers, pesticides, and farm machinery. In addition, the burden of borrowing at high interest rates has added to the cost of modernizing farming technology. Faced with a choice of modernizing industry or agriculture, most nations have opted to invest in costly projects that have little relation to their need to augment food production and feed all their people.

Pesticides are increasingly being used to kill insects and harmful plants. The dangers of longterm pesticide use on the environment are raising new questions about their benefits.

Health Issues

Advances made in public health services and medicine have lengthened life spans. Nevertheless, some sexually transmitted diseases, such as AIDS and other deadly illnesses, are devastating many developing nations in the 1990s. Unless there is more funded research to find medical cures and if changes do not occur in traditional social behavior, there will be an even higher death rate from AIDS and other diseases in the twenty-first century.

AIDS, or Acquired Immune Deficiency Syndrome, a disease that came to world attention in the 1980s, continues to spread. In some African countries, such as Uganda and Zaire, the percentage of affected individuals is alarmingly high. Traditional social customs that permit polygamy, having more than one wife, and the migration of men to cities to find work aggravate the spread of AIDS and other sexually communicable diseases. In Europe and the United States, the illegal use of injectable drugs such as heroin has facilitated the spread of this deadly disease, which destroys a person's immune system. AIDS is also increasing in Asia.

Cholera, tuberculosis, chronic diarrhea, and other diseases continue to devastate vulnerable malnourished populations in Africa, Asia, and Latin America. In parts of Eastern Europe and the Commonwealth of Independent States, the inefficient health system and lack of medical supplies threatens to increase the death rate from previously controllable diseases such as viral pneumonia.

In the 1990s, nations will have to invest more heavily in their public health systems if they are to insure present and future populations of a better chance for healthier and more productive lives. Adequate preventative health care can save public health programs a lot of money because fewer people will have to be treated for advanced illnesses.

Environmental Concerns

The Destruction of the Forests

Population pressures in Africa, Latin America, and Asia are a major cause of the growing destruction of the world's irreplaceable rain forests. In Brazil, the widespread conversion of primal Amazonian tropical forests to farms and cattle ranches has caused the loss of thousands of acres of land that previously supported complicated **ecosystems**, a community of animals and plants and the environment with which it is related. A multitude of plants and animal life have been destroyed. Presently, we can only estimate the ultimate cost of the deforestation of the world's tropical regions. However, it is certain that unless the destruction of these vital forests is halted soon, the consequences for humanity will be devastating.

The wholesale clearing and burning of the humid, densely overgrown areas of the Amazon region of Brazil contributes to a worsening world air quality. The enormous combustion of trees and plants adds to the carbon dioxide in the atmosphere. This ever larger amount of carbon dioxide in the air works to increase the warming trend known as the greenhouse effect. If allowed to continue unchecked, this will eventually lead to an alarming rise in average world temperatures. In addition, the loss of thousands of acres of vegetation reduces the ability of earth to cleanse its atmosphere by releasing oxygen.

In Europe and North America, industrial pollution of the atmosphere has led to the destruction of other types of forestland and the plant and animal life in lakes and ponds. The long-term effects of acid raid in developing nations such as

China and regions in Africa and South America demonstrate that the world's forests are in grave danger. Funding solutions to halt the destruction of forest lands will depend on international cooperation as the twentieth century ends. Allowed to continue at its present pace, the clearing of rain forests and other heavily wooded areas will eventually destroy one of the earth's most vital natural resources.

The Extinction of Animal Life

The growing destruction of the earth's environment has led to the extinction of numerous species of animal life. The world's largest land and sea mammals are increasingly endangered. Certain species of whales are on the verge of becoming extinct, and the once vast herds of African elephants have drastically declined because of the value of these animals' precious ivory tusks. Rhinoceroses, hunted for their horns, which are valued in Asia for medicinal purposes, have all but disappeared in most of their natural habitats.

The need to protect and conserve the wildlife of the earth has led to international, national, and private organizational efforts to reduce the slaughter. There is now an international agreement to restrict whaling. The use of drift nets by the tuna fishing industry is under attack because of the destruction their use causes to all sea life, particularly dolphins. Ivory importation has been restricted worldwide to protect elephants. Wildlife protection groups are also campaigning against the wearing of furs taken from such endangered species as leopards and tigers. In an effort to save endangered gorillas and other primates, stricter animal reserves policies are being enforced. The value of protecting animals for tourism programs that earn good profits is being encouraged in Africa and South America.

The choice is clear. Unless more is done to preserve the habitat of the world's wildlife, future generations will only know about most animals by looking at pictures in books or by visiting zoos. Greater international cooperation is needed to protect ecosystems that are the homes of irreplaceable animal and plant species.

The Pollution of the Earth

Uncontrolled pollution has caused heavy damage to the earth, its atmosphere, and the life that inhabits our planet. The growth in world population and industrialization has led to an enormous amount of waste. The sheer volume of garbage and industrial waste produced in the affluent developed nations has led to serious questions about how to dispose of such large amounts of material.

In the United States, the average American is responsible for more than 1,400 pounds of trash per year. This figure does not include waste and trash produced by industry, agriculture, and business. The trash goes into local dumps, is burned, and is taken by boat to be dumped into the sea. In the 1990s, landfills in the United States are overflowing and are shutting down. Dangerous chemicals are leaking into the ground water systems from barrels and cans that have corroded. The incineration of huge amounts of garbage adds to atmospheric pollution and the constant dumping of sludge and other waste-containing poisonous chemicals has killed plant and fish life and contaminated seafood.

Many nations have even worse pollution and water disposal problems than the United States. In Eastern Europe, the failure to properly dispose of waste and build industrial facilities with even a minimal concern for pollution control has devastated vast areas of the Czech Republic, Slovakia, Romania, and Poland. The Danube, which flows through Eastern Europe, is just one of the many rivers in Europe that have been totally contaminated and no longer supports plant or animal life. There are growing fresh water shortages caused by the dumping of toxic industrial wastes into the world's rivers and lakes.

In Ukraine, radioactive contamination resulting from the partial meltdown in 1986 of the Chernobyl' nuclear power plant, has poisoned a wide area of previously habitable and arable land. The growing threat of more nuclear accidents at poorly constructed and maintained atomic plants threatens the safety and well-being of nations that can no longer afford nuclear technology. In Sweden, an affluent, industrialized European country, a total ban on the use of nuclear power to generate energy has been declared, and in the United States, the construction of nuclear plants has practically ended.

The cleanup of toxic dump sites and bodies of water that have been poisoned is a worldwide concern. Industrialized nations, such as the United States, the Netherlands, and Germany have large ecology-oriented groups that are working to influence government policy in favor of safeguarding and cleaning up the environment. Nations are becoming more aware of the necessity of working together to solve some of the more threatening environmental problems caused by pollution. The international agreement of eighty-six nations in 1989 to ban chlorofluorocarbons used in refrigeration and air conditioning appliances is a reaction to the growing concern over the depletion of the ozone layer in the polar regions of the earth. The destruction of the ozone layer, a form of oxygen, by manmade chemicals, if allowed to continue, would eventually eliminate the natural protection against the sun's ultraviolet rays. Unless there is strict compliance with the ban by the major producers of these and other chemicals, the menace of increased cases of cancer and even the destruction of vital polar ecosystems is possible by the early twenty-first century.

Energy and Mineral Concerns

The major industrialized nations consume the lion's share of the earth's energy and mineral resources. For example, the United States, possessing less than 5 percent of the world's population, consumes about one quarter of its petroleum. This enormous use of oil to generate energy and other petroleum by-products results in a huge amount of nitrogen oxides and carbon dioxide emissions. Besides being wasteful, these emissions contribute heavily to polluting the environment and heating the atmosphere.

There has been rising concern over the environmental damage caused by energy pollution. The energy crisis involves not only how the mining of fuels and their use damages the environment, but also the consequences of exhausting the earth's reserves. In 1973, the industrialized nations learned how dependent they were on imported oil. The Organization of Petroleum Exporting Countries (OPEC), via an embargo, made people aware of the fact that the oil importing nations would have to pay more for this precious commodity. Secondly, the oil crisis clearly revealed that the world's petroleum reserves would someday be exhausted.

The sudden end of cheap energy led to many changes. The higher cost of energy affected the economies of all oil importing nations and the industrialized countries were forced to become more conservation conscious of these non-renewable resources and plan for alternative sources of energy to meet their growing needs.

For example, automobiles that were more fuel efficient became popular, and standards for the control of automobile emissions became a major concern in the United States. In Brazil and other developing countries, programs for gasoline substitution were introduced. The use of sugar cane to produce an alternative fuel, a mixture of gasoline and alcohol, became more widespread.

Researchers are seeking new ways to turn the enormous amount of garbage into energy. Solid waste (garbage and the remains of other materials) are more than ever being utilized to produce inexpensive fuels. Throughout the world, the search for cheaper and cleaner sources of energy has increased. There are research programs to better utilize the enormous potential of the sun and wind for power to run factories and provide energy for homes. Experiments with solar heating panels continue to demonstrate that the sun will become a viable source of energy if its potential can be harnessed. Other research involves the study of ocean tides and thermal springs as energy sources.

Summary

In June 1992, the United Nations sponsored a worldwide conference in Rio de Janeiro to decide on the fate of the earth's environment. Thousands of concerned representatives met at the Earth Summit to consider two themes that are in many ways incompatible with current economic and social systems: the well-being of the environment and the prosperity of all humankind. Worldwide, there is a growing awareness that environmental deterioration and widespread human poverty will lead to future disaster.

Representatives from the nations that attended the Rio de Janeiro conference could not agree on a united plan of action to resolve the many environmental issues facing an increasingly interdependent world; however, there was a worldwide agreement to continue working on problems that threaten the environment and our future on the planet earth.

Environmental and social issues are not easy to resolve. For reasons we have now seen, they have caused great concern to humankind in this century—in certain ways, more than in previous centuries. The need to resolve the problems caused by these issues requires increasingly greater cooperation among nations. Such cooperation, along with each person's awareness and concern, may make the world more livable in future years.

CHAPTER 38

Review Exercises

I. Multiple Choice

Directions: Find the *letter* of the correct answer.

1. The greenhouse effect may cause a dramatic

   (a) increase in the world's food production.
   (b) reduction in the level of the world's oceans.
   (c) rise in the temperatures of the earth in the twenty-first century.
   (d) decline in industrial pollution in the United States and Europe.

2. The destruction of tropical rain forests is most alarming on the continents of

   (a) South America and Africa.
   (b) Europe and Australia.
   (c) North America and Asia.
   (d) Africa and Antarctica.

3. World population is expected by the twenty-first century to reach

   (a) 3 billion.
   (b) 4 billion.
   (c) 5 billion.
   (d) 6 billion.

4. Lowering the birth rate has proven difficult because of all of the following *except*

   (a) traditional rural families prize many children.
   (b) knowledge of safe methods of contraception are often not available.
   (c) religious leaders often support the idea of family planning.
   (d) the concept of birth control remains a controversial issue.

5. Most developing nations have opted first to

   (a) invest in costly industrial projects.
   (b) expand the health care system for their people.
   (c) augment their agricultural production to feed their people.
   (d) expand programs that safeguard their environment.

6. Devastating sexually transmitted diseases such as AIDS are difficult to control because of all the following reasons *except*

(a) traditional social behavior is hard to change.
(b) many developing nations refuse to acknowledge the problem.
(c) the illegal use of injectable drugs is increasing.
(d) there is a need to reduce the birth rate in some religions.

7. The loss of tropical rain forests leads to

(a) animal and plant life being destroyed.
(b) a lessening of the greenhouse effect.
(c) less carbon dioxide in the atmosphere.
(d) the overall improvement of air quality.

8. The Bhopal and Chernobyl' incidents are examples of

(a) a nation's ability to control its industrial accidents.
(b) policies that governments should follow to control pollution.
(c) devastating accidents that can happen if safety is ignored.
(d) the need to build more chemical and nuclear plants.

9. The nation that consumes the greatest percentage of the world's energy is

(a) Japan.
(b) Russia.
(c) the United States.
(d) China.

10. The greatest source of the world's energy used today is

(a) natural gas.
(b) oil.
(c) coal.
(d) electricity.

II. Vocabulary

Directions: Define the following words, terms, or expressions and use them in a written sentence.

1. greenhouse effect—
2. birth rate—
3. malnutrition—
4. Green Revolution—
5. endangered species—
6. ecosystems—
7. industrial waste—
8. depletion of the ozone layer—
9. non-renewable resource—

III. Thought Questions

Directions: Answer the following questions in essay form.

1. The rate of world population growth is a cause for alarm.

   A. Give three reasons that cause this growth.
   B. Explain how you would solve each of these three causes.

2. World hunger is a growing problem.

   A. Give three reasons that cause this problem.
   B. Explain how you would try to find solutions for each cause.

3. AIDS and other sexually transmitted diseases are difficult to control.

   A. Give four reasons for the cause of sexually transmitted diseases.
   B. Explain how you would try to find solutions for each cause.

4. The rain forests are threatened with elimination.

   A. List four causes of the destruction of rain forests.
   B. Explain how you would work to solve each of these causes.

5. It is crucial to control industrial pollution.

   A. Give three causes of industrial pollution.
   B. Propose solutions for each of these causes.

IV. Activities

Directions: Complete the following activities.

1. You are assigned a research project on one of the problems listed below. Your task is to prepare a report on how the problem that you are assigned will become a threat to humanity in the twenty-first century unless a solution is found. Go to the library and complete your research.

   A. industrial pollution
   B. AIDS
   C. ozone layer depletion
   D. endangered species
   E. malnutrition
   F. rain forest destruction

2. As a member of a debate team, you are assigned to prepare a list of arguments for and against the controversial topics listed below.

   A. birth control
   B. legalization of drug use
   C. international control of multinational corporations
   D. the use of nuclear energy to create electric power
   E. closing rain forests to further exploitation

The Impact of Science and Technology

Have you ever used a computer? Have you heard about a person who has had a heart transplant or laser surgery to improve their vision? Did you recently listen to a television program that reported weather conditions based on information relayed by satellites? All of these questions can now be answered affirmatively because of the rapid advances made in science and technology in the past fifty years. In this chapter, you will examine how much your life has changed from that of your parents when they were your age because of the scientific and technological ideas that have now been put to use for the benefit of people.

After the Second World War, a technological and scientific revolution began that has far-reaching consequences for most nations. More than ever, the world is being drawn closer together by supersonic travel and rapid two-way electronic communication. This present period, called the **Post-Industrial Revolution**, refers to the recent changes in science and technology.

Advanced technology makes computers everyday business tools in industry. The use of personal computers has opened up the ability for individuals to bring state-of-the-art technology into their homes. Increasingly, nations and individuals depend on computers for research and to process information that aids in analyzing and forecasting political and economic events. Scientific research also greatly benefits from the use of computers.

Space exploration began in earnest in the 1950s as a result of the United States' and Soviet Union's competition for world leadership. After the successful launching of the Soviet Union's Sputnik in 1957, a space race began that has resulted in major technological advances. Satellites now circle the globe to provide better communications and weather information. Human beings are no longer confined to the inner atmosphere of the planet earth.

Advances in medical technology have prolonged and improved human life in many nations for those people who have access to its benefits. Biotechnology and genetic engineering hold both a promise and threat for the future. The prevention of diseases has also become a key medical concern. Increasingly, the relationship of longevity to life-styles, namely what we eat, drink, and do for physical activity, is being researched.

The Computer Revolution

Computers have had an enormous impact since their introduction in 1946 after World War II. There have been major changes in the gathering and storing of information, systems of communication, and the manufacturing of computer-related products. The growing computerization of transportation and communication systems in the industrialized nations and in a number of developing nations has promoted global interdependence.

What Computers Do

Today we consider computers to be common tools in the business world. The tiny low-cost **silicon chips**, nonmetallic chemical substances, make it possible to perform more than eight hundred million complicated calculations in seconds and store vast amounts, more than four million words, of information. This stored data can be retrieved at a moment's notice, transmitted to any location where there is a linking device, such as a telephone modem, to the computer. Data can be transmitted from one place on earth to another—and even into space.

International Competition. There has been aggressive competition for leadership in the international computer market. The United States and Japan are engaged in a race to develop and market the world's first "supercomputer." The

Chapter 39 Chronology

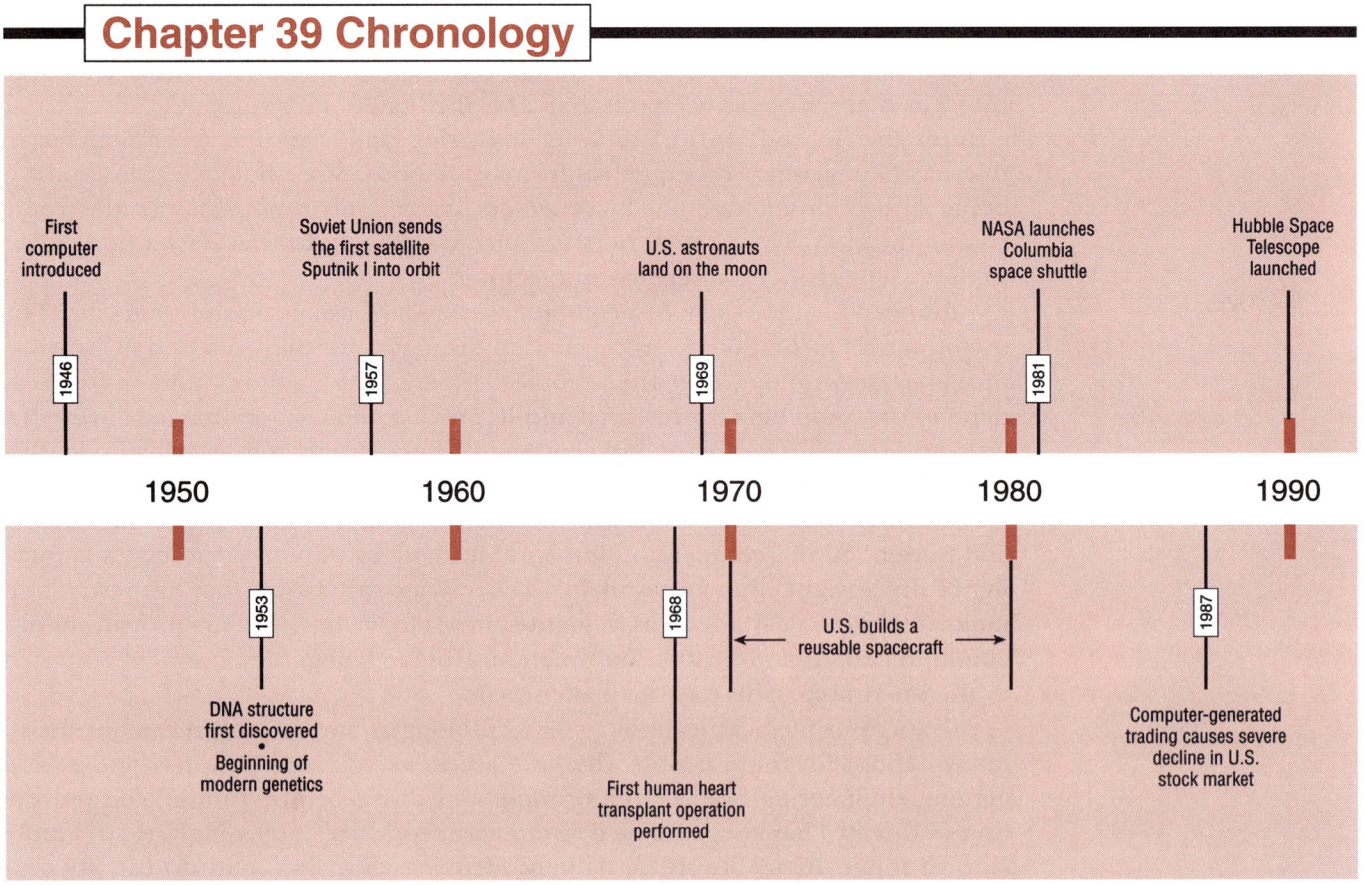

First computer introduced — 1946

Soviet Union sends the first satellite Sputnik I into orbit — 1957

U.S. astronauts land on the moon — 1969

NASA launches Columbia space shuttle — 1981

Hubble Space Telescope launched

1950   1960   1970   1980   1990

1953 — DNA structure first discovered • Beginning of modern genetics

1968 — First human heart transplant operation performed

U.S. builds a reusable spacecraft

1987 — Computer-generated trading causes severe decline in U.S. stock market

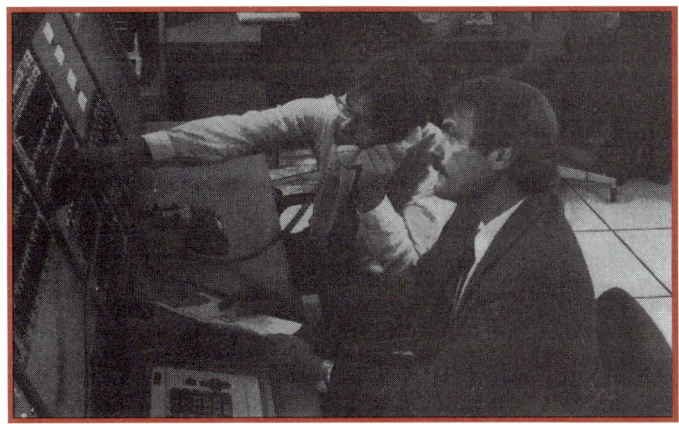

The use of computers helps link the Federal Reserve Bank with local institutions in other parts of the United States. Electronic banking is increasing worldwide.

There has been an enormous increase in the use of computers at home and in the office, which has led to the development of an international information network.

production and sale of silicon chips has become an international economic issue as well as a security issue for the industrialized nations.

Financial Transactions International financial and banking transactions and investments increasingly rely on the use of computers. The speed of transactions is so rapid that we have entered into an era of continuous economic activity. For example, computers are used to analyze stock and bond trends. Computer driven stock market trading is so prevalent today that regulations to control its negative impact have been adopted. For example, in 1987, the United States and other world markets declined drastically within a couple of days partly because of computer programs that called for heavy selling of stock.

Medical and Industrial Uses Many applications of computer technology are continuing to revolutionize the way we look at and complete different tasks. The microchip, or brain that drives the computer, is now used to make medical procedures easier and more reliable. For example, computer chips can now be inserted into the human body to power artificial limbs or regulate the heartbeat. In industry, robots have been developed and programmed to assemble machines and complete tasks such as painting and welding.

Communications Other important advances in **microchip technology** include the growing use of the cellular phone. Today, a person can travel with a portable cellular phone to isolated areas and remain in contact with the global communication network. Businesspeople can send a letter over a fascimile (fax) machine in a matter of minutes. The many millions of electronic communication signals that cross the world daily have furthered the growth of the global economy by increasing the possibility of doing business at all hours and in any place where this information can be received and used to send another message.

Weather forecasts, political opinion polls, and airport controller systems are additional examples of how computer technology affects our daily lives. Now we can more accurately predict weather patterns because of computer analysis of all determining factors that go into a forecast. Political campaigns and polls are more than ever dependent on computer analysis. It is now possible to predict winners on election evening before all ballots are counted and the polling locations close based on the computer's analysis of voting trends.

Use in Schools and at Home   In schools, we see an ever-growing use of computers in the educational process. Schools are increasingly offering students computer-related educational instruction. Students are encouraged to learn how to use computers at an early age. The knowledge of word processing is considered to be an important skill for future employment. The growing use of personal computers has brought computers into the home for use as hobbies, as educational tools for individuals and families, and as professional tools in working from the home. The growth of portable laptops is visible in the home, on airplanes, commuter trains, automobiles—just about anywhere—because of their high memory capabilities and versatility.

Laptop computers enable people to bring their work wherever they travel.

Space Exploration

From earliest times, human beings have been fascinated by the sun, moon, and stars. After World War II, the technology of rocket propulsion advanced rapidly. In the 1950s and 1960s, the United States and the Soviet Union became involved in a competition to be the leading nation in space exploration. Both superpower nations launched space programs that applied a more powerful rocket technology.

One goal of the space race for the United States and Soviet Union was to insure that their respective Cold War Era rival would not achieve military superiority. Commencing in the 1950s, the two superpowers launched hundreds of satellites into space. The military objectives were to improve their worldwide communication systems and to insure, by means of spy satellites using advanced photographic technology, that their ideological and technological rival would not gain any advantages.

The launching of satellites also had other objectives. There were weather satellites, scientific probes without passengers to gather information about the solar system, and experiments to see if human beings could adapt to long periods in space.

The 1960s   The first attempts by humans to boost themselves into space came in the 1960s. Yuri Gagarin, a Russian cosmonaut, and John Glenn, Jr., an American astronaut, were two of the space heroes of this phase of space exploration.

Towards the end of the 1960s, the challenge began to determine which nation would first put a human on the moon. This challenge was won by the American scientists at the **NASA (National Aeronautics and Space Administration)** at the end of the decade. In July 1969, two American astronauts, Neil Armstrong and Edwin Aldrin, Jr., were the first persons to walk on the surface of the moon. The world was transfixed by this great step forward in space exploration.

The 1970s and 1980s   Starting in the 1970s, the new challenges for NASA and the Soviet Union's space experts were to develop a reusable space shuttle and, ultimately, to construct a space station that would serve military and other scientific purposes. A program was also begun to utilize space-based technology to destroy intercontinental ballistic missiles (ICBM). During the Reagan administration in the 1980s, the United States started a Strategic Defense Initiative (SDI), nicknamed Star Wars, that applied satellite techniques for the purpose of knocking out launched ICBMs.

During the 1980s, the European Community developed a space program. The European Space Agency (ESA) involves France, Germany, Great Britain, and other EC (now EU) nations in a joint effort to improve the community's space capabilities. Canada and Japan are also each involved in space research programs.

In 1981, NASA successfully launched the United States' first completely operational space shuttle. The Columbia space shuttle opened a new era of travel beyond the earth's atmosphere. The United States continues to build space shuttles in part to conduct experiments in space. The goals of self-contained space stations that orbit the earth are within reach. There are also plans to continue the exploration of distant space by sending other space probes beyond our solar system.

The 1990s In the 1990s, our knowledge of space also grew from the boosting of the Hubble Space Telescope into orbit. This telescope, via satellite, enabled technicians and scientists to look into the depths of space without interference from the earth's atmosphere, which advanced our knowledge of our solar system and the far reaches of space. Astronomers now have the capability to more accurately analyze evidence retrieved from the deep reaches of the universe. In 1993, NASA made a series of critical repairs that will make the Hubble Telescope an even more effective instrument to record events in space.

The United States and Russia are also engaged in joint space ventures. Since the breakup of the Soviet Union, the United States has sought to work more closely with the Russian space industry. Presently, scientists from the United States, Russia, and other nations are working together on space exploration projects. In the 1990s, joint space projects have become more common. NASA, and its equivalents in Russia, Canada, Japan, and the ESA are working together on the Freedom Space Station. This is an international space project, scheduled to be orbited in 1995.

Advances in Medical Technology

Medical technology has advanced enormously since the turn of the century. Doctors now have medicines and the technology to combat diseases and better monitor human health. In the post-World War II Era, modern medicine has overcome the limitations that once hindered the medical profession from better serving humanity.

Diseases that were once untreatable have been virtually eradicated through the use of vaccines. Smallpox is no longer the threat it was at the turn of the century. The number of cases of other diseases, such as polio and tuberculosis, have been significantly reduced through the use of new drugs. Pneumonia and other infectious diseases have been controlled through the use of penicillin and other more recently discovered medicines.

Doctors are now utilizing diagnostic devices that are capable of identifying and curing problems that previously would have not been possible. The use of laser surgery technology permits doctors to perform delicate operations with a small chance of error. For example, the removal of cataracts that cloud the eyes has become so simple and commonplace that people no longer are threatened with a loss of vision from this frequent affliction once they become older.

The advent of delicate medicines to correct chemical imbalances in the brain has led to effective treatment for people who were condemned to a life of uncontrollable mental illness. The use of lithium to control manic depression is but one example of the wonders of modern medicine to help people better regulate their mental balance. Chemical therapy to combat formally incurable cancers is another example of how research has led to the use of special compounds to fight diseases that previously were untreatable.

New technologies have also brought about important breakthroughs in organ transplants. Liver and kidney transplants have become more common and successful because of the development of medicines that fight against the body's rejection of foreign organs. The search for an artificial heart that is durable continues unabated. It is conceivable that within this decade a dramatic breakthrough may occur that will make heart transplants commonplace. The first human heart transplant operation was performed in 1968.

The ramifications of the new medical technologies are multifold. There are ethical and moral questions raised over issues such as genetic engineering and the ability to prolong life by means of the latest medical technology. Do we have the right to genetically tinker with and alter the creation of life? Should society permit the creation of babies by artificial means? Do we have the moral and legal right to end life prematurely and "pull the plug" on life support systems when there is no hope for a patient's recovery and more suffering is all that can be reasonably expected? These are just some of the questions that are causing controversy.

In addition, advanced medical technology means that many people will live longer, and this will have an impact on the population explosion. There will be greater medical costs and more people to feed. The question we must answer is: Do we want to increase the quantity of life if we cannot improve its quality?

The rising costs of medical care for many families and individuals who can ill afford medical coverage or for those who lose whatever savings they have as a result of treating a major illness is impoverishing increasing numbers of people. Public health facilities are under increasing pressure and are less capable of providing quality services because of rising costs. Therefore, should the federal government step in to create a national health system and control health costs?

Genetics

An area that shows important promise in the field of medicine is genetics. In 1953, modern genetics started when a team of scientists, an American, James Watson, and an Englishman, Francis Crick, were able to decipher the structure of a genetic molecule. This discovery enabled scientists to better comprehend how cells reproduce themselves. The structure of **DNA**, deoxyribonucleic acid, opened the door to further research that promises to be a new frontier of medicine.

Through the understanding of DNA, additional molecular research can provide knowledge about the origins of and treatment for diseases, such as cancer, that are most likely related to people's genetic heritage. In the production of insulin, used to treat diabetes, DNA technology has already enabled research scientists to duplicate human insulin cells.

One controversial aspect in DNA technology involves genetic engineering, a process that involves the production of new life forms through cell alteration. Ethical questions about the idea of creating life artificially through genetic engineering and fears that this type of research might produce new strains of deadly diseases have led to criticism. Nevertheless, the promise of DNA techniques to fight and cure disease is a future medical frontier.

In the 1980s, an unknown illness, **AIDS**, became a major medical concern. The discovery of and research concerning Acquired Immune Deficiency Syndrome, by French and American medical researchers, revealed that this disease threatens to become an enormous killer of humanity by the twenty-first century. AIDS destroys a person's immunological system, thereby opening up the possibility for any opportunistic disease (any illness that takes advantage of the weakened immune system) to enter and spread within the body. At present, there is no known cure for AIDS, and death is an almost certain result if the HIV virus is contracted. The medications available can only slow its progression—not stop it. Blood and sexual secretions are the two major conduits in the spread of this deadly disease. AIDS has become an increasing worldwide concern, Africa, Europe, and the Americas were the continents most affected in the 1980s, but the relentless spread of AIDS into Asia and elsewhere has made it a problem that requires global research to find a cure. (Also see Chapter 38, "Global Environmental and Social Issues.")

Summary

The opportunities opened to humankind by the advances in science and technology have multiplied in the past fifty years. If used for peaceful purposes and for the benefit of the growing world population, these advances can lead to better and more productive lives for increasing numbers of people. We face a real choice today because much can be done to end world hunger and stamp out diseases that once were beyond the capabilities of the scientific and medical communities. The question is whether humankind will put aside its political, ethnic, and religious differences and allow scientists and medical personnel to solve some key problems that we face.

Change is increasing at an ever-expanding rate. In your parents' lifetime, people have walked on the moon, space shuttle trips are taken for granted, computers are an everyday tool, and you play video games. Even all the facts in this book can be placed on a chip and put into a watch!

While we enjoy the advantages of these advances, there are important questions that require discussing. While certain diseases have been eradicated, the world population continues to expand, causing a lowering of the standard of living in developing nations. Organ transplants raise the questions of, Who gets the organ and who pays for it? Life can now be created and altered artificially, but is this ethically right? Are we not only interested in the quantity of life but also the quality? Science alone cannot answer these questions. They touch on the very core of our beliefs. What is your position on these issues?

CHAPTER 39

Review Exercises

I. Multiple Choice

Directions: Find the *letter* of the correct answer.

1. The Post-Industrial Revolution refers to

   (a) a growth in mechanized production.
   (b) the era of airplane travel.
   (c) increased use of atomic power.
   (d) changes in science and technology.

2. The computer revolution has led to

   (a) the increasing high cost of producing silicon chips.
   (b) a decline in the use of computer generated stock trading.
   (c) enormous changes in the gathering of information.
   (d) a greater independence for industrialized nations.

3. All of the following are positive effects of the use of computers *except*

   (a) the increased use of computer-related instructional programs.
   (b) the improvement in the speed of financial and banking transactions.
   (c) the prediction of election results prior to the polls closing.
   (d) the ability to forecast worldwide weather conditions.

4. Space exploration began in earnest in the 1950s after the

   (a) United States launched the Columbia space shuttle.
   (b) Soviet Union launched the Sputnik I satellite.
   (c) United States developed the Strategic Defense Initiative.
   (d) Soviet Union developed the first operational space station.

5. All of the following are accepted medical advances *except*

   (a) laser surgery technology.
   (b) diagnostic services.
   (c) genetic engineering.
   (d) organ transplants.

II. Matching

Directions: Match the words in Column A with the correct description in Column B.

Column A
1. microchip
2. genetic molecule
3. penicillin
4. Strategic Defense Initiative
5. personal computer

Column B
(a) pneumonia
(b) deoxyribonucleic acid
(c) intercontinental ballistic missile
(d) laptop computer
(e) cellular phone

III. Vocabulary

Directions: Define the following words, terms, or expressions and use them in a written sentence.

1. NASA—
2. genetic engineering—
3. silicon chip—
4. AIDS—
5. insulin—

IV. Thought Questions

Directions: Answer the following questions in essay form.

1. The computer revolution has led to great changes in the way we do things.

   A. List three changes brought about by computers.
   B. Explain how these changes affect your life.

2. Recent medical advances have prolonged people's lives.

   A. List three recent medical advances.
   B. Explain how these advances have affected human longevity.

3. Some people object to genetic engineering on moral and ethical grounds. What is your position on this issue? Explain fully.

4. Space exploration has been an exciting part of American life the past three decades.

   A. List three benefits of space exploration.
   B. Explain how these benefits have improved people's lives.

5. Recent technological advances have promoted progress for society.

   A. List four technological advances.
   B. Explain why these advances are considered to be progress.

V. Activities

Directions: Complete the following activities.

1. Write a research paper about the technological changes that have taken place since 1945. In your report, explain how the following items have led to advances in communication and transportation.

   A. computers
   B. cellular phones
   C. jet engines
   D. satellites

2. You are a member of a group that will participate in a class discussion on advances in medical technology. To prepare for this discussion, be ready to speak on the following items by thinking about them and writing down a few complete thoughts about each:

   A. laser surgery
   B. organ transplants
   C. genetic engineering

CHAPTER 40

Global Cultural Patterns

Consider some of the following cultural facts. Rock singers from Africa and Europe go on tour in the United States and are enthusiastically received. American movies draw record crowds overseas. Basketball, an American sport initially, has become an increasingly popular game *worldwide* because of its television exposure during the 1992 Olympic Games and 1994 Goodwill Games. The 1994 World Cup Soccer competition was held in the United States, playing before record audiences in person and via television. These are examples of how our world has grown closer because of all the cultural and technological changes that have taken place since the end of the Second World War in 1945. Nations and peoples now have more contact than ever before, which has led to an increased exchange of ideas and exposure to different cultures. There is a growing global cultural interdependence in spite of the fact that nations and peoples are proud of their heritages and unique identities.

Today, it is quite common for people to have greater exposure to the arts, customs, music, sports, and literature of many diverse cultures from all over the world. Contact with different peoples and ideas influences the development of any culture. In spite of the efforts by some nations and peoples to maintain a traditional culture and ethnic identity, it is increasingly difficult to do so because of modern technological improvements. Television, radio, newspapers, and other means of communication, often referred to as the **mass media**, are readily available even to the most isolated peoples.

Today, we are living in a time in which a global culture is emerging. As the earth becomes more populated and people migrate to other areas in search of a better life and greater opportunity, national boundaries are no longer as clearly defined as they once were. Young people your age are especially influenced by these developments. Presently, we are witnessing a search for identity and meaning in a world that has changed in dramatic ways.

Since 1945, there have also been a number of negative consequences, which are directly related to the political, economic, social, and cultural changes that have taken place. In many nations, there has been an overall decline of ethical and moral constructs. Family values have declined. The divorce rate has greatly increased, and there is a growing abrogation of parental responsibility. This has been accompanied by a refusal by many to accept individual responsibility, the need for instant gratification, and the "greed is good" mentality. Consequently, more people—and at younger ages—are seeking to escape reality or ease their real or imagined pain by using drugs. Patriotism among youths is no longer an accepted moral obligation.

In this chapter, you will read about many of the positive and negative cultural changes that have taken place in recent decades and have affected your life.

Changing Values in the Post-World War II Era

Prior to World War II, cultural changes took place, but they were limited in scope and took a longer time to occur. The Industrial Revolution led to great political, economic, and social changes, but the transition from an agricultural and rural society to an industrial and urban one did not happen overnight. Although values changed as nations became more urbanized and new social classes emerged, the transition in terms of culture was more evolutionary than revolutionary. This means that changes have taken place slowly over time rather than in a sudden manner. The values that emerged in industrial societies guided people well into the twentieth century.

Chapter 40 Chronology

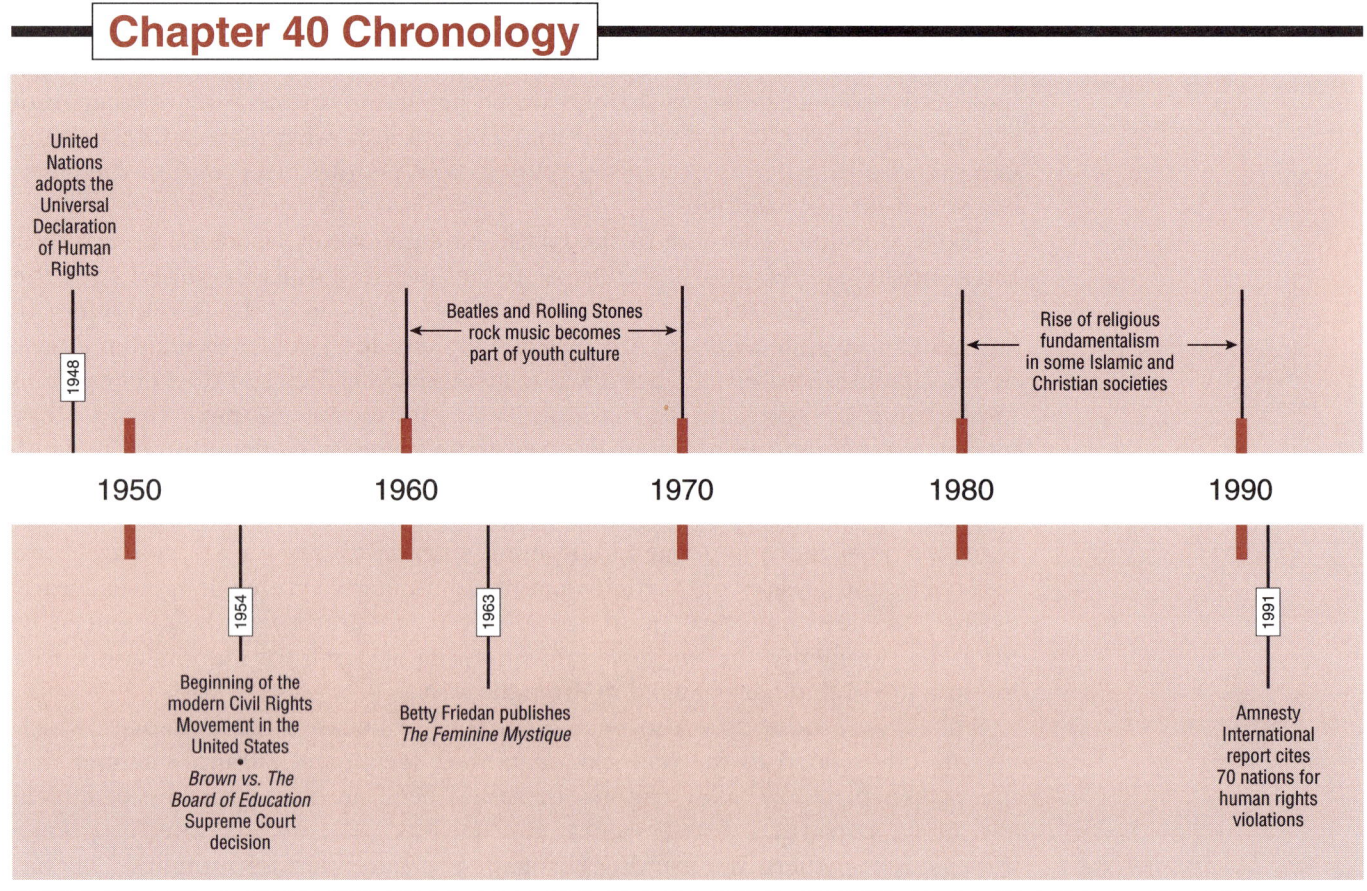

United Nations adopts the Universal Declaration of Human Rights

1948

Beatles and Rolling Stones rock music becomes part of youth culture

Rise of religious fundamentalism in some Islamic and Christian societies

1950   1960   1970   1980   1990

1954

1963

1991

Beginning of the modern Civil Rights Movement in the United States
•
Brown vs. The Board of Education Supreme Court decision

Betty Friedan publishes The Feminine Mystique

Amnesty International report cites 70 nations for human rights violations

After 1945, the world became increasingly fast-paced and complex. A world-wide communication and transportation system developed and has become extremely efficient. Today, people can travel faster worldwide than ever before, and communication is now practically instantaneous.

In the West, economic growth brought nations to new heights of prosperity. The United States was the first nation in the post-World War II Period to experience sustained economic growth that led to a better life in terms of material possessions for most people. After a period of post-war adjustment, the American economy began a time of sustained growth that lasted into the 1960s. Salaries gradually rose, and many more people became capable of affording "the good life." This meant that private homes, automobiles, televisions, washing machines, and other new technological products became more readily available to a growing number of people. These changes that first affected the United States spread to Western Europe, Japan, and elsewhere in the decades after countries recovered from the devastation of World War II.

New **technological advances** also resulted in a change in people's work patterns. More automation and reduced working hours allowed people to have a greater amount of leisure time in the United States and other industrialized nations. The prosperity of people living in the United States and other developed nations resulted in a growing materialistic attitude. **Consumerism** increased as people had more money available to purchase goods that they previously considered luxurious or unnecessary.

Despite the gains made by Westerners, particularly Americans, in terms of material goods and more time to enjoy life, there were growing signs that the **values** (beliefs or standards) that had previously guided people were no longer as clear as they once had been. To a large measure, this was a direct result of the growth of personal expression and individualism in the nations where increased numbers of people achieved economic liberation. This sense of a desire for self-expression and personal liberation led to new calls for changes concerning social concepts that had long governed people's lives.

Many of these demands for a society where greater freedom and a fairer system of social justice would be available to all citizens began in the United States. Commencing in the mid-1950s, a civil rights movement developed, which sought to finally resolve the issue of racial equality. The Civil Rights Movement sought to end the discriminatory practices that had for so long prevented African-Americans from fully participating in and enjoying the benefits of all aspects of American life. Campaigns began to insure that African-Americans could enjoy the privileges of voting and attending good schools. From legislation such as the *Brown vs. the Board of Education* decision in 1954, which sought to end segregated schools, to the Civil Rights Act of the 1960s, great strides were made to offer African-Americans the same rights that other Americans enjoyed.

The Status of Women

In the 1960s, American women also demanded changes in their traditional roles. In 1963, Betty Friedan's book, *The Feminine Mystique,* led to the rebirth of a women's movement in the United States. In the nineteenth century and prior to the 1920s, women in America fought for (and attained) voting rights equal to those of men and other feminine issues. More recently, women have demanded an end to sexual discrimination and gender stereotyping. Women have called for equal pay and access to jobs previously only available to men. They want the right to be construction workers, members of municipal fire and police departments, and fighter pilots, and to have greater accessibility to the highest executive positions in corporations. Many women rejected the ideas that they were born to be only housewives and mothers and should stay away from traditionally male roles. The Women's Liberation Movement spread to other countries in Western Europe and elsewhere. In each country, the movement took on a character of its own, depending on the culture of that nation and that society's acceptance of the right of women to expand their freedom and opportunities.

Religion

Religious ideas were also greatly affected by the changes in the Post-Industrial Era. Traditional religious views were increasingly rejected by those people who wanted more personal choice and individual freedom. The far-reaching political, economic, and social changes led many people to search for a new meaning to their lives. As people's thoughts, expectations, and actions were affected by a more materialistic, complex, and fast-paced world that surrounded them, mainstream religions, particularly in the West, lost followers.

Nevertheless, the decline in membership of mainstream religious denominations, such as Roman Catholicism and some established Protestant denominations, did not lead to vast numbers of people turning away from religion altogether in the industrial nations. To compensate for the general lack of interest in traditional teachings, religious leaders began to become involved in issues such as the environment, human rights, and nuclear disarmament.

In addition, **religious fundamentalism** experienced some growth. For example, in the United States during the 1980s, fundamentalist Christian groups grew rapidly as they attracted people who wanted a stricter interpretation of religious teachings. There was increased interest in the religions of the East among those who saw Buddhism and Hinduism as the answer to their search for religious values. Islam also attracted new adherents, particularly in urban areas. Islamic fundamentalism grew at a fast pace in North Africa and the Middle East in the 1980s and 1990s.

In the 1990s, because of the fall of the Communist regimes in the Soviet Union and Eastern Europe, traditional religion, suppressed for decades, is making a comeback. Churches are being reopened and numerous religious groups are seeking to propagate their faith among populations previously forbidden to openly practice their religious beliefs. The dismantling of the Communist governments has shown that, despite long years of repression and teaching, religion is the opiate of the people; it is impossible to completely eliminate religious faith. During their existence, Communist governments accepted the Marxist doctrine that the practice of religion was a harmful addiction for the people. If given the opportunity, human need for religious belief will revive and flourish once again.

Religious intolerance is also growing in today's world. The re-emergence of strong nationalist and religious feelings bordering on ethnocentricism is a continuing problem. Whereas in some countries progress had been made concerning religious freedom, in other nations religion remains a prime cause of bloody confrontations.

In Northern Ireland, for example, Catholics and Protestants have not been able to find a political solution that would allow these two Christian groups to live peacefully together in one nation. In former Yugoslavia, Christians and Muslims have battled for control of territory in Bosnia. The process of ethnic cleansing, in which peoples of different cultures and religions seek to drive each other out of mutually inhabited territories, has added to the suffering. In Iran, religious intolerance, particularly against adherents of the Baha'i faith, has resulted in the brutal repression of people who believe that the time for all humanity to unite and live in peace has come. These examples reflect the many controversies that surround religion.

The Struggle for Human Rights

The violation of **human rights** dates to prehistoric times. Throughout history, examples can be cited of people's human rights being violated. The existence of slavery throughout almost all of human history in all regions of the world is but one example of the mistreatment of people. The concern for human rights has only recently become a worldwide issue.

According to Amnesty International, an organization that monitors human rights, in the 135 nations where information could be gathered in 1991, over one half of the countries were guilty of human rights violations. People are still being imprisoned for having ideas that are different from the political leadership of their countries, for religious reasons, and for advocating ideas of national self-determination.

The increased monitoring of human rights abuses by numerous organizations has led to some improvements. In 1948, when the United Nations adopted the Universal Declaration of Human Rights, it sought to affirm the political, economic, and social rights of all people. Although the situation has been slow to change in many nations where the respect for even the most basic rights does not exist, there is hope for the future.

The United Nations and other international organizations have supported efforts to raise the overall quality of people's lives through education and other programs that provide for basic human needs and rights. Improved health and nutrition have resulted in a better quality of life for more of the world's growing population. Nevertheless, much remains to be done to achieve the goal of having all people live in a world where fear and hunger have been eliminated.

Art, Literature, Music, and Sports

The rapid changes that have taken place in the Post-Industrial Era have greatly facilitated the spread of different cultures and ideas. There has been a vast **cultural diffusion** of art, literature, and music since 1945. The end of the cultural isolation that existed prior to World War II had led to the creation of a global world culture that involves a mixing and blending of divergent ideas about art, literature, and music.

The Arts

After World War II, some artists radically altered their approach to the visual arts. In the 1950s, abstract expressionism became an artistic movement. Painters used colors to represent abstract forms and ideas. Artists used this revolutionary approach instead of the more traditional manner of representing objects realistically.

The rejection of realism in art also was seen in the Op Art (optical art) Movement that first developed in France in the 1950s and then spread elsewhere in Europe and to the United States. In op art, artists sought to plan arrangements of colors and patterns to demonstrate movement that was a vibrating visual illusion.

In the 1960s, pop art gained support in the United States and Europe. Artists, such as Andy Warhol, sought to use commonplace objects from everyday life as subjects in art to create a superrealistic effect. An example is Warhol's famous painting of cans of Campbell's soup. Photography also became more accepted as an art form in the post-1945 period. Realism, such as nature photography and photo journalism, became popular. For example, the photographer Richard Audubon influenced the development of the Environmental Movement in the United States with his vivid pictures of America's national park system. More people turned their attention to nature's problems as a result of his telling, realistic photography.

Literature and the Theater

The post-1945 period has seen a flowering of literature from many regions. More works of important authors are now being translated, thereby permitting a wider audience access to the growing volume of literature that transcends national and regional boundaries. Countries once isolated from the mainstream of world literature because of language barriers and political censorship have added their heritage to the global literary culture.

In the nations of the former Soviet Union and Eastern Europe, writers whose works were often repressed by Communist censors now have greater freedom to write and publish. In the former Communist bloc countries, the literature of Aleksandr Solzhenitzyn, the poetry of Andrey Voznesensky, and the plays of Vaclav Havel are increasingly available. Works of authors formerly banned are now being read because of the new artistic freedom.

The works of authors from developing countries in Africa, Asia, and Latin America are now available worldwide due to translation and less expensive publishing costs. The writings of African authors, such as Nigerian Chinua Achebe, and the Ghanian playwright Arma Ata Aidoo, and others reflect themes related to the continent's colonial heritage and problems of modernization in a world where tribal values are still strong.

A growing number of Latin American writers have also received worldwide recognition. The Colombian novelist Gabriel Garcia Marquez, the Peruvian novelist Mario Vargas Llosa, the Mexican writers Carlos Fuentes and Octavio Paz, the Brazilian novelist Jorge Amado, and the Argentinian writer Manuel Puig, have all had notable success in Latin America and their works are translated into foreign languages, especially English.

Music

Music also has become more international in scope since 1945. American jazz and rock and roll music are now played and listened to all over the globe. In the 1950s, the American rock and roll legend Elvis Presley became an international superstar. In the 1960s, rock music really took off and became a worldwide phenomenon when the British groups, the Beatles and the Rolling Stones, brought their version of rock and roll to the United States, Europe, and other regions. The development of a youth culture throughout the world that has elevated rock musicians into superstars continued into the following decades. The songs of Michael Jackson, Elton John, Billy Joel, Bruce Springsteen, and Aretha Franklin, among others, have thrilled audiences across the globe. The spectacular success of rock concerts that highlight the talents of rock superstars attract huge crowds of young people on all continents.

Rock music became more international as it spread to other continents and blended with regional music traditions. In the Caribbean, Jamaican reggae music gained a large following in the United States and Europe because of the music of Bob Marley and the Wailers, Jimmy Cliff, and other Caribbean musicians. The American songwriter Paul Simon produced two albums that drew upon African and Brazilian influences. In Africa, the growing popularity of Afro pop is another example of how regional music has blended into the global rock network.

Jazz, which originated in the United States, also became more international after World War II. The music of such American jazz artists as Louis Armstrong, Charlie Parker, Ella Fitzgerald, Miles Davis, and others spread to other continents. In Europe, regional jazz artists developed bands of their own and took jazz music into new directions, which reflect the cultural traditions of their roots.

More traditional forms of music continue to prosper. Classical music has remained very popular among those who appreciate symphonic and operatic type music. National symphonic orchestras continue to attract large audiences in Europe, the United States, and elsewhere. Older entertainers such as Frank Sinatra of the United States, Roberto Carlos of Brazil, and Julio Inglesias from Spain, continue to appeal to the populations in numerous nations who still enjoy ballads.

The ability of music to become international has been greatly facilitated by the continuous technological improvements in electronics. Transistor radios, stereo equipment, earphones, compact disc players, and tape recorders can be found almost anywhere. Smaller and longer-lasting batteries have even eliminated the need for electrical outlets.

Sports

Some sports have become more international as they receive a greater exposure on television and are increasingly played by young people of different nations. Sports that had little global popularity, such as basketball, have gained a worldwide acceptance and following. The United States "Dream Team," which won the gold medal at the Olympics in the summer of 1992 did much to popularize basketball. Michael Jordan, the game's most renowned player, whose professional team, the Chicago Bulls, won three consecutive championships, became an ambassador for the game. Today, basketball players from Europe and Africa compete as equals in the United States National Basketball Association. Soccer, called football elsewhere in the world, has finally caught on in the United States and is more than ever the global sport. In the summer of 1994, the world soccer championship games were held in the United States, and an American team competed for the World Cup.

Summary

In the past fifty years, as the world has grown closer because of the development of sophisticated communication and transportation networks, a global culture has emerged. Traditional national cultures continue to exist and flourish, but increasingly there is a commonality in terms of cultural developments that has resulted in the growth of international cultural patterns. Culturally, we are definitely moving in the direction of the concept of a global village.

You are probably more familiar with what is called a "global village" because of sports and music than the other aspects. Basketball and hockey stars from Europe are joining American professional teams. Colleges recruit for their teams in a number of nations. American baseball players often play out their careers in Japan to the cheers of the intense Japanese spectators who take their baseball very seriously. There are numbers of rock stars from Britain that have become even more popular in the United States. You would probably have little trouble discussing these areas (if you overcame the language barrier) with someone your age in London, Moscow, or Tokyo, because of similar interests.

The world has become a smaller place because of the rapidity of communication and transportation. People are talking about shuttle flights to other parts of the world. Your television set brings the world into your home and makes you familiar with faraway places. You will have to find the way to make these changes beneficial to mankind. That is your challenge!

CHAPTER 40

Review Exercises

I. Multiple Choice

Directions: Find the *letter* of the correct answer.

1. Cultural diffusion has increased because of

   (a) increased automation.
   (b) technological advances.
   (c) growing materialism.
   (d) renewed feminism.

2. The growth of materialism in the United States and elsewhere had led to

   (a) a questioning of values.
   (b) gender stereotyping.
   (c) women's liberation.
   (d) national self-determination.

3. New technological advances have resulted in all of the following *except*

   (a) increased automation.
   (b) reduced working hours.
   (c) declining consumerism.
   (d) more leisure time.

4. In the 1960s, the rebirth of the Women's Liberation Movement in the United States reflected

   (a) a demand for equal voting rights.
   (b) the enactment of a constitutional amendment for women's rights.
   (c) a desire to end all aspects of sexual discrimination.
   (d) the overall acceptance by men of the equality of women.

5. The disappearance of communism in the former Soviet Union and Eastern Europe has led to

   (a) greater numbers of people being employed.
   (b) a decline in ethnic and national consciousness.
   (c) a revival of religious practice in these areas.
   (d) more people having a better life materialistically.

II. Vocabulary

Directions: Define the following words, terms, or expressions and use them in a written sentence.

1. consumerism—
2. human rights—
3. materialistic—
4. values—
5. leisure time—
6. women's movement—
7. gender stereotyping—
8. religious fundamentalism—
9. Post-Industrial Era—
10. mass media—

III. Thought Questions

Directions: Answer the following questions in essay form.

1. Technological advances and political and economic changes after World War II have affected social values.

   A. List four technological advances or political and economic changes.
   B. Explain the way in which these technological advances or political and economic changes have affected social values.

2. Human rights is an increasing area of concern in the world today.

   A. Explain why human rights is a worldwide concern.
   B. Propose and explain three ways that human rights would be improved in the nations that violate them.

3. Changing values since World War II have had an important impact on religion.

   A. List examples of three religious values that have changed.
   B. Explain why these particular values have changed.

4. Feminism has inspired a rebirth of the women's movement.

   A. How have women fought for equality since the 1960s?
   B. What arguments do the opponents of feminism use?

5. Since World War II, a global culture has emerged involving art, literature, and music. Prove that this is true by explaining how each of these areas has influenced the emergence of a global culture.

IV. Activities

Directions: Complete the following activities.

1. You are a member of a debate team. You are assigned to prepare a list of arguments for or against the topics listed below.

   A. equality for women
   B. protection of human rights

C. materialistic life-styles

D. a return to traditional values

E. increased automation

2. You are assigned a research report on one of the topics listed below. For your report, go to the library and complete your research on the selected topic.

A. the Women's Liberation Movement

B. the rise of religious fundamentalism

C. the role of the mass media in creating a global culture

D. the role of materialism in changing traditional values

Glossary

A.D. Anno Dominum or "In the Year of Our Lord"; the basis of the modern calendar dating system beginning in the projected year of Christ's birth

absolutism the principle or the exercise of complete and unrestricted power of government

acropolis fortress on the highest point of an Ancient Greek city on which temples to the gods were built; it also served as both a treasury and an armory

Age of Exploration the period of history from the fifteenth to the seventeenth centuries when European nations explored the world in search of wealth and new trading routes

Age of Reason the period of history, the seventeenth century, when a logical explanation based on reason challenged faith as the accepted cause of an action or event

aggression an act of hostility, invasion, or attack

aghora the marketplace of an Ancient Greek city, which was the center of political and social, as well as economic life

agricultural economy an economy based primarily on farming and the raising of livestock

Agricultural Revolution the changes in agriculture brought about by the introduction of new technology and scientific methods of farming

AIDS Acquired Immune Deficiency Syndrome; the HIV virus, the virus that causes AIDS, destroys a person's ability to fight off infections and diseases and ultimately leads to death

alien a resident of a nation, who is not a citizen and who was born elsewhere

amphitheater a theater built with tiers (a series of rows rising behind one another) of seats around an open area

anarchy a state of disorder or lawlessness due to the absence of government

Anglican pertaining to the Church of England or any of the Churches connected to it

animism the belief that natural objects and phenomena possess spirits or souls

annals yearly records of events in chronological order

annex to add territory to a nation, usually by taking it over by force

annihilation a complete destruction, a wiping out

anschluss union; specifically, that between Germany and Austria in 1938

anthropologist a person who studies the origins and customs of humankind

anti-Semitism prejudice and hostility against Jews

apartheid racial segregation in the Republic of South Africa; separation of the races

apatheia apathy or a lack of feeling; the Stoics considered this the "perfect state" of mind, because it protected the individual from the pain of life

Appanage Russia the period during which Russia was under Mongol rule

appanages land granted to nobility

appeasement giving into a potential aggressor in the hope of achieving peace

aqueduct a structure that channels water over distances

archaeologist a person who studies historic or prehistoric people and their cultures by analysis of their artifacts or monuments

archipelago a large group of islands, in a particular formation or pattern

archon a leader in an Ancient Greek city-state

aristocracy the hereditary nobility who regard themselves as superior to other groups

armistice a truce; a temporary halt in fighting

artifact any object made or modified by humans especially one reflecting workmanship in ancient cultures

artisan a skilled craftsman

ascetic one who gives up all physical pleasure and luxury in pursuit of spiritual and/or religious development

ascetism the denial of worldly ways; avoidance of materialism in pursuit of spiritual and/or religious development

assembly line an arrangement of machines, tools, and workers in which a product is assembled by having each worker perform a specific operation as the unit passes by

assimilation the process whereby one group of people adopts the characteristics of another culture

astrolabe an ancient instrument for determining the position of the sun or the stars

astronomy the science that deals with the material universe beyond the earth's atmosphere

autocracy rule by one or the holding of power by an individual

auto-da-fé the public execution of heretics by Catholic Church officials during the Middle Ages, usually by burning at the stake

autonomy self-government

Axis powers the alliance of Germany, Italy, and Japan in World War II

B.C. Before Christ; term used to date the years before the projected year of Christ's birth in a descending order

balance of power a distribution of force among nations such that no one is strong enough to dominate the others

barbarian someone who was "not Greek" (had not adopted Greek civilization) or was "uncivilized"

bard a poet

baron title given to royal vassals in the Middle Ages; it later became the lowest rank of European nobility

belligerent (adj.) warlike and aggressive; (n.) a nation that is at war

Big Five the five original (1945) United Nations Security Council permanent members (China, France, Great Britain, the USSR, and the United States), who where the major victors in World War II

Big Four the four major victors in World War I (France, Great Britain, Italy, and the United States)

big lie a statement made by a government that claims the statement is true although the government knows it is false

Big Three Winston Churchill, Franklin D. Roosevelt, and Joseph Stalin (representing Great Britain, the United States, and the USSR, respectively)

bishop a high-ranking clergyman in the Christian Church who oversees many communities

Black Shirts original supporters of Benito Mussolini, who were fascist party members

blasphemy to speak of or use the name of God disrespectfully

blitzkrieg the quick, overpowering, lightning-like attack by German armed forces in World War II

blood and iron policy describing methods used by Bismarck to achieve German unification

Bolshevik extremist Russian Marxist or Communist

boom a period of rapid economic growth

bourgeoisie the middle class, whose values were considered materialistic and petty

boyar traditional title of Russian nobles

boycott organized refusal to buy products

Brown Shirts original supporters of Adolf Hitler, who were Nazi party members

bubonic plague a contagious disease that killed thousands of Europeans in the fourteenth century

bullion gold or silver bars or ingots

bureaucracy the division of responsibility in an organization, especially government

business cycle a recurring period of business in which certain events repeat themselves, e.g., boom, recession, depression

Byzantine chant music of the Byzantine and later Eastern Orthodox Church

Byzantium modern historical term used to identify the civilization of the Eastern Roman Empire (476–1453) based in the second Roman capital city of Constantinople; the name of the city of Constantinople before 325

cabinet group of official advisers to the head of a government

canon law ecclesiastical or Church law; rules of the Christian Church

canzoni Italian term for songs

capital wealth, whether in money or property, accumulated or employed in business

capitalism an economic system in which the means of production and distribution are owned and maintained chiefly by private individuals or corporations

capitalist system an economic system based on private ownership of the means of production and distribution

caravel a small Spanish or Portuguese sailing vessel of the fifteenth and sixteenth centuries

cartography the production of maps

cathedral the main church of a diocese or district under the administration of a bishop

catholic universal or for all people

Centuries an assembly of citizens in Ancient Rome that divided them into military units

chanson de geste "songs of warrior's deeds" or the earliest form of Medieval secular poetry

charter a government document outlining the conditions under which a corporation, colony, or city is organized

Chartist a member of a political reform movement in England in the nineteenth century

checks and balances a political system in which the different branches of government check the power of the other branches to prevent abuses of power

Cheka the Bolshevik secret police, replaced by the NKVD under Stalin

chiaroscuro a concept in painting that uses contrasting light and shade to give the illusion of depth

chronicle a yearly record of events

chronography the writing of yearly records of events or chronicles

Chunnel the tunnel under the English Channel connecting England and France

Church Slavonic the ancient language used in the liturgical practice and writings of the Slavic Orthodox Churches

circuit court system Medieval legal system of traveling judges

circumference the length of the outer boundary of a circle

civics the study of the city, citizenship, and citizens

civilization an advanced state of human society, in which a high level of culture and science has been reached

civilizing agent one that transmits an established culture to another

civitas the ancient Roman city-state

class struggle the Marxist idea of competing groups, e.g., bourgeoisie and proletariat, for the control of society

classic a work of lasting quality that does not become outdated

classics, the the literature of Ancient Greece and Rome

client a political supporter in the ancient Roman republic

Colbertism an economic system in France during seventeenth and eighteenth centuries in which the state regulated the economy for the benefit of the nation

Cold War the undeclared struggle between the USSR and the United States from the end of World War II until 1991; based on an ideological conflict between communism and democracy

collaboration to work together with another person, organization, or country

collective guilt holding a group of people responsible for the actions of one of its members

collectivization the Soviet policy of taking all private land away from farmers and forcing them to work on collective or state farms; the state would later decide how the products would be distributed

colony a group of people, or a territory, who form in a new land subject to government by a parent state

Cominform the Communist Information Bureau; established in 1947 to encourage cooperation between the Eastern European Communist parties

Comintern the Communist International; established in 1919 as an organization to coordinate the activities of Communist parties around the world; it was actually controlled by the USSR and abolished in 1943 as a sign of goodwill to the Allies

Commercial Revolution a period of history, during the seventeenth and eighteenth centuries, when the principles, practices, and spirit of commerce expanded

Common Market See **European Community**

commonwealth a group of sovereign states and their dependencies

communalism tension between Hindus and Muslims in South Asia

commune a system by which citizens share the responsibility of government

communism the theory and system of social organization based on the common ownership of all material wealth and property; it later became a political system in which all economic, political, and social organizations are controlled by a totalitarian state

compass an instrument for determining direction by means of a freely rotating magnetized needle that indicates magnetic north

computer revolution the post-World War II period in which electronic machines capable of accepting and processing results at high speeds were increasingly used in business, education, science, and the military

concentration camps places where prisoners (usually political opponents) of a government are kept

concession permission given to the nation by another one, to carry out some economic undertaking on land of the latter nation

Congress of Vienna the group of European nations (Great Britain, Russia, Prussia, and Austria-Hungary) that, guided by Prince Metternich, determined the course of European history after the defeat of Napoleon in 1815

conquistador one of the sixteenth-century conquerors in the Americas

conscription the drafting of civilians into a nation's armed forces

constitution a document that outlines the system of principles and laws according to which a nation or organization is governed

consul a president of the Roman Republic annually elected from the Senate

consulate the premises officially occupied by a consul or foreign service officer

consumerism a movement for the protection of the consumer against inferior or dangerous products and misleading advertising

contemplative life concern with salvation in the next world and spiritual development

continental system an economic plan developed by Napoleon to isolate and destroy the British economy

convent a nunnery or establishment where nuns reside

corporate state the economic system set up by Mussolini

corporation an association of individuals created by law and existing as an entity with powers and liabilities independent of those of its members

cosmopolitan free from local or national ideas, prejudices, and attachments

cossacks members of various tribes of warriors living mainly in southeast Russia

count royally appointed governor of a county in the Carolingian Empire; it later became an established title of European nobility

Counter Reformation attempts by the Catholic Church to stop the spread of the Protestant movement

coup d'état a sudden, often violent, seizure of government

crematory ovens or furnaces where Germans burned concentration and death camps prisoners' bodies

Cro-Magnon prehistoric people who developed after 100,000 B.C. and are the ancestors of modern people

crop rotation a system of alternating planting to increase crop yield

crucifixion a form of execution whereby one is put to death by being nailed to a cross

crusade an armed pilgrimage or war for religious reasons

cultural diffusion the mixing of different cultures to create a new one

culture the customary beliefs, social forms, and material features of an ethnic, religious, or social group

Curia Regis court of the king or the Medieval English assembly of barons and bishops that acted as advisers to the king

Curiae an assembly of citizens in Ancient Rome based on tribe or clan

Cyrillic an alphabet created for the Slavonic language by the Byzantine monk Cyril of Thessalonika; based on Greek and Coptic letters

czar the traditional title of a Russian ruler; literally, caesar, or emperor

czarevich the traditional title of a Russian royal prince

czarevna the traditional title of a Russian royal princess

czarina the traditional title of a female Russian ruler or the wife of a czar

death camps centers of intentional murder and planned extermination built by the Nazis

decolonization the change of an area's status from colony to free nation

deicide the killing of a god

demarcation line a boundary line separating territory or areas claimed

democracy a system of government characterized by popular sovereignty, with the people freely choosing those who govern, and by equality and respect for the individual

deportation forced removal of Jews in Nazi-occupied areas, to concentration camps and death camps

depression a period during which business and employment decline or remain at a low level of activity

Desert Fathers Christian monastic theologians who lived in isolation in the Egyptian desert for religious reasons; their collected writings became an important part of Christian theology

despot an absolute and often tyrannical ruler

Détente the policy of "understanding" or the improved relations between the Communist and democratic nations during the latter part of the Cold War

dialectic the art or practice of logical discussion

diameter the measurement of the width of a circle

dichotomy a division into two mutually opposed groups

dictator an individual who exercises absolute power, sometimes temporarily in a time of crisis

dictatorship of the proletariat the absolute power exercised in the name of the proletariat (workers) by the Communist party leadership

diktat a dictated peace; specifically the Nazi view of the Versailles treaty's provisions affecting Germany

direct rule a French policy of controlling its colonies in Africa and Asia

Directory a group that ruled France after the downfall of the radicals in 1795

divine right the belief that a ruler's right to govern comes directly from God

division of labor a system in which workers are assigned specific labor tasks to accomplish

DNA any of the class of nucleic acids found chiefly in the nucleus of cells and responsible for transmitting hereditary characteristics and for the building of protein

doctrine a position, principle, or point of view, taught or believed in by a government or religion

domestic system a premodern capitalist labor system of home production

Dow Jones Index a group of stocks that are used to measure the New York Stock Exchange's level of worth

drug cartel informal system of narcotics distributors based in drug-exporting nations, e.g., Colombia

Duce, Il Italian for "the leader" or "commander"; the title taken by Benito Mussolini

duchy a small territory, ruled by a duke or a member of a royal family

Duma the Russian parliament between 1905 and 1917

dynasty a sequence of rulers from the same family or group

Eastern Church the Greek or Eastern Orthodox Church, a federation of independent Churches recognizing a common tradition and the spiritual leadership of the Patriarch of Constantinople; the oldest and most conservative of Christian denominations

ecclesia an assembly of archons or leaders in an Ancient Greek city-state; after the establishment of the Christian movement, the Church or followers of Christianity became known as the Christian Ecclesia

ecclesiastical members of or matters concerning the Christian Church or its clergy

economic imperialism the economic control or policy of extending the rule of authority of an empire or nation over foreign countries

ecosystem a system formed by the interaction of a community of organisms with their environment

ecumenical pertaining to the whole world; any movement that involves all Christian denominations

Einsatzgruppen killing groups attached to the German army during World War II and trained mainly to find and murder Jews in Eastern Europe

emancipation freedom from slavery, influence, or restraint

emigré a person forced to leave his or her country because of political conditions

emperor   the monarch or hereditary ruler of an empire

empire   a group of nations or people ruled over by one sovereign

empiricism   the doctrine that all knowledge is derived from sense experience

enclosure movement   a movement in Great Britain to enclose land for sheep raising that forced farm laborers off the land in the early period of the Industrial Revolution

encyclopedia   books containing articles on all subjects arranged in alphabetical or topical order

enlightened despots   monarchs who tried to justify their absolutist rule by claiming to govern in the best interests of the people

Enlightenment, the   an eighteenth-century movement that rejected traditional ideas and emphasized reasoning and understanding

entrepreneur   a person who organizes, manages, and assumes responsibility for a business or other enterprise

erotic   dealing with sexual love or desire

Estates-general   a legislative body based on the system of three estates—clergy, nobility, and common people—in France prior to the French Revolution

ethics   a system of moral principles; the branch of philosophy that deals with values and morality

ethnic group   a group of people who have a common history and culture, and in some cases, common physical traits

ethnocentrism   the belief that one's own ethnic group or nation is superior to others

European Community   a group of European nations that seek political and economic unity to further their common interests. Later became the European Union. Also called the Common Market.

euthanasia   the mercy killing of people, to be done in a painless manner

evolution   a theory that all living things have acquired their present forms through successive generations

exploitation   to make use of the land or a resource of another for selfish reasons

extraterritoriality   the right of a person in a foreign country to be tried by the laws of his or own country

factory system   a system of manufacturing goods in a large facility using mass production techniques

fascism   a political philosophy, extremely conservative, nationalistic, violent, anti-Communist, anti-Semitic, and racist; specifically, the governmental system of Italy under Mussolini, 1922–1943

feminism   the doctrine advocating social, economic, and political rights for women equal to those of men

fervor   great zeal or an intense feeling of dedication and devotion

feudalism   a socioeconomic system based on local rule and mutual hereditary obligations in the absence of a strong central government

fief   a grant of land in return for service

final solution   the Nazi code phrase for the planned annihilation of the Jews of Europe

First Estate   the clergy in France prior to the French Revolution

foedorati   federates or barbarian tribes allied with Rome who protected the borders of the Roman Empire

forum   a marketplace or square in an Ancient Roman city

four-plus-two negotiations   discussions held in 1990 on plans for the reunification of Germany; participants included the four occupying powers (France, Great Britain, the USSR, and the United States) and the two German states (East and West Germany)

franchise   the right to vote

fraudulent   false or phony

free enterprise system   the economic system of the capitalist countries where private ownership predominates

French Revolution   the revolution that began in France in 1789 that resulted in the overthrow of the Old Regime

fresco   paintings on plaster surfaces, usually walls

führer, der   German for "the leader"; the title taken by Adolf Hitler

GATT   General Agreement on Tariffs and Trade

genetics   the science of heredity

genocide   the planned killing of a whole people because they belong to a hated or despised religion, race, ethnic group, or nation

geocentric   belief that the earth is the center of the universe

geography   the study of the earth's surface, climate, and topography

Gestapo   the secret police of the Nazi government

ghetto   the section of a city where Jews were required to live

Ghibelline   supporter of the German Holy Emperors in the Middle Ages

Girondists   a moderate political party during the French Revolution; it favored making France into a republic

glacier   an extended mass of ice formed by snow moving very slowly from high mountains

Glasnost   the policy of "openness" or greater political freedoms in the USSR and Eastern Europe during the rule of Mikhail Gorbachev

global interdependence   the idea that the nations of the world are mutually dependent

Glorious Revolution   the period in English history (1688–1689) when King James II was overthrown and Parliament's supremacy was recognized

Green Revolution   the increase in agricultural production resulting from modern science and technological improvements

greenhouse effect   a theory stating that the building up of gases in the atmosphere will cause the earth's temperature to gradually rise

Gregorian chant   religious music of the Medieval Roman Catholic Church

gross national product   the total value of goods and services produced in a country

Guelf   supporter of the papacy in the Middle Ages

guild   an association of merchants or artisans

haigiography   writings about saints' lives and their miracles

hedonism   the pursuit of pleasure

heliocentric   the belief that the sun is the center of the universe

Hellas   Greece

Hellenic   Greek

Hellenistic   a less ethnocentric identification of Greece, which included all people who adopted the language, culture, and learning of the Ancient Greeks

helot   enslaved peoples who farmed for the Ancient Spartans

hemophilia   a disease in which the sufferer is missing the clotting factor in the blood, which causes extensive bleeding

hereditary   that which is passed on from one generation to another

heresy   incorrect teaching or views that are outside of accepted beliefs

heretic   one who dissents publicly from the official beliefs of a religious body

historia   history or the "investigation of the past"; the analysis of past events in order to gain a better understanding of the present and future

Holocaust   the intentional murder of six million Jews and the attempt to destroy Judaism as a religion, as carried out between 1933 and 1945 by the Nazis and their collaborators

home rule   the practice of self-government in domestic matters in a dependent area

hominid   primate genus that includes modern human beings and a number of related species

hominocentrism   the concept that human beings are at the center of the universe and that they should be the measure of all things

hoplite   an Ancient Greek infantry regiment made up of citizen volunteers

hostile   feeling and showing of hatred and great unfriendliness

Huguenots   French Protestants of the sixteenth and seventeenth centuries

human rights   the fundamental rights of an individual; basic freedoms within limits

Humanism   a system of thought in which human interests or values and achievements are of primary importance

humanitarian   one who seeks to improve the daily life of people and the advancement of human rights

hymnography   the writing of hymns or religious music

icon   an image or picture; often used to mean holy images of Christ and the saints by Eastern Orthodox and Roman Catholic Christians

iconoclast   one who destroys images or pictures

imperator   an emperor or one who holds the executive authority

imperialism   the domination of one nation over a foreign area

imperium   executive authority

Impressionism   a movement in art, especially in painting, that attempts to convey general impressions rather than objective reality

indemnity   money paid for wrongful or damaging actions

Index   a list published by the Roman Catholic Church, restricting or forbidding the reading of certain books

indirect rule   British policy of controlling its colonies in Africa and Asia

indulgence   a Church pardon, purchased by worshippers to escape punishment for a sin

industrial labor   the workers in industries

industrial pollution   the waste materials, e.g., gases, produced as a by-product of industrial production that pollute the environment

Industrial Revolution   the changes in the economies of certain nations beginning in England in the late eighteenth century to production using the factory system

inevitable   certain to happen; unavoidable

infectious disease   a disease that can be transmitted from one person to another

inflation   an economic situation in which there is an increase in the supply of money and the price of goods; monetary value decreases

innovators   people who introduce new ideas

Inquisition   a court established in the Roman Catholic Church in order to put down heresy and dissent during the Middle Ages

interchangeable parts   parts that can be used in the place of others

internationalism   a willingness to have cooperative relations with other nations

interregnum   period of years without a king

intervention   to interfere with, especially with force or the threat of force

investment capital   money invested in an enterprise

iron curtain   the term created by Winston Churchill to describe the division of Europe due to Soviet aggression into two hostile parts: Communist and non-Communist

isolationism   a desire to have little or nothing to do with other nations

Jacobin   a radical during the period of the French Revolution, who took extreme positions

Jesuit   an order of priests in the Roman Catholic Church, founded in 1534 as part of the Counter Reformation

jingoism   policy of strongly supporting one's nation in its overseas activities

joint stock company   a business venture in which there is a sharing of risk by many investors

Judeo-Christian tradition   the combined basic beliefs and ideals of Jews and Christians

Junkers   wealthy, aristocratic landowners in Prussia

KGB   the Committee on State Security, or the Soviet secret police, which replaced the NKVD in 1953; abolished in 1991

knight   medieval warriors

Koine   the simple form of the Ancient Greek language developed during the Hellenistic and Roman periods

koura   statue of a young woman

kouros   statue of a nude young man

Kremlin   the "Citadel" or the fortress in Moscow that served as a palace for the czars and the chief offices of both the Soviet and later Russian governments

Kristallnacht   "night of the broken glass"; a pogrom carried out against Jews in Germany, November 1938

kulaks   wealthy peasants who, according to Communist ideology, "exploit their neighbors to gain their wealth"

kulturkampf   the struggle in Germany between the government and the Roman Catholic Church on issues involving marriage, schools, and Church appointments, 1872–1887

"L'étât, c'est moi"   French for "I am the state"; allegedly said by King Louis XIV, expressing his view of absolute monarchy

laissez-faire   the theory that government should intervene as little as possible in the direction of economic affairs

latitude   the distance north or south of the equator measured in degrees

lay investiture   the right of secular rulers to select and/or approve individuals for ecclesiastical positions

lebensraum   German for "living space"; one of Adolf Hitler's reasons for wanting to take over land in Eastern Europe

legend   a story based on truth, but greatly exaggerated

liberalism   favoring progress and reform, as in politics

liberalization   the opening of society in terms of politics, economics, and religion to change and reform

liturgy   the public worship (services and ritual) of the Christian Church

logic   the science of correct or reliable reasoning

longitude   the distance east or west between the meridian of a particular place and Greenwich, England measured in degrees

lord   a Medieval knight who gave pieces of land to other knights in return for service and loyalty; later became a European title of nobility

Magna Carta   the Great Charter or the agreement on the part of the English monarchy to share power

mandate   an order to do something; a territory temporarily administered, but not colonized, by a foreign power or international agency

Manhattan Project   secret and successful U.S. undertaking to develop an atomic bomb

manor   a large estate

manorialism   the system of self-sufficient agricultural estates under local nobles or the Church

March on Rome   the coming to Rome by followers of Mussolini, which eventually led to his taking over the government of Italy, October 1922

Marranos   Spanish Jews who converted to Catholicism but secretly practiced Judaism

mass media   the means of communication as in radio, newspapers, and television that reaches or influences very large numbers of people

mass production   making great quantities of an item

mass, the   the Roman Catholic term for the celebration of the Eucharist or service of Holy Communion

materialism   emphasis on material objects and needs, with disinterest in spiritual values

means of production   anything necessary to make possible a finished good (i.e., factories)

mechanization   using mechanical or technological methods of production as opposed to production by hand

medicant orders   the "begging orders" or monks who sought a more ascetic life-style by refusing to own property and living by begging

Medieval   the "Middle Ages" or time between the Roman Period and the Renaissance in Western Europe.

Menshevik   a moderate Russian Marxist

mercantilism an economic system that emphasizes a nation's control of trade and its colonies for its own self-interest and the accumulation of bullion

merchant a person who buys and sells goods for profit

messiah the "Annointed One," one who will arrive in the future to make the world better

metaphysical a concept of a phenomenon that deals with the spiritual rather than the physical; literally "beyond the physical"

metic term for foreigners (non-Athenians) in Ancient Athens

Metternich system political system established in Europe by Prince Metternich to restore order to Europe after the Napoleonic Era and prevent political change

microchip technology technology using small, relatively inexpensive chips and process to store data for computer use

microcosm the world in miniature or a small example of something that is equally true on a large scale

militarism glorification of armed power and a readiness to settle disputes by using force

millennium a period of one thousand years

mir a village commune in czarist Russia

miracle an act that is beyond natural or logical explanation and seen as the work of God

missi dominici imperial envoys or representatives of the Carolingian emperors

mission a group of persons, often clergy, sent to do religious work in foreign lands

missionaries religious officials who seek to bring their religion to people who are not members of that faith

mobilization getting ready for war by assembling troops and resources

monarchy government by a hereditary ruler such as a king, queen, or emperor

monastery an establishment where monks reside

monasticism a way of life for monks during the Middle Ages, involving religious and secular activities

Mongol an Asiatic person from Mongolia

monk a male ascetic who belongs to a religious order

Monophysite Christians who believe in a single nature of Christ (that He was only God) as opposed to the established Church teaching of two natures (the He was both fully God and fully man)

monopoly exclusive control of a commodity or service in a particular market that makes it possible to manipulate prices

Moriscos Spanish Muslims who converted to Catholicism

multicultural consisting of many cultures

multinational corporation a large corporation that operates in many countries

myth a fictional story that explains the unknown, usually natural phenomena

Napoleonic Code the system of law created in France by Napoleon Bonaparte

Napoleonic Era the period of history when Napoleon dominated the European world, 1801–1815

NASA National Aeronautics and Space Administration; the U.S. center for space research and exploration

nation a large body of people possessing its own territory ruled under a unified government

National Assembly the legislative body that was formed in France during the French Revolution

nationalism a devotion and loyalty to one's own nation, with primary emphasis on furthering its interests as opposed to those of other countries

nationality a group of people who feel they belong together because they share common cultural characteristics (i.e., history, language, religion, and traditions)

Native American the original inhabitants of the Americas prior to the arrival of Columbus

natural law laws formed by nature without human intervention

natural resources the resources formed naturally in and on the earth, such as fuels, metals, and trees

natural rights the rights that humans are born with and entitled to such as life, liberty, and justice

natural selection a process in nature resulting in the survival of forms of life that best adapt to their specific environment

Nazi a word formed by the abbreviation of National Socialist German Workers

Nazism the political philosophy and system of government in Germany under Adolf Hitler, 1933–1945, excessively ethnocentric, violent, nationalistic, anti-Communist, anti-Semitic, and racist

Neanderthal an extinct race of prehistoric people that lived in caves

Neolithic Period the period of history from about 10,000 B.C. to 3500 B.C.

nepotism the favoring of relatives for high positions

nike an Ancient Greek term for victory

95 Theses a written set of protests against Church practices, posted by Martin Luther in 1517

NKVD the People's Commissar of Internal Affairs, or Soviet secret police, during Stalin's rule; replaced by the KGB in 1953

nobility a body of nobles in a country; noble birth or rank; aristocracy

nomenklatura important positions in the Soviet and Eastern European satellite governments, the appointment to which needed the approval of the Communist party

North Atlantic Treaty Organization (NATO) the post–World War II alliance of the United States, Canada, and the non-Communist nations of Western Europe against Soviet aggression

novel a long work of fiction written in prose rather than poetry

objective without bias or prejudice

Official Nationality the policy in czarist Russia that all national minorities identify themselves as Russian and adopt Russian language, culture, and religion

Okhrana the secret police in czarist Russia

Old Regime French society prior to the French Revolution of 1789

oligarchy rule of the few or government by a small elite

Open Door Policy a U.S. proposal (1899) to establish equal trading rights in China for all nations

opportunist a person who changes opinions and takes advantage of any chance to achieve a goal, usually with little concern for moral ideals

oration a formal speech

orphanage an institution for the housing and care of children without parents

orthodox "right believing" or conforming to traditional and established beliefs, attitudes, and practices

Paleolithic Period the period of history from about 500,000 B.C. to 10,000 B.C.

pancration an ancient Greco-Roman sport that combined wrestling and boxing

panegyric a poem of praise

Pan-Slavism a movement started in the nineteenth century to unite all Slavic peoples for political and cultural reasons under the leadership of Russia

pantheism any philosophical doctrine that identifies God with the universe

papacy the institution and government of the pope

papal supremacy the belief that the pope of Rome is the supreme authority of the Christian Church

parity equality in regard to the quantity or status of something

parliament the legislature of certain countries, especially Great Britain

partition the division of land among nations or other groups of people who are competing to control it

partnership persons associated in business or joint ventures who share risks and profits

pasteurization the process of exposing milk to a high temperature to destroy certain microorganisms

paternalism a policy carried out by a colonial power, whereby it believes that the colonized people cannot govern themselves

patriarch the highest-ranking bishop in the Eastern Orthodox Church, usually administrating over a nation

patriarchate the city in which an Eastern Orthodox patriarch is based

patricians the aristocrats or elite class of Ancient Rome

patriotism love, support, and defense of one's country

patron providers and protectors in Ancient Rome

peasant a farmer or one who lives off the land

Perestroika the policy of "restructuring" or economic reform under Mikhail Gorbachev designed to transform the USSR from communism to a market economy

perioeci merchants and artisans in Ancient Spartan society

persecution a policy of persistent annoyment, harassment, or oppression of an individual or group

Petrine Reforms the reforms made under Czar Piotr (Peter) I (the Great) to Westernize and modernize Russia in the early eighteenth century

petrine theory the belief that the popes of Rome are direct successors of the Apostle Peter and derive their supreme authority over the Church from him

phalansteries communities proposed by Charles Fourier in which people would work as they wished and would share profits

phalanx the basic unit of Ancient Greek military organization, roughly the equivalent of the modern regiment

philanthropy the concern for human beings as expressed by work for the needy or donations to institutions advancing human welfare

philology the study of written texts, often to confirm their authenticity

philosophe a great thinker during the period of the Enlightenment in science and the humanities

philosophy the love of wisdom or the study of truths and principles of being, conduct, or knowledge

physiocrat person who believed that true wealth derived from agriculture

piazza an open square in a town

piers a support for a structure

pilgrim a person who travels to a sacred place as a sign of religious devotion

pilgrimage a journey made to a sacred place as a sign of religious devotion

plebians the "people" or all nonaristocrats in Ancient Rome

plebiscite a direct vote by the people of a country or state on some important public question

pogrom a violent attack on Jews by non-Jews

polis an Ancient Greek city-state

political repression to keep under political control or to put down

pope the title of respect in the Christian Church meaning "Father" bestowed to patriarchs; title by which the bishop or Patriarch of Rome is known

popular sovereignty independent and self-governing status of a people in a specific area

porphyroghenitos royalty or "born in the purple" (royal color)

posthumously occurring after a person's death

Post-Industrial Revolution the period after 1945 signifying the beginning of computer and other contemporary technology

praetor an Ancient Roman magistrate or judge

predestination a doctrine stated by John Calvin, in the 1500s, claiming that God has already chosen those who will be saved

prehistoric the period prior to recorded history

prejudice an attitude toward a group of people, based upon false information and unproven opinions

primogeniture the system of inheritance by the oldest son

proletariat the industrial working class

propaganda information or ideas spread to promote or attack a cause or belief

prose ordinary language without meter or rhyme such as in poetry

protagonist the leader of a movement; the leading character in a work of literature

protectorate an area controlled by a foreign nation, with the native ruler of the area allowed to hold some—at least nominal—power

provisional government a government that serves only until permanently replaced; specifically, the Democratic Provisional Government established in Russia in 1917

purge to get rid of someone or something regarded as undesirable

race a group of people having certain similar physical characteristics

racism a harmful, negative attitude toward a person or a group because of the person's (or group's) race

rain forest a tropical forest in an area of exceptionally high annual rainfall

raj the period of British rule in India

ratio a proportional relationship

rationalism the principle of accepting reason as the supreme authority in matters of opinion, belief, and conduct

reactionary describes a desire to restore a policy or idea that was once followed

recession a mild but widespread slowdown in business activity

Reformation a movement to change some of the ideas and practices of the Roman Catholic Church, beginning in the early 1500s

reich German word for empire

Reichstrat imperial parliament of the Austrian Empire

Reign of Terror period during the French Revolution when accused enemies of the state were executed, 1793–1794

religious fundamentalism a religious movement that stresses the infallibility of that religious doctrine in all matters of faith

renaissance rebirth

Renaissance man a multitalented, well-rounded individual

Renaissance, the the vigorous rebirth or revival of learning and art that occurred in Europe from the fourteenth to seventeenth centuries

repeal to change a previous policy or law by abolishing it

representative democracy the popular rule through elected representatives

republic a type of government in which the leaders are chosen by citizens eligible to vote

restoration the act of restoring the rightful ruler as the head of state

revanche French for "revenge," descriptive of France's attitude toward Germany after France lost Alsace-Lorraine in the Franco-Prussian War

revolution the forcible overthrow of an established government by the people governed; a complete or radical change

rhetoric the art and practice of argument and persuasion through public speech and the effective use of language

Risorgimento the nineteenth-century movement for Italian unification

robot the system of obligatory peasant labor in the Austrian Empire

romance Medieval poetry that combined epic and lyric traditions

romanticism a style of literature and art of the nineteenth century that encouraged freedom of form and emphasized imagination and emotion

royal capitulary order or regulation of the Carolingian emperors

royal chancery Medieval English government department to issue royal orders and compose correspondence

royal exchequer Medieval English government department for tax collection

Rus' the early Russian/Ukrainian state centered in the city of Kiev

Russification czarist policy of forcing minorities in the Russian Empire to adopt Russian culture, language, and religion

sacraments sacred rites given to believers by the Roman Catholic Church

samizdat "self-published" or literature censored by the Soviet government that was circulated privately in the USSR; underground writing

satellite nation a nation that is dominated by and/or dependent on another

scapegoat a person or group unjustly blamed for something bad that has happened

schism a division or split

scientific method a way to study nature, using experiments, observations, and mathematics

scientific socialism Marxist theory of the system of economic, political, and social organization

SEATO Southeast Asian Treaty Organization or the alliance of the United States and the non-Communist nations of Asia to prevent Communist aggression

Second Estate the nobility in France prior to the French Revolution

sect a small group led by a preacher, having broken away from a larger religious group

sectarian pertaining to or characteristic of a specific religious group or sect

secular uninvolved with religion; concerned with worldly things

semi-divine partly a god

Senate the ruling body of the Roman Republic

separation of powers the concept developed by Baron Montesquieu that the powers of government should be separated among the executive, legislative, and judicial branches of government

sepoys native Indian troops in the British army, during the Colonial Period

Septuagint the Greek version of the Old Testament

serf a peasant who is bound to a piece of land through hereditary obligation

sheriff Medieval English local official

silicon chip a nonmetallic chip used in computers and other electronic devices to transmit and store data

simony the buying and selling of Church positions in the Middle Ages

Slavonic the language of the early Slavic peoples. It is the root of Russian, Belarussian, Ukrainian, Polish, Serbian, Croatian, Slovene, Bulgarian, Czech, and Slovak

social class a group in society to which a person belongs, e.g., middle class

social contract an agreement by people to form a society based on agreed upon principles and rules

Social Darwinism the application of Charles Darwin's ideas on evolution and natural selection to human society

social structure the manner by which a society is organized in terms of its people

social unit an organized group in society

socialism a theory or system of social organization that advocates the ownership and control of industry, capital, and land by the community as a whole

socialist a person who supports the ideas and principles of socialism

socii the "allies" or Latin peoples of the Italian peninsula who became allied with the ancient Romans

sovereignty the independent power of authority in a state

Soviet Bloc the Eastern Europe nations that were dominated by the Soviet Union through puppet Communist governments

soviet a worker's council; the term was adopted by the Bolsheviks as the name of the Communist government of Russia

Spartan existence life based only on bare necessities and without any luxury

sphere of influence the area in which one nation dominates

stalemate an indecisive outcome to a contest, where no side has made any major gains

stereotype a fixed view or idea about the behavior of all members of a religion or race

stoa the front porch of an Ancient Greek home

stock the outstanding capital of a corporation represented by shares in the form of ownership certificates

Stoic a school of philosophy that teaches humans to accept their fate and overcome concern for the material world in order to be protected from the pain life can bring

subjective a view based on the individual's opinions and bias

subsidies direct financial aid to assist a government or business

suffrage the right to vote

sultan the traditional title of the emperor of the Ottoman Empire

superfluous more than sufficient or unnecessary

superpower a nation with greater military and economic power than most other nations; specifically, the United States or the USSR at the end of World War II

surplus value Marxist concept of profit above the cost of production

symmetry the concept of balance or proportion in art and architecture

synod a council, usually an assembly of Church officials or bishops

technological advance an advance in any branch of knowledge that deals with industrial arts, applied science, and engineering

telos the "end" or "purpose" of a person or object in Ancient Greek philosophy

terrorism the use of violence and threats to intimidate or coerce others, especially for political purposes

theocracy a system of government organized under religious rules and beliefs

theology the study of God and religious belief

Thermidorian reaction the time of the French Revolution that ended the Reign of Terror and saw the return of more moderate elements of society to power in France, post 1795

thesis a proposition to be proved or maintained through argument

Third Estate the people in France other than the clergy and nobility prior to the French Revolution; includes the middle class, peasants, and artisans

tithe Church taxes

topography the study of the natural surface features of a place or area

totalitarianism a system of government where those in power have complete control and do not permit any opposition or individual freedoms

trade union agreement by nations to join together to carry on trade to benefit these nations, also trading bloc

Transcaucasus the nations of Georgia, Armenia, and Azerbaijan, which are located in the area across from the Causasus mountain range

triangular trade the trade involving rum, slaves, sugar, molasses going between Europe, Africa, and the Americas between the fifteenth to nineteenth centuries

Triple Alliance the military alliance of Austria-Hungary, Germany, and Italy at the start of World War I

Triple Entente the military alliance of Britain, France, and Russia at the start of World War I

triumvirate a government of three individuals sharing power equally

troubadour traveling bards or singing poets in the Medieval Ages

tyrant a temporary absolute ruler in a time of crisis or emergency

ultimatum a final set of demands for the settlement of a dispute

ultraroyalist an extreme supporter of the idea of royal government or monarchy

unequal treaties treaties forced on China by Britain after the Opium Wars

universal applies to everyone or the whole group

universal history history written from the perspective that all events are part of a predetermined plan by God

universal suffrage the right of men and women to vote

utilitarianism theory emphasizing the usefulness of something rather than its beauty or ornamentation; developed by John Stuart Mill

utopia a place or state of political or social perfection

utopian socialism a visionary system of the economic and social organization of society based on belief of its possible perfection

values ideals or principles of a given society

Varangian a Russian term for the Scandanavian Vikings

vassal a Medieval term for a knight who took an oath of loyalty to a lord

vernacular the spoken or common language

versatility the ability to do many things well

vertical integration an economic organization to incorporate into a whole all goods and services required to produce a particular product

viceroy a person appointed to rule a country or province as the deputy of the sovereign, e.g., Spanish or Portuguese viceroy

villein free peasants (not serfs) who lived on a Medieval manor and were exempt from obligatory service to the lord

Warsaw Pact an alliance forced on the Eastern European Communist satellite states by the USSR in response to the creation of NATO and SEATO by the United States and its allies

Western Church the Roman Catholic Church, recognizing the spiritual leadership of the pope or bishop (patriarch) of Rome

Zemskii Sobor the Council of Nobles or a representative assembly called to end the time of troubles in seventeenth-century Russia

zemstvo elected rural assemblies in czarist Russia that were responsible for running local government

Zionism a movement to resettle Jews in the Middle East by re-establishing a Jewish national homeland

Zollverein a customs union in the German states in the 1800s

Zyklon B the gas used by Germans to kill Jews during the Holocaust

Index

Council of Constance, 119
Council of Florence, 102–103
Council of Nobles, 428
Council of Trent, 169–170
Count of Artois, 388
Counter Reformation, 169–170, 219
Courbet, Gustave, 366
Cranmer, Thomas, 168
Crassus, Marcus Licinius, 78
"Creation of Adam," 148
"Creationist science," 364
Crete, 36–37
Crick, Francis, 756
Crime and Punishment, 367, 436
Crimean War, 391–392, 432, 447–449
Croatia, 714–715
    independence of, 714
Cro-Magnons, 17–18
Crompton, Samuel, 317
Cromwell, Oliver, 244–245
Crop rotation, 315
Crusades, 121–123
Cuban Missile Crisis, 689
Curiae, 72
Cynics, 62
Cyprus, peacekeeping, United Nations, 618
Cyril, 101
Czech Republic, 711
Czech Revolution, 445
Czechoslovakia, 708, 710–712
    communism, collapse of, 708, 710–712
    division of, 711
    occupation of, 581
    Prague Spring, 710
    Soviet satellite, 710
    Velvet Revolution, 711
    World War I, 540
    World War II, 581
Czerniakow, Adam, 645

D

Dachau, 649–650
Dalton, John, 365
Danish War, 414
Dante *See* Alighieri, Dante, 149
Danton, Georges, 284–285
Darius I, 43–44
Darnley, Henry, 219
Darwin, Charles, 363–364
    Theory of Evolution, 364
Das Kapital, 354
Daumier, Honore, 366
"David," 148–149
David, Jacques-Louis, 261
Davis, Miles, 767
D-Day, 590
de Balzac, Honore, 367
de Gama, Vasco, 181
de Gaulle, Charles, 586, 620–621
de Klerk, Frederick W., 516
de Leòn, Ponce, 184
de Soto, Hernando, 189
de Stael, Madame, 367
de Vinci, Leonardo, 148
Death camps, Holocaust, 643, 648–650
Death marches, Holocaust, 667
Decameron, The, 149
Decembrist Revolt, 432
Declaration of Independence, 261
Decolonization of Asia and Africa, World War II, 595
Degas, Edgar, 366
Delacroix, Eugene, 366
Demjanjuk, John, 672
Democracy:
    development of, 40–41
        Athenian, 44–45
    in England, 237–254
    in Great Britain, 375–386
    House of Commons, 377

office holding requirements, 376
open ballot, 675
popular sovereignty, 375
representation, 376
voting restrictions, 375
Democritus, 43
Demography, 12, 14
Denmark:
    Fall of, World War II, 585
    Holocaust, 663–664
    Reformation, 169
Depression, 329
Descartes, René, 256, 266
Descent of Man, The, 364
Destruction of the European Jews, The, 636
Détente, 689–690
Devil's Island, 394
Dialectical materialism, 352
Dialogue Concerning the Two Chief Systems of the World, 263
Dialogues on Motion, 264
Diamonds, 200
"Diary of a Madman, A," 436
Diary of a Young Girl, The, 665
Dias, Bartolomeu, 181
Dickens, Charles, 367
Diderot, Denis, 257
Dimitrii, Prince, 428
Diocletian, 86
Diplomatic Revolution, 230
Discourse on Method, 266
"Disputa," 148
Disraeli, Benjamin, 378
Divine Comedy, The, 149
Divine right, 224, 241
Dmitrov, Georgi, 712–713
DNA, 756
"Doctor Faustus," 149
Doctor Zhivago, 699, 701
Domesday Book, 214
Domestic system, 201
    and development of woolen industry, 317
Domitian, 83
Don Quixote de la Mancha, 150, 229
Donatello, 148
Dostoievskii, Theodor, 367, 436
Draconian Laws, 45
Drake, Francis, 190
Dreyfus, Alfred, 394
Drug trade, global, 731
Dubček, Alexander, 710–711
Dudinstev, Vladimir, 699
Duke of Sully, 222
Duke of Wellington, 300
Dunkirk, World War II, 585–586
Dutch colonies, 189
Dutch East India Company, 200
Dutch East Indies, Japan's involvement, 584
Dutch West India Company, 189
Duties, 202
Dvorak, Antonin, 368
Dzhugashvili, Iosif *See* Stalin, Joseph

E

East Asia:
    imperialism, 485–488
    independence in, 513
Eastern Europe, Cold War in, 686
Eastern Orthodox Church, 101–104, 425–426
Ebert, Friederich, 562
Eck, John, 161
Economic:
    and Social Council, United Nations, 618
    geography, 8–12
    theories, 259, 348–350
Eden, Anthony, 662, 688

Edict of Expulsion, 227
Edict of Milan, 87
Edict of Nantes, 221–223
    revocation of, 225
Edict of Worms, 161
Edison, Thomas, 330
Edward I, 239
Edward VI, 168, 216
Efimovich, Grigorii, 434 *See also* Rasputin
Eichmann, Adolf, 645–646, 671
Einsatzgruppen, 646–648
Einstein, Albert, 365–366, 594
    Theory of Relativity, 366
Eisenhower, Dwight, 589–590, 667, 688–689
El Greco, 229
Elba, 301
Electricity, 330–331
Eliot, John, 242
Elizabeth, 240
Elizabeth I, 149, 168, 217, 220–221
Emancipation Edict, 433
Emile, 260
Empiricism, 256
Encyclopedia, 257–258
Encyclopedia Britannica, 257
Encyclopedias, 63
Energy concerns, 745–746
Engels, Friedrich, 351, 352, 354
England, 213–221 *See also* Great Britain
    banking system, 319–320
    Bill of Rights, 248
    Civil War, 243–244
    colonies, 190
    as a commonwealth, 244–246
    Commercial Revolution, 203
    democracy, 237–254
    nation-state, 213–221
    Reformation, 167–168
Enlightened despots, 231
Enlightenment, 211
    and the Scientific Revolution, 255–274
        See also Age of Reason
Entente Cordiale, 529
Enterprise Law of 1987, 701
Entrepreneurs, 200–201
Epicureans, 62
Epicurus, 85
Epitome of Copernican Astronomy, 263
Erasmus, Desiderius, 150, 165
Eratosthenes, 62
Erectheum, 48
Eroica, the, 358
Escorial, 228
Essay on the Principles of Population, 320, 349
Ethics, 62
Ethiopia, invasion by Italy, 579
Ethnic:
    cleansing, 672, 714
    groups, 707
Ethnocentrism, 399, 461, 564
Euclid, 62
"Eugene Onegin," 436
Eugénie, Empress, 391
Euripides, 42
European Community, 726–727
European Space Agency (ESA), 755
European Union, 9–10, 727
Evans, Mary Ann, 367
Evans, Sir Arthur, 36
Evian Conference, 641
Exploration, Age of, 179–196
Extinction of animal life, 744

F

Factories:
    assembly line system, 328

division of labor, 328
working condition in, 339
Faerie Queen, The, 150
Fascism in Italy, 559–561
    Black Shirts, 559
    economic factors, 559
    March on Rome, 560
    political factors, 559
    social factors, 559
Faure, Edgar, 688
Faure, Felix, 394
February Patent, 446
Ferdinand, Francis, assasination of, 530–532
Ferdinand I, 182, 226–228, 444–445
Ferdinand II, 223
Ferdinand of Aragon, 226
Fermi, Enrico, 594
Feudalism:
    decline of, 116–117
    destruction of, 304
    rise of, 115–116
Fichte, Johann, 411
Field, Cyrus, 330
Fifth Republic, France, 621
"Final solution," 645
First Estate, 276–277
First Socialist International, 354
First Triumvirate, 78–79
Fitzgerald, Ella, 767
Flavian Dynasty, 83
Flossenberg, 650
Foch, Ferdinand, 537
Food and Agriculture Organization (FAO), 618
Ford, Henry, 328
Fourier, Charles, 351
Fourteen Points, 538–539
France, 221–226, 387–398
    Bank of, 297
    Bourbon Restoration, 387–389
    bourgeoise, 389
    Chamber of deputies, 387
    Chamber of peers, 387
    Commercial Revolution, 203
    Committee of Public Safety, 287–288
    Congress of Vienna, 303–304
    Constitution of 1791, 282–283
    Constitution of 1875, 393
    creation of, 118–121
    decolonization by, 511, 514–515
    Directory, 288, 296–297
    economic problems, 277–278
    Enlightenment, 257–259
    entrepreneurs, 391
    Estates-general, 279–280
    expansionism, 226
    February Revolution, 390
    Fifth Republic, 621
    food shortages, 278
    Fourth Republic, 620–621
    House of Orléans, 389
    imperialism, 471, 474, 482–483, 492, 495–496
    industrialization, 326
    July Monarchy, 389–390
    July Ordinances, 388
    June Days of Terror, 390
    Legislative Assembly, 283–284
    liberal monarchy, 389–390
    nation-state, 221–226
    National Assembly, 279–280, 282, 392–393
    National Convention, 284–285
    National Day of Remembrance, 673
    political repression, 278
    Prussia, peace with, 392
    Reformation, 167
    Reign of Terror, 285–288
    Second Coalition, 298
    Second Empire, 391–393
        Fall of, 392